Carnegie Commission on Higher Education
Sponsored Research Studies

A STATISTICAL PORTRAIT OF HIGHER
EDUCATION
Seymour E. Harris

THE HOME OF SCIENCE:
THE ROLE OF THE UNIVERSITY
Dael Wolfle

EDUCATION AND EVANGELISM:
A PROFILE OF PROTESTANT COLLEGES
C. Robert Pace

PROFESSIONAL EDUCATION:
SOME NEW DIRECTIONS
Edgar H. Schein

THE NONPROFIT RESEARCH INSTITUTE:
ITS ORIGIN, OPERATION, PROBLEMS, AND
PROSPECTS
Harold Orlans

THE INVISIBLE COLLEGES:
A PROFILE OF SMALL, PRIVATE COLLEGES
WITH LIMITED RESOURCES
Alexander W. Astin and Calvin B. T. Lee

AMERICAN HIGHER EDUCATION:
DIRECTIONS OLD AND NEW
Joseph Ben-David

A DEGREE AND WHAT ELSE?:
CORRELATES AND CONSEQUENCES OF A
COLLEGE EDUCATION
*Stephen B. Withey, Jo Anne Coble, Gerald
Gurin, John P. Robinson, Burkhard Strumpel,
Elizabeth Keogh Taylor, and Arthur C. Wolfe*

THE MULTICAMPUS UNIVERSITY:
A STUDY OF ACADEMIC GOVERNANCE
Eugene C. Lee and Frank M. Bowen

INSTITUTIONS IN TRANSITION:
A PROFILE OF CHANGE IN HIGHER
EDUCATION
(INCORPORATING THE 1970 STATISTICAL
REPORT)
Harold L. Hodgkinson

EFFICIENCY IN LIBERAL EDUCATION:
A STUDY OF COMPARATIVE INSTRUCTIONAL
COSTS FOR DIFFERENT WAYS OF ORGANIZ-
ING TEACHING-LEARNING IN A LIBERAL ARTS
COLLEGE
Howard R. Bowen and Gordon K. Douglass

CREDIT FOR COLLEGE:
PUBLIC POLICY FOR STUDENT LOANS
Robert W. Hartman

MODELS AND MAVERICKS:
A PROFILE OF PRIVATE LIBERAL ARTS
COLLEGES
Morris T. Keeton

BETWEEN TWO WORLDS:
A PROFILE OF NEGRO HIGHER EDUCATION
Frank Bowles and Frank A. DeCosta

BREAKING THE ACCESS BARRIERS:
A PROFILE OF TWO-YEAR COLLEGES
Leland L. Medsker and Dale Tillery

ANY PERSON, ANY STUDY:
AN ESSAY ON HIGHER EDUCATION IN THE
UNITED STATES
Eric Ashby

THE NEW DEPRESSION IN HIGHER
EDUCATION:
A STUDY OF FINANCIAL CONDITIONS AT 41
COLLEGES AND UNIVERSITIES
Earl F. Cheit

FINANCING MEDICAL EDUCATION:
AN ANALYSIS OF ALTERNATIVE POLICIES
AND MECHANISMS
Rashi Fein and Gerald I. Weber

HIGHER EDUCATION IN NINE COUNTRIES:
A COMPARATIVE STUDY OF COLLEGES AND
UNIVERSITIES ABROAD
*Barbara B. Burn, Philip G. Altbach, Clark Kerr,
and James A. Perkins*

BRIDGES TO UNDERSTANDING:
INTERNATIONAL PROGRAMS OF AMERICAN
COLLEGES AND UNIVERSITIES
Irwin T. Sanders and Jennifer C. Ward

GRADUATE AND PROFESSIONAL EDUCATION
1980:
A SURVEY OF INSTITUTIONAL PLANS
Lewis B. Mayhew

THE AMERICAN COLLEGE AND AMERICAN
CULTURE:
SOCIALIZATION AS A FUNCTION OF HIGHER
EDUCATION
Oscar and Mary F. Handlin

RECENT ALUMNI AND HIGHER EDUCATION:
A SURVEY OF COLLEGE GRADUATES
Joe L. Spaeth and Andrew M. Greeley

CHANGE IN EDUCATIONAL POLICY:
SELF-STUDIES IN SELECTED COLLEGES AND
UNIVERSITIES
Dwight R. Ladd

STATE OFFICIALS AND HIGHER EDUCATION:
A SURVEY OF THE OPINIONS AND
EXPECTATIONS OF POLICY MAKERS IN NINE
STATES
Heinz Eulau and Harold Quinley

ACADEMIC DEGREE STRUCTURES:
INNOVATIVE APPROACHES
PRINCIPLES OF REFORM IN DEGREE
STRUCTURES IN THE UNITED STATES
Stephen H. Spurr

COLLEGES OF THE FORGOTTEN AMERICANS:
A PROFILE OF STATE COLLEGES AND
REGIONAL UNIVERSITIES
E. Alden Dunham

FROM BACKWATER TO MAINSTREAM:
A PROFILE OF CATHOLIC HIGHER
EDUCATION
Andrew M. Greeley

THE ECONOMICS OF THE MAJOR PRIVATE
UNIVERSITIES
William G. Bowen
(Out of print, but available from University Microfilms.)

THE FINANCE OF HIGHER EDUCATION
Howard R. Bowen
(Out of print, but available from University Microfilms.)

ALTERNATIVE METHODS OF FEDERAL
FUNDING FOR HIGHER EDUCATION
Ron Wolk

INVENTORY OF CURRENT RESEARCH ON
HIGHER EDUCATION 1968
Dale M. Heckman and Warren Bryan Martin

*The following technical reports are available from the Carnegie Commission on Higher Education, 1947
Center Street, Berkeley, California 94704.*

RESOURCE USE IN HIGHER EDUCATION:
TRENDS IN OUTPUT AND INPUTS, 1930–1967
June O'Neill

TRENDS AND PROJECTIONS OF PHYSICIANS
IN THE UNITED STATES 1967–2002
Mark S. Blumberg

MENTAL ABILITY AND HIGHER EDUCATIONAL
ATTAINMENT IN THE 20TH CENTURY
Paul Taubman and Terence Wales

SOURCES OF FUNDS TO COLLEGES AND
UNIVERSITIES
June O'Neill

MAY 1970:
THE CAMPUS AFTERMATH OF CAMBODIA
AND KENT STATE
Richard E. Peterson and John A. Bilorusky

The following reprints are available from the Carnegie Commission on Higher Education, 1947 Center Street, Berkeley, California 94704.

ACCELERATED PROGRAMS OF MEDICAL EDUCATION, by Mark S. Blumberg, reprinted from JOURNAL OF MEDICAL EDUCATION, vol. 46, no. 8, August 1971.

SCIENTIFIC MANPOWER FOR 1970–1985, by Allan M. Cartter, reprinted from SCIENCE, vol. 172, no. 3979, pp. 132–140, April 9, 1971.

A NEW METHOD OF MEASURING STATES' HIGHER EDUCATION BURDEN, by Neil Timm, reprinted from THE JOURNAL OF HIGHER EDUCATION, vol. 42, no. 1, pp. 27–33, January 1971.

REGENT WATCHING, by Earl F. Cheit, reprinted from AGB REPORTS, vol. 13, no. 6, pp. 4–13, March 1971.

COLLEGE GENERATIONS FROM THE 1930s TO THE 1960s, by Seymour M. Lipset and Everett C. Ladd, Jr., reprinted from THE PUBLIC INTEREST, no. 25, Summer 1971.

AMERICAN SOCIAL SCIENTISTS AND THE GROWTH OF CAMPUS POLITICAL ACTIVISM IN THE 1960s, by Everett C. Ladd, Jr., and Seymour M. Lipset, reprinted from SOCIAL SCIENCES INFORMATION, vol. 10, no. 2, April 1971.

THE POLITICS OF AMERICAN POLITICAL SCIENTISTS, by Everett C. Ladd, Jr., and Seymour M. Lipset, reprinted from PS, vol. 4, no. 2, Spring 1971.*

THE DIVIDED PROFESSORIATE, by Seymour M. Lipset and Everett C. Ladd, Jr., reprinted from CHANGE, vol. 3, no. 3, pp. 54–60, May 1971.

JEWISH ACADEMICS IN THE UNITED STATES: THEIR ACHIEVEMENTS, CULTURE AND POLITICS, by Seymour M. Lipset and Everett C. Ladd, Jr., reprinted from AMERICAN JEWISH YEAR BOOK, 1971.

THE UNHOLY ALLIANCE AGAINST THE CAMPUS, by Kenneth Keniston and Michael Lerner, reprinted from NEW YORK TIMES MAGAZINE, November 8, 1970 .

PRECARIOUS PROFESSORS: NEW PATTERNS OF REPRESENTATION, by Joseph W. Garbarino, reprinted from INDUSTRIAL RELATIONS, vol. 10, no. 1, February 1971.

. . . AND WHAT PROFESSORS THINK: ABOUT STUDENT PROTEST AND MANNERS, MORALS, POLITICS, AND CHAOS ON THE CAMPUS, by Seymour Martin Lipset and Everett C. Ladd, Jr., reprinted from PSYCHOLOGY TODAY, November 1970.*

DEMAND AND SUPPLY IN U.S. HIGHER EDUCATION: A PROGRESS REPORT, by Roy Radner and Leonard S. Miller, reprinted from AMERICAN ECONOMIC REVIEW, May 1970.*

RESOURCES FOR HIGHER EDUCATION: AN ECONOMIST'S VIEW, by Theodore W. Schultz, reprinted from JOURNAL OF POLITICAL ECONOMY, vol. 76, no. 3, University of Chicago, May/June 1968.*

INDUSTRIAL RELATIONS AND UNIVERSITY RELATIONS, *by Clark Kerr, reprinted from* PROCEEDINGS OF THE 21ST ANNUAL WINTER MEETING OF THE INDUSTRIAL RELATIONS RESEARCH ASSOCIATION, *pp. 15–25.**

NEW CHALLENGES TO THE COLLEGE AND UNIVERSITY, *by Clark Kerr, reprinted from Kermit Gordon (ed.),* AGENDA FOR THE NATION, *The Brookings Institution, Washington, D.C., 1968.* *

PRESIDENTIAL DISCONTENT, *by Clark Kerr, reprinted from David C. Nichols (ed.),* PERSPECTIVES ON CAMPUS TENSIONS: PAPERS PREPARED FOR THE SPECIAL COMMITTEE ON CAMPUS TENSIONS, *American Council on Education, Washington, D.C., September 1970.**

STUDENT PROTEST—AN INSTITUTIONAL AND NATIONAL PROFILE, *by Harold Hodgkinson, reprinted from* THE RECORD, *vol. 71, no. 4, May 1970.**

WHAT'S BUGGING THE STUDENTS?, *by Kenneth Keniston, reprinted from* EDUCATIONAL RECORD, *American Council on Education, Washington, D.C., Spring 1970.**

THE POLITICS OF ACADEMIA, *by Seymour Martin Lipset, reprinted from David C. Nichols (ed.),* PERSPECTIVES ON CAMPUS TENSIONS: PAPERS PREPARED FOR THE SPECIAL COMMITTEE ON CAMPUS TENSIONS, *American Council on Education, Washington, D.C., September 1970.**

INTERNATIONAL PROGRAMS OF U.S. COLLEGES AND UNIVERSITIES: PRIORITIES FOR THE SEVENTIES, *by James A. Perkins, reprinted by permission of the International Council for Educational Development, Occasional Paper no. 1, July 1971.*

FACULTY UNIONISM: FROM THEORY TO PRACTICE, *by Joseph W. Garbarino, reprinted from* INDUSTRIAL RELATIONS, *vol. 11, no. 1, pp. 1–17, February 1972.*

*The Commission's stock of this reprint has been exhausted.

A Statistical Portrait
of Higher Education

A Statistical Portrait
of Higher Education

by Seymour E. Harris

Lucius Littauer Professor of Political Economy Emeritus,
Harvard University,
and Professor of Economics and Medical Economics,
University of California, San Diego

A Report for

The Carnegie Commission on Higher Education

MCGRAW–HILL BOOK COMPANY

New York   St.Louis   San Francisco   Düsseldorf
London   Sydney   Toronto   Mexico   Panama
Johannesburg   Kuala Lumpur   Montreal
New Delhi   Rio de Janeiro   Singapore

The Carnegie Commission on Higher Education,
1947 Center Street, Berkeley, California 94704,
has sponsored preparation of this report as a
part of a continuing effort to obtain and present
significant information for public discussion.
The views expressed are those of the author.

A STATISTICAL PORTRAIT OF HIGHER EDUCATION

Library of Congress Cataloging in Publication Data

Harris, Seymour Edwin, date
A statistical portrait of higher education.

"A report for the Carnegie Commission on Higher
Education."
1. Education, Higher—U.S.—1965-   —Statistics.
2. Education—Economic aspects—U.S.—Statistics.
I. Carnegie Commission on Higher Education. II.   Title.
LA227.3.H25   378.73   72-38334
ISBN 0-07-010039-X

123456789MAMM798765432

Contents

ix

from 1840 to 1902 ▪ Enrollment in 30 major institutions in the early twentieth century ▪ Enrollment trends and projections, 1880 to 1978 ▪ Negro enrollment ▪ Enrollment trends by sex ▪ Graduate enrollment ▪ Rising share of public institutions in total enrollment ▪ Relative importance of professional degrees ▪ Professional schools ▪ Denominational schools ▪ Student mobility ▪ Summation

Tables

PART ONE: STUDENTS

1.1. Undergraduate Student Characteristics

1.2. Graduate Student Characteristics

1.6. Graduate Student Aid

PART TWO: ENROLLMENT

2.1. Population and Educational Attainment

2.2. Enrollment

2.4. Institutions: Various Aspects

PART THREE: FACULTY

3.1. Faculty: General Characteristics

3.2. Supply and Demand, Recruitment and Mobility of Faculty

PART FOUR: INCOME AND EXPENDITURES

4.1. Income

4.2. Government's Contribution

4.5. Expenditures: Library and Separately Budgeted Expenditures on Research

4.6. Physical Plant

4.7. Federal Funds for Scientific Activities

4.8. Expenditures: Various Aspects

4.9. The Burden of Educational Finance

PART FIVE: PRODUCTIVITY AND STRUCTURE

5.1. The Issue of Productivity

5.2. Structure of Higher Educational Enrollment

Foreword

During the last decade, interest in the economics of higher education has developed rapidly, but the growing band of scholars who have turned their attention to this subject in recent years all owe a great debt to Seymour Harris, who began his pioneering work on the economics of higher education nearly a quarter of a century ago. In the course of writing and editing innumerable books and papers on the economic and financial problems facing higher education, he has developed an encyclopedic knowledge of the sources of data on these issues — contemporary and historical, national and international — that is certainly unrivaled and is fully reflected in this volume. He has studied the early history of Harvard and other institutions, and I feel quite safe in saying that he has combed the data available in the late nineteenth and early twentieth century reports of the U.S. Commissioner of Education as no other scholar has ever done.

The present volume, *A Statistical Portrait of Higher Education,* has been designed as a statistical abstract, but it is actually far more than a statistical abstract. It is not confined to data available from official sources, but includes tables drawn from a wide variety of private surveys and research projects as well. In addition, Professor Harris has written an introduction to the volume and a summary of the data available in each of its chapters. Some of the chapters, notably that on productivity in higher education, reflect the results of the author's own extensive research.

Users of the volume, particularly those who are new to research on higher education, will find it especially valuable as a guide to sources of information. As the author points out in his prefatory note, the volume covers data relating to the economics of higher education more extensively than it does information on other aspects of the subject, but it is by no means confined to economic data. The historical data on enrollment, the tables relating to student characteristics, the comparative international data on enrollment rates, and the statistics on characteristics of institutions will be of interest to all those concerned with higher education, as well as to those who are conducting studies of higher education's economic aspects or wrestling with the unprecedentedly difficult financial problems facing colleges and universities today.

Clark Kerr

Chairman
The Carnegie Commission
on Higher Education

April 1972

Preface

In this volume I have tried to assemble useful tables dealing with higher education. In all, roughly 700 tables are included. Many brief tables are not listed. A substantial proportion of the tables were constructed for this volume. I have relied on books, periodicals, and government documents which contained records of congressional hearings and reports by congressional committees, and international, e.g., United Nations, documents. The 28 chapters cover problems relating to students, enrollment, faculty, income, and expenditures (see Contents). Originally we assembled about twice as many documents as we present here.

My debts are especially large to the U.S. Office of Education, which in recent years has increased the quantity of its output and greatly improved its quality. The American Council on Education (ACE) through its *Fact Book* and other publications has facilitated my task. Even as I write these lines, an excellent study, *Violence and Discipline on the U.S. Campus, 1968–1969*, by the American Council on Education appears. I have not dealt with this problem. The article, for example, reveals that 6 percent of the institutions of higher education had violent protests and 16 percent nonviolent protests in the year 1968–69. The results of the study, given by size and type of institution, include a classification of damage done and the issues over which protests emerged.

Aside from the tables and the relevant comments, this volume includes a brief summary of most chapters. I have also written a general introduction in which I have put together some interesting facts. To some extent, the introduction repeats material in the body of the book, but there are additional comments. I am not entirely satisfied with my choices and deletions, but I hope the introduction adds to the book.

Although, in general, I have refrained from taking positions on controversial issues, in commenting on such problems as tuition, aid, or physical plant, I have inadvertently exposed my prejudiced views. I may have raised a few controversial issues; I surely have not solved them.

The body of this book is divided into five parts: "Students," "Enrollment," "Faculty," "Income and Expenditures," and "Productivity and Structure." Much of the emphasis is on economic issues. But the coverage is wide, as one can glean from the contents pages. Thus in the six chapters of Part One ("Students"), we move from student characteristics to graduate student aid. Part Two ("Enrollment," seven chapters) treats population and educational attainment, institutions of higher education, degrees, dropouts, and international comparisons. Part Three ("Faculty," four chapters) includes such problems as recruitment, mobility, distribution by fields of specialization, supply and demand, and allocation of time. Part Four ("Income and Expenditures") required nine chapters. Included are government's contribution, endowment income, tuition, expenditures, and the burden of educational finance.

My greatest debt is to Bruce Barnett, without whose help this book could not have been written. An ideal research assistant, he offered many fruitful ideas and saved me from many mistakes. My debt is also great to Mrs. Myrtle Williams, an excellent typist, who assumed responsibility for duplicating thousands of sheets and was superb in keeping tabs on the location of the mountains of material. In every respect, she was outstanding, as was Mrs. Jane Nizyborski, who helped type the manuscript. Jay Marchand, also, was of much help as a research assistant.

I also owe a debt of gratitude to Margaret S. Gordon, associate director of the Carnegie Commission staff, who supervised the consolidation and conversion of an overly lengthy manuscript into a more publishable form, and to Mrs. Belle Cole and Mrs. Helen Cammarata, who ably assisted her. Mrs. Terry Y. Allen of the Commission's editorial staff efficiently carried out the time-consuming responsibility of the final detailed editing of the manuscript.

Further, it was a pleasure to work with Clark Kerr, who allowed his colleagues on the Carnegie project on higher education maximum freedom and gave them helpful guidance.

Seymour E. Harris

Introduction and Summary

The most striking aspect of higher education has been the enormous increase in enrollment, especially since World War II. During the 130 years from 1840 to 1970, enrollment in institutions of higher education rose 417 times, as compared with 12 times for population.

Roger Freeman estimates that in the last 20 years expenditures on education in constant dollars have risen 472 percent, while total consumption expenditures have risen 111 percent. Our educational outlays, in his view, may well equal those of the rest of the world.

What accounts for this tremendous rise in enrollment in higher education? The large increase in the percentage of the population graduating from high school has been a *sine qua non* for the spectacular escalation of enrollment in higher education. In the years from 1910 to 1968, the proportion of adults aged 25 and over who had graduated from high school increased from 13.5 to 52.6 percent, while the proportion who had graduated from college rose from 2.7 to 10.5 percent. The ratio of the former to the latter percentage was 5.0 both in 1910 and 1968.

The enormous increase in expenditures on higher education reflects the combined effects of enrollment increases and rising costs per student. One might expect a decline in the cost per student as the number of students per institution of higher education increased greatly. But this is not what happened. General inflationary trends in the economy contributed to rising costs per student. Moreover, higher education does not tend to experience gains in productivity, which might offset the inflationary pressures. In this respect, higher education resembles other service industries, in which price increases tend to be more pronounced than in goods industries. This is related to the fact that productivity increases have been much more pronounced in goods industries than in service industries.

1

Also relevant is the changing quality of the product. Over the years, colleges and universities have assumed increased responsibilities which have tended to raise overall expenditures. On a per-student basis, expenditures in higher education have tended to rise more rapidly than the cost of living, while total expenditures have tended to rise more rapidly than the gross national product. However, over a period of about 75 years, the cost per student has not risen as much as per capita income, an indication that higher education is not fully sharing the gains of the overall economy.

How does one explain the exceptionally rapid increase in enrollment from about one-half million after World War I to about 10 million estimated for the late 1970s? Clearly the increase in the college-age population is an important part of the explanation. But even more important is the increased percentage of the college-age population enrolled in institutions of higher education. The generally known fact that higher education contributes to lifetime incomes stimulates rising enrollment. Moreover, the amount by which the average income of college graduates exceeds that of high school graduates, on an annual or a lifetime basis, seems to be about as large as it was 20 years ago. This relationship may change in the future, however. As the annual number of college graduates approaches the million mark in the late 1970s, the ratio of the average income of college graduates to that of high school graduates may decline, reflecting reduced material gains from higher education. But the cultural gains may well tend to become a relatively more important part of the overall benefits of higher education.

There have been other factors, also, that have stimulated increases in enrollment. Family incomes are at a level which permits increased discretionary expenditures for education, medical care, travel, and the like. Increased expenditures for student aid have likewise played a role. Even as late as 1959–60, expenditures for student aid amounted to less than $200 million. By 1965–66, expenditures for this purpose had risen to almost one-half billion dollars. In a 1969 report to the President, an advisory committee to the Secretary of Health, Education and Welfare (Alice M. Rivlin, chairman) recommended $6.3 billion additional federal aid to higher education by 1976, with about two-thirds of this amount to be devoted to financial aid to students. The Carnegie Commission has recommended a similar expansion of student aid. The effectiveness of such funds can be greatly increased if the funds are allocated in such a manner as to make the maximum difference between enrolling and not enrolling.

Along with increased student aid, student loans are playing an increasingly important role. In fact, they are the fastest-growing ingredient in the student aid basket. Once the capital market becomes more normal, the long-term loan may well provide the means for any high school student of modest ability to go to the college of his choice. The student's four-year stint in college will be financed over 20, 30, or even 40 years—a period tending to match the period during which he or she benefits from higher education.

Other influences have also been significant. Increased support for public higher education has played an extremely important role. At the turn of the century, enrollment in public institutions of higher education was only 38 percent of total enrollment, but it is estimated that in the late 1970s public institutions will account for about 80 percent of total enrollment. In terms of numbers, this would represent an increase from 91,000 to 8,000,000 in public institutions. The increased tendency to go on to graduate education has been another important factor, with enrollment of graduate students approaching 1 million. Increased availability of junior colleges has helped stimulate a rapid increase in enrollment in two-year colleges, which by 1970 exceeded 2 million. Junior colleges attract students who want higher education but are unable or unwilling to make long-term commitments. Similarly, the rising importance of large urban universities, which especially cater to part-time students and are located in metropolitan areas in which population is rising rapidly, has played a significant role. Community colleges and urban institutions are within easy reach of students. It is well to recall that students living within 25 miles of a college are twice as likely to go to college as those living beyond 25 miles.

Recent evidence suggests that inadequacy of funds may not be the major deterrent to enrollment in higher education. An Office of Education study suggested that lack of motivation might be a more important factor. It showed that students in the lowest socioeconomic quartile enrolled in college in much smaller numbers than those in the top socioeconomic quartile. In view of the large public subsidy for students attending public institutions, this means that low-income groups are subsidizing those with high incomes through the taxes they pay. It is true that the student from a low-income family meets a much larger share of his needs through student aid programs, but the total amounts involved are far smaller than the public subsidies benefiting the large number of students from families in the highest socioeconomic quartile. Thus income is transferred from the poor to the rich.

A widely quoted study by Hansen and Weisbrod showed that, in the financing of public higher education in California, income is transferred from the poor to the rich. In 1964, the average income of the families of University of California students was $12,000; the subsidy made available to the student, who at that time paid no tuition, was the full cost of his education, estimated at $1,700; state and local taxes paid for all services by the student's family averaged $910; and thus the net transfer amounted to $790.

The difference in the cost of higher education for students in the highest socioeconomic quartile as compared with the costs for those in the lowest quartile is small indeed compared with the difference in average family income.

In the country as a whole, 18 percent of the families with students in college in 1966 had incomes of $15,000 or more, while 45 percent had incomes of $10,000 or more. Yet 46 percent of the college-age population in the top 18 percent of families attended public institutions of higher education and paid tuition of $500 or less — a bargain indeed.

In providing aid to higher education, the government may favor the student or the institution. Thus far students have been the recipients of more aid than institutions, but of course the major subsidies take the form of the excess of educational costs per student over tuition paid. In recent years tuition has amounted to about 40 percent of education costs in higher education as a whole.

In helping the student directly through student aid, government facilitates the financing of the student. If aid is channeled to institutions, the net result is to make institutions of higher education more viable. They may then improve the quality of their product, reduce tuition, increase admissions, and/or, in the case of private institutions, cut deficits. As institutions of higher education are increasingly confronted with budgetary crises, the pressure increases for the states to aid private institutions directly, while continuing to support public institutions, and for the federal government to provide institutional aid. As enrollments rise and costs increase more than tuition, the threat to the survival of institutions of higher education grows.

The difficulties of private institutions of higher education have become acute. Increased competition for students from public institutions of higher education, as the dollar gap between private and public tuition widens, is a major factor. Reduced relative help from endowment is another. As private institutions increasingly draw their students from low-income families, their capacity to attract gifts is impaired. All these factors help to explain the dilemma of the private institutions.

Moreover, private institutions suffer from a failure to increase the student-faculty ratio as enrollment expands and do not profit as much from economies of scale as do public institutions. A major reason for both of these phenomena is that graduate students, whose education is relatively costly, represent a larger proportion of all students in private institutions than in public institutions. But the absolute number of graduate students enrolled per institution is much smaller in private institutions than in public institutions. Hence unit costs of education are likely to be relatively high in private institutions.

Removal of financial constraints on students would increase costs of instruction by enabling more students to attend full time. An Office of Education study for 1966–67 estimated college tuition and fees at $500 and the cost of instruction per student at $1,500. If all potential students were to attend full time, class hours would rise by 40 percent, and tuition would have to rise to $780 or to more than half of the cost of instruction per student. Those not receving student aid would pay more in relation to educational costs.

An estimate by the author based largely on trends in enrollment and in per capita disposable income from 1940 to 1978–79 indicates that total revenue from tuition in 1978–79 would amount to $11.4 billion, subject to reductions for student aid, which is estimated to rise to $2 to $4 billion. Over this span of 38 to 39 years, average tuition would rise from $135 to $1,343, enrollment from 1.5 million to 10 million, and total tuition income from $200 million to $11.4 billion. In view of the projected rise in enrollment and increased capacity to finance higher education as per capita disposable income rises, a total net tuition bill of $8.4 billion ($11.4 billion minus $3 billion for aid) does not seem out of line.

The remainder of this introductory section will summarize the salient facts presented in successive sections of the volume.

The most important factors that determine enrollment in institutions of higher education are occupation and income of parents, aptitude and scholastic record at high school, and environmental conditions, including the size of the town in which the high school attended by the student is located.

Variations in some of these factors by type and control of institution are wide:

Variations in selected factors influencing enrollment, by type and control of institution, 1965–66

	Select private institutions	Other private institutions	Select public institutions	Other public institutions
Percentage of students with average grade of A in secondary schools	39	16	27	12
Percentage with fathers who were college graduates	27	21	24	16
Estimated median income of parents	$13,750	$10,500	$11,000	$8,500

The data show clearly that select institutions, and especially select private institutions, tend to attract relatively more able students and relatively more students from high-income families than less select institutions. In view of the fact that median income of all families in 1965–66 was less than $7,500, the data also indicate that college students tend to come from families with above-average incomes.[1]

The importance of high school grades is emphasized by a comparison of percentile rank in high school graduating class and probability of entering and of graduating from college.[2]

Percentile rank in high school graduating class	*Percentage of high school graduates who enter college*	*Percentage of college entrants who graduate*	*Percentage of high school graduates who graduate from college*
81–100	53	82	43
1–20	17	26	4

[1] College Entrance Examination Board, *The Economics of Higher Education,* New York, 1967, p. 150.

[2] D. Wolfle, *America's Resources of Specialized Talent,* report of the Commission on Human Resources and Advanced Training, Harper & Brothers, New York, 1954, p. 150.

The fathers' occupation greatly influences the probability of going to college. Among children with professional and semiprofessional parents, 67 percent of high school graduates enter college; among those with factory, craftsmen, and unskilled parents, only 26 percent enter.[3]

It is often said that highly talented students have no trouble in getting to college. Yet 12 separate studies have shown that substantial numbers of able students do not go to college. Thus Wolfle's study in the early 1950s showed that 45 percent of the top 8.8 percent of high school graduates in terms of ability did not attend college.

GRADUATE STUDENT CHARACTERISTICS

Graduate students in arts and science tend to come from families with lower incomes, lower occupational status, and lower educational achievement than law or medical students.[4]

Graduate students experience much the same financial problems as undergraduates. Lack of funds is probably the most important deterrent to going to graduate school and the most significant factor accounting for dropping out, as well as the most potent cause of the long period of preparation for the Ph.D. The long delays in getting the Ph.D. greatly increase the financial burden on graduate students and their families.[5]

PROFILE OF 1961 COLLEGE GRADUATES

The great majority of 1961 college graduates were white, single, native-born, and aged 21 or younger. Males accounted for 60 percent of the total. The proportion who were women was much smaller at the doctorate level than at the baccalaureate level.

The income and occupational distributions of the families of these 1961 graduates were similar to those of all college students. Their incomes were higher than average; the occupation of their fathers was especially likely to be in the professional or managerial

---

[3] A. H. Halsey, J. Flound, and C. A. Anderson (eds.), *Education, Economy and Society,* The Free Press of Glencoe, Inc., New York, 1961, pp. 230, 349; and C. C. Cole, Jr., *Encouraging Scientific Talent,* College Entrance Examination Board, New York, 1956, p. 147.

[4] B. Berelson, *Graduate Education in the United States,* McGraw-Hill Book Company, New York, 1960, p. 154.

[5] U.S. Office of Education, *Students and Buildings: An Analysis of Selected Federal Programs for Higher Education,* 1968, p. 64; and U.S. House of Representatives, Committee on Science and Astronautics, *Higher Education in the Sciences in the United States,* report of the Subcommittee on Science, Research and Development, prepared by the National Science Foundation, 1965, p. 7.

group; about 60 percent were Protestant, 25 percent were Roman Catholic, and 8 percent were Jewish. Incomes of families were correlated positively with parents' educational achievement.[6]

Most students — 94 percent — approved of their college. The major objective was to get a basic general education and an appreciation of ideas, but the typical student was also greatly interested in having a good time.[7]

Undoubtedly a similar poll in 1970 would reveal more dissatisfaction.

STUDENT EXPENSES

Student costs have not always varied consistently over time with capacity of families to pay. Thus from 1928 to 1940 costs rose relatively more than average family disposable income; from 1940 to 1952 costs lagged behind income; and from 1952 to 1964 major costs for state residents in public institutions rose somewhat less than family income, but costs in private institutions rose much more. In fact, costs in private institutions escalated. In 1952, the ratio of costs in private to costs in public institutions was 1.58, but by 1964 it had risen to 1.96, and there was much evidence of a declining competitive position of private institutions of higher education.[8]

However, some changes that were occurring tended to result in a reduced financial burden on students and their families that is not revealed by a comparison of changes in average income and costs. From 1940 to 1964, the proportion of students from families with incomes of $10,000 or more rose from one-half to three-fourths; and the number of students from families with incomes of $10,000 or more increased from 400,000 to 1,800,000. However, the impact of this last change on the financial burden was offset somewhat by an increase in the number of students per family in institutions of higher education.[9]

In 1966–67, costs of higher education per student in four-year private institutions varied from 1.10 times mean family income in the lowest socioeconomic quartile to 0.16 times in the highest quartile, while for four-year public institutions the corresponding variation was from 0.67 to 0.10 times.

[6] J. A. Davis, *Undergraduate Career Decisions: Correlates of Occupational Choice,* Aldine Publishing Company, Chicago, 1965, p. 193.

[7] Ibid., p. 199.

[8] College Entrance Examination Board, *The Economics of Higher Education,* New York, 1967, pp. 2, 8, and table 2.

[9] Ibid., table 2.

In 1965–66, graduate students accounted for 11 percent of enrollment, 19 percent of degrees, and 24 percent of student aid. In general, costs for graduate students were much higher in private than in public institutions of higher education. Living expenses tended to be higher for married than for unmarried graduate students. They were also higher for part-time than for full-time graduate students, reflecting the fact that part-time students were frequently employed full time and had higher incomes.[10]

In the years 1960–61, 1966–67, and 1976–77 (estimated), tuition accounted for nearly 20 percent of the income of public and 70 percent of the income of private institutions of higher education. The loss of competitive strength of private institutions of higher education is suggested by the rising dollar gap between private and public tuition in these three years— $672, $972, and $1,428, respectively.[11]

STUDENT AID Over a recent period of 25 years, the number of stipends to students increased three times, and the average amount of the stipend increased from $133 to $339.

A special committee of the U.S. Department of Health, Education and Welfare (Alice M. Rivlin, chairman) estimated in its 1969 report that enrollment could be increased by 795,000 if student aid were increased by $812 million. The Committee estimated the cost of 1.5 million federal awards at $892 million and recommended an increase by 1971 to 2.5 million awards at a cost of $1,815 million. At the time the committee's report was being prepared, in 1968, only one-fourth of the students in higher education were being helped. The committee recommended an increase in total federal aid to higher education of $6 billion by 1976, with about two-thirds of the increase going to students and one-third to institutions of higher education.[12]

In 1966–67, 44 percent of the financial needs of students from

[10] U.S. Office of Education, *Digest of Educational Statistics, 1968,* 1968, p. 72; and U.S. Office of Education, *Financial Statistics of Institutions of Higher Education: Current Funds, Revenues and Expenditures, 1965–66,* National Center for Educational Statistics, 1969, p. 4.

[11] U.S. Department of Health, Education and Welfare, *Accomplishments 1963–1968, Problems and Challenges, and a Look to the Future,* report to President Lyndon B. Johnson, December 1968, p. 8.

[12] U.S. Department of Health, Education and Welfare, *Toward a Long-range Plan for Federal Financial Support for Higher Education,* report to the President, Office of Assistant Secretary for Planning and Evaluation, January 1969, table 5.

families in the lowest socioeconomic quartile were covered by grants, 23 percent by work-study funds, and 27 percent by loans, with 94 percent of students in this socioeconomic quartile receiving one or more of these forms of aid. Among students from families in the second highest socioeconomic quartile, only 31 percent received aid in any of these forms.[13] All in all, about $1 billion of needs were not covered, but the extent of uncovered need was much smaller for students from families in the lowest socioeconomic quartile than for those from families in higher quartiles:[14]

	Amount per student	*Total amount*
Lowest socioeconomic quartile	$ 83	$ 25 million
Third socioeconomic quartile	$724	$480 million
Second socioeconomic quartile	$502	$575 million

In the mid-1960s, it was estimated that by 1970 total undergraduate costs would amount to $9.6 billion, ability to pay to $6.2 billion, and the deficit to $3.4 billion. The deficit was estimated at $2.25 billion for private four-year institutions, $1.09 billion for public four-year institutions, and $5 million for two-year colleges.[15] These estimates again tend to underscore the serious financial problems of private institutions of higher education.

Students from families in the lowest socioeconomic quartile accounted for 7 percent of the total full-time undergraduate population in 1966–67, while students from families in the highest socioeconomic quartile accounted for 48 percent. In terms of numbers the latter group was seven times as large as the former. Or, to put it differently, if students in all four quartiles were equally likely to enroll, the share of those from families in the highest socioeconomic quartile would be 25 percent as compared with the actual 48 percent, while the share of those from the lowest quartile would likewise be 25 percent as compared with the actual 7 per-

[13] U.S. Office of Education, *Students and Buildings: An Analysis of Selected Federal Programs for Higher Education,* 1968, pp. 17–18.

[14] Ibid., pp. 18–19, 59.

[15] U.S. House of Representatives, Committee on Education and Labor, *Higher Education Act of 1965, Hearings before the Special Subcommittee on Education,* February–May 1965, tables 4, 5, 6, and p. 727.

cent. If high school achievement is held constant, the rate of entry into higher education is related to ability to pay.[16]

In addition to the problem of inadequate funds for student aid, there is also a problem of maldistribution. A recent study revealed that 50 institutions of higher education, less than 3 percent of the total, accounted for 35 percent of the scholarship funds. Private institutions of higher education have disproportionate amounts of aid funds, which assists them in strengthening their position vis-à-vis public institutions, which are in a strong position to compete for students because of their low tuition charges. In 1963–64, private institutions of higher education, with 36 percent of the students, accounted for 55 percent of the expenditures on student aid.[17]

The Educational Opportunity Bank (EOB), as proposed by Zacharias and others, has great promise as an instrument for facilitating the financing of students. One of its great advantages is that it can spread the financing of higher education over a period of at least 30 to 40 years—the period over which benefits accrue—instead of concentrating the financing within two to seven years of attendance. On the basis of the experience of the 1960s, the annual average rate of increase of incomes was high enough to result in their increasing tenfold in 50 years. This means that the EOB greatly reduces the burden of financing because repayments are made out of rising incomes. Only if there is a return to a normal capital market, however, is there likely to be substantial use of the EOB type of plan.[18]

GRADUATE STUDENT AID Approximately 9 percent of the 2,000 graduate students had fellowships in 1890, as compared with 7 percent of the 314,000 in 1960. But when allowance is made for other types of aid, it is found that many more of the current graduate students receive aid. In 1968, 40 percent of the full-time graduate students had fellowships from

[16] Ibid., p. 22.

[17] Table 1.5-28; R. G. Moon, Jr., *Student Financial Aid in the United States: Administration and Resources,* College Entrance Examination Board, Princeton, N.J., 1963, p. 11; and U.S. Office of Education, *College Aid for Students,* 1963, p. 3.

[18] K. Shell et al., "The Educational Opportunity Bank: An Economic Analysis of a Contingent Repayment Loan Program for Higher Education," *National Tax Journal,* vol. 21, no. 1, March 1968, especially secs. 1, 4, 5, 6, and pp. 46–86.

federal sources, while 10 percent had help from other sources. With graduate education costing about $4,500 per student a year at present and an estimated $8,000 in 10 years, and in view of the large contribution of graduate training to the national welfare, the case for sizable increases in student aid to graduate students is strong. However, changing supply and demand conditions in the market for holders of advanced degrees must be kept in mind.[19]

The Office of Education has estimated the amount of stipends required to induce part-time graduate students to attend full time. It was found, for example, that 22 percent of the respondents (in 1963) would move to full-time status on receipt of a tuition scholarship and $4,000.[20]

Estimates indicated that in 1968, 1969, and 1974, graduate students would require $704, $980, and $1,330 in aid, with the federal government providing roughly two-thirds.[21]

Data for 1965 indicate that stipends were held disproportionately by males, the young, students without dependents, students in universities (three times the number in other institutions, relatively), students in large institutions, and foreigners.[22]

The distribution of fellowships in relation to the output of doctorates is uneven. Engineering, for example, received 11.1 percent of the value of fellowships and only 6.4 percent of earned doctorates in a recent year. Education, with only 4.6 percent of the value of fellowships, received 17 percent of the doctorates.[23]

ENROLLMENT POPULATION AND EDUCATIONAL ATTAINMENT In the next 30 years or so, the nonwhite population will increase substantially as a proportion of the total population, as will the population in metropolitan areas. Because the educational achievement of nonwhites is below that of whites, it might be assumed

[19] Association of American Universities, *The Federal Funding of Higher Education,* Washington, D.C., 1968, p. 16; cf. A. M. Cartter and R. L. Farrell, "Academic Labor Market Projections and the Draft," *The Economics and Financing of Higher Education in the United States,* a compendium of papers submitted to the Joint Economic Committee, U.S. Congress, 1969, pp. 357–396.

[20] U.S. Office of Education, *Students and Buildings: An Analysis of Selected Federal Programs for Higher Education,* 1968, pp. 26, 62.

[21] Ibid., p. 72.

[22] J. S. Hunter, *The Academic and Financial Status of Graduate Students, Spring, 1965,* U.S. Office of Education, 1967, pp. 25, 35.

[23] J. L. Chase, *Doctoral Study: Fellowships and Capacity of Graduate Schools,* U.S. Office of Education, 1961, p. 19.

that the relative rise of the nonwhite population would depress pressures on higher education. But there are some indications that the educational achievement of nonwhites has been rising relatively more than that of whites in the last 30 to 40 years, although this is not exactly clear at the more advanced levels. Educational facilities are more adequate in relatively populated areas, and thus the relative rise of the population of metropolitan areas tends to contribute to rising demands for higher education.[24]

That educational achievement is on the rise is revealed by the increase in the average number of years of schooling of the adult population, and by the much higher average educational achievement of sons than of their fathers and of the young than of the old. But in evaluating gains in educational achievement, we need to take into account the great advances in technology and capital, without which the contribution to economic growth would have been much smaller. These in turn are related to the steady rise of income and the changing attitude towards education.[25]

CHANGES IN ENROLLMENT Over a period of almost 100 years, resident degree-credit enrollment rose 27 times as much as the number of institutions and 17 times as much as the number of degrees. The resulting rise in the average size of institutions clearly contributed to a more economical level of operation.[26]

Between 1960 and 1970, graduate enrollment rose 1.7 times as much as undergraduate enrollment in four-year institutions of higher education, but the increase in enrollment in two-year institutions was even more spectacular: a rise of 2.6 times as much as undergraduate enrollment in four-year institutions.[27] However, the cost of graduate instruction per student is several times that for junior college students, and hence the relatively rapid rise in

---

[24] U.S. Bureau of the Census, *Statistical Abstract of the United States, 1967*, 1967, p. 10.

[25] J. K. Folger and C. B. Nam, *Education of the American Population*, a 1960 Census Monograph, U.S. Office of Education, 1967, pp. 132, 137–139, 147–148; U.S. Bureau of the Census, "Educational Attainment: March 1966 and 1965," *Population Characteristics, Current Population Reports*, ser. P-20, no. 158, 1966, p. 7; U.S. Office of Education, *Digest of Educational Statistics, 1968*, 1968, p. 9; and S. J. Mushkin (ed.), *Economics of Higher Education*, U.S. Office of Education, 1962, p. 101.

[26] U.S. Office of Education, unpublished tables on enrollment.

[27] The U.S. Office of Education enrollment reports classify all institutions as either two-year or four-year institutions.

graduate enrollment helps to account for large increases in educational costs per student.[28] Graduate enrollment rose from 356,000 in 1960 to an estimated 946,000 in 1970 and is projected by the Office of Education to rise to 1,640,000 by 1979. However, relatively more graduate students than undergraduates are enrolled on a part-time basis, and thus the increase in graduate enrollment relative to undergraduate enrollment has not been as great on a full-time equivalent basis.

The ratio of resident graduate students to population varies greatly by region. Thus, in 1954, the Northeast accounted for 37 percent and the South for 20 percent of graduate enrollment. Yet population was about one-third larger in the South than in the Northeast. The ratio of graduate enrollment to population in the South was only about 40 percent as large as the ratio in the Northeast.[29]

The capacity of institutions of higher education tends to be higher in heavily populated areas, i.e., in the standard metropolitan areas, than in less populated areas. However, the largest standard metropolitan areas tend to have relatively small capacity per 1,000 population. Deficient capacity in the ghettos undoubtedly contributes to this result.[30]

DEGREES   The ratio of the number of degrees awarded to enrollment (D/E ratio) has tended to decrease since the latter part of the nineteenth century. The D/E ratio depends on many factors: attrition, part-time enrollment as a proportion of the total, and relative enrollment in four-year undergraduate curricula as compared with graduate, professional, and two-year college curricula. An increase in part-time enrollment as a proportion of the total contributes to a decrease in D/E.[31]

Differentiation of product as indicated by the number of types of

[28] U.S. Office of Education, *Digest of Educational Statistics, 1968,* 1968, p. 20.

[29] National Science Foundation, *Graduate Student Enrollment and Support in American Universities and Colleges,* 1957, table III-3.

[30] U.S. Office of Education, *Students and Buildings: An Analysis of Selected Federal Programs for Higher Education,* 1968, p. 43.

[31] U.S. Office of Education, *Digest of Educational Statistics, 1968,* 1968, pp. 16, 69; U.S. Office of Education, *Projections of Educational Statistics to 1977–78,* National Center for Educational Statistics, 1968, pp. 19, 31; U.S. Office of Education, *Students Enrolled for Advanced Degrees, Fall 1967: Part A: Summary Data,* National Center for Educational Statistics, 1969, pp. 7, 11; and Table 2.2-13.

degrees indicates uneconomical operation. In a period of 318 years, institutions of higher education have awarded 2,452 different types of earned degrees; and there are more than 1,600 still being awarded. This proliferation of degrees must be exceedingly costly to the overall efficiency of higher education.

On the basis of projections of the proportion of the population with an elementary education in 1980, it is apparent that the proportion will have changed very little since 1950. However, the projections indicate large relative gains for those with a high school education and even larger gains for those with a college education. Rising educational achievement is explained in part by the changing occupational structure, which is associated with an increasing demand for higher levels of educational achievement.

INSTITUTIONS OF HIGHER EDUCATION

The ratio of student places to enrollment tends to be especially large for institutions with relatively small enrollments. In other words, the uneconomical operations of small institutions are suggested by their relatively high student place–enrollment ratios.

Ratios of percentages of enrollment to percentages of institutions vary greatly by type of institution and also point to the greater economies of the relatively large institutions. Thus in 1967 universities' share of total enrollment was 5.28 times as great as their share of the number of institutions; for liberal arts colleges, the share of enrollment was only 76 percent of the share of institutions.

Private institutions of higher education appeared to be benefiting less from economies of scale in 1967 than public institutions. Thus 27 percent of private institutions had enrollments of less than 500, and 47 percent had enrollments of less than 1,000. Among public institutions of higher education, only 17 percent had enrollments of less than 500.[32]

ENROLLMENT IN RELATION TO POPULATION

Enrollment rises both because of increases in the college-age population and because of a rise in the percentage of the college-age population enrolled in institutions of higher education. Over recent decades, the latter has accounted for a larger share of the rise in enrollment than the former.

How many attend institutions of higher education depends especially on the number of high school graduates as a proportion of the population aged 17. In a period of almost 100 years this

[32] U.S. Office of Education, *Digest of Educational Statistics, 1968,* 1968, p. 85.

proportion rose from 2 to 76 percent. From 1957–58 to 1967–68, the number of high school graduates increased 80 percent; but in the following 10 years the number of high school graduates is projected to increase only about 33 percent. This suggests reduced pressure on higher education.[33]

DROPOUTS The problem of dropouts is a matter of great concern because dropouts are screened out of opportunities for many types of jobs by employers' requirements for a bachelor's degree as a condition of eligibility. To some extent the problem has become more serious over the years because employers' education requirements have been rising—in some cases beyond what is genuinely needed.

In addition to the problem of deficiency of training in relation to requirements, a problem of a potential excess in the numbers seeking high level occupations is also relevant. If, for example, by the late 1970s a million B.A.'s are turned out in a year, a serious surplus may develop if the demand for B.A.'s does not increase commensurately with the supply. The result may then be relatively reduced incomes and forced acceptance of jobs at occupational levels below their expectations for the highly educated. Alternatively, the relative position of the highly educated might not deteriorate if educational requirements were to rise commensurately with the supply of B.A.'s. Still a third possibility would be a relative improvement in their position if educational requirements rose more rapidly than the supply of B.A.'s.[34]

ENROLLMENT AND EDUCATIONAL ATTAINMENT: INTERNATIONAL COMPARISONS In the 1950s enrollment in institutions of higher education throughout the world rose relatively more than the number of institutions. Increases in both the number of institutions and enrollment were especially large for underdeveloped countries. For example, in Asia there was a 240 percent increase in the number of institutions of higher education, as compared with 38 percent in Western Europe and 33⅓ percent in North America.[35]

A comparison of ratios of enrollment to population for years around 1960 shows that North America had an especially high ratio

[33] Ibid., p. 70; and Table 2.5-1.

[34] J. K. Folger and C. B. Nam, *Education of the American Population,* a 1960 Census Monograph, U.S. Bureau of the Census, 1967, pp. 71–72; and U.S. Bureau of the Census, *Statistical Abstract in the United States, 1968,* 1968, p. 113.

[35] F. Bowles, *Access to Higher Education,* UNESCO, Paris, 1963, vol. 1, p. 113.

in relation to other areas at the third (higher education) level and a considerably lower ratio at the first (primary) level. In the case of higher education, the ratio for North America was 3.25 times the ratio for the world as a whole, whereas at the primary level it was only 1.45 times the ratio for the world as a whole. The U.S.S.R. and Europe followed North America at the third level.[36]

With respect to proportions of the relevant age groups enrolled, the United States is far in the lead in higher education. Data for 1965 indicate that enrollment in higher education amounted to 41 percent of the relevant age group in the United States. Canada followed with 24 percent, and France was third with 17 percent. Other Western European countries, such as Belgium, Denmark, West Germany, Italy, the Netherlands, Sweden, and the United Kingdom, had proportions ranging from 10 to 15 percent.[37]

In one respect, the record of the United States is relatively disappointing. The proportion of qualified high school graduates who enter higher education is much lower in the United States than in Western Europe.[38] However, this reflects in part the far greater selectivity of secondary schools in Western Europe. In France and West Germany, for example, qualified secondary school leavers represent relatively small proportions of the relevant age group, but nearly all go on to higher education.

In comparison with four major Western European countries, the United States leads most decisively with respect to the ratio of the relevant age group qualified for admission to higher education — the United States ratio is 12 times that for these countries. However, for entrants the United States ratio is only seven times as large, and for first degrees only five to six times as large. These relationships indicate relatively large attrition rates for students moving through institutions of higher education in the United States.[39]

Plans for the development of higher education in the U.S.S.R. have called for a large increase in enrollments in higher education

[36] U.S. Office of Education, *Digest of Educational Statistics, 1968,* 1968, p. 121.

[37] Organization for Economic Cooperation and Development, *Development of Higher Education, 1960–1967: Analytical Report,* OECD Publications, Paris, 1970, p. 67.

[38] Organization for Economic Cooperation and Development, *Resources of Scientific and Technical Personnel in the O.E.C.D. Areas,* OECD Publications, Paris, 1959, p. 44.

[39] Ibid., p. 65.

between 1950 and 1985. An increase in average years of schooling from 6.5 years for 1967 to 7.9 years for 1985 was projected. But United States data showed average years of schooling of 9.3 years in 1950, 10.5 years in 1960, and 12 in early 1967.[40]

The ratio of enrollment in higher education in the United States to the population in the relevant age group is 4.45 times that of the U.S.S.R., but the United States leads the U.S.S.R. by a much smaller margin at the elementary level—there the United States ratio is only 1.11 times that of the Soviet Union.[41]

THE FACULTY IN HIGHER EDUCATION The number of faculty members per institution of higher education increased from 10 in 1870 to 279 in 1963. Part of the explanation of the fact that costs per student rose despite the rising average size of institutions—i.e., even though one would have expected increased average size to result in economies of scale—may be the rise in the number of schools within universities. However, a major factor was inflationary pressures.[42]

SCIENTIFIC MANPOWER The number of scientists has been increasing at a very rapid rate in the last few decades; and the share employed by institutions of higher education has risen steadily. Thus, from 1940 to 1963, the total labor force increased 35 percent, but the number of scientists increased 245 percent. The ratio of population to engineers has been estimated at 480 to 1 in 1940; 210 to 1 in 1960; 114 to 1 in 1980; and 71 to 1 in the year 2000.

Whereas from 1962 to 1966 the proportion of all scientists employed by institutions of higher education rose 30 percent, there was a decline of 25 percent in the proportion employed in industry and of 33⅓ percent in the proportion employed in government. Clearly, educational institutions were competing increasingly successfully for scientific talent. Ph.D.'s tend to be especially

[40] U.S. Bureau of the Census, *Estimates and Projections of Educational Attainment in the U.S.S.R., 1950–1985,* International Population Reports, ser. P-91, 1967, p. 9; and U.S. Office of Education, *Digest of Educational Statistics, 1968,* 1968, p. 9.

[41] Organization for Economic Cooperation and Development, *Economic Aspects of Higher Education,* OECD Publications, Paris, 1964, p. 137.

[42] American Council on Education, *A Fact Book on Higher Education,* Washington, D.C., 1967, p. 234; and R. E. Dunham and P. S. Wright, *Faculty and Other Professional Staff in Institutions of Higher Education, First Term 1963-64,* final report, U.S. Office of Education, 1966, p. 5.

interested in employment in institutions of higher education and in other nonprofit institutions, and to prefer that type of employment to government employment.

MOBILITY OF FACULTY

Younger faculty members tend to be much more mobile than older faculty members, just as younger persons in other occupations tend to be more mobile than older persons. One study showed that instructors were 10 times as mobile as full professors.[43]

In general, students receiving Ph.D.'s in highly pretigious institutions of higher education tend to find positions in less prestigious institutions, but this reflects the fact that the number of emerging Ph.D.'s exceeds the number of openings in prestigious institutions. There is a good deal of hiring of each other's products by the prestigious institutions. In 1964–65, the top 20 institutions supplied 5,000 emerging Ph.D.'s but hired only 1,300.[44]

SUPPLY AND DEMAND

As the rate of increase in the size of an institutions's faculty declines, replacement tends to account for a rising share of the numbers needed to meet both enrollment increases and replacement. The relative contribution of expanded demand to the creation of vacancies varied as follows in 1964:[45]

By size of institution	
5,000 or more students	61 percent
Less than 1,000 students	31 percent
By type of institution	
Universities	52 percent
Colleges	44 percent
By control of institution	
Public	51 percent
Private	42 percent
By quality of institution	
Top 20 percent	52 percent
Bottom 20 percent	46 percent

[43] D. G. Brown, *The Mobile Professors,* American Council on Education, Washington, D.C., 1967, p. 39.

[44] Ibid., pp. 99–101.

[45] Ibid., p. 31.

The percentage of doctoral recipients going into teaching ranged from 23 percent in chemistry to 89 percent in English in 1962–63 and 1963–64. The long-run trend showed a substantial decline in the percentage of all holders of doctorates employed in institutions of higher education from 1900 to 1958 but a rise more recently.[46]

The highest-rated institutions in terms of quality tend to have the largest percentages of faculty members who are Ph.D.'s. A study published in 1967 indicated that in the top 20 percent of the institutions, 71 percent of the faculty held Ph.D.'s, whereas in the bottom 20 percent, only 32 percent held Ph.D.'s.[47]

The general shortage of Ph.D.'s in the years from 1953–54 to 1964–65 is indicated by a decline in the proportion of all faculty members with Ph.D.'s from 31 to 27 percent. In the fields that have been characterized by rapid growth, the decline has been especially pronounced—e.g., in the social sciences, from 42 to 28 percent; and in psychology, from 68 to 31 percent.

As suggested earlier, the increase in the demand for scientists, especially for research work, was particularly rapid in the period from about 1950 to 1966. In these years total employment of scientists and engineers rose 156 percent, while employment of scientists and engineers in research rose 242 percent. The general intense demand for skilled professional workers contributed to this result, but institutions of higher education gained absolutely and relatively.

FACULTY PAY Among the important problems confronting administrators of institutions of higher education have been decisions concerning the appropriate pay of faculty. The narrow range between salary rates of instructors and full professors, which was related to inadequate resources; the decline in real salaries in the World War II and early postwar period, as well as the surprisingly small real income of faculty members compared with earnings generally; the question of the appropriate level of expenditures for fringe benefits in relation to basic pay—these are some of the troublesome prob-

---

[46] U.S. House of Representatives, Committee on Government Operations, *Conflicts between the Federal Research Programs and the Nation's Goals for Higher Education,* hearings before a subcommittee, June 1965, p. 91; and B. Berelson, *Graduate Education in the United States,* McGraw-Hill Book Company, New York, 1960, p. 50.

[47] D. G. Brown, *The Mobile Professors,* American Council on Education, Washington, D.C., 1967, p. 18.

lems. The losses in real income from 1940 to the middle 1950s were recouped in part by the late 1960s, though the gain in the year 1968–69 was disappointing. By 1968 (on a 1939=100 base), the index of consumer prices was 250; average salaries in institutions of higher education, 370; and average salaries adjusted for price changes, 148.[48]

Outside earnings of faculty are not as large as is generally assumed. A large proportion of the faculty have some outside earnings, e.g., 74 percent of all faculty members in the academic year 1961–62, but average outside earnings in the early 1960s were only a little over $2,000—a total which is of the order of one-fifth of average compensation in that year.[49]

ALLOCATION OF TIME A widely held view is that faculty members spend a disproportionate amount of time on research and public service. Yet a recent survey reveals that faculty members spend 3½ times as much time on teaching as on research and 17 times as much on instructional activities as on public service.

Instructional activity, as measured by hours spent, tends to vary inversely with rank, whereas research hours vary directly with rank.[50]

INCOME OF INSTITUTIONS OF HIGHER EDUCATION In the years from 1909–10 to 1963–64, educational and general income of institutions of higher education rose by 107 times, while income from auxiliary enterprises rose by 180 times and from plant by 128 times. Thus the relative importance of income from auxiliary enterprises and from plant increased. On the other hand, endowment, rising by 21 times, and private gifts and grants, by 73 times, lost ground relatively as sources of income.[51]

[48] U.S. Department of Health, Education and Welfare, *Toward a Long-Range Plan for Federal Financial Support for Higher Education,* report to the President, Office of Assistant Secretary for Planning and Evaluation, January 1969, p. 10; and American Association of University Professors, "The Threat of Inflationary Erosion: The Annual Report on the Economic Status of the Profession, 1968–69," *AAUP Bulletin,* vol. 55, no. 2, Summer 1969, p. 294.

[49] R. E. Dunham, P. S. Wright, and M. O. Chandler, *Teaching Faculty in Universities and 4-Year Colleges, Spring 1963,* U.S. Office of Education, 1966, p. 41.

[50] R. L. Williams, *The Administration of Academic Affairs,* University of Michigan Press, Ann Arbor, Mich., 1965, p. 89; and H. Orlans, *The Effects of Federal Programs on Higher Education,* The Brookings Institution, Washington, D.C., 1962, p. 63.

[51] U.S. Office of Education, *Digest of Educational Statistics, 1968,* 1968, p. 95.

From 1882 to 1964, the federal government's share as a source of income for institutions of higher education increased greatly, while the share of state and local governments also rose, but relatively slightly after 1930. The share of tuition rose and then declined. From 1910 on, the share of auxiliary enterprises rose especially sharply, whereas the share of endowment declined precipitously.[52]

Major private universities tend to receive the lion's share of voluntary gifts. In 1967–68, they received 45 percent of voluntary gifts, as compared with only 17 percent for public universities and colleges. However, in the 11 years ending 1967–68, the share of public institutions rose sharply, by 92 percent, while the share of private institutions declined 9 percent.[53]

Shares of gifts compared with shares of enrollment vary greatly among types of institutions, as the following data for 1966–67 indicates:[54]

<table>
<tr><td rowspan="3">**Ratio of share of gifts to share of enrollment**</td><td colspan="2"></td></tr>
<tr><td>*Major private universities*</td><td>1.95</td></tr>
<tr><td>*Private men's colleges*</td><td>1.30</td></tr>
<tr><td>*Municipal and urban universities*</td><td>0.10</td></tr>
</table>

The distribution of functions for which gifts are intended varies greatly from the relative importance of those functions in current expenditures. For example, relative voluntary giving for research and instruction was far below the relative importance of these functions in 1963–64. On the other hand, the percentages of voluntary gift amounts intended for plant and maintenance and for student aid were roughly four times the share of current expenditures on these items.[55]

[52] U.S. Office of Education, *Report of the Commissioner of Education, 1889–90,* pp. 762–763; *1902,* p. 1353; *1903,* p. 1178; *1910,* p. 868; and U.S. Office of Education, *Higher Education Finances: Selected Trend and Summary Data,* National Center for Educational Statistics, June 1968, p. 3.

[53] Council for Financial Aid to Education, American Alumni Council, and National Association of Independent Schools, *Voluntary Support of Education, 1967–68,* New York, 1969, pp. 64, 67.

[54] S. E. Harris, *Higher Education: Resources and Finance,* McGraw-Hill Book Company, New York, 1962, p. 462.

[55] U.S. Office of Education, *Digest of Educational Statistics, 1968,* 1968, p. 76; and Council for Financial Aid to Education and American Alumni Council, *Voluntary Support of Education, 1966–67,* New York, 1968, p. 66.

In the years from 1950 to 1968, total federal grants-in-aid for all purposes rose about four times, but for education nine times.[56]

From 1959–60 to 1964–65, the appropriation of state funds for operating expenses of higher education rose from $1.39 to $2.44 billion. In general, Eastern states, with limited involvement in the financing of higher education in the past, reflecting the predominance of private higher education in the East, increased their expenditures especially rapidly in this period.[57]

Despite the large increases in its appropriations in recent years, the federal government still accounts for a small share of outlays for education. Of $50 billion of expenditures on education in 1966–67, the federal government provided only $6.2 billion.[58]

Important projections of need suggest requirements for annual increases of $1 to $1½ billion of federal funds for higher education over the next six to nine years. In these estimates of need, aid to students and aid to institutions both play an important role. However, the recommendations call for federal funds to be divided between student aid and institutions on the basis of a 2 to 1 ratio in favor of the former.[59]

In the 10 years from 1955–56 to 1965–66, federal government aid to institutions of higher education was primarily for research and for student aid. Largely for this reason income received for these purposes rose as a proportion of the total. On the other hand, income from auxiliary enterprises declined relatively. It is estimated that, by 1977, there will be comparative declines in income destined for research and for construction, reflecting the relatively greater emphasis expected to be placed on increases in student aid and in institutional grants. An argument in support of the need for

[56] U.S. Department of Labor, *U.S. Economic Report of the President, 1969,* 1969, p. 306; and U.S. Bureau of the Census, *Statistical Abstract of the United States, 1968,* 1968, p. 419.

[57] National Association of State Universities and Land Grant Colleges, *Appropriation of State Tax Funds for Operating Expenses of Higher Education, 1964–1965,* Washington, D.C., 1964.

[58] U.S. Bureau of the Census, *Governmental Finances in 1966–67,* Government Finances Series GF 67, no. 3, 1968, p. 8.

[59] Carnegie Commission on Higher Education, *The Capitol and the Campus: State Responsibility for Postsecondary Education,* McGraw-Hill Book Company, New York, 1971, p. 8; and U.S. Department of Health, Education and Welfare, *Toward a Long-Range Plan for Federal Financial Support for Higher Education,* report to the President, Office of Assistant Secretary for Planning and Evaluation, January 1969, p. 36.

institutional grants is that, as increased federal aid stimulates increased enrollment, resulting deficits of institutions of higher education will have to be averted by federal institutional grants.[60]

ENDOWMENT INCOME AND INVESTMENT POLICY The total book value of endowment of institutions of higher education is around $10 billion, and market value is about $12 billion. Over the entire period from 1890 on, as well as from 1939–40 on, endowment has declined in relation to the total value of property owned by institutions of higher education. In 1963–64, total endowment was more than three times as high as in 1939–40, but the value of property was almost six times as high.[61]

It is not surprising to find that high-income groups tend to give larger amounts, relative to their incomes, to institutions of higher education than do lower-income groups. Thus, the proportion of adjusted gross income given to institutions of higher education rose from 0.1 percent for those with incomes of $10,000 to $15,000 to 2.4 percent for those with incomes of $1 million or more in a recent year. It is also interesting to note that business corporations provided 4 percent of gifts for all purposes, but 16 percent of gifts to higher education, in 1960.[62]

The Carnegie Commission has estimated, on the basis of need, that unit costs in higher education will rise 5 percent a year in the nine years ending 1976–77, or 55 percent compounded over the period as a whole. It will not be easy to increase the higher education bill by 5 percent a year, or from 2 to 3 percent of the GNP in 10 years.[63]

In 1963–64, 46 percent of educational and general income of institutions of higher education, and 40 percent of educational and

[60] U.S. Office of Education, *Higher Education Finances: Selected Trend and Summary Data,* National Center for Educational Statistics, June 1968, p. 3; U.S. Office of Education, *Students and Buildings: An Analysis of Selected Federal Programs for Higher Education,* 1968, p. 10; and Figure 1.5-2.

[61] U.S. Office of Education, *Report of the Commissioner of Education,* various years.

[62] American Alumni Council, *Symposium: Taxation and Education,* February 1966, pp. 17, 18.

[63] Carnegie Commission on Higher Education, *Quality and Equality: New Levels of Federal Responsibility for Higher Education,* McGraw-Hill Book Company, New York, 1968, p. 8; and U.S. Office of Education, *Projections of Educational Statistics to 1977–78,* National Center for Educational Statistics, 1968, p. 12. I have been informed that the Carnegie Commission is developing new estimates which will reflect reduced rates of increase in expenditures if all its policy recommendations, including a shift to a three-year B.A., are adopted.

general income plus capital funds, came from private sources.[64] The relative importance of endowment as a source of income has declined steadily since the turn of the century. In 1909–10, endowment accounted for 17 percent of educational and general income; by 1963–64, it accounted for only 3 percent, despite a rise of endowment income in dollar terms from $13 to $266 million in these years.[65]

Endowment is still of great importance as a source of income for the institutions that have relatively large endowments — notably the large private universities and the relatively selective liberal arts colleges. In 1967, nine institutions of higher education with endowments in excess of $200 million had endowments totaling more than half those of the 70 institutions that followed in terms of amount of endowment.[66]

From 1939–40 to 1963–64, private gifts rose at an annual average rate of 7 percent. If this rate of increase continues, private gifts will have risen from $1,175 million in 1963–64 to $3 billion in 1977–78. This may be optimistic. We should note, however, that in the competition for private gifts public institutions of higher education are rapidly improving their relative position, as indicated earlier. The large rise of the GNP and of family income should be a factor encouraging continued rapid increases in the amount of private giving.[67]

Institutions have been rather cautious in turning to equities as a type of investment. From 1955 to 1964, the value of common stocks rose 100 percent, but institutions of higher education maintained their investment in equities at 55 percent of total investment.[68]

Much is to be said against the traditional principle that endowment funds should be inviolate — i.e., that only the income from

---

[64] U.S. Office of Education, *Digest of Educational Statistics, 1968,* 1968, p. 95.

[65] Ibid.

[66] U.S. Office of Education, *College and University Endowment: Status and Management,* 1966, pp. 4–5, 74–75; and W. G. Bowen, *The Economics of the Major Private Universities,* Carnegie Commission on Higher Education, Berkeley, Calif., 1968, p. 35. See also S. E. Harris, *The Economics of Harvard,* McGraw-Hill Book Company, New York, 1970, passim.

[67] W. G. Bowen, *The Economics of the Major Private Universities,* Carnegie Commission on Higher Education, Berkeley, Calif., 1968, pp. 42–47; and U.S. Office of Education, *Digest of Educational Statistics, 1968,* 1968, p. 95.

[68] U.S. Office of Education, *College and University Endowment: Status and Management,* 1966, p. 55.

these funds should be spent. With some restrictions, institutions of higher education should be permitted to include capital gains as a part of income.

One of the most controversial issues in managing the endowments of institutions of higher education relates to the manner of allocating investment income. Should it be allocated on the basis of book value or market value? Allocation on the basis of book value favors current over past gifts in periods of rising values of equities. In periods of rising values, then, capital gains have the effect of increasing disproportionately the value of the gifts of recent donors.[69]

TUITION From 1955–56 to 1965–66, tuition and required fees increased 53 percent, and board charges 38 percent, the small rise in the latter explained by an increase in income from board of only 10 percent. Enrollment rose 112 percent, and the rise in enrollment accounted for two-thirds of the total increase in tuition income. That the annual rate of increase in tuition and fees of private institutions was twice that of public institutions helps to explain the declining competitive position of private institutions. Moreover, the shift to public institutions, with their much lower tuition charges, tends to slow down the rate of increase in total tuition income. In a recent year, tuition amounted to 44 percent of current income in private institutions but only to 13 percent in public institutions.

The relationship of tuition charges to costs of education per student varies greatly among curricula, departments, and universities. Tuition charges tend to be high when expected incomes of graduates are high. But it should be noted that in one university, the tuition-cost ratio was 0.2 for medicine, 0.8 for law, and 1.1 for business administration.[70] The high cost of medical education would mean exceptionally high tuition costs for medical students if these variations did not prevail.

[69] W. L. Cary and C. E. Bright, *The Law and Lore of Endowment Funds,* Ford Foundation, New York, March 1969, p. 66; U.S. Office of Education, *College and University Endowment Investments: A Survey,* 1959, p. 20; and U.S. Office of Education, *College and University Endowment: Status and Management,* 1966, p. 55.

[70] J. D. Millett, *Financing Higher Education in the United States,* Columbia University Press, New York, 1952, pp. 147–149; and U.S. Office of Education, *Basic Student Charges, 1963–64,* National Center for Educational Statistics, 1964, p. 11.

Tuition rose as a proportion of educational and general income from 1920 to 1950, but after that it declined.[71] However, from 1959–60 to 1965–66, the annual average rate of increase in tuition income per student was 4 percent for public and 8 percent for private institutions.

It is possible to increase the yield from tuition without increasing the burden of tuition on students and their families. A simple and rough guide to accomplishing this is to increase tuition charges commensurately with increases in per capita disposable income, i.e., income after direct taxes. Over the years, large increases in tuition income would then be explained by the increased capacity to pay and by increases in enrollment. It may be estimated that, by 1979, per capita disposable income will be 7½ times, tuition per student 7⅕ times, and enrollment less than 6 times the corresponding magnitudes in 1940. The estimated rise in tuition charges is justified on the basis of the corresponding increase in per capita disposable income. The associated rough figures for tuition income are $202 million in 1940, $1,899 million in 1964, $3,646 million in 1969, and $8,611 million in 1979. One important reservation is necessary. On the average, there will be more students per family at institutions of higher education as enrollment rises, but helping to offset this is the greatly improved level of income.

Data for years from 1958 on and projections to 1978 show much higher costs for students in private than in public institutions of higher education. Charges for tuition and room and board were 80 percent higher in private than in public institutions, while tuition charges were four times as high in private institutions. It is estimated that by 1978, tuition charges will be five times as high in private as in public institutions.

EXPENDITURES *Libraries* Library expenditures represent about 3 percent of educational outlays of institutions of higher education—a modest percentage indeed in view of the large contribution of libraries to higher education. However, in recent years, libraries of institutions of higher education have been in financial difficulties. From 1959 to 1965 prices of books doubled, as compared with a rise in the consumer price index of only 31 percent.[72] From 1959–60 to 1964–65 total operating expenditures of these libraries increased

[71] S. E. Harris, *Higher Education: Resources and Finance,* McGraw-Hill Book Company, New York, 1962, tables 8-1 and 8-3.

[72] U.S. Office of Education, *Digest of Educational Statistics, 1968,* 1968, p. 123.

133 percent. This increase was attributable primarily to a rise of 112 percent in expenditures on wages and salaries and a rise of 172 percent in expenditures on books and materials.

Research   In 1959–60, institutions of higher education spent more than $1 billion on organized research. Of total amounts spent on organized research, institutions provided from their own funds 28 percent in 1954, 26 percent in 1959, and 18 percent in 1964. During this period federal support of research, of course, was rising rapidly. Thus the data suggest that, as government sources provide more, other sources of support dry up to some extent. Basic research accounted for 55 percent of expenditures of institutions of higher education on research and development in 1959 and 79 percent of these expenditures by 1964.[73]

Another significant aspect of expenditures for separately budgeted research is that, in relation to their shares of population, relative expenditures on research were considerably higher in the Northeast and the West than in other regions in 1964:

	Percentage of total United States population	Percentage of expenditures on separately budgeted research in colleges and universities
Northeast	25	32
North Central	28	25
South	31	21
West	17	21

SOURCE: Table 4.5-19.

Concentration by fields also varies greatly by region.

Physical plant   In 1963–64 expenditures on buildings to be used for instruction represented 52 percent of all expenditures on construction by institutions of higher education. However, the percentage so invested varied greatly by region.

In 1958, instructional facilities could have accommodated about one-half million more students, but when allowance is made for

[73] National Science Foundation, *Scientific Activities at Universities and Colleges, 1964,* 1968, p. 40.

bottlenecks in residential and in other kinds of facilities, the excess capacity would be reduced considerably below this figure.[74]

For the years 1965 to 1970, total expenditures for buildings and campus improvements have been estimated at $17 billion, with public outlays twice as large as private expenditures. Government appropriations and grants have been estimated to provide 39.4 percent and bonds 34.4 percent of the total.[75] Federal support of construction expenditures greatly increased between 1959 and 1964, while the share of state and local governments dropped. Expenditures on residential buildings increased relatively more than on other types of facilities; public expenditures more than private; and expenditures in the West and Southwest more than in other regions.[76]

Revenue bonds and appropriations represented the most important sources of construction funds for public institutions, while gifts and grants and revenue bonds constituted the most important sources for private institutions in 1963–64:[77]

Sources of construction funds of institutions of higher education, by control, 1963–64 (major items)	*Public, percent*	*Private, percent*
Appropriations	31.0	6.0
Tax levy	1.3	—
General obligation bonds	14.0	1.1
Revenue bonds	43.7	28.2
Gifts and grants	2.6	38.3
Current funds and endowment	2.5	8.5
Borrowed, commercial sources	2.3	11.8

For most types of institutions except junior colleges, the share of construction expenditures exceeded the share of total enrollment. Sources of financing varied with the type of facility involved.

[74] U.S. Office of Education, *College and University Facilities Survey,* issued as Department of Health, Education and Welfare circulars, 1959–1965, part 1, 1959, p. 15; part 2, 1960, p. 4.

[75] U.S. Office of Education, *College and University Enrollment and Physical Facilities Survey, 1965–70,* 1970, p. 4; U.S. Office of Education, *College and University Facilities Survey,* issued as Department of Health, Education and Welfare circulars, 1959–1965, part 2, 1960, p. 24; and Table 4.6-19.

[76] Figure 4.6-1; and L. F. Robbins, *New Construction and Rehabilitation on College Campuses, 1961–62, 1962–63, and 1963–64,* U.S. Office of Education, 1966, p. 27.

[77] Robbins, 1966, p. 24.

Another interesting point is that expenditures for new construction per student from 1961 to 1965 were 2½ times as large for the smallest institutions of higher education as for the largest institutions. Economies of scale in connection with construction expenditures are clear.[78]

An inventory of buildings in all institutions of higher education in 1957 indicated that 47 percent were used for residential purposes and that 52 percent were in public institutions. The inventory also provided data on the condition of buildings, the number of student spaces, and assignable area for students. Unsatisfactory conditions were found in 27 percent of the areas in public, and 13.5 percent of the areas in private institutions. Universities accounted for four times as large a proportion of buildings as other institutions of higher education.[79]

The largest increases in the supply of buildings for initial occupancy occurred after 1939. Another survey in 1965 indicated that 63.0 percent of the buildings in public, and 77.8 percent of the buildings in private, institutions were in satisfactory condition; 9.3 and 8.7 percent, respectively, required rehabilitation; and 27.2 and 13.5 percent, respectively, required razing. In general, as might be expected, conditions of buildings tended to improve with recency of initial occupation.[80]

Another relationship that would be expected is that the ratio of the estimated value of buildings to investment (V/I ratio) tends to be higher the farther back in time its initial occupancy. Thus V/I was 215 percent for initial occupancy in years prior to 1900 and 110 percent for initial occupancy from 1950 to 1957. General inflation, rising costs of construction, and the rise of property values associated with the growth of college and university communities help to explain this relationship.[81]

The average book value of buildings per institution ranged from $1.5 million for junior colleges to $49.0 million for universities; and from $1,887 per student in junior colleges to $5,084 for universities. The average book value for public institutions was $11.1 million and for private institutions $4.4 million; while the

[78] U.S. Office of Education, *College and University Facilities Survey,* issued as Department of Health, Education and Welfare circulars, 1959–1965, part 5, 1965, p. 35.

[79] Ibid., part 3, 1964, Highlights, and table 1-1, p. 21.

[80] Ibid., pp. 34–35, and tables 17 and 18, pp. 42–43.

[81] Ibid., table 4-1, p. 99.

average book values per student were $4,248 and $4,139, respectively.

From 1960 to 1964 the total book value of buildings rose $2 billion a year, or 57 percent; and the book value per student rose 19 percent.[82] By 1966 total book value had increased to $27 billion. The value of buildings in public institutions was 45 percent higher than in private institutions, but on a per-student basis the value of buildings was one-third higher in private institutions — $6,050 as compared with $4,561.[83]

The ratio of shares of planned expenditures on construction to shares of enrollment varied greatly by type of institution for the period 1961–65 — for universities the shares were 59 and 51 percent, respectively, and for private liberal arts colleges, 38 and 48 percent, respectively.[84]

Some general comments on physical plant expenditures Government agencies have provided substantial funds for the building of dormitories as well as of academic facilities. The result may well be excessive spending for buildings against outlays for faculty. Any categorical program tends to encourage excessive outlays on the item involved.

On the other hand, if an argument can be made that there is excessive spending for buildings, on certain other grounds it can be argued that there is inadequate spending for buildings. Given the large and rising demand for higher education, many institutions of higher education underinvest in buildings. They have excessive fears of making commitments for financing over the next 20 to 40 years. They tend especially to leave out of account the steady rise of the GNP, which will facilitate long-term financing. In fact, there is little careful consideration given to the relationship between

[82] F. H. I. Lindsay, *Financial Statistics of Institutions of Higher Education: Receipts, Expenditures, and Property, 1959-60*, U.S. Office of Education, National Center for Educational Statistics, 1964, p. 68.

[83] U.S. Office of Education, *Digest of Educational Statistics, 1967*, 1967, table 124; P. Mertens, *Financial Statistics of Institutions of Higher Education: Property, 1965-66*, U.S. Office of Education, National Center for Educational Statistics, 1969, pp. 10, 11; and U.S. Office of Education, *Projections of Educational Statistics to 1977-78*, National Center for Educational Statistics, 1968, pp. 16, 19.

[84] U.S. Office of Education, *College and University Facilities Survey*, issued as Department of Health, Education and Welfare circulars, 1959-1965, part 4, 1965, p. 50.

needs for large investments in buildings and their financing. The projected rise in construction is much below what is needed and can be financed in the long run.

With total plant worth in excess of $30 billion, we may assume that, at a long-term interest rate of 5 percent and an average life of 30 years per building, about $2½ billion is involved each year. Should these costs not be considered as part of the aid given to students? At the present time subsidies of about $10 billion —the excess of costs over tuition—are to be compared with this additional item of $2½ billion. There are indeed tenable arguments for not passing some of the capital costs on to students —e.g., many of them cannot afford to pay this bill. Why should Harvard students pay an additional few hundred dollars a year to the House Plan which Harkness financed with a $15 million gift? However, more generally a characteristic of construction programs is that the benefits of any subsidies involved accrue to all students irrespective of need. Why should several billions of building subsidies be provided without consideration of who benefits?

The problem in the early 1970s is likely to be the difficulty of financing additions to plant as the government prunes its programs. Even if each additional student involves an outlay of only about $6,000, a sum of around $2 billion annually will be needed in the next 10 years. With the anti-inflation policies now in vogue and the resultant cuts in spending by the federal government, along with a record high level of interest rates, it is not easy for institutions to find the needed capital funds.[85]

FEDERAL FUNDS FOR RESEARCH, DEVELOPMENT, AND OTHER SCIENTIFIC ACTIVITIES, 1960s Federal funds for research and development in recent years have been highly correlated with amounts involved in Department of Defense basic science contracts. California, Massachusetts, and New York have ranked 1, 2, and 3 among the states on both items.[86] On the basis of regions, the Pacific states have been in the lead. In 1963, they accounted for 44 percent of federally financed research and development, 30 percent of total industrial research and development, and 16 percent of employed scientists and

---

[85] Cf. A. M. Cartter and R. L. Farrell, "Academic Labor Market Projections and the Draft," *The Economics and Financing of Higher Education in the United States,* a compendium of papers submitted to the Joint Economic Committee, U.S. Congress, 1969, pp. 77, 97–101.

[86] U.S. Senate, Committee on Labor and Public Welfare, *Impact of Federal Research and Development Policies on Scientific and Technical Manpower, Hearings before the Subcommittee on Employment and Manpower,* June and July 1965, p. 484.

engineers.[87] Highly concentrated aerospace operations on the West Coast help to explain the relatively large amounts of research funds going to this region, but educational achievements are also relevant. Furthermore, concentration of research funds is partly explained by the fact that prestigious institutions of higher education obtain large contracts, which result in increases of outstanding personnel and equipment which in turn induce further concentration.[88]

As compared with a national average of research and development funds per advanced degree of $14,300, the bottom 10 states averaged $3,500, while California, Massachusetts, and Maryland (plus Washington, D.C.) spent $47,000, $27,000, and $26,000, respectively, per advanced degree.[89]

California's share of federal R&D obligations far exceeded its share of population, personal income, or individual income and employment taxes in 1965:[90]

California's percentage of total, 1965

Federal R&D obligations	31.7
Population	9.6
Personal income	11.3
Individual income and employment taxes	10.5

Whereas industrial enterprises allocate most of their R&D funds to development, institutions of higher education allocate the bulk of their funds to basic or applied research:[91]

Industrial enterprises ($9.7 billion)	85% development 11% applied research 4% basic research
Institutions of higher education ($1.5 billion)	7% development 41% applied research 52% basic research

[87] The share of federal funds is generally based on prime contracts, but the share of industrial funds is based on total spending.

[88] U.S. Senate, Committee on Labor and Public Welfare, *Impact of Federal Research and Development Policies on Scientific and Technical Manpower, Hearings before the Subcommittee on Employment and Manpower,* June and July 1965, p. 131.

[89] Ibid., p. 96.

[90] U.S. Senate, *Equitable Distribution of R & D Funds by Government Agencies, Hearings before the Subcommittee on Government Research,* July 1967, pp. 649–650.

[91] National Science Foundation, *Federal Funds for Research, Development, and Other Scientific Activities, Fiscal Years 1967, 1968, and 1969,* vol. 17, 1968, p. 7.

Basic research obligations were estimated to rise 20 percent from fiscal year 1967 to fiscal year 1969. From 1958 to 1968, basic research funds multiplied six times; applied research funds, four times; and development funds, three times. The largest share of basic research funds is expended by institutions of higher education (37 percent), while the federal government spends 24 percent and industrial firms 19 percent.[92]

In recent years, industrial firms have lost much ground relatively as recipients of federal R&D funds, while federal government agencies and institutions of higher education have gained.[93]

From 1958 to 1968 federal obligations for R&D rose from $4,570 million to $16,230 million. Whereas funds for basic research accounted for only 9 percent of the $13.6 billion provided by the Department of Defense, the National Aeronautics and Space Agency, and the Atomic Energy Commission, basic research funds represented 34 percent of the $2.6 billion provided by all other agencies. Institutions of higher education received 40 percent of the total provided by these other agencies, while the Department of Health, Education and Welfare accounted for 50 percent of the total.[94]

Of the $1,468 million provided by five principal federal government agencies for research and science education in fiscal year 1964, the National Institutes of Health provided the largest amount. The Massachusetts Institute of Technology, with $115 million, was the largest recipient, followed by the University of California, Johns Hopkins, the University of Michigan, Stanford, Harvard, the University of Illinois, and Columbia.[95]

A comparison of the top 15 producers of science doctorates with the 15 leading recipients of funds for research and science education in fiscal year 1964 is of interest. The University of California, for example, was the largest producer of science doctorates and also the top recipient of funds from the National Institutes of Health. It ranked second on the Department of Defense list, first on the National Science Foundation list, second on the National Aero-

[92] Ibid., p. 10.

[93] Ibid., p. 15.

[94] Ibid., pp. 30, 33, 60–61.

[95] U.S. House of Representatives, Committee on Government Operations, *Conflicts between the Federal Research Programs and the Nation's Goals for Higher Education*, report of the Committee, 1965.

nautics and Space Agency list, and second on the Atomic Energy Commission list.[96]

EXPENDITURES OF INSTITUTIONS OF HIGHER EDUCATION — VARIOUS ASPECTS

From the mid-1950s to 1970–71, expenditures by institutions of higher education rose much more than those by public elementary and secondary schools. A decline in the student-faculty ratio contributed to this result, although of late that ratio has been rising.

Federal outlays tend to favor lower over higher education. The federal government increased its grants for education 86 percent in 1966 — 170 percent for elementary and secondary schools, but only 26 percent for higher education. In dollar terms the increases were $1,517 million and $694 million, respectively. However, from fiscal year 1963 to fiscal year 1967, federal expenditures on behalf of higher education rose by almost $900 million, or three-fifths.[97]

Over a long period — 1909–10 to 1963–64 — the relative importance of various sources of income changed greatly. The extremes were a rise of 451 times in the federal government's contribution to current income, as contrasted with increases of only 16 times for private gifts and grants and of only 20 times for endowment.[98]

Types of expenditures, for which data are available from 1929–30 to 1963–64, also changed greatly. The extremes were an increase of 108 times for organized research, 10 to 12 times for plant operations, and 12 times for instruction and departmental research.[99]

Projections of costs of higher education vary greatly. In part the explanation is the varying objectives of those making the projections — e.g., we should differentiate between *likely* outlays and *desired* outlays. The variations are also related to differing assumptions about the behavior of (1) the student-faculty ratio, (2) the supply and demand for teachers and the related factor of faculty salaries, (3) future increase in enrollments, and (4) changes in the socioeconomic composition of students. According to various

---

[96] Ibid., p. 38.

[97] U.S. Department of Health, Education and Welfare, *Trends,* 1966–67 edition, part 1, 1968; and National Science Foundation, *Federal Support to Universities and Colleges, Fiscal Year 1967,* 1968, p. 4.

[98] U.S. Office of Education, *Higher Education Finances: Selected Trend and Summary Data,* National Center for Educational Statistics, June 1968, p. 3.

[99] U.S. Department of Health, Education and Welfare, *Toward a Long-Range Plan for Federal Financial Support for Higher Education,* report to the President, Office of Assistant Secretary for Planning and Evaluation, January 1969, p. 13.

assumptions, the minimum projection of expenditures in 1975 is $30,958 million, while the maximum is $35,096 million.[100]

From 1956 to 1966, total expenditures of institutions of higher education rose from $4.2 to $15.0 billion. The increase in the federal contribution relatively was twice that of the states. The federal contribution for educational expenditures rose by 612 percent, as compared with 242 percent for all sources of funds. By categories, the percentage increase in the federal contribution was as follows: student aid, 749 percent; student education, 612 percent; and organized research, 444 percent. There was also an especially large percentage rise in the state contribution to student aid. Federal contributions for all purposes increased 440 percent, as compared with an increase of 258 percent for contributions from all sources.[101]

Relative federal increases in these 10 years were roughly twice those of four other sources of funds (combined). In fact, the rapid increase in federal contributions tended to some extent to discourage contributions from other sources.[102]

The ratio of expenditures to enrollment (E/E) varies greatly by type of institution. As E/E rises, unit costs increase. Extremes for the increase in this ratio from 1965–66 to 1966–67 were 16 to 4 for two-year private institutions and 3 to 5 for four-year private institutions other than universities.[103]

THE BURDEN OF EDUCATIONAL FINANCE Various criteria are available to measure state effort in supporting education. To some extent, the same measures tend to be used both for elementary and secondary schools and for institutions of higher education—e.g., percentage of income devoted to support of either schools or higher education. A more general indication is given by comparing state and local taxes in relation to personal income. In 1959, the extremes—in terms of states and local taxes as a percentage of personal income—were 11.67 percent for North Dakota and 4.90 percent for Delaware. Both capacity to pay and

---

[100] U.S. Office of Education, *Education in the Seventies,* planning papers of the Office of Program Planning and Evaluation, May 1968, p. 44.

[101] Ibid., p. 27.

[102] Ibid. Also see U.S. Department of Health, Education and Welfare, *Trends,* 1966–67 edition, part 1, 1968, p. S-78; and Table 4.8-20.

[103] U.S. Office of Education, National Center for Educational Statistics, *Financial Statistics of Institutions of Higher Education: Current Funds, Revenues, and Expenditures, 1966–67,* 1969, p. 10.

effort are measured by the revenues obtained—e.g., a rise of state and local government revenues from $7 billion in 1927 to $74 billion in 1966.[104]

I have put together a table (4.8-6) for 48 states in the late 1950s which, through recourse to 12 criteria, measures burdens, capacity, effort, and achievements. Each measure is graded from A+ to D.

In the 1950s sparsely populated states tended to spend relatively heavily on public higher education in relation to personal income. One explanation of this relationship is high unit costs where population is small. Another is heavy dependence on public support. Thus three sparsely populated states averaged 1.28 percent of personal income spent on higher education, whereas three rich industrial states with little help from state governments averaged only 0.16 percent.[105]

If we use state and local government expenditures on higher education in relation to personal income as a measure of effort, we again find relatively high expenditures in sparsely populated states and relatively low expenditures in four heavily industrialized states in the Northeast. The average for the four high states was 0.92 percent and for the four low states, 0.23 percent.[106]

Education competes with other welfare programs. In the health, education, and welfare areas as a whole, public outlays were twice private outlays in 1934–35 and in 1965–66. In education alone, the ratio of public to private outlays was roughly 5 to 1 in these years.[107]

In 1966–67, general revenues per capita varied from $310 to $1,067 among the 50 states. Expenditures by state and local governments on higher education varied from $3 per capita for the

[104] S. E. Harris, *Higher Education: Resources and Finance,* McGraw-Hill Book Company, New York, 1962, p. 349; and U.S. Congress, Joint Economic Committee, *Revenue Sharing and Its Alternatives: What Future for Fiscal Federalism?, Hearings before the Subcommittee on Fiscal Policy,* July and August 1967, p. 10.

[105] Ibid., pp. 354–356, 362; and Liaison Committee of the Regents of the University of California and the State Board of Education, *A Master Plan for Higher Education in California, 1960–1975,* Sacramento, Calif., 1960, p. 185.

[106] U.S. Office of Education, *Digest of Educational Statistics, 1968,* p. 101; and National Education Association, *Rankings of the States, 1968,* Washington, D.C., 1968, pp. 52–53.

[107] U.S. Congress, Joint Economic Committee, *Federal Programs for the Development of Human Resources,* a compilation of replies from departments and agencies of the U.S. Government to a questionnaire formulated by the Subcommittee on Economic Progress, 1966, p. 8.

lowest state to $109 for the highest. Even in relation to $1,000 of personal income the range was from $37 to $117 in expenditures for education. Income variations alone do not explain the wide range.[108]

Projections of expenditures by institutions of higher education from 1967–68 to 1977–78 indicate increases of 64 percent for public and 57 percent for private institutions. The large rise for private institutions is another suggestion of troubles for the private sector of higher education. However, large additional revenues of state and local governments are also projected: from $31 billion in 1965 to an estimated $117 billion in 1975.[109]

From 1889–90 to 1965–66, expenditures on all public social welfare programs rose from 2.4 to 12.3 percent of the GNP. The rise for education alone was less pronounced—from 1.1 to 4.5 percent of the GNP.

<table>
<tr><td>*Total public welfare expenditures*</td><td>28</td></tr>
<tr><td>*Education*</td><td>15</td></tr>
<tr><td>*Higher education*</td><td>31</td></tr>
</table>

Expenditure increases in terms of number of times, 1928–29 to 1967–68*

*Organization for Economic Cooperation and Development, *Higher Education and the Demand for Scientific Manpower in the United States,* OECD Publications, Paris, 1963, p. 17; and I. C. Merriam et al., "Social Welfare Expenditures, 1967–68," *Social Security Bulletin,* vol. 31, no. 12, pp. 14–27, December 1968.

Education depends much more heavily on public funds than does health. In 1969–70, public sources financed 35 percent of all expenditures on health, as compared with 82 percent of expenditures on education.[110]

With revenues rising by 12 percent and expenditures by 15 percent a year, we expect at least a doubling of expenditures of all governments in 10 years.[111]

[108] U.S. Bureau of the Census, *Governmental Finances in 1966–67,* Government Finances Series GF 67, no. 3, 1968, pp. 12–13.

[109] Table 4.8-15; and U.S. Congress, Joint Economic Committee, *Revenue Sharing and Its Alternatives: What Future for Fiscal Federalism?,* Hearings before the Subcommittee on Fiscal Policy, July and August 1967, p. 72.

[110] A. M. Skolnik and S. R. Dales, "Social Welfare Expenditures, 1969–70," *Social Security Bulletin,* vol. 33, no. 12, pp. 13, 15, December 1970.

[111] U.S. Congress, Joint Economic Committee, *Revenue Sharing and Its Alternatives: What Future for Fiscal Federalism?,* Hearings before the Subcommittee on Fiscal Policy, July and August 1967, p. 72.

THE ISSUE OF PRODUCTIVITY   In the chapter on productivity, a substantial part, at times changed a little or supplemented, comes from my *Higher Education: Resources and Finance.* [112] The material is reproduced, some 10 years since it was written, because it cannot be greatly improved. I have not repeated footnotes which appear in the original.

I should briefly indicate the coverage in this chapter.

1   I discuss the relationship of education to growth and productivity and the relationship of finance to output and to quality of output.

2   I consider the association of what the college offers and the students' receptivity to the product of higher education.

3   I examine the relationship of the numbers of baccalaureate degrees to the output of Ph.D.'s by institutions, which throws some light on the productivity of numerous institutions. Sociologists rate institutions of higher education according to the interaction of the institution and the student. It is clear, also, that if the maximum level of intelligence is reached before age 17, then the potential productivity of the college is clearly limited. However, increasing signs point to continued growth in intelligence for many even after age 21. Students with the most advanced intellectual orientation tend to go to the institutions of higher education which have the greatest impact in turning out productive scholars. Availability of resources contributes to productivity, but the critical questions have to do with the manner of allocating funds as well as the amounts available.

4   I consider, as one measure of the productivity of institutions of higher education, the rise of income for individuals associated with additional education.

5   I examine the relationship of prices and expenditures on higher education, and the related problem of productivity in education in comparison with other markets. Here, also, the expanding mix of services of institutions of higher education is relevant.

6   I review trends in enrollment, in number of institutions, in number of degrees, and in income over a period of 70 to 80 years as a way of shedding light on trends in unit costs. The fact that in 10 recent years enrollment rose six times as much as the number of institutions of higher education and yet unit costs rose greatly invites further study.

7   I find that over a period of about 70 years, educational expenditures rose much more than national income. But why should educational outlay per student lag far behind per capita national income?

[112] McGraw-Hill Book Company, New York, 1962.

8 I examine the troublesome problem of rising student aid. In view of rapidly increasing expenditures on student aid, study of the effectiveness of different kinds of aid and the manner of distributing each becomes all the more important.

9 The question of whether productivity should be measured on the basis of enrollment or of degrees is considered.

10 I review the data based on a helpful measure of productivity, skillfully used in a publication of the National Science Foundation, *The Dynamics of Academic Science* (1967), which involves reducing degrees at different levels to a common denominator, and accounting for the output of these degrees by types of institutions. Institutions offering doctorates are the major producers of degrees at the higher levels, as are public institutions of higher education. Private universities stand out in their commitments to graduate science and graduate degrees. The size of the budget is also an indication of results to be expected.

11 I find that productivity depends on the size of the unit and on the degree of utilization. The impact of these on costs needs study.

12 I consider the fact that one approach to holding down costs is cooperation and coordination among states and among institutions of higher education. Especially important in this context are the problems of sparsely populated states.

13 I point out that the optimum size of institutions requires study, taking account both of the *economic* gains of achieving the optimum and the impact on the kind of *product* turned out.

14 I examine the importance of the mobilization of economic measures — for example, maximizing use of low-paid assistants, making improved use of space, and increasing return on investment.

15 I consider the importance of class size as a factor in increasing costs. The case for small classes is overdone.

16 I examine the maldistribution of facilities among small and large and poor and rich institutions — a factor affecting the productivity of higher education.

17 I consider the question: How many institutions of higher education? The answer is related to the optimum size.

18 I point out that the proliferation of courses is an ancient academic disease. The impact of this tendency on student-faculty ratios and on costs of operation needs attention.

19 I consider whether institutions of higher education thrive in war and inflationary periods or in peacetime. We find, generally, that costs per student rise much more than the overall price level.

20 I analyze the questions of the location of new institutions and the estimation of potential enrollment. I point out that the methods generally used are far from ideal.

21 I find that, as institutions of higher education improve their financial management—e.g., with the use of capital gains—more funds are made available and hence increased productivity should follow.

22 I consider three interrelated questions: (1) whether the scale method of pay can be improved by merit pay; (2) how the institutions attain viability at the expense of the faculty; and (3) what fringe benefits should be provided and how these various fringes affect the output of faculty.

23 I examine the problem of joint costs and the neglect of cost-price considerations.

THE STRUCTURE OF HIGHER EDUCATION IN THE SECOND HALF OF THE NINETEENTH CENTURY AND IN MORE RECENT TIMES

There are wide discrepancies in the data available on enrollment for the second half of the nineteenth century. Data published by the Commissioner of Education at the time diverged greatly for various reasons from figures for those years compiled more recently by the Office of Education.

In 130 years (1840 to 1970), estimated enrollment rose 417 times, as compared with a population increase of 12 times. From 1872 to 1897–98, the largest rise relative to population was in graduate enrollment, which increased 14 times, compared with a gain of little more than one time for undergraduates and from 40 percent to 231 percent for the four most important types of professional schools.[113]

From the beginning of the twentieth century to 1963, resident degree-credit enrollment in relation to the population aged 18 to 24 rose more than in relation to the population aged 18 to 21. Rapidly rising graduate enrollment helped to explain this trend. From 1900 to 1963 the annual increase in relation to the population aged 18 to 21 was nine times; in relation to the population aged 18 to 24, 10 times.[114]

From 1900 to 1965, primary and secondary school enrollment rose 188 percent; enrollment in higher education, 2,226 percent; enrollment in public higher education, 3,897 percent; and enrollment in private higher education, 1,195 percent.

From 1900 to 1963, enrollment in K–8 (kindergarten to the

[113] U.S. Office of Education, *Report of the Commissioner of Education, 1897–98*, p. 1800.

[114] U.S. Office of Education, *Digest of Educational Statistics, 1968*, 1968, p. 70.

eighth grade) declined from 95 to 66 percent of total enrollment; enrollment in secondary schools (grades 9 to 12) rose from 4 to 24 percent; and enrollment in higher education rose from 1 to 10 percent of the total.[115]

Increases in selected items in terms of number of times, 1869–70 to 1963–64*	
Number of institutions of higher education	2.3
Resident degree-credit enrollment	80
Bachelor's and first professional degrees	52
General and educational income of institutions of higher education, 1889–90 to 1963–64 (compare enrollment rise of 26 times)	362

*U.S. Office of Education, *Digest of Educational Statistics, 1968,* 1968, p. 69.

From 1850 to 1902, the number of teachers increased about twice as much as the number of students, resulting in a large drop in the student-faculty ratio. This was a cost-increasing factor.

The rise in enrollment was much smaller in the second half of the nineteenth century than it has been in the years since 1900 (85,000 from 1840 to 1902, as compared with 5.3 million from 1940 to 1968).

In the years from 1880 to 1980 (estimated), the largest increases occurred in prosperous decades: the 1920s, the 1940s, and the 1960s. However, the Great Depression was an exception. In the 1960s, the increase was 124 percent and 4.7 million. The expected percentage rise for the 1970s is less than one-half that of the 1960s, but in terms of numbers the increase will be much closer to that of the 1960s.[116]

Women's share of enrollment rose from 21 percent in 1870 to 44 percent in 1930 and then declined to 35 percent in 1960. However, by 1970 it had risen to 41 percent and was projected to rise to 44 percent by 1980.

From 1900 to 1960, enrollment in public institutions of higher education rose from 38 to 59 percent of total enrollment, and by 1970 it had reached 75 percent of the total. What if the massive expansion of public enrollment's share beyond the 38 percent of 1900 had not occurred? The effects on enrollment would have

[115] Ibid., p. 3; cf. U.S. Office of Education, *Education in the Seventies,* planning papers of the Office of Program Planning and Evaluation, May 1968, p. 1.

[116] Ibid., pp. 3, 68–69; U.S. Office of Education, *Projections of Educational Statistics to 1977–78,* National Center for Educational Statistics, 1968, p. 12; and U.S. Office of Education, unpublished tables.

depended on the response of private institutions of higher education.[117]

In the late nineteenth century, 81 percent of enrollment was private; of major professional schools, 87 percent were private; and of normal schools, 15 percent were private. By 1963, public enrollment had reached 64 percent of total enrollment and a similar percentage of all students seeking a degree, but public institutions accounted for only 38 percent of first professional degrees and for 58 percent of graduate students. First professional enrollment accounted for only 3 percent and graduate students for only 10 percent of total enrollment. Compare 1891, when medicine, law, and theology accounted for 25 percent and normal schools for 27 percent. In 1891–92, professional degrees accounted for about 50 percent of all degrees awarded, as compared with only 6 percent of all bachelor and first professional degrees in 1965–66. The vast majority of law and medical schools in the 1890s were under private control.[118]

Student-faculty ratios varied greatly by institutions and also by type of school. Thus in 1889–90, among five institutions, there was a range from a ratio of 5 to 1 at Columbia to a ratio of 17 to 1 at Yale; and at Harvard from a ratio of 3 to 1 in the divinity school to a ratio of 26 to 1 in the law school. In medicine the range among the five institutions was from a ratio of 3 to 1 to a ratio of 18 to 1.[119]

[117] U.S. Office of Education, *Digest of Educational Statistics, 1968,* 1968, p. 69; U.S. Office of Education, *Projections of Educational Statistics to 1977–78,* National Center for Educational Statistics, 1968, pp. 16, 31, 217, 1178, 1903; and U.S. Office of Education, unpublished tables.

[118] U.S. Office of Education, *Report of the Commissioner of Education, 1891–92,* p. 13; vol. I, p. 2; and U.S. Office of Education, *Digest of Educational Statistics, 1968,* 1968, p. 86.

[119] U.S. Office of Education, *Report of the Commissioner of Education, 1889–90,* pp. 462–463.

Part One

Students

1.1. *Undergraduate* *Student* *Characteristics*

ENROLLMENT, APTITUDE, AND SOCIO-ECONOMIC STATUS Leading research universities and prestigious liberal arts colleges tend to attract students with relatively high scholastic aptitude test scores (Tables 1.1-1 and 1.1-2). In selecting an institution of higher education, students place the greatest emphasis on the qual-

TABLE 1.1-1 *Mean scholastic aptitude test scores of entering class, fall 1960, at 27 institutions**

| | Mean verbal score ranked by group | | | Mean mathematical score ranked by group | | | Mean mathematical score corresponding with verbal score in group | | |
	I	II	III	I	II	III	I	II	III
	650	620	681†	728	665	670	728	635	667†
	641	577	641†	675	635	667†	675	665	658†
	635	550	638	642	554	658†	637	554	670
	631	505‡	626	637	538‡	637	642	510‡	628
	597	505	612	596	520‡	628	596	489	637
	550‡	497‡	575	553‡	518‡	571	553‡	518‡	566
	528	494‡	566	526	510‡	566	526	469‡	571
	501‡	493‡	551	510‡	489	565	510‡	538‡	565
		480‡	535		469‡	542		520‡	534
			521			534			542
Median	614	505	594	617	520	600	617	520	600
Mean	592	525	595	608	555	604	608	555	604

*Scores were restricted, wherever possible, to students in colleges of liberal arts and sciences.
†Median.
‡Public university.

Group I includes 12 institutions of higher education chosen from 25 receiving $4 million or more from the federal government in 1957–58.

Group II includes 12 institutions of higher education chosen from 54 receiving $0.5 million to $1.9 million from the federal government in 1957–58.

Group III includes 12 liberal arts colleges — 6 prestigious ones and 6 of lesser prestige.

SOURCE: H. Orlans, *The Effects of Federal Programs on Higher Education*, The Brookings Institution, Washington, D.C., 1962, p. 148.

TABLE 1.1-2
Terman concept mastery test, mean total scores for selected ability groups

Group	Mean	SD*	Number
Writers	156.4	21.9	20
Subjects of Stanford gifted study	136.7	28.5	1,004
Women mathematicians	131.7	33.8	41
Graduate students	119.2	33.0	125
Research scientists	118.2	29.4	45
Architects	113.15	37.7	40
Undergraduate students	101.7	33.0	201
Spouses of gifted subjects	95.3	42.7	690
Air Force captains	60.1	31.7	344

*Standard deviation.

SOURCE: College Entrance Examination Board, *College Admissions,* New York, 1960, p. 22.

ity of training offered, while the cost of education seems to be the second most important consideration (Table 1.1-3). However, the importance of economic barriers becomes clearer when considering the percentage of young high school graduates (between ages 16 and 24) who do not enroll in college and who cite lack of money as the major reason for not enrolling (Table 1.1-4).

TABLE 1.1-3 *Probable reasons for selecting a college given by high-scoring students who plan to go to college*

	Boys		Girls	
Reason	Important	Most important	Important	Most important
Quality of training	88%*	33%	76%*	30%
Cost	46	17	42	15
Nearness to home	28	5	24	4
Availability of scholarships and financial aid	21*	4	13*	2
Admission requirements	18	4	13	2
Social factors	41*	3	47*	4
Religious factors	5	2	9	3
Miscellaneous		32		40
TOTAL		100%		100%

*Responses to several related choices of answer on the questionnaire have been combined to give these figures. In addition, because individual students gave multiple answers to the question, the percentages indicate the proportions of checked categories rather than individual student cases.

SOURCE: C. C. Cole, Jr., *Encouraging Scientific Talent,* College Entrance Examination Board, New York, 1956, p. 146.

TABLE 1.1-4
Percentage of high school graduates 16 to 24 years old not enrolled in college, by major reason reported for not enrolling and by sex, October 1959

Major reason reported for not enrolling in college	Male	Female
TOTAL	100.0	100.0
No desire to go	32.1	31.8
Not admitted	0.9	0.3
Lacked money	24.9	15.2
Took a job	18.5	22.9
Needed at home	1.4	0.3
Military service	12.5	0.2
Marriage	5.0	22.1
Other reason	2.7	6.3
Not reported	2.0	0.9

SOURCE: U.S. Department of Commerce, Bureau of the Census, and U.S. Department of Agriculture, Economic Research Service, Census-ERS, ser. P-27, no. 30, table 13, in C. C. Cole, Jr., *Encouraging Scientific Talent,* College Entrance Examination Board, New York, 1956, p. 146.

TABLE 1.1-5
Percentile rank in high school graduating class and probability of entering and of graduating from college

Percentile rank in high school graduating class	Percentage of high school graduates who enter college	Percentage of college entrants who graduate	Percentage of high school graduates who graduate from college
81–100	53	82	43
61–80	44	68	30
41–60	35	54	19
21–40	26	40	10
1–20	17	26	4

SOURCE: D. Wolfle, *America's Resources of Specialized Talent,* report of the Commission of Human Resources and Advanced Training, Harper & Brothers, New York, 1954, p. 150.

TABLE 1.1-6
Percentage of youths of high intelligence graduating from college

Ability level	AGCT score	Percent graduating from college
Top 0.1%	160 and higher	69
Top 1%	147 and higher	59
Top 5%	133 and higher	49
Top 10%	126 and higher	42
Top 20%	117 and higher	34

SOURCE: D. Wolfle, *America's Resources of Specialized Talent,* report of the Commission on Human Resources and Advanced Training, Harper & Brothers, New York, 1954, p. 149.

Attendance is also closely related to ability and, as may be seen from Tables 1.1-5 to 1.1-7, significant percentages of high-ability students either do not enter college or do not graduate from college. Table 1.1-7 shows, according to various tests that measure ability, the percentage of students of high ability who have not

TABLE 1.1-7 *Estimated proportion of students of high ability who do not go to college, selected samples, United States*

Source	Population	Date of high school graduation	Estimated percentage not attending college
National Merit Scholarship Program	Merit scholars ($N = 827$)	1957	0.2*
	Finalists ($N = 6,428$)	1957	3.1
	Semifinalists ($N = 7,690$)	1957	5.1
	Total ($N = 14,945$)	1957	3.9
Terman and Oden	Highest 1 or 2 percent by IQ, in California schools	1928	12
Phearman	Highest 2 percent, by achievement tests, among Iowa's high school graduates	1947	8
Wolfle	Highest 2.8 percent of high school graduates on intelligence test	1953	39
Phearman	Highest 9 percent of Iowa's high school graduates	1947	36
Iffert	Highest 10 percent in high school graduating class	1950	28
Corcoran and Keller	Highest 15 percent, by IQ, of Minnesota high school seniors	1950	33†
Wolfle	Highest 8.8 percent of high school graduates	1953	45
Educational Testing Service	Highest 10 percent, by aptitude test, of public high school seniors	1955	30
Iffert	Highest 30 percent in high school graduating class	1950	30
Wolfle	Highest 31 percent of high school graduates	1953	53
Educational Testing Service	Highest-scoring 30 percent of public high school seniors	1955	47

*Two students awarded scholarships are having their scholarships held over for one year.
†Percentage not attending college within four years of graduation.
SOURCE: Organization for Economic Cooperation and Development, *Financing of Education for Economic Growth,* OECD Publications, Paris, 1966, p. 232.

gone to college: out of the highest-scoring 30 percent of public high school seniors taking an Educational Testing Service examination in 1955, 47 percent did not attend college. When high scores on aptitude tests are accompanied by financial assistance, such as the National Merit Scholarship Program, a very small percentage

TABLE 1.1-8 *Ratios of immediate college entrants to high school graduates (in percentage, by high school class, comparing results of various studies)*

| | State studies | | | | National ETS-NSF sample¶ | National estimate |
	New York*	Kansas†	Wisconsin‡	Arkansas§		
High school class	1956	1955	1957	1957	1955	1956
Entire class:						
Total	43	40	30	26	32	37
Male	50	46	34	30	36	41
Female	36	34	26	22	27	32
Upper 30 percent:						
Total	64	65	54		53	58
Male	69	74	60		60	65
Female	59	54	44		46	50
Top 10 percent:						
Total	75		66	56	68	73
Male	80		72	60	75	80
Female	71		59	50	60	65
Other post–high school training:						
Total	8	6	15			
Male	5	2	9			
Female	10	10	21			
Military service:						
Male	20	11	23	22	19	17

*University of the State of New York, *Needs and Facilities in Higher Education in New York State,* State Education Department—data by sex unpublished.

† A. A. Daughtry, "A Report on the Post-graduation Activities of the 1955 Kansas High School Graduates," *Emporia State Research Studies,* vol. 5, no. 2, 1956, pp. 18, 51.

‡ J. Kenneth Little, *A State-wide Inquiry into Decisions of Youth about Education beyond High School,* School of Education, University of Wisconsin, Madison, 1958, pp. 8, 13.

§ Francis Stroup and Dean C. Andrews, *Barriers to College Attendance: Report of an Arkansas Study of Factors Related to Educational Discontinuance of High School Graduates,* Southern State College, Magnolia, Ark., 1959, pp. 29, 50, 55.

¶ Educational Testing Service, *Background Factors Relating to College Plans and College Enrollment among Public High School Students,* Princeton, N.J., 1957, appendix tables D-1, D-3.

SOURCE: In National Science Foundation, *The Duration of Formal Education for High-Ability Youth,* Washington, D.C., 1961, p. 19.

TABLE 1.1-9 *Percentages entering institutions of higher education within one year after completing grade 12, by aptitude and by income*

Percentages of male *high school graduates who did not enter college within 1 year after completing grade 12,* by aptitude percentile† and family income‡*

Aptitude level percentile	Less than $3,000	$3,000 to $5,999	$6,000 to $8,999	$9,000 to $11,999	$12,000 and up
98.0 to 100.0	0.0	3.9	4.8	4.1	1.5
90.0 to 97.9	12.1	13.3	11.4	7.5	3.3
75.0 to 89.9	24.6	26.7	19.4	16.1	9.9
50.0 to 74.9	51.8	47.5	40.3	33.2	20.3
0.0 to 49.9	80.4	72.7	68.1	59.8	50.3

*College attendance was reported by respondents to the mail questionnaire who constituted about 67 percent of the Project Talent sample of twelfth grade pupils.

†Academic aptitude was measured by a composite of nine Project Talent tests (C-002). Percentiles are based on a representative sample of pupils in grade 12 (March–April).

‡Family income for 1959, as estimated by twelfth-grade pupils on the Student Information Blank, item no. 173, in 1960.

NOTE: Data are taken from Project Talent in U.S. Office of Education cooperative research program, Project 2333.

Percentages of female *high school graduates who did not enter college within 1 year after completing grade 12,* by aptitude percentile† and family income‡*

Aptitude level percentile	Less than $3,000	$3,000 to $5,999	$6,000 to $8,999	$9,000 to $11,999	$12,000 and up
98.0 to 100.0	10.5	2.5	6.7	6.0	3.2
90.0 to 97.9	36.7	19.2	16.1	14.9	4.8
75.0 to 89.9	38.9	43.2	30.2	28.2	10.1
50.0 to 74.9	74.8	64.2	57.4	40.8	29.2
0.0 to 49.9	82.6	81.8	77.2	69.6	52.1

*College attendance was reported by respondents to the mail questionnaire who constituted about 67 percent of the Project Talent sample of twelfth-grade pupils.

†Academic aptitude was measured by a composite of nine Project Talent tests (C-002). Percentiles are based on a representative sample of pupils in grade 12 (March–April).

‡Family income for 1959, as estimated by twelfth-grade pupils on the Student Information Blank, item no. 173, in 1960.

NOTE: Data are taken from Project Talent in U.S. Office of Education cooperative research program, Project 2333.

SOURCE: In U.S. House of Representatives, Committee on Education and Labor, *Higher Education Act of 1965,* hearings before the Special Subcommittee on Education, February to May 1965, exhibits 10, 10-A.

of high-ability students do not attend college. For example, of the 827 merit scholars in 1957, only 0.2 percent, or about 17 students, did not attend college.

Aptitude and income influence *when* a student enters college as well as *whether* he enters at all. Table 1.1-8 compares various state studies and two national studies of college entry immediately after high school, showing that in 1956–57, of the total top 10 percent of high school seniors in New York, a high-income state, 75 percent entered college immediately, whereas in Arkansas, a low-income state, only 56 percent entered immediately. Table 1.1-9 shows by aptitude and family income the percentages of male and female high school graduates who did not enter college within one year after high school graduation. As may be expected, the percentages of females not attending college within one year of high school graduation are consistently greater than the percentages of males not attending. The highest percentages for nonattendance for both sexes occurred in the lowest-aptitude and lowest-income categories, and the lowest percentage of nonattendance occurred in the highest-aptitude categories, but not necessarily in the highest-income categories.

College enrollment data for 1955–56 indicate that 35 percent of students enrolled in public high schools entered public colleges in the fall of 1956, compared with 45 percent of students enrolled in Catholic schools. Total national statistics for 1956 measured 43 percent of all high school seniors entering college (Table 1.1-10).

TABLE 1.1-10 High school graduates of 1955–56 and those in college by fall 1956, by type of school (in thousands or percent)		*Public*	*Catholic*	*Other*	*Total*	*National statistics*
	Total:					
	Number of graduates	1,258	122	36	1,416	1,416
	Percentage in college	35	45	70	37	43
	Number in college	440	55	25	520	607
	Male:					
	Number of graduates	609	53	18	680	680
	Percentage in college	39	55	80	41	50
	Number in college	238	29	14	281	339
	Female:					
	Number of graduates	649	69	18	736	736
	Percentage in college	31	38	61	32	36
	Number in college	202	26	11	239	268

NOTE: Public and total high school graduates from U.S. Office of Education; Catholic high school graduates from National Catholic Welfare Conference, Department of Education, Washington, D.C. Number of graduates of "other" schools by subtraction of public and Catholic school graduates from the total. Other data derived as stated in preceding text.

SOURCE: National Science Foundation, *The Duration of Formal Education for High-Ability Youth,* Washington, D.C., 1961, p. 17.

The percentage of high school seniors enrolling immediately after high school graduation is also related to the students' socioeconomic background. Table 1.1-11 points to plans for attendance and actual enrollment according to father's education and occupation, and the number of children in the family. Similar data are presented in Table 1.1-12 for college freshmen in 1965–66, showing enrollment percentages for private and public colleges by type of secondary school attended, average grade in secondary school, father's educational attainment, and family income. The data suggest that the freshmen enrolling in private institutions (select group) had, on the average, higher grades in secondary school, and had fathers whose educational attainment was generally higher than that of their counterparts in public institutions (select group). In the

TABLE 1.1-11   *Percentages of high school seniors planning college and percentages actually en- rolling in the following fall according to father's education and occupation and number of children in family*

	Boys		Girls	
	Percentage planning to go to college	*Percentage enrolled*	*Percentage planning to go to college*	*Percentage enrolled*
Father's education:				
At least some college	73	68	72	60
Completed high school	48	36	40	26
Grade school only	36	24	26	16
Father's occupation:				
Professional	80	73	79	68
Business, supervisory	61	50	56	41
Business, nonsupervisory	61	51	51	42
Skilled labor	37	26	29	15
Semiskilled labor	35	23	27	15
Farm	35	28	32	21
Number of children in family:				
None	61	50	53	36
One	58	49	50	36
Two	51	39	42	33
Three or four	38	29	32	22
Five or more	29	17	25	10

SOURCE: Educational Testing Service, *Background Factors Related to College Plans and College Enrollment among High Aptitude Public High School Students,* Princeton, N.J., 1957; in College Entrance Examination Board, *College Admissions,* New York, 1960.

TABLE 1.1-12 *Some characteristics of 1965–66 freshmen in four categories of institutions of higher education (percentages)*

	Private institutions		Public institutions	
	Select group	Other	Select group	Other
Type of secondary school attended:				
Public	73.7%	74.2%	89.5%	88.7%
Denominational	10.9	20.1	5.4	7.5
Private	15.4	5.7	5.1	3.8
Average grade in secondary school:				
A	38.5	16.1	27.2	11.7
B+	23.7	17.7	22.9	18.8
B	17.6	21.9	22.2	26.4
B−	9.3	17.0	13.6	18.2
C	10.4	26.3	13.7	23.9
D	0.2	0.5	0.1	0.6
Father's educational attainment:				
Grammar school or less	4.1	7.4	5.0	8.3
Some high school	6.9	12.5	8.2	15.6
High school graduate	18.4	26.0	25.8	33.2
Some college	17.9	20.2	22.5	18.9
College graduate	26.6	20.8	23.5	16.2
Postgraduate degree	25.8	12.9	14.6	7.5
Estimated parents' income:				
$4,000 and below	4.0	5.4	3.9	6.7
$4,000–$8,000	18.8	26.5	26.4	36.6
$8,000–$15,000	36.6	42.5	40.5	40.7
$15,000–$25,000	22.5	16.7	18.6	11.6
$25,000 and above	17.6	8.4	10.2	4.0
Estimated median	$13,750	$10,500	$11,000	$8,500

SOURCE: Adapted from College Entrance Examination Board, *The Economics of Higher Education,* New York, 1967, table 4, p. 14.

category of estimated family income, the percentage of students in the income categories above $15,000 is significantly greater for private institutions (28.8 percent, select group).

The family income of students demonstrates that students from the highest family income levels ($10,000 and over) tend to be in the public and private four-year institutions, whereas a lesser percentage of students in two-year institutions are from this relatively high income group (Figure 1.1-1).

A high correlation exists between a student's socioeconomic background and the type of college attended. Table 1.1-13 shows that 64 percent of students in private universities have fathers who have gone to college and who have a family income of over $10,000, as compared with 49 percent of students in public universities.

FIGURE 1.1-1 *Income of families with heads aged 35 to 54 and family income of students, by type of college, United States, 1966*

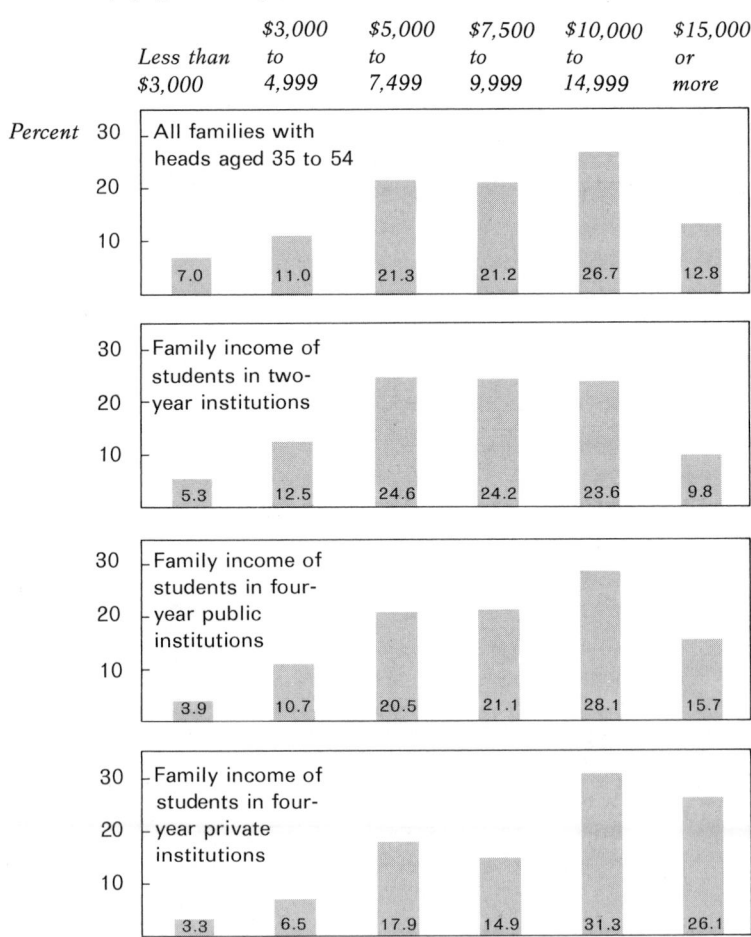

SOURCE: Adapted from U.S. Bureau of the Census data, in Carnegie Commission on Higher Education, *The Open-Door Colleges: Policies for Community Colleges,* McGraw-Hill Book Company, New York, 1970, p. 5.

TABLE 1.1-13
Relation between socioeconomic background and type of college attended

Type of college	Fathers with college, percent	Family income over $10,000, percent
Private university	64	64
Private four-year college	63	60
Catholic four-year college	54	54
Protestant four-year college	51	51
Public university	49	49
Private two-year college	39	42
Public four-year college	34	33
Public two-year college	34	40

SOURCE: Leland L. Medsker and Dale Tillery, *Breaking the Access Barriers: A Profile of Two-Year Colleges,* McGraw-Hill Book Company, New York, 1971.

A study of the occupational mobility aspirations of sons in 1953 indicated that there was a decided tendency for sons to aspire to higher occupational levels than the levels attained by their fathers (Table 1.1-14).

Father's occupation is an influential factor in the decision to attend college, as is the size of the high school attended. Table 1.1-15 shows the college plans of high-scoring seniors in relation to father's occupation and size of high school enrollment. The higher percentages of boys and girls planning to attend college immediately after high school are from families whose fathers are in the professional and top business positions. Students from high schools with large enrollments are more likely to plan to attend college immediately after high school than others.

Table 1.1-16 measures the percentage of students entering college immediately after high school by socioeconomic status and achievement quartile. The table shows almost consistently higher percentages of girls than boys in the high achievement quartile for all socioeconomic quartiles. If socioeconomic status only is considered, a greater percentage of girls (44 percent) than of boys (40 percent) is represented in the high quartile. The other socioeconomic quartiles have approximately the same percentage representations between the sexes (Table 1.1-17).

The probability of entering college within the year following high

(Text continued on p. 60)

		Percentage of sons who aspire to this level
TABLE 1.1-14 *Distribution of father's occupations and son's occupational aspirations; 3,971 cases* Occupational level	Percentage of fathers at this level	
Major white collar		
(e.g., doctor, lawyer, department store executive)	4	15
Middle white collar		
(e.g., office manager, schoolteacher, CPA)	14	29
Minor white collar		
(e.g., small storeowner, bookkeeper, postal clerk)	20	10
Skilled labor and service		
(e.g., highly skilled trades, policeman)	32	23
Other labor and service		
(e.g., semi- and unskilled factory workers, waiter)	21	5
Others:		
Indeterminate	9	7
Fantasy (baseball, FBI)		8
Military service only	___	3
TOTAL	100	100

SOURCE: A. H. Halsey, J. Flound, and C. Anderson (eds.), *Education, Economy, and Society,* The Free Press of Glencoe, Inc., New York, 1961, p. 349.

Halsey, Flound, and Anderson comment as follows on these data:

The questionnaire showed that the boys who had fairly clear occupational aims also had plans for an education that would appropriately prepare them for the jobs of their choice. About one-fourth of the boys were in the college preparatory course *and* were definitely planning a college career (and a later follow-up disclosed that most of them actually did go on to college). The IQ scores of the boys and the occupations of their fathers turned out to be of practically equal utility as predictors of the boys' educational ambitions. Most boys with high intelligence or from high status homes planned a college career, whereas most boys with low intelligence or from low status homes did not aspire to higher education.

TABLE 1.1-15 *Percentage of high-scoring seniors with college plans, by father's occupation and high school size*

Father's occupation	Going now		Going later		Interest only		No interest		Miscellaneous	
	Boys	Girls	Boys	Girls	Boys	Girls	Boys	Girls	Boys	Girls
Professional										
Scientific, nonmedical	65	69	25	10	1	3	4	10	5	8
Education, noncollege	61	70	34	20	0	1	4	3	1	6
Medical	83	84	12	10	0	2	4	2	1	2
Other	59	75	35	14	1	3	2	3	3	5
Business										
Supervising	61	55	24	16	2	4	6	13	7	12
Nonsupervising (high level)	63	63	28	11	2	7	3	10	3	9
Nonsupervising (low level)	56	50	29	20	3	5	6	14	6	11
Technical	55	49	31	22	2	2	7	12	5	15
Farm	38	38	29	22	6	9	11	19	16	12
Labor										
Skilled	32	24	37	25	5	11	15	26	10	14
Semiskilled	28	21	37	22	5	14	19	26	11	17
Unskilled	32	24	38	24	7	12	12	25	12	15
Other	33		35		6		14		11	
High school size by enrollment										
0–99	37	40	32	17	5	10	13	22	13	11
100–299	40	37	31	22	5	9	10	17	14	15
300–599	45	44	34	19	3	8	10	17	8	12
600–999	51	44	27	17	3	7	10	18	9	14
1,000–1,499	56	46	29	19	3	8	6	16	6	11
1,500 or more	43	39	33	24	4	6	12	19	8	12
Average	47	42	31	20	4	8	9	18	9	12

SOURCE: C. C. Cole, Jr., *Encouraging Scientific Talent,* College Entrance Examination Board, New York, 1956, pp. 147, 149.

TABLE 1.1-16 *Percentage of students entering college during the first year following high school graduation, by socioeconomic status quartile and high school achievement quartile: high school class of 1961*

Status quartile	Achievement quartile				
	High	*2d Q*	*3d Q*	*Low*	*Total*
Males:					
High socioeconomic status quartile	57	25	12	6	100
Second socioeconomic status quartile	46	32	15	7	100
Third socioeconomic status quartile	40	33	16	11	100
Low socioeconomic status quartile	26	30	23	21	100
Females:					
High socioeconomic status quartile	56	28	11	5	100
Second socioeconomic status quartile	54	27	15	4	100
Third socioeconomic status quartile	48	27	13	12	100
Low socioeconomic status quartile	28	29	22	21	100

SOURCE: Derived from Project Talent data. Implicit distribution from appendix tables A-8 and A-9; in U.S. Office of Education, *Students and Buildings: An Analysis of Selected Federal Programs for Higher Education,* 1968, p. 55.

school graduation closely reflects socioeconomic and achievement quartiles, but the probability for females is lower than for males in each quartile. However, Table 1.1-18 shows that for both sexes in all socioeconomic quartiles, as achievement level decreases, so

TABLE 1.1-17 *Percentage of students entering college during the first year following high school graduation, by socioeconomic status: high school class of 1961*

Socioeconomic status	*Male*	*Female*
High quartile	40	44
Second quartile	28	27
Third quartile	20	19
Low quartile	12	10
	100	100

SOURCE: Derived from Project Talent data. Implicit distribution from appendix tables A-8 and A-9; in U.S. Office of Education, *Students and Buildings: An Analysis of Selected Federal Programs for Higher Education,* 1968, p. 12.

TABLE 1.1-18
Probability of a high school graduate entering college in the year following graduation by family socioeconomic status quartile, student achievement quartile, and sex: high school class of 1961

Socioeconomic status quartile	Achievement quartile			
	High	Second	Third	Low
High	M 0.92 / 0.87 F	M 0.76 / 0.72 F	M 0.52 / 0.43 F	M 0.38 / 0.37 F
Second	0.81 / 0.75	0.55 / 0.44	0.38 / 0.26	0.21 / 0.09
Third	0.77 / 0.75	0.45 / 0.32	0.22 / 0.13	0.17 / 0.13
Low	0.61 / 0.42	0.31 / 0.26	0.19 / 0.13	0.10 / 0.08

SOURCE: Tables 5-1 and 5-2 in "One Year Follow-up Studies," *Project Talent*, American Institutes of Research, Pittsburgh, 1966, pp. 93, 94; in U.S. Office of Education, *Students and Buildings, An Analysis of Selected Federal Programs for Higher Education*, 1968, table A-8.

also does the probability that the person will enter college in the year following high school graduation.

Among college entrants who graduate from college, the relationship between socioeconomic status and graduation is not consis-

TABLE 1.1-19 *The relation between father's occupation and probability that a high school graduate will enter college and that a college entrant will graduate*

Father's occupation	Percentage of high school graduates who enter college	Percentage of college entrants who graduate from college	Percentage of high school graduates who also graduate from college
Professional and semiprofessional	67	60	40
Managerial	50	55	28
White collar (clerical, sales, service)	48	57	27
Farmer	24	44	11
Factory, craftsmen, unskilled, etc.	26	58	15

SOURCE: A. H. Halsey, J. Flound, and C. Anderson (eds.), *Education, Economy and Society*, The Free Press of Glencoe, Inc., New York, 1961, p. 230.

TABLE 1.1-20
Average
completed
levels of
education of
children, by
education of the
spending-unit
head (for
spending-unit
heads whose
children are no
longer in
school)

Education of spending-unit heads	Number of cases	Average years of children's education
No education	26	9.14
Elementary school	478	10.86
Some high school	177	12.01
High school diploma	92	12.81
High school diploma plus noncollege training	50	12.76
College, no degree	65	13.90
Bachelor's degree	35	14.70
Advanced degree	16	15.72

SOURCE: S. J. Mushkin (ed.), *Economics of Higher Education,* U.S. Office of Education, 1962, p. 28.

tent. Clearly, socioeconomic status has a more decisive influence on who enters college than on the proportion of entrants who graduate (Table 1.1-19). Table 1.1-20 shows that children tend to attain a higher level of education than the head of the "spending unit" up to the high school diploma level.

In countries other than the United States the father's occupational and educational background has a greater bearing upon vertical mobility of the children. For example, Table 1.1-21 shows, by father's occupation, the percentage of children born in Great Britain in 1940–41 who received full-time higher education. Only 33 percent of the children of fathers in the higher professional category and 1 percent of the children of semiskilled and unskilled workers received full-time higher education. Tables 1.1-22 and

TABLE 1.1-21 *Percentage of children within father's occupational category, born in Great Britain in 1940–41 who received full-time higher education*

Father's occupation	Degree level	Other
Higher professional	33	12
Managerial and other professional	11	8
Clerical	6	4
Skilled workers	2	2
Semi- and unskilled	1	1

SOURCE: Committee Appointed by the Prime Minister under the Chairmanship of Lord Robbins, *Higher Education,* Her Majesty's Stationery Office, London, October 1963, p. 50.

TABLE 1.1-22 *Percentage breakdown of National Service recruits to the Army and RAF, by age on leaving school and by father's occupation*

Father's occupation	Number	Recruit's age on leaving school			
		15 or under	*16*	*17*	*18 or over*
Professional or managerial	929	25%	24%	17%	34%
Skilled workers	3,666	78	15	3	4
Unskilled workers	852	92	6	1	1
All above, inclusive of clerical and semiskilled	7,275	72%	15%	5%	8%

SOURCE: *15 to 18: Report of the Central Advisory Council for Education,* England, vol. 2 (report), 1959; in Organization for Economic Co-operation and Development, *Financing of Education for Economic Growth,* OECD Publications, Paris, 1966, p. 227.

1.1-23 present more data on the socioeconomic origins of college students in other countries.

LIVING ARRANGE-MENTS, COMPLETION OF DEGREES, RESIDENCE AND MIGRATION A 1960 study showed that a higher percentage of male students (27.4 percent) than female students (13.7 percent), both graduate and undergraduate, were married and living with their spouses. However, the percentage of married students increased for both sexes with each additional year at college (Table 1.1-24).

The participation of college students and their spouses in the labor force is also an interesting social factor related to enrollment (Table 1.1-25). Folger and Nam have commented on the increase in marriages and participation in the labor force as follows:

One consequence of a higher marriage rate in each more advanced college class is that an extra burden is added to the already difficult task of procuring enough money for college. Married students in 1960 not only had

TABLE 1.1-23 Occupation of students' fathers, Austria (early 1950s)

Father's occupation	Per 1,000 students
Government officials and employees	267
Employees in industry and commerce	156
Farm owners and workers	60
Industrial workers	36

SOURCE: Organization for Economic Co-operation and Development, *Financing of Education for Economic Growth,* OECD Publications, Paris, 1966, p. 228.

TABLE 1.1-24 *Living arrangements of college students, by marital status, college class, and sex, 1960 (percentage distribution)*

Marital status, living arrangements, and sex	All college students	Fresh-men	Sopho-mores	Juniors	Seniors	Graduates or profes-sionals
Male	100.0	100.0	100.0	100.0	100.0	100.0
Married, spouse present	27.4	11.5	19.7	24.9	37.3	54.2
Household head	26.4	10.9	18.8	24.0	35.9	53.3
In parents' household*	0.8	0.5	0.8	0.8	1.2	0.8
In other relative's household	0.1	0.1	0.1	0.1	0.1	0.1
In nonrelative's household	0.0	0.0	0.0	0.1	0.1	0.1
Other marital status	72.6	88.5	80.3	75.1	62.7	45.8
Household head	5.1	2.4	4.1	5.0	6.3	9.3
In parents' household*	29.0	40.5	35.9	26.8	21.3	12.0
In other relative's household	2.0	2.6	2.4	2.0	1.6	1.1
In college dormitory†	24.4	32.5	26.3	27.5	20.3	10.5
In other living quarters	12.1	10.5	11.6	13.7	13.1	12.8
Female	100.0	100.0	100.0	100.0	100.0	100.0
Married, spouse present	13.7	7.6	10.4	12.7	24.9	36.7
Wife of head	13.2	7.3	9.9	12.2	24.1	35.8
In parents' household*	0.4	0.3	0.4	0.4	0.7	0.8
In other relative's household	0.1	0.1	0.1	0.0	0.0	0.1
In nonrelative's household	0.0	0.0	0.0	0.0	0.1	0.1
Other marital status	86.3	92.4	89.6	87.3	75.1	63.3
Household head	3.8	1.9	2.4	3.5	5.9	16.4
In parents' household*	29.0	33.9	31.3	24.3	23.6	18.1
In other relative's household	2.3	2.9	2.2	1.8	1.7	1.8
In college dormitory†	35.5	39.5	37.3	38.3	30.9	9.1
In other living quarters	15.7	14.2	16.3	19.4	12.9	17.8

*Includes parents-in-law.
†Includes sorority houses and fraternity houses.
SOURCE: *1960 Census of Population, Subject Reports, School Enrollment,* ser. PC(2)-5A, table 9; in J. K. Folger and C. B. Nam, *Education of the American Population,* a 1960 Census Monograph, U.S. Bureau of the Census, 1967, p. 69.

spouses to support; 17 percent of the college men (two-thirds of those who were married) and 8 percent of the college women (over half of those who were married) had children as well. It should be noted, however, that marriage made college attendance possible for many persons. Most of the

TABLE 1.1-25 *Percentage distributions of college students, by college class, family status, labor force status of student and spouse, and sex, 1960*

Family status, labor force status of student and spouse, and sex	All college students	Fresh-men	Sopho-mores	Juniors	Seniors	Graduates or profes-sionals
Male	100.0	100.0	100.0	100.0	100.0	100.0
Married, wife present	27.4	11.5	19.7	24.9	37.3	54.2
Labor force	22.5	10.3	17.1	19.8	29.2	44.1
Wife in labor force	9.2	4.2	6.7	8.7	12.2	17.6
With own children	3.7	1.8	2.9	3.5	4.7	7.0
Without own children	5.5	2.4	3.8	5.2	7.5	10.7
Wife not in labor force	13.3	6.1	10.5	11.1	17.0	26.5
With own children	11.4	5.1	8.9	9.5	14.5	23.2
Without own children	1.8	0.9	1.6	1.5	2.5	3.3
Not in labor force	4.9	1.2	2.5	5.2	8.0	10.1
Wife in labor force	3.0	0.8	1.6	3.4	5.0	5.9
With own children	1.0	0.3	0.5	1.1	1.7	1.8
Without own children	2.0	0.5	1.1	2.3	3.3	4.2
Wife not in labor force	1.9	0.5	1.0	1.8	3.1	4.2
With own children	1.3	0.3	0.6	1.1	2.1	3.1
Without own children	0.6	0.2	0.4	0.7	1.0	1.1
Other marital status	72.6	88.5	80.3	75.1	62.7	45.8
Labor force	34.2	37.5	38.1	34.6	30.8	26.6
Not in labor force	38.5	50.9	42.2	40.4	31.9	19.2
Female	100.0	100.0	100.0	100.0	100.0	100.0
Married, husband present	13.7	7.6	10.4	12.7	24.9	36.7
Labor force	5.9	2.7	3.9	5.1	10.7	22.9
Husband in labor force	5.5	2.5	3.6	4.7	9.7	21.3
With own children	2.4	1.2	1.7	2.1	4.4	7.9
Without own children	3.1	1.3	1.9	2.6	5.3	13.4
Husband not in labor force	0.5	0.2	0.3	0.4	1.0	1.6
With own children	0.1	0.1	0.0	0.1	0.2	0.2
Without own children	0.4	0.1	0.2	0.3	0.8	1.3
Not in labor force	4.9	4.9	6.5	7.6	14.2	13.9
Husband in labor force	3.0	4.6	5.9	6.9	12.6	12.5
With own children	4.8	3.5	4.3	4.4	7.9	8.0
Without own children	2.2	1.0	1.6	2.5	4.7	4.5

TABLE 1.1-25 *(continued)*

Family status, labor force status of student and spouse, and sex	All college students	Fresh-men	Sopho-mores	Juniors	Seniors	Graduates or profes-sionals
Female						
Married, husband present						
Not in labor force						
Husband not in labor force	0.7	0.3	0.6	0.7	1.6	1.4
With own children	0.2	0.2	0.2	0.2	0.4	0.4
Without own children	0.5	0.1	0.5	0.5	1.2	1.0
Other marital status	86.3	92.4	89.6	87.3	75.1	63.3
Labor force	34.5	31.0	36.0	37.7	33.2	43.0
Not in labor force	51.8	61.4	53.6	49.7	41.9	20.2

SOURCE: *1960 Census of Population, Subject Reports, School Enrollment,* ser. PC(2)-5A, table 8; in J. K. Folger and C. B. Nam, *Education of the American Population,* a 1960 Census Monograph, U.S. Bureau of the Census, 1967, p. 69.

TABLE 1.1-26 *Percentage distributions showing periods of attendance in four-year institutions by type, by sex, and by control; all in relation to institution of first registration*

Period of attendance	Grand total	Total by sex		Universities	
		Men	Women	Men	Women
Not beyond first registration period	10.7	13.0	7.2	11.3	6.8
Beyond first registration period, not more than 1 year	16.6	14.4	19.8	13.0	13.5
Beyond 1 year, not more than 2 years	15.0	12.2	19.1	12.8	19.0
Beyond 2 years, not more than 3 years	6.0	6.3	5.6	6.7	6.7
Entered fourth year, not graduated	7.3	9.8	3.7	12.1	5.6
Graduated in 1954	39.5	38.8	40.5	39.1	38.8
Others	4.9	5.5	4.1	5.0	4.6
Total number of students	12,667	7,503	5,164	3,802	1,973

*The percentages for 1,021 junior college students are as follows: Not beyond first registration period—12.0; beyond first registration period, not more than 1 year—28.3; beyond first year, not more than 2 years—56.8.

SOURCE: U.S. Office of Education, *Retention and Withdrawal of College Students,* 1957, p. 16.

college women with children had husbands in the labor force. Presumably many of these women attended school part time and their husbands worked full time so that financial needs could be met without too much difficulty. Among married college men, 87 percent of those with children and 74 percent of those without children were in the labor force. For about 27 percent of those with children and 76 percent of those without children, the wife was in the labor force. Among married couples where the husband was in college, in one-tenth of the cases both husband and wife were in the labor force and many of the couples had children.[1]

Data on periods of attendance in college show that only 39.5 percent of students who entered four-year institutions graduated in 1954 (four years later). About 27 percent had dropped out by the end of the first year and an additional 15 percent by the end of the second year (Table 1.1-26).

[1] J. K. Folger and C. B. Nam, *Education of the American Population,* a 1960 Census Monograph, U.S. Bureau of the Census, 1967, p. 69.

| Type of institution* | | | | | | Type of control | | | |
| Technological institutions | | Liberal arts colleges | | Teachers colleges | | | Private | | |
Men	Women	Men	Women	Men	Women	Totally public	Totally	Independent	Church related
9.9	6.4	14.1	6.5	21.3	9.2	12.5	8.2	7.8	9.2
12.8	8.5	14.6	20.2	22.0	21.6	18.4	14.2	12.0	20.1
10.2	6.4	11.7	21.1	12.3	16.3	15.7	14.2	14.0	14.7
7.1	8.5	6.1	4.7	4.4	5.3	6.0	6.0	6.5	4.8
11.8	10.6	6.5	2.5	6.1	2.2	8.7	5.4	6.3	3.0
42.0	53.2	40.8	41.8	28.8	40.7	33.0	48.0	49.6	43.7
6.2	6.4	6.2	3.1	5.1	4.7	5.7	4.0	3.8	4.5
736	47	2,191	2,006	774	1,138	7,179	5,488	3,996	1,492

To help explain the high percentage of students (60.5 percent) who do not remain at the institution where first registered, Table 1.1-27 indicates the general paths taken by students who leave. Of significance is that only 12 percent "transferred to another institution" whereas 41.5 percent are recorded as "dropped out with no record of transfer."

According to an Office of Education publication,

About 60 percent of the students who enter colleges eventually graduate, although fewer than 40 percent graduate from the institutions of first registration in normal progression. The 10 percent who transfer do so mainly because of general dissatisfaction, change in curricular interests, desire to be nearer home, and need to attend a less expensive institution. Students who take time out for military service, who are enrolled in programs requiring more than 4 years, and students who change to part-time status constitute the majority of the 10 percent in the delayed graduation group. The top fifth of the high school graduating class contributes 42 percent of college enrollees and 32 percent of college dropouts.[2]

Tables 1.1-28 to 1.1-30 show some of the stated reasons for discontinuing attendance at college. For example, 45.8 percent of students leaving college in a 1965 study indicated academic reasons as the one most important reason for leaving. However, the percentage of dropouts mentioning academic reasons for leaving was significantly greater in private colleges (58.7 percent) than in public colleges (35.8 percent) (Table 1.1-28).

A previous study in 1957 indicated that among male students the main reasons for discontinuing college attendance were the lack of interest in studies, military obligations, personal financial problems, and discouragement with low grades. For female students, the main reasons for leaving were marriage, taking a full-time job, and personal financial problems (Table 1.1-29).

Reasons for withdrawal from junior colleges are cited in a 1960 survey of 10,000 students: 28 percent of students stated full-time employment as the reason for withdrawal; 16 percent stated personal and health reasons; and 11 percent indicated moving or transferring, whereas only 9 percent reported academic difficulties (Table 1.1-30).

Another aspect of student attendance at college is the change of

[2] R. E. Iffert, *Retention and Withdrawal of College Students*, U.S. Office of Education, 1958, cover page.

TABLE 1.1-27 *Student records of graduation, transfer, and dropout, by types of four-year institutions*

	Percentage by type of institution				
Student record	Total for four-year institutions	Univer-sity	Tech-nological institution	Liberal arts college	Teachers college
Graduated in four years from institution of first registration	39.5	39.0	42.8	41.3	36.0
Not graduated but still attending after four years	11.2	13.1	13.3	9.3	8.6
Transferred to another institution	12.0	10.7	11.2	15.4	8.6
To smaller institution	4.8	7.0	3.3	3.1	2.7
To larger institution	5.5	2.3	5.4	10.3	4.8
Dropped out, no record of transfer	41.5	42.7	35.3	39.7	44.1
No information	1.4	.7	.8	.9	4.7
Total number of students	12,667	5,775	783	4,197	1,912

Percentages exceed 100 because some students fall into more than one category. For example, a student may have transferred and later returned with a loss of standing so that he would be counted in the "transfer" group as well as the "still attending" group. The excess is some indication of the relative student mobility within the four types of institutions. The total transfers also exceed the identifiable numbers transferring to smaller and larger institutions.

SOURCE: U.S. Office of Education, *Retention and Withdrawal of College Students,* 1957, p. 18.

TABLE 1.1-28 *Percentage distributions of dropouts naming the one most important reason for dropout in each category of reasons, percentages of mentions of contributing reasons in each category, and percentages of changed circumstances in each category, by control, 1956–57*

Category or reasons	Percentage of dropouts naming one reason as most important			Percentage of total mentions of other contributing reasons			Percentage of total mentions of changed circumstances		
	Total	Public	Private	Total	Public	Private	Total	Public	Private
Academic	45.8	35.8	58.7	40.5	38.7	42.7	40.0	34.6	49.5
Health and family	25.2	29.8	19.4	17.3	19.3	14.6	23.2	25.4	19.4
Financial	15.0	17.9	11.4	20.9	21.0	20.7	22.5	24.7	18.6
Dissatisfactions	6.1	8.0	3.5	12.3	13.5	10.8	5.3	6.1	3.9
Social and religious	2.3	1.9	2.9	2.2	0.0	5.0	2.2	1.8	2.8
Disciplinary	.5	.5	.6	.5	.2	.8	.2	.1	.3
Other	5.1	6.1	3.5	6.3	7.3	5.4	6.6	7.3	5.5
Total numbers	2,398	1,350	1,048	2,206	1,242	964	1,691	1,083	608

NOTE: The underlined percentages are significantly higher than the corresponding percentages for institutions under the other type of control.

SOURCE: R. E. Iffert and B. S. Clarke, *College Applicants, Entrants, Dropouts,* U.S. Office of Education, 1965, p. 28.

TABLE 1.1-29 Reasons for discontinuing college attendance— percentage comparisons between sexes and among reasons	Percentage rating "of some importance"	
Reasons for discontinuance	Men	Women
Academic		
(a) Lacked interest in studies	48.0	33.0
(b) Discouraged by low grades	40.0	22.9
(c) Found college work too difficult	26.5	19.9
(d) Placed on academic probation	21.2	10.4
(e) Dismissed for academic failure	18.1	6.9
Personal		
(a) Planned to be married soon	10.7	49.2
(b) Lonesome and unhappy	14.7	16.6
(c) Illness or physical disability	7.3	10.1
(d) Dismissal (nonacademic reasons)	2.8	1.1
(e) Placed on probation (nonacademic)	2.0	.4
(f) Suspended (disciplinary reasons)	1.7	.4
Family		
(a) Financial	29.7	32.3
(b) Needed at home	12.6	12.5
(c) Illness or physical disability	8.7	10.1
(d) Marital difficulties	3.6	3.3
Financial		
(a) Financial (self)	41.4	36.4
(b) Took a full-time job	24.2	37.2
Other		
(a) Military service (enlisted)	45.2	1.0
(b) Military service (drafted)	24.6	0.0
(c) Commuting took too long	6.6	6.6
(d) Housing situation caused trouble	6.4	5.3

SOURCE: U.S. Office of Education, *Retention and Withdrawal of College Students,* 1957, p. 91.

subject fields. For most of the major subject fields shown in Table 1.1-31, well over 50 percent of students have changed to a new interest. However, some fields of study seem to have greater stability in retaining students once enrolled, such as engineering and physical education, which show percentages of 60.5 and 53.4 respectively.

Data on the residence and migration of college students and the degree of student migration among states are presented in Table

TABLE 1.1-30 *Reasons stated for withdrawing from junior college reported by approximately 10,000 students enrolled in 20 two-year colleges between 1949 and 1957*

Reasons stated for withdrawal	No. of students	Percent
Full-time employment	2,734	28
Personal and health	1,554	16
Moved or transferred	1,084	11
Nonattendance	1,013	10
Academic or faculty action	860	9
To enter armed forces	832	8
Not interested in school or dissatisfied	763	8
Financial	549	6
Marriage	264	3
Educational goals completed	55	1
TOTAL	9,898	100

SOURCE: L. L. Medsker, *The Junior College: Progress and Prospect,* McGraw-Hill Book Company, New York, 1960, p. 48.

1.1-32. According to the 1963 study of residence and migration, of all student residents, 80 percent remained in their home states to attend college. California ranked first among the states, with 94 percent of the student residents remaining; Utah was second, with 92 percent; and Louisiana was third, with 91 percent.

Students enrolled outside their home states and doing work creditable toward a bachelor's or higher degree numbered 777,340, which is 18.2 percent of the total enrollment for the aggregate United States.

Five states (Connecticut, Illinois, New Jersey, New York, and Virginia) had a net out-migration of more than 10,000 students, whereas seven states (California, Indiana, Massachusetts, Missouri, North Carolina, Tennessee, and Utah and the District of Columbia) had a net in-migration of more than 10,000 students (Table 1.1-33).

As discussed in a study by the Organization for Economic Co-operation and Development (OECD), *(Financing of Education for Economic Growth):*[3]

"An indication of the greater vertical mobility in the United States as compared with Great Britain is obtained by comparing the ratios in the two

[3] Organization for Economic Co-operation and Development, *Financing of Education for Economic Growth,* OECD Publications, Paris, 1966, p. 227.

TABLE 1.1-31 *Analysis of changes in subject fields of interest by men students*

			Percentage maintaining				
Code	First interest (only first interests with frequencies of 100 or more)	Number	Accounting (1)	Agriculture (2)	Biology (10)	Business administration (12)	Chemistry (13)
(1)	Accounting	217	36.4	0.9		35.5	0.5
(2)	Agriculture	200	1.0	45.0	2.5	4.5	1.0
(10)	Biology	113			20.4	1.8	11.5
(12)	Business administration	487	7.8	1.2	.6	45.8	.8
(13)	Chemistry	245	.3	.8	2.0	2.9	21.2
(16)	Education	126	1.6	4.0	1.6	6.4	.8
(17)	Engineering	830	2.2	1.1	.5	6.4	2.7
(23)	English	113	.9		1.8	2.7	.9
(29)	History	143	1.4		1.4	3.5	.7
(36)	Mathematics	184	5.4	.5	1.6	7.6	5.4
(45)	Physical education	161	1.9	1.2	3.7	4.4	.6
(46)	Physics	116			1.7	4.3	6.9
(50)	Prelaw	158	7.7			14.7	.6
(51)	Premedicine	344	1.5	1.7	4.9	4.1	7.6

SOURCE: U.S. Office of Education, *Retention and Withdrawal of College Students*, 1957, p. 56.

countries of the percentage at college with a professional or management background to the percentage of those with a labour background. The ratio is roughly 2 to 1 in the United States, and about 20 to 1 (for higher professions) and about 8 to 1 (for managerial and other professions) in Great Britain."

In Great Britain, the economic factor is also shown to be very important: "Clearly the economic circumstances of the home are very influential: even in families of the same occupational level, the proportion of children reaching full-time higher education is four times as high for children from families with one or two children as from those where five or more children have claims on the family's resources. . . ."

In other countries of Western Europe, the economic and occupational status of the parents determines who does and who does not go to institu-

same interest (underlined) and percentage changing to a new interest

Education (16)	Engineering (17)	English (23)	History (29)	Mathematics (36)	Physical education (45)	Physics (46)	Prelaw (50)	Premedicine (51)	Other	Total
1.8	2.8	0.9	1.8	2.3	1.4	0.5	3.2		12.0	100
3.5	5.5	2.0	.5	.5	1.0		.5		32.5	100
5.3	1.8	1.8	4.4	4.4	3.5	1.8	1.8	6.2	35.4	100
2.5	5.3	1.2	3.9	.6	2.1		3.1	.2	24.9	100
2.9	18.0	3.3	4.1	7.8	.8	6.1	.8	4.9	28.7	100
_33.3_	3.2	4.8	9.5	6.4	1.6		1.6	.8	24.6	100
.7	_60.5_	.5	.8	4.0	.8	2.4	.6	.6	16.4	100
.9	.9	_24.8_	15.9	2.7	.9		6.2	4.4	37.2	100
4.9		6.3	_26.5_	2.1	3.5		4.9	.7	44.1	100
2.7	13.0	2.7	4.9	_19.6_	6.0	13.0		.5	16.9	100
6.2	2.5	1.9	5.6	1.2	_53.4_		.6	.6	15.2	100
	24.1	2.6	.9	9.5	.9	_28.5_	1.7	.9	18.1	100
4.5	3.2	2.6	4.5			.6	_27.6_	5.1	28.9	100
.9	4.1	3.5	2.3	1.5		2.0	1.5	_36.9_	27.6	100

tions of higher education. In Sweden, for example, the proportion of the working classes going to *gymnasium,* the major path to institutions of higher education, has been distressingly low. (Most graduates of a *gymnasium* go to institutions of higher education, and the percentage tends to rise.)

". . . In the first post-war years only 2–3 percent of all the children of manual workers—representing half of the labour force—entered the *gymnasium* whereas about ¾ of the children from families where the fathers were university graduates passed through the *gymnasium.* There have been big changes in the social recruitment to the *gymnasium* in the last decade. But still the more wealthy half of the population send four times as many children to the *gymnasium* as the other half of the population does."

(Text continued on p. 76)

TABLE 1.1-32 *Students enrolled, student residents, and students remaining in their home states to attend college, by level of enrollment and control of institutions, aggregate United States, fall 1963*

Thus New York, New Jersey, and Illinois are consistently among the top five States with the highest net outmigration in the all institutions, public institution, and private institution categories. Indiana is among the five States with the highest net inmigration for all, public, and private institutions.

There are marked differences in the pattern of student migration among the levels of enrollments. Twenty-three percent of the graduate students study outside their State of residence, while only 17 percent of the undergraduates do so. The rate of migration is highest at the first-professional level, with 33 percent of the students working toward the first-professional

Level of enrollment (1)	All institutions (2)	All four-year institutions (3)	Total (4)	Universities (5)
A. Students enrolled				
All students	4,265,864	3,644,667	2,108,250	1,187,879
Undergraduate	3,635,943	3,014,746	1,772,670	953,733
First-professional	151,149	151,149	56,776	51,440
Graduate	478,772	478,772	278,804	182,706
B. Student residents				
All students	4,192,489	3,575,903	2,074,008	
Undergraduate	3,593,680	2,977,094	1,755,707	941,980
First-professional	148,019	148,019	56,274	50,978
Graduate	450,790	450,790	262,027	167,010
C. Students remaining in their home states				
All students	3,415,149	2,843,386	1,819,652	982,399
Undergraduate	2,967,429	2,395,666	1,562,465	819,380
First-professional	99,183	99,183	47,034	42,585
Graduate	348,537	348,537	210,153	120,434
D. Ratio of students remaining to students enrolled				
All students	0.80	0.78	0.86	0.83
Undergraduate	0.82	0.79	0.88	0.86
First-professional	0.66	0.66	0.83	0.83
Graduate	0.73	0.73	0.75	0.66

degree leaving their State of residence to attend college. Many States have few private and no public professional schools.

Part-time undergraduate students migrate less than full-time undergraduate students. Only 5 percent of the part-time, as compared with 21 percent of the full-time, students leave their State of residence to attend institutions of higher education. For the Nation as a whole, the percent of women student migrants at all levels of enrollment is slightly less than the percent of all migrant students and of men migrant students. Seventeen percent of all women students migrate to other States to attend college.

| *Four-year institutions* | | | | *Junior colleges* | | |
| *Public* | | *Private* | | | | |
All other (6)	*Total* (7)	*University* *sities* (8)	*All other* (9)	*All junior colleges* (10)	*Public* (11)	*Private* (12)
920,371	1,536,417	558,367	978,050	621,197	547,826	73,371
818,937	1,242,076	363,614	878,462	621,197	547,826	73,371
5,336	94,373	55,452	38,921			
96,098	199,968	139,301	60,667			
914,040	1,501,895	542,436	959,459	616,586	544,282	72,304
813,727	1,221,387	357,212	864,175	616,586	544,282	72,304
5,296	91,745	53,990	37,755			
95,017	188,763	131,234	57,529			
837,253	1,023,734	367,768	655,966	571,763	520,522	51,241
743,085	833,201	244,259	588,942	571,763	520,522	51,241
4,449	52,149	31,261	20,888			
89,719	138,384	92,248	46,136			
0.91	0.67	0.66	0.67	0.92	0.95	0.70
0.91	0.67	0.67	0.67	0.92	0.95	0.70
0.83	0.55	0.56	0.54			
0.93	0.69	0.66	0.76			

TABLE 1.1-32
(continued)

Level of enrollment (1)	All institutions (2)	All four-year institutions (3)	Total (4)	Universities (5)
E. Ratio of students remaining to student residents				
All students	0.81	0.80	0.88	0.85
Undergraduate	0.83	0.80	0.89	0.87
First-professional	0.67	0.67	0.84	0.84
Graduate	0.77	0.77	0.80	0.72

SOURCE: M. C. Rice and P. L. Mason, *Residence and Migration of College Students, Fall 1963: State and Regional Data,* U.S. Office of Education, National Center for Educational Statistics, 1965, p. 2.

LEVELS OF ENROLLMENT

All Students in All Institutions.—As mentioned in the "Introduction", eighty percent of the students enrolled in work creditable toward a bachelor's or higher degree in the Nation's colleges in Fall 1963 were attending in their home States. However, the percents of the students enrolled in the individual States who are residents of the respective States vary widely. Only 24 percent of the students attending college in the District of Columbia are residents of the District; 92 percent of the students enrolled in California are residents who remain in their home State to

But the situation has improved. The percentage of manual workers among the fathers of the students at universities and colleges was 8 in 1947 and 14 in 1960.[4]

The British report *15 to 18*[5] states that the children of English professional or managerial parents stay in school much longer than the children of parents having other occupations [Table 1.1-22].

Of the National Service men entering the army, nine-tenths of the top 10 percent stayed in school voluntarily for at least one year. But more than four-tenths left by the time they were 16. Of men in ability group

[4] Organization for Economic Co-operation and Development, *Educational Policy and Planning in Sweden,* OECD Publications, Paris, January 1964.

[5] *15 to 18: Report of the Central Advisory Council for Education,* England, vol. 2, 1959, pp. 8–15.

| Four-year institutions | | | | Junior colleges | | |
| Public | | Private | | | | |
All other (6)	Total (7)	University sities (8)	All other (9)	All junior colleges (10)	Public (11)	Private (12)
0.92	0.68	0.68	0.68	0.93	0.96	0.71
0.91	0.68	0.68	0.68	0.93	0.96	0.71
0.84	0.57	0.58	0.55			
0.94	0.73	0.70	0.80			

attend college. . . . In 1963, eighteen States exceeded the percent for the Nation, with more than 80 percent of the students enrolled being residents of these respective States; in 1958, twenty-two States exceeded the percent for the Nation. Increases between 1958 and 1963 in the percent of enrollments represented by students who remained in their home States to attend college ranged from 1 to 11, with five States (Florida, Hawaii, Maryland, Rhode Island, and Virginia) having increases of 5 percent or more. Nine States had decreases.

1, 41 percent left school at 18 or later, but only 14 percent of the sons of manual workers.[6]

Similar statistics are available in other countries. In Austria in the early 1950s, fathers of sons at institutions of higher education were in the occupations shown in Table [1.1-23].

When allowance is made for the numbers in each occupation, the disproportionate percentage from higher occupations is even more evident.

Of 37,075 students in IHE [institutions of higher education] in Italy, more than 31,000 had parents who are in entrepreneurial, professional, managerial or salaried occupations; only 4,163 were children of wage earners.

In Sweden, entry to the *gymnasium* represents the greatest obstacle for

(Text continued on p. 80)

[6] Ibid., p. 9.

	Students enrolled	Student residents	Students remaining
State (1)	(2)	(3)	(4)
Aggregate United States	4,265,864	4,192,489	3,415,149
The 50 states and District of Columbia	4,233,501	4,159,075	3,383,877
Alabama	45,261	45,983	36,702
Alaska	1,663	3,077	1,419
Arizona	45,532	41,569	36,647
Arkansas	31,311	32,498	26,866
California	569,538	557,507	524,485
Colorado	49,194	40,614	32,636
Connecticut	60,251	73,269	45,187
Delaware	7,198	8,738	4,371
District of Columbia	48,785	18,024	11,622
Florida	100,646	109,258	87,211
Georgia	55,744	54,744	42,803
Hawaii	14,426	17,476	11,435
Idaho	14,736	17,478	11,736
Illinois	234,387	255,183	198,158
Indiana	116,971	96,610	80,506
Iowa	66,343	59,735	44,311
Kansas	62,329	59,290	48,813
Kentucky	55,873	51,173	41,737
Louisiana	69,090	66,156	59,990
Maine	13,088	12,711	8,237
Maryland	63,589	73,206	50,324
Massachusetts	154,854	129,192	101,394
Michigan	184,422	176,190	157,526
Minnesota	79,374	76,863	64,271
Mississippi	40,940	39,476	34,415
Missouri	91,709	81,344	64,252
Montana	15,623	17,069	13,160
Nebraska	38,063	34,251	28,099
Nevada	5,599	7,158	4,935
New Hampshire	13,384	10,249	5,788

TABLE 1.1-33
Residence and migration of all students: all institutions, fall 1963

	Ratio of students remaining to:						Migration of students		
	Students enrolled			Student residents					Net (col. 12− col. 11)
Total (5)	Men (6)	Women (7)	Total (8)	Men (9)	Women (10)	Out of (11)	Into (12)	(13)
0.80	0.79	0.82	0.81	0.80	0.83	777,340	850,715	+73,375
0.80	0.79	0.82	0.81	0.80	0.83	775,198	849,624	+74,426
0.81	0.80	0.83	0.80	0.79	0.81	9,281	8,559	−722
0.85	0.82	0.91	0.46	0.46	0.47	1,658	244	−1,414
0.80	0.79	0.82	0.88	0.88	0.89	4,922	8,885	+3,963
0.86	0.85	0.87	0.83	0.82	0.83	5,632	4,445	−1,187
0.92	0.91	0.94	0.94	0.94	0.95	33,022	45,053	+12,031
0.66	0.67	0.66	0.80	0.80	0.80	7,978	16,558	+8,580
0.75	0.71	0.82	0.62	0.60	0.64	28,082	15,064	−13,018
0.61	0.60	0.62	0.50	0.47	0.55	4,367	2,827	−1,540
0.24	0.22	0.27	0.64	0.63	0.66	6,402	37,163	+30,761
0.87	0.85	0.90	0.80	0.78	0.82	22,047	13,435	−8,612
0.77	0.74	0.81	0.78	0.77	0.80	11,941	12,941	+1,000
0.79	0.73	0.87	0.65	0.61	0.71	6,041	2,991	−3,050
0.80	0.78	0.82	0.67	0.67	0.67	5,742	3,000	−2,742
0.85	0.84	0.86	0.78	0.77	0.79	57,025	36,229	−20,796
0.69	0.66	0.75	0.83	0.82	0.85	16,104	36,465	+20,361
0.67	0.66	0.69	0.74	0.74	0.75	15,424	22,032	+6,608
0.78	0.77	0.81	0.82	0.81	0.85	10,477	13,516	+3,039
0.75	0.73	0.78	0.82	0.79	0.85	9,436	14,136	+4,700
0.87	0.84	0.90	0.91	0.90	0.92	6,166	9,100	+2,934
0.63	0.59	0.69	0.65	0.63	0.68	4,474	4,851	+377
0.79	0.79	0.79	0.69	0.69	0.69	22,882	13,265	−9,617
0.65	0.67	0.63	0.78	0.78	0.79	27,798	53,460	+25,662
0.85	0.84	0.88	0.89	0.89	0.91	18,664	26,896	+8,232
0.81	0.80	0.82	0.84	0.83	0.85	12,592	15,103	+2,511
0.84	0.83	0.86	0.87	0.86	0.89	5,061	6,525	+1,464
0.70	0.70	0.70	0.79	0.79	0.79	17,092	27,457	+10,365
0.84	0.82	0.89	0.77	0.78	0.76	3,909	2,463	−1,446
0.74	0.73	0.75	0.82	0.81	0.84	6,152	9,964	+3,812
0.88	0.87	0.90	0.69	0.68	0.70	2,223	664	−1,559
0.43	0.37	0.54	0.56	0.51	0.65	4,461	7,596	+3,135

TABLE 1.1-33
(continued)

State (1)	Students enrolled (2)	Student residents (3)	Students remaining (4)
New Jersey	108,453	164,960	93,789
New Mexico	20,852	20,239	15,540
New York	407,108	443,340	351,155
North Carolina	83,202	68,615	59,486
North Dakota	15,280	16,292	12,651
Ohio	207,616	199,397	165,569
Oklahoma	65,407	61,739	54,710
Oregon	45,466	42,219	34,569
Pennsylvania	224,493	223,391	172,527
Rhode Island	17,800	15,373	10,170
South Carolina	33,811	31,617	23,868
South Dakota	16,122	15,813	12,154
Tennessee	73,708	62,773	51,580
Texas	228,090	222,549	205,794
Utah	40,700	28,666	26,348
Vermont	11,104	6,245	3,755
Virginia	62,321	72,521	46,082
Washington	75,618	73,710	63,676
West Virginia	33,996	30,999	25,679
Wisconsin	90,816	84,585	70,394
Wyoming	7,164	7,991	5,345
United States service schools	14,451		
Outlying areas of the United States	32,363	33,414	31,272

SOURCE: M. C. Rice and P. L. Mason, *Residence and Migration of College Students, Fall 1963: State and Regional Data,* U.S. Office of Education, National Center for Educational Statistics, 1965, p. 29.

those from modest backgrounds; once this has been surmounted they do much better. We should also bear in mind that the recent improvements in the figures for children of working men are larger than they seem to be because the proportion of labourers in the working population is declining. In general, however, the children of parents in the lower paid occupations are far from proportionately represented in IHE.

Ratio of students remaining to:						*Migration of students*		
Students enrolled			*Student residents*					*Net (col. 12— col. 11)*
Total (5)	*Men* (6)	*Women* (7)	*Total* (8)	*Men* (9)	*Women* (10)	*Out of* (11)	*Into* (12)	(13)
0.86	0.84	0.91	0.57	0.55	0.60	71,171	14,664	−56,507
0.75	0.71	0.83	0.77	0.77	0.76	4,699	5,312	+613
0.86	0.86	0.87	0.79	0.77	0.83	92,185	55,953	−36,232
0.71	0.69	0.76	0.87	0.86	0.88	9,129	23,716	+14,587
0.83	0.80	0.88	0.78	0.80	0.74	3,641	2,629	−1,012
0.80	0.79	0.81	0.83	0.82	0.85	33,828	42,047	+8,219
0.84	0.82	0.86	0.89	0.88	0.89	7,029	10,697	+3,668
0.76	0.76	0.76	0.82	0.81	0.83	7,650	10,897	+3,247
0.77	0.76	0.79	0.77	0.76	0.80	50,864	51,966	+1,102
0.57	0.55	0.62	0.66	0.65	0.68	5,203	7,630	+2,427
0.71	0.67	0.76	0.75	0.73	0.79	7,749	9,943	+2,194
0.75	0.74	0.78	0.77	0.77	0.77	3,659	3,968	+309
0.70	0.69	0.72	0.82	0.82	0.83	11,193	22,128	+10,935
0.90	0.89	0.92	0.92	0.92	0.93	16,755	22,296	+5,541
0.65	0.66	0.63	0.92	0.91	0.94	2,318	14,352	+12,034
0.34	0.32	0.36	0.60	0.57	0.65	2,490	7,349	+4,859
0.74	0.74	0.74	0.64	0.61	0.68	26,439	16,239	−10,200
0.84	0.84	0.84	0.86	0.86	0.87	10,034	11,942	+1,908
0.76	0.73	0.79	0.83	0.81	0.85	5,320	8,317	+2,997
0.78	0.78	0.76	0.83	0.82	0.85	14,141	20,422	+6,281
0.75	0.71	0.81	0.67	0.67	0.67	2,646	1,819	−827
							14,451	+14,451
0.97	0.96	0.98	0.94	0.92	0.95	2,142	1,091	−1,051

A study in Germany in the late 1950's estimated that only one-sixth had sufficient income to meet room and board costs and fees. More than one-third of the students earned money during term time, and one-tenth worked more than 10 hours per week.

In Denmark, although the largest part of the population consists of workers, their sons represent only 8 per cent of the students at IHE; whereas the sons of university trained parents, a small part of the population, represent 25 percent of the students.

In the USSR, at first policy was to discriminate against the children of the upper classes, but it is now to provide aid on the basis of need and ability. The student receives a wage in addition to his expenses. Seventy-five to 97 per cent of these students receive financial aid from the government, the amount depending on the school, the subject and the quality of the work.

The fact that the number of children of well-to-do parents in higher education is relatively large does not mean that aid programmes would result in a proportionate number of children from the working classes attending IHE. Undoubtedly, the children of the more successful parents also have a higher level of intelligence, and possibly greater motivation. But few would deny that many children of outstanding ability are unable to profit from higher education because of financial difficulties.

An examination of the numbers graduating from secondary schools, entering IHE and graduating from IHE throws further light on this subject. Enrollment in IHE is relatively high in the United States; the greater availability of aid in some European countries, however, makes it possible for a larger proportion of the best students there to attend IHE than in the United States.[7]

[7] Organization for Economic Co-operation and Development, *Financing of Education for Economic Growth,* OECD Publications, Paris, 1966, pp. 228–229.

1.2. Graduate Student Characteristics

Table 1.2-1 contains data on a number of socioeconomic characteristics of graduate students, classified according to undergraduate academic achievement measures. It reveals the following: (1) A large proportion of the graduate students were married (61 percent), had dependents (41 percent), and were 29 years of age or above (46 percent). (2) Slightly more than half were enrolled on a part-time rather than a full-time basis.[1] (3) Outstanding academic performance was not a prerequisite to graduate school attendance. As many as two-fifths of graduate students had undergraduate grades of B— or below, and as few as 17 percent had undergraduate averages of A— or A. (4) Of all institutions offering graduate degrees, over three-fifths were under public control and nearly three-fourths were universities.

A table bearing on the social origins of graduate students shows that 29 percent had fathers who earned less than $5,000 and 72 percent had fathers whose income was less than $10,000. The occupations of the fathers of the graduate students were not as heavily concentrated in the professional or managerial class as might have been expected (57 percent of all fathers of graduate students were in these occupations and only about 36 percent of all fathers and 31 percent of all mothers of graduate students had some college education [Table 1.2-2]).

Table 1.2-3 provides information on prior employment of graduate students according to sex and broad academic field in 1965. Prior to entering graduate school, about one-half of all students had been teachers; 30 percent were from industry or business; and

(Text continued on p. 86)

[1] The proportion of full-time graduate students as a percentage of the total was higher than that ratio in the early 1960s. See U.S. Office of Education, *Enrollment for Advanced Degrees,* fall 1963, p. 10.

TABLE 1.2-1   *Profile variables, by undergraduate academic achievement (grade-point average) of graduate students, spring 1965*

Profile variables	Total Number	Total Percent	A, A—	B+, B	B—, C	Total, percent
All students	477,535		17	41	42	100
Sex		100				
Men	335,227	70	16	38	46	100
Women	142,308	30	20	48	32	100
Age		100				
23 and under	68,663	14	19	43	38	100
24–28	191,688	40	17	39	44	100
29 and over	217,183	46	16	43	41	100
Race		100				
White	425,323	96	15	41	44	100
Negro	12,141	3	11	38	51	100
Other (chiefly Oriental)	4,022	1	15	47	38	100
Citizenship		100				
United States	441,487	93	15	41	44	100
Other	36,048	7	39	45	16	100
Marital status		100				
Single, no dependents	168,225	35	20	43	38	100
Single, with dependents	18,132	4	15	46	39	100
Married, no dependents	96,199	20	18	40	42	100
Married, with dependents	194,977		14	40	46	
Enrollment status		100				
Full-time	210,130	48	23	43	34	100
Part-time	267,404	52	12	40	48	100
Control of institution		100				
Public	296,032	62	17	42	41	100
Private	181,503	38	17	39	43	100
Type of institution		100				
Universities	354,078	74	20	43	37	100
All other	123,457	26	7	37	56	100
Size of graduate enrollment		100				
Large	225,524	47	21	42	37	100
Small	252,010	53	13	41	46	100

SOURCE: J. S. Hunter, *The Academic and Financial Status of Graduate Students, Spring, 1965,* U.S. Office of Education, 1967, p. 14.

TABLE 1.2-2 *Social origins of graduate students—income, occupation, and education of the fathers and the education of the mothers, by sex, spring 1965*

		Sex	
Background characteristic	All students	Men	Women
Number of students	477,535	335,226	142,307
		Percent	
Total	100	100	100
Father's income (per annum)			
Less than $5,000	29	30	28
$5,000–$7,499	27	28	24
$7,500–$9,999	16	16	14
$10,000–$14,999	12	12	12
$15,000–$19,999	4	3	5
$20,000 and over	4	4	6
Do not know	8	6	12
Father's occupation			
Laborer	5	6	5
Service worker	4	4	3
Semiskilled operative	7	8	6
Skilled craftsman	18	19	16
Farm operator	8	7	8
Proprietor or manager	18	17	19
Semiprofessional	15	15	16
Professional (except educator)	19	19	21
Teacher or other educator	5	5	5
Father's education			
Did not complete grade school	13	13	11
Completed grade school but not high school	28	28	26
Completed high school but no college	23	24	23
One but less than four years of college	12	12	13
Completed college	12	12	13
Obtained master's degree	4	4	4
Obtained Ph.D. or other	8	7	10
Mother's education			
Did not complete grade school	9	9	8
Completed grade school but not high school	27	27	25
Completed high school but no college	34	35	32
One but less than four years of college	16	15	18
Completed college	11	10	12
Obtained master's degree	3	2	3
Obtained Ph.D. or other	1	1	1

SOURCE: J. S. Hunter, *The Academic and Financial Status of Graduate Students, Spring, 1965,* U.S. Office of Education, 1967, p. 7.

TABLE 1.2-3
Employment of graduate students prior to their entry into graduate school, by sex and broad academic field, spring 1965

Prior employment	*All students*	*Sex*	
		Men	*Women*
Number of students	477,535	335,227	142,308
Occupation			
Elementary school teacher	17	9	35
Secondary school teacher	23	20	27
Faculty of junior college	2	2	1
Faculty of four-year institution	8	8	6
Hospital, church, etc.	10	7	16
Self-employed	7	7	5
Industry or business	30	36	18
Professional partnership	1	1	1
Research organization	8	9	5
Federal government	16	20	5
State or local government	6	6	5
Other	7	6	9
No previous employment	16	17	15

SOURCE: J. S. Hunter, *The Academic and Financial Status of Graduate Students, Spring, 1965,* U.S. Office of Education, 1967, p. 16.

22 percent had been in government jobs. These proportions were not the same for different subject areas. For example, in the sciences approximately one-fifth of those starting graduate work had been teachers and 36 percent had been in industry and business, whereas for those entering the humanities as graduate students over half had been teachers and 23 percent had worked in industry and business.

For several years, graduate deans have attempted to reduce the time required to achieve the Ph.D. One common measure of the time required consists of the time it takes after receiving the B.A. to obtain the Ph.D. Another measure, which is shorter, is the time between beginning graduate work and completing Ph.D. requirements. The time difference in these two measures can be explained by frequent delays between the procurement of the B.A. and the beginning of graduate work.

Table 1.2-4 contains estimates of the lapse in time between receiving the baccalaureate and completing the doctoral degree in 10 fields of study. From 1920 to 1961 the mean number of years

		Broad academic fields			
Education	Humanities	Social & behavioral sciences	Professional fields	Sciences	Miscellaneous
133,478	53,231	73,540	65,906	135,887	15,493
Percent					
47	10	6	5	1	24
41	30	17	8	10	33
2	3	2	1	1	1
5	12	7	7	9	8
10	9	18	13	4	11
8	7	6	6	6	9
20	23	24	53	36	29
1	1	1	3	1	2
3	3	8	5	16	4
13	10	16	19	18	16
5	4	10	6	5	7
6	11	7	6	6	8
5	25	24	13	23	9

it took to obtain a doctoral degree after receiving the baccalaureate was 9.8. For 10-year periods the range was from 8.4 in 1920–1929 to 10.0 in 1950–1959. By fields the extremes were chemistry (6.5 years) and education (14.9 years). This information is plotted on a graph contained in Figure 1.2-1.

Table 1.2-5 provides data on the number of years elapsing between receipt of the baccalaureate degree and the beginning of graduate study for men and women in six academic fields classified by undergraduate grade-point average. It shows that 18 percent of all graduate students waited five years or more before entering graduate school after receiving a B.A.; 31 percent waited between one and four years; and over half waited less than one year after obtaining a B.A. before beginning graduate work. A larger proportion of graduate students in science, humanities, and social and behavioral sciences waited less than one year before entering graduate school than was true for graduate students in education and professional fields. Graduate students with the highest undergraduate grade-point averages were more likely to go directly to

(Text continued on p. 93)

TABLE 1.2-4 *Time lapse between baccalaureate and doctorate degrees in 10 fields: mean number of years and standard deviations for each decade, 1920–1960*

Period	Math	Physics	Chem- istry	Geo- physical sciences	Engi- neering	Total physical sciences
1920–1929:						
Number	337	632	1,902	326	219	3,416
Mean	8.1	7.4	6.2	7.8	6.9	6.8
S.D.	4.7	4.3	3.7	4.9	4.6	4.2
1930–1939:						
Number	774	1,305	3,917	604	780	7,380
Mean	7.7	7.1	6.2	7.8	7.4	6.8
S.D.	4.9	4.1	3.8	4.6	4.9	4.2
1940–1949:						
Number	829	1,469	5,309	563	1,406	9,576
Mean	8.3	7.5	6.3	8.9	8.1	7.1
S.D.	4.9	3.9	3.5	4.3	4.3	3.9
1950–1959:						
Number	2,317	4,962	10,221	1,700	5,923	25,123
Mean	8.3	7.4	6.6	8.1	8.1	7.4
S.D.	4.8	3.6	3.5	4.6	4.2	4.0
1960–1961:						
Number	643	1,160	2,231	506	1,826	6,366
Mean	8.5	7.6	7.0	8.6	8.3	7.8
S.D.	4.8	3.4	3.5	4.5	4.4	4.0
1920–1961:						
Number	4,900	9,528	23,580	3,699	10,154	51,861
Mean	8.2	7.4	6.5	8.2	8.0	7.2
S.D.	4.8	3.7	3.6	4.6	4.3	4.0

SOURCE: L. R. Harmon, et al., *Doctorate Production in the United States 1920–1962,* National Academy of Sciences, National Research Council, Washington, D.C., 1963, p. 40; in U.S. Office of Education, *Students and Buildings: An Analysis of Selected Federal Programs for Higher Education,* 1968, p. 64.

Biological sciences	Total natural sciences	Psy- chology	Social sciences (other than psy- chology	Arts and pro- fessions	Education	Social sciences, arts and pro- fessions, and education	Grand total
2,257	5,673	618	1,837	2,105	1,064	5,624	11,297
8.1	7.3	8.5	8.8	9.5	11.3	9.5	8.4
4.6	4.4	5.0	4.7	5.4	5.4	5.2	4.9
5,006	12,386	1,116	3,816	4,633	2,995	12,560	24,946
7.9	7.2	8.2	9.9	10.2	13.8	10.8	9.0
4.6	4.4	5.2	5.4	5.8	6.5	6.1	5.6
5,853	15,429	1,233	4,197	4,755	4,676	14,861	30,290
8.5	7.6	9.0	11.1	11.6	15.2	12.4	10.0
4.6	4.2	5.2	5.8	6.2	6.3	6.4	5.9
14,880	40,003	6,403	11,120	11,098	13,946	42,567	82,570
8.3	7.7	8.5	10.8	12.0	15.2	12.2	10.0
4.6	4.2	5.1	5.9	6.4	6.9	6.7	6.1
3,563	9,929	1,622	2,681	2,984	3,418	10,705	20,634
8.9	8.2	9.4	11.0	12.0	15.2	12.4	10.3
4.4	4.2	5.2	5.9	6.3	7.1	6.7	6.0
31,559	83,420	10,992	23,651	25,575	26,099	86,317	169,737
8.3	7.6	8.7	10.6	11.4	14.9	11.9	9.8
4.6	4.3	5.2	5.7	6.2	6.8	6.5	5.9

TABLE 1.2-5
Number of years elapsing between receipt of baccalaureate degree and the beginning of graduate study, by sex, broad academic fields, and undergraduate academic achievement (grade-point average), spring 1965

Sex, broad academic fields, and undergraduate grade-point average	All students		Less than one year
	Number	Percent	
Total	477,535	100	51
Sex			
Men	335,227	100	54
Women	142,308	100	45
Broad fields			
Education	133,478	100	38
Humanities	53,231	100	60
Social and behavioral sciences	73,540	100	60
Professional fields	65,906	100	41
Science	135,887	100	62
Miscellaneous	15,490	100	42
Undergraduate grade-point average			
A, A—	80,826	100	60
B+, B	196,749	100	53
B—, C	199,959	100	46

SOURCE: J. S. Hunter, *The Academic and Financial Status of Graduate Students, Spring, 1965,* U.S. Office of Education, 1967, p. 37.

| | Years elapsed, percent | | | | |
One year	Two years	Three years	Four years	Five to nine years	Ten and more years
13	8	6	4	9	9
12	9	6	5	9	6
15	7	4	3	9	16
16	10	6	4	11	15
14	6	4	3	6	7
12	7	5	3	7	7
11	8	8	7	13	11
11	8	5	4	7	4
16	8	8	5	11	11
12	7	4	3	8	7
12	7	5	4	9	9
14	10	7	5	9	9

FIGURE 1.2-1 *Mean B.A.-to-Ph.D. time lapse* in five major fields (two-year moving average)*

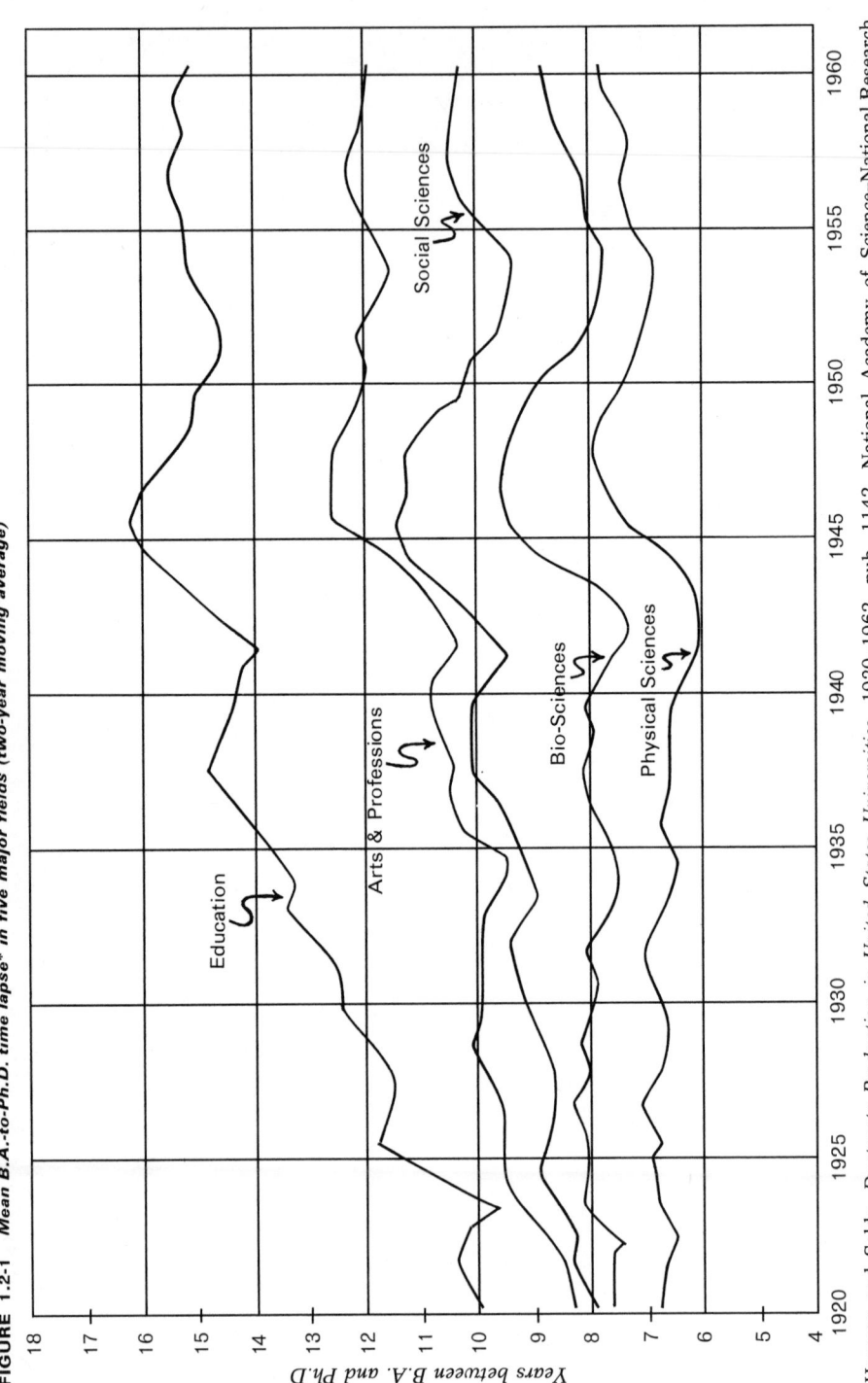

Education

Arts & Professions

Social Sciences

Bio-Sciences

Physical Sciences

Years between B.A. and Ph.D

1920 1925 1930 1935 1940 1945 1950 1955 1960

4 5 6 7 8 9 10 11 12 13 14 15 16 17 18

Harmon and Soldz, Doctorate Production in United States Universities, 1920–1962, pub. 1142, National Academy of Science–National Research Council, 1963; in U.S. House of Representatives, Committee on Science and Astronautics, Higher Education in the Sciences in the United States: ... prepared by the National Science Foundation, 1965, p. 7.

TABLE 1.2-6
*Average years
of graduate
attendance, by
field of study*

Field	Graduate attendance (years)*					
	All graduate institutions				Doctoral institution only	
	Mean	(P_{25})	Mdn.	(P_{75})	Mean	Median
Biosciences	4.7	(3.5)	4.4	(5.2)	3.7	3.6
Botany	4.4		4.2		3.5	3.4
Microbiology	4.7		4.5		3.9	3.5
Zoology	4.7		4.6		3.6	3.5
Other biosciences	4.9		4.6		4.0	3.8
Physical sciences	4.5	(3.7)	4.3	(5.2)	3.8	3.7
Mathematics	4.8		4.4		3.7	3.2
Physics	4.9		4.7		3.9	3.8
Chemistry	4.5		4.3		3.9	3.7
Engineering	4.2		4.0		3.7	3.4
Social sciences	4.1	(3.2)	3.8	(4.7)	3.2	3.1
Psychology	4.1		3.8		3.3	3.2
Sociology	3.9		3.8		2.9	3.0
Political science	4.3		4.0		3.5	3.1
Economics	4.0		3.7		3.1	3.0
Humanities	4.2	(3.2)	3.9	(4.8)	3.3	3.2
History	4.0		3.8		3.3	3.2
Foreign languages	4.4		4.3		3.4	3.4
English	4.2		3.9		3.7	3.1
All fields	4.4	(3.4)	4.2	(5.0)	3.6	3.5

* Reported as number of semesters and/or quarters of "attendance at a graduate institution" and converted into calendar-year equivalent. Includes both full- and part-time attendance and does not necessarily represent *continuous* attendance. In parentheses are the twenty-fifth and seventy-fifth percentiles, respectively, in distributions of total years of attendance, all graduate institutions for the major areas and the total sample of this; for example, 25 percent of biosciences graduates spent less than 3.5 years in attendance, and 25 percent spent more than 5.2 years in attendance.

SOURCE: K. M. Wilson, *Of Time and the Doctorate*, Southern Regional Education Board, Atlanta, Ga., 1965, p. 312.

graduate school from undergraduate education than graduate students with poorer undergraduate academic qualifications.

The average number of years of actual graduate attendance varied very little by subject area. The mean number of years graduate students spent in institutions offering the doctoral degree in all fields was 3.5. To get a doctorate it took approximately 3.1 years in the social sciences compared to 3.7 years in the physical sciences (Table 1.2-6).

Delays in getting the doctorate were related to a number of factors. For all broad fields of study covered in Table 1.2-7, the following were among the most significant factors contributing to slow progress in getting a Ph.D.: financial problems, working as a teaching assistant, the nature of the dissertation topic, and inadequate foreign language preparation.

Table 1.2-8 reports the Office of Education findings on the obstacles to more rapid completion of the requirements for an advanced degree. For the students covered in the survey, financial problems were most frequently regarded as an obstacle. The absolute and relative importance of financial problems as an explanation for delays in getting the doctorate had declined markedly by 1963–64 compared to earlier years.

TABLE 1.2-7 *Relative potency of various factors as "lengthening influences" in four major academic areas* *

Factor†	Biosciences	Physical sciences	Social sciences	Humanities
Discontinuity of attendance	Moderate	Moderate	Very high	Very high
Work as a teaching assistant	High	High	Low	High
Nature of dissertation topic	High	Moderate	High	High
Off-campus dissertation	Low	Low	Very high	Very high
Financial problems	Moderate	Moderate	High	High
Inadequate foreign language preparation	Moderate	Moderate	High	High
Lack of coordination between beginning and advanced study	Low	Moderate	High	Moderate
Family obligations	Low	Moderate	Moderate	Moderate
Inadequate undergraduate preparation in field of study	Moderate	Moderate	Moderate	Low
Transferring	Moderate	Moderate	Moderate	Moderate

* *Very high potency* — some lengthening influence for 35 percent or more and considerable lengthening influence for more than 20 percent.

High potency — some lengthening influence for 30–40 percent.

Moderate potency — some lengthening influence for 20–29 percent.

Low potency — some lengthening influence for less than 20 percent.

† Five additional factors were generally of low potency.

SOURCE: K. M. Wilson, *Of Time and the Doctorate,* Southern Regional Education Board, Atlanta, Ga., 1965, p. 57.

TABLE 1.2-8 Obstacles to more rapid completion of the requirements for an advanced degree reported by students expecting to earn a doctorate, by enrollment status and year graduate study began, spring 1965

Enrollment status and obstacles to completion of doctorate	Students expecting doctorate	Academic year graduate study began				
		Before 1961–62	1961–62	1962–63	1963–64	1964–65
Number of full-time students	72,337	35,365	9,676	12,918	8,035	6,263
		Percent				
Obstacles						
Financial problems	31	42	24	23	13	16
Personal responsibilities	13	16	10	12	7	9
Language requirements	9	10	10	10	6	2
Instruction of inferior quality	6	8	5	3	4	2
Making up prerequisites	6	8	6	4	5	2
Duties required of assistants	5	6	5	5	4	2
Uninteresting courses	4	4	5	4	9	2
Research and preparation of thesis	4	5	3	3	2	3
Limited stipends	3	3	4	4	3	
Academic restrictions	2	2	2	1	1	1
Inadequate early counseling	2	1	1	2	2	4
Preliminary examinations	1	1	1		1	
Comprehensive examinations	1	1	1		1	

SOURCE: J. S. Hunter, *The Academic and Financial Status of Graduate Students, Spring, 1965,* U.S. Office of Education, 1967, p. 42.

1.3. *Profile of the* *Current* *College Graduate*

Most of the material in this chapter is based on the book *Undergraduate Career Decisions* by J. A. Davis. Davis based his findings on a self-administered questionnaire completed in the spring of 1961 by 33,982 June graduates sampled from 135 colleges and universities.

Table 1.3-1 is a profile of the current (1961) college graduate based on a subsample of Davis's larger sample. (All the tables in the chapter are based on representative subsamples of the larger sample above.) Sixty percent of the graduates in this subsample were male and 40 percent female. Seventy-five percent of the graduates were single and 70 percent were 22 or younger at the time of graduation. With respect to race, 94 percent of the graduates were white, 3 percent were Negro, and 2 percent were Oriental. Ninety-seven percent of the graduates were born in the United States.

Table 1.3-2 gives selected social class characteristics of Davis's sample. About half of the families of graduates had incomes of $7,500 or more and 20 percent had incomes of less than $5,000. Nearly half of the heads of families of graduates were professional people or were managers and proprietors. Sixty percent of the fathers of graduates had at least a high school education, but only 25 percent had a bachelor's or higher degree. Sixty percent of the graduates came from families with a Protestant background, 25 percent had a Catholic background, and 8 percent had a Jewish background.

Table 1.3-3 gives several indices of the socioeconomic status of the graduates in this sample. Income of parents was clearly associated with type of occupation. Sixty-two percent of parents in the professional class had incomes of $10,000 or more, whereas only 10 percent of the parents who were skilled laborers had incomes of at least $10,000. Family income was also highly correlated

(Text continued on p. 100)

TABLE 1.3-1
Profile of the
college graduate
(representative
subsample)

	Percent	Cumulative
(a) Sex		
Male	60%	
Female	40	
	100%	
(b) Age at graduation		
19 or younger		
20	5%	
21	39	95%
22	26	56
23 to 24	12	30
25 to 29	12	18
30 or older	6	6
TOTAL	100%	
(c) Marital status		
Single	75%	
Expect to be married before fall 1961		13%
Other		62
Married	24	
Child or expecting a child		16
No children		8
Ex-married	1	
TOTAL	100%	
(d) Race		
White	94%	
Negro	3	
Oriental	2	
Other	1	
TOTAL	100%	
(e) Nativity		
United States–born	97%	
Foreign-born	3	
Naturalized		2%
Other, expect to stay in United States		1
Other, do not expect to stay		1
TOTAL	100%	

SOURCE: J. A. Davis, *Undergraduate Career Decisions: Correlates of Occupational Choice,* Aldine Publishing Company, Chicago, 1965, p. 193.

	Percent	Cumulative
(a) Annual income of parental family		
Less than $5,000	20%	
$ 5,000–$ 7,499	29	80%
$ 7,500–$ 9,999	19	51
$10,000–$14,999	15	32
$15,000–$19,999	6	17
$20,000 and over	11	11
TOTAL	100%	
(b) Occupation of head of parental family		
Professional	24%	
Manager or proprietor	25	
Sales	7	
Clerical	5	
Skilled	17	
Semiskilled	7	
Service	3	
Unskilled	4	
Farmer, farm worker	8	
TOTAL	100%	
(c) Father's education		
Eighth grade or less	22%	22%
Part high school	17	39
High school graduate	21	60
Part college	14	74
Bachelor's degree	12	86
Graduate or professional degree	13	
TOTAL	99%	
(d) Original religion		
Protestant	60%	
Roman Catholic	25	
Jewish	8	
Other	3	
None	3	
TOTAL	99%	

SOURCE: J. A. Davis, *Undergraduate Career Decisions: Correlates of Occupational Choice,* Aldine Publishing Company, Chicago, 1965, p. 196.

TABLE 1.3-3 *Socioeconomic status index: parental income, father's education, and parental occupation (representative subsample)*

(a) Parental income and parental occupation (percentage reporting parental income of $10,000 a year or more)

Professional	62
Proprietor, manager	52
Sales, clerical	21
Skilled	10
Semiskilled, service, unskilled	5
Farm, farm laborer	15

(b) Parental income and father's education (percentage reporting parental income of $10,000 a year or more)

Bachelor's degree or more	66
Part college	40
High school	25
Less than high school	14

(c) Parental occupation and father's education (percentage with given education level)

	Father's education				
	Bachelor's or more	Part college	High school	Less than high school	Total, percent
Professional	72	14	8	7	101
Proprietor, manager	21	21	28	30	100
Sales, clerical	16	24	27	33	100
Skilled	2	10	30	58	100
Semiskilled, service, unskilled	1	4	19	76	100
Farm, farm laborer	5	10	19	65	99

SOURCE: J. A. Davis, *Undergraduate Career Decisions: Correlates of Occupational Choice,* Aldine Publishing Company, Chicago, 1965, p. 207.

with father's education. For families whose fathers had a bachelor's degree or more, 66 percent earned $10,000 or more. For families whose fathers had less than a high school education, only 14 percent earned $10,000 a year or more. Fathers in the professional class had more education than fathers in any other occupational class. Seventy-two percent of the professional families had fathers with a bachelor's degree or more, whereas only 21 percent of the fathers of families in the proprietors and managers class and only 16 percent of the fathers of families in sales and clerical occupations had a bachelor's degree or more.

FUTURE PLANS In the spring of 1961 approximately 19 percent of the graduates in this sample intended to go to graduate or professional schools and had been accepted by one or more schools, 12 percent expected to attend graduate school the next year but had not been accepted yet, and 45 percent expected to go after 1961 (Table 1.3-4). With respect to anticipated careers, 33 percent expected to go into education, 18 percent into business, 11 percent into social sciences and humanities, and 17 percent into science and engineering. Only 3 percent expected to go into medicine and 4 percent into law.

TABLE 1.3-4
Graduate or professional school plans for fall 1961

Going to graduate or professional school and accepted by one or more schools	19%
Going to graduate or professional school and not yet accepted by one or more schools	12
Going to graduate or professional school after fall 1961 and have a definite date in mind	30
Going to graduate or professional school after fall 1961 but no definite date in mind	15
Not going to graduate or professional school but would like to if there were no obstacles	6
Not going to graduate or professional school and would not like to	18
TOTAL	100%

Anticipated career field	
Science	8%
Social science and humanities	11
Medicine	3
Law	4
Engineering	9
Education	33
Business	18
Other professions	15
TOTAL	100%

SOURCE: J. A. Davis, *Undergraduate Career Decisions: Correlates of Occupational Choice*, Aldine Publishing Company, Chicago, 1965, pp. 201–202.

Table 1.3-5 gives anticipated career employers. Twenty-seven percent of these graduates expected to work for a private company with 100 or more employees. Forty-six percent expected to work for educational institutions—33 percent for elementary and secondary schools, 12 percent for institutions of higher education, and 1 percent for other educational institutions. Fourteen percent expected to work for the federal government and 6 percent for state and local governments.

With respect to anticipated career activities, 50 percent expected to go into teaching, 33 percent into administration, 24 percent into research, and 24 percent into service to patients or clients.

Table 1.3-6 gives characteristics which would be very important to these graduates in choosing a job or a career. Sixty-five percent chose opportunity to be helpful to others or useful to society, while

TABLE 1.3-5
Anticipated career employer

Private company with 100 or more employees	27%
Private company with fewer than 100 employees or professional partnership	11
Family business	2
Self-employed	8
Research organization or institute	7
College, university, or junior college	12
Elementary or secondary school or school system	33
Other educational institutions	1
United States government	14
State or local government	6
Hospital, church, clinic, welfare organization, etc.	8
Other	3
Anticipated career activities	
Teaching	50%
Research	24
Administration	33
Service to patients or clients	24
None of these	7

NOTE: Some planned two career activities.

SOURCE: J. A. Davis, *Undergraduate Career Decisions: Correlates of Occupational Choice,* Aldine Publishing Company, Chicago, 1965, p. 203.

TABLE 1.3-6
Characteristics which would be very important in picking a job or career

Opportunities to be helpful to others or useful to society	65%
Opportunity to work with people rather than things	56
Opportunity to be original and creative	51
A chance to exercise leadership	41
Living and working in the world of ideas	39
Opportunities for moderate but steady progress rather than the chance of extreme success or failure	33
Making a lot of money	24
Freedom from supervision in my work	18
Avoiding a high-pressure job which takes too much out of you	16
Getting away from the city or area in which I grew up	13
Remaining in the city or area in which I grew up	7

SOURCE: J. A. Davis, *Undergraduate Career Decisions: Correlates of Occupational Choice,* Aldine Publishing Company, Chicago, 1965, p. 202.

56 percent chose opportunity to work with people rather than things. Only 24 percent of the graduates in this sample chose making a lot of money.

Students planning for a professional degree vary greatly in the extent to which they expect to delay beginning their professional training. Whereas 90 percent of those planning on a medical career expected to begin their study for a professional degree the following year, only 52 percent of those interested in the social sciences as a career and 25 percent of those interested in education would begin to study the following year. Variations in this respect among four fields were as follows:

Plans to begin study for a professional degree

	Next year	*Later*	*Never*	*Total (percent)*
Medicine	90	7	2	100
Physics	65	30	5	100
Engineering	33	46	21	100
Business	17	42	41	100

SOURCE: J. A. Davis, *Undergraduate Career Decisions: Correlates of Occupational Choice,* Aldine Publishing Company, Chicago, 1965, p. 200.

The attitudes of this group of graduates toward the prospect of being a college professor were also worthy of note:

	Percent
Would be very interesting	42
Do not have the ability	65
Takes too much time; want more time with family	22
Personality not suitable	31

SOURCE: J. A. Davis, *Undergraduate Career Decisions: Correlates of Occupational Choice,* Aldine Publishing Company, Chicago, 1965, p. 200.

TABLE 1.3-7
Distribution of reasons for not attending graduate or professional school next year

Specific reasons
(Percentage circling item as answer to the question: Which of the following best explains why you do not anticipate going to graduate or professional school next year?)

Response	Percent of . . . *	
	Total sample	Those not going
I want to get practical experience first.	22	33
Financial obstacles.	20	30
I'm tired of being a student.	18	27
I can get a desirable job without further schooling.	16	23
No desire to do so.	15	22
Family responsibilities.	12	19
I would rather get married.	8	12
Military service.	7	11
Low grades in college.	7	10
I will be in a company training program which provides the equivalent.	2	4
I do not think I have the ability.	2	4
I lack the necessary undergraduate course prerequisites.	1	2

*Percentages total more than 100 because of multiple answers.
SOURCE: J. A. Davis, *Great Aspirations: Career Decisions and Educational Plans During College,* National Opinion Research Center, The University of Chicago Press, vol. 1, 1963, p. 321.

Also of considerable interest were the reasons given for not planning to attend graduate or professional school next year (Table 1.3-7). Of the total sample, 22 percent wanted practical experience first, 20 percent were short of funds, 16 percent could get a job without more schooling, and 8 percent would rather get married.

ATTITUDES TOWARD COLLEGE In general, these graduates seemed to approve of their colleges (Table 1.3-8). A relatively small 6 percent disapproved. Thirty-two percent felt a very strong attachment to their colleges. About two-thirds of the graduates felt that the purpose of college was a basic general education and appreciation of ideas, while about one-third felt that the purpose of college was career training.

SEXUAL DIFFERENCES Reflecting the fact that relatively fewer women than men begin graduate work and complete the training for a Ph.D., the proportion of women among college graduates was much greater than among Ph.D. recipients in the early 1950s. In the labor market the

TABLE 1.3-8
College experience (representative subsample)

(a) Attachment to present college

Very strong attachment	32%
Like it, but not strongly	43
Mixed feelings	19
Do not like it, but not strongly	4
Thoroughly dislike it	2
TOTAL	100%

(b) Perceived purpose of college

	Myself	*The typical student here*
A basic general education and appreciation of ideas	67%	38%
Having a good time while getting a degree	3	25
Career training	32	39
Developing the ability to get along with different kinds of people	16	9

SOURCE: J. A. Davis, *Undergraduate Career Decisions: Correlates of Occupational Choice,* Aldine Publishing Company, Chicago, 1965, p. 199.

Field	Percentage of women among:		
	College graduates*	Ph.D. recipients†	Persons with four or more years of college in labor force in 1950
Natural sciences	25	6	11
Psychology	51	14	
Social sciences	35	10	28‡
Humanities and arts	60	15	
Engineering	§	§	1
Applied biology			
Agriculture	2	2	
Home economics	99	86	99
Health fields			
Medicine	6		5
Dentistry	1		2
Nursing	99		97
Business and commerce	14	7	6
Education	71	16	69
General	76	16	71
Physical	35	23	28
Other fields			
Law	4	2	4
Social work	80	25	70

*Based on recent graduating classes, but adjusted to correct for the unusually high number of male (veteran) students.

† Actual percentages, 1948–1949 through 1951–1952.

‡ Including psychology.

§ Less than 0.5 percent.

SOURCE: Office of Education and United States Census in D. Wolfle, *America's Resources of Specialized Talent,* report of the Commission on Human Resources and Advanced Training, Harper & Brothers, New York, 1954, p. 188.

proportion of women was especially large in home economics, nursing, social work, and education—in that order (Table 1.3-9). Women also represented an exceptionally large percentage of Ph.D. recipients in home economics.

Whereas there were only rather minor differences between male college graduates and all men in the life cycle in employment rates, female college graduates were considerably more likely to be employed than all women in every adult age group in the early 1950s (Figure 1.3-1).

FIGURE 1.3-1
Employment of women college graduates compared with nongraduates and with men

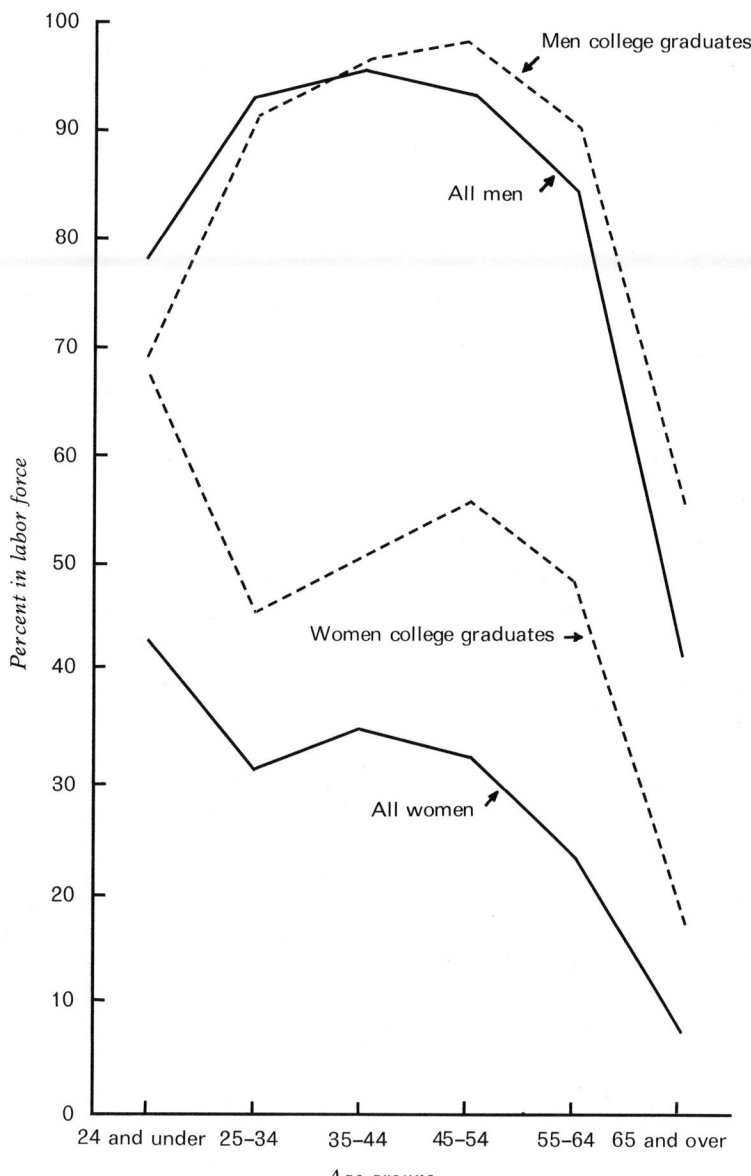

SOURCE: D. Wolfle, *America's Resources of Specialized Talent,* report of the Commission on Human Resources and Advanced Training, Harper & Brothers, New York, 1954, p. 227.

1.4. Student Expenses

Expenses incurred by students vary greatly by type of institution attended. A 1965 study showed that the total expenses of a typical student varied from $3,350 a year at high-cost private universities to $750 a year at public junior colleges (Table 1.4-1). This wide difference is explained in large part by the difference in average tuition and fees—from $50 at public junior colleges to $1,750 at high-cost private universities. A second major factor is the saving on room and board for students who commute to public junior colleges. However, the data should properly include an allowance for the cost of room and board at home for the junior college student.

TABLE 1.4-1   *Expenses of the typical student, by type of institution, 1965*

	High-cost private university	High-cost private liberal arts college	State university	State college (commuters)	Public junior college (commuters)	Private technical institute (commuters)
Total expenses	$3,350	$3,100	$1,700	$850	$750	$1,200
Tuition and fees	1,750	1,500	250	150	50	500
Room and board	800	800	800			
Books and supplies	100	100	100	100	100	100
Transportation	300	300	150	200	200	200
Personal expenses and miscellaneous	400	400	400	400	400	400

SOURCE: U.S. House of Representatives, Committee on Education and Labor, *Higher Education Act of 1965, Hearings before the Special Subcommittee on Education,* February to May 1965, p. 101.

STUDENT
COSTS AND
CAPACITY TO
PAY

From 1928 to 1964, major student expenses did not vary consistently with capacity to pay:

Indexes of student costs and average disposable family income, 1928–1964

	Major student costs in public institutions (for state residents)	Major student costs in private institutions	Average disposable family income
1928	100	100	100
1940	112	115	79
Percentage change, 1928–1940	+12	+15	−21
1952	180	185	205
Percentage change, 1940–1952	+61	+61	+159
1964	268	346	322
Percentage change, 1952–1964	+49	+87	+57

SOURCE: Table 1.4-2.

TABLE 1.4-2
Indexes of income and college costs (tuition and fees, room and board), 1928–1964

Year	Public in-state major costs	Public out-of-state major costs	Private major costs	Per-capita disposable income	Pre-tax average family income
1928	100	100	100	100	100
1932	108	112	111	58	n.a.*
1936	102	112	109	77	73
1940	112	121	115	86	80
1948	152	170	159	193	187
1952	180	205	185	226	228
1956	200	233	218	260	265
1960	238	286	279	287	303
1964	268	333	346	336	356

* n.a. indicates "not available."
SOURCE: College Entrance Examination Board, *The Economics of Higher Education,* New York, 1967, p. 8.

From 1928 to 1940, when average disposable family income fell substantially, student costs rose at both public and private institutions, and thus student capacity to pay declined. Between 1940 and 1952, however, average disposable family income rose sharply, while student costs also rose substantially, but not as much as disposable income. In the years from 1952 to 1964, a different relationship emerged. Student costs at public institutions of higher education rose less than average disposable family income, but costs at private institutions rose much more rapidly than family income.

Table 1.4-3 compares the changes in median family income, for families with heads aged 35 to 56 (the age bracket of parents with children in college), with changes in the consumer price index and in tuition and fees at public and private institutions of higher education. By 1961, family income was 95 percent higher than in 1949, while charges at public institutions had increased 93 percent and charges at private institutions 125 percent over the same period. However, during the greater part of the period, the increase in tuition and fees lagged behind the rise in family income, especially at public institutions. It was in the years from 1957 on that

Post-tax average family income	*Ratio of private to public (in-state) cost*	*Ratio of private to public (out-of-state) cost*
100	1.53	1.37
n.a.	1.58	1.37
72	1.63	1.35
79	1.57	1.30
171	1.58	1.27
205	1.58	1.24
240	1.65	1.28
276	1.78	1.33
322	1.96	1.42

TABLE 1.4-3 *Comparison of median income of families with heads aged 35–56, the Consumer Price Index and mean annual institutional charges, 1949–1961*

| | Median income of families with heads aged 35–56* | | Comsumer Price Index* (annual average) | Mean institutional tuition and required fees† | | | |
| | | | | Public institutions | | Private institutions | |
Year	Amount	Percent relative to 1949		Amount	Percent relative to 1949	Amount	Percent relative to 1949
1961	$6,618	195	128	$216	193	$1,045	225
1960	6,450	190	127	207	185	938	202
1959	6,140	181	125	194	175	890	191
1958	5,772	169	124	179	160	820	176
1957	5,560	164	120	168	150	741	159
1956	5,383	159	116	155	138	690	148
1955	4,987	147	115	147	131	638	137
1954	4,719	139	115	135	121	590	127
1953	4,735	140	114	130	116	565	122
1949	3,393	100	100	112	100	465	100

* Summarized from reports of the U.S. Department of Commerce and the U.S. Department of Labor and from an article by Lanore G. Lewis, "Median Family Income, the Cost of Living and Tuition Charges," *College and University Business*, vol. 27, pp. 19–21, December 1959.

† For the academic session beginning in September of the years indicated. Mean tuition charges of 196 representative institutions for 1949 and 1954 are taken from Herbert S. Conrad and Ernest V. Hollis, "Trends in Tuition Charges and Fees," *Annals of the American Academy of Political and Social Science*, vol. 301, pp. 148–164, September 1955. Data for 1955 through 1961 are calculated for the *same* institutions.

SOURCE: S. E. Harris and A. Levensohn, eds., *Education and Public Policy*, McCutchan Publishing Corporation, Berkeley, Calif., 1965, p. 266.

the rate of increase in tuition and fees at private institutions began to exceed the rate of increase in family income.

Table 1.4-2 shows a very sharp rise after 1952 in the ratio of costs at private institutions to costs for state residents at public institutions—from 1.58 in 1952 to 1.96 in 1964.

However, in the years from 1940 to 1964, the percentage of families with incomes of $10,000 or more (in 1964 dollars) rose from 9 to 20 percent. As the proportion of families in this income group increased, so also did the percentage of college students from families with incomes of $10,000 or more—from one-half in 1940 to three-fourths in 1964—while the number of college students from such families rose from 400 thousand to 1.8 million.[1]

[1] College Entrance Examination Board, *The Economics of Higher Education*, New York, 1967, table 2.

Table 1.4-4 shows the relationship between family income and family contributions to student expenses in 1966–67. The first point to be noted is that the number of students from families in the highest income quartile was more than six times the number from families in the lowest quartile. Estimated student expenses declined slightly with declining family income, reflecting the fact that students from high-income families were more likely than those from low-income families to attend high-cost institutions. The data also indicate, as would be expected, that the average family contribution declined sharply with declining income, and that, for students from families in the lowest income quartile, nearly all expenses had to be met from other sources.

The average amount required from other sources for these students was $1,477. Other data from the same study showed that, on the assumption that average summer earnings per student amounted to $300, the average family contribution (including these student earnings) varied from $660 for families with incomes between $5,000 and $7,499 to $5,700 for families with incomes of $20,000 and over.[2]

As the data in Table 1.4-4 indicate, student expenses decline somewhat with declining family income, but the difference between expenses of students from families in the lowest and highest income quartiles is not nearly as wide as the difference in average income. Another way of expressing this relationship is that student costs represent a larger percentage of family income in low-income than in high-income brackets (Table 1.4-5). Student expenses in private four-year institutions, for example, varied from 110 percent of mean family income in the lowest income quartile to 16 percent in the highest quartile. In public four-year institutions, the corresponding range was from 67 percent for the lowest income quartile to 10 percent for the highest.

Estimates of the gap between total family contributions for a college education and the total costs of alternative enrollment patterns are of considerable interest (Table 1.4-6). The assumptions underlying the projections are as follows:

- *Low enrollment pattern*—continuation of the recent enrollment pattern by achievement and socioeconomic quartile.

(Text continued on p. 116)

[2] U.S. Office of Education, *Students and Buildings: An Analysis of Selected Federal Programs for Higher Education,* 1968, p. 57.

TABLE 1.4-4
Average family income, average student cost, average family contribution, and average annual financial need for degree-credit undergraduates at all institutions of higher education by size of family income, 1966–67

Approximate family income quartile	Average family income (1)	Undergraduate students enrolled, full-time (in thousands) (2)
High	$16,016	1,940
Second	8,359	1,145
Third	5,549	671
Low	2,321	302
TOTAL	10,745	4,058

*Based on College Scholarship Service tabulation of family-financial plans filed by scholarship recipients. Excludes expenditures not directly related to formal education.

† Not estimated.

SOURCE: U.S. Office of Education, *Students and Buildings: An Analysis of Selected Federal Programs for Higher Education,* 1968, table 9, p. 17.

TABLE 1.4-5
Student costs of higher education relative to family income

	1st quartile (lowest)	2nd quartile	3rd quartile	4th quartile (highest)
Mean family income	$2,321	$5,549	$8,359	$16,016
Student cost				
Public, four-year	.67	.28	.19	.10
Private, four-year	1.10	.46	.31	.16
Public, two-year	.48	.20	.13	.07
Private, two-year	.89	.37	.25	.13

SOURCE: U.S. Office of Education, *Students and Buildings: An Analysis of Selected Federal Programs for Higher Education,* 1968, pp. 16–18.

Average cost tuition, fees, books, and personal expenses required for full-time study (3)	Average family contribution* (4)	Average student financial need for full-time study (3) — (4) (5)
$1,984	†	†
1,788	$1,060	$ 728
1,660	489	1,171
1,553	76	1,477
1,843	†	†

TABLE 1.4-6 The gap between estimated total family contributions for the college education of their child and the total costs of alternative enrollment patterns by socioeconomic status quartile for 1966, 1968, and 1972 (in thousands of dollars)†

Enrollment pattern	Socioeconomic status quartile				
	High	2d	3d	Low	Total
1966:					
Low	*	834	786	446	2,066
Medium	*	881	860	523	2,264
High	*	902	977	798	2,677
1968:					
Low	*	950	888	491	2,329
Medium	*	1,110	1,132	706	2,948
High	*	1,166	1,481	1,492	4,139
1972:					
Low	*	1,165	1,082	584	2,831
Medium	*	1,540	1,623	930	4,093
High	*	1,632	2,292	2,321	6,245

* Not estimated.

† This is apparently in error and should be "(in millions of dollars)."

SOURCE: U.S. Office of Education, *Students and Buildings: An Analysis of Selected Federal Programs for Higher Education,* 1968, p. 15.

- *Medium enrollment pattern*—an enrollment pattern like the present pattern but adjusted for differences in motivation found among persons of different socioeconomic status.

- *High enrollment pattern*—an enrollment pattern for all socioeconomic quartiles based solely on the present pattern for persons in the highest socioeconomic status quartile.

On the assumption of the medium enrollment pattern, the gap would be $4.1 billion in 1972, while, on the assumption of the high enrollment pattern, the gap would be $6.2 billion.

The cost of a college education to a student includes more than the outlay for his educational costs. In fact, the largest element in his total cost is foregone income—income that could have been earned if the student had been employed full-time rather than attending college. Table 1.4-7 provides estimates of foregone earnings (Text continued on p. 120)

TABLE 1.4-7 *Annual earnings foregone by students attending high school, college, or university, 1900–1956*

Year	Average weekly earnings, all manufacturing (dollars)	Annual earnings foregone (adjusted for unemployment) per student in		Number of students attending		Total earnings foregone by all students attending		High schools, colleges, and universities
		High school	College or university	High school	College or university	High school	College or university	
		(Dollars)		*(Millions)*		*(Millions of dollars)*		
1900	8.37	84	192	0.7	0.238	59	46	105
1910	10.74	113	259	1.1	0.355	124	92	216
1920	26.12	275	626	2.5	0.598	688	374	1,062
1930	23.25	224	509	4.8	1.101	1,075	560	1,635
1940	25.20	236	537	7.1	1.494	1,676	802	2,478
1950	59.33	626	1,422	6.4	2.659	4,006	3,781	7,787
1956	80.13	855	1,943	7.7	2.996	6,584	5,821	12,405

SOURCES: Theodore W. Schultz, "Capital Formation by Education," *Journal of Political Economy,* vol. 68, 1960, p. 575. Also "Education and Economic Growth," in Herman Richey (ed.), *Forces Influencing American Education,* University of Chicago Press, Chicago, 1960; in F. Machlup, *The Production and Distribution of Knowledge in the United States,* Princeton University Press, Princeton, N.J., 1962, p. 96.

TABLE 1.4-8 **Educational costs per student and average tuition and fees, in public and private institutions of higher education, actual, 1959–60 and 1966–67, and projected, 1976–77 (in 1966–67 dollars)**

	Public institutions		Private institutions	
	Costs per student	Tuition and fees	Costs per student	Tuition and fees
1959–60	$1,275	$250	$1,373	$ 922
1966–67	1,388	268	1,782	1,240
1976–77	1,558	329	2,450	1,757

SOURCE: U.S. Department of Health, Education and Welfare, *Accomplishments, 1963–1968, Problems and Challenges and a Look to the Future,* report to President Lyndon B. Johnson, December 1968, p. 87.

TABLE 1. 4-9 *Hypothetical annual cash outlays and economic cost for an undergraduate student, 1965–66*

Annual cash outlays			
Tuition and fees			$ 400
Board and room (academic year)			1,000
Expenses incident to education (books, supplies, transportation, club memberships, etc.)			400
Other expenses (clothing, health care, recreation, etc.)			300
TOTAL			$2,100
Annual economic cost			
(a) Assignable to the student			
Expenses incident to education (books, supplies, transportation, club memberships, etc.)		$ 400	
Board and room (including summer)	$1,200		
Minus cost of board and room if he were employed and not in college	1,000	200	
Estimated earnings if not in college	$4,500		
Minus summer and part-time earnings while in college	1,000	3,500	$4,100
(b) Assignable to the institution Costs covered by tuition and fees (paid by student)		$ 400	
Costs covered by appropriation, gifts, etc.		800	1,200
			$5,300

SOURCE: H. R. Bowen, *The Finance of Higher Education,* Carnegie Commission on Higher Education, Berkeley, Calif., 1968, p. 9.

TABLE 1.4-10
Living expenses
of graduate
students, by
enrollment
status, sex
and marital
status, and
living
arrangements,
spring 1965

Enrollment status, sex and marital status, and living arrangements	Total		Less than $1,000
	Number	Percent	
Full-time students	172,433	100	8
Men			
Single men, no dependents	57,493	100	14
Single men, dependents	2,396	100	11
Married men, no dependents	28,055	100	1
Married men, dependents	42,101	100	0
Women			
Single women, no dependents	24,176	100	18
Single women, dependents	2,698	100	4
Married women, no dependents	9,375	100	6
Married women, dependents	6,135	100	9
Living arrangements			
With parents	17,691	100	32
University unit	31,371	100	8
Room or apartment	85,403	100	6
Rented house	16,356	100	2
Owned house	18,551	100	5
Other	3,058	100	10
Part-time students	252,237	100	7
Men			
Single men, no dependents	31,922	100	11
Single men, dependents	3,751	100	6
Married men, no dependents	25,743	100	4
Married men, dependents	99,456	100	3
Women			
Single women, no dependents	29,377	100	10
Single women, dependents	6,911	100	4
Married women, no dependents	26,079	100	14
Married women, dependents	28,995	100	16
Living arrangements			
With parents	30,840	100	14
University unit	5,830	100	6
Room or apartment	75,290	100	5
Rented house	26,316	100	3
Owned house	109,111	100	8
Other	4,847	100	8

SOURCE: J. S. Hunter, *The Academic and Financial Status of Graduate Students, Spring, 1965,* U.S. Office of Education, 1967, p. 20.

Living expenses, percent								
$1,000 to 1,999	$2,000 to 2,999	$3,000 to 3,999	$4,000 to 4,999	$5,000 to 5,999	$6,000 to 6,999	$7,000 to 7,999	$8,000 to 8,999	$9,000 and over
23	21	15	12	7	5	3	2	
43	30	8	2	1	0	0	0	0
29	32	10	5	5	7	1		
5	16	29	23	12	7	3	2	1
3	9	22	22	14	11	6	5	7
42	27	8	3	1	1	0	0	0
18	16	12	17	6	14	8	1	4
13	20	17	17	8	8	3	2	5
6	9	10	11	11	13	7	6	16
30	24	8	3	2	1	0	0	0
27	18	19	16	6	3	1	1	1
26	25	17	11	7	4	2	1	2
13	17	17	16	11	11	6	5	3
5	6	10	13	12	13	10	10	16
32	18	12	11	5	7	2	1	2
7	8	11	14	15	11	8	6	13
26	22	14	12	9	3	1	1	2
7	12	11	17	20	6	9	3	8
3	6	14	21	18	12	9	7	7
1	2	6	12	17	15	14	11	20
16	20	20	20	11	2	1	1	0
5	6	13	17	20	12	7	6	10
4	10	13	12	16	10	6	4	11
4	3	5	8	12	10	9	6	27
17	19	16	17	10	4	1	1	1
28	14	18	14	11	5	2		1
9	12	15	17	17	9	5	4	6
5	8	13	19	19	13	9	5	5
2	3	5	9	14	13	13	10	24
10	8	14	16	13	13	6	5	7

for students attending high school and college from 1900 to 1956. Average foregone earnings per college student rose from $192 in 1900 to $1,943 in 1956. Total foregone earnings for all college and university students increased from $46 million to $5.8 billion during the same period.

In 1966–67, tuition amounted to 19 percent of educational costs per student in public institutions and to 70 percent in private institutions of higher education. Average tuition in public institutions is projected to rise 23 percent and educational costs 12 percent in constant dollars from 1966–67 to 1976–77 (Table 1.4-8). In private institutions the projected increases are 42 percent for tuition and 37 percent for educational costs per student. The data show clearly that costs of education per student are rising much more rapidly in private than in public institutions and that the dollar gap is steadily widening. The difference was only $98 in 1960–61 (in constant dollars) but is projected to rise to $892 in 1976–77.

Table 1.4-9 compares hypothetical cash outlays and annual economic costs for a typical undergraduate student in 1965–66. Cash outlays, estimated at $2,100, are expenditures actually incurred by the student. Economic costs, estimated at $5,300, are total societal costs of his education, regardless of who pays for them. Societal costs include the student's foregone earnings, estimated at $4,100—the largest component of cost, as suggested earlier.

GRADUATE STUDENT EXPENSES Educational expenses of graduate students vary according to the type and control of the institution they attend. More than half of all full-time graduate students had educational expenses of less than $800 in 1965, and 69 percent spent less than $1,200. However, expenses were much higher in private than in public universities. Forty percent of the graduate students in private universities incurred annual educational expenses of $1,700 or more, as compared with only 3 percent of the graduate students in public universities.

Related to the higher educational costs of graduate students is the larger share of student aid, in relation to enrollment and degrees, received by graduate students as compared with undergraduates:

Share of enrollment, degrees, and student aid, 1965–66, by levels	*Undergraduate and first professional*	*Graduate*
Enrollment (1963)	89	11
Degrees	81	19
Student aid	76	24

SOURCE: My calculations from U.S. Office of Education, *Financial Statistics of Institutions of Higher Education: Student Financial Aid, 1965–66,* National Center for Educational Statistics, 1968, table 2, p. 2; U.S. Office of Education, *Digest of Educational Statistics, 1968,* p. 72; and U.S. Office of Education, *Financial Statistics of Institutions of Higher Education: Current Funds, Revenues, and Expenditures, 1965–66,* National Center for Educational Statistics, 1969, p. 4.

In 1965, 31 percent of all full-time graduate students had annual living expenses of less than $2,000 while nearly four-fifths had living expenses of less than $5,000 (Table 1.4-10). However, as would be expected, the living expenses of married students tended to be considerably higher than those of single students. Moreover, part-time students tend to have higher living expenditures than full-time students. This is explained by the fact that part-time students have higher incomes because they frequently hold full-time jobs.

TABLE 1.4-11 *Distribution of total expenses and sources of funds for unmarried college students, 1959–60 (percentage distribution of students now in college)*

Dollars	Total expenses	Scholar-ships	Parents' contribution	Students' earnings	Other sources
0–49	*	75	13	44	83
50–499	6	15	17	21	8
450–949	8	8	23	24	6
950–1,449	28	1	23	7	3
1,450–1,949	31	*	10	1	*
1,950–2,449	16	*	8	1	*
2,450–2,949	5	*	3	*	*
2,950–3,449	4	*	2	1	*
3,450 and over	2	*	*	*	*
TOTAL	100	99	99	99	100

*Less than 0.5 percent.

SOURCE: J. B. Lansing, T. Lorimer, and C. Moriguchi, *How People Pay for College,* Institute for Social Research, University of Michigan, Ann Arbor, 1960, p. 21.

Table 1.4-11 shows the distribution of total expenses and sources of funds for unmarried college students in 1959–60. Three-fourths of the undergraduates received less than $50 in scholarships and 90 percent received less than $500. Thirty percent received less than $500 from parents' contributions, while, at the other end of the scale, 13 percent received $1,950 or more. Earnings amounted to less than $50 for 44 percent of the students, but 34 percent earned $450 or more.

TABLE 1.4-12 *Weighted mean percentage of college expenses defrayed with funds from several sources by active students and dropouts, by control, 1956–57*

Source of funds	Total		Public control		Private control	
	Active students	Drop-outs	Active students	Drop-outs	Active students	Drop-outs
Family, including relatives	51.2	50.7	53.9	47.3	47.8	55.1
Personal savings	18.9	23.7	20.7	27.7	16.7	17.7
On-campus work	3.9	3.1	4.3	2.6	3.2	3.9
Off-campus work	10.2	9.4	8.3	9.5	12.7	9.1
Church	.3	.2	.2	.1	.5	.5
Civic organizations	.3	.5	.3	.7	.2	.1
College scholar-ship(s)	4.1	1.8	2.5	1.4	6.1	2.9
Other scholar-ship(s)	3.7	1.8	2.5	1.8	5.4	1.6
College loan funds	.4	.5	.3	.4	.5	.8
Other loan(s)	.6	.7	.6	.4	.6	1.7
Other funds	6.4	7.6	6.4	8.1	6.3	6.6
Number reporting source and per-centage	9,410	1,495	4,778	838	4,632	657
Number reporting source	10,983	1,859	5,423	1,098	5,560	761
Percent reporting both	85.7	80.4	88.1	76.3	83.3	86.3

NOTE: The weighted mean percentage of expenses defrayed from each source was derived by multiplying the mean percentage defrayed per student by the percentage using it.

SOURCE: R. E. Iffert and B. S. Clarke, *College Applicants, Entrants, Dropouts,* U.S. Office of Education, 1965, p. 51.

TABLE 1.4-13   *Sources of student income as determined by questionnaire, 1957–1960*

| | Most important source | | All sources used | |
	Third-year	First-year	Third-year	First-year
Regular income	35.1	26.4	83.3	81.9
Savings specifically set aside for education	4.5	5.2	19.2	17.1
General savings and other assets	5.3	7.8	28.1	31.1
Loan from bank, etc.	3.1	3.6	15.6	18.1
Mother went to work for this purpose	10.2	9.9	29.8	24.9
Father took extra job or worked longer hours	1.7	5.2	14.1	16.6
Other	1.0	0.5	4.5	4.7
None listed as most important	40.5	44.5		
No response	(3.7)	(1.5)	(3.7)	(1.5)

SOURCE: N. Cliff and R. Ekstrom, *Practices and Attitudes in Paying for College,* Educational Testing Service, Princeton, N.J., 1962, p. 95.

More light is shed on the relative importance of various sources of college expenses by the data in Table 1.4-12. Slightly more than half of all expenses of active students were defrayed by family contributions. Other sources included personal savings, earnings, and scholarships, in order of relative importance. Students in private institutions tended to meet relatively more of their expenses from earnings and considerably more from scholarships than those in public institutions, whereas family contributions and personal savings contributed relatively less.

Of interest, also, are 1957–60 data on the sources of parents' contributions (Table 1.4-13). Regular income, as would be expected, was by far the most important source, but perhaps less to be expected is that the next most important source was income resulting from mothers joining the labor force. Savings and loans also played a significant role.

Data from the 1960 Census indicated that large proportions of both male and female college students received earnings in 1959, but amounts earned tended to be low, especially in the case of women. As Folger and Nam have pointed out:

TABLE 1.4-14 *Income of* *college students* *by college* *class and sex,* *1959*	*Income in 1959 by type and sex*	*All* *college* *students*	*Fresh-* *men*	*Sopho-* *mores*

Income in 1959 by type and sex	*All college students*	*Fresh-men*	*Sopho-mores*
Male	100.0	100.0	100.0
Earnings only	63.8	69.8	67.1
Under $1,000	27.9	39.7	31.6
$1,000–$1,999	14.7	14.7	16.3
$2,000 and over	21.2	15.4	19.2
Earnings and other income	23.8	15.1	20.3
Under $1,000	4.2	5.1	4.3
$1,000–$1,999	5.2	3.4	4.9
$2,000 and over	14.5	6.5	11.2
Other income only	2.5	1.5	2.0
Under $1,000	1.3	1.0	1.1
$1,000 and over	1.2	0.5	0.9
Not an income recipient	9.9	13.6	10.6
Female	100.0	100.0	100.0
Earnings only	59.2	57.5	58.9
Under $1,000	42.3	45.8	45.6
$1,000–$1,999	7.0	6.1	6.6
$2,000 and over	9.3	5.7	6.6
Earnings and other income	9.1	8.0	8.4
Under $1,000	4.9	5.1	5.1
$1,000–$1,999	1.7	1.3	1.6
$2,000 and over	2.5	1.5	1.7
Other income only	3.2	2.8	3.0
Under $1,000	2.1	2.1	2.1
$1,000 and over	1.0	0.7	0.9
Not an income recipient	28.5	31.7	29.7

SOURCE: J. K. Folger and C. B. Nam, *Education of the American Population,* U.S. Bureau of the Census (a 1960 Census Monograph), 1967, table 11–22, p. 72.

Of all male students with earnings during the year, slightly more than one-third had made less than $1,000, and some had received part of this income from sources other than earnings. About half of the college men with earnings during the year had incomes of $2,000 or more, but two-fifths of these men had incomes other than earnings to help bring them

uniors	*Seniors*	*Graduates or profes- sionals*
100.0	100.0	100.0
63.1	58.7	55.7
27.6	21.6	11.6
16.9	14.6	10.4
18.7	22.6	33.7
25.4	29.9	34.4
4.5	3.9	2.7
6.4	7.0	5.1
14.4	19.0	26.6
2.6	3.5	3.5
1.3	1.7	1.5
1.3	1.8	1.9
8.9	7.9	6.4
100.0	100.0	100.0
60.2	60.3	64.3
44.8	36.6	16.6
7.4	8.2	10.1
7.9	15.4	37.6
9.0	9.9	17.1
5.2	4.4	2.6
2.1	2.2	2.6
1.7	3.3	11.9
3.0	3.8	4.6
2.0	2.4	1.9
1.0	1.4	2.7
27.8	26.0	14.0

over the $2,000 mark. Of the female students with annual earnings, fully 70 percent made less than $1,000, and only one-sixth made $2,000 or more.[3]

[3] J. K. Folger and C. B. Nam, *Education of the American Population,* U.S. Bureau of the Census (a 1960 Census Monograph), 1967, pp. 71–72.

1.5. Student Aid

In a report to the President in December of 1968, officials of the Department of Health, Education and Welfare estimated that under four important federal programs, 1.5 million financial awards were made to college students in 1968 — at a cost of $892 million to the federal government. By 1971 federal aid to college students is projected to increase to $1,815 million, consisting of 2.5 million awards (Figure 1.5-1).

In an early 1969 report to the President, a committee chaired by Alice Rivlin, assistant secretary of Health, Education and Welfare, urged increased federal aid to higher education in the amount of $6.3 billion by fiscal year 1976. Most of this increased aid would go for programs of student aid and educational allowances to institutions. About $1.6 billion of the increase would be in the form of cost-of-education allowances to institutions. These allowances are intended to cover the additional institutional costs associated with increased enrollment of low-income students induced by the more generous federal aid program.[1] The Rivlin Committee estimated that by fiscal year 1976 about two-thirds of this $6.3 billion increase in federal aid would go directly to students and one-third directly to institutions.[2]

The committee recommended making financial aid available to a larger number of students and increasing the amount of individual stipends. In 1968 federal programs aided one out of four undergraduates, but this was inadequate to help all those who would

[1] See Table 4.2-11 in Chapter 4.2, "Government's contribution."
[2] U.S. Department of Health, Education and Welfare, *Toward a Long Range Plan for Federal Financial Support for Higher Education,* Report to the President, Office of Assistant Secretary for Planning and Evaluation, January 1969, pp. 31–36.

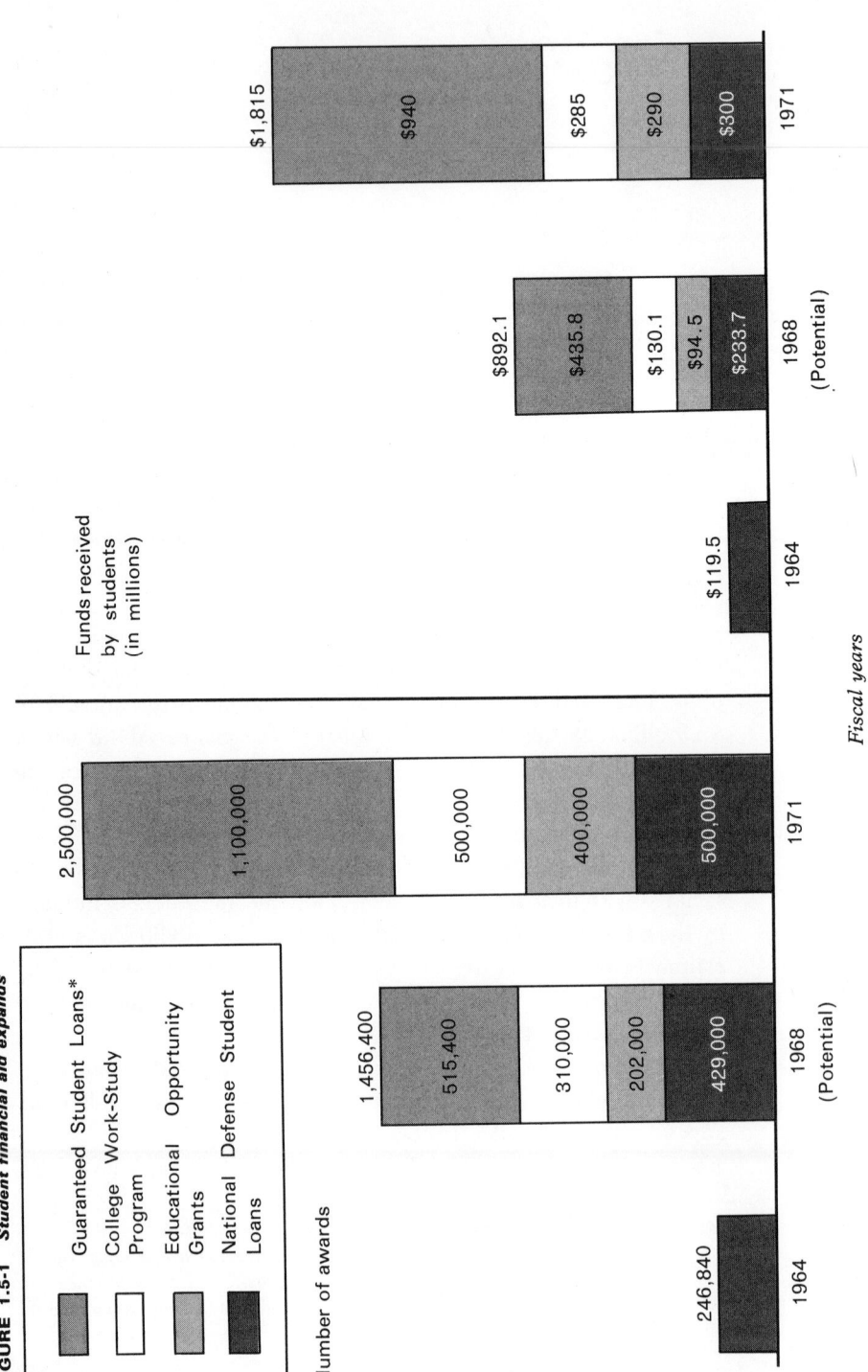

FIGURE 1.5-1 *Student financial aid expands*

Guaranteed Student Loans*

College Work-Study Program

Educational Opportunity Grants

National Defense Student Loans

Number of awards

246,840 — 1964

1,456,400 — 1968 (Potential)
- 515,400
- 310,000
- 202,000
- 429,000

2,500,000 — 1971
- 1,100,000
- 500,000
- 400,000
- 500,000

Fiscal years

Funds received by students (in millions)

$119.5 — 1964

$892.1 — 1968 (Potential)
- $435.8
- $130.1
- $94.5
- $233.7

$1,815 — 1971
- $940
- $285
- $290
- $300

* Loans made to vocational and college students.

SOURCE: U.S. Department of Health, Education and Welfare, *Accomplishments, 1963–1968, Problems and Challenges and a Look to the Future.*

benefit from a college education but could not attend because of financial need. In addition the committee considered the maximum Educational Opportunity Grant of $1,000 inadequate, because by 1971 tuition would have increased 50 percent since the introduction of the Educational Opportunity Grant program in 1965.[3]

Howard Bowen has also proposed a large increase in the number of federal grants, but he advises caution in raising the amounts of individual awards. Under his proposals, institutions would be helped by federal contributions related to costs per student.[4]

Care must be taken in the allocation of federal funds between student aid and institutional aid. The former concentrates on providing equality of opportunity and the latter on making the institution viable. Students benefit from institutional aid if the funds received by the institution are used to reduce tuition or to keep it from rising. However, many students who do not need financial assistance also benefit from these institutional subsidies.[5]

Clark Kerr, chairman of the Carnegie Commission on Higher Education, has noted five alternatives for aiding higher education: categorical programs, student aid, institutional aid, tax relief to parents, and federal grants to states. The emphasis in the past has been on the first three alternatives.[6]

The Carnegie Commission stresses in particular the need for student aid. In 1967–68 student aid accounted for 18 percent and institutional aid for 13 percent of estimated federal obligations for higher education and related activities. Of course, research and development received the largest share of federal aid to higher education—42 percent. The Carnegie Commission has recommended $13.2 billion in federal aid to higher education by 1976–77, with student aid accounting for 27 percent and institutional aid and cost-of-education supplements accounting for 23 percent. Research and construction would experience relative decreases of 11 and 7 percent, respectively, in their shares of federal aid obligations

---

[3] Ibid., pp. 7–8.

[4] H. R. Bowen, *The Finance of Higher Education,* Carnegie Commission on Higher Education, Berkeley, Calif., 1968.

[5] C. Kerr, "New Challenges to the College and University," in Kermit Gordon, ed., *Agenda for the Nation,* The Brookings Institution, Washington, D.C., 1968, pp. 269–270 contain a discussion of this issue.

[6] Ibid., p. 267.

FIGURE 1.5-2 *Percentage of federal aid to higher education by purpose, 1967–68 and 1976–77*

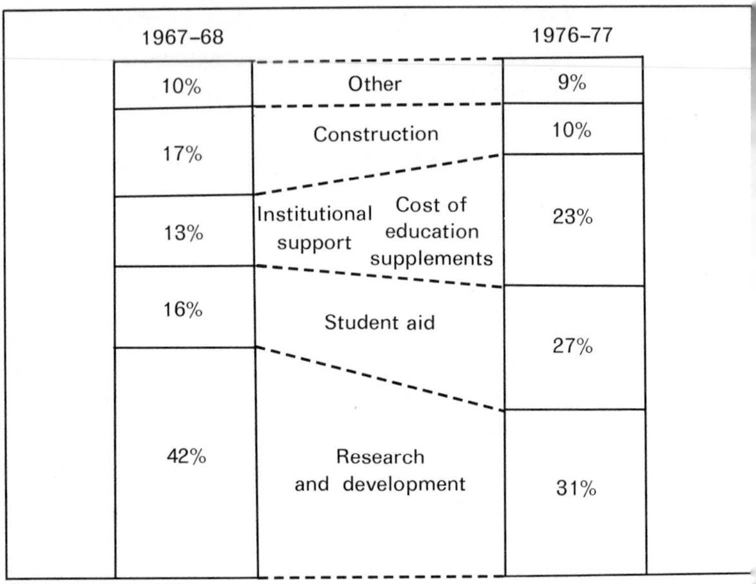

| | 1967–68 | 1976–77 |
	1967–68 ($ billions)	1976–77 ($ billions)
Research and development	1.45	4.05
Student aid	0.62	3.60
Institutional support cost of education supplements	0.44	3.06
Construction	0.57	1.26
Other	0.37	1.25
TOTAL	3.45	13.22

NOTE: The total of $13.22 billion for 1976–77 includes federal expenditures for Commission proposals and as estimated $250 million for certain programs of federal support to higher education institutions not covered in Commission proposals but expected to be continued. The 1967–68 institutional support figure includes an estimated amount for fellowship and traineeship program expenditures through institutions of higher education which are retained by institutions to defray partially the costs of the training programs.

SOURCE: Carnegie Commission on Higher Education, *Quality and Equality: New Levels of Federal Responsibility for Higher Education,* McGraw-Hill Book Company, New York, 1968, p. 53.

(Figure 1.5-2). Obviously, a large part of the increased federal aid to higher education would go for student aid, but the projected rise of private contributions from $9 billion to $21 billion between 1967–68 and 1976–77 suggests heavy dependence on increased tuition, although the private sector's share of funds for higher education is projected to decrease from 52 to 51 percent between 1967–68 and 1976–77 (Figure 1.5-3).[7]

OVERALL TRENDS, 1955–56 TO 1965–66
Before turning to the specific aspects of student aid, we will briefly review some recent trends in higher education. From 1955–56 to 1965–66, income and expenditures of institutions of higher education rose about 3.5 times, but enrollment increased only 2.1 times, with non-degree-credit enrollment rising more than degree-credit enrollment (Table 1.5-1). In this period the rise of institutional expenditures per student was much larger than the rise in the cost

[7] These recommendations have been revised somewhat in Carnegie Commission on Higher Education, *Quality and Equality: Revised Recommendations: New Levels of Federal Responsibility for Higher Education,* McGraw-Hill Book Company, New York, 1970.

FIGURE 1.5-3 *Sources of funds expended by institutions of higher education, 1957–58, 1967–68, and 1976–77*

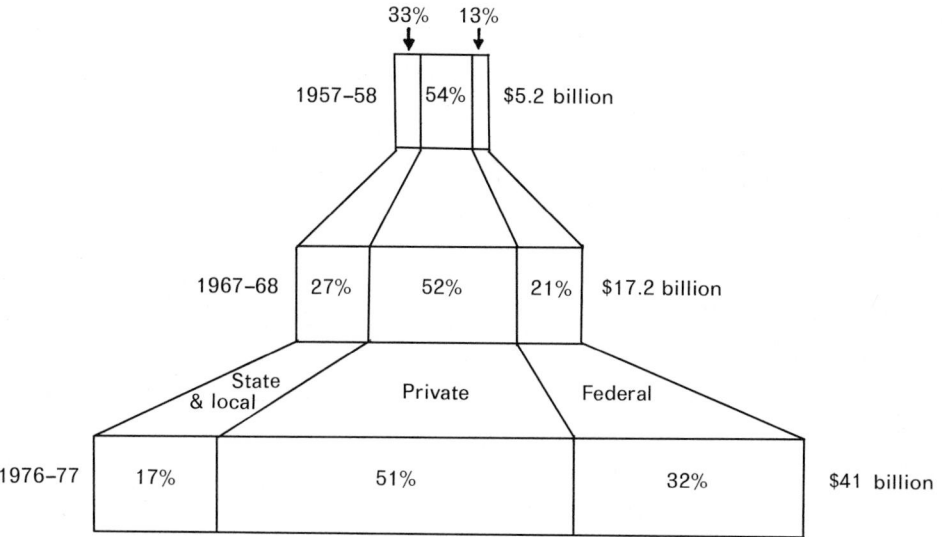

	1957–58		*1967–68*		*1976–77*	
	$ billions	*%*	*$ billions*	*%*	*$ billions*	*%*
State and local	1.7	33	4.7	27	7	17
Private	2.8	54	9.0	52	21	51
Federal	0.7	13	3.5	21	13	32
TOTAL	5.2	100	17.2	100	41	100

SOURCE: Carnegie Commission on Higher Education, *Quality and Equality: New Levels of Federal Responsibility for Higher Education,* McGraw-Hill Book Company, New York, 1968, p. 8.

TABLE 1.5-1
*Major changes
in the
postsecondary
educational
system of the
United States,
1955–56 to
1965–66*

Item	1955–56
Number of institutions	1,858
Opening fall enrollment	2,811,000
Degree	2,660,000
Nondegree	151,000
Instructional and other professional staff (FTE)	236,000
Instructional	195,000
Other professional	41,000
Earned degrees	377,698
Income (thousands) (current dollars)	$4,445,000
Current	3,629,000
Plant fund	826,000
Expenditures (thousands) (current dollars)	$4,190,000
Current	3,379,000
Plant fund	811,000

SOURCE: U.S. Office of Education, *Students and Buildings: An Analysis of Selected Federal Programs for Higher Education,* 1968, table 1, p. 7.

of living. It is also of some interest that other professional staff increased relatively more than instructional staff.

ENROLLMENT PROJECTIONS FOR 1968 AND 1972 In order to interpret some of the tables in this chapter, we must understand the Office of Education's alternative projections of undergraduate enrollment for 1968 and 1972. The assumptions underlying these projections may be summarized as follows:

Low: Continuation of the recent enrollment pattern by achievement and socioeconomic quartile.

Medium: An enrollment pattern adjusted for all persons based on the present pattern adjusted for differences in motivation found among persons of different socioeconomic status. The purpose of this projection is to ascertain the effect on enrollments if financial barriers were removed but present motivational barriers continued.

High: An enrollment pattern for all socioeconomic quartiles based solely on the present pattern for persons in the highest socioeconomic status

1965–66	Increase	Ratio: 1965–66 to 1955–56
2,230	372	1.20
5,967,000	3,156,000	2.12
5,570,000	2,910,000	2.09
394,000	243,000	2.61
465,000	229,000	1.97
359,000	164,000	1.84
106,000	65,000	2.59
679,600	301,902	1.80
$15,395,000	$10,940,000	3.46
12,343,000	8,714,000	3.40
3,052,000	2,226,000	3.69
$15,018,000	$10,828,000	3.58
11,993,000	8,614,000	3.55
3,026,000	2,215,000	3.73

quartile. The purpose of this projection is to measure the effect of removing both financial and motivational barriers.

The results of the projections may be summarized as follows:

- Full-time undergraduate enrollments by 1968 would be 604,000 higher under the medium projection than under the low projection. If the general population went to postsecondary school solely in accordance with the highest socioeconomic status quartile pattern, undergraduate enrollments would exceed the low projection pattern by more than 1½ million.

- In 1972 total enrollments in the medium projection are approximately 1.1 million above those of the low projection while the high projection results in 2.7 million more students than the low.

- In terms of percentages, by 1968, 14 percent more students would attend postsecondary institutions under the medium-projection pattern and 37 percent under the high-projection pattern. By 1972 the number of students would increase by 22 percent (medium projection) and 54 percent (high projection) when compared with the low-projection pattern.

- With the low-projection pattern the socioeconomic compositions of the students would scarcely change. With the medium-projection pattern the proportion of higher socioeconomic status students would decline to 42 percent by 1968 and would further drop to 40 percent in 1972. Under the high-projection pattern the proportion of children from higher socioeconomic status families would decline to 35 percent in 1968 and 31 percent in 1972.

· By contrast, the share of 1968 enrollments claimed by the low socioeconomic status children would increase from 7 percent under the low projection to 9 percent under the medium pattern to 16 percent under the high. In 1972 these figures would be 9 percent and 19 percent respectively.

· The change in attendance by socioeconomic status quartile would have important effects on the quality of students going on to postsecondary education. For instance, under the low-projection pattern roughly 57 percent of all students in 1972 would have ranked in the top quarter of their class. With the medium-projection assumptions their share would decline to 53–54 percent. Under the high-projection assumptions this reduction would be even more dramatic: the share of students in the upper achievement quartile of the class would be reduced to 45 percent.

· By contrast, the share of students in the lowest half of the high school graduating class attending postsecondary educational institutions would increase from 16 percent in 1968 and 1972 under the low-projection pattern to 18 percent under the medium-projection pattern and 25 percent under the high-projection pattern by 1972. In other words, increasing the participation of children from lower income families in postsecondary education is likely to decrease the average quality of entering freshmen.

Estimates of student financial needs. The financial needs of students for each enrollment projection pattern have been estimated according to the procedures described above. The total gap based upon the low-projection pattern is likely to increase from $2.1 billion in 1966 to $2.3 billion in 1968 and grow to $2.8 billion in 1972. Under the medium-projection pattern the financial gap will be $2.9 billion in 1968 and $4.1 billion in 1972. Under the high-projection assumption the gap could grow to $4.1 billion in 1968 and $6.2 billion in 1972.[8]

[8] U.S. Office of Education, *Students and Buildings: An Analysis of Selected Federal Programs for Higher Education,* 1968, pp. 14–15.

The distribution of this gap by income quartile is shown in Table 1.4-6.

THE
INSTITUTIONAL
DEFICIT

By comparing tuition income and total institutional costs, we can estimate the institutional deficit on the current educational account; in other words, that part of institutional costs not covered by tuition income. (This, of course, is a special kind of deficit.) In 1966–67 the net institutional deficit was $3.7 billion—tuition income covered a little more than 40 percent of total institutional costs. (Tuition income and total educational costs may be obtained from Table 1.5-2 by multiplying the per capita figures for tuition and total outlay by the figures for full-time equivalent enrollment.)

The Office of Education estimates that by 1972–73 the net institutional deficit will rise to $7,171 million on the assumption of a maintenance (low) enrollment projection or to $7,759 million on the assumption of a medium enrollment projection (Table 1.5-2).

A case can be made for increased federal aid to institutions on the ground that approximately $1.3 billion of the projected 1972–73 institutional deficit will be related to the effects of federal student aid programs. Private institutions, with a declining student-faculty ratio, will especially feel the effects of rising enrollment. Their resources will fall short of projected requirements by $1 billion in 1972–73.[9]

This discussion relates largely to current expenditures and income of institutions, to the tuition costs and the funds available to students, and to the need for additional aid. However, the financial status of institutions of higher education is further impaired by the large amount of money needed for construction—a problem dealt with fully in Chapter 4.6. In 1966–67, estimated federal obligations for construction and rehabilitation were approximately $1.4 billion.[10]

[9] Ibid., pp. 40–41.

[10] Ibid., p. 66. These figures apply to expenditures made under Titles I and II of the Higher Education Facilities Act of 1963.

TABLE 1.5-2	Year, projection	Full-time equivalent enrollment (thousands)	Instructional cost	Student aid	Per capita Total outlay
Projected institutional deficit on current educational account, 1968–69 and 1972–73	1966–1967	4,937	$1,300	$65	$1,365
	1968–1969:				
	Maintenance	5,771	1,447	62	1,509
	Medium	5,988	1,447	67	1,514
	1972–1973:				
	Maintenance	6,750	1,793	63	1,856
	Medium	7,237	1,793	69	1,862

SOURCE: U.S. Office of Education, *Students and Buildings: An Analysis of Selected Federal Programs for Higher Education,* 1968, p. 40.

One peculiarity of the system of federal aid to higher education is that institutions with large enrollments receive a smaller proportion of available aid relative to their share of total enrollment than institutions with small enrollments. In 1967, institutions with enrollments of 20,000 or over (which enroll 12 percent of all full-time equivalent students) received 5 percent of federal aid funds, whereas institutions with less than 1,000 students (and only 6 percent of total enrollment) received 20 percent of all federal aid to higher education.

PRESENT PROGRAMS OF STUDENT AID   In 1966–67 student aid was available in the following forms:

1 Institutional aid, which includes scholarships, fellowships, the matching parts of the educational opportunity grant and the work-study programs, and other programs administered by institutions on behalf of private businesses and state governments

2 Work-study and educational opportunity grant programs

3 Veterans' benefits

4 National defense student loans

5 Guaranteed loans

The average aid per recipient varied considerably according to the program under which the aid was extended:

Tuition	Deficit	Total deficit (millions)	Grants for graduate study (millions)	Net deficit (millions)
$567	$ 798	$3,940	$214	$3,726
624	885	5,107	225	4,882
624	890	5,329	225	5,104
738	1,118	7,546	375	7,171
738	1,124	8,134	375	7,759

Average annual aid available to individuals under various programs, 1966–67		
Work-study programs		$826
Educational opportunity grants		433
Veterans' benefits		990
National defense student loans		588
Guaranteed loans		837
Freshmen		716
Sophomores		817
Juniors		869
Seniors		870

SOURCE: U.S. Office of Education, *Students and Buildings: An Analysis of Selected Federal Programs for Higher Education,* 1968, p. 17.

The average annual aid per recipient varied from $990 for veterans' benefits to $433 for educational opportunity grants. Average institutional aid (excluding the educational opportunity grant and work-study programs) was $400.[11]

STUDENT AID AND FAMILY INCOME Table 1.5-3 shows undergraduate student financial need and funds extended by major student aid programs by family income quartile for 1966–67. The figures in this table are approximations on two counts: (1) the allocation by income quartile is not precise, and (2) an assumption was made that all the aid went to full-time students.

[11] U.S. Office of Education, *Students and Buildings: An Analysis of Selected Federal Programs of Higher Education,* 1968, pp. 17–18.

TABLE 1.5-3 *Undergraduate student financial need and funds extended under major student aid programs by student family income, 1966–67*

Line	Approximate family income quartile	Number of full-time undergraduates (thousands) (1)	Student financial need for full-time study (millions) (2)	Total aid received by full-time students (millions) (3)	Institutional* (millions) (4)
1	High	1,940	‡	$ 232	$ 14
2	Second	1,145	$ 834	259	28
3	Third	671	786	300	77
4	Low	302	446	421	145
5	TOTAL	4,058	‡	$1,212	$264
6	Total excluding highest income group	2,118	$2,066	$ 980	$250

*Includes state and private aid administered by institutions of higher education.

† Except for the high income quartile, equals amount shown in column (2) minus amount shown in column (3).

‡ Not estimated.

SOURCE: U.S. Office of Education, *Students and Buildings: An Analysis of Selected Federal Programs for Higher Education,* 1968, p. 18.

One way of looking at the adequacy of present programs of student aid is to examine the extent to which student need in each income quartile is covered by present aid programs. Looking at Table 1.5-3, we see that:

Forty-four percent of the financial need of students from the lowest-income quartile was covered by grants, 23 percent by work-study wages, and 27 percent by loans. Therefore, 94 percent of the total student financial gap was covered. By contrast, for the third quartile, 15 percent of the student needs not covered by family contributions was provided by grants, 5 percent by work-study wages, 18 percent by loans. Thus, a total of only 38 percent was covered by all programs. In the second highest-income quartile, 14 percent was covered by outright grants, 1 percent through work-study, and an additional 16 percent by loans. Thus, a total of 31 percent was covered in this manner.

It is very likely that part of the remaining financial need of students was met through part-time work. U.S. Bureau of the Census reports published by the Bureau of Labor Statistics show that in October 1966, 30 percent of full-time college students were engaged in part-time work. These full-time college students, numbering about 1.2 million would have been

| *Major student aid program* | | | | | |
Work-study (millions) (5)	Educational opportunity grants (millions) (6)	Veterans' benefits (millions) (7)	NDEA student loan (millions) (8)	Guaranteed loans (millions) (9)	Other non-federal and personal sources† (millions) (10)
$ 6	$ 1	$ 32	$ 40	$139	‡
8	6	81	40	96	$ 575
36	18	24	72	73	486
102	33	20	69	52	25
$152	$58	$157	$221	$360	‡
$146	$57	$125	$181	$221	$1,086

required to work an average of only 15 hours per week at an average rate of $1.88 per hour for 36 weeks in order to completely account for both the work-study program and the entire remaining financial gap. . . . Alternatively these students could have worked an average of 19 hours per week at an average rate of $1.50 per hour to accomplish the same result. In all probability some of the students with parents in the upper quartile worked. Since no estimate of the socioeconomic distribution of working students is available, undoubtedly some of the gap in need was still covered by savings of their families or the reduction of living standards.

Roughly $232 million in student aid, most of it in loans, went to children whose parents belonged to the highest-income quartile. Since the lower limit of family income in that quartile is $10,000, it is likely that children of parents with numerous offspring qualified for outright grant aid and that a large number of students found loans an attractive way of financing their education at more expensive institutions.

[As shown in Tables 1.5-3 and 1.5-4], the student financial gap *not* covered by the major Federal and institutional programs was:

1 $83 per student or a total of $25 million for the lowest quartile of income recipients.

Approximate family income quartile	Number of full-time under-graduates (thousands) (1)	Student financial need for full-time study (2)	Total aid received by full-time students (3)	Institu-tional* (4)
High	1,940	†	$ 120	$ 7
Second	1,145	$ 728	226	24
Third	671	1,171	447	115
Low	302	1,477	1,394	480
Total	4,058	†	299	65
Total excluding highest income group	2,118	$ 975	$ 463	$118

* Includes state and private aid administered by institutions of higher education.
† Not estimated.
SOURCE: U.S. Office of Education, *Students and Buildings: An Analysis of Selected Federal Programs for Higher Education,* 1968, table A-20, p. 59.

2 $724 per student, or a total of $486 million for the third-income quartile.

3 $502 per student, or a total of $575 million for the second-income quartile.

In other words, an additional $1 billion would have been needed if the financial gap for full-time students had been filled through institutional and government channels.

Approximate family income quartile	Number of full-time undergraduates (1)	Approximate unduplicated total number of students receiving aid (2)	Institu-tional* (3)
High	1,940	274	83
Second	1,145	356	106
Third	671	256	240
Low	302	285	231
Total	4,058	1,171	660
Total excluding highest income group	2,118	897	577

*Includes state and private aid administered by institutions of higher education.
SOURCE: U.S. Office of Education, *Students and Buildings: An Analysis of Selected Federal Programs for Higher Education,* 1968, table A-21, p. 59.

Major student aid program

Work-study (5)	Educational opportunity grant (6)	Veterans' benefits (7)	Student loans, NDEA (8)	Guar-anteed loans (9)	Other nonfederal and personal sources (10)
$ 3	$ 1	$16	$ 21	$ 72	†
7	5	71	35	84	$502
54	27	36	107	109	724
338	109	66	228	172	83
37	14	39	54	89	†
$ 69	$ 27	$59	$ 85	$104	$513

A somewhat different view of student aid may give some insight into the desirability of different forms of student aid. If we look at the extent to which outright grants helped students in each quartile, and then examine how much of the remaining need was filled by work-study and how much by loans, we gain further insight into how the programs operated. In the lowest quartile 44 percent of the gap in student need was filled by outright

Major student aid program

Work-study (4)	Educational opportunity grant (5)	Veterans' benefits (6)	Student loans, NDEA (7)	Guaranteed loans (8)
13	4	32	63	159
14	20	81	66	116
60	54	24	122	90
97	56	20	125	65
184	134	157	376	430
171	130	125	313	271

grants, and 41 percent of the remainder was taken up by work-study. Following this, 83 percent of the remaining gap was filled by loans. In the third lowest quartile, only 15 percent was available in grants, only 5 percent of the remainder was covered by work-study, and 23 percent of the rest was covered by loans. Roughly the same situation was evidenced in the second quartile: 14 percent from grants, 1 percent from work-study closed the remaining gap, and finally loans took up 19 percent of what remained.

Loans thus played a much more important part in financing the children of the poor than in financing those from other income quartiles where the smaller financial need occurred. The average NDSL loan per borrower from the lowest-income quartile was $557 and for guaranteed loans about $800. [Table 1.5-5 shows that] roughly two out of three students from this income group resorted to a loan to finance their higher education. For the third quartile the average loan per borrower was slightly higher, and roughly one out of three students took out a loan. For the second highest quartile, roughly one student out of six took out a loan. In the highest income quartile roughly one student out of nine borrowed.

If students from the lowest-income quartile borrowed only as much on the average as students from the very highest quartile, the average remaining financial gap for that group would have increased more than 4½ times to $391. The average remaining financial gaps in the two other quartiles would have also risen to $846 and $528 for the third and second quartiles respectively. Conversely, if students from the third- and second-income quartiles borrowed as much as those from the lowest quartile, the gap would be reduced to $539 and $221 respectively [see Table 1.5-4]. . . .[12]

Another indication of student financial need is the percentage of students from different income quartiles who received aid. Surprisingly, as John Morse has shown, the percentage aided is not tied to income as might be expected. In the early 1960s, 59 percent of the students from families with incomes of $3,000 or less received financial aid, while 57 percent of the students from families with incomes of $11,000 to $13,000 received aid (Table 1.5-6). Morse pointed out that students from higher-income groups receive better grades and have higher aptitude scores than students from low-income groups.

ABILITY TO PAY AND STUDENT FINANCIAL NEED The ability to pay for a college education varies directly with family income. In 1970 families were estimated to be able to pay a total of $299 million for two-year colleges, $3.2 billion for public four-year colleges, and $2.7 billion for private four-year colleges (Table

[12] Ibid., pp. 17–19, 59.

	Percentage to whom
TABLE 1.5-6 *Family income*	*aid given*

TABLE 1.5-6
*Aid to students—
breakdown by
family income,
early 1960s*

Family income	Percentage to whom aid given
Less than $3,001	59
$ 3,001–$ 5,000	63
$ 5,001–$ 7,000	66
$ 7,001–$ 9,000	65
$ 9,001–$11,000	62
$11,001–$13,000	57
More than $13,000	38

SOURCE: Organization for Economic Cooperation and Development, *Financing of Education for Economic Growth,* OECD Publications, Paris, 1966, table 19, p. 242.

1.5-7). The excess of student costs over ability to pay was then estimated to be $3.3 billion in 1970 (Table 1.5-8), and student aid available in 1970 was estimated to be $1.9 billion (Table 1.5-9). Hence, undergraduate students were expected to carry a deficit in excess of $1.4 billion in 1970.

The average amount of money needed by students from families with different incomes is shown in Table 1.4-4.

The student population is divided into four quartiles. For purposes of the analysis, students from the upper quartile are assumed, on the average, not to need outside financial help. Where the maximum cost per student is set at $1,984 per year, the average need for all students from the upper income group would be quite low, but has not been estimated. Those from the lowest quartile need an average of roughly $1,477 from sources outside the family to cover the living and tuition costs of full-time study. These figures have been derived by taking into account the different types of colleges attended by students from different income quartiles, and the standard parent contribution expected from each income group according to the College Scholarship Service standards of need. . . .

Estimates in column (3) [of Table 1.4-4] show that average student costs for lower-income students are lower than for upper-income students because the former generally attend lower-cost institutions. The difference between the average cost of full-time study to the student and the average family-student contribution toward this cost can be defined as the student need gap. It is shown in column (5). Average student financial need is not estimated for the highest family income quartile, [but] this does not mean that the same number of students from that group necessarily would have attended college in the absence of student aid.[13]

[13] Ibid., pp. 16–18.

TABLE 1.5-7
Possible
distribution of
4,049,734
full-time
undergraduate
students by
family income
level for the
year 1970 and
by their ability
to pay

| | | | Two-year colleges | |
Family income	Percentage	Ability to pay	Number	Ability to pay
Less than $2,999	8.0	$ 400	48,597	$ 19,438,800
$ 3,000–$ 3,999	4.8	500	29,158	14,579,000
$ 4,000–$ 4,999	4.6	870	27,943	13,971,500
$ 5,000–$ 5,999	12.4	1,150	75,325	36,662,500
$ 6,000–$ 6,999	8.2	1,430	49,812	24,906,000
$ 7,000–$ 7,999	9.9	1,565	60,138	30,069,000
$ 8,000–$ 8,999	9.9	1,745	60,138	30,069,000
$ 9,000–$ 9,999	9.9	2,215	60,138	30,069,000
$10,000–$14,999	20.0	2,990	121,492	60,746,000
$15,000–$19,999	9.0	(4,440)	54,672	27,336,000
$20,000 and over	3.3	(5,000)	20,046	10,023,000
TOTAL	100.0		607,459	$298,869,800

NOTE: Income frequencies for over $7,000 were assigned arbitrarily.
SOURCE: U.S. House of Representatives, Committee on Education and Labor, *Higher Education Act of 1965, Hearings before the Special Subcommittee on Education,* February–May 1965, table 4, p. 727.

COST OF
HIGHER
EDUCATION
AND
INCOME

"Even though children of parents from lower-income groups do attend cheaper colleges, the cost of college, relative to the income of parents, is still very much higher for persons in the lower income bracket."[14] We saw in Table 1.4-5 that for the lowest income quartile, the cost of the cheapest two-year college is equal to 48

[14] Ibid., pp. 16–18.

TABLE 1.5-8
Total cost of
higher education
to American
families in
relation to their
total ability to
pay in the
year 1970

Type of institution	Percentage	Number of students	Per-student cost
Two-year college	15	607,459	$ 500
Public four-year college	50	2,024,867	2,112
Private four-year college	35	1,417,408	3,519
TOTAL	100	4,049,734	

SOURCE: U.S. House of Representatives, Committee on Education and Labor, *Higher Education Act of 1965, Hearings before the Special Subcommittee on Education,* February–May 1965, table 5.

Public (four-year)		Private (four-year)	
Number	Ability to pay	Number	Ability to pay
161,989	$ 64,795,600	113,393	$ 45,357,200
97,194	48,597,000	68,036	34,018,000
93,144	81,035,280	65,201	56,724,870
251,084	288,746,600	175,759	202,122,850
166,038	237,434,340	116,227	166,204,610
200,462	313,723,030	140,323	219,605,495
200,462	349,806,190	140,323	244,863,635
200,462	423,375,744	140,323	310,815,445
404,973	855,302,976	283,482	847,611,180
182,238	384,886,656	127,567	448,908,273
66,821	141,125,952	46,774	164,597,706
2,024,867	$3,188,829,368	1,417,408	$2,740,829,264

percent of average family income. For the highest income quartile, however, the cost of a private four-year college—the most expensive alternative—is only 16 percent of average family income.

FINANCIAL AID FOR LOW-INCOME STUDENTS The Office of Education seems to have some doubts about the success of the Upward Bound and Talent Search programs, which were introduced primarily to attract more students from minority

Total student cost	Ability to pay	Deficit—1970
$ 303,729,500	$ 298,869,800	$ 4,859,700
4,276,519,104	3,188,829,368	1,087,689,736
4,987,858,752	2,740,829,264	2,247,029,438
$9,568,107,356	$6,228,528,432	$3,339,578,924

TABLE 1.5-9 *Student aid available or needed for the support of full-time undergraduate education, actual for 1955 and 1960, projected for 1970*

Source and type	1955	1960	1970 (?)
College scholarships		($100,000,000	$ 425,381,000
College jobs	$144,000,000	{ 100,000,000	425,381,000
College loans		(15,000,000	64,131,000
NDEA loans		70,000,000	297,881,000
Veteran's benefits	706,000,000	70,000,000	
Federal work-study program			297,881,000
ROTC	11,000,000	11,500,000	49,256,000
Federal government miscellaneous	None	500,000	2,506,000
State scholarships	5,000,000	20,000,000	85,381,000
State miscellaneous	10,000,000	30,000,000	127,881,000
Corporations and others	15,000,000	30,000,000	127,881,000
TOTAL	$891,000,000	$447,000,000	$1,903,560,000
Full-time undergraduate	1,920,000	2,527,000	4,049,734
Average aid per student	$ 464	$ 177	$ 470

SOURCE: Rexford G. Moon, Jr., *Student Aid in the United States: Administration and Resources,* College Entrance Examination Board, New York, 1963; in U.S. House of Representatives, Committee on Education and Labor, *Higher Education Act of 1965, Hearings before the Special Subcommittee on Education,* February–May 1965, table 6, p. 727.

groups to college. The small percentage of these students going on to receive a college degree has been disappointing. Lack of motivation may be a more serious deterrent to enrollment and completion of a college program than financial need. The results of federal subsidies to developing institutions have also been disappointing. The institutions chosen are too small, the amount of aid has been inadequate, and the dependence on tuition by these institutions has been excessive.

Programs to recruit college freshmen. The Federal Government is making a substantial effort to increase the proportion of youth from the lowest socioeconomic classes who attend college. Much of the student aid program is oriented toward helping children of poor parents to enroll in school. In addition, the Upward Bound program, administered by the Office of Economic Opportunity, and the Talent Search program, administered by the Office of Education, are aimed at informing disadvantaged youth about (and motivating them to take advantage of) the opportunities of attending college. There can be little doubt that there will be a great desire to increase the funding of both programs in future years. However, there appears to be little awareness of how the recruitment program fits into the total aid picture, what the uncertainties of these investments are, and what the potential scope of the program as a whole may be.[15]

The table below contrasts the percentage of students from the two lowest socioeconomic quartiles who are likely to be helped by additional financial aid with the percentage of students who still will not attend college because they lack the motivation of children of equivalent ability in the highest socioeconomic quartile.

Potential share of students aided by removal of financial barriers and residual share who will not attend college because of lack of motivation; by family socioeconomic status quartile	*Socioeconomic status*	*Percentage of twelfth-grade students in each quartile*
	Third	
	Financial	13.3
	Motivation	17.7
	Low	
	Financial	7.2
	Motivation	25.8

SOURCE: U.S. Office of Education, *Students and Buildings: An Analysis of Selected Federal Programs for Higher Education,* 1968, p. 32.

The Office of Education concludes:

It is obvious that the number of students who could be motivated to go to college is still very large, even after financial barriers are removed. Almost four times as many students in the lower socioeconomic quartile would not attend college because of motivational factors as are likely to be helped by the removal of financial barriers. In the third-lowest socioeconomic quartile, about 25 percent more students would not attend college because of motivational factors, compared to those who would attend if financial barriers were removed.

The majority of students not enrolling are in the two lowest ability quartiles. [The following table] shows the percentage distribution by socioeconomic class and ability quartile of potential college students who do not enroll because of lack of motivation. Over two-thirds of the potential

[15] Ibid., p. 32.

students who could be helped through motivational efforts are found in the lowest half of the class.[16]

Students who fail to enroll because of lack of motivation as a percentage of all students who fail to enroll by achievement quartiles for the third and low socioeconomic status quartiles

Socioeconomic	*Achievement quartile*			
status	*High*	*Second*	*Third*	*Low*
Third	0	34.3	38.9	26.8
Low	7.1	35.4	25.0	42.5
TOTAL	4.2	29.0	30.7	36.1

SOURCE: U.S. Office of Education, *Students and Buildings: An Analysis of Selected Federal Programs for Higher Education,* 1968, p. 33.

While increasing the number of students going to college from low-income households would, at least in appearance, indicate an improvement in the distribution of educational opportunity, it is neither a necessary nor sufficient condition for improvement in the distribution of income. A change in the earning capacity of a disadvantaged youth must be preceded by improvements in his productive ability. If students drop out prior to the end of their second year in college, the benefits to their future productivity from their attendance are likely to be small. In fact, failure in college may offset whatever improvements in the disadvantaged students' self-image had been brought about by efforts to motivate them to enter college. Currently, there are indications that few of these youths will be able to successfully complete

[16] U.S. Office of Education, *Students and Buildings: An Analysis of Selected Federal Programs for Higher Education,* 1968, pp. 32–33.

TABLE 1.5-10
Funds disbursed under current student aid programs and estimated cost of proposed programs by student family income, 1966–67 (in millions of dollars)

	Current programs			
	Grant programs			
Quartile	*Institutional* (1)	*Work-study* (2)	*Educational opportunity grants* (3)	*Veterans' benefits* (4)
High	14	6	1	32
Second	28	8	6	81
Third	77	36	18	24
Low	145	102	33	20
TOTAL	264	152	58	157

*Not estimated.

SOURCE: U.S. Office of Education, *Students and Buildings: An Analysis of Selected Federal Programs for Higher Education,* 1968, p. 22.

their 2- or 4-year programs even though they attend relatively low quality institutions.

Upward Bound. Upward Bound is a program which is aimed at low achievers from the lowest socioeconomic classes. Most of the participants (over 73 percent) have averaged C or less in high schools where general achievement levels are low. Upward Bound attempts to change the achievement level and motivation of the students through remediation and a change in environment by offering them a summer program of study and other aid for the last 2 years of school. The cost is approximately $1,200 per year for each student prior to entrance into college.

Of the first group of Upward Bound students, 762 out of 953, or 80 percent, went to college and 388 of the 762, or 50 percent, entered the sophomore year.

Data from *Project Talent* show that only about 75 percent of all 10th graders from the lowest socioeconomic quartile and the lowest one-half by achievement finish high school. Thus, Upward Bound did increase somewhat the chances of these deprived children to graduate from high school. The dropout rate of 59 percent per year for freshmen is very close to the estimated rate in the model for youths in the lowest ability quartile of the lowest socioeconomic group. The current experience indicates that very few will finish more than 2 years of college. First indications are, therefore, that Upward Bound will successfully motivate the disadvantaged youth to enter college, but that the students will have difficulty completing their programs.[17]

[17] Ibid., p. 33.

Loans		Proposed programs, amounts net of current grants			
NDSL (5)	Guaranteed loans (6)	Ribicoff tax credit (7)	Prouty tax credit (8)	$1,000 taxable grants to parents (9)	Federal scholarships according to need (10)
40	139	524	256	1,214	*
40	96	301	285	801	719
72	73	122	143	445	667
69	52	0	0	74	248
221	360	947	684	2,534	1,634

SOURCES OF STUDENT AID In 1966–67 total student aid disbursed under current programs was $1.2 billion (Table 1.5-10). The following table shows the percentage distribution of the sources of this aid.

Percentage distribution of sources of student aid, 1966–67

Guaranteed loans	30
Institutional aid	22
National defense student loans	18
Veterans' benefits	13
Work-study programs	13
Educational opportunity grants	5

SOURCE: Table 1.5-10.

In 1966–67, students from the highest income quartile received $232 million in student aid or 19 percent of the total of $1.2 billion. Students from the lowest income quartile received $421 million in student aid—35 percent of the total (Table 1.5-10).

The Office of Education has estimated student aid requirements of $1.9 billion in 1968–69 and $2.7 billion in 1972–73 (using the medium enrollment projection based on the removal of all financial barriers to attending college), as compared with budget obligations of $1.1 billion and $2.1 billion in 1968–69 and 1972–73, respectively (Table 1.5-11).

TABLE 1.5-11 Total student aid requirements, Office of Education, 1968–69 and 1972–73 (dollars in millions)

	1968–69 Medium projection	1968–69 Maintenance-of-effort projection	1972–73 Medium projection
Guaranteed loans	$ 743	$ 661	$ 942
NDSL	450	393	552
Subtotal loans	$1,193	$1,054	$1,494
Work-study programs	$ 221	$ 188	$ 273
Educational opportunity grants	475	145	875
Other	50	50	80
TOTAL	$1,939	$1,437	$2,722

SOURCE: U.S. Office of Education, *Students and Buildings: An Analysis of Selected Federal Programs for Higher Education,* 1968, table 18, p. 39.

STUDENT AID
AND FAMILY
CONTRIBU-
TIONS

The amount of student aid provided by an institution depends upon the contributions of the students' families. Standards for parents' contributions are determined by family income and number of dependents. In addition, students' summer earnings and savings are included as part of the family contribution. Table 1.5-12 shows estimated 1970 family contributions for families with two children (one in college). For example, such a family with an income of $9,000 to $10,000 will be expected to contribute $1,215 from income, $200 from assets, and $800 in student summer work and savings—a total of $2,215 toward the expenses of the student for one year.

When no parental aid is available, financial assistance varies from an average of $750 for a public junior college to $3,350 for a high-cost private university. The mix of the aid provided varies according to the student costs of the various types of institutions. High-cost private universities provide six categories of student aid, and they depend especially on national defense student loans and on institutional grants-in-aid. State universities, with half the costs of high-cost private universities, have recourse to only four categories of student aid, three of which are federally funded: national defense student loans, federal scholarships, and the college work-study program (Table 1.5-13).

Table 1.5-14 shows expected family contributions for different income levels and different numbers of dependent children for

	Budget obligations				
	1968–69			1972–73	
Maintenance-of-effort projection	*Medium projection*	*Maintenance-of-effort projection*	*Medium projection*	*Maintenance-of-effort projection*	
$ 849	$ 88	$ 81	$ 136	$ 122	
480	217	190	267	232	
$1,329	$ 295	$271	$ 403	$ 354	
$ 228	$ 221	$188	$ 273	$ 228	
343	475	145	875	343	
80	50	50	80	80	
$1,980	$1,051	$654	$2,113	$1,005	

TABLE 1.5-12 *Estimated two-child family yearly purchasing power for higher education for one child in 1970*

	Parents' contribution		Student summer work and savings	Family able to pay
Income ranges	From income	From assets		
Less than $2,999			$400	$ 400
$ 3,000–$ 3,999			500	500
$ 4,000–$ 4,999	$ 270		600	870
$ 5,000–$ 5,999	450		700	1,150
$ 6,000–$ 6,999	630		800	1,430
$ 7,000–$ 7,999	765		800	1,565
$ 8,000–$ 8,999	945		800	1,745
$ 9,000–$ 9,999	1,215	$200	800	2,215
$10,000–$14,999	1,890	300	800	2,990
$15,000–$19,000	3,240	400	800	4,440
$20,000 and over	3,600	600	800	5,000

SOURCE: U.S. House of Representatives, Committee on Education and Labor, *Higher Education Act of 1965, Hearings before the Special Subcommittee on Education,* February–May 1965, table 3, p. 726.

TABLE 1.5-13 *Packaging of student assistance in six types of institutions of higher education: composition of assistance to a needy student with no parental support, by type*

	High-cost private university	High-cost private liberal arts college	State university
National Defense Education Act loans	$ 800	$ 800	$ 350
Federal scholarship	500	500	500
College work-study	600	600	600
Student summer work (freshman and sophomore)	250	250	250
Institutional grants-in-aid	800	800	
Other	400	*50	
Total assistance	$3,350	$3,100	$1,700

* This is apparently in error and should be "$1,100."

SOURCE: U.S. House of Representatives, Committee on Education and Labor, *Higher Education Act of 1965, Hearings before the Special Subcommittee on Education,* February–May 1965, table A, p. 101 (data about 1964).

Annual family income	Number of dependent children in family				
	1	*2*	*3*	*4*	*5*
$ 2,000	$ 240	$ 185	$ 145	$ 120	$ 105
4,000	555	445	370	305	240
6,000	885	685	615	525	435
8,000	1,250	965	840	755	660
10,000	1,750	1,370	1,165	1,020	915
12,000	2,300	1,805	1,535	1,350	1,210

SOURCE: John F. Morse, *An Aid to Administrators of National Defense Student Loans,* College Entrance Examination Board, New York, 1959; in D. M. Keezer (ed.), *Financing Higher Education: 1960–70,* McGraw-Hill Book Company, New York, 1959, table 4, p. 177.

1959. Expected family contributions are positively related to family income and negatively related to the number of dependents. For example, for a family income of $10,000 the expected family contribution varied from $1,750 for one dependent to $915 for five dependents. Table 1.5-15 shows actual annual contributions of families by income level for the late 1960s. For family incomes of less than $2,500 there was no family contribution. For family incomes from $5,000 to $7,499, the average parental contribution was $330 and the average student summer earnings were $300,

State college (commuters)	Public junior college (commuters)	Private technical institute (commuters)
$350		$ 300
500	$500	500
250	250	250
		150
$850*	$750	$1,200

TABLE 1.5-15
Actual annual
contributions
of families to
college expense
financing, by net
income range

Net income range	Average* parent contribution	Average† student summer earnings	Average total family contribution
Less than $2,499	0	0	0
$ 2,500–$ 4,999	$ 160	0	$ 160
$ 5,000–$ 7,499	330	$300	630
$ 7,500–$ 9,999	1,050	300	1,350
$10,000–$12,499	1,660	300	1,960
$12,500–$14,999	2,160	300	2,460
$15,000–$17,499	2,820	300	3,120
$17,500–$19,999	5,120	300	5,420
Over $20,000	5,400	300	5,700

*From James L. Bowman, and Gertrude S. Weiss, "A Proposal for Modification of the Curves of Expectations," unpublished manuscript, p. 7, from a tabulation of parents' confidential statements supplied to the College Scholarship Service.
† Estimated.
SOURCE: U.S. Office of Education, *Students and Buildings: An Analysis of Selected Federal Programs for Higher Education,* 1968, table A-15, p. 57.

for a total family contribution of $630. For families with incomes of $15,000 to $17,499, the average total family contribution was $3,120.

Scholarship awards are also based on family income and number of dependents. Thus, for family income under $3,000 the student typically received an $800 scholarship in 1965, regardless of the number of children in his family. For family incomes of $5,401 to $6,000 no scholarships were offered to a student from a family with three or fewer children; $200 would be the average scholarship for families with four children; and so forth (Table 1.5-16).

A 1959 survey stresses the fact that a large proportion of parents (38 percent of the sample) found financing their children's higher education difficult. Of course, the percentage of parents who found college financing difficult varied inversely with income. Only 39 percent of the parents in the sample found college financing easy.[18]

AID AND ENROLLMENT It was estimated that if an additional $812 million in student aid had been available for full-time undergraduates in 1966–67, enroll-

[18] J. B. Lansing, T. Lorimer, and C. Moriguchi, *How People Pay for College,* Institute for Social Research, University of Michigan, Ann Arbor, 1960, p. 58.

ment would have risen by 795,000 students—an increase of 20 percent over actual enrollment.[19]

The statement that current student aid programs produce the desired results . . . does not imply that more aid, effectively distributed, would not produce additional students and additional future benefits to society. The proportion of low-income students in the total full-time undergraduate population was estimated to be 7 percent. The proportion from the highest family income quartile was 48 percent. There is evidence . . . that when high school achievement levels are held constant, the rate at which students enter college is influenced by ability to pay. Virtually every item represented in the socioeconomic index is correlated with family income. . . .

If the high school graduates from the three lowest socioeconomic quartiles entered college at the rates . . . for their own achievement levels, but at just one socioeconomic quartile higher than their own, then one could expect that the proportion of full-time undergraduates from the lowest-income quartile would be raised from 7 percent to 9 percent and the proportion from the highest-income quartile would be lowered from 48 to 40 percent. This would imply an additional 795,000 full-time undergraduates in 1966–67. . . . This would have required approximately $812 million in additional student aid last year. There is hence a strong presumption that the current terms of the loan programs were not attractive enough to

[19] U.S. House of Representatives, Committee on Education and Labor, *Higher Education Act of 1965, Hearings before the Special Subcommittee on Education,* February–May 1965, p. 22.

TABLE 1.5-16 *Typical scholarship awards by income level and family size*

	Number of children							
	1	*2*	*3*	*4*	*5*	*6*	*7*	*8+*
Less than $3,000	$800	$800	$800	$800	$800	$800	$800	$800
$3,000–$3,600	600	600	800	800	800	800	800	800
$3,601–$4,200	400	400	600	800	800	800	800	800
$4,201–$4,800	200	200	400	600	800	800	800	800
$4,801–$5,400	0	0	200	400	600	800	800	800
$5,401–$6,000	0	0	0	200	400	600	800	800
$6,001–$6,600	0	0	0	0	200	400	600	800
$6,601–$7,200	0	0	0	0	0	200	400	600
$7,201–$7,800	0	0	0	0	0	0	200	400
$7,801–$8,400	0	0	0	0	0	0	0	200

SOURCE: U.S. House of Representatives, Committee on Education and Labor, *Higher Education Act of 1965, Hearings before the Special Subcommittee on Education,* February–May 1965, p. 100.

reach all potential students in the absence of more grant and work-study seed money.[20]

For students from the second, third, and lowest family income quartiles, the financial need for full-time undergraduate study in 1966–67 was $834 million, $786 million, and $446 million, respectively. The financial aid actually received in 1966–67 was $259 million by the second, $300 million by the third, and $412 million by the lowest income quartile. Clearly, the aid tends to go where it is most needed—to the lowest family income quartile. Nevertheless, a serious gap is evident. Against expressed total needs of $2.1 billion for the second, third, and lowest income quartiles, only $980 million in aid was provided in 1966–67— less than half of total need. Total institutional aid (excluding the highest income quartile) was $250 million, with 55 percent going to students from the lowest income quartile. Students from the lowest income quartile also received the major share of work-study funds—70 percent (excluding the high income quartile). The higher income groups also received substantial aid, largely in loans (Table 1.5-3).

Financial need per undergraduate student in 1966–67 was $728 for the second, $1,171 for the third, and $1,477 for the lowest in-

[20] Ibid., p. 22.

TABLE 1.5-17
Undergraduate student financial need and average amount per recipient extended under major student aid programs, by student family income quartile, 1966–67 (average amount per recipient)

Approximate family income quartile	Student financial need for full-time study (1)	Institutional* (2)
High	†	$169
Second	$ 728	264
Third	1,171	321
Low	1,477	628
Total	†	$400
Total, excluding highest income group	$975	$433

*Includes state and private aid administered by institutions of higher education.
† Not estimated.
SOURCE: U.S. Office of Education, *Students and Buildings: An Analysis of Selected Federal Programs for Higher Education,* 1968, table A-18, p. 58.

come quartile (Table 1.5-17). Average student aid per recipient for 1966–67 is also shown in Table 1.5-17. Under six major student aid programs, the ratio of aid per recipient from the lowest income quartile to aid per recipient from the highest income quartile varied by type of aid. This ratio was almost 4 to 1 for institutional aid and more than 2 to 1 for work-study programs and educational opportunity grants. Apparently institutions of higher education allocate funds more favorably to the poor than do poverty programs. The level of veterans' benefits was not related to family income. Veterans' benefits averaged $990 per recipient for all income quartiles.

In 1966–67 the number of undergraduates was 4.1 million. Only 1.7 million, or 41 percent, received financial aid. Fourteen percent of the students from the highest income quartile received aid,[21] as compared with 94 percent of the students from the lowest income quartile (Table 1.5-18).

PROJECTED STUDENT NEED AND FINANCIAL AID

For 1968–69 the average per-student financial need for full-time undergraduates was estimated to be $585, but the estimated average aid per student was only $469, creating a per-student financial need of $116. The average aid received by students from the lowest income quartile is projected to equal the average need. For all other

[21] U.S. Office of Education, *Students and Buildings: An Analysis of Selected Federal Programs for Higher Education,* 1968, p. 59.

Major student aid program				
Work-study (3)	Educational opportunity grants (4)	Veterans' benefits (5)	Student loans, NDEA (6)	Guaranteed loans (7)
$ 462	$250	$990	$635	$874
571	300	990	606	828
600	333	990	590	811
1,052	589	990	552	800
$ 826	$433	$990	$588	$837
$ 854	$438	$990	$578	$815

TABLE 1.5-18
Percentage
distribution by
source of
funds for
undergraduate
student financial
need, by student
family income
quartile,
1966–67
(percentage
distribution by
source)

Approximate family income quartile	Student financial need for full-time study (1)	Total aid received by full-time students (2)	Institutional (3)
High			
Second	100	31	3
Third	100	38	10
Low	100	94	33
Total excluding the highest quartile	100	47	11

SOURCE: U.S. Office of Education, *Students and Buildings: An Analysis of Selected Federal Programs for Higher Education,* 1968, p. 59.

income quartiles, however, the estimated per-student need is larger than the estimated aid per student. The projected per-student national defense loan varies with income level—from $20 per student for the highest to $220 per student for the lowest income quartile (Table 1.5-19, medium enrollment projection).

For 1972–73 per capita undergraduate student need is estimated to be $663 and per capita undergraduate student aid is estimated to be $516, creating a gap of $147. Estimated per-student need in 1972–73 varies from $803 for the second highest to $1,623 for

TABLE 1.5-19
Per capita
undergraduate
student
financial need
and funds
extended under
major student
aid programs,
by student
family income
quartile,
1968–69
medium
projection
(dollars per
capita)

Approximate family income quartile	Number of full-time under-graduates (thousands) (1)	Student financial need for full-time study (2)	Total aid received by full-time students (3)	Institutional (4)
High	2,134	*	$ 129	$ 6
Second	1,505	$ 738	368	22
Third	938	1,207	882	101
Low	462	1,528	1,528	427
TOTAL	5,039	$ 585	$ 469	$ 67

*Not estimated.
SOURCE: U.S. Office of Education, *Students and Buildings: An Analysis of Selected Federal Programs for Higher Education,* 1968, p. 70.

Major student aid program					
Work-study *(4)*	*Educational opportunity grants* *(5)*	*Veterans' benefits* *(6)*	*Student loans, NDEA* *(7)*	*Guaranteed loans* *(8)*	*Other non-federal and personal sources* *(9)*
1	1	10	5	11	69
5	2	3	9	9	62
23	7	4	15	12	6
7	3	6	9	11	53

the lowest income quartile, while estimated financial aid per student varies from $141 for the highest to $1,623 for the lowest income quartile (Table 1.5-20, medium enrollment projection). For 1972–73 projected aid per student is 78 percent of projected financial need per student, down from 80 percent in 1968–69.

In 1972–73 total financial need for full-time undergraduates is projected to be $4.1 billion and total student aid is projected to be $3.2 billion (Table 1.5-21). The projected distribution of sources of student aid for 1972–73 is given in the table on page 160.

Major student aid program					
Work-study *(5)*	*Educational opportunity grants* *(6)*	*Veterans' benefits* *(7)*	*Student loans, NDEA* *(8)*	*Guaranteed loans* *(9)*	*Other nonfederal and personal sources* *(10)*
$ 3		$ 30	$ 20	$ 70	*
6	$ 27	108	35	170	$370
50	310	51	200	170	325
315	309	87	220	170	0
$ 41	$ 94	$ 62	$ 77	$128	$116

Major student
aid programs,
1972–73
(estimated)

Type of aid	Amount (millions of dollars)	Percentage of total
Institutional	$ 426	13
Work-study programs	260	8
Educational opportunity grants	875	27
Veterans' benefits	314	10
National defense student loans	488	15
Guaranteed loans	842	26
TOTAL	$3,205	99

SOURCE: Table 1.5-21.

The distribution of aid among family income quartiles in 1972–73 is projected to follow the pattern of the recent past. Students from the higher income quartiles will rely mainly on loans for financial aid, whereas students from the lowest income quartile will rely on institutional aid, educational opportunity grants, work-study programs, and national defense student loans, in that order (Table 1.5-21).

DISTRIBUTION OF STUDENT AID BY STATES, 1963–64   Table 1.5-22 shows the distribution by state of institutional scholarship, service grants-in-aid, loan, and employment programs for 1963–64. For the country as a whole, scholarship aid totaled $130 million, service grants-in-aid totaled $32 million, loans totaled $24

TABLE 1.5-20
Per capita undergraduate student financial need and funds extended under major student aid programs, by student family income quartile, 1972–73 medium projection (dollars per capita)

Approximate family income quartile	Number of full-time under-graduates (thousands) (1)	Student financial need for full-time study (2)	Total aid received by full-time students (3)	Institu-tional (4)
High	2,451	*	$ 141	$ 6
Second	1,918	$ 803	393	22
Third	1,228	1,322	957	101
Low	573	1,623	1,623	427
TOTAL	6,170	$ 663	$ 516	$ 69

*Not estimated.
SOURCE: U.S. Office of Education, *Students and Buildings: An Analysis of Selected Federal Programs for Higher Education,* 1968, p. 70.

million, and employment aid totaled $145 million. By state, the largest number and amount of scholarships were awarded in New York. The largest number and amount of loans were awarded in California, the largest number and amount of service grants-in-aid in Texas, and the largest amount of employment aid in Michigan.

It is interesting to compare the mix of student aid in such different states as California, New York, Mississippi, with that in the country as a whole:

Percentage distribution of types of student aid for three states, 1963–64

Type of aid	Aggregate United States	California	New York	Mississippi
Scholarships	39	34	67	25
Service grants-in-aid	10	8	4	29
Loans	7	12	7	4
Employment	44	46	21	43

SOURCE: Table 1.5-22.

New York students depend relatively less on employment aid than students in the nation as a whole, while California and Mississippi students approach the national level for relative dependence on employment aid. As might be expected, scholarships and loans contribute relatively more to student aid in California than in

Major student aid program

Work-study (5)	Educational opportunity grants (6)	Veterans' benefits (7)	Student loans, NDEA (8)	Guaranteed loans (9)	Other nonfederal and personal sources (10)
$ 3		$26	$ 20	$ 86	*
6	$ 76	84	35	170	$410
50	397	39	200	170	365
315	421	70	220	170	0
$ 39	$142	$51	$ 79	$136	$147

		Student financial need for full-time study	Total aid received by full-time students	Institu-tional
	Approximate family income quartile	*(1)*	*(2)*	*(3)*
	High	*	$ 345	$ 15
	Second	$1,540	755	42
	Third	1,623	1,176	124
	Low	930	929	245
	TOTAL	$4,093	$3,206	$426

TABLE 1.5-21 *Undergraduate student financial need and funds extended under major student aid programs by student family income quartile, 1972–73 medium projection (millions of dollars)*

*Not estimated.

SOURCE: U.S. Office of Education, *Students and Buildings: An Analysis of Se-lected Federal Programs for Higher Education*, 1968, p. 71.

Mississippi. Service grants-in-aid contribute relatively more in Mississippi than in California and New York. (Poor states with little money for higher education tend to rely heavily on service grants-in-aid.) The contrast in scholarship aid between New York and California is also striking. The heavy recourse to scholarships in New York is necessary mainly because of the relatively small contribution of the New York state government to the financing of higher education.

SCHOLARSHIPS AND GRANTS

Over the years scholarships have become more numerous and the average stipend has increased. From 1959–60 to 1963–64, the total amount spent on scholarships and service grants rose by 66 percent, while the total number of scholarship and service grant recipients rose by only 35 percent. In 1963–64 the total amount of scholarships and service grants was $163 million and the number of recipients totaled 388,000. The average scholarship stipend in 1963–64 was $409 and the average service grant was $474. From 1959–60 to 1963–64, financial assistance in the form of student employment aid increased by 47 percent, or about 70 percent of the relative increase in the amount of scholarships and service grants (Table 1.5-23).

Table 1.5-24 shows financial aid to undergraduates for 1934–35, 1949–50, 1955–56, and 1959–60. From 1934–35 to 1959–60, the number of scholarships granted by institutions of higher educa-tion rose by 4.3 times while the amount of scholarship aid rose by 11.0 times. The average scholarship stipend was $133 in 1934–35

Major student aid program

Work-study (4)	Educational opportunity grants (5)	Veterans' benefits (6)	Student loans, NDEA (7)	Guaranteed loans (8)
$ 7		$ 64	$ 49	$210
12	$146	162	67	326
61	488	48	246	209
180	241	40	126	97
$260	$875	$314	$488	$842

and $340 in 1959–60. But the relative increase in the average stipend was only about one-half of the relative increase in per capita disposable income during this period. In relation to prices the average scholarship stipend rose about one-third more than the consumer price index from 1934–35 to 1959–60.[22]

Scholarships in amounts larger than $1,000 have been relatively scarce. In 1963–64 only 2 percent of the scholarships awarded by public institutions and only 15 percent of the scholarships awarded by private institutions amounted to $1,000 or more. On the other hand, 83 percent of the scholarships awarded by public and 48 percent of the scholarships awarded by private institutions amounted to less than $400 (Table 1.5-25).

Table 1.5-26 shows a series of estimates of scholarship needs for 1960 if different student aid programs had been put into effect. These estimates of scholarship needs vary from $16 million (the Eisenhower proposals of 1958) to $2 billion (Munro's proposal of $500 per student).

INSTITUTIONAL AID In 1963–64 institutional aid was dispensed primarily through employment aid (44 percent) and scholarships (40 percent). Student employment aid was the major form of financial aid in public

(Text continued on p. 166)

[22] R. G. Moon, Jr., *Student Financial Aid in the United States: Administration and Resources,* College Entrance Examination Board, Princeton, N.J., 1963, pp. 10–11. N. Cliff and R. Ekstrom, *Practices and Attitudes in Paying for College,* Educational Testing Service, Princeton, N.J., 1962, p. 91, puts the average stipend for third-year students at $410 in 1959–60.

TABLE 1.5-22
Number of
students aided
and funds
disbursed in
institutional
scholarship,
service grants-
in-aid, loan,
and employment
programs, by
state,
aggregate
United States,
1963-64

State or outlying part (1)	Number of institutions with financial assistance programs (2)	Scholarships	
		Number of students (3)	Total amount (4)
Aggregate United States	1,854	320,085	$130,851,256
Alabama	26	4,331	1,117,158
Alaska	3	228	93,929
Arizona	6	2,842	1,101,609
Arkansas	19	2,888	621,415
California	148	15,637	7,213,142
Canal Zone	1	12	3,108
Colorado	19	5,092	1,443,515
Connecticut	24	4,390	2,853,341
Delaware	4	1,173	292,430
District of Columbia	14	2,428	1,324,627
Florida	45	4,785	1,316,416
Georgia	43	4,352	1,391,804
Guam	1		
Hawaii	4	894	224,002
Idaho	7	1,329	335,760
Illinois	87	19,153	6,673,994
Indiana	38	10,659	3,700,122
Iowa	48	8,330	2,576,021
Kansas	42	5,195	1,231,890
Kentucky	33	5,036	1,440,347
Louisiana	18	8,891	1,822,029
Maine	20	2,267	1,010,506
Maryland	39	3,436	1,682,071
Massachusetts	88	15,045	11,729,531
Michigan	56	14,365	4,102,358
Minnesota	40	6,558	2,160,033
Mississippi	36	2,746	611,314
Missouri	55	6,662	2,457,835
Montana	11	1,354	295,465
Nebraska	21	4,183	873,700
Nevada	1	167	44,000

Service grants-in-aid		Loans		Employment	
Number of students (5)	*Total amount* (6)	*Number of students* (7)	*Total amount* (8)	*Number of students* (9)	*Total amount* (10)
67,934	$32,181,113	61,918	$23,760,272	438,019	$144,574,306
2,105	607,921	366	180,763	5,717	1,452,651
		95	23,329	406	240,048
525	294,916	1,016	513,987	2,734	1,369,673
1,237	432,365	212	56,568	3,496	958,657
3,522	1,724,673	6,285	2,562,599	36,614	9,985,255
				18	5,805
1,707	568,701	473	314,123	4,305	1,534,789
425	195,476	2,107	781,502	5,281	1,131,099
392	122,500	2	450	378	91,476
937	676,065	614	306,504	2,748	742,160
2,249	1,426,430	1,883	544,587	6,614	2,156,336
1,528	656,824	710	292,869	6,602	1,626,213
				20	4,880
30	4,834	110	58,482	1,116	552,830
236	207,316	160	32,396	3,522	597,079
1,918	1,112,551	1,510	621,443	25,868	9,473,350
1,520	639,722	1,020	478,788	17,206	5,535,993
2,592	1,151,367	1,114	436,714	13,478	6,854,360
2,347	579,816	438	179,756	10,521	7,928,129
1,705	897,648	508	160,444	7,136	1,504,667
2,990	1,405,334	831	267,928	7,038	2,017,278
385	100,310	263	98,528	2,809	593,155
2,081	565,594	264	125,677	4,623	1,405,464
932	760,066	3,242	1,754,112	19,589	7,468,400
2,350	1,125,755	4,456	1,767,746	27,230	11,025,150
1,180	259,005	1,612	644,112	11,600	8,696,894
1,879	708,066	221	91,845	4,917	1,056,714
1,442	500,127	1,504	434,398	12,151	4,004,271
639	268,877	165	99,010	1,852	839,783
829	367,733	597	218,932	3,733	1,167,417
100	60,000	31	13,751	430	375,000

TABLE 1.5-22
(continued)

State or outlying part (1)	Number of institutions with financial assistance programs (2)	Scholarships Number of students (3)	Scholarships Total amount (4)
New Hampshire	11	2,280	1,544,232
New Jersey	29	4,777	3,029,052
New Mexico	9	1,651	382,955
New York	154	29,216	19,550,862
North Carolina	57	10,079	2,936,511
North Dakota	14	1,055	249,948
Ohio	64	15,547	7,048,851
Oklahoma	28	4,190	1,091,683
Oregon	28	6,436	2,487,487
Pennsylvania	114	21,082	12,509,596
Puerto Rico	5	4,768	1,708,876
Rhode Island	11	1,905	1,182,608
South Carolina	26	1,912	669,036
South Dakota	15	1,515	277,154
Tennessee	47	5,596	1,787,689
Texas	86	15,977	3,514,827
Utah	8	5,126	871,968
Vermont	16	1,287	747,964
Virginia	41	6,845	2,722,943
Washington	27	4,247	1,303,291
West Virginia	21	2,110	623,228
Wisconsin	41	6,686	2,538,324
Wyoming	5	1,370	328,699

SOURCE: R. C. McKee, *Financial Assistance for College Students; Undergraduate and First Professional,* U.S. Office of Education, 1965, pp. vi–vii.

institutions (28 percent), and scholarships were the major form of financial aid in private institutions (30 percent) (Table 1.5-27). This direct aid to students was in addition to the subsidies provided by institutions because the cost of educating a student is greater than the tuition charged.

A 1963 study revealed that 50 institutions (or less than 3 per

Service grants-in-aid		Loans		Employment	
Number of students	*Total amount*	*Number of students*	*Total amount*	*Number students*	*Total amount*
(5)	*(6)*	*(7)*	*(8)*	*(9)*	*(10)*
42	11,880	461	175,985	1,790	482,878
593	303,847	727	274,142	7,056	1,529,679
431	227,792	635	326,187	2,362	989,577
2,133	1,273,166	4,060	2,147,353	25,133	6,139,647
2,098	1,232,499	1,558	696,563	11,274	3,050,073
343	148,697	1,102	430,780	2,133	465,126
3,044	1,762,996	2,604	739,952	25,360	7,086,919
1,000	511,047	1,189	534,772	6,876	2,542,411
943	495,093	3,774	699,731	4,861	1,816,426
3,083	1,852,577	2,473	1,153,937	17,513	4,836,081
59	10,930	43	6,278	1,410	159,739
108	37,938	180	77,235	2,515	535,161
1,441	712,300	1,358	362,409	4,287	1,005,109
281	91,502	336	88,322	4,081	1,026,755
2,336	1,360,647	971	344,849	7,331	1,903,032
6,390	2,516,624	2,133	818,750	21,484	6,681,455
343	61,357	3,072	500,695	8,231	2,439,592
174	166,975	289	106,161	1,437	277,783
1,154	716,042	1,051	375,161	6,081	1,627,193
790	435,241	560	239,575	11,503	3,897,819
305	110,371	738	260,152	3,446	1,005,822
660	449,158	795	339,940	11,028	2,242,919
401	272,442			1,075	438,134

cent of the total number) controlled about 35 percent of the scholarship funds awarded by all institutions.[23]

A breakdown of student aid for 1963–64 by type of aid and by

[23] R. G. Moon, Jr., *Student Financial Aid in the United States: Administration and Resources,* College Entrance Examination Board, Princeton, N.J., 1963, p. 11.

		Students aided* (thousands)		
TABLE 1.5-23 *Financial assistance awarded by colleges and universities* Category		1959–60	1963–64	Percentage increase
Total, all programs		†	†	†
Employment		341.4	438.0	28
Scholarships and service grants		287.6	388.0	35
Scholarships			320.1	
Service grants		‡	67.9	‡
Loans		52.3	61.9	18

*Includes undergraduate and first professional degree students.

† Neither totals nor mean amounts are shown for all programs, since a given student may receive more than one type of aid.

‡ Service grants were included with scholarships in 1939–1960.

SOURCE: U.S. Office of Education, *College Aid for Students*, 1963, p. 2.

institutional control shows that, although students in private institutions accounted for 36 percent of all undergraduate and first professional students, they received 55 percent of total financial aid. Students in private institutions also received more than their proportionate share of scholarships and service grants-in-aid. In the average size of the scholarship stipend, private institutions were more generous than public institutions. Private institutions granted scholarships averaging $519, as compared with $247 for public institutions (Table 1.5-28). (Remember, however, the tuition is much higher at private than at public institutions. Private institutions receive a higher proportion of their operating costs from tuition income than do public institutions.)

	1934–35		1949–50	
TABLE 1.5-24 *Financial aid to undergraduates by colleges and universities*	Number of awards	Total value	Number of awards	Total value
Scholarships	66,708	$8,863,000	124,223	$27,000,000
Loans	*	*	*	*
Employment	*	*	*	*
TOTAL	*	*	*	*

*Data not available for these years.

SOURCES: Mattingly, 1962; Ratcliffe; Wilkins, 1958; Wilkins, 1954; in R. G. Moon, Jr., *Student Financial Aid in the United States: Administration and Resources*, College Entrance Examination Board, Princeton, N.J., 1963, p. 10.

Amount (millions of dollars)			Mean amount (dollars)		
1959–60	*1963–64*	*Percentage increase*	*1959–60*	*1963–64*	*Percentage increase*
$211.0	$331.4	57	†	†	†
98.5	144.6	47	$289	$330	14
98.2	163.0	66	341	420	23
	130.9			409	
‡	32.2	‡	‡	474	‡
14.4	23.8	65	275	384	40

STATE AID TO STUDENTS In 1960–61 state aid to students provided 210,219 awards totaling $51.6 million. The average award was $246. Scholarships and fellowships accounted for 44 percent of all state aid to students, guaranteed and other loans accounted for 16 percent, and grants-in-aid accounted for 9 percent (Table 1.5-29).

EMPLOYMENT AID By fiscal year 1967 obligations under the federal college work-study program had reached $134 million—aiding 191,000 students with average earnings per student of $815 (Table 1.5-30). The allocation of work-study funds tends to help low-income states comparatively more than high-income states in relation to their share of national income. The percentage of national income and the percentage of

1955–56		1959–60	
Number of awards	*Total value*	*Number of awards*	*Total value*
237,370	$ 65,732,000	288,521	$ 98,000,000
77,107	12,463,000	56,432	14,800,000
288,479	65,932,000	347,678	98,900,000
302,956	144,132,000	692,631	210,900,000

TABLE 1.5-25
Distribution of
college
scholarship and
loan recipients,
1963–64

Amount of scholarship or loan (in dollars)	Students aided (percent)			
	Scholarships		Loans	
	Public	Private	Public	Private
Total	100	100	100	100
Over 1,000	2	15	2	18
600–999	5	17	6	19
400–599	10	20	11	19
200–399	34	27	38	25
100–199	34	16	32	14
1– 99	15	5	11	5

SOURCE: U.S. Office of Education, *College Aid for Students,* 1963, p. 6.

aid received under the work-study program for three low-income states (Mississippi, Arkansas, and West Virginia) and three high-income states (New York, California, and Illinois) are compared in the table below.

Percentages of
national income
and aid received
under the
federal college
work-study
program for
three high-
income and
three low-
income
states, 1966

	Percentage of national income	Percentage of work-study aid
Three high-income states	29	23.9
Three low-income states	0.21	7.4

SOURCE: Adapted from U.S. House of Representatives, Committee on Education and Labor, *Study of the United States Office of Education,* report of the Committee, 1967, table G, p. 159.

Institutions in the state of California received almost twice as much work-study aid as institutions in the state of New York (which has almost the same share of national income as California) (Table 1.5-31). The three high-income states received an amount of work-

TABLE 1.5-26
College and
university aid
in amounts
and
percentages,
1963–64
(amounts are
in millions
of dollars)

	Public and private			
		Percentage of all aid		
Category	Total	Total	Public	Private
All aid	$331.4	100	45	55
Employment	144.6	44	28	16
Scholarships	130.9	40	10	30
Service grants	32.1	9	4	5
Loans	23.8	7	3	4

SOURCE: U.S. Office of Education, *College Aid for Students,* 1963, table 3.

TABLE 1.5-27 *Estimates of annual scholarship needs, United States, 1960 (millions of dollars)*

1. *The President's Commission on Education beyond the High School*	750*
2. *To save 50,000–100,000 able students now lost each year*	400
3. *Item 2 plus aid for students in need now in college, not receiving help*	600
4. *Monro's proposal, $500 for each student*	2,000
5. *Application of scholarships on the basis of CSS formula under which allocation is according to need based on family income*	900
6. *National scholarship funds allowing the same per capita amount to be paid throughout the country as is now paid by the 23 IHL granting the largest scholarships*	600†
7. *Application of the British policy to the United States*	1,500‡
8. *Eisenhower administration proposals, 1958*	16
9. *Kennedy proposals, 1961 (average five years)*	30

Presumably largely nonfederal government.
Part-time students excluded.
Part-time students excluded, and allowing $500 per student for employment earnings.
SOURCES: Organization for Economic Cooperation and Development, *Financing of Education for Economic Growth,* OECD Publications, Paris, 1966, p. 247; and S. E. Harris, *Higher Education: Resources and Finance,* McGraw-Hill Book Company, New York, 1962, p. 105.

study funds roughly proportional to their share of national income. The three low-income states, however, received work-study funds in an amount 35 times greater than their share of national income. In dollar amounts California received the largest amount of work-study funds ($13 million) and Alaska received the smallest ($113,-228) for the 50 states.

NATIONAL DEFENSE STUDENT LOANS AND OTHER LOANS In 1959 the federal government provided $9.5 million in loans to 24,831 students under the national defense student loan program. By 1964, the $119.5 million was being provided to 246,840 students—approximately 5 percent of total enrollment. In the latter

Public		Private	
Amount	*Percent*	*Amount*	*Percent*
$149.0	100	$182.4	100
92.3	61	52.2	28
32.3	22	98.6	54
14.5	10	17.6	10
9.9	7	13.9	8

TABLE 1.5-28 *College and university aid to undergraduate and first professional degree students, 1963–64*

Category	Total	Public	Private	Percent private
Total institutions	2,117	752	1,365	64
Total students (thousands)	4,091.4	2,629.5	1,461.9	36
Institutions with aid programs	1,852	677	1,175	64
All aid (millions)	$331.4	$149.0	$182.4	55
Employment				
Institutions with programs	1,660	624	1,036	62
Students aided (thousands)	438.0	256.8	181.2	41
Amount (millions)	$144.6	$92.3	$52.2	36
Mean amount	$330	$359	$288	
Scholarships				
Institutions with programs	1,706	581	1,125	66
Students aided (thousands)	320.1	130.5	189.6	59
Amount (millions)	$130.9	$32.3	$98.6	75
Mean amount	$408	$247	$519	
Service grants				
Institutions with programs	844	292	552	65
Students aided (thousands)	67.8	31.1	36.7	54
Amount (millions)	$32.1	$14.5	$17.6	55
Mean amount	$472	$464	$479	
Loans				
Institutions with programs	773	229	544	70
Students aided (thousands)	61.8	29.8	32.0	52
Amount (millions)	$23.8	$9.9	$13.9	58
Mean amount	$384	$331	$434	

SOURCE: U.S. Office of Education, *College Aid for Students,* 1963, p. 3.

year, undergraduates received 92.4 percent of all national defense student loans, with the remainder going to graduate and professional students.

Future teachers receiving loans were offered special financial incentives (in the form of canceling some portion of the repayment for each year taught). These future teachers accounted for 55 percent of the value of national defense student loans in 1959 and 46 percent in 1964. By 1964, $9.6 million had been repaid by teachers aided by these loans (Table 1.5-32).

TABLE 1.5-29   *State programs of student aid in the United States*

Program	1958-59		1960-61	
	Number of awards	*Total value*	*Number of awards*	*Total value*
Scholarships and fellowships	81,756	$11,728,000	53,711	$22,789,000
Grants-in-aid	16,009	4,558,000	16,009	4,558,000
Service loans	7,413	3,283,000	7,413	3,283,000
Guarantee and other loans	7,238*	4,594,000*	13,086	8,000,000*
Total:				
Without New York state Scholar Incentive Program	62,416	24,163,000	90,219	38,630,000
With New York state Scholar Incentive Program			210,219	51,630,000

*Estimated.

SOURCES: Goldthorpe; University of State of New York; correspondence with Maine Higher Education Assistance Foundation; with New York Higher Education Assistance Corporation; with Rhode Island Higher Education Assistance Corporation; with Department of Public Instruction, Bismark, N.D.; with New Jersey State Scholarship Commission; with Massachusetts Higher Education Assistance Corporation; with Wisconsin State Department of Public Welfare; in R. G. Moon, Jr., *Student Financial Aid in the United States: Administration and Resources,* College Entrance Examination Board, Princeton, N.J., 1963, table 8, p. 34.

Of the $436 million principal in the national defense student loan program in 1963-64, $211 million went to public and $225 million went to private institutions. The principal on all loan funds of institutions of higher education (other than national defense

TABLE 1.5-30   *College work-study program data*

	Fiscal year 1965 (first year of program)	*Fiscal year 1966*	*Fiscal year 1967**
Appropriation	$55,710,000	$99,123,000	$134,100,000
Number of institutions:			
Applying for participation	†	†	1,731
Approved for operation	1,120	1,540	1,700
Obligations	$55,708,880	$99,121,828	$134,100,000
Students aided*	107,525	190,000	191,000
Average earnings per student*	$567	$714	$815

*Estimated.

Not available.

SOURCE: U.S. House of Representatives, Committee on Education and Labor, *Study of the United States Office of Education,* report of the Committee, 1967, table G, p. 159.

TABLE 1.5-31
College
work-study
program,
obligations by
state, fiscal
year 1966

New England:		Kentucky	$ 2,137,929
Connecticut	$ 921,307	Louisiana	2,072,416
Maine	449,607	Mississippi	3,370,691
Massachusetts	4,129,880	North Carolina	3,195,841
New Hampshire	329,943	South Carolina	729,246
Rhode Island	150,368	Tennessee	3,120,212
Vermont	244,299	Virginia	1,063,831
Mideast:		West Virginia	1,080,248
Delaware	150,700	Southwest:	
District of Columbia	596,138	Arizona	838,616
Maryland	901,851	New Mexico	859,951
New Jersey	1,295,483	Oklahoma	1,827,436
New York	7,072,207	Texas	4,634,808
Pennsylvania	3,172,908	Rocky Mountains:	
Great Lakes:		Colorado	1,511,160
Illinois	3,473,330	Idaho	422,808
Indiana	1,250,419	Montana	970,852
Michigan	2,478,155	Utah	1,076,766
Ohio	2,135,904	Wyoming	307,722
Wisconsin	2,754,775	Far West:	
Plains:		Alaska	113,228
Iowa	882,888	California	13,172,578
Kansas	1,554,123	Hawaii	357,669
Minnesota	2,286,193	Nevada	356,262
Missouri	1,581,625	Oregon	2,878,761
Nebraska	851,296	Washington	1,807,953
North Dakota	754,875	Outlying areas:	
South Dakota	543,654	Guam	104,522
Southeast:		Puerto Rico	674,686
Alabama	3,288,366	Virgin Islands	10,059
Arkansas	2,915,889		
Florida	2,502,301		
Georgia	1,757,093	TOTAL	99,121,828

SOURCE: U.S. House of Representatives, Committee on Education and Labor, *Study of the United States Office of Education,* report of the Committee, 1967, table G, p. 159.

student loans) was $135 million in 1963–64, with $51 million going to public and $84 million to private institutions (Table 1.5-33).

Table 1.5-34 shows characteristics of borrowers of national defense student loans. In 1964 the size of the average loan was $494. Most of the borrowers were single. The distribution of income of parents of borrowers was as follows: 41 percent had incomes less than $4,000, 71 percent had incomes less than $6,000, and 86 percent had incomes of less than $8,000.

Table 1.5-35 compares the graduated versus the equal annual installment approaches for repayment of national defense student loans. The repayment schedules of a $1,000 loan at 3 percent interest are given in the table. For a loan financed by equal annual payments over 10 years, the total cost is $1,171.92. Annual payments are $117.50 until the tenth year, when $114.42 is due. Under this plan the total net interest cost is $171.92. Under the graduated payments plan the net interest cost is $214.50. The repayment of principal begins at $10 in the first year, as compared with a repayment of principal of $87.50 in the first year under the equal annual payments plan.

Amounts borrowed under the National Defense Student Loan Act vary greatly by type of institution. In 1959–60 loans varied from an average of $480 per borrower at teachers colleges to $184 per borrower at theological schools (Table 1.5-36).[24]

Table 1.5-37 shows average annual interest rates for college loans in 1963–64. Interest rates varied greatly, but were substantially higher after the borrower left college. A large proportion of borrowers (48 percent in public and 62 percent in private institutions) paid no interest while in college.

TAX CREDIT TO FAMILIES   Table 1.5-38 gives some details of both the Ribicoff and Prouty tax credit proposals, which are intended to ease the burden of financing a college education. Under these proposals, parents are

(Text continued on p. 178)

---

[24] See U.S. House of Representatives, Committee on Education and Labor, *Study of the United States Office of Education,* Report of the Committee, 1967, p. 84 and U.S. House of Representatives, Committee on Education and Labor, *Higher Education Act of 1965, Hearings before the Special Subcommittee on Education,* February–May 1965, p. 106 for statistics on guaranteed loans by states. By March 1, 1967, 283,106 students had guaranteed loans amounting to $217 million.

TABLE 1.5-32 Defense educational activities, student loans (lending activity 1959–64)	*Fiscal year*	*1959*	*1960*	*1961*
	Number of institutions par-ticipating	1,181	1,357	1,410
	Number of student loans	24,831	115,450	151,068
	Average loan per borrower	$383	$438	$470
	Total amount of loans	$9,500,000	$50,200,000	$71,000,000
	Number of loans to:			
	Undergraduates	22,200	103,200	137,500
	Percentage	89.2	89.4	91.0
	Freshmen			40,200
	Percentage			26.6
	Sophomores			33,100
	Percentage			21.9
	Juniors			30,000
	Percentage			19.9
	Seniors			34,200
	Percentage			22.6
	Graduates and profes-sionals	2,700	12,200	13,600
	Percentage	10.8	10.6	9.0
	Loans to subsequent teachers	13,700	52,500	69,600
	Total loans	$4,000,000	$27,400,000	$31,600,000
	Percentage of total loans (number)	55.1	45.4	46.0
	Teacher cancellations:			
	Number		346	4,100
	Amount (principal only)		$12,700	$220,300
	Cash repayments:			
	Number		2,900	12,800
	Amount (collection of principal)		$467,000	$1,500,000
	Sec. 208 repayments:†			
	Teacher cancellations (principal plus interest)			$12,900
	Payments to institutions			$1,300
	Number of institutions			123

1962	1963	1964*
1,468	1,526	1,589
186,465	216,930	246,840
$478	$478	$484
$89,100,000	$103,700,000	$119,535,958
171,500	200,400	228,080
92.0	92.4	92.4
49,400	54,600	62,204
26.5	25.2	25.2
43,100	49,500	56,280
23.1	22.8	22.8
39,100	48,000	54,551
21.0	22.1	22.1
39,900	48,300	55,045
21.4	22.3	22.3
14,900	16,500	18,760
8.0	7.6	7.6
88,300	101,100	116,015
$41,100,000	$47,400,000	$54,900,000
47.3	45.7	46.0
16,800	34,000	63,000
$1,100,000	$2,300,000	$3,539,664
37,000	75,000	132,000
$3,200,000	$ 5,800,000	$9,600,000
$240,600	$1,418,000	$4,000,000
$24,400	$142,000	$264,000
470	853	1,037

TABLE 1.5-32 *(continued)*	Fiscal year	1959	1960	1961
	Sec. 207 loans:			
	Number of institutions	44	46	58
	Total amount of loans	$91,400	$271,000	$490,000
	Average loan	$ 2,100	$ 5,900	$ 8,400

*Preliminary estimate. Actual data not yet available.

† Repayments are made in year following actual teacher cancellations.

SOURCE: U.S. House of Representatives, Committee on Education and Labor, *Higher Education Act of 1965,* hearings before the Special Subcommittee on Education, February-May 1965, p. 104.

allowed tax deductions on a percentage of the costs of tuition and books. Since tax credits are related primarily to tuition payments, students in private institutions (with relatively high tuition) would be helped more than those in public institutions. Institutions that are hard pressed financially are likely to react to the introduction of tax credits by increasing tuition. Hence even the modest aid provided to parents in this manner would yield less aid than anticipated.

Compared with costs of $1,212 million for student aid in 1966–67, the Ribicoff tax credit proposal would cost $947 million, the

TABLE 1.5-33 *Student loan operations of institutions of higher education, by control: United States and outlying areas, 1963–64*

Item (1)	All institutions (2)	Publicly controlled institutions (3)	Privately controlled institutions (4)
National Defense Student Loan Funds:			
Federal capital contributions during year	$107,608,046	$ 51,402,289	$ 56,205,757
Principal of fund at end of year	436,993,693	211,512,886	225,480,807
Loans granted during year	120,601,593	57,980,184	62,621,409
Loans repaid during year	11,549,414	5,630,893	5,918,52
Loans outstanding, end of year	412,402,251	199,731,232	212,671,019
Unloaned funds, end of year	25,325,593	11,958,902	13,366,69
All other loan funds:			
Principal at beginning of year	121,393,733	44,125,806	77,267,92

SOURCE: U.S. Department of Health, Education and Welfare, Office of Education, survey of "Financial Statistics of Institutions of Higher Education, 1963–64"; in U.S. Office of Education, *Digest of Educational Statistics, 1968,* p. 103.

1962	1963	1964*
85	89	80
$671,600	$773,400	$898,975
$ 7,900	$ 8,700	$ 11,238

Prouty tax credit proposal would cost $683 million, a $1,000 taxable grant to parents would cost $2,534 million, and federal scholarships awarded on the basis of need would cost $1,639 million (Table 1.5-10).

Neither the Ribicoff nor the Prouty tax credit proposal would give any help to families of students in the lowest income quartile. And families of students in the third income quartile would receive only $122 million under the Ribicoff proposal and $143 million under the Prouty proposal. As can be seen from Table 1.5-38, both plans tend to favor high-income groups — in part because low-

em / 1)	All institutions (2)	Publicly controlled institutions (3)	Privately controlled institutions (4)
dditions to principal during ear	17,587,713	8,571,243	9,016,470
Of these additions, private gifts and grants amounted to	8,836,206	4,184,478	4,651,728
rincipal at end of year	135,337,498	50,960,623	84,376,875
oans granted during year	35,402,584	17,370,718	18,031,866
oans repaid during year	26,754,376	14,560,460	12,193,916
oans outstanding, end of ar	81,185,642	26,205,975	54,979,667
nloaned funds, end of year	54,203,390	24,778,562	29,424,828

	National Defense Education Act
TABLE 1.5-34 **Characteristics** **of college** **student** **borrowers under** **National** **Defense** **Education Act**	
1. Size of average loan	$494
	Percent
2. Male borrowers	61
Female borrowers	39
3. Married	18
Single	82
4. Proportion of loans made to:	
Freshmen*	30
Sophomores	21
Juniors	19
Seniors	23
Graduate students	7
5. Income of parents:	
Under $4,000	41
Under $6,000	71
Under $8,000	86
Over $8,000	14
6. Curriculum of borrowers:	
Education	37
Science	16
Engineering	10
Mathematics	6
Language	3
Liberal arts	
Professional	
Business	
Other	28

*Loans will be made to freshmen in the school year beginning September 1963.

SOURCE: U.S. Senate, Committee on Labor and Public Welfare, *Education Legisla*
tion, 1963, Hearings before the Subcommittee on Education, June 1963, *appendi*
C, p. 3363.

income families have relatively limited income tax liabilities and
in part because relatively more students from the first and second
income quartiles go to college than students from the third and
low-income quartiles. Moreover, students from the higher-income

TABLE 1.5-35 *Payment schedules*

The following payment schedules demonstrate the
graduated versus equal annual installment approaches:
equal annual payments, $1,000 at 3% over 10 years

Year	Net interest	Principal payment	Balance of loan	Total payment
1	$ 30.00	$ 87.50	$912.50	$ 117.50
2	27.38	90.12	822.38	117.50
3	25.67	92.83	729.55	117.50
4	21.89	95.61	633.94	117.50
5	19.02	98.48	535.46	117.50
6	16.06	101.44	434.02	117.50
7	13.02	104.48	329.54	117.50
8	9.89	107.61	221.93	117.50
9	6.66	110.84	111.09	117.50
10	3.33	111.09		114.42
	$171.92	$1,000.00		$1,171.92

Graduated annual payments, $1,000 at 3% over 10 years —
$10 for year 1 to $195.70 for year 10

Payment no.	Net interest	Principal payment	Balance of loan	Total payment
1	$ 30.00	$ 10.00	$990.00	$ 40.00
2	29.70	30.00	960.00	59.70
3	28.80	50.00	910.00	78.80
4	27.30	70.00	840.00	97.30
5	25.20	90.00	750.00	115.20
6	22.50	110.00	640.00	132.50
7	19.20	130.00	510.00	149.20
8	15.30	150.00	360.00	165.30
9	10.80	170.00	190.00	180.00
10	5.70	190.00		195.70
	$214.50	$1,000.00		$1,214.50

SOURCE: H. D. Babbidge, Jr., *Student Financial Aid,* American College Personnel Association, Washington, D.C., 1960, p. 23.

quartiles tend to go to higher-cost institutions than students from the lower-income quartiles. Under the Ribicoff proposal, the 1.9 million students from the highest-income quartile, who have average expenditures on tuition and books (less grants received) of $948

TABLE 1.5-36
Comparison of institutional types, amounts borrowed, and average amounts per borrower under the National Defense Student Loan Fund (1959–60)

		National Defense Student Loan Program 1959–60, all institutions	
Type of institution	*No. of institutions*	*Amount borrowed*	*Average amount per borrower*
Universities	145	$19,203,166	$419
Liberal arts colleges	640	19,383,712	464
Teachers colleges	176	8,260,019	480
Technological schools	31	1,208,661	453
Theological schools	42	180,547	184
Other professional schools	42	235,714	204
Junior colleges	241	1,539,664	331
TOTAL	1,317	$50,011,483	$437

SOURCE: R. C. Hall and S. Craigie, *The National Defense Student Loan Program. Student Borrowers, Their Needs and Resources,* U.S. Office of Education, 1962, p 16.

per student, would receive $524 million in tax credits—$270 per student. In contrast, the 302,000 students from the low-income quartile would receive no tax credit aid.

THE EDUCA-TIONAL OPPORTUNITY BANK One approach to financing college students is to rely heavily on loans based to some extent on the house mortgage principle. The Panel on Educational Innovation first recommended that the federal government establish an Educational Opportunity Bank which

TABLE 1.5-37
Average annual interest rates for college loans, 1963–64 (percentage)

Interest rate	*While in school*		*After leaving school*	
	Public	*Private*	*Public*	*Private*
Total	100	100	100	100
0	48	62	12	11
1	3	5	1	
2	7	5	2	5
3	15	10	26	36
4	11	7	25	20
5	4	3	11	12
6	12	8	22	16
Over 6			1	

SOURCE: U.S. Office of Education, *College Aid for Students,* 1963, table 6.

would be authorized to borrow money at government rates and to lend money to college students regardless of the students' resources. Students should be able to borrow an amount sufficient to cover tuition, fees, and living expenses. In exchange for the loan, a borrower would pledge a given percentage of his gross income for a fixed number of years after graduation (which would be collected by the Internal Revenue Service with his other taxes).[25]

How much the student will have to repay depends partly on the rate of interest and on the length of the repayment period. It is assumed that the Educational Opportunity Bank will charge less than the market rate of interest, in part because society as a whole benefits from an increased flow of college graduates.

Loans made by the Educational Opportunity Bank would have an "opt-out provision" by which a borrower can treat his loan as a conventional 6 percent (or other reasonable market rate) loan if it is to his advantage. If the borrower decides to opt out, his previous repayment taxes would be credited toward payment of interest (at 6 percent) and reduction of the principal. In the absence of an opt-out provision, there would be a tendency for EOB loans to be concentrated among students with less than average income prospects.[26]

An Educational Opportunity Bank loan could also provide life insurance, health insurance, and income insurance features. As incomes rise in the future, students entering the program in later years should be able to borrow under more favorable terms than current students.

In a brilliant study, M.I.T. economists K. Shell, F. Fisher, and others analyzed the impact of the Educational Opportunity Bank under varying assumptions of the rate of growth of the economy, interest rates, years of repayment, and opt-out interest rates. The rate of return to the Educational Opportunity Bank is an increasing function of the repayment tax rate. "The rate of return can be thought of as that interest rate at which each cohort of borrowers pays back its borrowings plus interest charges. To the economist, the rate of return should serve as a crude estimate of the marginal *private* 'profitability' of investment in higher education to be

---

[25] K. Shell, et al., *The Educational Opportunity Bank: An Economic Analysis of a Contingent Repayment Loan Program for Higher Education,* Department of Economics, Massachusetts Institute of Technology, Cambridge, Mass., November 1967, pp. 1–2. (Working paper.)

[26] Ibid., p. 6.

TABLE 1.5-38 *Tax-credit proposals for expenditures on tuition and books*

Ribicoff plan	Prouty plan
1. The amount of the credit is 75 percent of the first $200 of allowable expenses (tuition and fee charges plus expenditures on books); plus 25 percent of the next $300; plus 10 percent of the next $1,000.	1. The amount of the credit is 100 percent of allowable expenses; plus 10 percent of the next $300; plus 5 percent of the next $1,000.
2. The total amount of credit is reduced by 1 percent of the amount by which a taxpayer's adjusted gross income exceeds $25,000.	2. The total amount of credit is reduced by 2 percent of the amount by which a taxpayer's adjusted gross income exceeds $10,000.
3. The eligible amount would be reduced by the amount of grant student aid received.	3. Any excess of allowable credit over the taxpayer's tax liability is treated as an overpayment of tax, refundable in cash to the taxpayer.
	4. The eligible amount would be reduced by the amount of grant student aid received.

In effect, the proposals would cover the following expenditures by the type of college:

Average of:	Public four-year	Private four-year	Public two-year	Private two-year
Tuition and fees	$278	$1,168	$103	$754
Books	100	100	100	100
Total	$378	$1,268	$203	$854
Ribicoff tax credit	$195	$ 302	$151	$260
Prouty tax credit	$217	$ 268	$200	$247

Estimated benefits from Ribicoff and Prouty proposals for full-time undergraduates by family income quartile: 1966–1967

			Tax credit			
			Ribicoff		Prouty	
Family income quartile	Number of full-time students (thousands)	Average expenditure on tuition and books less grants received*	Average	Total (millions)	Average	Total (millions)
High†	1,940	$948	$270	$524	$132	$256
Second	1,145	876	263	301	249	285
Third	671	330	182	122	213	143
Low	302	0	0	0	0	0
TOTAL	4,058			$947		$684

*From table 9 column (3), reduced to exclude student living expenses and average grants received shown in appendix table A-20.

† All families in the upper quartile receive incomes of $10,000 or more, the mean income is estimated to be slightly more than $16,000. Thus, under the Prouty proposal the average credit is reduced by 2 percent of $6,000 or $120.

$1,000 taxable benefits to parents of full-time students and net after-tax benefits by income quartile

Family income quartile	Average net after-tax benefit	Number of students (thousands)	Cost of program		
			Gross cost (millions)	Less: current grants, percent (millions)	Net cost (millions)
Highest	$650	1,940	$1,261	$ 47	$1,214
Second	800	1,145	916	115	801
Third	840	671	564	119	445
Lowest	900	302	272	198	74
TOTAL		4,058	$3,013	$479	$2,534

SOURCE: U.S. Office of Education, *Students and Buildings: An Analysis of Selected Federal Programs for Higher Education,* 1968, tables A-22, A-23, A-24, p. 60.

expected after the adoption of the Ed Op Bank."[27] Table 1.5-39 gives estimated implicit rates of return for different repayment tax rates, assuming a $1,000 loan with a repayment period of 40 years, an annual growth rate of income of 4.5 percent, and an opt-out interest rate of 6.5 percent. Under these assumptions the rate of return varies from 2.9 percent for a repayment tax rate of 0.20 percent to 5.5 percent for a repayment tax rate of 1.00 percent.

The M.I.T. paper also dealt with the difficult problem of covering women, who ordinarily could not get large loans without collateral because of their limited attachment to the labor market.

Women on the average have life-time incomes which are about one-third that of the average man. This is mostly a reflection of their low labor participation rates due to child-rearing, etc. If women are subject to the same repayment tax rates as men, then the men will be heavily subsidizing female education. Under this scheme, the woman planning to spend her life as a housewife would be able to obtain a college education at no cost to herself. On the other hand, if women had a separate Ed Op Bank, then women planning to have careers would have to subsidize those not planning to have careers.[28]

One possible solution would be to have all borrowers pledge a percentage of their future *family* income. Shell and his colleagues propose a scheme in which fully employed women pay only on their

[27] Ibid., p. 8.

[28] Ibid., pp. 6–7.

TABLE 1.5-39 *Rate of return r (percentage) as a function of the tax rate* τ

Repayment period T set at 40 years
Cut-off salary for married women $\overline{W}$ set at mean college-educated female income*
Annual growth rate of incomes assumed to be 4.5 percent
Opt-out interest rate set at 6.5 percent

| College class entering in | Tax rate τ per $1,000 borrowed | | | | |
	τ = 0.20%	τ = 0.25%	τ = 0.33%	τ = 0.50%	τ = 1.00%
1969	2.9	3.6	4.3	5.1	5.5
1970	3.0	3.7	4.4	5.1	5.5
1971	3.1	3.8	4.4	5.1	5.5
1972	3.2	3.8	4.5	5.2	5.5
1973	3.3	3.9	4.6	5.2	5.6
1974	3.4	4.0	4.6	5.2	5.6
1975	3.5	4.1	4.7	5.3	5.6
1976	3.6	4.1	4.7	5.3	5.6
1977	3.7	4.2	4.8	5.3	5.6
1978	3.7	4.3	4.8	5.3	5.6
1979	3.8	4.3	4.8	5.3	5.6
1980	3.9	4.4	4.8	5.3	5.7
1981	4.0	4.4	4.8	5.3	5.7

* $4,075 \ (1.045)^{t \ - \ 1,965}$.

SOURCE: K. Shell et al., *The Educational Opportunity Bank: An Economic Analysis of a Contingent Repayment Loan Program for Higher Education,* Department of Economics, Massachusetts Institute of Technology, Cambridge, Mass., November 1967, table N.1, p. 46. (Working paper.)

own incomes, and married women not participating in the labor force pay on family income.[29] The M.I.T. study also considered the fiscal impact of the Educational Opportunity Bank, because the effect of a large amount of borrowing on the economy—especially at high levels of output—is the same as the effect of an increase in government expenditures; in other words, the loans will stimulate the nation's demand for goods and services. In periods of full employment, restrictive monetary and fiscal policies will be required to offset the inflationary effects of the rise in spending due to increased loans to college students. The government will have to raise taxes (or forgo a tax cut) to prevent inflation. The total increase in aggregate

[29] Ibid., p. 7.

demand attributable to the Educational Opportunity Bank—the size of the tax increase needed to prevent inflation—is estimated at $2.1 billion in 1969, $15.2 billion in 1977 (maximum), and $9.5 billion in 1984.[30]

Table 1.5-40 shows a proposed loan and repayment schedule (and fiscal impact) for the Educational Opportunity Bank. New loans would begin at $1.6 billion in 1969, and rise to $16.8 billion in 1984. In 1984 repayments would total $12.3 billion, with outstanding loans of $132 billion.

An earlier government report on the proposed Educational Opportunity Bank suggested beginning with total loans of $0.7 billion in 1968–69 and reaching a level of $5.9 billion in new loans by 1979–80. Repayments would total $0.5 billion and outstanding

(Text continued on p. 190)

[30] Ibid., especially sections 1, 4, 5, and 6.

TABLE 1.5-40 *Educational Opportunity Bank: proposed loan and repayment schedule, with fiscal impact, 1969–1984 (billions of dollars)*

Year	New loans	Repayments	Outstanding loans	Fiscal impact
1969	$ 1.620	$ 0.000	$ 1.620	$ 2.106
1970	3.435	0.000	5.054	4.465
1971	5.510	0.008	10.556	7.154
1972	7.886	0.045	18.397	10.206
1973	10.557	0.177	28.777	13.546
1974	11.245	0.415	39.606	14.202
1975	11.950	0.797	50.759	14.738
1976	12.630	1.326	62.063	15.093
1977	13.290	2.042	73.311	15.234
1978	13.968	2.936	84.344	15.223
1979	14.664	4.058	94.950	15.005
1980	15.301	5.405	104.845	14.485
1981	15.892	6.876	113.862	13.783
1982	16.382	8.626	121.617	12.670
1983	16.605	10.715	127.507	10.871
1984	16.796	12.331	131.972	9.503

SOURCE: K. Shell et al., *The Educational Opportunity Bank: An Economic Analysis of a Contingent Repayment Loan Program for Higher Education*, Department of Economics, Massachusetts Institute of Technology, Cambridge, Mass., November 1967, p. 86. (Working paper.)

TABLE 1.5-41 *Federal financial aid to students in any field of study*

Program	Student eligibility	Assistance to students
National Defense Student Loans (National Defense Education Act of 1958, as amended)	Undergraduates may borrow up to $1,000 per year to a total of $5,000. Graduate or professional students may borrow up to $2,500 a year, with the total of undergraduate and graduate loans not to exceed $10,000.	Students must carry at least one-half of normal college workload in eligible colleges or universities, accredited postsecondary business schools, or proprietary and vocational institutions. Students must be able to demonstrate financial need for the loan.
College work-study (Higher Education Act of 1965, as amended)	Students are employed for an average of 15 hours weekly during the academic year, and a maximum of 40 hours weekly during summer or vacations. Work may be on or off campus in public or private nonprofit institutions or agencies.	Students must be enrolled full-time and be in good standing at participating colleges, universities, postsecondary business schools, or area vocational schools.
Educational opportunity grants (Higher Education Act of 1965, as amended)	Grants provide $200 to $1,000 a year for four years of undergraduate study. They must be matched by other help from schools such as NDSL or a college work-study job.	Students must be enrolled or accepted in participating junior colleges, colleges, universities, or postsecondary institutions. Only full-time, undergraduate students from low-income families who would not otherwise be able to continue their education are eligible. These are opportunity grants and as such are awarded to students from all ranges of academic ability with varying degrees of preparation for college.
Guaranteed student loans (Higher Education Act of 1965, as amended)	This loan program is designed to make it possible for students to borrow from private lenders to help pay educational costs. Up to $1,500 per academic year may be borrowed ($7,500 aggregate maximum) from eligible lenders in most states. For a student whose adjusted family income is less than $15,000 a year, the federal government will pay the lender the total interest due (up to 7 percent) on the unpaid principal balance while the student is in school or during other periods of deferment. If a borrower dies or becomes permanently disabled, his loan will be cancelled.	Any student may apply who has been accepted for enrollment in an eligible school or who is already in attendance and in good standing and who is a citizen or national of the United States or is in the United States for other than a temporary purpose. In many states half-time students are eligible, but some require full-time attendance.

SOURCE: V. Trimble, "Student Financial Aid: What, Where, How," *American Education,* February 1969, pp. 7–8.

Student financial obligations	*How to obtain assistance*
Students make no payment on interest or principal until nine months after completion of study. Payment may be extended up to ten years with three years deferment for military, Peace Corps, or VISTA service. Partial or total loan "forgiveness" for teaching service is another benefit.	Apply to the financial aid officer of the educational institution the student attends or which has accepted him for enrollment.
Students are required to perform their jobs satisfactorily. Generally, they are paid no less than $1.30 per hour. Specialized workers usually receive higher wages. Average earnings are approximately $450 per annum.	Apply to the financial aid officer of the educational institution the student attends or which has accepted him for enrollment.
Students make no repayments. These are outright grants to low-income students who demonstrate academic or creative potential.	Apply to the financial aid officer of the institution which the student wishes to attend.
Students make no payment while attending an eligible institution. Repayment may also be deferred while the borrower is a member of the Armed Forces or a full-time volunteer in Peace Corps or VISTA. The repayment period will usually begin from 9 to 12 months after a student ceases or completes his studies. Repayment will normally be made in installments over a period from 5 to 10 years. The student will be required to pay a minimum of $360 per year on all the guaranteed loans he has received during his school years.	Applications for loans may be obtained from banks, savings and loan associations, credit unions, pension funds, schools, colleges, insurance companies, and similar institutions which participate and qualify as eligible lenders. Students desiring loan assistance should contact their own local lending institutions first. Loans are approved or denied at the discretion of the lender. State or private nonprofit guarantee agencies, regional offices of the Office of Education, or school officials will also provide assistance.

loans would be $46.6 billion (an estimated 3.7 percent of GNP) in 1979–80. In this report it is estimated that if college enrollment and population stabilize and repayments are equal to new loans, then the total Educational Opportunity Bank credit for one year's loans would be $11.8 billion with a 20-year repayment period and $21.2 billion with a 40-year repayment period. For a 30-year repayment period and loans equal to one-third of the student costs of higher education, total loans outstanding would be 8 percent of GNP. (Nonfarm mortgage credit is now 30 percent of GNP.)[31]

[31] U.S. Office of the President, Panel on Educational Innovation, *The Educational Opportunity Bank,* report to the Commissioner of Education, Director of National Science Foundation, and Special Assistant to the President for Science and Technology, 1967, pp. 20–21.

TABLE 1.5-42
Net cost of student aid as percentage of educational and general income, 1957–58

	Number of colleges	Percentages of educational and general income			
		Median	Average	High	Low
All colleges	55	4.5	4.2	18.5	0.1
Type					
Men	10	4.0	4.2	11.2	0.3
Women	9	3.4	2.1	7.8	0.1
Coed	36	5.2	5.0	18.5	0.3
Size of Enrollment					
200–600	10	7.2	6.3	12.5	2.9
601–1,000	26	4.1	4.7	18.5	0.3
1,001–1,400	11	4.5	4.2	10.4	0.3
1,401 and up	8	3.8	3.2	8.3	0.1
Associations					
American	11	5.8	5.4	12.5	0.6
Central	12	4.8	4.7	15.4	2.2
Eastern	12	2.5	2.7	8.3	0.1
Southern	12	5.4	5.6	18.5	0.3
Western	8	6.0	5.8	8.1	2.4

SOURCE: National Federation of College and University Business Officers Association, *The Sixty College Study . . . A Second Look, A Comparison of Financial Operating Data for 1957–58,* 1960, p. 25.

Table 1.5-41 is a compilation of the various federal programs for student aid in 1968. The table contains the types of aid provided, student eligibility, student financial obligations, and how to obtain financial assistance.

In 1957–58 student aid as an average percentage of educational and general income of institutions of higher education was 4.2 percent (in a sampling of 60 small private liberal arts colleges). Student aid as an average percentage of tuition income was 7.6 percent. The average percentages of student aid relative to educational and general income were especially high in coeducational colleges (5.0 percent), in colleges with enrollments of 200 to 600 (6.3 percent), and in Western associations of colleges (5.8 percent). The average percentage of aid relative to tuition income was also high in coeducational institutions (8.7 percent) (Table 1.5-42).

Percentages of tuition income

Median	Average	High	Low
8.9	7.6	33.8	0.0
9.6	8.6	27.6	0.6
5.1	3.7	19.5	0.1
8.6	8.7	33.8	0.0
19.4	16.6	33.8	6.4
9.2	8.8	33.5	0.6
6.3	7.0	18.1	0.0
5.7	5.4	12.3	0.1
19.3	14.2	33.8	1.9
8.4	8.2	33.5	4.1
5.0	4.5	12.3	0.1
11.2	13.8	32.2	0.0
8.6	8.1	11.5	3.4

1.6. Graduate Student Aid

There have been large relative increases in the number of graduate students and graduate programs in recent years. Has graduate student aid grown with enrollment and income? To answer this question, a comparison of graduate enrollment and graduate fellowships for the years 1890 and 1960 is useful.

Number of graduate students and number of fellowships, 1890 and 1960	*Year*	*Number of graduate students*	*Number of fellowships*	*Number of fellowships as a percentage of graduate enrollment*

	Number of graduate students	Number of fellowships	Number of fellowships as a percentage of graduate enrollment
Year			
1890	2,000	172	8.6
1960	314,349	20,811 (1958–59)	6.6

SOURCES: U.S. Office of Education, *Report of the Commissioner of Education, 1889–90*, p. 762; U.S. Department of the Interior, *Annual Report of the Secretary of the Interior,* 1890, p. 819; U.S. Office of Education, *Digest of Educational Statistics, 1968,* p. 73; and J. L. Chase, *Doctoral Study: Fellowships and Capacity of Graduate Schools,* U.S. Office of Education, 1961, p. 19.

In view of the economic advances over the 70 years from 1890 to 1960, the fellowship record for 1960 does not seem particularly generous. But fellowships, it should be emphasized, accounted for only 8.6 percent of the income of graduate students in 1965. When other forms of aid are added, we must conclude that graduate students today receive much more aid than in 1890.

Because of graduate education's contribution to the national welfare, the federal government has incurred special obligations to finance graduate students. Furthermore, with the average annual institutional costs of educating one graduate student estimated at $4,500 in 1968 and $8,000 by 1975–76, the federal government also has obligations to help finance institutions with graduate programs. In 1966–67 the federal government provided $441 million in various forms of aid directly to graduate students.[1] The table below gives the distribution of federal support of graduate education (both institutional aid and student aid) for fiscal years 1966 and 1967.

Federal support of graduate education, fiscal years 1966 and 1967 (in millions of dollars)

Type of support	Fiscal year 1966	Fiscal year 1967
Institutional grants	164	244
Fellowships and traineeships	265	329
Federal schools and training of personnel	556	576
Research and development in colleges and universities	1,350	1,430

SOURCE: Adapted from U.S. Office of Education, *Education in the Seventies*, planning papers of the Office of Program Planning and Evaluation, May 1968, table 23, pp. 34–37.

The 1958 National Defense Education Act provided for graduate fellowships and grants to the sponsoring institutions. The following table shows the appropriations for graduate fellowships under the National Defense Education Act for fiscal years 1966, 1967, and 1968.

Graduate fellowships under the National Defense Education Act of 1958

Fiscal year	Authorization	Appropriations (in millions)
1966	Not specified	$56
1967	Not specified	81
1968	Not specified	87

SOURCE: U.S. Office of Education, *Fact Book, Office of Education Programs*, prepared by the Office of Administration, Management Evaluation Branch, January 1967, p. 26.

In considering financial aid to higher education, one must realize that the greater the stress on student aid, the greater the emphasis on equality of opportunity; the greater the stress on institutional aid, the greater the emphasis on improved conditions of institutions of higher education. Institutional aid may lead to an improvement in the financial position of the institution, an improvement in the

[1] Association of American Universities, *The Federal Funding of Higher Education*, Washington, D.C., 1968, p. 6.

quality of output, and/or an increase in the number of students serviced.[2]

Growing graduate programs increase the financial problems of institutions of higher education because rising unit costs are associated with increases in graduate enrollment. The following table shows the large increase in graduate enrollment relative to total enrollment from 1957 to 1967 and the projected increase from 1967 to 1977. Graduate enrollment is projected to increase by 344 percent from 1957 to 1977, as compared with a projected increase of 218 percent in total enrollment.

Total and graduate enrollment, 1957, 1967, and 1977 (projected)	Year	Total degree-credit enrollment (thousands)	Graduate enrollment (thousands)
	1957	3,047	288
	1967	6,348	688
	1977	9,684	1,279

SOURCE: U.S. Office of Education, *Projections of Educational Statistics to 1977–78*, National Center for Educational Statistics, 1968, p. 12.

SOCIAL ORIGINS OF GRADUATE STUDENTS On the whole, parents of graduate students have smaller incomes, less education, and "lower-status" occupations than parents of undergraduates. A summary of the social origins of graduate student for spring 1965 is given in Table 1.6-1. Note that 56 percent of the fathers of graduate students had incomes of less than $7,500. Only 42 percent of the fathers of graduate students had jobs which could be classified as professional (including educators), proprietary, or managerial. Only 24 percent of the fathers and 15 percent of the mothers of graduate students had completed at least four years of college.

A BREAK-DOWN OF GRADUATE AID There is much need for expansion of the National Defense Education Act fellowships. The Rivlin Committee recommended that the number of fellowships under the National Defense Education Act be doubled to 30,000 by 1975, at which time they would still support only 6 percent of all full-time graduate students. The Rivlin Committee also proposed that the institutional grant accompanying each graduate fellowship be increased to $5,000 by 1975—an amount much below projected institutional costs for that year. If the Rivlin Committee proposals were accepted, the expanded

[2] U.S. Department of Health, Education and Welfare, *Toward a Long-range Plan for Federal Support for Higher Education,* report to the President, Office of Assistant Secretary for Planning and Evaluation, January 1969, pp. 33–35.

TABLE 1.6-1 *Social origins of graduate students—income, occupation, and education of the fathers and the education of the mothers, by sex, spring 1965*

Background characteristic	All students	Sex	
		Men	Women
Number of students	477,535	335,226	142,307
		Percent	
TOTAL	100	100	100
Father's income (per annum)			
Less than $5,000	29	30	28
$ 5,000–$7,499	27	28	24
$ 7,500–$9,999	16	16	14
$10,000–$14,999	12	12	12
$15,000–$19,999	4	3	5
$20,000 and over	4	4	6
Do not know	8	6	12
Father's occupation			
Laborer	5	6	5
Service worker	4	4	3
Semiskilled operative	7	8	6
Skilled craftsman	18	19	16
Farm operator	8	7	8
Proprietor or manager	18	17	19
Semiprofessional	15	15	16
Professional (except educator)	19	19	21
Teacher or other educator	5	5	5
Father's education			
Did not complete grade school	13	13	11
Completed grade school but not high school	28	28	26
Completed high school but no college	23	24	23
One but less than four years of college	12	12	13
Completed college	12	12	13
Obtained master's degree	4	4	4
Obtained Ph.D. or other	8	7	10
Mother's education			
Did not complete grade school	9	9	8
Completed grade school but not high school	27	27	25
Completed high school but no college	34	35	32
One but less than four years of college	16	15	18
Completed college	11	10	12
Obtained master's degree	3	2	3
Obtained Ph.D. or other	1	1	1

SOURCE: J. S. Hunter, *The Academic and Financial Status of Graduate Students, Spring, 1965,* U.S. Office of Education, 1967, p. 7.

National Defense Education Act fellowships and cost-of-education allowances would provide $470 million in aid by fiscal year 1976.[3]

In 1965–66 student aid totaled $1.01 billion, with federal aid accounting for 44 percent ($442 million) and nonfederal aid accounting for 56 percent ($568 million). Graduate students accounted for a little more than 10 percent of total enrollment in this year, but they received 26 percent of all student aid.[4] The following table shows the distribution of total student aid among work assignments, grants, and loans for 1965–66. Work assignments accounted for 31 percent, grants for 41 percent, and student loans for 28 percent of total student aid.

Distribution of total student aid, by type, 1965–66

Type of aid	Millions of dollars	Percentage
Work assignments	316	31
Grants	416	41
Loans	281	28

SOURCE: U.S. Office of Education, *Financial Statistics of Institutions of Higher Education: Student Financial Aid 1965–66,* National Center for Educational Statistics, 1968, p. 1.

The proportion of nonfederal student aid received by graduate students varies by type of aid. In 1965–66 graduate students received 27 percent of the nonfederal work assignments, 23 percent of the nonfederal grants, and 20 percent of the nonfederal student loans. In terms of total student aid, graduate students received 35 percent of all grants, 27 percent of all work assignments, and 12 percent of all loans. Hence, the federal contribution to graduate aid was relatively large for grants and relatively small for loans. These figures are shown in the table below.

Nonfederal and total student aid, distribution among types of aid, and percentage received by graduate students, 1965–66

Type of aid	Nonfederal aid (in millions)	Percentage received by graduate students	Total aid (in millions)	Percentage received by graduate students
Work assignments	$209	27	$316	27
Grants	315	23	416	35
Loans	44	20	281	12

SOURCE: U.S. Office of Education, *Financial Statistics of Institutions of Higher Education: Student Financial Aid 1965–66,* National Center for Educational Statistics, 1968, p. 4.

[3] Ibid.

[4] U.S. Office of Education, *Financial Statistics of Institutions of Higher Education: Student Financial Aid 1965–66,* National Center for Educational Statistics, 1968, p. 1. Another source estimates that graduate students received 27.7 percent of all student aid in 1965–66.

A comparison of nonfederal and total student aid in public and private institutions can be shown in a similar table. In 1965–66 graduate students at public institutions received relatively more nonfederal aid in the form of work assignments (31 percent versus

Nonfederal and total student aid in public and private institutions and percentage received by graduate students, 1965–66

	Nonfederal aid				Total aid			
	Public		Private		Public		Private	
	Mil-lions of dollars	Percentage received by graduate students	Mil-lions of dollars	Percentage received by graduate students	Mil-lions of dollars	Percentage received by graduate students	Mil-lions of dollars	Percentage received by graduate students
Work assignments	$148	31	$ 61	20	$216	27	$100	26
Grants	103	26	212	21	157	43	258	29
Loans	23	18	21	22	140	14	141	11

SOURCE: U.S. Office of Education, *Financial Statistics of Institutions of Higher Education: Student Financial Aid 1965–66,* National Center for Educational Statistics, 1968, p. 4.

20 percent) and grants (26 percent versus 21 percent) than graduate students at private institutions. Graduate students at private institutions received relatively more nonfederal aid in the form of loans than graduate students at public institutions (22 percent versus 18 percent). Apparently graduate students at public institutions receive more favorable treatment from nonfederal sources of aid than graduate students at private institutions. But this difference is to some extent related to the larger graduate enrollment of public institutions. For total student aid (both federal and nonfederal), there is a marked difference in the percentage of grants received by graduate students at public and private institutions. Forty-three percent of all grants in public institutions went to graduate students, as compared with 29 percent of all grants in private institutions.

According to the Office of Education, graduate students were estimated to require $704 million of support in 1966, $980 million in 1969, and a projected $1,330 million in 1973. In each of these years the federal government's contribution represents approximately two-thirds of total support. Federal support of graduate students is composed of veterans' benefits and Office of Education programs. The major source of nonfederal aid in each of these years is teaching assistantships (Table 1.6-2).

TABLE 1.6-2
Graduate
student support
requirements
(in millions
of dollars)

Graduate student financing	1966	1969	1973
TOTAL	704	980	1330
Subtotal, nonfederal	227	357	467
Nonfederal fellowships	5	5	5
Research assistantships	5	6	7
Teaching assistantships	144	230	302
Faculty appointments	73	116	153
Subtotal, federal	477	623	863
Veterans Administration	102	204	204
Office of Education (total)	140	179	247
National Defense Student Loan	36	50	64
Guaranteed Loans	49	70	100
College Work-Study	7	9	13
Other Office of Education	50	50	80
Other federal	235	240	412

SOURCE: U.S. Office of Education, *Students and Buildings: An Analysis of Selected Federal Programs for Higher Education,* 1968, p. 72.

FEDERAL SUPPORT OF GRADUATE STUDENTS Table 1.6-3 shows federal support of graduate students by agency for 1966–67. Total federal aid to graduate students in that year was $441 million, with the Department of Health, Education and Welfare providing approximately half. Table 1.6-4 gives a breakdown of graduate stipends by source of funds for 1963–64 and 1966–67. In 1966–67 the federal government provided $296 million in fellowships and scholarships and $90 million in research assistantships. Total graduate stipends were provided by fellowships and scholarships, teaching assistantships, research assistantships, and faculty appointments, in that order.

Determining the need
In order to determine the total financial aid needed for graduate students to pursue their studies, it is necessary to determine the number of full-time equivalent (FTE) graduate students. This determination is complicated by several factors.

First, OE has not taken a census of graduate students since 1963–64. Estimates published currently are projections of past trends and do not take into account the recent infusion of nearly $200 million per year for graduate student support from VA and OE programs.

Another complication results from the flow of students into and through graduate programs. Studies of the National Opinion Research Center (NORC)[a] and the Bureau of Social Science Research for the National Science Foundation[b] have documented the complexity of graduate student

TABLE 1.6-3 Federal support for graduate	Agency	Amount*
students, estimates by	Total federal student aid	$441.4
agency,	Stipends	386.4
1966–67 (in millions)	Department of Health, Education and Welfare	167.7
	National Institutes of Health	95.4
	Office of Education†	56.8
	Other	15.5
	Veterans Administration	102.0
	National Science Foundation	44.1
	Department of Defense	37.2
	National Aeronautics and Space Administration	22.9
	Atomic Energy Commission	12.1
	Department of the Interior	.5
	Loans	55.0
	Department of Health, Education and Welfare	55.0
	Office of Education:	
	National Defense Student Loans	25.0
	Guaranteed Loans	30.0

*Estimates for predoctoral academic year programs. Estimates are for funds for student use only, exclusive of cost-of-education payments to institutions. Estimates of payments to graduate research assistants are included in agency totals.

† Includes estimated graduate student support from work-study program: $7 million.

SOURCE: U.S. Office of Education, *Students and Buildings: An Analysis of Selected Federal Programs for Higher Education,* 1968, p. 25.

study patterns at great length. Besides students who attend full-time until they receive their degree, there are students who alternate between full- and part-time study or between full-time and no study. The majority of students seem to interrupt their studies between the master's degree and the doctorate.

Finally, the present use of course load to distinguish between part-time and full-time students in graduate work leaves much to be desired. Some part-time students do not carry a full load of courses because they are writing dissertations or preparing for comprehensive or language examinations; others are precluded by their institution from taking a full course load because they hold teaching or research assistantships.

Two methods may be used to approximate the number of FTE graduate students. The traditional method is to assume that part-time students study one-third of the time. Based on current projections of full-time and part-time students, this method produces a figure of 404,000 FTE graduate students in 1967. Thus, as projected by NCES, graduate students could be expected to increase to 492,000 in 1969 and 617,000 in 1973.[c]

TABLE 1.6-4
Graduate student stipends, by source of funds, 1963–64 and 1966–67 (in millions)

Type of stipend	Total	Source Federal	Nonfederal
1963–64:			
TOTAL	$394.4	$230.2	$164.2
Fellowships and scholarships	162.4	157.5	4.9
Research assistantships	77.4	72.7	4.7
Teaching assistantships	102.7		102.7
Faculty appointment	51.9		51.9
1966–67:			
TOTAL	612.7	386.4	226.3
Fellowships and scholarships	300.9	295.9	5.0
Research assistantships	95.5	90.5	5.0
Teaching assistantships	143.6		143.6
Faculty appointment	72.7		72.7

SOURCE: OPPE estimates based on agency fiscal reports, NORC and BSSR studies on sources of student stipends, and agency estimates on research assistantships from R & D funds; in U.S. Office of Education, *Students and Buildings: An Analysis of Selected Federal Programs for Higher Education,* 1968, p. 62.

An alternative is to assume that the FTE level in a given year is proportional to the number of master's and Ph.D. degrees awarded in that year, plus the total number of master's degrees and Ph.D.'s awarded in the following year and the number of Ph.D.'s awarded in the third subsequent year. Estimates based on this method would result in 331,000 FTE graduate students in 1967, 443,000 in 1969, and 512,000 in 1973.

Both estimates indicated that the number of graduate students was likely to increase by some 20 percent between 1967 and 1969 and that it would grow by some 50 percent over the base figure by 1973.

An additional number of students could be expected to enroll full-time if additional aid were available. For instance, in 1963 NORC asked part-time graduate students what inducements were needed to have them go to school full time. Up to 56 percent of the students would have gone to school full time if they had had additional stipend money [Table 1.6-5].

Rationale for graduate student aid
Graduate student aid has usually been justified in terms of the American economy's need for highly trained talent. It has been argued that student aid increases the number of individuals with graduate degrees by permitting students to start graduate careers earlier and reducing the likelihood that they will drop out before completion because of financial pressures.

TABLE 1.6-5		
Stipends required to induce part-time graduate students to attend school full-time (1963)	*Stipend and level of support*	*Percentage of total respondents*
	Tuition scholarship	1
	Tuition scholarship plus $500 stipend with no obligations	1
	Tuition scholarship plus $1,000 stipend with no obligations	4
	Tuition scholarship plus $2,000 stipend with no obligations	14
	Tuition scholarship plus $3,000 stipend with no obligations	14
	Tuition scholarship plus $4,000 stipend with no obligations	22
	None of the above	44

SOURCE: *Graduate Student Finances, 1963,* National Opinion Research Center, The University of Chicago Press, Chicago, September 1965, p. 113; in U.S. Office of Education, *Students and Buildings: An Analysis of Selected Federal Programs for Higher Education,* 1968, p. 62.

All these arguments have some verisimilitude. For example, in the natural sciences, of the 1958 bachelor degree recipients who attended graduate school, 55 percent held a stipend, and 35.6 percent obtained a graduate degree by 1963. By contrast in social sciences and education, where the percentage of graduate students receiving stipends was only 36 and 17 percent respectively, the percentage of graduate degree recipients during the 6-year period was lower: 29 and 16 percent for the two disciplines. The availability of stipends was also closely correlated with the percentage of students engaged in full-time study. Natural sciences, with the highest proportion of students benefiting from stipends, had the highest percentage of full-time students, and education and business were in the cellar in terms of both the share of students supported and the share of students who studied full time. . . .

The correlation between the proportion of graduates in full-time study and the proportion of degree recipients by discipline was .73. The correlation between the proportion of students who received stipends and those who studied full time by discipline was .71. The correlation between stipend recipients and degree recipients was .78.

Thus the availability of stipends accounts for approximately one-half of the variation in the number of degrees received by field of study. An independent study by NORC of graduate student patterns in 1963 came to essentially the same conclusion.

If data are controlled for academic level and grade-point average, rates of full-time study are at least twice as high for stipend holders as for others.[d]

There appears to be a fair relationship between the availability of aid and the number of candidates for master's and Ph.D. degrees. A relationship also exists between the availability of aid and the length of time between completion of one degree and the start of work towards a higher degree. The amount of aid, it appears, serves to increase the number of persons who obtain degrees in a given period rather than to shorten the average time between a B.A. and a Ph.D.

During the period 1920–61, the length of time between the receipt of a bachelor's degree and a doctorate was not much affected by the aid available. In major disciplines roughly 10 years elapsed between the award of a bachelor's degree and a Ph.D. This figure scarcely changed between 1920 and 1961. . . .

This finding is relevant to the policy of financing Ph.D. candidates. A preliminary analysis of NDEA fellowships awards . . . indicates that a disappointingly low number of NDEA grant holders who received fellowships at the beginning of their Ph.D. studies completed their degree within the 3-year period. On the other hand, those who received grants when they were further along with their Ph.D. studies did complete their work during or soon after the grant period. Most degrees, it appears, will be received well after the NDEA grant expired.

Rates of return
The level of subsidies to graduate students probably is not high enough to make the returns from the student's investment in graduate study as high as the returns to individuals who stopped their education at the bachelor's level. For instance, Hanoch[e] has estimated that the average internal rate of return to white males in the Northeast from undergraduate education was 9.6 percent, compared to 8.7 percent for those who had had some graduate school work.

An estimate, using 1960 census data, indicates that at age 22 the present value of graduate study is $15,000, if the student's income stream is discounted at 6 percent. If we assume that it takes the equivalent of 2 full-time years of graduate study to get a master's degree and an additional 3 years to get a doctorate, the average degree recipient in 1966–67[f] had spent the equivalent of 2.1 years of effort in graduate work. His foregone income, according to 1960 data, was $13,200. The average Federal subsidy provided to him, at $1,963 per year, was $4,123 for the 2.1 year period. Hence his net income loss was about $9,100. The rate of return which will equate his future income with the value of his net outlay is 7.9 percent. This is not an exceptionally high rate of return, if one takes into account the risks of failure and the labor involved. Obviously psychic returns play an important role in the decision to obtain a graduate degree. (SOURCES: (*a*) National Opinion Research Center, *Graduate Student Finances, 1963*, The University of Chicago Press, Chicago, 1965; (*b*) Bureau of Social Science Research, Inc., *Five Years After the College Degree*, Washington,

D.C., 1966; (c) U.S. Office of Education, *Projections of Educational Statistics to 1975–76,* National Center for Educational Statistics, 1966, p. 17; (d) National Opinion Research Center, *Graduate Student Finances, 1963,* The University of Chicago Press, Chicago, 1965, p. 106; (e) Giora Hanoch, *Personal Earnings and Investment in School,* The University of Chicago Press, Chicago, December 1965 [dissertation]; and (f) degree recipient data in U.S. Office of Education, *Projections of Educational Statistics to 1975–76,* National Center for Educational Statistics, 1966, pp. 27–36.)[5]

FELLOWSHIPS AND OTHER RESOURCES OF GRADUATE STUDENTS

In 1965 fellowships, assistantships, and faculty appointments provided only one-fourth of the income of graduate students. Other employment provided one-half and savings, spouse's earnings, gifts, and loans provided most of the remaining income. Many graduate students believe the financial aid they receive is insufficient. In a recent study 30 percent of the first-year graduate students, 37 percent of the second-year students, and 32 percent

[5] U.S. Office of Education, *Students and Buildings: An Analysis of Selected Federal Programs for Higher Education,* 1968, pp. 27–28.

TABLE 1.6-6
Sources of income of graduate students, 1965

Source of income	Percentage distribution of total income by source		
	All students	*Full-time students*	*Part-time students*
All sources	100.0	100.0	100.0
Scholarship	1.5	2	1
Fellowship	8.6	19	1
Teaching assistant	6.2	11	3
Research assistant	4.8	9	2
Faculty appointment	3.2	2	4
Other employment	51.5	18	74
NDEA loan	.6	1	
Commercial loan	.7	1	
University loan	.3	1	
Savings	3.6	7	2
Spouse's earnings	12.6	17	9
Gifts, loans from relatives	4.2	8	1
Other	2.1	3	1

SOURCE: Office of Education survey, "Academic and Financial Status of Graduate Students, Spring 1965"; in U.S. Office of Education, *Students and Buildings: An Analysis of Selected Federal Programs for Higher Education,* 1968, p. 26.

of the third-year students thought the financial aid they received was inadequate.[6]

Income of graduate students varies by sex, by amount of time devoted to study, and by marital status. In 1965, 39 percent of all full-time graduate students had incomes of $5,000 or more, whereas 72 percent of all part-time graduate students had incomes this high. Of the single men who had no dependents and were part-time students, 38 percent had incomes of $5,000 or more, whereas 52 percent of the single women in this category had incomes of $5,000 or more (Table 1.6-7).

TYPES OF EMPLOYERS   Table 1.6-8 gives a percentage breakdown of the employers of science graduate students in the mid 1960s. Seventy-one percent of the engineering students, fifty-two percent of the physical science students, fifty-eight percent of the behavioral science students, and forty-two percent of the life science students were employed on a nonstipend basis. The largest employer of engineering and physical science students was private companies, while the largest employer of behavioral and life science students was colleges and universities.

DISTRIBUTION OF STIPENDS BY FIELD OF STUDY   In 1963 the percentage of full-time graduate students holding stipends ranged from 89 percent in the life sciences to 64 percent in the humanities. For part-time graduate students, the percentage holding stipends varied from 62 percent for the life sciences to 32 percent for the humanities (Table 1.6-9). (These figures refer to a 1963 follow-up of the 1961 college graduates. Five years after college graduation the percentage of these students holding stipends was less than the 1963 estimates.)

A distribution of fellowships that is far from optimum probably increases the cost of an adequate graduate program. The Rivlin Committee pointed out an imbalance in administrative and institutional arrangements; for example, excessive emphasis on research versus teaching and on the sciences versus all other disciplines.[7]

[6] W. G. Bowen, *The Federal Government and Princeton University,* Princeton University Press, Princeton, N.J., January 1962, p. 201.

[7] U.S. Department of Health, Education and Welfare, *Toward a Long-Range Plan for Federal Financial Support for Higher Education,* report to the President, Office of Assistant Secretary for Planning and Evaluation, January 1969, pp. 17–19.

TABLE 1.6-7
*Annual income
of graduate
students, by
enrollment
status, sex,
and marital
status, spring
1965*

Enrollment status sex and marital status	Total		Less than $2,000	$2,000 2,999
	Number	Percent	Percent	Percent
Full-time students	172,433	100	10	18
Men				
Single men—no dependents	57,493	100	17	32
Single men—dependents	2,396	100	17	16
Married men—no dependents	28,055	100	2	5
Married men—dependents	42,101	100	1	3
Women				
Single women—no dependents	24,176	100	20	34
Single women—dependents	2,698	100	7	9
Married women—no dependents	9,375	100	7	9
Married women—dependents	6,135	100	10	7
Part-time students	252,237	100	9	5
Men				
Single men—no dependents	31,922	100	15	19
Single men—dependents	3,751	100	8	4
Married men—no dependents	25,743	100	5	1
Married men—dependents	99,456	100	3	1
Women				
Single women—no dependents	29,377	100	11	10
Single women—dependents	6,911	100	5	5
Married women—no dependents	26,079	100	15	5
Married women—dependents	28,995	100	17	3

SOURCE: J. L. Chase, *Doctoral Study: Fellowships and Capacity of Graduate Schools,* U.S. Office of Education, 1961, p. 21.

Table 1.6-10 shows the percentage of graduate students in public and private institutions receiving aid in the early 1960s—by field of study and institutional quality. The proportion of graduate students in public institutions receiving aid in the natural sciences ranged from 48 percent for the highest-quality institutions to 66 percent for the lowest-quality institutions. Although the percentage of natural science students receiving aid was higher in the less prestigious than in the more prestigious institutions, the percentage

			Income group				
$3,000– *3,999*	*$4,000–* *4,999*	*$5,000–* *5,999*	*$6,000–* *6,999*	*$7,000–* *7,999*	*$8,000–* *8,999*	*$9,000–* *9,999*	*$10,000* *and* *over*
Percent	*Percent*	*Percent*	*Percent*	*Percent*	*Percent*	*Percent*	*Percent*
19	15	11	9	6	5	2	6
27	13	6	2	1	1	1	0
32	17	2	2	6	2	2	3
14	17	16	17	10	10	4	5
9	18	17	15	12	8	4	12
24	12	6	2	1	1	0	0
17	14	12	10	16	4	4	6
17	17	12	13	6	5	4	10
7	9	7	10	11	9	3	25
6	8	16	13	11	8	6	18
16	11	16	8	5	5	1	3
8	4	20	13	17	12		12
4	10	17	14	12	8	7	22
2	6	13	16	15	12	9	24
12	15	31	13	4	2	1	1
4	10	24	17	11	10	5	10
7	8	17	10	8	4	5	20
4	5	9	10	10	6	4	32

of humanities students receiving aid was highest for the top-quality institutions (for both public and private institutions).

Table 1.6-11 gives the percentage of science graduate students holding one, two, or three stipends in 1962–63. Eighty percent of the graduate students in the life sciences held a first stipend, twenty percent held a second, and four percent held a third. Table 1.6-12 shows the distribution of stipends by type of aid and by field of study for 1962–63. Eighty percent of the life science students,

TABLE 1.6-8 *Nonstipend employment and income, by area of graduate study and source of employment*

	Engi-neering	Physical sciences	Behavioral sciences	Life sciences
Percentage of graduate students employed				
Percentage of graduate students employed (nonstipend)	71	52	58	42
Percentage of employed students				
Source of employment:				
Private company	59	39	19	13
Research organization	12	14	8	11
College or university*	17	17	20	32
Other college or university†	4	9	12	10
Elementary or secondary school	‡	7	4	11
Government employee§	12	14	17	17
Hospital, clinic, other nonprofit organization	‡	2	17	10
Other	4	6	14	5
Monthly income:				
$800 or more	34	17	9	4
$400 to $799	56	63	58	62
Less than $400	10	21	34	34

*But not a "stipend."
† Includes junior college or technical school.
‡ Less than 0.5 percent.
§ Federal, state, or local.
SOURCE: U.S. House of Representatives, Committee on Science and Astronautics, *Higher Education in the Sciences in the United States,* report of the Subcommittee on Science, Research and Development, prepared by the National Science Foundation, 1965, p. 70.

seventy-four percent of the physical science students, sixty-three percent of the behavioral science students, and sixty-one percent of the engineering students held stipends. The highest percentage of students (by field of study) holding each type of stipend was as follows: twenty-four percent of the engineering students held scholarships, twenty-four percent of the behavioral science students held fellowships and twenty-four percent held research assistantships, thirty-two percent of the physical science students held teaching assistantships, and thirty-one percent of the life science students held research assistantships (Table 1.6-12).

In the spring of 1965 more than half of the graduate students in most fields of study held some kind of stipend. Eighty percent of students in agriculture and forestry held stipends, seventy-four

TABLE 1.6-9 *Behavior of graduate students and availability of stipends*

A. 1963 follow-up of 1961 graduates (men and women)

Field of study	Percentage of B.A.'s enrolled full-time	Percentage of full-time students holding stipends	Percentage of part-time students holding stipends	Percentage of all students holding stipends	Mean value of stipend	Percentage of stipends duty-free	Percentage enrolled within 1 year for next highest degree
Life sciences	72	89	62	80	$2,700	39	61
Physical sciences	61	88	54	74	2,646	35	68
Behaviorial sciences	55	83	48	63	2,350	41	66
Engineering	40	77	42	46	2,200	n.a.*	57
Humanities	50	64	32	46	2,000	39	58

B. Five years after the college degree (males)

	Percentage enrolled full-time	Percentage holding stipends	Percentage degree recipients	Percentage candidate for degree
Natural sciences	58.4	55.5	35.6	18.4
Engineering	41.1	46.0	16.5	12.3
Social sciences	45.0	36.2	29.1	20.6
Humanities and arts	38.8	50.0	18.9	25.8
Health	85.7	n.a.	18.4	8.3
Agriculture	38.9		31.2	16.9
Business and commerce	36.4	10.0	6.2	6.9
Education	19.7	17.1	15.7	5.7
Other	73.0	21.7	3.3	6.6
Unknown	44.2			

n.a. indicates "not available."

SOURCE: *Five Years After the College Degree, Part I,* Bureau of Social Science Research, Inc., Washington, D.C., 1968; in U.S. Office of Education, *Students and Buildings: An Analysis of Selected Federal Programs for Higher Education,* 1968, p. 63.

percent in the biological sciences, seventy-three percent in the physical sciences, seventy-two percent in social work administration, and seventy-one percent in the health professions; only fourteen to twenty-eight percent in educational fields held stipends and twenty-seven percent in library science (Table 1.6-13).

The different types of stipends as percentages of all stipends received by graduate students also vary by fields. In the spring of

TABLE 1.6-10
*Percentage of graduate students receiving aid, by institutional control and quality**

Stratum	Natural sciences	Social sciences	Humanities	Total
	Private			
	(a) Universe (history classified as a social science)			
I.	40	35	25	100%
II.	40	35	25	100
III.	43	39	18	100
	(b) Sample (history classified as a social science)			
I.	42	32	26	100% (480)
II.	40	37	23	100 (562)
III.	41	55	4	100 (383)
	(c) Sample (history classified as a humanity)			
I.	42	19	39	100% (480)
II.	40	26	34	100 (562)
III.	41	29	30	100 (383)

* See Council for Financial Aid to Education, American Alumni Council, and National Association of Independent Schools, *Voluntary Support of Education, 1967–68,* New York, 1965, for criteria for rating institutional quality. Category I includes the highest quality institutions and Category III includes the lowest.

SOURCE: J. A. Davis, *Stipends and Spouses, The Finances of American Arts and Science Graduate Students,* The University of Chicago Press, Chicago, 1962, p. 151.

1965 teaching assistantships as a percentage of total stipends ranged from 45 percent for foreign languages to 0 percent for social work administration. Research assistantships as a percentage of total stipends ranged from 60 percent for agriculture and forestry to 1 percent for religion, and fellowships as a percentage of total

TABLE 1.6-11
Stipend holding by field of graduate study, 1962–63

Field of graduate study	Percentage of graduate students in discipline holding—		
	A first stipend	A second stipend	A third stipend
Engineering	61	16	3
Physical sciences	74	24	5
Behavioral sciences	63	20	4
Life sciences	80	20	4

SOURCE: U.S. House of Representatives, Committee on Science and Astronautics, *Higher Education in the Sciences in the United States,* report of the Subcommittee on Science, Research and Development, prepared by the National Science Foundation, 1965, p. 71.

	Public		
Natural sciences	*Social sciences*	*Humani- ties*	*Total*
48	29	23	100%
54	27	19	100
66	22	12	100
46	33	21	100% (337)
55	30	15	100 (713)
55	30	15	100 (359)
46	24	30	100% (337)
55	22	23	100 (713)
55	21	24	100 (359)

stipends ranged from 69 percent for social work administration to 14 percent for elementary education (Table 1.6-14).

One possible classification of graduate student aid is as follows: (1) support from outside the family requiring no work (fellow-ships), (2) support requiring a kind of work that helps in achieving

(Text continued on p. 214)

TABLE 1.6-12   *Percentage distribution of science graduate student recipients of stipends, by field and type of stipend, 1962–63*

		Percentage holding stipend of indicated type			
				Assistantship	
Field	*All types*	*Scholar- ship*	*Fellow- ship*	*Teaching*	*Research*
Engineering	61	24	17	13	17
Physical sciences	74	14	21	32	24
Behavioral sciences	63	11	24	17	24
Life sciences	80	9	29	23	31

SOURCE: U.S. House of Representatives, Committee on Science and Astronautics, *Higher Education in the Sciences in the United States,* report of the Subcommittee on Science, Research and Development, prepared by the National Science Foundation, 1965, p. 71.

TABLE 1.6-13
Stipend status of graduate students, by academic field of specialization, spring 1965

	Total		Stipend status	
			Held stipends	Did not hold stipends
Academic field	*Number*	*Percent*	*Percent*	*Percent*
Education				
Elementary education	28,146	100	14	86
Secondary education	14,430	100	18	82
Educational administration	19,320	100	16	84
Counseling and guidance	17,399	100	22	78
All other education	54,181	100	28	72
Humanities				
English and journalism	22,660	100	40	60
Fine and applied arts	15,015	100	40	60
Foreign languages	12,105	100	59	41
Philosophy	3,449	100	62	38
Social and behavioral sciences				
Psychology	13,732	100	58	42
History	14,565	100	44	56
Social work administration	8,901	100	72	28
Other social sciences	36,340	100	49	51
Professional fields				
Business and commerce	43,997	100	31	69
Health professions	8,234	100	71	29
Library science	7,563	100	27	73
Religion	6,110	100	61	39
Science				
Biological science	23,660	100	74	26
Physical science	34,061	100	73	27
Mathematics and statistics	18,226	100	60	40
Agriculture and forestry	5,621	100	80	20
Engineering	54,318	100	51	49
Miscellaneous	15,450	100	30	70

SOURCE: J. S. Hunter, *The Academic and Financial Status of Graduate Students, Spring, 1965,* U.S. Office of Education, 1967, p. 26.

TABLE 1.6-14 *Types of stipends awarded graduate students, by academic field of specialization, spring 1965*

	Total		Type of stipend			
			Teaching assistantship	Research assistantship	Fellowship	Scholarship
Academic field	Number	Percent	Percent	Percent	Percent	Percent
Education						
Elementary education	4,279	100	8	4	14	73
Secondary education	2,889	100	24	3	26	46
Educational administration	3,545	100	21	13	35	32
Counseling and guidance	4,175	100	22	12	30	36
All other education	17,334	100	24	13	29	34
Humanities						
English and journalism	11,363	100	43	4	31	22
Fine and applied arts	7,307	100	43	7	22	28
Foreign languages	8,612	100	45	6	32	16
Philosophy	2,717	100	31	7	43	19
Social and behavioral sciences						
Psychology	9,977	100	27	32	30	10
History	7,816	100	34	8	39	20
Social work administration	7,109	100	0	3	69	28
Other social sciences	22,556	100	23	22	36	19
Professional fields						
Business and commerce	14,899	100	16	13	15	56
Health professions	6,346	100	9	27	52	12
Library science	2,252	100	12	5	20	62
Religion	4,517	100	10	1	47	41
Science						
Biological science	22,421	100	29	27	33	11
Physical science	34,126	100	34	31	22	13
Mathematics and statistics	13,150	100	37	11	30	22
Agriculture and forestry	5,414	100	9	60	24	9
Engineering	32,745	100	14	27	30	29
Miscellaneous	5,388	100	22	14	31	34

SOURCE: J. S. Hunter, *The Academic and Financial Status of Graduate Students, Spring, 1965,* U.S. Office of Education, 1967, p. 32.

a degree (research assistantships), and (3) support requiring the kind of work that helps little in getting a degree (teaching assistant-ships). In the late 1950s, 44 percent of all graduate students held fellowships, 33 percent held research assistantships, and 61 percent held teaching assistantships (Table 1.6-15).

GRADUATE STIPENDS BY PROFILE VARIABLES, 1965 Stipends were held by 43 percent of all graduate students in 1965. By sex, 49 percent of the males and 37 percent of the females held stipends. The percentage of graduate students holding stipends decreased with age. Foreign students received relatively more

TABLE 1.6-15 *Support, by type and field*

	Support, outside my own family, requiring no work from me, e.g., a fellowship	Support requiring work that contrib-uted greatly to my degree, e.g., a research assis-tantship used for dissertation	Support requiring work that did not contribute directly to the degree, e.g., a teaching assistantship	Any of these
Physical sciences	51%	53%	75%	97%
Biological sciences	45	47	62	97
Social sciences	45	28	64	87
Humanities	53	7	63	83
Engineering	48	52	62	95
Education	28	13	48	72
Total arts and sciences	48	37	67	92
Total professional fields	35	27	51	80
GRAND TOTAL	44	33	61	88

For those who receive these forms of support, the duration in different fields is roughly the same. The average fellowship support runs two years, the average research assistantship nearly two and a half, the average teaching assistantship nearly three. When all forms of support are summated, students in the natural sciences and engineering receive stipends over an average of four years, those in the social sciences and humanities for about three and a half, and those in education for about two and a half. When these figures are compared with the duration of doctoral study, in elapsed time from start to finish, it turns out that the sciences and engineering have such support for virtually the entire time, the social sciences and humanities for about 60% of the time.

SOURCE: B. Berelson, *Graduate Education in the United States,* McGraw-Hill Book Company, New York, 1960, p. 149.

TABLE 1.6-16
Stipend status
of graduate
students, by
profile
variables,
spring 1965

	Total		Stipend status	
			Held stipends	Did not hold stipends
Profile variables	Number	Percent	Percent	Percent
All students	477,535	100	43	57
Sex				
Men	335,227	100	49	51
Women	142,308	100	37	63
Age				
23 and under	68,663	100	54	46
24–28	191,688	100	51	49
29 and over	217,183	100	34	66
Race				
White	425,323	100	41	59
Negro	12,141	100	44	56
Other (chiefly Oriental)	4,022	100	42	58
Citizenship				
United States	441,487	100	41	59
Other	36,048	100	70	30
Marital status				
Single, no dependents	168,225	100	53	47
Single, with dependents	18,132	100	38	62
Married, no dependents	96,199	100	45	55
Married, with dependents	194,977	100	35	65
Enrollment status				
Full-time	210,130	100	66	44
Part-time	267,404	100	26	74
Control of institution				
Public	296,032	100	43	57
Private	181,503	100	44	56
Type of institution				
Universities	354,078	100	52	48
All other	123,457	100	18	82
Size of graduate enrollment				
Large	225,524	100	52	48
Small	252,010	100	36	64

SOURCE: J. S. Hunter, *The Academic and Financial Status of Graduate Students, Spring, 1965,* U.S. Office of Education, 1967, p. 25.

stipends than American students—70 percent of all foreign students held stipends, as compared with 41 percent of all American students. Students with dependents received relatively fewer stipends than students without dependents.

Fifty-two percent of the graduate students in universities held stipends, as compared with only eighteen percent of the graduate students in other types of institutions. Institutions with large graduate enrollments gave relatively more stipends than institutions with small graduate enrollments. Fifty-two percent of the graduate students at institutions with large graduate enrollments received stipends, as compared with thirty-six percent of the graduate students at institutions with small graduate enrollments (Table 1.6-16).

STIPENDS AND ABILITY AND CONTROL Table 1.6-17 shows the percentage of graduate students holding stipends by ability of the student and by control. Fellowships and

TABLE 1.6-17 Stage, division, control, ability, and stipend holding (percentage with a fellowship or assistantship)

Control	Division	Beginning		
		Low ability	*Medium ability*	*High ability*
		Division		
Public	Natural sciences	62	73	86
	Sociology–humanities	38	50	70
Private	Natural sciences	42	60	71
	Sociology–humanities	18	36	36
		Data rearranged to show effect of control		
Natural sciences	Public	62	73	86
	Private	42	60	71
Sociology–humanities	Public	38	50	70
	Private	18	36	36
		Data rearranged to show effect of stage		
		Public		
Natural sciences	Advanced	78	88	84
	Beginning	62	73	86
Sociology–humanities	Advanced	45	73	88
	Beginning	38	50	70

SOURCE: J. A. Davis, *Stipends and Spouses, The Finances of American Arts and Science Graduate Students,* The University of Chicago Press, Chicago, 1962, p. 204.

assistantships are available in relatively larger numbers for the more able than for the less able students. Stipends are relatively more numerous in public than in private institutions. In both public and private institutions, natural science graduate students receive relatively more stipends than graduate students in the social sciences and the humanities. A larger percentage of graduate students receive stipends in advanced than in beginning stages of study.

Graduate students in the best private universities (I) were more likely to receive aid than graduate students in public institutions or in other private graduate schools (Table 1.6-18). However, graduate students at public institutions received relatively more teaching assistantships and fellowships combined than graduate students at all private institutions. In general, top private universities give aid to a larger percentage of their graduate students than other private institutions. For all types of institutions, relative-

Stage		
	Advanced	
Low ability	Medium ability	High ability
78	88	84
45	73	88
55	61	74
32	33	48
78	88	84
55	61	74
48	72	80
32	33	48
	Private	
55	61	74
39	60	70
32	33	48
18	36	36

TABLE 1.6-18	Division			
Percentage of graduate students with fellowships and assistantships, by control and institutional quality	Social science and humanities		Natural science	
	Stage			
School	Beginning	Advanced	Beginning	Advanced
(a) Fellowships (percentage with a fellowship)				
Private I	20	21	35	47
Public	18	19	20	36
Private II–III	14	24	19	30
(b) Research assistantships (percentage with a research assistantship)				
Public	8	9	19	34
Private I	2	5	15	26
Private II–III	3	6	7	17
(c) Teaching assistantships (percentage with a teaching assistantship)				
Public	30	51	37	36
Private I	50	27	37	28
Private II–III	9	16	21	22
(d) High aid (percentage with a fellowship and/or assistantship)				
Public	51	71	69	84
All private	24	43	53	68
Private I	26	48	80	85
Private II–III	24	39	41	58

SOURCE: J. A. Davis, *Stipends and Spouses, The Finances of American Arts and Science Graduate Students,* The University of Chicago Press, Chicago, 1962, p. 202.

ly more stipends are available in the natural sciences than in the social sciences and the humanities.

DISTRIBUTION OF FELLOWSHIPS The relation between stipends for male graduate students and fathers' incomes is not what might be expected. In the spring of 1965 the percentage of male graduate students receiving stipends ranged from 43 percent for those with fathers' incomes of less than $5,000 to 53 percent for those with fathers' incomes between $10,000 and $15,000. For fathers' incomes of $20,000 and over, 42 percent of the male graduate students received stipends. Stipends for female graduate students in relation to fathers' income followed a similar pattern.

The relation between stipends and fathers' occupation is more nearly the expected. The proportion of male graduate students receiving stipends varied from 35 percent for fathers who were laborers to 56 percent for fathers who were professionals. On the basis of fathers' education, the proportion of male graduate students receiving stipends rose steadily from 39 percent for fathers who did not complete grade school to 57 percent for fathers with Ph.D.'s (Table 1.6-19).

As we have seen, fellowships are not evenly divided among fields of study. Table 1.6-20 shows the percentage of the total dollar value of fellowships received by graduate students in different fields in 1959–60. Fellowships from all sources totaled $35 million. The sciences received relatively more support than any other field. (The figures in this table are for 1959–60. The maldistribution of graduate aid today is even greater.)

A glance at the fields leading the list shows the customary concentration of support in a small number of fields. Chemistry, for example, has over 10 percent of the total; and while its share of support is not out of line with its share in the number of earned doctorates, the proportion of support for physics and mathematics exceeds their percentage of earned doctorates by significant amounts. Together the top three fields awarded 18.6 percent of the doctorates, and received 24.7 percent of the total fellowship support.

Together, the top 10 fields awarded 56.1 percent of the doctorates, and received 53.3 percent of all fellowship support. The top 20 fields awarded 73.7 percent of the doctorates, and received 71.6 percent of all fellowship support. And the top 30 fields awarded 82.5 percent of all earned doctorates, and received 81.1 percent of all fellowship support.

The total of 24.7 percent of all fellowship support for the top three fields may be compared with the following percentages for certain other groups of subject-matter fields: 15.3 percent for all of the social sciences listed, excluding business and commerce; 4.5 percent for all foreign languages, including classics and linguistics; and 13.7 percent for the language group plus English, philosophy, religion, music, and fine arts. And the latter group, comprising the major humanities in the liberal arts tradition, may be compared with 11.1 percent of the total support for engineering and metallurgy. In the first 30 fields, the greatest discrepancies between percent of doctorates and percent of support are in these fields: chemical engineering (number 9), which received almost twice as much support as its share of doctorates; civil engineering (number 16), which received more than twice as much support as its share of doctorates; education (number 6), which awarded over 3.7 times as many doctorates as its share of fellowship support; agriculture (number 20), which awarded over 2.5 times as many doctorates as its share of support; religion (number 25), which awarded over 3 times as many doctorates as its share of support;

(Text continued on p. 225)

TABLE 1.6-19				
Stipend status of graduate students, by social origins and sex, spring 1965			*Men*	
			Held stipend	
		All men		*Yes*
Background characteristic	*Number*	*Percent*		*Percent*
Father's income (per annum)				
Less than $5,000	99,538	100		43
$ 5,000– 7,499	94,760	100		44
$ 7,500– 9,999	53,989	100		49
$10,000–14,999	41,320	100		53
$15,000–19,999	11,337	100		50
$20,000 and over	12,654	100		42
Do not know	21,620	100		51
Father's occupation				
Laborer	18,645	100		35
Service worker	13,533	100		38
Semiskilled operative	26,344	100		37
Skilled craftsman	63,378	100		39
Farm operator	24,134	100		49
Proprietor or manager	58,543	100		47
Semiprofessional	50,992	100		49
Other professional	62,489	100		56
Teacher, other educator	17,160	100		55
Father's education				
Did not complete grade school	43,946	100		39
Completed grade school but not high school	95,467	100		40
Completed high school but not college	79,834	100		48
One but less than four years college	39,512	100		49
Completed college	40,920	100		53
Obtained master's degree	12,905	100		56
Obtained Ph.D. or other	22,635	100		57
Mother's education				
Did not complete grade school	31,005	100		43
Completed grade school but not high school	91,348	100		40
Completed high school but not college	117,769	100		48

Sex				
	Women			
			Held stipend	
No	*All women*		*Yes*	*No*
Percent	*Number*	*Percent*	*Percent*	*Percent*
57	39,156	100	32	68
56	33,610	100	37	63
51	20,578	100	42	58
47	16,643	100	39	61
50	7,035	100	43	57
58	8,821	100	35	65
49	16,457	100	38	62
65	6,454	100	40	60
62	4,845	100	38	62
63	7,952	100	40	60
61	22,928	100	32	68
51	11,721	100	30	70
53	27,525	100	32	68
51	23,017	100	39	61
44	30,277	100	43	57
45	7,578	100	46	54
61	15,928	100	30	70
60	36,703	100	33	67
52	32,137	100	36	64
51	19,177	100	38	62
47	18,172	100	42	58
46	5,734	100	48	52
43	14,452	100	43	57
57	11,741	100	33	67
60	35,814	100	32	68
52	45,663	100	38	62

TABLE 1.6-19
(continued)

Background characteristic	All men		Men — Held stipend — Yes
	Number	Percent	Percent
Mother's education cont.:			
One but less than four years college	51,338	100	48
Completed college	33,641	100	52
Obtained master's degree	7,689	100	52
Obtained Ph.D. or other	2,430	100	57

SOURCE: J. S. Hunter, *The Academic and Financial Status of Graduate Students, Spring, 1965,* U.S. Office of Education, 1967, p. 35.

TABLE 1.6-20 *Total dollar value of fellowship support awarded by responding institutions from all sources (1959–60) in descending order by field, by percentage of total fellowship support, and by percentage of doctorates awarded in 1958–59*[*]

Field (in order of dollar support) (1)	Total dollar value for fellowships from all sources, 1959–1960 (2)	Percentage of total dollar support by field, 1959–1960 (3)	Percentage of all doctorates awarded by field, 1958–1959 (4)
1. Chemistry	$ 3,594,327	10.3	10.8
2. Physics	2,560,789	7.3	5.1
3. Mathematics	2,469,314	7.1	2.7
4. English and dramatic art	1,913,430	5.5	4.1
5. Psychology	1,797,381	5.1	6.8
6. Education	1,616,906	4.6	17.2
7. History	1,482,357	4.2	3.5
8. Economics	1,202,818	3.4	2.4
9. Chemical engineering	1,066,781	3.0	1.5
10. Political science or government	995,041	2.8	2.0
11. Electrical engineering	963,394	2.8	2.0
12. Biology (general)	734,622	2.1	1.6
13. Geology	696,997	2.0	2.0
14. Biochemistry	606,597	1.7	1.5
15. Sociology	586,975	1.7	1.7
16. Civil engineering	568,390	1.6	0.7
17. Philosophy	567,339	1.6	1.1
18. Business and commerce	553,712	1.6	1.5
19. Zoology	550,116	1.6	1.5

Sex				
		Women		
			Held stipend	
No	All women		Yes	No
Percent	Number	Percent	Percent	Percent
52	25,919	100	38	62
48	16,766	100	41	59
48	4,557	100	51	49
43	1,842	100	60	40

Field (in order of dollar support) (1)	Total dollar value for fellowships from all sources, 1959–1960 (2)	Percentage of total dollar support by field, 1959–1960 (3)	Percentage of all doctorates awarded by field, 1958–1959 (4)
20. Agriculture	546,092	1.6	4.0
21. Mechanical engineering	538,186	1.5	0.9
22. French	365,832	1.0	0.6
23. Bacteriology	359,555	1.0	1.3
24. Metallurgical engineering	327,345	0.9	0.7
25. Religion and theology	326,457	0.9	2.8
26. Botany	302,576	0.9	1.1
27. Aeronautical engineering	288,759	0.8	0.3
28. International relations	285,319	0.8	0.3
29. Anthropology	281,563	0.8	0.6
30. Classics	280,029	0.8	0.2
31. Pharmacology	273,543	0.8	0.3
32. Slavic	258,687	0.7	0.1
33. Area and regional studies	241,716	0.7	0.3
34. Music	236,821	0.7	1.2
35. Physiology	201,217	0.6	0.7
36. Fine arts	200,838	0.6	1.8
37. Chinese and Japanese	190,669	0.5	†
38. German	173,420	0.5	0.4

TABLE 1.6-20 *(continued)*

Field (in order of dollar support) (1)	Total dollar value for fellowships from all sources, 1959–1960 (2)	Percentage of total dollar support by field, 1959–1960 (3)	Percentage of all doctorates awarded by field, 1958–1959 (4)
39. Spanish and Portuguese	168,734	0.5	0.4
40. Anatomy	164,217	0.5	0.4
41. Biophysics	150,605	0.4	0.2
42. American civilization and culture	130,435	0.4	0.2
43. Home economics	120,535	0.3	0.2
44. Astronomy	108,831	0.3	0.2
45. Entomology	108,642	0.3	0.8
46. Linguistics	107,236	0.3	0.2
47. Geography	106,258	0.3	0.5
48. Pathology	74,886	0.2	†
49. Statistics	74,541	0.2	0.3
50. Metallurgy	68,770	0.2	0.2
51. Genetics	67,565	0.2	0.5
52. Industrial engineering	65,298	0.2	0.1
53. Plant pathology	60,938	0.2	0.7
54. Law	59,210	0.2	0.3
55. Public administration	54,617	0.2	0.2
56. Architecture	38,634	0.1	†
57. Library science	37,398	0.1	†
58. Meteorology	22,115	0.1	0.1
59. Italian	17,980	0.1	†
60. Oceanography	11,520	†	0.11
TOTAL	$32,025,420	91.4	93.0
All "other"	3,015,158	8.6	7.0
Grand total	$35,040,578	100.0	100.0

* Totals for the individual fields are the sums of the figures on the questionnaire. Percentages of doctorates taken from *Advance Report: Survey of Earned Degrees Granted During Year 1958–59* (OE-54010), U.S. Department of Health, Education and Welfare, June 1960; and *Engineering Enrollments and Degrees 1959* (OE-54006, Circular No. 617), Office of Education, U.S. Department of Health, Education and Welfare, 1960. Although not all the fields for which degree figures are available are identical with the other fields listed, they are very largely the same.

† Less than one-tenth of one percent.

SOURCE: J. L. Chase, *Doctoral Study: Fellowships and Capacity of Graduate Schools*, U.S. Office of Education, 1961, p. 18.

aeronautical engineering (number 27), which received over 3 times as much support as its share of earned doctorates; and classics (number 30), which received nearly 4 times as much support as its percent of earned doctorates.[8]

What is surprising is that the distribution of tuition fellowships follows the same pattern as the distribution of other fellowships administered by institutions. In view of the maldistribution of nontuition fellowships in favor of the sciences and the usual freedom from restriction of tuition fellowships, it might be expected that institutions would try to offset maldistribution of other fellowships by awarding tuition fellowships to graduate students in fields that receive relatively little support.[9] To some extent institutions have used assistantships to try to balance the aid by departments.

Table 1.6-21 shows the distribution of tuition fellowships by field for 1959–60. Table 1.6-22 shows the ranking of the top and bottom 10 fields for tuition fellowships and other university fellowships. Chemistry was the top-ranked field for both tuition and other university fellowships, while metallurgy ranked lowest in support for tuition fellowships. In 1959–60 university tuition fellowships of $3.6 million were distributed as follows: 25 percent (of the dollar value) went to the physical sciences, 24 percent to the social sciences, 24 percent to the humanities, 13 percent to the biological sciences, and 10 percent to engineering (Table 1.6-23).

University fellowships other than tuition fellowships were concentrated in the sciences, as we have seen (Table 1.6-24).[10] The physical, social, and biological sciences together received 74 percent of all nontuition fellowships in 1959–60. These three fields also received 65 percent of the dollar value of all nontuition fellowships. The physical sciences received 28 percent, the social sciences received 20 percent, and the biological sciences received 16 percent of the dollar value of all university fellowships in 1959–60 (Table 1.6-25).

(Text continued on p. 231)

[8] J. L. Chase, *Doctoral Study: Fellowships and Capacity of Graduate Schools,* U.S. Office of Education, 1961, p. 18.

[9] In 1959–60, however, tuition fellowships averaged only $602 per stipend for almost 6,000 tuition fellowships (Table 1.6-21).

[10] For a detailed breakdown of nontuition fellowships by field, see J. L. Chase, *Doctoral Study: Fellowships and Capacity of Graduate Schools,* U.S. Office of Education, 1961, table 3.

Field* (in order of total dollar support) (1)	Total number of tuition fellow-ships (2)	Total dollar value of tuition fellow-ships (3)	Average size of tuition fellow-ships (4)
1. Chemistry	531	$ 337,000	$ 635
2. English and dramatic art	480	264,080	550
3. Physics	390	256,738	658
4. History	409	247,634	605
5. Psychology	249	144,418	580
6. Mathematics	229	143,894	628
7. Education	337	133,967	398
8. Economics	188	120,755	642
9. Political science and government	185	112,555	608
10. Geology	165	106,560	646
11. Philosophy	143	100,302	701
12. Sociology	136	88,594	651
13. Religion and theology	147	84,025	572
14. Biology—general	110	80,982	736
15. Electrical engineering	108	80,601	746
16. Civil engineering	91	76,512	841
17. Chemical engineering	137	72,608	530
18. International relations	70	70,600	1,009
19. French	107	70,441	658
20. Music	144	61,473	427
21. Aeronautical engineering	81	56,219	694
22. Business and commerce	104	46,545	448
23. Classics	66	46,328	702
24. Fine arts	84	44,481	530
25. Anthropology	66	44,480	674
26. German	57	36,988	649
27. Area and regional studies	36	34,552	960
28. Zoology	96	32,280	336
29. Biochemistry	54	31,756	588
30. Mechanical engineering	45	29,575	657
31. Agriculture	93	28,329	305
32. Spanish and Portuguese	41	25,513	622
33. Botany	46	25,173	547
34. Bacteriology	28	24,917	890
35. Geography	38	24,614	648

226

Field* (in order of total dollar support) (1)	Total number of tuition fellow-ships (2)	Total dollar value of tuition fellow-ships (3)	Average size of tuition fellow-ships (4)
36. American civilization and culture	35	22,289	637
37. Linguistics	36	21,333	593
38. Anatomy	19	20,040	1,055
39. Astronomy	23	18,841	819
40. Industrial engineering	18	13,715	762
41. Biophysics	14	13,168	941
42. Slavic	17	10,476	616
43. Metallurgical engineering	17	9,918	583
44. Law	17	9,860	580
45. Physiology	23	9,414	409
46. Public administration	25	8,288	332
47. Plant pathology	8	7,914	989
48. Statistics	14	7,783	556
49. Genetics	12	7,677	640
50. Chinese and Japanese	12	7,064	589
51. Italian	11	6,850	623
52. Pathology	10	4,982	498
53. Pharmacology	12	4,708	392
54. Architecture	4	4,261	1,065
55. Home economics	13	3,958	304
56. Library science	11	3,737	340
57. Meteorology	8	3,335	417
58. Entomology	5	2,066	413
59. Oceanography	2	500	250
60. Metallurgy	0	0	0
TOTAL	5,657	$3,407,666	$ 602
All "other"	327	196,774	602
Grand total	5,984	$3,604,440	$ 602

*No special instructions about the definitions of "fields" were included in the questionnaire, because it was felt that at the most advanced graduate level the possibilities of confusion were slight. This did, however, leave the matter of precise definition to the judgment of the deans who supplied the data, but the limitation, if any, is not thought to be serious.

SOURCE: J. L. Chase, *Doctoral Study: Fellowships and Capacity of Graduate Schools,* U.S. Office of Education, 1961, p. 2.

TABLE 1.6-22
Ranking of top 10 fields, 1959–60, university tuition fellowships

Ranking of top ten fields*	
Tuition fellowships	*Other university fellowships*
1. Chemistry‡	1. Chemistry‡
2. English and dramatic art‡	2. Mathematics‡
3. Physics‡	3. Physics‡
4. History‡	4. English and dramatic art‡
5. Psychology‡	5. Psychology‡
6. Mathematics‡	6. Chemical engineering
7. Education‡	7. Economics‡
8. Economics‡	8. History‡
9. Political science	9. Education‡
10. Geology	10. Electrical engineering

* There is, of course, no magic in the figure 10. A rather sharp break in fellowship support did occur between philosophy, the eleventh field, and sociology, the twelfth.
† In each of the lowest 18 fields, total fellowship support was less than $10,000.
‡ Indicates presence in both categories, tuition and other university fellowships.
SOURCE: J. L. Chase, *Doctoral Study: Fellowships and Capacity of Graduate Schools,* U.S. Office of Education, 1961, p. 6.

TABLE 1.6-23 *University tuition fellowships awarded by responding institutions, number and total dollar value, percentage of the total number, percentage of the total value, and average (mean) size of tuition fellowships, by academic area, 1959–60**

Academic areas (1)	Number of fellowships (2)	Dollar value of fellowships (3)	Percentage of total number (4)	Percentage of total value (5)	Average (mean) size of fellowships (6)
Engineering fields	538	$ 355,133	8.9	9.9	$600
Physical sciences	1,397	900,996	23.4	25.0	645
Biological sciences	825	468,396	13.8	13.0	568
Social sciences	1,355	858,972	22.6	23.8	634
Humanities	1,431	850,474	23.9	23.6	594
Education	393	148,653	6.6	4.1	378
Other fields	45	21,816	0.8	0.6	485
TOTAL	5,984	$3,604,440	100.0	100.0	$602

* Includes in all columns the entries under "other" on the questionnaire.
SOURCE: J. L. Chase, *Doctoral Study: Fellowships and Capacity of Graduate Schools,* U.S. Office of Education, 1961, p. 3.

Ranking of fields — Lowest ten†	
Tuition fellowships	*Other university fellowships*
51. Italian‡	51. Genetics
52. Pathology‡	52. Architecture‡
53. Pharmacology	53. Metallurgy‡
54. Architecture‡	54. Library science‡
55. Home economics	55. Slavic
56. Library science‡	56. Pathology‡
57. Meteorology‡	57. Public administration
58. Entomology	58. Oceanography‡
59. Oceanography‡	59. Italian‡
60. Metallurgy‡	60. Meteorology‡

TABLE 1.6-24 *Other university fellowships awarded by responding institutions, number and total dollar value, percentage of the total number and value, and average (mean) size of tuition fellowships, by academic areas, 1959–60*

Academic areas (1)	Number of fellowships (2)	Dollar value of fellowships (3)	Percentage of total number (4)	Percentage of total value (5)	Average (mean) size of fellowships (6)
Engineering fields	1,206	$ 2,538,310	13.1	15.0	$2,146
Physical sciences	2,302	5,010,106	24.9	29.0	2,176
Biological sciences	1,524	2,941,312	16.5	17.0	1,930
Social sciences	2,053	3,304,749	22.2	10.0	1,610
Humanities	1,580	2,315,416	17.1	13.4	1,809
Education	476	960,149	5.2	5.6	2,017
Other fields	90	165,634	1.0	1.0	1,840
TOTAL	9,231	$17,285,676	100.0	100.0	$1,873

SOURCE: J. L. Chase, *Doctoral Study: Fellowships and Capacity of Graduate Schools,* U.S. Office of Education, 1961, p. 8.

TABLE 1.6-25
Percentages of dollar support of university fellowships, by major academic area, 1959–60

Areas	Percent
Physical sciences	28.3
Social sciences	19.9
Biological sciences	16.3
Humanities	15.2
Engineering	14.1
Education	5.3
Other	.9

SOURCE: J. L. Chase, *Doctoral Study: Fellowships and Capacity of Graduate Schools*, U.S. Office of Education, 1961, p. 8.

TABLE 1.6-26
Total university fellowship support awarded by responding institutions, in dollars and percentages, by major academic area, 1959–60

Major academic areas	Total dollar value of support	Percentage of total dollar support
Engineering fields	$ 2,943,443	14.1
Physical sciences	5,911,102	28.3
Biological sciences	3,409,708	16.3
Total, all sciences and engineering	$12,264,253	58.7
Social sciences	4,163,721	19.9
Humanities	3,165,890	15.2
Total, social sciences and humanities	$ 7,329,611	35.1
Education	1,108,802	5.3
Other	187,450	.9
Grand total	$20,890,116	100.0

To summarize, the biological and physical sciences together received 44.6 percent of the total, the social sciences and humanities together, 35.1 percent. The scientific and engineering areas combined received 58.7 percent of the total, the social sciences, humanities, and education together, 40.4 percent of the total. The biological and physical sciences together received more than twice as much (e.g., 44.6 percent) as the social sciences alone, and almost three times as much as the humanities alone.

SOURCE: J. L. Chase, *Doctoral Study: Fellowships and Capacity of Graduate Schools*, U.S. Office of Education, 1961, p. 9.

The presumed excess demand for scientists and engineers relative to the supply may help explain the favored treatment of science graduate students in the distribution of fellowships. In 1959–60 the biological and physical sciences together received more than twice as much in fellowship aid as the social sciences alone and almost three times as much aid as the humanities alone (Table 1.6-26).

Table 1.6-27 shows the top and bottom 15 fields in graduate fellowship support for 1959–60. Chemistry ranked first in both tuition fellowships and other university fellowships, while physics ranked first in government fellowships. Metallurgy ranked last in tuition fellowships, meteorology ranked last in other university fellowships, and public administration ranked last in government fellowships. The National Science Foundation and the National Institutes of Health awarded most of their fellowships to graduate students in science. The major social sciences received relatively less support from government fellowships than from university fellowships.

In fiscal year 1967 the biological, physical, and engineering sciences together received 70 percent of all government fellowships, with the social sciences, the humanities, and education receiving the remaining 30 percent. The biological, physical, and engineering sciences together received an even larger share of the dollar value of government fellowships (74 percent) than of the number of government fellowships, reflecting the higher average stipends of science graduate students.[11]

Details of federal fellowships, traineeships, and training grants for fiscal year 1969 are given in Table 1.6-28. Table 1.6-29 shows the dollar value and percentage distribution of government fellowships by academic area for 1959–60. The physical sciences received 36 percent, the biological sciences received 27 percent, and engineering received 11 percent of the dollar value of all government fellowships in that year, while the humanities received 10 percent, education 9 percent, and the social sciences 8 percent of the dollar value of all government fellowships.

The humanities and the social sciences received more favorable treatment from private sources than from either institutions or government. Private foundations gave 55 percent of their support

(Text continued on p. 237)

[11] J. L. Chase, *Doctoral Study: Fellowships and Capacity of Graduate Schools,* U.S. Office of Education, 1961, p. 13.

TABLE 1.6-27   *Graduate fellowship support*

| Top 15 fields in total dollar support | | |
Tuition fellowships	Other university fellowships	Government fellowships
1. Chemistry*	1. Chemistry*	1. Physics*
2. English and dramatic art*	2. Mathematics*	2. Mathematics*
3. Physics*	3. Physics*	3. Chemistry*
4. History*	4. English and dramatic art*	4. Psychology*
5. Psychology*	5. Psychology*	5. Education*
6. Mathematics*	6. Chemical engineering	6. English and dramatic art*
7. Education*	7. Economics	7. Biochemistry
8. Economics	8. History*	8. Zoology
9. Political science	9. Education*	9. Electrical engineering*
10. Geology*	10. Electrical engineering*	10. Slavic
11. Philosophy	11. Political science	11. Geology*
12. Sociology	12. Biology*	12. Biology*
13. Religion and theology	13. Business and commerce	13. History*
14. Biology*	14. Geology*	14. Chemical engineering
15. Electrical engineering*	15. Mechanical engineering	15. Bacteriology

Of the top 10 fields, 6—chemistry, physics, mathematics, psychology, English, and education—appear on all three lists.

Of the top 15 fields, 10 fields—biology, electrical engineering, history, and geology, in addition to the first 6—appear on all 3.

Anyone familiar with government fellowship programs administered by the National Science Foundation and the National Institutes of Health would expect to find a number of scientific fields among those most heavily supported. This expectation is borne out by an examination of the table, which shows that 7 of the top 10, 11 of the top 15, and 14 of the top 20 are scientific fields (counting psychology as one of the sciences). It is probably only because of the National Defense Education Act that Slavic (10th) and Chinese and Japanese (19th) rank in the top 20 fields.

It is noticeable that the major social sciences rank lower in the list of government fellowships than they did in the list of university fellowships. History, economics, and political science all ranked in the top 11 of both university lists, but history is 13th, economics 21st, and political science 27th in the government list.

Shown below are the 15 lowest fields in each classification of support, marked as before.

| Lowest 15 fields in total dollar support | | |
Tuition fellowships	Other university fellowships	Government fellowships
46. Public administration*	46. Astronomy	46. Fine arts
47. Plant pathology	47. Statistics	47. German
48. Statistics	48. Chinese and Japanese	48. Plant pathology

Lowest 15 fields in total dollar support		
Tuition fellowships	Other university fellowships	Government fellowships
49. Genetics	49. Biophysics	49. Music
50. Chinese and Japanese	50. Industrial engineering	50. Geography
51. Italian*	51. Genetics	51. Industrial engineering
52. Pathology	52. Architecture*	52. American civilization and culture
53. Pharmacology	53. Metallurgy	53. Italian*
54. Architecture*	54. Library science*	54. Religion and theology
55. Home economics	55. Slavic	55. Architecture*
56. Library science*	56. Pathology	56. Law*
57. Meteorology*	57. Public administration*	57. Library science*
58. Entomology	58. Oceanography*	58. Meteorology*
59. Oceanography*	59. Italian*	59. Oceanography*
60. Metallurgy	60. Meteorology*	60. Public administration*

*Indicates all three types of fellowships received by graduate students in the field.

SOURCE: J. L. Chase, *Doctoral Study: Fellowships and Capacity of Graduate Schools,* U.S. Office of Education, 1961, p. 11.

TABLE 1.6-28 *Fellowship, traineeship, and training grant programs of federal agencies; expenditures and number of participants, fiscal year 1969 (amounts in thousands of dollars)*

Agency and program 1	Fellowships and traineeships		Training grants	
	Amount 2	Number of participants 3	Amount 4	Number of participants 5
Department of Health, Education and Welfare				
Office of Education:				
College personnel development	$70,337	15,000		
Strengthening developing institutions*	26,944	655		
Strengthening graduate schools of education	5,492			
Library training			$ 1,709	
State training grants			2,085	45,000
Teacher training—Education Professions Development Act			25,852	14,830
Personnel training programs			8,401	15,000
Civil rights activities			8,239	40,000
Institutes for teachers			9,201	

TABLE 1.6-28 *(continued)*

Agency and program 1	Fellowships and traineeships		Training grants	
	Amount 2	Number of par-ticipants 3	Amount 4	Number of par-ticipants 5
Office of Education: cont.:				
Research training			4,470	3,232
Librarian training			1,296	3,703
Teacher education (handicapped)			21,680	18,864
Language training			12,595	
Public Health Service:				
Consumer protection and environmental health:				
Fellowships—environmental health	74	17		
Air pollution control training and fellowships	1,424	98		
Graduate and professional training grants—environmental health			2,470	235
Air pollution control training grants			795	489
Health Services and Mental Health Administration:				
National Institute of Mental Health fellowships	8,267	1,185		
Research and development training grants and fellowships	700			
Comprehensive health, mental retardation training grants			984	280
National Institute of Mental Health training grants, undergraduate			7,774	1,811
National Institute of Mental Health training grants, graduate and professional			40,627	6,292
Comprehensive health, curriculum development			79	
Comprehensive health, cancer			3,337	3,156
Comprehensive health, neurology			456	161
Comprehensive health, radiology			1,794	185
Comprehensive health, graduate and professional short-term			973	1,000

Agency and program	Fellowships and traineeships		Training grants	
	Amount	*Number of participants*	*Amount*	*Number of participants*
	2	3	4	5
Maternal and child health			16,289	789
National Institute of Mental Health, postdoctoral training grants			35,059	2,858
National Institutes of Health:				
Child health fellowships	3,549	282		
Research resources fellowships	139	15		
Strengthening institutions	42,461	8,661		
Neurology postdoctoral fellowships	3,556	244		
Cardiology postdoctoral fellowships	6,933	405		
Cancer fellowships	3,570	319		
Neurology traineeships	2,263	234		
Allergy fellowships	3,578	280		
Dental research fellowships	1,553	121		
Arthritis fellowships	6,075	451		
Child health training grants			9,274	1,208
Dental grants			45	10
Dental research training			4,829	420
Dental service grants			270	
Dental grants			14	23
Allergy training			7,936	1,331
Cardiology training grants			17,491	1,596
Arthritis training			14,645	852
Environmental health grants			4,125	380
Cancer training			10,774	1,057
Nursing service grants			1,650	
Neurology graduate training grants			15,514	1,461
Research resources training grants			418	34
Fogarty scholarships				8
Howard University:				
Freedman's health training			5,000	
Freedman's nurse training			4,517	

TABLE 1.6-28 *(continued)*

Agency and program	Fellowships and traineeships		Training grants	
	Amount	Number of participants	Amount	Number of participants
1	2	3	4	5
Public Health Service: cont.:				
Social and Rehabilitation Service:				
Training, research and teaching			25,555	15,000
Training grants and contracts			1,347	363
Education research training grants			6	
Atomic Energy Commission				
Graduate fellowships and traineeships	6,198	3,054		
Postdoctoral fellowships	328	32		
Faculty institutes of college teachers			609	335
National Aeronautics and Space Administration				
Summer undergraduate fellowships	213	106		
Summer faculty fellowships	1,338	360		
Graduate training grants			13,369	1,262
National Foundation on the Arts and the Humanities				
Fellowships, humanities	647	201		
National Science Foundation				
Fellowships, postdoctoral	2,037	90		
Graduate fellowships and traineeships	45,948	8,292		
Science faculty fellowships	2,905	210		
Senior foreign science fellowships	808			
Institutes, precollege			39,182	32,864
Faculty institutes, high school teachers			188	316
Preservice teacher education			580	
Institutes and research — college teachers			4,887	2,965
Department of Housing and Urban Development				
Urban fellowships	503	107		
Office of Economic Opportunity				
Head Start training			16,000	50,000

*Program amount includes portions for purposes other than fellowships, traineeships, and training grants.

SOURCE: Compiled by the National Center for Educational Statistics, Office of Education, U.S. Department of Health, Education and Welfare, from information obtained from the Bureau of the Budget for *Special Analyses, Budget of the United States, Fiscal Year 1971;* in U.S. Office of Education, *Digest of Educational Statistics, 1970,* 1970, p. 111.

TABLE 1.6-29 Government fellowships awarded by responding institutions, number, total dollar value, percentage of the total number and value, and average (mean) size of tuition fellowships, by academic areas, 1959–60

Academic areas 1	Number of fellowships 2	Dollar value of fellowships 3	Percentage of total number 4	Percentage of total value 5	Average (mean) size of fellowships 6
Engineering fields	359	$1,006,691	10.5	10.9	$2,804
Physical sciences	1,173	3,339,107	34.3	36.0	2,847
Biological sciences	854	2,491,982	24.9	26.9	2,918
Social sciences	347	705,006	10.1	7.6	2,032
Humanities	398	900,685	11.6	9.7	2,263
Education	284	792,201	8.3	8.6	2,780
Other fields	10	29,047	.3	.3	2,905
TOTAL	3,425	$9,264,719	100.0	100.0	$2,705

SOURCE: J. L. Chase, *Doctoral Study: Fellowships and Capacity of Graduate Schools,* U.S. Office of Education, 1961, p. 13.

(by dollar value) to the social sciences and the humanities and 42 percent to the combined sciences in 1959–60 (Table 1.6-30).

GRADUATE STUDENT SUPPORT BY FEDERAL AGENCIES Seven federal agencies and departments provide the majority of federal stipends to graduate students. The federal government's contribution is especially large for the life sciences—46 percent of the graduate stipends in the life sciences are provided by the federal government. Nonfederal sources provided 71 percent of the stipends in engineering, as compared with 54 percent in the life sciences (Table 1.6-31). Table 1.6-31 also shows the hours per week devoted to graduate study by field of science. Thirty-five percent of the engineering students, 22 percent of the physical science students, 19 percent of the behavioral science students, and 14 percent of the life science students spent less than 20 hours a week in academic study in the mid-1960s.

NATIONAL DEFENSE STUDENT FELLOWSHIPS Graduate student fellowships under Title IV of the National Defense Student Act totaled 10,210 in the period 1959–60 — 1965–66. The humanities, education, and the social sciences received 59 percent of these fellowships, while the biological, physical, and

(Text continued on p. 242)

TABLE 1.6-30 *Noninstitutional nongovernmental fellowships awarded at responding institutions, number, total dollar value, percentage of the total number and value, and average (mean) size of fellowships, by academic area, 1959–60*

Academic area 1	Number of fellowships 2	Dollar value of fellowships 3	Percentage of total number 4	Percentage of total value 5	Average (mean) size of fellowships 6
Engineering fields	243	$ 503,594	11.2	10.0	$2,072
Physical sciences	444	1,017,587	20.4	21.0	2,292
Biological sciences	212	514,635	10.0	11.0	2,428
Social sciences	644	1,498,761	30.0	31.0	2,327
Humanities	552	1,176,270	25.4	24.0	2,131
Education	62	135,616	3.0	3.0	2,187
Other fields	14	39,280	*	*	2,806
TOTAL	2,171	$4,855,743	100.0	100.0	$2,250

*Less than one-tenth of one percent.

The support given the major scientific areas by the private foundations is especially striking when compared with the Government's support of the same areas. Government support of the physical sciences was 36.0 percent of the total dollar value; by contrast, private foundations allocated only 21.0 percent of their support to this area. Government support for engineering and the physical sciences together was 46.9 percent of the total; private support was only 31.0 percent of the total—the same percent given to the social sciences alone. Government support for all scientific areas combined was nearly three-quarters (e.g. 73.8 percent) of the total, and for the social sciences and humanities combined, only 17.3 percent. By contrast, private foundations gave 55.0 percent of their support to the social sciences and humanities, and 42.0 percent to the combined scientific areas.

SOURCE: J. L. Chase, *Doctoral Study: Fellowships and Capacity of Graduate Schools*, U.S. Office of Education, 1961, p. 16.

TABLE 1.6-31 *Percentage distribution of graduate students with stipends by source of first stipend and field of graduate study*

Donor or grantee	Percentage of stipend holders in—			
	Engineering	Physical sciences	Behavioral sciences	Life sciences
United States government agencies:				
Atomic Energy Commission	3	7		1
Department of Defense	6	4	2	1
National Science Foundation	7	15	5	16
National Aeronautics and Space Administration	3	1	*	*
Office of Education, NDEA	2	3	7	3
Public Health Service, NIH	2	3	20	23

TABLE 1.6-31 (*continued*)

Donor or grantee	Percentage of stipend holders in—			
	Engineering	Physical sciences	Behavioral sciences	Life sciences
Other federal government	5	3+	6	2
Total, United States government	— 29	— 37	— 39	— 46
Non–United States government sources:				
Private philanthropic organizations	4	3	5	2
Industry	32	10	2	2
Institution attended	27	40	39	32
State-local governments	2	3	6	6
Other	6	8	9	11
Total, non–United States government	— 71	— 63	— 61	— 54

* Less than 0.5 percent.

It is clear that in each of the science areas, the percentages of graduate students *(a)* employed (i.e., receiving *nonstipend* income) and *(b)* receiving some form of stipend, add up to over 100 percent—indicating that an appreciable number of graduate students obtain support of both kinds. Since, except for fellowships and scholarships, these forms of support require service on the part of the student, the result will be reduced time available for pursuit of his graduate program. The amount of time spent in *actual graduate* study is given, for the four broad science areas. . . . If one assumes that to carry a full graduate program requires the investment of at least 40 hours per week in academic study, then it appears that somewhat less than half (42 percent) of the engineering graduate students can be looked upon as full-time students, while more than half of the students in the other three areas can be so classified.

Hours per week devoted to graduate study, by field of science

Hours per week in academic work	Percentage working in—			
	Engineering	Physical sciences	Behavioral sciences	Life sciences
Less than 10	15	9	7	4
10 to 19	20	13	12	10
20 to 39	22	22	27	19
40 to 59	26	34	35	33
60 to 69	9	13	13	18
70 or more	7	9	6	15

SOURCE: U.S. House of Representatives, Committee on Science and Astronautics, *Higher Education in the Sciences in the United States,* report of the Subcommittee on Science, Research and Development, prepared by the National Science Foundation, 1965, p. 72.

TABLE 1.6-32 *Approved Title IV programs and fellowships*

Approved Title IV programs by academic area

	1959–60		1960–61		1961–62		1962–63
Academic area	Number	Percent	Number	Percent	Number	Percent	Number
Humanities	59	22	91	23	112	21	105
Education	15	6	30	7	42	8	54
Social sciences	60	22	92	23	133	26	129
Biological sciences	50	18	63	16	86	17	100
Physical sciences	64	23	83	20	101	19	110
Engineering	24	9	45	11	47	9	67
TOTAL	272	100	404	100	521	100	565
Subtotals:							
Humanities, education, social sciences	134	49	213	53	287	55	288
Biological and physical sciences and engineering	138	51	191	47	234	45	277

Title IV fellowships allotted by academic area

	1959–60		1960–61		1961–62		1962–63
Academic area	Number	Percent	Number	Percent	Number	Percent	Number
Humanities	258	26	416	28	389	26	316
Education	48	5	109	7	122	8	143
Social sciences	250	25	420	28	411	27	376
Biological sciences	161	16	160	11	195	13	243
Physical sciences	203	20	254	17	239	16	256
Engineering	80	8	141	9	144	10	166
TOTAL	1,000	100	1,500	100	1,500	100	1,500
Subtotals:							
Humanities, education, social sciences	556	56	945	63	922	61	835
Biological and physical sciences and engineering	444	44	555	37	578	39	665

*These figures do not include the 1,290 fellowships allocated in February 1965, since these awards were allocated to institutions and not to specific study programs.

SOURCE: U.S. House of Representatives, Committee on Government Operations, *Conflicts Between the Federal Research Programs and the Nation's Goals for Higher Education,* hearings before a subcommittee, June 1965, p. 88.

Percent	1963-64		1964-65		1965-66		Initial program, 1959-66	
	Number	Percent	Number	Percent	Number	Percent	Number	Percent
19	105	17	133	19	200	22	325	21
9	58	9	59	9	66	7	112	7
23	150	24	167	24	238	27	368	23
18	110	18	98	14	137	15	269	17
19	120	20	129	19	169	19	309	20
12	75	12	104	15	95	10	198	12
100	618	100	690	100	905	100	1,581	100
51	313	51	359	52	504	56	805	51
49	305	49	331	48	401	44	776	49

Percent	1963-64		1964-65		1965-66*		Total	
	Number	Percent	Number	Percent	Number	Percent	Number	Percent
21	324	22	357	24	361	21	2,421	24
10	154	10	135	9	155	9	866	9
25	344	23	385	25	479	28	2,665	26
16	269	18	208	14	218	13	1,454	14
17	247	16	252	17	305	18	1,756	17
11	162	11	163	11	192	11	1,048	10
100	1,500	100	1,500	100	1,710	100	10,210	100
56	822	55	877	58	995	58	5,952	58
44	678	45	623	42	715	42	4,258	42

engineering sciences received the remaining 41 percent (Table 1.6-32). [12]

NATIONAL DEFENSE STUDENT LOANS The average National Defense Student Loan from July to November 1960 was $494. In 1960, 31 percent of the freshmen, 21 percent of the sophomores, 19 percent of the juniors, and 23 percent of the seniors received loans. In contrast, only 7 percent of all graduate students received loans in 1960. Most of the National Defense Student Loans go to students from low- and middle-income families. [13] The table below gives the distribution of student borrowers by parents' income for fall 1960.

Percentage distribution of National Defense Student Loan borrowers in relation to parents' income, fall 1960

Income of parents	Percentage of all borrowers
$ 0-$ 4,000	40.96
4,001– 6,000	30.40
6,001– 8,000	15.07
8,001– 10,000	6.26
10,001– 12,000	2.44
12,001 or more	1.10
No parents or guardians	3.58

SOURCE: Adapted from R. C. Hall and S. Craigie, *National Defense Student Loan Program: Student Borrowers, Their Needs and Resources,* U.S. Office of Education, 1962, p. 54.

The following table shows the indebtedness that borrowers of National Defense Student Loans felt able to bear in the fall of 1960.

Indebtedness borrowers felt able to bear, fall 1960

Amount of indebtedness	Percentage of all borrowers
$ 500 or less	5.04
501–1,000	17.76
1,001–2,000	29.37
2,001–3,000	24.41
3,001–6,000	18.65
6,001 or more	4.65

SOURCE: R. C. Hall and S. Craigie, *National Defense Student Loan Program: Student Borrowers, Their Needs and Resources,* U.S. Office of Education, 1962, p. 65.

[12] For a breakdown of these fellowships by state, see U.S. House of Representatives, Committee on Government Operations, *Conflicts Between the Federal Research Programs and the Nation's Goals for Higher Education,* hearings before a subcommittee, held June 1965, p. 89.

[13] R. C. Hall and S. Craigie, *National Defense Student Loan Program: Student Borrowers, Their Needs and Resources,* U.S. Office of Education, 1962, pp. 1–3.

Part Two
Enrollment

2.1. Population and Educational Attainment

The educational attainment of the population has advanced steadily during the twentieth century, and there has been a tendency for the rate of increase to accelerate in the last few decades. For purposes of comparison, adjustments must be made for the fact that the number of days per year spent in school by the average pupil has increased greatly since the beginning of the century. The "equivalent 1940" years of schooling completed per member of the labor force, on the basis of such adjustments, increased from 4.14 years in 1900 to 10.45 years in 1957 (Table 2.1-1).

However, the rise in educational attainment has been much more pronounced among those under 45 years of age than among older persons. Whereas, in 1900, the decline in educational attainment with advancing age was relatively slight, by 1957 the gap in educational attainment between persons under 45 years of age and those in the older age brackets was wide (Table 2.1-2). Indeed, the major factor underlying the gain in educational attainment has "been the death of older persons, who as a class had lower than average education, and entrance into adulthood of younger persons with higher than average amounts of schooling."[1]

In 1960, only 8.3 percent of the population aged 25 years and older had had less than five years of schooling, 41.1 percent had had four years of high school or more, and 7.7 percent had had four years of college or more (Table 2.1-3). These percentages were projected to rise substantially in the following two decades. Recent data indicate that gains have occurred in the 1960s at a more rapid rate than Bureau of the Census projections suggested. By 1968,

(Text continued on p. 248)

---

[1] J. K. Folger and C. B. Nam, *Education of the American Population*, U.S. Bureau of the Census (a 1960 Census Monograph), 1967, p. 137.

TABLE 2.1-1
Equivalent 1940 years of schooling completed by the population 14 years and older and by the labor force 18–64 years of age, United States, 1900–1957

Year and index 1957	Population		
			Total
		Equivalent	equivalent
		1940 years	1940 years
		of schooling	of schooling
	Number	completed	completed
	(millions)	per person	(millions)
1900	51.2	4.13	212
1910	64.3	4.65	299
1920	74.5	5.21	388
1930	89.0	6.01	535
1940	101.1	7.07	715
1950	112.4	8.46	951
1957	117.1	10.02	1,173
Index 1957 (1900 = 100)	229	243	553

SOURCE: S. J. Mushkin (ed.), *Economics of Higher Education,* U.S. Office of Education, 1962, p. 97.

TABLE 2.1-2
Years of schooling completed by members of the labor force, by age group, 1900 and 1957

Age group	Number of years of schooling		Increase between 1900 and 1957, index 1957 (1900 = 100)
	1900	1957	
14–19	4.2	11.0	262
20–24	4.6	12.8	273
25–44	4.2	12.2	290
45–64	3.8	7.8	205
65 and over	3.3	5.6	170

SOURCE: S. J. Mushkin (ed.), *Economics of Higher Education,* U.S. Office of Education, 1962, p. 101.

Number (millions)	Labor force	
	Equivalent 1940 years of schooling completed per person	Total equivalent 1940 years of schooling completed (millions)
28.1	4.14	116
35.8	4.65	167
41.4	5.25	217
48.7	6.01	293
52.8	7.24	382
60.1	8.65	520
70.8	10.45	740
252	252	638

TABLE 2.1-3 Selected measures of educational attainment, for the population 25 years old and over, 1910 to 1980

Year*	Median school years completed	Percentage with—		
		Less than 5 years of school	High school, 4 years or more	College, 4 years or more
Estimate:†				
1910	8.1	23.8	13.5	2.7
1920	8.2	22.0	16.4	3.3
1930	8.4	17.5	19.1	3.9
Census:				
1940	8.6	13.7	24.5	4.6
1950	9.3	11.1	34.3	6.2
1960	10.5	8.3	41.1	7.7
Projection:				
1970	11.9	5.7	49.3	10.2
1980	12.3	3.4	58.9	13.3

*Figures for 1910 to 1930 are estimates based on retrojection of 1940 Census data on education by age. Figures for 1970 to 1980 are projections. All other figures are from Census reports. Figures for 1950 to 1980 include Alaska and Hawaii; those for earlier years do not.

† Based on retrojection of reported 1940 Census data on education by age.

SOURCE: Series A (high) projections are shown for 1970 and 1980; *1960 Census of Population,* vol. I, *Characteristics of the Population,* part 1, U.S. Summary, table 173; and *Current Population Reports—Population Estimates,* ser. P-25, no. 305, table 1; *1950 Census of Population,* vol. II, *Characteristics of the Population,* part 1, U.S. Summary, table 115; in J. K. Folger and C. B. Nam, *Education of the American Population,* U.S. Bureau of the Census (a 1960 Census Monograph), 1967, p. 132.

		Persons 25 years old and over (1,000)	Years of school completed		
			Elementary school		
	Year, race, and sex		Less than 5 years*	5–7 years	8 years
TABLE 2.1-4 **Years of school completed, persons 25 years old and over, by race and sex, 1960 and 1968**	Total, all races, 1960	99,438	8.3	13.8	17.5
	Male	47,931	9.4	14.6	17.8
	Female	51,508	7.4	13.1	17.3
	White	89,581	6.7	12.8	18.1
	Male	43,259	7.4	13.7	18.4
	Female	46,322	6.0	11.9	17.8
	Negro	9,054	23.8	24.2	12.9
	Male	4,240	28.3	23.9	12.3
	Female	4,814	19.8	24.5	13.4
	Total, all races, 1968	106,469	5.9	9.8	14.1
	Male	50,510	6.5	10.3	14.3
	Female	55,959	5.3	9.4	13.9
	White	95,696	4.6	9.0	14.4
	Male	45,526	4.9	9.5	14.7
	Female	50,170	4.3	8.5	14.1
	Negro	9,769	17.6	18.3	11.9
	Male	4,474	21.0	18.3	10.8
	Female	5,295	14.7	18.3	12.8

*Includes persons reporting no school years completed.

SOURCE: Department of Commerce, Bureau of the Census; *U.S. Census of Population: 1960*, vol. I, and *Current Population Reports*, ser. P-20, no. 181; in U.S. Bureau of the Census, *Statistical Abstract of the United States, 1969*, 1969, p. 106.

52.1 percent of the population had had four years of high school or more, while 10.5 percent had had four years of college or more (Table 2.1-4).

By 1980, adults who were aged 25 to 44 in 1960 will have moved into the 45 to 54 and 55 to 64 age brackets, with the result that median years of school completed in these older age groups will be substantially higher than for the comparable groups in 1960. Only those aged 65 and older will continue to have had appreciably fewer years of schooling than the population as a whole (Table 2.1-5).

percentage distribution)				Median
High school		College		school years
1–3 years	4 years	1–3 years	4 years or more	com- pleted
19.2	24.6	8.8	7.7	10.6
18.7	21.2	8.6	9.7	10.3
19.7	27.8	9.0	5.8	10.9
19.3	25.8	9.3	8.1	10.9
18.9	22.2	9.1	10.3	10.7
19.6	29.2	9.5	6.0	11.2
19.0	12.9	4.1	3.1	8.2
17.3	11.3	4.1	2.8	7.7
20.5	14.3	4.1	3.3	8.6
17.6	32.5	9.6	10.5	12.1
17.0	28.9	9.8	13.3	12.1
18.2	35.7	9.5	8.0	12.1
17.2	33.7	10.1	11.0	12.1
16.6	29.9	10.3	14.1	12.1
17.7	37.2	10.0	8.3	12.1
22.2	20.7	5.1	4.3	9.3
21.0	19.7	5.5	3.7	9.0
23.2	21.5	4.7	4.8	9.6

The gradually rising level of educational attainment in the population is also reflected in comparisons of years of schooling for
sons and their fathers. In March 1962, for example, 22.9 percent of
sons aged 25 to 64 had had at least one year of college, as contrasted
with only 7.9 percent of their fathers (Table 2.1-6).

The gap in educational attainment between whites and nonwhites
historically has been very wide, but in recent years it has been
narrowing appreciably, as youthful nonwhites have benefited from
improved opportunities for education at all levels. By March 1967,
median years of schooling for whites and nonwhites aged 25 to 29

(Text continued on p. 253)

TABLE 2.1-5 *Selected measures of educational attainment, for the population 25 years old and over, by age, 1920 to 1980*

Age and year		Median school years completed	Percentage with—		
			Less than 5 years of school	High school, 4 years or more	College, 4 years or more
25 to 34 years old					
Estimate:	1920	8.4	16.8	19.6	4.0
Census:	1940	10.0	6.5	35.7	6.1
	1960	12.2	3.1	58.1	11.0
Projection:	1980	12.6	1.0	68.0	18.3
35 to 44 years old					
Estimate:	1920	8.3	19.7	16.7	3.4
Census:	1940	8.7	10.9	25.4	5.1
	1960	12.1	4.3	51.7	8.8
Projection:	1980	12.4	1.7	66.4	17.1
45 to 54 years old					
Estimate:	1920	8.1	23.5	13.6	2.8
Census:	1940	8.4	16.8	19.6	4.0
	1960	10.2	6.7	37.9	7.3
Projection:	1980	12.2	3.1	58.2	11.8
55 to 64 years old					
Estimate:	1920	8.0	26.0	11.7	2.4
Census:	1940	8.3	19.7	16.8	3.4
	1960	8.7	11.7	26.7	5.6
Projection:	1980	12.1	4.1	51.9	8.7
65 years old and over					
Estimate:	1920	7.9	28.6	9.9	1.8
Census:	1940	8.1	24.2	13.1	2.6
	1960	8.3	20.5	19.1	3.7
Projection:	1980	9.5	8.4	34.1	6.6

SOURCE: *1960 Census of Population,* vol. I, *Characteristics of the Population,* part 1, U.S. Summary, table 173; and *Current Population Reports—Population Estimates,* ser. P-25, no. 305, table 1; *1950 Census of Population,* vol. II, *Characteristics of the Population,* part 1, U.S. Summary, table 115; and estimates; in J. K. Folger and C. B. Nam, *Education of the American Population,* U.S. Bureau of the Census (a 1960 Census Monograph), 1967, p. 137.

TABLE 2.1-6 *Selected measures of educational attainment, for sons 25 to 64 years old, by age, and for their fathers, March 1962*

Educational attainment of sons and their fathers	Age of son				
	Total, 25 to 64 years old	*25 to 34 years old*	*35 to 44 years old*	*45 to 54 years old*	*55 to 64 years old*
Percentage with less than 8 years of school					
Sons	16.3	8.8	13.0	19.0	28.0
Fathers*	48.1	37.4	48.2	52.4	56.9
Percentage with 4 years of high school or more					
Sons	50.3	64.7	54.3	44.2	30.3
Fathers*	19.1	24.8	19.0	16.7	14.2
Percentage with 1 year of college or more					
Sons	22.9	30.3	24.8	19.2	14.5
Fathers*	7.9	10.5	8.0	7.0	5.5

Folger and Nam comment as follows on these data:

One problem in interpreting these findings is that the educational structure of the United States has undergone considerable change over the past decades. There has been a proliferation of educational institutions and broadened facilities, educational opportunities have been made more readily available to all people and all areas of the country, and public attitudes toward education have improved considerably. As a result, the national educational structure has been upgraded. Even apart from these changes, there has been some educational mobility between generations. In effect, the net educational movement between the fathers' and sons' generations can be ascribed to two major factors: first, changes in the relative size of the educational strata over time resulting from increased educational opportunities and an increasing demand for educated persons; and second, the educational mobility of sons as a result of personal and family factors.

---

*Includes fathers whose education was not reported. Allocation was based on fact that such fathers were distributed, with regard to other characteristics, much like those fathers who had less than 8 years of school. Of the 48.1 percent in the total column, 12.0 percent were not reported. The percentage not reported varied from 7.1 for the youngest age group to 17.4 for the oldest.

SOURCE: Unpublished tabulations from the U.S. Bureau of the Census, *Current Population Survey;* in J. K. Folger and C. B. Nam, *Education of the American Population,* U.S. Bureau of the Census (a 1960 Census Monograph), 1967, p. 139.

TABLE 2.1-7 Level of school completed by persons 25 years old and over and 25 to 29 years old, by color; United States, 1910 to 1967		Percentage by level of school completed			
Date, age, and color (1)		Less than 5 years of elementary school (2)	4 years of high school or more (3)	4 or more years of college (4)	Median school years com- pleted (5)
White and nonwhite					
25 years old and over:					
1910*		23.8	13.5	2.7	8.1
1920*		22.0	16.4	3.3	8.2
1930*		17.5	19.1	3.9	8.4
April 1940		13.5	24.1	4.6	8.6
April 1950		10.8	33.4	6.0	9.3
April 1960		8.3	41.1	7.7	10.5
March 1964		7.1	48.0	9.1	11.7
March 1967		6.1	51.1	10.1	12.0
25 to 29 years old:					
April 1940		5.9	37.8	5.8	10.4
April 1950		4.6	51.7	7.7	12.1
April 1960		2.8	60.7	11.1	12.3
March 1964		2.1	69.2	12.8	12.4
March 1967		1.1	72.5	14.6	12.5
White					
25 years old and over:					
April 1940		10.9	26.1	4.9	8.7
April 1950		8.7	35.5	6.4	9.7
April 1960		6.7	43.2	8.1	10.8
March 1964		5.8	50.3	9.6	12.0
March 1967		4.8	53.4	10.6	12.1
25 to 29 years old:					
1920*		12.9	22.0	4.5	8.5
April 1940		3.4	41.2	6.4	10.7
April 1950		3.2	55.2	8.1	12.2
April 1960		2.2	63.7	11.8	12.3
March 1964		1.6	72.1	13.6	12.5
March 1967		1.0	74.8	15.5	12.6

Date, age, and color (1)	Percentage by level of school completed			Median school years completed (5)
	Less than 5 years of elementary school (2)	4 years of high school or more (3)	4 or more years of college (4)	
Nonwhite				
25 years old and over:				
April 1940	41.8	7.7	1.3	5.7
April 1950	31.4	13.4	2.2	6.9
April 1960	23.5	21.7	3.5	8.2
March 1964	18.6	27.5	4.7	8.9
March 1967	17.4	31.5	5.0	9.4
25 to 29 years old:				
1920*	44.6	6.3	1.2	5.4
April 1940	26.7	12.1	1.6	7.1
April 1950	15.4	23.4	2.8	8.7
April 1960	7.2	38.6	5.4	10.8
March 1964	5.3	48.0	7.0	11.8
March 1967	1.6	55.7	8.3	12.1

*Estimate based on retrojection of 1940 Census data on education by age.

NOTE: Prior to 1950, data exclude Alaska and Hawaii.

SOURCE: U.S. Department of Commerce, Bureau of the Census, *1960 Census of Population*, vol. 1, part 1; *Current Population Reports*, ser. P-20, nos. 138 and 169; ser. P-19, no. 4; and 1960 Census Monograph, *Education of the American Population*, by John K. Folger and Charles B. Nam; in U.S. Office of Education, *Digest of Educational Statistics, 1968*, 1968, p. 9.

were 12.6 and 12.1, respectively. However, the percentage of whites in this age group who had had four or more years of college (15.5 percent) was nearly twice as high as the corresponding percentage of nonwhites (8.3 percent—Table 2.1-7).

Reflecting the differential influence of environmental factors, achievement test scores for minority group children, other than Oriental Americans, were lower than for whites in the first grade in 1965, and the differences were slightly wider among twelfth graders (Table 2.1-8).

More detailed comparisons based on the 1960 Census reveal

TABLE 2.1-8 *Estimated median test scores for first- and twelfth-grade pupils, United States, fall 1965*

			Racial or ethnic group			
Test (1)	Puerto Ricans (2)	Indian Americans (3)	Mexican Americans (4)	Oriental Americans (5)	Negro (6)	White (7)
First grade:						
Nonverbal	45.8	53.0	50.1	56.6	43.4	54.1
Verbal	44.9	47.8	46.5	51.6	45.4	53.2
Twelfth grade:						
Nonverbal	43.3	47.1	45.0	51.6	40.9	52.0
Verbal	43.1	43.7	43.8	49.6	40.9	52.1
Reading	42.6	44.3	44.2	48.8	42.2	51.9
Mathematics	43.7	45.9	45.5	51.3	41.8	51.8
General information	41.7	44.7	43.3	49.0	40.6	52.2
Average of the 5 tests	43.1	45.1	44.4	50.1	41.1	52.0

NOTE: This table presents the results of standard achievement tests of certain intellectual skills such as reading, writing, calculating, and problem solving. The tests were designed to measure the skills which are the most important in our society for getting a good job and moving up to a better one, and for full participation in an increasingly technical world.

The scores in each test were standardized so that the average over the national sample equaled 50 and the standard deviation equaled 10. This means that for all pupils in the nation, about 16 percent would score below 40 and about 16 percent would score above 60.

SOURCE: U.S. Department of Health, Education and Welfare, Office of Education, Commissioner's report on "Equality of Educational Opportunity," July 2, 1966; in U.S. Office of Education, *Digest of Educational Statistics, 1968,* 1968, p. 129.

striking differences in educational attainment by ethnic group, especially for relatively young adults aged 25 to 34. Japanese Americans and Chinese Americans, for example, were considerably more likely to have had four years of high school or more, and were also more likely to have had at least one year of college than whites. Moreover, in this same age group, whites of Northern or Western European foreign stock tended to have higher levels of educational attainment than whites of native parentage, and, with respect to completion of four years of high school or more, whites of Central or Eastern European foreign stock also ranked high (Table 2.1-9).

Educational attainment tends to be high in heavily populated areas, in part because incomes are higher and educational facilities more adequate. As the proportion of population in metropolitan

TABLE 2.1-9 *Selected measures of educational attainment for men in specified ethnic groups, 25 to 34 years old and 45 to 64 years old, 1960*

Ethnic group	25 to 34 years old, percentage with—			45 to 64 years old, percentage with—		
	Less than 5 years of school	High school, 4 years or more	College, 1 year or more	Less than 5 years of school	High school, 4 years or more	College, 1 year or more
Native white of native parentage	3	59	27	7	34	16
Northern or Western European foreign stock	1	67	35	3	33	16
Central or Eastern European foreign stock	1	68	21	8	32	18
Southern European foreign stock	2	54	23	15	18	8
Mexican, Central or South American foreign stock	10	31	15	43	16	7
Puerto Rican stock	19	20	6	33	11	5
Negro	12	30	11	36	11	5
American Indian	18	24	8	31	14	5
Japanese	1	82	40	9	38	15
Chinese	6	71	51	37	25	13

SOURCE: J. K. Folger and C. B. Nam, *Education of the American Population,* U.S. Bureau of the Census (a 1960 Census Monograph), 1967, p. 151.

areas rises, continued increases in educational attainment may be expected (Table 2.1-10).

There are also wide differences in educational attainment among the states, reflecting differences in per capita income, racial composition of the population, and other factors (Table 2.1-11). Another manifestation of these state-by-state differences was the pronounced difference in selective service test scores in 1951, with the percentage of registrants scoring 70 or more ranging from 31 in Mississippi to 79 in New Hampshire (Table 2.1-12).

Educational attainment tends to be closely related to occupational level (Table 2.1-13). However, as education level has increased, employers have tended to raise their hiring standards, and the educational attainment of persons employed in various occupation groups tended to rise from 1940 to 1960 (Table 2.1-14).

| | Years of school completed | | |
| | Elementary school | | |
Residence and age	Popula-tion (1,000)	Less than 5 years*	5 to 7 years	8 years
Metropolitan†				
Total, 14 and over	90,846	3.8	8.2	13.3
14 to 17 years	9,080	0.6	14.4	26.6
18 and 19 years	4,276	0.4	1.4	2.0
20 to 24 years	9,204	0.7	2.2	3.0
25 years and over	68,288	4.9	8.7	13.6
25 to 29 years	7,749	0.9	3.1	4.6
30 to 34 years	7,129	1.5	4.2	5.4
35 to 44 years	16,033	2.4	5.2	7.6
45 to 54 years	14,786	3.1	7.4	13.0
55 to 64 years	11,189	6.0	13.0	20.8
65 years and over	11,402	14.5	17.6	27.2
Nonmetropolitan				
Total, 14 and over	48,747	6.5	12.3	16.4
14 to 17 years	5,393	0.9	17.8	26.6
18 and 19 years	2,415	0.6	4.0	3.5
20 to 24 years	4,361	1.3	4.1	5.5
25 years and over	36,576	8.4	13.0	17.0
25 to 29 years	3,885	1.5	5.2	6.3
30 to 34 years	3,625	2.5	6.9	8.7
35 to 44 years	7,832	4.9	9.9	11.7
45 to 54 years	7,670	7.1	13.1	16.8
55 to 64 years	6,277	10.7	17.2	21.9
65 years and over	7,287	18.1	19.7	28.4

TABLE 2.1-10 Years of school completed, by metropolitan and nonmetropolitan residence and age (persons 14 years old and over as of March 1967)

*Includes persons reporting no school years completed.

† Covers 212 standard metropolitan statistical areas as defined in 1960.

SOURCE: U.S. Bureau of the Census, *Current Population Reports*, ser. P-20, no. 169; in U.S. Bureau of the Census, *Statistical Abstract of the United States 1968*, 1968, p. 111.

(percentage distribution)

High school		College		Median school years completed
1 to 3 years	4 years	1 to 3 years	4 years or more	
22.4	31.6	11.2	9.5	12.1
57.5	0.8	0.1	0	9.4
33.3	48.8	14.0	0	12.3
15.5	43.1	26.4	9.1	12.7
18.0	33.1	10.4	11.4	12.1
16.4	43.2	15.9	16.0	12.6
17.7	42.3	13.5	15.4	12.5
20.0	39.6	11.6	13.7	12.4
20.1	36.0	10.0	10.4	12.2
18.5	24.2	8.4	9.2	10.7
13.1	16.1	5.6	5.9	8.7
22.6	27.7	8.4	6.2	11.0
54.2	0.5	0.1	0	9.3
38.3	42.4	11.2	0	12.1
18.4	42.0	23.3	5.4	12.5
17.4	29.0	7.7	7.6	11.0
19.6	44.6	10.9	11.7	12.4
19.8	42.6	9.1	10.4	12.3
19.5	37.1	7.8	9.2	12.1
18.6	30.4	7.6	6.4	11.1
16.9	19.7	7.3	6.2	9.0
11.9	11.6	5.5	4.8	8.4

TABLE 2.1-11
Percentage of
population 25
years old and
over with at
least 4 years
of high school
and with at least
4 years of
college,
by state,
1960

State (1)	4 years of high school or more (2)	4 years of college or more (3)
United States	41.1	7.7
Alabama	30.4	5.7
Alaska	54.7	9.5
Arizona	45.7	9.1
Arkansas	28.9	4.8
California	51.5	9.8
Colorado	52.0	10.7
Connecticut	43.9	9.5
Delaware	43.4	10.1
District of Columbia	47.8	14.3
Florida	42.6	7.8
Georgia	31.9	6.2
Hawaii	46.1	9.0
Idaho	48.6	7.2
Illinois	40.4	7.3
Indiana	41.8	6.3
Iowa	46.3	6.4
Kansas	48.2	8.2
Kentucky	27.6	4.9
Louisiana	32.3	6.7
Maine	43.3	5.5
Maryland	40.0	9.3
Massachusetts	47.0	8.8
Michigan	40.9	6.8
Minnesota	43.9	7.5
Mississippi	29.8	5.6
Missouri	36.6	6.2
Montana	47.8	7.5
Nebraska	47.7	6.8
Nevada	53.3	8.3
New Hamphsire	42.9	7.1
New Jersey	40.7	8.4
New Mexico	45.4	9.8

State (1)	4 years of high school or more (2)	4 years of college or more (3)
New York	40.8	8.9
North Carolina	32.3	6.3
North Dakota	38.9	5.6
Ohio	42.0	7.0
Oklahoma	40.5	7.9
Oregon	48.4	8.5
Pennsylvania	38.1	6.4
Rhode Island	35.0	6.6
South Carolina	30.4	6.9
South Dakota	42.1	5.7
Tennessee	30.4	5.5
Texas	39.6	8.0
Utah	55.8	10.2
Vermont	42.8	7.3
Virginia	37.9	8.4
Washington	51.5	9.3
West Virginia	30.5	5.2
Wisconsin	41.6	6.7
Wyoming	52.1	8.7

SOURCE: U.S. Bureau of the Census, *U.S. Census of Population: 1960,* PC(1)C series; in U.S. Office of Education, *Digest of Educational Statistics, 1968,* 1968, p. 12.

TABLE 2.1-12
College-level ability by states as indicated by score on the Selective Service College Qualification Test, 1951*

State	Registrants scoring 70 or above
Alabama	39%
Arizona	62
Arkansas	38
California	65
Colorado	63
Connecticut	76
Delaware	66
District of Columbia	70
Florida	53

State	Registrants scoring 70 or above
Georgia	42
Idaho	56
Illinois	65
Indiana	66
Iowa	66
Kansas	61
Kentucky	42
Louisiana	43
Maine	66
Maryland	62
Massachusetts	76
Michigan	69
Minnesota	73
Mississippi	31
Missouri	60
Montana	60
Nebraska	61
Nevada	62
New Hamphsire	79
New Mexico	53
New Jersey	70
New York	72
North Carolina	46
North Dakota	59
Ohio	65
Oklahoma	48
Oregon	64
Pennsylvania	66
Rhode Island	59
South Carolina	33
South Dakota	59
Tennessee	48
Texas	46
Utah	56

State	Registrants scoring 70 or above
Vermont	59
Virginia	50
Washington	66
West Virginia	41
Wisconsin	69
Wyoming	63
Continental United States	64

*Percentage of registrants for the tests who scored 70 or above listed only for the College Qualification Test given from May through July, 1951.

SOURCE: Educational Testing Service, *A Summary of Statistics on the Selective Service College Qualification Test of May 26, 1951; June 16, 1951; June 30, 1951; July 12, 1951,* p. 38; in C. C. Cole, Jr., *Encouraging Scientific Talent,* College Entrance Examination Board, New York, 1956, p. 83.

TABLE 2.1-13 *Median years of school completed by the employed civilian labor force 18 years old and over, by occupation group and color, United States, March 1967*

Occupation group (1)	Total (2)	White (3)	Nonwhite (4)
All occupation groups	12.3	12.4	10.8
Professional and managerial workers	14.7	14.6	16.0
Professional and technical workers	16.3	16.2	16.3
Managers, officials, and proprietors	12.7	12.7	12.2
Farmers and farm laborers	8.9	9.0	6.2
Farmers and farm managers	9.1	9.3	6.7
Farm laborers and foremen	8.6	8.9	6.0
Clerical and sales workers	12.5	12.5	12.5
Clerical workers	12.5	12.5	12.5
Sales workers	12.5	12.5	12.3
Craftsmen, operatives, and laborers	11.1	11.2	9.9
Craftsmen and foremen	12.0	12.0	10.2
Operatives	10.8	10.9	10.4
Nonfarm laborers	9.5	10.0	8.6
Service workers	11.0	11.5	9.8
Private household workers	8.9	9.8	8.5
Other service workers	11.5	11.7	10.7

SOURCE: U.S. Office of Education, *Digest of Educational Statistics, 1968,* 1968, p. 9.

TABLE 2.1-14 **Percentage of white males 35 to 54 years old in the experienced civilian labor force who have completed specified levels of school, by major occupation group, 1960 and 1940**

Major occupation group	Less than 5 years of school		High school graduates		College, 1 year or more	
	1960	1940*	1960	1940*	1960	1940*
Professional, technical, and kindred workers	0.2	0.4	91.3	84.7	74.5	72.7
Farmers and farm managers	6.1	13.4	32.5	9.5	7.5	4.1
Managers, officials, and proprietors, except farm	1.0	2.2	68.0	46.7	35.4	23.5
Clerical, sales, and kindred workers	0.8	1.2	65.6	47.1	28.0	20.4
Craftsmen, foremen, and kindred workers	3.0	4.9	36.4	15.8	8.0	4.4
Operatives and kindred workers	5.7	8.1	24.9	10.9	4.0	2.9
Service workers	5.2	5.4	34.0	15.2	8.1	4.4
Farm laborers and foremen	29.2	21.2	12.1	6.3	2.7	1.9
Laborers, except farm and mine	12.3	13.5	17.2	7.3	2.8	2.0

*Data for 1940 are for employed native white males only.

SOURCE: Data for 1960 are from *1960 Census of Population, Subject Reports, Educational Attainments*, series PC(2)-5B; for 1940 from *1940 Census of Population, Special Report, Educational Attainment by Economic Characteristics and Marital Status*; in J. K. Folger and C. B. Nam, *Education of the American Population*, U.S. Bureau of the Census (a 1960 Census Monograph), 1967, p. 170.

According to Folger and Nam:

What can be said about the factors which affect the education-occupation relationship, and which may help to explain the declining association? Katz followed one approach to analyze changes in educational attainment levels within occupational groups for the 1952 to 1959 period, using data from the Census Bureau's Current Population Survey. Computing an "expected" occupational distribution for 1959 that would have been obtained if the "demand for workers at each attainment level had remained the same in the various occupational groups as in 1952" and comparing it to the actual 1959 occupational distribution, he concluded that "The differences between the 'expected' and the actual 1959 occupation structure mainly depict an increasing demand for better educated workers." The data and analysis presented by Katz do not, however, really answer the question: Did the "demand" rise because the supply increased, or did the "demand" really stimulate the growth of the supply?

Some insight into this question, and the relative strength of demand factors, can be obtained by analyzing the extent to which the rise in the educational level of workers can be accounted for by shifts in the occupational distribution. How much of the rise in the educational level of the labor force is due to shifts from jobs requiring little education to those requiring more education, and how much of it can be attributed to rises in educational attainment within occupations? This is the question posed by Denison. The analysis again is confined to employed white males 35 to 54 years old, an age group for which shifts in and out of the labor force, as well as occupational and educational changes, should be minimal. The changes considered took place between 1940 and 1960.

During this period, the population in the age group increased from 10.6 million to 18.5 mil-

TABLE 2.1-14 *(continued)*

ion, and its median level of educational attainment increased from 8.5 to 11.5 years of school completed. The group grew in size about twice as fast from 1940 to 1950 as from 1950 to 1960, but its educational attainment rose more rapidly in the second decade. The rise in educational attainment was subdivided into a component due to changes in occupational composition and a component due to increases in educational attainment within occupational groups.

Most of the educational change that occurred in the 1940 to 1960 period for the age group considered could be attributed to a rise in the level of educational attainment within occupational groups. Overall, about 85 percent of the rise in educational attainment may be attributed to increased educational levels within occupations, and only 15 percent to shifts in the occupational structure from occupations requiring less education to occupations requiring more. This was true to about the same extent in the 1940 to 1950 period as in the 1950 to 1960 period, even though the labor force was expanding at a more rapid rate, relative to increases in educational attainment, during the earlier period than in the later period.

2.2. Enrollment

Historical data on the expansion of higher education are available from the U.S. Office of Education for the years from 1869–70 to 1963–64:[1]

	1869–1870	1929–1930	1963–1964
Number of institutions	563	1,409	2,132
Resident degree-credit enrollment	52,286	1,100,737	4,234,092
Degrees, bachelor's and first professional	9,371	122,484	498,654

Over this period of 94 years the number of institutions rose nearly 4 times, resident degree-credit enrollment 80 times, and bachelor's and first professional degrees 53 times.

A useful classification of enrollment in 1959–60 is presented in Figure 2.2-1. Undergraduate enrollment represented 67.4 percent of the total and graduate enrollment 7.9 percent; the remainder consisted of enrollment in extension courses, courses by mail, and the like. Whereas more than three-quarters of undergraduate enrollment was full time, only 38 percent of graduate enrollment was full time.

VARYING ESTIMATES OF FUTURE ENROLLMENT Actual increases in enrollment from 1955 to 1965 and official projections to 1970 and 1975 appear in Table 2.2-1. The projections indicate that, by 1975, graduate school enrollment is likely to amount to 1,086,000, or 12 percent of the total, as compared with 9 percent in 1955. In 1963, there were 151,000 professional

[1] U.S. Office of Education, *Digest of Educational Statistics, 1968,* 1968, p. 69.

FIGURE 2.2-1 *Classification and percentage distribution of enrollment in institutions of higher education, by type and level: United States and outlying parts, first term, 1959–1960*

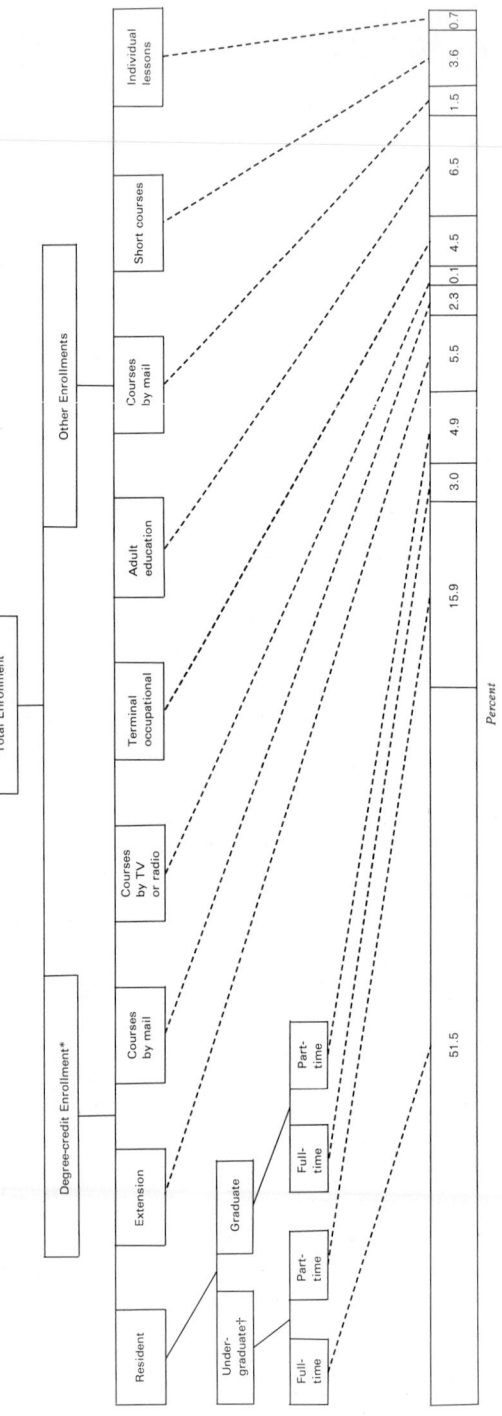

*Students enrolled in work wholly or principally creditable toward a bachelor's or higher degree.

†Includes students enrolled for first professional degree.

SOURCE: U.S. Department of Health, Education and Welfare, Office of Education, Circular No. OE-54024, *Advance Report, Total Enrollment in Institutions of Higher Education: First Term, 1959–60*; in U.S. Senate, Committee on Labor and Public Welfare, *Education Legislation, 1963, Hearings before the Subcommittee on Education,* June 1963, p. 97.

TABLE 2.2-1 **Total and full-time equivalent fall enrollments in higher education, 1955 and 1965, with projections to 1970 and 1975 (in thousands)**

	Total degree-credit enrollments, NCES			*Total enrollments, census, all institutions*	*Full-time equivalent enrollments (degree credit)*		
		Undergraduate and first	*Graduate*			*OPPE*	
Year	*All institutions*	*professional*	*school*		*NCES*	*A*	*B*
1955	2,660	2,418	242		2,122	2,122	2,122
1965	5,526	4,945	582	5,675	4,443	4,443	4,443
1970	7,296	6,481	816	7,424	5,829	6,240	6,644
1975	9,088	8,002	1,086	9,459	7,235	7,515	7,928

SOURCES: U.S. Office of Education, NCES, *Projection of Educational Statistics to 1976–77* (in process); U.S. Bureau of Census, *Current Population Reports,* series P-25, no. 365, May 5, 1967; U.S. Office of Education, Office of Program Planning and Evaluation (OPPE); in U.S. Office of Education, *Education in the Seventies,* planning papers of the Office of Program Planning and Evaluation, May 1968, p. 10.

students with preprofessional training, and, by 1967, there were 207,000 enrolled in programs leading to first professional degrees.[2]

The reliability of enrollment projections depends on the assumptions and methods used in developing the projections. In the past, underestimates of the increase in enrollment in higher education have been revealed, as a rule. In projecting to the 1970s, the Office of Education used the trend in enrollment in 1957–67 as a percentage of the population aged 18 to 21 in these years. Since the ratio of enrollment to the number of 18- to 24-year-olds was rising more rapidly than the ratio of enrollment to 18- to 21-year-olds, this method contributed to underestimates. In estimating full-time equivalent enrollment for the 1970s, the OE relied on the experience in 1966. In estimating the distribution of students by sex and control (public or private) of institutions, the OE used the trend for 1957–67 of the percentage of males and of the numbers in public institutions.

In view of the differences in methods used by various government agencies, it is not surprising that there have been large differences in their estimates. For 1975, the full-time equivalent enrollment projection of the OE National Center of Education Statistics (NCES) was 7,235,000. The NCES projected total enrollment in

[2] Ibid., p. 72; and U.S. Office of Education, *Students Enrolled for Advanced Degrees, Fall 1967: Part A: Summary Data,* National Center for Educational Statistics, 1969, Highlights and Addendum.

1975 at 9,088,000, as compared with a Census Bureau projection of 9,459,000.[3]

Another branch of the OE projected full-time equivalent enrollment in 1975 as 7,515,000 (A) and 7,928,000 (B). Projection A assumes that "the present attendance pattern by socioeconomic composition of the student population will continue," whereas projection B assumes that "financial deterrents on lower socioeconomic groups will be eliminated." Another illustration of differing results stemming from varying assumptions is indicated by a comparison of enrollment estimates prepared by the OE and the Ford Foundation for 1975 in terms of the percentage increase over 1965:[4]

Percentage increase in enrollment, 1965–1975 (projected)	*Office of Education*	*Ford Foundation*
Public	74	87
Private	47	29

The OE estimates a gain in full-time equivalent enrollment of 3.5 million from 1965 to 1975, as compared with an increase of 2.3 million from 1945 to 1955. It is assumed that 50 percent of high school graduates will be enrolled in *four-year institutions of higher education* and 60 percent of high school graduates will be enrolled in *college* in 1975, a difference which reflects the anticipated doubling of two-year college enrollment in the 10 years. An alternative assumption that current admission standards will be maintained and that enrollment by lower economic groups will equal that of the highest economic group (in terms of percentages of high school graduates) yields an estimate that the entering class in 1975 is likely to include 75 percent of high school graduates.[5]

[3] For the Census Bureau projection, which may already be too low, see M. O. Chandler, *Opening Fall Enrollment in Higher Education, 1968, Part A: Summary Data,* U.S. Office of Education, National Center for Educational Statistics, 1969, p. 5.

[4] See especially U.S. Office of Education, *Education in the Seventies,* planning papers of the Office of Program Planning and Evaluation, May 1968, p. 10; U.S. Office of Education, National Center for Educational Statistics, *Projections of Educational Statistics to 1977–78,* 1968, pp. 16–17; and H. Doermann, *Crosscurrents in College Admissions, Institutional Response to Student Ability and Family Income,* Teachers College Press, Columbia University, New York, 1968, pp. 100–105.

[5] U.S. Office of Education, *Projections of Educational Statistics to 1977–78,* National Center for Educational Statistics, 1968, p. 10.

An interesting aspect of the graduate component is that graduate degrees are projected to account for roughly twice as large a share of all degrees as of enrollment, e.g., about 10 percent of enrollment and 20 percent of degrees. The explanation seems to be largely that most undergraduate degrees require four years, whereas, in the graduate field, the requirements are from one to four years.

ENROLLMENT BY SEX, TYPE OF ENROLLMENT, AND CONTROL OF INSTITUTION Enrollment has been rising much more rapidly in public institutions of higher education than in private institutions in the postwar period, and by 1963 enrollment in public institutions represented about 65 percent of total enrollment (Table 2.2-2). However, public institutions accounted for smaller percentages of first professional and graduate enrollment than private institutions:

Professional and graduate degree-credit enrollment as a percentage of total enrollment in public and private institutions, 1963

	Public	*Private*
First professional	2	6
Graduate	9	12

These differences may well help to explain the higher costs per student in private institutions.

Enrollment increased much more rapidly from 1957 to 1967 than it did in the preceding decade or than it is projected to increase from 1967 to 1977.[6]

Percentage rise of enrollment, 1946–1977	*1946–1956*	*1957–1967*	*1967–1977 (projected)*
Degree-credit enrollment total	40	108	53
Men	35	91	44
Women	52	141	65
Full-time	N.A.*	120	50
Part-time	N.A.	84	60
Public	44	144	65
Private	6	59	26

* N.A.= not available.

[6] Calculated from U.S. Office of Education, *Digest of Educational Statistics, 1968,* 1968, table 80, and Table 2.2-3.

TABLE 2.2-2 *Enrollment in institutions of higher education, by six, type of enrollment, and control of institution; United States and outlying areas, fall 1963*

Type of enrollment and control of institution (1)	Number of students		
	Total (2)	*Men* (3)	*Women* (4)
All institutions:			
All resident and extension students	4,814,933	2,979,206	1,835,727
Students taking work chiefly creditable toward a bachelor's or higher degree	4,543,117	2,796,389	1,746,728
Resident students	4,266,455	2,639,290	1,627,165
Undergraduate and first-professional students	3,787,683	2,304,780	1,482,903
Undergraduate students	3,636,441	2,172,561	1,463,880
Full-time	2,765,683	1,649,567	1,116,116
Part-time	870,758	522,994	347,764
First-professional students*	151,242	132,219	19,023
Graduate students	478,772	334,510	144,262
Extension students	276,662	157,099	199,563
Students in occupational or general studies programs not chiefly creditable toward a bachelor's degree	271,816	182,817	88,999
Resident students	209,886	139,118	70,768
Extension students	61,930	43,699	18,231
Publicly controlled institutions			
All resident and extension students	3,105,968	1,905,858	1,200,110
Students taking work chiefly creditable toward a bachelor's or higher degree	2,888,213	1,757,325	1,130,888
Resident students	2,656,076	1,628,085	1,027,991
Undergraduate and first-professional students	2,377,272	1,438,053	939,219
Undergraduate students	2,320,496	1,388,756	931,740
Full-time	1,760,441	1,058,335	702,106
Part-time	560,055	330,421	229,634
First-professional students*	56,776	49,297	7,479
Graduate students	278,804	190,032	88,772
Extension students	232,137	129,240	102,897
Students in occupational or general studies programs not chiefly creditable toward a bachelor's degree	217,755	148,533	69,222
Resident students	164,496	109,233	55,263
Extension students	53,259	39,300	13,959

Type of enrollment and control of institution (1)	Number of students		
	Total (2)	*Men* (3)	*Women* (4)
Privately controlled institutions:			
All resident and extension students	1,708,965	1,073,348	635,617
Students taking work chiefly creditable toward a bachelor's or higher degree	1,654,904	1,039,064	615,840
Resident students	1,610,379	1,011,205	599,174
Undergraduate and first-professional students	1,410,411	866,727	543,684
Undergraduate students	1,315,945	783,805	532,140
Full-time	1,005,242	591,232	414,010
Part-time	310,703	192,573	118,130
First-professional students*	94,466	82,922	11,544
Graduate students	199,968	144,478	55,490
Extension students	44,525	27,859	16,666
Students in occupational or general studies programs not chiefly creditable toward a bachelor's degree	54,061	34,284	19,777
Resident students	45,390	29,885	15,505
Extension students	8,671	4,399	4,272

*Includes only first-professional students with preprofessional training.

SOURCE: U.S. Department of Health, Education and Welfare, Office of Education, fall 1963; and "Opening Fall Enrollment in Institutions of Higher Education, 1963"; in U.S. Office of Education, *Digest of Educational Statistics, 1968,* 1968, p. 72.

In each of the decades beginning in 1946, enrollment of women increased, or is projected to increase, considerably more rapidly than that of men. However, despite the pronounced upward trend in the enrollment of women, they constituted only 40 percent of all students in the fall of 1968.[7]

From 1957 to 1977 (projected), the increase in elementary and secondary school enrollment is estimated at 36 percent, as compared with 231 percent, or six times as much, for higher education.

[7] M. O. Chandler, *Opening Fall Enrollment in Higher Education, 1968: Part A— Summary Data,* U.S. Office of Education, National Center for Educational Statistics, 1969, p. 5.

TABLE 2.2-3 *Total degree-credit enrollment in all institutions of higher education, by sex, by attendance status, and by institutional control; United States, fall 1957 to 1977 (resident and extension opening fall enrollment)*

Year (fall) (1)	Total degree-credit enrollment (2)	Sex		Attendance status*		Control	
		Men (3)	Women (4)	Full-time (5)	Part-time (6)	Public (7)	Private (8)
1957	3,047,373	1,991,411	1,055,962	2,077,000	970,000	1,762,726	1,284,647
1960	3,582,726	2,256,877	1,325,849	2,466,000	1,117,000	2,115,893	1,466,833
1965	5,526,325	3,374,603	2,151,722	3,910,848	1,615,477	3,624,442	1,901,883
1966†	5,885,000	3,554,000	2,331,000	4,230,000	1,655,000	3,897,000	1,988,000
1967†	6,348,000	3,800,000	2,548,000	4,560,000	1,788,000	4,305,000	2,043,000
Projected‡							
1968	6,758,000	4,019,000	2,739,000	4,845,000	1,913,000	4,629,000	2,129,000
1969	6,906,000	4,080,000	2,825,000	4,941,000	1,964,000	4,775,000	2,131,000
1970	7,181,000	4,217,000	2,965,000	5,129,000	2,052,000	5,009,000	2,172,000
1971	7,530,000	4,393,000	3,137,000	5,368,000	2,162,000	5,297,000	2,233,000
1975	9,056,000	5,166,000	3,889,000	6,410,000	2,646,000	6,559,000	2,497,000
1977	9,684,000	5,470,000	4,214,000	6,830,000	2,854,000	7,102,000	2,581,000

* Attendance status for 1957 to 1961 and for 1966 and 1967 is estimated from first-term enrollment by attendance status reported in comprehensive enrollment surveys, 1959, 1961, and 1966.

† Estimates based on 1966 and 1967 opening fall surveys of total degree-credit and non-degree-credit enrollment not reported separately, and on preliminary data from the 1966 comprehensive survey of total degree-credit and total non-degree-credit enrollment reported separately.

‡ The projection of total degree-credit enrollment in all institutions by sex and institutional control is based on the assumption that enrollment in these institutions, expressed as a percentage of population aged 18 to 21 years, will follow the 1957–67 trend to 1977 in each enrollment category.

The projection of total degree-credit enrollment in all institutions by attendance status is based on the assumption that in each enrollment category the ratio of full-time enrollment to total enrollment reported in the 1966 comprehensive enrollment survey, with minor adjustments, will remain constant to 1977.

Veterans attending college through aid provided by the Veterans' Readjustment Benefits Act of 1966 are included in the trend projections.

NOTE: Data are for 50 states and the District of Columbia for all years. Because of rounding, detail may not add to totals.

SOURCE: Enrollment data and estimates are based on U.S. Department of Health, Education and Welfare, Office of Education circulars: (1) "Opening (Fall) Enrollment in Higher Education," annually, 1957 through 1967; (2) "Resident and Extension Enrollment in Institutions of Higher Education," biennially, first-term 1957 to 1963; and (3) unpublished preliminary data from "Resident and Extension Enrollment in Institutions of Higher Education," fall 1966; in U.S. Office of Education, *Projections of Educational Statistics to 1977–78*, National Center for Educational Statistics, 1969, p. 16.

The relative rise for enrollment in higher education for this period, however, is not as large as its relative increase over the entire period since 1900, when it increased, it will be recalled, 7½ times faster than enrollment at all levels.

Enrollment on the basis of three different definitions should be distinguished:[8]

	1957	1967	1977
1. Total resident and extension degree credit and non-degree-credit	3,224	6,912	10,667
2. Total opening fall degree-credit enrollment and extension	3,047 (5)	6,348 (8)	9,684 (9)
3. Full-time equivalent of total full-time and part-time resident and extension enrollment	2,499 (22)	5,476 (16)	8,340 (16)

The numbers in parentheses give the percentage difference from row (1) to rows (2) and (3) respectively. Elimination of non-degree-credit reduces row (2) below row (1); and adjusting to full-time equivalent accounts for the decline in row (3) vis-à-vis row (1). By 1976, the difference between rows (1) and (3) is expected to be in excess of 2 million.

From 1957 to 1967, enrollment rose much more rapidly in two-year institutions of higher education than in four-year institutions, while graduate enrollment rose more rapidly than undergraduate enrollment in four-year institutions. These same relationships are expected to prevail for the period from 1957 to 1977.[9]

Percentage increases in degree-credit enrollment in two- and four-year institutions, and in graduate enrollment; actual, 1957 to 1967, and projected, 1957 to 1977

	1957–1967	1957–1977
Degree-credit enrollment, four-year institutions	97	192
Degree-credit enrollment, two-year institutions	191	404
Graduate enrollment (resident)	139	344

RECENT CHANGES IN ENROLLMENT, 1960 TO 1965

From 1960 to 1965, total enrollment increased 54.3 percent, but there were substantially higher gains for women than for men, for two-year than for four-year institutions, for public than for private

[8] U.S. Office of Education, *Projections of Educational Statistics to 1977–78,* National Center for Educational Statistics, 1968, pp. 12, 16, and 24. The estimate of FTE enrollment 1957–1967 is the sum of full-time enrollment and full-time equivalent. See footnote to table 8, ibid., for explanation of procedures followed in estimating and projecting FTE enrollment.

[9] Calculated from Table 2.2-4.

TABLE 2.2-4 Total degree-credit enrollment in all institutions of higher education, by level and institutional type; United States, fall 1957 to 1977* (resident and extension opening fall enrollment— in thousands)

Year (fall) (1)	Total degree-credit enrollment			Estimated total graduate (resident only)†	Estimated total undergraduate and first professional		
	Total (2)	Four-year (3)	Two-year (4)	Four-year (5)	Total (6)	Four-year (7)	Two-year (8)
1957	3,047	2,678	369	288	2,760	2,391	369
1960	3,583	3,131	451	356	3,227	2,776	451
1965	5,526	4,685	841	582	4,945	4,103	841
1966	5,885‡	4,941‡	945‡	624	5,261	4,317	945
1967	6,348‡	5,272‡	1,075‡	688	5,659	4,584	1,075
				Projected§			
1968	6,758	5,595	1,164	749	6,010	4,846	1,164
1969	6,906	5,698	1,207	781	6,125	4,918	1,207
1970	7,181	5,908	1,273	828	6,353	5,080	1,273
1975	9,056	7,351	1,705	1,152	7,904	6,199	1,705
1977	9,684	7,825	1,859	1,279	8,405	6,546	1,859

* Total degree-credit enrollment by level was estimated from first-term enrollment by level reported in comprehensive enrollment surveys, biennially, 1957 to 1963, and from first-professional and graduate enrollment reported separately in the 1963 comprehensive enrollment survey, and together in the 1967 opening fall enrollment survey.

† Resident students are students who take their college work on main campus or on a branch campus. Living quarters (on campus or off) and legal domicile are irrelevant.

‡ Estimates based on 1966 and 1967 opening fall surveys of total degree-credit and non-degree-credit enrollment not reported separately, and on 1966 comprehensive survey of total degree-credit and total non-degree-credit enrollment reported separately.

§ The projection of resident graduate enrollment in four-year institutions was made separately by sex and by institutional control and is based on the assumption that in each enrollment category the proportion of total enrollment at the graduate level will continue the 1956–67 trend to 1977.

The projection of undergraduate and first-professional degree-credit enrollment in four-year institutions is the difference between projected total degree-credit enrollment in four-year institutions . . . and resident graduate enrollment in four-year institutions. . . . Veterans attending college through aid provided by the Veterans' Readjustment Benefits Act of 1966 are included in the trend projection.

NOTE: Data are for 50 states and the District of Columbia for all years. Because of rounding, detail may not add to totals.

SOURCES: Enrollment data and estimates are based on U.S. Department of Health, Education and Welfare, Office of Education publications: (1) *Opening (Fall) Enrollment in Higher Education,* annually, 1957 to 1967; (2) *Resident and Extension Enrollment in Institutions of Higher Education,* biennially, 1957 to 1963, and (3) unpublished preliminary data from *Resident and Extension Enrollment in Institutions of Higher Education,* fall 1966; in U.S. Office of Education, *Projections of Educational Statistics to 1977-78,* National Center for Education Statistics, 1968, p. 19.

institutions, and for liberal arts colleges than for universities (Table 2.2-5).

Graduate enrollment increased 70 percent, but there were wide differences by fields of study. The three fields in which graduate enrollment increased most rapidly were library science, foreign languages and literature, and broad general curriculums and miscellaneous fields, in that order (Table 2.2-6). Other fields in which pronounced increases occurred (80 percent or more) were architecture, biological sciences, business and commerce, English and journalism, fine and applied arts, geography, and social sciences.

ENROLLMENT BY STATE In 1967, eight major industrial states—California, New York, Pennsylvania, Illinois, Texas, Michigan, Ohio, and Massachusetts, in that order—accounted for 52 percent of all enrollment in higher education (Table 2.2-7). This percentage did not, however, greatly exceed the proportion (48 percent) of the total population represented by these states.[10]

The geographic distribution of enrollment in 1963, and projections for 1970 and 1975, are presented in Table 2.2-8. The most pronounced estimated state increases and declines, relative to the national total, from 1963 to 1975 are as follows:[11]

States with the largest estimated increases and declines in enrollment relative to the national total, 1963–1975

Largest relative increases		Largest relative declines	
Nevada	+100%	Montana	−25%
Florida	+ 37	Oregon and South Dakota	−25
Arizona	+ 36	Utah	−20
Idaho	+ 33	Oklahoma	−20
New Jersey	+ 12	Alabama	−20

The contribution of public enrollment to the increases from 1955 to 1960 varied greatly among states. The states with the largest contributions from public institutions of higher education to the increase in opening fall enrollments for 1955 to 1960 were Alaska, Nevada, Wyoming, Arizona, North Dakota, Louisiana, New

[10] Calculated from Table 2.2-7 and U.S. Bureau of the Census, *Statistical Abstract of the United States, 1968,* 1968, p. 12.

[11] Adapted from S. J. Mushkin and E. P. McLoone, *Public Spending for Higher Education, 1970,* Council of State Governments, Chicago, February 1965, p. 5. Based on changes in the percentage share of each state in the total from 1963 to 1975 (estimated).

TABLE 2.2-5
Enrollment in institutions of higher education, by sex, and by type and control of institution, United States and outlying areas, fall 1965 and fall 1960

| Type and control of institution | Number of students, 1965 | |
(1)	*Total* *(2)*	*Men* *(3)*
Total, public and private		
All institutions	5,570,271	3,396,574
Two-year institutions	845,244	523,532
Four-year institutions	4,725,027	2,873,042
Universities	2,303,777	1,510,551
Liberal arts colleges	1,553,783	845,348
Independently organized professional schools:		
Teachers colleges	571,695	276,168
Technological schools	134,455	121,398
Theological, religious	49,604	37,297
Schools of art	21,119	10,328
Other professional	90,594	71,952
Public		
All institutions	3,654,578	2,205,652
Two-year institutions	739,918	466,019
Four-year institutions	2,914,660	1,739,633
Universities	1,633,870	1,050,319
Liberal arts colleges	642,769	347,730
Independently organized professional schools:		
Teachers colleges	555,271	273,336
Technological schools	67,085	58,128
Theological, religious		
Schools of art	790	315
Other professional	14,875	9,805
Private		
All institutions	1,915,693	1,190,922
Two-year institutions	105,326	57,513
Four-year institutions	1,810,367	1,133,409
Universities	669,907	460,232
Liberal arts colleges	911,014	497,618
Independently organized professional schools:		
Teachers colleges	16,424	2,832
Technological schools	67,370	63,270
Theological, religious	49,604	37,297

	Number of students, 1960			Percentage change, 1960 to 1965		
Women (4)	Total (5)	Men (6)	Women (7)	Total (8)	Men (9)	Women (10)
,173,697	3,610,007	2,270,640	1,339,367	+54.3	+49.6	+62.3
321,712	453,617	283,292	170,325	+86.3	+84.8	+88.9
,851,985	3,156,390	1,987,348	1,169,042	+49.7	+44.6	+58.4
793,226	1,550,902	1,071,688	479,214	+48.5	+41.0	+65.5
708,435	1,027,567	560,050	467,517	+51.2	+50.9	+51.5
295,527	359,227	171,021	188,206	+59.1	+61.5	+57.0
13,057	106,978	99,479	7,499	+25.7	+22.0	+74.1
12,307	41,817	32,723	9,094	+18.6	+14.0	+35.3
10,791	15,166	8,241	6,925	+39.3	+25.3	+55.8
18,642	54,733	44,146	10,587	+65.5	+63.0	+76.1
,448,926	2,135,690	1,326,545	809,145	+71.1	+66.3	+79.1
273,899	393,553	253,565	139,988	+88.0	+83.8	+95.7
,175,027	1,742,137	1,072,980	669,157	+67.3	+62.1	+75.6
583,551	991,716	672,271	319,445	+64.8	+56.2	+82.7
295,039	345,926	182,207	163,719	+85.8	+90.8	+80.2
281,935	345,906	167,542	178,364	+60.5	+63.1	+58.1
8,957	46,063	42,950	3,113	+45.6	+35.3	+187.7
				0.0	0.0	0.0
475	257	130	127	+207.4	+142.3	+274.0
5,070	12,269	7,880	4,389	+21.2	+24.4	+15.5
724,771	1,474,317	944,095	530,222	+29.9	+26.1	+36.7
47,813	60,064	29,727	30,337	+75.4	+93.5	+57.6
676,958	1,414,253	914,368	499,885	+28.0	+24.0	+35.4
209,675	559,186	399,417	159,769	+19.8	+15.2	+31.2
413,396	681,641	377,843	303,798	+33.7	+31.7	+36.1
13,592	13,321	3,479	9,842	+23.3	−18.6	+38.1
4,100	60,915	56,529	4,386	+10.6	+11.9	−6.5
12,307	41,817	32,723	9,094	+18.6	+14.0	+35.3

TABLE 2.2-5
(continued)

	Number of students, 1965	
Type and control of institution (1)	Total (2)	Men (3)
Independently organized professional schools:		
Schools of art	20,329	10,013
Other professional	75,719	62,147

NOTE: Includes resident and extension degree-credit students.

SOURCE: U.S. Department of Health, Education and Welfare, Office of Education, *Opening Fall Enrollment in Higher Education, 1965;* and unpublished data, in U.S. Office of Education, *Digest of Educational Statistics, 1968,* 1968, p. 67.

**TABLE 2.2-6
Enrollment for
advanced
degrees in
institutions of
higher
education, by
field of study,
United States
and outlying
areas, fall
1960 and 1965**

Field of study (1)	Fall 1960 (2)	Fall 1965 (3)	Percentage increase, 1960–1965 (4)
All fields	314,349	535,332	70.3
Agriculture	3,852	5,405	40.3
Architecture	585	1,085	85.5
Biological sciences	14,775	27,165	83.9
Business and commerce	25,342	50,920	100.9
Education	94,993	150,300	58.2
Engineering	36,636	57,516	57.0
English and journalism	13,463	25,991	93.1
Fine and applied arts	9,255	17,792	92.2
Foreign languages and literature	6,310	14,299	126.6
Forestry	560	1,021	82.3
Geography	1,041	1,972	89.4
Health professions	5,842	8,909	52.5
Home economics	1,580	2,358	49.2
Law	1,651	2,465	49.3
Library science	1,360	8,597	532.1
Mathematical subjects	11,770	20,198	71.6
Philosophy	2,258	3,862	71.0
Physical sciences	25,707	36,506	42.0
Psychology	10,677	15,551	45.6
Religion	5,314	7,028	32.3
Social sciences	37,317	67,802	81.7
Broad general curriculums and miscellaneous fields	4,061	8,590	111.5

SOURCE: U.S. Department of Health, Education and Welfare, Office of Education, circulars on "Enrollment for Master's and Higher Degrees"; in U.S. Office of Education, *Digest of Educational Statistics, 1968,* 1968, p. 73.

	Number of students, 1960			Percentage change, 1960 to 1965		
Women (4)	Total (5)	Men (6)	Women (7)	Total (8)	Men (9)	Women (10)
0,316	14,909	8,111	6,798	+36.4	+23.4	+51.8
3,572	42,464	36,266	6,198	+78.3	+71.4	+119.0

Mexico, Colorado, Oklahoma, and California, in that order. The 10 with the lowest contribution from public institutions of higher education were the District of Columbia, New York, Massachusetts, Connecticut, Iowa, Pennsylvania, Texas, Arkansas, Ohio, and Georgia (from low to high). Large contributions came especially from states that had neglected public support in the past and from Southern states which have experienced relatively rapid economic growth in recent decades.

THE TWO-YEAR COLLEGE It is clear from earlier discussion that two-year colleges are experiencing much more rapid growth than other institutions of higher education. Enrollment in two-year colleges increased from 100 in 1900–01 to 622,864 in 1953–54, with public enrollment in the latter year accounting for 86 percent of the total (Table 2.2-9). However, there were wide variations in two-year college development and expansion among the states (Table 2.2-10).

By 1968, according to estimates developed by the staff of the Carnegie Commission on Higher Education, there were 1,072 two-year institutions of higher education, enrolling 1,871,000 students (Table 2.2-11). Public two-year colleges and specialized institutes accounted for about 64 percent of the number of two-year institutions and for about 89 percent of enrollment in two-year institutions. The enrollment data include both degree-credit and non-degree-credit enrollment.

GRADUATE ENROLLMENT Since the 1870s, enrollment in graduate work has increased more rapidly than the population of college age, and its rate of increase has exceeded by an even larger margin the rate of increase in undergraduate enrollment (Table 2.2-13).

According to the U.S. Office of Education projections, graduate enrollment is estimated to rise about three times from 1957 to 1977, a much larger increase than for undergraduates (Table 2.2-14).

(Text continued on p. 293)

TABLE 2.2-7
Total enrollment
in institutions
of higher
education, by
control of
institution and
by state, fall
1967

State (1)	Total (2)	Public		Independent of church (5)
		State* (3)	Local† (4)	
United States	8,911,748	3,349,518	1,468,510	1,120,093
Alabama	88,575	71,348		4,821
Alaska	5,836	5,180		
Arizona	78,549	55,175	22,191	506
Arkansas	48,505	35,334	1,887	3,994
California	974,426	333,223	529,916	60,589
Colorado	93,309	71,908	7,417	2,928
Connecticut	95,796	48,615		39,343
Delaware	15,173	12,781		1,466
District of Columbia	65,104		2,371	32,310
Florida	179,847	59,170	79,336	31,323
Georgia	98,476	69,591	4,640	7,296
Hawaii	27,847	25,584		177
Idaho	26,372	13,240	7,271	
Illinois	343,292	120,340	85,265	78,039
Indiana	163,393	109,097	2,244	18,446
Iowa	99,072	44,208	14,233	17,333
Kansas	89,069	58,168	15,628	98
Kentucky	90,211	56,509	9,577	4,817
Louisiana	104,171	84,807		9,333
Maine	25,519	17,299		6,754
Maryland	115,510	61,967	20,580	22,505
Massachusetts	252,638	73,325	2,578	151,086
Michigan	317,466	187,565	78,660	19,403
Minnesota	138,239	109,510		4,833
Mississippi	64,716	39,817	16,915	1,344
Missouri	153,281	78,395	23,567	19,609
Montana	23,175	19,762	901	533
Nebraska	54,955	29,997	11,756	2,146
Nevada	8,575	8,575		
New Hampshire	25,793	13,810		9,039
New Jersey	152,548	74,188	16,233	38,448
New Mexico	33,767	29,916	1,076	113
New York	677,251	104,268	222,693	272,203

ivate		
Denominational		
otestant (6)	Roman Catholic (7)	Other‡ (8)
82,211	447,531	45,885
10,222	2,184	
656		
677		
7,290		
22,942	24,389	3,367
8,850	2,206	
279	7,559	
926		
14,147	16,276	
6,854	3,164	
16,949		
	848	1,238
2,345	19	3,497
24,630	34,590	428
17,905	15,701	
14,379	7,746	1,173
9,674	5,501	
11,316	7,992	
3,373	6,658	
617	849	
2,479	7,732	247
2,024	23,505	120
16,132	15,706	
14,212	9,684	
6,600	40	
13,584	18,126	
	1,979	
5,936	5,120	
	2,944	
6,625	17,054	
	2,662	
8,700	68,756	631

TABLE 2.2-7
(continued)

| State | Total | Public | | Independent of church |
| | | State* | Local† | |
(1)	(2)	(3)	(4)	(5)
North Carolina	134,979	70,572	16,800	11,241
North Dakota	26,501	23,990	1,600	
Ohio	313,956	145,294	72,935	32,781
Oklahoma	100,352	81,490	1,462	8,216
Oregon	90,305	55,521	21,311	3,833
Pennsylvania	347,894	126,829	20,795	120,233
Rhode Island	36,909	19,521		12,359
South Carolina	51,812	31,819	583	6,485
South Dakota	27,483	20,765		1,271
Tennessee	112,583	75,388	203	16,264
Texas	348,481	202,536	75,620	13,435
Utah	75,773	40,411		977
Vermont	16,407	7,912		6,575
Virginia	117,531	89,147	299	8,399
Washington	144,496	62,168	61,707	2,795
West Virginia	52,688	41,023		5,669
Wisconsin	156,553	109,828	12,303	8,725
Wyoming	12,010	8,053	3,957	
U.S. Service Schools	14,579	14,579		
Outlying areas	51,939	34,302		10,703
Canal Zone	1,284	1,284		
Guam	1,597	1,597		
Puerto Rico	47,725	30,088		10,703
Virgin Islands	1,333	1,333		

* Includes institutions under federal control (U.S. Service Schools and Canal Zon
College).

† Includes institutions under the joint control of state and local governments.

‡ Includes Jewish, Latter Day Saints, Greek Orthodox, Russian Orthodox, and Uni
tarian.

NOTE: Includes students whose programs of study are creditable toward a bache
lor's or higher degree and also students in one-, two-, or three-year undergraduat
programs which are not creditable toward a bachelor's degree but which are designe
to prepare for immediate employment or to provide general education.

SOURCE: U.S. Department of Health, Education and Welfare, Office of Educa
tion, "Opening Fall Enrollment in Higher Education, 1967"; "Education Directory
1966–67: Part 3, Higher Education"; and unpublished data, in U.S. Office of Educa
tion, *Digest of Educational Statistics, 1968,* 1968, p. 66.

Private		
Denominational		
Protestant (6)	*Roman Catholic* (7)	*Other‡* (8)
35,188	1,178	
607	304	
31,071	30,417	1,458
8,620	564	
6,568	3,072	
26,790	53,070	177
	5,029	
12,925		
4,671	776	
19,331	1,397	
46,926	9,964	
836		33,549
	1,920	
18,914	772	
9,983	7,843	
5,177	819	
4,281	21,416	
	6,934	
	6,934	

		Total degree-credit enrollment		
		1963		
State and region	Number	Percentage of United States total	Number	
United States	4,479.7	100.0	7,689.4	
New England	292.0	6.5	516.6	
Maine	16.5	0.4	33.5	
New Hamphsire	14.1	0.3	23.1	
Vermont	11.1	0.2	17.3	
Massachusetts	163.3	3.6	285.4	
Rhode Island	23.5	0.5	44.5	
Connecticut	63.5	1.4	112.8	
Mideast	892.8	19.9	1,575.9	
New York	415.2	9.3	749.6	
New Jersey	108.9	2.4	212.2	
Pennsylvania	229.5	5.1	375.4	
Delaware	10.2	0.2	18.3	
Maryland	73.0	1.6	133.6	
District of Columbia	56.0	1.3	86.8	
Great Lakes	865.5	19.3	1,416.8	
Michigan	195.4	4.4	307.6	
Ohio	214.8	4.8	359.8	
Indiana	117.9	2.6	164.9	
Illinois	242.4	5.4	426.6	
Wisconsin	95.0	2.1	157.9	
Plains	402.4	9.0	681.9	
Minnesota	95.9	2.1	177.1	
Iowa	68.2	1.5	109.7	
Missouri	103.1	2.3	180.0	
North Dakota	16.1	0.4	26.9	
South Dakota	17.1	0.4	27.3	
Nebraska	38.7	0.9	60.7	
Kansas	63.3	1.4	100.2	
Southeast	721.2	16.1	1,261.8	
Virginia	71.2	1.6	112.2	
West Virginia	35.2	0.8	52.9	
Kentucky	57.1	1.3	110.9	
Tennessee	76.5	1.7	131.9	
North Carolina	87.9	2.0	163.3	

TABLE 2.2-8 Total degree-credit enrollment in colleges and universities, by state, fall 1963, 1970, and 1975 (in thousands)

970 Percentage of nited States total	1975	
	Number	Percentage of United States total
100.0	9,479.9	100.0
6.7	611.5	6.5
0.4	40.5	0.4
0.3	27.7	0.3
0.2	20.7	0.2
3.7	335.4	3.5
0.6	53.1	0.6
1.5	134.1	1.4
20.5	1,895.5	20.0
9.7	914.5	9.6
2.8	255.2	2.7
4.9	441.4	4.7
0.2	22.4	0.2
1.7	161.6	1.7
1.1	100.4	1.1
18.4	1,720.8	18.2
4.0	375.2	4.0
4.7	435.4	4.6
2.1	206.8	2.2
5.5	511.9	5.4
2.1	191.5	2.0
8.9	828.6	8.7
2.3	215.8	2.3
1.4	130.6	1.4
2.3	220.0	2.3
0.3	33.2	0.4
0.4	33.1	0.3
0.8	73.6	0.8
1.3	122.3	1.3
16.4	1,599.8	16.9
1.5	143.4	1.5
0.7	64.0	0.7
1.4	134.2	1.4
1.7	159.2	1.7
2.1	197.2	2.1

		Total degree-credit enrollment	
		1963	
State and region	Number	Percentage of United States total	Number
South Carolina	35.5	0.8	66.7
Georgia	60.3	1.3	99.2
Florida	106.6	2.4	201.7
Alabama	45.5	1.0	66.4
Mississippi	42.3	0.9	70.2
Louisiana	70.7	1.6	131.6
Arkansas	32.4	0.7	54.8
Southwest	372.7	8.3	613.2
Oklahoma	67.6	1.5	96.4
Texas	232.7	5.2	362.7
New Mexico	22.7	0.5	35.8
Arizona	49.7	1.1	118.3
Rocky Mountain	139.4	3.1	215.5
Montana	16.0	0.4	22.7
Idaho	15.6	0.3	28.6
Wyoming	7.8	0.2	11.8
Colorado	57.4	1.3	94.2
Utah	42.6	1.0	58.2
Far West	774.9	17.3	1,373.6
Washington	85.0	1.9	148.8
Oregon	55.7	1.2	73.1
Nevada	5.6	0.1	16.3
California	628.6	14.0	1,135.4
Alaska	4.4	0.1	8.4
Hawaii	14.4	0.3	25.6

TABLE 2.2-8 *(continued)*

NOTE: Detail may not add to totals due to rounding.

SOURCE: 1963 data, U.S. Department of Health, Education and Welfare, *Opening (Fall) Enrollment in Higher Education, 1963: Institutional Data;* in S. J. Mushkin and E. P. McLoone, *Public Spending for Higher Education, 1970,* Council of State Governments, Chicago, Ill., February 1965, p. 45.

| 1970 | | 1975 | |
Percentage of United States total	Number	Percentage of United States total
0.9	80.3	0.8
1.3	119.9	1.3
2.6	309.0	3.3
0.9	80.1	0.8
0.9	85.0	0.9
1.7	160.4	1.7
0.7	66.2	0.7
8.0	787.2	8.3
1.3	117.3	1.2
4.7	480.0	5.1
0.5	43.6	0.5
1.5	146.3	1.5
2.8	271.0	2.9
0.3	29.0	0.3
0.4	34.8	0.4
0.2	14.6	0.2
1.2	121.3	1.3
0.8	71.3	0.8
17.9	1,722.2	18.2
1.9	181.8	1.9
1.0	88.9	0.9
0.2	20.1	0.2
14.8	1,431.4	15.1
0.1	12.0	0.1
0.3	31.7	0.3

TABLE 2.2-9
Growth in junior college enrollment, 1900-1953

Year	Total enrollment	Public	Private
1900-1901	100	0	100
1915-1916	2,363	592	1,771
1921-1922	16,031	8,349	7,682
1925-1926	35,630	20,145	15,485
1929-1930	74,088	45,021	29,067
1933-1934	107,807	74,853	32,954
1938-1939	196,710	140,545	56,165
1947-1948	500,536	378,844	121,692
1951-1952	572,193	495,766	76,427
1952-1953	560,732	489,563	71,169
1953-1954	622,864	533,008	69,856

SOURCE: J. P. Bogue, *American Junior Colleges,* 4th ed., American Council on Education, Washington, D.C., 1956, table 2.

TABLE 2.2-10 *Total enrollment and number of public and private junior colleges by year and state, and percentage of increase of 1954 over 1930*

State	1929-1930 Number of colleges	1929-1930 Enrollment	1934-1935 Number of colleges	1934-1935 Enrollment	1939-1940 Number of colleges	1939-1940 Enrollment
Alabama	5	286	8	556	8	1,173
Arizona	2	641	2	863	2	1,184
Arkansas	11	1,864	10	2,433	9	2,692
California	50	17,072	55	36,977	64	86,357
Colorado	5	792	5	743	7	2,106
Connecticut	3	182	5	388	14	3,170
Delaware	0		0		0	
District of Columbia	7	314	10	645	11	3,049
Florida	3	256	7	902	7	1,908
Georgia	12	1,083	19	3,345	20	5,635
Idaho	2	859	5	1,940	4	2,110
Illinois	18	8,222	21	9,904	24	19,589
Indiana	3	268	6	542	5	623
Iowa	37	2,357	37	3,066	36	3,768
Kansas	18	2,413	19	3,494	24	5,798
Kentucky	17	2,021	17	3,012	14	3,514
Louisiana	4	194	7	702	3	876

1944–1945		1949–1950		1953–1954		Percentage of increase over 1930	
Number of colleges	*Enrollment*	*Number of colleges*	*Enrollment*	*Number of colleges*	*Enrollment*	*Number of colleges*	*Enrollment*
9	1,010	9	2,719	10	1,702	100	495
2	1,086	2	2,410	2	3,138	0	390
9	1,792	7	4,077	5	2,181	—55	17
74	120,685	78	246,708	73	294,508	46	1,625
7	3,222	8	7,605	8	7,605	60	852
13	3,586	10	8,562	7	8,472	133	4,554
1	124	1	147	1	179		
6	852	6	8,475	6	2,377	—14	657
9	1,481	9	3,245	10	4,815	233	1,781
20	4,637	19	12,472	18	14,832	50	1,270
4	1,634	3	2,030	2	2,514	0	193
24	9,192	26	28,943	22	32,455	22	295
4	462	3	472	8	9,983	167	3,625
22	1,446	26	6,512	23	8,278	—38	251
20	2,368	21	5,719	23	6,068	28	151
15	1,947	15	4,545	14	3,453	—18	71
2	839	3	1,127	1	239	—75	23

TABLE 2.2-10 *(continued)*

State	1929–1930 Number of colleges	1929–1930 Enroll-ment	1934–1935 Number of colleges	1934–1935 Enroll-ment	1939–1940 Number of colleges	1939–1940 Enroll-ment
Maine	3	137	3	245	4	517
Maryland	5	314	6	518	8	1,163
Massachusetts	10	593	9	831	23	5,994
Michigan	9	2,158	12	2,785	13	4,187
Minnesota	10	1,540	9	2,068	16	3,326
Mississippi	14	1,574	21	4,117	22	5,205
Missouri	23	5,275	22	4,537	24	8,143
Montana	2	859	5	1,940	4	2,110
Nebraska	10	718	7	727	5	800
New Hamphsire	1	120	3	368	3	530
New Jersey	2	125	10	2,097	11	2,900
New Mexico	1	235	2	520	2	1,319
New York	11	1,053	6	859	12	2,936
North Carolina	16	1,975	23	3,584	25	6,602
North Dakota	2	402	2	239	4	912
Ohio	5	1,381	8	2,865	8	2,203
Oklahoma	14	1,908	24	3,281	30	5,409
Oregon	2	112	2	164	2	758
Pennsylvania	7	923	10	1,167	24	4,844
Rhode Island	0		0		0	
South Carolina	2	311	4	405	11	1,553
South Dakota	5	267	4	472	4	363
Tennessee	12	1,785	12	2,727	14	2,860
Texas	44	8,473	43	10,558	43	15,085
Utah	5	815	5	1,537	6	3,299
Vermont	0		1	162	3	454
Virginia	11	1,349	13	2,205	16	3,166
Washington	6	558	10	1,021	8	1,398
West Virginia	5	455	5	1,117	4	1,052
Wisconsin	2	91	6	1,129	7	4,273
Wyoming	0		0		0	
Grand Total	436	74,088	518	122,311	610	236,162

SOURCE: J. P. Bogue, *American Junior Colleges,* 4th ed., American Council on Education, Washington, D.C., 1956, table 3.

1944–1945		1949–1950		1953–1954		Percentage of increase over 1930	
Number of colleges	*Enroll-ment*	*Number of colleges*	*Enroll-ment*	*Number of colleges*	*Enroll-ment*	*Number of colleges*	*Enroll-ment*
6	413	4	1,285	4	595	33	334
5	1,951	9	2,445	10	2,286	100	229
20	3,129	22	7,723	18	6,225	80	950
13	3,168	13	11,286	17	17,937	89	731
14	1,658	12	5,157	11	7,702	10	400
22	3,674	23	11,670	23	8,859	64	463
23	6,953	24	11,450	22	10,016	− 4	90
4	1,634	3	2,039	2	2,514	50	242
5	1,137	6	3,350	5	2,183	−50	190
1	360	1	395	1	459	0	283
9	1,732	14	7,998	10	3,292	80	2,534
1	93	0				0	0
19	8,176	28	20,981	31	23,415	182	2,124
24	4,419	24	7,357	24	8,127	50	311
5	345	4	1,540	4	1,484	100	269
8	2,255	8	5,631	7	4,979	40	261
17	1,452	19	6,023	16	5,072	14	166
2	787	2	3,908	5	5,870	60	5,141
20	2,472	21	8,042	25	12,722	257	1,278
2	342	2	604	1	547		
11	1,199	8	1,534	7	1,358	250	337
5	446	4	347	3	335	−40	25
13	1,984	11	4,134	9	2,360	−25	32
48	15,221	58	53,931	45	47,332	2	459
6	15,521	4	4,847	4	6,266	−20	669
3	412	2	559	2	467		
15	4,374	15	5,215	14	6,084	27	351
8	1,568	10	14,181	10	18,762	67	3,262
4	620	4	2,475	4	1,168	−20	157
9	6,210	16	5,986	12	6,722	500	7,287
1	198	4	1.658	4	2,793		
591	251,290	634	562,786	598	622,864	37	741

TABLE 2.2-11 *Two-year institutions of higher education, by type and enrollment, United States, fall 1968*

			Enrollment*	
Institutions	Number	Percent	Number, in thousands	Percent
Public community colleges	584	54.6	1,599.5	85.5
Private junior colleges	258	24.0	123.1	6.6
Two-year branches of universities	127	11.8	78.7	4.2
Specialized two-year institutions				
Public	73	6.8	47.0	2.5
Private	30	2.8	22.7	1.2
TOTAL	1,072	100.0	1,871.0	100.0

*Includes all full-time and part-time students.

SOURCE: Carnegie Commission on Higher Education, *The Open-Door Colleges: Policies for Community Colleges*, McGraw-Hill Book Company, New York, 1970, p. 13.

TABLE 2.2-12 *Total degree-credit enrollment in two-year institutions of higher education, by sex, attendance status, and institutional control, United States, fall 1957 to 1977 (resident and extension opening fall enrollment)*

Year (fall) (1)	Total degree-credit enrollment (2)	Sex		Attendance status*		Control	
		Men (3)	Women (4)	Full-time (5)	Part-time (6)	Public (7)	Private (8)
1957	369,162	237,679	131,483	206,000	163,000	315,990	53,172
1960	451,333	282,155	169,178	247,000	205,000	392,310	59,023
1965	841,437	521,846	319,591	495,454	345,983	737,890	103,547
1966†	945,000	577,000	367,000	568,000	377,000	840,000	105,000
1967†	1,075,000	653,000	422,000	630,000	445,000	967,000	109,000
			Projected‡				
1968	1,164,000	705,000	458,000	681,000	483,000	1,047,000	117,000
1969	1,207,000	730,000	477,000	706,000	501,000	1,087,000	121,000
1970	1,273,000	768,000	505,000	745,000	529,000	1,147,000	127,000
1975	1,705,000	1,019,000	686,000	995,000	710,000	1,539,000	166,000
1977	1,859,000	1,107,000	751,000	1,084,000	775,000	1,679,000	180,000

*Attendance status for 1957 to 1961 and for 1966 and 1967 is estimated from first-term enrollment by attendance status reported in comprehensive enrollment surveys, biennially, 1957 to 1963, and 1966.

† Estimate based on 1966 and 1967 opening fall surveys of total degree-credit and non-degree-credit enrollment not reported separately, and on preliminary data from the 1966 comprehensive survey of total degree-credit and total non-degree-credit enrollment reported separately.

‡ The projection of total degree-credit enrollment in two-year institutions by sex and institutional control is based on the assumption that enrollment in these institutions, expressed as a percentage of population aged 18 to 21 years, will follow the 1957–1967 trend to 1977 in each enrollment category.

The projection of total degree-credit enrollment in two-year institutions by attendance status is based on the assumption that in each enrollment category the ratio of full-time enrollment to total enrollment reported in the 1966 comprehensive survey, with minor adjustments, will remain constant to 1977. Veterans attending college through aid provided by the Veterans' Readjustment Benefits Act of 1966 are included in the trend projections.

NOTE: Data are for 50 states and the District of Columbia for all years. Because of rounding, detail may not add to totals.

SOURCES: Enrollment data and estimates are based on U.S. Department of Health, Education and Welfare, Office of Education circulars: (1) "Opening (Fall) Enrollment in Higher Education," annually, 1957 to 1967; (2) "Resident and Extension Enrollment in Institutions of Higher Education," biennially, first-term 1957 to 1963; and (3) unpublished preliminary data from "Resident and Extension Enrollment in Institutions of Higher Education," fall 1966; in U.S. Office of Education, *Projections of Educational Statistics to 1977–78,* National Center for Educational Statistics, 1968, p. 18.

The projections also indicate that the proportion of women in graduate education is likely to rise from 28 to 38 percent, that the proportion of graduate students attending full time will increase from 39 to 44 percent, and that the proportion of graduate enrollment in public institutions is likely to increase from 50 to 72 percent (author's calculations).

In the fall of 1964, the types of institutions in which graduate students were enrolled, and their distribution by year of enrollment and full-time status, were as follows:[12]

Enrollment for master's and higher degrees by type of institution, control, level of study, and attendance status, fall 1964

Number of institutions	704
Public	299
Private	405
Liberal arts	249
Universities	155
Other	300

Enrollment in universities = 71 percent of total

Percentage of total enrollment by year of enrollment*

First year	67
Intermediate years	30
Terminal	4

Percentage of students in full-time attendance

First year	36
Intermediate years	51
Terminal	59

*Percentages do not add to 100 because of rounding.

(Text continued on p. 297)

[12] U.S. Office of Education, *Enrollment for Master's and Higher Degrees, Fall 1964,* Final Report, National Center for Educational Statistics, 1966, p. 5 (author's calculations).

TABLE 2.2-13 *Graduate student enrollment, 1871–1954*

Year	Enrollment (1)	Percentage increase over previous decade (2)
1871	44	
1880	411	
1890	2,382	480
1900	5,831	145
1910	9,153	57
1920	15,612	71
1930	47,255	203
1940	105,748	124
1950	237,208	124
1952	233,778	
1954	278,261	

SOURCE: U.S. Office of Education publications, especially *Statistics of Higher Education: Faculty, Students and Degrees, 1953–54,* 1956, p. 78. There are minor differences in OE figures for the same year in different publications.

According to a report by the National Science Foundation:*

But the event during this period that decisively influenced the future of graduate education was the founding in 1876 of Johns Hopkins University as an institution devoted exclusively to education and research at the graduate level. Europe had long set the highest standards of scholarship for American emulation; German institutions in particular attracted large numbers of advanced American students who went abroad each year to complete their education. The rising industrial nation of the Old World offered many lessons to the rising industrial nation of the New, and not least among them was the way its higher educational institutions bolstered its technology and skilled labor force. In Germany, higher education was devoted not only to the transmission but also to the pursuit of knowledge; the Ph.D. signified not just the acquisition of existing knowledge, but a positive addition thereto; instruction and research were merged, and professors and graduate students alike participated actively in the research process. This is essentially the modern American conception of graduate education at the Ph.D. level, and it was first realized forcefully at Johns Hopkins University, which became the leading American center for graduate and professional education, its methods and standards being extensively copied by existing and new institutions throughout the country.

* National Science Foundation, *Graduate Student Enrollment and Support in American Universities and Colleges,* Washington, D.C., 1957, p. 2.

TABLE 2.2-13 *(continued)*

However, the experiment of creating at Johns Hopkins University—and, in 1889, at Clark University—an independent institution devoted solely to graduate education did not succeed, partly for financial reasons and partly because of the pressure to make available for other educational programs the outstanding scholars who had been gathered together for a narrower purpose. Both institutions subsequently extended their operations to the undergraduate sphere and Johns Hopkins established schools of medicine, engineering, education, public health, and nursing. The major organizational form which developed in the rapid burgeoning of graduate education at the end of the last century was that of the "university", which designated an institution offering graduate and professional programs in addition to undergraduate instruction in liberal arts. The other and increasingly important form came from professional schools and institutes—engineering, medical, law, and teachers colleges—that sprang up in great numbers and gradually extended their programs to the graduate level. The 25 institutions offering graduate programs in 1876 thereby increased to 270 in the 1920's, and 615 in 1955–56.

The rate of increase of graduate enrollment has been even greater. Over the last eighty years, graduate enrollment has doubled or more than doubled in every decade except the first two of this century (judging from indications thus far available, expansion will also be at a somewhat reduced rate in the 1950's). . . . This phenomenal expansion has greatly exceeded the proportionate increases in the U.S. population, the population of college age, and even the large increase in undergraduate enrollment. . . . Its motivating force has come from countless sources—the continually raised standards required for admission into and advancement in the independent professions, academic careers, and the upper levels of industry and Government; the increased role of women, and of Negroes and other minority groups in the technical and professional labor force; and the greater abundance of leisure and money. Underlying all these causes have been the increasing wealth and complexity of the Nation. . . .

TABLE 2.2-14 *Estimated graduate degree-credit enrollment in four-year institutions of higher education by sex, attendance status, and institutional control, United States, fall 1957 to 1977* (resident opening fall enrollment—in thousands)*

Year (fall) (1)	Resident graduate degree-credit enrollment† (2)	Sex		Attendance status‡		Control	
		Men (3)	Women (4)	Full-time (5)	Part-time (6)	Public (7)	Private (8)
1957	288	208	80	113	174	145	142
1960	356	253	103	143	213	187	169
1967	688	453	236	298	390	435	254
Projected§							
1968	749	489	259	325	424	481	268
1969	781	507	273	339	442	509	272
1970	828	535	293	360	468	548	280
1975	1,152	725	427	503	649	811	341
1977	1,279	798	481	560	719	919	360

* Graduate enrollment by sex and institutional control was estimated from first-term graduate enrollment reported in comprehensive enrollment surveys, biennially, 1957 to 1963, and from first-professional and graduate enrollment reported separately in the 1963 comprehensive enrollment survey, and together in the 1967 opening fall enrollment survey.

† Resident students are students who take their college work on the main campus or on a branch campus. Living quarters (on campus or off) and legal domicile are irrelevant.

‡ Graduate enrollment by attendance status was estimated from first-term graduate enrollment by attendance status reported in the 1959 and 1961 comprehensive enrollment surveys. These estimates together with similar estimates for undergraduate enrollment were adjusted to agree with total enrollment by attendance status reported in the opening fall enrollment surveys, annually, 1962 to 1967 and in the 1966 comprehensive enrollment survey.

§ The projection of graduate enrollment by sex and by control of institution is based on the assumption that in each enrollment category the proportion of total enrollment at the graduate level will continue the 1957–67 trend to 1977.
   The projection of graduate enrollment by attendance status is based on the assumption that in each enrollment category the estimated ratio of full-time enrollment to total enrollment reported in the 1966 comprehensive enrollment survey, with minor adjustments, will remain constant to 1977. Veterans attending college through aid provided by the Veterans' Readjustment Act of 1966 are included in the trend projection.

NOTE: Data are for the 50 states and the District of Columbia for all years. Because of rounding, detail may not add to totals.

SOURCES: Enrollment data and estimates are based on U.S. Department of Health, Education and Welfare, Office of Education publications: (1) *Opening (Fall) Enrollment in Higher Education,* annually, 1957 to 1967; (2) *Resident and Extension Enrollment in Institutions of Higher Education,* biennially, 1957 to 1963; and (3) unpublished preliminary data from *Resident and Extension Enrollment in Institutions of Higher Education,* fall 1966, in U.S. Office of Education, *Digest of Educational Statistics, 1968,* 1968, p. 20.

These data are presented in greater detail in Table 2.2-15. More recent figures for 1968 provide less detail on types of institutions and present enrollment in first-professional-degree programs separately from enrollment in master's and doctoral programs (Table 2.2-16 and 2.2-17). All told, enrollment in master's and other advanced degree programs increased 47 percent in the four years from 1964 to 1968. The proportion of enrollment in universities declined slightly—from 71 to 69 percent, while the percentage of enrollment in public institutions increased from 59 to 61 percent. These changes probably largely reflect the rapid growth of graduate enrollment in state colleges.

Data on average enrollment for higher degrees by institution suggest some inefficiencies. Among the 100 leading institutions of higher education offering graduate instruction, average graduate enrollment in the public institutions was 939, and average enrollment in the private institutions was 486.[13] The latter may therefore be producing a relatively costly product. Liberal arts colleges and teachers colleges are also probably operating at an uneconomical level,[14] as the following table suggests:[15]

Average number of graduate students, by type of institution, 1964	
Public	939
Private	486
Universities	2,199
Liberal arts	319
Teachers colleges	284

Graduate students are unevenly distributed by regions. The Northeast led in 1954, with 37 percent of resident graduate students (Table 2.2-18). The contrasts are even greater within fields

(Text continued on p. 304)

[13] Graduate enrollment in the 100 institutions ranged from 12,040 for New York University to 1,095 for Tulane (National Science Foundation, *The Dynamics of Academic Science,* 1967, table B-5).

[14] See also U.S. Office of Education, *Students Enrolled for Advanced Degrees, Fall 1967: Part A: Summary Data,* National Center for Educational Statistics, 1969, referred to earlier in the chapter, in which the breakdown for fall 1967 is given.

[15] U.S. Office of Education, *Enrollment for Master's and Higher Degrees, Fall 1964,* Final Report, National Center for Educational Statistics, 1966, table 2 (author's calculations).

TABLE 2.2-15 *Enrollment for master's and higher degrees by type and control of institution, level of study, attendance status, aggregate United States, fall 1964*

Type and control of institution (1)	Number of institu- tions (2)	All students Total (3)	First- year students* (4)	Inter- mediate students† (5)	Terminal- year students‡ (6)
TOTAL	704	477,535	317,808	142,112	17,615
Universities	155	340,096	198,018	125,760	16,318
Liberal arts colleges	249	79,480	72,727	6,266	487
Independently organized professional schools:					
Teachers colleges	128	36,348	34,403	1,896	49
Technological schools	30	14,360	7,591	6,207	562
Theological, religious	89	3,313	2,005	1,204	104
Schools of art	23	882	762	117	3
Other professional	30	3,056	2,302	662	92
Public	299	280,716	192,417	77,973	10,326
Universities	90	199,608	117,283	72,166	10,159
Liberal arts colleges	66	41,795	39,609	2,175	11
Independently organized professional schools:					
Teachers colleges	119	34,794	33,092	1,679	23
Technological schools	15	3,763	1,945	1,741	77
Schools of art	1	53	40	13	
Other professional	8	703	448	199	56
Private	405	196,819	125,391	64,139	7,289
Universities	65	140,488	80,735	53,594	6,159
Liberal arts colleges	183	37,685	33,118	4,091	476
Independently organized professional schools:					
Teachers colleges	9	1,554	1,311	217	26
Technological schools	15	10,597	5,646	4,466	485
Theological, religious	89	3,313	2,005	1,204	104
Schools of art	22	829	722	104	3
Other professional	22	2,353	1,854	463	36

*Includes students who have completed less than 1 full year of required work for an advanced degree.

†Includes all except first-year and terminal-year students.

‡Estimated number of students who were expected to complete all doctoral requirements by June 30, 1965.

SOURCE: U.S. Office of Educational, *Enrollment for Master's and Higher Degrees, Fall 1964,* Final Report, National Center for Educational Statistics, 1966, table 2.

First-year students*		Intermediate students†		Terminal-year students‡	
Full-time (7)	Part-time (8)	Full-time (9)	Part-time (10)	Full-time (11)	Part-time (12)
113,784	204,024	72,569	69,543	10,467	7,148
92,670	105,348	66,952	58,808	9,624	6,694
11,667	61,060	2,262	4,004	299	188
4,443	29,960	268	1,628	39	10
2,369	5,222	1,663	4,544	379	183
1,361	644	879	325	48	56
536	226	67	50	3	
738	1,564	478	184	75	17
69,413	123,004	43,624	34,349	6,193	4,133
58,330	58,953	42,472	29,694	6,103	4,056
5,561	34,048	287	1,888	4	7
4,063	29,029	165	1,514	19	4
1,111	834	529	1,212	26	51
39	1	13			
309	139	158	41	41	15
44,371	81,020	28,945	35,194	4,274	3,015
34,340	46,395	24,480	29,114	3,521	2,638
6,106	27,012	1,975	2,116	295	181
380	931	103	114	20	6
1,258	4,388	1,134	3,332	353	132
1,361	644	879	325	48	56
497	225	54	50	3	
429	1,425	320	143	34	2

TABLE 2.2-16 ***Enrollment for master's and doctor's degrees, by level of enrollment, sex of student, attendance status, and institutional control and level, aggregate United States, fall 1968***

		First-year students*			
		Men		Women	
Institutional control and level (1)	*All students* (2)	*Full-time* (3)	*Part-time* (4)	*Full-time* (5)	*Part-time* (6)
Total, public and private					
All institutions	703,745	113,976	164,881	60,639	118,838
Universities	476,741	86,189	79,442	45,873	47,123
All other four-year	227,004	27,787	85,439	14,766	71,715
Public					
All institutions	456,095	75,167	104,133	41,341	87,628
Universities	305,869	58,401	45,765	31,440	31,518
All other four-year	150,226	16,766	58,368	9,901	56,110
Private					
All institutions	247,650	38,809	60,748	19,298	31,210
Universities	170,872	27,788	33,677	14,433	15,605
All other four-year	76,778	11,021	27,071	4,865	15,605

* Students who had completed less than one full year of required study for an advanced degree or its equivalent in part-time study are designated as first-year students.

† Students who had completed at least one full year of required study for an advanced degree but who were not expected to complete all doctoral requirements by June 30, 1969, are designated as intermediate students.

‡ Students who were expected to complete all doctoral requirements by June 30, 1969, are designated as terminal-year students.

SOURCE: U.S. Office of Education, *Students Enrolled for Advanced Degrees, Fall 1968,* National Center for Educational Statistics, 1970, table 1.

| Intermediate students† | | | | Terminal-year students‡ | | | |
| Men | | Women | | Men | | Women | |
Full-time (7)	Part-time (8)	Full-time (9)	Part-time (10)	Full-time (11)	Part-time (12)	Full-time (13)	Part-time (14)
99,538	61,439	26,439	23,655	19,059	9,886	3,285	2,110
89,656	51,545	24,502	20,462	17,648	9,233	3,084	1,984
9,882	9,894	1,937	3,193	1,411	653	201	126
62,173	34,373	15,696	14,385	11,489	6,740	1,599	1,371
59,400	30,980	14,963	12,770	11,180	6,598	1,523	1,331
2,773	3,393	733	1,615	309	142	76	40
37,365	27,066	10,743	9,270	7,570	3,146	1,686	739
30,256	20,565	9,539	7,692	6,468	2,635	1,561	653
7,109	6,501	1,204	1,578	1,102	511	125	86

TABLE 2.2-17
Enrollment for
first
professional
degrees in
selected fields,
by level
of enrollment,
sex of student,
attendance
status, and
institutional
control and
level,
aggregate
United States,
fall 1968

Institutional control and level (1)	All students (2)	First-year students*			
		Men		Women	
		Full-time (3)	Part-time (4)	Full-time (5)	Part-time (6)
Total, public and private					
All institutions	137,877	39,798	4,169	2,744	333
Universities	100,054	29,212	1,919	2,203	184
All other four-year	37,823	10,586	2,250	541	149
Public					
All institutions	59,737	17,826	758	1,245	81
Universities	56,379	16,877	704	1,174	72
All other four-year	3,358	949	54	71	9
Private					
All institutions	78,140	21,972	3,411	1,499	252
Universities	43,675	12,335	1,215	1,029	112
All other four-year	34,465	9,637	2,196	470	140

* Students who had completed less than one full year of required study in a professional school or its equivalent in part-time study are designated as first-year students.

† Students who had completed at least one full year of required study in the professional school but who were not expected to complete all requirements for the professional degree by June 30, 1969, are designated as intermediate students.

‡ Students who were expected to complete all requirements for the professional degree by June 30, 1969, are designated as terminal-year students.

SOURCE: U.S. Office of Education, *Students Enrolled for Advanced Degrees, Fall 1968,* National Center for Educational Statistics, 1970, table 2.

TABLE 2.2-18
Resident
graduate
students in
major fields,
by region,
April 1954

Field	Total* (1)	Percentage distribution			
		Northeast (2)	North Central (3)	South (4)	West (5)
Physical sciences	18,984	37	26	20	6
Life sciences	12,993	23	37	20	8
Engineering	14,248	51	23	14	3
Psychology	5,434	31	31	19	8
Social sciences	15,375	37	23	22	4
Education	51,042	32	17	23	8
Humanities	14,061	33	29	19	6
Professional fields	19,509	56	20	13	3
TOTAL	151,646	37	23	20	6

* Nine students in Alaska and 188 in Hawaii omitted.

NOTE: Detail may not add to total because of rounding.

SOURCE: National Science Foundation, *Graduate Student Enrollment and Support in American Universities and Colleges,* Washington, D.C., 1957, table III-3

| Intermediate students† | | | | Terminal-year students‡ | | | |
| Men | | Women | | Men | | Women | |
Full-time (7)	Part-time (8)	Full-time (9)	Part-time (10)	Full-time (11)	Part-time (12)	Full-time (13)	Part-time (14)
49,611	4,696	2,930	298	29,662	2,082	1,429	125
36,845	2,461	2,295	139	22,622	1,010	1,102	62
12,766	2,235	635	159	7,040	1,072	327	63
22,799	869	1,375	65	13,723	341	625	30
21,424	842	1,275	62	13,018	318	587	26
1,375	27	100	3	705	23	38	4
26,812	3,827	1,555	233	15,939	1,741	804	95
5,421	1,619	1,020	77	9,604	692	515	36
1,391	2,208	535	156	6,335	1,049	289	59

| | Number | | | | |
Pacific (6)	Northeast (7)	North Central (8)	South (9)	West (10)	Pacific (11)
11	6,968	5,014	3,706	1,190	2,106
13	2,947	4,746	2,561	1,075	1,664
9	7,330	3,274	1,941	449	1,254
11	1,679	1,686	1,053	410	606
14	5,764	3,483	3,353	668	2,107
19	16,324	8,660	11,943	4,214	9,901
13	4,653	4,035	2,608	905	1,860
7	11,042	3,838	2,635	673	1,321
14	56,707	34,736	29,800	9,584	20,819

of concentration. Thus, in 1954, maximum and minimum percentages by fields and regions were as follows:[16]

Distribution of resident graduate students, by fields and regions, percentage of total, 1954

Region	Maximum	Minimum
Northeast	Professional fields, 56	Life sciences, 23
North Central	Life sciences, 37	Educational, 17
South	Education, 23	Professional fields, 13
West	3 fields (life sciences, psychology, education), 8 each	Professional and engineering, 3
Pacific	Education, 19	Professional fields, 7

FOREIGN STUDENTS From 1948–49 to 1966–67, the number of foreign students enrolled in American institutions of higher education rose from 25,464 to 100,262 (Table 2.2-19). The rate of increase of foreign-student enrollment was substantially greater than the overall rate of increase in enrollment for degrees in this country. In these 17 years, the proportion of students from the Western Hemisphere dropped substantially, and there was a less pronounced relative decline for Western Europe. The Near, Middle, and Far East provided 8,218 students in 1948–49 and 46,400 in 1966–67, a rise of 4.6 times. Africa's rate of increase was even greater.

The largest enrollments of foreign students in 1966–67 were in engineering (21,619), humanities (20,080), physical and natural sciences (17,058), and social sciences (14,852). Enrollment in all fields rose 73 percent from 1961–62 to 1966–67, with roughly comparable increases occurring in most major fields, except for medical sciences, in which the increase was only 32 percent (Table 2.2-20).

In 1963, 11 states, most of them with distinguished institutions of higher education, accounted for almost two-thirds of foreign students enrolled in the United States. Four states—California,

[16] National Science Foundation, *Graduate Student Enrollment and Support in American Universities and Colleges,* 1957, table III-3.

TABLE 2.2-19 *Number of foreign students enrolled in American institutions of higher education, by area of origin, 1948–49 to 1966–67*

Academic year (1)	Total (2)	Western hemisphere (3)	Europe (4)	Africa (5)	Near, Middle, and Far East (6)	Pacific (7)	Other (8)
1948–1949	25,464	11,070	4,065*	888	8,218	845†	378
1949–1950	26,433	10,444	5,574*	904	8,313	938†	260
1950–1951	29,813	10,962	7,157*	1,027	9,411	1,110†	146
1951–1952	30,474	11,034	7,220*	1,072	9,737	1,227†	184
1952–1953	33,675	12,258	7,856	1,081	11,547†	316	617*
1953–1954	33,833	13,297	6,171	1,163	12,766†	354	82*
1954–1955	34,232	13,160	5,196	1,234	14,254	337	51*
1955–1956	36,494	13,516	5,502	1,231	15,864†	353	28*
1956–1957	40,666	14,554	5,996	1,424	18,192†	424	76*
1957–1958	43,391	14,566	6,816	1,515	19,901†	495	98*
1958–1959	47,245	15,761	6,601	1,735	22,442†	612	94*
1959–1960	48,486	15,189	6,362	1,959	24,285†	568	123*
1960–1961	53,107	15,754	6,686	2,831	27,084†	658	94*
1961–1962	58,086	16,554	6,833	3,930	29,845†	796	128*
1962–1963	64,705	18,110	7,888	4,996	32,615†	948	148*
1963–1964	74,814	21,430	9,348*	6,144	36,662†	1,080	150
1964–1965	82,045	22,995	10,108*	6,855	40,617†	1,265	205
1965–1966	82,709	23,849	10,226*	6,896	40,266†	1,325	147
1966–1967	100,262	30,412	14,207*	7,170	46,400†	1,635	438

*Includes students from U.S.S.R.

†Includes students from the Philippines.

SOURCE: Institute of International Education, New York. Education for One World, 1948–49 to 1953–54; and Open Doors, 1954–55 to 1967; in U.S. Office of Education, *Digest of Educational Statistics, 1968,* 1968, p. 120.

New York, Illinois, and Michigan—were the choice of 36 percent of the foreign students.[17]

Host institutions of higher education with more than 400 foreign students in 1958–59 are indicated in Table 2.2-21. The university with the largest enrollment of foreigners in that year was the University of California (1,693). In terms of foreign students as a percentage of total enrollment, M.I.T. led, with 12.4 percent.

(Text continued on p. 308)

[17] For a breakdown by state, see U.S. Office of Education, *Digest of Educational Statistics, 1968,* 1968, p. 119.

Major field of interest and year (1)	World total (2)	Far East (3)	Near East (4)	Europe (5)
Total				
1961–1962	58,086	21,568	8,277	6,833
1966–1967	100,262	33,570	12,830	14,152‡
Agriculture:				
1961–1962	1,893	535	346	126
1966–1967	3,290	966	396	293
Business administration:				
1961–1962	5,085	1,961	499	570
1966–1967	9,879	3,188	986	1,206
Education:				
1961–1962	3,042	1,012	354	217
1966–1967	5,533	1,473	504	524‡
Engineering:				
1961–1962	13,031	4,954	3,031	1,240
1966–1967	21,619	8,447	4,593	2,392
Humanities:				
1961–1962	11,163	3,506	1,086	1,896
1966–1967	20,080	5,163	1,607	4,449
Medical sciences:				
1961–1962	4,109	1,461	495	424
1966–1967	5,429	1,749	560	623
Physical and natural sciences:				
1961–1962	9,414	4,347	1,167	1,049
1966–1967	17,058	7,791	1,960	1,966
Social sciences:				
1961–1962	8,443	3,114	1,039	1,085
1966–1967	14,852	4,091	1,803	2,243
All other fields:				
1961–1962	661	202	84	47
1966–1967	1,174	365	228	140
No information:				
1961–1962	1,245	476	176	179
1966–1967	1,348	337	193	316

* South America, Mexico, Central America, and Caribbean areas.
† Bermuda and Canada only.
‡ Includes 1 student from the "Arctic."
SOURCE: Institute of International Education, "Open Doors," 1962 and 1967; in U.S. Office of Education, *Digest of Educational Statistics, 1968,* 1968, p. 120.

Latin America* (6)	North America† (7)	Africa (8)	Oceania (9)	U.S.S.R. (10)	Stateless or country unknown (11)
,915	6,639	3,930	796	37	91
,182	12,230	7,170	1,635	56	437
523	113	218	32		
697	308	556	71		3
985	742	246	77		5
144	1,467	691	165	4	28
409	670	292	88		
852	1,464	511	193	1	11
339	874	497	53	15	28
704	1,178	1,082	124	15	84
115	1,741	602	197	3	17
332	3,133	831	371	22	172
316	506	313	91	1	2
116	799	427	147		8
28	888	686	123	5	21
267	1,526	1,191	289	6	62
37	952	979	113	11	13
582	2,073	1,746	250	6	58
39	52	31	6		
06	144	77	13		1
24	101	66	16	2	5
82	138	58	12	2	10

TABLE 2.2-21
United States institutions with more than 400 foreign students, 1958–59

Institution	Total enrollments	Number of foreign students	Percentage of total enrollment
University of California	41,598	1,693	4.0
New York University	31,068	1,670	2.2
Columbia University	26,787	1,380	5.2
University of Michigan	26,370	1,139	4.3
University of Minnesota	35,852	1,136	3.2
University of Illinois	25,920	908	3.5
University of Southern California	17,950	814	4.5
Massachusetts Institute of Technology	6,137	762	12.4
Harvard University	13,131	716	5.5
University of Wisconsin	24,873	709	2.9
Cornell University	11,102	708	6.4
University of Texas	18,563	542	2.9
Indiana University	21,609	462	2.1
Yale University	7,229	430	5.9
American University	6,456	428	6.6
Louisiana State University	10,558	414	3.9
University of Chicago	6,509	407	6.3
University of Washington	18,876	405	2.1

SOURCE: Figures taken from the *Education Directory, 1958–59* (Part III, Higher Education) of the U.S. Office of Education; in American Council on Education, *American Universities and Colleges, 1966,* Washington, D.C., 1966, p. 72.

UNITED STATES COLLEGE STUDENTS ABROAD

About 25,000 American students were studying abroad in 1965–66, less than one-quarter of the number of foreign students studying in institutions of higher education in this country (Table 2.2-22). In 1966–67, there were 4,674 faculty studying abroad. The largest number of students—more than half—were attending European institutions of higher education. Among countries France, with 17 percent, and Mexico, with 14 percent, were in the lead.

OTHER ASPECTS OF THE ENROLLMENT PROBLEM

Trends by type of institution From 1928 to 1956, the largest percentage increases in enrollment among six types of institutions of higher education occurred in 23 large Catholic and 40 large urban

TABLE 2.2-22
*United States
college students
abroad,
1965–66,
and college
faculty abroad,
1966–67, by
geographical
area and country*

Geographical area and country (1)	Students* Number (2)	Students* Percent (3)	Faculty† Number (4)	Faculty† Percent (5)
All areas	24,900	100.0	4,674	100.0
Europe	14,679	59.0	2,271	48.6
Latin America	3,946	15.8	722	15.4
North America‡	3,146	12.6	49	1.0
Far East	1,979	7.9	590	12.6
Near and Middle East	713	2.9	279	6.0
Africa	270	1.1	489	10.5
Oceania	167	0.7	80	1.7
Other areas or general assignment			194	4.2
All countries	24,900	100.0	4,674	100.0
France	4,223	17.0	260	5.6
Mexico	3,434	13.8	103	2.2
Canada	3,146	12.6	44	0.9
Germany, Federal Republic of	2,392	9.6	252	5.4
United Kingdom	2,040	8.2	537	11.5
Italy	1,504	6.0	195	4.2
Spain	1,182	4.7	86	1.8
Japan	1,003	4.0	112	2.4
Philippines	737	3.0	42	0.9
Switzerland	643	2.6	89	1.9
Belgium	594	2.4	21	0.4
Austria	559	2.2	55	1.2
Vatican City State	497	2.0		
Israel	406	1.6	58	1.2
Colombia	328	1.3	43	0.9
Sweden	312	1.3	51	1.1
Other countries or general assignment	1,900	7.6	2,726	58.3

* Includes students reported by 564 institutions in 83 countries.

† The faculty came from 578 institutions of higher education in the United States and went to 108 countries.

‡ Excludes Mexico and the Central American countries, which are included in Latin America.

NOTE: Because of rounding, percentages may not add to totals.

SOURCE: Institute of International Education, New York, "Open Doors 1967"; in U.S. Office of Education, *Digest of Educational Statistics, 1968,* 1968, p. 118.

TABLE 2.2-23   *Enrollment* by type of institution: percentage rise, 1928–1956*

	Average of all cases					
				Percentage rise		
College groups	*1928*	*1940*	*1956*	*1928–* *1940*	*1940–* *1956*	*1928–* *1956*
8 Ivy League	6,949	7,839	9,832	13.0	25.5	41.8
6 other private universities	6,070	4,904	7,899	−19.3	59.4	29.8
10 women's colleges	1,132	982	1,137	−13.2	15.3	0.5
20 liberal arts	641	701	942	9.4	34.2	46.8
40 large urban	6,175	7,438	11,067	20.4	48.5	79.4
23 large Catholic	2,677	2,632	5,009	− 1.7	90.0	87.4

*Excluding summer and extension schools.
SOURCE: *American Universities and Colleges,* 1928, 1940, 1956, compiled and calculated by S. E. Harris; in S. E. Harris, *Higher Education: Resources and Finance,* McGraw-Hill Book Company, New York, 1962, p. 35.

TABLE 2.2-24
Estimated higher education enrollment per 1,000 of total population in standard metropolitan statistical areas (SMSA), fall 1965[a]

SMSA size category	*Population of universe[b]* *(in thousands)*	*Enrollment[c]*	
		Total[d]	*Full-time[e]*
3,000,000 or more	36,598	746,000	360,000
1,000,000 to 3,000,000	35,444	698,500	437,500
500,000 to 1,000,000	18,804	577,000	294,000
250,000 to 500,000	17,073	526,000	391,500
100,000 to 250,000	14,150	821,000	647,000
50,000 to 100,000	2,121	60,000	47,000
Outside SMSAs	68,372	2,312,000	1,850,500
Total United States	192,562	5,740,500	4,027,500

[a] Based on 20 percent sample of all institutions of higher education.
[b] 1965 estimates used where available; otherwise, based on 1960 census.
[c] Estimate based on sample.
[d] Includes full-time and part-time degree-credit plus non-degree-credit enrollment.
[e] Degree credit.
[f] Full-time equivalent degree-credit enrollment; estimate based on assumption that 3 part-time students equal 1 full-time student.
SOURCE: U.S. Office of Education, *Students and Buildings: An Analysis of Selected Federal Programs for Higher Education,* 1968, p. 43.

institutions (Table 2.2-23).[18] The smallest relative increase was in women's colleges.

Earlier we noted the more rapid rise of enrollment in public than in private institutions of higher education. From 1900 to 1960, the proportion of enrollment in private institutions declined from 61 to 42 percent, and one study estimates that it will decline to 20 percent by 1985 (Figure 2.2-2).

Standard metropolitan areas have greater capacity in higher education (student places per 1,000 population) than areas outside of metropolitan areas (Table 2.2-24). However, there is a tendency for the largest standard metropolitan areas to have substantially less capacity than smaller standard metropolitan areas. Clearly, capacity is note equitably divided between the poor living in large urban areas and others.

[18] In their admirable book on higher education, Jencks and Riesman revealed that, although the Irish accounted for only 16 percent of the adult Catholic population, they constituted 46 percent of Catholic college alumni (C. Jencks and D. Riesman, *The Academic Revolution,* Doubleday and Company, Garden City, N.Y., 1968, p. 397).

	Places per 1,000 population		
Full-time equivalent	*Total*	*Full-time*	*Full-time equivalent*
454,000	20.4	9.8	12.4
521,667	19.7	12.3	14.7
371,167	30.7	15.6	19.7
429,833	30.8	22.9	25.2
696,333	58.0	45.7	49.2
51,000	28.3	22.2	24.0
2,004,300	33.8	27.1	20.3
4,528,300	29.8	20.9	23.5

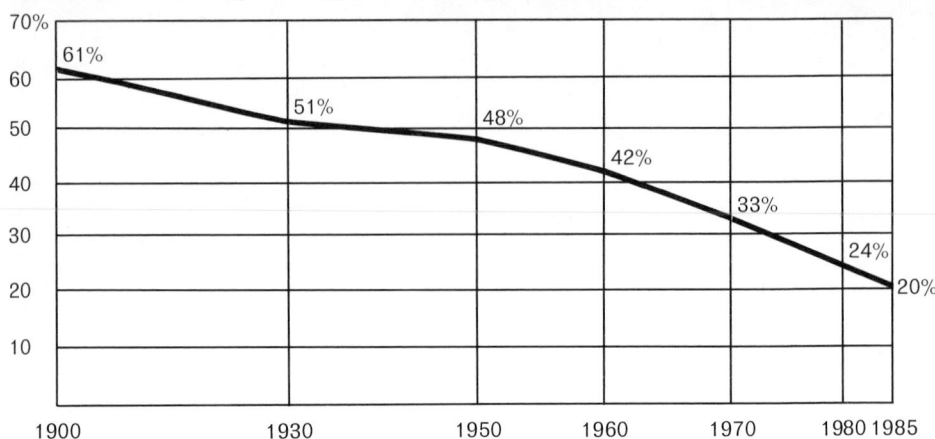

FIGURE 2.2-2   *Percentage of college and university enrollments in private institutions, 1900–1985*

SOURCE: S. E. Harris and A. Levensohn, eds., *Education and Public Policy,* McCutchan Publishing Corporation, Berkeley, Calif., 1965, p. 226.

The reliability of forecasts   I noted earlier that the increase in enrollment in higher education in this country from 1960 to 1968 was more than twice that *forecast* from 1959 to 1970. Throughout the Western world, forecasts have tended to be far below actual increases in enrollment.

Another example of this tendency is a series of five forcasts made from 1950 to 1965 of enrollment in higher education in 1970 in the Netherlands. Predicted enrollment rose from 50,000 in the 1950 forecast to 95,000 in the 1965 forecast:[19]

Forecasts and actual total enrollment in higher education, in thousands, the Netherlands, selected years, 1950–1965

Year in which forecast was made	Actual enrollment in base year	Predicted enrollment in 1970
1950	29	50
1955	29	56
1959	32	65
1963	52	80
1965	65	95

Alternative projects of enrollment prepared by the U.S. Bureau of the Census indicate much more rapid increases in enrollment in higher education than in grades 1 to 12 from 1965 to 1985[20]:

[19] Organization for Economic Co-operation and Development, *Curriculum Improvement and Educational Development,* OECD Publications, Paris,1966,p. 28.

[20] My calculations from U.S. Bureau of the Census, "Revised Projections of School and College Enrollment in the United States to 1985," *Population Estimates, Current Population Reports,* series P-25, no. 365, May 5, 1967, pp. 4–5. Projections differ because of different assumptions about population and enrollment increases: B-1, high population and enrollment growth; B-2, high population growth, low enrollment growth; D-1, low population growth, high enrollment growth; and D-2, low population and enrollment growth.

312

Percentage increase in enrollment, 1965–1985, by levels of education, United States, alternative projections

Level of education	B-1	B-2	D-1	D-2
Grades 1 to 12	35	33	4	2
Higher education	109	75	104	71

This table suggests an increase of enrollment in higher education two to three times as large as the increase in grades 1 to 12 on the basis of two projections, and 26 times as large on the basis of a third. The far greater margin in the third projection is explained by the relative stability of school enrollment from 1965 to 1985 under projection D-1, which assumes a relatively low rate of population increase and a high rate of increase in ratios of enrollment to population.

In terms of numbers, the alternative projections indicate the following increases in college enrollment:[21]

Estimated college enrollment, in thousands, United States, alternative projections, 1965, 1975, and 1985

	B-1	B-2	D-1	D-2
1965	5,675	5,675	5,675	5,675
1975	9,459	8,565	9,459	8,564
1985	11,846	9,927	11,588	9,695

Upper-division enrollment In the fall of 1967, there were more than 1.5 million students enrolled in upper-division work in four-year institutions, with public institutions of higher education accounting for 64.5 percent and private institutions for 35.5 percent (Table 2.2-25). However, publicly controlled universities enrolled more than three times as many in the upper division as did privately controlled universities. Total undergraduate resident enrollment amounted to 4.3 million.

In interpreting these data, three points should be kept in mind. First, the upper-division survey asked for total resident and extension enrollment, whereas the undergraduate totals in the opening fall enrollment survey were limited to resident students. Second, the 4.3 million undergraduate total shown in the last column of Table 2.2-26 does not include about 1.5 million undergraduates, all "lower-division" or "unclassified," in two-year institutions. Third, while the upper-division undergraduate data include only degree-credit enrollments, the total undergraduate enrollment data include students in non-degree-credit programs.

[21] Adapted from ibid., pp. 4–5.

TABLE 2.2-25 *Enrollments of upper-division undergraduate students and of total undergraduate students in universities and other four-year institutions, by institutional control and level, aggregate United States, fall 1967*

Institutional control and level (1)	Upper-division enrollment (resident and extension)				Total undergraduate enrollment (resident only)*	
	Total upper division					
	Number (2)	Percent (3)	Juniors (4)	Seniors (5)	Number (6)	Percent (7)
All institutions	1,560,298	100.0	844,517	715,781	4,271,257	100.0
Universities	669,898	42.9	362,458	307,440	1,867,325	43.7
Other four-year	890,400	57.1	482,059	408,341	2,403,932	56.3
Publicly controlled	1,006,858	64.5	551,408	455,450	2,729,851	63.9
Universities	504,623	32.3	276,466	228,157	1,422,867	33.3
Other four-year	502,235	32.2	274,942	227,293	1,306,984	30.6
Privately controlled	553,440	35.5	293,109	260,331	1,541,406	36.1
Universities	165,275	10.6	85,992	79,283	444,458	10.4
Other four-year	388,165	24.9	207,117	181,048	1,096,948	25.7

*From *Opening Fall Enrollment in Higher Education, 1967,* OE 54003-67.

SOURCE: U.S. Office of Education, *Upper Division Enrollment, Fall 1967,* 1969, table 1.

2.3. Degrees

TYPE, LEVEL,
AND SEX OF
STUDENTS During the past 318 years, 2,452 different types of earned degrees and 235 types of honorary degrees have been conferred in the United States. In 1960 as many as 1,620 types of earned degrees were offered, consisting of 693 bachelor's degrees, 585 master's degrees, and 119 doctor's degrees (Table 2.3-1). The question that can justifiably be raised is whether this variety of offerings constitutes excessive differentiation.

During the academic year 1966, approximately three-quarters of a million degrees were awarded by higher educational institutions. This represents an eightyfold increase since 1869, with the major rise beginning in 1919–20. A comparison of the number of degrees awarded in 1919 and 1966 indicates an increase in the total number of degrees conferred and particularly rapid rates of increase associated with higher-level degrees (Table 2.3-2).

Changes in degrees conferred from 1920 to 1967

Degree	Number of degrees conferred		Increase from 1919–20 to 1966–67 (number of times)	Percentage distribution of degrees by level	
	1919–20	*1966–67*		*1919–20*	*1966–67*
TOTAL	55,516	750,200	13	100.0	100.0
B.A. and first professional	48,622	583,100	11	91.0	78.0
Master's	4,279	147,300	33	8.0	20.0
Doctor's	615	19,800	31	1.0	2.0

SOURCE: Table 2.3-2.

Projections of earned degrees made by the U.S. Office of Education for 1977, as well as the actual number of degrees awarded in 1957 and 1967, are presented in Table 2.3-3. These data indicate that for the decade beginning in 1956, advanced degrees continued

(This tabulation refers to different kinds of degrees offered, e.g.: A.B., B.S., M.S., LL.M., Ph.D., Sc.D., etc., not to number of institutions offering each degree or to number of persons taking each degree. It is to be read thus: A total of 2,452 different earned degrees has been offered by American institutions of higher education since 1642; of these 1,620 were offered in 1960 and 832 have been discontinued.)

Item (1)	Total (2)	Current* (3)	Noncurrent† (4)
Earned degrees:			
Total	2,452	1,620	832
Associate	146	134	12
Bachelor's	913	693	220
Master's	792	585	207
Doctor's	374	119	255
Other	227	89	138
Honorary degrees:			
Total	235	120	115
Associate	3	3	0
Bachelor's	27	13	14
Master's	56	24	32
Doctor's	144	78	66
Other	5	2	3

* Offered by one or more institutions in 1960.
† Not offered by any institution in 1960.
SOURCE: U.S. Office of Education, *Academic Degrees,* Bulletin 1960, no. 28, 1960, pp. 18, 47.

to rise more than baccalaureates and that these trends are expected to persist. Between 1966 and 1976 the forecast is for close to a 50 percent increase in the total number of degrees conferred, resulting in a total degree output of over 1 million. The estimated rise in the number of B.A.'s that would be granted in 1977 is approximately one-half that expected for M.A.'s. The largest anticipated increase is in doctor's degrees, which are projected to increase between 1966 and 1976 by almost 100 percent (Table 2.3-3).

Female degree recipients increased their share of total degrees between 1957 and 1967 and are expected to obtain the following proportion of these degree levels by 1977: bachelor's, 46 percent; master's, 32 percent; and doctor's, 11 percent. Between 1966 and 1976 the rate of increase in baccalaureates received by women is expected to be higher than the increase received by men. The proportion of women receiving advanced degrees will be approxi-

TABLE 2.3-2
Earned degrees conferred by institutions of higher education, United States, 1869-70 to 1966-67

		Earned degrees conferred		
		Bachelor's and first	Master's except first	
Year (1)	All degrees (2)	professional (3)	professional (4)	Doctor's (5)
1869-70	9,372	9,371	0	1
1879-80	13,829	12,896	879	54
1889-90	16,703	15,539	1,015	149
1899-1900	29,375	27,410	1,583	382
1909-10	39,755	37,199	2,113	443
1919-20	53,516	48,622	4,279	615
1929-30	139,752	122,484	14,969	2,299
1939-40	216,521	186,500	26,731	3,290
1941-42	213,491	185,346	24,648	3,497
1943-44	141,582	125,863	13,414	2,305
1945-46	157,349	136,174	19,209	1,966
1947-48	317,607	271,019	42,400	4,188
1949-50	496,661	432,058	58,183	6,420
1951-52	401,203	329,986	63,534	7,683
1953-54	356,608	290,825	56,788	8,995
1955-56	376,973	308,812	59,258	8,903
1957-58	436,979	362,554	65,437	8,938
1959-60	476,704	392,440	74,435	9,829
1961-62	514,323	417,846	84,855	11,622.
1963-64	614,194	498,654	101,050	14,490
1964-65	663,622	535,031	112,124	16,487
1965-66	709,832	551,040	140,555	18,237
1966-67*	750,200	583,100	147,300	19,800

*Estimated by Office of Education.

NOTE: Beginning in 1959-60, includes Alaska and Hawaii.

SOURCE: U.S. Office of Education, "Biennial Survey of Education in the United States," and circulars on "Earned Degrees Conferred"; in U.S. Office of Education, *Digest of Educational Statistics, 1968,* 1968, p. 89.

mately the same as in 1967, which means that, at these levels, overall increases in the number of projected degrees will be divided more or less evenly between men and women (Table 2.3-3).

FIELD OF STUDY AND INSTITUTIONAL CONTROL

Historical comparisons

Historical data on the change in the proportion of degrees conferred by field of specialization for bachelor's, first professional,

TABLE 2.3-3 *Earned degrees by level and by sex, actual, 1957–58 and 1967–68, and projections, 1977–78*

	Numbers of earned degrees, in thousands			Actual increase, 1957–58 and 1967–68, percent	Projected increase, 1967–68 and 1977–78, percent
	Actual		*Projected,*		
	1957–58	*1967–68*	*1977–78*		
Bachelor's and first professional					
Total	363.5	685.0	980.0	0.88	0.43
Men	241.6	401.0	530.0	0.66	0.32
Women	121.9	283.0	450.0	1.32	0.59
Master's (except first professional)					
Total	65.6	148.8	273.7	1.27	0.84
Men	44.2	99.3	186.8	1.25	0.88
Women	21.3	49.5	86.9	1.25	0.76
Doctor's					
Total	8.9	22.2	43.9	1.48	0.98
Men	8.0	19.7	39.0	1.47	0.98
Women	0.9	2.6	4.9	1.70	0.88
Grand total					
Total	438.0	856.0	1,297.6	0.95	0.52
Men	293.8	520.0	755.8	0.76	0.45
Women	144.2	335.1	541.8	1.32	0.62

SOURCE: U.S. Office of Education, *Projections of Educational Statistics to 1977–78,* National Center for Educational Statistics, 1968, p. 31.

TABLE 2.3-4 *Bachelor's and first professional degrees in the United States by fields, 1901–1953, percentage of total*

Field	1901–1905	1906–1910	1911–1915	1916–1920	1921–1925
Natural sciences	13.3	14.1	14.3	13.9	12.7
Psychology	0.3	0.5	0.6	0.7	0.9
Social sciences (history, economics, other)	3.8	5.3	6.4	6.9	7.9
Humanities and arts	25.3	24.7	23.7	22.3	18.5
Engineering	3.3	4.3	6.0	9.3	10.3
Applied biology (agriculture, home economics)	0.2	0.4	2.0	6.7	5.1
Health (medicine, dentistry)	33.2	27.9	23.2	16.1	12.1
Business and commerce	0.2	0.4	0.7	2.2	5.8
Education	0.4	0.2	1.3	3.1	7.5
Law	11.2	11.3	10.7	7.4	8.2
Other	8.8	10.9	11.1	11.4	11.0

SOURCE: D. Wolfle, *America's Resources of Specialized Talent,* report of the Commission on Human Resources and Advanced Training, Harper & Brothers, New York, 1954. Summarized from table B.1, appendix B, pp. 292–293.

TABLE 2.3-5 Degrees awarded by subject field and level of degree for 1911–1915 and 1951–1953, percentage

All subjects	Bachelor of arts and first professional		Doctor's	
	1911–1915	1951–1953	1911–1915	1951–1953
Natural sciences	14.3	9.8	44.2	36.9
Psychology	0.6	2.0	4.8	6.6
Social sciences	6.4	11.2	16.8	12.0
Humanities and arts	23.7	12.0	26.9	12.0
Engineering	6.0	9.6	0.4	6.7
Applied biology	2.0	5.3	1.6	5.8
Health fields	23.2	6.0		1.0
Law	10.7	3.7		
Business and commerce	0.7	14.4		1.3
Education	1.3	19.4	4.9	16.2
Other	11.1	6.6	0.4	1.5
TOTAL	100.0	100.0	100.0	100.0

SOURCE: D. Wolfle, *America's Resources of Specialized Talent,* report of the Commission on Human Resources and Advanced Training, Harper & Brothers, New York, 1954, pp. 292–293 and 298–299.

and doctor's degrees pertaining to the period 1901–1958 are summarized in Tables 2.3-4 and 2.3-5 and Figures 2.3-1 and 2.3-2. Between 1901 and 1915 at the bachelor's and first-professional-degree level, the fields of humanities and arts, health (medicine and dentistry), natural sciences, and law accounted for over 70 percent of all degrees conferred. By 1951–1953 the number of

1926–1930	1931–1935	1931–1940	1941–1945	1946–1950	1951–1953
12.4	10.4	10.4	10.9	10.7	10.8
1.1	1.3	1.5	1.7	2.2	2.0
8.9	8.9	9.7	10.1	11.6	11.2
18.6	16.1	13.8	12.9	11.6	12.0
7.0	8.0	7.6	8.8	11.3	9.6
3.9	4.2	5.6	6.5	5.3	5.3
9.5	7.0	6.1	7.4	5.9	6.0
5.6	6.9	8.8	8.6	14.6	14.4
14.0	20.1	23.1	22.4	14.8	19.4
7.7	6.1	4.6	2.4	3.4	3.7
11.3	11.0	8.8	8.3	8.6	6.6

FIGURE 2.3-1   *Distribution of doctoral degrees, by field*

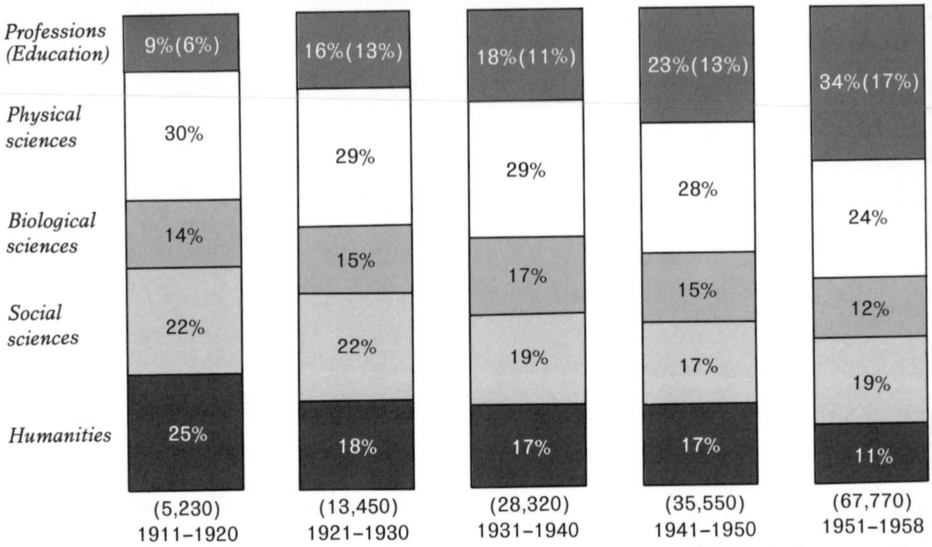

Professions (Education) 9%(6%)	16%(13%)	18%(11%)	23%(13%)	34%(17%)
Physical sciences 30%	29%	29%	28%	24%
Biological sciences 14%	15%	17%	15%	12%
Social sciences 22%	22%	19%	17%	19%
Humanities 25%	18%	17%	17%	11%
(5,230) 1911–1920	(13,450) 1921–1930	(28,320) 1931–1940	(35,550) 1941–1950	(67,770) 1951–1958

SOURCE: B. Berelson, *Graduate Education in the United States,* McGraw-Hill Book Company, New York, 1960, p. 37.

degrees awarded to those in natural sciences, education, business and commerce, humanities and arts, and the social sciences exceeded all other fields and represented about 60 percent of all degrees granted (Tables 2.3-4 and 2.3-5). The trend has been toward a decline in the share of total baccalaureate and first-professional degrees accounted for by health, law, and humanities and art, and a rise in the proportion of other fields, e.g., education, business and commerce, psychology, and applied biology.

The data on doctor's degrees revealed a much higher concentration of degrees in relatively few fields than was the case at the bachelor's and first-professional-degree level (Figure 2.3-1 and Table 2.3-5).[1] This was a result, in part, of the fact that compared to undergraduate and first-professional-degree programs, the Ph.D. was offered in fewer fields and that a considerable proportion of all doctor's degrees was accounted for by one field—the natural sciences. In 1911–1915 and 1951–1953 natural sciences rep-

[1] This figure and table cover different periods and the subject areas in the latter are more disaggregated than in the former. However, the results are consistent when it is realized that natural sciences, in Table 2.3-5, is the same as fields of physical science and biological sciences combined, in Figure 2.3-1, and that social sciences, in Figure 2.3-1, consists of both social science and psychology in Table 2.3-5.

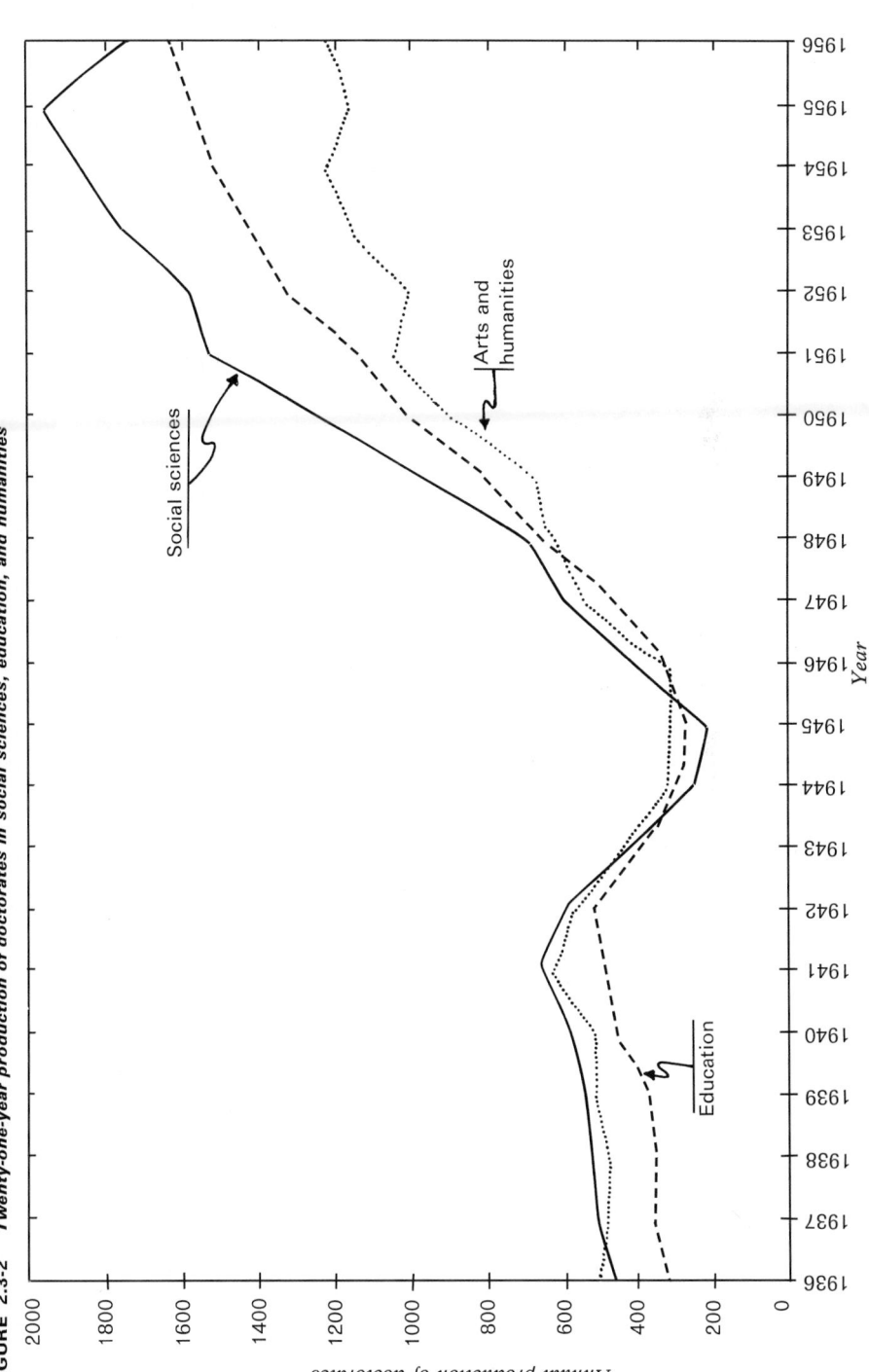

FIGURE 2.3-2 *Twenty-one-year production of doctorates in social sciences, education, and humanities*

SOURCE: National Academy of Sciences and National Research Council, *Doctorate Production in United States Universities, 1936–56*, Washington, D.C., 1958, p. 4.

resented approximately 44 percent and 37 percent, respectively, of all Ph.D. degrees granted in those years.

There has been a change in the absolute and relative shares of all fields that accounted for the largest proportion of degrees at this level. Between 1911 and 1915 about 90 percent of all Ph.D. degrees were awarded in three fields: natural sciences, humanities and arts, and social sciences, whereas in 1951–53 four fields— these three plus education—accounted for about 10 percent less of the total. Proportional declines occurred in the humanities and arts, and to a lesser extent in the social sciences. Proportional increases took place in education, engineering, and applied biology (Table 2.3-5).

There were major increases in the absolute number of doctor's degrees received by students specializing in social sciences, education, and humanities and arts between 1936 and 1956 (Figure 2.3-2).

During both periods, 1911–1915 and 1951–1953, in the natural sciences, psychology, and social sciences, the proportion that Ph.D. degrees represented of total degrees exceeded the proportion of the total accounted for by bachelor's degrees. However, from 1951 to 1953 the share of degrees in the social sciences doubled at the B.A. level and declined somewhat at the Ph.D. level. At this time the proportions accounted for by Ph.D. and B.A. degrees were about the same. From 1911 to 1915 the proportion of doctorates compared to baccalaureates was slightly higher in humanities and arts and education. By 1951–1953, humanities and arts degrees at both levels were one-half as important as in the earlier period, while the relative position of education increased nineteenfold at the B.A. level and about fourfold at the Ph.D. level. The effect of this was to raise the proportion of total bachelor's degrees accounted for by degrees in education above the share that education-related degrees represented of doctorates (Table 2.3-5).

The change in the distribution of degrees conferred by institutions according to type of control is brought out in Table 2.3-6. At all levels, and particularly at the M.A. and Ph.D. levels, the trend has been for an increase in the proportion of degrees conferred by institutions under public control and a corresponding decline in the proportion conferred by those under private control. In 1930, around two-fifths of B.A. and M.A. degrees and one-third of doctoral degrees were granted at public institutions. By 1966–67 approximately three-fifths of the degrees conferred at each of these levels were at publicly controlled institutions.

TABLE 2.3-6 Percentage of earned degrees conferred, by level and institutional control, selected years, 1931–1967	Bachelor's and first professional		Master's		Doctorate	
	Public	Private	Public	Private	Public	Private
1930–31*	45.5	54.5	40.1	59.9	33.2	66.8
1947–48*	50.0	50.0	41.7	58.3	39.6	60.4
1957–58*	54.3	45.7	57.8	42.2	51.6	48.4
1963–64†	56.1	43.9	61.7	38.3	56.5	43.5
1966–67‡	59.9	40.1	61.7	38.3	60.3	39.7

*SOURCE: D. Keezer, ed., *Financing Higher Education: 1960–70*, McGraw-Hill Book Company, New York, 1959, p. 107.

†SOURCE: P. Wright, *Earned Degrees Conferred, 1963–64: Bachelor's and Higher Degrees*, U.S. Office of Education, National Center for Educational Statistics, 1966, p. 5.

‡SOURCE: U.S. Office of Education, *Earned Degrees Conferred, 1966–67: Part A—Summary Data*, 1968, p. 5.

Recent developments

Table 2.3-7 includes data pertaining to four levels of degrees granted in 1963–64 according to field of specialization, type of institutional control, and type of institution. The following is a summary of some features of this table applicable to 10 fields of study.[2]

More students at the B.A. and M.A. levels received degrees in education than in any other subject field. At the Ph.D. level the proportion of all doctoral degrees made up of degrees in education was only slightly below the share represented by degrees in physical science. The proportion of total degrees at the B.A., M.A., and Ph.D. levels at all institutions accounted for by degrees awarded to those specializing in education was 24 percent, 40 percent, and 16 percent, respectively. Other fields of specialization that accounted for a large proportion of total degrees granted at the B.A. and M.A. levels included the social sciences, engineering, business and commerce, and English and journalism. Additional important areas of concentration on the doctoral level were social sciences, engineering, and biological sciences, each of which represented approximately 12 percent of the total number of doctoral degrees granted.

Degrees received by students preparing for the medical and legal professions at the first-professional-degree level accounted for about three-fifths of all such degrees conferred.

---

[2] Information on types of institution is covered below, pp. 325–333.

	Percentage of bachelor's degrees			Percentage of first professional degree		
Degrees conferred in selected areas of study as a percentage of total degrees conferred, all and public and private institutions, 1963–64	All	Public	Private	All	Public	Priv
All areas of study	100.0	100.0	100.0	100.0	100.0	100
Education	24.4	30.4	16.4	1.0	0.9	1
Social sciences	16.7	14.2	20.2	6.8	6.9	6
Business and commerce	12.1	11.4	13.3	6.9	2.3	9
English and journalism	7.7	6.6	9.1	0.2	*	0
Engineering	7.2	7.9	6.3	4.5	9.1	1
Biological sciences	5.0	4.3	5.9	*	0.1	*
Physical sciences	3.8	3.3	4.6	*	0.1	*
Health	2.5	2.8	2.8	33.2	43.0	27
Law	*	*	*	26.0	26.0	26
Religion	0.8	*	*	12.1	0	19
Others (14 fields)	19.8	19.1	21.4	9.3	11.6	7
Combined share— three highest†	33.2	56.0	49.9	71.3	78.1	72

* Less than 0.05 percent.
† Obtained by summing the shares of the three subject fields which account for the highest proportion of the total in each column.
SOURCE: Table 2.3-7.

Education majors, at the B.A. and M.A. levels in particular, received a considerably higher proportion of degrees from publicly controlled institutions than from those under private authority. At these levels, the proportion of total degrees conferred at public institutions was around 15 percent higher than the corresponding share at private institutions. There were proportionately more doctoral degrees awarded to those specializing in biological science by public colleges and universities than by private institutions.

Those specializing at the B.A. level in the social sciences and English and journalism, at the M.A. level in social sciences, engineering, and business and commerce, and at the Ph.D. level in social sciences received proportionately more degrees from private institutions than from public ones. There was a fairly even distribution of degrees between public and private institutions for undergraduate degree recipients in engineering, business and commerce, physical and biological sciences; for those obtaining M.A.

Percentage of master's degrees			Percentage of doctor's degrees		
All	*Public*	*Private*	*All*	*Public*	*Private*
100.0	100.0	100.0	100.0	100.0	100.0
40.3	45.8	31.4	16.2	19.0	12.6
9.4	8.1	11.4	12.3	9.4	16.0
6.3	5.1	8.2		2.1	1.6
4.8	4.2	5.7	3.9	3.2	4.8
10.7	9.4	12.8	11.7	11.1	12.4
3.3	3.8	2.4	11.2	13.1	8.8
4.5	4.5	4.5	16.9	17.1	16.8
2.3	2.3	2.2	1.3	1.7	0.8
0.6	0.1	1.5	0.2	0	0.5
1.3	*	3.5	2.1	*	4.8
16.5	16.7	16.4	24.2	23.3	20.9
60.4	63.3	55.6	45.4	49.2	45.4

degrees in English and journalism, physical and biological sciences; and for Ph.D. holders in engineering, business and commerce, and English and journalism.

For all institutions at each level the extent to which a large share of degrees awarded was concentrated in a few subject fields varied. The following represents the proportion of the total at four degree levels accounted for by combined shares of the three largest subject areas: bachelor's, 53 percent; first professional, 71 percent; master's, 60 percent; and doctor's, 45 percent. The relative shares of the three top subject areas at all levels were highest at institutions under public control.

The Office of Education groups institutions of higher education into seven basic types: universities, liberal arts, teachers colleges, technological schools, theological schools, schools of art, and other professional schools. The summary on the percentage of degrees accounted for by principal subject areas by type of institution (pp. 332–333) was based on data included in Table 2.3-7.

TABLE 2.3-7
Degrees
conferred in
each area of
study as a
percentage of
total degrees
at each level,
by institutional
control and
type,
aggregate
United States,
1963–64

Area of study	All institutions	Institutional control	
		Public	Private
Four-year bachelor's	100.0	100.0	100.0
Agriculture	1.0	1.6	0.2
Architecture	0.1	0.2	0.1
Biological sciences	5.0	4.3	5.9
Business and commerce	12.2	11.4	13.3
Education	24.4	30.4	16.4
Engineering	7.2	7.9	6.3
English and journalism	7.7	6.6	9.1
Fine and applied arts	3.5	3.1	4.0
Foreign languages and literature	2.7	2.2	3.4
Forestry	0.3	0.5	*
Geography	0.3	0.4	0.1
Health professions	2.5	2.3	2.8
Home economics	1.1	1.3	0.7
Law	*	*	*
Library science	0.1	0.2	*
Mathematical subjects	4.1	4.2	3.8
Military, naval, or air force science	0.5	0.9	*
Philosophy	1.0	0.3	2.0
Physical science	3.8	3.3	4.6
Psychology	2.9	2.4	3.6
Religion	0.8	*	1.9
Social sciences	16.7	14.2	20.2
Trade and industrial training	0.4	0.5	0.4
Miscellaneous fields	1.6	2.0	1.1
Five-or-more-year first professional	100.0	100.0	100.0
Agriculture	0	0	0
Architecture	3.5	6.2	1.9
Biological sciences	*	0.1	*
Business and commerce	6.9	2.3	9.8
Education	1.0	0.9	1.1
Engineering	4.5	9.1	1.7
English and journalism	0.2	*	0.3
Fine and applied arts	0.5	0.1	0.7
Foreign languages and literature	*	*	*
Forestry	0.2	0	0.3

326

			Type of institution			
versities	*Liberal arts*	*Teachers colleges*	*Technological*	*Theological*	*Schools of art*	*Other professional schools*
00.0	100.0	100.0	100.0	100.0	100.0	100.0
1.8	0.4	0.4	1.4	0	0	0
0.3	*	0	0.2	0	0	0.5
5.1	5.9	3.2	1.5	1.1	0	4.6
14.6	11.3	5.1	9.3	0.2	0	64.4
16.6	23.6	60.6	2.5	5.8	21.3	4.7
10.5	2.3	0	49.3	0	0	4.8
7.5	9.2	6.4	1.1	1.8	0	1.3
3.7	3.4	1.3	2.8	1.4	75.9	3.4
2.8	3.4	1.3	0.2	1.6	0	0.1
0.5	0.1	*	0.3	0	0	2.3
0.3	0.2	0.6	0	0	0	0
3.7	2.0	0.4	0.2	0.8	0	8.3
1.5	0.9	0.3	0.7	0	0	0
0.1	*	0	0	0	0	0
0.1	0.1	0.3	0	0	0	0
3.5	4.5	5.2	3.2	0.4	0	0.1
0.2	0.1	0	12.2	0	0	0
0.7	1.2	*	*	38.1	0	0
3.8	4.2	2.3	8.0	0.3	0	0.7
3.2	3.8	0.5	0.4	1.0	0	0.9
0.2	1.2	*	*	39.6	0	0
17.1	20.4	10.8	2.7	7.3	0	3.3
0.5	0.3	0.3	2.5	0	0	0
1.7	1.7	1.2	1.7	0.6	2.9	0.6
00.0	100.0	100.0	100.0	100.0	100.0	100.0
0	0	0	0	0	0	0
4.1	1.2	0	30.0	0	15.2	0
*	*	4.5	0	0	0	0
8.1	6.2	0	0	0	0	6.9
0.5	2.1	60.9	0	0	30.5	0
5.2	3.0	0	38.6	0	0	0
0.2	0.3	2.1	0	0	0	0
0.2	0.7	3.8	0	1.0	54.3	0
0	0	0.3	0	*	0	0
0.2	0	0	0	0	0	0

TABLE 2.3-7
(continued)

Area of study	All institutions	Institutional control Public	Priva
Five-or-more-year first professional			
Geography	0	0	0
Health professions	33.2	43.0	27.2
Home economics	0	0	0
Law	26.0	26.0	26.(
Library science	4.9	5.1	4.7
Mathematical subjects	0.1	0.2	*
Military, naval, or air force science	0	0	0
Philosophy	0	0	0
Physical sciences	*	0.1	*
Psychology	0	0	0
Religion	12.1	0	19.6
Social sciences	6.8	6.9	6.7
Trade and industrial training	0	0	0
Miscellaneous fields	*	*	*
Master's (except first professional)	100.0	100.0	100.(
Agriculture	1.1	1.8	0.1
Architecture	0.4	0.2	0.7
Biological sciences	3.3	3.8	2.4
Business and commerce	6.3	5.1	8.2
Education	40.3	45.8	31.4
Engineering	10.7	9.4	12.8
English and journalism	4.8	4.2	5.7
Fine and applied arts	3.6	3.3	4.2
Foreign languages and literature	2.3	1.7	3.2
Forestry	0.2	0.3	*
Geography	0.3	0.4	0.2
Health professions	2.3	2.3	2.2
Home economics	0.6	0.8	0.2
Law	0.6	0.1	1.5
Library science	0.7	0.9	0.3
Mathematical subjects	3.6	3.7	3.3
Military, naval, or air force science	0	0	0
Philosophy	0.5	0.2	1.(
Physical science	4.5	4.5	4.5
Psychology	2.0	1.9	2.3

32

		Type of institution				
Universities	Liberal arts	Teachers colleges	Technological	Theological	Schools of art	Other professional schools
0	0	0	0	0	0	0
37.5	11.6	0	0	0	0	59.5
0	0	0	0	0	0	0
28.7	33.8	0	0	0	0	33.6
5.0	11.9	10.0	30.4	0	0	0
0	0.1	8.7	0	0	0	0
0	0	0	0	0	0	0
0	0	0	0	0	0	0
*	0.1	4.2	0	0	0	0
0	0	0	0	0	0	0
2.2	18.9	0	0	99.0	0	0
8.3	9.9	5.5	1.0	0	0	0
0	0	0	0	0	0	0
*	0.2	0	0	0	0	0
00.0	100.0	100.0	100.0	100.0	100.0	100.0
1.6	0.1	0.1	0	0	0	0
0.5	*	0	1.0	0	0.6	0.2
3.9	2.2	1.7	0.7	0	0	15.8
7.1	5.6	0.5	12.4	0	0	23.7
31.6	59.1	81.6	3.8	0	23.8	2.6
12.0	1.9	0	63.4	0	0	0
5.2	5.5	2.7	0.4	0	0	0.2
4.1	2.7	0.8	0.9	9.9	75.7	0.9
2.7	2.6	0.2	0.1	0.7	0	0
0.2	0	0	0	0	0	6.7
0.4	0.3	0.2	0	0	0	0
3.2	0.3	0	0	0	0	20.9
0.8	0.3	*	0.4	0	0	0.9
0.9	*	0	0	0	0	11.6
0.6	0.4	1.8	0	0	0	0
4.1	2.5	2.7	3.5	0	0	0
0	0	0	0	0	0	0
0.6	0.3	*	0	6.2	0	0
5.2	3.3	0.9	9.6	0	0	0
2.1	3.0	0.7	0.1	0	0	5.3

TABLE 2.3-7
(continued)

Area of study	All institutions	Institutional control	
		Public	Private
Master's (except first professional)			
Religion	1.3	*	3.5
Social sciences	9.4	8.1	11.4
Trade and industrial training	*	*	*
Miscellaneous fields	1.2	1.4	0.9
Doctor's	100.0	100.0	100.0
Agriculture	3.4	5.6	0.5
Architecture	*	0	*
Biological sciences	11.2	13.1	8.8
Business and commerce	1.9	2.1	1.6
Education	16.2	19.0	12.6
Engineering	11.7	11.1	12.4
English and journalism	3.9	3.2	4.8
Fine and applied arts	2.9	2.8	3.0
Foreign languages and literature	2.6	2.0	3.3
Forestry	0.5	0.7	0.2
Geography	0.5	0.5	0.5
Health professions	1.3	1.7	0.8
Home economics	0.3	0.5	*
Law	0.2	0	0.5
Library science	0.1	0.1	*
Mathematical subjects	4.1	3.9	4.4
Military, naval, or air force science	0	0	0
Philosophy	0.9	0.4	1.7
Physical science	16.9	17.1	16.8
Psychology	6.5	6.4	6.6
Religion	2.1	*	4.8
Social sciences	12.3	9.4	16.0
Trade and industrial training	0.1	0.1	0.1
Miscellaneous fields	0.4	0.4	0.4

*Less than 0.05 percent.

SOURCE: P. Wright, *Earned Degrees Conferred, 1963–64, Bachelor's and Higher Degrees,* U.S. Office of Education, National Center for Educational Statistics, 1966, pp. 16–17.

			Type of institution			
Universities	Liberal arts	Teachers colleges	Technological	Theological	Schools of art	Other professional schools
0.7	1.5	0	0	82.3	0	0
11.2	7.5	4.3	1.2	0.9	0	10.7
*	*	0	0.2	0	0	0
1.2	0.9	1.8	2.2	0	0	0.5
100.0	100.0	100.0	100.0	100.0	100.0	100.0
3.7	0	0	0	0	0	0
*	0	0	0	0	0	0
11.8	7.1	0	2.6	0	0	52.4
2.0	0	0	2.0	0	0	0
16.9	9.1	89.1	0	0	0	2.4
9.8	11.7	0	49.2	0	0	0
4.2	4.3	0.8	0	0	0	0
3.2	0.3	0	0	4.0	100.0	0
2.7	3.7	0	0.1	1.6	0	0
0.4	0	0	0	0	0	22.0
0.5	1.7	0	0	0	0	0
1.5	0	0	0	0	0	1.2
0.3	0.6	0	0	0	0	0
0.2	0	0	0	0	0	12.2
0.1	0	0	0	0	0	0
3.9	5.1	2.3	7.9	0	0	0
0	0	0	0	0	0	0
1.0	1.1	0	0	0	0	0
16.2	25.9	0	33.2	0	0	6.1
6.9	9.4	5.5	0.5	0	0	0
1.3	4.3	0	0	92.0	0	2.4
13.0	15.4	1.6	3.8	2.4	0	1.2
0.1	0	0	0.5	0	0	0
0.4	0.3	0.8	0	0	0	0

Principal subject areas of concentration at four degree levels for seven types of institutions, 1963–64

Universities		Liberal arts schools		Teachers colleges		Technological
Field	*Percent*	*Field*	*Percent*	*Field*	*Percent*	*Field*
						Four-year bachelor's
Social sciences	17	Education	24	Education	61	Engineering
Educational	17	Social sciences	20	Social sciences	11	Military science
Business and commerce	15	Business and commerce	11			
TOTAL	49		55		72	
						Five-year (or more) first professional
Health	38	Health	12	Education	61	Engineering
Law	29	Law	34	Library science	10	Library science
		Religion	19			Architecture
TOTAL	67		65		71	
						Master's, except first professional
Education	32	Education	59	Education	82	Engineering
Engineering	12					Business and commerce
Social sciences	11					
TOTAL	55		59		82	
						Doctorate
Education	17	Physical sciences	26	Education	89	Engineering
Physical sciences	16	Social sciences	15			Physical sciences
Social sciences	13	Engineering	12			
TOTAL	46		53		89	

Undergraduates at both universities and liberal arts colleges received the largest number of degrees in the same fields, viz., social sciences, education, and business and commerce, even though at each type of institution the relative shares varied. At the first-professional-degree level, health professions accounted for 38 percent

chools	Theological schools		Schools of art		Other profes-sional schools	
Percent	*Field*	*Percent*	*Field*	*Percent*	*Field*	*Percent*
49	Religion	40	Fine and applied arts	76	Business and commerce	64
12	Philosophy	38	Education	21		
61		78		97		64
39	Religion	99	Fine arts	54	Health	60
30			Education	31	Law	34
30			Architecture	15		
99		99		100		94
63	Religion	82	Fine arts	76	Business and commerce	24
12	Fine arts	10	Education	24	Health	21
					Law	11
75		92		100		56
49	Religion	92	Fine arts	100	Biological sciences	52
33					Forestry	22
					Law	12
82		92		100		86

and 12 percent of all degrees provided by universities and liberal arts colleges, respectively. The distribution of degrees according to subject areas between universities and liberal arts colleges at the master's degree level was quite different: education, engineering, and social science together accounted for 55 percent of total master's degrees granted at universities, and education alone constituted 55 percent of all master's degrees conferred at liberal arts colleges. Universities and liberal arts schools had in common the fact that physical sciences and social sciences were two of the three leading subject areas of concentration at the Ph.D. level. At this level in universities, degrees in education were the most numerous, accounting for about 17 percent of the total, and at liberal arts colleges, engineering was the third most important field of specialization.

At all levels, teachers colleges specialized in providing degrees in education. In technological schools at all levels, engineering was the principal subject area. For undergraduates who received degrees from theological schools, the highest number of degrees was divided about equally between religion and philosophy. At the advanced degree stage in schools of theology, religion was the principal subject. Schools of art offered most of their degrees in fine and applied art, and, secondarily, except at the doctoral level, in education.

At the baccalaureate level, about two–thirds of the degrees conferred by other professional schools were in business and commerce, while at the first-professional-degree level, degrees from other professional schools were concentrated in the health professions and law. The majority of doctor's degrees granted at other professional schools were in the biological sciences.

RECENT CHANGES IN SUBJECT FIELDS A comparison of changes in the number of degrees granted in different subject fields by level of degree over the decade ending in 1966–67 appears in Table 2.3-8. In the discussion that follows all comparisons are between 1955–56 and 1966–67. The number of M.A. degrees granted increased most rapidly, by 166 percent; the number of B.A. degrees least rapidly, by 91 percent; and Ph.D production rose by 132 percent. At the B.A. level, the largest increases were in mathematical subjects and foreign languages and literature, and the only area which experienced a decline was library science. However, at the M.A. level, the number of degrees in library science grew astronomically by almost 2,500 percent. Other subject areas producing considerably more degrees by 1966–67 were mathematical subjects, social sciences, business and commerce, and foreign languages and literature. The largest percentage increase at the Ph.D. level was in architecture, which started from a low base. In law there was no increase at all.

Table 2.3-9 provides data on the absolute number of degrees conferred during 1965–66 and 1966–67 at the bachelor's, first professional, master's, and doctoral levels for 50 states. In the latest year, 1966–67, the largest numbers of degrees were conferred by three states—New York, California, and Pennsylvania—each of which accounted for over 40,000 degrees. In six states—Illinois, Ohio, Texas, Michigan, Massachusetts, and Indiana—the number of degrees conferred ranged from 24,000 to 44,000. The total number of degrees conferred in these nine states accounted for more than half of the total number of degrees granted in the United States. The distribution of degrees by states for 1966–67 was as follows:

Earned degrees at three levels, by state, 1966–67

	Number of states	*All levels of degrees* *Percent, total*	*B.A.* *Percent, total*	*Ph.D.* *Percent, total*
	15	65	64	73
	23	31	31	25
	12	4	5	2
TOTAL	50	100	100	100

SOURCE: Table 2.3-9.

The 15 states that accounted for slightly less than two-thirds of the sum of all degrees and B.A. degrees represented an even larger proportion of the country's Ph.D. output. This was in contrast to the 23 states whose share of the sum of all degrees and B.A. degrees amounted to about 30 percent but whose share of Ph.D. degrees was somewhat less. The 12 states producing the fewest number of degrees accounted for less than 5 percent of the total at all three degree levels.

What is evident when states are grouped according to size of population and degree output is that in most cases the number of degrees conferred is a function of the size of the state. For example, in all states where the population was over 10 million, more than 35,000 degrees of all types were granted, while the average number of degrees produced in states with less than 1 million in population was below 4,000.

As an aid to evaluating the production of degrees by state, the

(Text continued on p. 340)

	Bachelor's and first professional		
Area of study	1956–57	1963–64	1966–67
All areas	9.3	61.3	91.1
Agriculture	6.8	−7.7	21.7
Architecture	3.5	42.7	98.7
City planning	†	†	†
Biological sciences	10.4	81.7	130.7
Business and commerce	10.8	39.7	65.2
Computer science and systems analysis	†	†	†
Education	10.1	59.9	71.2
Engineering	18.6	33.9	37.5
English and journalism	6.9	109.7	172.8
Fine and applied arts	5.1	44.3	92.2
Folklore	†	†	†
Foreign languages and literature	8.6	210.8	327.9
Forestry	15.7	48.3	67.1
Geography	7.4	99.1	232.3
Health professions	3.1	13.6	31.2
Home economics	−2.0	4.2	34.6
Law	6.6	33.1	85.1
Library science	−3.1	59.0	−56.0
Mathematical subjects	19.0	300.8	357.3
Military science	14.6	55.8	22.4
Miscellaneous fields	−0.4	11.9	5.1
Philosophy	6.2	80.3	103.1
Physical sciences	10.8	50.2	52.5
Psychology	9.3	135.8	244.1
Records management	†	†	†
Religion	1.9	7.0	0.3
Social sciences	9.6	97.9	160.0
Trade and industrial training	36.6	104.6	†

TABLE 2.3-8 Percentage change in degrees conferred in 1956–57, 1963–64, and 1966–67, at each level in each area of study based upon number of degrees conferred during 1955–56*

* The percentage rise is from 1955–56. Thus, for all areas, 61.3 is the percentage rise from 1955–56 to 1963–64.

† No degrees in 1955–56.

SOURCE: P. Wright, *Earned Degrees Conferred, 1963–64, Bachelor's and Higher Degrees,* U.S. Office of Education, National Center for Educational Statistics, 1966 pp. 8–9, 11; and U.S. Office of Education, *Earned Degrees Conferred, 1966–67: Part A — Summary Data,* 1968, p. 9.

evel of degree

	Master's			Doctor's	
1956–57	*1963–64*	*1966–67*	*1956–57*	*1963–64*	*1966–67*
4.5	70.5	166.3	− 1.7	62.8	131.6
13.6	36.5	74.4	−16.2	41.4	63.5
4.5	92.5	122.7	50.0	50.0	400.0
†	†	†	†	†	†
2.7	88.0	185.2	7.6	58.5	120.1
5.3	105.2	393.8	−23.1	127.3	261.2
†	†	†	†	†	†
3.2	35.6	86.0	− 3.2	48.3	122.9
10.8	129.2	193.9	− 2.3	177.5	328.5
9.0	132.3	285.9	− 8.8	46.9	42.8
1.4	56.0	146.8	4.7	79.6	114.5
†	†	†	†	†	†
−2.0	158.2	373.8	−15.0	47.8	128.5
−15.1	0.0	49.7	52.9	97.1	114.7
13.0	90.1	187.6	2.2	45.7	41.1
9.1	81.2	169.3	4.2	33.3	73.6
6.7	32.2	88.5	39.4	24.2	100.0
6.8	50.1	91.6	14.8	11.1	0.0
14.5	301.7	2495.8	−40.0	−13.3	6.7
8.2	303.9	492.4	6.0	153.6	254.0
†	†	†	†	†	†
8.6	231.8	319.1	4.8	−30.1	19.3
9.4	92.5	126.2	3.7	67.1	203.7
1.9	72.1	18.3	0.4	47.3	107.7
12.5	111.6	222.5	−13.2	48.1	94.2
†	†	†	†	†	†
2.3	24.4	108.6	13.4	41.0	43.8
3.5	115.7	325.3	− 2.3	58.3	123.0
†	†	†	†	†	†

		1965–66	
TABLE 2.3-9 *Earned degrees conferred by institutions of higher education, by level and by state, 1965–66 and 1966–67*			

State (1)	Bachelor's (requiring four or five years) (2)	First professional (requiring at least six years) (3)	Second level (master's) (4)
United States	519,804	31,236	140,555
Alabama	7,567	345	1,367
Alaska	212	0	44
Arizona	4,925	112	1,820
Arkansas	4,855	202	843
California	43,508	2,669	13,049
Colorado	7,268	382	2,541
Connecticut	6,762	440	2,690
Delaware	851	0	284
District of Columbia	4,342	1,358	3,458
Florida	10,456	513	2,300
Georgia	8,303	681	1,510
Hawaii	1,540	0	427
Idaho	1,744	34	276
Illinois	24,268	1,949	8,378
Indiana	15,810	696	6,233
Iowa	9,511	508	1,681
Kansas	8,481	359	2,228
Kentucky	7,289	712	1,247
Louisiana	8,347	667	2,062
Maine	2,843	19	350
Maryland	7,512	746	1,501
Massachusetts	20,441	1,687	8,208
Michigan	22,855	1,016	8,607
Minnesota	12,107	758	1,811
Mississippi	6,127	175	888
Missouri	12,061	1,192	2,950
Montana	2,668	32	342
Nebraska	6,553	315	817
Nevada	512	0	110
New Hamphsire	2,801	0	370
New Jersey	12,840	514	3,461
New Mexico	2,425	23	861

		1966–67*		
Doctor's (Ph.D., Ed. D., etc.) (5)	*Bachelor's (requiring four or five years)* (6)	*First professional (requiring at least six years)* (7)	*Second level (master's)* (8)	*Doctor's (Ph.D., Ed. D., etc.)* (9)
18,237	550,000	33,100	147,300	19,800
106	8,000	370	1,400	120
3	200		†	‡
174	5,200	120	1,900	190
65	5,100	210	900	70
2,011	46,100	2,830	13,600	2,190
396	7,700	400	2,700	430
399	7,200	470	2,800	430
46	900		300	50
295	4,600	1,440	600	320
337	11,100	540	2,400	370
179	8,800	720	1,600	190
29	1,600		400	30
22	1,800	40	300	20
1,244	25,700	2,070	8,800	1,350
824	16,800	740	6,500	900
433	10,100	540	1,800	470
225	9,000	380	2,300	240
96	7,700	750	1,300	100
221	8,800	710	2,200	240
13	3,000	20	400	10
309	7,900	790	1,600	340
1,161	21,700	1,790	8,600	1,260
919	24,200	1,080	9,000	1,000
396	12,800	800	1,900	430
55	6,500	190	900	60
329	12,800	1,260	3,100	360
31	2,800	30	400	30
135	6,900	330	900	150
1	500		100	‡
31	3,000		400	30
451	13,600	540	3,600	490
57	2,600	20	900	60

TABLE 2.3-9 (continued)				
				1965–66

State (1)	Bachelor's (requiring four or five years) (2)	First professional (requiring at least six years) (3)	Second level (master's) (4)
New York	48,268	3,389	19,037
North Carolina	12,980	702	2,421
North Dakota	2,567	80	431
Ohio	26,558	1,388	5,447
Oklahoma	8,511	404	2,260
Oregon	6,612	428	1,772
Pennsylvania	31,481	1,977	7,467
Rhode Island	3,171	0	740
South Carolina	5,028	146	551
South Dakota	2,868	40	406
Tennessee	10,159	751	2,082
Texas	25,939	1,961	5,339
Utah	5,994	102	1,143
Vermont	1,984	45	538
Virginia	8,445	702	1,343
Washington	10,084	323	1,952
West Virginia	4,763	145	991
Wisconsin	13,147	514	3,108
Wyoming	916	35	271
U.S. Service Schools	2,545	0	542
Outlying areas:			
Guam	27	0	0
Puerto Rico	4,286	260	217

* Estimated.
† Less than 50.
‡ Less than 5.
SOURCE: U.S. Office of Education, "Earned Degrees Conferred, 1965–66," in U.S. Office of Education, *Digest of Educational Statistics, 1968,* 1968, p. 86.

data contained in Table 2.3-10 were assembled. The table provides information for 23 states on population, personal income per capita and absolute and relative population-degree ratios at three degree levels. The population-degree ratio measures the relationship during a given year between the number of people in a state and the num

Doctor's Ph.D., Ed. D., etc.) (5)	1966-67* Bachelor's (requiring four or five years) (6)	First professional (requiring at least six years) (7)	Second level (master's) (8)	Doctor's (Ph.D., Ed. D., etc.) (9)
2,122	51,100	3,600	19,900	2,310
420	13,700	740	2,500	460
37	2,700	80	500	40
629	28,100	1,480	5,700	690
306	9,000	430	2,400	330
279	7,000	450	1,900	300
935	33,300	2,100	7,800	1,020
113	3,400		800	120
48	5,300	150	600	50
13	3,000	40	400	10
262	10,700	800	2,200	280
704	27,400	2,080	5,600	770
184	6,300	110	1,200	200
12	2,100	50	600	10
163	8,900	740	1,400	180
354	10,700	340	2,000	380
43	5,000	150	1,000	50
566	13,900	540	3,300	620
50	1,000	40	300	50
4	2,700		3,600	‡
0				
2	4,500	280	200	‡

ber of earned degrees conferred in that state by all institutions of higher education. When the numerical estimate, which represents the number of people per degree, is relatively low, it is favorable, and when it is high, it is less favorable. The method used for comparing population-degree ratios among states was to compute the

(Text continued on p. 344)

Size categories of selected states	Population, thousands[a]	Personal income per capita[b]	Total number of degrees conferred[c]	Total number of B.A. degrees[d]	Total number of Ph.D. degrees[d]	Total number of other degrees[e]
United States	195,936	$3,159	749,400	550,000	19,000	180,400
18 million +						
California	18,990	3,697	64,720	46,100	2,190	16,430
New York	18,023	3,824	76,910	51,100	2,310	23,500
8–12 million						
Pennsylvania	11,672	3,176	44,220	33,300	1,020	9,900
Illinois	10,887	3,752	37,920	25,700	1,350	10,870
Texas	10,857	2,747	27,400	770	7,680	302
Michigan	8,608	3,387	35,280	24,200	1,000	10,080
3.0–6.0 million						
Florida	6,035	2,834	14,410	11,100	370	2,940
Massachusetts	5,434	3,533	33,350	21,700	1,260	10,390
North Carolina	5,059	2,606	17,400	13,700	460	3,240
Georgia	4,490	2,552	11,310	8,800	190	2,320
Wisconsin	4,194	3,152	18,360	13,900	620	3,840
Tennessee	3,936	2,367	13,980	10,700	280	3,000
Minnesota	3,625	3,079	15,930	12,800	430	2,700
Alabama	3,583	2,167	9,890	8,000	120	1,700
Washington	3,201	3,389	13,420	10,700	380	2,340
1.0–2.9 million						
Connecticut	2,918	3,978	10,900	7,200	430	3,270
South Carolina	2,638	2,339	6,100	5,300	50	750
Mississippi	2,344	2,057	7,650	6,500	60	1,090
Oregon	1,981	3,325	9,650	7,000	300	2,350
Arkansas	1,972	2,304	6,280	5,100	70	1,110
Below 1 million						
District of Columbia	808	4,516	6,960	4,600	320	2,040
Idaho	701	2,728	2,160	1,800	20	340
Delaware	524	3,888	1,250	900	50	300

[a] SOURCE: U.S. Bureau of the Census, *Statistical Abstract of the United States, 1969,* 1969, p. 12.
[b] SOURCE: Ibid., p. 320.
[c] SOURCE: Table 2.3-12. Sum of four levels presented in the table.
[d] SOURCE: Table 2.3-12.
[e] Obtained by dividing population by total number of degrees conferred for each state. Data were then computed as multiples of United States average (United States = 1.00).

Population proportion of United States total, percent[a]	Personal income, multiple United States	Ratio population/ total degrees, multiple United States[e]	Ratio population/ B.A. degrees, multiple United States[f]	Ratio population/ Ph.D. degrees, multiple United States[g]
100.000	1.00	1.00	1.00	1.00
0.097	1.17	1.12	1.15	0.84
0.092	1.21	0.90	0.99	0.76
0.060	1.01	1.00	0.98	1.11
0.056	1.19	1.10	1.19	0.78
0.055	0.87	1.16	1.11	1.37
0.044	1.07	0.93	1.00	0.83
0.031	0.90	1.60	1.53	1.58
0.028	1.12	0.62	0.70	0.42
0.026	0.83	1.11	1.04	1.07
0.023	0.81	1.52	1.43	2.29
0.021	1.00	0.87	0.85	0.66
0.020	0.75	1.08	1.03	1.36
0.019	0.97	0.87	0.80	0.82
0.018	0.69	1.37	1.26	2.86
0.016	1.07	0.91	0.84	0.82
0.015	1.26	1.02	1.14	0.66
0.014	0.74	1.66	1.40	5.12
0.012	0.65	1.17	1.01	3.79
0.010	1.05	0.79	0.79	0.64
0.010	0.73	1.20	1.08	2.73
0.004	1.43	0.44	0.49	0.25
0.004	0.86	1.24	1.09	3.40
0.003	1.23	1.61	1.63	1.02

Obtained by dividing population by total number of B.A. degrees conferred for each state. Data were then computed as multiples of United States average (United States = 1.00).

Obtained by dividing population by total number of Ph.D. degrees conferred for each state. Data were then computed as multiples of United States average (United States = 1.00).

Ranking of states with most and least favorable population-degree ratios at three levels and according to per capita income and size of population, 1966–67	States with most favorable population-degree ratios	Population-degree ratio, total degrees, multiple of United States (United States = 100)	Population-degree ratio, B.A., multiple of United States (United States = 100)
	District of Columbia	0.44	0.49
	Massachusetts	0.62	0.70
	Oregon	0.79	0.79
	Wisconsin	0.87	0.85
	States with least favorable population-degree ratios:		
	Georgia	1.52	1.43
	Florida	1.60	1.53
	Delaware	1.61	1.63
	South Carolina	1.66	1.40

SOURCE: Table 2.3-10.

multiple each state's individual ratio represented of the United States average ratio. Except for Wisconsin at the bachelor's level, the four states with the most favorable population-degree rankings were the same at each of the three degree levels. The population of these four states ranged from less than 1 million (District of Columbia) to 5.4 million (Massachusetts). Per capita income of these states was equal to or exceeded the national average by the following proportions: District of Columbia, 43 percent; Massachusetts, 12 percent; and Oregon, 5 percent. The states experiencing the least favorable population-degree ratios were different at the doctor's level from those at aggregate and bachelor's degree levels. Except for South Carolina, at the most advanced level the multiple of the Ph.D.-population ratio was higher in Alabama, Idaho, and Mississippi than it was in states with the highest average population-degree ratios. There appeared to be about the same range in population in the four states with the most satisfactory and the least favorable population-degree ratios. Except for Delaware, in which per capita income was the second highest in the country, the other states reported per capita incomes that were

›pulation- ›gree ratio, ›.D., ultiple United States ›nited States = 100)	Per capita personal income, multiple of United States (United States = 100)	Size of state population, proportion of United States (United States = 100%)
0.25	1.43	0.004
0.42	1.12	0.028
0.64	1.05	0.010
0.66	1.00	0.021
2.29	0.81	0.023
1.58	0.90	0.031
1.02	1.23	0.003
5.12	0.74	0.014

below the national average by the following percentages: Georgia, 19 percent; Florida, 10 percent, and South Carolina, 26 percent.

One conclusion is that favorable population-degree ratios are usually associated with relatively high economic status, and this is particularly true at the doctor's level. Less satisfactory population-degree ratios seem to occur in states with relatively low per capita income. The only exception to this, as mentioned above, is Delaware, which has one of the poorest population-degree ratios but which is one of the richest states in the country.

FEDERAL FINANCE AND PH.D. PRODUCTION The distribution of doctor's degrees and of population in 1940–49 and 1960–61 are compared in Table 2.3-11. The rise between the 1940s and early 1960s in the ratio of shares of Ph.D. degrees produced to the share of population in the South Central and Mountain regions, areas which had relatively unfavorable ratios in the earlier period, is thought to be related to increased federal research and development funds made available to these regions during this period. In addition this table reveals the extremely favorable ratio of Ph.D.'s to population in the New England region at both dates,

TABLE 2.3-11 *Comparison of Ph.D. production and population*

	1940–1949			1960–1961		
Region	*Percent of total Ph.D.'s*	*Percent of total population*	*Ratio*	*Percent of total Ph.D.'s*	*Percent of total population*	*Ratio*
New England: Maine, New Hampshire, Vermont, Massachusetts, Rhode Island, Connecticut	12.6	6.4	1.97	9.8	5.9	1.66
Middle Atlantic: New York, New Jersey, Pennsylvania	22.5	20.8	1.08	20.1	19.1	1.05
East North Central: Ohio, Indiana, Illinois, Michigan, Wisconsin	31.8	20.6	1.55	28.1	20.2	1.39
West North Central: Minnesota, Iowa, Missouri, North Dakota, South Dakota, Kansas, Nebraska	11.8	10.8	1.09	9.8	8.6	1.14
South Atlantic: Delaware, Maryland, West Virginia, North Carolina, District of Columbia, South Carolina, Georgia, Florida	7.3	12.9	0.57	8.8	14.5	0.67
South Central: Kentucky, Tennessee, Alabama, Mississippi, Arkansas, Oklahoma, Texas, Louisiana	2.5	17.9	0.14	6.5	16.2	0.40
Mountain: Montana, Wyoming, Nevada, Colorado, New Mexico, Arizona, Utah, Idaho	0.8	3.0	0.27	2.7	3.8	0.71
Pacific: Washington, Oregon, California, Alaska, Hawaii	10.6	7.0	1.52	14.3	11.8	1.27

SOURCE: U.S. Senate, Committee on Labor and Public Welfare, *Impact of Federal Research and De* *velopment Policies on Scientific and Technical Manpower;* hearings before Subcommittee on Employmen and Manpower, June and July 1965, p. 44.

as well as the fact that the ratio for this region and the two othe most productive areas (Middle Atlantic and East North Centra regions) declined somewhat over this period.

DEGREES AND ENROLLMENT One approach to analyzing the performance of higher educationa institutions is to regard the output of graduates with degrees as a principal product of such institutions and to consider the ratio o degrees produced to degree-credit enrollment (D/E) as a measure o an institution's economic efficiency. The goal, then, of higher edu cational institutions would be to achieve as high a D/E ratio a possible, i.e., to increase the proportion of degree recipients in the total higher educational population. A high ratio can be achieved when the largest part of the student body is working toward a degree on a full-time basis, intending to graduate in as short a time as possible, and when the institution has a high retention rate (relatively few students leave before graduation). The inverse of the D/E ratio is the ratio of enrollment to degrees (E/D) which represents the average number of years required to obtain the degree in question. The lower the E/D ratio, the more efficient the institution. Data pertaining to both the D/E and the E/D ratios covering selected years between 1870 and 1968 and projections for 1978 for all degrees and for bachelor's and first professional degrees are set forth in Table 2.3-12.

During the period 1870–1968 the D/E ratio fluctuated. It declined between 1869 and 1900 and rose gradually afterwards. The ratio in 1968 for all degrees was 0.162 and for bachelor's and first professional degrees, 0.130. The Office of Education's prediction for 1977–78 is for the D/E ratio for all degrees to be comparable to that prevailing in 1967–68, but for some decline at the bachelor's and first-professional-degree level (Table 2.3-12).

It is important in interpreting the D/E ratio to be aware of the specific composition of the enrolled population. For example, in the case of the D/E ratio for bachelor's and first professional degrees, if enrollment includes graduate as well as undergraduate students, the ratio will be lower than it would be if graduate enrollment were

TABLE 2.3-12
Ratio of all degrees, and bachelor's and first professional degrees, to total four-year degree-credit enrollment, selected years 1870 to 1966–67 and projections for 1977–78

Year	Proportion of all degrees to enrollment	Proportion of B.A. and first professional degree to enrollment	Average number of years required for degree (enrollment/degrees)
1869–70*	0.179%	0.179%	5.6
1899–1900*	0.124	0.115	8.1
1929–30*	0.136	0.119	7.4
1963–64*	0.159	0.129	6.3
1967–68†	0.162	0.130	6.2
1977–78†	0.166	0.125	6.0

* SOURCE: U.S. Office of Education, *Digest of Educational Statistics, 1968,* 1968, p. 69. Enrollment data during this period refer to degree-credit resident students.

† SOURCE: U.S. Office of Education, *Projections of Educational Statistics to 1977–78,* National Center for Educational Statistics, 1968, pp. 19, 31. Enrollment data include all categories of degree-credit enrolled students.

TABLE 2.3-13
School retention rates — fifth grade through college entrance, 1926–1934 to 1959–1967

(Prior to 1962, excludes Alaska and Hawaii. Rates for the eighth grade through high school graduation are based on enrollments in successive grades in successive years in public elementary and secondary schools and are adjusted to include estimates for nonpublic schools. Rates for first-time college enrollment are based on data supplied by institutions of higher education.)

Year of entrance into fifth grade	Retention per 1,000 pupils who entered 5th grade					
	Fifth grade	Sixth grade	Seventh grade	Eighth grade	Ninth grade	Tenth grade
1926	1,000	919	824	754	677	552
1928	1,000	939	847	805	736	624
1930	1,000	943	872	824	770	652
1932	1,000	935	889	831	786	664
1934	1,000	953	892	842	803	711
1936	1,000	954	895	849	839	704
1938	1,000	955	908	853	796	655
1940	1,000	968	910	836	781	697
1942	1,000	954	909	847	807	713
1944	1,000	952	929	858	848	748
1946	1,000	954	945	919	872	775
1948	1,000	984	956	929	863	795
1950	1,000	981	968	921	836	809
1952	1,000	974	965	936	904	835
1954	1,000	980	979	948	915	855
1956	1,000	985	984	948	930	871
1958 (preliminary)	1,000	985	978	960	940	906
1959 (preliminary)	1,000	990	983	976	968	928

* Not calculated because of the influx of veterans in institutions of higher education.
SOURCE: U.S. Office of Education, *Digest of Educational Statistics, 1966, 1967,* and unpublished data.

removed. The 1963–64 data used in computing the bachelor's and first-professional-degree enrollment ratio in Table 2.3-12 included all categories of students, and worked out to 0.129. When enrollment was limited to B.A. students exclusively, the D/E ratio rose to 0.146. In the same year, the D/E ratio for graduate students was 0.25. In a study prepared in 1952, based on a special sample

Eleventh grade	*Twelfth grade*	*High school grad- uates*	*Year of high school grad- uation*	*First- time college students*
453	400	333	1934	129
498	432	378	1936	137
529	463	417	1938	148
570	510	455	1940	160
610	512	467	1942	129
554	425	323	1944	121
532	414	419	1946	*
566	507	481	1948	*
604	539	505	1950	205
650	549	522	1952	234
641	583	553	1954	283
706	619	581	1956	301
709	632	582	1958	303
746	667	621	1960	328
759	684	642	1962	343
790	728	676	1964	302
833	782	717	1966	394
853	785	721	1967	400

of higher educational institutions, D/E values ranged from 0.16 in 1930 to 0.22 in 1940, to 0.21 in 1950. Out of total enrollment in this sample, nonsectarian enrollment accounted for 8 percent. If nonsectarian and sectarian institutions differed, for example, in terms of average retention rates or degree-enrollment patterns, and if the performance of sectarian institutions was generally superior to that of nonsectarian ones, it would be reasonable to relate these high ratios to the composition of the sample of institutions.

The D/E ratio can be expected to increase when enrollment is stationary if the proportion of degrees to enrollment increases, and, under conditions of rising levels of enrollment, if the rise is accompanied by a proportionately larger increment in the number of degrees conferred. The latter can be achieved if, among other things, the proportion of students enrolled on a part-time basis declines, retention levels improve, and the residence requirements of the category of students who are enrolling at a faster rate are comparatively short.

Probably the most important reason for the rise in the D/E ratio since 1930 is the increase in graduate enrollment at the master's and first-professional-degree levels. However, an interpretation of the experience depicted in Table 2.3-12 reveals conflicting trends. On the one hand, over the long period there have been developments that would cause the D/E ratio to decline: there has been a rise over the long run in part-time attendance and non-degree-credit enrollment, an expansion of graduate enrollment in fields requiring comparatively long residence requirements, and a fairly high incidence of attrition at the college level. On the other hand, in recent years the proportion of students enrolled on a part-time basis has declined somewhat; the number of students enrolled in master's and first-professional-degree programs, where resident requirements are below the undergraduate norm, has increased significantly; and a smaller proportion of those entering school drop out than in the past (Table 2.3-13). These phenomena would have the effect of raising the D/E ratio.

More specific observations about part-time attendance and attrition illustrate the point just raised concerning the difficulty in interpreting trends. With the growth of metropolitan areas and large urban institutions, part-time attendance has grown absolutely and relatively. However, in 1967, part-time enrollment, which amounted to about 25 percent of total enrollment, accounted for a somewhat lower percentage than in 1957. The prediction of the Office of Education is for a slight relative rise in part-time enrollment by 1977. There has been, as suggested above, an improvement in school retention rates over the past 30 years. The greatest gain has been in those enrolling as first-time college students.

FIGURE 2.3-3 *School retention rates, fifth grade through college graduation, 1959–1971*

For every 10 pupils in the fifth grade in 1959–60

9.7 entered the ninth grade in 1963–64

8.5 entered the eleventh grade in 1965–66

7.2 graduated from high school in 1967

4.0 entered college in fall 1967

2.0 are likely to earn four-year degrees in 1971

SOURCE: U.S. Office of Education, *Digest of Educational Statistics, 1968,* 1968, p. 8.

School retention rates, 1926 and 1959; retention per 1,000 pupils who entered fifth grade		Year		Percentage rise, 1926–1959
Level	*1926*	*1959*		
Eighth grade	754	976		29
Twelfth grade	400	784		96
First-time college student	129	400		210

SOURCE: Table 2.3-12.

Nevertheless, additional Office of Education information indicates that, for every 10 pupils in the fifth grade in 1959–60, 4 were expected to enter college in the fall of 1967 and 2 were likely to earn four-year degrees in 1971. This meant that only about half of the entrants would graduate in four years. On the average, then, even if the assumption were that enrollment was stationary, the number of graduates with baccalaureates would account for about one-eighth rather than one-fourth of those enrolled (Figure 2.3-3).

Further data on the E/D ratio, that is, the average number of years experienced in obtaining a degree covering eight subject areas in 1954, are contained in Table 2.3-14. It appears that at the master's level the lowest ratio was in education (2.7) and the highest

TABLE 2.3-14 Ratio of graduate degrees to resident enrollment in major fields, April 1954*	Resident enroll-ment April 1954 (1)	Master's degrees, 1953–54 (2)	Ratio of column 1 to column 2 (3)	Doctor's degrees, 1953–54 (4)
Field				
Physical sciences	18,996	3,262	5.8	2,065
Life sciences	13,042	3,065	4.3	1,570
Engineering	14,249	3,295	4.3	482
Psychology	5,444	951	5.7	594
Social sciences	15,405	3,044	5.1	1,004
Education	51,053	18,735	2.7	1,092
Humanities	14,098	3,869	3.6	767
Professional fields	19,556	6,279	3.1	140
TOTAL	151,843	42,500	3.6	7,714

* Estimates made by department heads in April and May 1954 of the graduate degrees they expected to award during the academic year 1953–54.

SOURCE: National Science Foundation, *Graduate Student Enrollment and Support in American Universities and Colleges,* 1957, p. 17.

in physical sciences (5.8). At the doctor's level, the range was much greater. The average of 9 for the three lowest fields—life sciences, psychology, and physical sciences—was in sharp contrast to the ratio for professional fields of about 140. One explanation for the extremely unfavorable ratios of the Ph.D. degrees to resident enrollment in education and the professions is that, although a large number of students in these fields were enrolled in master's degree programs, a very small proportion were seeking Ph.D. degrees.

	All degrees, 1953–54	
Ratio of column 1 to column 4 (5)	*Number* (6)	*Percentage of doctor's degrees* (7)
9.2	5,327	39
8.3	4,635	34
29.6	3,777	13
9.2	1,545	38
15.3	4,048	25
46.8	19,827	6
18.4	4,636	17
139. 7	6,419	2
19.7	50,214	15

2.4. Institutions: Various Aspects

A presentation of the number of institutions of higher education granting degrees at three levels by type of institution is contained in Table 2.4-1. The following comments, which are based on this table, summarize the changes that occurred at each of these levels over the decade 1953–54 to 1963–64.

At the first level (bachelor's and first professional), these developments occurred: (1) the number of public universities more

(Text continued on p. 358)

TABLE 2.4-1
Number of institutions of higher education conferring earned degrees, by level, institutional control, and type, 1953–54 and 1963–64

| | Total I.H.E. | First level (bachelor's and first professional) | | | |
| | | Public | | Private | |
		University	Other	University	Other
1953–54	1,315	69	297	62	887
(%)		(5.2)	(22.6)	(4.7)	(67.5)
1963–64	1,745	160	313	113	1,159
(%)		(9.2)	(17.9)	(6.5)	(66.4)
		Master's (except first professional)			
1953–54	522	68	140	60	254
(%)		(13.0)	(26.9)	(11.5)	(48.7)
1963–64	650	88	193	58	311
(%)		(13.5)	(29.7)	(9.0)	(47.8)
		Doctors			
1953–54	158	51	16	40	51
(%)		(32.3)	(10.1)	(25.3)	(32.3)
1963–64	212	83	19	48	62
(%)		(39.2)	(9.0)	(22.6)	(29.2)

SOURCE: P. Wright, *Earned Degrees Conferred, 1963–64: Bachelor's and Higher Degrees,* U.S. Office of Education, National Center for Educational Statistics, 1966, pp. 3–4.

355

TABLE 2.4-2 *Number of degrees conferred by institutions of higher education, by level, aggregate United States, 1963–64 (largest institutions ranked in descending order of size)*

Rank	4-year-bachelor's Institution	Number	5-or-more-year first professional Institution	Number
1	City University of New York (all institutions)	9,083	Harvard University	1,389
2	University of California (all campuses)	8,214	University of California (all campuses)	1,311
3	State University of New York (all institutions)	7,721	Columbia University	1,211
4	Michigan State University of Agriculture & Applied Science	4,399	Ohio State University	780
5	University of Wisconsin	4,059	University of Southern California	754
6	University of Minnesota	3,781	University of Michigan	739
7	University of Illinois	3,768	University of Chicago	718
8	Pennsylvania State University	3,670	New York University	713
9	University of Michigan	3,448	University of Minnesota	699
10	University of Texas	3,259	University of Illinois	687
11	Ohio State University	3,131	Cornell University	669
12	New York University	2,974	University of Texas	622
13	University of Missouri	2,917	University of Florida	595
14	San Jose State College	2,831	University of Pittsburgh	559
15	University of Washington	2,717	State University of New York (all institutions)	540
16	University of Maryland	2,593	University of Pennsylvania	535
17	Indiana University	2,577	Western Reserve University	532
18	Purdue University	2,482	University of Tennessee	470
19	Rutgers University	2,381	Northwestern University	459
20	University of Puerto Rico	2,278	University of Puerto Rico	454
21	San Francisco State College	2,236	University of Washington	445
22	Boston University	2,184	Georgetown University	441
23	LA State College of Applied Arts & Science	2,160	Yale University	424
24	Syracuse University	2,121	Rutgers University	401

Master's (except first professional)		Doctor's	
Institution	*Number*	*Institution*	*Number*
University of California (all campuses)	2,899	University of California (all campuses)	865
New York University	2,582	Columbia University	602
University of Michigan	2,550	University of Illinois	495
Columbia University	2,347	Harvard University	483
State University of New York (all institutions)	2,053	University of Wisconsin	458
University of Illinois	1,814	University of Michigan	403
Indiana University	1,809	New York University	362
City University of New York (all institutions)	1,755	Ohio State University	341
University of Wisconsin	1,586	Indiana University	322
George Washington University	1,288	University of Minnesota	316
Michigan State University of Agriculture & Applied Science	1,174	Massachusetts Institute of Technology	306
University of Minnesota	1,139	Michigan State University of Agriculture & Applied Science	303
Stanford University	1,132	Purdue University	302
University of Pennsylvania	1,123	Stanford University	301
Harvard University	1,088	University of Chicago	273
University of Missouri	1,065	Cornell University	259
Purdue University	1,013	Yale University	253
University of Southern California	984	University of Texas	243
Ohio State University	958	University of Iowa	223
Boston University	944	University of Pennsylvania	212
Wayne State University	833	State University of New York (all institutions)	203
Syracuse University	779	Iowa State University of Science & Technology	201
Massachusetts Institute of Technology	774	Pennsylvania State University	201
Yale University	738	Northwestern University	198

TABLE 2.4-2 *(continued)*

	4-year-bachelor's		5-or-more-year first professional	
Rank	Institution	Number	Institution	Number
25	Wayne State University	2,048	Stanford University	389
26	University of Colorado	1,985	Indiana University	380
27	Florida State University	1,969	Emory University	371

NOTE: The City University of New York is comprised of four separate degree-granting institutions; the State University of New York, 19.

SOURCE: P. Wright, *Earned Degrees Conferred, 1963–64; Bachelor's and Higher Degrees*, U.S. Office of Education, National Center for Educational Statistics, 1966, p. 20.

than doubled, raising the share they represented of all higher educational institutions from 5.2 percent to 9.2 percent, (2) the share accounted for by private universities increased from 4.7 percent to 6.5 percent, (3) the number of other public institutions remained about the same, which meant that they represented a smaller proportion of the total, and (4) other private institutions were the most numerous, accounting for approximately two-thirds of all first-level institutions in both years.

The number of institutions offering the master's degree rose by one-quarter during this period. The share of these institutions accounted for by public universities (around 13 percent) was about the same in both years. The largest number of schools at this level were other private institutions and other public institutions, accounting for approximately 50 percent and 30 percent, respectively, of all institutions granting the master's degree in both years.

Doctoral degrees were earned at 212 institutions in 1963–64, a one-third increase over 1953–54. In 1963–64, public universities offering the doctor's degree accounted for two-fifths of all institutions providing degrees at this level, which represented a 7 percentage point increase over the decade. This rise was accompanied by relative declines in the shares of all other public and private institutions.

SEPARATE INSTITUTIONS The Office of Education annually compiles statistics on the number of degrees at four levels conferred by each institution of higher education. In Table 2.4-2, 27 of the institutions that conferred the largest number of degrees at four levels in 1963–64 are listed. At

Master's (except first professional)		Doctor's	
Institution	*Number*	*Institution*	*Number*
University of Washington	736	Princeton University	192
Pennsylvania State University	705	University of Washington	182
University of Iowa	687	University of Southern California	175

TABLE 2.4-3   *State and land-grant institutions awarding the most doctorates, 1958–59 and 1964–65*

Institution	1958–59	1964–65	Percentage of increase from 1958–59 to 1964–65
University of California	453	1,048*	131
University of Wisconsin	373	531	42
University of Illinois	332	493	48
Ohio State University	253	397	57
Michigan State University	145	368	159
University of Minnesota	240	366	53
University of Michigan	307	364	19
Indiana University	182	342	88
Massachusetts Institute of Technology	192	335	74
Purdue University	177	322	82
Cornell University	211	312	48
University of Texas	142	249	75
Pennsylvania State University	129	232	80

University of California: combined 1964–65 total for seven campuses—Berkeley (585 degrees), Los Angeles (306), Davis (87), San Francisco (22), San Diego (21), and Santa Barbara (6).
SOURCE: University of California, *Growth and Distinction: The University of California 1958–66,* University of California Press, Berkeley, 1967.

TABLE 2.4-4 *Number of institutions of higher education, by type of program and highest level of offering, aggregate United States, 1963–64*

Type of program	Total	Highest level of offering				
		I Two but less than four years of work beyond the twelfth grade	*II* Only bachelor's and/or first professional degree	*III* Master's and/or second professional degree	*IV* Doctor of philosophy and equivalent degree	*V* Other
TOTAL	2,139	644	792	455	223	25
a—*Terminal-occupational (below bachelor's degree)*	52	50				2
b—*Liberal arts and general*	153	63	71	17		2
c—*Liberal arts and general, and terminal-occupational*	380	357	22			1
d—*Primarily teacher preparatory*	99	31	31	35	1	1
e—*Liberal arts, general, and teacher preparatory*	561	33	367	151	10	
f—*Liberal arts, general, terminal-occupational, and teacher preparatory*	244	93	109	40	2	
g—*Professional only (not including teacher-preparatory)*	202	5	80	65	43	9
h—*Professional and teacher preparatory*	74	6	21	28	14	5
i—*Professional and terminal-occupational*	40	5	25	5	2	3
j—*Liberal arts and general with one or two professional schools*	143	1	62	64	14	2
k—*Liberal arts and general with three or more professional schools*	191		4	50	137	

SOURCE: U.S. Office of Education, *Education Directory, 1963–64, Part 3: Higher Education,* 1964, p. 9.

each of these levels, the university providing the largest number of degrees was as follows: bachelor's—City University of New York, 9,083 degrees; first professional—Harvard University, 1,389 degrees; master's—University of California (all campuses), 2,899 degrees; and doctor's—University of California (all campuses), 865 degrees.

A summary of the number of doctorates awarded by public institutions (state and land-grant institutions) in 1958–59 and 1964–65 and the percentage change over this period are contained in Table 2.4-3. The growth of doctoral degrees over this period ranged from less than 100 percent for the University of Michigan, Ohio State University, M.I.T., Cornell, and the University of Wisconsin, to over 100 percent for the University of California and Michigan State University.

PROGRAM AND LEVEL OF OFFERING A breakdown of the total number of institutions of higher education in 1963–64 by type of program and highest level of offering appears in Table 2.4-4. Of all institutions, the largest number offered bachelor's degrees, first professional degrees, or both as their highest-level degree. Another large group of institutions, chiefly two-year colleges, offered two but less than four years of work beyond the twelfth grade. Institutions with master's degrees and doctor's degrees as their highest offerings together accounted for around one-third of the total; there were about twice as many institutions offering master's degrees as doctor's degrees.

The Office of Education lists 11 types of programs offered by all institutions of higher education. These consist of different combinations of programs, including degrees below the bachelor's (terminal occupational), and degrees at liberal arts, teacher preparatory, and professional levels. Institutions with the following programs were the most numerous (proportion of total in parentheses): both liberal arts and general and teacher preparatory (26 percent); liberal arts and general and terminal occupational (18 percent); liberal arts and general, terminal occupational, teacher preparatory (12 percent). Approximately two-thirds of those institutions with programs defined as "both liberal arts and general and teacher preparatory," which accounted for the majority of institutional programs, had as their highest level of offering the bachelor's degree, the first professional degree, or both (Table 2.4-4).

INSTITUTIONAL CONTROL AND SEX OF STUDENT BODY Table 2.4-5 provides data on the distribution of higher educational institutions according to institutional control, sex of student body, and highest level of offering in 1969–70. For breakdown of institutions on the basis of institutional control, see page 364.

(Text continued on p. 364)

					Public	
TABLE 2.4-5 Number of institutions of higher education, by highest level of offering, sex of student body, and institutional control; aggregate United States, 1969–70	Highest level of offering and sex of student body (1)	Total (2)	Federal (3)	State (4)
	TOTAL	2,551	8	707
	Two but less than four years beyond high school	903	1	304
	Coeducational	823	1	302
	Men only	22		2
	Women only	58		
	Four- or five-year baccalaureate degree	754	5	73
	Coeducational	559		69
	Men only	63	5	3
	Women only	132		1
	First professional degree	81		6
	Coeducational	61		6
	Men only	20		
	Women only			
	Master's degree	425		136
	Coeducational	346		131
	Men only	43		1
	Women only	36		4
	Beyond master's but less than doctorate	92		58
	Coeducational	83		58
	Men only	9		
	Women only			
	Doctorate	296	2	130
	Coeducational	276	2	129
	Men only	17		
	Women only	3		1

* Includes 1 Greek Orthodox, 1 Interdenominational, 19 Jewish, 5 Latter Day Saints, 1 Russian Orthodox, 2 Unitarian-Universalist, and 2 "other."

† Includes one undergraduate non-degree-granting institution.

‡ Includes two undergraduate non-degree-granting institutions.

§ Includes one graduate non-degree-granting institution.

SOURCE: U.S. Office of Education, *Education Directory, 1969–70,* 1970, p. 16.

Local (city, county, or district) (5)	Independent of religious group (6)	Private		
		Religious group		
		Protestant (7)	Catholic (8)	Other (9)
364	637	486	318	31*
345	120	78	53	2
345	81	74	18	2
	9		11	
	30	4	24	
5	253	261	152	5
5	194†	240‡	47	4
	14	7	33	1
	45	14	72	
	36	22	10	7
	34	17	3	1
	2	5	7	6
3	125	88	67	6
3	103§	83	24	2
	6	5	27	4
	16		16	
3	12	6	11	2
3	11	6	5	
	1		6	2
8	91	31	25	9
8	82	30	19	6
	7	1	6	3
	2			

Type of control	Proportion of total
All institutions	1.00
Public	0.42
State	0.28
Local	0.14
Private	0.58
Independent of religious group	0.25
Protestant	0.19
Roman Catholic	0.13
Other	0.01

SOURCE: Table 2.4-5.

About 35 percent of all institutions had two but less than four years beyond high school as their highest level of offering, and 30 percent had four- or five-year baccalaureate degrees as their highest level of offering. Approximately 17 percent and 12 percent of all institutions had as their highest level of offering the master's degree and the doctorate, respectively.

The highest level of offering of practically all local public institutions was two to four years beyond the twelfth grade. About 40 percent of state public institutions had two to four years beyond twelfth grade as the highest level of offering; 20 percent had the master's degree, and another 20 percent had the doctorate as their highest level of offering. Two-fifths of private independent institutions counted as their highest level of offering the bachelor's degree, the first professional degree, or both. All institutions at all levels were predominately coeducational.

TYPES AND INSTITUTIONAL CONTROL

Historical trends

A summary of the growth of higher educational institutions over the decade ending in 1965 is contained in Table 2.4-6. During this period, the number of institutions of higher education increased by 20 percent from 1,858 in 1955 to a total of 2,230 in 1965. The gains were greater for public institutions (25 percent) than for private ones (17 percent). Approximately one-half of the rise in the number of institutions was accounted for by the growth of junior colleges. In the latter, the number of institutions under public control increased twice as fast as the number under private authority. Increases of the following order of magnitude occurred in different

TABLE 2.4-6
Number of
postsecondary
institutions by
type and
control, 1955
and 1965

Institutions by type	1955*	1965†	Change	Ratio: 1965 : 1955
All	1,858	2,230	+372	1.20
Public	655	821	+166	1.25
Private	1,203	1,409	+206	1.17
Universities	141	154	+ 13	1.09
Public	81	89	+ 8	1.10
Private	60	65	+ 5	1.08
Liberal arts colleges	732	815	+ 83	1.11
Public	82	116	+ 34	1.41
Private	650	699	+ 49	1.08
Teachers colleges	192	186	− 6	.97
Public	168	158	− 10	.94
Private	24	28	+ 4	1.17
Technological schools	44	55	+ 11	1.25
Public	22	26	+ 4	1.18
Private	22	29	+ 7	1.32
Theological schools				
Private	124	207	+ 83	1.67
Other professional schools	120	134	+ 14	1.18
Public	10	12	+ 2	1.20
Private	110	122	+ 12	1.11
Junior colleges	505‡	679§	+174	1.34
Public	292	420	+128	1.44
Private	213	259	+ 46	1.22

* Office of Education, National Center for Educational Statistics, *Statistics of Higher Education: 1955–56,* chap. 4, sec. 1, table V, p. 14.

† Office of Education, National Center for Educational Statistics, *Digest of Educational Statistics, 1966,* table 99, p. 78.

‡ Includes community colleges, technical institutes, and county teachers colleges (normal schools) offering at least two but fewer than four years of college-level work immediately beyond the high school.

§ Includes 57 (28 public, 29 private) "technical institutes and semiprofessional schools" separately classified in 1965. These types of institutions were included, as per above note, with junior colleges in 1955.

SOURCE: U.S. Office of Education, *Students and Buildings: An Analysis of Selected Federal Programs for Higher Education,* 1968, table A-1.

types of institutions: theological schools, 67 percent; technological schools, 25 percent; other professional schools, 18 percent; liberal arts colleges, 11 percent; and universities, 9 percent. There was a decline in the number of teachers colleges over this period.

(Text continued on p. 368)

TABLE 2.4-7 *Total enrollment and number of public and private junior colleges by year and state, and the percentage of increase of 1954 over 1930*

State	1929–30 Number of colleges	1929–30 Enroll-ment	1934–35 Number of colleges	1934–35 Enroll-ment	1939–40 Number of colleges	1939–40 Enroll-ment
Alabama	5	286	8	556	8	1,173
Arizona	2	641	2	863	2	1,184
Arkansas	11	1,864	10	2,443	9	2,692
California	50	17,072	55	36,977	64	86,357
Colorado	5	792	5	743	7	2,106
Connecticut	3	182	5	388	14	3,170
Delaware	0		0		0	
District of Columbia	7	314	10	645	11	3,049
Florida	3	256	7	902	7	1,908
Georgia	12	1,083	19	3,345	20	5,635
Idaho	2	859	5	1,940	4	2,110
Illinois	18	8,222	21	9,904	24	19,589
Indiana	3	268	6	542	5	623
Iowa	37	2,357	37	3,066	36	3,768
Kansas	18	2,413	19	3,494	24	5,798
Kentucky	17	2,021	17	3,012	14	3,514
Louisiana	4	194	7	702	3	876
Maine	3	137	3	245	4	517
Maryland	5	314	6	518	8	1,163
Massachusetts	10	593	9	831	23	5,994
Michigan	9	2,158	12	2,785	13	4,187
Minnesota	10	1,540	9	2,068	16	3,326
Mississippi	14	1,574	21	4,117	22	5,205
Missouri	23	5,275	22	4,537	24	8,143
Montana	2	859	5	1,940	4	2,110
Nebraska	10	718	7	727	5	800
New Hampshire	1	120	3	368	3	530
New Jersey	2	125	10	2,097	11	2,900
New Mexico	1	235	2	520	2	1,319
New York	11	1,053	6	859	12	2,936
North Carolina	16	1,975	23	3,584	25	6,602
North Dakota	2	402	2	239	4	912

1944–45		1949–50		1953–54		Percentage of increase over 1930	
Number of colleges	*Enroll-ment*	*Number of colleges*	*Enroll-ment*	*Number of colleges*	*Enroll-ment*	*Number of colleges*	*Enroll-ment*
9	1,010	9	2,719	10	1,702	100	495
2	1,086	2	2,410	2	3,138	0	390
9	1,792	7	4,077	5	2,181	−55	17
74	120,685	78	246,708	73	294,508	46	1,625
7	3,222	8	7,605	8	7,605	60	852
13	3,586	10	8,562	7	8,472	133	4,554
1	124	1	147	1	179		
6	852	6	8,475	6	2,377	−14	657
9	1,481	9	3,245	10	4,815	233	1,781
20	4,637	19	12,472	18	14,832	50	1,270
4	1,634	3	2,030	2	2,514	0	193
24	9,192	26	28,943	22	32,455	22	295
4	462	3	472	8	9,983	167	3,625
22	1,446	26	6,512	23	8,278	−38	251
20	2,368	21	5,719	23	6,068	28	151
15	1,947	15	4,545	14	3,453	−18	71
2	839	3	1,127	1	239	−75	23
6	413	4	1,285	4	595	33	334
5	1,951	9	2,445	10	2,286	100	229
20	3,129	22	7,723	18	6,225	80	950
13	3,168	13	11,286	17	17,937	89	731
14	1,658	12	5,157	11	7,702	10	400
22	3,674	23	11,670	23	8,859	64	463
23	6,953	24	11,450	22	10,016	− 4	90
4	1,634	3	2,039	2	2,514	50	242
5	1,137	6	3,350	5	2,183	−50	190
1	360	1	395	1	459	0	283
9	1,732	14	7,998	10	3,292	80	2,534
1	93	0				0	0
19	8,176	28	20,981	31	23,415	182	2,124
24	4,419	24	7,357	24	8,127	50	311
5	345	4	1,540	4	1,484	100	269

TABLE 2.4-7 *(continued)*

State	1929–30 Number of colleges	1929–30 Enroll-ment	1934–35 Number of colleges	1934–35 Enroll-ment	1939–40 Number of colleges	1939–40 Enroll-ment
Ohio	5	1,381	8	2,865	8	2,203
Oklahoma	14	1,908	24	3,281	30	5,409
Oregon	2	112	2	164	2	758
Pennsylvania	7	923	10	1,167	24	4,844
Rhode Island	0		0		0	
South Carolina	2	311	4	405	11	1,553
South Dakota	5	267	4	472	4	363
Tennessee	12	1,785	12	2,727	14	2,860
Texas	44	8,473	43	10,558	43	15,085
Utah	5	815	5	1,537	6	3,299
Vermont	0		1	162	3	454
Virginia	11	1,349	13	2,205	16	3,166
Washington	6	558	10	1,021	8	1,398
West Virginia	5	455	5	1,117	4	1,052
Wisconsin	2	91	6	1,129	7	4,273
Wyoming	0		0		0	
Grand total	436	74,088	518	122,311	610	236,162

SOURCE: L. L. Medsker, *The Junior College: Progress and Prospect,* McGraw-Hill Book Company, New York, 1960, table 3.

Junior colleges

The number of junior colleges rose from 8 in 1901 to 598 in 1954. Between 1929–30 and 1953–54, increases in the number and enrollment of junior colleges were 37 percent and 741 percent, respectively (Table 2.4-7). In 1953–54 there were 73 junior colleges in California (12 percent of all junior colleges in the country), reporting an enrollment of about 247,000 (47 percent of total junior college enrollment). Other states with junior college enrollment exceeding 10,000 were: Texas, 47,332; Illinois, 32,455; New York, 23,415; Washington, 18,762; Michigan, 17,937; Georgia, 14,832; Missouri, 10,016; and Pennsylvania, 12,722. Of the nine states that accounted for the largest proportion of junior college enrollment, only Georgia could be classified as a relatively low-income

1944–45		1949–50		1953–54		Percentage of increase over 1930	
Number of colleges	Enroll-ment	Number of colleges	Enroll-ment	Number of colleges	Enroll-ment	Number of colleges	Enroll-ment
8	2,255	8	5,631	7	4,979	40	261
17	1,452	19	6,023	16	5,072	14	166
2	787	2	3,908	5	5,870	60	5,141
20	2,472	21	8,042	25	12,722	257	1,278
2	342	2	604	1	547		
11	1,199	8	1,534	7	1,358	250	337
5	446	4	347	3	335	−40	25
13	1,984	11	4,134	9	2,360	−25	32
48	15,221	58	53,931	45	47,332	2	459
6	15,521	4	4,847	4	6,266	−20	669
3	412	2	559	2	467		
15	4,374	15	5,215	14	6,084	27	351
8	1,568	10	14,181	10	18,762	67	3,262
4	620	4	2,475	4	1,168	−20	157
9	6,210	16	5,986	12	6,722	500	7,287
1	198	4	1,658	4	2,793		
591	251,290	634	562,786	598	622,864	37	741

state. The junior college, it seems, is attractive to the more affluent states because it represents an efficient solution to the problem of providing an opportunity for those living in cities to obtain some education beyond high school at convenient urban locations.

More recent data indicate that in the 14-year interval between 1954 and 1968, the number of two-year institutions almost doubled and enrollment at such institutions tripled (Table 2.4-8).

Recent patterns for all types of institutions

Presented in Table 2.4-9 are estimates of the number of institutions of higher education by type, control, and state in 1964–65. For the country as a whole, liberal arts and junior college institutions

		Enrollment*
	Number of	(numbers in
State	institutions	thousands)
United States	1,072	1,871.0
Alabama	19	19.9
Alaska	7	0.7
Arizona	9	32.1
Arkansas	5	3.8
California	90	600.8
Colorado	10	13.2
Connecticut	25	20.4
Delaware	4	4.5
District of Columbia	5	3.9
Florida	33	95.4
Georgia	21	19.6
Hawaii	8	6.3
Idaho	5	6.6
Illinois	58	113.7
Indiana	9	7.4
Iowa	25	18.9
Kansas	21	14.1
Kentucky	23	11.9
Louisiana	6	6.6
Maine	4	0.4
Maryland	20	27.1
Massachusetts	40	40.2
Michigan	42	99.7
Minnesota	24	16.3
Mississippi	28	22.0
Missouri	20	28.6
Montana	3	1.2
Nebraska	9	3.6
Nevada	0	0.0
New Hampshire	4	1.2
New Jersey	22	24.2
New Mexico	6	3.0
New York	67	168.0
North Carolina	60	37.4

TABLE 2.4-8 Total enrollment and number of public and private two-year institutions by state, 1968

TABLE 2.4-8
(continued)

State	Number of institutions	Enrollment* (number in thousands)
North Dakota	6	5.0
Ohio	35	43.3
Oklahoma	18	10.9
Oregon	16	25.1
Pennsylvania	58	56.1
Rhode Island	3	5.7
South Carolina	27	13.1
South Dakota	2	0.3
Tennessee	12	9.0
Texas	51	97.0
Utah	6	4.9
Vermont	4	1.9
Virginia	30	22.7
Washington	22	66.8
West Virginia	9	4.2
Wisconsin	35	27.1
Wyoming	6	4.8

* 1968 enrollments, which include both degree-credit and non-degree-credit enrollments, are based on U.S. Office of Education data; enrollments on two-year campuses of public four-year institutions are not included in OE data, but have been added. 1.87 million students enrolled on these two-year campuses in 1968.

SOURCE: Carnegie Commission on Higher Education, *The Open-Door Colleges: Policies for the Community Colleges,* McGraw-Hill Book Company, New York, 1970, pp. 58–61.

accounted for about three-fifths of all institutions, and of these, the former were predominately private and the latter, though more evenly divided, were largely public.

Among states, the variation in the structure of institutions is the product of, among other things, differing traditions, economic status, and governing public policies. To illustrate the impact of these differences, Table 2.4-10 was constructed. It includes data for the United States and four states—Alabama, California, New York, and Kansas. In 1964–65, liberal arts institutions and junior colleges accounted for over half of all higher educational institutions in each of these states.

(Text continued on p. 378)

TABLE 2.4-9   *Number of institutions of higher education, by type, control, and state, fall 1965*

State (1)	All institu- tions (2)	Universities		Liberal arts colleges		Teachers colleges	
		Public (3)	Private (4)	Public (5)	Private (6)	Public (7)	Private (8)
United States	2,230	89	65	116	699	158	28
Alabama	37	2		3	12	5	
Alaska	3	1			1		
Arizona	11	2			1	1	
Arkansas	19	1		5	8	2	
California	182	1	3	14	38	2	1
Colorado	21	2	1	2	4	3	
Connecticut	41	1	1		13	4	1
Delaware	4	1		1			
District of Columbia	22		5		3	1	
Florida	49	3	1	2	11		
Georgia	51	1	1	10	16	2	
Hawaii	4	1			2		
Idaho	9	1		3	2		
Illinois	115	3	5	1	35	4	4
Indiana	42	2	2		23	2	1
Iowa	51	2	1		24	1	
Kansas	46	3		2	17	2	
Kentucky	38	2		1	16	4	
Louisiana	22	1	2	8	5	1	1
Maine	22	1			8	5	
Maryland	44	1	1	2	11	5	
Massachusetts	103	1	7		29	9	2
Michigan	74	3	1	5	19	1	
Minnesota	49	1			16	5	1
Mississippi	43	2		3	9	3	
Missouri	65	1	2	1	20	6	
Montana	11	2		1	3	2	
Nebraska	24	1	1	1	8	4	1
Nevada	1	1					
New Hampshire	17	1			7	2	
New Jersey	42	1	2		11	6	

Technological schools		Theological schools, private	Other professional schools		Junior colleges		Technical institutes and semiprofessional schools	
Public (9)	Private (10)	private (11)	Public (12)	Private (13)	Public (14)	Private (15)	Public (16)	Private (17)
26	29	207	12	122	392	230	28	29
		1			9	5		
						1		
				1	6			
		1				2		
2	5	23	1	14	72	3	2	1
1		3			5			
	1	5		1	2	7	4	1
						2		
		6		2		3		2
	2	1			24	4		1
1		4	1		7	8		
						1		
					1	2		
	3	16		12	18	13		1
	3	5		2	1	1		
		2		1	16	4		
		3			15	4		
		5			1	9		
		2				2		
1		1		3		2		1
		4		5	12	2		1
3	1	11	1	8	10	16	1	4
1	2	9		7	19	5		2
		9		3	11	2		1
					17	9		
		10		6	9	9		1
1					2			
		1			5	2		
		2		2			3	
1	1	6	1	3	1	8	1	

TABLE 2.4-9 *(continued)*

State (1)	All institutions (2)	Universities Public (3)	Universities Private (4)	Liberal arts colleges Public (5)	Liberal arts colleges Private (6)	Teachers colleges Public (7)	Teachers colleges Private (8)
New Mexico	10	2		1	2	2	1
New York	194	2	11	6	51	10	7
North Carolina	63	2	2	7	24	6	
North Dakota	13	2			2	4	
Ohio	77	8	1	2	39		1
Oklahoma	35	2	1	4	6	5	
Oregon	33	2	1	2	8	3	1
Pennsylvania	132	1	6	1	56	13	
Rhode Island	14	1			5	1	1
South Carolina	33	2		2	17		
South Dakota	15	2			6	4	
Tennessee	48	1	1	4	26	2	1
Texas	97	6	4	11	26	4	
Utah	9	2	1	2	1		
Vermont	17	1			9	3	
Virginia	48	2		4	17	3	
Washington	33	2			9	3	1
West Virginia	21	1		3	7	6	
Wisconsin	62	1	1	2	16	7	3
Wyoming	6	1					
U.S. service schools	8						
Outlying areas	8	1		1	3		
Canal Zone	1						
Guam	1			1			
Puerto Rico	5	1			3		
Virgin Islands	1						

SOURCE: U.S. Office of Education, "Opening Fall Enrollment in Higher Education, 1965"; in U.S. Office of Education, *Digest of Educational Statistics, 1966,* 1967, p. 78.

Technological schools		Theological schools, private	Other professional schools		Junior colleges		Technical institutes and semiprofessional schools	
Public (9)	Private (10)	private (11)	Public (12)	Private (13)	Public (14)	Private (15)	Public (16)	Private (17)
1					1			
2	6	19	5	14	24	26	10	1
		2			3	15	1	1
					4	1		
	1	8		9	2	3		3
		2		1	12	2		
		4		1	7	3	1	
	1	20		16	1	15		2
		1		2	1	2		
1		2	1			5	2	1
1						2		
		3		3		6	1	
1	1	6		1	30	7		
					1			2
				1		1	1	1
1	1	4	2	1		10	1	2
		2			16			
					1	3		
	1	4		3	21	3		
					5			
8								
					2	1		
					1			
						1		
					1			

TABLE 2.4-10 Types and institutional control of institutions of higher education for the United States and four selected states, 1964–65		United States	Alabama
	Total institutions (number)	2230	37
	Total institutions (percent)	100.00*	100.00
		(percent of total)	(percent of total)
University			
	Total	0.07	0.05
	Public	0.04	0.05
	Private	0.03	
Liberal arts			
	Total	0.36	0.40
	Public	0.05	0.08
	Private	0.31	0.32
Teachers colleges			
	Total	0.08	0.14
	Public	0.07	0.14
	Private	0.01	
Technological schools			
	Total	0.02	
	Public	0.01	
	Private	0.01	
Theological schools			
	Total	0.09	0.03
	Public		
	Private	0.09	0.03
Other professional			
	Total	0.06	
	Public	†	
	Private	0.05	
Junior colleges			
	Total	0.28	0.38
	Public	0.18	0.24
	Private	0.10	0.14
Technical and semiprofessional			
	Total	0.02	
	Public	0.01	
	Private	0.01	

*Totals may not sum to 100.00 percent because of rounding.

† Less than 0.01.

SOURCE: U.S. Office of Education, *Digest of Educational Statistics, 1966*, 1967, p. 78.

California	New York	Kansas
182	194	46
100.00	100.00	100.00
percent of total)	(percent of total)	(percent of total)
0.03	0.07	0.07
0.01	0.01	0.07
0.02	0.06	
0.29	0.29	0.41
0.08	0.03	0.04
0.21	0.26	0.37
0.01	0.09	0.04
0.01	0.05	0.04
†	0.04	
0.04	0.04	
0.01	0.01	
0.03	0.03	
0.12	0.10	0.07
0.12	0.10	0.07
0.08	0.10	
†	0.03	
0.08	0.07	
0.42	0.25	0.42
0.40	0.12	0.33
0.02	0.13	0.09
0.02	0.06	
0.01	0.05	
0.01	†	

Area	Total: liberal arts and junior colleges (proportion of all institutions)	Liberal arts (proportion of all institutions)	Junior colleges (proportion of all institutions)
United States	0.63	0.36	0.27
Alabama	0.78	0.40	0.38
California	0.71	0.29	0.42
New York	0.54	0.29	0.25
Kansas	0.83	0.41	0.42

SOURCE: Table 2.4-10.

In Alabama, which is relatively poor compared to New York and California, the share represented by teachers colleges was almost two times the national average, and other professional schools, technical institutions, and semiprofessional schools were non-existent. In the more affluent states, such as California and New York, other professional schools and technical institutions were of significance, while teachers colleges represented a very small pro-portion of all institutions. Kansas shared some of the same struc-tural features as California—a heavy investment in public junior colleges and minimal reliance on teachers colleges. It had in common with Alabama the absence of other professional and technical institutions and an abundance of liberal arts institu-tions.

CONCENTRA-TION OF HIGHER DEGREES Over the decade ending in 1963–64, the percentage rise in the number of institutions offering bachelor's and doctor's degrees was about the same (33 percent) and was somewhat lower for master's degrees (25 percent) (Table 2.4-1). However, the relative increase in the number of students seeking doctor's degrees is considerably in excess of that for those obtaining first-level and master's degrees. These additional numbers have been absorbed by the increased capacity of existing institutions for offering doctoral degrees. The conferring of the Ph.D. has become the responsibility of increasing numbers of institutions of higher education. The average institu-tion awards a rising number of Ph.D.'s.

Concentration of doctoral degrees by institution and average number of degrees offered per institution, 1908, 1928, 1958, and 1964			

Year	Number of institutions offering doctoral degrees	Number of Ph.D. degrees awarded	Average number of degrees offered per institution
1908	38	394	10
1928	69	1,447	21
1958	175	8,942	51
1964	212	14,490	68

SOURCE: Figure 2.4-1 for 1908, 1928, and 1958. The sources for 1964 are Table 2.4-1 and U.S. Office of Education, *Digest of Educational Statistics, 1966,* 1967, p. 82.

FIGURE 2.4-1　*Concentration of doctorates by institution — 1908, 1928, 1958*

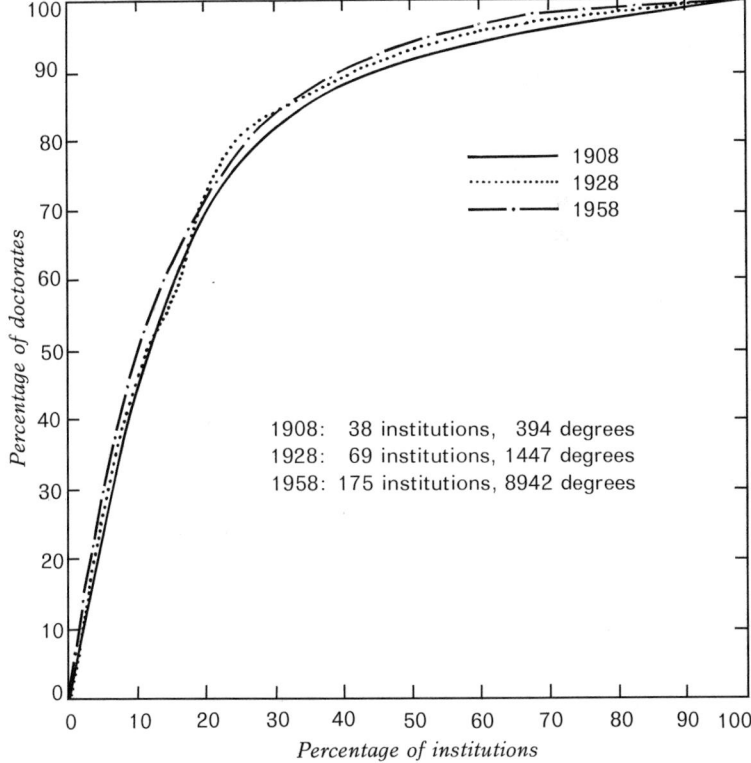

SOURCE: B. Berelson, *Graduate Education in the United States,* McGraw-Hill Book Company, New York, 1960, p. 95.

The distribution of doctorates according to the quality of educational institutions has changed over time. The proportion of the output of doctorates accounted for by the better universities has declined (Figure 2.4-2). The top five universities in 1925, 1939, and 1957 accounted for the following proportion of all doctorates conferred: 1925, 41 percent; 1934, 29 percent; and 1957, 20 percent. The quality of these top institutions has not changed but, as doctoral programs have spread to an increasing number of institutions, the relative share of the highest-ranking schools has been reduced. This conclusion is borne out by Table 2.4-11, which presents four decades of degree history for 105 universities that are grouped according to an overall quality index established in 1964. The top four, for example, conferred around one-quarter of the doctorates in 1960–62, compared with nearly 45 percent 40 years earlier. The growth of the number of institutions providing education at the Ph.D. level is depicted in Table 2.4-12.

A summary of the concentration of Ph.D. production by institu-

TABLE 2.4-11
Earned doctorates* awarded by institutions, grouped by 1964 faculty quality rating, percentage distribution, 1920–1962

Institutions, by faculty quality group	1960–62
"Top 10"	27
"Next 15"	26
Number of institutions awarding Ph.D. in period indicated	15
"Next 25"	21
Number of institutions awarding Ph.D. in period indicated	25
"Next 55"	21
Number of institutions awarding Ph.D. in period indicated	55
All institutions in 1964 survey	95
Number of institutions awarding Ph.D. in period indicated	105
Total number of earned doctorates	26,793

* Doctorates in education have been excluded.

† Percentages for 1960–62 calculated from data in Allan M. Cartter (ed.), *American Universities and Colleges*, 9th ed., American Council on Education, Washington, D.C. 1964; and Wayne E. Tolliver, *Earned Degrees Conferred, 1959-60, 1960-61, 1961-62*, U.S. Office of Education Circulars 687, 721, and 719, Washington, Government Printing Office, 1962, 1963. Percentages for 1920–59 calculated from data in Lindsey R. Harmon and Herbert Soldz (compilers), *Doctorate Production in United States Universities, 1920-62.* NAS—NRC Publication No. 1142 National Academy of Sciences—National Research Council, Washington, D.C., 1963.

SOURCE: A. M. Cartter, *An Assessment of Quality in Graduate Education,* American Council on Education, Washington, D.C., 1966, p. 120.

FIGURE 2.4-2
*Doctorates,
three years, by
quality of
institution*

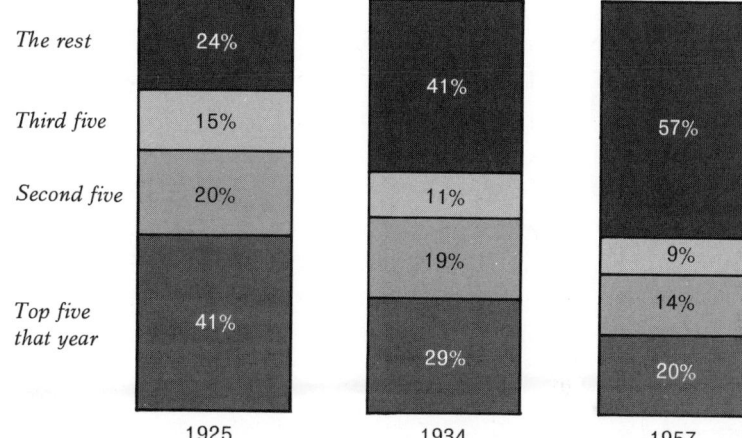

The rest	24%	41%	57%
Third five	15%		
Second five	20%	11%	9%
		19%	14%
Top five that year	41%	29%	20%
	1925	1934	1957

SOURCE: B. Berelson, *Graduate Education in the United States,* McGraw-Hill Book Company, New York, 1960, p. 97.

Percent distribution†			
1950–59	*1940–49*	*1930–39*	*1920–29*
29	35	38	44
28	29	30	32
15	14	13	12
22	20	19	13
25	24	21	20
19	14	12	10
54	49	39	26
98	98	99	99
104	97	83	68
68,813	25,817	22,482	10,743

TABLE 2.4-12
Dates of first
doctorates from
1900–1965
and number of
doctorates in
1965–66

By 1900			
Chicago	306	Northwestern	241
Columbia	427	Pittsburgh	169
Cornell	209	By 1940	
Harvard	491	North Carolina	259
Johns Hopkins	141	Penn State	258
Pennsylvania	251	Purdue	345
Yale	285	Southern California	241
By 1920		Texas	336
California	645	By 1950	
Illinois	545	Indiana	383
Wisconsin	543	UCLA	311
By 1925		By 1955	
Cal Tech	104	Boston	111
Catholic	130	Maryland	166
Iowa	225	Michigan State	355
Iowa State	208	Syracuse	131
Michigan	439	Washington, Seattle	252
Minnesota	396	By 1965	
NYU	385	Colorado	189
Ohio State	362	Florida	185
Princeton	222	Illinois—Chicago Circle	525
Stanford	403	Columbia Teachers College	203
By 1930			
MIT	360		

SOURCE: B. Berelson, *Graduate Education in the United States,* McGraw-Hill Book Company, New York, 1960, p. 93.

tions and field of study is presented in Table 2.4-13. This shows that in 1957–58 the number of institutions conferring varying proportions of Ph.D.'s in 15 fields of study was as follows: one or two institutions of higher education accounted for 10 percent of all doctorates conferred in all fields; between three and six institutions provided 25 percent of the total in these subject areas; and 100 percent of all doctorates were conferred by as few as 23 institutions (business and commerce) and as many as 100 institutions (physical sciences).

Table 2.4-14 gives an overall view of the number of universities offering the Ph.D. in 39 subject fields in 1958. The range of university offerings was considerable. For example, of all universities covered in this table, two-thirds offered Ph.D.'s in chemistry, whereas there were very few universities providing doctorates in such fields as archeology and geochemistry.

TABLE 2.4-13
Concentration of Ph.D. production, 1957–58, by institutions and field of study

Field of study*	Number of institutions conferring Ph.D.'s		
	10%	25%	100%
Agriculture	1	3	27
Biological	1	4	99
Business and commerce	1	2	23
Education	1	3	94
Engineering	1	3	60
English and journalism	2	5	61
Fine and applied arts	1	3	34
Foreign language and literature	2	4	43
Health professions	1	3	31
Maths and statistics	2	4	60
Philosophy	1	3	34
Physical sciences	2	6	100
Psychology	2	6	73
Religion	1	3	39
Social sciences	2	4	82
All degrees	2	6	175

* List includes only fields with more than 100 Ph.D.'s awarded in 1957–58.

SOURCE: U.S. Office of Education, *Earned Degrees Conferred by Higher Educational Institutions, 1957–58;* in OECD, *Higher Education and the Demand for Scientific Manpower in the United States,* Paris, 1963, p. 48.

TABLE 2.4-14 *Number of universities offering Ph.D.'s by specific field, 1958 (N = 140)*

Field	Yes	No	No infor-mation	Field	Yes	No	No infor-mation
Chemistry	111	26	3	Classics	29	110	1
Modern languages (any)	89	51		Entomology	28	111	1
Physics	89	50	1	Musicology	27	113	
Psychology	83	56	1	Biology, general	27	112	1
Mathematics	80	59	1	Pathology	23	113	4
History	79	60	1	Genetics	21	118	1
English	76	62	2	Biophysics	20	117	3
Economics	65	75		Astronomy, astrophysics	20	119	1
Zoology	63	76	1	Comparative literature	17	123	
Physiology	62	76	2	Art history	17	121	2
Political science	62	77	1	Linguistics	13	126	1
Biochemistry	61	76	3	Meteorology	9	131	
Sociology	59	80	1	International relations	9	131	
Botany	56	83	1	Geophysics	8	132	
Geology	55	85		Oceanography	5	135	
Anatomy	52	85	3	Biometrics	3	136	1
Philosophy	48	90	2	Archeology, other than classical	2	137	1
Microbiology	47	91	2	Geochemistry	2	138	
Bacteriology	44	93	3				
Anthropology	36	103	1				
Geography	33	107					

SOURCE: J. A. Davis, *Stipends and Spouses: The Finances of American Arts and Science Graduate Students,* The University of Chicago Press, Chicago, 1962, table 2.3.

Table 2.4-15 presents data on the number of institutions of higher education by type, control, and size of enrollment in 1967. The following summarizes the data for public and private institutions.

Distribution of numbers and enrollment of all public and private institutions by size of enrollment, 1967

	Public and private institutions		Public institutions		Private institutions	
	Number (proportion of total)	Enrollment (proportion of total)	Number (proportion of total)	Enrollment (proportion of total)	Number (proportion of total)	Enrollment (proportion of total)
0–999	0.49	0.08	0.27	0.03	0.64	0.19
1,000–4,999	0.36	0.27	0.45	0.21	0.30	0.38
5,000–9,999	0.09	0.20	0.15	0.22	0.03	0.16
10,000–19,999	0.04	0.20	0.08	0.23	0.02	0.14
20,000 or more	0.02	0.25	0.05	0.31	0.01	0.13
TOTAL	1.00	1.00	1.00	1.00	1.00	1.00
Less than 9,999	0.94	0.55	0.87	0.46	0.97	0.73
10,000 or more	0.06	0.45	0.13	0.54	0.03	0.27
TOTAL	1.00	1.00	1.00	1.00	1.00	1.00

SOURCE: Table 2.4-15.

Approximately half of the total of public and private institutions enrolled fewer than 1,000 students with the proportions for public and private institutions 27 and 64 percent, respectively. The largest number of public and private institutions enrolled less than 5,000 students, a size category characteristic of 72 percent of public institutions and 94 percent of privately controlled institutions. About 3 percent of private institutions and 13 percent of public institutions enrolled 10,000 or more students. The proportion of aggregate enrollment in institutions with fewer than 5,000 students was 35 percent for all institutions; for public institutions, 35 percent; and for private institutions, 57 percent. At the other extreme, the small proportion of institutions enrolling more than 10,000 students accounted for 54 and 27 percent of enrollment at public and private institutions, respectively.

There is some experience to show that an enrollment of less than 1,000 results in high unit costs and a limited curriculum. If the objective is to maximize all available resources entering into higher education institutions, it may be necessary to have an enrollment

(Text continued on p. 388)

TABLE 2.4-15
Number of
institutions of
higher
education, by
type, control,
and size of
enrollment;
United States,
fall 1967

Control of institution and size of enrollment (1)	All institutions	
	Number (2)	Enrollment (3)
Public and private institutions	2,374	6,911,748
Under 200	291	31,562
200 to 499	345	120,484
500 to 999	531	387,672
1,000 to 2,499	590	900,079
2,500 to 4,999	269	950,825
5,000 to 9,999	193	1,392,163
10,000 to 19,999	100	1,389,873
20,000 or more	55	1,739,090
Public institutions	934	4,816,028
Under 200	21	2,268
200 to 499	79	28,421
500 to 999	148	109,776
1,000 to 2,499	230	369,093
2,500 to 4,999	184	669,205
5,000 to 9,999	147	1,061,418
10,000 to 19,999	79	1,104,415
20,000 or more	46	1,471,432
Private institutions	1,440	2,095,720
Under 200	270	29,294
200 to 499	266	92,063
500 to 999	383	277,896
1,000 to 2,499	360	530,986
2,500 to 4,999	85	281,620
5,000 to 9,999	46	330,745
10,000 to 19,999	21	285,458
20,000 or more	9	267,658

NOTE: Includes students whose programs of study are creditable toward a bachelor's or higher degree and also students in one-, two-, or three-year undergraduate programs which are not creditable toward a bachelor's degree but which are designed to prepare for immediate employment or to provide general education.

SOURCE: U.S. Office of Education, *Digest of Educational Statistics, 1968,* 1968, p. 85.

Universities		All other four-year institutions		Two-year institutions	
Number (4)	*Enrollment (5)*	*Number (6)*	*Enrollment (7)*	*Number (8)*	*Enrollment (9)*
156	2,589,009	1,432	2,809,977	786	1,512,762
0	0	186	20,637	105	10,925
0	0	187	65,709	158	54,775
0	0	354	260,079	177	127,593
1	1,751	412	628,447	177	269,881
11	43,016	157	545,229	101	362,580
49	367,575	106	767,171	38	257,417
53	775,675	20	264,370	27	349,828
42	1,400,992	10	258,335	3	79,763
92	1,873,277	322	1,570,698	520	1,372,053
0	0	1	192	20	2,076
0	0	12	4,532	67	23,889
0	0	29	22,182	119	87,594
0	0	79	137,506	151	231,587
2	8,637	87	320,669	95	339,899
20	150,089	89	653,912	38	257,417
36	541,703	16	212,884	27	349,828
34	1,172,848	9	218,821	3	79,763
64	715,732	1,110	1,239,279	266	140,709
0	0	185	20,445	85	8,849
0	0	175	61,177	91	30,886
0	0	325	237,897	58	39,999
1	1,751	333	490,941	26	38,294
9	34,379	70	224,560	6	22,681
29	217,486	17	113,259	0	0
17	233,972	4	51,486	0	0
8	228,144	1	39,514	0	0

as high as 2,500. The optimum size will vary with the type of institution. An enrollment of 1,000 may be too large for certain professional schools and too small for a junior college or university. The ratio of available physical plant to the number of students enrolled measures the extent to which physical capacity is effectively utilized. Table 2.4-16 includes such data for both private and public institutions of different sizes. It appears from this that excess capacity declines with the size of the institution.

Some of the main features of Tables 2.4-17 and 2.4-18, both of which bear on the distribution of institutions by size of faculty, were: (1) Approximately two-fifths of the smallest faculty size category for all institutions, consisting of between 1 and 49 faculty members, were found at junior colleges. In addition, for over half of all institutions of higher education, the average size of faculty was between 1 and 49. (2) Liberal arts colleges represented about 65 percent of institutions with faculties between 50 and 99, and 50 percent of those with faculties of 100 to 199. A faculty of between 50 and 99 was characteristic of 39 percent of all liberal arts colleges and 21 percent of all technical schools. (3) Faculties of over 500 were found predominantly at universities.

GEOGRAPHIC DISTRIBUTION   The number of institutions of higher education in 1963–64 was fairly evenly divided among the four regions indicated in Table 2.4-19. The North Atlantic and the Great Lakes each accounted for 29 percent of the total, and the Southeast, and the West and Southwest, each accounted for 21 percent of the nation's institutions.

TABLE 2.4-16
Ratio of student spaces to number of students enrolled for public and private institutions by size of enrollment

Enrollment size of institution	Public	Private
0 to 499	2.11	1.76
500 to 999	1.52	1.63
1,000 to 2,499	1.32	1.34
2,500 to 4,999	1.26	1.08
5,000 to 9,999	1.06	0.95
10,000 and over	1.08	0.85

SOURCE: John Bishop, Office of Program Coordination, Department of Health, Education and Welfare, unpublished memorandum on costs of higher education; in U.S. Office of Education, *Students and Buildings: An Analysis of Selected Federal Programs for Higher Education*, 1968, p. 42.

Each region's proportion of total enrollment differed from its share of the number of institutions. The relative importance of certain regions with respect to the distribution of enrollment between public and private institutions varied considerably. Around 30 percent of all students and 40 percent of those in public institutions were in the West and Southwest; only 13 percent of all students in privately controlled institutions were enrolled in this region. The North Atlantic region accounted for 26 percent of total enrollment at all institutions., 16 percent of enrollment at public institutions, and 43 percent of enrollment at private colleges and universities.

Relative to the number of universities, enrollment at universities is high, particularly at private institutions. At private liberal arts colleges and at all two-year institutions, the relative share each type of institution represented of the number of institutions was higher than the proportion they accounted for of total enrollment.

Table 2.4-20 presents a regional distribution of graduate schools in 1958. It reveals, among other things, that, of private institutions regarded as major producers of graduate degrees, 62 percent were located in the East, 27 percent in the Midwest or on the West Coast, and 12 percent in the South or the Mountain States. The geographic distribution of major public producers of graduate degrees differed in that 13 percent of such schools were in the East; 70 percent in the Midwest or on the West Coast; and 17 percent in the South or the Mountain states. These figures support our observation that, with respect to schools offering the Ph.D., there was a concentration of private institutions in the East and a concentration of public institutions in the Midwest or on the West Coast.

ACCREDITA-TION Nonaccredited institutions accounted for 12.8 percent of all degree-granting institutions and 41 percent of non-degree-granting institutions in 1962–63. However, enrollment at nonaccredited degree-granting institutions amounted to about 2 percent of total enrollment and 0.2 percent of enrollment for graduate degrees. Enrollment at accredited institutions accounted for the remainder. Since relatively few students were enrolled at nonaccredited institutions, the effect of accreditation could not have been to elevate standards of higher education; it might, however, have served to prevent serious abuses of these standards (Table 2.4–21).

(Text continued on p. 395)

TABLE 2.4-17
Percentage of institutions by size of faculty for resident instruction in degree-credit courses (FT + FTE), type, and institutional control; aggregate United States, fall 1963

Type of institution (1)	1–49 (2)	50–99 (3)	100–199 (4)
All institutions	100.0	100.0	100.0
Universities			2.1
Liberal arts colleges	27.6	64.8	50.4
Teachers colleges	4.8	10.8	26.3
Technological schools	1.3	2.5	4.2
Theological (all private) schools	17.4	1.5	
Art schools	3.3	1.5	0.8
Other professional schools	4.6	2.7	3.4
Junior colleges	41.0	16.2	12.7
Public institutions	(26.7)	(31.2)	(58.5)
Universities			1.3
Liberal arts colleges	0.9	5.2	15.3
Teachers colleges	2.7	10.4	25.4
Technological schools	0.5	1.0	2.5
Art schools	0.2		
Other professional schools	0.1	0.2	1.3
Junior colleges	22.3	14.4	12.7
Private institutions	(73.3)	(68.7)	(41.5)
Universities			0.8
Liberal arts colleges	26.7	59.6	35.2
Teachers colleges	2.1	0.4	0.8
Technological schools	0.8	1.5	1.7
Theological schools	17.4	1.5	
Art schools	3.1	1.5	0.8
Other professional schools	4.5	2.5	2.1
Junior colleges	18.7	1.9	

SOURCE: R. E. Dunham and P. S. Wright, *Faculty and Other Professional Staff in Institutions of Higher Education, First Term, 1963–64,* final report, U.S. Office of Education, 1966, p. 20.

Percentage of institutions by faculty size (FT + FTE)

200–499 (5)	500–749 (6)	750–999 (7)	1,000–1,499 (8)	1,500 + (9)
100.0	100.0	100.0	100.0	100.0
36.4	76.7	88.5	95.0	100.0
27.2	16.3	11.5		
12.6				
11.3	4.7		5.0	
4.0	2.3			
8.6				
(65.6)	(65.1)	(57.7)	(65.0)	(63.6)
21.9	46.5	46.2	65.0	63.6
16.6	11.6	11.5		
12.6				
4.6	4.7			
1.3	2.3			
8.6				
(34.4)	(34.9)	(42.3)	(35.0)	(36.4)
14.6	30.2	42.3	30.0	36.4
10.6	4.7			
6.6			5.0	
2.6				

TABLE 2.4-18 *Institutions of higher education: types and numbers; median and mean number of faculty; number of faculty (50–99), and percentage they represent of total faculty, fall 1963*

All institutions of higher education		Number of faculty		Faculty of 50–99	
Type	Number	Median	Mean	Number of institutions	Percentage of total faculty
All institutions of higher education*	2,080	46	121	480	23
Universities	146	598	752	0	0
Liberal arts colleges	788	63	89	311	39
Technological schools	57	115	127	12	21
Junior colleges	577	32	45	78	13
Other professional schools	79	38	78	13	16

*Includes other categories of institutions not listed here.
SOURCE: Adapted from R. E. Dunham and P. S. Wright, *Faculty and Other Professional Staff in Institutions of Higher Education, First Term 1963–64*, final report, U.S. Office of Education, 1966, p. 19.

TABLE 2.4-19 Total numbers of colleges and universities and of undergraduate and first professional degree students, by geographic region and type of institution, 1963–64 (enrollment in thousands)

	Public and private			
	Institutions		Enrollment	
Category	Number	Percent	Number	Percent
United States	2,117	100	4,091	100
Region				
North Atlantic	611	29	1,050	26
Great Lakes	613	29	1,115	27
Southeast	446	21	658	16
West and Southwest	439	21	1,236	30
Outlying areas	8		33	1
Type of institution				
University	146	7	1,496	37
Liberal arts	781	37	1,149	28
Teachers	186	9	373	9
Technological	49	2	107	3
Theological	201	9	43	1
Other professional	121	6	86	2
Two-year institution	633	30	838	20

SOURCE: U.S. Office of Education, *College Aid for Students*, 1963, p. 8.

Public				Private			
Institutions		Enrollment		Institutions		Enrollment	
Number	Percent	Number	Percent	Number	Percent	Number	Percent
752	100	2,630	100	1,365	100	1,462.	100
147	19	420	16	464	34	630	43
196	26	707	27	417	31	408	28
164	22	438	16	282	21	220	15
241	32	1,042	40	198	14	193	13
4	1	23	1	4		10	1
88	12	1,073	41	58	4	423	29
100	13	411	15	681	50	737	51
159	21	361	14	27	2	12	1
20	3	44	2	29	2	63	4
				201	15	43	3
9	1	10		112	8	76	5
376	50	730	28	257	19	108	7

TABLE 2.4-20   *Geographic patterning of graduate schools*

(a) Percentage of graduate schools located in the central city of a standard metropolitan area	Private	Public
Major producers	69 (26)	35 (23)
Other	80 (44)	38 (47)

	I. East*		II. Midwest or West Coast†		III. South or Mountain states‡	
(b) Percentage of graduate schools located in	Private	Public	Private	Public	Private	Public
Major producers	62 (26)	13 (23)	27 (26)	70 (23)	12 (26)	17 (23)
Other	61 (44)	11 (47)	25 (44)	21 (47)	14 (44)	68 (47)

	. . . In central city of an Eastern standard metropolitan area		. . . Outside central city of a standard metropolitan area and not in the East	
(c) Percentage of graduate schools located	Private	Public	Private	Public
Major producers	42 (26)	0 (23)	12 (26)	52 (23)
Other	50 (44)	0 (47)	18 (44)	55 (47)

*East is defined as the census regions New England and Middle Atlantic plus Maryland, Delaware, and the District of Columbia.

† Midwest is defined as the census regions West North Central and East North Central. West Coast is defined as the census region Pacific.

‡ South is defined as the census regions West South Central, East South Central, and South Atlantic other than Maryland, Delaware, and the District of Columbia. Mountain is defined as the census region Mountain.

NOTE: Explanation of numbers in parentheses is not provided in the source.

SOURCE: J. A. Davis, *Stipends and Spouses: The Finances of American Arts and Science Graduate Students,* The University of Chicago Press, Chicago, 1962, p. 149.

Proportion of all applicants accounted for by those admitted and registered, 1957	Proportion of applicants admitted— range, percent	Proportion of applicants registered— range, percent
10 public	50–95	39–75
10 private	28–90	20–79
Universities	40–79	30–52

SOURCE: Table 2.4-22.

ABLE 2.4-21 *Enrollment and degrees granted by all United States institutions of higher education* *n academic year 1962–63*

	Number of institutions	Enrollment Total	Enrollment Graduate degrees
All institutions of higher education	2,136	4,400,030	375,118
Degree-granting	1,442	3,585,110	375,118
Accredited, included in study	1,063	3,425,456	369,964
Accredited, excluded from study	194	83,213	4,506
Nonaccredited, excluded from study	185	76,441	648
Non-degree-granting (excluded from study)	694	815,190	0
Accredited	410		
Nonaccredited	284		
Percentage			
Degree-granting institutions—percentage of all higher education	67.5	81.5	100.0
Accredited, included in study:			
Percentage of degree-granting	73.7	95.6	98.6
Percentage of all higher education	49.7	77.8	98.6
Accredited, excluded from study:			
Percentage of degree-granting	13.5	2.3	1.2
Percentage of all higher education	9.1	1.9	1.2
Nonaccredited, excluded from study:			
Percentage of degree-granting	12.8	2.1	0.2
Percentage of all higher education	8.7	1.7	0.2
Non-degree-granting (excluded from study)	32.5	18.5	0
Accredited—percentage of non-degree-granting	59.1		
Nonaccredited—percentage of non-degree-granting	40.9		

SOURCE: National Science Foundation, *The Dynamics of Academic Science,* 1967, p. 40.

APPLICATIONS AND ADMISSIONS   Estimates by the Office of Education for 1956 and 1957 on the proportion of persons applying to colleges and universities who were admitted, the percentage of those admitted who were registered, and the ratio of those applying to those registered are contained in Table 2.4-22. There appeared to be considerable variability in the experience of both public and private institutions (see facing table).

TABLE 2.4-22 Percentage of applicants admitted and registered in individual institutions, by control and by multipurpose and single-purpose institutions, fall 1956 and 1957	Institutions by control	Percentage of applicants admitted		Percentage of admittants registered		Percentage of applicants registered	
		1956	1957	1956	1957	1956	1957
	TOTAL	61.1	63.5	71.4	68.5	43.6	43.5
	Public	74.6	76.8	73.6	68.4	54.9	52.6
	Private	44.3	45.3	66.8	68.8	29.6	31.2
	Public:						
	A	97.8	94.6	84.0	79.0	82.2	74.8
	B	93.8	93.1	88.2	82.6	82.7	76.9
	C	90.8	90.1	76.2	75.0	69.1	67.5
	D	86.7	81.2	82.4	75.7	71.5	61.4
	E	83.4	72.6	77.0	72.2	64.3	52.4
	F	82.8	80.9	70.0	70.0	57.9	56.6
	G	77.8	72.4	64.1	56.5	49.9	40.9
	H	72.3	77.5	70.1	58.5	50.7	45.3
	I	61.6	73.4	67.3	60.4	41.4	44.3
	J	51.1	49.9	77.2	78.9	39.5	39.4
	Private:						
	K	92.0	89.5	74.3	88.8	68.3	79.5
	L	90.9	86.1	61.5	58.8	55.9	50.6
	M	71.2	67.2	62.7	58.3	44.6	39.2
	N	66.1	65.5	61.8	77.5	40.9	50.8
	O	56.2	53.3	70.9	74.5	39.9	39.7
	P	53.8	55.8	46.9	48.3	25.2	26.9
	Q	51.1	45.6	66.8	55.2	34.1	25.2
	R	44.9	48.7	50.9	58.2	22.9	28.3
	S	41.2	42.8	51.0	47.9	21.0	20.5
	T	25.4	27.5	96.2	95.8	24.5	26.3
	Universities:						
	Public	73.6	78.7	71.7	66.0	52.8	51.9
	Private	38.5	39.5	70.8	76.0	27.2	30.0
	Single-purpose institutions:						
	Public	90.4	87.4	78.6	75.2	71.1	65.7
	Private	54.7	55.7	59.8	62.4	32.7	34.8

SOURCE: R. E. Iffert and B. S. Clarke, *College Applicants, Entrants, Dropouts* U.S. Office of Education, 1965, p. 9.

TABLE 2.4-23		*(a) Numbers*			
Distribution of schools and students by stratum and control			*Control*		
		Private		*Public*	
		Schools	*Students*	*Schools*	*Students*
I. Keniston Ranks 1–10 + *MIT, Cal. Tech**		8	9,920	4	7,273
II. Others, AGS and/or high producers†		18	13,376	19	16,015
III. Other		44	8,566	47	8,037

(b) Percentage

		Of all students (universe)			*Of all schools*		
		Private	*Public*	*Total*	*Private*	*Public*	*Total*
I.		16	11	27	6	3	9
II.		21	25	46	13	14	27
III.		14	13	27	31	33	64
	TOTAL	51	49	100	50	50	100
		$N = 63,187$			$N = 140$		

Of all students (sample)

		Private	*Public*	*Total*
I.		17	12	29
II.		20	25	45
III.		14	13	27
	TOTAL	51	50	101

* Refers to schools with ranks 1 to 10 in the Keniston survey plus M.I.T. and California Institute of Technology.

† Other members of the Association of Graduate Schools (AGS).

‡ All other graduate schools.

SOURCE: J. A. Davis, *Stipends and Spouses: The Finances of American Arts and Science Graduate Students,* The University of Chicago Press, Chicago, 1962, p. 148.

RANKING: VARIOUS APPROACHES *Distribution of enrolled students by quality of institution* The data in Table 2.4-23 are based on a sample survey by J. A. Davis covering 140 institutions offering the Ph.D. in at least one traditional arts and science field in 1958.[1] *Stratem* in this study is a comprehensive term referring to a combination of institutional

[1] J. A. Davis, *Stipends and Spouses: The Finances of American Arts and Science Graduate Students,* The University of Chicago Press, Chicago, 1962.

prestige and the size and variety of institutional offerings. There are three stratem levels specified. The first (I) pertains to the most prestigious schools—those that ranked 1 to 10 in the Keniston survey (1957)[2] plus the Massachusetts Institute of Technology and the California Institute of Technology, which were not included in the Keniston survey. The second (II) refers to other members of the Association of Graduate Schools, an organization of leading graduate institutions, or institutions which granted 400 or more arts and science Ph.D.'s between 1936 and 1956. The third stratem (III) consists of all other graduate schools.

In 1958, Table 2.4-23 shows: (1) The approximately 17,000 students enrolled for the Ph.D. in the 12 schools included in Stratem I accounted for 27 percent of total enrollment in the institutions covered in this survey, while Ph.D. students enrolled at public institutions in this group accounted for 16 percent and those at private institutions for 11 percent of the total. (2) The 37 schools in Stratem II had an aggregate enrollment of around 29,000 Ph.D. students, representing 46 percent of total enrollment, while those in public institutions in this group included 25 percent and those in private institutions 21 percent of the total. (3) Stratem III included 91 institutions, with 16,600 Ph.D. students, who made up 27 percent of total Ph.D. enrollment in the schools included in the survey, with a more or less even distribution between public and private institutions. The average number of enrolled students at public and private institutions in each of these institutional classifications was as follows:

Average number of Ph.D. students per institution of higher education by stratem and control, 1958	*Enrollment*	
Stratem level	*Per private institution*	*Per public institution*
I	1240	1810
II	743	843
III	195	170

The top 12 institutions had on the average as many as 1½ times the number of enrolled Ph.D. students as the 37 Stratem II institutions and 6 times as many as the average of 91 schools included in Stratem III.

[2] H. Keniston, *Graduate Study and Research in the Arts and Sciences at the University of Pennsylvania,* University of Pennsylvania Press, Philadelphia 1959.

TABLE 2.4-24   *Number of faculty at 36 institutions with various scholarly distinctions, 1939–1961*

Institutions and ratios	Guggenheim fellows			Members of National Academy of Sciences			Members of American Philosophical Society		
	1941	1951	1961	1940	1950	1960	1939	1949	1959
Group I	6	27	69	73	115	167	113	120	126
Group II	0	5	11	6	6	9	3	6	7
Group III	0	1	3	1	1	0	5	3	1
Ratio of									
Group I:II		5.4	6.3	12.2	19.2	18.6	37.7	20.0	18.0
Group II:III		5.0	3.7	6.0	6.0		0.6	2.0	7.0

The ratio of all faculty in Group I to all in Group II ranges from about 2:1 to 4:1, depending on the measure employed. The ratio of all faculty in Group II to those in Group III ranges more widely, from 2:1 to 6.5:1.

SOURCE: H. Orlans, *The Effects of Federal Programs on Higher Education,* The Brookings Institution, Washington, D.C., 1962, p. 18.

Effects of federal grants on quality

Another approach to measuring the quality of institutions of higher education was that followed by H. Orlans.[3] He compared distinctions achieved over three decades by three groups of institutions. These included: (1) those with large grants for research from the federal government; (2) those with smaller grants; and (3) those considered to be good liberal arts schools. The three types of scholarly distinctions he specified were: (1) number of Guggenheim fellows; (2) number of members of the National Academy of Sciences; and (3) number of members of the American Philosophical Society. The principal conclusion was that institutions that received substantial federal financial support had considerably more distinguished faculty members than less well financed institutions. This was especially true in 1959–60 compared with earlier years (Table 2.4-24).

The ratio in 1957 of graduate enrollment totals in Orlans' heavily financed institutions (Group I) to those in well-supported institutions (Group II) was 4 to 1, as compared to a 3 to 1 ratio 10 years earlier. Between 1936 and 1956, Group I institutions produced 4.5 times the number of doctorates as Group II institutions, with the ratio even higher in the case of science doctorates. When other

[3] H. Orlans, *The Effects of Federal Programs on Higher Education,* The Brookings Institution, Washington, D.C., 1962.

TABLE 2.4-25
Comparisons
of two groups
of institutions;
graduate
students

	Group I	Group II	Ratio I : II
Graduate enrollment			
Fall 1957	48,823	11,992	4.1
Fall 1947	20,980	6,749	3.1
Graduate students in sciences, April 1958*	16,220	3,493	4.6
Doctorates, 1936–56	29,993	6,669	4.5
Sciences†	16,627	3,160	5.3
Percentage in sciences	55.4%	47.4%	
Science doctorates, 1956–59‡	4,669	900	5.2
National Science Fellows, 1960	520	44	11.8
Woodrow Wilson Fellows, 1959–60 to 1961–62	1,229	143	8.6
Ph.D's and M.D.'s starred in American Men of Science 1903–43§	603	35	17.2

*SOURCE: National Academy of Sciences, *Census of Graduate Students in Basi and Applied Natural Sciences,* 1958. Sciences include engineering, psychology and anthropology, as well as physical and biological sciences;

† SOURCE: National Academy of Sciences, *Doctorate Production in United State Universities 1936–1956,* 1958. Sciences include engineering and physical and bio logical sciences;

‡ SOURCE: National Science Foundation. Same fields as in footnote †, with additio of psychology;

§ SOURCE: Stephen S. Visher, *Scientists Starred 1903–1943 in "American Men Science,"* The Johns Hopkins Press, Baltimore, 1947, pp. 270–271; in H. Orlan *The Effects of Federal Programs on Higher Education,* The Brookings Institutio Washington, D.C., 1962, p. 154.

criteria of distinction were introduced, Group I institutions ap peared to be even more prestigious. For example, between 190 and 1943, for every Ph.D. or M.D. in Group II starred in America Men of Science, there were 17.2 such persons from Group I. Fur thermore, the ratio of Group I to Group II was 11.8 to 1 for Nationa Science Fellows in 1960 and 8.6 to 1 for Woodrow Wilson Fellow in 1959–60 to 1961–62 (Table 2.4-25).

Ranking of separate institutions

A comparison of the overall rankings of graduate schools in 192 and in 1957[4] is presented in Table 2.4-26. The American Counc

[4] American Council on Education, *American Universities and Colleges, 196* Washington, D.C., 1966; H. Keniston, *Graduate Study and Research in th Arts and Sciences at the University of Pennsylvania,* University of Pennsy vania Press, Philadelphia, 1959.

TABLE 2.4-26				
Overall standing of institutions of higher education (total scores)				

1925		1957	
1. Chicago	1543	1. Harvard	5403
2. Harvard	1535	2. California	4750
3. Columbia	1316	3. Columbia	4183
4. Wisconsin	886	4. Yale	4094
5. Yale	885	5. Michigan	3603
6. Princeton	805	6. Chicago	3495
7. Johns Hopkins	746	7. Princeton	2770
8. Michigan	720	8. Wisconsin	2453
9. California	712	9. Cornell	2239
10. Cornell	694	10. Illinois	1934
11. Illinois	561	11. Pennsylvania	1784
12. Pennsylvania	459	12. Minnesota	1442
13. Minnesota	430	13. Stanford	1439
14. Stanford	365	14. U.C.L.A.	1366
15. Ohio State	294	15. Indiana	1329
16. Iowa	215	16. Johns Hopkins	1249
17. Northwestern	143	17. Northwestern	934
18. North Carolina	57	18. Ohio State	874
19. Indiana	45	19. N.Y.U.	801
		20. Washington	759

SOURCE: H. Keniston, *Graduate Study and Research in the Arts and Sciences at the University of Pennsylvania,* University of Pennsylvania Press, Philadelphia, 1959, p. 119.

on Education relied on panels of experts for its survey, and Keniston's findings consisted of the composite ratings of department chairmen from 25 institutions throughout the country. He identified approximately 20 outstanding institutions.

The most recent study, that of Cartter,[5] updated and enlarged upon the Keniston survey. It was based on usable questionnaires received from approximately 4,000 scholars consisting of department chairmen and senior and junior scholars at 106 universities. The respondents were asked to judge both the quality of the graduate faculty in terms of schooling competence and present achievement, and the effectiveness of the doctoral program. The ratings of leading universities by broad subject field according to the quality

[5] A. M. Cartter, *An Assessment of Quality in Graduate Education,* American Council on Education, Washington, D.C., 1966.

TABLE 2.4-27
The leading universities, by general area of study, as measured by quality of faculty, 1964*

Humanities		Social sciences		Biological sciences	
Harvard	4.36	Harvard	4.66	Harvard	4.42
California, Berkeley	4.27	California, Berkeley	4.48	California, Berkeley	4.33
Yale	4.17	Chicago	4.39	Rockefeller Institute	3.97
Princeton	3.91	Yale	4.12		
Columbia	3.79	Princeton	3.98	California Institute of Technology	3.95
Michigan	3.69	Wisconsin	3.91	Stanford	3.92
		Columbia	3.77	Michigan	3.85
		Michigan	3.75	Wisconsin	3.76
		Stanford	3.75	Illinois	3.73
				Yale	3.68

Rating categories and numerical ranges of institutions according to quality of graduate faculty:

Rating category	Numerical range
Distinguished	4.01–5.00
Strong	3.01–4.00
Good	2.51–3.00
Adequate plus	2.00–2.50
Not grouped	Below 2.00

SOURCE: A. M. Cartter, *An Assessment of Quality in Graduate Education,* American Council on Education, Washington, D.C., 1966, pp. 15, 107.

of the graduate faculty are presented in Table 2.4-27. The subject areas included humanities, social sciences, biological sciences, physical sciences, and engineering. The schools listed had the highest average scores within each of these general areas of study and could claim at least two "distinguished" departments.

Relative standings of leading universities

Universities in leading group (total 12)	Number of areas of study in which university is listed (maximum 5)
University of California, Berkeley	5
Harvard, Stanford	4
Columbia, Yale, Illinois, Princeton, Michigan, California Institute of Technology	3
Chicago, Wisconsin	2
Rockefeller Institution	1

SOURCE: Table 2.4-27.

Physical sciences		Engineering	
Harvard	4.60	M.I.T.	4.48
California, Berkeley	4.55	California, Berkeley	4.23
California Institute of Technology	4.46	Stanford	4.02
M.I.T.	4.33	California Institute of Technology	3.94
Princeton	4.33	Illinois	3.91
Stanford	4.22		
Chicago	3.98		
Illinois	3.82		
Columbia	3.78		

Other ranking criteria

The Cartter study also introduced what Cartter referred to as "objective" criteria for rating and evaluating institutions. These criteria included the following: different types of fellowships held by students; faculty salaries; library resources; number of doctorates produced; and faculty and student honors and awards. Several years earlier, A. Bowker[6] ranked universities according to a number of indices of faculty quality and institutional attractiveness. He developed separate rankings, one for social sciences and humanities and another for the sciences. Student quality was measured by the number of Woodrow Wilson Fellows and National Science Foundation awardees attending an institution. In estimating faculty excellence, Bowker's evaluation was in terms of the numbers of faculty who had received Guggenheim Fellowships, who were members of the National Academy of Learned Societies and of the Na-

---

[6] A. H. Bowker, "Quality and Quantity in Higher Education," *Journal of the American Statistical Association,* vol. 60, no. 309, pp. 1–15, March 1965.

tional Academy of Sciences, and who were Nobel laureates. Some of these measures and institutional rankings are covered in Tables 2.4-28 to 2.4-32. The latter two tables provide measures for ranking undergraduate institutions.

ESTIMATING NEED FOR A COLLEGE OR CURRICULUM   In the late 1950s, I sent out questionnaires to heads of over 500 new institutions founded in a recent 10-year period to determine how the need for new colleges and curricula was established. Out

TABLE 2.4-28   *Institutional ranking, social science and humanities, 1961–62 (institutions listed in rank order)*

Institution	Rank	Institution	Rank
Columbia University	1	Duke University	26
Harvard University	2	Northwestern University	27
Yale University	3	Washington University (St. Louis)	28
University of California (Berkeley)	4	State University of Rutgers	29
University of Chicago	5	State University of New York	30
Stanford University	6	University of Oregon	31
University of Michigan	7.5	Boston University	32
Princeton University	7.5	Michigan State University	33
Indiana University	9	Brandeis University	35
University of Pennsylvania	10	University of Virginia	35
University of Wisconsin	11	Vanderbilt University	35
Cornell University	12.5	University of Iowa	37
University of California (Los Angeles)	12.5	Tufts University	38
University of Illinois	14	University of Connecticut	39
University of Minnesota	15	University of Notre Dame	40
Brown University	16.5	Dartmough	41
City University of New York	16.5	Catholic University	42
University of Washington (Seattle)	18	Wayne State University	43
New York University	19	University of Missouri	44.5
University of Texas	20	University of Rochester	44.5
Massachusetts Institute of Technology	21	Williams	46
Johns Hopkins University	22	University of Kentucky	47.5
Ohio State University	23	University of Nebraska	47.5
Tulane University	24	Emory University	49.5
University of North Carolina	25	Georgetown University	49.5

SOURCE: A. H. Bowker, "Quality and Quantity in Higher Education," *Journal of the American Statistical Association,* vol. 60, no. 309, p. 8, March 1965.

of the 253 usable replies, more than half had enrollments of less than 500. These results indicated that the need for new colleges was established principally by studies (56 percent), but that requests of interested students, and of professional, business, and church groups were also influential (Table 2.4-33). The replies to a questionnaire on the manner of estimating likely enrollment revealed that studies of intent, of applications, and of occupational interest were especially important in anticipating enrollment needs. About one-third of the replies reflected lack of significant study of the problem (Table 2.4-34). In estimating enrollment, respon-

(Text continued on p. 410)

TABLE 2.4-29 *Institutional ranking, science, 1961–62 (institutions listed in rank order)*

Institution	Rank	Institution	Rank
Harvard University	1	Carnegie Institute of Technology	25.5
University of California (Berkeley)	2	Washington University (St. Louis)	25.5
Stanford University	3	Ohio State University	27
Princeton University	4	University of Colorado	28
Massachusetts Institute of Technology	5	Pennsylvania State University	29
California Institute of Technology	6	Brown University	30
Columbia University	7	University of Washington (Seattle)	31
University of Chicago	8	University of North Carolina	32.5
University of Wisconsin	9.5	Rice University	32.5
Yale University	9.5	University of Kansas	34
Cornell University	11	University of Arizona	35
University of Illinois	12	University of Virginia	36
New York University	13	State University of Rutgers	38
University of Michigan	14.5	St. Louis University	38
University of California (Los Angeles)	14.5	Western Reserve University	38
Indiana University	16	University of Notre Dame	40
University of Texas	17	Florida State University	44.5
University of Minnesota	18.5	University of Iowa	44.5
Purdue University	18.5	Lehigh University	44.5
Northwestern University	20.5	University of Maryland	44.5
University of Rochester	20.5	Michigan State University	44.5
Duke University	23	Oklahoma State University	44.5
Iowa State University	23	University of Tennessee	44.5
University of Pennsylvania	23	Yeshiva University	44.5

SOURCE: A. H. Bowker, "Quality and Quantity in Higher Education," *Journal of the American Statistical Association,* vol. 60, no. 309, p. 10, March 1965.

TABLE 2.4-30
One of the
criteria used
to compile
science ranking:
National Science
Foundation
awardees
choosing
school, 1962

Institution	Number	Rank
Harvard University	240	1
Massachusetts Institute of Technology	182	2
University of California (Berkeley)	171	3
Princeton University	139	4
Stanford University	131	5
California Institute of Technology	82	6
Yale University	61	7
University of Chicago	57	8
University of Wisconsin	56	9
Columbia University	47	10.5
University of Illinois	47	10.5
University of Michigan	41	12
Cornell University	32	13
Johns Hopkins University	26	14
New York University	22	15
Purdue University	21	16
Northwestern University	19	17
University of California (Los Angeles)	18	18
Indiana University	14	20
Ohio State University	14	20
Pennsylvania State University	14	20

SOURCE: National Science Foundation, *12th Annual Report 1962,* Washington, D.C., 1962, pp. 347–351; in A. H. Bowker, "Quality and Quantity in Higher Education," *Journal of the American Statistical Association,* vol. 60, no. 309, p. 9, March 1965.

	Number of Woodrow Wilson Fellowships granted to baccalaureate recipients from school, 1945–46	
TABLE 2.4-31 Possible criterion for ranking of undergraduate institutions: Top 20 institutions of baccalaureate origin of Woodrow Wilson Fellows, 1945–46 through 1963–64 (schools listed in rank order)		
Institution	*to 1963–64*	*Rank*
Harvard University	295	1
Princeton University	274	2
Columbia University	202	3
Yale University	185	4
City University of New York	176	5
Cornell University	148	6
University of Michigan	139	7
University of California (Berkeley)	122	8
Chicago University	114	9
Oberlin	109	10
Swarthmore	99	11
Stanford University	97	12
University of Kansas	95	13
University of Notre Dame	93	14
University of Texas	84	15.5
University of Wisconsin	84	15.5
Tulane University	81	17
Reed	80	18
University of California (Los Angeles)	74	19
University of Minnesota	73	20

SOURCE: Woodrow Wilson National Fellowship Foundation, report for 1962–1963, pp. 26–45; in A. H. Bowker, "Quality and Quantity in Higher Education," *Journal of the American Statistical Association,* vol. 60, no. 309, p. 11, March 1965.

TABLE 2.4-32 *Possible criterion for ranking of undergraduate institutions: leading 20 baccalaureate origins, institutions of doctorate production, 1960 and 1961*

Baccalaureate source	Number of students who received baccalaureates at institution and earned doctorate in 1960 and 1961	Percentage of all sources	Rank
City University of New York	791	3.80	1
University of California (Berkeley)	359	1.73	2
University of Illinois	356	1.71	3
Harvard University	287	1.38	4
University of Michigan	275	1.32	5
University of Wisconsin	271	1.30	6
New York University	261	1.25	7
University of Minnesota	258	1.24	8
University of California (Los Angeles)	255	1.23	9
Cornell University	248	1.19	10
Massachusetts Institute of Technology	232	1.11	12
University of Chicago	231	1.11	12
Columbia University	231	1.11	12
Yale University	212	1.02	14
Ohio State University	191	0.92	15
Pennsylvania State University	170	0.82	16
Purdue University	167	0.80	17
University of Texas	143	0.69	18
University of Washington	139	0.67	19
Michigan State University	131	0.63	20

SOURCE: National Academy of Sciences, *Doctorate Production in United States Universities, 1920–1962*, report prepared by the National Research Council, National Academy of Sciences, Washington, D.C., 1963, pp. 120–136; in A. H. Bowker, "Quality and Quantity in Higher Education," *Journal of the American Statistical Association*, vol. 60, no. 309, p. 12, March 1965.

TABLE 2.4-33 *Manner of estimating need for a college or a curriculum (e.g., law)*

Manner of estimating	Number	Percent*
State survey of population, demand for higher education	36	14.2
Local or institutional survey of population, demand for higher education	49	19.4
Estimate of job needs	42	16.6
Cursory examination population, jobs, etc.	14	5.5
Total studies	141	55.7
Requests from professional and business groups	37	14.6
Requests from prospective students	44	17.4
Requests related to church needs	39	15.4
Elections and similar public demand	8	3.2
Total requests	128	50.6
Allow continued segregation in higher education	5	2.0
Other	22	8.7
No answer or unknown	6	2.4

The total percentages add to more than 100 because a number of respondents cited more than one basis for determining need.

SOURCE: S. E. Harris, *Higher Education: Resources and Finance,* McGraw-Hill Book Company, New York, 1962, p. 603.

TABLE 2.4-34 *Manner of estimating likely enrollment*

Manner of estimating	Number	Percent
High school population and intent survey	86	34.0
Job opportunity survey	20	7.9
Applications	35	13.8
Total studies	141	55.7
Cursory examination available data	41	16.2
Guess	27	10.7
None	22	8.7
Total superficial or nonexistent estimate	90	35.6
Facilities available as limit	16	6.3
No answer or unknown	6	2.4

SOURCE: S. E. Harris, *Higher Education: Resources and Finance,* McGraw-Hill Book Company, New York, 1962, p. 604.

TABLE 2.4-35
Enrollment:
Determined
how?

Determinant	Number	Percent
Purely educational issues	137	54.2
Both educational issues and cost considered	82	32.4
Primarily cost considerations	13	5.1
Neither	1	0.4
Unknown, no answer	20	7.9

SOURCE: S. E. Harris, *Higher Education: Resources and Finance,* McGraw-Hill Book Company, New York, 1962, p. 605.

TABLE 2.4-36 *Manner of determining particular location*

Determinant	Number	Percent	Percentage of those selecting new location (156 IHL)*
Central location in terms of proposed student body	77	30.4	49.4
Site and/or buildings available	57	22.5	36.5
Staff available	11	4.3	7.1
Professional advice	7	2.8	4.5
Donors' wishes	9	3.6	5.8
Other	13	5.1	8.3
Existing institution determined choice of site	111	43.9	
No answer	6	2.4	

* Adds to more than 100 because some mentioned two criteria.
SOURCE: S. E. Harris, *Higher Education: Resources and Finance,* McGraw-Hill Book Company, New York, 1962, p. 605.

dents generally considered purely educational issues and costs, with the larger proportion concentrating on educational issues (Table 2.4-35). The most important guides in determining location were: the central location in relation to residence of students (49 percent) and availability of sites or buildings (36 percent). Availability of staff and donors' wishes seemed relatively unimportant[7] (Table 2.4-36).

[7] S. E. Harris, *Higher Education: Resources and Finance,* McGraw-Hill Book Company, New York, 1962, pp. 602–608.

2.5. Enrollment in Relation to Population

HISTORICAL
AND
PROJECTED
RELATIONSHIP
OF
ENROLLMENT
TO
POPULATION

The most relevant population data for assessing future demand for higher education are those published by the Bureau of the Census applicable to age groups 15 to 19 and 20 to 24. The ratio of the population aged 15 to 24 to total population in 1960 was 0.14; the projected ratio for 1975 and 1980 was approximately 0.18.[1] This trend indicates an increasing burden on high schools and institutions of higher education.

The American Council on Education published estimates on the ratio of population aged 15 to 24 to total population covering the period 1900–1990. These data point to a considerable decline in the ratio between 1900 and 1960, a projected increase between 1960 and 1980, and a leveling off after that date.

Proportion of total United States population accounted for by population aged 15 to 24

Year	Ratio
1900	0.20
1960	0.14
1980*	0.17
1990*	0.16

* Forecasts consist of Bureau of the Census Series B projections.

SOURCE: American Council on Education, *A Fact Book on Higher Education,* Washington, D.C., 1967.

Since 1870 the rate of growth of enrollment in institutions of higher education has greatly exceeded the growth rate of the entire population, but the proportion that enrolled students represented of the population aged 18 to 21 and 18 to 24 grew even more rapidly (Table 2.5-1).

(Text continued on p. 414)

[1] U.S. Bureau of the Census, *Statistical Abstract of the United States, 1967,* 1967, p. 8. Projections were based on current estimates and projections of the population by age and sex for July 1, 1966, and imply an annual net immigration of 400,000. Fertility projections based on Census Series C data.

TABLE 2.5-1 *Resident degree-credit enrollment in institutions of higher education related to total population and to age groups 18 to 21 and 18 to 24; United States, 1869–70 to fall 1963*

	Population*		
	---	---	---
Year (1)	Total† (2)	Ages 18 to 21‡ (3)	Ages 18 to 24‡ (4)
Academic year:			
1869–70	39,818,449	3,116,000	4,574,000
1879–80	50,155,783	4,253,000	7,092,000
1889–90	62,947,714	5,160,000	8,820,000
1899–1900	75,994,575	5,931,000	10,357,000
1909–10	90,492,000	6,934,000	12,300,000
1919–20	104,512,000	7,386,000	12,830,000
1929–30	121,770,000	8,862,000	15,280,000
1939–40	131,028,000	9,582,000	16,458,000
1941–42	133,402,000	9,703,000	16,715,000
1943–44	136,739,000	9,706,000	16,914,000
1945–46	139,928,000	9,557,000	16,790,000
1947–48	144,126,000	9,276,000	16,419,000
1949–50	149,188,000	8,990,000	16,120,000
1951–52	154,283,000	8,742,000	15,709,000
1953–54	159,559,000	8,441,000	15,221,000
First term of academic year:			
November 1953	159,559,000	8,441,000	15,221,000
November 1955	165,276,000	8,508,000	14,966,000
First term, 1957–58	171,278,000	8,844,000	15,118,000
First term, 1959–60	177,865,000	9,225,000	15,693,000
First term, 1961–62	183,742,000	10,246,000	16,954,000
Fall 1963	189,278,000	11,129,000	18,153,000

* Armed Forces overseas are excluded from 1869–70 to 1929–30; they are included in 1939–40 and subsequent years.

† Data are actual census counts as of June 1 from 1870 to 1900; for later years they are estimates by the Bureau of the Census as of July 1 preceding the fall term of each school year.

‡ Data from 1869–70 to 1930–40 are estimates by the Office of Education from figures for broad age groups supplied by the Bureau of the Census; data for later years are estimates by the Bureau of the Census.

	Resident degree-credit enrollment		Ratios			
			Total resident degree-credit students to a 100 of—			Undergraduate resident degree-credit students to 100 of population 18–21
			Total population	Population 18–21	Population 18–24	
Total (5)	Undergraduate (6)	Graduate (7)	(8)	(9)	(10)	(11)
52,286	§	§	0.13	1.63	1.14	§
115,817	§	§	0.23	2.72	1.63	§
156,756	154,374	2,382	0.25	3.04	1.78	2.99
237,592	231,761	5,831	0.31	4.01	2.29	3.91
355,213	346,050	9,153	0.39	5.12	2.89	4.99
597,880	582,268	15,612	0.57	8.09	4.66	7.88
1,100,737	1,053,482	47,255	0.90	12.42	7.20	11.89
1,494,203	1,388,455	105,748	1.14	15.59	9.03	14.49
1,403,990	1,318,547¶	85,443¶	1.05	14.47	8.40	13.59
1,155,272	1,098,041¶	59,231¶	0.84	11.90	6.83	11.29
1,676,851	1,555,599	121,252	1.20	17.55	9.99	16.28
2,616,262	2,441,830	174,432	1.82	28.20	15.93	26.32
2,659,021	2,421,813	237,208	1.78	29.58	16.50	26.94
2,301,884	2,068,557	233,327	1.49	26.33	14.65	23.68
2,514,712	2,237,713	276,999	1.58	29.79	16.52	26.51
2,199,972	1,976,863	223,109	1.38	26.06	14.45	23.42
2,597,670	2,347,656	250,014	1.57	30.53	17.36	27.59
2,899,565	2,621,919	277,646	1.69	32.79	19.18	29.65
3,215,544	2,873,724	341,820	1.81	34.86	20.49	31.15
3,726,114	3,328,288	397,826	2.03	36.37	21.98	32.43
4,234,092	3,755,515	478,577	2.24	35.05	23.33	33.75

§ Data not available.

¶ Distribution by level estimated.

SOURCE: U.S. Department of Health, Education and Welfare Office of Education, "Biennial Survey of Education in the United States"; and comprehensive surveys of enrollment in institutions of higher education, in U.S. Office of Education, *Digest of Educational Statistics, 1968,* 1968, p. 70.

	Rise from 1869–70 to 1963 (number of times)	Rise from 1889–1900 to 1963 (number of times)
Enrollment in relation to population	16	8
Enrollment in relation to population 18 to 21	22	12
Enrollment in relation to population 18 to 24	19	12
Undergraduate resident degree-credit students to 100 of population 18 to 21		10

SOURCE: Table 2.5-1.

Between 1955 and 1964, undergraduate enrollment as a proportion of the college-age group (18 to 24) at two-year institutions increased by about 35 percent, which was approximately five times
the rate of increase at four-year institutions (Table 2.5-2).

Contained in Table 2.5-3 are percentages of enrollment to population for different age groups (5 to 34 years) for the years 1947 to
1966. The following are some of the conclusions that can be drawn
from this table: (1) There has been little change over this period
in the percentage of children aged 6 to 13 enrolled in elementary
school (by 1947 virtually all children in this age range were already
enrolled in school). (2) The proportion of 16- and 17-year-olds who
were enrolled in high school rose from 68 percent in 1947 to 89
percent in 1966. (3) In 1966, 47 percent of the college-age group
consisting of 18- and 19-year-olds were enrolled in institutions of

TABLE 2.5-2 Ratio of undergraduate enrollment to the eligible population age 18–24; United States, 1955 and 1964*

Type of institution	1955	1964	Increase	Percentage increase
Four-year institutions†	0.305	0.326	0.021	6.9
Two-year institutions‡	0.051	0.069	0.018	35.3
TOTAL	0.356	0.395	0.039	11.0

* The eligible population is defined as those in the age group who hold a high school
diploma, are not in the armed forces, and are not college graduates.

† Excludes graduate enrollment.

‡ Includes an indeterminate number of two-year enrollees who do not hold a high
school diploma.

SOURCE: Robert Campbell and B. N. Siegel, "Demand for Higher Education in
the United States," *American Economic Review*, vol. 62, no. 3, pp. 482–494, June
1967; in U.S. Office of Education, *Students and Buildings: An Analysis of Selected
Federal Programs for Higher Education*, 1968, p. 8.

FIGURE 2.5-1   *Two factors in booming enrollments: More college-age people (18–24 years) and larger percent in college*

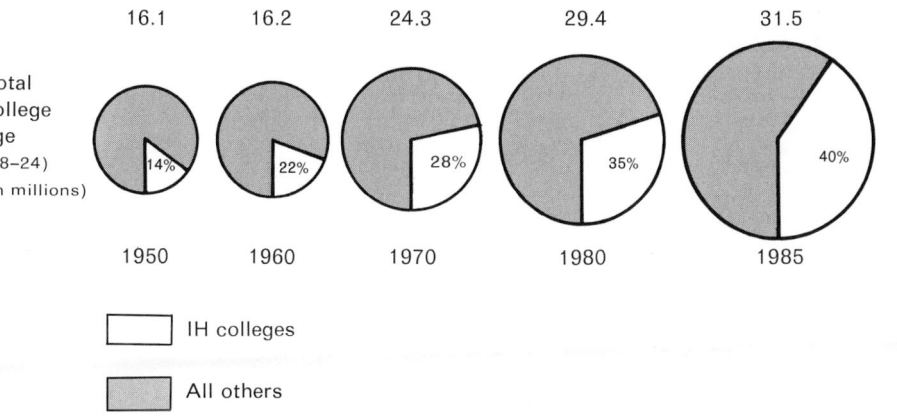

Total
college
age
(18–24)
(in millions)

| 16.1 | 16.2 | 24.3 | 29.4 | 31.5 |

| 14% | 22% | 28% | 35% | 40% |

| 1950 | 1960 | 1970 | 1980 | 1985 |

☐ IH colleges

▨ All others

SOURCE: S. E. Harris and A. Levensohn, eds., *Education and Public Policy,* McCutchan Publishing Corporation, Berkeley, Calif., 1965, p. 227.

higher education, compared to 24 percent in 1947. (4) In 1966, 20 percent of the population aged 20 to 24 were enrolled as students, compared to 10 percent in 1947.

Since high school students serve as reservoirs from which colleges draw their students, the relationship of high school graduates to the population aged 17 is of special interest to a study of enrollment-population trends at institutions of higher education. Between 1869–70 and 1966–67, a period of 97 years, the number of high school graduates per 100 persons 17 years of age rose from 2.0 to 76.2, an average annual increase of 0.76 percent. Between 1955–56 and 1966–67, this ratio of high school graduates to population aged 17 rose by around 1.26 percent a year, representing a cumulative increase over this period of 14 percent. The highest average annual increase of 2.2 percent took place between 1929–30 and 1939–40, the period of the Depression (Table 2.5-4). More schooling seemed to be a way out of the severe conditions of unemployment.

A summary of my estimates of the projected growth of college-age population (18 to 24) and of the proportion of the population attending college between 1950 and 1985 is contained in Figure 2.5-1.[2] It was expected that during this 35-year period the college-

(Text continued on p. 418)

[2] S. E. Harris and A. Levensohn, eds., *Education and Public Policy,* McCutchan Publishing Corporation, Berkeley, Calif. 1965, p. 227. Projections were made in 1959.

	Year (1)	Total, 5 to 34 years (2)	5 years* (3)	6 years* (4)	7 to 9 years (5)	10 to 13 years (6)	14 and 15 years (7)
TABLE 2.5-3 Percentage of the population 5 to 34 years old enrolled in school, by age; United States, October 1947 to 1966	1947	42.3	53.4	96.2	99.4	98.6	91.6
	1948	43.1	55.0	96.2	98.3	98.0	92.7
	1949	43.9	55.1	96.2	98.5	98.7	93.5
	1950	44.2	51.8	97.0	98.9	98.6	94.7
	1951	45.4	53.8	96.0	99.0	99.2	94.8
	1952	46.8	57.8	96.8	98.7	98.9	96.2
	1953	48.8	58.4	97.7	99.4	99.4	96.5
	1954	50.0	57.7	96.8	99.2	99.5	95.8
	1955	50.8	58.1	98.2	99.2	99.2	95.9
	1956	52.3	58.9	97.0	99.4	99.2	96.9
	1957	53.6	60.2	97.4	99.5	99.5	97.1
	1958	54.8	63.8	97.3	99.5	99.5	96.9
	1959	55.5	62.9	97.5	99.4	99.4	97.5
	1960	56.4	63.7	98.0	99.6	99.5	97.8
	1961	56.8	66.3	97.4	99.4	99.3	97.6
	1962	57.8	66.8	97.9	99.2	99.3	98.0
	1963	58.5	67.8	97.4	99.4	99.3	98.4
	1964	58.7	68.5	98.2	99.0	99.0	98.6
	1965	59.7	70.1	98.7	99.3	99.4	98.9
	1966	60.0	72.8	97.6	99.3	99.3	98.6

* Includes children enrolled in kindergarten.

SOURCE: U.S. Department of Commerce, Bureau of the Census, "Current Population Reports," Series P-20, No. 162; in U.S. Office of Education, *Digest of Educational Statistics, 1968,* 1968, p. 4.

16 and 17 years (8)	*18 and 19 years* (9)	*20 to 24 years* (10)	*25 to 29 years* (11)	*30 to 34 years* (12)
67.6	24.3	10.2	3.0	1.0
71.2	26.9	9.7	2.6	0.9
69.5	25.3	9.2	3.8	1.1
71.3	29.4	9.0	3.0	0.9
75.1	26.3	8.3	2.5	0.7
73.4	28.7	9.5	2.6	1.2
74.7	31.2	11.1	2.9	1.7
78.0	32.4	11.2	4.1	1.5
77.4	31.5	11.1	4.2	1.6
78.4	35.4	12.8	5.1	1.9
80.5	34.9	14.0	5.5	1.8
80.6	37.6	13.4	5.7	2.2
82.9	36.8	12.7	5.1	2.2
82.6	38.4	13.1	4.9	2.4
83.6	38.0	13.7	4.4	2.0
84.3	41.8	15.6	5.0	2.6
87.1	40.9	17.3	4.9	2.5
87.7	41.6	16.8	5.2	2.6
87.4	46.3	19.0	6.1	3.2
88.5	47.2	19.9	6.5	2.7

TABLE 2.5-4 *Number of high school graduates compared with population 17 years of age; United States, 1869–70 to 1966–67*

School year (1)	Population 17 years old† (2)	High school graduates* Total (3)	Boys (4)	Girls (5)	Number graduated per 100 persons 17 years of age (6)
1869–70	815,000	16,000	7,064	8,936	2.0
1879–80	946,026	23,634	10,605	13,029	2.5
1889–90	1,259,177	43,731	18,549	25,182	3.5
1899–1900	1,489,146	94,883	38,075	56,808	6.4
1909–10	1,786,240	156,429	63,676	92,573	8.8
1919–20	1,855,173	311,266	123,684	187,582	16.8
1929–30	2,295,822	666,904	300,376	366,528	29.0
1939–40	2,403,074	1,221,475	578,718	642,757	50.8
1941–42	2,425,574	1,242,375	576,717	665,658	51.2
1943–44	2,410,389	1,019,233	423,971	595,262	42.3
1945–46	2,254,738	1,080,033	466,926	613,107	47.9
1947–48	2,202,927	1,189,909	562,863	627,046	54.0
1949–50	2,034,450	1,199,700	570,000	629,000	59.0
1951–52	2,040,800	1,196,500	569,200	627,300	58.6
1953–54	2,128,600	1,276,100	612,500	663,600	60.0
1955–56	2,270,000	1,414,800	679,500	735,300	62.3
1957–58	2,324,000	1,505,900	725,500	780,400	64.8
1959–60	2,862,005	1,864,000	898,000	966,000	65.1
1961–62	2,768,000	1,925,000	941,000	984,000	69.5
1963–64	3,001,000	2,290,000	1,121,000	1,169,000	76.3
1965–66	3,522,000	2,672,000	1,326,000	1,346,000	75.9
1966–67‡	3,518,000	2,679,000	1,331,000	1,348,000	76.2

*Includes graduates of public and nonpublic schools.
† Data from the Bureau of the Census.
‡ Preliminary data.
NOTE: Beginning in 1959–60, includes Alaska and Hawaii.
SOURCE: U.S. Department of Health, Education and Welfare, Office of Education, "Biennial Survey of Education in the United States," chapters on statistical summary of education; in U.S. Office of Education, *Digest of Educational Statistics, 1968,* 1968, p. 52.

age population would double and that 40 percent of students aged 18 to 24 would be enrolled in institutions of higher education, compared to a proportion of 14 percent in 1950. The growth of enrollment in the future is expected to result more from the relative rise in numbers at universities and colleges than from increases in the size of the college-age population.

HISTORICAL AND RECENT EXPERIENCE OF STATES
The ranking of states according to the ratio of the state's population per resident enrolled in college anywhere for 1875, 1890, and 1958 appears in Table 2.5-5. In 1958 the state with the most favorable ratio was Oklahoma (1 college student per 50 of the population) and the one with the least desirable ratio was Virginia (1 college student per 117 of the population). Over this period the most impressive improvements were in Oklahoma, Arizona, Utah, and North Dakota, where population growth invited the opening of an increasing number of institutions of higher education. The rankings over this period of certain New England states—namely, Vermont,

TABLE 2.5-5 *Population per resident in college anywhere 1875, 1890, and 1958*

State	Rank in 1958	Populations per student			Rank in 1890	Changes in rank, 1890–1958	
		1958	1890	1875		Upward	Downward
Oklahoma	1	50	15,458	*	49	48	
Arizona	2½	51	5,962	*	45	42½	
Utah	2½	51	4,077	*	44	41½	
North Dakota	4	52	2,900	*	42	38	
Kansas	5	54	1,449	3,919	24	19	
California	6	56	1,001	835	12	6	
South Dakota	7	57	1,797	*	30	23	
Wyoming	8	58	2,828	*	40	32	
Connecticut	9½	61	930	686	7		2½
New York	9½	61	1,089	1,562	15	5½	
Idaho	12½	62	6,027	*	46	33½	
Montana	12½	62	2,240	*	34	21½	
Nebraska	12½	62	1,911	2,921	31	18½	
Washington	12½	62	2,393	*	36	23½	
Massachusetts	15	63	858	951	4		11
Oregon	16	64	894	641	5		11
New Mexico	17½	65	13,963	*	48	30½	

TABLE 2.5-5 *(continued)*

State	Rank in 1958	Populations per student			Rank in 1890	Changes in rank, 1890–1958	
		1958	1890	1875		Upward	Downward
Texas	17½	65	2,433	2,310	38	20½	
New Jersey	19½	66	1,438	1,446	23	3½	
Minnesota	19½	66	1,257	3,903	17		2½
Michigan	21	67	1,383	1,702	21		
Colorado	22½	68	2,181	*	33	10½	
Iowa	22½	68	908	1,496	6		16½
Louisiana	24½	69	1,011	15,420	13½		11
Illinois	24½	69	1,292	1,821	18		6½
Wisconsin	26	75	1,364	1,733	20		6
West Virginia	27	77	2,871	3,277	41	14	
District of Columbia	28½	78	789	1,365	2½		26
Indiana	28½	78	1,409	1,406	22		6½
Ohio	30	80	986	1,315	10		20
Arkansas	31	81	7,374	6,072	47	16	
Mississippi	33	82	2,401	5,201	37	4	
Nevada	33	82	789	*	2½		30½
Pennsylvania	33	82	1,506	1,751	25		8
Alabama	36	83	2,275	3,635	35		1
Florida	36	83	2,943	*	43	7	
Kentucky	36	83	1,557	1,660	27		9
New Hampshire	38½	84	934	1,346	8		30½
Vermont	38½	84	757	1,917	1		37½
Tennessee	40	85	1,194	1,362	16		24
Missouri	41	87	1,518	2,077	26		15
Maryland	42	94	1,335	1,216	19		23
North Carolina	43	96	1,968	3,279	32		11
Georgia	44½	98	2,698	2,843	39		5½
Rhode Island	44½	98	996	1,142	11		33½
Delaware	46	107	952	3,355	9		37
Maine	47½	110	1,011	1,763	13½		34
South Carolina	47½	110	1,659	2,471	28		19½
Virginia	49	117	1,754	1,389	29		20

* Data not available.

SOURCE: *Report of U.S. Commissioner of Education for 1887–1888,* pp. 751–753; *Report for 1890–1891,* vol 2, p. 827; American Council on Education, "A Fact Book on Higher Education," p. 116.

Maine, New Hampshire, and Rhode Island—and Delaware declined, a phenomenon related to worsening relative economic conditions in these states and to out-migration of young people.

When states were ranked according to the relationship of fall enrollment to the college-age population 18 to 21 years of age, the results were similar to those in Table 2.5-6. The ratio of fall enrollment to this age group was especially favorable in sparsely populated states. Of the first ten states with the highest ratios, six fall into this category. Utah, with over 77 percent of its college-age population enrolled at institutions of higher education, had the highest ratio (Table 2.5-6).

In 1962–63, the ratio among states of college entrants to high

ABLE 2.5-6 *Fall enrollments related to total college-age populations in order of rank by percentage f total college-age population enrolled, 1964, 50 states*

'tate	18- to 21-year-olds	Fall enrollment	Percentage	Rank
Jtah	64,035	49,373	77.1	1
Arizona	88,274	59,690	67.6	2
Massachusetts	301,180	180,795	60.0	3
Oklahoma	131,455	75,672	57.6	4
Colorado	112,516	63,916	56.8	5
Minnesota	185,114	104,943	56.7	6
California	1,204,863	667,902	55.4	7
Kansas	132,483	71,832	54.2	8
Nebraska	79,058	42,798	54.1	9
South Dakota	37,299	19,580	52.5	10
Vermont	22,743	11,927	52.4	11
Montana	33,906	17,623	52.0	12
North Dakota	35,263	18,138	51.4	13
Iowa	146,565	74,519	50.8	14
Oregon	116,506	59,137	50.8	15
New York	900,574	454,349	50.5	16
Wyoming	18,105	9,148	50.5	17
Michigan	438,445	219,537	50.1	18
Wisconsin	214,528	107,482	50.1	19
Illinois	554,106	269,341	48.6	20
Connecticut	146,311	70,216	48.0	21
Missouri	242,501	116,103	47.9	22
New Hampshire	33,308	15,779	47.4	23

TABLE 2.5-6 *(continued)*

State	18- to 21-year-olds	Fall enrollment	Percentage	Rank
Indiana	282,163	127,362	45.1	24
Idaho	38,016	17,043	44.8	25
Rhode Island	60,874	26,790	44.0	26
Pennsylvania	581,743	252,047	43.3	27
New Mexico	60,608	25,992	42.9	28
Ohio	568,251*	241,835	42.6	29
Washington	218,570	90,513	41.4	30
Delaware	28,029	11,550	41.2	31
West Virginia	96,677	39,095	40.4	32
Louisiana	209,544	82,864	39.5	33
Maryland	210,493	82,660	39.3	34
Texas	661,354	256,003	38.7	35
Nevada	18,221	6,814	37.4	36
Florida	312,821	115,841	37.0	37 .
Kentucky	179,370	65,534	36.5	38
New Jersey	329,518	118,514	36.0	39
Arkansas	100,013	35,810	35.8	40
Tennessee	245,717	87,397	35.6	41
Mississippi	137,696	46,567	33.8	42
Maine	58,516	17,683	30.2	43
North Carolina	316,679	93,579	29.6	44
Hawaii	54,407	15,880	29.2	45
Virginia	292,777	78,041	26.7	46
Alabama	210,098	56,091	26.7	47
Georgia	270,445	67,457	24.9	48
South Carolina	175,561	38,282	21.8	49
Alaska	20,673	4,147	20.1	50
Service schools, District of Columbia, and outlying parts	58,820 (D.C.)	106,676		
Total United States	11,029,249	4,987,867	45.2	

*Revised from estimate of 560, 708 used by Thompson.

SOURCE: Data for 18- to 21-year-olds from Ronald B. Thompson, *Enrollment Projections for Higher Education, 1961–1978,* American Association of Collegiate Registrars and Admissions Officers, 1961. Data for fall enrollments from U.S. Office of Education, *Opening (Fall) Enrollment in Higher Education, 1964,* 1964; in Ohio Board of Regents, *Provisional Master Plan for Public Higher Education in Ohio,* Columbus Blank Book Company, Columbus, Ohio, 1965, p. 6.

school graduates varied greatly. The aggregate for the United States was 0.51 with the ratio for California (0.81) far ahead of any other state. Other states with ratios above 0.60 were Nevada, Wyoming, Florida, Idaho, Illinois, and Arizona. More than one-quarter of the states had less than 45 percent of their high school graduates registered to enter college that year. These included Maine, Alabama, South Carolina, Vermont, North Carolina, West Virginia, New Hampshire, Pennsylvania, Georgia, Tennessee, Indiana, Michigan, and Ohio (Table 2.5-7).

TABLE 2.5-7
College entrance to high school graduation ratios, by states

Ratio of college registrants, fall 1963,* to high school graduates, 1962–63	
Aggregate United States	0.51
The fifty states and the District of Columbia	0.51
Alabama	0.32
Alaska	0.47
Arizona	0.61
Arkansas	0.47
California	0.81
Colorado	0.55
Connecticut	0.58
Delaware	0.45
District of Columbia	0.60
Florida	0.62
Georgia	0.39
Hawaii	0.49
Idaho	0.62
Illinois	0.62
Indiana	0.44
Iowa	0.48
Kansas	0.54
Kentucky	0.47
Louisiana	0.47
Maine	0.31
Maryland	0.52
Massachusetts	0.53
Michigan	0.44

TABLE 2.5-7 *(continued)*

Ratio of college regis- trants, fall 1963* to high school graduates, 1962–63	
Minnesota	0.46
Mississippi	0.52
Missouri	0.49
Montana	0.58
Nebraska	0.54
Nevada	0.70
New Hamsphire	0.38
New Jersey	0.53
New Mexico	0.49
New York	0.47
North Carolina	0.36
North Dakota	0.50
Ohio	0.44
Oklahoma	0.54
Oregon	0.54
Pennsylvania	0.38
Rhode Island	0.45
South Carolina	0.34
South Dakota	0.51
Tennessee	0.42
Texas	0.57
Utah	0.56
Vermont	0.34
Virginia	0.47
Washington	0.57
West Virginia	0.37
Wisconsin	0.43
Wyoming	0.63
Outlying parts of the United States	0.44

*For each state: Number of first-time college registrants in the United States giving that state as the state of their permanent residence, divided by the number of students graduating from that state's high schools.

SOURCE: U.S. House of Representatives, Committee on Science and Astronautics, *Higher Education in the Sciences in the United States,* report of the Subcommittee on Science, Research and Development, prepared by the National Science Foundation, 1965, p. 18.

2.6. International Comparisons

Table 2.6-1 contains data on world enrollment at three levels of education for 1950, 1960, and 1966; estimates of average annual increases in enrollment for each level over this period; and the percentage distribution of enrollment by level in each of these years. By far the largest number of persons in the world were enrolled at the primary level although the proportion of the total accounted for by primary enrollment dropped from 80 percent in 1950 to around 73 percent in 1966. This decline resulted from increases in the proportion of total enrollment represented by both secondary and higher education. Between 1950 and 1966 the following occurred: (1) The shares accounted for by secondary and higher education increased by 31 and 64 percent, respectively. (2) The proportion that secondary-level enrollment represented of enrollment at all levels increased by 5.4 percentage points—from 17.2 to 22.6 percent. (3) The ratio of enrollment of the third level to total enrollment increased from 2.8 percent to 4.6 percent. The largest gains in enrollment were in higher education, which grew at the average rate of approximately 10 percent a year between 1950 and 1966. This compares with average annual growth rates of enrollment over this period of 3.9 and 7.2 percent at the first and second levels of education, respectively.

Table 2.6-2 presents the same information as that contained in Table 2.6-1 for six major areas of the world.[1] Between 1950 and 1966, average annual enrollment at all levels grew most rapidly in Africa (13.6 percent) and Asia (8 percent), and least rapidly in the U.S.S.R. (2.6 percent) and Europe (2.4 percent). At the first, second, and third levels, the rise in numbers in African countries exceeded the increases occurring in all other areas of the world.

---

[1] See Table 2.6-3 for definition of world areas.

TABLE 2.6-1
World
enrollment at all
educational
levels,* 1950,
1960, and 1966

	Enrollment, thousands			*Average annual increase (percentage)*	
	1950	*1960*	*1966*	*1950–1966*	*1960–1966*
Primary school	177,145	248,486	311,700	4.4	3.9
Secondary school	38,041	63,927	96,713	9.1	7.2
Higher education	6,317	11,174	19,992	12.7	10.2
TOTAL	221,503	323,587	428,405	5.5	4.8

	Percentage distribution		
	1950	*1960*	*1966*
Primary school	80.0	76.8	72.8
Secondary school	17.2	19.8	22.6
Higher education	2.8	3.4	4.6
TOTAL	100.0	100.0	100.0

* See Table 2.6-3 for definition of each level of education.
SOURCE: UNESCO, *Statistical Yearbook, 1968,* Paris, 1969, p. 54.

From 1950 to 1966, the average rate of growth of enrollment for major world areas at the third level was as follows: Africa (22 percent), Asia (19 percent), Oceania (16 percent), U.S.S.R. (14 percent), America[2] (11 percent), and Europe (9 percent). Clearly, less developed countries and others with relatively low levels of enrollment in higher education in 1950 recorded the fastest rates of growth over this period.

Table 2.6-3 contains information on the distribution of world population, school-age population, enrollment at three levels by major areas of the world in 1965, and the percentage of the population aged 5 to 24 enrolled at all levels. The proportion of school-age population enrolled at all levels ranged from a low of around 20 percent in Asia and Africa to a high of approximately 75 percent in North America. Two additional tables (2.6-4 and 2.6-5) were constructed using data from Table 2.6-3. The subject of Table 2.6-4 is the proportion that school-age population (5 to 24 years of age) and enrollment at three levels represents of total population for major areas of the world. Table 2.6-5 provides a distribution of world enrollment by school-age population and by three levels of education for these areas.

[2] Includes North America, South America, Central America, and the Caribbean.

The population of the world aged 5 to 24 (school-age population) consisted of more than a billion persons and accounted for about 40 percent of the world's population in 1965. The ratio of an area's school-age population to its total population was below the world average in the case of Europe, U.S.S.R., Oceania, and North America and above the world average in Middle America and Africa, South America, and the Caribbean (Table 2.6-4).

Approximately 13 percent of the world population was enrolled at all levels in 1965: 9 percent at the first level, 2.7 percent at the second level, and 0.6 percent at the third level. The ratio of enrollment to population at all levels was higher than the world average in all areas except Asia and Africa. At the third level, enrollment-population ratios in Middle America, South America, and the Caribbean were below the world average. The proportion of North America's population enrolled in school was the highest at all levels (Table 2.6-4).

About one-third of the world's school-age population was enrolled at all levels in 1965. The differences in the distribution of the school-age population and of enrollment at each level among major areas of the world reflected the stage of economic development of the majority of countries within an area. Asia and Africa, with large school-age populations, had disproportionately low levels of enrollment. Asia, for example, with over half of the world's school-age population, accounted for about 36 percent of world enrollment at all levels and about 20 percent of world enrollment at the third level. Enrollment in Africa, which includes about 11 percent of the world's school-age population, amounted to 7.2 percent of world enrollment at all levels and 1.8 percent of global enrollment at the third level. At the other extreme were North America, U.S.S.R., and Europe, where the relationship between school-age population and enrollment was reversed. These areas, accounting for relatively low proportions of the world's school-age population, had considerably higher shares of total enrollment at all levels. North America and the Soviet Union, for example, each had school-age populations that amounted to no more than 6 percent of the world total. However, the proportions of total world enrollment at the third level represented by third-level enrollment in North America and the Soviet Union were 32 and 21 percent, respectively (Table 2.6-5).

(Text continued on p. 433)

		1950		1960	
TABLE 2.6-2 Estimated total enrollment by level of education and by major areas (1950, 1960, and 1966) and average annual increases in enrollment between 1950–1966 and 1960–1966		Number (thousands)	Percent-age total	Number (thousands)	Percent-age total
Africa					
	TOTAL	9,328	100.0	21,238	100.0
	First level	8,511	91.2	18,931	89.1
	Second level	745	8.0	2,115	10.0
	Third level	71	0.8	192	0.9
*America**					
	TOTAL	50,441	100.0	80,144	100.0
	First level	39,146	77.6	60,810	75.9
	Second level	8,638	17.0	15,042	18.7
	Third level	2,657	5.3	4,292	5.4
Asia					
	TOTAL	66,967	100.0	110,691	100.0
	First level	53,303	79.6	87,236	78.8
	Second level	12,658	18.9	21,325	19.3
	Third level	1,007	1.5	3,722	1.9
Europe					
	TOTAL	56,966	100.0	70,453	100.0
	First level	42,899	75.3	49,106	69.7
	Second level	12,786	22.5	19,285	27.4
	Third level	1,280	2.2	2,061	2.9
Oceania					
	TOTAL	2,058	100.0	3,306	100.0
	First level	1,584	76.9	2,403	72.7
	Second level	419	20.4	801	24.2
	Third level	55	2.7	102	3.1
U.S.S.R.					
	TOTAL	35,743	100.0	37,755	100.0
	First level	31,702	88.7	30,000	79.5
	Second level	2,794	7.8	5,359	14.2
	Third level	1,247	3.5	2,396	6.3

* Includes North America, South America, Central America and the Caribbean. For countries included, see footnotes to Table 2.6-3.

SOURCE: UNESCO, *Statistical Yearbook, 1968,* Paris, 1969, pp. 54–55. According-ing to this source, the breakdown and percentage distribution by level of education are affected by the length of schooling at each level, which, in turn, depends on the criteria applied in the national definition of levels. Since these criteria, particularly

1966		Average annual percentage increase	
Number (thousands)	*Percentage total*	*1950– 1966*	*1960– 1966*
30,975	100.0	13.6	6.5
26,748	86.3	12.5	5.9
3,895	12.6	24.9	10.7
334	1.1	21.8	9.7
104,286	100.0	6.2	4.5
70,259	67.4	4.6	2.4
26,323	25.2	11.9	9.8
7,704	7.4	11.1	10.2
157,802	100.0	8.0	6.1
121,516	77.0	7.5	5.7
32,105	20.3	9.1	7.1
4,181	2.7	18.5	11.9
79,876	100.0	2.4	2.1
51,400	64.4	1.1	.8
25,034	31.3	5.6	4.4
3,442	4.3	9.9	8.9
4,105	100.0	5.8	3.7
2,719	66.2	4.2	2.1
1,178	28.7	10.6	6.6
208	5.1	16.4	12.6
51,361	100.0	2.6	5.3
39,058	76.1	1.4	4.5
8,180	15.9	11.4	7.3
4,123	8.0	13.6	9.5

with respect to primary and secondary education, vary from country to country, caution should be exercised in making comparisons between areas and also in interpreting changes observed within a given area over a period of time. They may be a result of a reorganization of the school system in one or more countries of that area (ibid., p. 54).

TABLE 2.6-3
Estimated population and enrollment by level in major areas of the world, 1965 (in thousands)

Major area (1)	Population	
	All ages (2)	Between 5 and 24 years of age[b] (3)
World total	3,269,154	1,297,937
Africa	306,173	138,901
Asia (excluding U.S.S.R.)	1,816,812	749,735
Europe (excluding U.S.S.R.)	440,301	139,027
Oceania	17,166	5,991
U.S.S.R.	231,000	79,382
Western hemisphere:		
North America[f]	213,150	77,365
Middle America[g]	54,843	25,412
South America	167,017	72,229
Caribbean	22,692	9,895

[a] Does not include data for the mainland of China, North Korea, and North Vietnam.

[b] Does not include data for North Korea, Ryukyu Islands, Israel, Cyprus, Polynesia and Micronesia. The total population of these areas in 1965 is estimated at 16,084,000.

[c] First level includes elementary school enrollment the main function of which is to provide basic instruction in the tools of learning. Preschool, kindergarten, and special education enrollment are excluded.

[d] Second level includes general, vocational, and teaching-training enrollments at the secondary school level. Entrance to secondary schools requires at least four years of previous instruction at the first level. Special and adult education enrollments are excluded.

[e] Third level includes colleges and universities that require the successful completion of education at the second level of education as a minimum entrance requirement. Adult education enrollments are excluded.

[f] Includes United States, Canada, Bermuda, Greenland, and St. Pierre and Miquelon.

[g] Includes Mexico, British Honduras, Canal Zone, and the Central American countries.

SOURCE: United Nations Educational, Scientific, and Cultural Organization, "Statistical Yearbook 1967," Paris; in U.S. Office of Education, *Digest of Educational Statistics, 1969,* 1969, p. 115.

| | Enrollment[a] | | | Percentage of population |
| | First level of education[c] | Second level of education[d] | Third level of education[e] | 5 to 24 enrolled at all levels |
All levels (4)	(5)	(6)	(7)	(8)
413,101	304,004	91,032	18,015	31.8
29,861	25,924	3,615	322	21.5
148,301	113,876	30,703	3,722	19.7
80,677	51,570	25,946	3,161	50.8
3,967	2,649	1,128	190	66.2
50,862	38,343	8,459	3,880	63.8
57,325	36,938	14,537	5,850	74.0
10,098	8,751	1,181	166	39.7
27,916	22,480	4,776	660	38.6
4,294	3,473	737	84	43.3

TABLE 2.6-4
*Population 5 to
24 years of age
and enrollment
at three levels
of education
as a percentage
of total
population for
the world and
for different
areas, 1965*

	Population 5 to 24 years of age	Enrollment			
		All levels	First	Second	Third
World total	39.7	12.6	9.3	2.7	0.6
Africa	45.3	9.8	8.5	1.2	0.1
Asia (excluding U.S.S.R.)	41.2	8.2	6.3	1.7	0.2
Europe (excluding U.S.S.R.)	31.5	18.3	11.7	5.9	0.7
Oceania	34.9	23.1	15.4	6.6	1.1
U.S.S.R.	34.3	22.0	16.6	3.7	1.7
North America	36.2	26.9	17.3	6.8	2.7
Middle America	46.3	18.4	16.0	2.1	0.3
South America	43.2	16.7	13.5	2.8	0.4
Caribbean	43.6	18.9	15.3	3.2	0.4

SOURCE: U.S. Office of Education, *Digest of Educational Statistics, 1969,* 1969, p. 115.

TABLE 2.6-5
*Distribution of
world
enrollment for
school-age
population and
for three levels
of education by
major areas of
the world, 1965*

	Population 5 to 24 years of age	Levels of education			
		All levels	First	Second	Third
World					
Number (thousands)	1,297,937	413,101	304,004	91,082	18,015
Percent	100.0	100.0	100.0	100.0	100.0
		Percent			
Africa	10.7	7.2	8.5	4.0	1.8
Asia	57.8	35.9	37.5	33.7	20.7
Europe	10.7	19.5	17.0	28.5	17.5
Oceania	0.5	0.9	0.9	1.2	1.1
U.S.S.R.	6.1	12.3	12.6	9.3	21.4
North America	5.9	13.9	12.1	16.0	32.4
Middle America	2.0	2.4	2.9	1.3	0.9
South America	5.6	6.8	7.4	5.2	3.7
Caribbean	0.7	1.1	1.1	0.8	0.5

SOURCE: Table 2.6-3.

The countries with the largest enrollment at the third level in 1966 were as follows:

	Number (in thousands)
United States*	6,390
U.S.S.R.*	4,123
India†	1,682
Japan*	1,270

* Data taken from UNESCO, *Statistical Yearbook, 1968,* Paris, 1969.
† Data do not include preuniversity and intermediate course. Taken from Institute of Applied Manpower Research, *Fact Book on Manpower, Part II: Education and Training,* A. J. A. Touro, New Delhi, 1969, p. 107.

Table 2.6-6 provides estimates of the number of enrolled students at the third level per 100,000 inhabitants for countries in the world which had the highest ratios in 1966. These give some indication of the relative magnitude of higher education for different world areas. With the exception of Canada and the U.S.S.R., the United States ratio of 3,245 was between two and three times higher than that of all other countries covered in the table.

Table 2.6-7 includes estimates of the growth of enrollment in institutions of higher education in selected European countries. Be-

TABLE 2.6-6
Number of enrolled students per 100,000 inhabitants, selected countries, 1950 and 1966

	1950	1966
United States	1,508	3,245
Canada	593	1,857
U.S.S.R.	693	1,769
Israel	403	1,488
Philippines	902	1,441
Netherlands	603	1,310
Japan	471	1,285
Australia	441	1,256
Bulgaria	381	1,124
New Zealand	742	1,104
Denmark	428	1,101
Argentina	483	1,092
France	334	1,076

SOURCE: UNESCO, *Statistical Yearbook, 1968,* Paris, 1969, pp. 185–199.

	Enrollment at the third level[a]		
TABLE 2.6-7 **Growth of** **enrollment at** **institutions of** **higher education** **in selected** **European** **countries from** **1950 to 1966**	*1950* *(numbers)*	*1960* *(relatives:* *1950 = 100)*	*1966* *(relatives:* *1950 = 100)*
Austria	24,793	155	200
Belgium	35,033[b]	148	259[c]
Denmark	18,283	155	289
France[d]	145,865	186	294
Germany, Federated Republic	246,090	166	208[c]
Italy	145,170	132	235
Netherlands	61,036	174	267
Norway	7,537	122	279
Spain	55,272	158	279
Sweden[e]	16,887	219	353[c]
Switzerland	16,550	129	203
Turkey	24,815	263	455
Yugoslavia	60,395	234	324
United Kingdom (England *and Wales)*	106,691[f]	166[g]	291

[a] Except where noted, the source of enrollment data was UNESCO, *Statistical Year book, 1968,* Paris, 1969, pp. 195–199.

[b] Refers to 1952.

[c] Refers to 1965.

[d] Refers to enrollment in universities exclusively. Data taken from OECD, *Case Studies on Innovation in Higher Education: French Experience Before 1968,* Paris, 1970, p. 19.

[e] Data taken from OECD, *Development of Secondary Education: Trends and Implications,* Paris, 1969, p. 129.

[f] Refers to universities and degree-granting institutions exclusively.

[g] Refers to 1961.

tween 1950 and 1966, countries experiencing the largest increases were Turkey, Sweden, and Yugoslavia; those whose enrollment was growing at the slowest rates were Austria, Switzerland, and Germany.

It is common practice to measure the relative important of higher education in a country by estimating the ratio of enrollment at the third level to an age cohort that roughly corresponds to the typical ages of people attending universities or colleges. Among the difficulties in making such estimates in coverage of institutions of higher education among countries are the lack of uniformity from country to country and changes over time. Another has to do with relating total numbers of enrolled students in higher education to a specific age cohort. Ideally, the ratio should apply to enrolled students who are the same age as those in the selected age cohort. These reservations should be kept in mind when interpreting the data contained in Table 2.6-8.

What is apparent from this table regarding the ratio of enrollment at the third level to the population age group 20 to 24 is the following: (1) The United States had a ratio that was three to four times that of all other countries covered in the table in 1950 and in 1965. The United States ratio in 1950 (around 20 percent) exceeded the ratios of all other countries except Canada in 1965. By 1965 the United States ratio had more than doubled, rising to over 40 percent. (2) The countries which experienced the highest percentage rates of increase in their ratios between 1950 and 1965 were Canada, Sweden, and Belguim. (3) Over this period, Italy recorded the least change in the proportion of its college-age population attending colleges or universities.

TABLE 2.6-8
Total enrollment in higher education as a percentage of population 20 to 24 years of age, for selected countries, 1950 and 1965*

Country	1950, percentage	1965, percentage
Austria	4.1	8.5
Belgium	5.3	13.7
France†	4.4	10.9 (14.9)
Germany, Federated Republic	3.5	8.6
Italy	5.4	9.4
Netherlands	7.6	16.5
Sweden†	3.7	10.5 (12.5)
United Kingdom (England and Wales)‡	3.5	7.6
United States	19.5	41.2
Canada	7.1	23.8

* Except where noted, the source of data on population aged 20 to 24 and enrollment in higher educational institutions in both years was OECD, *Development of Secondary Education: Trends and Implications,* Paris, 1969, pp. 128 and 129. The enrollment data refer to persons of all ages enrolled at degree-granting and non-degree-granting institutions of higher education of all types (universities, higher technical schools, teacher training colleges, theological schools, etc.).

† Enrollment data refer to persons enrolled at universities exclusively. The figures in parentheses under 1965 represent the ratio of total enrollment to population aged 20 to 24.

‡ Enrollment refers to persons enrolled at universities, degree-granting institutions, and teacher training colleges only.

During the 1950s, the proportion of new entrants in higher education to secondary school graduates was considerably higher in
most Western European countries than in the United States (Table
2.6-9). The principal reason for this was the much larger proportion
of the relevant age group graduating from high school in the United
States compared with Western Europe. In 1959 about half of the
high school graduates in the United States went on to higher education compared to a proportion of more than 70 percent in Denmark,
United Kingdom, France, Germany, and Italy. Only Norway,
Greece, Ireland and Canada, of the countries covered in this table,
had ratios of new entrants to high school graduates lower than that
of the United States. The process of attrition from completion of
primary school to entry into higher education for selected countries
in the 1950s is depicted in Figure 2.6-1.

TABLE 2.6-9 New entrants to higher education in relation to secondary school graduates qualified for admission to higher education, 1950, 1955, and 1959			
Country*	1950	1955	1959
Italy†	100	100	99
Germany, Federated Republic	84	95	81
France	94	87	81
United Kingdom‡		85	78
Denmark	73	60	71
Sweden	63	62	67
Netherlands	53	58	67
Belgium	52	52	62
Austria	43	53	56
Spain	73	53	50
United States	43	50	50
Norway	41	37	47
Greece		39	41
Ireland	47	29	40
Canada			40

* Data are not available for Switzerland, Turkey, and Yugoslavia. For United Kingdom
they are not comparable.
† Taking into account the total number of "abilitazione tecnica" and "abilitazione
magistrale" graduates instead of only those entering higher education (as was done
in this table) the following ratios are relevant:

1950	1955	1959	1963	1970
65	60	60	61	65

‡ Great Britain only.
SOURCE: OECD, *Resources of Scientific and Technical Personnel in the O.E.C.D
Area,* Paris, 1959, p. 44.

FIGURE 2.6-1 *The admissions process in the 1950s*

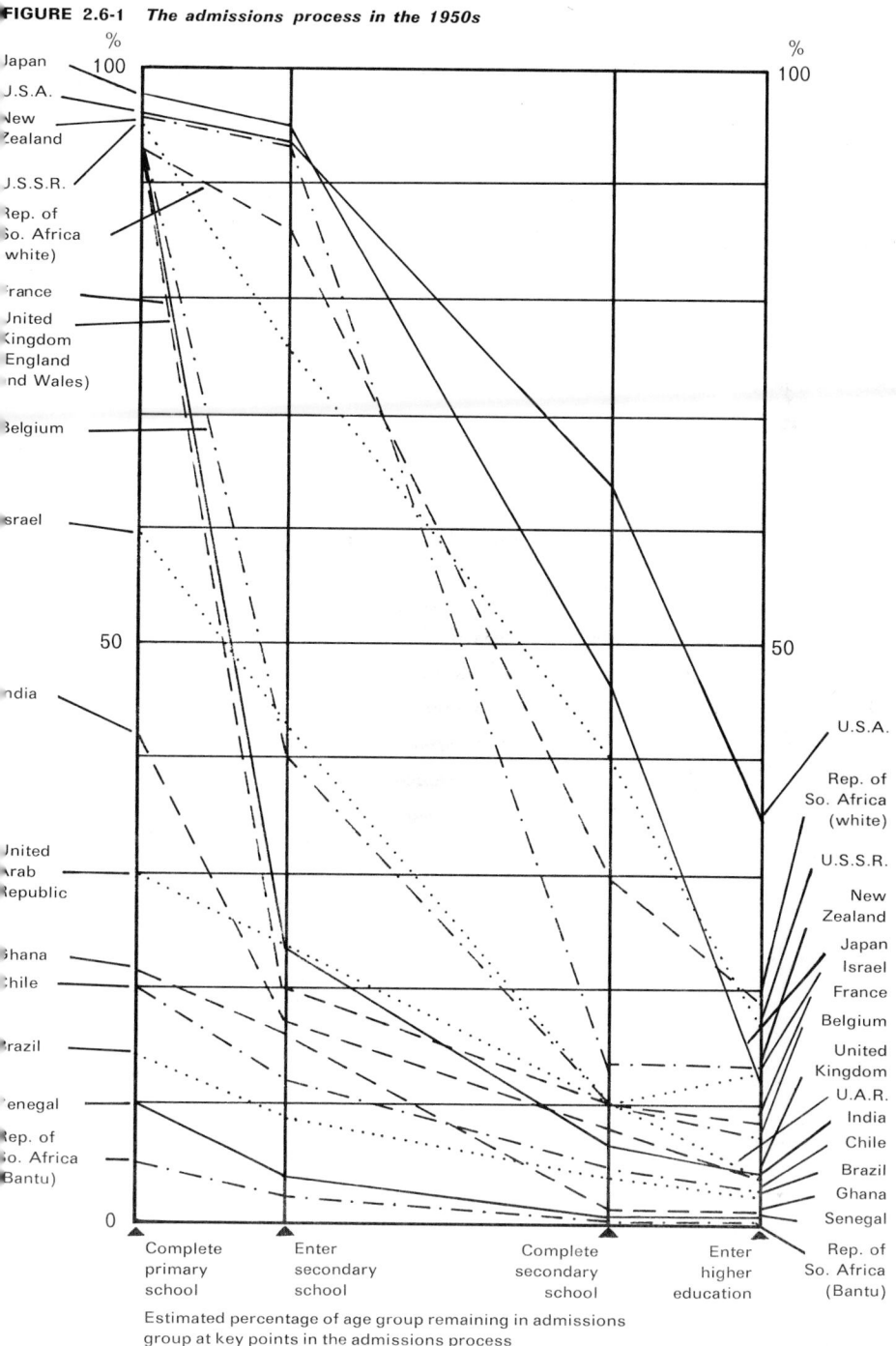

Japan
U.S.A.
New
Zealand

U.S.S.R.
Rep. of
So. Africa
(white)

France
United
Kingdom
(England
and Wales)

Belgium

Israel

India

United
Arab
Republic

Ghana
Chile

Brazil

Senegal
Rep. of
So. Africa
(Bantu)

U.S.A.

Rep. of
So. Africa
(white)

U.S.S.R.

New
Zealand

Japan

Israel

France

Belgium

United
Kingdom

U.A.R.

India

Chile

Brazil

Ghana

Senegal

Rep. of
So. Africa
(Bantu)

Complete
primary
school

Enter
secondary
school

Complete
secondary
school

Enter
higher
education

Estimated percentage of age group remaining in admissions
group at key points in the admissions process

SOURCE: F. Bowles, *Access to Higher Education,* UNESCO, Paris, 1963, vol. 1, p. 77.

TABLE 2.6-10
Percentage of students in institutions of higher education, for selected years; by method of study, U.S.S.R.

Year	Full-time (day) students	Part-time students			All students
		Evening	Correspondence	All part-time	
1940	68.8	3.3	27.9	31.2	100.0
1950	65.7	2.2	32.1	34.3	100.0
1955	61.5	4.3	34.1	38.5	100.0
1956	58.8	5.0	36.2	41.2	100.0
1957	56.8	6.1	37.1	43.2	100.0
1958	54.2	7.2	38.6	45.8	100.0
1959	50.6	8.7	40.7	49.4	100.0

SOURCE: Great Britain, *Higher Education,* report of the Committee Appointed by the Prime Minister under the Chairmanship of Lord Robbins, Her Majesty's Stationery Office, London, 1963, p. 289.

TABLE 2.6-11
Enrollments of aspirants (graduate students), by type of instruction; U.S.S.R., selected years, 1940–1961

Type of instruction	Number of aspirants			
	1940	1950	1955	1960
TOTAL	16,863	21,905	29,362	36,754
In higher educational institutions	13,169	12,487	16,774	20,406
Training with interruption from production	11,506	11,199	13,212	13,463
Training without interruption from production	1,663	1,288	3,562	6,943
In scientific organizations	3,694	9,418	12,588	16,348
Training with interruption from production	2,919	6,944	8,145	9,515
Training without interruption from production	775	2,474	4,443	6,833

SOURCE: S. M. Rosen, *Higher Education in the U.S.S.R.,* U.S. Office of Education, 1969, p. 106.

SOME COMPARISONS BETWEEN THE UNITED STATES AND THE SOVIET UNION	Tables 2.6-10, 2.6-11, 2.6-12, and 2.6-13 contain information which is used for comparing certain features of higher education in the United States and the U.S.S.R. Between 1940 and 1960, enrollment in American and Russian higher educational institutions was as follows:

Year	United States	U.S.S.R.
1940–41	1,494*	812
1949–50	2,659	1,032
1959–60	3,215	2,267

* Refers to enrollment in 1939–40. United States enrollment data for all years covered here refer to degree-credit enrollment.

SOURCES: U.S. Office of Education, *Digest of Educational Statistics, 1968*, 1968, p. 9; and S. M. Rosen, *Higher Education in the U.S.S.R.*, U.S. Office of Education, 1969, p. 100.

1960 as percentage (or multiple of)

1940	1950	1955	1961
218	168	125	47,560
155	163	122	27,066
177	120	102	17,367
(4.2 times)	(5.4 times)	195	9,699
(4.4 times)	174	130	20,494
(3.3 times)	137	117	11,308
(8.8 times)	276	154	9,186

	Thousands of specialists			
	1928	Jan. 1, 1941	Jan. 1, 1946	July 1, 1950
Total specialists with higher education working in the national economy	233.0	909.0	896.9	1,442.8
	(100)	(100)	(100)	(100
Engineers	47.0	289.9	277.5	392.4
	(20.2)	(31.9)	(30.9)	(27.2
Agronomists, zootechnicians, veterinarians, and foresters	28.0	69.6	59.4	109.5
	(12.0)	(7.7)	(6.6)	(7.6
Economists, economist-statisticians		57.0	48.3	72.8
	13.0	(6.2)	(5.4)	(5.1
	(5.6)			
Commodities experts		2.3	1.8	4.7
		(.3)	(.2)	(.3
Lawyers	13.0	20.9	15.6	25.1
	(5.6)	(2.3)	(1.7)	(1.7
Doctors (excluding dentists)	63.2	141.8	126.2	232.4
	(27.0)	(15.6)	(14.1)	(16.1
Teachers and university graduate librarians and cultural educational workers	59.0	300.4	333.3	556.7
	(25.3)	(33.1)	(37.2)	(38.6

TABLE 2.6-12
Number of specialists with higher education working in the national economy, by specialty: U.S.S.R., selected years, 1928–1960

SOURCE: S. M. Rosen, *Higher Education in the U.S.S.R.*, U.S. Office of Education 1969, p. 99.

figures in parentheses are percentage of total)

Apr. 1, 1954	July 1, 1955	Dec. 1, 1957	Dec. 1, 1959	Dec. 1, 1960
?,008.5	2,184.0	2,805.5	3,235.7	3,545.2
(100)	(100)	(100)	(100)	(100)
530.2	585.9	816.1	986.6	1,115.5
(26.4)	(26.8)	(29.1)	(30.5)	(31.5)
134.5	158.7	193.1	222.4	241.8
(6.7)	(7.3)	(6.9)	(6.9)	(6.8)
96.0	105.2	145.2	177.6	197.7
(4.8)	(4.8)	(5.2)	(5.5)	(5.6)
7.8	8.6	12.3	16.3	19.3
(.4)	(.4)	(.4)	(.5)	(.5)
40.7	47.1	57.8	65.5	69.8
(2.0)	(2.2)	(2.1)	(2.0)	(2.0)
280.4	299.0	346.0	378.6	400.6
(14.0)	(13.7)	(12.3)	(11.7)	(11.3)
867.8	906.4	1,144.9	1,278.9	1,378.1
(43.2)	(40.5)	(40.8)	(39.5)	(38.9)

	Jan. 1,
	1941
Specialties	
Total women specialists with higher education working in national economy	312.3
Engineers	43.2
Agronomists, zootechnicians, veterinarians, and foresters	17.6
Economists, economists-statisticians, commodities experts	18.1
Lawyers	3.1
Doctors (excluding dentists)	85.4
Teachers, university graduate librarians, and cultural-educational workers	144.5

TABLE 2.6-13 *Number and percentages of women specialists with higher education working in national economy, by specialty; U.S.S.R., 1941, 1954, and 1960*

SOURCE: S. M. Rosen, *Higher Education in the U.S.S.R.*, U.S. Office of Education, 1969, p. 99.

Enrollment in the U.S.S.R. rose from 54 percent of the United States total in 1940–41 to 71 percent of the United States figure in 1959–60.

A larger proportion of students in the U.S.S.R. compared to those in the United States were enrolled on a part-time basis. The majority of these part-time students in the Soviet Union were in correspondence courses. Between 1940 and 1959, the proportion of all students in the Soviet Union accounted for by those enrolled on a part-time basis rose from approximately 30 percent to around half (Table 2.6-10). In 1960 part-time students in the United States represented approximately 25 percent of all enrolled students.

In 1960 there were more than seven times as many graduate students enrolled in the United States as in the Soviet Union. The total for the United States was 356,000,[3] compared to 48,000 in the Soviet Union (Table 2.6-11).

The number of specialists in the working population of the Soviet Union rose from 233,000 in 1928 to 1,442,000 in 1950 and 3,545,000 in 1960. The corresponding totals in the United States for professional and technical workers were 4,490,000 in 1950

[3] U.S., Office of Education, *Projections of Educational Statistics to 1977–78*, National Center for Educational Statistics, 1968, p. 12.

		Women as percentage of total specialists	
Thousands of women			
Apr. 1, 1954	*Dec. 1, 1960*	*Jan. 1, 1941*	*Dec. 1, 1960*
1,098.3	1,864.6	34	53
151.5	320.1	15	29
54.9	94.5	25	39
56.3	112.7	31	57
13.0	22.3	15	32
214.3	302.0	60	75
581.0	901.3	49	65

and 7,475,000 in 1960.[4] The numbers for the U.S.S.R. rose from about one-third of the American figure in 1950 to almost half in 1960 (Table 2.6-12).

In 1960 the ratio of persons per physician was 4,000 in the U.S.S.R. and 7,000 in the United States.[5] With respect to lawyers, the position of the two countries was reversed. In 1960 there were 286,000 and 7,000 lawyers in the United States and U.S.S.R., respectively. In the Soviet Union, participation of women in the professions and technical fields far exceeded that of the United States. In 1960, Soviet women accounted for 53 percent of all specialists, 75 percent of all physicians, and 32 percent of the total in law. In the United States, the proportion of total physicians and lawyers accounted for by women was 7 percent[7] and 3 percent,[8] respectively.

[4] U.S. Bureau of the Cenus, *Statistical Abstract of the United States, 1969,* 1969, p. 222.

[5] Ibid., p. 835.

[6] Ibid., p. 151.

[7] S. M. Rosen, *Higher Education in the U.S.S.R.,* U.S. Office of Education, 1969, p. 93.

[8] U.S. Bureau of the Census, *Statistical Abstract of the United States, 1969,* 1969, p. 151.

2.7. Dropouts

In view of the strong demand for educated members of the labor force, and the declining demand for uneducated workers, it is not surprising that much attention has been given to the dropout problem. In the 1930s and 1940s, there was great concern over a potential excess supply of highly educated men and women.[1] But in the face of the technological gains of a highly prosperous economy in the 1960s, the problem seemed to be more one of finding men and women sufficiently educated, rather than the problem of a proletariat of the A.B. or Ph.D.

The danger of an excess supply of college graduates is still a threat, however. By the mid-1970s, United States institutions of higher education may graduate a million persons per year. An official study estimates that by 1975, 8 million professional, technical, and kindred workers and 8 million managers, officials, and proprietors (exclusive of farming) will be needed. And many of these jobs will not be at a high level. Even if 10 million jobs in these categories were assured by 1975, it is clear that an output of 1 million college graduates a year may be excessive, given the number and kinds of openings sought by college graduates. The possibility of a future shortage of jobs for college graduates would be more serious if educational requirements for many jobs were not greatly in excess of the amount of education actually needed in the job. Why must all nurses and secretaries be college graduates?

Studying the period 1940 to 1960, Folger and Nam concluded: "Overall, about 85 percent of the rise in educational attainment may be attributed to increased educational levels within occupations, and only 15 percent to shifts in the occupational structure

[1] See S. E. Harris, *The Market for College Graduates,* Harvard University Press, Cambridge, Mass., 1949.

TABLE 2.7-1
Percentage
change in
educational
attainment
attributable
to changes in
occupational
structure, for
employed
white males
35 to 54
years old,
1940 to 1960

Years of school completed	1940 to 1960	1940 to 1950	1950 to 1960
None	51	45	20
Elementary:			
1 to 4 years	36	60	17
5 to 8 years	12	9	14
High school:			
1 to 3 years	13	15	5
4 years	2	4	3
College:			
1 to 3 years	15	11	19
4 years or more	57	60	54

SOURCE: J. K. Folger and C. B. Nam, *Education of the American Population,* U.S. Bureau of the Census (a 1960 Census Monograph), 1967, table VI-5, p. 172.

TABLE 2.7-2
Main reason for
dropping out of
school, by color
and sex,
February 1963
(persons 16 to
21 years old)

Color and sex	Number (thousands)	Total	Not interested in school	Poor grades	Difficulties with school authorities
TOTAL	3,046	100.0	21.3	8.1	4.6
Men	1,371	100.0	24.4	13.2	7.4
Women	1,675	100.0	18.9	4.3	2.4
White	2,450	100.0	24.1	8.2	3.5
Men	1,105	100.0	28.9	13.1	6.2
Women	1,345	100.0	20.3	4.4	1.5
Nonwhite	596	100.0	10.1	8.1	8.6
Men	266	100.0	6.3	13.9	12.3
Women	330	100.0	13.0	3.6	5.8

* Includes unemployment in family, to support family, could not afford to go to school, needed money, and similar reasons.

NOTE: Detail may not add to totals due to rounding.

SOURCE: U.S. Department of Labor, *Manpower Report of the President and a Report on Manpower Requirements, Resources, Utilization, and Training,* Employment Security Bureau, 1966, p. 93.

from occupations requiring less education to occupations requiring more."[2] At the college level, however, there seems to be a greater percentage change attributable to changes in occupational structure than for other levels of education (except for those with less than four years of school) (Table 2.7-1). It may well be that disaster will not accompany excessive years of schooling in relation to qualified job openings if increased emphasis is placed on education as a consumption rather than an investment good.

SCHOOL
RETENTION
RATES

Table 2.3-13 in the chapter on degrees showed school retention rates for the fifth grade through college entrance for the years 1926–1934 to 1959–1967. For every 10 pupils in the fifth grade in 1959–60, 4 were expected to enter college in the fall of 1967, and 2 were likely to earn four-year degrees in 1971. This means that only half of the college entrants in 1967 would graduate in four years (Figure 2.3-3). For every 10 pupils who entered the fifth grade in 1926, 1 went to college in the fall of 1934.

[2] J. K. Folger and C. B. Nam, *Education of the American Population,* U.S. Bureau of the Census (a 1960 Census Monograph), 1967, pp. 171–172.

Percentage distribution

Wanted to go to work	Economic*	Marriage or pregnancy	Own illness	Other
7.7	18.2	23.9	5.5	10.8
12.1	26.2	2.8	4.0	9.9
4.3	12.1	40.0	6.6	11.5
7.5	17.8	22.9	5.4	10.6
11.1	24.8	3.5	3.5	8.9
4.8	12.4	37.8	6.9	11.9
8.2	19.8	27.7	5.8	11.7
16.3	31.3		6.0	13.9
2.1	10.9	48.8	5.8	10.0

Why do students drop out of school? In 1963 the main reasons were financial need, marriage or pregnancy, and lack of interest. Twenty-four percent of the dropouts gave marriage or pregnancy as a reason, 21 percent were not interested in school, and 18 percent quit because of economic reasons. Only 8 percent gave poor grades as a reason for dropping out (Table 2.7-2).

In general, high school graduates tend to obtain more desirable employment than high school dropouts. But the advantages of a

TABLE 2.7-3 *Employed high school graduates and school dropouts—major occupation group, by color, 1966*
(Percentage distribution of persons 16 to 21 years old. Excludes Armed Forces and inmates of institutions. As of October. Data for high school graduates relate to those not enrolled in college; data for dropouts to persons who completed 3 years of high school or less. Based on a sample and subject to sampling variability.)

Major occupation group	Graduates			Dropouts		
	Total	*White*	*Nonwhite*	*Total*	*White*	*Nonwhite*
All occupation groups, 1,000	3,455	3,116	339	1,548	1,230	318
Percentage	100.0	100.0	100.0	100.0	100.0	100.0
Professional, technical, and kindred workers	6.5	6.9	2.5	0.7	0.9	*
Farmers and farm managers	0.5	0.5	0.6	0.6	0.6	0.6
Managers, officials, and proprietors, except farm	1.3	1.4		1.3	1.6	*
Clerical and kindred workers	41.3	42.7	28.1	6.5	5.6	9.8
Sales workers	4.4	4.7	1.5	2.0	1.7	3.2
Craftsmen, foremen, and kindred workers	5.8	5.7	7.1	8.2	8.8	5.7
Operatives and kindred workers	21.2	20.8	25.3	38.8	42.8	24.0
Private household workers	1.2	0.9	4.0	4.5	4.3	5.0
Service workers, except private household	9.5	8.6	17.3	14.4	12.8	20.8
Farm laborers and foremen	1.8	2.0	0.6	8.8	7.7	12.9
Laborers, except farm and mine	6.3	5.6	13.0	14.3	13.3	18.0

* Represents zero.

SOURCE: U.S. Department of Labor, Bureau of Labor Statistics; *Employment of High School Graduates and Dropouts in 1966,* Special Labor Force Report, No. 85, in U.S. Bureau of the Census, *Statistical Abstract of the United States, 1967,* 1967, p. 119.

high school diploma are larger for whites than for blacks. In 1966 high school graduates accounted for 6.5 percent of the employment in the professional, technical, and kindred workers group. Dropouts accounted for only 0.7 percent of the employment of this group. Almost 7 percent of the white high school graduates were employed as professional, technical, and kindred workers, but only 2.5 percent of the nonwhite high school graduates were so employed (Table 2.7-3).

Part Three

Faculty

3.1. *Faculty: General Characteristics*

NUMBER, DISTRIBUTION, RANK, AND EMPLOYMENT The average number of faculty at institutions of higher education rose as follows between 1870 and 1963:

Year	Number of faculty per institution of higher education
1870	10
1909	38
1963	279

Between 1939 and 1963 the growth of professional staff in public institutions of higher education was approximately two times that of comparable private institutions (Figure 3.1-1).

In 1963, there were 503,000 faculty positions at four-year institutions. Universities accounted for 61 percent of these positions and liberal arts colleges 23 percent. The proportion of total staff consisting of faculty available for resident instruction in degree-credit courses varied among different types of institutions. The ratio was 0.61 at universities and 0.69 and 0.72 at teachers colleges and liberal arts colleges, respectively. Differences in the ratios reflect the relative importance of research at these types of institutions (Table 3.1-1).

The proportions of total professional staff working in different types of four-year and other higher educational institutions are presented graphically in Figure 3.1-2.

Men and women in faculty positions differed in, among other things, absolute numbers, fields of specialization, highest degree held, and marital status. (1) In 1963, men outnumbered women by as much as 4½ to 1 on the average for all teaching areas. The only fields in which women faculty predominated were nursing, home

453

FIGURE 3.1-1 *Percentage change in number of professional staff employed in publicly and privately controlled institutions; aggregate United States, 1939–1963*

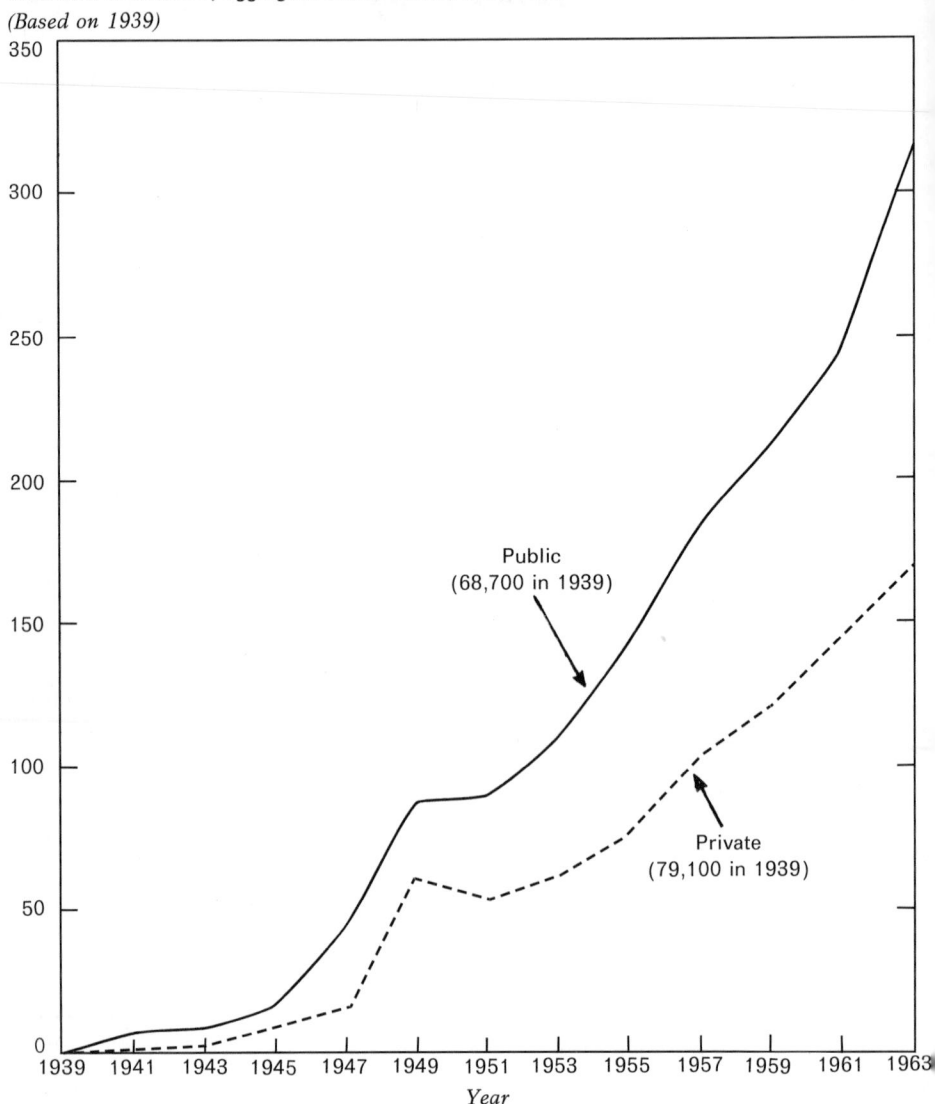

(Based on 1939)

SOURCE: R. E. Dunham and P. S. Wright, *Faculty and Other Professional Staff in Institutions of Higher Education, First Term 1963–64,* final report, U.S. Office of Education, 1966, p. 4.

economics, library science, business education, and social work (Table 3.1-2). (2) More men in teaching had doctorates than their female counterparts. In 1963 and 1966 the doctorate was the highest degree held by close to one-half of the male faculty and approximately one-fifth of the female faculty (Table 3.1-6). (3) About 86

IGURE 3.1-2 *Percentage of professional staff employed in each type of institution; aggregate ▮nited States, fall 1963*

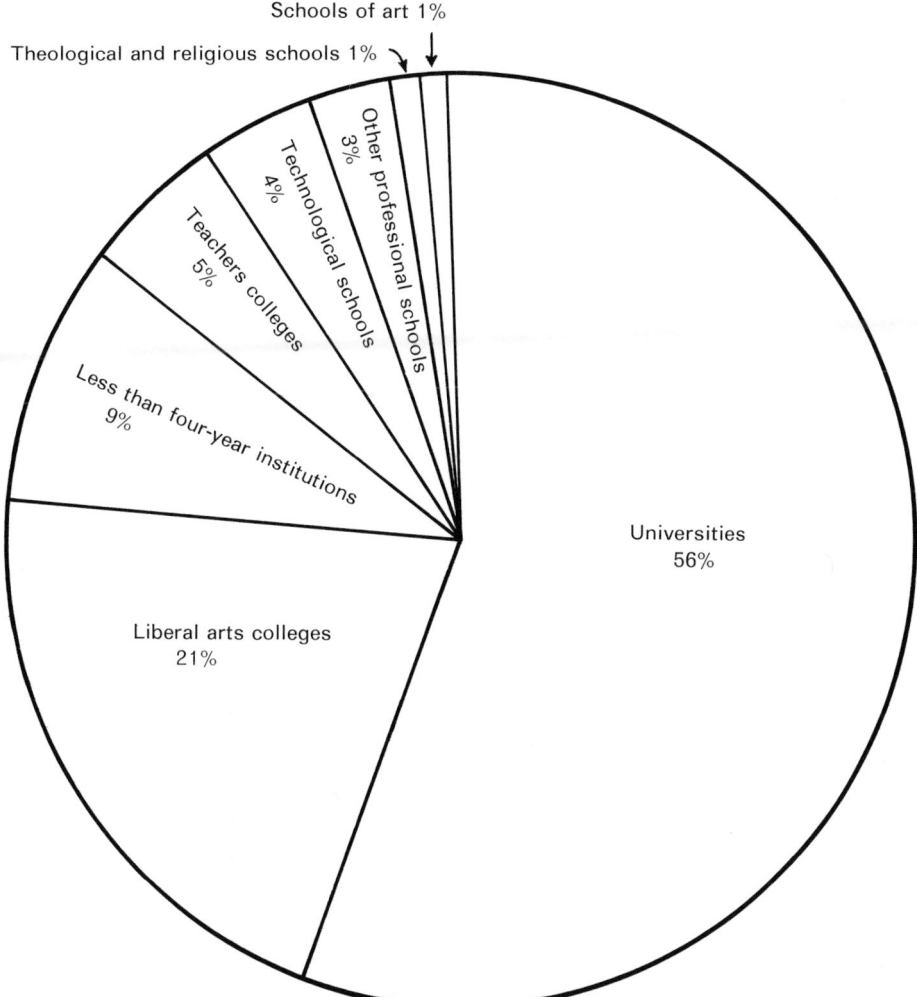

Schools of art 1%

Theological and religious schools 1%

Other professional schools 3%

Technological schools 4%

Teachers colleges 5%

Less than four-year institutions 9%

Universities 56%

Liberal arts colleges 21%

▮OURCE: R. E. Dunham and P. S. Wright, *Faculty and Other Professional Staff in Institutions of ▮igher Education, First Term 1963–64,* final report, U.S. Office of Education, 1966, p. 5.

percent of the male faculty and 31 percent of the female faculty were married.[1]

From Table 3.1-3, it appears that between 1953–54 and 1963–64

(Text continued on p. 460)

[1] R. E. Dunham, P. S. Wright, and M. O. Chandler, *Teaching Faculty in Universities and Four-year Colleges, Spring 1963,* U.S. Office of Education, 1966, p. 4.

	Total four-year institutions	Universities	Libera arts college
TABLE 3.1-1 *Positions for faculty and other professional staff by type of institution, type of position, and institutional control; aggregate United States, fall 1963* — *Type of position* (1)	(2)	(3)	(4)
All institutions			
Number of institutions	1,503	146	78
Number of different persons	451,820	278,968	102,25
Full-time	298,035	168,017	79,73
Part-time	153,785	110,951	22,51
Number of positions	503,307	308,054	113,63
Professional staff for general administration	22,179	8,215	9,15
Professional staff for student personnel services	18,141	7,684	7,09
Faculty for resident instruction in degree-credit courses	325,930	188,823	82,20
Instructor or above	273,387	144,227	78,48
Full-time	185,626	90,567	60,16
Part-time	87,761	53,660	18,32
Full-time equivalent of part-time	28,783	17,622	6,41
Junior instructional staff	52,543	44,596	3,71
Faculty for resident instruction in non-degree-credit courses	4,373	1,897	1,37
Extension staff	36,135	29,821	3,92
Giving courses	19,696	13,785	3,57
Other extension staff	16,439	16,036	34
Other faculty, including instructional staff for courses by mail, radio, or TV, short courses, and individual lessons	13,853	10,011	1,86
Professional library staff	11,380	5,483	3,86
Professional staff for organized research	64,957	54,428	2,28
Instructional staff for elementary or secondary instruction	6,359	1,692	1,86

SOURCE: R. E. Dunham and P. S. Wright, *Faculty and Other Professional Staf in Institutions of Higher Education, First Term 1963–64,* final report, U.S. Offic of Education, 1966, p. 10.

Four-year institutions					Less than four-year institutions (10)
Independently organized professional schools					
Teachers colleges (5)	Techno- logical schools (6)	Theo- logical and religious schools (7)	Schools of art (8)	Other profes- sional schools (9)	
186	57	201	46	79	637
26,664	20,700	5,867	3,330	14,033	46,539
23,777	14,880	4,396	1,632	5,594	28,172
2,887	5,820	1,471	1,698	8,439	18,367
30,998	23,565	7,299	4,033	15,721	53,597
1,684	999	1,176	336	617	3,334
1,525	718	631	163	322	2,593
21,437	14,120	4,346	2,613	12,388	32,223
20,778	11,416	4,185	2,534	11,759	32,072
18,414	8,705	2,940	1,128	3,706	18,935
2,364	2,711	1,245	1,406	8,053	13,137
863	1,020	451	576	1,836	4,023
659	2,704	161	79	629	151
85	448	130	97	339	10,742
1,796	281	125	135	52	1,633
1,753	275	119	135	52	1,593
43	6	6			40
905	259	138	518	157	639
1,006	347	412	78	186	1,159
163	6,390	54	6	1,630	131
2,397	3	287	87	30	1,143

TABLE 3.1-2
Percentage of
teaching
faculty in each
basic profile by
primary teaching
field, aggregate
Unites States,
spring 1963

Primary teaching field	Grand total	Total	Men	Women
Grand total	138,149	100.0	82.2	17.8
Agriculture and related fields	2,986	100.0	99.3	0.7
Agricultural fields	2,096	100.0	99.5	0.5
Related fields	890	100.0	98.8	1.2
Agricultural economics	445	100.0	100.0	0
Forestry	445	100.0	97.6	2.4
Biological sciences	10,818	100.0	89.3	10.7
Bacteriology	362	100.0	85.3	14.7
Biochemistry	1,273	100.0	94.2	5.8
General biology	1,761	100.0	83.2	16.8
General botany	977	100.0	89.2	10.8
General zoology	1,461	100.0	87.7	12.3
Genetics	587	100.0	92.8	7.2
Microbiology	917	100.0	86.2	13.8
Pharmacology	473	100.0	97.7	2.3
Physiology	1,035	100.0	91.8	8.2
Other biological sciences	1,973	100.0	90.8	9.2
Business and commerce	6,932	100.0	82.9	17.1
Accounting	2,005	100.0	91.5	8.5
Business education	1,024	100.0	38.1	61.9
Finance	375	100.0	94.4	5.6
General business	1,368	100.0	93.0	7.0
Management	329	100.0	100.0	0
Other business and commerce	1,832	100.0	85.5	14.5
Education and related fields	10,632	100.0	77.0	23.0
Educational psychology	1,535	100.0	73.8	26.2
Elementary education	2,769	100.0	50.8	49.2
Foundations: history, sociology, philosophy	782	100.0	94.6	5.4
Industrial arts	1,074	100.0	99.0	1.0
Secondary education	1,959	100.0	88.1	11.9
Services: administrative, supervisory	753	100.0	91.6	8.4
Services: student personnel, counseling and guidance	489	100.0	80.3	19.7
Other education fields	1,271	100.0	81.6	18.4

TABLE 3.1-2
(continued)

Primary teaching field	Grand total	Total	Men	Women
Engineering	9,455	100.0	99.7	0.3
Aeronautical	403	100.0	100.0	0
Agricultural	307	100.0	100.0	0
Chemical	669	100.0	100.0	0
Civil	1,727	100.0	100.0	0
Electrical	2,017	100.0	99.5	0.5
Engineering science fields	413	100.0	100.0	0
Graphics	341	100.0	100.0	0
Industrial	287	100.0	100.0	0
Materials	372	100.0	100.0	0
Mechanical	2,136	100.0	99.0	1.0
Other engineering	783	100.0	100.0	0
English and journalism	11,723	100.0	73.8	26.2
English and literature	11,140	100.0	73.0	27.0
Journalism	583	100.0	89.1	10.9
Fine arts	13,329	100.0	77.5	22.5
Art	3,283	100.0	74.9	25.1
Dramatics and speech	3,232	100.0	79.1	20.9
Music	6,253	100.0	78.0	22.0
Other fine arts	562	100.0	77.4	22.6
Foreign languages and literature	7,504	100.0	72.9	27.1
Classical: Hebrew, Greek, Latin	971	100.0	81.4	18.6
French	2,307	100.0	64.2	35.8
German	1,542	100.0	84.8	15.2
Spanish	1,649	100.0	64.0	36.0
Russian	427	100.0	77.6	22.4
Other (including philology)	609	100.0	82.5	17.5
Health fields	7,480	100.0	64.7	35.3
Dentistry	536	100.0	86.0	14.0
Medicine	3,474	100.0	93.8	6.2
Nursing	2,071	100.0	1.5	98.5
Pharmacy	416	100.0	89.8	10.2
Other health fields	982	100.0	72.8	27.2
Home economics	1,946	100.0	3.8	96.2
Law	1,458	100.0	97.1	2.9

TABLE 3.1-2
(continued)

Primary teaching field	Grand total	Total	Men	Women
Mathematics	7,640	100.0	85.7	14.3
Philosophy	2,214	100.0	92.8	7.2
Physical and health education	6,270	100.0	62.9	37.1
Physical sciences	11,755	100.0	94.6	5.4
Chemistry	5,238	100.0	91.5	8.5
Geology and other earth sciences	1,687	100.0	99.4	0.6
Physics	4,225	100.0	97.5	2.5
Other physical sciences	605	100.0	87.8	12.2
Psychology	3,838	100.0	86.7	13.3
Clinical	736	100.0	87.0	13.0
Counseling and guidance	446	100.0	83.2	16.8
Experimental	1,033	100.0	92.8	7.2
General psychology	413	100.0	79.5	20.5
Social	404	100.0	89.4	10.6
Other psychology	808	100.0	83.0	17.0
Religion and theology	2,148	100.0	91.1	8.9
Social sciences	16,952	100.0	90.0	10.0
Anthropology	736	100.0	92.8	7.2
Economics	3,203	100.0	98.7	1.3
History	5,851	100.0	88.8	11.2
Political sciences and government	2,900	100.0	94.5	5.5
Social work	695	100.0	49.2	50.8
Sociology	2,399	100.0	85.9	14.1
Other social sciences	1,169	100.0	92.7	7.3
All other fields	3,070	100.0	82.4	17.6
Architecture	670	100.0	98.4	1.6
Library science	487	100.0	26.1	73.9
Military science	564	100.0	100.0	0
All other fields	1,348	100.0	87.4	12.6

SOURCE: R. E. Dunham, P. S. Wright, M. O. Chandler, *Teaching Faculty in Universities and Four-year Colleges, Spring 1963,* U.S. Office of Education, 1966.

faculty in administration and organized research grew most rapidly (178 percent) and faculty for resident instruction increased by considerably less (74 percent).

Presented in Table 3.1-4 are numbers of full-time and part-time instructional staff at all institutions of higher education for the period 1957–58 to 1967–68, and projections to 1977–78. During the decade from 1957–58 to 1967–68, the number of faculty with the rank of instructor or above rose by 81 percent, and the percentage increase in the number of junior instructional staff was 112 percent. Projected increases over the decade 1968–69 to 1977–78 for both senior and junior instructional staff, of about one-third each, are considerably below past levels of growth.

The differences between total instructional staff and full-time equivalent staff for 1957–58, 1967–68, and for a projected year, 1977–78, are brought out below:

Instructional staff, part-time instructional staff, and full-time equivalent*	Year	Total instructional staff (thousands)	FTE (thousands)	Part-time instructional staff as percentage of total instructional staff
	1957–58	259	187	28
	1967–68	478	339	29
	1977–78	665	472	29

*FTE (full-time equivalent) expresses the number of full-time staff plus part-time staff on an equivalent basis. If, for example, 300,000 staff operated on the average at one-third time, their contribution, or FTE, would be 100,000.
SOURCE: U.S. Office of Education, *Projections of Educational Statistics to 1977–78*, National Center for Educational Statistics, 1968, pp. 55–56.

Table 3.1-5 provides a breakdown of faculty and other professional staff by type of position and institutional control for 1959, 1961, and 1963. Between 1959 and 1963, the percentage of the total faculty engaged in resident instruction in degree-credit courses declined by two percentage points from 66 percent in 1959 to 64 percent in 1963, with almost all the decline occurring at privately controlled institutions. Over the four-year period the proportion accounted for by staff in organized research rose from 8.7 to 11.7 percent.

Office of Education data are available for 1966 and past years on numbers of professional personnel by primary function and the number of full-time teaching and research personnel by their highest educational level. This source provides the following breakdown of the distribution of full-time teaching and research personnel according to academic rank in 1966 for all institutions which are classified by institutional control (see Table 3.1-6).

(Text continued on p. 466)

TABLE 3.1-3
Faculty in
colleges and
universities, by
position,
selected years,
1953–54 to
1963–64, and
percentage
change between
1953–54 and
1963–64

Type of position*	Number of faculty and other professional staff positions*	
	1953–54	*1959–60*
Total number of different persons	(268,028)	(382,664
Total number of positions	302,904	431,720
General administration	16,608	19,063
Student personnel services		15,299
Faculty for resident instruction	214,107	297,215
Degree-credit courses	(208,547)	(283,080
Instructor or above	(182,028)	(244,461
Junior instructional staff	(26,519)	(38,619
Non-degree-credit courses	(5,560)	(14,135
Extension staff	24,623	31,439
Other faculty†	8,819	11,877
Library staff	7,875	9,939
Organized research	23,374	37,099
Elementary and secondary instruction‡	7,498	9,789

* Positions are those held by persons serving at a professional level and do not include clerical or other nonprofessional personnel, staff on leave without pay, or staff in emeritus or retired status. Included are full- and part-time faculty and other professional staff, those rendering "contributed" services, and those on sabbatical leave. All data for the United States and outlying parts. 1953–54 figures are for November 1953; later data are as of the "first term" or "fall term" (semester or quarter) of the academic year indicated.

† Includes instructional staff for courses by mail, radio or TV, short courses and individual lessons.

‡ Professional staff in elementary and secondary schools conducted by institutions of higher education.

NOTE: Numbers in parentheses relate to persons or to courses but are not related to the total number of positions in row 2.

SOURCES: (1) U.S. Office of Education, *Statistics of Higher Education: Faculty, Students, and Degrees, 1953–54,* 1956, p. 83 and (2) U.S. Office of Education, *Faculty and Other Professional Staff in Institutions of Higher Education, Fall Term 1963–64,* final report, 1966, p. 9; in American Council on Education, *A Fact Book on Higher Education,* Washington, D.C., 1967, p. 196.

1961–62	1963–64	Percentage change, 1953–54 to 1963–64
427,833)	(498,359)	85.9
475,810	556,904	83.8
20,686	25,513	
16,722	20,734	178.4
326,319	373,268	74.3
312,687)	(358,153)	
266,624)	(305,459)	
(46,063)	(52,694)	
(13,632)	(15,115)	
31,409	37,768	53.3
11,771	14,492	64.3
11,025	12,539	59.2
50,058	65,088	178.4
7,820	7,502	0

		Instructor or above			Junior
Year (fall) (1)	Total (2)	Total (3)	Full-time (4)	Part-time (5)	instructional staff (6)
1957–58	258,848	224,930	153,150	71,780	33,918
1958–59*	272,000	237,000	160,000	77,000	36,000
1959–60	281,506	242,914	162,292	80,622	38,592
1960–61*	294,000	253,000	169,000	84,000	42,000
1961–62	310,772	264,749	177,052	87,697	46,023
1962–63*	334,000	285,000	190,000	95,000	49,000
1963–64	355,542	302,896	202,396	100,500	52,646
1964–65*	387,000	329,000	220,000	109,000	58,000
1965–66†	427,000	363,000	243,000	120,000	64,000
1966–67†	449,000	382,000	255,000	127,000	67,000
1967–68†	478,000	406,000	271,000	135,000	72,000
Projected‡					
1968–69	503,000	428,000	286,000	142,000	75,000
1969–70	509,000	433,000	289,000	144,000	76,000
1970–71	524,000	446,000	298,000	148,000	79,000
1971–72	545,000	463,000	309,000	154,000	82,000
1972–73	568,000	483,000	323,000	160,000	85,000
1973–74	593,000	504,000	337,000	167,000	89,000
1974–75	614,000	522,000	349,000	173,000	92,000
1975–76	633,000	538,000	360,000	179,000	95,000
1976–77	651,000	553,000	370,000	183,000	98,000
1977–78	665,000	565,000	378,000	187,000	100,000

TABLE 3.1-4 *Full-time and part-time instructional staff for resident degree-credit courses in all institutions of higher education, by professional rank: United States, first term, 1957–58 to 1977–78*

*Interpolated.

† Estimated.

‡ The projection of total full-time and part-time instructional staff for resident degree-credit courses was computed separately by institutional control and type categories, and summed for all institutions.

The projection of total instructional staff for resident degree-credit courses employed as full-time instructor or above, part-time instructor or above, and as junior instructor, is based on the percentage each was of total full-time and part-time instructional staff for resident degree-credit courses in 1963–64. These percentages were 57, 28, and 15 percent, respectively, and are assumed to remain at the 1963–64 level to 1977–78.

NOTE: Data are for 50 states and the District of Columbia for all years. Because of rounding, detail may not add to totals.

SOURCES: U.S. Office of Education publications: "Faculty and Other Professional Staff in Institutions of Higher Education," biennially, first term 1957–58 to 1963–64; in U.S. Office of Education, *Projections of Educational Statistics to 1977–78,* National Center for Educational Statistics, 1968, p. 55.

TABLE 3.1-5 Percentage of positions for faculty and other professional staff by type of position and institutional control; aggregate United States, fall 1959–1963

Type of position (1)	Total			Public			Private		
	1963 (2)	1961 (3)	1959 (4)	1963 (5)	1961 (6)	1959 (7)	1963 (8)	1961 (9)	1959 (10)
All positions	100.0	100.0	100.0	100.0	100.0	100.0	100.0	100.0	100.0
Professional staff for general administration	4.6	4.3	4.5	3.2	2.9	2.9	6.5	6.2	6.3
Professional staff for student personnel services	3.7	3.5	3.6	3.1	3.0	2.8	4.5	4.2	4.4
Faculty for resident instruction in degree-credit courses	64.3	65.7	66.2	61.4	62.2	61.1	68.4	70.2	71.1
Instructor or above	54.8	56.0	57.2	50.9	51.7	51.8	60.3	61.4	62.5
Full-time	36.7	37.5	38.3	35.7	37.1	37.8	38.2	38.1	38.1
Part-time	18.1	18.5	18.9	15.2	14.6	14.1	22.1	23.4	24.5
Full-time equivalent of part-time	5.9	6.2	5.9	5.0	7.1	4.6	7.1	7.5	7.6
Junior instructional staff	9.5	9.7	9.0	10.5	10.4	9.2	8.1	8.7	8.6
Faculty for resident instruction in non-degree-credit courses	2.7	2.9	3.3	3.5	3.6	4.1	1.6	2.0	2.3
Extension staff	6.8	6.6	7.4	10.4	10.6	11.6	1.9	1.5	1.9
Giving courses	3.8	3.2	3.6	5.4	4.8	5.2	1.6	1.2	1.5
Other extension staff	3.0	3.4	3.8	4.9	5.9	6.4	0.3	0.3	0.4
Other faculty, including instructional staff for courses by mail, radio or TV, short courses and individual lessons	2.6	2.5	2.8	3.1	3.2	3.5	1.9	1.5	1.9
Professional library staff	2.3	2.3	2.3	2.0	2.1	2.1	2.6	2.6	2.6
Professional staff for organized research	11.7	10.5	8.7	11.8	10.5	9.4	11.6	10.5	7.6
Instructional staff for elementary or secondary instruction	1.3	1.6	2.3	1.5	1.8	2.6	1.2	1.4	1.9

SOURCE: R. E. Dunham and P. S. Wright, *Faculty and Other Professional Staff in Institutions of Higher Education, First Term 1963–64*, final report, U.S. Office of Education, 1966, p. 10.

TABLE 3.1-6
Estimated number of full-time senior teaching and research personnel, by highest degree held, sex, and rank; aggregate United States, fall 1966, all institutions

	All degree levels		
Rank	*Total*	*Men*	*Women*
(1)	*(2)*	*(3)*	*(4)*
Academic dean	4,036	3,679	357
Professor	65,642	59,730	5,912
Associate professor	59,724	50,811	8,913
Assistant professor	84,727	67,967	16,760
Instructor	67,085	45,166	21,919
Other or no rank	20,571	14,895	5,676
TOTAL	301,785	242,248	59,537

SOURCE: R. Beazley, *Numbers and Characteristics of Employees in Institutions of Higher Education, Fall 1966,* U.S. Office of Education, National Center for Educational Statistics, February 1969, p. 11.

	All institutions,* *percent*	*Public,†* *percent*	*Private,†* *percent*
All positions	100.0	100.0	100.0
Academic dean	1.3	1.1	1.6
Professor	21.8	20.4	23.9
Associate professor	19.8	19.6	20.0
Assistant professor	28.1	28.2	27.8
Instructor	22.2	23.6	20.1
Other or no rank	6.8	7.1	6.6

* Includes universities, other four-year institutions, and two-year institutions. SOURCE Table 3.1-6.

† SOURCE: R. Beazley, *Numbers and Characteristics of Employees in Institutions of Higher Education, Fall 1966,* U.S. Office of Education, National Center for Educational Statistics, February 1969, pp. 12–14.

At all institutions, which include junior colleges as well as universities and other four-year institutions, the largest proportions of total faculty were at the ranks of assistant professor (28 percent) and of instructor (22 percent). The principal difference between public and private institutions was that at the former relatively more faculty were ranked as instructors and at the latter a larger proportion of the faculty were classified as professors. In general it appeared that proportionately more faculty were in lower-ranking

Bachelor's degree or lower		Selected first professional degree		Master's degree		Doctor's degree	
Men (5)	Women (6)	Men (7)	Women (8)	Men (9)	Women (10)	Men (11)	Women (12)
57	5	225	3	735	147	2,662	202
,340	139	4,333	150	7,921	1,428	46,136	4,195
,654	201	3,329	201	14,675	4,964	31,153	3,547
,981	704	4,822	422	30,153	11,816	29,011	3,818
,604	4,824	3,016	503	31,106	15,826	2,440	766
,080	1,478	1,228	119	7,890	3,439	2,697	640
,716	7,351	16,953	1,398	92,480	37,620	114,099	13,168

jobs (assistant professor and instructor) than in higher-ranking positions (professor and associate professor) and that the rankings were more evenly divided at private institutions.

At public and private universities a larger proportion of faculty were full professors and associate professors than was the case for the average of all institutions. At other four-year institutions and two-year institutions, the largest proportions of faculty were in lower-ranking positions.[2] These results are consistent with the theory that established institutions growing at slow rates tend to promote staff from within according to traditional procedures and to hire lower-ranking staff for replacement. Newer, more rapidly growing institutions, on the other hand, are likely to have a smaller base of senior faculty and to hire increasing numbers of lower-ranking faculty.

The data in Table 3.1-7 pertain to the prior status of faculty in 1962–63. They indicate that over a third of the faculty came to their present jobs from employment in other institutions of higher education; 28 percent were previously students; and the rest either taught elementary or secondary school or had been employed in

[2] R. Beazley, *Numbers and Characteristics of Employees in Institutions of Higher Education, Fall 1966,* U.S. Office of Education, National Center for Educational Statistics, February 1969, pp. 12–14.

TABLE 3.1-7 *Percentage of faculty according to status immediately prior to accepting their presen position, by primary teaching area*

Primary teaching area	Total	Student	Higher education	Elementary or secondary education*	All other
TOTAL	100	28	35	13	24
Agriculture	100	33	31	5	31
Biological sciences	100	36	37	5	22
Business and commerce	100	22	33	14	31
Education and related fields	100	16	35	38	11
Engineering	100	26	25	3	46
English and journalism	100	29	41	16	14
Fine arts	100	28	36	15	21
Foreign languages and literature	100	26	45	14	15
Health fields	100	29	28	1	42
Home economics	100	20	30	28	22
Law	100	14	30	1	55
Mathematics	100	30	33	16	21
Philosophy	100	37	38	6	19
Physical and health education	100	20	29	37	14
Physical sciences	100	35	32	6	27
Psychology	100	34	38	2	26
Religion and theology	100	30	28	13	29
Social sciences	100	34	40	7	19
All other fields	100	17	24	8	51

"Percentage of faculty by status immediately prior to accepting present position"

* For the total group, secondary education accounted for 11 percent and elementary education for 2 percen Among education faculty, elementary accounted for 15 percent; in all other teaching fields, the percentag from elementary was 2 percent or less.

† "All other" included the following percentages within the total group: private business, 7 percent; gov ernment and nonprofit organizations, 4 percent each; active military service and "other," 3 percent eac self-employed, 2 percent; and homemaker, 1 percent.

SOURCE: R. E. Dunham, P. S. Wright, and M. O. Chandler, *Teaching Faculty in Universities an Four-year Colleges, Spring 1963*, U.S. Office of Education, 1966, p. 27.

other activities. The previous experience of faculty varied co siderably among different subject areas. For example, the pe centage of the faculty that had been students prior to entering t ranks of the faculty ranged from a maximum in philosophy (3 percent) to a minimum in law (17 percent). Over two-fifths of the faculty in foreign languages and literature, English and journalism, and social sciences had worked previously in higher educational institutions. In engineering, religion and theology, and physical health education, the proportion of faculty with experience in other institutions of higher education was much lower.

On the question of specific types of prior work experience, the survey pointed out that over half of the respondents reported that they had worked as teaching assistants or teaching fellows while in graduate school, about 30 percent had been secondary school teachers, and 29 percent had been employed in part-time or full-time research not on federal grant or contract (Table 3.1-8).

DISTRIBUTION OF FACULTY BY FIELDS OF SPECIAL-IZATION   The distribution of faculty among various subject areas reflects the demand for these specialties in the nation at large. Because of unique characteristics of the educational process, such as the relatively long period of time involved in training specialists, the tenure system, etc., there is a lag in adjusting faculty distribution to changes in demand. Tables 3.1-9 and 3.1-10 provide data on the distribution of faculty according to field of specialization for 1953 and 1963, respectively. In Table 3.1-11 the distributions for the two years are compared. The latter table reveals that the subject areas attracting the largest number of faculty, viz., humanities,

TABLE 3.1-8
Percentage of faculty having selected types of employment experience

Type of employment experience	Percentage of faculty having each type of experience*
Full-time teacher or administrator in:	
Elementary school	12
Secondary school	30
Junior college	7
Part-time teaching assistant or teaching fellow while in graduate school	51
Part-time or full-time research:	
Federal grant or contract	22
Not on federal grant or contract	29

* Percentages add to more than 100 since respondents were permitted to check more than one type of experience.

SOURCE: R. E. Dunham, P. S. Wright, and M. O. Chandler, *Teaching Faculty in Universities and Four-year Colleges, Spring 1963,* U.S. Office of Education, 1966, p. 27.

Field of specialization	Percent
All fields	100
Natural sciences	(19)
Chemistry	4
Physical science	8
Earth science	2
Biological science	5
Psychology	2
Social sciences	(11)
Economics	3
History	3
Other	5
Humanities and arts	(25)
English	8
Language	7
Philosophy	3
Fine arts	7
Engineering	7
Applied biology	(6)
Agriculture	4
Home economics	2
Health fields	(8)
Medicine	4
Dentistry	1
Other	3
Business and commerce	3
Education	(11)
General	7
Physical	4
Other fields	(8)
Law	1
Other professions	7

TABLE 3.1-9 *Estimated percentage distribution of all college and university faculty members by fields of specialization, early 1950s*

SOURCE: J. F. Wellemeyer, Jr., American Council of Learned Societies; in D. Wolfle, *America's Resources of Specialized Talent,* report of the Commission on Human Resources and Advanced Training, Harper & Brothers, New York, 1954, p. 125.

natural sciences, social sciences, and education, were the same in both years. By 1963 the shares accounted for by faculty in natural sciences, social sciences, and education had increased somewhat, and the proportion represented by faculty in agriculture and health fields had declined.

In 1963 on the average, 95 percent of the faculty were teaching in the same broad areas as their specialization, and 90 percent had received their highest degree in the same general areas as their specialization (Table 3.1-10).

DEGREES Information on the highest degrees held by faculty in various academic ranks in 1966 is summarized below.

Percentage distribution of faculty by academic rank according to highest degree held, 1966	*All degree levels*	*Bachelor's degree or below*	*Selected first pro- fessional degree*	*Master's degree*	*Doctor's degree*
All ranks	100	9	6	43	42
Academic dean	100	2	6	22	71
Professor	100	2	7	14	77
Associate professor	100	3	6	33	58
Assistant professor	100	6	6	50	39
Instructor	100	20	5	70	5
Other or no rank	100	22	7	55	16

SOURCE: Table 3.1-6.

According to this source, in 1966 at institutions of higher education the doctorate was the highest-level degree for 42 percent of the faculty and the master's degree was the top credential for 43 percent. The proportion of faculty with doctor's degrees was positively correlated with rank. Around 77 percent of full professors had doctorates, compared to 58 percent of associate professors, 39 percent of assistant professors, and 5 percent of instructors. The master's degree was the highest-level degree for a majority of instructors and assistant professors, for less than a third of associate professors, and for 14 percent of full professors.

In 1966 the master's degree was the highest degree held by almost three-quarters of faculty teaching at junior colleges. One-fifth of the faculty at these two-year institutions had no degree

TABLE 3.1-10
Number and
percentage of
faculty with
primary teaching
assignment or
highest degree
in same broad
area as area of
specialization,
1963

Area (1)	Number with specialization in specified area (2)	Percentage of total (3)
Median for 19 areas		
Agriculture	2,521	1.3
Biological sciences	12,065	8.7
Business and commerce	6,103	4.4
Education	11,241	8.1
Engineering	9,210	6.7
English and journalism	11,205	8.1
Fine arts	13,596	9.8
Foreign languages	7,152	5.2
Health fields	6,902	5.0
Home economics	1,734	1.3
Law	1,691	1.2
Mathematics	7,259	5.3
Philosophy	2,193	1.6
Physical and health education	5,784	4.2
Physical sciences	11,895	8.6
Psychology	4,168	3.0
Religion and theology	2,210	1.6
Social sciences	17,899	13.0
All other	3,322	2.4

SOURCE: R. E. Dunham, P. S. Wright, and M. O. Chandler, *Teaching Faculty in Universities and Four-year Colleges, Spring 1963,* U.S. Office of Education, 1966, p. 10.

higher than a bachelor's degree and 6 percent held doctorates (Table 3.1-12).

The data in a table prepared by Berelson[3] on the sources of highest degrees held by faculty in 1959 at universities and colleges, which he groups according to Keniston's ranking criteria, are reproduced in Table 3.1-13. They reveal the following: (1) Over four-fifths (85 percent) of the faculty at the top 12 universities received

[3] B. Berelson, *Graduate Education in the United States,* McGraw-Hill Book Company, New York, 1960, p. 115.

Teaching in same broad area as specialization		Highest degree in same broad area as specialization	
Number (4)	*Percent* (5)	*Number* (6)	*Percent* (7)
	95		90
2,394	95	2,182	87
10,455	87	10,473	87
5,923	97	4,658	76
9,521	85	10,045	89
8,736	95	8,256	90
10,728	96	10,495	94
12,864	95	12,715	94
6,855	96	6,453	90
6,655	96	6,204	90
1,681	97	1,575	91
1,436	85	1,574	93
7,006	97	6,635	91
1,992	91	1,989	91
5,699	99	5,139	89
11,099	93	11,165	94
3,510	84	3,627	87
1,934	88	1,719	78
16,475	92	16,522	92
2,233	67	1,533	46

their highest degree from these top 12 universities, and 9 percent of the faculty at these same 12 universities obtained their highest-level degree from the next 10 universities. (2) With respect to the faculty teaching at the next 10 universities, 47 percent received their highest degree from the top 12 universities and 38 percent from the next 10 universities. (3) Forty-seven percent of the faculty at the top 12 universities received their highest degree from their own institution. This "inbreeding" was more pronounced at the highest-ranking schools (Table 3.1-13).

Figure 3.1-3 and Tables 3.1-14 to 3.1-16 pertain to the proportion

(Text continued on p. 478)

TABLE 3.1-11
Estimated percentage distribution of all college and university faculty members by fields of specialization, 1953 and 1963

	1953	1963
All fields	100	100
Natural sciences (including mathematics)	19	22
Psychology	2	3
Social sciences	11	13
Humanities	25	25
Engineering	7	7
Agriculture	4	2
Home economics	2	1
Health fields	8	5
Business and commerce	3	4
Education	11	12
Law	1	1
Other fields	7	6

SOURCE: D. Wolfle, *America's Resources of Specialized Talent,* report of the Commission on Human Resources and Advanced Training, Harper & Brothers, New York, 1954, p. 125 and Table 3.1-12.

TABLE 3.1-12 *Distribution of faculty at two-year institutions by academic rank and highest degree held, 1966*

	All degree levels	Bachelor's degree or below	Selected first pro- fessional degree	Master's degree	Doctor's degree
Academic dean	100	5	1	58	36
Professor	100	8	1	69	21
Associate professor	100	9	1	75	15
Assistant professor	100	13	*	82	5
Instructor	100	25	1	71	3
Other or no rank	100	19	1	75	5
TOTAL	100	20	1	73	6

* Less than 0.05 percent.
SOURCE: R. Beazley, *Numbers and Characteristics of Employees in Institutions of Higher Education, Fall 1966,* U.S. Office of Education, National Center for Educational Statistics, February 1969, p. 14.

TABLE 3.1-13 *Sources of highest degrees by faculties, 1958–59*

Received highest earned degree from:	*Present faculties of:**						
	Top 12 universities	Next 10 universities	Other AGS, plus	Other universities	Best colleges	Better colleges	Other colleges
Top 12 universities	85%	47%	44%	31%	44%	33%	21%
Next 10 universities	9	38	13	15	19	16	11
Other AGS, plus	2	8	31	17	15	19	23
Other universities	1	6	7	28	7	12	23
Other	3	1	5	9	15	20	22
Total number of cases (= 100%)	187	253	297	274	261	354	347
In-breeding (i.e., highest earned degree from own institution)	47	27	20	15	5	6	4

These data were secured primarily from the faculty lists in college and university catalogues. Incidentally, just as William James implied nearly sixty years ago, it is the lesser institutions that are quicker to list the degrees of their faculty members.

SOURCE: B. Berelson, *Graduate Education in the United States,* McGraw-Hill Book Company, New York, 1960, p. 115.

TABLE 3.1-14 *Science faculty, rank of instructor or above, spring 1963*

Field	Total	Percentage with doctorate	Percentage of males	*Principal teaching level*		
				Lower division, percent	Upper division, percent	Graduate, percent
Agriculture	2,986	66	99	25	50	25
Biological sciences	10,892	78	89	37	26	36
Engineering	9,497	39	100	20	57	22
Mathematics	7,640	48	86	55	30	15
Physical sciences	11,829	75	95	52	32	16
Psychology	3,849	82	87	29	40	31
Social sciences	16,984	66	90	42	44	14
Total sciences	63,677	64	92	40	39	21
Total nonsciences	74,525	40	73	44	41	15
TOTAL	138,202	51	82	42	40	18

SOURCE: U.S. House of Representatives, Committee on Science and Astronautics, *Higher Education in the Sciences in the United States,* report of the Subcommittee on Science, Research and Development, prepared by the National Science Foundation, 1965, p. 33.

TABLE 3. 1-15 Total staff and teachers by degrees, 1953–54 to 1964–65

Year and group (1)	Doctor's degree		Master's degree plus at least one year		Master's degree		Less than master's degree		Total	
	Number (2)	Percent (3)	Number (4)	Percent (5)	Number (6)	Percent (7)	Number (8)	Percent (9)	Number (10)	Percent (11)
Total staff in 1953–54[a]	23,768	40.5	12,266	20.9	16,582	28.2	6,103	10.4	58,719	100.0
New teachers in 1953–54[b]	1,329	31.4	770	18.2	1,363	32.2	770	18.2	4,232	100.0
New teachers in 1954–55[b]	1,333	28.4	878	18.7	1,577	33.6	906	19.3	4,694	100.0
New teachers in 1955–56[c]	1,692	26.7	1,128	17.8	2,243	35.4	1,274	20.1	6,337	100.0
New teachers in 1956–57[c]	1,952	23.5	1,504	18.1	2,933	35.3	1,919	23.1	8,308	100.0
New teachers in 1957–58[d]	2,354	25.3	1,505	16.2	3,409	36.7	2,025	21.8	9,293	100.0
New teachers in 1958–59[d]	2,161	23.8	1,703	18.7	3,339	36.7	1,897	20.8	9,100	100.0
New teachers in 1959–60[e]	2,650	25.9	2,034	19.9	3,788	37.1	1,749	17.1	10,221	100.0
New teachers in 1960–61[e]	2,886	25.8	2,234	20.0	4,116	36.8	1,918	17.4	11,184	100.0
New teachers in 1961–62[f]	2,851	27.3	1,920	18.4	4,178	40.0	1,490	14.3	10,439	100.0
New teachers in 1962–63[g]	3,092	25.4	2,479	20.3	4,799	39.4	1,816	14.9	12,186	100.0
New teachers in 1963–64	3,833	28.3	2,831	20.9	5,188	38.3	1,710	12.6	13,562	100.0
New teachers in 1964–65[g]	4,361	27.2	3,381	21.1	6,306	39.3	2,011	12.5	16,059	100.0

[a] Based on reports from 637 universities and colleges.
[b] Based on reports from 656 universities and colleges.
[c] Based on reports from 827 universities and colleges.
[d] Based on reports from 936 universities and colleges.
[e] Based on reports from 1,085 universities and colleges.
[f] Based on reports from 1,009 universities and colleges.
[g] Based on reports from 1,084 universities and colleges.

SOURCE: U.S. House of Representatives, Committee on Government Operations, *Conflicts Between the Federal Research Programs and the Nation's Goals for Higher Education*, hearings before a subcommittee, June 1965, p. 92.

TABLE 3.1-16   *Characteristics of newly hired faculty, by institutional prestige*

Prestige of the current institution	Percentage with doctorate*	Percentage of big publishers*	Percentage with last degree from top 20 percent*
Top 10 percent	74	67	80
10 to 20 percent	67	52	64
20 to 40 percent	54	47	49
40 to 60 percent	52	24	34
60 to 80 percent	39	31	43
Bottom 20 percent	32	28	28

Means that the differences among groups are significant by a chi-square test at the 0.05 level.
SOURCES: Survey data, Prestige Index, and Productivity Index, in D. G. Brown, *The Mobile Professors,* American Council on Education, Washington, D.C., 1967, p. 97.

FIGURE 3.1-3   *Percentage of faculty with doctorates in 18 subject areas, 1963*

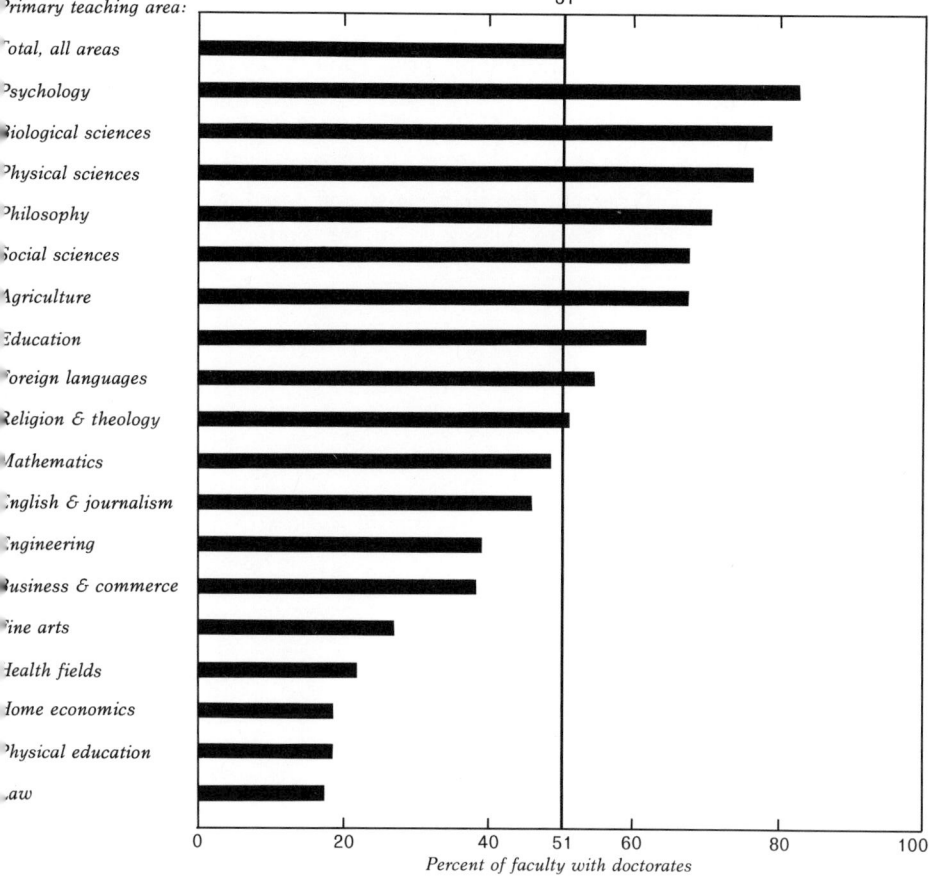

SOURCE: R. E. Dunham, P. S. Wright, and M. O. Chandler, *Teaching Faculty in Universities and Four-year Colleges, Spring 1963,* U.S. Office of Education, 1966. p. 9.

of faculty with doctorates in a variety of subject areas at different types of institutions. The proportion of faculty with doctorates teaching at universities and other four-year institutions varied from a low of 20 percent to a high of 80 percent with an average in all primary teaching areas of 51 percent (Figure 3.1-3). In the sciences, the proportion of faculty holding doctor's degrees varied considerably. Less than two-fifths of engineering faculties had doctorates and more than four-fifths of those teaching in psychology had this high-level degree. In biological science and physical science, somewhat over three-quarters of the faculty held doctorates (Table 3.1-14).

Over the decade 1953–54 to 1963–64, the proportion of all new faculty accounted for by those who held doctor's degrees declined somewhat, while the share of the new professional staff with master's degrees increased. New faculty with less than a master's degree represented a declining proportion of the total (Table 3.1-15). There were more newly hired faculty with doctorates at prestigious institutions than there were at schools with lower quality rankings. Approximately 74 percent of new faculty at institutions ranked in the top 10 percent had doctorates, compared to 32 percent of the newly hired faculty classified in the bottom 20 percent (Table 3.1-16).

TABLE 3.1-17
Trends in the employment of scientists and engineers in universities and colleges, by employment status and function, 1958, 1961, and 1965

	Thousands	
Employment status and function	*March 1958**	*March 1961**
Number of scientists and engineers in all activities	148.8	175.4
Full-time	96.2	112.2
Part-time	22.6	26.9
Employed graduate students	30.0	36.3
Full-time-equivalent scientists and engineers in all activities	119.5	138.4
Teaching	73.0	84.5
Research and development	36.5	42.4
Other activities	10.0	11.5

* Estimates based on NSF surveys of universities and colleges conducted in 1958 and 1961.

SOURCE: National Science Foundation, *Scientific Activities at Universities and Colleges, 1964,* 1968, p. 15.

Table 3.1-17 provides information on the number of scientists and engineers in universities and colleges by employment status and function for the years 1958, 1961, and 1965. During this period the following occurred: (1) The number of scientists and engineers in all activities at universities and colleges rose from 148,800 in 1953 to 250,000 in 1965 representing an annual rate of increase (compounded) of 7.7 percent. (2) Those in part-time positions increased more rapidly than those with full-time jobs (8.8 percent compared to 6.4 percent). (3) The number of scientists and engineers on an FTE basis rose faster in teaching than in research.

In summarizing the data contained in Table 3.1-18, it seems that in 1965 the largest number of scientists and engineers employed in universities and colleges had jobs in the field of life sciences (40 percent) and the second largest number were in physical sciences (25 percent). Over three-fifths of all scientists and engineers employed in universities and colleges were working at publicly controlled institutions. The educational qualifications of scientists and engineers working in universities and colleges differed among fields of specialization. The doctorate was the highest-level degree for approximately three-quarters of all scientists, with the proportion of life scientists with doctorates (88 percent) higher than any other scientific or engineering field (Table 3.1-19).

January 1965	*Compound annual rate of increase, 1958–1965, percent*
250.0	7.7
148.8	6.4
40.8	8.8
60.4	10.5
192.6	7.1
117.7	7.1
54.9	6.0
19.9	10.4

TABLE 3.1-18
Selected characteristics of scientists and engineers employed in universities and colleges, January 1965 (thousands)

Selected characteristics	Total	Institutions granting graduate degrees in the sciences and engineering*
TOTAL	250.0	210.2
Employment status:		
Full-time	148.8	118.1
Part-time	40.8	31.9
Employed graduate students	60.4	60.2
Field of science:		
Engineers	32.4	28.2
Physical scientists	62.4	49.6
Life scientists	100.7	93.6
Psychologists	12.7	9.3
Social scientists	40.7	29.0
Other scientists	1.1	.5
Institutional control:		
Public	152.9	132.5
Private	97.1	77.8

*Includes medical schools and agricultural experiment stations.
† Fewer than 0.05 (50).
‡ All agricultural experiment stations are under public control.

SOURCE: National Science Foundation, *Scientific Activities at Universities and Colleges, 1964,* 1968, p. 16.

TABLE 3.1-19
Scientists and engineers employed in universities and colleges classified by highest degree granted in the sciences and engineering, by broad field of science, January 1965 (thousands)

Institutions classified by highest degree granted in the sciences and engineering	Total	Engineers	Physical scientists	Life scientists
Doctorate	185.3	25.2	40.9	88.7
Master's	24.9	3.0	8.7	4.8
Bachelor's	22.6	1.6	7.6	3.9
No science degree	17.2	2.6	5.1	3.3
TOTAL	250.0	32.4	62.4	100.7

SOURCE: National Science Foundation, *Scientific Activities at Universities and Colleges, 1964,* 1968, table A-15, p. 51.

Other institutions	Selected components of graduate schools	
	Medical schools	Agricultural schools and experiment stations
39.8	51.1	22.4
30.6	30.9	15.8
8.9	16.0	1.2
.2	4.2	5.4
4.1	†	.7
12.7	.2	.4
7.1	50.4	19.0
3.4	.3	
11.7	.1	2.0
.6		.3
20.4	21.9	22.4
19.3	29.2	‡

Psychologists	Social scientists	Other scientists
7.1	22.9	0.5
2.2	6.1	
1.9	7.2	0.4
1.5	4.5	0.3
12.7	40.7	1.1

3.2. Supply and Demand, Recruitment and Mobility of Faculty

Recent trends in faculty hiring

Between 1949–50 and 1967–68, the use of faculty for residential instruction in degree-credit courses increased by approximately 150 percent. During the decade 1957–58 to 1967–68, all faculty for residential instruction in degree-credit courses rose from 260,-486 to 481,000, an increase of 85 percent (Table 3.2-1). On the average, faculty for residential instruction in degree-credit courses accounted for about 65 percent of all positions available to faculty and other professional staff between 1959–60 and 1963–64 (Table 3.2-2). Over this three-year period, the relative numbers of the faculty in different positions changed. Professional staff for organized research experienced the highest rate of growth. It accounted for approximately 9 percent of all types of positions in 1959–60 and 12 percent of the total in 1963–64.

Future requirements for instructional staff

From 1962–63 to 1967–68, the full-time equivalent (FTE) instructional staff rose from 281,000 to 407,000. A total of 225,000 estimated vacancies occurred during this period: 126,000 to satisfy expansion demand and 99,000 to meet replacement needs. The Office of Education projected a total of 572,000 FTE instructional staff by 1977–78. The estimates of projected total vacancies between 1968–69 and 1977–78 amounted to 454,000, of which 35 percent were for increased enrollment and 65 percent for replacement. This represented a change from the experience of the five years prior to 1967–68, when replacement and expansion demand accounted for 44 and 56 percent, respectively, of total vacancies (Table 3.2-3). In short, the Office of Education predicts a slackening off of the rate of increase of future enrollment, which means that faculty will grow at a slower rate and that replacement demand

483

TABLE 3.2-1 *Faculty for resident instruction in degree-credit courses in institutions of higher education: United States and outlying areas, 1949–50 to 1967–68*

Year (1)	Total (2)	Instructor or above			Junior instructional staff (6)
		Total (3)	Full-time (4)	Part-time (5)	
1949–50 (academic year)	191,396	*	*	*	*
1951–52 (academic year)	184,826	*	*	*	*
November 1953	208,547	182,028	*	*	26,519
November 1955	227,929	197,791	*	*	30,138
First term of the academic year:					
1957–58	260,486	226,536	154,602	71,934	33,950
1959–60	283,080	244,461	163,656	80,805	38,619
1961–62	312,687	266,624	178,632	87,992	46,063
1963–64	358,153	305,459	204,561	100,898	52,694
1965–66†	430,000	365,000	244,000	121,000	65,000
1966–67†	453,000	385,000	257,000	128,000	68,000
1967–68†	481,000	409,000	273,000	136,000	72,000

* Data not available.
† Estimated by Office of Education.
SOURCE: U.S. Office of Education, "Biennial Survey of Education in the United States;" and circulars on "Faculty and Other Professional Staff in Institutions of Higher Education;" in U.S. Office of Education, *Digest of Educational Statistics, 1968*, 1968, p. 79.

will be the most important factor determining the number of new faculty positions.

On the basis of survey data in the mid-1960s developed by Brown,[1] the relative importance of expansion and replacement demand differed for institutions of varying sizes, levels, types of control, and quality. In 1964–65 expansion demand accounted for over half of all vacancies at large public universities rated in the top 20 percent in terms of quality, whereas replacement demand made up over half of all vacancies at small private colleges in the lowest quality category (Table 3.2-4). Although the average annual expansion rate at all four-year institutions was 8.5 percent, the expansion

[1] D. G. Brown, *The Mobile Professors,* American Council on Education, Washington, D.C., 1967.

TABLE 3.2-2		*Number of positions*	
Faculty and other professional staff in institutions of higher education, by type of position; United States and outlying areas, first term 1959-60 to 1963-64	*Type of position* *(1)*	*1959-60* *(2)*	*1961-62* *(3)*	*1963-64* *(4)*

Type of position (1)	*1959-60* (2)	*1961-62* (3)	*1963-64* (4)
*All types**	431,720	475,810	556,904
Professional staff for general administration	19,063	20,686	25,513
Professional staff for student personnel services	15,299	16,722	20,734
Faculty for resident instruction in degree-credit courses	283,080	312,687	358,153
Instructor or above	244,461	266,624	305,459
Full-time	163,656	178,632	204,561
Part-time	80,805	87,992	100,898
Full-time equivalent of part-time†	25,600	29,645	32,806
Junior instructional staff	38,619	46,063	52,694
Faculty for resident instruction in other than degree-credit courses	14,135	13,632	15,115
Extension staff	31,439	31,409	37,768
Giving courses	15,348	15,236	21,289
Other extension staff	16,091	16,173	16,479
Other faculty, including instructional staff for courses by mail, radio, or TV, short courses, and individual lessons	11,877	11,771	14,492
Professional library staff	9,939	11,025	12,539
Professional staff for organized research	37,099	50,058	65,088
Instructional staff for elementary or secondary instruction	9,789	7,820	7,502

*The sum of the number of persons in all types of positions exceeds the number of different persons because some professional staff serve in more than one capacity. "Total number of positions" represents the sum in all types of positions as classified in the survey questionnaires.

† Rounded.

SOURCE: U.S. Office of Education, circulars on "Faculty and Other Professional Staff in Institutions of Higher Education;" in U.S. Office of Education, *Digest of Educational Statistics, 1968,* 1968, p. 80.

rate was not even throughout higher education. This is brought out in Table 3.2-5, which contains estimates of hiring rates for expansion, replacement, shifting jobs, and temporary replacement at four-year institutions that are classified according to size, type of control, and quality.

TABLE 3.2-3 *Estimated demand for full-time equivalent instructional staff in institutions of higher education, by primary function; United States, first term 1962–63 to 1977–78*

Year (fall) (1)	Total full-time equivalent instructional staff			Additional full-time equivalent instructional staff needed		
	Total (2)	For resident degree-credit courses (3)	Other instructional staff (4)	Total (5)	For increased enrollment (6)	For replacement (7)
1962–63*	281,000	237,000	44,000			
1963–64	299,000	252,000	47,000	35,000	18,000	17,000
1964–65*	327,000	275,000	52,000	46,000	28,000	18,000
1965–66†	362,000	303,000	59,000	55,000	35,000	20,000
1966–67†	382,000	319,000	62,000	41,000	19,000	22,000
1967–68†	407,000	339,000	67,000	48,000	25,000	23,000
1962–1968	1,776,000	1,489,000	287,000	225,000	126,000	99,000
Projected‡						
1968–69	429,000	358,000	71,000	47,000	22,000	24,000
1969–70	435,000	362,000	73,000	32,000	6,000	26,000
1970–71	448,000	373,000	76,000	40,000	13,000	26,000
1971–72	466,000	387,000	79,000	45,000	18,000	27,000
1972–73	486,000	403,000	83,000	48,000	20,000	28,000
1968–1973	2,265,000	1,882,000	382,000	211,000	80,000	131,000
1973–74	508,000	421,000	87,000	51,000	22,000	29,000
1974–75	527,000	436,000	91,000	49,000	18,000	31,000
1975–76	544,000	450,000	94,000	49,000	17,000	32,000
1976–77	559,000	462,000	97,000	48,000	16,000	33,000
1977–78	572,000	472,000	100,000	46,000	13,000	34,000
1973–1978	2,711,000	2,242,000	469,000	243,000	86,000	158,000

* Interpolated.

† Estimated.

‡ The projection of additional full-time equivalent instructional staff for increased enrollment was computed as the difference between the total full-time equivalent instructional staff employed in two successive years.

The projection of additional full-time equivalent instructional staff for replacement of those leaving the profession, temporarily or permanently, was estimated at 6 percent of the total full-time equivalent professional staff employed in the previous year.

NOTE: Data are for 50 states and the District of Columbia for all years. Because of rounding, detail may not add to totals.

SOURCE: U.S. Office of Education publications: "Faculty and Other Professional Staff in Institutions of Higher Education," biennially, first term, 1957–58 to 1963–64; in U.S. Office of Education, *Projections of Educational Statistics to 1977–78,* National Center for Educational Statistics, 1968, p. 63.

TABLE 3.2-4
Importance
of expansion
and
replacement
demands,
compared by
institutional
size, level,
control, and
quality, 1964–65

Characteristic of institution	*Percentage of all vacancies created by expansion demand*
*Size**	
Over 5,000 students	61
Under 1,000 students	36
*Level**	
University	52
College	44
*Control**	
Public	51
Private	42
Quality	
Top 20%	52
Bottom 20%	46

* Means that by a chi-square test at the 0.05 level, the difference in matched pairs is significant.

SOURCE: D. G. Brown, *The Mobile Professors,* American Council on Education, Washington, D.C., 1967, p. 31.

Future requirements for faculty in science and engineering

The National Science Foundation has estimated requirements for FTE teaching staff in science and engineering in universities and colleges from 1964–65 to 1974–75 (Table 3.2-6). The projected increased requirements in FTE teaching staff over this period for different types of scientists and engineers were as follows: all scientists and engineers, 105 percent; physical scientists, 142 percent; engineers, 47 percent; life scientists, 79 percent; and social scientists and psychologists, 121 percent. For the same period the NSF has estimated requirements of science and engineering staff in teaching, research, and other activities in universities and colleges. The results are contained in Table 3.2-7. Over this decade, the demand for FTE staff in teaching was expected to be slightly greater than the estimated requirements of such staff in research.

Faculty shortages

During the late 1950s and through the first half of the 1960s, there were existing or impending shortages of faculty for university and

TABLE 3.2-5
Hiring rates,
by selected
institutional
characteristics,*†
1964–65

Characteristics of schools	Percentage expansion rate*	Percentage replacement rate†
All four-year institutions	8.5	3.4
Size		
Under 1,000 students	6.8	4.7
1,000–5,000 students	9.1	4.3
Over 5,000 students	9.2	2.4
Control		
Public	11.2	4.2
Private	7.3	3.8
Quality		
Top 20%	7.6	1.9
Middle 60%	8.6	3.4
Bottom 20%	9.2	4.8

*Expansion rate = the number of faculty hired into newly created positions for fall 1964 divided by the total number of faculty in spring 1964.

† Replacement rate = the number of faculty hired to replace persons who were teaching in the spring of 1964, but had left college teaching altogether as of the fall of 1964 divided by the same denominator.

‡ Shift rate = the number of faculty hired to replace persons who switched from one faculty to another between the 1963–64 and 1964–65 academic years divided by the same denominator.

§ Temporary rate = the number of faculty hired in the fall of 1964 as temporary, one-year replacements for persons on leave and so forth divided by the same denominator.

¶ The accession rate is the sum of columns 1 to 4. It may be computed independently by dividing the total number of newly appointed faculty members as of fall 1964 by the total number of faculty members as of spring 1964.

SOURCE: D. G. Brown, *The Mobile Professors,* American Council on Education, Washington, D.C., 1967, p. 30.

college teaching. One indication of such shortages was the rapid rise in faculty salaries between 1960 and 1965; faculty earnings increased at a considerably more rapid rate than the manufacturing wage level.[2] Brown attempted to measure relative scarcity of faculty in 23 disciplines (Table 3.2-8). He selected seven factors bearing on the condition of excess demand in the academic market and gave ratings to each of the disciplines according to these factors. The following were the measures used: (1) starting salaries to

[2] Ibid., p. 12.

Percentage shift rate‡	Percentage temporary rate§	Percentage accession rate¶
4.4	1.4	17.7
5.9	1.7	19.1
4.9	1.6	19.9
2.4	1.1	15.1
5.1	1.5	22.0
4.7	1.6	17.4
4.0	1.2	14.7
4.5	1.4	17.9
4.6	1.3	19.9

newly graduated Ph.D.'s, (2) extent of salary increase, (3) salaries paid to full professors in 1962–63, (4) academic rank of newly graduated Ph.D.'s, (5) unfilled positions as percentages of all positions, (6) percentage of newly graduated Ph.D.'s entering college teaching, and (7) expansion demand as a percentage of all hiring. The data revealed a wide range in the relative scarcity of faculty among disciplines. In shortest supply were electrical engineers, teachers of educational service and administration, and mechanical engineers. The subject areas experiencing the least scarcity were French, history, and English language and literature.

TABLE 3.2-6 *Estimated requirements for full-time-equivalent teaching staff* in science and engineering in universities and colleges,† 1964–65 to 1974–75 (in thousands)*

Academic year	Total	Physical scientists‡	Engineers	Life scientists§	Social scientists and psychologists
1964–65	117.7	33.4	15.5	35.4	33.4
1965–66	138.3	40.7	17.6	40.1	39.9
1966–67	153.1	46.4	18.8	43.2	44.7
1967–68	156.4	48.1	18.5	43.5	46.3
1968–69	163.8	50.8	18.3	45.5	49.2
1969–70	177.1	55.2	19.4	49.9	52.6
1970–71	188.7	59.9	20.0	52.2	56.6
1971–72	201.5	65.0	20.7	54.8	61.1
1972–73	213.4	70.2	21.5	56.1	65.5
1973–74	225.5	75.4	22.2	58.7	69.2
1974–75	240.8	80.9	22.8	63.4	73.7

* Includes full-time and part-time staff and employed graduate students.
† Excludes Federal Contract Research Centers administered by these institutions.
‡ Includes mathematicians.
§ Includes medical scientists.
NOTE: Detail may not add to totals because of rounding.
SOURCE: National Science Foundation, *The Prospective Manpower Situation for Science and Engineering Staff in Universities and Colleges 1965–75,* 1967, p. 18.

According to Brown, the situation had changed by the late 1960s when it seemed that excess demand no longer characterized the market for college teachers.[3]

A recent study prepared for the Joint Economic Committee of the Congress by Cartter and Farrell[4] deals with the market for college teachers. The authors attempt to clarify past trends with respect to demand and supply of college teachers and to predict future market conditions for professional academics. They have this to say about the future:

[3] Ibid., p. 12.

[4] A. M. Cartter and R. L. Farrell, "Academic Labor Market Projections and the Draft," *The Economics and Financing of Higher Education in the United States,* a compendium of papers submitted to the Joint Economic Committee, U.S. Congress, Washington, D.C., 1969, pp. 357–374.

TABLE 3.2-7 *Estimated requirements for science and engineering staff for teaching, research, and other activities in universities and colleges,* 1964–65 to 1974–75 (in thousands)*

Academic year	FTE staff† engaged in—			FTE total, all activities	Number employed‡
	Teaching	Research	Other activities		
1964–65	117.7	54.9	20.0	192.6	189.6
1965–66	138.3	63.7	22.8	224.8	220.7
1966–67	153.1	69.9	24.6	247.6	242.5
1967–68	156.4	71.1	24.7	252.2	246.4
1968–69	163.8	74.3	25.6	263.7	257.4
1969–70	177.1	80.8	27.9	285.9	279.1
1970–71	188.7	85.4	29.3	303.4	295.7
1971–72	201.5	91.3	30.7	323.9	315.0
1972–73	213.4	95.2	31.5	340.1	330.1
1973–74	225.5	100.6	32.8	358.9	347.7
1974–75	240.8	106.1	34.3	381.2	368.8

Excludes Federal Contract Research Centers administered by these institutions.
Full-time and part-time staff and employed graduate students.
"Head count" of full-time and part-time staff only; does not include employed graduate students.
NOTE: Detail may not add to totals because of rounding.
SOURCE: National Science Foundation, *The Prospective Manpower Situation for Science and Engineering Staff in Universities and Colleges, 1965–75*, 1967, p. 21.

We can look forward to the 1970s with confidence that there will be an adequate supply of available manpower to meet most critical needs in teaching, research and other specialized employment fields. Whereas for the last decade we have needed to channel out half of all persons receiving the doctorate into college teaching to maintain the quality of our staffs, in the 1970s less than a third will be required, and fifteen years from now it may require only one in five.[5]

They present a persuasive statement in support of the position that the shortage of doctorates between 1954 and 1964 was not as serious as some claimed and that, in any event, in the future there would not be a shortage of college teachers. They based their conclusions on the experience of the last 15 years. Their assessment

[5] Ibid., p. 357.

TABLE 3.2-8 *Measures of shortage in 23 disciplines,* 1964–65*

Discipline (in order of overall shortage)	Shortage index	Mean salary, new Ph.D.'s	Salaries of new Ph.D.'s versus assistant professor
Electrical engineering	1	1	1
Educational service and administration‡	2	2	2
Mechanical engineering	3	3	3
Mathematics	4	6	5
Physics	5	8	11
Economics	6	5	6
Civil engineering	7	4	10
Chemistry	8	14	15
Counseling and guidance‡	9	7	4
Clinical psychology	10	13	19
Sociology	11	15	16
Art	12	9	8
Secondary education	13	10	9
Political science	14	16	20
Earth science and geology	15	19	18
General biology	16	17	13
Biochemistry	17	12	23
Physical education and health	18	11	12
Music	19	18	7
General zoology	20	20	22
English and literature	21	21	14
History	22	23	17
French	23	22	21

* The rank of "1" means that excess demand is greatest in that discipline.
† Information unavailable.
‡ Teachers.
SOURCE: D. G. Brown, *The Mobile Professors,* American Council on Education, Washington, D.C., 1967, p. 13.

of the past differed from the results of earlier studies.[6] They claimed that past projections of demand for college teachers were misleading indicators of actual development because of the inaccuracy of the basic data. They argued that the studies conducted by the Na-

[6] Cartter and Farrell, op. cit., pp. 358–359.

Rank of discipline by various measures

Hire in rank, new Ph.D.'s	Percentage of new Ph.D.'s entering academia	Fields with most rapid expansion	Mean salary, full professor	Unfilled positions divided by total positions
1	†	3	6	6
3	†	8	1	†
7	†	2	4	8
15	7	1	10	2
14	2	4	7	1
6	9	15	9	7
5	†	12	8	12
12	1	7	12	5
2	†	11	23	11
18	3	6	2	†
4	11	16	11	3
16	8	9	17	16
10	†	14	21	†
19	12	10	3	10
13	4	13	5	20
9	5	23	22	4
8	†	5	14	19
11	13	18	18	17
20	10	22	19	18
17	6	20	15	15
21	15	17	16	13
22	14	19	13	14
23	†	21	20	9

tional Educational Association exaggerated future faculty shortages by using Ph.D. enrollment projections that were too low, a student-faculty ratio that was too low, and a replacement ratio that was too high by a factor of 3. Table 3.2-9 contains Office of Education and Cartter and Farrell Ph.D. enrollment projections; Table 3.2-10

			Projection	
Year	Actual	OE (1967)	OE (1969)	Cartter and Farrell
1957–58	8,942			
1958–59	9,360			
1959–60	9,829			
1960–61	10,575			
1961–62	11,622			
1962–63	12,822			
1963–64	14,490			
1964–65	16,467			
1965–66	18,237	17,500		
1966–67	20,621	18,800	19,800	20,600
1967–68		21,000	22,200	22,600
1968–69		23,600	25,100	24,500
1969–70		24,800	26,500	26,400
1970–71		24,900	27,000	28,200
1971–72		26,800	29,200	31,100
1972–73		32,000	34,900	32,700
1973–74		35,500	38,900	34,800
1974–75		35,800	39,300	36,900
1975–76		36,900	40,600	39,100
1976–77		38,700	42,000	41,600
1977–78			43,900	44,800
1978–79				47,200
1979–80				49,100
1980–81				50,900
1981–82				52,700
1982–83				54,600
1983–84				56,200
1984–85				57,700
1985–86				59,200

TABLE 3.2-9 Doctorates awarded and projected to 1986

SOURCE: A. M. Cartter and R. L. Farrell, "Academic Labor Market Projections and the Draft," *The Economics and Financing of Higher Education in the United States,* a compendium of papers submitted to the Joint Economic Committee, U.S. Congress, Washington, D.C., 1969, p. 361.

presents estimates of average and marginal faculty coefficients for selected years between 1953–54 and 1963–64. Cartter and Farrell use in their own model an incremental student-faculty ratio of 20 to 1 and an annual replacement ratio of 2 percent.[7]

[7] Ibid., p. 362.

TABLE 3.2-10
Average and marginal faculty coefficients 1953–54 to 1963–64

	E^*	ΔE	$F\dagger$	ΔF	F/E	$\Delta F/\Delta E$	$\Delta E{:}\Delta F$
1953–54	2,236		182.0		0.084		
1955–56	2,660	424	197.8	15.8	0.076	0.037	26.8:1
1957–58	3,047	387	226.5	28.7	0.074	0.074	13.5:1
1959–60	3,377	330	244.5	18.0	0.072	0.055	18.2:1
1961–62	3,861	484	266.6	22.1	0.069	0.046	21.7:1
1963–64	4,495	634	298.9	32.3	0.066	0.051	19.6:1
1953–54 to 1963–64		2,259		116.9		0.0517	19.3:1

$^*E =$ enrollment.

$\dagger F =$ faculty.

SOURCE: "Projections of Educational Statistics to 1973-74" (OE-10030, 1964), pp. 8, 24. Faculty considered here are members of the instructional staff at the level of instructor or above. The extreme high and low ratios for 1955–56 and 1957–58 may result from errors in reporting by institutions. In A. M. Cartter, "The Supply and Demand for College Teachers," *Journal of Human Resources,* Summer 1966, p. 27.

TABLE 3.2-11
Percentage of doctors' degrees graduates of 77 universities going into college teaching by fields, 1962–63 and 1963–64*

Field	Number	Percent in college teaching
English	885	88.6
History	701	87.6
Foreign languages	411	87.3
Political science	386	79.0
Sociology	329	76.6
Music	275	75.6
Mathematics	906	66.4
Economics	578	65.9
Education (Ed.D. and Ph.D.)	3,497	48.5
Biological sciences	2,114	40.9
Psychology	1,436	37.2
Engineering	2,533	36.0
Agriculture	1,036	33.5
Physics	1,338	28.7
Chemistry	2,192	22.8

* It is clear also that the percentage going into teaching has risen in recent years.

NOTE: Of all doctor's degree graduates reported for 1962–63 and 1963–64 (22,269), college teaching gained the services of 48.4 percent. Of all doctor's degree graduates reported for 1960–61 and 1961–62 (18,545), college teaching attracted 46.7 percent. Of all doctor's degree graduates reported for 1958–59 and 1959–60 (16,252), just 45.6 percent were engaged in college teaching. Of all doctor's degree graduates reported for 1956–57 and 1957–58 (12,378), college teaching claimed 44.5 percent. Of all doctor's degree graduates reported for 1954–55 and 1955–56 (8,955), 45.2 percent were in the occupation of college teaching.

SOURCE: U.S. House of Representatives, Committee on Government Operations, *Conflicts Between the Federal Research Programs and the Nation's Goals for Higher Education,* hearings before a subcommittee, June 1965, p. 91.

TABLE 3.2-12 *Percentage of doctorates in institutions of higher education, 1900–1958*

Date	Approximate percentage of employed doctorates in college and university posts	From
Around 1900	70 to 80	Ryan on early doctorates from Johns Hopkins, Chicago, and Clark Walcott on Ph.D. recipients from 1885 to 1904 Chase on early Harvard doctorates Haggerty on early Chicago doctorates
Late 1920s	70 to 75	John on a sample of doctorates after 1924 Haggerty on Ph.D.'s from seven major universities
1930s	65	Hollis on Ph.D.'s of the 1930s
1958	60	NRC data on all doctorates

Two important points emerge at once: first, holders of the doctorate are not now employed overwhelmingly in colleges and universities, but only a slight majority of them; and second, the long-run trend is running against the employment of doctorates in higher education. On the overall picture, then, the market argument, that was not persuasive enough to change the situation in the past, is even weaker today. If it was a good argument earlier, it is not as good now; if it was bad then, it is worse now.

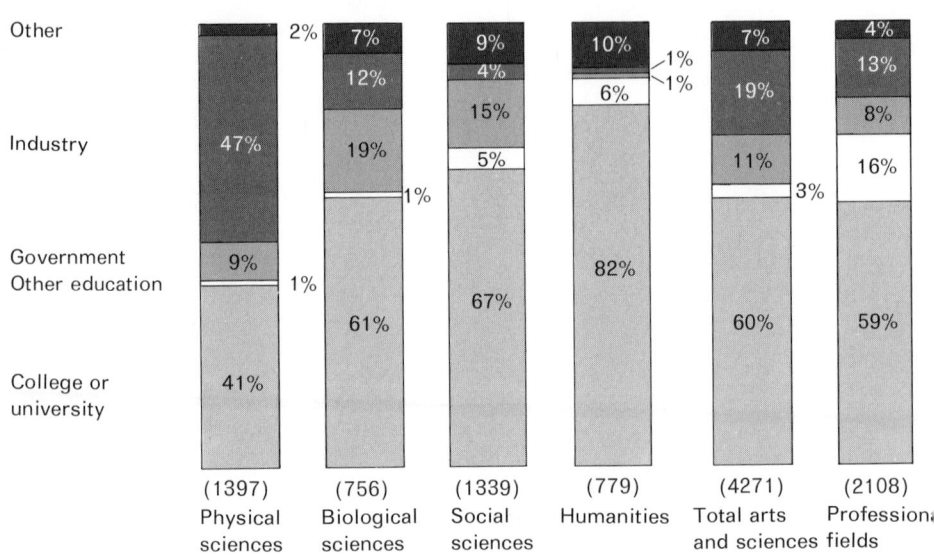

Type of employment of 1958 recipients of the doctorate

SOURCE: NRC data; in B. Berelson, *Graduate Education in the United States,* McGraw-Hill Book Company, New York, 1960, p. 50.

They set the proportion of newly trained students entering teaching at 50 percent, which was the approximate proportion experienced in the recent past. Each year from 1955 to 1969, between 45 and 50 percent of all Ph.D. holders selected teaching as a profession.[8] According to another source, this ratio differed considerably among different fields of specialization.[9] Data that are available on the proportion of graduates with Ph.D.'s in 15 subject areas for 1962–63 indicate that over three-quarters of those with doctorates in music, sociology, political science, foreign languages, history, and English went into college teaching whereas less than a third of those with doctorates in agriculture, physics, and chemistry chose teaching as a career (Table 3.2-11). The longer-run trend seems to be toward a decreasing proportion of doctorates seeking academic employment in colleges and universities (Table 3.2-12).

Table 3.2-13 provides data, developed by Cartter and Farrell, on the percentage of faculty with doctoral degrees in private and public colleges and universities for selected years from 1950–51 to 1966–67. It shows a gradual rise in the proportion of faculty

	Private	*Public*
Colleges:		
1950–51	29.7	23.2
1954–55	32.5	30.1
1958–59	33.7	32.0
1962–63	35.4	33.5
1966–67	37.5	34.7
Universities:		
1950–51	37.3	36.0
1954–55	40.0	40.7
1958–59	40.7	41.7
1962–63	43.8	44.9
1966–67	45.6	48.4

TABLE 3.2-13 *Percentage of faculty with doctoral degree, private and public colleges and universities*

SOURCE: A. M. Cartter and R. L. Farrell, "Academic Labor Market Projections and the Draft," *The Economics and Financing of Higher Education in the United States,* compendium of papers submitted to the Joint Economic Committee, U.S. Congress, Washington, D.C., 1969, p. 367.

[8] Ibid., p. 360.

[9] U.S. House of Representatives, Committee on Government Operations, *Conflicts Between the Federal Research Programs and the Nation's Goals for Higher Education,* hearings before subcommittee, June 1965, p. 91.

with doctoral degrees in both colleges and universities, and a larger proportion of faculty with doctorates at universities than at colleges. Cartter and Farrell settled on an estimate of 44 percent as the proportion of teaching faculty with doctorates. Brown[10] points out that the proportion of new faculty with doctorates is more than twice as high at schools with the best quality rating as at those in the lowest quality bracket (Table 3.2-14).

Cooperation of government and private interests has solved the problem of Ph.D.'s which in the 1950s seemed insoluble to many. In the future a substantial part of the flow of the Ph.D.'s is likely to be used to increase the proportion of faculty members with doctoral degrees, that is, in improving the quality of teaching.

Cartter and Farrell conclude: ". . . the arguments for support of graduate students as an inducement to enter a field in short supply are no longer as compelling as they were in the immediate post-sputnik period. . . ."[11] Government support, however, is necessary to reduce the heavy cost burden of private and public institutions of higher education that train doctoral students.

RECRUITMENT   The discussion that follows about faculty recruitment is based primarily on two sources: Brown's study, *The Mobile Professors*[12] and Caplow and McGee's *The Academic Marketplace*.[13] According

[10] Brown, op. cit., p. 18.

[11] Cartter and Farrell, op. cit., p. 374.

[12] Brown, op. cit.

[13] T. Caplow and R. J. McGee, *The Academic Marketplace,* Basic Books, Inc., Publishers, New York, 1958.

TABLE 3.2-14   *Characteristics of new faculty, by quality of schools, 1963–64*

Quality of school	Percentage with Ph.D.'s*	Percentage hired as instructors†	Percentage hired directly from graduate school	Percentage hired from primary and secondary schools
Top 20 percent	71	30	36	3
20 to 40 percent	54	36	44	6
40 to 60 percent	53	36	41	8
60 to 80 percent	40	40	39	12
Bottom 20 percent	32	46	44	16

* The percentage of Ph.D.'s on the faculty is one of the variables used to calculate the prestige index. Therefore, it is not surprising to learn that "prestige" and "percentage with Ph.D.'s" are positively related. What is surprising is the strength of the relationship.

† Means that differences are statistically significant by a chi-square test at the 0.05 level.

SOURCE: D. G. Brown, *The Mobile Professors,* American Council on Education, Washington, D.C., 1967, p. 18.

TABLE 3.2-15 *Faculty search for jobs: role of market liaisons (1964–65)*

Type of liaison	Method of search of all candidates	Mean number of jobs found per candidate	Method of finding current job of all candidates
Informal			
Graduate professor	40%	1.41	12%
Graduate department office	32	1.72	6
Undergraduate professor	16	0.82	3
Graduate school classmate	17	0.61	3
Faculty colleague	20	1.07	7
Other professional friend	25	1.01	8
Publisher's representative	2	0.86	*
Did nothing and was recruited	23	1.82	26
TOTAL	†	†	65%
Formal			
Blind letters	46	2.14	19
College placement office	36	2.75	6
Church-related placement service	5	1.30	1
Professional association‡	14	1.96	2
Advertisement: "Candidate Available"	3	2.56	*
Advertisement: "Position Available"	9	1.73	2
Convention placement service	14	2.42	2
Public employment service‡	3	1.65	*
Commercial teacher's agency	7	3.05	3
TOTAL	†	†	35%

* Less than 0.5 percent.
† Totals are not meaningful, for one person could pursue jobs by several methods.
‡ Excluding convention placement service and advertisements in professional journals.

SOURCE: D. G. Brown, *The Mobile Professors,* American Council on Education, Washington, D.C., 1967, p. 119.

to Brown, 65 percent of faculty members surveyed found their current jobs through informal methods (Table 3.2-15). These included reliance on graduate professors (12 percent) and "did nothing and were recruited" (26 percent). A summary of the results of 13 studies bearing on methods of finding jobs in the academic labor market, including Brown's findings cited above, is included in Table 3.2-16. On the basis of seven studies, informal methods were the principal

(Text continued on p. 503)

TABLE 3.2-16 *Percentage of faculty members or institutions reporting selected methods of finding jobs in the academic labor market in 13 studies*

Method	Brown: all college teachers (1964–65)	Brown: South-eastern social scientists (1962–63)	Marshall: economists (1960–64)	Klugh: psycho-logists (1958–63)[a]	Stecklein and Lathrop: U. of Minn. faculty (1956–57)
Informal					
Former professor	15	11	3[f]	[g]	
Graduate department office	6	23	20		
Professional acquaintance	18	46[l]	26[m]	37[g]	25[n]
Publisher's representative	*		1		
Did nothing and was recruited	26		8		33
TOTAL	65	80	58	37	58
Formal					
College placement office	6	4	3	13	
Convention placement service	2	[l]	26[q]	16	
U.S. Employment Service	*		4		
Advertised in a journal	*			3[r]	
Answered a journal advertisement	2	2	1[s]	12[r]	
Church-related bureau	1				
Commercial teacher's agency	3	1	*	3	
Blind letters	19	7	9	15	22[v]
Professional association	2				10
TOTAL	35	20[aa]	42	62	42[bb]

[a] The Klugh article reported only the methods used to search for jobs. For purposes of this summary, it is assumed that the methods by which the job was actually found are distributed in the same proportion that the various methods were used.

[b] The data were given as "Percentages of institutions indicating various sources of prospective staff members as most useful." Also see footnote *e*.

[c] Sample included only AAUP members. Also see footnote *e*.

[d] Sample included responses from faculty of Amherst, Brown, Dartmouth, Harvard, Wesleyan, Williams, and Yale. Also see footnote *e*.

[e] Employees were surveyed rather than candidates.

[f] Category was "Other professors."

[g] Category was "Friends or major professor."

[h] Category was "Recommendations of graduate faculty at higher institutions."

[i] Category was "Deans and chairmen of departments."

[j] Category was "Recommendations of our own faculty member."

[k] This includes the categories listed in footnotes *h* and *j*.

[l] Convention placement service is included in "Professional acquaintance" category.

[m] Category was "Friends."

[n] This classification was "Known or met Minnesota faculty who indicated opening."

[o] Category was "Outside offers."

Anantaraman: "well-established" economists (1960)	Bosley: all college teachers (1946)	Haggerty and Works: North Central Association colleges (1936–37)[b]	Craig: 80 institutions (1927–28)[c]	Hill: 7 New England colleges (1926–27)[d]	Poorman: California junior colleges (1962–63)[e]	Gleazer: junior colleges (1961)[e]	Brown: junior colleges (1964–65)
	23[h]			28	12		6
29[i]	2[j]	62	42[k]	8			2
29[m]		21	22	31	25		21
							1
15[o]	—	—	—	11	—	—	18
73	25	83	71	40	37	40[p]	48
	28		11	4	21	29	16
				6			*
						0	1
							*
			3[t]	1			2
		2		2			*
	18	13[u]	5			10	4
13[w]	23[x]		10[x]	11	38	12	27
	6[y]	1[z]			4	9	2
37[cc]	75	16	29	23	63	60	52

Since his survey referred only to "formal methods," it is assumed that the 40 percent not accounted for were informal.

This includes two categories listed as "Informal contacts at annual meetings" and "Regional meetings."

Advertisements in the *APA Journal* only.

Advertisements were only in the *American Economic Review*.

Category was "Lists from graduate schools."

This includes "Teacher's agency" and "Similar institutions."

Category was "Appointee initiated contact."

Category was "Direct contacts."

Category was "Direct applications."

Category was "Scientific societies."

Category was "Office of AAUP."

"Other" methods account for 6 percent.

"Other" methods account for 10 percent.

Due to the nature of the report, the 14 percent unaccounted for is assumed to be formal methods.

Less than 0.5 percent.

SOURCE: D. G. Brown, *The Mobile Professors,* American Council on Education, Washington, D.C., 1967, pp. 122–123.

TABLE 3.2-17 *Evaluation of various market intermediaries in faculty search for jobs, 1964–1965*

Market intermediary	Frequency (percentage who used) Percentage (rank in column) (1)	Efficiency (number found/ number used) Percentage (rank in column) (2)	Desirability (number of jobs accepted/ number of jobs found) Percentage (rank in column) (3)	Importance [average of ranks in columns (1)–(3)] (4)
Informal				
Faculty colleague	20 (6)	35 (3)	31 (1)	3.3
Other professional friend	25 (5)	32 (4)	30 (2)	3.7
Graduate professor	40 (2)	30 (5)	21 (5)	4.0
Graduate department	32 (4)	19 (8½)	11 (9)	7.1
Undergraduate professor	16 (8)	19 (8½)	25 (4)	6.8
Graduate classmate	17 (7)	18 (10)	29 (3)	6.8
Publisher's representative	2 (16)	10 (14½)	11 (10)	13.5
Formal				
Blind letters	46 (1)	41 (2)	20 (6)	3.0
Commercial agency	7 (12)	43 (1)	13 (7)	6.7
Answered an advertisement	9 (11)	22 (6)	12 (8)	8.3
College placement office	36 (3)	17 (11)	7 (13)	9.0
Church-related service	5 (13)	20 (7)	10 (11)	10.3
Convention placement service	14 (9½)	14 (12½)	6 (14)	12.0
Professional association	14 (9½)	14 (12½)	9 (12)	13.3
Advertised availability	3 (14½)	10 (14½)	4 (16)	15.0
Public employment service	3 (14½)	7 (16)	5 (15)	15.1

SOURCE: D. G. Brown, *The Mobile Professors,* American Council on Education, Washington, D.C., 1967, p. 140.

TABLE 3.2-18 *Percentage of active participants in the recruitment of a faculty member, by separate stages**

Participants	Search for candidates	Evaluation of credentials	Selection of candidates	Consulted before offer	Making offer	Closing contract
Higher administration	5	3	8	15	27	8
Deans and committees	76	60	48	85	67	34
Chairman and senior colleagues	91	87	83	48	75	75
Whole department	17	29	40	25	5	

* A cell value of 100 would equal involvement of the given participants in the given stage of recruitment in 100% of the replacements studied.

SOURCE: T. Caplow and R. J. McGee, *The Academic Marketplace,* Basic Books, Inc., Publishers, New York, 1958, p. 183.

type of search. In the case of psychologists, studied in 1958–63, and junior college teachers, surveyed in 1961 and 1962–63, formal procedures of search were relatively more frequent.

Brown also provides data evaluating these various market intermediaries (Table 3.2-17). According to column 1 of this table, blind letters, graduate professors, and college placement offices were the most popular ways for faculty to get jobs. From column 2, which measures efficiency, it is clear that the commercial employment agency and blind letters, more than any other informal or formal intermediary, provided the faculty job seeker with the most job opportunities. From the point of view of qualitatively desirable jobs, as measured by column 3, informal intermediaries were more

TABLE 3.2-19
Determinants of job choice for recently hired faculty (1964–65)

Choice variable	Choice index*
Courses taught	3.7
Teaching load	3.4
Research facilities and opportunities	3.3
Competency of colleagues	3.3
Salary	3.2
Future salary prospects	3.2
Reputation of school	3.1
Quality of students	3.1
Administration and administrators	3.0
Cultural opportunities	2.9
Congeniality of colleagues	2.9
Academic rank	2.8
Fringe benefits	2.4
Nearness to graduate school	2.4
Climate	2.1
Nearness to friends and relatives	2.1
Moonlighting opportunities	1.8

* In response to the question, "How important were each of these factors in your decision to choose your current job instead of your next best alternative?" three options were given: "very important," "important," and "not important." For each of the seventeen factors, five times the number of "very important's," three times the "important's," and one times the "not important's" were summed. By dividing the summed products by the total number of answers, the "choice index" was obtained. (For example, if 50 persons were surveyed about the importance of salary, and ten answered "very important," 35 answered "important," and five "not important," then the index would be 3.2.) Thus, the most important variables are assigned the higher choice-index values.

SOURCE: D. G. Brown, *The Mobile Professors,* American Council on Education, Washington, D.C., 1967, p. 150.

effective than formal methods. Column 4, which consists of the average ranks of intermediaries from columns 1 to 3, indicates the overall relative importance of blind letters, friends, contemporaries, and former teachers in getting jobs.

Recommendations, records, and publications were the most important criteria used in the selection of faculty at all ranks, while interviews and visits were considerably less important.[14]

The most active participants in the search for faculty candidates, in evaluation of credentials, and in the selection of candidates included department chairmen, senior colleagues, and deans and

[14] Ibid., p. 129.

TABLE 3.2-20
Mobility of teaching faculty in universities and four-year colleges (1962–63), by selected disciplines

Principal teaching field	Total	At the same institutions in 1961–62	
		Number	Percent
Agriculture and related fields	2,986	1,629	55
Biological sciences	10,892	7,122	65
Engineering	9,497	7,175	76
Mathematics	7,640	5,894	77
Physical sciences	11,829	8,332	70
Psychology	3,849	2,848	74
Social sciences	16,984	13,422	79
Total, sciences	63,677	46,432	73
Health fields	7,205	5,276	70
Selected nonscience fields*			
Business and commerce	6,974	5,765	83
Education	10,717	9,289	87
English and journalism	11,798	9,859	84
Foreign language and linguistics	7,514	6,216	83
Philosophy	2,214	1,872	85
Total, all fields	138,203	108,215	78
Universities	68,925	51,244	74
Colleges	62,084	51,768	83
Technical institutes	7,194	5,203	72

* Not shown separately.
SOURCE: U.S. House of Representatives, Committee on Science and Astronautics, *Higher Education in the Sciences in the United States,* report of the Subcommittee on Science, Research and Development, prepared by the National Science Foundation, 1965, p. 36.

committees (Table 3.2-18). The most important determinant of job choice, as summarized in Brown's job choice index, from a total of 17 possible determinants, were courses taught and teaching load. The least significant conditions affecting job choice were environmental and personal factors and moonlighting opportunities (Table 3.2-19).

MOBILITY   The data in this section on faculty mobility were taken from the two studies referred to above.[15] Faculty mobility is measured by the number of faculty who remain employed in the same institution of

[15] Brown, op. cit.; and Caplow and McGee, op. cit.

At different institutions in 1961–62		Not in higher education in 1961–62	
Number	Percent	Number	Percent
1,167	39	190	6
2,964	27	807	7
1,389	15	933	10
737	10	1,008	13
2,287	19	1,211	10
683	18	319	8
1,493	9	2,068	12
10,620	17	6,536	10
1,272	17	953	13
542	8	667	10
497	5	931	9
638	5	1,301	11
469	6	830	11
118	5	224	10
15,782	12	14,205	10
11,383	17	6,297	9
3,219	5	7,079	11
1,180	16	811	11

TABLE 3.2-21 *Mobility of teaching faculty* in universities and four-year colleges (1962–1963), by faculty rank*

Rank	Total	At the same institution in 1961–62 Number	Percent	At a different institution in 1961–62 Number	Percent	Not in higher education in 1961–62 Number	Percent
Professor	37,513	31,681	84.5	4,779	12.7	1,053	2.8
Associate professor	32,840	27,262	83.1	3,890	11.8	1,688	5.1
Assistant professor	40,361	30,815	76.3	4,701	11.7	4,844	12.0
Instructor	22,430	14,287	63.7	1,788	7.9	6,355	28.4
Other	5,060	4,170	82.5	625	12.4	262	5.2
Doctorate holders	69,949	53,666	77.0	11,409	16.0	4,872	7.0
Nondoctorates	68,254	54,549	80.0	4,373	6.0	9,332	14.0

* Includes all faculty, science and nonscience.
SOURCE: U.S. House of Representatives, Committee on Science and Astronautics, *Higher Education in the Sciences in the United States,* report of the Subcommittee on Science, Research and Development, prepared by the National Science Foundation, 1965, p. 37.

higher education in successive years. Presented in Table 3.2-20 are data on numbers of teaching faculty in universities and four-year colleges by selected disciplines in 1962–63 and 1961–62. The proportion of the faculty in 1962–63 who were in the same institution in 1961–62 was as low as 55 percent in agriculture and related

TABLE 3.2-22
Rank and mobility of faculty, 1964–65

Rank before move	Percentage of faculty moving from one institution to another*	Percentage of all college faculty	Probability of moving†
Instructor	40	16	0.137
Assistant professor	42	25	0.079
Associate professor	10	24	0.021
Full professor‡	7	28	0.012

* These data exclude all newly hired professors who were not also full-time faculty members in the previous year.
† For example, 0.137 means that in any given year it is 13.7 percent likely that a full-time faculty member who holds the rank of instructor will leave to accept an appointment on another faculty. Persons who leave to pursue a noncollege teaching job are not considered.
‡ The figures in columns 1 and 2 do not total 100 percent because some professors are not assigned an academic rank.
SOURCE: COLFACS data; in D. G. Brown, *The Mobile Professors,* American Council on Education, Washington, D.C., 1967, p. 39.

Subject matter specialty	Number moving from one faculty to another*	All college faculty	Probability of moving†
Sciences‡	1,190	29,600	0.040
Engineering	150	9,500	0.015
Humanities§	3,050	38,500	0.079
Social sciences	1,750	17,000	0.103

* These data exclude all college professors who did not hold a full-time faculty position during the previous year.

† Means that differences are significant by a chi-square test at the 0.05 level.

‡ Sciences = agriculture and related fields, biological sciences, physical sciences, and psychology, in the COLFACS study.

§ Humanities = English and journalism, fine arts, foreign languages and literature, law, philosophy, religion and theology, in the COLFACS study.

SOURCE: COLFACS data, in D. G. Brown, *The Mobile Professors,* American Council on Education, Washington, D.C., 1967, p. 42; ibid., p. 39, for description of COLFACS.

fields and as high as 87 percent in education, with the average for all fields 78 percent. The overall proportion for universities was 74 percent and for colleges 83 percent. The percentage of faculty in 1962-63 at the same institution in 1961-62 differed also according to rank. There was, as might be expected, less mobility among professors and associate professors than there was among instructors (Table 3.2-21).

The probability of a faculty member's moving in a given year was related to rank, subject matter specialty, and age. The probability of moving was considerably greater for instructors than it was for full professors (Table 3.3-22); for faculty teaching in the social sciences compared to those in engineering (Table 3.2-23); and for faculty under 30 years of age, since the likelihood of moving decreased with age (Table 3.2-24).

In Table 3.2-25, institutions of higher education were classified according to prestige ratings, and for each prestige group the proportions were given of the previous year's faculty that moved from that prestige group to an institution in the same prestige group. No one prestige category drew a majority of its faculty from within its own ranks. The ratio for the top 20 percent was 36 percent and for the bottom quintile 44 percent.

A majority of graduate students entering teaching took their first job at institutions of lower prestige than the one at which they received their graduate degree. The conclusion that can be drawn

TABLE 3.2-24
Age and mobility of faculty, 1964–65

Age	Percentage of faculty moving from one faculty to another*	Percentage of all college faculty	Probability of moving†
Under 30	25	7	0.195
30 to 39	37	33	0.061
40 to 49	17	30	0.031
50 to 59	9	20	0.024
60 and over	2	10	0.012

*These data exclude all newly hired professors who were not also full-time faculty members in the previous year.

† Probabilities are computed by dividing the number of movers in each age group by the number of faculty members in that group.

SOURCES: Survey data; and Ralph E. Dunham, Patricia S. Wright, and Marjorie Chandler, *Teaching Faculty in Universities and Four-Year Colleges: Spring, 1963,* (Washington, D.C.: OE-53022-63, U.S. Government Printing Office, 1966), p. 5. The latter study is subsequently cited as COLFACS, in D. G. Brown, *The Mobile Professors,* American Council on Education, Washington, D.C., 1967, p. 38.

from Table 3.2-26 is that 64 percent of all students entering the academic labor market moved to institutions of lower prestige, 26 percent to institutions with the same prestige ratings as that of their graduate school, and 10 percent to higher-prestige institutions. Upward movement, however, characterized those starting at the least prestigious institutions (Table 3.2-27) and those at the least prestigious institutions who published prodigiously (Table 3.2-28). The majority of associate professors and full professors leaving one institution for another reported that they were dissatisfied (Table 3.2-29). However, slightly more than half of the assistant professors leaving reported that they were not dissatisfied. The

(Text continued on p. 512)

TABLE 3.2-25
Intragroup hirings of faculty by prestige of institution, 1964–65

Prestige of the previous institution	Percentage moving between faculties of schools in the same prestige group*
Top 20 percent†	36
20 to 40 percent	18
40 to 60 percent	26
60 to 80 percent	31
Bottom 20 percent	44
Weighted average	28

*For example, 36 percent of the last year's college teachers who moved from the top 20 percent of schools went to a top 20 percent school.

† The percentage for the top 10 percent only is 27.

SOURCE: D. G. Brown, *The Mobile Professors,* American Council on Education, Washington, D.C., 1967, p. 99.

TABLE 3.2-26 Direction of interprestige movements of last year's students

Prestige of graduate institution	Percentage prestige of present institution*		
	Higher	Same	Lower
Top 10 percent		16	84
10 to 20 percent	4	8	88
20 to 40 percent	7	23	70
40 to 60 percent	18	28	54
Bottom 20 percent	28	72	
Weighted average	10	26	64

*Means that the distributions for the various "prestige groups" differ significantly by a chi-square test at the 0.05 level.

SOURCE: D. G. Brown, *The Mobile Professors,* American Council on Education, Washington, D.C., 1967, p. 100.

TABLE 3.2-27 Direction of interprestige movements of last year's faculty

Prestige of previous institution	Prestige of present institutions*		
	Percentage higher	Percentage same	Percentage lower
Top 10 percent		27	73
10 to 20 percent	14	11	75
20 to 40 percent	24	18	58
40 to 60 percent	31	26	43
60 to 80 percent	40	31	29
Bottom 20 percent	56	44	
Weighted average	32	28	40

*Means that the distributions for the various "prestige groups" differ significantly by a chi-square test at the 0.05 level.

SOURCE: D. G. Brown, *The Mobile Professors,* American Council on Education, Washington, D.C., 1967, p. 101.

TABLE 3.2-28 Direction of interprestige movements and extent of publication

Prestige of previous institution	Probability of moving up		Probability of moving down	
	Big publishers*	Others	Big publishers*	Others
Top 20 percent†			67	79
20 to 40 percent†	33	20	30	62
40 to 60 percent†	46	25	41	41
60 to 80 percent†	42	38	12	30
Bottom 20 percent†	72	53		

†Big publishers are defined as persons who have published 10 or more journal articles or at least one book.

*Means that for each "prestige group," big publishers and others are significantly different by a chi-square test at the 0.05 level.

SOURCE: D. G. Brown, *The Mobile Professors,* American Council on Education, Washington, D.C., 1967, p. 101.

TABLE 3.2-29
Percentage of dissatisfaction before departure by rank of vacancy

Reported dissatisfied	Assistant professor	Associate professor	Full professor
No	52	33	45
Yes	48	67	55

SOURCE: T. Caplow and R. J. McGee, *The Academic Marketplace,* Basic Books, Inc., Publishers, New York, 1958, p. 80.

TABLE 3.2-31
Age of compulsory retirement from full-time teaching service, by type of institution

Age (1)	All institutions* (2)	State universities (3)	Nonpublic universities (4)
60 years	1		
65 years	262	22	29
66 years	5		1
67 years	15	3	2
68 years	80	10	11‡
69 years	1		1
70 years	421	46	27‡
72 years	10	1	
75 years	1		
Institutions having compulsory retirement age limits	796	82	71
Institutions having no compulsory retirement age limit	147	1	14
Institutions not reporting	142	7	15

* Individual items do not add to this total because the 47 state universities and the 2 nonpublic universities which are also land-grant colleges have been included under both categories.

† In one of these institutions the age shown is for men; for women, 62 years.

‡ In one of these institutions the age shown is for men; for women, 65 years.

§ In one of these institutions the age shown is for men; for women, 68 years.

SOURCE: National Education Association, *Teacher Supply and Demand in Universities, Colleges, and Junior Colleges, 1959–60 and 1960–61,* Washington, D.C., 1961, p. 26.

TABLE 3.2-30
Rank of vacancy by cause of termination

Type of termination	Assistant professor	Associate professor	Full professor	Total number	Percent
Resignation	60	32	31	123	57
Died	2	6	13	21	10
Retired	4	5	26	35	16
Dismissed	34	2	___	36	17
TOTAL	100	45	70	215	
Percent	47	22	31		100

SOURCE: T. Caplow and R. J. McGee, *The Academic Marketplace,* Basic Books, Inc., Publishers, New York, 1958, p. 41.

Municipal universities (5)	Land-grant colleges (6)	State colleges (7)	Teachers colleges (8)	Nonpublic colleges (by enrollment):		
				1,000 and over (9)	500–999 (10)	Under 500 (11)
						1
4	22	38	8	36	73	49†
			2	1	1	
	2	3	2	2	1	2
	2	8	1	16	16	18
9	26	97	50	44	74§	68‡
	1		2	1	4	1
						1
13	53	146	65	100	169	140
	1	5	2	14	33	78
	5	17	3	15	23	62

TABLE 3.2-32   *Characteristics of newly hired faculty by control of institution, 1964–65*

Control of institution	Percentage of non- Ph.D.s*	Percentage teaching- oriented*	Percentage with no publications†	Percentage who were students last year	Percentage at bottom 20 percent institutions†
Public	54	77	54	40	30
Nondenominational	43	63	44	39	15
Catholic	65	78	64	41	40
Baptist	77	86	79	47	40
Presbyterian	54	86	69	43	25
Methodist	49	91	51	38	26
Lutheran	76	86	71	49	58

* Spend more time teaching than researching.
† Means that differences among four groups (public, nondenominational, Catholic, and all Protestant institutions) are statistically significant by a chi-square test at the 0.05 level.
SOURCE: D. G. Brown, *The Mobile Professors,* American Council on Education, Washington, D.C., 1967, p. 86.

results of a sample of 10 major universities investigating reasons for faculty turnover indicated that over half of all faculty leaving institutions resigned, 10 percent died, 16 percent retired, and 17 percent were dismissed. The reasons for faculty turnover varied according to faculty rank. A smaller proportion of full professors resigned and a larger proportion retired, compared to assistant professors (Table 3.2-30). The compulsory retirement age varied from 60 to 75. The largest number of institutions required retirement at age 70 (Table 3.2-31).

Characteristics of newly hired faculty differed among institutions grouped according to type of control. For example, the percentage of newly hired faculty who did not have a Ph.D. ranged from 43 percent for nondenominational institutions to 77 percent for Baptist institutions (Table 3.2-32).

3.3. Faculty Pay, Outside Earnings, and Allocation of Time

FACULTY PAY The best studies on faculty salaries have been those undertaken by the American Association of University Professors (AAUP). This section is based largely on the 1968–69 AAUP report concerning the economic status of the academic profession.[1]

Table 3.3-1 provides data for the period 1939–40 to 1968–69 on the following: changes in the consumer price index, changes in a combined index of average salaries for 36 institutions of higher education, movement of average faculty salaries adjusted for price changes, and average annual increases in the index of real salary levels. Prior to 1957, the rise in faculty salaries lagged behind prices and income. Taking 1939 as the base year, in 1948 the consumer price index had risen to 173.1 while the faculty salary index stood at 133. By 1968 the situation had changed and the indices of average faculty salaries and of consumer prices were 370.3 and 250.4, respectively.

The ratio of the index of salaries to the index of consumer prices was 148, which means that between 1939 and 1968 real faculty salaries rose by nearly 50 percent. The average annual increase in academic salaries from 1959–60 to 1965–66 was higher than the general increase in wages for the economy.[2] However, the average annual increase from 1967 to 1968 of 2 percent was less than one-half the average rate experienced since 1959. This slowdown in growth of academic salaries affected some of the most prestigious institutions.

[1] American Association of University Professors, "The Threat of Inflationary Erosion: The Annual Report on the Economic Status of the Profession, 1968–69," *AAUP Bulletin,* vol. 55, no. 2, pp. 192–253, summer 1969.

[2] U.S. Department of Health, Education and Welfare, *Toward a Long-range Plan for Federal Financial Support for Higher Education,* report to the President, Office of Assistant Secretary for Planning and Evaluation, January 1969, p. 10.

	Year	Relatives of consumer price index	Relatives of average salaries for 36 biennial-survey institutions	Relatives of average salaries adjusted for price changes	Average annual increase in index of real salary levels
TABLE 3.3-1 Relatives showing trends in average salaries of all ranks combined in the 36 biennial-survey institutions* and in the consumer price index,† 1939–40 to 1968–69, and the average increase in real salary levels since 1957 (1939 = 100)‡	1939	100.0	100.0	100.0	
	1948	173.1	133.3	77.1	
	1949	171.5	139.7	81.5	
	1953	192.6	169.0	87.7	
	1955	192.8	178.6	92.6	
	1957	202.5	204.1	100.8	4.1
	1959	209.7	227.9	108.7	4.0
	1961	215.3	254.6	118.3	4.8
	1963	220.5	280.3	127.1	4.4
	1965	227.1	311.5	137.2	5.0
	1967	240.3	350.6	145.9	4.4
	1968	250.4	370.3	147.9	2.0

*Statistics for the 36 biennial-survey institutions are calculated from data in the *AAUP* report and published in the *AAUP Bulletin,* winter issue, 1961; spring issue, 1962; and summer issues, 1964 and 1966.

† Data for the consumer price index obtained from the *Federal Reserve Bulletins* and from the *Monthly Labor Review.*

‡ Relatives calculated using 1939 as a base.

SOURCE: American Association of University Professors, "The Threat of Inflationary Erosion: The Annual Report on the Economic Status of the Profession, 1968–69," *AAUP Bulletin,* vol. 55, no. 2, p. 194, summer 1969.

In recent years, increases in faculty compensation have brought faculty salaries more in line with income received by other occupational groups. The AAUP has contributed to this improvement through the effectiveness of its studies and publications. From 1960–61 to 1967–68, the average annual percentage increase in earnings for all faculty ranks was 6.5 percent.[3] The most impressive gains were for professors, whose average annual earnings for this seven-year period increased by 6.8 percent and, for the year 1967–68 to 1968–69, by 7.7 percent. However, from 1968–69 to 1969–70, average compensation levels of faculty increased by a percentage rate lower than that of the previous year (Table 3.3-2).

[3] The Office of Education reported an annual average increase of 5.5 percent between 1957–58 and 1967–68. U.S. Office of Education, *Digest of Educational Statistics, 1968,* 1968, p. 82.

TABLE 3.3-2 *Annual increases in average salary plus benefits (nine-month basis)**

Academic rank	This year	Last year	Two years ago	Three years ago	Four years ago	Five years ago	Six years ago	Seven years ago
				Dollar increase				
Professor	$1,181	$1,205	$1,024	$1,035	$832	$677	$ 703	$775
Associate professor	941	874	746	760	612	471	497	529
Assistant professor	749	702	598	610	445	350	405	405
Instructor	574	524	438	445	364	282	320	351
Lecturer	907	848	1,617	901	774	692	1,362	259
All ranks	875	839	723	728	571	460	507	529
				Percentage increase				
Professor	7.0%	7.7%	6.9%	7.5%	6.4%	5.5%	5.9%	7.2%
Associate professor	7.5	7.4	6.7	7.3	6.2	5.0	5.5	6.3
Assistant professor	7.2	7.2	6.5	7.1	5.4	4.5	5.5	5.8
Instructor	7.0	6.9	6.0	6.5	5.3	4.5	5.3	6.2
Lecturer	9.3	9.4	20.1	11.4	10.3	9.5	22.5	4.0
All ranks	7.2	7.4	6.8	7.3	6.0	5.0	5.8	6.5

* Average annual dollar and percentage increases in compensation for institutions reporting comparable data for one-year periods — this year, last year, and two, three, four, five, six, and seven years ago — by academic rank and weighted average for all ranks.

Data for last year (1966–67 to 1967–68), two years ago (1965–66 to 1966–67), three years ago (1964–65 to 1965–66), four years ago (1963–64 to 1964–65), five years ago (1962–63 to 1963–64), six years ago (1961–62 to 1962–63), and seven years ago (1960–61 to 1961–62) are taken from *AAUP Bulletin*, table 2, p. 188, summer 1968. In calculating these figures, we used what amounts to a Paasche index, since numbers of persons who are currently in the various ranks were employed as weights. Thus we computed as a base what average compensation would have been last year if relative numbers in the different ranks had been what they are currently.

SOURCE: American Association of University Professors, "The Threat of Inflationary Erosion: The Annual Report on the Economic Status of the Profession, 1968–69," *AAUP Bulletin*, vol. 55, no. 2, p. 193, summer 1969.

Details on faculty pay

Table 3.3-3 provides a breakdown of salaries, adjusted for changes in the rate of increase in consumer prices, for faculty of different ranks at various types of public and private institutions, covering two periods, 1963–64 to 1964–65, and 1967–68 to 1968–69. From this the following was observed: from 1963 to 1964, earnings of faculty teaching at universities increased by 4.3 percent, and from 1967 to 1968, the average annual increase for such faculty was only 1.4 percent. The trend was similar at liberal arts colleges and technical institutions. What the AAUP refers to as "inflationary

TABLE 3.3-3
Percentage increase in average salary adjusted for changes in the rate of increase in consumer prices, for a constant sample of institutions reporting comparable data for both periods, 1963–64 to 1964–65 and 1967–68 to 1968–69, by type of control and academic ranks (nine-month basis)

Academic rank	All combined		Public	
	1963 to 1964	*1967 to 1968*	*1963 to 1964*	*1967 to 1968*
				Universities
Professor	4.6%	1.4%	4.9%	1.5%
Associate professor	4.5	1.7	4.7	1.8
Assistant professor	4.0	1.1	4.2	1.2
Instructor	3.5	1.3	3.4	1.4
Lecturer	4.3	0.6	4.8	1.1
All	4.3	1.4	4.5	1.5
				Liberal arts colleges
Professor	5.1	3.0	5.1	3.5
Associate professor	4.5	2.7	4.1	2.9
Assistant professor	3.3	2.5	2.7	2.8
Instructor	3.2	1.2	2.6	1.1
Lecturer	4.0	6.5	4.2	8.3
All	4.1	2.5	3.7	2.8
				Technical institutions
Professor	7.6	0.7	8.8	0.4
Associate professor	6.5	2.3	8.3	2.2
Assistant professor	6.8	1.5	8.2	1.1
Instructor	5.0	1.2	5.1	1.3
Lecturer	19.5	5.1	21.5	5.1
All	6.9	1.4	8.1	1.2

SOURCE: American Association of University Professors, "The Threat of Inflationary Erosion: The Annual Report on the Economic Status of the Profession, 1968–69," *AAUP Bulletin,* vol. 55, no. 2, p. 195, summer 1969.

erosion" was particularly pronounced in private institutions compared to public institutions.[4]

Table 3.3-4 gives average compensation of full-time faculty members in 1968–69 at 54 institutions of higher education in which average annual compensation was $15,000 or more. According to this source, compensation levels were highest at Harvard Univer-

[4] American Association of University Professors, "The Threat of Inflationary Erosion: The Annual Report on the Economic Status of the Profession, 1968–69," *AAUP Bulletin,* vol. 55, no. 2, p. 193, summer 1969.

Private independent		Church-related	
1963 to 1964	1967 to 1968	1963 to 1964	1967 to 1968
4.0%	0.7%	6.4%	4.1%
4.0	1.1	5.2	2.2
3.3	0.8	3.4	1.4
3.9	0.7	3.2	1.1
2.5	−1.5	6.7	14.3
3.8	0.8	4.9	2.5
4.3	2.3	5.9	1.9
4.5	2.7	5.8	1.9
4.1	2.1	4.7	1.7
3.8	1.3	4.3	1.3
2.5	0.8	5.2	−1.0
4.2	2.1	5.3	1.7
5.9	1.2		
3.7	4.1		
3.7	4.4		
4.7	1.1		
4.8	1.7		

TABLE 3.3-4 How institutions pay—names of institutions listed in descending order of average compensations for full-time faculty members, 1968–69 (where data are authorized for publication)

Range and institution	Average compensation	Range and institution	Average compensation
$19,500 to $19,999		**$16,000 to $16,499**	
Harvard University	$19,800	Duke University	16,494
$19,000 to $19,499		University of Pennsylvania	16,297
California Institute of Technology	19,313	U.S. Naval Postgraduate School	16,287
$18,500 to $18,999		State University of N.Y. at Buffalo	16,240
University of Chicago	18,735		
$18,000 to $18,499		Teachers College (Columbia)	16,170
CUNY–City College	18,247	Rice University	16,123
Claremont Graduate School and University Center	18,230	Princeton Theological Seminary	16,115
Stanford University	18,195	State University of N.Y. at Binghamton	16,096
CUNY–Brooklyn College	18,121	**$15,500 to $15,999**	
New School for Social Research	18,108	Air Force Institute of Technology	15,773
$17,500 to $17,999		State University of N.Y. at Albany	15,711
Northwestern University	17,975	Haverford College	15,700
Union Theological Seminary (N.Y.)	17,749	Brandeis University	15,674
Massachusetts Institute of Technology	17,737	Vanderbilt University	15,672
		University of Virginia	15,622
Johns Hopkins University	17,682	CUNY–N.Y. City Community College	15,608
CUNY–Hunter College	17,617		
$17,000 to $17,499		University of California	15,600
CUNY–Queensborough Community College	17,423	**$15,000 to $15,499**	
		State University of N.Y. at Stony Brook	15,483
Yale University	17,414	University of Iowa	15,462
Cornell University	17,325	Wesleyan University	15,376
University of Rochester	17,120	Washington University (Mo.)	15,355
$16,500 to $16,999		Syracuse University	15,256
Princeton University	16,920	Rutgers State University	15,224
CUNY–Queens College	16,898	New York University	15,174
Amherst College	16,854	Ohio State University	15,115
Brown University	16,835	Purdue University	15,113
CUNY–Herbert H. Lehman College	16,740	Colgate University	15,069
		San Jose State College	15,069
Hebrew Union College (Ohio)	16,730	Newark College of Engineering	15,056
University of Michigan	16,729	Oberlin College	15,056
Columbia University	16,610		

SOURCE: American Association of University Professors, "The Threat of Inflationary Erosion: The Annual Report on the Economic Status of the Profession, 1968–69," *AAUP Bulletin,* vol. 55, no. 2, p. 197, summer 1969.

	AA	A	B	C	D	E	F
	\multicolumn{7}{c}{Average compensation scale}						
ofessor	$27,000	$21,500	$17,000	$13,600	$10,900	$9,000	$8,000
ssociate professor	15,500	13,500	11,900	10,400	9,000	7,900	7,200
ssistant professor	12,000	10,700	9,560	8,580	7,760	7,100	6,600
structor	9,000	8,300	7,680	7,140	6,680	6,300	6,000
	\multicolumn{7}{c}{Minimum compensation scale}						
ofessor	$18,180	$15,260	$12,700	$10,620	$ 8,950	$7,700	$6,880
ssociate professor	13,250	11,490	9,940	8,610	7,540	6,690	6,080
ssistant professor	9,840	8,750	7,800	6,990	6,310	5,780	5,370
structor	7,400	6,810	6,320	5,880	5,500	5,160	5,000

URCE: American Association of University Professors, "The Threat of Inflationary Erosion: The nnual Report on the Economic Status of the Profession, 1968–69," *AAUP Bulletin*, vol. 55, no. 2, p. 206, mmer 1969.

sity, the California Institute of Technology, and the University of Chicago.

The AAUP standards of average compensation for different ranks of faculty in 1968–69 are presented in Table 3.3-5. The average compensation for a professor at the AA scale was $27,000, at the A scale $21,500, and at the B scale $17,000. According to Table 3.3-6, only three institutions, or 0.3 percent of the total, and about 2,000 full-time faculty members, slightly less than 1 percent of the total, qualified for the AA classification. The A rating was achieved by 36 institutions (3.7 percent of all institutions) and 22,358 full-time faculty members (10.1 percent of total full-time faculty members).

Approximately 24 and 44 percent of institutions and 43 and 36 percent of full-time faculty members were given the B rating and C rating, respectively.

In general, terms of employment were more favorable at larger compared to smaller institutions. Table 3.3-7 shows that at institutions with over 5,000 students compared to those with less than 1,000 students, the work load was less, the mean salary was more, and the proportion teaching in more than one field was less.

Table 3.3-8. provides a comparison of compensation and salary (compensation minus fringe benefits) for eight public and eight private institutions for the years 1965–66 and 1966–67. The designation AA to B indicates how average compensation would be rated in accordance with AAUP standards.[5] Average compensation for the eight private institutions was $16,452, which was about 20

[5] See Table 3.3-5.

TABLE 3.3-6 Average compensation grades this year and last year—number and percentage of institutions and full-time faculty members, 1968–69, and percentage of institutions and full-time faculty members, 1967-1968, classified by grade of average compensation scale

Grade of average scale	Institutions			
	Number, 1968–69	Percentage, 1968–69	Number, 1967–68*	Percentage, 1967–68*
AA	3	0.3%		
A	36	3.7	34	3.7%
B	235	24.0	188	20.3
C	432	44.0	350	37.8
D	218	22.2	275	29.7
E	31	3.2	54	5.8
F and below†	6	0.6	7	0.8
Other‡	20	2.0	17	1.8
TOTAL	981	100.0%	925	100.0%

* Data for 1967–1968 were taken from "On the Financial Prospects for Higher Education: The Economic Status of the Profession, 1967–68," *AAUP Bulletin*, appendix table 4, p. 198, summer 1968.

† Includes two institutions with a grade of G.

‡ Includes 20 institutions in which the rank of professor is not utilized and therefore no overall grade is assigned.

NOTE: Percentages may not total 100 because of rounding.

SOURCE: American Association of University Professors, "The Threat of Inflationary Erosion: The Annual Report on the Economic Status of the Profession, 1968–69," *AAUP Bulletin*, vol. 55, no. 2, p. 207, summer 1969.

TABLE 3.3-7 *Terms of employment, by size of institution*

	Size of institution	
Terms applied to newly hired faculty	Less than 1,000 students	More than 5,000 students
Percentage teaching in only 1 field*	71	86
Percentage teaching and researching in the same field*	80	88
Average teaching load*	12 hrs.	9 hrs.
Mean salary (last year's students)*	$6,550	$7,350
Mean salary (last year's faculty)*	$8,050	$9,550

* Means that the difference is significant by a chi-square test at the 0.05 level.

SOURCE: D. C. Brown, *The Mobile Professors*, American Council on Education, Washington, D.C., 1967, p. 104.

Full-time faculty members			
Number, 1968–69	*Percentage, 1968–69*	*Number, 1967–68**	*Percentage, 1967–68**
1,951	0.9%		
22,358	10.1	21,865	10.9%
94,947	43.0	74,301	37.2
80,037	36.3	68,106	34.1
17,776	8.1	30,827	15.4
2,023	0.9	3,152	1.6
363	0.2	510	0.3
1,307	0.6	924	0.5
220,762	100.0%	199,685	100.0%

percent above the average compensation of $13,452 characteristic of public institutions. However, since rapidly growing public institutions tend to have relatively more faculty members at lower ranks, this difference would probably be reduced on the basis of comparisons standardized by rank.

From 1965–66 to 1966–67, the average rise in compensation for 16 institutions of higher education was 6⅔ percent with a low of 3 percent at the University of California and a high of 10 percent at Purdue University. Full-time compensation per student varied greatly from $406 at Minnesota to $2,548 at the California Institute of Technology (Table 3.3-8).

Fringe benefits

For all institutions covered in Table 3.3-8, except for the City College of New York and the University of Wisconsin, excess compensation over salary (fringe benefits) ranged from 11 percent to 19 percent of total compensation. Average fringe benefits for all institutions listed in Table 3.3-8 accounted for approximately 14 percent of total compensation. This compared with an average ratio

TABLE 3.3-8 *Comparison of compensation, salary, average and minimum compensation, rise of compensation, 1966–67 over 1965–66 and other comparisons, 1965–66, 1966–67, 8 public and 8 independent universities*

| | | | 1966–67 | | | |
| | | | | Grade of average compensation* | | |
Institution	Grade average compensation	Grade minimum compensation	Professor	Associate professor	Assistant professor	Instructor
University of California	B	A	B	A	A	A
Harvard University	A	A	A	AA	AA	AA
Stanford University	A	A	A	A	A	A
California Institute of Technology	A	A	A	A	A	A
Massachusetts Institute of Technology	A	A	A	A	A	A
University of Chicago	A	A	A	AA	AA	AA
Yale University	A	A	A	A	A	A
Columbia University	A	A	A	A	AA	A
Princeton University	A	A	A	A	A	A
Minnesota University	B	B	B	B	A	A
Michigan University	A	B	A	A	AA	A
CUNY City College	A	A	A	AA	AA	AA
Ohio State University	B	B	B	A	A	A
Wisconsin University	B	C	B	A	A	AA
Indiana University	B	B	B	A	AA	AA
Purdue University	B	B	B	A	A	AA

* See Tables 3.3-4 and 3.3-6 and also American Association of University Professors, "The Threat of Inflationary Erosion: The Annual Report on the Economic Status of the Profession, 1968–69," *AAUP Bulletin*, vol. 55, no. 2, pp. 202–204, summer 1969, for breakdown of institutions according to average minimum compensation grades.

† Salary is equivalent to compensation less fringe benefits.

SOURCE: Author's calculations based on AAUP data.

Average compensation, full-time faculty		Average salary,† full-time faculty		Excess compensation over salary, 1966-67	Percentage rise, average compensation, 1966-67	Full-time compensation per student equivalent, 1966-67
1966-67	1965-66	1966-67	1965-66			
13,348	$12,952	$11,933	$11,899	12%	3	$ 857
18,700	17,600	15,700	14,800	19	6	1,087
16,947	15,894	15,120	14,254	12	7	980
16,489	15,916	14,129	13,699	17	4	2,548
16,203	14,868	13,953	12,797	16	9	1,805
17,376	16,377	15,445	14,557	13	6	1,607
14,976	14,289	13,124	12,451	14	5	1,605
15,573	14,302	13,500	12,609	15	9	No response
15,356	14,797	13,259	12,762	16	4	1,866
12,600	11,585	11,277	10,486	12	9	406
15,060	14,130	13,236	12,482	14	7	No response
13,938	12,737	13,459	12,460	4	9	606
13,245	12,413	11,879	11,158	11	7	468
12,541	11,592	11,517	10,776	9	8	606
13,361	12,672	11,468	10,958	17	5	No response
13,523	12,346	11,561	10,622	17	10	686

TABLE 3.3-9
*Average
compensation,
salary and
benefits —
number of
full-time faculty,
total and
average
compensation,
average salary
and average
fringe benefits
by rank,
1968–69
(nine-month
basis)*

	Total full-time faculty members	*Total compensation*	*Average compensation*
I. 981 institutions with professorial rank			
Professor	53,768	$ 967,910,367	$18,001
Associate professor	51,446	696,469,743	13,537
Assistant professor	73,880	824,264,195	11,156
Instructor	38,577	338,292,555	8,769
Lecturer	3,242	34,467,055	10,631
All ranks	220,913	$2,861,403,915	$12,951
II. 79 institutions without professorial rank			
One rank only	8,212	$ 92,485,929	$11,262
Total reporting	229,125	$2,953,889,844	$12,892

SOURCE: American Association of University Professors, "The Threat of Inflationary Erosion: The Annual Report on the Economic Status of the Profession, 1968–69," *AAUP Bulletin,* vol. 55, no. 2, p. 207, summer 1969.

of fringe benefits to total compensation for a larger sample of institutions (981 institutions and 220,913 faculty) of 9.2 percent (Table 3.3-9). The difference between the 14 percent, applicable to the most prestigious institutions, and the 9 percent, pertaining to an average for a large number of institutions, suggests that the former institutions tended to devote more than average resources to fringe benefits.

Material assembled here on fringe benefits is based primarily on two comprehensive sources.[6] Table 3.3-10 provides some examples of waiver of college tuition for faculty children and college health services for 1960–61.

One of the most important fringe benefits is retirement income. The relative benefits from retirement depend on years of service, age of retirement, and the institution's contribution as a percentage of salary. Table 3.3-11 represents an illustration of benefits provided by various contribution rates for single males entering teach-

[6] W. C. Greenough and F. P. King, *Retirement and Insurance Plans in American Colleges,* Columbia University Press, New York, 1959; M. H. Ingraham, *The Outer Fringe: Faculty Benefits Other Than Annuities and Insurance,* University of Wisconsin Press, Madison, 1965.

Average salary	Average fringe benefits	Fringe benefits as percentage of average compensation
$16,312	$1,689	9.4%
12,296	1,241	9.2
10,130	1,053	9.4
8,010	759	8.7
9,522	1,109	10.4
$11,760	$1,191	9.2%
$10,704	$ 558	5.0%
$11,722	$1,170	9.1%

ing at age 30 and retiring at age 65. According to these data for the late 1950s, it was estimated that, for example, with a final salary of $12,000, a contribution of 15 percent at entrance age 30 and retirement at 65, the retired faculty member could expect to receive $6,584 or 54.9 percent of his last pay. Annuities would be substantially higher in the late 1960s since average salaries increased by 62 percent from 1955 to the late 1960s (Table 3.3-11).

Structure of faculty pay

Table 3.3-9 also provides data on average compensation, salary, and benefits for faculty from different ranks in 1968–69. The average salary ranged from $16,312 for professors to $8,010 for instructors, a difference of 104 percent. Table 3.3-12 gives approximate ratios of salaries between professors and instructors for 1920, 1960, 1968–69, and the AAUP goals for 1968–69. Professors earned about 2½ times as much as instructors in 1920 on the average in public and private institutions, and less than 2 times as much as instructors in 1960. The earnings differential between professor and instructor rose in 1968–69 to 2.3, although this was below the goal of 3.0 set at the AAUP. During the lean years, institutions

TABLE 3.3-10 Some examples of fringe benefits, 1960-61	Proportion of all institutions in category, percent
Mortgage loans	
Institutions making mortgage loans to faculty	14.4
Public	4.6
Private	18.4
Institutions with outstanding second-mortgage loans	8.7
Sabbatical leaves*	
Institutions granting leave	57.0
Faculty taking sabbatical, 1962-63	3.4
Faculty taking leave with pay other than sabbatical	2.3
College tuition waived†	
Institutions waiving tuition	69.7
Participating in student exchanges	19.3
College health service—doctor's consultation	
Numbers:	
496 of 745 have service	
214 have service available to faculty	

* In 1960–61, 4.6 percent of the faculty were on leave. The minimum was 3.9 percent in state colleges; the maximum 4.7 percent in state universities and land-grant colleges. See National Education Association, *Teacher Supply and Demand in Universities, Colleges, and Junior Colleges, 1959-60 and 1960-61*, Washington, D.C., 1961, p. 26.

† For faculty children.

SOURCE: M. H. Ingraham, *The Outer Fringe: Faculty Benefits Other Than Annuities and Insurance*, University of Wisconsin Press, Madison, 1965, pp. 227, 239, 257.

improved the status of their faculty through the use of "dry increases" that resulted in raises in rank but not in pay. The unavailability of financial resources explains the narrowness of the earnings differential in 1960, and improvement in resource availability contributed to the widening of earnings between professors and instructors in 1968–69.

A comparison of earnings of scientists in 14 subject areas according to type of employer in 1966 can be made by referring to Table 3.3-13. All data in this source refer to those reporting to the National Register of Scientific and Technical Personnel. Average earnings for all such scientists of $12,000 were the same as average

ABLE 3.3-11 *Illustration of benefits provided by various contribution rates*: Single male, entrance ▮e 30, retirement age 65; including percentage of final salary, 1957–58*

al- ▮y ▮ale	Final sal- ary	Annual retirement benefit					
		Annuity		OASDI†		Total	
		Dollars	Percent	Dollars	Percent	Dollars	Percent
		Contribution of 10 percent on all of salary					
	4,000	1,236	30.9	1,272	31.8	2,508	62.7
	8,000	2,366	29.5	1,524	19.1	3,890	48.6
	12,000	3,373	28.1	1,524	12.7	4,897	40.8
		Contribution of 12 percent on all of salary					
	4,000	1,483	37.1	1,272	31.8	2,755	68.9
	8,000	2,839	35.4	1,524	19.1	4,363	54.5
	12,000	4,047	33.7	1,524	12.7	5,571	46.4
		Contribution of 15 percent on all of salary					
	4,000	1,854	46.4	1,272	31.8	3,126	78.2
	8,000	3,550	44.3	1,524	19.1	5,074	63.4
	12,000	5,060	42.2	1,524	12.7	6,584	54.9
		Step-rate plan of 10 percent annuity contributions on first *$4,800 of salary and 15 percent above $4,800*					
	4,000	1,236	30.9	1,272	31.8	2,508	62.7
	8,000	2,699	33.7	1,524	19.1	4,223	52.8
	12,000	4,180	34.8	1,524	12.7	5,704	47.5

eachers Insurance and Annuity Association of America deferred annuity rates without dividends, ▮suming all contributions go into Teachers Insurance and Annuity Association of America, none to ▮ollege Retirement Equities Fund.
▮ld Age Social Disability Insurance.
▮OURCE: W. C. Greenough and F. P. King, *Retirement and Insurance Plans in American Colleges,* ▮olumbia University Press, New York, 1959, p. 98.

calendar year earnings of those working in educational institutions —a result, in part, of the large proportion of those in the sample who worked in educational institutions. Average earnings of those working in industry and business were higher, on the average ($13,000), and for self-employed scientists, of whom there were relatively few, salaries were the highest of all ($17,000).

OUTSIDE EARNINGS Table 3.3-14 provides data on outside earnings in 1963 of faculty who were teaching on an academic year contract in 1961–62. Approximately 75 percent of the faculty had outside earnings, with

(Text continued on p. 532)

TABLE 3.3-12   *Ratio of salaries: professors to instructors; 1920, 1960, and 1968–69*

	Ratio
1920:	
Public	2.0
Private	2.7
1960:	
Public	1.8
Private	1.8
1968–69:	
A.A. goal* of AAUP	3.0
Actual, AAUP	2.3

* "A.A. goal" refers to highest grade of compensation in AAUP index.

SOURCES: L. A. D'Amico, "Salaries of College and University Professors by Rank, Institutional Size, and Control," *Educational Record,* vol. 41, pp. 300–305, October 1960; American Association of University Professors, "The Threat of Inflationary Erosion: The Annual Report on the Economic Status of the Profession, 1968–69," *AAUP Bulletin,* vol. 55, no. 2, pp. 206, 207, summer 1969.

TABLE 3.3-13   *Number and median salaries of scientists, by field and type of employer; United States, 1966*

			Type of employer		
Scientific and technical field (1)	Total (2)	Educational institutions (3)	Federal government (4)	Other governments (5)	Military (6)
					Number
All fields	242,763	87,315	24,689	8,268	5,89⬛
Chemistry	65,917	14,770	3,983	834	68⬛
Earth sciences	19,749	4,686	2,667	886	25⬛
Meteorology	6,283	812	1,837	114	2,34⬛
Physics	29,130	13,135	3,145	116	57
Mathematics	22,806	9,308	1,413	270	46⬛
Agricultural sciences	10,038	2,554	3,690	1,680	4⬛
Biological sciences	29,633	16,650	3,300	1,057	79⬛
Psychology	19,027	9,791	1,379	2,205	20⬛
Statistics	3,042	937	614	125	4⬛
Economics	13,150	5,599	1,348	490	9⬛
Sociology	3,640	2,748	163	141	1
Anthropology	919	721	41	14	
Linguistics	1,269	889	58	18	
Other fields	18,160	4,715	1,051	318	37⬛

Nonprofit organizations (7)	Industry and business (8)	Self-employed (9)	Other (10)	Not employed (11)	Type of employer not reported (12)
9,813	83,990	4,914	1,309	14,783	1,791
1,884	37,033	553	347	5,352	472
235	8,226	1,512	57	1,129	95
197	662	18	25	242	27
1,023	8,287	112	40	2,538	163
1,074	8,901	147	109	1,001	119
106	1,524	192	20	188	38
2,185	3,185	673	135	1,348	310
1,714	1,350	1,116	266	749	252
149	1,012	23	23	100	16
460	4,073	228	45	719	98
211	86	26	51	135	68
33	2	6	54	41	6
84	43	4	8	146	15
458	9,606	304	129	1,095	112

TABLE 3.3-13 *(continued)*

Scientific and technical field (1)	Total (2)	Educational institutions (3)	Federal government ment (4)	Other governments ments (5)	Military (6)
					Type of employer
					Median salary
		Academic year	*Calendar year*		
All fields	$12,000	$9,600	$12,000	$12,100	$9,900
Chemistry	12,000	9,500	11,000	12,000	9,700
Earth sciences	11,400	9,500	11,000	11,800	9,500
Meteorology	11,700	10,100	12,000	11,700	10,100
Physics	12,500	9,600	11,000	12,900	9,300
Mathematics	12,000	9,100	11,000	12,900	10,400
Agricultural sciences	10,000	9,000	12,000	10,000	8,200
Biological sciences	12,000	9,500	13,100	12,500	10,400
Psychology	11,500	10,000	12,000	13,400	10,400
Statistics	12,800	10,000	13,000	14,300	10,800
Economics	13,100	10,500	13,000	14,700	13,000
Sociology	11,300	10,000	12,500	14,700	11,500
Anthropology	11,500	10,600	13,000	15,800	
Linguistics	10,000	10,000	10,500	12,000	
Other fields	12,000	8,600	10,600	13,400	10,700

NOTE: Medians were not computed for groups with fewer than 25 registrants reporting salary. All data relate to those persons reporting to the National Register of Scientific and Technical Personnel.

SOURCE: National Science Foundation, National Register of Scientific and Technical Personnel, 1966; in U.S. Office of Education, *Digest of Educational Statistics, 1968,* 1968, p. 126.

onprofit ›gani- ›tions (7)	Industry and business (8)	Self- employed (9)	Other (10)	Not employed (11)	Type of employer not reported (12)
$8,300	$13,000	$13,000	$17,000	$11,500	$12,000
6,700	12,000	12,800	15,000	11,500	12,000
8,000	12,000	12,000	13,200	11,500	
7,800	14,000	12,000			
7,800	14,400	14,600	20,000	10,000	12,000
9,000	14,800	13,500	20,500	11,300	
6,200	12,000	10,000	11,000		
11,300	14,000	13,900	20,000	11,000	15,000
9,500	11,500	15,100	20,000	11,500	11,100
9,500	13,800	13,000			
8,600	16,200	15,300	18,000	15,000	15,000
	14,000	15,000		14,000	
				10,600	
	6,000	13,800			
7,400	14,500	13,000	17,500	10,800	12,000

TABLE 3.3-14   *Outside earnings of faculty in 1961–62 by principal teaching area 1962–63*

| | Faculty teaching in spring 1963 and were in higher education in 1961–62 | | | |
| | On academic year contract in 1961-62 | | On calendar year contract in 1961-62 | |
Principal teaching area in 1962–63	Percentage with outside earnings	Average amount of outside earnings	Percentage with outside earnings	Average amount of outside earnings
All areas	74	$2,165	51	$2,248
Agriculture and related fields	71	2,756	33	1,054
Biological sciences	80	2,074	45	2,061
Business and commerce	78	2,924	61	2,885
Education and related fields	80	2,090	57	1,983
Engineering	83	3,197	60	2,286
English and journalism	63	1,598	45	1,276
Fine arts	74	1,588	59	1,768
Foreign languages and literature	62	1,465	53	1,405
Health fields	56	2,270	46	3,928
Home economics	44	1,094	41	1,317
Law	78	5,297	64	4,800
Mathematics	75	2,378	54	1,891
Philosophy	74	1,485	64	1,292
Physical and health education	63	1,322	34	1,576
Physical sciences	80	2,853	55	3,317
Psychology	85	2,655	72	2,102
Religion and theology	78	1,335	46	1,729
Social sciences	74	1,907	58	1,589
All other fields	77	2,309	46	1,629

SOURCE: R. E. Dunham, P. S. Wright, and M. O. Chandler, *Teaching Faculty in Universities and Four year Colleges, Spring 1963*, U.S. Office of Education, 1966, p. 41.

the average of such earnings equivalent to $2,165. Law teacher earned the highest average amount of outside compensatio ($5,297) and home economists earned the lowest ($1,094). Ap proximately 44 percent of the faculty on academic contract i 1961–62 obtained their outside earnings from summer teaching 13 percent relied on consultant fees, and another 13 percent de pended on other teaching for outside remuneration (Table 3.3-15).

TABLE 3.3-15   *Outside earnings of faculty in 1961–62 by sources*

| | Faculty teaching in spring 1963 who were employed in higher education in 1961–62 | | | |
| | On academic year contract 1961–62 | | On calendar year contract 1961–62 | |
Source	Percentage of total	Average amount (mean)	Percentage of total	Average amount (mean)
Summer teaching	44	$1,269	10	$1,389
Other summer employment	11	1,744	4	1,533
Other teaching	13	935	7	949
Royalties	8	1,173	9	1,574
Speeches	9	243	9	258
Consultant fees	13	1,429	16	1,604
Retirement	1	3,386	1	3,120
Research	7	1,836	4	2,540
Other professional earnings	10	1,287	10	2,280
Nonprofessional earnings	8	1,698	6	1,569

SOURCE: R. E. Dunham, P. S. Wright, and M. O. Chandler, *Teaching Faculty in Universities and Four-year Colleges, Spring 1963,* U.S. Office of Education, 1966, p. 41.

ALLOCATION OF FACULTY TIME   In 1968 it was estimated that faculty at the University of California spent an average of 60 hours a week working in all activities. Of this time, about 50 percent was spent teaching (regular courses and supervision of independent study); 32 percent was devoted to research; 12 percent was spent on administration; and 5 and 2 percent went into student affairs and public service, respectively.

TABLE 3.3-16 *Comparison of time spent in major activities in 1960 and 1968, total faculty appointments*

| | Numbers | | Percentage distribution | |
Activity	1960	1968	1960	1968
Regular courses	24	21	41.4	35.0
Supervision of independent study	7	9	12.1	15.0
Research	17	19	29.3	31.7
Student affairs	3	3	5.2	5.0
Administration	6	7	10.3	11.7
Public service	1	1	1.7	1.6
TOTAL	58	60	100.0	100.0

SOURCE: University of California, Office of the President, *Faculty Effort and Output Study,* University of California Press, Berkeley, 1970, p. 11.

TABLE 3.3-17 *Average number of hours per week spent by typical full-time equivalent faculty member, by rank, 1961–62*

Type of activity	Average number of hours per week						
	Professor	Associate professor	Assistant professor	Instructor	Lecturer	Teaching fellow	All ranks
Instruction							
Formal classes	10.98	12.06	11.52	13.12	12.33	15.18	12.46
Supervision— teaching	0.86	0.82	1.06	0.67	1.91	0.03	0.73
Supervision— research	2.50	2.33	1.69	0.74	0.52	0.05	1.52
*Other Instructional activity**	14.41	16.02	17.42	19.84	23.74	23.06	18.10
Total Instruction	28.75	31.23	31.69	34.37	38.50	38.32	32.81
Administration	9.32	6.06	5.24	2.16	3.48	0.32	5.08
Research	11.75	12.78	12.39	9.29	10.36	0.38	9.23
Public service	3.52	2.53	1.52	0.54	1.17	0.27	1.88
TOTAL	53.34	52.60	50.84	46.36	53.51	39.29	49.00

*Paper-grading, student conferences, and class preparation.

SOURCE: R. L. Williams, *The Administration of Academic Affairs,* University of Michigan Press, Ann Arbor, 1965, p. 89.

TABLE 3.3-18 Actual and desired allocation of working time by Group 1* scientists, by rank, 1960–61†				
Activity	Professor	Associate professor	Assistant professor	Instructor
Mean time spent				
Teaching and preparation	43.2%	47.3%	48.9%	54.8%
Undergraduates	20.6	25.8	31.8	46.9
Graduate students	22.6	21.5	17.1	7.9
Research	30.8	37.7	39.5	42.1
Administration	21.2	10.5	8.3	2.1
Other academic activities	4.8	4.5	3.3	0.9
TOTAL	100.0%	100.0%	100.0%	100.0%
Number	364	166	203	63
Mean time desired				
Teaching and preparation	42.7%	43.3%	42.8%	48.1%
Undergraduates	18.2	20.1	19.7	27.0
Graduate students	24.5	23.2	23.1	21.1
Research	49.3	51.5	54.0	48.2
Administration	6.3	3.1	1.7	2.7
Other academic activities	1.7	2.0	1.5	1.0
TOTAL	100.0%	100.0%	100.0%	100.0%
Number	358	161	197	62

*Refers to 12 universities receiving large sums from the federal government.

† From replies to two questions: "How did you *actually* spend your working time this academic year—September 1960 to date? (Enter percent of time you devoted to each activity. Rough approximations will do but totals should come to 100%.)" and "If you were free to choose, how would you like to spend your working time?"

SOURCE: H. Orlans, *The Effects of Federal Programs on Higher Education,* The Brookings Institution, Washington, D.C., 1962, p. 63.

Eight years earlier, in 1960, faculty at the University of California devoted about the same amount of time a week to their work, and the distribution of time among these activities was similar to the division of time in 1968 (Table 3.3-16).

A survey of faculty at the University of Michigan in 1961–62 is the source of another set of data on the distribution of time for faculty at different ranks.[7] Table 3.3-17 indicates that the number of hours spent on instruction was considerably lower for professors than it was for instructors (29 hours per week compared to 34). Consequently, professors allocated proportionately more time

[7] R. L. Williams, *The Administration of Academic Affairs,* University of Michigan Press, Ann Arbor, 1965, p. 89.

TABLE 3.3-19 *Percentage of faculty teaching undergraduate or/and graduate students, 1960–61*

Field and institution group	Faculty teaching only Under- graduates	Graduate students	Faculty teaching both undergraduates and graduate students	Total	Number
Total					
Group I*	23%	14%	63%	100%	1,782
Group II†	22	10	69	100	1,084
Group III‡	94	§	5	100	523
Sciences					
Group I	20	18	62	100	799
Group II	15	14	71	100	437
Group III	94	1	6	100	173
Social Sciences					
Group I	15	17	68	100	480
Group II	14	12	74	100	290
Group III	94		6	100	123
Humanities					
Group I	36	5	59	100	503
Group II	36	2	62	100	357
Group III	95		5	100	227

* Refers to 12 universities receiving large amounts of research support from the federal government.
† Refers to 12 other universities receiving smaller sums from the federal government.
‡ Refers to 12 liberal arts colleges.
§ 0.2 percent.

NOTE: The question was "How did you actually spend your working time this academic year—September 1960 to date? (Enter percent of time you devoted to each activity. Rough approximations will do but totals should come to 100%.)" Only faculty who devoted some time to teaching are included in the tabulation.

SOURCE: H. Orlans, *The Effects of Federal Programs on Higher Education,* The Brookings Institution, Washington, D.C., 1962, p. 50.

to activities other than teaching than did instructors. The average distribution for all faculty ranks was as follows: total instruction, 67 percent; administration, 10 percent; research, 19 percent; and public service, 4 percent. Orlans provides estimates of actual and preferred allocation of working time for four ranks of academic scientists teaching in his Group I category.[8] The mean time pro-

[8] Group I consists of 12 universities receiving large research grants from the federal government.
H. Orlans, *The Effects of Federal Programs of Higher Education,* The Brookings Institution, Washington, D.C., 1962, p. 63.

TABLE 3.3-20 *Proportion of teaching done by each academic grade in all schools and colleges, fall semester, 1961–62*

School or college	Total hours taught	Professor	Associate professor	Assistant professor	Instructor	Lecturer and teaching fellow
A	1,108	27.71	29.78	16.43	10.38	15.70
B	451	37.47	19.07	14.64	9.09	19.73
C	285	2.81	18.25	21.75	20.70	36.49
D	1,492	29.83	17.49	14.28	15.08	23.32
E	476	47.90	17.23	16.81	7.56	10.50
F	3,027	33.20	20.61	16.06	11.99	18.14
G	242	14.88	41.73	27.27		16.12
H	251	66.14	10.35	11.56	11.95	
	9,524	21.18	12.11	11.88	9.62	45.21
	1,273	26.55	21.84	19.01	1.10	31.50
K	308	44.48	31.17	15.26		9.09
L	783	0.77	6.13	27.84	52.23	13.03
M	158	36.08	35.44	27.21		1.27
N	444		20.05	15.99	29.95	34.01
O	362	33.70	28.73	24.03	1.38	12.16
P	276	31.16	22.83	30.80		15.21
Total hours	20,460	5,137	3,449	3,108	2,346	6,420
Percent of total	100.00	25.11	16.86	15.19	11.46	31.38

SOURCE: R. L. Williams, *The Administration of Academic Affairs,* University of Michigan Press, Ann Arbor, 1965, p. 86.

fessors spent in teaching and preparation was more or less evenly divided between teaching of undergraduate and graduate students. Faculty at lower ranks spent proportionately more time teaching undergraduates and doing research than their professorial colleagues. All ranks of faculty preferred to reduce the time they spent in teaching and increase the time they spent on research (Table 3.3-18).

Orlans also estimated the proportion of faculty in each of his three groupings of institutions who taught undergraduate students and graduate students exclusively and who taught both types of students in 1960–61. The proportion of faculty teaching graduate students was small at all types of institutions and particularly at liberal arts colleges. The proportion of faculty available for teaching

TABLE 3.3-21
Average teaching load based on full-time equivalent (FTE) faculty positions, 1961–62

	Professors	Associate professors	Assistant professors	Instructors
Hours taught	5,137	3,449	3,108	2,346
Number of FTE hours	473.84	284.6	258.66	177.89
Average hours per FTE	10.84	12.12	12.02	13.17

SOURCE: Adapted from R. L. Williams, *The Administration of Academic Affairs*, University of Michigan Press, Ann Arbor, 1965, pp. 87–88.

graduate students exclusively was considerably higher in the sciences and social sciences than it was in the humanities (Table 3.3-19).

The results of a survey conducted in 1961–62 of the proportion of teaching by each academic grade in 16 institutions are contained in Table 3.3-20. The number of hours spent in teaching for each professorial rank and among universities varied considerably. The range among universities for professors was between 66 percent and zero.

Relative workload,[9] too, differed for faculty at different ranks. Table 3.3-21 provides estimates of average teaching loads for professors, associate professors, assistant professors, and in-

[9] Total hours divided by total FTE.

TABLE 3.3-22
Cumulative distributions of weekly course contact hours—teaching faculty appointments only

Discipline (1)	Percentage of teaching faculty appointments whose weekly course contact hours are:			
	12 or more (2)	9 or more (3)	6 or more (4)	3 or more (5)
Biological sciences	10.4%	25.4%	65.7%	94.0%
Mathematics	5.2	53.4	86.2	96.6
Physical sciences	5.3	22.1	59.0	91.0
Engineering	19.2	43.3	79.8	94.2
Social sciences	24.1	55.5	82.2	97.9
Arts and letters	34.3	63.6	86.6	98.3
Professions	34.5	55.8	89.4	100.0
Universitywide	22.0%	48.8%	79.2%	96.3%

SOURCE: University of California, Office of the President, *Faculty Effort and Output Study*, University of California Press, Berkeley, 1970.

TABLE 3.3-23
Faculty time
devoted to
research during
the academic
year September
1960–June 1961

Field	Percentage devoting 25% or more of working time to research in institution group			Percentage devoting no time to research in institution group		
	I*	*II†*	*III‡*	*I*	*II*	*III*
Total	55%	41%	14%	10%	15%	35%
Sciences	68	54	10	6	11	39
Social sciences	57	43	24	7	12	25
Humanities	32	24	11	18	22	37

* Refers to 12 universities receiving large amount of research support from federal government.

† Refers to 12 other universities receiving smaller sums from the federal government.

‡ Refers to 12 liberal arts colleges.

SOURCE: H. Orlans, *The Effects of Federal Programs on Higher Education,* The Brookings Institution, Washington, D.C., 1962, p. 59.

structors in 1961–62. These results show that higher faculty ranks tend to have lighter workloads.

A comparison of faculty contact hours [10] for a number of universities and subject areas is contained in Table 3.3-22. About half of the teaching faculty appointments had 9 or more contact hours per week, and 22 percent of the faculty had 12 or more contact hours per week. Over one-third of teaching faculty appointments in the professions and arts and letters had 12 or more contact hours a week.

The Orlans study also points out that the proportion of faculty devoting 25 percent or more of working time to research was as high as 55 percent in his Group I universities and as low as 14 percent in his Group III institutions. A much larger proportion of faculty in the sciences and social sciences devoted time to research than faculty in the humanities (Table 3.3-23).

[10] Contact with students includes contact during scheduled class hours in lectures, labs, sections, field trips, concerts, dramatic productions, etc., and also contacts with enrolled students outside class, as in office hours and other informal meetings. University of California, Office of the President, *Faculty Effort and Output Study,* University of California Press, Berkeley, 1970, p. 12.

3.4. Scientific Manpower

SOME FACTS
ON
SCIENTISTS
AND THE
LABOR
MARKET

In 1968 there were 297,942 registered scientists in the country; 91 percent were male and 9 percent were female.[1] Chemistry accounted for the largest share of registered scientists in 1968 (32 percent), followed by the biological sciences with 16 percent and physics with 11 percent. From 1962 to 1968 the number of registered scientists increased by 39 percent. There were significant increases in the share of all registered scientists accounted for by chemistry (from 25 to 32 percent) and by the biological sciences (12 to 16 percent) in this period.

From 1962 to 1968 the proportion of scientists with Ph.D.'s increased from 31 to 37 percent, while the proportion of scientists with only bachelor's degrees decreased from 37 to 30 percent. The median age of registered scientists was 38 in both 1962 and 1968.

The share of scientists employed by educational institutions appears to be increasing. In 1968 educational institutions employed 40 percent of all registered scientists, as compared with 28 percent in 1962. During this same period the share of registered scientists employed by government (including the military) decreased from 20 to 15 percent, and the share employed by industry decreased from 42 to 32 percent.

In 1962 research and development accounted for 35 percent of the primary work activity of registered scientists, as compared with 32 percent in 1968. Teaching accounted for 16 percent of the primary work activity in 1962 and 21 percent in 1968. From 1962 to

(Text continued on p. 548)

[1] A national register of American science manpower is available for the years 1960, 1962, 1966, and 1968: National Science Foundation, *American Science Manpower, A Report of the National Register of Scientific and Technical Personnel, 1960, 1962, 1966, and 1968.*

541

Characteristics	Number	Percent
Registered scientists:	214,940	100
Men	200,362	93
Women	14,578	7
Field of science:		
Agricultural sciences	12,389	6
Biological sciences	25,554	12
Psychology	16,791	8
Earth sciences	18,725	9
Meteorology	5,379	3
Mathematics and statistics	18,189	8
Physics and astronomy	25,725	12
Chemistry	54,130	25
Sanitary engineering	4,923	2
Other fields	33,135	15
Highest degree:		
Bachelor's	78,574	37
Master's	56,660	26
Professional medical	5,693	3
Ph.D.	66,133	31
Less than bachelor's	5,767	3
No report	2,113	1
Age (median age, 38):		
20–29 years	39,145	18
30–39	81,143	38
40–49	56,177	26
50–59	26,705	12
60 and over	11,288	5
No report	482	
Employment status:		
Full-time civilian employed	185,191	86
Active military duty and Public Health Service	5,325	2
Students	13,085	6
Other	11,339	5

TABLE 3.4-1 General characteristics of United States scientists in the National Register of Scientific and Technical Personnel, 1962

NOTE: Percentages may not add to total because of rounding.

SOURCE: National Science Foundation, *American Science Manpower, A Report of the National Register of Scientific and Technical Personnel, 1962,* June 1964, p. 5.

Characteristics	Number	Percent
Type of employer:		
Educational institutions	60,319	28
Government organizations, including military and Public Health Service	43,488	20
Nonprofit organizations	9,445	4
Industry and business	90,800	42
Self-employed	5,095	2
Other	5,793	3
Work activity:		
Research, development, or design	75,679	35
Teaching	33,907	16
Management or administration	48,226	22
Other	57,128	27
Years of professional experience:		
1 year	5,508	3
2–4	32,261	15
5–9	43,563	20
10–14	44,454	21
15–19	21,537	10
20 or more	50,608	24
No report	17,009	8

1962 salary		
Salary distribution of full-time employed scientists:		
Lower decile	$6,000	
Lower quartile	8,000	
Median	10,000	
Upper quartile	13,000	
Upper decile	16,000	

	Characteristics	Number	Percent*
TABLE 3.4-2 **Characteristics** **of scientists** **in the** **United States,** **1968**	Registered scientists	297,942	100
	Men	270,109	91
	Women	27,833	9
	Field of science		
	Chemistry	93,788	32
	Earth and marine sciences	23,746	8
	Atmospheric and space sciences	5,745	2
	Physics	32,491	11
	Mathematics	24,477	8
	Computer sciences	6,972	2
	Agricultural sciences	12,740	4
	Biological sciences	46,183	16
	Psychology	23,077	8
	Statistics	2,639	1
	Economics	11,510	4
	Sociology	6,638	2
	Political science	5,176	2
	Anthropology	1,219	
	Linguistics	1,541	1
	Highest degree		
	Doctorate	111,206	37
	Professional medical	7,455	3
	Master's	86,717	29
	Bachelor's	89,141	30
	Less than bachelor's	353	
	No report	3,070	1
	Age (median age 38)		
	24 or under	9,759	3
	25–29	51,661	17
	30–34	51,751	17
	35–39	47,199	16
	40–44	43,162	14
	45–49	35,336	12
	50–54	24,439	8
	55–59	15,971	5

Characteristics	Number	Percent*
Type of employer		
Educational institutions	117,746	40
Federal government	29,666	10
Other government	10,031	3
Nonprofit organizations	11,204	4
Industry and business	95,776	32
Self-employed	6,462	2
Military	7,155	2
Other	1,729	1
Not employed	12,707	4
No report	5,466	2
Primary work activity		
Research and development	96,036	32
Basic research	46,177	15
Applied research	38,841	13
Management or administration	62,870	21
Management or administration of research and development	28,568	10
Teaching	62,087	21
Production and inspection	16,847	6
Consulting	12,334	4
Exploration, forecasting, reporting	14,365	5
Other	8,416	3
Not employed	12,707	4
No report	12,280	4
Years of professional experience		
1 or less	11,312	4
2–4	44,308	15
5–9	55,645	19
10–14	42,590	14
15–19	39,352	13
20–24	22,729	8
25–29	17,030	6
30–34	12,294	4
35–39	6,458	2
40 or more	5,422	2

	Characteristics	Number	Percent*
TABLE 3.4-2 **(continued)**	*Age (median age 38)*		
	60–64	9,919	3
	65–69	4,748	2
	70 or over	3,050	1
	No report	947	
	Employment status		
	Full-time employed	258,536	87
	Civilian	251,555	84
	Military	6,981	2
	Part-time employed	17,476	6
	Not employed	12,707	4
	No report	9,223	3

Salary distribution of scientists, by field, 1968

Scientific and technical field	Lower decile	Lower quartile
All fields	8,500	10,400
Chemistry	8,500	10,500
Earth and marine sciences	9,000	10,500
Atmospheric and space sciences	9,600	11,400
Physics	9,000	11,000
Mathematics	8,000	10,000
Computer sciences	10,300	12,000
Agricultural sciences	7,600	9,000
Biological sciences	7,500	10,000
Psychology	9,400	11,000
Statistics	10,200	12,000
Economics	9,800	11,700
Sociology	8,000	9,500
Political science	8,400	9,600
Anthropology	9,500	10,500
Linguistics	8,000	9,500

*Percentages may not add to total because of rounding.

SOURCE: National Science Foundation, *American Science Manpower, A Report of the National Register of Scientific and Technical Personnel, 1968,* December 1969, p. 49.

Characteristics	Number	Percent*
Years of professional experience		
No report	40,802	14
Federal support status		
Receiving support	127,415	43
No support	137,181	46
Status unknown	10,192	3
No report	23,154	8

Median	Upper quartile	Upper decile
13,200	17,000	21,500
13,500	17,000	21,000
12,900	16,000	20,000
13,400	15,800	19,600
14,000	18,000	22,500
13,000	17,500	22,300
14,100	17,000	20,300
11,000	13,500	16,900
13,000	17,600	23,000
13,200	16,200	20,200
14,900	18,200	22,000
15,000	19,000	24,000
12,000	15,500	19,500
12,000	16,000	21,000
12,700	16,900	20,400
11,500	15,000	19,000

1968 the median salary of registered scientists rose from $10,000 to $13,200 (Tables 3.4-1 and 3.4-2).[2]

Table 3.4-3 compares the increase in the number of scientists, engineers, and technicians with increases in population and the labor force for the years 1940 to 1963. It is clear that the relative increase in scientific personnel was much larger than the relative increases in population and the labor force. From 1940 to 1963, the number of scientists rose by 245 percent while the size of the labor force increased by only 35 percent and the population increased by only 44 percent.

ENGINEERS The demand for engineers for the year 2000 can be estimated on the basis of a relationship between gross national product and the number of engineers needed for this production. On this basis, the number of engineers needed should rise from 854,000 in 1960 to 4,700,000 in the year 2000, or from $\frac{1}{210}$ to $\frac{1}{71}$ of the United States population.[3]

Projections of needs for engineers are necessary to the planning of engineering education. That they are affected by acknowledged uncertainties in the projections of population and gross national product, of peace and prosperity, and of the character of society makes them no less desirable if utilized with this understanding. The numbers of engineers, as used herein, are based on the U.S. Census definition of "Engineers—Technical, Male." Female engineers have constituted less than 1% in the past.

A projection of United States needs for engineers in 1970 and 1975 has

---

[2] For more details on salaries by field and educational training, see U.S. Congress, Joint Economic Committee, *Federal Programs for the Development of Human Resources,* a compilation of replies from departments and agencies of the United States government to a questionnaire formulated by the Subcommittee on Economic Progress, 1966; U.S. Office of Education, *Digest of Educational Statistics, 1968,* 1968, table 156; U.S. Senate, Committee on Labor and Public Welfare, *Impact of Federal Research and Development Policies on Scientific and Technical Manpower,* hearings before the Subcommittee on Employment and Manpower, June and July 1965, tables 4 and 5; and National Science Foundation, *American Science Manpower, A Report of the National Register of Scientific and Technical Personnel, 1966,* December 1967, p. 2.

In 1966 the median salary for different types of employment varied from $8,300 for the military to $17,000 for self-employed scientists. By type of degree, the median salary varied from $10,700 for an A.B. to $17,200 for a professional medical degree.

[3] Also see comparisons of job openings and applications for 1965 and 1966 by State Employment Security Agencies.

TABLE 3.4-3 Population, labor force, scientists, engineers, and technicians, 1940–1963	*Millions*			
	1940	*1950*	*1960*	*1963 (est)*
United States population	132.0	152.3	180.7	190
Labor force	56.2	64.7	73.1	76
	Thousands			
Scientists*	145	245	435	500
Engineers	300	545	840	935
Technicians	300	550	875	1,000
Doctoral scientists and engineers	28 {27.5 / 0.5†}	45 {43.5 / 1.5}	89.2 {81.7 / 7.5}	106 {96.0 / 10.0}

* Includes natural and social scientists.
† Upper number = scientists, lower = engineers.
SOURCE: National Science Foundation, in U.S. Senate, Committee on Labor and Public Welfare, *Impact of Federal Research and Development Policies on Scientific and Technical Manpower*, hearings before the Subcommittee on Employment and Manpower, June and July 1965, p. 143.

been made recently by Colm and Lecht of the National Planning Association. They utilized economic guidelines and determined need figures on the basis of the trends of the past decade. They also computed the needs based on achieving the higher U.S. National Goals previously described. . . .

Another projection has been made for 1970 by the Bureau of Labor Statistics. This carefully executed study resulted in a projected 1970 employment of engineers of 1,375,000, which falls within the 1970 range of Colm and Lecht. Slightly higher 1970 projections appear in two other reports.

The approach used in the Report to project United States needs for engineers beyond 1975 is based on the conviction that the U.S. gross national product represents a fairly good overall measure of the effects of the work of engineers. [Table 3.4-4] analyzes past data as a guide to the projection.

TABLE 3.4-4 *Engineers in the United States*

Year	GNP, billions of 1960 dollars	Numbers of United States engineers	Engineers per millions of dollars of GNP	Engineers in population
1940	236	275,000	1.16	1/480
1950	364	525,000	1.44	1/290
1960	502	854,000	1.70	1/210
1980	1,060	2,100,000	2.00	1/114
2000	2,200	4,700,000	2.15	1/71

SOURCE: Engineering Advisory Council, *An Engineering Master Plan Study for the University of California*, University of California, Berkeley, 1965, p. 60.

TABLE 3.4-5
Earned doctor's (except first professional) degrees, by science field, actual 1957–58 and 1967–68, and projected, 1977–78

Year	Total	Mathematics and statistics	Engineering	Physical sciences	Biological sciences
1957–58	5,324	247	647	1,655	1,125
1967–68	14,240	1,060	3,120	3,630	2,520
1977–78	29,080	2,790	8,960	6,490	4,620

SOURCE: U.S. Office of Education, *Projections of Educational Statistics to 1977–78*, National Center for Educational Statistics, 1968, pp. 38–39.

The projections of numbers of engineers to 1980 and 2000 were obtained by projecting the ratio of "Engineers per $Million GNP" . . . based on the historical ratios shown and guided by the 1970 and 1975 projections of Colm and Lecht.[4]

EARNED DOCTORATES IN THE NATURAL SCIENCES AND THE SOCIAL SCIENCES

The relative increase in earned doctorates from 1957–58 to 1967–68 and the projected relative increase from 1967–68 to 1977–78 vary by scientific field. Thus, from 1957–58 to 1967–68 earned doctorates in all fields of science (except social science) increased by 2.7 times, as compared with a relative increase of 4.8 times for engineering and about 0.75 times for the health professions. The number of earned doctorates in all sciences is projected to increase relatively by 5.5 times from 1957–58 to 1977–78, as compared with projected relative increases of 14 times for engineering, 11 times for mathematics and statistics, and about 0.75 times for the health professions (Table 3.4-5).

PROFILE OF SCIENTIFIC MANPOWER, 1960

In 1960 there were 2,370,000 specialists in United States scientific manpower. Roughly 4 percent of these held doctorates. Scientists and engineers accounted for 1,275,000, or more than one-half of all scientific manpower in 1960. In addition, there were 220,000 teachers of mathematics and science in secondary schools (9 percent of all scientific manpower) and 875,000 technicians (37 percent of all scientific manpower). In 1960 research employed 175,-000, development employed 490,000, and production employed 780,000 scientific personnel.

Relatively more research scientists held doctorates (45 percent)

[4] Engineering Advisory Council, *An Engineering Master Plan Study for the University of California,* University of California, Berkeley, 1965, p. 60.

Agriculture and Forestry	Health professions	Science, general program	Social sciences
353	147	6	1,144
720	270	20	2,900
1,150	260	50	4,760

than any other type of scientist. Only 7 percent of the scientists working in development and only 7 percent of all scientists and engineers held doctorates in 1960 (Table 3.4-6).

Industry employed the largest share of scientists, engineers, and technicians in 1960—63 percent. Government employed 14 percent, and colleges and universities employed 8 percent of all scientific personnel (Table 3.4-7). In 1960 scientific personnel accounted for 12 percent of all industry employment, 22 percent of all government employment, and 67 percent of the employment of colleges and universities. The share of total employment holding doctorates was 2 percent for industry, 1 percent for government, and 26 percent for institutions of higher education.

The percentage of scientific personnel employed in a particular sector of the economy differs greatly from the percentage of scientific personnel supported by that sector. Thus, the percentage of all research and development scientists and engineers employed by industry in 1960 (75 percent) was much larger than the percentage of scientific research and development workers supported by industry (35 percent). The same is true of institutions of higher education; they employed 12 percent of all R&D scientists and engineers but supported only 2 percent. These differences in support were provided mainly by the federal government, which employed only 11 percent of all R&D scientists and engineers while supporting 62 percent. As Table 3.4-8 shows, institutions of higher education employed six times as many R&D scientists in 1960 as they supported, and industry employed about two times as many R&D scientists as it supported. In contrast, government supported almost six times as many R&D scientists and engineers as it employed.

In 1960 there were 110,000 full-time equivalent scientists em-

(Text continued on p. 554)

TABLE 3.4-6
Scientific
manpower by
types of work,
1960

Persons working in	All, thousands	Doctoral, thousands	Percentage holding doctorates
Research	175	47.5	27.1
Scientists	100	45.0	45.0
Engineers	35	2.5	7.1
Technicians	40		
Development	490	6.0	1.2
Scientists	75	5.5	7.3
Engineers	215	0.5	0.2
Technicians	200		
Production, operations	780	1.3	0.2
Scientists	105	1.0	1.0
Engineers	290	0.3	0.1
Technicians	385		
Administration, management	140	4.5	3.2
Scientists	40	4.0	10.0
Engineers	85	0.5	0.6
Technicians	15		
Teaching	310	28.5	9.2
Scientists	70	23.0	32.9
Engineers	10	3.5	35.0
Technicians	10		
Teachers of science and mathematics in secondary schools	220	2.0	0.9
Other work	475	3.4	0.7
Scientists	45	3.2	7.1
Engineers	205	0.2	0.1
Technicians	225		
All scientists and engineers	1,275	89.2	7.0
All technicians	875		
Teachers of science and mathematics in secondary schools	220	2.0	0.9
All specialized manpower in science and technology	2,370	91.2	3.8

SOURCE: U.S. Senate, Committee on Labor and Public Welfare, *Impact of Federal Research and Development Policies on Scientific and Technical Manpower,* hearings before the Subcommittee on Employment and Manpower, June and July 1965, p. 182.

TABLE 3.4-7 *Employment profile by sectors of the economy: scientists, engineers, technicians, 1960*

Persons employed by	All, thousands	Doctoral, thousands
Industry	1,495	28.0
Scientists	185	26.0
Engineers	680	2.0
Technicians	630	
Federal, state, and local government	340	4.0
Scientists	75	3.5
Engineers	110	0.5
Technicians	155	
Colleges and universities	195	50.4
Scientists	130	46.0
Engineers	25	4.4
Technicians	40	
Other	120	6.8
Scientists	45	6.2
Engineers	25	0.6
Technicians	50	
All scientists and engineers	1,275	89.2
All technicians	875	

SOURCE: U.S. Senate, Committee on Labor and Public Welfare, *Impact of Federal Research and Development Policies on Scientific and Technical Manpower,* hearings before the Subcommittee on Employment and Manpower, June and July 1965, p. 184.

TABLE 3.4-8 **Employment profile by sectors of the economy, 1960**

Scientists and engineers working in research and development	Employed in sector	Supported by sector
Industry	75%	35%
Government	11	62
Colleges and universities	12	2
Other	2	1
All sectors	100%	100%

SOURCE: U.S. Senate, Committee on Labor and Public Welfare, *Impact of Federal Research and Development on Scientific and Technical Manpower,* hearings before the Subcommittee on Employment and Manpower, June and July 1965, p. 188.

TABLE 3.4-9
*Scientists and
engineers
employed in
colleges
and
universities,
1960*

Throughout this book figures for employment of scientists and engineers relate to persons "primarily employed," which means they spend at least one-half of their time in the employment specified. Because some scientists and engineers, especially in colleges and universities, divide their time among different types of work or employment, planners and policy makers sometimes need to use the alternative methods of counting manpower demonstrated here.

	Thousands		
	Scientists	*Engineers*	*Total*
Number primarily employed	130	25	155
Total count of persons	139	28	167
Full-time equivalent number	110	23	133
Teaching	62	12	74
Research and development	42	9	51
Other work	6	2	8

Of the 155 thousand persons primarily employed as scientists and engineers in colleges and universities, about 109 thousand were employed full-time and 46 thousand part-time. However, another 12 thousand persons spent some, but less than one-half of their time doing similar work. Added together these numbers give a total count of about 167 thousand individual scientists and engineers. A third method of counting sums up all full-time and part-time efforts, measured in the proportion of time spent by each person on each type of work, and yields the full-time-equivalent number: the hypothetical number of full-time persons who would contribute the same total effort.

[Of the 133,000 full-time equivalent scientists and engineers, scientists numbered 110,000 and engineers only 23,000.]

The last three lines of the table show how scientists and engineers employed in colleges and universities divided their time, in terms of full-time equivalents, among types of work.

SOURCE: U.S. Senate, Committee on Labor and Public Welfare, *Impact of Federal Research and Development Policies on Scientific and Technical Manpower,* hearings before the Subcommittee on Employment and Manpower, June and July, 1965, p. 189.

ployed by institutions of higher education. Fifty-six percent were engaged primarily in teaching and 38 percent were engaged primarily in research (Table 3.4-9).

**GROWTH OF
PH.D.'s**

The number of Ph.D.'s rose at an increasing rate from 1958 to 1964. In the years 1960 to 1964, Ph.D. output rose by 48 percent.

The following letter submitted to a subcommittee of the House of Representatives testifies to the increased rate of Ph.D. production:

Executive Office of the President
Office of Science and Technology
Washington, D.C., June 25, 1965

Hon. Henry S. Reuss
Chairman, Research and
Technical Programs Sub-
committee, Committee on
Government Operations,
House of Representatives,
Washington, D.C.

Dear Mr. Reuss:

I am writing to amplify and comment on a matter which you raised in the question and answer period at the testimony of Dr. MacLeod of this Office. You pointed out a chart on the rate of growth of Ph.D. production which showed that the rate of growth of Ph.D.'s was falling behind the 7 percent, long-term growth rate. The situation has changed markedly since the graph you referred to was published. The rate of growth of Ph.D.'s has in fact been substantially greater than the long-term, 7 percent rate over the last 4 years.

I obtained today the most recent figures from Dr. Lindsay Harmon of the National Academy of Sciences who prepared the chart you referred to which included data up until 1962. The table shows the number of Ph.D.'s per year and the growth rate over the previous years for the past few years.

Year	Total Ph.D.'s	Percentage change	Natural science Ph.D.'s	Percentage change
1958	8,840	+ 2.8	4,143	− 5.1
1959	9,358	+ 5.9	4,473	+ 8.0
1960	10,002	+ 6.9	4,820	+ 7.8
1961	10,801	+ 8.0	5,169	+ 7.2
1962	11,944	+10.6	5,941	+15.0
1963	13,512	+13.1	6,660	+12.1
1964	14,856*	+10.0	†	†

* Estimated.
† Not available.

I believe that this information is further objective evidence that Federal research programs have not been harmful to the education system as a whole. An increase of almost 50 percent between 1960 and 1964 for both science and nonscience fields is quite heartening.[5]

The production of doctorates in the physical and biological sciences rose by 7 percent a year from 1936 to 1956. But by 1956 the annual production of doctorates in the biological sciences was still much lower than the annual production of doctorates in the physical sciences (Figure 3.4-1).

During the period 1936 to 1956 the increase in Ph.D. production varied greatly by field of science, as shown by the following table.

Trends in the increase of Ph.D.'s in science, 1936-1942 to 1950-1956 and 1943-1949 to 1950-56		*Especially large increases (in order, high to low)*	*Especially small increases (in order, high to low)*
	1936-1942 to 1950-1956	Agriculture	Biochemistry
		Engineering	Physiology
		Bio-science miscellany	Botany and phytopathology
		Physics and astronomy	Genetics
	1943-1949 to 1950-1956	Bio-science miscellany	Botany and phytopathology
		Engineering	Biochemistry
		Physics and astronomy	Genetics
			Chemistry
			Agriculture

SOURCE: Adapted from Table 3.4-10.

EDUCATIONAL ATTAINMENT OF SCIENTISTS As might be expected, the number of bachelor's degrees as a percentage of all earned degrees is projected to decline from 1957–58 to 1977–78, while the percentage of earned degrees accounted for by master's and doctorates is projected to increase. The number of Ph.D.'s awarded in the natural sciences as a percentage of all

[5] U.S. House of Representatives, Committee on Government Operations, *Conflicts Between the Federal Research Programs and the Nation's Goals for Higher Education,* hearings before a subcommittee, June 1965.

IGURE 3.4-1 *Production of doctorates in physical and biological sciences*

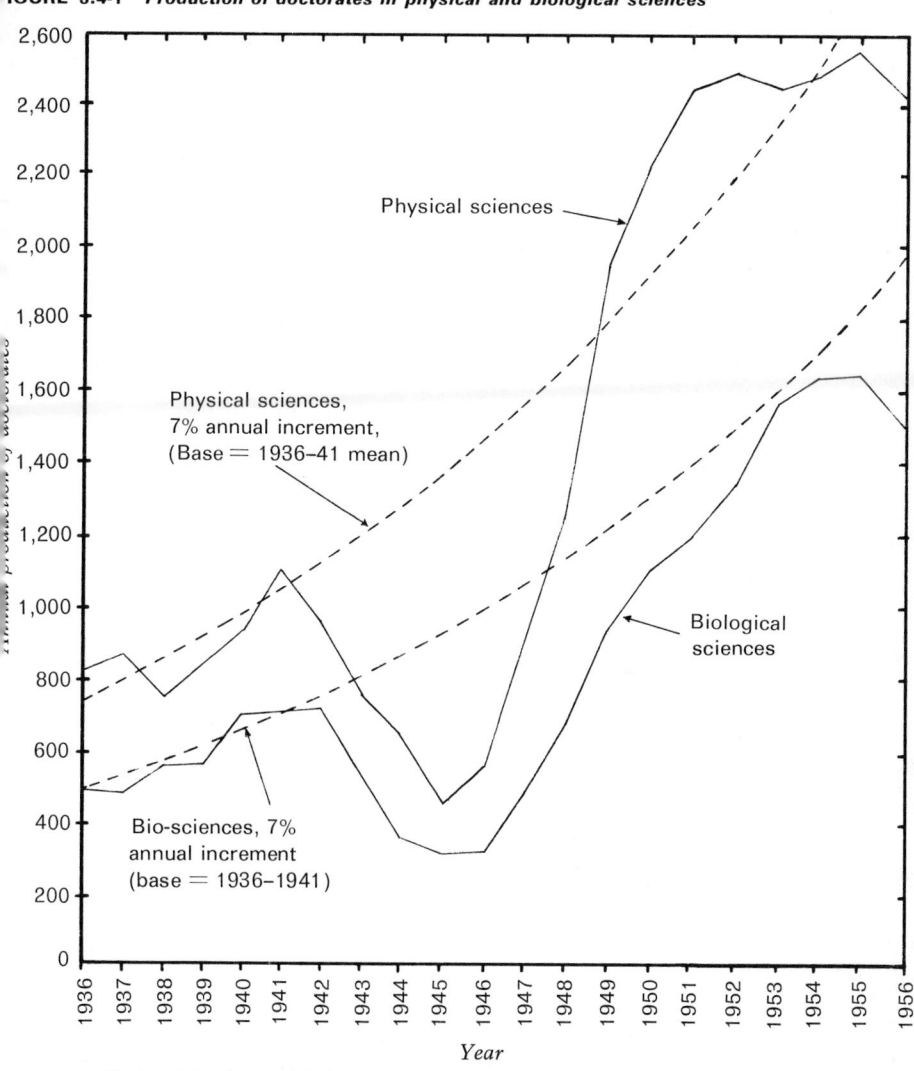

OURCE: National Academy of Sciences and National Research Council, *Doctorate Production in e United States Universities, 1936–1956,* Washington, D.C., 1958, p. 3.

Ph.D.'s is projected to rise from 46.7 to 55.2 percent—a substantial increase. There are sizable variations in the projections of other degrees and in different fields. Bachelor's degrees in mathematics and statistics are projected to increase from 1.9 to 6.6 percent of all bachelor's degrees. Master's degrees in forestry and agriculture are projected to decline from 2.3 to 0.3 percent of all master's de-

(Text continued on p. 561)

TABLE 3.4-10   *The yearly production of doctorates in the natural sciences, 1936-1956*

	Mathematics	*Physics and astronomy*	*Chemistry*	*Earth sciences*	*Engineering*	*Total physical sciences*
1936	78	140	447	72	68	805
1937	73	159	503	54	90	879
1938	61	154	406	69	65	755
1939	90	156	465	59	61	831
1940	102	144	524	63	97	930
1941	96	186	648	67	110	1,107
1942	75	155	591	66	83	970
Total, 1936-42	575	1,094	3,584	450	574	6,277
1943	41	130	506	42	49	768
1944	40	63	469	18	61	651
1945	38	43	292	24	65	462
1946	53	71	320	37	101	582
1947	116	148	425	61	116	866
1948	117	224	605	67	252	1,265
1949	144	319	940	121	446	1,970
Total, 1943-1949	549	998	3,557	370	1,090	6,564
1950	174	422	1,051	130	469	2,246
1951	204	501	1,035	148	586	2,474
1952	204	519	1,062	149	569	2,503
1953	226	523	1,006	166	565	2,486
1954	247	527	1,018	161	560	2,513
1955	243	506	1,009	179	648	2,585
1956	226	484	979	156	576	2,421
Total, 1950-1956	1,524	3,482	7,160	1,089	3,973	17,228
Grand total, 1936-1956	2,648	5,574	14,301	1,909	5,637	30,069

National Academy of Sciences and National Research Council, *Doctorate Production in United States Universities, 1936-1956,* Washington, D.C., 1958, p. 6.

Agriculture	*Botany and phytopathology*	*Biochemistry*	*Genetics*	*Microbiology*	*Physiology and related fields*	*Zoology*	*Biosciences, miscellaneous*	*Medical sciences*	*Total biological sciences*	*Total natural sciences*
6	95	9	19	47	107	125	83	22	513	1,318
6	97	22	15	50	103	97	97	11	498	1,377
4	99	108	26	39	95	98	84	25	578	1,333
9	100	116	22	52	87	96	90	16	588	1,419
8	111	128	27	59	100	128	119	28	708	1,638
5	107	104	25	68	125	115	135	29	713	1,820
10	115	136	24	66	100	118	126	28	723	1,693
48	724	623	158	381	717	777	734	159	4,321	10,598
9	87	114	25	52	79	88	84	15	553	1,321
3	47	97	11	42	39	58	51	28	376	1,027
4	44	72	8	26	43	27	67	18	309	771
42	60	30	8	29	38	68	22	19	316	898
82	106	43	18	71	44	92	45	18	519	1,385
06	113	90	36	70	79	122	41	20	677	1,942
72	137	123	27	102	97	159	79	33	929	2,899
18	594	569	133	392	419	614	389	151	3,679	10,243
33	186	127	21	116	111	170	98	48	1,110	3,356
12	156	140	33	144	146	176	342	49	1,198	3,672
21	145	152	50	147	179	213	379	59	1,345	3,848
36	215	179	33	192	217	269	390	45	1,576	4,062
15	223	202	49	158	213	261	439	85	1,645	4,158
16	166	210	30	181	220	238	479	105	1,645	4,230
58	158	179	52	152	208	172	407	110	1,496	3,917
91	1,249	1,189	268	1,090	1,294	1,499	2,534	501	10,015	27,243
57	2,567	2,381	559	1,863	2,430	2,890	3,657	811	18,015	48,084

TABLE 3.4-11
Percentage distribution of earned degrees, by field of study and level; United States, 1957–58 to 1977–78

			Natural sciences and related professions		
Year (1)	Total number of degrees (2)	Total natural sciences (3)	Mathematics and statistics (4)	Engineering (5)	Physical sciences (6)
			Bachelor's and first professional		
1957–58	363,502	28.8	1.9	9.7	3.9
1967–68	685,000	24.5	4.2	6.0	3.0
1977–78	980,000	24.1	6.6	4.1	2.7
					Master's
1957–58	65,576	23.3	1.9	8.8	4.6
1967–68	149,000	25.3	4.2	10.4	3.6
1977–78	274,000	31.1	6.8	13.4	3.7
				Doctor's (except first professional)	
1957–58	8,942	46.7	2.8	7.2	18.6
1967–68	23,100	51.0	4.7	14.1	16.3
1977–78	42,900	55.2	6.3	20.4	14.7

SOURCE: U.S. Office of Education, *Projections of Educational Statistics to 1977-78*, National Center for Educational Statistics, 1968, p. 32.

TABLE 3.4-12
Age distribution of scientists, 1968

		Ph.D. degree holders		
Age	Total registrants	Number	Percentage of total	Percen.
All ages	297,942	111,206	37	100
24 or under	9,759	58		
25–29	51,661	9,854	19	9
30–34	51,751	20,433	39	18
35–39	47,199	20,836	44	19
40–44	43,162	18,584	43	17
45–49	35,336	15,269	43	14
50–54	24,439	10,267	42	9
55–59	15,971	6,751	42	6
60–64	9,919	4,715	48	4
65–69	4,748	2,501	53	2
70 or over	3,050	1,649	54	1
No report	947	289	30	

SOURCE: National Science Foundation, *American Science Manpower, A Report of the National Register of Scientific and Technical Personnel, 1968,* December 1969, p. 26.

Biological ciences (7)	*Agriculture and forestry* (8)	*Health professions* (9)	*Science, general program* (10)	*Social sciences* (11)
3.9	2.3	6.6	0.5	12.8
5.0	1.2	4.5	0.5	17.6
5.5	0.3	4.2	0.6	20.4
2.8	2.3	2.6	0.3	8.0
3.1	1.3	2.0	0.7	9.7
3.5	0.3	1.9	1.5	11.7
12.6	3.9	1.6	0.0	12.8
11.3	3.3	1.2	0.1	11.6
10.5	2.6	0.6	0.1	10.8

grees. The share of all bachelor's degrees accounted for by forestry and agriculture is also projected to decline from 2.3 to 0.3 percent. From 1957–58 to 1977–78, the share of all doctorates accounted for by the physical sciences is projected to decrease from 18.6 to 14.7 percent. The share of all doctorates accounted for by the social sciences is also projected to decrease—from 12.8 to 10.8 percent (Table 3.4-11).

Of the 297,942 registered scientists in 1968, 37 percent had Ph.D.'s and 29 percent had master's degrees.[6] The percentage of scientists holding Ph.D.'s rises with age. For ages 25 to 29, 19 percent of the scientists had Ph.D.'s. For ages 70 and over, 54 percent of the scientists had Ph.D.'s (Table 3.4-12).

In what way do holders of Ph.D. and master's degrees differ? The percentages of scientists holding Ph.D.'s and master's degrees vary by scientific field (Table 3.4-13). Especially conspicuous is the following contrast: 95 percent of anthropologists held doctor-

[6] National Science Foundation, *American Science Manpower, A Report of the National Register of Scientific and Technical Personnel, 1968,* December 1969, pp. 23, 25.

TABLE 3.4-13 Scientists with Ph.D.'s and M.A.'s by fields, primary work and type of employers, 1968		*Percentage with* *Ph.D.'s*	*Percentage with* *M.A.'s*
	I. Field		
	All fields	37	29
	Anthropology	95	3
	Sociology	51	38
	Psychology	64	35
	Biology	48	22
	Economics	53	37
	Physics	44	33
	Chemistry	31	21
	Mathematics	28	49
	Earth and marine sciences	21	32
	Atmospheric and space sciences	9	27
	II. Primary work		
	Research and development	38	30
	Teaching	30	24
	Management and administration	19	19
	III. Type of employers		
	Educational institutions	55	30
	Nonprofit institutions	44	28
	Federal government	28	28
	Industry and business	25	27
	Other government	23	34
	Military	13	30

SOURCE: National Science Foundation, *American Science Manpower, A Report of the National Register of Scientific and Technical Personnel, 1968*, December 1969, pp. 23–26.

ates, as compared with only 9 percent of atmospheric and space scientists. In general, the percentage of scientists holding Ph.D.'s (in a particular field) exceeds the percentage holding only master's but mathematics, earth and marine sciences, and atmospheric and space sciences are exceptions.

With respect to the primary work of scientists, 38 percent of doctorate holders were engaged in research and development and 30 percent of doctorate holders were engaged in teaching. By type of employer, Ph.D.'s tend to concentrate in educational institutions

ABLE 3.4-14   *Scientists employed in educational institutions, by field, 1968*

ʾield	Total registrants	Registrants in educational institutions		
		Number	*Percentage of total*	*Percent*
All fields	297,942	117,746	40	100
ʿhemistry	93,788	20,510	22	17
ʿarth and marine sciences	23,746	5,890	25	5
ʾtmospheric and space sciences	5,745	757	13	1
ʾhysics	32,491	15,522	48	13
ʿathematics	24,477	12,837	52	11
ʿomputer sciences	6,972	921	13	1
ʾgricultural sciences	12,740	2,933	23	2
ʿiological sciences	46,183	27,141	59	23
ʾsychology	23,077	12,810	56	11
ʿtatistics	2,639	889	34	1
ʿconomics	11,510	6,681	58	6
ʿociology	6,638	4,827	73	4
ʾolitical science	5,176	3,921	76	3
ʾnthropology	1,219	986	81	1
inguistics	1,541	1,121	73	1

Scientific Field

ɾimary employment for about three-fourths of the registrants in sociology, political science, ɪthropology, and linguistics was in educational institutions; less than one-fourth of the ɾgistrants in chemistry, atmospheric and space sciences, computer sciences, and agricultural ɪences were employed in educational institutions.

ɔURCE: National Science Foundation, *American Science Manpower, A Report of the National Register Scientific and Technical Personnel, 1968*, December 1969, p. 29.

and other nonprofit organizations, with relatively less interest in government.

Of the 117,746 scientists employed by educational institutions in 1968, biological sciences accounted for 23 percent; chemistry, 17 percent; physics, 13 percent; psychology, 11 percent; and economics, 6 percent (Table 3.4-14).

GEOGRAPHIC ᴅISTRIBUTION ꜰ SCIENTISTS   The geographic distribution of scientists varies greatly by field, as the following table suggests:

Percentage of scientists in four states, 1964		Population	All scientists	Chemists
	California	9.1	11.7	8.9
	Massachusetts	2.8	4.3	4.1
	New York	9.4	10.0	11.1
	Mississippi	1.2	0.4	0.2

SOURCE: Adapted from Table 3.4-15.

TABLE 3.4-15 *Number of scientists, by geographic location and field, 1964*

		Scientific and technical field				
Geographic location	Total	Chem- istry	Earth sciences	Meteor- ology	Physics	Mathe- matics
All locations	223,854	63,053	17,907	5,510	26,698	17,41?
Alabama	1,887	536	54	64	222	18?
Alaska	452	25	129	70	14	1?
Arizona	1,768	255	202	88	197	17?
Arkansas	770	168	72	16	33	3?
California	26,645	5,620	2,036	630	4,536	3,16?
Colorado	3,656	538	988	156	425	22?
Connecticut	4,149	1,424	121	78	610	34?
Delaware	2,387	1,550	17	10	113	4?
District of Columbia	7,175	977	666	323	1,043	51?
Florida	3,708	729	226	200	374	29?
Georgia	2,238	485	95	82	154	15?
Hawaii	742	105	64	63	30	4?
Idaho	814	131	59	24	70	3?
Illinois	11,537	3,888	496	238	1,253	78?
Indiana	4,628	1,567	194	24	467	37?
Iowa	2,351	551	76	26	263	16?
Kansas	2,088	447	363	43	136	15?
Kentucky	1,545	513	129	21	96	7?
Louisiana	3,172	772	988	59	150	14?
Maine	589	139	31	28	39	4?
Maryland	7,005	1,651	235	251	1,006	68?
Massachusetts	9,540	2,577	358	284	1,978	90?
Michigan	7,573	2,435	297	100	724	51?
Minnesota	3,811	1,081	149	51	359	32?

Physicists	Mathematicians	Biologists
17.0	18.2	10.4
7.4	5.2	3.9
12.2	12.3	10.9
0.1	0.2	0.6

Agricultural sciences	Biological sciences	Psychology	Statistics	Economics	Sociology	Linguistics	Other fields
9,526	27,135	16,804	2,843	12,143	2,703	1,351	20,770
174	222	84	19	75	22	5	222
99	61	6	2	8		2	18
186	228	135	18	100	21	9	151
145	140	50	5	44	6	1	52
825	2,827	2,321	297	1,171	254	156	2,805
272	359	241	35	97	26	10	288
60	429	336	37	207	51	36	418
19	94	53	19	149	5	1	315
184	669	495	297	1,206	128	106	566
294	640	381	43	154	38	11	324
268	475	195	36	130	26	5	135
66	161	52	8	45	13	25	62
226	115	42	1	33	3	3	73
229	490	976	151	816	163	81	969
153	685	353	44	272	67	41	386
155	456	250	41	166	43	11	147
107	328	208	15	105	22	9	148
95	251	114	11	68	44	5	124
169	369	97	18	110	26	8	264
68	96	47	8	34	9	1	44
207	1,512	374	182	192	78	16	621
84	1,068	721	92	470	129	63	815
304	952	712	82	485	137	82	753
259	601	370	58	201	43	13	304

TABLE 3.4-15 *(continued)*

		Scientific and technical field			
Geographic location	Total	Chem-istry	Earth sciences	Meteor-ology	Physics	Mathe-matics
Mississippi	978	140	256	15	33	40
Missouri	3,722	1,180	215	125	304	243
Montana	797	64	170	44	19	41
Nebraska	1,118	156	83	101	77	114
Nevada	430	80	72	40	46	21
New Hampshire	650	135	50	20	71	46
New Jersey	11,844	5,819	156	87	1,486	775
New Mexico	2,023	319	332	92	530	206
New York	24,510	7,015	675	348	3,267	2,143
North Carolina	3,118	920	113	87	244	221
North Dakota	460	90	66	16	20	29
Ohio	10,135	4,124	412	104	1,150	625
Oklahoma	3,112	726	1,028	75	154	171
Oregon	2,253	342	163	55	131	121
Pennsylvania	12,813	4,898	500	97	1,572	805
Rhode Island	895	247	57	7	164	66
South Carolina	1,203	428	22	52	109	71
South Dakota	463	60	38	19	27	34
Tennessee	3,108	1,155	115	42	429	183
Texas	10,660	2,509	3,231	264	793	601
Utah	1,570	293	240	64	113	107
Vermont	343	71	15	3	21	33
Virginia	3,741	1,010	182	134	483	413
Washington	3,717	794	221	125	427	297
West Virginia	1,513	776	67	15	65	52
Wisconsin	3,912	1,133	174	50	384	336
Wyoming	717	84	327	8	13	20
Puerto Rico	355	88	19	27	26	14
Foreign	3,464	226	863	465	248	187

SOURCE: National Register of Scientific and Technical Personnel, 1954; in C. V. Kidd, *American Universities and Federal Research,* The Belknap Press, Harvard University Press, Cambridge, Mass., 1959, pp. 32–33.

Agricultural sciences	Biological sciences	Psychology	Statistics	Economics	Sociology	Linguistics	Other fields
162	169	61	1	35	14	1	51
159	490	248	32	280	73	7	357
209	131	20	8	35	7	3	46
119	201	97	11	80	16	3	60
43	37	22	1	21	2	2	43
65	121	30	3	40	14	2	53
100	796	684	136	427	61	24	1,293
159	119	64	24	36	7	5	130
310	2,965	2,713	400	1,793	372	162	2,347
231	635	212	55	146	66	12	176
87	63	37		27	3		22
176	937	729	122	510	128	35	1,083
102	252	120	24	104	17	4	335
576	380	179	10	101	39	7	149
256	1,428	992	133	641	135	59	1,297
25	92	64	4	49	18	12	90
140	131	46	8	48	12	2	134
93	89	37	5	28	9	2	22
162	439	168	24	100	21	6	264
313	866	466	86	343	67	54	1,067
166	231	105	27	48	20	12	144
35	78	28	1	25	5	2	26
199	413	241	68	169	36	15	378
408	554	275	42	164	38	22	350
76	135	45	9	64	18	4	187
257	601	295	42	222	68	31	319
111	67	32	3	14	2		36
11	68	19	4	22	5	16	38
128	419	162	41	233	76	147	269

The distribution of scientists is very much out of proportion with the distribution of population and income by state. California and Massachusetts are especially strong in mathematics and physics. Mississippi is weak in every important scientific field. It is clear that California and Massachusetts are richly endowed with scientists relative to their share of the population and that Mississippi is poorly endowed. New York has a slightly larger percentage of scientists in the major fields than it has of the national population. Table 3.4-16 shows the geographic distribution of federally funded scientists in 1962. Federally supported scientists are heavily concentrated in the Northeast (30 percent) and in the Pacific states (15 percent). A relatively small percentage of federally funded scientists work in the South or in the Mountain states (except the South Atlantic). The federal government employs over half of all scientists in the Mountain, the South Atlantic, the Pacific, the East South Central, and the New England states (in order from high to low).

TABLE 3.4-16
Percentage of scientists whose work is funded by the federal government, by geographic division, 1962

Geographic division	Scientists in federal government work		Percentage of total scientists in the geographic region in federal government work
	Number	*Percent*	
New England	7,889	7	52
Middle Atlantic	25,653	23	33
East North Central	18,610	16	37
West North Central	7,141	6	46
South Atlantic	16,813	15	62
East South Central	3,890	3	54
West South Central	9,369	8	27
Mountain	6,564	6	64
Pacific	17,582	15	58
Foreign	1,484	1	47
TOTAL	114,995	100	46

SOURCE: "National Register of Scientific and Technical Personnel," preliminary tabulation; Resources Analysis Branch, Office of Program Planning, NIH, May 1965; in U.S. Senate, Committee on Labor and Public Welfare, *Impact of Federal Research and Development Policies on Scientific and Technical Manpower,* hearings before the Subcommittee on Employment and Manpower, June and July 1965, p. 698.

TABLE 3.4-17 The direct and indirect effects of R&D expenditures

The available evidence suggests that subcontracting does not lead to the geographic diffusion of federal R&D expenditures. Does this mean that the economic impacts of such expenditures are limited to the areas of prime contracts and grants? The answer is, definitely not. This is because research contracts and grants generate further "rounds" of economic activity which benefits areas that might be quite remote from the major research centers of the Nation.

Location	R&D* Number	R&D* Percentage of Ten areas	R&D* Percentage of United States	Administration Number	Administration Percentage of Ten areas	Administration Percentage of United States	Total Number	Total Percentage of Ten areas	Total Percentage of United States	Ratio of R&D to administration
New York, New York	4,637	15.9	6.0	3,367	20.1	7.2	8,004	17.4	6.5	1.38
Washington, D.C., Maryland, and Virginia	4,801	16.5	6.2	3,811	22.7	8.2	8,612	18.7	6.9	1.26
Los Angeles and Long Beach, California	3,584	12.3	4.6	2,032	12.1	4.4	5,616	12.2	4.5	1.76
Chicago, Illinois	2,901	9.9	3.7	1,608	9.6	3.5	4,509	9.8	3.6	1.80
Boston, Massachusetts	3,466	11.9	4.5	1,181	7.0	2.5	4,647	10.1	3.7	2.93
San Francisco and Oakland, California	2,850	9.8	3.7	1,116	6.7	2.4	3,966	8.6	3.2	2.55
Philadelphia, Pennsylvania, and New Jersey	2,518	8.6	3.2	1,304	7.8	2.8	3,822	8.3	3.1	1.93
Newark, New Jersey	1,993	6.8	2.6	1,127	6.7	2.4	3,120	6.8	2.5	1.77
Pittsburgh, Pennsylvania	1,258	4.3	1.6	558	3.3	1.2	1,816	4.0	1.5	2.25
Wilmington, Delaware, New Jersey, and Maryland	1,166	4.0	1.5	660	3.9	1.4	1,826	4.0	1.5	1.77
TOTAL	29,174	100.0		16,764	100.0		45,938	100.0		1.74
Ten areas as percentage of United States			37.5			36.0			37.1	

* Basic and applied.

SOURCE: "Summary of American Science Manpower, 1964," National Register of Scientific and Technical Personnel, National Science Foundation, March 1966; in U.S. Senate, Committee on Government Operations, *Equitable Distribution of R&D Funds by Government Agencies*, hearings before the Subcommittee on Government Research, July 1967, p. 733.

Scientists are mainly concentrated in leading research areas. In 1964, 10 leading research areas accounted for 37.1 percent of all research and development scientists. The Washington, D.C.–Maryland–Virginia area leads the list with 6.9 percent of all research and development scientists (Table 3.4-17). Seven of these leading scientific areas are on the East Coast, two are on the West Coast, and one is in the Midwest. Not one is in the South.

MOBILITY PROBLEMS   There are large variations in the geographic distribution of scientists at different stages in their careers (Table 3.4-18). Compare, for example, New England and the Pacific states. New England has a larger share of Ph.D.'s granted to scientists and engineers than it has of high school students who go on to become scientists and engineers. But after training these Ph.D.'s, New England loses many of them to other parts of the country. In 1964 New England granted 10.7 percent of all Ph.D.'s in science, but only 7.7 percent of the scientific and engineering jobs were located in New England. Many Ph.D.'s from Harvard and M.I.T. found jobs outside New England. The Pacific states allow others to educate much of their scientific manpower, as do the South Atlantic states. The table

TABLE 3.4-18   *Geographic distribution of a sample of Ph.D. scientists and engineers, about 1964*

Region	1960 percentage of nation's population	Percentage of Ph.D. sample			Percentage of engineers sample job location
		High school origin	*Ph.D.'s granted*	*Job location*	
New England	5.9	7.1	10.7	7.7	6.9
Middle Atlantic	19.0	23.8	21.2	23.3	21.9
East North Central	20.2	19.6	28.6	17.6	19.2
West North Central	8.6	10.6	10.4	6.4	5.9
South Atlantic	14.5	6.3	7.7	15.6	12.0
East South Central	6.7	2.5	1.2	3.1	3.8
West South Central	9.5	4.3	3.3	5.4	8.0
Mountain	3.8	3.9	1.6	4.7	4.5
Pacific	11.8	7.9	11.2	15.0	16.3
Foreign	*	7.2	3.8	1.1	1.1

* Not available.

SOURCE: National Science Foundation, in U.S. Senate, Committee on Labor and Public Welfare, *Impact of Federal Research and Development Policies on Scientific and Technical Manpower,* hearings before the Subcommittee on Employment and Manpower, June and July 1965, p. 42.

below compares the share of national population, high school origin, location of Ph.D.-granting institution, and job location of Ph.D. scientists and engineers in 1964 for the Northeast and the Pacific states.

Percentage of Ph.D. sample	*Share of United States population*	*High school origin*	*Ph.D.'s granted*	*Job location*
New England	5.9	7.1	10.7	7.7
Pacific states	11.8	7.9	11.2	15.0

SOURCE: Table 3.4-18.

Table 3.4-19 shows the regional migration of doctorates in the physical and the life sciences at selected points in time. The last entries in the table for 1960, 1962, and 1964 refer to employment of Ph.D. scientists in each of these three years. The gains and losses by region differ to some extent for the physical and life sciences. By comparing the share of Ph.D. scientists in a region at different times in a man's career, we see that the mobility of scientists varies with age. New England produced 10.7 percent of all Ph.D.'s in the life and physical sciences in 1964, but employed 7.8 percent of all Ph.D.'s in the life and physical sciences in 1960, 7.8 percent in 1962, and 7.1 percent in 1964. For the Pacific states (which granted 11.2 percent of all Ph.D.'s in the life and physical sciences in 1964), there are increases in the employment of Ph.D. scientists as their careers develop. The Pacific states employed 14.0, 14.7, and 15.0 percent of all Ph.D.'s in the life and physical sciences in 1960, 1962, and 1964, respectively.[7]

Both New England and the Pacific states import large numbers of students: the number of Ph.D.'s granted exceeds the number of high school graduates who eventually get Ph.D.'s in science. The employment figures show that New England exports Ph.D. recipients and the Pacific states import them (Table 3.4-20). The regions that were the largest net exporters of Ph.D.'s in science were the East North Central, the West North Central, and foreign countries, in that order. The regions that were the largest net importers of

(Text continued on p. 575)

---

[7] The material in Table 3.4-19 can be put in terms of absolute numbers, with similar results. See U.S. Senate, Committee on Labor and Public Welfare, *Impact of Federal Research and Development Policies on Scientific and Technical Manpower,* hearings before the Subcommittee on Employment and Manpower, June and July 1965, p. 129.

				East	West
					Regions
				East	*West*
		New	*Middle*	*North*	*North*
Selected points in time	*Total*	*England*	*Atlantic*	*Central*	*Central*
Total, life sciences, and physical sciences:					
Birth	99.9	6.6	23.0	19.3	11.5
High school	99.9	7.1	23.8	19.6	10.6
Ph.D.	99.8	10.7	21.2	28.6	10.4
1960	100.0	7.8	23.7	18.3	6.5
1962	99.8	7.8	23.7	17.8	6.5
1964	99.9	7.7	23.3	17.6	6.4
Life sciences:					
Birth	100.0	7.2	24.0	19.0	12.6
High school	100.0	7.5	25.0	19.1	11.6
Ph.D.	100.0	7.9	22.5	28.7	13.2
1960	99.9	7.3	20.7	18.5	8.4
1962	100.1	7.2	20.9	18.2	8.4
1964	99.9	7.1	20.6	17.9	8.3
Physical sciences:					
Birth	100.0	6.3	22.3	19.6	10.7
High school	99.9	7.0	23.1	20.0	9.9
Ph.D.	100.6	12.1	20.4	28.6	8.8
1960	99.9	8.1	25.4	18.2	5.2
1962	100.0	8.2	25.3	17.7	5.3
1964	99.9	8.0	24.8	17.6	5.3

NOTE: Cohort totals 34,870 of whom 12,841 were in the life sciences and 19,972 were in the physical sciences including mathematics. Percentages may not add to 100.0 because of rounding.

SOURCE: National Register of Scientific and Technical Personnel; Resources Analysis Branch, Office of Program Planning, NIH, May 1965; in U.S. Senate, Committee on Labor and Public Welfare, *Impact of Federal Research and Development Policies on Scientific and Technical Manpower,* hearings before the Subcommittee on Employment and Manpower, June and July 1965, p. 699.

South Atlantic	East South Central	West South Central	Mountain	Pacific	Foreign	No response
5.9	2.7	4.2	4.0	6.0	10.6	6.1
6.3	2.5	4.3	3.9	7.9	7.2	6.7
7.7	1.2	3.3	1.6	11.2	3.8	0.1
14.8	3.2	5.5	4.6	14.0	0.8	0.8
15.2	3.1	5.5	4.7	14.7	0.8	
15.6	3.1	5.4	4.7	15.0	1.1	
5.8	2.7	4.5	4.6	5.8	7.8	6.0
6.3	2.5	4.4	4.6	7.8	4.7	6.5
7.4	1.5	3.6	1.9	11.0	2.2	0.1
15.4	3.4	5.4	4.5	14.1	1.0	1.2
15.7	3.5	5.5	4.8	14.9	1.0	
16.0	3.4	5.4	4.8	15.3	1.1	
5.9	2.7	4.1	3.7	6.1	12.3	6.3
6.2	2.5	4.2	3.4	8.1	8.7	6.8
7.9	1.1	3.2	1.9	11.6	4.9	0.1
14.3	3.1	5.6	4.7	13.9	0.8	0.6
14.9	3.0	5.6	4.8	14.5	0.7	
15.2	3.0	5.4	4.8	14.8	1.0	

TABLE 3.4-20
Location of
cohort of
doctoral
scientists* at
selected career
points by
geographic
division

Geographic division	Birth	Secondary school completion	Doctoral award	Employment		
				1960	1962	1964
New England	2,289	2,492	3,721	2,726	2,733	2,694
Middle Atlantic	8,026	8,317	7,405	8,263	8,271	8,120
East North Central	6,737	6,821	9,956	6,370	6,222	6,149
West North Central	4,004	3,705	3,639	2,269	2,266	2,246
South Atlantic	2,065	2,212	2,702	5,154	5,315	5,426
East South Central	930	835	427	1,106	1,090	1,087
West South Central	1,474	1,498	1,161	1,929	1,926	1,881
Mountain	1,407	1,346	569	1,602	1,652	1,648
Pacific	2,087	2,762	3,923	4,872	5,111	5,238
Foreign	3,712	2,528	1,331	285	284	381
No report	2,139	2,324	36	294		

* Includes 34,870 doctoral degree holders, who reported in each of the 1960, 1962, and 1964 registrations.

SOURCE: National Register of Scientific and Technical Personnel; in U.S. Senate, Committee on Labor and Public Welfare, *Impact of Federal Research and Development Policies on Scientific and Technical Manpower,* hearings before the Subcommittee on Employment and Manpower, June and July 1965, p. 129.

TABLE 3.4-21
Mobility of
cohort of
doctoral
scientists
between
geographic
division of
doctoral
awarded and
1960
employment
location

Geographic division	Doctoral award	Losses from	Gains into	Net mobility
New England	3,721	2,710	1,715	−985
Middle Atlantic	7,405	3,709	4,567	858
East North Central	9,956	6,564	2,978	−3,586
West North Central	3,639	2,759	1,389	−1,370
South Atlantic	2,702	1,498	3,950	2,452
East South Central	427	277	956	679
West South Central	1,161	638	1,406	768
Mountain	569	363	1,396	1,033
Pacific	3,923	1,838	2,787	949
Foreign	1,331	1,314	268	−1,046
No report	36	36	294	258
TOTAL	34,870	21,706	21,706	

SOURCE: National Register of Scientific and Technical Personnel; in U.S. Senate, Committee on Labor and Public Welfare, *Impact of Federal Research and Development Policies on Scientific and Technical Manpower,* hearings before the Subcommittee on Employment and Manpower, held June and July 1965, p. 130.

science Ph.D.'s were the South Atlantic, the Mountain, and the Middle Atlantic states, in that order (Table 3.4-21).

Table 3.4-22 gives the birth rate of scientists per 100,000 children under 1 year of age. The states with the 10 highest birth rates of scientists (from 48 to 68 per 100,000 births) include both rural and industrial states. The 10 states with the lowest birth rates of scientists (9 to 14 per 100,000) are all Southern states.

An interesting study compares the shares of population and engineers in the two leading states—California and New York— for the period 1940 to 2000 (estimated). From 1940 to 1960 the number of engineers in California increased from 21,900 to 124,-700—a gain of about six times. The corresponding increase for New York was from 37,100 to 86,700—a gain of only 2.3 times. By the year 2000, California is projected to have about 680,000 engineers (Table 3.4-23).

(Text continued on p. 579)

TABLE 3.4-22
Scientists' birthplaces by states

Rank	State	Index number*	Rank	State	Index number*
1	Colorado	68	39	West Virginia	14
2	Utah	61	40	Texas	13
3	Massachusetts	57	41	Louisiana	13
4	Connecticut	56	42	Florida	12
5	New Hampshire	55	43	Kentucky	12
6	Montana	54	44	New Mexico	11
7	Wyoming	53	45	Alabama	11
8	Vermont	51	46	Tennessee	10
9	California	49	47	Georgia	10
10	Washington	48	48	Arkansas	9

*Births of scientists per 100,000 children under one year of age at the census nearest the date of birth.
NOTE: Only the 10 highest and the 10 lowest ranking states in productivity of scientists are given here.

In addition, according to Knapp and Goodrich, the small centers of population and the semi-rural areas of the country appear to have been fertile breeding grounds for scientists. Although there is less evidence on this point, it would also appear that the public school tended to produce proportionately more scientists than the private school.

SOURCE: E. Huntington, *Mainsprings of Civilization,* John Wiley and Sons, Inc., New York, 1945, p. 82; in C. C. Cole, Jr., *Encouraging Scientific Talent,* College Entrance Examination Board, New York, 1956, p. 15.

TABLE 3.4-23
Population and
engineers, New
York and
California, 1940
to 2000

	1940	Percentage increase	1950
California	6,910,000	53%	10,590,000
New York	13,480,000	10%	14,830,000
Continental United States	131,700,000	15%	150,700,000
California/United States	5.3%		7.0%
New York/United States	10.1%		9.8%

		Engineers—technical, male	
California	21,900	134%	51,400
New York	37,100	67%	61,700
Continental United States	275,000	91%	525,000
California/United States	8.0%		9.8%
New York/United States	13.5%		11.8%

		Percentages of engineers in population	
California	0.32	0.17	0.49
New York	0.28	0.14	0.42
Continental United States	0.21	0.14	0.35

		Engineers in California	
Year	Number of engineers	Engineers in population
1940	21,900	1:330
1950	51,400	1:210
1960	124,000	1:130
1970	225,000	1:95
1980	360,000	1:80
2000	680,000	1:60

	Needed annual increments of California engineers	
Year	Net increase	Attrition
1960	8,500	2,500
1970	12,500	4,500
1980	14,500	7,000
2000	16,000	13,500

SOURCE: Engineering Advisory Council, *An Engineering Master Plan Study for the University of California,* University of California, Berkeley, 1965, p. 63.

Percentage increase	1960
48%	15,720,000
13%	16,780,000
18%	178,500,000
	8.8%
	9.4%

143%	124,700
41%	86,700
63%	854,000
	14.5%
	10.2%

0.30	0.79
0.10	0.52
0.13	0.48

Basis
U.S. census
U.S. census
U.S. census
Projected
Projected
Projected

Gross increase
11,000
16,500
21,500
29,500

TABLE 3.4-24 *Immigration of scientists, engineers, and physicians compared with immigration of all professional, technical, and kindred workers, fiscal years 1956 and 1962–66**

Fiscal year	Immigration of professional, technical, and kindred workers Number	Index (1956 = 100)	Immigration of scientists, engineers, and physicians Number	Index (1956 = 100)	Percentage, scientists, etc. of professional, technical, and kindred workers
1956	18,995	100.0	5,373	100.0	28.3
1962	23,710	124.8	5,956	110.8	25.1
1963	27,930	147.0	7,896	147.0	28.3
1964	28,756	151.4	7,810	145.4	27.2
1965	28,790	151.6	7,198	134.0	25.0
1966	30,039	158.1	9,534	177.4	31.7

* For a breakdown by countries for 1962, 1963, and 1966, see U.S. Senate, Committee on Labor and Public Welfare, *Impact of Federal Research and Development Policies on Scientific and Technical Manpower,* hearings before the Subcommittee on Employment and Manpower, held June and July 1965, table I; and U.S. House of Representatives, Committee on Government Operations, *The Brain Drain into the United States of Scientists, Engineers, and Physicians,* a staff study for the Research and Technical Programs Subcommittee, 1967, p. 18.

NOTE: "Scientists" do not include social scientists; "physicians" include surgeons and dentists. "Scientists, engineers, and physicians" include college- or university-level instructors of science, engineering, and medicine.

SOURCE: Annual reports of the Immigration and Naturalization Service, in U.S. House of Representatives, Committee on Government Operations, *The Brain Drain into the United States of Scientists, Engineers, and Physicians,* a staff study for the Research and Technical Programs Subcommittee, 1967, p. 2.

TABLE 3.4-25 *Immigration into the United States of scientists, engineers, and physicians, fiscal years 1956 and 1962–1966**

Fiscal year	Total Number	Index (1956 = 100)	Scientists Number	Index (1956 = 100)
1956	5,373	100.0	1,022	100.0
1962	5,956	110.8	1,104	108.0
1963	7,896	147.0	1,612	157.7
1964	7,810	145.4	1,676	164.0
1965	7,198	134.0	1,549	151.6
1966	9,534	177.4	1,852	181.2

* For a breakdown by countries for 1962 and 1963 and 1966 see U.S. Senate, Committee on Labor and Public Welfare, *Impact of Federal Research and Development Policies on Scientific and Technical Manpower,* hearings before the Subcommittee on Employment and Manpower, June and July 1965, table I; and U.S. House of Representatives, Committee on Government Operations, *The Brain Drain into the United States of Scientists, Engineers, and Physicians,* a staff study for the Research and Technical Programs Subcommittee, 1967, p. 18.

SOURCE: U.S. House of Representatives, Committee on Government Operations, *The Brain Drain into the United States of Scientists, Engineers, and Physicians,* a staff study for the Research and Technical Programs Subcommittee, 1967, p. 2.

TABLE 3.4-26 Immigration into the United States of scientists, engineers, and physicians, by geographic areas, fiscal years 1956 and 1962–1966	Geographic area	1956	1962	1963	1964	1965	1966
	Europe	2,419	2,267	2,915	3,092	2,997	3,612
	Asia*	535	772	1,658	1,265	824	2,736
	North America	1,940	2,328	2,550	2,562	2,704	2,591
	South America	512	695	866	1,051	871	807
	Africa	69	86	138	123	106	129
	TOTAL	5,475	6,148	8,127	8,093	7,502	9,875

*Includes Oceania.

SOURCE: U.S. House of Representatives, Committee on Government Operations, *The Brain Drain into the United States of Scientists, Engineers, and Physicians,* a staff study for the Research and Technical Programs Subcommittee, 1967, p. 4.

THE BRAIN DRAIN: INTERNATIONAL ASPECTS   Immigration of scientists, engineers, and physicians has been increasing in recent years. In the 10 years from 1956 to 1966, the annual immigration of professional, technical, and kindred workers rose from 18,995 to 30,039 (an increase of 58 percent), while the annual immigration of scientists, engineers, and physicians rose from 5,373 to 9,534 — an increase of 77 percent (Tables 3.4-24 and 3.4-25).

The abandonment of national origins quotas contributed to the large increase in immigration in the 1960s — particularly for Asians (Table 3.4-26). From 1956 to 1966, immigration of scientists, engineers, and physicians from Asia increased by more than 400 percent.

Engineers		Physicians	
Number	Index (1956 = 100)	Number	Index (1956 = 100)
2,804	100.0	1,547	100.0
2,940	104.8	1,912	123.6
4,014	143.2	2,270	146.7
3,725	132.8	2,409	155.7
3,455	123.2	2,194	141.8
4,921	175.5	2,761	178.5

TABLE 3.4-27 *Immigration into the United States of scientists, engineers, and physicians, by type of country of emigration, fiscal years 1956 and 1962–1966*

Fiscal year	Total, all countries		Developed countries		Developing countries	
	Number	Percentage of total	Number	Percentage of total	Number	Percentage of total
1956	5,373	100.0	3,604	67.1	1,769	32.9
1962	5,956	100.0	3,573	60.0	2,383	40.0
1963	7,896	100.0	4,534	57.4	3,362	42.6
1964	7,810	100.0	4,607	59.0	3,203	41.0
1965	7,193	100.0	4,548	63.2	2,650	36.8
1966	9,534	100.0	5,144	54.0	4,390	46.0

NOTE: Developed countries include the European countries, Canada, Japan, South Africa, Australia, and New Zealand. Developing countries are all other countries.

SOURCE: U.S. House of Representatives, Committee on Government Operations, *The Brain Drain into the United States of Scientists, Engineers, and Physicians,* a staff study for the Research and Technical Programs Subcommittee, 1967, p. 5.

TABLE 3.4-28 Comparisons of annual additions to scientific manpower by United States educational institutions and by immigration into the United States, fiscal years 1956 and 1962–1966

	Scientists				
		Immigrants			
Fiscal year	Graduates of United States institutions*	Number	Percentage of United States graduates	Graduates of United States institutions*	
1956	45,948	1,022	2.2	31,646	
1962	71,307	1,104	1.5	44,851	
1963	77,149	1,612	2.1	44,471	
1964	86,574	1,676	1.9	47,746	
1965	93,368	1,549	1.6	50,975	
1966‡	99,145	1,852	1.9	51,785	

* Baccalaureate or higher degrees.

† Doctorates in medicine and dentistry.

‡ 1966 figures for scientists and physicians are Office of Education estimates.

SOURCE: Figures on U.S. graduates from "Scientific and Technical Manpower Resources," National Science Foundation, NSF 64–28, tables V-13, V-16, and V-19 for 1956, 1962, and 1963. Data for 1964 and 1965 furnished by the Office of Economic and Manpower Studies, National Science Foundation. Data for 1966 furnished by the Division of Statistical Analysis, Office of Education; in U.S. House of Representatives, Committee on Government Operations, *The Brain Drain into the United States of Scientists, Engineers, and Physicians,* a staff study for the Research and Technical Programs Subcommittee, 1967, p. 3.

Immigration of scientific personnel from developing countries has tended to rise in recent years. From 1956 to 1966, total immigration of scientific personnel rose 77 percent, immigration from developed countries rose 43 percent, and immigration from developing countries rose 148 percent (Table 3.4-27).

Table 3.4-28 shows immigration of foreign scientific personnel as a percentage of new United States scientific manpower graduates. For 1966 the foreign contribution was especially large for engineers (9.5 percent) and physicians (26.1 percent).

Foreign student enrollment in United States institutions is an important offset (but perhaps also an inducement) to immigration. From 1956 to 1966, foreign student enrollment in United States institutions of higher education rose by about 18,500 while immigration of scientists, engineers, and physicians rose by about 2,600 (Table 3.4-29).

An interesting characteristic of these scientific immigrants is that the proportion going into research and development and teaching exceeds the proportion of United States scientists going into these fields. The educational achievements of the immigrants also exceed those of United States scientists (Table 3.4-30).

ngineers		*Physicians*		
Immigrants			*Immigrants*	
Number	*Percentage of United States graduates*	*Graduates of United States institutions†*	*Number*	*Percentage of United States graduates*
2,804	8.9	9,862	1,547	15.7
2,940	6.6	10,392	1,912	18.4
4,014	9.0	10,469	2,270	21.7
3,725	7.8	10,538	2,409	22.9
3,455	6.8	10,482	2,194	20.9
4,921	9.5	10,580	2,761	26.1

TABLE 3.4-29 Comparison of foreign student enrollments in United States, college enrollment in United States (students majoring in physical sciences, medical sciences, and engineering) and immigration of scientists, engineers, and physicians

Year	Foreign student enrollment*	Immigration*
1956	10,856	1,769
1962	19,955	2,383
1963	22,510	3,362
1964	25,972	3,203
1965	28,751	2,650
1966	28,419	4,390

*Enrollments include only those students majoring in the physical sciences, medical sciences, and engineering; immigration figures include only scientists, engineers, and physicians.

SOURCE: Enrollment figures from Institute of International Education annual issues of Open Doors; in U.S. House of Representatives, Committee on Government Operations, *The Brain Drain into the United States of Scientists, Engineers, and Physicians,* a staff study for the Research and Technical Programs Subcommittee, 1967, p. 9.

TABLE 3.4-30 *Percentage of foreign-origin scientists and engineers from developing countries in R&D and teaching and their degree qualifications compared with all United States scientists and engineers, 1964*

	Scientists		Engineers	
	Foreign origin	United States total	Foreign origin	United States total
Percentage in R&D	53	35	41	27
Research	50	30	12	6
Development or design	3	5	29	21
Percentage in teaching	19	18	6	4
Degree qualifications:				
Ph.D.	53	38	15	5
Master's	32	27	28	17
Bachelor's	12	32	38	63
Other	3	2	19	15

NOTE: The data on scientists are for persons whose secondary school was in such countries while those on engineers are for individuals born in such countries.

SOURCE: Data for U.S. scientists from National Science Foundation, American Science Manpower, 1964, (NSF 66–29); for U.S. engineers from Engineers Joint Council, Engineering Manpower in Profile; for foreign-origin scientists and engineers from special tabulations by NSF of data on individuals from non-OECD countries; in U.S. House of Representatives, Committee on Government Operations, *The Brain Drain into the United States of Scientists, Engineers, and Physicians,* a staff study for the Research and Technical Programs Subcommittee, 1967, p. 11.

Part Four

Income and Expenditures

4.1. *Income*

From 1889–90 to 1956–57, general and educational income of higher education increased steadily as a percentage of GNP—from 0.23 to 0.70 percent (Table 4.1-1). Over this 70-year period enrollment increased almost 20 times, while prices rose about 2½ times. General and educational income per resident student increased 6⅓ times, but income per student increased less than per capita GNP (Table 4.1-2) This indicates a lag in the rise of educational income per student in relation to the gains in the economy. From 1889–90 to 1919–20, for example, the rise in income

NOTE: For more detailed treatment of specific subjects, see Chapters 4.3 and 4.4

TABLE 4.1-1   *Higher education income in relation to GNP and other variables, 1889–90 to 1956–57*

Period	Proportion of general income to GNP, percent	Consumer prices, 1923 = 100	Resident enrollment, thousands	Education and general income per resident	Value of physical property, millions	Endowment, millions
1889–90	0.23	48	157	$ 137	$ 95	$ 579
1919–20	0.28	108	598	289	741	569
1929–30	0.51	98	1,101	439	1,925	1,512
1939–40	0.58	85	1,494	382	2,753	1,764
1949–50	0.66	142	2,659	689	5,275	2,644
1953–54	0.63	158	2,407	979	8,033	3,313
1956–57	0.70*	163	3,000*	1,000*	10,000*	4,000*

*Estimated.

SOURCE: U.S. Census, *Historical Statistics of the United States, 1789–1845;* Department of Health, Education and Welfare, *Statistics of Higher Education: Receipts, Expenditures and Property and Faculty, Students and Degrees,* various issues; and *Economic Report of the President,* Jan. 1, 1959. Estimates and computations are the author's; in S. E. Harris, *Higher Education: Resources and Finance,* McGraw-Hill Book Company, New York, 1962, p. 7.

TABLE 4.1-2		1889–90	1919–20	1929–30	1939–40	1949–50
Percentage rise		to	to	to	to	to
in higher						
educational	*Income*	*1919–20*	*1929–30*	*1939–40*	*1949–50*	*1957–58*
income per						
capita and	*Education*	+111	+52	−13	+ 80	+54
national income						
per capita	*National*	+283	+35	− 5	+149	+36

SOURCE: S. E. Harris, *Higher Education: Resources and Finance,* McGraw-Hill Book Company, New York, 1962, table 1-8, p. 14.

per student was only 39 percent of the rise in per capita GNP, although total educational income rose substantially more than total GNP. In the last 20 years, however, income per student has increased faster than per capita GNP (Table 4.1-3).

The following table compares the number of times (total and per capita) that higher educational income and GNP increased from 1889–90 to 1959–60:

Number of		*Total*	*Per capita*
times,			
1959–60 in			
relation to	*Educational and general income*	175	8.4
1889–90	*GNP*	53	18.5

SOURCE: Table 4.1-4.

Educational and general income increased more than three times as much as GNP, but income per resident student rose less than half as much as per capita GNP.

SOURCES OF INCOME From 1909–10 to 1963–64, income from different sources rose at uneven rates. The table on page 587 shows some trends for this period.

TABLE 4.1-3	*Year*	*Rise*
Percentage		
increase in		
educational	*1889–90 to 1919–20*	39
income per	*1919–20 to 1929–30*	149
resident student		
as percent of	*1929–30 to 1939–40*	(260)*
percentage		
increase in	*1939–40 to 1949–50*	54
national		
per capita	*1949–50 to 1953–54*	200
income	*1953–54 to 1957–58*	129

*Larger decline (− 13 and −5).

SOURCE: S. E. Harris, *Higher Education: Resources and Finance,* McGraw-Hill Book Company, New York, 1962, table 1-6, p. 12.

Higher educational income, for selected purposes and from selected sources, 1909–10 to 1963–64	Number of times	
	1963–64/1909–10	*1963–64/1949–50*
Educational and general	107	4.2
Auxiliary	180	3.1
Plant funds	128	4.8
Fees	98	4.8
State government	101*	4.3
Endowment	21	2.8
Private gifts and grants	155	4.6

*Current fund only.
SOURCE: Table 4.1-5.

The largest relative gains from 1909–10 to 1963–64 were in auxiliary income (room and board), private gifts and grants, and plant funds. The smallest gains were in endowment and student fees. In 1910 auxiliary income amounted to 46 percent of tuition; in 1964, about 85 percent. One explanation of this relative increase is undoubtedly the increasing tendency of students to live in college- and university-owned housing.[1]

From 1882 to 1964, major changes occurred in the distribution of sources of income (Table 4.1-6). Federal support increased greatly in relative importance, especially after 1940. State and local government support increased substantially in the early years, but has been relatively stable and has even declined somewhat in relative importance since 1940. Endowment income has suffered a large relative decline since 1900. Tuition income experienced a large relative decrease from 1882 to 1910, a relative increase from 1910 to 1940, and a relative decrease from 1940 to 1964.[2]

Statistics for federal government support in the early years are

(Text continued on p. 592)

[1] U.S. Office of Education, *Report of the Commissioner of Education, 1910,* p. 868; and U.S. Office of Education, *Higher Education Finances: Selected Trend and Summary Data,* National Center for Educational Statistics, June 1968, p. 3.

[2] See also American Council on Education, *A Fact Book on Higher Education,* Washington, D.C., 1967, p. 63. Here the relative amounts received from various income sources are revealed for 14 recent years. The share of tuition and federal income tends to rise.

TABLE 4.1-4 *Trends of finance in higher education, national income, and prices, 1889–90 to 1959–60*

Variable	1889–90 (1)	1919–20 (2)	Percentage change 1889–90 to 1919–20 (3)	1929–30 (4)	Percentage change 1919–20 to 1929–30 (5)	1939–40 (6)
Resident college enrollment (thousands)	157	598	+280	1,101	+ 84	1,494
Degrees (thousands)†	15.5	48.6	+214	122	+151	186.5
Educational and general income (millions of dollars)	21.5	173	+704	483	+179	571
Educational and general expenditures (millions of dollars)†				378		522
Educational and general income per resident student (dollars)†	137	289	+111	439	+ 52	382
Value of physical property (millions of dollars)†	95.4	741	+677	1,925	+106	2,753
Endowment and other nonexpendable funds (millions of dollars)†	78.8	569	+622	1,512	+166	1,764
National income (GNP, millions of dollars)†	9,410	61,000	+548	95,000	+ 56	97,400
National income (GNP) per capita (dollars)†	150	575	+283	774	+ 35	740
Consumers prices (1923 = 100)†	48	107.8	+125	98	− 9	85

*Interpolation 1951 to 1956 estimates and related to annual figures of fall enrollment of U.S. Department of Health, Education and Welfare.

† Columns 3, 5, 7, 9, 11, 13, 15 = percentage changes.

‡ 1957–1958.

SOURCES: U.S. Department of Health, Education and Welfare, *Statistical Summary of Education, 1951–52,* 1955, and *Summary of 1953–54 Financial Statistics of Higher Education,* 1956; ibid., *Statistics of Higher Education, 1955–56: Receipts, Expenditures and Property, 1955–56,* 1959, and *Faculty,*

Per-centage change 1929-30 to 1939-40 (7)	1949-50 (8)	Percentage change 1939-40 to 1949-50 (9)	1953-54 (10)	Percentage change 1949-50 to 1953-54 (11)	1955-56 (12)	Percentage change 1953-54 to 1955-56 (13)	1959-60 (14)	Percentage change 1955-56 to 1959-60 (15)
+36	2,659	+ 78	2,407*	− 9	2,661	+11	3,402	+28
+53	432	+132	357	−17	379	+ 6		
+18	1,834	+221	2,357	+29	2,882	+22	3,762‡	+31‡
+38	1,706	+227	2,288	+34	3,525	+22	3,634‡	+ 3‡
−13	689	+ 80	979	+42	1,083	+11	1,154‡	+ 7‡
+43	5,273	+ 92	8,033	+52	9,485	+18	11,180‡	+18‡
+17	2,644	+ 50	3,313	+25	3,837	+16	4,648‡	+21‡
+ 3	279,000	+186	364,000	+30	412,000	+13	496,000	+20
− 5	1,846	+149	2,242	+21	2,467	+10	2,771	+12
−13	141.7	+ 67	158	+12	159.5	+ 1	161.9	+ 1½

tudents and Degrees, 1955–56, 1958; *Economic Report of the President, January, 1957*, 1960; and .S. Department of Commerce, *Historical Statistics of the United States, 1789–1945*, 1949; also see .S. Office of Education: Memo to the Board, 1960, series no. 4, National Education Series, *Teacher upply . . . 1960–61, Research Report 1961-R12*, and R. Walters, *Four Decades of U.S. Collegiate nrollments*, 1960; in S. E. Harris, *Higher Education: Resources and Finance*, McGraw-Hill Book Com-any, New York, 1962, p. 19.

TABLE 4.1-5 Income of institutions of higher education, United States and outlying areas, 1909–10 to 1963–64 (thousands of dollars)

Item (1)	1909–10 (2)	1919–20 (3)	1929–30 (4)	1939–40 (5)	1949–50 (6)	1959–60 (7)	1961–62 (8)	1963–64 (9)
Current fund income	$82,007	$200,136	$556,845	$720,095	$2,390,079	$5,812,759	$7,466,461	$9,591,330
Educational and general	73,041	173,143	485,348	575,796	1,846,825	4,712,548	6,072,219	7,830,033
Student tuition and fees[a]	19,426	42,263	144,624	201,831	395,855	1,161,753	1,505,329	1,899,455
Federal government:								
Veterans' tuition and fees					308,432	3,483		
Land-grant institutions[b]	2,998	4,709	16,389	31,889	48,245	88,297	103,135	119,756
Research[b]	c	c	c	c	c	828,734	1,274,364	1,797,095
Other purposes	1,815	8,074	4,269	7,648	170,356	120,384	164,557	253,898
State governments[d]	21,203[e]	61,864[e]	152,335[e]	153,690	500,289	1,389,271	1,689,086	2,133,665
Local governments	e	e	e	24,392	61,378	151,715	191,188	240,355
Endowment earnings	12,681	26,485	68,620	71,364	96,370	206,666	232,341	266,214
Private gifts and grants	3,551[f]	7,585	26,203	40,576	118,705	383,186	450,764	551,507
Related activities	c	c	c	32,894	112,437	244,894	304,129	363,584
Sales and services of educational departments	c	c	c	c	c	45,425	52,415	65,063
Other educational and general	11,367	22,163	72,908	11,512	34,758	88,739	104,911	139,441
Auxiliary enterprises	8,966	26,993	60,470	144,299	513,096	1,005,963	1,274,026	1,610,426
Student-aid income[g]	c	c	c	c	16,288	94,248	120,216	150,871
Other current income			11,027		13,870			
Plant-fund receipts	19,855[f]	19,219	82,831	66,306	530,435	1,311,907	1,820,747	2,534,182
Federal government				{ 22,987	12,362	57,599	70,501	134,215
State governments	11,476	11,319	31,374	{ 18,486	285,234	320,401	515,897	632,100
Local governments				{ 2,154	19,373	36,304	35,495	62,694

59•

		1,300	31,451	22,019	12,029	190,464	226,529	314,569
Loans—noninstitutional sources	c	c	c	c	c	363,514	504,749	744,451
Loans—institutional sources	c	c	c	c	c	31,873	43,249	64,132
Transfers from other funds	c	c	c	c	c	288,597	319,894	422,777
Miscellaneous receipts	c	c	c	c	60,914	77,155	104,433	159,243
Other fund receipts	h	h	h	h	79,923	499,005	508,319	629,605
Private gifts and grants	11,156	51,514	63,514	36,366	117,190[i]	209,147	258,509	308,693
Other resources	h	h	h	5,778	50,251	289,858	249,809	320,911
Net increase in principal of funds	h	h	h	h	66,939	419,356	409,918	484,111
Endowment funds[j]						375,179	379,707	444,817
Annuity funds						11,854	16,636	25,350
Student loan funds						32,324	13,576	13,944

[a] Tuition and fees received from veterans under Public Law 550 are reported under student fees and not under income from the federal government.

[b] Income from the federal government for research at agricultural experiment stations administered by land-grant institutions were reported under land-grant institutions and not under research.

[c] Data not separately collected.

[d] Includes federal aid received through state channels and regional compacts.

[e] Income from state and local governments tabulated under state.

[f] Does not include separately organized professional schools, for which data were not collected.

[g] Specifically designated or earmarked funds.

[h] Data not collected.

[i] Does not include interfund transfers.

[j] Includes funds functioning as endowment.

SOURCE: U.S. Department of Health, Education and Welfare, Office of Education, surveys of "Financial Statistics of Institutions of Higher Education"; in U.S. Office of Education, *Digest of Educational Statistics, 1968,* 1968, p. 95.

TABLE 4.1-6 *Trends of income, institutions of higher education, several years from 1882 to 1964, percentage of total*

Year	Federal government	State and local government	Endowment income	Student tuition and fees	Private gifts and grants	Other
1882	6	13 (state)	19	61		
1902	9	19	24	39		9
1910*	7	30	17	27‡	5	16
1940*	7	31	6	35	7	14
1964*	28†	27	3	24	7	11

* Percentage of educational and general income.

† Organized research accounts for 1.8 billions of 2.13 billions total for federal government.

‡ Of tuition fees and other educational services, $1.22 million are for room rent and $3.31 million for board and other noneducational services.

SOURCE: U.S. Office of Education, *Report of the Commissioner of Education, 1889–1890*, pp. 762–763; *1902*, p. 1353; *1903*, p. 1178; *1910*, p. 868, and U.S. Office of Education, *Higher Education Finances: Selected Trend and Summary Data*, National Center for Educational Statistics, June 1968, p. 3 (author's calculations).

inadequate, but a Carnegie Commission study shows projected federal outlays as follows:[3]

Period	Federal expenditures on higher education, billions of dollars	Federal expenditures as a percentage of total expenditure on higher education
1957–58	0.7	13
1967–68	3.5	21
1976–77	13.0	32

Federal support is projected to increase from 13 to 32 percent of total expenditure in 20 years if the Carnegie Commission recommendations for increased federal aid are adopted.

From 1963–64 to 1968–69, estimated expenditures from federal sources rose steadily, but they were projected to rise relatively more for private than for public institutions of higher education (Table 4.1-7). Total federal expenditures were expected to increase by 17 percent during this period, but federal support as a source of expenditures of private institutions was expected

(Text continued on p. 598

[3] Carnegie Commission on Higher Education, *Quality and Equality: New Levels of Federal Responsibility for Higher Education*, McGraw-Hill Book Company, New York, 1968, p. 8.

Total expenditures of higher educational institutions, by source of funds, United States, 1963–64 to 1968–69 (amounts in billions)

Source of funds control of institution (1)	1964-65 Amount (2)	Percent (3)	1965-66 Amount (4)	Percent (5)	1966-67 Amount (6)	Percent (7)	1967-68 Amount (8)	Percent (9)	1968-69 Amount (10)	Percent (11)
Institutions of higher education:										
Total public and private	13.1	100.0	15.0	100.0	16.9	100.00	18.8	100.0	20.4	100.0
Federal	2.8	21.4	3.3	21.7	3.9	23.1	4.5	24.0	5.1	25.0
State	3.1	23.6	3.5	23.7	3.9	23.0	4.3	22.9	4.6	22.5
Local	.3	2.3	.4	2.6	.4	2.4	.5	2.6	.5	2.5
All other	6.9	52.7	7.8	52.0	8.7	51.5	9.5	51.5	10.2	50.0
Total public	7.6	100.0	8.8	100.0	9.9	100.0	11.2	100.0	12.2	100.0
Federal	1.4	17.7	1.6	18.4	1.9	19.0	2.2	19.7	2.5	20.4
State	3.0	39.6	3.4	39.0	3.8	38.5	4.2	37.9	4.5	37.3
Local	.3	4.3	.4	4.2	.4	4.1	.5	4.0	.5	3.8
All other	2.9	38.4	3.4	38.4	3.8	38.4	4.3	38.4	4.7	38.5
Total private	5.5	100.0	6.2	100.0	7.0	100.0	7.6	100.0	8.2	100.0
Federal	1.4	25.2	1.7	26.8	2.0	28.3	2.3	29.9	2.6	31.5
State	.1	1.3	.1	1.3	.1	1.4	.1	1.4	.1	1.4
Local		.2		.2		.2		.2		.2
All other	4.0	73.3	4.4	71.7	4.9	70.1	5.2	68.5	5.5	66.9

Total expenditures are defined as the expenditure of all money from both loans and grants and exclude only the funds used for reducing debt and transfers of funds. Expenditures from feder, state, and local sources are defined as institutional expenditures of all grants (but not loans) of funds received from those sources. Expenditures from all other sources include all funds received by the institutions that were not received as a grant from federal, state, and local governments. Loans from any source are included in this category. (It was estimated that in 1967–68, about $504 million in federal loans to institutions of higher education was included in the all other category shown here.)

SOURCE: U.S. Office of Education, *Digest of Educational Statistics, 1968,* 1968, p. 18.

TABLE 4.1-8   *Current-fund income by institutions of higher education, by source and by state, 1963–64 (in thousands)*

State (1)	Total current-fund income (2)	Total educational and general (3)	Student fees (4)	Federal government Research (5)	Other (6)
				Educational and general income	
United States	$9,543,514	$7,788,446	$1,892,839	$1,796,710	$364,179
Alabama	99,233	75,579	15,858	6,892	5,338
Alaska	13,914	12,452	748	3,924	1,087
Arizona	66,053	51,879	11,722	5,731	2,228
Arkansas	57,108	42,900	8,184	3,383	3,520
California	1,432,304	1,299,612	122,169	628,175	15,697
Colorado	125,058	96,749	21,204	14,005	8,863
Connecticut	132,139	104,537	32,426	19,932	2,361
Delaware	18,211	13,949	3,538	995	907
District of Columbia	114,404	87,512	40,145	18,991	12,330
Florida	168,789	138,009	33,257	17,301	6,291
Georgia	128,722	103,305	23,704	10,478	7,680
Hawaii	32,323	29,447	2,735	3,985	8,791
Idaho	27,295	21,584	4,491	475	1,758
Illinois	598,001	506,018	101,528	152,543	9,858
Indiana	265,538	191,270	51,991	21,132	3,953
Iowa	171,635	130,707	35,054	17,099	5,789
Kansas	111,302	87,172	16,759	6,970	5,070
Kentucky	95,562	77,096	16,312	4,075	4,877
Louisiana	129,402	100,034	15,122	12,406	2,804
Maine	35,012	24,696	10,725	114	1,615
Maryland	195,193	172,370	26,935	77,926	2,590
Massachusetts	531,241	437,526	137,630	183,535	8,473
Michigan	395,800	300,237	69,951	51,059	12,439
Minnesota	188,035	145,579	34,431	19,341	10,107
Mississippi	69,011	48,746	11,253	2,710	4,796
Missouri	191,570	152,925	44,894	18,730	5,031
Montana	30,084	21,968	4,040	2,339	1,309
Nebraska	65,352	51,894	13,692	2,114	3,848
Nevada	10,863	9,937	1,410	391	1,107
New Hampshire	41,743	31,538	12,340	4,089	1,673

State governments (7)	Local governments (8)	Private gifts and grants (9)	Other (10)	Auxiliary enterprise Income (11)	Student-aid income (12)
$2,110,981	$239,851	$550,684	$833,201	$1,606,974	$148,093
28,398	897	3,730	14,466	23,114	540
4,846		857	990	1,399	63
26,353	1,899	2,035	1,911	13,607	566
20,988	1	2,689	4,135	13,841	367
304,287	115,361	53,149	60,774	122,712	9,980
35,360	1,610	5,346	10,362	26,603	1,706
19,215	1,570	10,186	18,848	24,614	2,987
6,046		990	1,474	3,666	596
223	921	7,184	17,717	14,074	2,819
62,836	3,200	7,475	7,649	28,333	2,447
32,129	1,675	6,918	20,720	24,009	1,409
11,184		1,906	846	2,663	213
11,534	751	1,426	1,149	5,458	253
142,180	9,091	36,258	54,559	83,631	8,352
73,822	652	13,568	26,152	66,656	7,613
47,677	727	9,364	14,997	37,516	3,411
39,037	4,122	5,146	10,068	22,770	1,360
32,847	2,698	7,113	9,173	17,636	830
55,554	737	5,449	7,963	27,874	1,495
7,116	60	2,612	2,453	9,317	999
34,777	1,739	10,770	17,633	20,224	2,599
21,126	366	38,603	47,794	75,080	18,635
117,405	3,438	27,065	18,880	92,453	3,110
47,669	914	13,135	19,983	39,901	2,555
17,694	3,867	3,192	5,234	19,700	565
43,100	1,714	14,663	24,792	36,749	1,896
12,363	138	798	981	7,750	367
18,728	1,696	4,600	7,216	12,789	669
6,141		451	436	830	96
5,215	20	3,496	4,705	9,296	910

TABLE 4.1-8 *(continued)*

				Educational and general income	
	Total current fund income	Total educational and general	Student fees	Federal government	
State (1)	(2)	(3)	(4)	Research (5)	Other (6)
New Jersey	185,900	153,378	54,362	33,320	2,731
New Mexico	48,713	37,370	4,483	10,532	2,093
New York	981,375	846,668	290,150	171,913	19,199
North Carolina	220,665	166,478	41,485	23,317	10,378
North Dakota	29,529	23,031	4,832	1,130	1,604
Ohio	380,611	290,236	114,373	35,740	6,393
Oklahoma	110,092	77,779	16,419	10,784	4,270
Oregon	102,667	82,328	21,288	12,192	2,913
Pennsylvania	498,785	406,328	171,533	61,888	10,517
Rhode Island	50,516	39,092	14,975	7,447	1,365
South Carolina	64,696	45,097	14,420	1,722	3,046
South Dakota	33,811	23,296	6,484	2,196	1,695
Tennessee	141,389	112,528	30,672	12,370	8,138
Texas	360,150	277,680	51,563	32,015	9,368
Utah	74,072	57,455	11,003	11,410	3,109
Vermont	33,471	23,942	12,566	1,814	1,747
Virginia	145,718	115,055	33,243	7,784	5,155
Washington	160,475	130,840	22,150	25,735	3,348
West Virginia	57,533	44,048	8,598	1,439	3,336
Wisconsin	188,838	154,752	41,767	20,388	9,333
Wyoming	16,384	12,810	2,228	270	1,691
United States service schools	117,226	91,032		464	90,562
Outlying areas	47,816	41,587	6,616	385	9,475
Canal Zone	359	359	161		197
Guam	582	532	28		
Puerto Rico	46,822	40,660	6,414	385	9,278
Virgin Islands	54	36	13		

SOURCE: U.S. Office of Education, *Digest of Educational Statistics, 1968,* 1968, p. 92.

State govern- ments (7)	*Local govern- ments* (8)	*Private gifts and grants* (9)	*Other* (10)	*Auxiliary enterprise income* (11)	*Student- aid income* (12)
34,898	380	12,418	15,267	28,083	4,440
16,012	273	1,056	2,921	10,690	654
135,221	46,858	69,981	113,346	122,553	12,155
44,613	360	13,468	32,859	50,291	3,895
12,581	214	776	1,893	5,841	658
58,037	14,639	23,246	37,806	84,992	5,384
34,535	16	5,495	6,260	30,606	1,708
35,331	1,370	4,965	4,270	17,322	3,016
69,235	814	31,359	60,981	85,137	7,320
8,292		4,350	2,664	10,592	832
19,000	268	3,506	3,135	18,980	620
10,168		1,150	1,603	10,192	323
29,082	324	9,511	22,432	27,345	1,515
110,457	10,745	26,925	36,608	78,758	3,712
19,358	135	10,808	1,632	16,008	609
5,276	109	947	1,484	8,848	682
35,419	40	7,735	25,680	27,779	2,883
66,835	235	4,850	7,687	27,804	1,831
25,265	68	1,429	3,914	13,022	463
49,048	2,276	16,177	15,763	32,163	1,923
6,467	864	361	929	3,392	182
			5	12,315	13,879
22,685	503	823	1,100	3,452	2,778
	503		1	47	3
22,662		823	1,100	3,387	2,774
23				18	

to increase by 25 percent but only 15 percent for public institutions. State support as a percentage of total expenditures was projected to decrease by 5 percent for all institutions from 1963–64 to 1968–69.

Sources of income vary widely from state to state (Table 4.1-8). Below are comparisons of sources of income for California, New York, Mississippi (a poor state), and Iowa (a rich agricultural state):

Sources of income, several important categories, four states, 1963–64, as a percentage of total income

State	Student fees	Federal research	State	Local	Private gifts and grants
California	9	44	21	8	4
New York	30	18	14	5	7
Mississippi	16	4	26	6	5
Iowa	20	10	28	1/2	5

SOURCE: Table 4.1-8.

Note especially the contrast in values between California and New York respecting student fees; the importance of federal research in California—as compared with Mississippi; the extent to which Mississippi and Iowa depend on fees and state government; the relative lack of state and federal government support in New York as compared with California.

TABLE 4.1-9 *Overall voluntary support, 1958–59 to 1967–68*

These facts indicate clearly that the increase of overall voluntary support of higher education in 1967–68 was the largest since 1964–65. The total amount of private gifts and grants received by the nation's colleges and universities in 1967–68 is estimated by CFAE to have been $1.570 billion, up 8.3% from the revised estimate of $1.450 billion in 1966–67. Revised estimates for the prior years are as follows (in billions):

1965–66	$1.410	*1961–62*	$0.950
1964–65	1.400	*1960–61*	0.900
1963–64	1.215	*1959–60*	0.815
1962–63	1.050	*1958–59*	0.760

SOURCE: Council for Financial Aid to Education, American Alumni Council, and National Association of Independent Schools, *Voluntary Support of Education, 1967–68*, New York, 1969, p. 4.

TABLE 4.1-10 *Total support by source, all colleges and universities reporting*

	1966–67		1967–68		*Percent change*
Foundations	$ 289,533	(22.8)	$ 320,982	(23.4)	+10.9
Nonalumni	319,918	(25.2)	349,459	(25.5)	+ 9.2
Alumni	277,747	(21.9)	307,477	(22.4)	+10.7
Business corporations	213,194	(16.8)	213,787	(15.6)	+ 0.3
Religious denominations	91,536	(7.2)	102,014	(7.4)	+11.4
Other	78,041	(6.1)	77,838	(5.7)	− 0.3
TOTAL	$1,269,969	(100.0)	$1,371,557	(100.0)	+ 8.0

SOURCE: Council for Financial Aid to Education, American Alumni Council, and National Association of Independent Schools, *Voluntary Support of Education, 1967–68,* New York, 1969, p. 6.

VOLUNTARY SUPPORT The following discussion is based primarily on the 1966–67 report sponsored by the Alumni Council for Financial Aid to Education and the National Association of Independent Schools.[4] Voluntary support increased from $760 million in 1958–59 to about $1,570 million in 1967–68 (Table 4.1-9). Nonalumni, welfare foundations, alumni, and corporations, in that order, gave the largest amounts in 1967–68 (Table 4.1-10). Average voluntary support per institution rose at varying rates by sources, 1956–57 to 1967–68. Alumni's contributions increased the most

[4] See the following: Council for Financial Aid to Education, *Voluntary Support of America's Colleges and Universities, 1964–65,* New York, 1966; Council for Financial Aid to Education and American Alumni Council, *Voluntary Support of Education, 1965–66 and 1966–67,* New York, 1967, 1968; and Council for Financial Aid to Education, American Alumni Council, and National Association of Independent Schools, *Voluntary Support of Education, 1967–68,* New York, 1969.

TABLE 4.1-11
Growth of voluntary support per institution, 1956–57 to 1967–68

	Average annual percentage rate of increase
Alumni	9.2
Business corporations	8.3
General welfare foundations	8.0
Nonalumni individuals	7.7
Above sources, as a group	8.3
Other sources (not shown)	3.5
Total voluntary support	7.5

SOURCE: Council for Financial Aid to Education, American Alumni Council, and National Association of Independent Schools, *Voluntary Support of Education, 1967–68,* New York, 1969, p. 5.

(Table 4.1-11 and Figure 4.1-1). Alumni giving to annual funds and general alumni support continue to rise. The number of donors to the alumni funds rose by more than 20 percent from 1962–63 to 1967–68. Gifts to alumni funds increased by about 50 percent and all alumni giving by 40 percent (Table 4.1-12).

From 1954–55 to 1967–68, the relative contributions of the main groups of donors changed to some extent (Table 4.1-13). Notice particularly the relative increases of 34 percent for general

FIGURE 4.1-1. *Voluntary support per institution, principal sources of support*

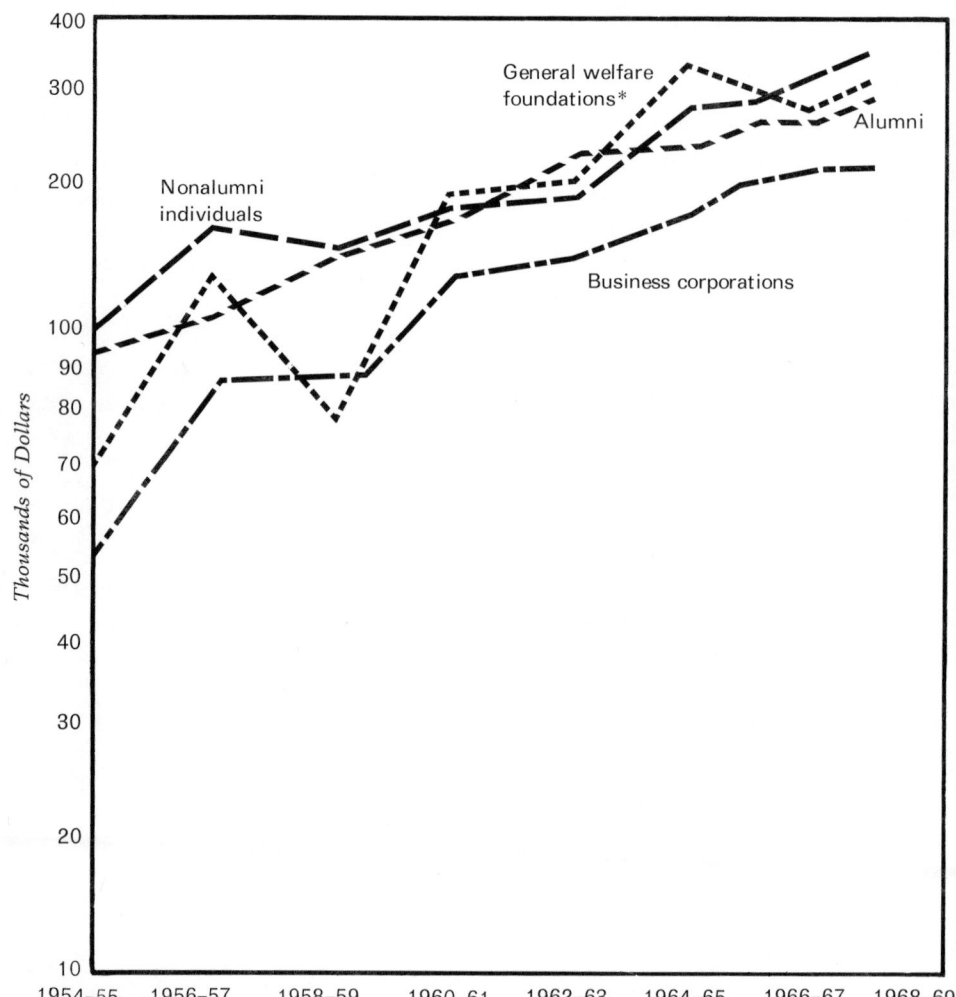

*Excludes Ford Foundation Faculty Salary Grants.

SOURCE: Council for Financial Aid to Education, American Alumni Council, and National Association of Independent Schools, *Voluntary Support of Education, 1967–68,* New York, 1969, p. 5.

TABLE 4.1-12 *Six years of annual giving and alumni support*

Year	Institutions reporting	Number of alumni donors to annual fund	Alumni gifts to annual fund	Average alumni gift to annual fund	Effectiveness of annual fund solicitation	Total of all alumni giving
1962-63	1,113	1,631,127	$62,973,669	$38.40	21.5%	$237,191,052
1963-64	750	1,701,366	70,681,938	44.14	21.8	220,056,148
1964-65	1,278	1,774,956	78,129,685	44.01	22.7	284,122,334
1965-66	1,109	1,872,565	88,771,329	47.41	20.2	283,093,503
1966-67	1,133	1,857,292	91,477,401	49.25	20.0	291,555,233
1967-68	1,396	1,990,164	98,242,540	49.36	20.0	332,719,578

SOURCE: Council for Financial Aid to Education, American Alumni Council, and National Association of Independent Schools, *Voluntary Support of Education, 1967-68*, New York, 1969, p. 6.

TABLE 4.1-13 *Amounts contributed by the various groups of donors, nine survey years (including percentage of grand total)*

Source	1954-55 (728 institutions)	1966-67 (1,042 institutions)	1967-68 (1,043 institutions)	Percentage changes, 1966-67 to 1967-68
Alumni	$67,766,515 (23.4%)	$277,746,466 (21.9%)	$307,477,335 (22.4%)	+10.7
Nonalumni individuals	71,921,913 (24.8%)	319,917,809 (25.2%)	349,458,619 (25.5%)	+ 9.2
*General welfare foundations**	50,247,321 (17.4%)	289,532,440 (22.8%)	320,982,109 (23.4%)	+10.9
Business corporations	39,432,625 (13.6%)	213,194,423 (16.8%)	213,786,718 (15.6%)	+ 0.3
Religious denominations	26,220,190 (9.1%)	91,536,257 (7.2%)	102,013,918 (7.4%)	+11.4
Nonalumni, nonchurch groups	18,681,898 (6.4%)	59,947,561 (4.7%)	60,749,625 (4.4%)	+ 1.3
Other sources	15,271,058 (5.3%)	18,093,580 (1.4%)	17,088,525 (1.3%)	− 5.6
TOTAL	$289,541,520 (100%)	$1,269,968,536 (100%)	$1,371,556,849 (100%)	+ 8.0

*Includes $199,522,710 in nonrecurring faculty salary endowment grants received from the Ford Foundation.

SOURCE: Council for Financial Aid to Education, American Alumni Council, and National Association of Independent Schools, *Voluntary Support of Education, 1967-68*, New York, 1969, p. 65.

welfare foundations and 15 percent for corporations. A drop of other sources from 5.3 to 1.4 percent is considerable but may be largely explained by changes in definitions. Support from religious sources also decreased substantially as a percentage of total voluntary support.

Table 4.1-14 shows the distribution of voluntary gifts from different sources among different types of institutions for 1967–68. Major private universities received 45 percent of total voluntary gifts, in contrast to 17 percent for state colleges and universities. The main beneficiaries of voluntary gifts in 1967 were major private universities, private coeducational colleges, and state-controlled

TABLE 4.1-14 *Voluntary support received in 1967–68 by 861 institutions participating both in the 1966–67 and the 1967–68 surveys, by various groups of donors (figures in parentheses are percentage changes in 1967–68 as compared with 1966–67)*

Group	Grand total of support	Business corporations	Religious denominations
Major private universities (59)	$ 591,704,337 (+11.7)	$ 72,877,040 (+ 4.0)	$27,731,013 (+15.0)
Private men's colleges (56)	58,561,558 (+ 9.0)	7,641,611 (+ 3.8)	2,526,250 (+51.8)
Private women's colleges (124)	68,595,069 (+10.6)	5,950,778 (+ 1.1)	4,190,184 (+17.8)
Private coeducational colleges (334)	261,101,111 (+ 2.4)	35,848,656 (− 2.2)	45,398,310 (+ 7.6)
Professional and specialized schools (53)	82,122,623 (+ 9.9)	29,821,914 (+ 0.5)	7,322,517 (+34.4)
Public institutions, state-controlled (141)	220,880,645 (+ 6.7)	52,058,599 (+ 1.5)	454,508 (−42.4)
Municipal colleges and universities (5)	9,808,691 (− 5.4)	1,939,943 (+45.8)	0
Junior colleges (89)	14,913,851 (+ 4.3)	1,550,288 (+23.7)	3,345,341 (− 7.8)
TOTAL (861)	$1,307,687,885 (+ 8.3)	$207,688,829 (+ 2.1)	$90,968,123 (+11.8)

NOTE: The year-to-year changes shown in this table are not all of equal significance. The total amount reported by any one class of institution from any one class of donor is subject to erratic behavior due to major fund-raising drives, the timing of corporate and foundation programs, large bequests and other nonrecurring influences. This is particularly true of the smaller groups of institutions and the smaller dollar figures. Thus, 19 out of the 48 entries in the body of this table show changes of plus or minus 20% or more; of these 19 large changes, 17 of them involve amounts less than $10 million in 1966–67. In many of these instances, the year-to-year change is primarily the result of one large gift to a single institution from a single donor. On the other hand, at least half of all the entries are sufficiently large, and the number of schools involved is sufficiently big, to ensure that the percentage change is meaningful. The row and column totals are likewise statistically significant.

SOURCE: Council for Financial Aid to Education, American Alumni Council, and National Association of Independent Schools, *Voluntary Support of Education, 1967–68*, New York, 1969, p. 67.

institutions, in decreasing order. This group accounted for over 80 percent of total voluntary support.

Business corporations favored major private universities (35 percent of total corporate gifts), state colleges and universities (25 percent), private coeducational colleges (17 percent), and professional and specialized schools (14 percent). Alumni supported major private universities (55 percent), private coeducational colleges (14 percent), and public institutions (12 percent). Nonalumni supported major private universities (41 percent), private coeducational colleges (27 percent), and public institutions (12 percent). Welfare foundations also concentrated on the major

Alumni	*Nonalumni individuals*	*General welfare foundations*	*Other groups and sources*
$163,827,128 (+30.3)	$131,902,592 (− 4.0)	$172,093,378 (+14.6)	$23,273,186 (+ 3.9)
23,989,391 (+23.3)	12,706,362 (− 1.5)	10,625,567 (− 8.7)	1,072,377 (+46.9)
22,203,635 (− 2.5)	22,416,948 (+16.3)	11,147,360 (+22.7)	2,686,164 (+86.3)
41,696,750 (−11.7)	87,357,901 (+18.0)	41,796,608 (− 3.4)	9,002,886 (−22.4)
12,597,759 (+15.2)	18,840,823 (+ 7.7)	10,899,814 (+43.6)	2,639,796 (−26.9)
35,417,429 (0.0)	38,704,854 (+12.7)	61,556,794 (+ 9.0)	32,688,461 (+14.0)
936,344 (+42.4)	3,614,156 (−34.2)	657,821 (−34.6)	2,660,427 (+41.3)
1,505,227 (−42.0)	5,479,281 (+17.3)	2,441,337 (+52.2)	592,377 (+ 7.7)
$302,173,663 (+14.1)	$321,022,917 (+ 5.0)	$311,218,679 (+10.8)	$74,615,674 (+ 5.3)

TABLE 4.1-15
Number of
institutions of
higher education
receiving $1
million or more
of private
support

	1958–59	1960–61	1962–63
Major private universities	37	46	44
Private coeducational colleges	31	37	54
State universities	22	27	35
Professional and specialized institutions	16	13	11
Private men's colleges	10	13	15
Private women's colleges	9	7	11
Municipal colleges and universities	2	1	2
Junior colleges	0	1	2
	127	145	174

SOURCE: Council for Financial Aid to Education and American Alumni Council, *Voluntary Support of Education, 1966–67*, New York, 1968, p. 8.

private universities (55 percent), public institutions (20 percent), and private coeducational colleges (13 percent).

The number of institutions of higher education receiving $1 million or more of private support from 1958–59 to 1966–67 is shown in Table 4.1-15. The 20 institutions receiving the largest

TABLE 4.1-16   *Institutions reporting highest 20 totals of voluntary support, 1967–68*

Institution	Voluntary support	Institution	Voluntary support
Harvard University	$66,025,694	University of Pennsylvania	$18,423,580
Yale University	33,382,106		
Columbia University	32,076,647	Johns Hopkins University	16,440,285
University of Chicago	30,710,641	University of Texas (system)	15,755,121
University of California (10 campuses)	30,128,408	University of Wisconsin	15,434,663
Stanford University	29,719,695		
Brigham Young University	29,194,411	Washington University	15,228,147
Massachusetts Institute of Technology	25,881,024	Vanderbilt University	14,664,874
		University of Rochester	14,461,179
Cornell University	24,294,996	Case Western Reserve University	14,241,994
New York University	23,556,551		
University of Michigan	21,018,600	Northwestern University	14,223,298

SOURCE: Council for Financial Aid to Education, American Alumni Council, and National Association of Independent Schools, *Voluntary Support of Education, 1967–68*, New York, 1969, p. 9.

1964-65	1965-66	1966-67
49	49	47
91	78	85
47	52	53
15	22	25
21	20	19
13	15	15
2	2	2
2	1	1
240	239	247

amounts of voluntary support in 1967–68 are shown in Table 4.1-16. Harvard is first with gifts of $66 million, almost twice as much as its nearest competitor.

Table 4.1-17 compares the proportion of voluntary gifts to the proportion of enrollment for 1956–57. The maximum ratio was 1.95 for major private universities; the minimum, 0.10 for municipal and urban institutions.

The change in the relative distribution of voluntary support from 1956–57 to 1967–68 gives a useful indication of the relative growth and decline of voluntary support of educational institutions by type. Of great significance is an average increase of 92 percent in the share of state universities and colleges as compared with a decline of 9 percent for major private universities, of 27 percent

TABLE 4.1-17
Ratio of proportion of gifts to proportion of enrollment, 1956–57

Group	Ratio
Major private universities	1.95
Private women's colleges	1.9
Professional and technical	1.7
Private men's colleges	1.3
Private coeducational	1.3
State universities and land-grant colleges	0.25
Junior colleges	0.25
Municipal and urban universities	0.10

SOURCE: S. E. Harris, *Higher Education: Resources and Finance,* McGraw-Hill Book Company, New York, 1962, p. 462.

for private women's colleges, and of 15 percent for private coeducational colleges. Voluntary support of municipal colleges and universities, a relatively small item, grew by 133 percent (Table 4.1-18). In general, the private schools lost ground to the public colleges and universities.

VOLUNTARY SUPPORT VIS-À-VIS BUDGET STRUCTURE   The distribution of voluntary gifts by type of expenditure seems to be much out of line with the current allocation of expenditures. For example, the following rough estimates can be made for 1963–64 (see page 607):[5]

[5] U.S. Office of Education, *Digest of Educational Statistics, 1968,* 1968, p. 96; and Council for Financial Aid to Education and American Alumni Council, *Voluntary Support of Education, 1966–67,* New York, 1968, p. 66.

TABLE 4.1-18
Comparison of grand totals of voluntary support (including percentage of grand total, and average per institution)

Group*	1956–57
Major private universities	$356,813,827 (48.4%) (65) Av. $5,489,443
Private coeducational colleges	176,477,880 (23.9%) (327) Av. $539,688
State universities and colleges	65,251,252 (8.8%) (109) Av. $598,635
Professional and specialized schools	39,756,632 (5.4%) (61) Av. $651,748
Private women's colleges	51,642,395 (7.0%) (129) Av. $400,329
Private men's colleges	36,819,993 (5.0%) (66) Av. $557,879
Junior colleges	9,124,556 (1.2%) (138) Av. $66,120
Municipal universities and colleges	2,231,570 (0.3%) (9) Av. $247,952
	$738,118,105 (100%)† (904) Av. $816,502 minus Ford $595,792

* In every survey, each institution is classified in the category appropriate to its status in that year. Since the statuses of many institutions have changed over the years, the data by category is not strictly comparable from one survey to another.

† Minus Ford Foundation faculty salary endowment grants, the total is $538,595,395.

SOURCE: Council for Financial Aid to Education, American Alumni Council, and National Association of Independent Schools, *Voluntary Support of Education, 1967–68,* New York, 1969, p. 64.

Comparisons of structure of expenditures and gifts, 1963–64		Percentage of current expenditures, 1963–64	Voluntary giving,* 1963–64
	Instruction and departmental research	30.6	5.3 (faculty)
	Organized research	21.5	12.3
	Physical plant operation and maintenance	7.5	26.0
	Student aid	3.3	12.0

* Estimated.

1966–67	1967–68
$481,364,776 (37.9%) (55) Av. $8,752,086	$605,367,781 (44.1%) (61) Av. $9,924,061
289,426,642 (22.8%) (375) Av. $771,804	277,439,374 (20.2%) (372) Av. $745,804
233,130,557 (18.4%) (186) Av. $1,253,390	231,713,305 (16.9%) (195) Av. $1,188,273
114,280,236 (9.0%) (75) Av. $1,523,736	99,067,994 (7.2%) (77) Av. $1,286,597
65,232,959 (5.1%) (143) Av. $456,174	69,986,152 (5.1%) (136) Av. $514,604
57,154,250 (4.5%) (64) Av. $893,035	58,692,377 (4.3%) (57) Av. $1,029,690
18,745,193 (1.5%) (137) Av. $136,826	19,422,586 (1.5%) (137) Av. $141,770
10,633,923 (0.8%) (7) Av. $1,519,131	9,867,235 (0.7%) (8) Av. $1,233,404
$1,269,968,536 (100%) (1,042) Av. $1,218,779	$1,371,556,849 (100%) (1,043) Av. $1,315,011

Clearly, instruction and organized research are underfinanced through voluntary giving, and physical plant and student aid are treated relatively generously. Roughly one-half of all voluntary gifts goes to capital.[6] But capital includes much more than plant; it includes endowment, for example.

PURPOSES OF SUPPORT In nine surveys covering the period 1954–55 to 1967–68, voluntary support rose from $290 million to $1,372 million (Table 4.1-19). But there was not much variation in the percentage of total support going for each purpose (Figure 4.1-2). In 1967–68, the largest amounts went to:

Purpose of support, 1967–68	Percentage of total support
Unrestricted	33.5
Physical plant	23.3
Basic research	12.5
Student financial aid	12.9
Faculty compensation	5.5
Other	12.3

SOURCE: Table 4.1-19.

[6] Council for Financial Aid to Education, American Alumni Council, and National Association of Independent Schools, *Voluntary Support of Education, 1967–68,* New York, 1969, p. 10.

TABLE 4.1-19 *Comparison of purposes of support, nine survey years (including percentage of grand total)*

Purposes	1954–55	1966–67	1967–68
Unrestricted	$82,456,728 (28.6%)	$380,769,833 (30.0%)	$460,028,463 (33.5%)
Physical plant	66,481,431 (23.0%)	312,537,142 (24.6%)	319,357,604 (23.3%)
Basic research	36,267,510 (12.5%)	156,732,635 (12.4%)	171,736,023 (12.5%)
Student financial aid	35,604,446 (12.2%)	174,024,883 (13.7%)	176,819,768 (12.9%)
Faculty compensation	21,470,718 (7.4%)	84,405,599 (6.6%)	75,240,919 (5.5%)
Other purposes	47,260,687 (16.3%)	161,498,444 (12.7%)	168,374,072 (12.3%)
TOTAL	$289,541,520 (100%)	$1,269,968,536 (100%)	$1,371,556,849 (100%)

SOURCE: Council for Financial Aid to Education, American Alumni Council, and National Association of Independent Schools, *Voluntary Support of Education, 1967–68,* New York, 1969, p. 66.

FIGURE 4.1-2. *Voluntary support per institution, principal purposes of support*

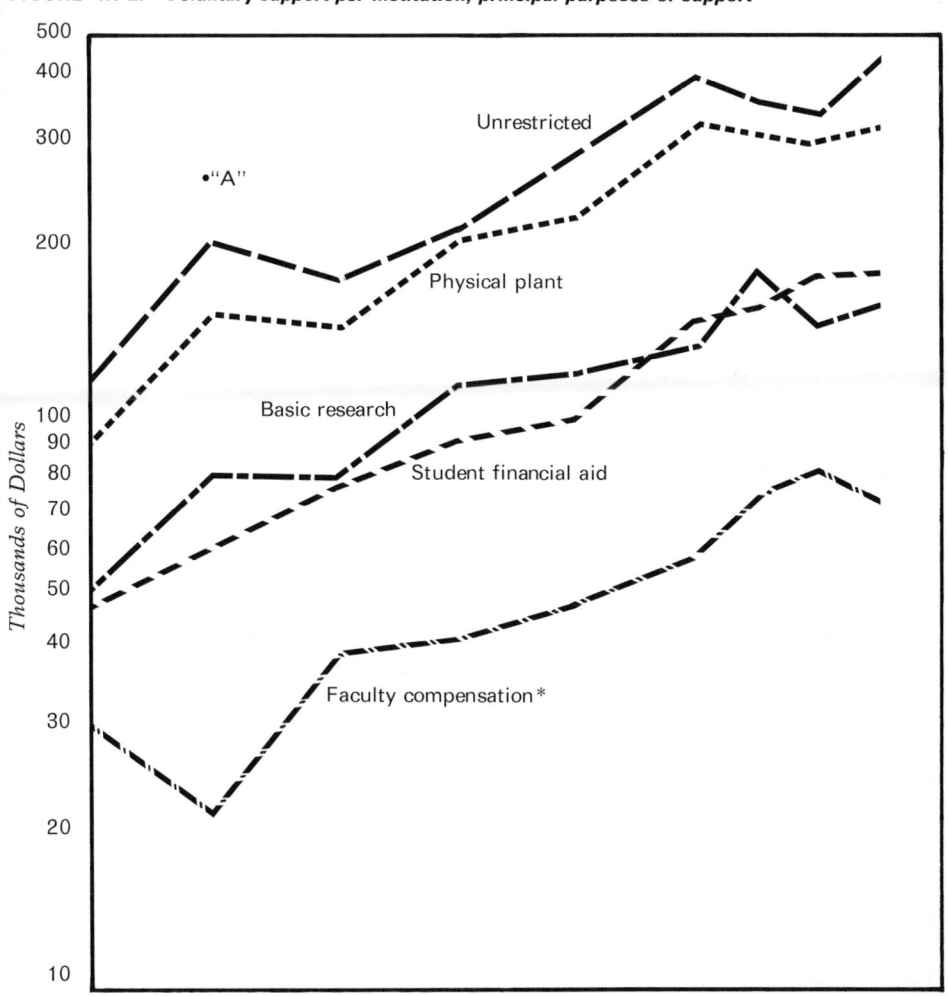

*Excludes Ford Foundation Faculty Salary Grants

SOURCE: Council for Financial Aid to Education, American Alumni Council, and National Association of Independent Schools, *Voluntary Support of Education, 1967–68,* New York, 1969, p. 62.

In relation to current expenditures, gifts were relatively too large for physical plant and student aid and too small for faculty compensation.[7] In recent years unrestricted support has been growing faster than restricted support. From 1966–67 to 1967–68, unrestricted gifts increased by 20.8 percent, while restricted gifts increased by 2.5 percent.

[7] Ibid., p. 66. See also J. L. Chase, *Doctoral Study: Fellowships and Capacity of Graduate Schools,* U.S. Office of Education, 1961, p. 250.

Figure 4.1-3 shows large relative gains in voluntary support for educational and general expenditures from 1919–20 to 1955–56. Educational and general income increased from 11.3 percent of total voluntary support to 41.9 percent in 1955–56. Plant funds rose from 1.7 to 24.5 percent of voluntary gifts, while endowment support decreased from 76.0 percent to 33.6 percent of total support in 1955–56.

GENERAL ISSUES   A large decline in foundation grants as a proportion of voluntary support of education in recent years points to serious financial problems in the future.[8] A possible remedy is to continue increasing relative support from corporations. Corporate support increased from 13.4 percent of total voluntary support in 1947 to 39.1 per-

[8] American Council on Education, *A Fact Book on Higher Education,* Washington, D.C., 1967, p. 125.

FIGURE 4.1-3. *Percent of private gifts and grants contributed for endowment, plant, and educational and general purposes, from 1919–20 to 1955–56*

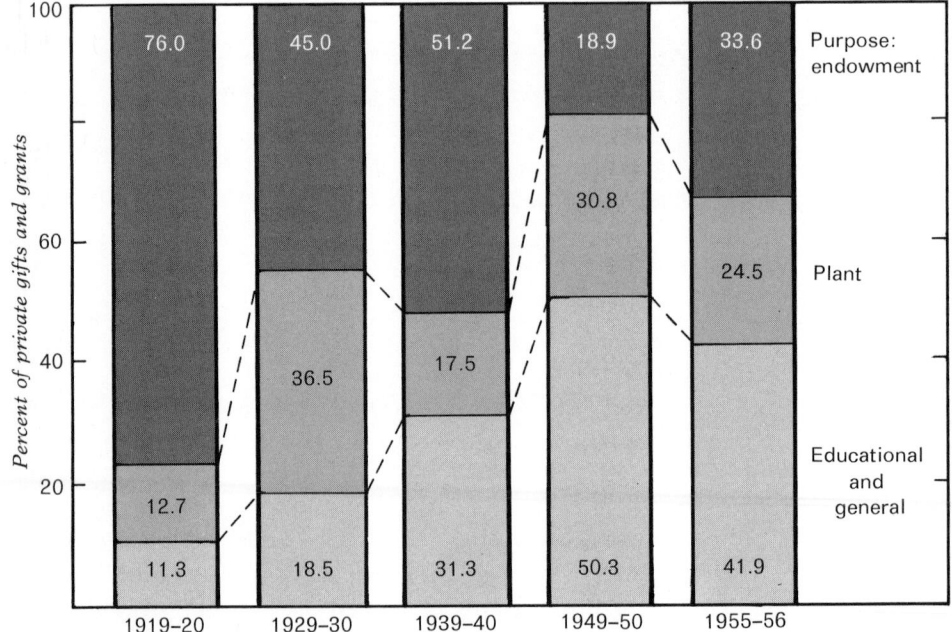

SOURCE: U.S. Office of Education, *College and University Endowment Investments: A Survey,* 1959, p. 4.

TABLE 4.1-20 *Data relating to college and university attendance and completion for the leading 24 donors of each of 19 institutions*

	Donor group		
College and university attendance and completion	*Top 24*	*Top 10*	*Top 5*
College attendance:			
Known to have attended college	342	137	67
Known not to have attended college	32	18	9
No information	82	35	19
Known to have attended "beneficiary" college	276	106	56
College completion:			
Known to have attended and received a college degree	303	119	57
Known to have attended without receiving college degree	39	18	10
Completion of a higher degree:			
Known to have completed a higher degree	115	45	22
Known to have completed a higher degree at "beneficiary" institution	64	19	7
Total number of donors	456	190	95

SOURCE: S. E. Harris, *Higher Education: Resources and Finance,* McGraw-Hill Book Company, New York, 1962, p. 474.

cent in 1959. Moreover, business corporations are much more generous to education than to all other charitable objectives.[9]

My 1958 study of 456 top donors in 19 institutions of higher education revealed that more than 80 percent of the top donors who attended college were alumni of the college to which they contributed. A surprising fact is the large percentage of the top donors who completed a higher degree at the beneficiary institution (Table 4.1-20). Table 4.1-21 shows the occupational distribution of these top donors; 49 percent were businessmen.

ACCUMULA-TION OF PRODUCTIVE FUNDS[10] Over the past 330 to 340 years, institutions of higher education have accumulated about $10 billion of endowment. The growth has been uneven over the years and among institutions. In the last few years, Harvard's endowment has fluctuated around $1 billion (market value), but it took more than two centuries to accumulate the first million. Harvard's relative position has

[9] See also Chapter 4.3.

[10] See also Chapter 4.3.

TABLE 4.1-21 The occupational distribution of the 24 leading donors of 19 institutions

Occupation	Top 24		Top 10		Top 5	
	Number	Mean percentage for 19 IHL*	Number	Mean percentage for 19 IHL*	Number	Mean percentage for 19 IHL*
Business	222	48.9	109	57.4	62	65.2
Lawyer	44	9.6	15	7.8	11	11.3
Engineer	33	7.2	10	5.2	3	3.1
Physician	26	5.7	10	5.2		
Educator	20	4.4	3	1.6	2	2.1
Government	4	0.9	1	0.5		
Dentist	1	0.2	1	0.5		
Subtotal	350	76.7	149	77.5	77	81.2
Other	31	6.8	9	4.7	3	3.1
Women (not otherwise classified)	17	3.7	8	4.2	3	3.1
Retired (not otherwise classified)	6	1.3	1	0.5	1	1.1
No occupation	10	2.2	6	3.1	4	4.1
No information	42	9.2	17	8.8	7	7.2
TOTAL	456	100.1	190	100.1	95	99.8

* Institutions of higher learning.

SOURCE: S. E. Harris, *Higher Education: Resources and Finance*, McGraw-Hill Book Company, New York, 1962, p. 476.

TABLE 4.1-22
Gifts to institutions of higher education, various years (figures in thousands of dollars)

Year	Institution of higher education		Total
1898–99	Stanford	= $11,100	$21,925
	Harvard	= 1,544	
1902	= 31 gifts > $100,000		17,100
	University of Chicago	= 2,983	
	Harvard University	= 1,095	
	University of Pennsylvania	= 936	
1912	= 54 gifts > $100,000		18,527
	5 gifts > $1,000,000		
	Princeton	= 1,707	
	University of California	= 1,239	
	University of Chicago	= 1,144	
	Harvard University	= 447	
1928–1930	= 167 gifts > $100,000		
	17 gifts > $1,000,000		
	Yale	= 26,520	
	Harvard	= 12,659	
	University of Chicago	= 14,515	
	Northwestern	= 8,062	
	Columbia	= 5,097	
	Cornell	= 2,723	

SOURCE: *Educational Report, 1898–99*, p. 1564; *1902*, p. 1354; *1912*, p. 250; *Biennial Survey of Education, 1928–1950*, pp. 378–379; in Council for Financial Aid to Education and American Alumni Council, *Voluntary Support of Education, 1965–66*, New York, 1967, pp. 4, 9. Cf. S. E. Harris, *The Economics of Harvard*, McGraw-Hill Book Company, New York, 1970, chaps. 35–39.

also fluctuated over the years. From 1776 to 1865, Harvard received $340,000 for five endowment chairs, but Yale obtained seven such gifts, bringing in $750,000. In 1967–68, however, Harvard received $68 million from private sources—twice as much as any competitor.

The relatively high level of gifts before World War II as compared with recent years and the varying results experienced by different institutions is evident from Table 4.1-22. These figures might be compared to gifts of about $1.5 billion in 1967–68. Twenty institutions received $500 million, or one-third of the total.

4.2. *Government's* *Contribution*

Government at all levels provided 48 percent of institutional expenditures for higher education in 1967–68 and is projected by the Carnegie Commission to supply 49 percent in 1976–77.[1]

[1] Carnegie Commission on Higher Education, *Quality and Equality: New Levels of Federal Responsibility for Higher Education,* McGraw-Hill Book Company, New York, 1968. The 1976–77 estimate is based on need rather than actual outlays.

VARIATION IN STATE GOVERNMENT INCOME AND XPENDITURES Governments of poor states have smaller per capita incomes and make fewer per capita expenditures than do governments of rich states. But poor states receive more federal aid per capita than rich states (Table 4.2-1). In 1958 per capita income from the federal government of the 12 poorest states was more than double the federal income per capita of the 12 richest states. Per capita

ABLE 4.2-1 *State and local governments' income, federal grants, taxes, expenditures, 12 richest ates* and 12 poorest states† per capita, 1958*

ates	Income	Income from federal government	Taxes per $1,000 income	All taxes	Property taxes	Total expenditures	Expenditures for education	Expenditures per institution of higher learning
2 richest	$2,133	$12.25	$83.49	$198.85	$94.14	$303.87	$103.47	$14.00
2 poorest	1,186	26.63	90.91	136.82	48.22	213.72	77.24	14.11

ichest states in order: Delaware (highest), Connecticut, Nevada, New Jersey, California, New York, linois, Michigan, Washington, Massachusetts, Maryland, Ohio.

oorest states in order: Mississippi (lowest), Arkansas, South Carolina, Alabama, North Carolina, ennessee, Kentucky, Georgia, North Dakota, Louisiana, South Dakota, New Mexico.

OURCES: *Survey of Current Business,* August, 1959, and U.S. Census, *Governmental Finances in 958* (author's calculations); in S. E. Harris, *The Market for College Graduates,* Harvard University Press, ambridge, Mass., 1949, table 15.

expenditures on education in the 12 poorest states, however, were only three-fourths of the per capita expenditures on education in the 12 richest states.

The following table compares federal grants-in-aid to state governments with federal grants-in-aid for education in 1950 and 1968:[2]

	1950	1968
Total state governments	$2.75	$13.6*
For education	0.35	3.5

* 1967.

[2] U.S. Department of Labor, *U.S. Economic Report of the President, 1969,* 1969, p. 306; and U.S. Bureau of the Census, *Statistical Abstract of the United States, 1968,* 1968, p. 419.

Year	Veterans' services and benefits	Health, welfare, and labor	Education and general research	Agriculture and agricultural resources
1902	$ 1,005		$ 1,210	$ 786
1912	1,152		2,510	1,593
1920	1,095	$ 1,759	4,637	5,912
1925	706	1,509	8,473	7,300
1929	560	1,482	9,426	11,003
1930	575	746	10,010	11,875
1931	453	21,199	10,617	12,990
1932	786	59,908	11,158	12,990
1933	758	63,133	10,349	12,966
1934	522	1,817,427	9,623	12,710
1935	499	2,243,671	12,622	12,694
1936	568	2,248,197	13,055	21,656
1937	610	2,546,757	13,800	21,954
1938	674	1,972,366	24,213	32,942
1939	720	2,622,480	24,678	92,370
1940	1,368	2,066,362	24,444	143,113
1941	1,432	1,771,307	25,213	110,129
1942	1,375	1,506,514	25,521	77,519
1943	1,176	902,582	26,056	47,690
1944	1,181	616,151	25,479	66,319
1945	1,194	570,176	24,956	81,862
1946	20,238	567,873	25,308	92,427

Federal grants-in-aid for education as a percentage of grants-in-aid to state governments rose from 13 to 26 percent from 1950 to 1968. From 1902 to 1962, however, the share of grants-in-aid to state and local government going to education and general research declined from 40 to 4 percent (Table 4.2-2).

STATE GOVERNMENT SUPPORT From 1959–60 to 1964–65, appropriations of state tax funds for operating expenses of institutions of higher education rose from $1,390 million to $2,439 million—a gain of 75 percent (Table 4.2-3). The states with the smallest percentage increases in support for higher education in these five years were Montana (19

Other natural resources	Commerce, housing, transportation, communication	Total*
		$ 3,001
		5,255
	$ 20,483	33,886
$ 346	95,412	113,746
1,133	85,999	109,603
1,318	79,839	104,363
1,623	138,128	185,010
1,664	132,006	218,512
1,523	104,237†	192,966
1,516	444†	1,842,242
1,511	326†	2,271,323
1,473	27,565†	2,312,514
1,539	79,168†	2,663,828
1,528	143,103	2,174,826
2,474	161,277	2,903,999
6,392	153,519	2,395,198
4,120	170,647	2,082,848
4,518	204,127	1,819,574
9,005	299,847	1,286,356
7,359	286,670	1,003,159
7,473	218,201	903,862
8,274	180,505	894,625

TABLE 4.2-2
(continued)

Year	Veterans' services and benefits	Health, welfare, and labor	Education and general research	Agriculture and agricultural resources
1947	59,182	902,093	32,170	65,116
1948	84,977	1,024,488	37,154	70,940
1949	31,587	1,231,538	36,921	86,631
1950	15,277	1,562,252	38,614	106,276
1951	8,998	1,637,185	48,814	98,344
1952	6,656	1,661,957	122,234	83,865
1953	6,326	1,811,136	230,958	97,337
1954	6,863	1,890,389	203,210	213,173
1955	7,686	1,854,170	239,303	247,730
1956	8,091	2,109,270	208,672	389,277
1957	8,217	2,178,892	204,570	381,786
1958	8,326	2,523,430	165,881‡	278,195
1959	8,316	2,777,160	296,747‡	322,470
1960	7,880	2,923,591	363,558‡	275,268
1961 *(est.)*	9,096	3,105,400	384,525‡	297,937
1962 *(est.)*	9,024	3,243,596	306,417‡	322,632

* Data in this table are drawn from tabulations made in prior years by the Labor and Welfare Division, Bureau of the Budget and for more recent years from special analyses dealing with grants-in-aid and accompanying the President's Budget.

† Federal aid highway program financed for these years out of emergency relief funds.

‡ Includes $5 to $7 million for services to Indians embracing both education and welfare functions.

SOURCE: U.S. Senate, Committee on Government Operations, *Research in the Service of Man, Hearings before Subcommittee on Government Research,* February and March 1967, pp. 172–173.

percent), Nebraska (24 percent), and Oklahoma (24 percent). The states with the largest percentage increases were New York (191 percent), Maine (189 percent), and Kentucky (186 percent). In general, Eastern states with little support of public higher education in the past experienced large increases. California, with a massive, state-supported system already in operation, expanded its outlays by 87 percent.

State aid for operating expenses of public junior colleges rose by 147 percent from 1959–60 to 1964–65—from $53 million to $131 million (Table 4.2-4). The number of states appropriating

Other natural resources	*Commerce, housing, transportation, communication*	*Total**
9,754	601,881	1,670,196
11,473	387,461	1,616,493
13,997	442,225	1,842,899
16,957	475,006	2,214,382
17,740	433,970	2,245,051
19,755	481,699	2,376,166
22,771	594,384	2,762,912
24,938	630,299	2,968,872
25,932	723,634	3,098,455
26,606	873,715	3,615,631
26,577	1,016,359	3,816,401
31,330	1,723,940	4,731,102
34,481	2,877,781	6,316,955
35,335	3,241,641	6,847,273
33,108	3,273,917	7,103,983
33,742	3,481,610	7,397,021

substantial amounts for public junior colleges grew from 17 to 23 in this period. In 1964–65 California accounted for $48 million, or 37 percent of total state support for public junior colleges. Five states—California, Florida, New York, Washington, and Texas—together accounted for almost 75 percent of total public junior college support in 1964–65.

In 1961–62 state and local government funds for student higher education only were estimated at $1,216 million. On the assumption of increases in support reflecting probable economic growth, these outlays would increase to $1,973 million by 1970. In order

(Text continued on p. 622)

TABLE 4.2-3
Appropriations of state tax funds for operating expenses of higher education for six consecutive fiscal years (in thousands of dollars), with total change over a five-year period shown in dollar gains and percentage gains

States (1)	1959–60 (2)	1960–61 (3)	1961–62 (4)	1962–63 (5)
Alabama	21,823	22,397	20,535	22,659
Alaska	2,111	2,323	3,023	3,301
Arizona	14,042	16,218	18,305	21,007
Arkansas	13,551	13,551	16,599	16,599
California	188,604	221,592	247,172	277,708
Colorado	17,271	24,332	27,149	31,255
Connecticut	12,273	13,080	14,855	15,948
Delaware	3,731	3,734	4,368	5,094
Florida	40,392	41,412	51,438	53,452
Georgia	24,058	26,605	29,046	32,162
Hawaii	4,958	5,825	7,254	8,515
Idaho	8,799	8,800	10,137	10,137
Illinois	90,289	90,290	116,293	116,293
Indiana	45,463	50,163	55,316	62,709
Iowa	34,630	34,861	39,682	39,705
Kansas	25,036	27,938	30,172	35,423
Kentucky	14,954	19,672	24,491	29,573
Louisiana	40,062	44,557	48,316	46,760
Maine	3,356	5,599	7,238	7,429
Maryland	23,818	25,166	27,208	30,678
Massachusetts	12,167	13,361	15,281	16,503
Michigan	95,599	101,836	102,816	109,759
Minnesota	36,173	38,920	43,908	45,117
Mississippi	15,118	18,347	18,347	19,863
Missouri	24,744	25,641	29,251	33,603
Montana	11,230	11,231	10,660	10,661
Nebraska	15,217	15,218	17,077	17,078
Nevada	3,682	4,107	4,863	5,325
New Hamphshire	3,973	4,106	4,717	4,733
New Jersey	21,982	24,457	28,421	34,179
New Mexico	11,165	11,239	13,002	14,372
New York	78,546	94,115	116,879	163,656
North Carolina	28,419	30,574	36,087	36,815
North Dakota	9,368	9,368	10,505	10,505
Ohio	43,331	45,326	52,014	55,620

1963–64 (6)	1964–65 (7)	Five-year gain (8)	Percentage gain (9)
29,133	30,421	8,598	39%
4,817	5,300	3,189	151%
25,683	29,742	15,700	112%
20,369	20,369	6,818	50%
301,304	351,982	163,378	87%
35,279	35,837	18,566	107%
18,585	19,706	7,433	61%
5,831	6,493	2,762	74%
68,143	75,695	35,303	87%
35,270	41,770	17,712	74%
10,867	12,580	7,622	154%
11,203	11,203	2,404	27%
148,170	148,170	57,881	64%
70,866	80,134	34,671	76%
48,275	48,328	13,698	40%
38,390	44,583	19,547	78%
32,164	42,782	27,828	186%
55,847	65,031	24,969	62%
9,099	9,709	6,353	189%
34,812	39,177	15,359	64%
19,874	28,415	16,248	134%
115,604	138,063	42,464	44%
49,710	55,059	18,886	49%
19,873	25,931	10,813	72%
44,526	46,847	22,103	89%
12,177	13,367	2,137	19%
18,820	18,820	3,603	24%
6,042	6,518	2,836	77%
5,146	5,104	1,131	28%
40,020	45,816	23,834	108%
15,960	18,636	7,471	67%
182,918	228,614	150,068	191%
46,768	51,431	23,012	81%
12,079	12,109	2,741	29%
60,670	67,670	24,339	56%

TABLE 4.2-3
(continued)

States (1)	1959–60 (2)	1960–61 (3)	1961–62	1962–63 (5)
Oklahoma	27,014	27,020	30,014	30,020
Oregon	28,719	28,719	34,796	34,263
Pennsylvania	43,471	43,472	46,431	56,187
Rhode Island	4,477	5,271	5,826	7,697
South Carolina	12,113	13,141	14,449	15,440
South Dakota	8,078	8,128	8,675	8,702
Tennessee	17,022	17,023	21,522	22,359
Texas	71,021	72,133	84,873	90,282
Utah	13,139	13,139	15,580	15,580
Vermont	3,264	3,399	3,759	3,750
Virginia	19,943	23,187	23,983	34,625
Washington	46,909	47,441	58,733	58,387
West Virginia	14,791	16,919	19,938	20,743
Wisconsin	34,834	37,417	40,895	44,670
Wyoming	4,935	4,935	5,916	5,916
TOTAL	1,389,665	1,507,305	1,717,815	1,892,817

SOURCE: National Association of State Universities and Land-grant Colleges, *Appropriation of State Tax Funds for Operating Expenses of Higher Education, 1964–65,* Washington, D.C., 1964, Sept. 15, 1964 release.

to finance a balance of expenditures for higher education, however, state and local government support would have to increase to $3,034 million by 1970 (Table 4.2-5).

GOVERNMENT REVENUE AND EXPENDITURE TRENDS

The following table shows the distribution of tax revenue among the three levels of government for 1966–67:[3]

Revenue, three levels of government, 1966–67

	Revenue from own sources		Revenue, allowing for intergovernmental transfers	
	Billions of dollars	Percent	Billions of dollars	Percent
Total	$253	100.0	$253	100.0
Federal	161	63.7	146	57.6
State	47	18.5	43	16.8
Local	45	17.8	65	25.6

[3] U.S. Bureau of the Census, *Governmental Finances in 1966–67,* Government Finance Series GF67, no. 3, 1968, p. 2.

1963–64 (6)	1964–65 (7)	Five-year gain (8)	Percentage gain (9)
33,505	33,505	6,491	24%
39,923	39,998	11,279	39%
66,064	68,819	25,348	58%
7,963	10,283	5,806	130%
17,360	19,286	7,173	59%
10,133	12,338	4,260	53%
28,324	31,892	14,870	87%
114,924	114,156	43,135	61%
19,154	19,154	6,015	46%
4,986	5,445	2,181	67%
35,858	39,527	19,584	98%
69,913	71,973	25,064	53%
22,286	23,761	8,970	61%
51,490	60,410	25,576	73%
6,707	6,707	1,772	36%
182,884	2,438,666	1,049,001	75.4%

In 1966–67 the federal government received 63.7 percent of total tax revenue, state government received 18.5 percent, and local government received 17.8 percent. Intergovernmental transfers took money away from federal and state governments and added to the revenue of local government.

The federal government depends heavily on taxes that are based on ability to pay and productive of large revenues. This contrasts strikingly with the tax structure of state and local governments. In 1966–67 the federal government received 83 percent of its tax revenue from income taxes, whereas state governments received only 22 percent of their revenue from this source, and local governments received only 3 percent of their revenue from income taxes (Table 4.2-6).

Most expenditures on education are by state and local governments. In 1966–67 the federal government spent only $6.2 billion on education, of which $3.9 billion was used in intergovernmental transfers. State governments spent $21.2 billion on education in 1966–67, and local government spent $28.9 billion. Direct outlays

(Text continued on p. 631)

TABLE 4.2-4 *Appropriations of state tax funds for operating expenses of local public community-junior colleges for fiscal years 1959–60 to 1964–65*

Five years ago the aggregate of state aid for operating expenses of local public community-junior colleges was about $53 million for the year. Currently it is nearly 2½ times that sum. The number of states appropriating substantial amounts has grown from 17 to 23.

States (1)	1959–60 (2)	1960–61 (3)	1961–62 (4)	1962–63 (5)	1963–64 (6)
California	$26,539	$26,280	$33,189	$33,900	$ 37,460
Florida	3,129	4,149	5,395	7,409	12,900
New York	3,450	4,610	5,690	7,100	9,500
Washington	4,902	5,433	6,976	6,630	9,270
Texas	5,178	5,178	7,000	7,000	8,256
Michigan	3,620	3,820	4,382	5,677	6,272
Illinois	2,150	2,150	3,250	3,250	6,759
Arizona	300	400	453	585	2,273
Mississippi	1,638	2,147	2,147	2,363	2,362
Minnesota	605	670	878	1,059	1,607
Missouri	NR†	NR	350	350	1,519
New Jersey	30	30	130	100	200
Colorado	475	1,050	1,050	1,339	1,346
Maryland	405	432	554	869	1,254
Oregon	NR	NR	426	840	1,350
North Carolina	150	234	409	462	388
Iowa	400	631	768	791	787
Pennsylvania	0	0	0	0	NR
Kansas	0	0	325	385	466
Ohio	0	0	0	0	220
Wyoming	200	200	317	317	360
Georgia	NR	NR	NR	NR	NR
North Dakota	115	115	119	119	220
TOTAL	$53,286	$57,529	$73,808	$80,545	$104,769

Weighted average (approximate)

* The Minnesota junior colleges are to become state institutions, and no longer to derive any tax support for operating expenses from the local taxing subdivisions.

† NR = no response.

It appears that in seven of these states the state aid for operating expenses has been doubled within the two years since fiscal year 1962–63.

SOURCE: National Association of State Universities and Land-grant Colleges, *Appropriation of State Tax Funds for Operating Expenses of Higher Education, 1964–65*, Washington, D.C., 1964, p. 3.

1964–65 (7)	Two-year gain (8)	Percentage gain (9)
48,000	$14,100	$41\frac{1}{4}$
15,767	8,358	113
12,711	5,611	79
11,330	4,700	71
8,284	1,284	$18\frac{1}{4}$
6,905	1,228	$21\frac{1}{2}$
6,759	3,509	108
3,858	3,272	$559\frac{1}{2}$
2,850	487	$20\frac{1}{2}$
2,188*	1,129	$106\frac{1}{2}$
1,839	1,489	$425\frac{1}{2}$
1,700	1,600	1600
1,523	184	$13\frac{1}{2}$
1,512	643	74
1,425	585	70
850	388	84
840	49	$6\frac{1}{4}$
500	500	
480	95	$24\frac{1}{2}$
461	461	
360	43	$13\frac{1}{2}$
300	300	
250	131	110
130,692	$50,147	
		$62\frac{1}{4}$

TABLE 4.2-5
Illustrative estimates of state and local funds for student higher education only, fiscal year 1962 and calendar year 1970 (millions of dollars)

State and region	State and local government funds, 1962	1970 Illustration I Increased to reflect economic growth	Illustration II Required to finance balance of expenditures
United States	$1,216.0	$1,972.7	$3,033.7
New England	37.1	57.5	143.2
Maine	3.6	5.2	13.1
New Hampshire	3.2	4.7	6.4
Vermont	2.4	3.5	5.7
Massachusetts	11.6	18.1	64.3
Rhode Island	4.8	7.0	16.7
Connecticut	11.5	19.0	37.0
Mideast	154.7	257.7	515.4
New York	95.9	162.8	347.9
New Jersey	16.8	26.0	55.1
Pennsylvania	19.6	28.2	56.8
Delaware	2.7	4.8	8.2
Maryland	18.8	34.3	42.9
District of Columbia	0.9	1.6	4.5
Great Lakes	277.0	458.5	654.2
Michigan	75.0	137.3	160.4
Ohio	49.9	69.7	136.7
Indiana	41.1	72.6	76.7
Illinois	85.4	127.0	225.0
Wisconsin	25.6	51.9	55.4
Plains	126.2	197.1	255.5
Minnesota	28.2	51.8	71.0
Iowa	26.4	39.5	41.2
Missouri	22.0	35.2	51.2
North Dakota	8.8	12.0	15.7
South Dakota	5.4	8.8	11.0
Nebraska	11.5	15.9	22.2
Kansas	23.9	33.9	43.2
Southeast	218.1	343.7	513.7
Virginia	19.2	28.6	28.6
West Virginia	16.6	23.2	30.9
Kentucky	18.4	29.9	50.7

Amount of increase 1962 to 1970	
lustration I	*Illustration II*
$756.7	$1,817.7
20.4	106.1
1.6	9.5
1.5	3.2
1.1	3.3
6.5	52.7
2.2	11.9
7.5	25.5
103.0	360.7
66.9	252.0
9.2	38.3
8.6	37.2
2.1	5.5
15.5	24.1
0.7	3.6
181.5	377.2
62.3	85.4
19.8	86.8
31.5	35.6
41.6	139.6
26.3	29.8
70.9	129.3
23.6	42.8
13.1	14.8
13.2	29.2
3.2	6.9
3.4	5.6
4.4	10.7
10.0	19.3
125.6	295.6
9.4	9.4
6.6	14.3
11.5	32.3

TABLE 4.2-5
(continued)

State and region	State and local government funds, 1962	1970 Illustration I — Increased to reflect economic growth	Illustration II — Required to finance balance of expenditure
Tennessee	13.3	20.8	30.7
North Carolina	23.5	40.4	61.9
South Carolina	11.0	17.8	31.2
Georgia	12.0	19.6	26.1
Florida	33.4	58.8	95.5
Alabama	12.1	14.2	14.2
Mississippi	12.5	19.1	24.7
Louisiana	37.5	58.2	104.5
Arkansas	8.6	13.1	14.7
Southwest	97.3	143.9	220.9
Oklahoma	17.7	25.3	29.2
Texas	58.8	79.7	133.2
New Mexico	7.9	14.7	16.9
Arizona	12.9	24.2	41.6
Rocky Mountain	43.2	64.0	86.3
Montana	6.7	9.8	10.5
Idaho	7.3	11.7	16.5
Wyoming	4.1	5.7	6.4
Colorado	12.9	19.9	36.0
Utah	12.2	16.9	16.9
Far West	257.1	440.6	623.9
Washington	38.5	53.6	94.2
Oregon	20.3	26.8	26.8
Nevada	3.1	5.9	10.6
California	195.2	354.3	492.3
Alaska	1.9	4.2	7.5
Hawaii	3.5	5.5	14.0

NOTE: Detail may not add to totals due to rounding.

SOURCE: 1961–62 data computed from U.S. Department of Health, Education
and Welfare, *Financial Statistics of Institutions of Higher Education, 1961–62*
in S. J. Mushkin and E. P. McLoone, *Public Spending for Higher Education, 1970*
Council of State Governments, Chicago, February 1965, p. 58.

Amount of increase	
1962 to 1970	
Illustration I	*Illustration II*
7.5	17.4
16.9	38.4
6.8	20.2
7.6	14.1
25.4	62.1
2.1	2.1
6.6	12.2
20.7	67.0
4.5	6.1
46.6	123.6
7.6	11.5
20.9	74.4
6.8	9.0
11.3	28.7
20.8	43.1
3.1	3.8
4.4	9.2
1.6	2.3
7.0	23.1
4.7	4.7
183.5	366.8
15.1	55.7
6.5	6.5
2.8	7.5
159.1	297.1
2.3	5.6
2.0	10.5

TABLE 4.2-6
Tax revenue,
1966–67

		Amount (millions of dollars)			

Item	All governments	Federal government	State governments	Local governments	All governments
Total taxes	176,362	115,121	31,926	29,315	100.0
Income	103,559	95,497	7,136	926	58.7
Individual	67,361	61,526	4,909	926	38.2
Corporation	36,198	33,971	2,227	*	20.5
Property	26,280	*	862	25,418	14.9
Sales, gross receipts, and customs	36,360	15,806	18,575	1,979	20.6
Customs duties	1,901	1,901	*	*	1.1
General sales and gross receipts	10,143	*	8,923	1,220	5.8
Selective sales and gross receipts	24,316	13,905	9,652	759	13.8
All other	10,163	3,818	5,354	992	5.8

* Represents zero or rounds to zero.
NOTE: Because of rounding, detail may not add to totals.
SOURCE: U.S. Bureau of the Census, *Governmental Finances in 1966–67,* Government Finances Series GF67, no. 3, 1968, table B.

TABLE 4.2-7
Educational expenditures, by level of government, total and intergovernmental, 1966–67 (in millions)

Item	Federal government	State governments	Local governments
Total education expenditure	$6,214	$21,229	$28,867
Intergovernmental expenditure	3,920	11,845	18
Direct expenditure	2,295	9,384	28,849
Local schools	*	300	27,766
Institutions of higher education	*	7,728	1,082
Other	2,295	1,357	*

* Represents zero or rounds to zero.
SOURCE: U.S. Bureau of the Census, *Governmental Finances in 1966–67,* Government Finances Series GF67, no. 3, 1968, p. 8.

Percentage			Percentage increase from prior fiscal year		
Federal govern-ment	State govern-ments	Local govern-ments	All govern-ments	Federal govern-ment	State and local govern-ments
100.0	100.0	100.0	9.7	10.6	8.1
83.0	22.4	3.2	12.2	11.7	18.6
53.4	15.4	3.2	11.9	11.0	22.6
29.5	7.0	*	12.7	13.0	9.3
*	2.7	86.7	6.5	*	6.5
13.7	58.2	6.8	7.8	8.0	7.7
1.7	*	*	7.6	7.6	*
*	27.9	4.2	10.0	*	10.0
12.1	30.2	2.6	7.0	8.0	5.6
3.3	16.8	3.4	1.3	−3.0	4.2

for higher education were $7.7 billion by state governments and $1.1 billion by local governments (Table 4.2-7).

Table 4.2-8 shows that from 1962–63 to 1966–67, per capita government expenditures on education rose much more than all per capita government expenditures. During this period per capita public expenditures on education increased 58 percent, while

TABLE 4.2-8 *Per capita expenditures, total and educational, 1962–63, 1964–65, 1966–67*

All governments	1962–63	1964–65	1966–67	Percent rise 1962–63 to 1966–67	Percent rise 1964–65 to 1966–67
Total	$981	$1,061	$1,306	33	23
Education	130	153	205	58	34

SOURCE: U.S. Bureau of the Census, *Governmental Finances in 1966–67*, Government Finances Series GF67, no. 3, 1968, p. 15 (author's calculations).

total public expenditures per capita increased by 33 percent. From 1963–64 to 1966–67, state aid to education rose by 45 percent, while state aid to higher education rose by 67 percent. The $5 billion increase in intergovernmental expenditures from 1963–64 to 1966–67 is due mainly to the large increases in federal subsidies to education on behalf of state and local governments (Table 4.2-9).

PROJECTED INCREASES IN FEDERAL SUPPORT Both the Rivlin Committee and the Carnegie Commission have recommended large increases in federal support of higher education. The Rivlin Committee recommended increases in federal support from $5.4 billion in 1970–71 to $14.7 billion in 1976–77.[4] This means that federal support of higher education would increase from 18 to 25 percent of total estimated income of higher education from 1959–60 to 1975–76, while combined state and local government support was projected to decline from 27 to 22 percent of higher education income in this period (Table 4.2-10). If the Carnegie Commission recommendations were followed, federal

[4] U.S. Department of Health, Education and Welfare, *Toward a Long-Range Plan for Federal Financial Support for Higher Education,* report to the President, Office of Assistant Secretary for Planning and Evaluation, January 1969, p. 36.

TABLE 4.2-9
Total governmental and educational expenditures, 1963–64 to 1966–67 (billions of dollars)

	1963–64	1966–67	Percentage rise, 1963–64 to 1966–67
Federal total expenditures	$125.9	$166.8	32
Total expenditures per capita	658.27	843.25	28
Federal intergovernmental	10.1	15.0	49
Intergovernmental per capita	52.77	75.95	44
Federal education, direct	1.056	2.295	117
State and local, total expenditures	80.6	106.7	32
State education	26.3	38.2	45
State institutions of higher education	5.28	8.81	67

SOURCE: U.S. Bureau of the Census, *Governmental Finances in 1966–67,* Government Finances Series GF67, no. 3, 1968, pp. 17–18.

TABLE 4.2-10
Percent
distribution of
income of
institutions of
higher
education by
source of funds,
1959–60 to
1975–76

Year	Federal govern-ment*	State and local gov-ernment	Student charges†	Private giving	Other private	Total
1959–60	18	27	37	7	11	100
1965–66	21	26	38	5	10	100
1975–76	25	22	40	4	9	100

*Federal expenditures for higher education not dispensed through institutions are excluded from the table. The primary categories of spending excluded are VA assistance, SSA payments for students 18–22, the proposed national student loan bank, and the proposed educational opportunity grant program.

† Tuition and fees plus income from auxiliary enterprises.

SOURCE: U.S. Department of Health, Education and Welfare, *Toward a Long-Range Plan for Federal Financial Support for Higher Education,* report to the President, Office of Assistant Secretary for Planning and Evaluation, January 1969, p. 17.

aid to higher education would increase from 21 to 32 percent of total expenditures on higher education from 1967–68 to 1976–77.[5] The projected relative increases in the importance of government funding are partly due to the projected relative decreases in endowment income and in private gifts and grants.

Plans and programs for the future stress student aid and institutional grants. The Carnegie Commission proposes large increases in federal funds for student aid, research, and cost-of-education supplements. The Commission recommends federal expenditures on student aid of $1.90 billion in 1970–71 and $3.56 billion in 1976–77. These recommended figures may be compared with total student aid of $474 million in 1965–66 and federal aid to students of $620 million in 1967–68. Federal aid to institutions is recommended to increase from $440 million in 1967–68 to $3.06 billion in 1976–77. If these recommendations are accepted, direct aid to students would rise from 18 to 27 percent of total federal aid to higher education. Institutional grants and cost-of-education supplements together would increase from 13 to 23 percent of total federal support. The Commission also projects

[5] Carnegie Commission on Higher Education, *Quality and Equality: New Levels of Federal Responsibility for Higher Education,* McGraw-Hill Book Company, New York, 1968, p. 8. Revised recommendations have more recently been made by the Carnegie Commission in *Quality and Equality: Revised Recommendations New Levels of Federal Responsibility for Higher Education,* McGraw-Hill Book Company, New York, 1970.

that support of organized research will decline relatively from 42 to 31 percent of total federal support from 1967–68 to 1976–77.[6] The Rivlin Committee recommends that the federal government provide $6.3 billion in new aid programs by fiscal year 1976. Roughly two-thirds of this sum would go to student aid and one-third to institutions. The most costly program would be direct grants to students (educational opportunity grants) paying from $200 to $1,500 per student in need.[7] The major items in the Rivlin Program are given in Table 4.2-11. To implement these recommendations, large increases in federal support would be needed to found a National Student Loan Bank and to provide for educational opportunity grants, cost-of-education allowances, and doubled expenditures on research.

INSTITUTIONAL GRANTS Many authorities support an increase in federal grants to institutions, rather than increases in categorical grants or direct aid to

[6] Carnegie Commission on Higher Education, *Quality and Equality: New Levels of Federal Responsibility for Higher Education*, McGraw-Hill Book Company, New York, 1968, pp. 52–53 and table 1.5-3.

[7] U.S. Department of Health, Education and Welfare, *Toward a Long-Range Plan for Federal Financial Support for Higher Education*, report to the President, Office of Assistant Secretary for Planning and Evaluation, January 1969, pp. 31–35.

TABLE 4.2-11
Illustrative projections of federal funds for higher education, fiscal years 1970 and 1976 (in billions)

	Fiscal year 1970	Fiscal year 1976
Present programs dispensed through institutions	2.8	3.9
Present programs directly to students (V.A. and S.S.A.) *	0.9	0.9
National Student Loan Bank		0.7
Proposed Educational Opportunity Grants (E.O.G.)		3.1
Proposed cost-of-education allowance		1.2
Other proposed funding dispensed through institutions		1.4
Proposed research	1.7	3.5
Total federal support	5.4	14.7

* Veteran's Administration and Social Security Administration.
SOURCE: U.S. Department of Health, Education and Welfare, *Toward a Long-Range Plan for Federal Financial Support for Higher Education*, report to the President, Office of Assistant Secretary for Planning and Evaluation, January 1969, p. 36.

TABLE 4.2-12 *Major federal programs intended to provide direct aid for development of academic institutions*

Agency	Program description	Fiscal year 1967 funds
NSF	University science development: Relatively large grants to a limited number of carefully selected academic institutions that are not among the very foremost, but are judged to have the greatest potential for development.	$ 35,600,000
NSF	Departmental science development: To improve the quality of science education and academic research in specific areas of science in graduate level institutions which have significant strength in at least one field, but are not yet ready to move into the top ranks of excellence on a broad front.	15,000,000
NSF	College science improvement: For the improvement of the science capabilities of predominantly undergraduate-level educational institutions.	10,000,000
PHS/HEW	Health professions education improvement program: To improve the educational quality of schools of medicine, dentistry, osteopathy, optometry, and podiatry.	30,000,000
PHS/HEW	Allied health professions personnel training: To improve the educational quality of schools providing training in medical technology, occupational therapy, dental hygiene, etc.	4,000,000
OE/HEW	Strengthening developing institutions: To assist in upgrading the academic standards of developing institutions of higher learning.	30,000,000
NIH/HEW	Health sciences advancement award program: To accelerate the advancement of existing capabilities in health research and related graduate research education activities within institutions of higher education which already have demonstrated some achievement in the health-related sciences; support of the advancement of new health research and training in emerging and less well-developed academic institutions.	4,000,000
NIH/HEW	Biomedical science support grants: To encourage the most effective and rapid evolution of institution's health-related research and research training capabilities in non-health professional schools.	6,000,000*
NIH/HEW	General research support grants: To encourage the most effective and rapid evolution of institutions' health-related and research training capabilities.	41,700,000*
DOD	Project Themis: To support research programs in defense-related fields at institutions of higher education not now heavily engaged in federal research and development.	20,500,000
TOTAL		196,800,000

* Formula based.

SOURCE: U.S. House of Representatives, Committee on Science and Astronautics, *A National Program of Institutional Grants for Science and Science Education,* a study for the Subcommittee on Science, Research and Development, 1968, p. 17.

students. They feel that categorical aid tends to cause excessive outlays in the favored items, such as housing or research fellowships. The Bundy Committee study of private institutions in New York state emphasizes the institutional grant as a mechanism for discouraging direct appeals for financial aid to the state legislature.[8] The Carnegie Commission study recommends that the "Federal government grant cost-of-education supplements to colleges and universities, based on the number and levels of students holding grants enrolled in the institutions."[9] The Rivlin Committee stresses the increased flexibility and greater freedom of allocation that would result from general grants to institutions. Block grants for research "would give institutions more fiscal flexibility and thus promote autonomy."[10]

Table 4.2-12 shows the magnitude of federal grants to institutions in fiscal year 1967. Total grants to institutions were $197 million, with the largest shares funded through the National Science Foundation, the National Institutes of Health, and the Office of Education. Table 4.2-13 gives estimated National Institutes of Health and Office of Education programs for funding institutional development in fiscal 1967 and 1968. Total support for these programs is estimated to increase by 32 percent from 1967 to 1968.[11]

Many college and university administrators favor supplemental payments to the institution on the ground that the costs of higher education greatly exceed tuition income. The gap between costs and tuition income is often widened by an increase in federal aid which causes large increases in enrollment.[12] The Rivlin Committee

[8] Select Committee on the Future of Private and Independent Higher Education in New York State, *New York State and Private Higher Education,* Bureau of Publications, Albany, N.Y., January 1968, pp. 58–59.

[9] Carnegie Commission on Higher Education, *Quality and Equality: New Levels of Federal Responsibility for Higher Education,* McGraw-Hill Book Company, New York, 1968, p. 30.

[10] U.S. Department of Health, Education and Welfare, *Toward a Long-Range Plan for Federal Financial Support for Higher Education,* report to the President, Office of Assistant Secretary for Planning and Evaluation, January 1969, pp. 28–37.

[11] For National Institutes of Health grants itemized by institution for 1962–67, see U.S. House of Representatives, Committee on Science and Astronautics, *A National Program of Institutional Grants for Science and Science Education,* a study for the Subcommittee on Science, Research and Development, 1968, pp. 62–69.

[12] U.S. Office of Education, *Students and Buildings: An Analysis of Selected Federal Programs for Higher Education,* 1968, p. 40. See also Chapter 1.5.

TABLE 4.2-13
National Institutes of Health and Office of Education funding of institutional development programs

	Estimated fiscal year 1967	*Estimated fiscal year 1968*
Health professions educational improvement program	$30,000,000	$49,750,000*
Allied health professions educational improvement program	3,285,000†	9,750,000
General research support grant program	41,700,000	43,200,000
Biomedical sciences support grant program	6,000,000	7,500,000
Health sciences advancement award program	4,000,000	11,000,000
Developing institutions program	30,000,000‡	30,000,000‡

* The original approved figure of $52,500,000 for fiscal year 1968 was reduced in accordance with budget reductions directed by the President to $49,750,000.

† $500,000 was transferred to this program from allied health traineeship funds, raising the original $2,785,000 available for grants to $3,285,000.

‡ $26,250,000 was available for cooperative arrangements; the balance for national teaching fellowships. This information was obtained from Senate appropriation hearings on the fiscal year 1968 HEW budget request, "Labor—Health, Education, and Welfare appropriations for fiscal year 1968" 90th Cong., 1st Sess., on H.R. 10196, at p. 502.

SOURCE: U.S. House of Representatives, Committee on Science and Astronautics, *A National Program of Institutional Grants for Science and Science Education,* a study for the Subcommittee on Science, Research and Development, 1968, p. 26.

recommends that the federal government make available to the institution a cost-of-education allowance of $100 per student plus 25 percent of each individual student grant in excess of $100. This allowance should also be tied to the National Defense Education Act loan program, with each institution receiving an allowance of 25 percent of the funds made available to students under these programs. If the Rivlin Committee recommendations for student aid are adopted, enrollment is predicted to increase by 800,000 above the Office of Education projection of 6.3 million for fiscal 1972.[13] Table 4.2-14 shows the additional sums that would be provided by the federal government under the Rivlin Committee proposals by fiscal 1976.

[13] U.S. Department of Health, Education and Welfare, *Toward a Long-Range Plan for Federal Financial Support for Higher Education,* report to the President, Office of Assistant Secretary for Planning and Evaluation, January 1969, pp. 31–35, 331–332, 335. Enrollment has increased more rapidly than earlier Office of Education projections indicated. The Office of Education's most recent projection estimates total enrollment at 8.7 million by 1971–72.

TABLE 4.2-14
Proposed increases in federal funding, fiscal year 1976, by the Rivlin Committee— major items (millions of dollars)

Grants to students	$2,925
Cost-of-education allowance (graduate)	1,200
Student loans	740
Developing institutions	125
NDEA Fellowships and cost-of-education allowances	470
Sustaining grants	400
Other	440
TOTAL	$6,300

SOURCE: U.S. Department of Health, Education and Welfare, *Toward a Long-Range Plan for Federal Financial Support for Higher Education,* report to the President, Office of Assistant Secretary for Planning and Evaluation, January 1969, p. 35.

One of the objections often made about noncategorical grants to institutions is that these funds may be used to reduce tuition (or keep it from rising) rather than to improve the quality of education. The result is that much money is wasted. Any relative reduction in tuition provides help to many students who do not need it. Direct aid through scholarships, the argument runs, yields more returns per dollar spent than noncategorical institutional aid.

An institutional grant may be of several types. The government may offer the institution money with no constraint on the manner of spending. Grants for expanding graduate instruction are of this kind. National Institutes of Health grants to health and medical schools are categorical but allow much latitude for spending within this category. More generally, the government ties the funds to a specific program.[14] Table 4.2-15 shows the percentage distribution by use of institutional grants in fiscal years 1964, 1965, and 1966. Perhaps too much of this money was spent on equipment and supplies—53 percent in 1964 and 48 percent in 1966—and too little on students—4.4 percent in 1964 and 6.0 percent in 1966.

Table 4.2-16 gives the distribution of federal obligations by size of federal program for 1967. More than two-fifths of the institutions getting federal aid received less than $100,000 per institution, while 4.13 percent received $10 million or more. Table 4.2-17 shows how the 50 states and the District of Columbia

[14] U.S. House of Representatives, Committee on Science and Astronautics, *A National Program of Institutional Grants for Science and Science Education,* a study for the Subcommittee on Science, Research and Development, 1968, pp. 17, 28.

TABLE 4.2-15 *Uses of institutional grant funds* (percentages)*

	Fiscal year 1964	Fiscal year 1965	Fiscal year 1966
Equipment and supplies:			
General	44.5	41.7	41.0
Library	8.6	6.6	7.0
Subtotal	53.1	48.3	48.0
Facilities:			
General	6.9	9.5	7.0
Computers	6.4	8.0	7.0
Subtotal	13.3	17.5	14.0
Personnel:			
Faculty salaries	9.9	10.0	13.0
Student stipends	4.4	5.4	6.0
Visiting lecturers and consultants	1.0	1.2	1.0
Subtotal	15.3	16.6	20.0
Research projects:			
Faculty research projects	15.1	13.4	13.0
Undergraduate research projects	0.2	0.6	†
Research services	0.7	0.4	†
Subtotal	16.0	14.4	14.0
Miscellaneous:			
Travel	1.3	1.1	2.0
Curriculum development	0.4	0.4	1.0
Manuscript preparation and publication	0.3	0.2	†
Other	0.3	1.5	†
Subtotal	2.3	3.2	4.0
TOTAL	100.0	100.0	100.0

* U.S. National Science Foundation. Justification of estimates of appropriations, salaries, and expenses, fiscal year 1969, p. 176.
† Approximately 0.5% or less.
SOURCE: U.S. House of Representatives, Committee on Science and Astronautics, *A National Program of Institutional Grants for Science and Science Education,* a study for the Subcommittee on Science, Research and Development, 1968, p. 21.

ranked according to amount of federal aid to higher education in several recent years. California ranked first and New York second, while Nevada and Delaware ranked fiftieth and fifty-first, respectively.

TABLE 4.2-16
Number of universities and colleges receiving federal obligations, ranked by size of federal program, 1967

Size of federal program	Number of institutions	Percentage distribution
$10 million or more	85	4.13
$5 million to $9.9 million	53	2.58
$1 million to $4.9 million	222	10.80
$500,000 to $999,000	213	10.36
$100,000 to $499,000	611	29.72
Less than $100,000	872	42.41
TOTAL	2,056	100.00

SOURCE: National Science Foundation, *Federal Support to Universities and Colleges, Fiscal Year 1967,* 1968, table 11, p. 23.

TABLE 4.2-17
Rankings of federal obligations to universities and colleges, population and selected educational data, by state, various years

States (in order of total federal obligations, 1967)*	Population July 1, 1967	Earned degrees awarded, all levels, 1965–66	Student enrollment — All levels, fall 1966	Student enrollment — Advanced degrees, fall 1965
1. California	1	2	1	2
2. New York	2	1	2	1
3. Massachusetts	10	8	8	4
4. Illinois	4	4	4	6
5. Pennsylvania	3	3	3	3
6. Michigan	7	7	6	5
7. Texas	5	6	5	8
8. Ohio	6	5	7	7
9. North Carolina	11	13	16	20
10. Indiana	12	9	10	9
11. Maryland	18	23	18	15
12. Wisconsin	16	10	12	14
13. Florida	9	15	9	18
14. Missouri	13	12	11	13
15. New Jersey	8	11	13	10
16. Washington	23	17	14	23
17. Connecticut	24	26	24	12
18. Minnesota	20	14	15	16
19. Tennessee	17	16	17	25

EDUCATIONAL OBJECTIVES OF GOVERNMENT Congress seems to prefer categorical to general or institutional aid. For example, if $1 billion is available, Congress prefers to decide whether the money is to be used for housing, research, or student aid. In distributing public funds, the government tends to resort to formulas. Congressmen, of course, seek formulas which favor their constituencies. Where enrollment is high, the distribution of funds is urged on the basis of numbers. Where incomes are low, help is sought inversely to income. Enrollment is a frequently used guide for the distribution of grants. But the Bundy Committee prefers the number of degrees granted per institution rather than enrollment as a guide to the distribution of grants.

(Text continued on p. 644)

Academic science obligations, 1967	*Earned degrees in the sciences and engineering 1965–66*				*Student enrollment, advanced degrees in sciences and engineering, fall 1965*
	Total	*Doctor's†*	*Master's*	*Bachelor's*	
2	2	2	2	2	2
1	1	1	1	1	1
3	5	5	3	8	4
4	4	4	4	7	5
5	3	3	6	3	3
6	7	7	5	6	7
7	8	6	8	5	8
9	6	8	7	4	6
8	13	15	22	12	18
12	9	9	9	9	9
10	25	14	31	25	14
11	10	11	11	10	12
16	19	23	18	19	22
13	12	10	12	14	13
17	11	17	10	11	10
14	15	21	17	15	16
19	27	27	15	29	17
15	14	16	25	13	15
20	16	13	19	16	24

TABLE 4.2-17
(continued)

States (in order of total federal obligations, 1967)*	Population July 1, 1967	Earned degrees awarded, all levels, 1965–66	Student enrollment All levels, fall 1966	Advanced degrees, fall 1965
20. Alabama	21	28	28	31
21. District of Columbia	40	27	31	11
22. Georgia	15	25	23	27
23. Colorado	31	20	27	17
24. Louisiana	19	21	20	21
25. Oregon	30	30	29	29
26. Kentucky	22	29	26	33
27. Iowa	25	18	21	24
28. Virginia	14	24	19	28
29. Kansas	29	22	25	22
30. Arizona	34	34	30	26
31. Oklahoma	27	19	22	19
32. Utah	36	32	32	30
33. South Carolina	26	37	35	39
34. Mississippi	28	33	33	37
35. West Virginia	33	36	36	36
36. New Mexico	37	40	39	35
37. Nebraska	35	31	34	32
38. Arkansas	32	35	37	38
39. Hawaii	41	47	45	42
40. Rhode Island	39	38	38	34
41. New Hampshire	44	42	41	40
42. Montana	42	44	46	45
43. South Dakota	45	39	40	46
44. North Dakota	46	43	44	43
45. Vermont	49	45	47	49
46. Wyoming	50	48	49	48
47. Maine	38	41	43	44
48. Alaska	51	51	51	51
49. Idaho	43	46	42	47
50. Nevada	48	50	50	50
51. Delaware	47	49	48	41

*Includes the District of Columbia; excludes United States service schools.
† Includes M.D. and D.D.S.
‡ Duplicate numbers indicate "tie" for place; e.g., same number of doctor's degrees

Academic science obligations, 1967	Earned degrees in the sciences and engineering 1965-66				Student enrollment, advanced degrees in sciences and engineering, fall 1965
	Total	Doctor's†	Master's	Bachelor's	
23	28	32	32	26	31
26	29	12	16	31	11
21	20	22	27	20	27
18	21	30	20	21	20
22	24	20	23	23	25
25	26	18	26	27	28
30	31	28‡	38	30	35
24	17	19	21	18	21
27	18	24	28	17	29
28	23	28‡	14	24	23
32	32	35	24	37	26
31	22	25‡	13	22	19
29	30	31	29	28	30
38	37	36	41‡	34	38
34	35	38	33	33	37
39	34	34	36	32	36
33	39	41	30	42	32
37	33	25‡	34	36	34
40	36	33	37	35	42
35	46	43	40	47	41
36	38	37	35	38	33
41	40	42	41‡	39	40
42	44	46	44	44	43
44	42	49	43	41	45
46	43	44‡	39	43	44
43	45	39	50	45	50
47	49	44‡	46	48	46
48	41	48	48	40	49
45	51	50	51	51	51
50	47	47	47	46	47
49	50	51	49	50	48
51	48	40	45	49	39

were awarded in Kentucky and Kansas, in Oklahoma and Nebraska, and in North Dakota and Wyoming; of master's degrees, in South Carolina and New Hampshire.

SOURCE: National Science Foundation, *Federal Support to Universities and Colleges, Fiscal Year 1967,* 1968, p. 19.

Degrees measure institutional achievement better than enrollment does because the emphasis is on productivity, not numbers.[15]

In many fields the guide to the offer of funds is the quality of the institution. But a policy of distributing funds on the basis of quality results in a heavy concentration of funds among the prestigious schools. The political results are likely to be unfortunate. To avoid the pitfalls of excessive concentration of grants among distinguished schools, Congress seeks special appropriations for institutions not favored by existing formulas.[16]

The amount of money that the federal government makes available to higher education depends in part on the competition from other claimants of federal funds. This issue is discussed elsewhere.[17] The types of federal grants to higher education are also determined by educational policy. The federal government seems more disposed to aid students directly than to help institutions. As noted before, proposed programs of federal aid yield twice as much to students directly as to institutions. Perhaps the political gains are greater per dollar spent on students, since aid to institutions is less visible than direct aid to students. Government officials are unsure what institutions would do with noncategorical grants. The tendency may be to reduce tuition rather than improve quality. However, the Bundy Committee seems to believe that the amounts given as student aid may have less impact than direct subsidies to private institutions of higher education.[18]

Because government officials are more aware than formerly that increases in federal aid can induce rising enrollment and lead to increasing costs and appeals for public funds, the federal government's enthusiasm for aid to higher education is being dulled somewhat. The Office of Education puts it this way:

[15] Select Committee on the Future of Private and Independent Higher Education in New York State, *New York State and Private Higher Education*, Bureau of Publications, Albany, N.Y., January 1968, p. 55.

[16] c.f., U.S. Department of Health, Education and Welfare, *Toward a Long-Range Plan for Federal Financial Support for Higher Education*, report to the President, Office of Assistant Secretary for Planning and Evaluation, January 1969, p. 27.

[17] See Chapter 4.8.

[18] Select Committee on the Future of Private and Independent Higher Education in New York State, *New York State and Private Higher Education*, Bureau of Publications, Albany, N.Y., January 1968, p. 59.

Increased attendance is going to place further strain on the finances of higher education institutions. By 1968–69 about $0.5 billion of the incremental deficit is projected as a result of increased enrollment resulting from federal aid programs. This amount is projected to increase to $1.4 billion in 1972–73.[19]

AID TO DEVELOPING INSTITUTIONS Under Title III of the Higher Education Act of 1965, the federal government is attempting to help developing institutions through development grants. In practice, this has meant aiding small institutions with low faculty salaries (less than $6,000 average) and, to a considerable extent, institutions that spend less than $1,000 per student a year and charge less than $400 a year for tuition. The inadequacy of this development program is shown by Table 4.2-18. The number of institutions aided rose from 127 in 1966 to 411 in 1967, while the average grant increased from $39,370 to $72,933. But, surely, grants of less than $100,000 per institution will not be highly productive.

In general, poor and especially Negro institutions have been helped under this program. The average enrollment of the aided institutions was slightly over 770 students in 1966 and 929 in 1967. Such small enrollments mean either high unit costs or poor quality. The money spent under Title III has been used primarily for encouraging consortia (or cooperative arrangements) which tie a weak institution to a strong one for the purposes of cutting costs and improving quality, and providing teaching fellowships in order to increase the proportion of the faculty with doctorates.

The Office of Education has expressed dissatisfaction with the results of the developing institutions program. Faculty doctorates are not being attained in large numbers, and when they are attained, the recipients tend to move to better schools. In the view of the

(Text continued on p. 648)

[19] U.S. Office of Education, *Students and Buildings: An Analysis of Selected Federal Programs for Higher Education,* 1968, p. 37.

TABLE 4.2-18 Aid to developing institutions, fiscal years 1966, 1967

	Fiscal 1966	Fiscal 1967
Number of awards	127	411
Grants	$5 million	$30 million
Average grant	$39,370	$70,993

SOURCE: U.S. Office of Education, *Students and Buildings: An Analysis of Selected Federal Programs for Higher Education,* 1968, pp. 34, 67.

TABLE 4.2-19 *Number and percentage of responses acknowledging certain favorable characteristics of consortiums as applicable to a specific existing consortium, 1965–66 (1,314 responses* = 100 percent)*

Characteristic	Number of responses to the question	Percentage of the 1,314 responses
1. Makes better use of specialized or unique facilities and/or staff	938	71.4
2. Strengthens, enriches, or upgrades institutions concerned	858	65.3
3. Makes possible programs or quality otherwise impracticable	828	63.0
4. Broadens perspective of institutions	780	59.4
5. Avoids unnecessary duplication by pooling of resources	758	57.7
6. Broadens range of courses	734	55.8
7. Provides additional incentives for students and teachers	711	54.1
8. Enables small institutions to enjoy advantages of large ones	690	52.5
9. Facilitates degree programs in interdisciplinary areas	427	32.5
10. Coordinated approach better serves region with graduate courses	412	31.4
11. Has proved to be an overall economy measure	267	20.3
12. Presents a united front in negotiations with other agencies	260	19.8
13. Other	106	8.1

* A total of 708 institutions returned 1,314 evaluative responses (part II, sec. D of the survey questionnaire). Each evaluative response was confined to a single, specific consortium. Two or more institutions of course could have responded independently to a given question in regard to the same specific consortium.

SOURCE: U.S. Office of Education, *Consortiums in American Higher Education, 1965–66,* report of an exploratory study, 1968, table 23.

TABLE 4.2-20 *Summary of conclusions, indirect costs*

The chief conclusions which can be drawn from our study of these six universities can be summarized as follows:

A. The costs recovered by universities for federally sponsored research are less than the costs incurred. The causes are:

1. The cost allocation principles applied by the federal government uniquely to institutions of higher education militate against full indirect cost allocation to government sponsored research projects. This is in addition to costs which are unallowed as with other types of contractors.
2. Individual federal agencies impose limitations on indirect cost recovery. This is caused by authorizing legislation, agency administrative regulations or by negotiation.

TABLE 4.2-20 *(continued)*

3. The majority of universities studied voluntarily contributed to the support of federally sponsored research. This practice stemmed generally from institutional policy.

B. The many variations in rate computations among the six universities generally were permitted under the cost principles established by BoB A-21. The differences in rates were found to be attributable generally to:

1. Charging certain activities as indirect rather than direct costs.

2. Use of different bases for allocation of indirect costs to individual research projects.

3. Differences in construction of indirect cost pools.

4. Differences in bases used to allocate pool costs.

5. Differences in the level of supporting services.

6. Results of audit and negotiation.

C. The variations in indirect cost rates found among the six universities has little to do with any comparative evaluation of research efforts.

D. The treatment of the cost of an activity as a direct rather than an indirect charge in theory should have no effect on reimbursement. In practice direct charging results in higher total reimbursement to the university and a lower indirect cost rate.

E. Studies to develop special formulas and weighting factors for use in distributing indirect cost pools to organized research could be conducted by any university. Changes in the bases for distributing pool costs would result.

F. Use of a more standardized approach to indirect cost rate determination and presentations might be helpful to the universities, auditors and negotiators. Indirect cost rates, nevertheless, still would be diverse.

G. Any set of cost principles, formulas, procedures used or limitations imposed must give cognizance to fundamental differences among educational institutions. Failure to recognize and recover full costs could be damaging to a university's ability to sustain a desirable research capability and thus adversely affect the nation as a whole.

SOURCE: U.S. Senate, Committee on Government Operations, *Federal Support of Project Grants: Indirect Costs and Cost Sharing, Hearings before the Subcommittee on Government Research,* April-June 1969, vol. 2, pp. 187–188.

Office of Education, consortia have many weaknesses. But the participants in the consortia are more optimistic,[20] as shown by Table 4.2-19. A large majority of the respondents to a 1965–66 survey felt that consortia make better use of specialized or unique faculties and/or staff and that they strengthen, enrich, or upgrade the institutions concerned. The Carnegie Commission recommends that the program for developing institutions be increased to $100 million by 1976–77.[21]

INDIRECT COSTS Many college and university administrators are unhappy at their failure to obtain full coverage of overhead costs on government contracts. They object to a ceiling on overhead rates, but they could adjust to ceilings by changing their accounting systems and tying more costs to direct costs. They find little support for the recourse to foundation practices by the government, where the objective for the foundation is to provide seed money. The univer-

[20] U.S. Office of Education, *Students and Buildings: An Analysis of Selected Federal Programs for Higher Education,* 1968, pp. 34–35.

[21] Carnegie Commission on Higher Education, *Quality and Equality: New Levels of Federal Responsibility for Higher Education,* McGraw-Hill Book Company, New York, 1968, p. 42.

TABLE 4.2-21 *Distribution of indirect cost rates*

Negotiated indirect cost rate ranges based on salaries and wages	*Number of institutions*	*Percentage of institutions*
Below 25	0	0
25 to 30	2	2.7
30 to 35	8	11.0
35 to 40	6	8.1
40 to 45	10	13.7
45 to 50	10	13.7
50 to 55	13	17.9
55 to 60	11	15.0
60 to 65	10	13.7
Over 65	3	4.2
TOTAL	73	100.0

SOURCE: U.S. Senate, Committee on Government Operations, *Federal Support of Project Grants: Indirect Costs and Cost Sharing, Hearings before the Subcommittee on Government Research,* April–June 1969, vol. 1, p. 33.

TABLE 4.2-22 *Variation caused by using different basis to compute overhead rate*

The rates, shown below, were negotiated in recent years with the schools indicated and, in each case, the overhead rate was computed on a different basis.

School	Main campus overhead rate (percent)	Basis of computation
Columbia	35.39	Total direct salaries and wages
Montana	27.83	Total direct salaries and wages, plus fringe benefits
Harvard	36.42	Total direct costs

The large majority of institutions use total direct salaries and wages as a basis. For the purposes of comparison, the above overhead rates were recomputed using this basis for all three schools. The results are as follows (in percent):

School	Negotiated overhead rate	Adjusted to basis: of total direct salaries and wages
Columbia	35.39	35.39
Montana	27.83	31.52
Harvard	36.42	55.65

When a same basis is used, it may be expected that similar overhead rates may result. Although this was true for the rates of Columbia and Montana, substantial differences resulted between these two schools and Harvard. This situation arises because there are many other factors; in addition to the use of different bases, which contribute to the overall differences in the above overhead rates, including the treatment of research costs as direct or indirect, the nature of the university and the research performed, as well as the location of the university and its research facilities.

SOURCE: U.S. Senate, Committee on Government Operations, *Federal Support of Project Grants: Indirect Costs and Cost Sharing, Hearings before the Subcommittee on Government Research,* April–June 1969, p. 18.

sity adminstrators claim they do not have the resources to share costs.[22]

Table 4.2-20 gives a summary of the conclusions of a Senate subcommittee hearing on indirect costs. The costs recovered by

[22] See U.S. Senate, Committee on Government Operations, *Federal Support of Project Grants: Indirect Costs and Cost Sharing, Hearings before the Subcommittee on Government Research,* April–June 1969, vol. 2, pp. 189–193; and Circular A-1, ibid., vol. 1.

universities for federally sponsored research are less than the costs incurred. Table 4.2-21 shows that the range of indirect costs tied to salaries and wages varies widely. Table 4.2-22 shows that this varying rate is related to the base on which indirect costs are calculated.

4.3. Endowment Income and Investment Policy

In 1963–64 total endowment of institutions of higher education was almost $7 billion. By 1967–68 total endowment had risen to $10 billion. The following table shows the book and market value of total endowment of higher education in 1966–67 and 1967–68. In both years market value was higher than book value.

Endowment, book and market value, 1966–67 and 1967–68 (millions of dollars)

	1966–67	1967–68
Book value	$8,200	$8,734
Market value	9,879	10,647

SOURCE: Council for Financial Aid to Education, American Alumni Council, and National Association of Independent Schools, *Voluntary Support of Education, 1967–68,* New York, 1969, p. 63.

Although endowment income has been declining relatively as a share of total income of higher education, total endowment has been rising at a rapid rate in the last 84 years (Table 4.3-1). From 1880 to 1963–64, total endowment increased by 182 times. Total endowment and property values of institutions of higher education were roughly equal in 1890, but by 1963–64, property values were more than four times as large as endowment. In the shorter period of 1939–40 to 1963–64, total endowment increased by four times, while property values rose more than six times.

Of 188 institutions in 1895–96, 54 had endowments of less than $25,000, and only four had endowments of more than $1 million. Even in 1910 only 250 out of 494 institutions had endowments in excess of $100,000.[1]

In general, private institutions have larger endowment funds and larger endowment-per-student ratios than public institutions.

[1] U.S. Office of Education, *Report of the Commissioner of Education, 1910,* p. 865.

651

TABLE 4.3-1 **Endowment and property values of institutions of higher education, various years (millions of dollars)**		

Year	Endowment funds	Property values
1880	$ 38	$ 0
1890	74	69
1902	164	0
1939–40	1,687	4,534
1959–60	5,322	20,225
1963–64	6,955	30,229

SOURCE: U.S. Office of Education, *Report of the Commissioner of Education*, various years, 1880–81 to 1920–21, before 1940; and U.S. Office of Education, *Higher Education Finances: Selected Trend and Summary Data*, National Center for Educational Statistics, June 1968, p. 3.

In 1962 public institutions had endowment funds totaling slightly more than $1 billion compared to almost $5 billion for private institutions. By 1964 total endowment of public institutions had increased to $1.3 billion, while endowment of private institutions increased to $5.7 billion. In 1964 endowment per student was only $480 for public institutions, as compared with $3,527 for private ones (Table 4.3-2).

DECLINE OF ENDOWMENT INCOME

Endowment income has declined relatively as a share of total income of higher education since the turn of the century. In 1909–10 endowment income provided 17 percent of total educational income; in 1963–64, it provided only 3 percent. Yet, in this period endowment income increased from $13 million to $266 million per year.[2]

Why has the relative contribution of endowment declined so much? Endowment income responds to rises in prices and national income only in part and with a time lag. Since the early 1950s, colleges and universities have been responding (more than in the past) to the losses caused by inflation by investing increasingly in equities, whose market value rises in times of inflation. Another reason for the relative decline in endowment income is that gifts for current use have been relatively more important than gifts to endowment funds. In periods of financial stress a gift for current use provides more income in the immediate future than if the gift were made to endowment.

Large increases in enrollment over the years have caused large declines in the endowment-per-student ratio for most institutions.

[2] U.S. Office of Education, *Digest of Educational Statistics, 1968*, 1968, p. 95.

TABLE 4.3-2 *Endowment funds of institutions of higher education, by control and level, United States and outlying areas, 1962 and 1964*

Type of institution, by control and level (1)	Number (2)	Enrollment* (3)	Endowment funds†	
			Total‡ (4)	Per student (5)
1962:				
All institutions	2,044	3,752,448	$6,080,724	$1,620
Four-year institutions	1,458	3,215,995	6,017,865	1,871
Two-year institutions	586	536,453	62,859	117
Publicly controlled institutions	724	2,233,189	1,086,124	486
Four-year institutions	376	1,760,223	1,077,756	612
Two-year institutions	348	472,966	8,368	18
Privately controlled institutions	1,320	1,519,259	4,994,600	3,288
Four-year institutions	1,082	1,455,772	4,940,109	3,393
Two-year institutions	238	63,487	54,491	858
1964:				
All institutions	2,140	4,266,455	6,954,696	1,630
Four-year institutions	1,503	3,644,760	6,882,977	1,888
Two-year institutions	637	621,695	71,720	115
Publicly controlled institutions	765	2,656,076	1,275,669	480
Four-year institutions	387	2,108,250	1,260,857	598
Two-year institutions	378	547,826	14,812	27
Privately controlled institutions	1,375	1,610,379	5,679,027	3,527
Four-year institutions	1,116	1,536,510	5,622,120	3,659
Two-year institutions	259	73,869	56,907	770

Resident degree-credit enrollment, full time and part time, first term 1961–62 and 1963–64.
Including funds functioning as endowment.
In thousands of dollars.
SOURCE: U.S. Department of Health, Education and Welfare, Office of Education, surveys of "Financial Statistics of Institutions of Higher Education"; in U.S. Office of Education *Digest of Educational Statistics, 1968*, 1968, p. 103.

College and university administrators often try to restrict enrollment in order to prevent this ratio from decreasing even more. All of this does not mean that endowment is unimportant. It is much more important for private than for public institutions. And, for some institutions, endowment income is a substantial percentage of total income. At Harvard, endowment income provided about one-half of total income in the nineteenth century and in recent years has provided about one-third of total income (exclusive of gifts and grants).[3]

Endowment income of all private universities decreased from 13.2 percent of educational income in 1955–56 to 8.8 percent in 1963–64. For Princeton, Vanderbilt, and the University of Chicago, endowment income as a percentage of educational and general income decreased from 43.5 percent in 1924–25 to 13.4 percent in 1965-66.[4]

ENDOWMENT BY TYPE OF INSTITUTION Trends in endowment in recent years vary by type of institution. From 1958 to 1962, among institutions with endowments of $500,000 or more, the largest relative gains in endowment per student accrued to theological schools and the smallest to private professional schools (Table 4.3-3). A study by the author of 107 institutions of higher education for the years 1928, 1940, and 1956 reveals varying rates of growth of endowment, both total and per student, for several different categories of institutions (Table 4.3-4). From 1928 to 1956, the largest percentage increase in total endowment (345 percent) accrued to eight Ivy League institutions,

[3] S. E. Harris, *The Economics of Harvard*, McGraw-Hill Book Company, New York, 1970.

[4] W. G. Bowen, *The Economics of the Major Private Universities*, Carnegie Commission on Higher Education, Berkeley, Calif., 1968, p. 35.

TABLE 4.3-3 *Endowment per student for all institutions (in selected categories) having $500,000 endowment, 1958 to 1962*

Institution type and control	Estimated market value* of endowment per degree-credit student	
	1958	*1962*
61 *public universities*	$ 1,374	$ 1,545
55 *private universities*	5,650	6,819
353 *private liberal arts colleges*	5,721	6,247
17 *private technological schools*	14,866	17,041
48 *theological schools*	18,984	24,153
24 *private professional schools including two-year institutes*	12,107	12,408
558 *all institutions*	6,933	7,924

*Estimated market value equals reported book value times 1.3. The 1.3 factor represents the average ratio of endowment market values to book values in 1958 and 1963.

SOURCE: U.S. Office of Education, *College and University Endowment: Status and Management*, 1965, table 1.

TABLE 4.3-4 *Endowment (millions of dollars)*

College groups	1928	1940	1956	1928–1940	1940–1956	1928–1956
			Average of all cases			
				Percentage rise		
Total United States	1,372*	1,764	3,837	29	118	181
8 Ivy League	21.5	52.6	95.4	147	82	345
5 other private	24.9	35.4	51.6	44	45	107
10 women's	4.4	5.1	10.2	16	98	132
20 liberal arts	3.5	5.6	9.4	61	66	170
40 large urban	9.8	15.5	22.6	57	47	130
23 large Catholic	1.6	1.3	2.7		111	68
			Endowment per student			
Total United States	1,245*	1,180	1,442	−5	22	16
8 Ivy League	4,326	8,334	12,103	93	45	180
5 other private	6,168	9,397	7,738	52		26
10 women's	4,501	4,864	7,704	8	60	71
20 liberal arts	6,247	7,500	9,765	21	30	56
40 large urban	1,590	2,080	2,050	31		29
23 large Catholic	606	490	542		11	−11

This figure is for the year 1930.

SOURCE: *American Universities and Colleges,* 1928, 1940, 1956 (compiled and calculated by S. E. Harris); in S. E. Harris, *Higher Education: Resources and Finance,* McGraw-Hill Book Company, New York, 1962, p. 460.

and the smallest percentage increase (68 percent) accrued to 23 large Catholic institutions. Endowment per student increased by 180 percent for the Ivy League group and decreased by 11 percent for the Catholic schools.

CONCENTRA-
TION OF
ENDOWMENT

A large percentage of total endowment is held by relatively few institutions. Table 4.3-5 shows the percentage distribution of 70 college and university endowment funds, each in excess of $8.9 million for 1967. Nine institutions, each with an endowment of $200 million or more, owned more than half of the total endowment of the 70 institutions. Thirty-one institutions, with endowments of $50 million or more, owned 85 percent of the endowment of these 70 institutions. In 1962, 1,365 institutions had endowments of less than $500,000 each, but only 46 institutions had endowments worth more than $25 million (Figure 4.3-1). In the early 1960s, 180

TABLE 4.3-5   *Percentage distribution of 70 college and university endowment funds, 1967*

Seventy colleges and universities are included in this study with endowments ranging in size from some $8,900,000 to over $1,038,000,000. The distribution in size is as follows:

Size of endowment based on market value, end of fiscal year	Number of endowment funds	Percentage of total value of 70 endowment funds
$200,000,000 and over	9	50.5
$100,000,000 to $200,000,000	9	19.2
$50,000,000 to $100,000,000	13	15.2
$25,000,000 to $50,000,000	17	9.2
$10,000,000 to $25,000,000	21	5.8
Under $10,000,000	1	0.1

SOURCE: Boston Fund, *The 1967 Study of College and University Endowment Funds,* Boston Management and Research Company, Inc., Boston, Mass., 1968, p. 2.

institutions, each with an endowment of $5 million or more, owned 84 percent of all endowment funds.[5]

The concentration in endowment is also evident in the endowment-per-student ratio. In 1962 the average endowment per student was $24,153 for theological schools, $1,545 for public universities, and $6,819 for private universities.[6] In the same year, among 65 public universities, 33 had endowment-per-student ratios of less than $500. Only three public universities had endowment per student of $10,000 or more, while 51 private liberal arts colleges, 13 private universities, 14 private professional schools, and 42 theological schools had endowment per student of $10,000 or more (Figure 4.3-2).[7] In 1963, among 37 private universities, endowment per student varied from $67,925 for Harvard to $826 for George Washington University. For a group of 58 private liberal arts

[5] U.S. Office of Education, *College and University Endowment: Status and Management,* 1965, pp. 4–5.

[6] Ibid., p. 5.

[7] See ibid., pp. 8–9, for endowment income in relation to basic educational expenditures.

FIGURE 4.3-1 *Distribution of all institutions of higher education by size of endowment,** 1962.

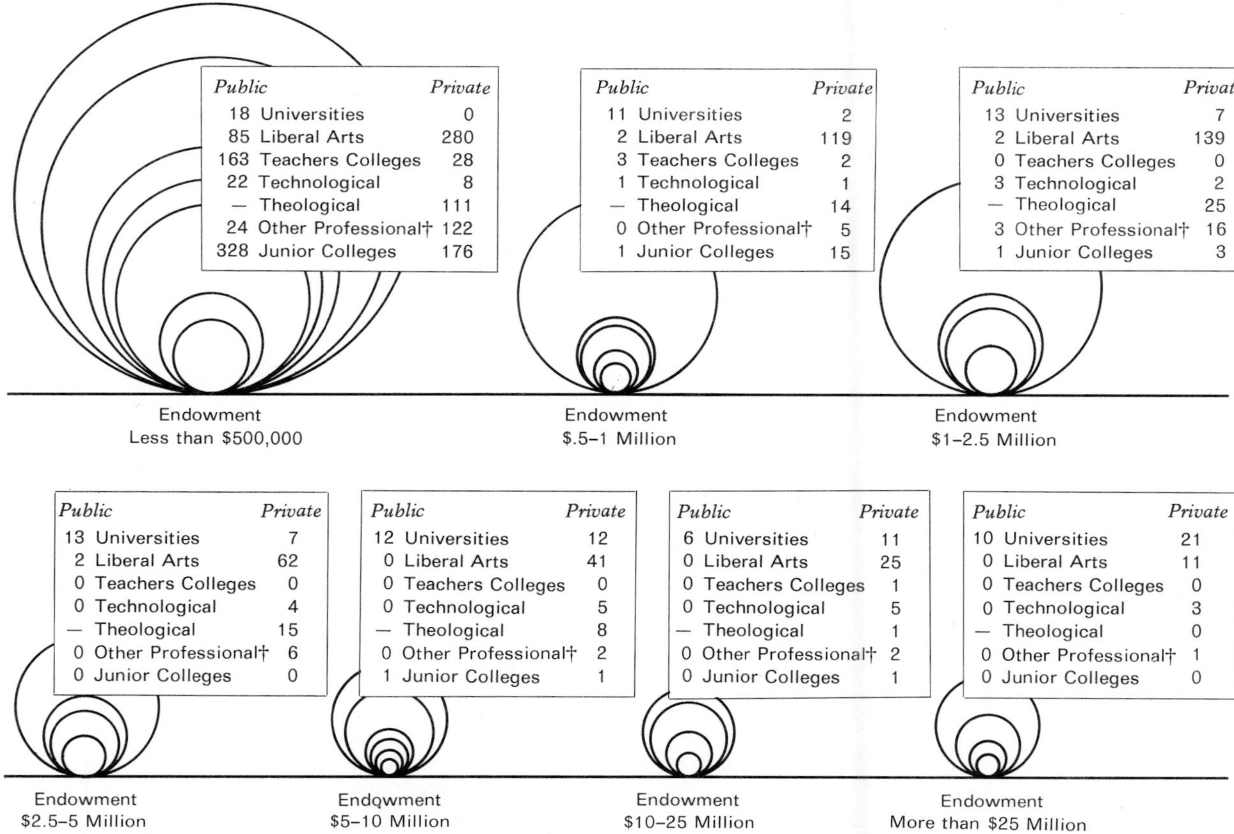

Endowment Less than $500,000

Public		Private	
18	Universities	0	
85	Liberal Arts	280	
163	Teachers Colleges	28	
22	Technological	8	
—	Theological	111	
24	Other Professional†	122	
328	Junior Colleges	176	

Endowment $.5–1 Million

Public		Private	
11	Universities	2	
2	Liberal Arts	119	
3	Teachers Colleges	2	
1	Technological	1	
—	Theological	14	
0	Other Professional†	5	
1	Junior Colleges	15	

Endowment $1–2.5 Million

Public		Private	
13	Universities	7	
2	Liberal Arts	139	
0	Teachers Colleges	0	
3	Technological	2	
—	Theological	25	
3	Other Professional†	16	
1	Junior Colleges	3	

Endowment $2.5–5 Million

Public		Private	
13	Universities	7	
2	Liberal Arts	62	
0	Teachers Colleges	0	
0	Technological	4	
—	Theological	15	
0	Other Professional†	6	
0	Junior Colleges	0	

Endowment $5–10 Million

Public		Private	
12	Universities	12	
0	Liberal Arts	41	
0	Teachers Colleges	0	
0	Technological	5	
—	Theological	8	
0	Other Professional†	2	
1	Junior Colleges	1	

Endowment $10–25 Million

Public		Private	
6	Universities	11	
0	Liberal Arts	25	
0	Teachers Colleges	1	
0	Technological	5	
—	Theological	1	
0	Other Professional†	2	
0	Junior Colleges	1	

Endowment More than $25 Million

Public		Private	
10	Universities	21	
0	Liberal Arts	11	
0	Teachers Colleges	0	
0	Technological	3	
—	Theological	0	
0	Other Professional†	1	
0	Junior Colleges	0	

*Based on book values.

† Included with other professional schools are two-year semiprofessional schools and technological institutions.

SOURCE: U.S. Office of Education, *College and University Endowment: Status and Management,* 1965, p. 6.

FIGURE 4.3-2 *Distribution of institutions based on endowment per student,* 1962

The institutions in each category are all those with more than $500,000 endowment at book value. These 637 institutions held 97 percent of all higher education endowment in 1962.

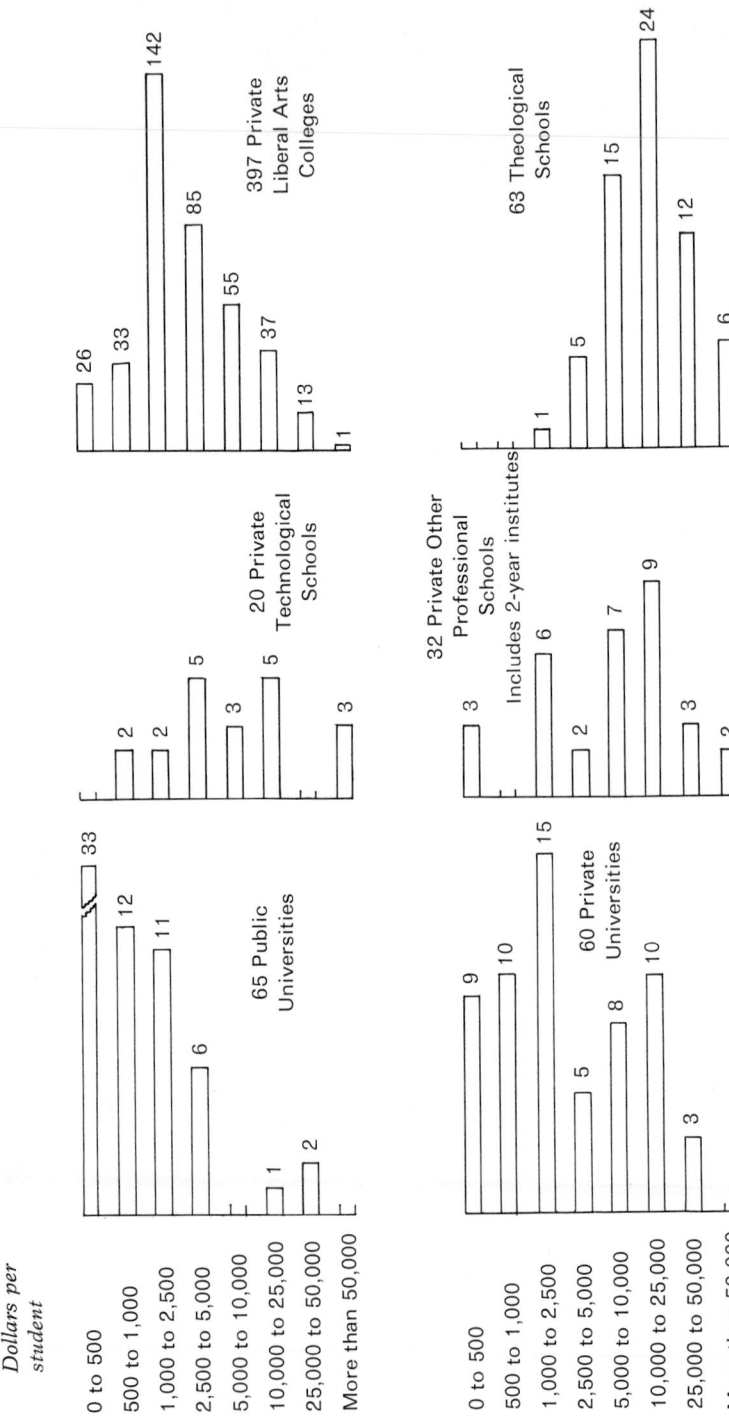

*Endowment is estimated market value and enrollment is fall degree credit. Estimated market value equals reported book value times 1.3. The 1.3 factor represents the average ratio of endowment market value to book value in 1958 and 1963.

SOURCE: U.S. Office of Education, *College and University Endowment: Status and Management*, 1965, p. 7.

colleges, endowment per student varied from $67,833 for Rice University to $2,924 for the University of Richmond.[8]

STRUCTURE OF INVESTMENT The structure of investment of endowment funds has been changing over the last 40 years. Statistics on investments over a long period are not available for large groups of institutions. However, Table 4.3-6 shows the percentage distribution of endowment funds according to type of investment for eight institutions from 1926 to 1958. This table indicates the general trend since 1926 for all institutions. A disposition to reduce the holdings of government bonds resulted in a large drop in the total bond portfolio until 1958, when bond holdings were sharply increased. Investment in common stocks increased more than six times from 1926 to 1957, but turned downward in 1958.

A study by the American Council on Education, based on a private compilation, shows a rise in the share of common stocks from 14.0 to 42.5 percent of endowment investment in the years 1929 to 1965. Investment in bonds declined from 48.8 to 40.5 percent and investment in real estate and mortgages declined from 28.8 to 6.6 percent of total endowment investment in this period.[9]

[8] U.S. Office of Education, *College and University Endowment: Status and Management,* 1965, pp. 74–75.

[9] American Council on Education, *A Fact Book on Higher Education,* Washington, D.C., 1967, p. 129.

TABLE 4.3-6 *Percentage distribution of funds according to type of investment for eight institutions**

	At book value					Book	Market
Investments	*1926*	*1939*	*1950*	*1952*	*1957*	*1958*	
TOTAL	100.0	100.0	100.0	100.0	100.0	100.0	100.0
Bonds	59.7	49.3	44.7	41.5	27.1	48.8	35.6
Preferred stocks	9.0	8.6	7.2	6.9	3.8	4.0	3.2
Common stocks	9.2	24.8	33.7	34.9	57.1	33.9	52.1
Mortgages	10.1	4.3	2.2	1.5	2.4	1.8	1.3
Real estate	5.3	9.7	6.8	7.0	5.8	5.8	4.3
Institutional plant and loans to other funds	5.5	1.6	3.3	2.5	1.7	2.7	2.0
Other investments and cash	1.2	1.7	2.1	5.7	2.1	3.0	1.5

Carnegie Institute of Technology, University of Chicago, Dartmouth College, Harvard University, Massachusetts Institute of Technology, Oberlin College, Stanford University, and Vanderbilt University.

SOURCE: U.S. Office of Education, *College and University Endowment Investments: A Survey,* 1959, p. 34.

A study for the year 1967 shows that 70 institutions with a total of $6 billion of investment had 58 percent invested in common stocks (market value) and 29 percent in bonds.[10] Figure 4.3-3 shows the percentage of the endowment of 35 institutions that was invested in government bonds from 1948 to 1958 (at both book and market values). The percentage of endowment that these same institutions invested in nongovernment bonds is shown in Figure 4.3-4. Investment in nongovernment bonds increased relatively in this period, while investment in government bonds declined.

An Office of Education study for the years 1925 to 1963 points to the steady rise in the percentage of endowment invested in

[10] Boston Fund, *The 1967 Study of College and University Endowment Funds,* Boston Management and Research Company, Inc., Boston, Mass., 1968, p. 4.

FIGURE 4.3-3 *Percentage of endowment fund of 34 institutions invested in government bonds, 1948-1958*

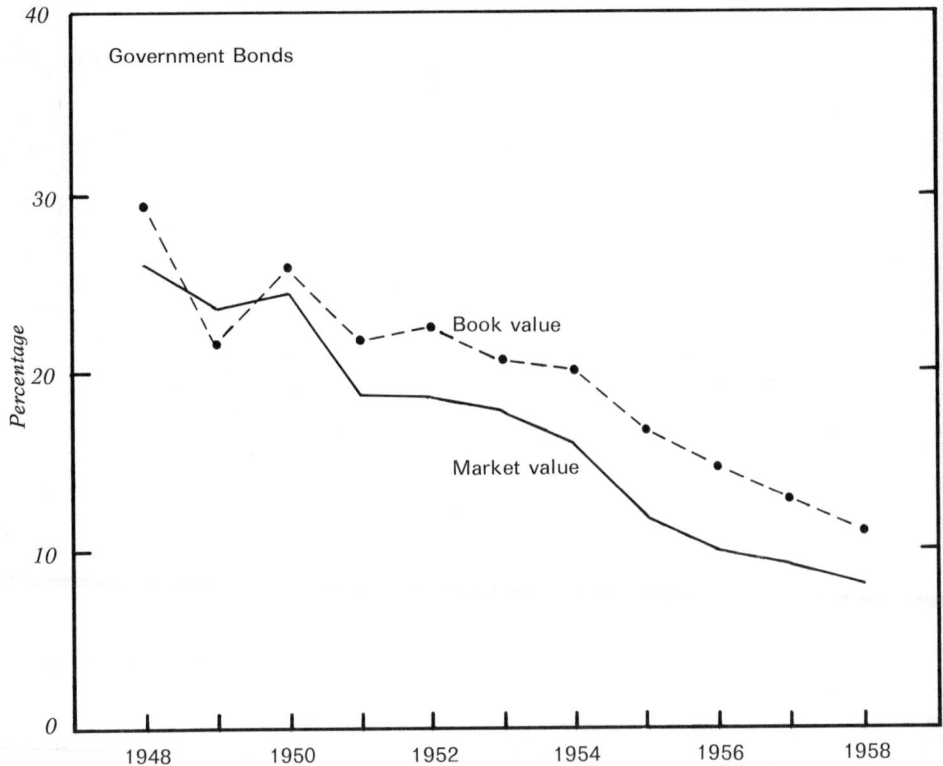

SOURCE: U.S. Office of Education, *College and University Endowment Investments: A Survey,* 1959, p. 36.

FIGURE 4.3-4 *Percentage of endowment fund of 35 institutions invested in nongovernment bonds, 1948–1958*

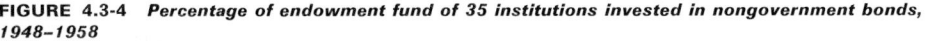

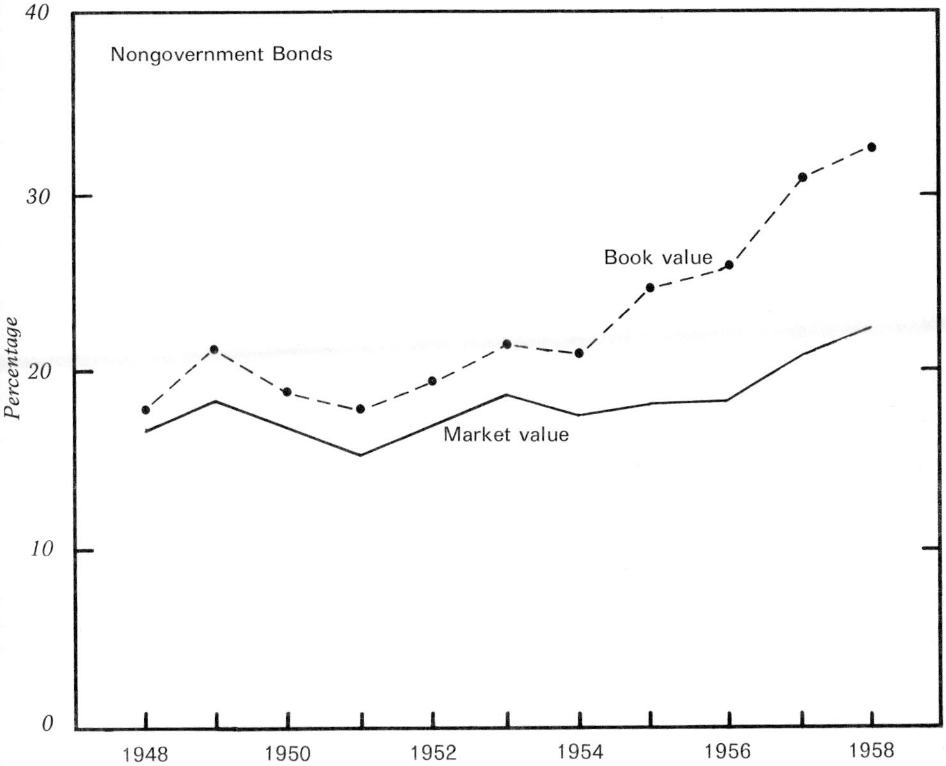

SOURCE: U.S. Office of Education, *College and University Endowment Investments: A Survey,* 1959, p. 37.

common stocks and to the large increase in market value over book value (Figure 4.3-5). In the late 1950s common stocks in endowment portfolios were valued at $1.2 billion book value and $2.3 billion market value. In this period common stocks accounted for 46 percent of endowment income, 32 percent of the book value of endowment, and 48 percent of market value.[11]

The distribution of investment by type of institution in 1962–63 is shown in Figure 4.3-6. Eighty-eight public universities held 17 percent of the $9.7 billion of investment. Fifty-eight private universities held 43 percent of total investment, and 684 private liberal arts colleges held 25 percent.

[11] U.S. Office of Education, *College and University Endowment: Status and Management,* 1965, pp. 9, 17.

FIGURE 4.3-5   *Percentage of endowment funds invested in common stocks, 1926–1963*

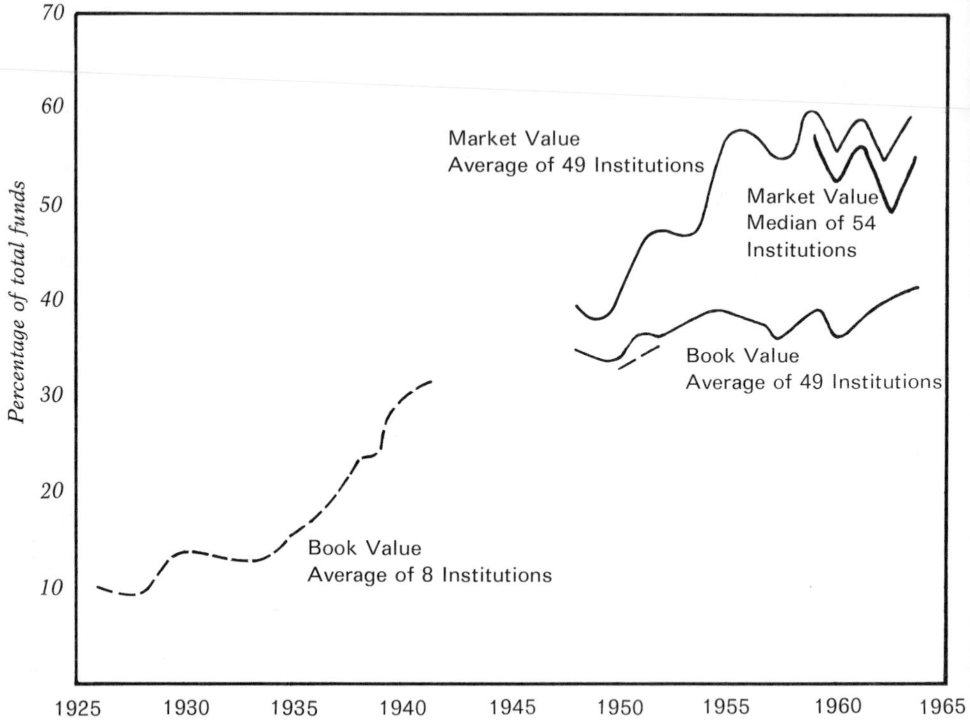

Market Value
Average of 49 Institutions

Market Value
Median of 54
Institutions

Book Value
Average of 49 Institutions

Book Value
Average of 8 Institutions

Percentage of total funds

NOTE: The term average is arithmetic mean.

SOURCE: U.S. Office of Education, *College and University Endowment: Status and Management,* 1965, p. 31.

Table 4.3-7 compares the percentage of investments held in common stock for institutions of higher education and other investment groups. Educational institutions held a much smaller percentage of their investments in common stock than open-end investment companies, but a much larger percentage than national bank trust departments, foundations, or church board funds. The percentage invested in common stocks was approximately the same for educational institutions and common trust funds.

INVESTMENT PERFORMANCE OF ENDOWMENT FUNDS   A recent study by the Ford Foundation Advisory Committee on Endowment Management reveals large differences in the rate of return on investments of 15 institutions of higher education. The average rate of return for the 15 schools was 8.7 percent for the 10 years ending June 30, 1968, but the extremes ranged from 6.2 to 13.0 percent. The average return for the five years ending June

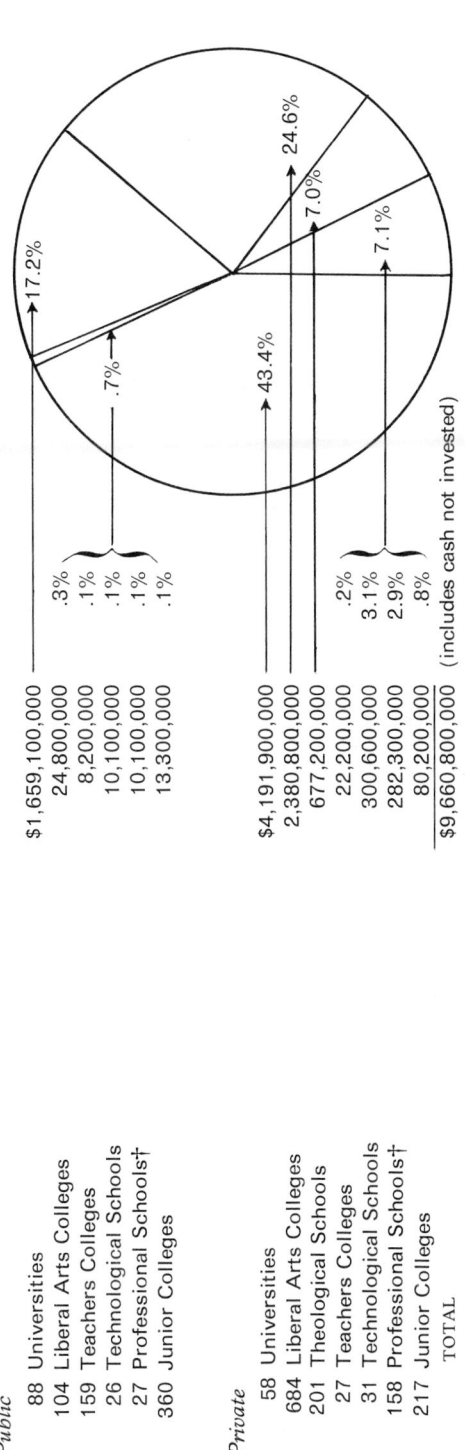

FIGURE 4.3-6 *The structure of investments, 1962–63**

Public

88	Universities	$1,659,100,000	17.2%
104	Liberal Arts Colleges	24,800,000	.3%
159	Teachers Colleges	8,200,000	.1%
26	Technological Schools	10,100,000	.1%
27	Professional Schools†	10,100,000	.1%
360	Junior Colleges	13,300,000	.1%

Private

58	Universities	$4,191,900,000	43.4%
684	Liberal Arts Colleges	2,380,800,000	24.6%
201	Theological Schools	677,200,000	7.0%
27	Teachers Colleges	22,200,000	.2%
31	Technological Schools	300,600,000	3.1%
158	Professional Schools†	282,300,000	2.9%
217	Junior Colleges	80,200,000	.8%
	TOTAL	$9,660,800,000	(includes cash not invested)

* Estimated 1963 market values. Distribution based on 1962 book values for all institutions in the United States.

† Included with other professional schools are two-year semiprofessional schools and technological institutions.

SOURCE: U.S. Office of Education, *College and University Endowment: Status and Management*, 1965, p. 28.

TABLE 4.3-7
A comparison
of percentage
invested in
common stock,
institutions of
higher
education and
other
categories, late
1950s

Category	Percentage
200 colleges and universities	48.0
277 common trust funds	47.6
Open-end investment companies	80.0
National bank trust departments	26.5
Foundations	23.6
Church board funds	26.8

SOURCE: U.S. Office of Education, *College and University Endowment Investments: A Survey,* 1959, p. 30.

TABLE 4.3-8 *Investment performance of college endowments*

	Total return			
	Ten years to June 30, 1968		Five years to June 30, 1968	
	Cumulative	Annual average	Cumulative	Annual average
I. Fifteen educational institutions				
A	240%	13.0%	85%	13.1%
B	196	11.5	68	11.0
C	176	10.7	72	11.5
D	146	9.4	46	7.8
E	135	8.9	53	8.9
F	133	8.8	51	8.6
G	131	8.7	47	8.1
H	120	8.2	30	5.3
I	117	8.0	42	7.3
J	116	8.0	39	6.8
K	113	7.8	38	6.6
L	108	7.6	43	7.5
M	100	7.2	32	5.7
N	94	6.8	25	4.6
O	83	6.2	28	5.1
Average	134%	8.7%	47%	7.9%
II. The University of Rochester	283%	14.4%	127%	17.9%

GENERAL NOTE: Total return includes both (1) appreciation, and (2) interest and dividends, which are assumed to have been reinvested. . . . The annual average return is on a compound basis.

SPECIAL NOTES: 1. In the case of educational institutions, there may in certain cases be moderate inaccuracies owing to inclusion of some nonmarketable assets and to relative infrequency of unit calculations. In a few cases, the fiscal year ends on August 31 rather than June 30. However, we do not believe that the resulting inaccuracies are substantial. 2. The University of Rochester is shown separately because it is a well-known example of an educational institution that almost 20 years ago adopted the objective of long-term growth for most of its endowment fund.

SOURCE: Advisory Committee on Endowment Management, *Managing Educational Endowments,* Ford Foundation, New York, 1969, p. 57.

TABLE 4.3-9
Performance
of various
funds, annual
average return

	Ten years to June 30, 1968	Five years to June 30, 1968
15 institutions of higher education	8.7	7.9
21 balanced funds	9.2	8.8
Standard and Poors Index of 500 Common Stocks	14.0	11.0
Ten growth funds	14.6	16.6

SOURCE: Advisory Committee on Endowment Management, *Managing Educational Endowments*, Ford Foundation, New York, 1969, pp. 57–59.

30, 1968 was 7.9 percent, with extreme values of 13.1 and 4.6 percent (Table 4.3-8). Some schools obviously had a more remunerative investment policy than others. The Ford study also showed that noneducational investment groups seemed to perform better than these 15 institutions of higher education (Table 4.3-9). The average return for 21 balanced funds over the 10 years prior to June 30, 1968 was 9.2 percent. For Standard and Poors Index of 500 Common Stocks, the average return was 14.0 percent, and for 10 growth stocks, 14.6 percent.

Table 4.3-10 gives a summary of the yields on endowment investments for various years from 1926 to 1958. During this period the highest yield was 5.69 percent in 1929; the lowest was 3.90 percent in 1946 (based on book value). In 1967 the yield on investments for 67 institutions varied from 7.61 to 2.49 percent. Thirty-four institutions had yields of more than 4 percent on their investments and 60 had yields of 3.5 percent or higher. Only 6 institutions received more than 5 percent (Table 4.3-11).

Table 4.3-12 shows the investment earnings of 90 institutions with more than $5 million of endowment each for fiscal year 1963. Income from common stocks was $70.7 million at a rate of return of 3.4 percent. Bond income was $53.4 million at a rate of return of 4.1 percent. Total dollar income from stocks was much larger than bond income because most of these institutions had nearly twice as much of their endowment invested in stocks as in bonds. Capital gains (realized and unrealized) amounted to $488 million for stocks and $8 million for bonds.

No clear evidence is available to suggest that large institutions earn a higher rate of return than small ones. Table 4.3-13 shows that in 1958 the average rate of return was 3.64 percent for institutions with endowments of less than $2 million each and 3.65 percent for institutions with over $50 million of endowment each. The highest average rate of return was 3.82 percent for institutions with endowment funds of $2 to $3 million.

(Text continued on p. 669)

TABLE 4.3-10
Returns on investment

Year	Number of IHL*	Total yield (based on book value unless designated market)
1926[a,d]	45	5.14
	59	4.99
1929[a,b]	45	5.08
	22	5.69
1930[a,c]	45	5.16
	19–20	4.97 market
1933[a,b]	45	4.58
	22	4.15
1936[h,d]	22	4.15
	59	4.25
1940[a,c]	45	4.42
	19–20	4.50 market
1946[d]	59	3.90
	59	3.33 market
1950[c]	19–20	4.37 market
1953[e]	26	4.75
	21	4.00 market
1956[f,g]	39	3.36 market
	904	4.12
1958[h]	200	3.84 market
	200	4.91

*Institutions of higher learning.

SOURCE: (a) J. H. Cain, *What Is Happening to College and University Investments and Income?*, American Council on Education Studies, Washington, 1941, p. 29. (b) C. R. Sattgast, *The Administration of College and University Endowments*, 1940, p. 54. (c) "College Investments," *Barron's*, June 25, 1951. (Based on market value.) (d) Scudder, Stevens and Clark, *Survey of University and College Endowment Funds*, New York, 1947, p. 21. (e) S. H. F. Goldstein, "Investing Returns by Endowment Funds," *Commercial and Financial Chronicle*, no. 5224, 1953. (Includes some foundations.) (f) Boston Fund, *A Study of College and University Endowment Funds*, 1956, p. 24. (g) Adjusted 1956 market figures by ratio of market to book values, given in *Voluntary Support of America's Colleges and Universities, 1956–1957*, Council for Financial Aid to Education, New York, pp. 38–39. (h) U.S. Department of Health, Education and Welfare, *College and University Endowment Investments: A Survey as of June 30, 1958*, p. 12; in S. E. Harris, *Higher Education: Resources and Finance*, McGraw-Hill Book Company, New York, 1962, p. 490.

TABLE 4. 3-11   *Yield statistics*

To determine the yield for each of the sixty-seven colleges and universities . . . we have related the total income on bonds, preferred stocks and common stocks to an average of the market values of these classifications as of the beginning and end of the 1967 fiscal year. The following table shows a yield figure for each endowment, in declining order, without identification of the institution.

Endowment	Yield	Endowment	Yield
1	7.61%	29	4.04%
2	5.19	30	4.03
3	5.16	31	4.02
4	5.15	32	4.01
5	5.06	33	4.01
6	5.04	34	4.01
7	4.91	35	3.99
8	4.76	36	3.99
9	4.72	37	3.97
10	4.64	38	3.97
11	4.54	39	3.95
12	4.39	40	3.90
13	4.38	41	3.90
14	4.38	42	3.89
15	4.37	43	3.86
16	4.35	44	3.83
17	4.34	45	3.77
18	4.30	46	3.74
19	4.30	47	3.71
20	4.26	48	3.70
21	4.17	49	3.69
22	4.16	50	3.69
23	4.14	51	3.68
24	4.13	52	3.64
25	4.11	53	3.62
26	4.10	54	3.56
27	4.10	55	3.55
28	4.10	56	3.55

TABLE 4.3-11 *(continued)*

Endowment	Yield	Endowment	Yield
57	3.55%	63	3.33%
58	3.54	64	3.27
59	3.54	65	3.15
60	3.53	66	2.97
61	3.36	67	2.49
62	3.34		

SOURCE: Boston Fund, *The 1967 Study of College and University Endowment Funds,* Boston Management and Research Company, Inc., Boston, Mass., 1968, p. 25.

TABLE 4.3-12 *Earnings for 90 institutions, each having more than $5,000,000 in endowment, fiscal year 1963*

Ninety colleges and universities reported their investment returns for fiscal year 1963. The $4.68 billion endowment held by these institutions represents about one-half the total endowment for all higher education. A summary of these returns is presented. While stocks yielded less than bonds, the total amount of dollar income from stock dividends was substantially larger than the income from bond interest. This was due to the fact that most institutions had nearly twice as much of their endowment funds invested in equities as in bonds (an average of 54.2 versus 28.8 percent of the portfolio total).

Investment	Income (dividends, interest, rent)			Capital gains† (realized and unrealized)		
	Median yield* (percent)	Amount (thousands)	Percentage of total	Median appreciation rate* (percent)	Amount (thousands)	Percentage of total
Stocks	3.4	$70,714	43.3	21	$488,200	93.6
Bonds	4.1	53,370	32.7	1	8,183	1.6
All other	4.3	39,242	24.0		25,639	4.9
TOTAL	3.7	$163,326	100.0	12	$522,022	100.0

* Relative to average of beginning and end-of-fiscal-year investment market values.

† Both realized and unrealized capital gains equal: (end-of-year minus beginning-of-year market values) plus (sale price of holdings sold minus purchase price of holdings bought during fiscal year).

SOURCE: U.S. Office of Education, *College and University Endowment: Status and Management,* 1965, p. 45.

Higher returns could be earned on endowment if investment policy improved. Policies in the past have been too conservative. Since endowment income is a relatively declining source of income for higher education, endowment managers should be willing to take more risks to increase endowment income and the value of endowment funds.

Greater use of capital gains could lead to a relative increase in the contribution of endowment income. Investment managers tend to be overly conservative in this area. Many insist that the original gift plus any capital gains are inviolate and cannot be used as current income. A minority, however, would make part of realized capital gains available as current income.[12]

Cary and Bright, in their excellent volume for the Ford Foundation, *The Law and Lore of Endowment Funds,* have shed much light on the subject of capital gains. Realized capital gains have been an increasing source of income for charitable trusts since the late 1940s. Failure of institutions of higher education to consider realized capital gains as income has resulted in investments yielding high current incomes, but incomes much below what would have been attained had they invested relatively more in equities and used some of the capital gains as income. Cary and Bright insist that colleges and universities wrongly assume that they are not allowed to consider realized capital gains as income. These authors exclude unrealized capital gains from income because of court rulings, but they recommend putting aside part of the realized capital gains to protect endowment funds against inflation and possible declines in the market value of securities. They conclude that the law does not hamper the development of sound investment policies and that ". . . subject to the standards which prudence dictates, the expenditures of gains should lie within the discretion of the institution's directors."[13]

A policy which concentrates heavily on growth stocks raises some questions, too. If extreme emphasis is placed on the growth of the endowment fund, some present income will be sacrificed for future income. This is, of course, necessary to some extent to prevent endowment from declining further as a percentage of higher

(Text continued on p. 673)

---

[12] U.S. Office of Education, *College and University Endowment: Status and Management,* 1965, p. 55.

[13] W. L. Cary and C. E. Bright, *The Law and Lore of Endowment Funds,* Ford Foundation, New York, March 1969.

			Bonds	
		Cash and short-term invest-ments	United States govern-ment	Other gov-ernments, including foreign
TABLE 4.3-13 Distribution of cash and securities included in portfolios of 200 institutions showing market value, income, and rate of return, 1957–58, by size of endowment (dollar figures are in thousands)	*Number of responses*	*Size of endowment fund*			
17	Over $50 million			
	Market value	$61,238	$422,724	$68,246
	Income	537	11,954	2,218
	Rate of return	0.88	2.83	3.25
31	$15 to $50 million			
	Market value	$11,124	$72,093	$18,280
	Income	88	2,122	570
	Rate of return	0.79	2.94	3.12
21	$11 to $15 million			
	Market value	$2,807	$20,341	$5,409
	Income	9	568	158
	Rate of return	0.32	2.79	2.92
32	$6 to $11 million			
	Market value	$5,165	$23,304	$5,997
	Income	34	670	251
	Rate of return	0.66	2.88	4.19
29	$4 to $6 million			
	Market value	$3,557	$12,903	$7,434
	Income	23	427	174
	Rate of return	0.65	3.31	2.34
22	$3 to $4 million			
	Market value	$3,325	$9,117	$2,345
	Income	75	300	76
	Rate of return	2.26	3.29	3.24
23	$2 to $3 million			
	Market value	$1,698	$4,853	$891
	Income	31	134	29
	Rate of return	1.83	2.76	3.25
25	Under $2 million			
	Market value	$518	$5,446	$375
	Income	9	141	11
	Rate of return	1.74	2.59	2.93
200	Total			
	Market value	$89,432	$570,781	$108,977
	Income	806	16,316	3,487
	Rate of return	0.90	2.86	3.20

SOURCE: U.S. Office of Education, *College and University Endowment Investments: A Survey,* 1959, p. 13.

Nongov-ernment	Stocks		Investment companies	Total cash and securities
	Preferred	*Common*		
$526,507	$71,204	$1,198,720	$1,275	$2,349,914
23,197	3,509	44,389	35	85,839
4.41	4.93	3.70	2.75	3.65
$233,504	$51,134	$602,424	$1,359	$989,918
9,243	2,476	21,282	84	35,865
3.96	4.84	3.53	6.18	3.62
$62,456	$18,599	$182,724	$39	$292,375
2,659	928	6,811	2	11,135
4.26	4.99	3.73	5.13	3.81
$61,378	$17,637	$167,754	$733	$281,968
2,252	870	6,596	29	10,702
3.67	4.93	3.93	3.96	3.80
$28,902	$9,999	$76,922	$2,344	$142,061
1,050	446	3,174	88	5,382
3.63	4.46	4.13	3.75	3.79
$18,875	$4,312	$44,847	$1,494	$84,315
616	195	1,750	37	3,049
3.26	4.52	3.90	2.48	3.62
$12,773	$4,170	$31,236	$421	$56,042
481	211	1,240	15	2,141
3.77	5.06	3.97	3.56	3.82
$5,775	$1,764	$18,933	$328	$33,139
194	74	767	10	1,206
3.36	4.20	4.05	3.05	3.64
$950,170	$178,819	$2,323,560	$7,993	$4,229,732
39,692	8,709	86,009	300	155,319
4.18	4.87	3.70	3.75	3.67

TABLE 4.3-14   *Investment policies and administration (1958)*

On a questionnaire form, . . . a series of policy questions were asked of the 200 institutions. . . . These questions and [their] answers follow:

1. For investment advice on whom do you primarily depend?

	Responses
a. Own institutional investment staff	19
b. Outside investment counsel	68
c. A trust company	49
d. Committee of governing board	64
TOTAL	200

A number of institutions reported a combination of methods. It is obvious that the governing board has the final responsibility, but the trend seems to be for more institutions to seek expert advice.

2. Do you use the market value method of endowment fund accounting?

Yes, 60; no, 140

Of the institutions holding more than $4 million in endowment funds, 46 answered "yes," 84 answered "no." Only in the category of over $50 million did more than half (9 of 17) of the respondents indicate that the market value of endowment fund accounting was used. . . .

3. Have you established an income reserve account for the purpose of stabilizing the amount available for budgetary appropriations from year to year?

Yes, 54; no, 146

This account is usually designated as "Reserve for stabilization of endowment income." An estimate of income is prepared at the beginning of a fiscal period. For budgetary purposes, a difference is almost certain to exist between the estimated and actual receipts. The reserve account is not used to accumulate unnecessarily large surpluses, but merely to distribute the income on a pro rata basis to all funds, or to take care of all budgetary appropriations at as uniform a percentage rate as feasible.

4. Do you have an established policy on investing in common stocks? If "yes," what is the maximum percent of endowment and nonexpendable funds that may be invested in common stocks?

TABLE 4.3-14 *(continued)*

Yes, 75; no, 125

. . . Of the 200 institutions, 75 indicated that a policy existed which limited the portion of their endowment funds which could be invested in common stocks. For the 75 having a limiting policy, the range was from 35 to 100 percent, with an average of 56 percent.

SOURCE: U.S. Office of Education, *College and University Endowment Investments: A Survey,* 1959, p. 20.

educational income. In periods of financial stress, however, institutions should concentrate on investments which bring high current income rather than future income. The trade-off between these two positions will have to be determined by the directors of the institution.

In an important study, *Managing Educational Endowment,* a Ford Foundation committee examines past endowment policies and proposes measures that would increase the rate of return on endowment.[14] The main suggestion of the Ford Committee is for each institution to seek the highest return over the long run rather than the highest current income. To achieve this goal the Ford Committee advises placing more responsibility on a hired investment manager—with corresponding incentives to him, use of some realized capital gains as income, reduced emphasis on liquidity, greater disposition to risk taking, less diversification, and increased study of small, young corporations which are more likely to achieve a record of substantial growth than are old, established firms.

Improved yields could certainly be obtained by hiring professional investment managers who understand the issues raised by the Ford Committee. But there are limits to this improvement. Improved management will generally result in increased emphasis on stocks with rapidly rising prices, thus reducing yields. Also, there are managers and trustees who continue to favor the objective of high current income over growth, and others who will not allow capital gains to be used as income.

[14] For a complete discussion of this topic, see Advisory Committee on Endowment Management, *Managing Educational Endowments,* Ford Foundation, New York, 1969.

Of the 200 respondents to a 1958 survey on investment policies and administration, 34 percent depended primarily on outside investment council for advice, 25 percent invested through a trust company, 32 percent depended mainly on a committee of the governing board, and 9 percent on their own institutional investment staff (Table 4.3-14).

4.4. Tuition

Tuition[1] has grown steadily as a percentage of educational and
general income of higher education in recent years—in part because
of increases in enrollment and in part because of increases in
tuition necessitated by increasing costs of higher education per
student. Tuition in private institutions has been rising relatively
faster than tuition in public institutions. From 1955–56 to 1965–
66, tuition charged by private institutions rose by 116 percent,
while tuition charged by public institutions rose by 53 percent.
Public institutions are becoming comparatively less expensive for
the student than private institutions. Tuition is a relatively more
important source of revenue for private than for public institutions,
amounting to 44 percent of current fund revenue per student for
private institutions, as compared with only 13 percent for public
institutions, in 1965–66. From 1955–56 to 1965–66, tuition
increased more rapidly than current fund revenue, especially in
private institutions (Table 4.4-1).

From 1955–56 to 1965–66, enrollment increased by 112 percent
and tuition by 53 percent. Increases in enrollment, therefore,
accounted for roughly two-thirds of the increase in tuition income
and increases in tuition per student for the remaining one-third.
(These calculations are in current dollars. In dollars of stable
purchasing power, the increase in tuition was only 30 percent.)[2]
With tuition increasing more rapidly for private than for public

---

[1] Tuition in this chapter will refer to both tuition and student fees, but not to
room and board charges.

[2] U.S. Office of Education, *Students and Buildings: An Analysis of Selected
Federal Programs for Higher Education,* 1968, pp. 7, 10; and U.S. Office of
Education, *Financial Statistics of Institutions of Higher Education: Current
Funds, Revenues, and Expenditures, 1965–66,* National Center for Educa-
tional Statistics, 1969, p. 10 (author's calculations).

TABLE 4.4-1
Average current fund revenue per full-time equivalent student and estimated average charges per full-time resident degree student by control, 1955–56 and 1965–66 (in current dollars)

Item	1955–56 amount
Public	
*Average current fund revenue per FTE student**	$1,466
Total tuition, board and room	710
Tuition and required fees	164
Board (seven-day basis)	401
Dormitory rooms	141
Private	
*Average current fund revenue per FTE student**	$1,425
Total tuition, board and room	1,168
Tuition and required fees	527
Board (seven-day basis)	436
Dormitory rooms	205

*Excluding revenue from organized research.
SOURCE: Supplementary table to *Projections of Educational Statistics to 1975–76;* in U.S. Office of Education, *Students and Buildings: An Analysis of Selected Federal Programs for Higher Education,* 1968, p. 10.

institutions, we conclude that a shift of enrollment from private to public institutions would mean substantial savings on student expenses.

TRENDS OVER A LONGER PERIOD Table 4.4-2 presents estimated tuition and total cost of attending both public and private institutions from 1930–31 to 1980–81. Tuition is projected to increase by 10.7 times for public and 7.2 times for private institutions from 1930–31 to 1980–81. The relatively larger increase in tuition projected for public institutions over this period hides the more recent trend toward relatively larger increases in tuition for private institutions.

TABLE 4.4-2
Estimated costs for tuition and required fees and total costs of attending college, per student, 1930–31 to 1980–81, by control

	Tuition and required fees			
	Tuition and fees		Total costs	
Year	Public	Private	Public	Private
1930–31	$ 71	$ 252	$ 730	$ 960
1960–61	179	676	1,400	2,090
1970–71	353	1,115	1,840	2,780
1980–81	760	1,815	2,400	3,640

SOURCE: U.S. House of Representatives, Committee on Education and Labor, *The Federal Government and Education,* report of a subcommittee, 1963, p. 165.

1965–66 amount	Percentage change	Annual rate of increase
$1,971	34.4	3.0
979	37.9	3.3
251	53.0	4.4
442	10.2	1.0
286	102.8	7.3
$2,603	82.7	6.2
1,982	69.7	5.4
1,141	116.5	8.0
496	13.8	1.2
345	68.3	5.3

The following table shows the estimated differences in tuition and in total cost of attending college, per student, between public and private institutions from 1930–31 to 1980–81:

Estimated differences in total cost and in tuition, private over public	1930–31	1960–61	1980–81
Tuition	181	497	1,055
Total cost	230	690	1,240

SOURCE: U.S. House of Representatives, Committee on Education and Labor, *The Federal Government and Education,* report of a subcommittee, 1963, p. 165.

The excess of private over public costs and tuition has been increasing since 1930–31 and is projected to continue to increase.

ROOM AND BOARD The cost of room and board varies greatly by type of institution and by location. In 1962–63 overall differences in room and board charges between public and private institutions were relatively small. Private dormitory rates were 13 percent and private board rates 7 percent higher than public rates. By type of institution and by region, the differences were much larger. For private institutions (at the fiftieth percentile) the annual rates for rooms ranged from $154 for junior colleges to $333 for universities. For public insti-

TABLE 4.4-3
Dormitory and board rates, by control, region, and type of institution, 1962–63 (fiftieth percentile)

| | Dormitory rates | | Board rates | |
Type of institution	Public	Private	Public	Private
All	$199	$224	$389	$417
University	242	333	444	492
Liberal arts college	188	236	361	429
Teachers college	196	225	367	412
Technological institution	213	319	454	442
Theological institution		170		363
Other professional institution	250	308	450	506
Junior college	175	154	376	381
Region				
North Atlantic	276	290	406	474
Great Lakes and Plains	218	235	427	418
Southeast	177	164	339	363
West and Southwest	205	215	427	393

SOURCE: U.S. Bureau of the Census, *Basic Student Charges, 1962–63*, 1963, tables 7 and 8.

tutions, the annual rates for rooms varied from $175 for junior colleges to $250 for other professional schools. By region, the highest charges for room and board were in the North Atlantic states, and the lowest charges in the Southeast. A public junior college in the Southeast would provide the student with the minimum possible room and board charges and a private university in the North Atlantic states with the highest (Table 4.4-3).

DIFFERENTIAL CHARGES TO RESIDENT AND NONRESIDENT STUDENTS

One of the major complaints about tuition policy in recent years has been the higher tuition charged by public institutions to out-of-state students. Table 4.4-4 shows that from 1939–40 to 1954–55 the percentage difference between resident and out-of-state tuition rates rose by 159 percent. For universities, the percentage difference increased by 137 percent and for teachers colleges, 288 percent. Note, however, that most of the increase in the difference between in-state and out-of-state tuition occurred in the 1940–1950 period, and only a small increase can be attributed to the 1950–1955 period.

OTHER VARIATIONS IN TUITION

On the whole, tuition in private institutions was about four times as high as tuition charged to in-state students by public institutions in both 1958–59 and 1962–63. Liberal arts colleges ex-

40, 1949-50, and 1954-55 (catalogue study— U.S. Office of Education)

Curricular-organizational classification (1)	Number of institutions (2)	Average difference between in-state and out-of-state tuition rates in —			Amount of increase in difference from —			Percentage increase in difference from —		
		1939-40 (3)	1949-50 (4)	1954-55 (5)	1940 to 1950[a] (6)	1940 to 1955[b] (7)	1950 to 1955[c] (8)	1940 to 1950[d] (9)	1940 to 1955[e] (10)	1950 to 1955[f] (11)
Publicly controlled	120	$ 66	$146	$171	$ 80	$105	$ 25	121	159	17
Universities	69	81	182	192	101	111	10	125	137	6
Liberal arts colleges	19	38	84	119	46	81	35	121	213	42
Technological schools	4	82	100	265	18	183	165	22	223	165
Teachers colleges	17	41	120	159	79	118	39	193	288	33
Other professional schools	1	200	300	300	100	100	0	50	50	0
Junior colleges	10	34	59	86	25	52	27	74	153	46

[a] Column 4 minus column 3.

[b] Column 5 minus column 3.

[c] Column 5 minus column 3.

[d] Column 6 divided by column 3, times 100. The first entry in this column is to be read: The *increase* in the difference between average in-state and out-of-state tuition rate from 1939-40 to 1949-50 (viz., $80, column 6) was 121 percent of the average difference existing in the school year 1939-40 (viz., $66, column 3).

[e] Column 7 divided by column 3, times 100. The first entry in this column is to be read: The *increase* in the difference between average in-state and out-of-state tuition rate from 1939-40 to 1954-55 (viz., $105, column 7) was 159 percent of the average difference existing in the school year 1939-40 (viz., $66, column 3).

[f] Column 8 divided by column 4, times 100. The first entry in this column is to be read: The *increase* in the difference between average in-state and out-of-state tuition rate from 1949-50 to 1954-55 (viz., $25, column 8) was 17 percent of the average difference existing in the school year 1949-50 (viz., $146, column 4).

SOURCE: "Higher Education Under Stress," *The Annals of the American Academy of Political and Social Science*, vol. 301, September 1955, table 8.

TABLE 4.4-5 *Tuition and fees for full-time undergraduates by institutional type and control, fiftieth percentile, 1958–59 and 1962–63*

	Public resident 1958–59	Public resident 1962–63	Percentage change	Private 1958–59	Private 1962–63	Percentage change
TOTAL	$134	$183	+37	$534	$ 740	+39
Universities	208	257	+24	750	1,000	+33
Liberal arts colleges	143	181	+27	543	788	+45
Teachers colleges	134	211	+57	500	600	+20
Technological institutions	200	226	+13	776	1,089	+40
Junior colleges	84	109	+30	392	526	+34
Theological institutions				290	397	+37
Other professional				646	795	+23

SOURCE: Adapted from L. A. D'Amico and W. R. Bokelman, *Changes in Tuition Charges to Full-Time Undergraduate Students, 1958–59 to 1962–63,* U.S. Office of Education, March 1964, p. 1.

perienced the largest relative increase in tuition among private schools, and private teachers colleges experienced the smallest. For public institutions, teachers colleges experienced the largest relative increase in tuition, and technological schools had the smallest (Table 4.4-5).

Table 4.4-6 shows that in 1962–63 there were large variations in tuition charged by private institutions of the same type and in the same region. Table 4.4-7 shows some of the same information

TABLE 4.4-6 *Percentile values of tuition and required fees charged for full-time undergraduate students in private institutions for the academic year, by type of institution and region, aggregate United States, 1962–63*

Type of institution, by region	Number reporting	Percentile Tenth	Percentile Twenty-fifth	Percentile Fiftieth	Percentile Seventy-fifth	Percentile Ninetieth
All institutions	1,210	$290	$ 470	$ 690	$ 944	$1,245
University	55	663	798	1,038	1,412	1,556
Liberal arts college	637	439	616	751	981	1,281
Teachers college	29	365	463	575	1,088	1,355
Technological school	28	40	700	1,050	1,350	1,610
Theological school	161	72	213	361	495	696
Other professional school	94	500	620	794	999	1,184
Junior college	206	208	344	502	740	1,025
North Atlantic	411	306	645	855	1,162	1,471
University	27	793	1,019	1,375	1,532	1,591

TABLE 4.4-6 *(continued)*

Type of institution, by region	Number reporting	Percentile Tenth	Twenty-fifth	Fiftieth	Seventy-fifth	Ninetieth
Liberal arts college	189	$681	$ 782	$ 968	$ 1,214	$1,475
Teachers college	12	554	600	1,100	1,350	1,540
Technological school	13	15	1,071	1,275	1,394	1,670
Theological school	53	0	163	335	516	735
Other professional school	42	500	725	925	1,075	1,200
Junior college	75	230	450	736	967	1,370
Great Lakes and Plains	375	273	485	673	835	1,100
University	15	688	770	838	1,113	1,275
Liberal arts college	206	463	591	725	906	1,215
Teachers college	10*			468		
Technological school	10*			725		
Theological school	53	59	182	335	494	743
Other professional school	33	490	616	713	817	1,030
Junior college	48	221	344	519	669	965
Southeast	251	275	389	508	674	831
University	6*			975		
Liberal arts college	153*	367	453	559	675	837
Teachers college	2*			300		
Technological school	1*			1,050		
Theological school	21*	127	228	306	422	525
Other professional school	3*			750		
Junior college	65	223	310	396	517	740
West and Southwest	173	318	475	641	886	1,140
University	7*			638		
Liberal arts college	89	448	564	717	925	1,160
Teachers college	5*			563		
Technological school	4*			900		
Theological school	34	170	313	438	525	640
Other professional school	16	580	775	867	1,000	1,410
Junior college	18	163	225	400	525	630

* In cases where the number of institutions reporting is 10 or less, only the medians (fiftieth percentile) are shown.

SOURCE: U.S. Office of Education, *Basic Student Charges, 1962–63,* 1963, p. 11.

TABLE 4.4-7
Range of tuition for public institutions 1962–63

	Tenth percentile	Fiftieth percentile	Ninetieth percentile
All institutions	$ 20	$170	$295
Universities	165	268	399
Technological schools	74	259	440
North Atlantic	107	244	419
Southeast	47	172	310

SOURCE: Adapted from U.S. Office of Education, *Basic Student Charges, 1962–63*, 1963, tables 2, 3.

for public institutions. For private, church-supported institutions, tuition varies according to the denominational affiliation of the institution (Table 4.4-8). At the fiftieth percentile, tuition in 1962–63 varied from $464 for Jewish institutions to $726 for Presbyterian institutions to $939 for independent institutions.

Tuition also varies considerably for students seeking first professional degrees (Table 4.4-9). At the fiftieth percentile level in 1963–64, charges by public resident institutions varied from $229 for agriculture to $550 for medicine. Charges to nonresidents by public institutions varied from $595 for education to $989 for dentistry. Charges by private institutions at the fiftieth percentile

TABLE 4.4-8   *Percentile distribution of tuition and fees charged full-time undergraduate students in private four-year institutions, by denominational affiliation of institution, 1962–63 academic year*

Denominational affiliation	Number of institutions	Percentile*				
		Tenth	Twenty-fifth	Fiftieth	Seventy-fifth	Ninetieth
Independent	357	$453	$663	$939	$1,261	$1,486
Baptist	62	256	373	488	661	891
Lutheran	42	254	339	684	882	1,041
Methodist	88	370	486	637	831	987
Presbyterian	62	331	482	726	908	1,096
Catholic	248	212	460	660	794	956
Other Christian	136	297	459	630	782	978
Jewish	5	413	432	464	495	651

* This table is read: Of 357 independent institutions, approximately 36 had academic year charges of $453 or under, 89 had charges of $663 or under, 178 had charges of $939 or under, 267 had charges of $1,261 or under, 321 had charges of $1,486 or under, and 36 had charges over $1,486.

SOURCE: U.S. Office of Education, *Variations in Tuition and Fees Charged Full-Time Undergraduate Students by Denominationally Affiliated Institutions, 1962–63*, 1964, p. 3.

level varied from $850 for pharmacy to $1,389 for medicine. Table 4.4-10 shows the tuition charges for education, law, and medicine at the tenth and ninetieth percentile levels for public resident, public nonresident, and private institutions. Education is the least expensive and medicine the most expensive first-professional degree in terms of charges for tuition and fees per year.

TUITION AND CURRENT EDUCATIONAL INCOME　Income from tuition as a percentage of general and educational income of institutions of higher education increased from 24 to 38 percent from 1920 to 1950 and then declined to 25 percent in 1958 (Table 4.4-11). The contribution of tuition to general and educational income also varies by type of institution (Table 4.4-12). In 1956 tuition at Catholic universities provided 78 percent of educational income, while tuition at state universities provided only 24 percent of income. In recent years tuition income has tended to rise faster than total educational income, and the ratio of tuition to general educational income has tended to rise more for private than for public institutions (Table 4.4-13).

Large variations are found, both among schools and among departments, in the ratio of tuition to educational costs per student. For six distinguished private universities, tuition varied from 27 percent of educational costs at the University of Chicago to 48 percent at Stanford (Table 4.4-14). One also finds large differences in the ratio of tuition to educational expenditures among different departments in the same institution. Table 4.4-15 shows the ratios of tuition to the relevant expenditures of different departments at Harvard for 1954–55 and 1958–59. Tuition covers almost half the costs of an arts and sciences education, but less than 10 percent of the costs of an education in public health.

A comparison of tuition with faculty salaries is one of some interest. In 1955–56 the average faculty salary was $5,200. In the same year average tuition was $350, or 7 percent of average faculty pay. At a ratio of 14 students per faculty member, tuition would almost cover the cost of faculty salaries. But outlays on instructional and departmental research (of which faculty salaries form the major part) account for only 42 percent of educational and general expenditures.[3]

(Text continued on p. 688)

[3] S. E. Harris, *Higher Education: Resources and Finance,* McGraw-Hill Book Company, New York, 1962, p. 59.

TABLE 4.4-9
Percentile values of tuition and required fees charged full-time students in first professional degree programs in public (resident and nonresident charges) and private universities and liberal arts colleges, aggregate United States, 1963–64

Program	Number reporting	Tenth	Twenty-fifth	Fiftieth	Seventy-fifth
					University
					Percentile
				Public—resident	
Total programs	326	$ 181	$ 225	$ 290	$ 401
Agriculture	47	146	182	229	303
Dentistry	20	350	425	525	734
Education	71	176	219	274	315
Engineering	71	172	222	278	323
Law	48	185	225	293	368
Medicine	32	356	445	550	675
Pharmacy	37	190	236	286	318
				Public—nonresident	
Total programs	304	472	545	663	846
Agriculture	45	459	510	617	798
Dentistry	19	579	845	989	1,007
Education	64	457	511	595	750
Engineering	67	468	525	617	786
Law	45	503	536	639	799
Medicine	30	750	857	950	1,120
Pharmacy	34	481	532	600	789
					Private
Total programs	180	682	883	1,156	1,410
Agriculture	1				
Dentistry	25	875	992	1,239	1,370
Education	29	662	806	920	1,320
Engineering	32	652	910	1,164	1,500
Law	45	670	815	1,020	1,273
Medicine	34	1,154	1,190	1,389	1,526
Pharmacy	14	656	764	850	1,107

SOURCE: U.S. Office of Education, *Basic Student Charges, 1963–64,* 1964, p. 11.

		Liberal arts				
			Percentile			
	Number					
Ninetieth	*reporting*	*Tenth*	*Twenty-fifth*	*Fiftieth*	*Seventy-fifth*	*Ninetieth*
$ 581	84	$92	$142	$189	$ 243	$ 304
405	19	85	99	170	207	290
825						
417	41	96	156	196	235	300
437	13	91	154	195	270	322
581	5	189	257	307	323	364
749						
408	6	90	114	150	189	196
1,005	69	350	435	490	619	698
873	13	334	407	489	681	717
1,211						
864	35	339	431	487	532	685
884	12	406	475	500	625	691
914	4	481	489	500	601	740
1,215						
841	5	414	445	482	492	689
1,567	205 3	464	605	757	941	1,282
1,563						
1,504	152	367	559	718	868	1,211
1,621	28	608	750	950	1,264	1,456
1,505	16	616	707	757	900	1,056
1,661						
1,209	6	464	657	700	1,014	1,361

TABLE 4.4-10
Tenth and
ninetieth
percentile values
of tuition
and required
fees charged
full-time
students in the
first
professional
degree
programs of
education, law,
and medicine,
by public
(resident and
nonresident)
and private
institutions,
1963–64

	Tenth percentile	Ninetieth percentile
Public resident		
All	$ 181	$ 581
Education	176	417
Law	185	581
Medicine	356	749
Public nonresident		
All	472	1,005
Education	457	864
Law	503	914
Medicine	750	1,215
Private		
All	682	1,567
Education	662	1,504
Law	670	1,505
Medicine	1,154	1,661

SOURCE: U.S. Office of Education, *Basic Student Charges, 1963–64*, 1964, p. 1⬛

TABLE 4.4-13
Average annual
percentage
increase in
current income
per student
1959–60
to 1965–66

Type of institution	Total income	Tuition and fees	Organized research (federal)	Other federal	State government
All institutions	5.5	7.0	7.6	12.3	5.3
Public	4.0	7.4	5.7	7.0	3.4
Private	8.1	9.1	10.8	26.5	10.0
Public:					
Universities	4.3	7.0	6.3	9.6	3.2
Other four-year	3.6	7.9	8.9	1.9	3.5
Two-year	7.8	12.7	*	31.3	11.0
Private:					
Universities	9.0	9.1	10.4	26.9	11.9
Other four-year	8.1	9.7	13.6	29.3	6.8
Two-year	2.5	4.4	*	29.0	*

*The change in this income source is not particularly relevant for this type of institution.

SOURCE: U.S. Department of Health, Education and Welfare, *Toward a Long-Range Plan for Federal Financial Support for Higher Education,* report to the President, Office of Assistant Secretary for Planning and Evaluation, January 1969, p 46.

TABLE 4.4-11   *Tuition and ratio of tuition income to general and educational income (GEI) and to GEI adjusted, per resident student, 1920 to 1956*

Tuition item	1920	1930	1940	1950	1956	1958
Fees per resident student	$70	$131	$133	$265	$279	
Tuition income to GEI	24%	30%	35%	38%	26%	25%
Tuition income to GEI adjusted		33%*	41%	50%	39%	

*Related activities estimated.

SOURCE: Calculated from U.S. Department of Health, Education and Welfare, *Statistics of Higher Education, 1955–56: Receipts, Expenditures and Property,* and *Faculty, Students and Degrees.* 1958 estimated on basis of HEW preliminary figures; in S. E. Harris, *Higher Education: Resources and Finance,* McGraw-Hill Book Company, New York, 1962, tables 8-1, 8-3.

TABLE 4.4-12   *Tuition and fees as percentage of general and educational income, 1956*

	Percentage	Local government	Endowment earnings	Private gifts and grants	Auxiliary enterprises
Private IHL	62.5	4.5	−1.1	0.6	4.6
Universities	57.2	2.8	−3.1	0.5	3.3
Liberal arts colleges	71.8	3.5	2.1	3.3	7.0
Nonsectarian universities	52.4	*	−3.1	0.7	4.6
Catholic universities	78.1	1.7	2.1	7.1	2.6
Public IHL	25.1	2.9	5.5	−6.7	−0.7
Municipal	39.2	3.4	4.9	6.3	8.1
State	24.4	6.9	0.0	1.8	6.8
		*	−4.2	−3.3	1.2

SOURCE: S. E. Harris, *Higher Education: Resources and Finance,* McGraw-Hill Book Company, New York, 1962, tables 8-1, 8-3.

TABLE 4.4-14
Tuition as a percentage of educational costs per student, major universities, 1954–55

University	Percent tuition	University	Percent tuition
Princeton	42	Chicago	27
Stanford	48	Cornell	44
Yale	40	Harvard	34

*Figures are adjusted to some extent to make them comparable. The Yale figure is higher than the one shown above because of the elimination of some costs in this table.

SOURCE: *New York Times,* June 25, 1956; in S. E. Harris, *Higher Education: Resources and Finance,* McGraw-Hill Book Company, New York, 1962, p. 57.

INCREASES IN TUITION: VIEWS

Despite the trend of rising tuition in recent years, most of the spokesmen of institutions of higher education have not been enthusiastic supporters of increasing tuition. The 1968 report of the Association of American Universities stressed the adverse effect of higher tuition on low-income groups.[4] Provost William Bowen of Princeton has warned of the probable small net gains from increasing tuition. He envisages large increases in student aid which would absorb a substantial portion of the additional income derived from higher tuition. In a study of three major universities from 1962 to 1966, Bowen found that of an increase in tuition of $404, the increase in net tuition income per student was only $87 (Table 4.4-16). In other words, almost 80 percent of the increase in tuition was offset by increases in student aid. I have not found this to be the case for all institutions over a longer period of time. From 1949–50 to 1963–64, tuition income increased by $1,503 million and student aid by $135 million. Only 9 percent

[4] Association of American Universities, *The Federal Funding of Higher Education,* Washington, D.C. 1968, p. 12.

TABLE 4.4-15
Ratio of tuition to educational costs, Harvard, 1954–55 and 1958–59, by schools

Field	1954–55	1958–59
Arts and science	47	45
Medicine	18	19
Public health	9	7
Law	58	66
Business	52	44
Education	27	40
Divinity	22	24

SOURCE: S. E. Harris, *Higher Education: Resources and Finance,* McGraw-Hill Book Company, New York, 1962, p. 58.

TABLE 4.4-16
*Rise of current
educational
expenditures
per student,
gross and net
fee income
per student,
1962–1966*

	1962	1966	*Amount of change*
Estimated current educational expenditures per student	$2,880	$3,500	+ $620
Gross fee income per student	1,186	1,590	+ 404
Net fee income per student	824	911	+ 87

SOURCE: W. G. Bowen, *The Economics of the Major Private Universities,* Carnegie Commission on Higher Education, Berkeley, Calif., 1968, p. 39.

of the increase in tuition during this period was offset by increases in student aid.[5]

Howard Bowen, chancellor of Claremont University Center, is against large increases in tuition, although he would tolerate increases in tuition at private institutions as long as low-cost public institutions were available.[6]

TUITION POTENTIAL We may anticipate a large additional income from tuition if reasonable assumptions are made concerning the rise in enrollment and the increase in students' ability to pay. In the following discussion I tie probable future increases in tuition to past increases (since 1940) and anticipate a steady increase in per capita disposable income—a useful index of ability to pay. (Disposable income is income remaining after direct taxes.)

In 1963–64 tuition provided about $1,900 million, or one-fourth of educational and general income of institutions of higher education. It is possible to greatly increase the receipts from tuition, although value judgments will come into play in choosing tuition policies. Perhaps as good a guide as any to the possibilities of increasing tuition is the trend of per capita disposable income over the years. As per capita disposable income rises, we may assume that the ability to finance higher education grows. In general, the increase in tuition since 1940 has been roughly the same as the

[5] A. M. Cartter and R. L. Farrell, "Academic Labor Market Projections and the Draft," *The Economics and Financing of Higher Education in the United States,* a compendium of papers submitted to the Joint Economic Committee, U.S. Congress, Washington, D.C., 1969, p. 473.

[6] Bowen, H. R., The *Finance of Higher Education,* Carnegie Commission on Higher Education, Berkeley, Calif., 1968, pp. 6, 26–29.

Period	Per capita disposable income	Tuition per student
1940-1964	4.0	4.2
1964-1969	1.3	1.2
1969-1979	1.63	1.63*
1940-1979	8.5	8.2

* Projection assumes tuition will represent a constant percentage of per capita disposable income (63 percent) from 1969 to 1979.

SOURCE: U.S. Office of Education, *Digest of Educational Statistics, 1968,* 1968, and U.S. Office of Education, *Projections of Educational Statistics to 1977-78,* National Center for Educational Statistics, 1968, various pages (author's calculations).

increase in per capita disposable income. Since per capita disposable income in the 1960s was rising at about 5 percent a year and the economy was booming, tuition could have been increased more than per capita disposable income, but it increased slightly less (Table 4.4-17).

By 1979 enrollment is projected to be almost seven times the 1940 figure and tuition per student more than eight times 1940 tuition. Tuition income is projected to increase from $202 million in 1940 to $8,611 million in 1979. When the tuition charged students who are not pursuing degrees is added, tuition income is projected to rise to about $9,500 million by 1979. The projected increase of almost $5 billion in tuition income from 1969 to 1979

TABLE 4.4-18   *Tuition per student, per capita disposable income, enrollment and tuition receipts, 1940-1979, various years*

Year	Per capita disposable income	Tuition per student	Enrollment degree credit (thousands)	Tuition income* (millions)
1940	$ 573	$ 135	1,499	$ 202
1964	2,280	572	4,234	1,899
1969	3,000	677	6,906	3,646
1979	4,890	1,104	10,000	8,611 (projected)†

* Tuition projections are based on tuition per student times enrollment, minus a 22 percent estimated adjustment for non-full-time students.

† Rises to about $9.5 billion if omissions are included.

SOURCE: U.S. Office of Education, *Digest of Educational Statistics, 1968,* 1968, and U.S. Office of Education, *Projections of Educational Statistics to 1977-78,* National Center for Educational Statistics, 1968, various pages (author's calculations).

TABLE 4.4-19
Charges to students, 1958–59 and 1968–69

Year	Tuition, room, and board	Tuition	Board	Room
1958–59				
Public	$ 797	$ 192	$415	$190
Private	1,435	729	456	250
1968–69				
Public	1,133	298	482	353
Private	2,395	1,436	544	415
Percentage change, 1958–59 to 1968–69				
Public	42	55	16	86
Private	67	97	19	66

SOURCE: U.S. Office of Education, *Digest of Educational Statistics, 1968,* 1968, p. 95 (author's calculations).

is associated with an increase in enrollment of more than three million, or 40 percent (Table 4.4-18). The increase in tuition per student and the increase in enrollment contribute approximately equally to the total expected gain in tuition income. The $5 billion increase from 1969 to 1979 stems from the assumptions that per capita disposable income increases by 63 percent and that tuition increases in the same proportion.[7]

It will be possible to increase tuition by 63 percent from 1969 to 1979 without seriously affecting the socioeconomic composition of the student body. With incomes of parents of college students averaging about $11,000 (and about $16,000 for the top income quartile of student families), many students could afford the increased tuition. Colleges and universities could then use $2 billion to $4 billion a year of the increased tuition income to aid students who would be seriously affected by projected increases in tuition and by the acceleration of the upward movement of rates.

In assessing the burden of rising tuition, one should allow for a more moderate increase in the cost of board. Charges for board rose by 16 percent for public and 19 percent for private institutions from 1958–59 to 1968–69. During this period tuition increased by 55 percent for public and 97 percent for private institutions (Table 4.4-19).

[7] U.S. Office of Education, *Projections of Educational Statistics to 1977–78,* National Center for Educational Statistics, 1968, pp. 95–97.

4.5. Expenditures: Library and Separately Budgeted Expenditures on Research

Institutions of higher education spend a surprisingly small proportion of their general and educational income on libraries—slightly more than 3 percent since 1960. Table 4.5-1 contains much general

TABLE 4.5-1 *General statistics of college and university libraries, United States and outlying areas, 1959–60, 1963–64, and 1965–66*

Item (1)	1959–60 (2)	1963–64 (3)	1965–66* (4)
Number of libraries	1,951	2,140	2,207
Number of students enrolled, total (thousands)†	3,800	5,320	6,438
Enrolled for bachelor's and higher degrees	3,610	4,988	5,991
Enrolled in undergraduate occupational programs	190	333	447
Collections (thousands of units)			
Number of volumes at end of year	176,721	227,000	265,000
Volumes per student (number of volumes divided by total number of students enrolled)	46.5	42.7	41.2
Number of volumes added during year	8,415	13,600	18,000
Number of periodical titles received	1,271	1,760	2,700
Library staff in terms of full-time equivalents			
Total staff	18,000	25,200	29,000
Professional librarians	9,000	11,900	13,000
Other library staff‡	9,000	13,300	16,000
Hours of student and other assistance (thousands)	12,062	16,400	19,000
Library operating expenditures (excluding capital outlay) in thousands of dollars			
Operating expenditures, total	$137,245	$246,000	$320,000
Salaries (including contributed service)	72,495	126,000	155,000

TABLE 4.5-1 *(continued)*

Item (1)	1959–60 (2)	1963–64 (3)	1965–66* (4)
Hourly wages	$11,680	$19,000	$ 23,500
Binding	4,852	9,000	11,500
Books and other library materials	40,760	79,000	111,000
Other library operating expenditures	7,458	13,000	19,000
Operating expenditures in percentages, total	100.0	100.0	100.0
Salaries (including contributed service)	52.8	51.2	48.4
Hourly wages	8.5	7.7	7.3
Binding	3.6	3.7	3.6
Books and other library materials	29.7	32.1	34.7
Other library operating expenditures	5.4	5.3	6.0
Library operating expenditures as percentage of total institutional expenditures for educational and general purposes	3.0	3.3	3.3

* Library data estimated by American Library Association.

† Each enrollment figure is for the fall term which follows the specified year (e.g., approximately 3,800,000 students were enrolled in fall term 1960). Enrollment in undergraduate occupational programs is estimated for fall 1960 and fall 1966.

‡ Includes nonprofessional staff and professional staff other than librarians.

SOURCE: U.S. Department of Health, Education and Welfare, Office of Education, "Library Statistics of College and Universities"; in U.S. Office of Education, *Digest of Educational Statistics, 1968,* 1968, table 151, p. 123.

TABLE 4.5-2
Average price and price index for books, periodicals, and serial services, United States, 1957–1959 to 1967

Item (1)	1957–1959 (2)	1960 (3)	1961 (4)	1962 (5)
	Average price			
Hardcover books*	$ 5.29	$ 5.24	$ 5.81	$ 5.90
Mass market paperbacks	†	†	†	.53
Trade paperbacks	†	†	†	2.12
Periodicals	4.92	5.32	5.63	5.92
Serial services‡	39.80	50.00	43.88	46.18
	Price index (1957–1959 = 100.0)			
Hardcover books*	100.0	99.1	109.8	111.5
Periodicals	100.0	108.1	114.4	120.3
Serial services‡	100.0	125.6	110.3	116.0

* Excludes texts, United States documents, and encyclopedias.

† Data not available.

‡ Includes business, law, science and technology, United States documents, Soviet translations, and miscellaneous areas.

information about college and university libraries. From 1959–60 to 1965–66, total operating expenditures of these libraries increased by 133 percent. This increase was attributable primarily to a rise of 112 percent in expenditures on wages and salaries and a rise of 172 percent in expenditures on books and materials.

Although the number of volumes per student decreased by 11 percent from 1959–60 to 1965–66, the total number of volumes rose from 177 million to 265 million. Increasing financial problems of these libraries have resulted in a relative decrease in professional staff from 50 to 45 percent of total staff and a relative increase in nonprofessional staff (Table 4.5-1).

In the brief period from 1957–59 to 1967, the price of hardcover books (excluding textbooks) rose by 51 percent, and the prices of periodicals and serial materials by 63 and 68 percent, respectively (Table 4.5-2). In this same period consumer prices rose only 13 percent. Since expenditures on books and material now exceed 35 percent of total library operating expenses, it is clear that the substantial inflation in book prices contributes significantly to rising library expenditures.

The increases in price by category of book are shown in Table 4.5-3. The price of art books increased 13 percent, while the price for general literature books increased by 106 percent. Some of the variation in prices among different categories of books can be

1963 (6)	1964 (7)	1965 (8)	1966 (9)	1967 (10)
$ 6.55	$ 6.93	$ 7.65	$ 7.94	$ 7.99
.58	.59	.63	.64	.69
2.27	2.41	2.50	2.95	3.09
6.31	6.64	6.95	7.44	8.02
47.94	50.85	58.78	63.64	66.98
123.8	131.0	144.5	150.0	151.0
128.3	135.0	141.3	151.2	163.0
120.5	127.8	147.7	159.9	168.3

SOURCES: "Publisher's Weekly," Jan. 29, 1968, and late winter issues of previous years; "Library Journal," July 1967, and midsummer issues of previous years; in U.S. Office of Education, *Digest of Educational Statistics, 1968,* 1968, table 154, p. 125.

TABLE 4.5-3
Average price and price index for selected hardcover books,* by category, United States, 1957-1959 to 1967

Category (1)	1957-1959 Average price (2)	Index (3)	1962 Average price (4)	Index (5)
TOTAL	$ 5.29	100.0	$ 5.90	111.5
Agriculture	6.01	100.0	6.39	106.3
Art	10.89	100.0	8.57	78.7
Biography	5.02	100.0	5.94	118.3
Business	7.21	100.0	8.70	120.7
Children's books	2.63	100.0	2.77	105.3
Economics	6.24	100.0	6.59	105.6
Education	4.78	100.0	5.64	118.0
History	6.25	100.0	6.72	107.5
Law	8.86	100.0	10.60	119.6
Literature, fiction	3.48	100.0	3.97	114.1
Literature, general†	3.32	100.0	4.76	143.4
Literature, poetry	3.16	100.0	4.03	127.5
Literature, drama	3.86	100.0	4.62	119.7
Medicine	8.20	100.0	9.87	120.4
Music	5.95	100.0	6.74	113.3
Religion	3.73	100.0	4.42	118.5
Science	8.14	100.0	10.30	126.5
Sports	4.68	100.0	5.12	109.4
Technology	8.33	100.0	10.46	125.6

* Excludes paperbacks, government documents, and encyclopedias.
† The general literature category includes the poetry and drama figures, also shown separately.
SOURCE: "Publisher's Weekly," Jan. 29, 1968, and late winter issues of previous years; in U.S. Office of Education, *Digest of Educational Statistics, 1968,* 1968, table 155, p. 125.

explained by differences in cost, but low prices for children's books and books for education reflect to some extent differences in capacity to pay. Figure 4.5-1 shows that the price of books almost doubled from 1950 to 1965, while consumer prices increased only 31 percent.

Table 4.5-4 contains selected data on the 40 largest academic libraries in 1964-65. Harvard had the largest library, with 7.44 million volumes and operating expenses of $5.76 million. The University of Colorado had the smallest library in this group — 946,000 volumes and operating expenditures of $1.45 million.

1964		1966		1967	
Average price (6)	Index (7)	Average price (8)	Index (9)	Average price (10)	Index (11)
$ 6.93	131.0	$ 7.94	150.0	$ 7.99	151.0
7.69	128.0	8.37	139.2	8.90	148.1
10.68	98.1	14.73	135.4	12.32	113.1
6.65	132.5	7.57	150.9	8.52	169.7
9.74	135.1	9.74	131.2	9.77	135.5
3.06	116.3	3.46	131.6	3.41	129.7
7.63	122.3	9.08	145.5	8.65	138.6
5.50	115.0	5.61	117.4	5.61	117.4
7.73	123.7	8.56	137.0	9.02	144.3
9.96	112.4	10.95	123.6	12.52	141.3
4.14	118.5	4.52	130.0	4.80	137.9
5.16	155.4	6.67	201.0	6.84	206.0
4.11	130.1	4.74	150.0	5.49	173.7
5.91	153.1	6.67	172.0	6.49	168.1
11.22	136.8	12.37	150.8	12.78	155.9
6.98	117.3	8.15	137.0	8.69	146.1
4.63	124.1	5.38	144.2	5.66	151.7
10.99	135.0	11.72	144.0	12.15	149.3
6.13	131.0	6.28	134.0	7.25	154.9
11.02	132.3	12.51	150.5	12.86	154.4

Although enrollment has been increasing relatively faster in public than in private institutions, the number of volumes in the libraries of public institutions increased by only 2 percent from 1959–60 to 1963–64, as compared with an increase of 18 percent in the number of volumes in the libraries of private institutions. In this same period library expenditures increased by 34 percent in public and by 100 percent in private institutions.[1]

(Text continued on p. 701)

[1] T. Samore, *Library Statistics of Colleges and Universities, 1963–64,* U.S. Office of Education, 1968, pp. 13–14.

TABLE 4.5-4
*Selected data
for the 40
largest academic
libraries,
United States,
1964–65
[institutions
ranked by size
of collection
(column 3)]*

Rank (1)	Institution (2)	Total volumes (3)	Volumes added (4)
1.	Harvard University	7,445,072	257,631
2.	Yale University	4,826,148†	128,281
3.	University of Illinois	3,888,983	150,049
4.	Columbia University	3,569,565	123,311
5.	University of Michigan	3,376,076	135,533
6.	University of California—Berkeley	3,113,024	165,594
7.	Cornell University	2,725,624	152,822
8.	Stanford University	2,560,220	181,745
9.	University of Chicago	2,406,142	109,390
10.	University of Minnesota	2,405,797†	88,896
11.	University of California—Los Angeles	2,197,175	193,576
12.	University of Wisconsin	1,901,048	137,399
13.	University of Pennsylvania	1,894,480	89,880
14.	Indiana University	1,771,900	
15.	Princeton University	1,769,699	65,934
16.	Ohio State University	1,748,943	88,173
17.	University of Texas	1,724,332	76,023
18.	Duke University	1,716,855	70,465
19.	Northwestern University	1,709,172	68,796
20.	New York University	1,535,583	68,439
21.	Johns Hopkins University	1,399,700†	76,342
22.	University of Washington	1,390,636	69,741
23.	University of North Carolina	1,314,359	79,763
24.	Louisiana State University	1,237,171	74,861
25.	University of Iowa	1,226,254	51,864
26.	University of Virginia	1,221,353	65,798
27.	Rutgers University	1,207,350†	72,781
28.	University of Missouri	1,167,000†	58,777
29.	Michigan State University	1,147,188	97,660
30.	University of Southern California	1,138,812	47,177
31.	University of Kansas	1,122,158	54,417
32.	Wayne State University	1,116,620	65,490
33.	Brown University	1,111,240	34,197
34.	University of Florida	1,087,665	52,268
35.	University of Kentucky	1,069,908†	38,345
36.	University of Oregon	1,057,879†	79,835
37.	University of Oklahoma	981,012†	51,666
38.	Massachusetts Institute of Technology	959,212	64,367
39.	Joint University Libraries	947,941†	40,370
40.	University of Colorado	946,435	70,119

* Includes binding.
† Includes microform.

SOURCE: T. Samore, *Library Statistics of Colleges and Universities, 1963–64,* U.S. Office of Education, 1968, p. 7.

Total staff in FTE (5)	Total library operating expenditures (6)	Staff salaries and wages (7)	Books and other library materials* (8)
486	$5,760,585	$3,382,583	$1,433,351
434	3,029,624	2,249,059	642,291
348	3,418,200	2,083,646	1,183,408
360	3,173,973	1,969,369	997,960
428	3,552,508	2,477,578	897,109
373	4,588,759	2,947,622	1,381,015
330	3,281,869	2,041,505	1,047,226
267	2,626,046	1,611,474	814,131
206	2,110,586	1,230,173	692,648
209	2,160,561	1,358,365	726,999
299	4,132,807	2,380,077	1,475,737
230	2,551,913	1,431,174	964,822
218	1,824,686	1,171,498	580,125
241	2,423,999	1,308,600	1,051,056
202	1,597,881	881,283	595,666
215	2,019,516	1,304,521	580,732
180	4,838,097	957,664	3,813,068
148	1,417,431	798,915	560,578
140	1,438,691	840,329	496,735
192	1,584,079	932,727	484,939
105	1,005,272	605,744	306,295
279	2,452,199	1,614,557	679,417
134	1,513,317	812,235	600,924
150	1,741,033	930,301	701,644
119	1,275,624	661,860	569,131
102	865,983	496,742	329,241
121	1,508,467	839,176	610,587
112	1,240,910	607,911	523,793
115	1,460,133	815,290	587,218
124	1,169,192	758,539	339,335
120	1,206,368	646,903	485,975
118	1,552,434	898,316	546,093
126	1,007,934	631,574	313,391
153	1,418,317	853,263	480,646
100	1,060,677	604,696	419,015
105	1,056,789	655,988	343,825
71	701,604	370,949	301,116
141	1,003,942	724,287	240,649
97	800,736	457,337	289,442
136	1,451,715	944,768	451,212

FIGURE 4.5-1   *Prices of library materials*

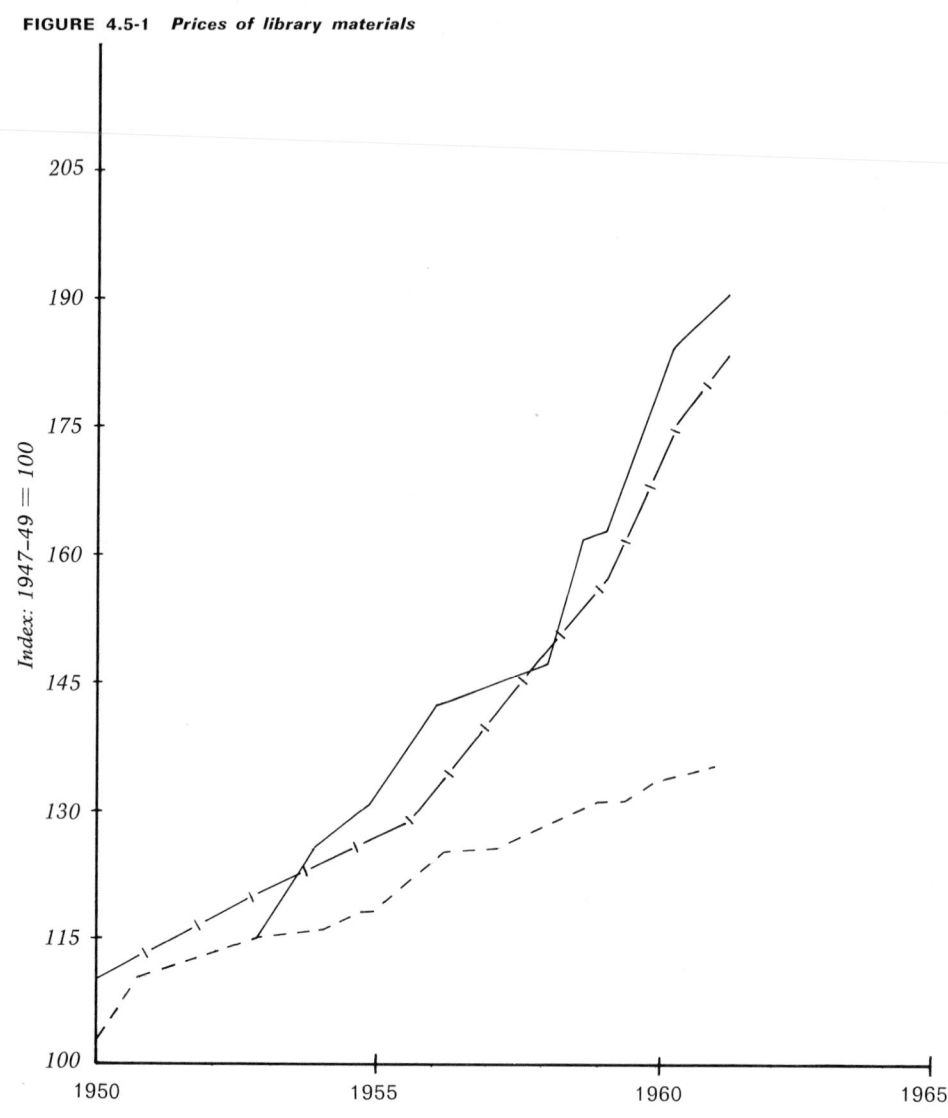

The Price of Books
The Price of Periodicals
Consumer Price Index

SOURCE: U. S. House of Representatives, Committee on Education and Labor, *Higher Education Act of 1965, Hearings before the Special Subcommittee on Education,* February–May 1965, p. 95.

From 1954 to 1958 operating expenditures for separately budgeted research and development at colleges and universities[2] increased from $410 million to $741 million—an increase of 81 percent. The smallest relative increase in research and development expenditures (10 percent) was in engineering and the largest (137 percent) was in medicine (Table 4.5-5).

In 1958 operating expenditures for separately budgeted research and development in 369 colleges and universities proper (excluding agricultural experiment stations and federal contract research centers) were only $329 million. Expenditures on basic research were 74 percent of total research and development expenditures of colleges and universities proper. The federal government provided 67 percent of this $329 million in 1958. By field of science the federal government provided 39 percent of the research and development expenditures on the social sciences and 80 percent of the research and development expenditures on the physical sciences (Table 4.5-6).

The next two tables tell the story of the large increase in federal support of separately budgeted research and development in colleges and universities in the early 1960s. From 1954 to 1958 the

(Text continued on p. 704)

[2] For a discussion of research and development on a wider front, see Chapter 4.7, "Federal Funds for Scientific Activities."

TABLE 4.5-5 *Operating expenditures for separately budgeted research and development in colleges and universities, 1954 and 1958 (dollar amounts in millions)*

| | 1954 | | 1958* | | Percentage increase, |
Organizational unit	Amount	Percent	Amount	Percent	1954–1958
TOTAL	$409.7	100	$740.7	100	81
Colleges and universities proper	203.5	50	329.3	44	62
Medical	45.3	11	107.3	14	137
Engineering	64.4	16	70.9	10	10
All other	93.8	23	151.1	20	61
Agricultural experiment stations (including colleges of agriculture)	76.2	19	122.3	17	60
Federal contract research centers	130.0	32	289.1	39	122

*The total includes the 377 colleges and universities reporting research and development expenditures in 1958.

NOTE: Detail may not add to totals because of rounding.

SOURCE: National Science Foundation, *Scientific Research and Development in Colleges and Universities: Expenditures and Manpower, 1958,* 1963, p. 8.

TABLE 4.5-6
Operating expenditures for separately budgeted research and development in 369 colleges and universities proper, by field of science, character of work and source of support, 1958 (dollar amounts in millions)

Field of science	Total expenditures R&D	Basic research	Basic research as percentage of total R&D funds	Federal support R&D	Basic research
TOTAL	$329.3	$244.0	74	$219.1	$166.5
Life	141.2	112.3	80	88.0	71.5
Physical	97.2	77.8	80	77.5	61.9
Engineering	67.5	36.1	54	44.6	26.5
Social	23.3	17.8	76	9.0	6.5

*Other sources include institutions' own funds, foundations, voluntary health agencies, industry, gifts and grants, and other outside sources.

NOTE: Detail may not add to totals because of rounding.

SOURCE: National Science Foundation, *Scientific Research and Development in Colleges and Universities: Expenditures and Manpower, 1958*, 1963, p. 21.

TABLE 4.5-7
Estimated current expenditures for research and development in universities and colleges, by source of funds, 1954–1964 (millions of dollars)

Separately budgeted R&D expenditures

Year*	Total, all sources	Total	Federal government Percent	Dollars	Industry Percent	Dollars
1954	$ 377	$ 290	55.2	$160	7.6	$22
1955‡	409	312	54.2	169	8.0	25
1956‡	480	372	57.2	213	7.8	29
1957‡	531	410	55.9	229	8.3	34
1958	592	456	55.7	254	8.6	39
1959‡	682	526	58.2	306	7.4	39
1960‡	825	646	62.7	405	6.2	40
1961‡	969	763	65.5	500	5.2	40
1962‡	1,143	904	67.8	613	4.4	40
1963‡	1,359	1,081	70.3	760	3.8	41
1964	1,595	1,272	72.1	917	3.2	41

*Academic year ending in the year shown; for example, 1954 refers to "academic year 1953–54."

† Includes estimates for departmental research and for other research activities for which universities and colleges do not maintain separate records.

‡ Estimate derived from related information; no sector survey took place this year.

SOURCE: National Science Foundation, *Scientific Activities at Universities and Colleges, 1964*, 1968, p. 40.

Basic research as percentage of R&D funds	Other sources of support*		Basic research as percentage of R&D funds
	R&D	Basic research	
76	$110.2	$77.5	70
81	53.3	40.8	77
80	19.7	15.9	81
59	22.9	9.6	42
72	14.4	11.3	78

Other nonprofit institutions		Institutions' own funds		
Percent	Dollars	Percent	Dollars	Other†
9.7	$28	27.6	$ 80	$ 87
9.6	30	28.2	88	97
9.1	34	25.8	96	108
9.3	38	26.6	109	121
9.2	42	26.5	121	136
8.9	47	25.5	134	156
8.0	52	23.1	149	179
7.6	58	21.6	165	206
7.3	66	20.5	185	239
6.8	73	19.1	207	278
6.5	83	18.2	232	323

TABLE 4.5-8 *Percentage increase, separately budgeted current expenditures for research and development in universities and colleges, by source of funds*

	Total	Federal government	Industry	Other nonprofit	Institution's own funds
1954–1959	81	91	77	68	68
1959–1964	142	200	5	77	73

SOURCE: Table 4.5-9.

federal share of support for separately budgeted research and development was relatively constant at a little over 55 percent Beginning in 1959, however, federal support increased rapidly — reaching 72 percent of total research and development support in 1964. The relative shares of all other sources of research and development declined accordingly (Table 4.5-7). In the five years from 1959 to 1964, federal support of separately budgeted research and development increased by 200 percent, as compared with a 91 percent rise during the previous five years (Table 4.5-8). Note also the rapid leveling off of industry support of research and

TABLE 4.5-9 *Estimated current expenditures for research and development in universities and colleges, by character of work, 1954–1964* (dollar amounts in millions)*

Year†	Total	Basic research Amount	Basic research Percentage of total	Applied research Amount	Applied research Percentage of total	Development Amount	Development Percentage of total
1954	$377	$206	54.6	$154	40.8	$17	4.5
1955‡	409	237	57.9	155	37.9	17	4.2
1956‡	480	286	59.6	169	35.2	25	5.2
1957‡	531	337	63.5	169	31.8	25	4.7
1958	592	390	65.9	175	29.6	27	4.6
1959‡	682	468	68.6	186	27.3	28	4.1
1960‡	825	576	69.8	215	26.1	34	4.1
1961‡	969	701	72.3	233	24.0	35	3.6
1962‡	1,143	850	74.4	253	22.1	40	3.5
1963‡	1,359	1,036	76.2	283	20.8	40	2.9
1964	1,595	1,261	79.1	294	18.4	40	2.5

* Includes estimates for departmental research and for other research activities for which most universities and colleges do not maintain separate records.

† Academic year ending in year shown; for example, 1954 refers to "academic year 1953–54."

‡ Estimates derived from related information; no sector survey took place this year.

SOURCE: National Science Foundation, *Scientific Activities at Universities and Colleges, 1964,* 1968 p. 40.

development. From 1959 to 1964 (and this period includes some boom years) industry support increased only 5 percent—as compared with a 77 percent increase in the previous five years. A pronounced trend, which continued unabated in the decade 1954 to 1964, was a shift away from applied research and development toward more basic research. In 1954 expenditures on basic research were 54.6 percent of current expenditures on research and development in colleges and universities; by 1964 they had risen to 79.1 percent. During this same period expenditures on applied research fell from 40.8 to 18.4 percent of total expenditures on research and development, and development expenditures fell from 4.5 to 2.5 percent (Table 4.5-9).

TABLE 4.5-10 *Current expenditures for separately budgeted basic and applied research in universities and colleges, detailed field of science, 1964 (millions of dollars)*

				Selected components of graduate institutions	
Field of science	*Total*	*Institutions granting graduate degrees in the sciences and engineering**	*Other institutions*	*Medical schools*	*Agricultural schools and experiment stations*
All sources	$1,234.8	$1,222.5	$12.3	$345.9	$196.8
Engineering	156.6	155.8	0.8		3.5
Physical sciences	293.5	289.5	4.0	†	3.6
Chemistry	68.5	67.0	1.6	†	3.1
Earth sciences	52.4	52.2	0.2		0.2
Physics	117.4	115.8	1.6		0.1
Mathematics	28.3	27.8	0.6	†	0.2
Other physical sciences	26.8	26.8	0.1		
Life sciences	660.1	655.9	4.2	345.5	179.1
Agricultural sciences	161.9	161.9	*		146.8
Biological sciences	183.1	180.2	2.9	76.4	26.4
Medical sciences	315.1	313.8	1.3	269.0	5.9
Psychology	31.3	29.7	1.6	0.4	0.2
Social sciences	78.9	77.8	1.1	†	9.4
Other sciences	14.4	13.8	0.6		0.4

* Includes medical schools and agricultural experiment stations.
† Less than $50,000.
SOURCE: National Science Foundation, *Scientific Activities at Universities and Colleges, 1964*, 1968, p. 42.

TABLE 4.5-11 Capital expenditures for research, development, and instruction in the sciences and engineering in universities and colleges, by broad field of science, 1964 (millions of dollars)

				Selected components of graduate institutions	
Field of science	Total	Institutions granting graduate degrees in the sciences and engineering*	Other institutions	Medical schools	Agricultural schools and experiment stations
All sources	$529.5	$450.6	$78.9	$105.6	$29.4
Engineering	71.7	58.1	13.6		0.7
Physical sciences	153.5	121.1	32.4	†	1.2
Life sciences	232.0	210.2	21.8	105.6	26.9
Social sciences	32.6	24.8	7.8		0.4
Other sciences	39.7	36.3	3.4	†	0.2

* Includes medical schools and agricultural experiment stations.
† Less than $50,000.
SOURCE: National Science Foundation, *Scientific Activities at Universities and Colleges, 1964*, 1968, p. 48.

TABLE 4.5-12 Percentage distribution of number of colleges and universities and their operating expenditures for separately budgeted research and development, by size (based on research and development expenditures) and source of support, 1958

Colleges and universities with R&D expenditures of— (thousands of dollars)	Number of colleges and universities	Total R&D expenditures	Federal support — Number of colleges and universities
(Total numbers and amounts)	(377)	($740.7 million)	(316)
TOTAL	100	100	100
Less than $25	40	*	31
$25–$249	24	1	25
$250–$999	10	3	12
$1,000–$4,999	19	22	23
$5,000 or more	7	74	8

* Less than 0.5 percent.
NOTE: Detail may not add to totals because of rounding.
SOURCE: National Science Foundation, *Scientific Research and Development in Colleges and Universities: Expenditures and Manpower, 1958*, 1963, tables 2 and 4.

An important feature of scientific expenditures of colleges and universities is the relatively heavy orientation toward the life sciences. Table 4.5-10 shows expenditures for separately budgeted basic and applied research by field of science in 1964. Life sciences received 53 percent of total expenditures on research and development, while engineering and the physical sciences combined received 37 percent. The life sciences also received the largest share of capital expenditures for research, development, and instruction in the sciences and engineering in 1964—44 percent (Table 4.5-11).

Total expenditures for separately budgeted research and development were $741 million in 1958. Seven percent of the 377 institutions accounted for 96 percent of total expenditures on separately budgeted research and development (Table 4.5-12). Table 4.5-13 shows a smaller degree of concentration in research and development expenditures for colleges and universities proper than for all institutions. Five percent of the 369 colleges and universities proper accounted for 57 percent of total outlays of $329 million in 1958. Of the $741 million total spent on separately budgeted research and development in 1958, colleges and universities proper spent 44 percent, federal contract research centers spent 39 percent, and agricultural experiment stations spent 17 percent (Table 4.5-14).

	Other sources of support	
Amount	*Number of colleges and universities*	*Amount*
($538.9 million)	(321)	($201.8 million)
100	100	100
*	31	*
1	26	2
2	12	5
17	23	36
80	8	57

TABLE 4.5-13
Percentage distribution of number of colleges and universities proper and their operating expenditures for separately budgeted research and development, by size (based on research and development expenditures) and source of support, 1958

Colleges and universities proper with R&D expenditures of— (thousands of dollars)	Number of colleges and universities proper	Total R&D expenditures	Federal support — Number of colleges and universities proper
(Total numbers and amounts)	(369)	($329.3 million)	(308)
TOTAL	100	100	100
Less than $25	41	*	32
$25–$249	28	3	30
$250–$999	12	8	14
$1,000–$4,999	14	32	17
$5,000 or more	5	57	6

* Less than 0.5 percent.
NOTE: Detail may not add to totals because of rounding.
SOURCE: National Science Foundation, *Scientific Research and Development in Colleges and Universities: Expenditures and Manpower, 1958,* 1963, tables 2 and 4.

TABLE 4.5-14
Comparison of operating expenditures for separately budgeted research and development and number of R&D scientists and engineers employed in 377 colleges and universities, by field of science and organizational unit, 1958 (dollar amounts in millions)

Organizational unit	Total — R&D expenditures	Total — R&D scientists and engineers	Life — R&D expenditures	Life — R&D scientists and engineers
TOTAL	$740.7	69,900	$256.3	32,600
Colleges and universities proper	329.3	50,300	141.2	22,300
Medical	107.3	15,600	107.1	15,600
Engineering	70.9	9,800	0.2	
All other	151.1	24,900	33.9	6,700
Agricultural experiment stations (includes colleges of agriculture)	122.3	11,300	104.2	9,800
Federal contract research centers	289.1	8,300	10.9	500

	Other sources of support	
Amount	Number of colleges and universities proper	Amount
($219.1 million)	(313)	($110.2 million)
100	100	100
*	32	1
3	31	4
7	14	10
32	17	32
58	6	53

Field of science

Physical		Engineering		Social	
R&D expenditures	R&D scientists and engineers	R&D expenditures	R&D scientists and engineers	R&D expenditures	R&D scientists and engineers
$260.9	18,000	$187.9	12,200	$35.6	7,000
97.2	13,600	67.5	8,500	23.3	5,900
0.2					
10.3	1,600	60.0	8,100	0.3	100
86.7	12,000	7.5	400	23.0	5,800
6.0	200	3.2	400	8.8	1,000
157.7	4,300	117.1	3,300	3.4	100

TABLE 4.5-14
(continued)

Organizational unit	Total		Life	
	R&D expenditures	R&D scientists and engineers	R&D expenditures	R&D scientists and engineers
TOTAL	100	100	100	100
Colleges and universities proper	44	72	55	68
Medical	14	22	42	48
Engineering	10	14		
All other	20	36	13	21
Agricultural experiment stations (includes colleges of agriculture)	17	16	41	30
Federal contract research centers	39	12	4	2

NOTE: Detail may not add to totals because of rounding.

SOURCE: National Science Foundation, *Scientific Research and Development in Colleges and Universities: Expenditures and Manpower, 1958,* 1963, Summary, table III.

Colleges and universities employ many more scientists and engineers than might be expected from their share of research and development expenditures. Physics and engineering departments in particular command large numbers of scientists and engineers in relation to their share of expenditures on research and development. Agricultural experiment stations and federal contract research centers use relatively fewer scientists and engineers than might be inferred from their share of research and development expenditures (Table 4.5-15). Table 4.5-16 shows that expenditures on research and development and the number of scientists and engineers engaged in research and development are concentrated among relatively few institutions. In 1958, 16 institutions ac-

TABLE 4.5-15
Percentage of expenditures on research and development and percentage of scientists and engineers

	Percentage of expenditures	Percentage of scientists and engineers
Colleges and universities proper	44	72
Agricultural experiment stations	17	16
Federal contract research centers	39	12

SOURCE: Table 4.5-15.

| Field of science | | | | | |
| Physical | | Engineering | | Social | |
R&D expenditures	R&D scientists and engineers	R&D expenditures	R&D scientists and engineers	R&D expenditures	R&D scientists and engineers
Percentage distribution					
100	100	100	100	100	100
37	76	36	70	65	84
4	9	32	66	1	1
33	67	4	3	65	83
2	1	2	3	25	14
60	24	62	27	10	1

TABLE 4.5-16 *Distribution of R&D scientists and engineers and operating expenditures for separately budgeted research and development in 377 colleges and universities, by size (based on number of R&D scientists and engineers), 1958*

| R&D scientists and engineers, by size class | Number of institutions | R&D scientists and engineers | R&D expenditures (millions of dollars) | Percentage distribution | | |
				Number of institutions	R&D scientists and engineers	R&D expenditures
TOTAL	377	69,900	$740.7	100	100	100
Less than 25	206	1,000	8.6	55	1	1
25–99	52	2,700	12.7	14	4	2
100–299	59	11,400	87.5	16	16	11
300–499	24	9,500	64.1	6	14	9
500–999	20	14,000	139.6	5	20	19
1,000 or more	16	31,300	428.2	4	45	58

NOTE: Detail may not add to totals because of rounding.

SOURCE: National Science Foundation, *Scientific Research and Development in Colleges and Universities: Expenditures and Manpower, 1958,* 1963, table IV.

TABLE 4.5-17
Current
expenditures for
separately
budgeted basic
and applied
research in
universities and
colleges,
compared to
population, by
region,
percentage,
1964

	Population, percent	Expenditure, percent
United States	100.0	100.0
Northeast	24.6	32.1
New England	5.7	11.5
Middle Atlantic	18.9	20.6
North Central	28.0	25.3
East North Central	19.7	18.3
West North Central	8.3	7.0
South	31.0	21.2
South Atlantic	14.8	11.8
East South Central	6.6	3.4
West South Central	9.6	6.0
West	16.5	21.0
Mountain	4.0	5.5
Pacific	12.5	15.4
United States territories	1.4	0.5

SOURCES: Table 4.5-19; and U.S. Bureau of the Census, *Statistical Abstract of the United States, 1967,* 1967, p. 12.

TABLE 4.5-18
Current
expenditures
for separately
budgeted basic
and applied
research in
universities
and colleges,
by geographic
location and
broad field of
science, 1964
(millions of
dollars)

Geographic region and division	Total	Engineering		Physical sciences	
		Percent	Dollars	Percent	Dollars
United States total	$1,234.8	12.7	$156.6	23.8	$293.5
Northeast	396.7	13.9	55.0	26.9	106.8
New England	141.9	16.0	22.7	30.4	43.1
Middle Atlantic	254.7	12.7	32.3	25.0	63.7
North Central	311.9	13.9	43.2	21.9	68.4
East North Central	225.6	16.5	37.2	22.6	50.9
West North Central	86.2	6.8	5.9	20.2	17.4
South	261.8	8.7	22.9	15.8	41.4
South Atlantic	145.6	9.8	14.2	18.2	26.5
East South Central	42.3	7.8	3.3	5.2	2.2
West South Central	74.0	7.4	5.5	17.3	12.8
West	258.9	13.6	35.2	29.4	76.1
Mountain	68.2	20.4	13.9	27.0	18.4
Pacific	190.7	11.2	21.3	30.3	57.7
United States territories	5.7	5.3	0.3	14.0	0.8

SOURCE: National Science Foundation, *Scientific Activities at Universities and Colleges, 1964,* 1968, p. 45.

counted for 58 percent of total research and development expenditures and 45 percent of all research and development scientists and engineers.

Expenditures on separately budgeted research by colleges and universities tend to be concentrated in the more industrialized areas of the country. Table 4.5-17 compares regional distribution of research and development expenditures with the regional distribution of population. Research and development expenditures are most concentrated in the Northeast and in the West—in relation to the population. Variations in regional concentration of research and development expenditures differ among the sciences (Table 4.5-18). Table 4.5-19 gives expenditures for separately budgeted research and development by state for the year 1964. Table 4.5-20 shows regional distribution of capital expenditures for research, development, and instruction in the sciences and engineering in 1964.

Life sciences		*Psychology*		*Social sciences*		*Other sciences*	
Percent	*Dollars*	*Percent*	*Dollars*	*Percent*	*Dollars*	*Percent*	*Dollars*
53.5	$660.1	2.5	$31.3	6.4	$78.9	1.2	$14.4
48.2	191.4	2.7	10.8	6.8	27.1	1.4	5.5
40.0	56.7	3.2	4.5	7.4	10.5	3.1	4.4
52.9	134.7	2.5	6.3	6.5	16.6	0.4	1.1
51.8	161.7	3.2	9.9	8.4	26.3	0.8	2.5
47.8	107.8	3.0	6.8	9.3	21.0	0.8	1.9
62.4	53.8	3.6	3.1	6.1	5.3	0.7	0.6
68.7	179.8	2.6	6.8	3.6	9.5	0.5	1.3
65.4	95.2	3.0	4.3	2.8	4.1	0.8	1.2
79.7	33.7	2.8	1.2	4.7	2.0		
68.8	50.9	1.9	1.4	4.6	3.4		
47.7	123.4	1.4	3.7	5.9	15.2	2.0	5.1
44.3	30.2	1.8	1.2	5.6	3.8	1.0	0.7
48.9	93.2	1.3	2.5	6.0	11.5	2.3	4.4
70.2	4.0			12.3	0.7		

TABLE 4.5-19
Geographic
distribution of
current
expenditures
for separately
budgeted
research and
development in
universities and
colleges, by
source of funds,
1964 (millions
of dollars)

Geographic location	Total	Federal government	State and local governments	Other
United States, total	$1,272.4	$917.3	$173.2	$181.9
Northeast	403.2	317.1	30.4	55.7
New England	146.1	118.6	6.4	21.1
Maine	2.7	1.5	0.9	0.3
New Hampshire	5.1	4.4	0.4	0.3
Vermont	2.9	2.3	0.5	0.1
Massachusetts	99.4	81.4	1.7	15.3
Rhode Island	8.9	7.7	0.6	0.6
Connecticut	27.0	21.3	2.2	3.5
Middle Atlantic	257.1	198.5	24.0	34.6
New York	149.5	120.3	10.6	18.6
New Jersey	36.6	23.4	8.0	5.2
Pennsylvania	71.0	54.8	5.4	10.8
North Central	322.8	230.2	42.0	50.7
East North Central	230.7	172.3	21.2	37.2
Ohio	39.3	29.0	3.3	7.0
Indiana	26.5	19.3	2.7	4.5
Illinois	77.5	59.3	7.5	10.7
Michigan	52.2	42.5	0.5	9.2
Wisconsin	35.3	22.2	7.1	6.0
West North Central	92.0	57.8	20.8	13.4
Minnesota	23.4	17.1	3.1	3.2
Iowa	17.8	11.2	4.0	2.6
Missouri	22.8	14.9	4.4	3.5
North Dakota	3.6	1.9	1.1	0.6
South Dakota	3.6	2.2	1.2	0.2
Nebraska	7.0	3.0	3.2	0.8
Kansas	13.9	7.6	3.9	2.4
South	270.5	177.7	47.2	45.7
South Atlantic	146.2	99.2	20.6	26.4
Delaware	2.9	1.6	0.4	0.9
Maryland	36.0	28.7	2.5	4.8
District of Columbia	12.8	11.2	*	1.6

* Less than $50,000.

SOURCE: National Science Foundation, *Scientific Activities at Universities and Colleges, 1964*, 1968, p. 44.

Geographic location	Total	Federal government	State and local governments	Other
Virginia	$14.1	$ 9.3	$ 2.4	$ 2.4
West Virginia	3.5	1.9	1.0	.6
North Carolina	27.1	18.2	4.3	4.6
South Carolina	4.7	2.6	1.3	.8
Georgia	18.1	9.9	1.6	6.6
Florida	27.1	15.8	7.1	4.2
East South Central	45.0	28.6	12.0	4.4
Kentucky	8.7	4.8	3.1	0.8
Tennessee	18.6	13.0	3.8	1.8
Alabama	11.0	6.9	3.2	0.9
Mississippi	6.7	4.0	2.0	0.7
West South Central	79.3	49.8	14.6	14.9
Arkansas	6.6	3.4	1.9	1.3
Louisiana	18.2	11.7	4.2	2.3
Oklahoma	10.8	6.6	2.4	1.8
Texas	43.6	28.2	6.1	9.3
West	270.2	188.9	51.7	29.7
Mountain	73.7	47.0	18.2	8.5
Montana	3.8	1.6	1.8	0.4
Idaho	3.8	1.5	2.1	0.2
Wyoming	3.1	1.0	0.7	1.4
Colorado	20.3	15.9	1.6	2.8
New Mexico	14.6	11.4	2.5	0.7
Arizona	14.4	6.6	5.9	1.9
Utah	11.1	7.8	2.5	0.8
Nevada	2.6	1.2	1.1	0.3
Pacific	196.5	141.8	33.5	21.2
Washington	24.3	16.3	5.5	2.5
Oregon	15.8	10.8	3.2	1.8
California	144.8	108.3	21.8	14.7
Alaska	4.2	2.3	0.5	1.4
Hawaii	7.3	4.2	2.4	0.7
United States territories	5.8	3.5	1.9	0.4

TABLE 4.5-20 Geographic distribution of capital expenditures for research, development, and instruction in the sciences and engineering in universities and colleges, by source of funds, 1964	*Geographic region and division*	*Total*	*Federal government*	*Non-federal*

Geographic region and division	Total	Federal government	Non-federal
	Millions of dollars		
United States, total	$529.5	$134.4	$395.1
	Percent of total amount		
Northeast	27.8	28.9	27.4
New England	7.5	9.8	6.7
Middle Atlantic	20.3	19.1	20.7
North Central	28.9	29.2	28.7
East North Central	20.6	21.9	20.1
West North Central	8.3	7.3	8.7
South	19.9	23.2	18.9
South Atlantic	8.3	9.4	7.9
East South Central	5.3	6.0	5.0
West South Central	6.4	7.7	5.9
West	23.3	18.5	24.9
Mountain	3.5	4.1	3.2
Pacific	19.8	14.4	21.6
United States territories	0.1	0.2	0.1

SOURCE: National Science Foundation, *Scientific Activities at Universities and Colleges, 1964*, 1968, p. 14.

4.6. Physical Plant

Table 4.6-1 (although rather old) shows the number and cost of buildings completed by public institutions of higher education during the period 1951–1955. Fifty-three percent of total building funds of public institutions were spent on instructional buildings, 24 percent on residential buildings, and 5 percent on research facilities. By geographic region, the proportion of total building funds spent for each type of facility varied. For example, the Northeast spent only 34 percent of its building funds on instructional buildings, as compared with 62 percent for the West, which was growing fast.

In 1956 the instructional facilities of 1,335 institutions of higher education could have accommodated 445,249 more students than were actually enrolled (Table 4.6-2). Inadequate residential and other facilities might restrict enrollment below what could be accommodated by instructional facilities, but these 1,335 institutions could have accommodated 49,063 more students in residences in 1956 than were actually accommodated. "This computation indicates a 92.9 percent saturation in the use of residence facilities by those institutions at that time."[1]

In 1956 colleges and universities housed 37 percent of their students on campus. By regions, the South accommodated 50 percent of its students in college residences, and the West accommodated 22 percent. Public institutions housed 33 percent of their students, as compared with 42 percent for private institutions. Thirty-two percent of all male students and 47 percent of all female

(Text continued on p. 722)

[1] U.S. Office of Education, *College and University Facilities Survey,* issued as Department of Health, Education and Welfare circular, 1960, part 2, p. 4.

TABLE 4.6-1
Number and
cost of buildings
completed by
public
institutions of
higher
education, by
function of
buildings,
grouped by
geographic
regions and by
spring 1956
full-time
enrollments,
aggregate
United States,
1951–1955
(cost figures are
in thousands
of dollars)

Region and enrollment (1)	Total		Instructional	
	Number (2)	Cost (3)	Number (4)	Cost (5)
Aggregate United States	1,744	$1,094,577	732	$576,257
Below 200	28	6,277	8	1,445
200–499	115	35,931	57	25,163
500–999	243	114,690	103	65,217
1,000–1,999	304	147,616	103	61,989
2,000–4,999	497	302,176	236	167,358
5,000–9,999	399	245,906	153	113,964
10,000–19,999	120	193,438	56	124,386
20,000 and more	38	48,543	16	16,735
Northeast	162	121,759	47	40,988
Below 200	3	771	1	200
200–499	8	3,528	4	2,929
500–999	52	31,435	11	6,755
1,000–1,999	29	24,988	12	12,061
2,000–4,999	27	19,028	7	8,589
5,000–9,999	24	29,496	4	2,833
10,000–19,999	19	12,513	8	7,621
20,000 and more				
North Central	383	343,765	147	162,087
Below 200				
200–499	18	4,190	8	1,505
500–999	27	13,730	12	8,082
1,000–1,999	56	21,857	18	7,607
2,000–4,999	105	85,094	38	43,682
5,000–9,999	82	69,547	33	32,769
10,000–19,999	57	100,804	22	51,707
20,000 and more	38	48,543	16	16,735
South	762	352,697	332	201,743
Below 200	11	1,355	4	810
200–499	75	24,158	36	18,214
500–999	95	38,574	48	26,144
1,000–1,999	138	51,463	43	19,647
2,000–4,999	206	114,591	107	70,028
5,000–9,999	223	106,444	86	56,642
10,000–19,999	14	16,112	8	10,258
20,000 and more				

Research		General		Auxiliary		Residential	
Number (6)	*Cost* (7)	*Number* (8)	*Cost* (9)	*Number* (10)	*Cost* (11)	*Number* (12)	*Cost* (13)
136	$51,066	309	$128,051	143	$78,080	424	$261,123
2	2,667	8	760	4	663	6	742
2	65	22	5,514	7	1,013	27	4,176
4	634	52	19,123	17	3,310	67	26,406
20	15,931	47	15,279	42	13,167	92	41,250
34	5,015	77	25,674	34	19,262	116	84,867
48	10,344	78	42,695	30	22,867	90	56,036
22	9,627	14	6,412	7	14,244	21	38,769
4	6,783	11	12,594	2	3,554	5	8,877
15	4,115	46	38,493	11	8,109	43	30,054
		1	186			1	385
		2	80			2	519
		21	13,873	5	1,658	15	9,149
		7	3,793			10	9,134
4	756	3	1,689	3	2,401	10	5,593
5	1,794	9	18,398	2	1,512	4	4,959
6	1,565	3	474	1	2,538	1	315
28	16,848	67	31,772	22	25,035	119	108,023
		7	2,230			3	455
		4	798			11	4,850
2	1,337	9	2,483	5	2,252	22	8,178
8	475	17	5,775	5	2,629	37	32,533
3	2,227	12	4,973	8	8,458	26	21,120
11	6,026	7	2,919	2	8,142	15	32,010
4	6,783	11	12,594	2	3,554	5	8,877
49	9,458	118	30,946	69	24,926	194	85,624
		3	367	2	147	2	31
2	65	10	1,780	7	1,013	20	3,086
1	256	18	2,671	6	1,048	22	8,455
5	1,601	17	4,785	23	7,087	50	18,343
8	2,566	28	7,467	17	6,457	46	28,073
33	4,970	41	13,095	13	7,745	50	23,992
		1	781	1	1,429	4	3,644

TABLE 4.6-1 (continued)	Total		Instructional	
Region and enrollment (1)	Number (2)	Cost (3)	Number (4)	Cost (5)
West	416	$ 257,094	198	$158,124
Below 200	14	4,151	3	435
200–499	14	4,055	9	2,515
500–999	68	22,251	31	15,536
1,000–1,999	81	49,308	30	22,674
2,000–4,999	149	76,899	82	43,531
5,000–9,999	60	36,421	25	18,633
10,000–19,999	30	64,009	18	54,800
20,000 and more				
U.S. service academies	8	13,171	2	8,980
Below 200				
200–499				
500–999	1	8,700	1	8,700
1,000–1,999				
2,000–4,999	7	4,471	1	280
5,000–9,999				
10,000–19,999				
20,000 and more				
Outlying parts of the United States	13	6,091	6	4,335
Below 200				
200–499				
500–999				
1,000–1,999				
2,000–4,999	3	2,093	1	1,248
5,000–9,999	10	3,998	5	3,087
10,000–19,999				
20,000 and more				

SOURCE: U.S. Office of Education, *College and University Facilities Survey,* issued as Department of Health, Education and Welfare circular, 1959, part 1, p. 16.

Research		General		Auxiliary		Residential	
Number (6)	*Cost* (7)	*Number* (8)	*Cost* (9)	*Number* (10)	*Cost* (11)	*Number* (12)	*Cost* (13)
42	$20,223	74	$ 25,097	38	$18,905	64	$ 34,745
2	2,667	4	207	2	516	3	326
		3	1,424			2	116
3	378	9	1,781	6	604	19	3,952
13	12,993	14	4,218	14	3,828	10	5,595
13	824	26	9,100	7	6,798	21	16,646
6	1,325	15	6,129	6	5,024	8	5,310
5	2,036	3	2,238	3	2,135	1	2,800
		3	1,643	2	977	1	1,571
		3	1,643	2	977	1	1,571
2	422	1	100	1	128	3	1,106
1	394					1	451
1	28	1	100	1	128	2	655

TABLE 4.6-2
Estimated gross additional full-time students who could have been accommodated in instructional facilities, spring 1956, by type of control and geographic region

Region (1)	Total Institutional response		
	Number reporting no additional students (2)	*Number reporting gross additional students* (3)	*Gross additional students* (4)
Aggregate United States	211	1,124	445,249
Northeast	74	260	86,749
North Central	39	353	147,199
South	63	357	135,880
West	31	146	73,490
United States service academies	2	3	781
Outlying parts	2	5	1,150

SOURCE: U.S. Office of Education, *College and University Facilities Survey,* issued as Department of Health, Education and Welfare circular, 1960, part 2, p. 3.

students were accommodated in residential facilities in 1956.[2] Table 4.6-3 shows the proportion of students houses on public campuses in each region for the year 1960–61.

Although there is no clear correlation between the percentage of students accommodated in residential facilities and the size of the institution, the Office of Education has stated that ". . . at both public and private institutions, the larger the size of the institution, the smaller the percent of the students that can be housed in its student residences; the smaller the institution, the larger the percent that can be accommodated."[3] Table 4.6-4 shows the average and median number of acres in developed campuses in 1956.

PROPOSED EXPENDITURES ON CONSTRUCTION AND REHABILITATION, 1956–1970

According to projections made in 1956, the average annual cost of new construction and rehabilitation projects from 1956 to 1970 would be $1.2 billion (Table 4.6-5). This was clearly an underestimate in the light of rising construction costs since 1956. The Office of Education has estimated the increase in the value of

[2] U.S. Office of Education, *College and University Facilities Survey,* issued as Department of Health, Education and Welfare circular, 1960, part 2, pp. 4–5.

[3] U.S. Office of Education, *College and University Facilities Survey,* issued as Department of Health, Education and Welfare circular, 1964, part 3, p. 455.

Public			Private		
Institutional response			Institutional response		
Number reporting no additional students	Number reporting gross additional students	Gross additional students	Number reporting no additional students	Number reporting gross additional students	Gross additional students
(5)	*(6)*	*(7)*	*(8)*	*(9)*	*(10)*
84	391	219,648	127	733	225,601
20	50	15,527	54	210	71,222
14	108	65,559	25	245	81,640
23	158	84,530	40	199	51,350
24	69	52,651	7	77	20,839
2	3	781			
1	3	600	1	2	550

TABLE 4.6-3 Regional percentage distribution of full-time students in public institutions and of full-time students housed on campus; also for each region the percentage of its full-time students housed on campus, 1960–61

	Full-time students in public institutions		
Region	Percentage enrolled	Percentage housed	Percentage of regional enrollment housed
All regions	100.0	100.0	33.4
North Atlantic	12.0	12.2	33.8
Great Lakes and Plains	32.6	33.2	34.1
Southeast	19.7	31.1	52.8
West and Southwest	34.8	23.4	22.4
Outlying parts	0.9	0.1	4.2

SOURCE: U.S. Office of Education, *College and University Facilities Survey,* issued as Department of Health, Education and Welfare circular, 1965, part 4, p. 34.

physical plant to have been $2.3 billion a year from 1962 to 1964— almost double the figure projected in 1956.[4]

Almost half of the proposed expenditures on facilities from 1956 to 1970 were for instructional facilities—52 percent for public and 45 percent for private institutions. Proposed expenditures on

[4] U.S. Office of Education, *Digest of Educational Statistics, 1967,* 1967, table 124.

TABLE 4.6-4
Average and
median number
of acres in
developed
campus in
random
sampling of 146
institutions,
by size of
enrollment,
1956

	Number of acres			
	Average		Median	
Enrollment	*Public*	*Private*	*Public*	*Private*
Enrollment below 1,000	14	38	10	30
1,000–4,999	172	97	69	68
5,000 and over	597	599	270	92

SOURCE: U.S. Office of Education, *College and University Facilities Survey,* issued as Department of Health, Education and Welfare circular, 1960, part 2, p. 29.

facilities were almost twice as large for public as for private insti tutions. For all institutions, instructional facilities absorbed 5(percent of the planned outlay, residential facilities absorbed 29 percent, and research facilities absorbed 4 percent (Table 4.6-6)

NEW CON-STRUCTION AND REHABIL-ITATION, 1959-1964

From 1959 to 1964 expenditures for new construction and rehabili tation of facilities increased by 81 percent—from $625 million to $1,131 million. Public institutions increased their expenditures for new construction and rehabilitation by 83 percent, as compared with 76 percent for private institutions (Table 4.6-7).[5]

There were large regional variations in the percentage increase of expenditures on plant in this period. Expenditures on facilities increased by 124 percent in the West and Southwest, but only 4(percent in the Great Lakes and Plains states (Tables 4.6-8 and 4.6-9). From 1961 to 1965, California and New York consistently ranked either first or second in construction expenditures for higher education (Table 4.6-10).

NEW CON-STRUCTION AND REHABIL-ITATION, 1963-1964

Expenditures on new construction and rehabilitation projects totaled $1,131 million in 1963–64. Public institutions spent $74(million on facilities, and private institutions spent $391 million (Table 4.6-11). Tables 4.6-12 and 4.6-13 give the cost per square foot of new construction projects for 1963–64. The cost of construction per square foot was the lowest in the Southeast ($17.30

[5] L. F. Robbins, *New Construction and Rehabilitation on College Campuses 1961–62, 1962–63, and 1963–64,* U.S. Office of Education, 1966, p. 26 Figures cited from this source are for reporting institutions only (88 to 95 percent of the total). If these figures are extrapolated to 100 percent, expenditures on facilities increased from $710 to $1,285 million from 1959 to 1964

TABLE 4.6-5 *Projections of funds needed for new construction and rehabilitation, 1956–1970*

New construction for increased enrollments, 1956–1970		
Instructional, research, general, and auxiliary facilities	$ 7,057,500,000	
Residential facilities	5,307,240,000	
	12,364,740,000	
Divided by 15 (years) = per year		$ 824,316,000
Replacement, rehabilitation, and depreciation from 1958 through 1970		
Replacement	1,404,030,000	
Rehabilitation	504,577,000	
Depreciation	2,874,043,000	
	4,782,650,000	
Divided by 12 (years) = per year		398,554,000
Total amount needed	17,147,390,000	
Average per year		1,222,870,000

SOURCE: U.S. Office of Education, *College and University Facilities Survey,* issued as Department of Health, Education and Welfare circular, 1960, part 2, p. 24.

and highest in the North Atlantic ($23.40). By building function, the cost per square foot was lowest for residential facilities ($18.50) and highest for research facilities ($26.70).

PHYSICAL FACILITIES PLANNED FOR 1965–1970 Table 4.6-14 shows the planned percentage increase in instructional facilities from 1965–1970. The largest relative increases were planned for graduate rather than undergraduate facilities, for full-time rather than part-time students, and for public rather than private institutions. Residential accommodations were expected to increase by 58 percent in this period and about two-thirds more for public than for private institutions (Table 4.6-15).

SOURCES OF FUNDS FOR CONSTRUC-TION, 1959–1964 Sources of funds for construction showed large variations from 1959 to 1964. Appropriations of state governments as a percentage of total construction funds of public institutions decreased during this period. The federal government increased its share of contribution to research plant but decreased relatively its Housing and Home Financing Agency lending to public institutions (Table

(Text continued on p. 728)

TABLE 4.6-6
Distribution of proposed facilities expenditures, by functional groups, 1956–1970 (cost figures are in thousands of dollars)

	Totals			
Functional groups *(1)*	*Number* *(2)*	*Percent* *(3)*	*Cost* *(4)*	*Percent* *(5)*
Aggregate	6,333	100.0	$5,469,771	100.0
Buildings:				
Instructional	2,657	42.0	2,726,065	49.8
Research	228	3.6	231,641	4.2
General	771	12.2	472,812	8.6
Auxiliary	572	9.0	355,265	6.5
Residential	1,843	29.1	1,588,376	29.1
Campus improvements	262	4.1	95,612	1.8

SOURCE: U.S. Office of Education, *College and University Facilities Survey,* issued as Department of Health, Education and Welfare circular, 1960, part 2, p. 46.

TABLE 4.6-7
Distribution of expenditures for new construction and rehabilitation at institutions of higher education by control, aggregate United States, 1959–1964

	Public		Private	
Year	*Amount* *(thousands)*	*Percent*	*Amount* *(thousands)*	*Percent*
1958–59	$403,732	64.5	$221,760	35.5
1959–60	531,423	64.2	296,808	35.8
1960–61	482,448	59.4	329,475	40.6
1961–62	493,187	55.1	401,554	44.9
1962–63	605,095	56.8	459,355	43.2
1963–64	739,665	65.4	390,842	34.6

SOURCE: L. F. Robbins, *New Construction and Rehabilitation on College Campuses, 1961–62, 1962–63, and 1963–64,* U.S. Office of Education, 1966, p. 28.

TABLE 4.6-9
Distribution of expenditures for new construction and rehabilitation at institutions of higher education, by region, aggregate United States, 1959–1964

	North Atlantic		Great Lakes and Plains	
Year	*Amount* *(thousands)*	*Percent*	*Amount* *(thousands)*	*Percent*
*1958–59**	$166,711	26.7	$224,883	35.9
*1959–60**	236,074	28.5	223,032	26.9
*1960–61**	221,378	27.3	257,682	31.7
*1961–62**	269,517	30.1	256,115	28.6
*1962–63**	276,365	25.9	324,212	30.5
*1963–64**	320,995	28.4	328,801	29.1

*These details do not add to 100 percent because outlying areas and United States service academies contributed small percentages.

SOURCE: L. F. Robbins, *New Construction and Rehabilitation on College Campuses, 1961–62, 1962–63, and 1963–64,* U.S. Office of Education, 1966, p. 29.

Public				Private			
Number (6)	*Percent (7)*	*Cost (8)*	*Percent (9)*	*Number (10)*	*Percent (11)*	*Cost (12)*	*Percent (13)*
3,593	100.0	$3,538,716	100.0	2,740	100.0	$1,931,055	100.0
1,611	44.8	1,850,403	52.3	1,046	38.2	875,662	45.3
156	4.3	145,509	4.1	72	2.6	86,132	4.5
440	12.3	278,423	7.9	331	12.1	194,389	10.1
298	8.3	205,820	5.8	274	10.0	149,445	7.7
874	24.3	973,532	27.5	969	35.4	614,844	31.8
214	6.0	85,029	2.4	48	1.7	10,583	0.6

TABLE 4.6-8
Percentage increase in expenditures for new construction and rehabilitation, by region, 1959–1964

North Atlantic	93
Great Lakes and Plains	46
Southeast	83
West and Southwest	124

SOURCE: Table 4.6-9.

Southeast		West and Southwest	
Amount (thousands)	*Percent*	*Amount (thousands)*	*Percent*
$107,178	17.1	$125,715	20.1
134,120	16.2	235,005	28.4
118,337	14.6	212,532	26.2
146,636	16.4	216,558	24.2
184,019	17.3	279,094	26.2
195,762	17.3	280,985	24.9

TABLE 4.6-10 *Construction, institutions of higher education, order of expenditures by state, top 10 (in millions)*

1960–61		1961–62		1962–63		1963–64	
California	$105	New York	$92	California	$137	California	$131
New York	56	California	86	New York	86	New York	131
Pennsylvania	55	Pennsylvania	58	Illinois	82	Illinois	66
Ohio	49	Ohio	48	Ohio	52	Pennsylvania	60
Illinois	40	Illinois	39	Massachusetts	51	Indiana	58
Indiana	31	Michigan	35	Pennsylvania	47	Michigan	47
Texas	29	Massachusetts	35	Indiana	39	Texas	41
Massachusetts	27	Texas	34	Texas	37	Massachusetts	39
Michigan	25	North Carolina	32	Wisconsin	32	Louisiana	34
Missouri	22	New Jersey	31	New Jersey	31	Wisconsin	34

SOURCE: L. F. Robbins, *New Construction and Rehabilitation on College Campuses, 1961–62, 1962–63, and 1963–64,* U.S. Office of Education, 1966, p. 29.

4.6-16). Figure 4.6-1 shows some trends in sources of funds for new construction at public institutions. State appropriations accounted for a declining share of the expenditures on instructional facilities but an increasing share of the expenditures on research facilities. The relative increase in the federal funding of research facilities is clearly shown in this figure.

Private institutions also expanded research facilities in this period with the help of the federal government. Federal funding of research facilities at private institutions increased relatively by almost five times. Private institutions relied heavily on gifts and grants to finance instructional, research, and general facilities and on revenue bonds to finance residential facilities. Some of the money spent on instructional, research, and general facilities was borrowed from endowment funds—a practice generally frowned upon (Table 4.6-17). Some general trends in the sources of funds for new construction at private institutions are shown in Figure 4.6-2.

Table 4.6-18 gives the percentage distribution of sources of funds for new construction at public and private institutions by type of facility for 1963–64. Public institutions received 31 percent of their construction funds from government appropriations, as compared with 6 percent for private institutions. Private insti-

(Text continued on p. 732)

FIGURE 4.6-1 *Trends in sources of funds for new construction at public institutions, 1959–1964*

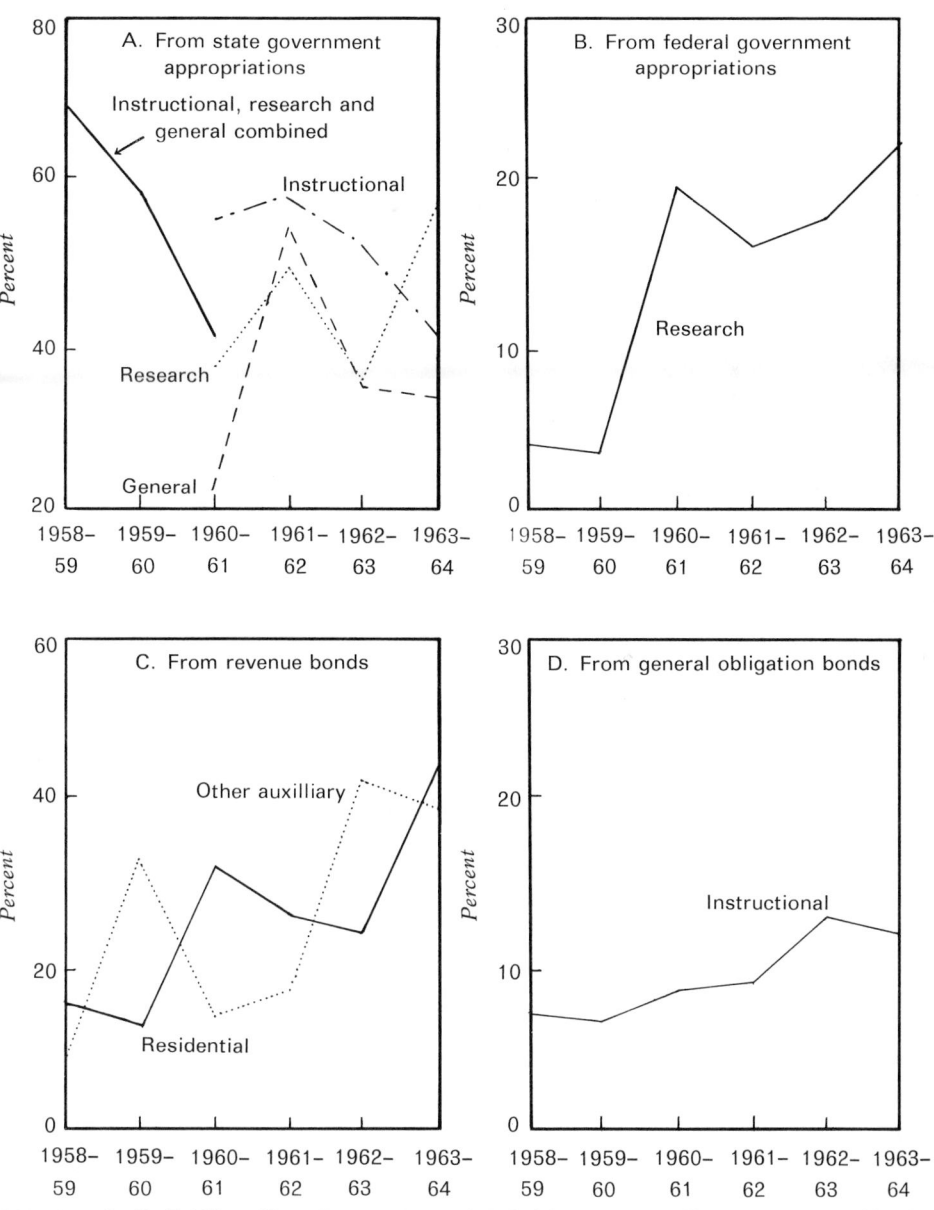

SOURCE: L. F. Robbins, *New Construction and Rehabilitation on College Campuses, 1961–62, 1962–63 and 1963–64*, U.S. Office of Education, 1966, p. 31.

TABLE 4.6-11 *Number and cost of new construction and rehabilitation projects completed by higher education institutions, by control, region, and state, aggregate United States, 1963–64*

Region and state	Total Number of projects	Total Amount (thousands)	Public Number of projects	Public Amount (thousands)	Private Number of projects	Private Amount (thousands)
TOTAL	1,549	$1,130,507	885	$739,665	664	$390,842
North Atlantic	365	320,995	137	146,918	228	174,077
Connecticut	18	20,524	13	4,324	5	16,200
Delaware	4	6,397	4	6,397		
District of Columbia	5	8,637			5	8,637
Maine	21	9,428	15	8,511	6	917
Maryland	24	11,053	16	6,092	8	4,961
Massachusetts	56	39,300	8	11,209	48	28,091
New Hampshire	2	716	1	466	1	250
New Jersey	28	23,820	8	9,859	20	13,961
New York	115	130,613	43	75,904	72	54,709
Pennsylvania	74	60,193	24	18,759	50	41,434
Rhode Island	9	5,638	4	3,502	5	2,136
Vermont	9	4,676	1	1,895	8	2,781
Great Lakes and Plains	392	328,801	225	240,984	167	87,817
Illinois	72	65,752	45	50,596	27	15,156
Indiana	34	57,865	14	40,152	20	17,713
Iowa	38	18,541	15	11,118	23	7,423
Kansas	29	14,352	21	12,383	8	1,969
Michigan	47	47,362	28	37,110	19	10,252
Minnesota	18	10,139	9	4,041	9	6,098
Missouri	52	29,830	24	15,934	28	13,896
Nebraska	13	9,279	11	8,812	2	467
North Dakota	9	6,305	9	6,305		
Ohio	39	29,385	17	17,666	22	11,719
South Dakota	10	6,140	7	5,122	3	1,018
Wisconsin	31	33,851	25	31,745	6	2,106
Southeast	374	195,762	219	134,692	155	61,070
Alabama	13	9,307	7	8,306	6	1,001
Arkansas	31	13,282	25	12,091	6	1,191
Florida	42	17,500	35	14,272	7	3,228
Georgia	25	17,462	18	13,665	7	3,797
Kentucky	17	8,696	9	6,423	8	2,273

Region and state	Total		Public		Private	
	Number of projects	Amount (thousands)	Number of projects	Amount (thousands)	Number of projects	Amount (thousands)
Southeast—continued:						
Louisiana	23	$ 34,300	13	$ 15,561	10	$ 18,739
Mississippi	51	14,598	46	13,448	5	1,150
North Carolina	54	25,251	14	10,143	40	15,108
South Carolina	16	4,952	8	3,021	8	1,931
Tennessee	48	19,112	16	11,354	32	7,758
Virginia	43	29,011	22	24,413	21	4,598
West Virginia	11	2,291	6	1,995	5	296
West and Southwest	415	280,985	301	213,107	114	67,878
Alaska	7	10,245	7	10,245		
Arizona	14	10,869	14	10,869		
California	170	130,744	117	97,656	53	33,088
Colorado	15	8,962	11	7,193	4	1,769
Hawaii	6	5,333	6	5,333		
Idaho	8	8,296	7	8,153	1	143
Montana						
Nevada	1	624	1	624		
New Mexico	7	5,021	6	4,538	1	483
Oklahoma	24	7,111	14	4,787	10	2,324
Oregon	34	9,593	23	8,167	11	1,426
Texas	84	41,021	60	27,855	24	13,166
Utah	11	13,133	8	1,523	3	11,610
Washington	33	29,941	26	26,072	7	3,869
Wyoming	1	92	1	92		
United States service schools	1	3,546	1	3,546		
Outlying areas	2	418	2	418		
Guam	1	287	1	287		
Virgin Islands	1	131	1	131		

SOURCE: L. F. Robbins, *New Construction and Rehabilitation on College Campuses. 1961–1962, 1962–63, and 1963–64,* U.S. Office of Education, 1966, p. 19.

TABLE 4.6-12
Gross square foot cost for higher education new construction projects which reported area, by control and region, aggregate United States, 1963–64

Region	*Total*				
	Number of projects	*Gross square feet (hundreds)*	*Cost (thousands)*	*Cost per square foot*	*Number of projects*
*All regions**	1,080	487,702	$1,002,030	$20.50	641
North Atlantic	246	122,240	285,613	23.40	105
Great Lakes and Plains	271	148,341	295,780	19.90	167
Southeast	279	97,882	169,053	17.30	169
West and Southwest	282	118,610	247,751	20.90	198

*Totals include two projects in outlying areas and United States service academies not meaningful for unit cost patterns.

SOURCE: L. F. Robbins, *New Construction and Rehabilitation on College Campuses, 1961–62, 1962–63, and 1963–64*, U.S. Office of Education, 1966, p. 23.

tutions received 38 percent of their construction funds from gifts and grants, as compared with 3 percent for public institutions. Revenue bonds provided a large proportion of the construction funds of both groups — 44 percent for public and 28 percent for private institutions.

SOURCES OF FUNDS FOR PROPOSED CONSTRUCTION AND REHABILITATION, 1965–1970   Government appropriations were expected to provide 26 percent of the funds for new construction and rehabilitation projects from 1965 to 1970. Federal government grants were expected to provide 14 percent, revenue bonds 18 percent, and general obligation bonds 16 percent. Public institutions expected to receive 35 percent of their construction funds from government appropriations, as compared with 6 percent for private institutions (Table 4.6-19).

PHYSICAL FACILITIES COMPLETED AND PLANNED BY NEW INSTITUTIONS, 1961–1965   From 1961 to 1965, 181 new institutions of higher education (including branch campuses) reported 718 physical facilities projects completed or planned at an estimated cost of $442 million.[6] Expenditures for instructional, research, and general facilities accounted for 72.1 percent of this $442 million and outlays on residential facilities for 11.3 percent. The allocation of construction and rehabilitation expenditures of new institutions varied

[6] U.S. Office of Education, *College and University Facilities Survey,* issued as Department of Health, Education and Welfare circular, 1965, part 5, p. 15.

Public			Private			
Gross square feet (hundreds)	*Cost (thousands)*	*Cost per square foot*	*Number of projects*	*Gross square feet (hundreds)*	*Cost (thousands)*	*Cost per square foot*
330,509	$666,368	$20.20	439	157,193	$335,662	$21.40
63,057	135,916	21.60	141	59,183	149,697	25.30
112,551	225,254	20.00	104	35,790	70,526	19.70
69,681	118,455	17.00	110	28,201	50,598	17.90
84,591	182,910	21.60	84	34,019	64,841	19.10

by control and by type of institution. New public institutions planned to spend 79.5 percent of their construction funds on instructional, research, and general facilities and 3.9 percent on residential facilities. The corresponding figures for new private institutions were 57.3 percent for instructional, research and general facilities and 26.2 percent for residential facilities (Figure 4.6-3). Expenditures on instructional, research, and general facilities accounted for 83 percent of the construction expenditures of new junior colleges, but for only 60 percent of the construction expenditures of new four-year liberal arts colleges.[7]

Construction expenditures tend to be low for new junior colleges and technical institutes compared to the share of enrollment involved. New junior colleges and technical institutes accounted for 66 percent of the enrollment of new institutions, but for only 43 percent of the construction expenditures (Table 4.6-20).

SOURCES OF FUNDS FOR CONSTRUCTION AT NEW INSTITUTIONS, 1961–1965 In financing institutional, research, and general facilities, new public institutions relied on governmental appropriations (50 percent) and general obligation bonds (37 percent) as sources of funds. In financing residential and other auxiliary facilities, they depended primarily on revenue bonds (49 percent) and general

(Text continued on p. 744)

[7] U.S. Office of Education, *College and University Facilities Survey,* issued as Department of Health, Education and Welfare circular, 1965, part 5, p. 21.

FIGURE 4.6-2 *Trends in sources of funds for new construction at private institutions, 1959–1964*

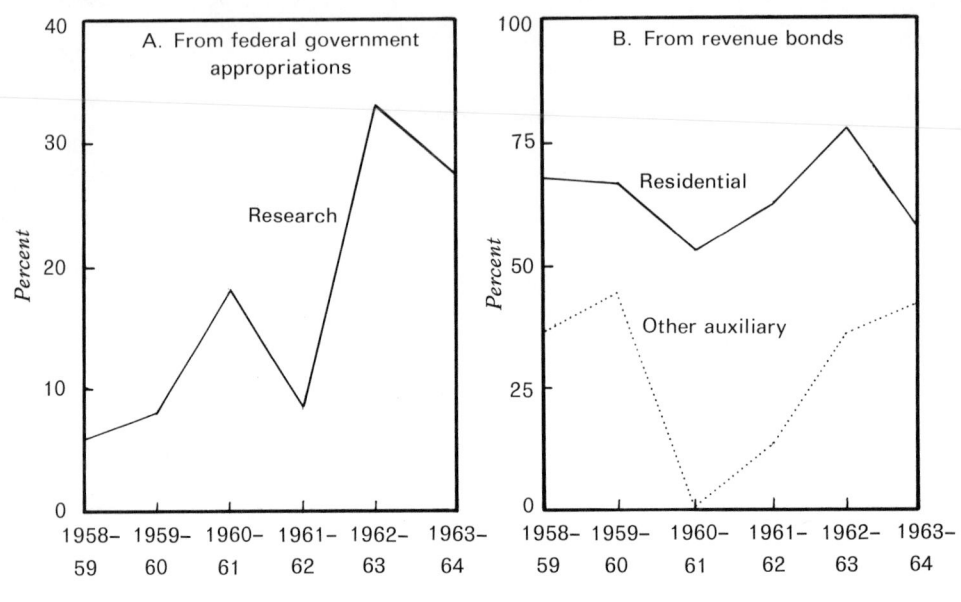

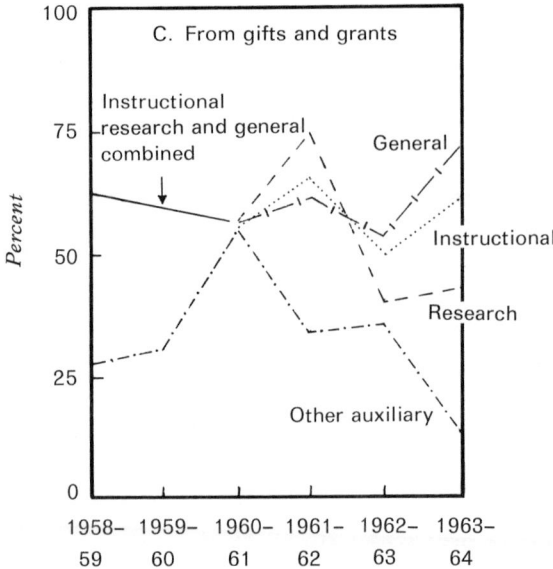

SOURCE: L. F. Robbins, *New Construction and Rehabilitation on College Campuses, 1961–62, 1962–63 and 1963–64,* U.S. Office of Education, 1966, p. 32.

FIGURE 4.6-3 *Expenditures for facilities at new institutions of higher education, by control and functional group, 1961–1965*

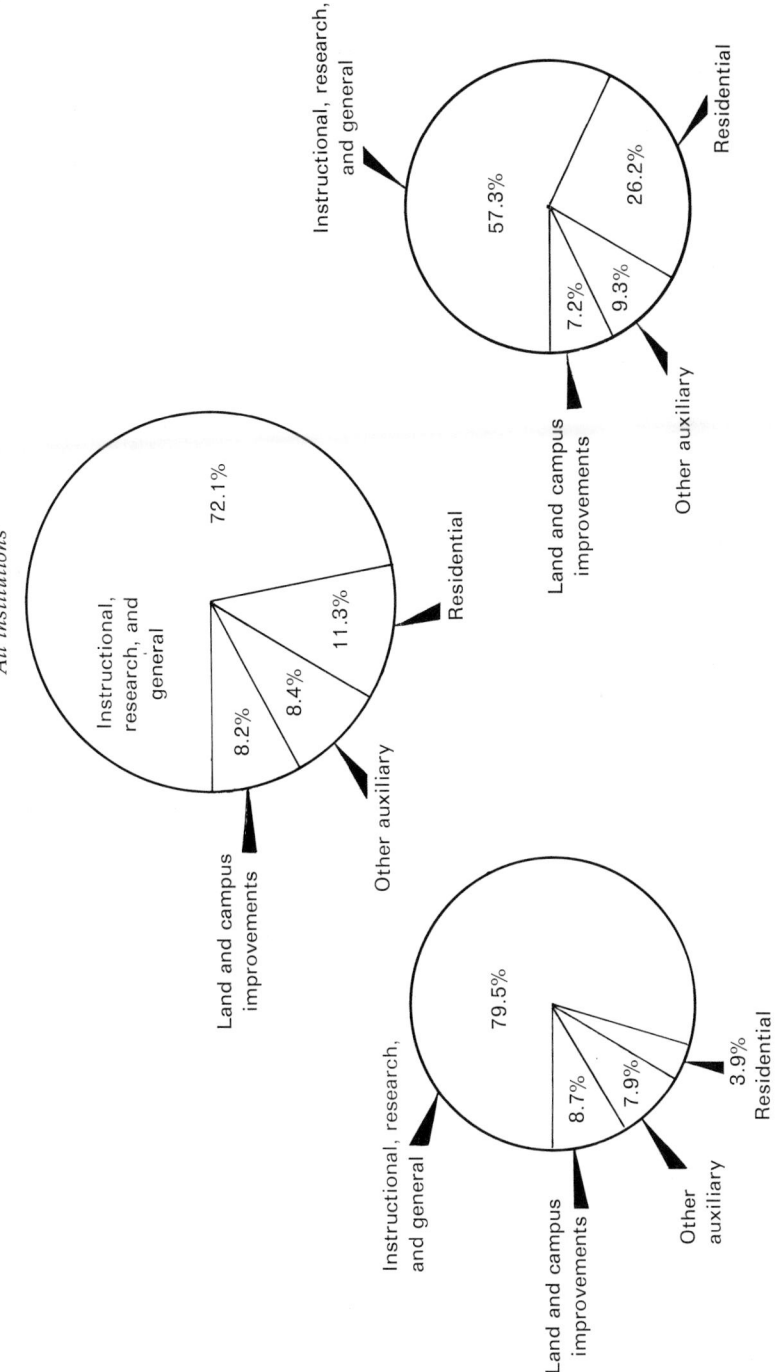

All institutions

Private

Public

SOURCE: U.S. Office of Education, *College and University Facilities Survey*, issued as Department of Health, Education and Welfare circular, 1965, part 5, p. 15.

TABLE 4.6-13 *Gross square foot cost for total higher education new construction projects which reported area, by primary function, aggregate United States, 1963–64*

Primary function	Number of projects	Gross square feet (hundreds)	Cost (thousands)	Cost per square foot
TOTAL	1,080	487,702	$1,002,030	$20.50
Total instructional	383	194,375	411,316	21.20
Demonstration school	8	6,604	13,312	20.20
Fieldhouse	8	5,141	8,461	16.50
Gymnasium	42	21,836	43,958	20.10
Home management laboratory	4	1,205	2,493	20.70
Instructional classroom	194	95,840	201,530	21.00
Library	56	29,535	60,074	20.30
Museum	2	393	1,159	29.50
Instructional laboratory	46	27,059	63,736	23.60
Swimming pool	5	799	1,863	23.30
Teaching hospital	4	1,021	2,750	26.90
Other instructional	14	4,942	11,980	24.20
Total research	107	37,110	99,017	26.70
Agriculture research	29	3,614	6,872	19.00
Astronomy research	1	45	105	23.30
Biological research	11	2,072	6,484	31.30
Chemistry research	7	4,429	14,007	31.60
Mathematical and statistical research	4	804	2,398	29.80
Physics research	7	3,306	9,151	27.70
Other physical sciences research	13	4,754	11,956	25.10
Social science research	6	1,852	4,720	25.50
Dentistry research	1	160	795	49.70
Engineering research	7	1,175	2,612	22.20
Medical research	21	14,899	39,917	26.80
Total general	90	19,029	40,534	21.30
Administration building	25	5,973	11,827	19.80
Armory	2	603	908	15.10
Auditorium	7	2,034	5,243	25.80
Chapel	8	2,322	8,314	35.80
Extension and experiment station	1	48	139	29.00
Faculty club	3	553	1,622	29.30

Primary function	Number of projects	Gross square feet (hundreds)	Cost (thousands)	Cost per square foot
Garage	4	1,720	1,202	7.00
Maintenance shops	22	1,935	2,355	12.20
Multipurpose	1	264	719	27.20
Education office building	8	1,242	4,870	39.20
Theater	1	199	605	30.40
Warehouse	4	1,501	1,269	8.50
Other general	4	635	1,461	23.00
Total residential	400	206,025	382,015	18.50
Faculty apartments	5	307	460	15.00
Faculty-staff houses	27	759	911	12.00
Fraternity and sorority houses	14	1,724	2,399	13.90
Married students apartments	39	24,183	36,038	14.90
Men's residence halls	131	62,264	120,196	19.30
Women's residence halls	135	69,203	126,709	18.30
President's home	7	251	376	15.00
Residence halls with separate units for men and women	39	46,788	94,018	20.10
Other residential	3	546	908	16.60
Total other auxiliary	100	31,163	69,148	22.20
College union	44	19,876	42,314	21.30
Food facilities	36	9,130	22,176	24.30
Infirmary	10	1,508	3,640	24.10
Other auxiliary	10	649	1,018	15.70

SOURCE: L. F. Robbins, *New Construction and Rehabilitation on College Campuses, 1961–62, 1962–63, and 1963–64,* U.S. Office of Education, 1966, p. 22.

TABLE 4.6-14 *Planned percentage increase in accommodations in instructional facilities of responding higher education institutions between fall 1965 and fall 1970, by kind of student and institutional control, aggregate United States*

Control	Attendance status	Percentage increase Undergraduate	Graduate
Public	Full-time	53.7	74.5
	Part-time	49.3	53.6
Private	Full-time	32.3	40.6
	Part-time	25.7	19.4
TOTAL	Full-time	46.8	61.7
	Part-time	42.1	38.6

SOURCE: U.S. Office of Education, *College and University Enrollment and Physical Facilities Survey, 1965–70,* 1970, p. 2.

TABLE 4.6-16 *Selected trends in sources of construction funds at public institutions of higher education, by percentage, aggregate United States, 1958–59 to 1963–64*

	1958–59 (1)	1959–60 (2)	1960–61 (3)
From state government appropriations:			
For instructional facilities			53.3
For research facilities	68.2	57.5	38.5
For general facilities			24.4
From federal government appropriations: for research facilities	3.9	3.1	19.3
From state general obligation bonds: for instructional facilities	6.5	6.3	8.4
From gifts and grants:			
For instructional facilities			3.8
For research facilities	4.1	5.0	8.5
For general facilities			25.1
Borrowed from commercial lenders:			
For residential facilities	7.8	2.6	3.2
For other auxiliary facilities	4.4	1.0	12.7
Borrowed from Housing and Home Finance Agency:			
For residential facilities	57.1	56.4	44.2
For other auxiliary facilities	29.8	23.3	21.4
From revenue bonds other than HHFA:			
For residential facilities	16.2	13.2	30.5
For other auxiliary facilities	9.7	33.1	13.4

NOTE: Since these are selected sources and selected functional types of buildings, they cannot add up to 100 percent for any year or any type. Each percentage figure represents the portion of the total expenditure for the respective year derived from the indicated source for the indicated functional type.

SOURCE: L. F. Robbins, *New Construction and Rehabilitation on College Campuses, 1961–62, 1962–63, and 1963–64,* U.S. Office of Education, 1966, p. 30.

TABLE 4.6-15 *Percentage increase, fall 1965 to fall 1970, in number of higher-education student residential accommodations for respondents, by kind of student and institutional control, aggregate United States*

Control		Total	Single men	Single women	Married couples
Public		70.2	75.2	67.9	46.6
Private		42.1	45.0	38.4	51.8
	TOTAL	57.6	62.6	54.3	48:0

SOURCE: U.S. Office of Education, *College and University Enrollment and Physical Facilities Survey, 1965–70,* 1970, p. 3.

961–62 (4)	1962–63 (5)	1963–64 (6)
56.2	53.0	42.3
47.5	35.7	55.6
52.5	34.8	33.9
15.8	17.8	21.9
9.2	13.2	12.1
2.6	6.3	2.8
13.5	14.8	9.6
7.0	1.0	6.6
8.5	2.6	3.0
1.2	0.7	5.2
43.4	55.6	45.3
40.3	20.4	29.2
25.4	24.4	42.8
17.2	42.0	39.0

TABLE 4.6-17
Selected trends in sources of construction funds at private institutions of higher education, by percentage, aggregate United States, 1959–1964

	1958–59 (1)	1959–60 (2)	1960–61 (3)
From federal government appropriations:			
for research facilities	5.7	7.4	17.8
From gifts and grants:			
For instructional facilities	} 61.0	} 58.8	56.2
For research facilities			55.6
For general facilities			53.9
For residential facilities	13.1	12.4	26.0
For other auxiliary facilities	27.4	31.0	53.9
Borrowed from Housing and Home Finance Agency:			
For residential facilities	64.3	63.7	51.9
For other auxiliary facilities	41.2	45.4	
From revenue bonds other than HHFA:			
For residential facilities		0.5	0.2
For other auxiliary facilities	2.1	0.2	
From current funds:			
For instructional facilities	} 11.5	} 7.1	8.2
For research facilities			18.9
For general facilities			13.9
For other auxiliary facilities	7.2	5.7	13.9
Borrowed from endowment funds:			
For instructional facilities	} 5.4	} 6.2	1.6
For research facilities			3.6
For general facilities			0.3
Borrowed from commercial lenders:			
For instructional facilities	} 6.1	} 8.3	15.4
For research facilities			2.0
For general facilities			16.2
For residential facilities	7.0	3.3	6.0
For other auxiliary facilities	13.0	10.9	16.2

NOTE: Since these are selected sources and selected functional types of buildings, they cannot add up to 100 percent for any year or any type. Each percentage figure represents the portion of the total expenditure for the respective year derived from the indicated source for the indicated functional type.

SOURCE: L. F. Robbins, *New Construction and Rehabilitation on College Campuses, 1961–62, 1962–63, and 1963–64,* U.S. Office of Education, 1966, p. 33.

1961–62 (4)	1962–63 (5)	1963–64 (6)
7.7	33.6	27.3
66.0	50.9	63.6
72.8	40.3	43.3
63.6	53.9	69.4
18.4	9.7	14.6
34.0	35.0	14.3
57.6	75.7	60.6
13.6	35.3	38.2
0.1	0.8	0.4
	0.9	2.5
4.2	20.5	5.1
8.9	7.6	0.8
12.0	4.3	7.7
27.1	6.3	10.4
1.8	3.7	5.8
8.6	7.1	7.5
	1.0	9.4
12.8	6.5	13.1
		2.4
12.9	11.3	7.1
7.3	3.3	15.0
10.1	3.7	7.2

TABLE 4.6-18
Percentage distribution of fund sources for new construction completed by institutions of higher education, by functional group and control, aggregate United States, 1963-64
(L = Less than 0.05 percent)

Source	All functional groups		Instructional		Research	
	Public	Private	Public	Private	Public	Private
TOTAL	100.0	100.0	100.0	100.0	100.0	100.0
Total appropriations	31.1	5.9	44.7	5.1	77.6	38.9
State	27.4	0.6	42.3	0.2	55.6	4.8
Local	0.7	0.7	1.1		0.1	6.8
Federal	3.0	4.6	1.3	4.9	21.9	27.3
Total tax levy	1.3		2.5			
State	0.4		0.6		L	
Local	0.9		1.9			
Total general obligation bonds	14.0	1.1	25.0	2.6	7.7	
Local	2.3		3.9			
State	6.4		12.1		2.9	
State authority	4.1		6.2		4.8	
Institutional	1.2	1.1	2.8	2.6		
Total revenue bonds	43.7	28.2	17.4	0.2	0.5	
Other than HHFA	25.7	0.4	17.4	0.2	0.5	
HHFA	18.0	27.8				
Total other sources	9.9	64.8	10.4	92.1	14.2	61.1
Gifts and grants	2.6	38.3	2.8	63.6	9.6	43.3
Current funds	2.4	4.5	3.5	5.1	1.3	0.8
Endowment funds	0.1	4.0	L	5.8	1.0	7.5
Borrowed from other college funds	1.3	1.4	2.3	2.5	1.3	0.1
Borrowed from commercial sources	2.3	11.8	0.9	13.1	0.5	2.4
Other	1.2	4.8	0.9	2.0	0.5	7.0

SOURCE: L. F. Robbins, *New Construction and Rehabilitation on College Campuses, 1961-62, 1962-63, and 1963-64,* U.S. Office of Education, 1966, p. 24.

General		Residential		*Other auxiliary*	
Public	*Private*	*Public*	*Private*	*Public*	*Private*
100.0	100.0	100.0	100.0	100.0	100.0
44.1	0.2	3.7		14.7	
33.9		3.6		12.7	
0.2		0.1		2.0	
10.0	0.2				
1.2		0.5		0.2	
		0.5			
1.2		L		0.2	
20.4	0.9	2.5	0.3	4.9	
6.1				3.6	
7.8		0.8		1.3	
6.3		1.7			
0.2	0.9		0.3		
4.7	2.0	88.1	61.0	68.2	40.7
3.8	0.2	42.8	0.4	39.0	2.5
0.9	1.8	45.3	60.6	29.2	38.2
29.6	96.9	5.2	38.7	12.0	59.3
6.6	69.4	0.3	14.6	0.8	15.3
3.6	7.7	1.0	3.4	3.5	10.4
	9.4	0.1	1.2		0.9
2.4	3.0		0.8	0.7	
9.9	7.1	3.0	15.0	5.2	7.2
7.1	0.3	0.8	3.7	1.8	25.5

TABLE 4.6-19 *Percentage distribution by basic source of funds of estimated cost of new construction and rehabilitation projects and campus improvement projects, fall 1965 to fall 1970, by institutional control, aggregate United States*

Source of funds	Total	Public	Private
All sources	100.0	100.0	100.0
Governmental appropriations	25.6	34.7	6.3
Federal government grants	13.8	12.6	16.2
Direct tax levy	0.8	1.2	0.2
General obligation bonds	16.3	19.1	10.3
Revenue bonds	18.1	19.7	14.9
Other	25.4	12.7	52.1

SOURCE: U.S. Office of Education, *College and University Enrollment and Physical Facilities Survey, 1965–70,* 1970, p. 4.

obligation bonds (26 percent). New private institutions relied on gifts and grants (68 percent) and private lenders (18 percent) to finance instructional, research, and general facilities, and on revenue bonds (51 percent) and gifts and grants (32 percent) to finance residential and other auxiliary facilities (Figure 4.6-4). Table 4.6-21 gives the cost of new construction and rehabilitation projects planned or completed by new public institutions from 1961 to 1965.

INVENTORY OF COLLEGE AND UNIVERSITY PHYSICAL FACILITIES, 1957

Table 4.6-22 gives the number of buildings at public and private institutions of higher education in 1957. Public institutions owned 22,446 buildings, as compared with private institutions, which owned 18,570. Only 14 percent of all public institutions were universities, but they owned 58 percent of the buildings of public institutions. Only 6 percent of all private institutions were private universities, but they owned 23 percent of the buildings. In contrast, public junior colleges made up 40 percent of all public institutions, but they owned only 11 percent of the buildings of public institutions.

CONDITION OF BUILDINGS, 1957

In 1957 the Office of Education classified buildings at institutions of higher education as (I) satisfactory, (II) requiring major rehabilitation now, and (III) razing recommended. For the country as a whole, 63.5 percent of the buildings at public institutions were rated as in satisfactory condition, compared with 77.8 percent of the buildings at private institutions. For public institutions,

(Text continued on p. 749)

FIGURE 4.6-4 **Sources of funds for facilities at new institutions of higher education, by control, 1961–1965**

Instructional, research, and general

Residential and other auxiliary

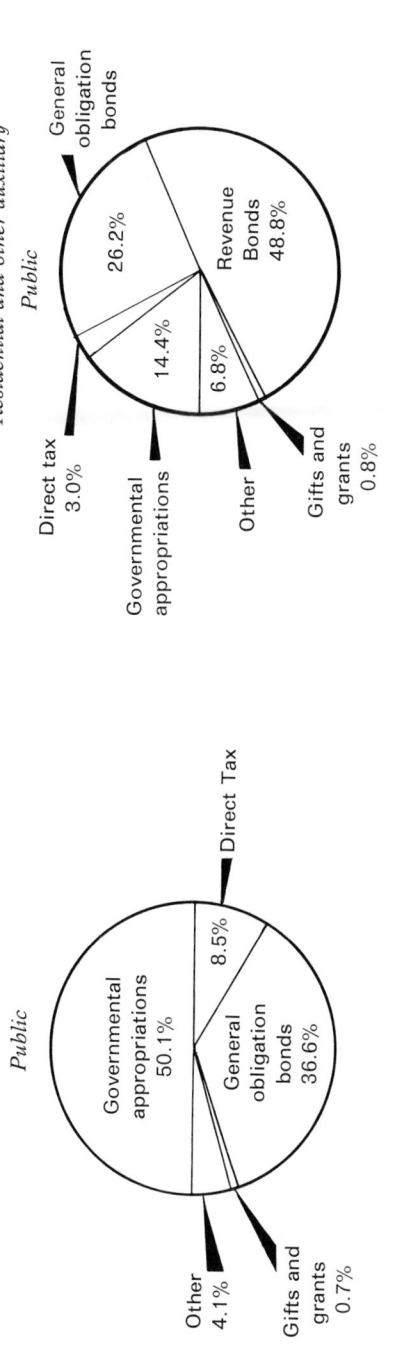

Public

General obligation bonds

Revenue Bonds 48.8%

26.2%

14.4%

6.8%

Direct tax 3.0%

Governmental appropriations

Other

Gifts and grants 0.8%

Public

Direct Tax

8.5%

Governmental appropriations 50.1%

General obligation bonds 36.6%

Other 4.1%

Gifts and grants 0.7%

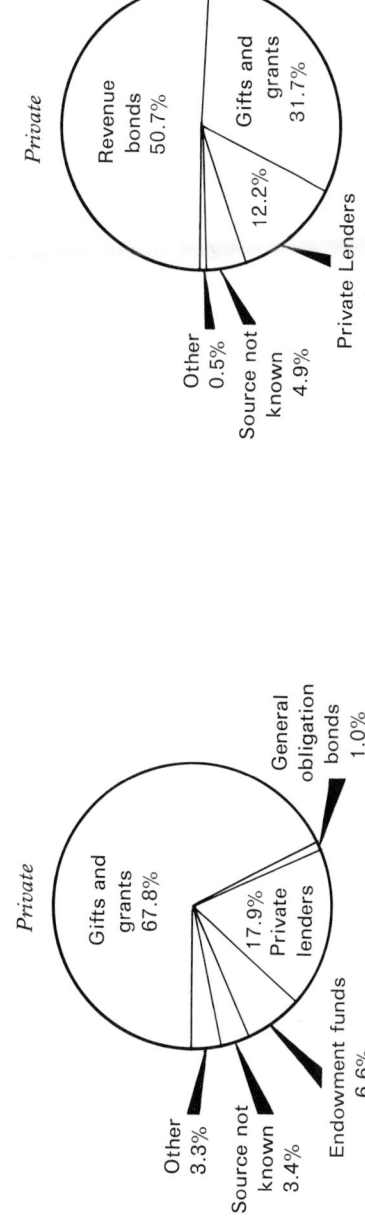

Private

Revenue bonds 50.7%

Gifts and grants 31.7%

12.2%

Private Lenders

Other 0.5%

Source not known 4.9%

Private

Gifts and grants 67.8%

17.9% Private lenders

General obligation bonds 1.0%

Endowment funds 6.6%

Other 3.3%

Source not known 3.4%

SOURCE: U.S. Office of Education, *College and University Facilities Survey*, issued as Department of Health, Education and Welfare circular, 1965, part 5, p. 24.

TABLE 4.6-20
Cost of new
construction and
rehabilitation
projects
completed and
planned by new
institutions
of higher
education, by
functional
group, type of
institution, and
control,
1961–1965 (cost
figures in
thousands)

Control and type	Enrollment 1965–66 (FTE)	Total expenditures	Instructional
Total, public and private	141,081	$441,762	$282,627
Junior colleges and technical institutes	93,517	190,728	147,674
Four-year liberal arts colleges	22,335	95,757	52,006
All other types	25,229	155,277	82,947
Total, public and private	100.0	100.0	100.0
Junior colleges and technical institutes	66.3	43.2	52.3
Four-year liberal arts colleges	15.8	21.7	18.4
All other types	17.9	35.1	29.3
Total, public	118,087	$294,636	$205,983
Junior colleges and technical institutes	87,426	150,923	125,445
Four-year liberal arts colleges	9,738	20,679	15,286
All other types	20,923	123,034	65,252
Total, public	100.0	100.0	100.0
Junior colleges and technical institutes	74.0	51.2	60.9
Four-year liberal arts colleges	8.3	7.0	7.4
All other types	17.7	41.8	31.7
Total, private	22,944	$147,126	$ 76,644
Junior colleges and technical institutes	6,091	39,805	22,229
Four-year liberal arts colleges	12,597	75,078	36,720
All other types	4,306	32,243	17,695
Total, private	100.0	100.0	100.0
Junior colleges and technical institutes	26.5	27.1	29.0
Four-year liberal arts colleges	54.8	51.0	47.9
All other types	18.7	21.9	23.1

SOURCE: U.S. Office of Education, *College and University Facilities Survey,* issued as Department of Health, Education and Welfare circular, 1965, part 5, p. 20.

Research	General	Residential	Other auxiliary	Land and campus improvements
$9	$35,909	$50,077	$36,926	$36,214
9	10,315	7,854	12,615	12,261
	5,207	23,810	9,300	5,434
	20,387	18,413	15,011	18,519
Percent				
100.0	100.0	100.0	100.0	100.0
100.0	28.7	15.7	34.2	33.9
	14.5	47.5	25.2	15.0
	56.8	36.8	40.6	51.1
$9	$28,243	$11,547	$23,199	$25,655
9	7,739	1,282	9,619	6,829
	1,780	2,475	561	577
	18,724	7,790	13,019	18,249
Percent				
100.0	100.0	100.0	100.0	100.0
100.0	27.4	11.1	41.5	26.6
	6.3	21.4	2.4	2.3
	66.3	67.5	56.1	71.1
	$ 7,666	$38,530	$13,727	$10,559
	2,576	6,572	2,996	5,432
	3,427	21,335	8,739	4,857
	1,663	10,623	1,992	270
Percent				
	100.0	100.0	100.0	100.0
	33.6	17.0	21.8	51.4
	44.7	55.4	63.7	46.0
	21.7	27.6	14.5	2.6

TABLE 4.6-21 *Cost of new construction and rehabilitation projects completed and planned by new public institutions of higher education, by functional group and source of funds, 1961–1965 (cost figures in thousands)*

Source of funds	Total Cost	Percent	Instructional, research, and general Cost	Percent	Residential Cost	Percent
TOTAL	$294,636	100.0	$234,235	100.0	$11,547	100.0
Appropriations	130,418	44.3	117,336	50.1	1,580	13.7
State government	105,674	35.9	94,323	40.3	1,545	13.4
Local government	23,176	7.9	21,461	9.2	35	0.3
Federal government	1,568	0.5	1,552	0.6		
Direct tax levy	20,928	7.1	19,898	8.5		
State government						
Local government	20,928	7.1	19,898	8.5		
General obligation bonds	110,910	37.7	85,801	36.6	3,346	29.0
Local government	42,650	14.5	35,371	15.1	687	5.9
State government	51,296	17.4	38,623	16.5	285	2.5
State authority	473	0.2	473	0.2		
Institutional	16,491	5.6	11,334	4.8	2,374	20.6
Revenue bonds	17,771	6.0			6,421	55.6
Other than HHFA	10,925	3.7			75	0.6
HHFA	6,846	2.3			6,346	55.0

SOURCE: U.S. Office of Education, *College and University Facilities Survey,* issued as Department of Health, Education and Welfare circular, 1965, part 5, p. 23.

TABLE 4.6-22 Number of buildings at public and private institutions, by type of institution, United States, 1957

Type of institution (1)	Public Institutions Number (2)	Percent (3)	Buildings Number (4)	Percent (5)
All types	633	100.0	22,446	100.0
University	91	14.4	12,901	57.5
Liberal arts college	79	12.5	2,745	12.2
Teachers college	163	25.8	3,557	15.8
Independent technological school	18	2.8	600	2.7
Theological and religious school				
Other independent professional school	24	3.8	213	0.9
Junior college	256	40.4	2,426	10.8
Technical institute	2	0.3	4	*

*Less than 0.05 percent.

SOURCE: U.S. Office of Education, *College and University Facilities Survey,* issued as Department of Health, Education and Welfare circular, 1964, part 3, table 1-1, p. 21.

27.2 percent of the buildings needed to be razed, compared with 13.5 percent of the buildings at private institutions (Table 4.6-23).

INVESTMENT IN BUILDINGS, 1957 In 1957 investment in buildings amounted to $3,316 million at public institutions and $2,554 million at private institutions (Table 4.6-24). Public institutions invested relatively more than private institutions in instructional, research, and auxiliary facilities; private institutions invested relatively more than public in residential facilities (Table 4.6-25).

Investment in buildings varies according to the functions of the different types of institutions. Community colleges need little beyond instructional buildings. Universities with large science departments and research programs spend heavily for plant, as do independent technological schools.

ESTIMATED VALUE OF BUILDINGS, 1957 In 1957 the estimated value of buildings owned by institutions of higher education was $9 billion. University buildings accounted for about half of this amount, while buildings owned by liberal arts colleges accounted for 27.4 percent, teachers colleges for 8.9 percent, and junior colleges for 4.8 percent.[8] In general, the earlier

[8] U.S. Office of Education, *College and University Facilities Survey,* issued as Department of Health, Education and Welfare circular, 1964, part 3, p. 84.

Private			
Institutions		*Buildings*	
Number (6)	*Percent (7)*	*Number (8)*	*Percent (9)*
1,020	100.0	18,570	100.0
59	5.8	4,220	22.7
566	55.5	10,727	57.8
20	2.0	130	0.7
21	2.1	539	2.9
93	9.1	890	4.8
94	9.2	485	2.6
158	15.5	1,548	8.3
9	0.9	31	0.2

TABLE 4.6-23 *Number of buildings at public and private institutions, by condition, and region, United States, 1957*

Region (1)	Total (2)	Condition 1		Condition 2		Condition 3	
		Number (3)	Percent (4)	Number (5)	Percent (6)	Number (7)	Percent (8)
Public institutions							
United States	22,213*	14,108	63.5	2,066	9.3	6,039	27.2
Northeast	2,105	1,476	70.1	174	8.3	455	21.6
North Central	5,492	3,065	55.8	445	8.1	1,982	36.1
South	9,060	6,335	69.9	1,119	12.4	1,606	17.7
West	5,556	3,232	58.2	328	5.9	1,996	35.9
Private institutions							
United States	18,473†	14,381	77.8	1,607	8.7	2,485	13.5
Northeast	5,893	4,751	80.6	451	7.7	691	11.7
North Central	4,445	3,264	73.4	428	9.6	753	16.9
South	6,090	4,792	78.7	555	9.1	743	12.2
West	2,045	1,574	77.0	173	8.5	298	14.6

*Exclusive of 233 buildings for which the condition was not reported.
† Exclusive of 97 buildings for which the condition was not reported.
SOURCE: U.S. Office of Education, *College and University Facilities Survey,* issued as Department of Health, Education and Welfare circular, 1964, part 3, table 1-4, p. 23.

the initial occupancy of a building, the higher is the ratio of the estimated value of the building to the money actually invested in it (the V/I ratio). For buildings first occupied before 1899, the V/I ratio is 2.15 for public and 1.75 for private institutions. For buildings first occupied in 1950–57, the V/I ratio is 1.10 for public and 1.07 for private institutions (Table 4.6-26). The V/I ratio is usually a maximum for instructional and a minimum for residential buildings.[9] The large V/I ratio for older buildings can be explained primarily by inflation, rising construction costs, and increases in building value associated with the growth of the college community.

In general, the more recent the initial occupancy date of a building, the lower is the equipment investment to building investment ratio, but this is not uniformly true, as Figure 4.6-5 shows for public institutions. In recent years there have been greater economies in producing equipment than in producing buildings. Addition or subtraction of equipment after a building is completed also affects this ratio.

[9] Ibid., p. 103.

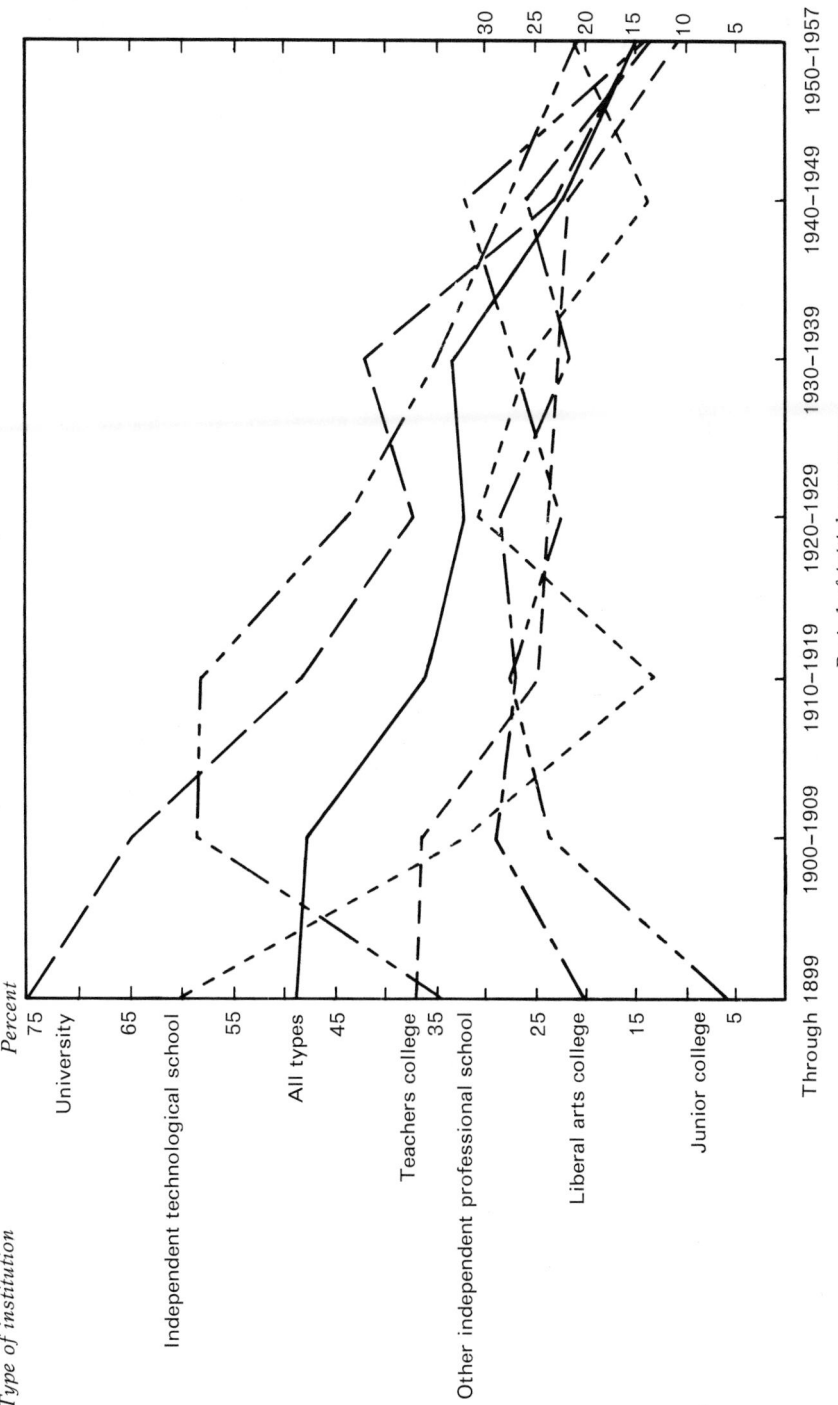

Type of institution

Percent

Period of initial occupancy

SOURCE: U.S. Office of Education, *College and University Facilities Survey*, issued as Department of Health, Education and Welfare circular, 1964, part 3, table 8-1.

TABLE 4.6-24 *Investment in buildings* at public and private institutions, by type of institution, and facilities category, United States, 1957 (thousands of dollars)*

Facilities category (1)	All types Amount (2)	Per-cent (3)	University Amount (4)	Per-cent (5)	Liberal arts college Amount (6)	Per-cent (7)	Teachers college Amount (8)	Pe cer (9
							Public institutio	
All categories	$3,316,310	100.0	$1,886,307	100.0	$434,430	100.0	$541,561	10(
Instructional	1,573,140	47.4	762,874	40.4	230,316	53.0	287,546	5:
Research	426,697	12.9	331,603	17.6	30,854	7.1	2,411	(
General	244,808	7.4	162,263	8.6	26,723	6.2	35,754	(
Auxiliary	210,562	6.3	129,415	6.9	29,711	6.8	31,408	:
Residential	861,103	26.0	500,152	26.5	116,826	26.9	184,442	3.
							Private institutio	
All categories	$2,554,052	100.0	$836,469	100.0	$1,276,094	100.0	$20,748	10(
Instructional	1,088,989	42.6	334,574	40.0	556,220	43.6	11,963	5:
Research	218,707	8.6	165,620	19.8	22,050	1.7		
General	182,694	7.1	77,208	9.2	81,606	6.4	1,588	:
Auxiliary	119,628	4.7	35,350	4.2	66,280	5.2	559	:
Residential	944,034	37.0	223,717	26.8	549,938	43.1	6,638	3:

* Exclusive of 21 buildings (public, 1; private, 20) for which neither facilities category nor investment was reported, and one private building for which the facilities category was not reported.

SOURCE: U.S. Office of Education, *College and University Facilities Survey,* issued as Department of Health, Education and Welfare circular, 1964, part 3, p. 60.

TABLE 4.6-25 Investment in buildings by type of facility, 1957

	Public institutions (percentage of total)	Private institutions (percentage of total)
All categories	100.0	100.0
Instructional	47.4	42.6
Research	12.9	8.6
General	7.4	7.1
Auxiliary	6.3	4.7
Residential	26.0	37.0

SOURCE: Table 4.6-24.

Independent technological school		Theological and religious school		Other independent professional school		Junior college		Technical institute	
Amount (10)	Per-cent (11)	Amount (12)	Per-cent (13)	Amount (14)	Per-cent (15)	Amount (16)	Per-cent (17)	Amount (18)	Per-cent (19)
$96,683	100.0			$131,517	100.0	$225,779	100.0	$33	100.0
53,922	55.8			54,992	41.8	183,457	81.3	33	100.0
3,277	3.4			57,991	44.1	561	0.2		
4,505	4.6			5,038	3.8	10,525	4.7		
4,141	4.3			3,647	2.8	12,240	5.4		
30,838	31.9			9,849	7.5	18,996	8.4		
$95,567	100.0	$100,193	100.0	$105,608	100.0	$113,703	100.0	$5,670	100.0
48,772	51.0	25,991	26.0	64,666	61.2	41,275	36.3	5,528	97.5
8,378	8.8			20,101	19.1	2,558	2.3		
5,770	6.0	4,534	4.5	5,915	5.6	6,062	5.3	11	0.2
4,084	4.3	5,148	5.1	1,714	1.6	6,486	5.7	7	0.1
28,563	29.9	64,520	64.4	13,212	12.5	57,322	50.4	124	2.2

RESIDENTIAL ACCOMMODA-TIONS In 1957 accommodations for single men accounted for 50.3 percent of the residential accommodations of public institutions, those for single women for 42.3 percent, and those for married students for 7.4 percent. In private institutions, accommodations for single men constituted 50.3 percent of residential accommodations, those for single women 46.5 percent, and those for married students 3.2 percent (Table 4.6-27).

In 1957 investment in residential facilities amounted to $861 million for public institutions and to $944 million for private institutions. In all regions of the country except the Northeast, however, public investment in residential facilities was larger than private investment (Table 4.6-28).

(Text continued on p. 758)

TABLE 4.6-26
Ratio of estimated value to investment in buildings at public and private institutions, by region, and period of initial occupancy, United States (percentages)

Period of initial occupancy (1)	Public institutions				
	United States (2)	North-east (3)	North Central (4)	South (5)	West (6)
Through 1899	215.1	258.3	182.9	237.1	188.3
1900–1909	208.2	191.2	251.5	179.6	172.1
1910–1919	201.5	183.0	222.8	189.6	177.6
1920–1929	169.0	137.7	182.4	158.8	188.3
1930–1939	183.7	168.0	185.3	188.2	183.1
1940–1949	143.0	133.4	128.9	151.9	150.6
1950–1957	109.6	108.2	105.6	109.8	114.9
Not reported	103.2	104.4	174.6	110.8	44.4

SOURCE: U.S. Office of Education, *College and University Facilities Survey,* issued as Department of Health, Education and Welfare circular, 1964, part 3, table 4-1, p. 99.

TABLE 4.6-27
Design capacity of student residential accommodations at public and private institutions, by kind of student, and type of institution, United States, 1957

Design capacity, by type of institution (1)	Public institutions			
	Kind of student			
	All (2)	Married (3)	Single men (4)	Single women (5)
All types				
Number	364,525	27,087	183,117	154,321
Percent	100.0	7.4	50.3	42.3
University				
Number	197,518	20,101	109,112	68,305
Percent	100.0	10.2	55.2	34.6
Liberal arts college				
Number	56,325	1,665	23,640	31,030
Percent	100.0	2.9	42.0	55.1
Teachers college				
Number	84,336	3,855	32,353	48,128
Percent	100.0	4.6	38.4	57.0

SOURCE: U.S. Office of Education, *College and University Facilities Survey,* issued as Department of Health, Education and Welfare circular, 1964, part 3, p. 455.

		Private institutions		
United States (7)	*North-east* (8)	*North Central* (9)	*South* (10)	*West* (11)
174.6	171.6	180.5	180.4	174.7
185.9	195.0	171.8	175.6	204.4
184.9	198.9	186.6	160.2	195.1
158.1	156.1	159.8	157.5	167.0
174.6	176.5	194.4	147.5	184.0
132.2	132.6	141.8	126.6	125.2
106.6	105.5	106.3	106.6	115.5
160.2	162.4	128.8	190.7	195.2

	Private institutions		
	Kind of student		
All (6)	*Married* (7)	*Single men* (8)	*Single women* (9)
334,839	10,698	168,528	155,613
100.0	3.2	50.3	46.5
71,055	3,411	44,020	23,624
100.0	4.8	62.0	33.2
205,641	4,251	94,007	107,383
100.0	2.1	45.7	52.2
2,990	292	853	1,845
100.0	9.8	28.5	61.7

TABLE 4.6-28		United States		Northeast	
Investment in residential buildings at public and private institutions, by region, and primary function, United States, 1957 (thousands of dollars)	Primary function (1)	Amount (2)	Percent (3)	Amount (4)	Percent (5)
		Public institutions			
	All functions	$861,103*	100.0	$83,956	100.0
	Faculty and staff apartments	22,700	2.6	2,204	2.6
	Faculty and staff houses	13,778	1.6	1,233	1.5
	Fraternity and sorority houses	5,526	0.7	49	0.1
	Hotel-type accommodations	8,911	1.1	1,904	2.3
	Married-student apartments	102,692	11.9	2,115	2.5
	Residence halls for single men	364,459	42.3	36,412	43.4
	Residence halls for single women	336,022	39.0	39,239	46.7
	Presidents' houses	7,015	0.8	800	0.9
		Private institutions			
	All functions	$944,034†	100.0	$335,811	100.0
	Faculty and staff apartments	42,687	4.5	16,037	4.8
	Faculty and staff houses	25,356	2.7	8,167	2.4
	Fraternity and sorority houses	8,715	0.9	1,933	0.6
	Hotel-type accommodations	5,152	0.6	241	0.1
	Married-student apartments	26,650	2.8	4,092	1.2
	Residence halls for single men	415,096	44.0	158,440	47.2
	Residence halls for single women	412,460	43.7	143,834	42.8
	Presidents' houses	7,918	0.8	3,067	0.9

*Exclusive of investment figures for 1,034 buildings for which figures were not reported.

† Exclusive of investment figures for 1,325 buildings for which figures were not reported.

‡ Less than 0.05 percent.

SOURCE: U.S. Office of Education, *College and University Facilities Survey,* issued as Department of Health, Education and Welfare circular, 1964, part 3, p. 61.

North Central		South		West	
Amount (6)	*Percent* (7)	*Amount* (8)	*Percent* (9)	*Amount* (10)	*Percent* (11)
$310,240	100.0	$350,234	100.0	$116,673	100.0
6,634	2.1	11,143	3.2	2,719	2.3
1,844	0.6	8,325	2.4	2,376	2.0
100	‡	4,163	1.2	1,214	1.1
1,071	0.3	5,871	1.7	65	0.1
50,098	16.2	36,999	10.6	13,480	11.6
126,229	40.7	151,494	43.2	50,324	43.1
122,850	39.6	128,295	36.6	45,638	39.1
1,414	0.5	3,944	1.1	857	0.7
$262,864	100.0	$261,567	100.0	$83,792	100.0
13,605	5.2	9,545	3.6	3,500	4.2
5,137	2.0	10,527	4.0	1,795	2.1
5,356	2.0	1,202	0.5	224	0.3
3,698	1.4	930	0.4	283	0.3
7,933	3.0	11,369	4.3	3,256	3.9
104,706	39.8	119,235	45.5	32,715	39.1
120,866	46.0	106,185	40.6	41,575	49.6
1,563	0.6	2,844	1.1	444	0.5

TABLE 4.6-29 *Book value of physical plant, by control and type of institution, aggregate United States, end of fiscal year 1960 (amounts in thousands of dollars)*

Type of institution (1)	Total (2)	*Amount* Publicly controlled (3)	Privately controlled (4)	Total (5)	*Percent* Publicly controlled (6)	Privately controlled (7)
All institutions	$13,588,360	$7,848,415	$5,739,945	100.0	57.8	42.2
Universities	6,961,472	4,787,395	2,174,076	51.2	35.2	16.0
Liberal arts colleges	3,351,554	840,249	2,511,305	24.7	6.2	18.5
Teachers colleges	1,101,829	1,054,693	47,136	8.1	7.8	0.3
Technological schools	774,522	489,042	285,480	5.7	8.6	2.1
Theological schools	315,293	In*	315,293	2.3	In*	2.3
Other professional schools	197,337	42,197	155,141	1.5	0.3	1.2
Junior colleges	764,449	545,787	218,662	5.6	4.0	1.6
Technical institutes and semiprofessional schools	121,904	89,052	32,852	0.9	0.7	0.2

*In = Inapplicable.

NOTE: Detail may not add to total because of rounding.

SOURCE: F. H. I. Lindsay, *Financial Statistics of Institutions of Higher Education: Receipts, Expenditures, and Property, 1959–60,* U.S. Office of Education, National Center for Educational Statistics, 1964, p. 66.

BOOK VALUE OF PLANT In 1959–60 the total book value of property owned by institutions of higher education (including endowment funds) was $20.2 billion.[10] In the same year the book value of physical plant was $13.6 billion (Table 4.6-29). Universities and liberal arts colleges accounted for 51 and 25 percent of book value of plant, respectively.

Book value of plant per institution and book value per student varied with the control and type of institution. The average book value of plant of public institutions was about 2½ times that of private institutions. But on the basis of book value per student, there was little difference between public and private institutions. Universities had the largest book value of plant, while technological schools had the largest book value of plant per student.

From 1962 to 1964, book value of plant rose from $16.7 billion to $21.3 billion—a 28 percent increase. This increase in book value is largely explained by additional construction during these years.

[10] F. H. I. Lindsay, *Financial Statistics of Institutions of Higher Education: Receipts, Expenditures, and Property, 1959-60,* U.S. Office of Education, National Center for Educational Statistics, 1964, p. 66.

Book value of plant rose by 30 percent for public institutions and bv 24 percent for private institutions.

By 1966 book value of plant had increased to almost $27 billion. Book value of plant of public institutions was almost $16 billion, as compared with $11 billion for private institutions. But book value per student of private institutions exceeded book value per student of public institutions by almost one-third.

UTILIZATION For public institutions in 1960–61, utilization of instructional facilities is estimated to have been 93.8 percent of capacity. By regions, the Southeast had the lowest utilization rate (92 percent) and the North Atlantic had the highest (96.5 percent). A similar pattern prevails for private institutions, although utilization rates are higher for small private than for small public institutions, whereas utilization rates are lower for the largest private institutions (94 percent) than for the largest public institutions (99 percent).[11]

[11] U.S. Office of Education, *College and University Facilities Survey,* issued as Department of Health, Education and Welfare circular, 1965, part 4, p. 16.

4.7. Federal Funds for Scientific Activities

GEOGRAPHIC
DISTRIBUTION
OF FEDERAL
FUNDS FOR
RESEARCH
AND
DEVELOPMENT

In 1967 the ten most populous states accounted for approximately 54 percent of the population of the United States, 57 percent of college students, 64 percent of graduate students, and 61 percent of federal funding of university research. Illinois and California received the two largest shares of federal funding of university research—12.3 and 10.1 percent, respectively (Table 4.7-1). Table 4.7-2 shows the ranking by states of numbers of members of the National Academy of Sciences and the ranking by states of Department of Defense basic research contracts to educational institutions in 1964. California, Massachusetts, and New York (in that order) headed both lists.

The geographic distribution of federal funds for industrial research and development is shown in Table 4.7-3. The Pacific states accounted for 44 percent of the federally financed research and development (R&D) in 1963, reflecting the concentration of the missile and aircraft industries on the West Coast.

In fiscal year 1965, the Pacific states received 34 percent of total federal obligations for R&D, with California alone receiving 32 percent. Other regions of the country receiving substantial shares of total federal obligations for R&D were the Middle Atlantic (16 percent) and the South Atlantic (15 percent) (Table 4.7-4). Table 4.7-5 compares the percentage of federal R&D obligations to the percentage of population for each state in fiscal year 1965. The East North Central states accounted for 6 percent of federal R&D obligations and 20 percent of the population, while the Pacific states accounted for 34 percent of the federal R&D obligations and 13 percent of the population.

In 1966 one-half of the scientists employed by educational institutions and 21 percent of those employed in industry and business reported doing federally supported work (Table 4.7-6). The proportion of scientists receiving federal support varied by field of

(Text continued on p. 774)

State	Percentage of representatives, 1960–1970 (approximate percentage of population)	Percentage of congressmen (representatives and senators)	Percentage of land area
New York	9.4	8.0	1.3
California	8.7	7.5	4.4
Pennsylvania	6.2	5.4	1.2
Illinois	5.5	4.9	1.6
Ohio	5.5	4.9	1.2
Texas	5.3	4.7	7.4
Michigan	4.4	3.9	1.6
New Jersey	3.5	3.2	0.2
Massachusetts	2.8	2.6	0.2
Florida	2.8	2.6	1.5
Indiana	2.5	2.4	1.0
North Carolina	2.5	2.4	1.4
Missouri	2.3	2.2	1.9
Virginia	2.3	2.2	1.1
Wisconsin	2.3	2.2	1.5
Georgia	2.3	2.2	1.6
Tennessee	2.1	2.0	1.2
Minnesota	1.8	1.9	2.2
Alabama	1.8	1.9	1.4
Louisiana	1.8	1.9	1.3
Maryland	1.8	1.9	0.3
Kentucky	1.6	1.7	1.1
Washington	1.6	1.7	1.9
Iowa	1.6	1.7	1.6
Connecticut	1.4	1.5	0.1
South Carolina	1.4	1.5	0.9
Oklahoma	1.4	1.5	1.9
Kansas	1.1	1.3	2.3
Mississippi	1.1	1.3	1.3
West Virginia	1.1	1.3	0.7
Arkansas	0.9	1.1	1.5
Oregon	0.9	1.1	2.7

TABLE 4.7-1
United States educational and research-funding percentages

Percentage of college students (for B.S./B.A. or higher, 1963)	Percentage of graduate students (U.S. Office of Education, 1963)	Percentage of federal funding of university research (Industrial Research Survey, 1967)	Relative funding (percentage of federal funding 1967) (percentage of congressmen)
9.4	15.6	7.4	−0.6
14.2	11.9	10.1*	+2.6
5.2	6.4	6.7	+1.3
5.5	5.4	12.3*†	+7.4
4.8	4.5	3.2	−1.7
5.3	3.9	3.9	−0.8
4.4	5.7	4.6	+0.7
2.4	3.1	2.5	−0.7
3.7	5.9	9.1*	+6.5
2.4	1.4	1.5	−1.1
2.7	3.1	2.2	−0.2
2.0	1.6	2.6	+0.2
2.3	2.1	2.2	0
1.6	0.8	0.7	−1.5
2.1	2.0	2.0	−0.2
1.4	0.9	1.2	−1.0
1.7	1.2	0.8	−1.2
2.2	2.0	1.9	0
1.0	0.8	1.0	−0.9
1.6	1.4	0.4	−1.5
1.7	2.0	5.7‡	+3.8
1.3	0.7	0.6	−1.1
1.9	1.3	1.9	+0.2
1.5	1.3	1.7	0
1.4	2.6	1.6	+0.1
0.8	0.4	0.3	−1.2
1.5	1.6	0.7	−0.8
1.4	1.4	0.4	−0.9
1.0	0.3	0.3	−1.0
0.8	0.5	§	(?)
0.7	0.4	0.3	−0.8
1.3	0.9	1.2¶	+0.1

TABLE 4.7-1
(continued)

State	Percentage of repre-sentatives, 1960–1970 (approxi-mate percentage of population)	Percentage of congress-men (rep-resentatives and senators)	Percentage of land area
Colorado	0.9	1.1	2.9
Nebraska	0.7	0.9	2.1
Arizona	0.7	0.9	3.2
Maine	0.5	0.8	0.9
New Mexico	0.5	0.8	3.4
Utah	0.5	0.8	2.3
Rhode Island	0.5	0.8	0.03
South Dakota	0.5	0.8	2.2
Montana	0.5	0.8	4.1
Idaho	0.5	0.8	2.3
Hawaii	0.5	0.8	0.2
North Dakota	0.5	0.8	2.0
New Hampshire	0.5	0.8	0.3
Delaware	0.2	0.5	0.1
Vermont	0.2	0.5	0.3
Wyoming	0.2	0.5	2.7
Nevada	0.2	0.5	3.1
Alaska	0.2	0.5	16.4

* Does not include University Managed Federal Research Labs.
† Includes nonfederal funding at University of Chicago.
‡ Includes APL at Johns Hopkins.
§ No data.
¶ Estimated.
SOURCE: U.S. Senate, Committee on Government Operations, *Equitable Distribution of R&D Funds by Government Agencies, Hearings before Subcommittee on Government Research,* July 1967, p. 467.

Percentage of college students (for B.S./B.A. or higher, 1963)	Percentage of graduate students (U.S. Office of Education, 1963)	Percentage of federal funding of university research (Industrial Research Survey, 1967)	Relative funding (percentage of federal funding 1967) (percentage of congressmen)
1.3	1.2	1.8	+0.7
0.9	0.6	0.7	−0.2
1.1	1.1	0.7	−0.2
0.4	0.1	0.1	−0.7
0.5	0.7	1.1¶	+0.3
1.0	0.9	1.1¶	+0.3
0.5	0.5	0.7	−0.1
0.4	0.2	0.2¶	−0.6
0.4	0.2	0.2	−0.6
0.4	0.1	0.1	−0.7
0.3	0.2	0.4	−0.4
0.4	0.2	0.1	−0.7
0.3	0.2	0.4	−0.4
0.2	0.4	0.2	−0.3
0.3	0.1	0.2	−0.3
0.2	0.1	0.1	−0.4
0.1	0.1	0.4	−0.1
0.1	0.03	0.5	0

TABLE 4.7-2
Ranking by
states of the
members of the
National
Academy of
Sciences
(July 1, 1964)
and ranking
by states of
Department of
Defense basic
research
contracts (fiscal
year 1964) to
educational
institutions

State	National Academy of Sciences members	Department of Defense basic research contracts
1. California	158	1. California
2. Massachusetts	117	2. Massachusetts
3. New York	109	3. New York
4. New Jersey	44	4. Illinois
5. Illinois	38	5. Pennsylvania
6. District of Columbia	31	6. Texas
7. Maryland	27	7. Maryland
8. Wisconsin	24	8. New Jersey
8. Connecticut	24	9. Rhode Island
10. Pennsylvania	20	10. North Carolina
11. Texas	12	11. Michigan
12. Minnesota	10	12. Florida
12. Missouri	10	13. Ohio
14. Indiana	9	14. District of Columbia
15. Colorado	8	15. Wisconsin
16. Michigan	7	16. Washington
16. Ohio	7	17. Connecticut
16. North Carolina	7	18. Indiana
19. Virginia	6	19. Minnesota
19. Arizona	6	20. Alaska
21. Iowa	4	21. Iowa
21. Tennessee	4	22. Georgia
23. Florida	3	23. Virginia
23. Rhode Island	3	24. Oregon
23. New Hampshire	3	25. Missouri
26. Delaware	2	26. New Mexico
26. Utah	2	27. Colorado
26. Hawaii	2	28. Louisiana
29. Louisiana	1	29. Utah
29. Georgia	1	30. Oklahoma
29. Maine	1	31. Arizona
29. Oregon	1	32. New Hampshire
29. Washington	1	33. Tennessee
29. New Mexico	1	34. Kansas
29. Nevada	1	35. Hawaii
29. Montana	1	36. Kentucky
37. Kentucky	0	37. Delaware
37. Mississippi	0	38. Mississippi

TABLE 4.7-2
(continued)

State	National Academy of Sciences members	Department of Defense basic research contracts
37. South Carolina	0	39. South Carolina
37. Vermont	0	40. Vermont
37. Oklahoma	0	41. Montana
37. Alabama	0	42. Alabama
37. Nebraska	0	43. Nebraska
37. Idaho	0	44. Idaho
37. South Dakota	0	45. South Dakota
37. West Virginia	0	46. West Virginia
37. Kansas	0	47. Maine
37. Arkansas	0	48. Arkansas
37. Alaska	0	49. Nevada
37. Wyoming	0	50. Wyoming
37. North Dakota	0	51. North Dakota

SOURCE: U.S. Senate, Committee on Labor and Public Welfare, *Impact of Federal Research and Development Policies on Scientific and Technical Manpower, Hearings before Subcommittee on Employment and Manpower,* June and July 1965, p. 484.

	Industrial R&D, 1963		Government R&D, fiscal year 1964, obligations for selected	Scientists and engineers, 1960
Geographic division	Federally financed	Total	agencies*	
TOTAL	100	100	100	100
New England	8	8	5	7
Middle Atlantic	16	22	15	22
East North Central	6	17	6	20
West North Central	5	5	4	6
South Atlantic	9	9	14	12
East South Central	3	2	4	4
West South Central	4	4	7	7
Mountain	5	4	8	4
Pacific	44	30	37	16
Unallocated			2	

* Includes Departments of Agriculture; Commerce; Defense; Interior; and Health, Education and Welfare; Atomic Energy Commission; National Aeronautics and Space Administration; National Science Foundation.

NOTE: Percentages do not add to totals because of rounding.

SOURCE: U.S. Senate, Committee on Labor and Public Welfare, *Impact of Federal Research and Development Policies on Scientific and Technical Manpower, Hearings before Subcommittee on Employment and Manpower,* June and July 1965, p. 131.

Divisions and states	Total all agencies	Agri-culture	Com-merce	Defense	HEW
United States total	100.0	1.50	0.42	47.08	5.92
New England, total	6.91	0.04	0.01	5.06	0.57
Maine	0.03	0.01		*	0.01
New Hampshire	0.20	0.01	*	0.12	0.02
Vermont	0.03	0.01		*	0.01
Massachusetts	5.11	0.01	0.01	3.93	0.43
Rhode Island	0.26	*	*	0.21	0.02
Connecticut	1.29	0.01	0.01	0.79	0.08
Middle Atlantic, total	15.52	0.12	0.04	8.78	1.20
New York	8.98	0.05	0.03	4.91	0.80
New Jersey	2.86	0.01	*	1.91	0.08
Pennsylvania	3.68	0.07	0.01	1.96	0.32
East North Central, total	6.43	0.17	0.01	3.02	0.82
Ohio	2.64	0.02	*	1.54	0.22
Indiana	0.50	0.02	*	0.29	0.07
Illinois	1.34	0.07	*	0.35	0.25
Michigan	1.08	0.02	*	0.72	0.18
Wisconsin	0.88	0.04	*	0.12	0.11
West North Central, total	2.85	0.16	*	0.62	0.33
Minnesota	0.74	0.03	*	0.23	0.12
Iowa	0.20	0.05	*	0.03	0.05
Missouri	1.61	0.02	*	0.26	0.10
North Dakota	0.03	0.02		*	0.01
South Dakota	0.02	0.01		*	*
Nebraska	0.05	0.01	*	*	0.02
Kansas	0.18	0.01	*	0.10	0.04
South Atlantic, total	15.01	0.45	0.26	7.56	1.61
Delaware	0.05	*		0.03	0.01
Maryland	6.11	0.17	0.02	3.23	1.02
District of Columbia	2.61	0.11	0.23	1.03	0.21
Virginia	1.98	0.01	*	1.15	0.06
West Virginia	0.14	0.01		0.07	0.02
North Carolina	0.40	0.04	*	0.20	0.10
South Carolina	0.12	0.02		0.01	0.01
Georgia	0.41	0.05		0.13	0.10
Florida	3.20	0.03	0.01	1.73	0.08

TABLE 4.7-4 Percentage distribution of federal research and development obligations to all performers by state and agency, fiscal year 1965 (percentage of federal total)

Interior	AEC	NASA	NSF
0.79	8.61	34.48	1.20
0.05	0.36	0.69	0.14
0.01	*	*	*
*	*	0.05	0.01
*	*	*	*
0.03	0.16	0.44	0.10
*	*	0.01	0.01
0.01	0.18	0.19	0.02
0.10	1.37	3.69	0.23
0.02	0.67	2.39	0.13
0.01	0.10	0.70	0.04
0.07	0.60	0.60	0.06
0.03	0.71	1.46	0.20
*	0.13	0.68	0.04
*	0.05	0.04	0.03
0.01	0.49	0.11	0.06
0.01	0.03	0.09	0.04
0.01	0.03	0.54	0.03
0.05	0.09	1.54	0.05
0.01	0.02	0.32	0.01
*	0.05	0.02	0.01
0.01	*	1.20	0.02
0.01	*	*	*
0.01	*	*	*
*	0.01	*	*
*	*	0.01	0.01
0.15	0.20	4.57	0.20
*	*	0.01	*
0.04	0.04	1.57	0.02
0.04	0.03	0.85	0.11
*	0.02	0.72	0.01
0.02	*	*	0.02
0.02	0.01	0.01	0.01
*	0.08	*	*
0.01	*	0.11	0.01
0.01	0.02	1.30	0.02

Divisions and states	Total all agencies	Agri-culture	Com-merce	Defense	HEW
East South Central, total	4.38	0.10	*	1.15	0.17
Kentucky	0.12	0.02		0.03	0.04
Tennessee	1.42	0.01	*	0.64	0.06
Alabama	2.58	0.02		0.45	0.05
Mississippi	0.26	0.04	*	0.03	0.02
West South Central, total	7.96	0.15	0.02	3.47	0.28
Arkansas	0.05	0.01		*	0.02
Louisiana	2.63	0.07	*	0.01	0.07
Oklahoma	0.20	0.01	*	0.08	0.04
Texas	5.09	0.05	0.02	3.37	0.16
Mountain, total	6.90	0.11	0.06	3.04	0.15
Montana	0.06	0.02		0.01	0.02
Idaho	0.44	0.02		*	*
Wyoming	0.03	0.01		*	*
Colorado	1.48	0.02	0.06	1.10	0.06
New Mexico	2.96	0.01		1.32	0.01
Arizona	0.53	0.02	*	0.33	0.02
Utah	0.31	0.02	*	0.23	0.03
Nevada	1.08	0.01		0.04	*
Pacific, total	33.78	0.19	0.01	14.34	0.76
Washington	1.49	0.02	*	0.71	0.09
Oregon	0.18	0.03		0.01	0.08
California	31.72	0.12	0.01	13.51	0.56
Alaska	0.10	0.01	*	0.04	0.01
Hawaii	0.29	0.01	*	0.08	0.01

TABLE 4.7-4 (continued)

* Less than 0.005 percent.

NOTE: Percentages may not add to total because of rounding. Detail does not add to totals because territories and offices abroad have been excluded.

SOURCE: National Science Foundation; in U.S. Senate, Committee on Government Operations, *Equitable Distribution of R&D Funds by Government Agencies, Hearings before Subcommittee on Government Research,* July 1967, pp. 652–653.

Interior	AEC	NASA	NSF
0.03	0.61	2.31	0.01
0.01	*	0.01	0.01
0.01	0.61	0.08	*
0.01	*	2.05	*
*	*	0.16	*
0.04	0.04	3.92	0.04
*	0.01	*	*
*	*	2.46	*
0.01	*	0.04	0.01
0.02	0.03	1.41	0.03
0.17	2.95	0.29	0.13
0.01	*	*	*
0.01	0.41	*	*
0.02		*	*
0.07	0.01	0.08	0.07
0.01	1.51	0.09	0.01
0.02	0.03	0.08	0.03
0.02	0.01	*	0.01
0.02	0.98	0.03	*
0.17	2.28	15.84	0.20
0.04	0.23	0.39	0.02
0.03	*	*	0.02
0.06	1.90	15.43	0.14
0.03	*	0.01	0.01
0.02	0.15	0.01	0.01

TABLE 4.7-5 *Percentage distribution of federal R&D obligations, population, personal income, and federal tax collections, fiscal year 1965*

Divisions and states	Total federal R&D obligations	Population	Personal income	Individual income and employment taxes
United States total (in millions)	$14,357	194	$532,147	$70,765
	Percentage distribution			
New England, total	6.91	5.74	6.25	5.84
Maine	0.03	0.51	0.42	0.28
New Hampshire	0.20	0.35	0.32	0.25
Vermont	0.03	0.20	0.17	0.12
Massachusetts	5.11	2.76	3.07	2.98
Rhode Island	0.26	0.46	0.47	0.46
Connecticut	1.29	1.46	1.80	1.75
Middle Atlantic, total	15.52	18.76	21.26	24.54
New York	8.98	9.32	11.15	14.62
New Jersey	2.86	3.50	4.12	3.44
Pennsylvania	3.68	5.94	5.99	6.48
East North Central, total	6.44	19.68	21.41	22.86
Ohio	2.64	5.29	5.44	5.99
Indiana	0.50	2.52	2.61	2.40
Illinois	1.34	5.49	6.55	7.54
Michigan	1.08	4.24	4.70	5.14
Wisconsin	.88	2.14	2.11	1.79
West North Central, total	2.85	8.18	7.78	6.65
Minnesota	0.74	1.83	1.78	1.69
Iowa	0.20	1.42	1.38	0.89
Missouri	1.61	2.32	2.24	2.37
North Dakota	0.03	0.34	0.27	0.15
South Dakota	0.02	0.36	0.28	0.16
Nebraska	0.05	0.76	0.72	0.63
Kansas	0.18	1.15	1.11	0.76
South Atlantic, total	15.01	14.81	12.73	10.53
Delaware	0.05	0.26	3.2	0.63
Maryland	6.11	1.82	1.99	2.84
District of Columbia	2.61	0.41	0.55	*
Virginia	1.98	2.30	2.00	1.41
West Virginia	0.14	0.93	0.69	0.42
North Carolina	0.40	2.54	1.89	1.37
South Carolina	0.12	1.31	0.88	0.55

Divisions and states	Total federal R&D obligations	Population	Personal income	Individual income and employment taxes
South Atlantic cont.:				
Georgia	0.41	2.25	1.78	1.38
Florida	3.20	2.99	2.63	1.93
East South Central, total	4.38	6.61	4.60	3.06
Kentucky	0.12	1.64	1.21	0.79
Tennessee	1.42	1.98	1.45	1.09
Alabama	2.58	1.79	1.25	0.80
Mississippi	0.26	1.20	0.69	0.38
West South Central, total	7.96	9.55	7.75	6.02
Arkansas	0.05	1.01	0.67	0.39
Louisiana	2.63	1.82	1.38	0.99
Oklahoma	0.20	1.28	1.05	0.82
Texas	5.09	5.44	4.65	3.82
Mountain, total	6.89	4.02	3.58	3.35
Montana	0.06	0.36	0.32	0.20
Idaho	0.44	0.36	0.31	.023
Wyoming	0.03	0.18	0.15	0.11
Colorado	1.48	1.02	0.99	1.49
New Mexico	2.96	0.53	0.41	0.28
Arizona	0.53	0.83	0.70	0.48
Utah	0.31	0.51	0.43	0.33
Nevada	1.08	0.23	0.27	0.23
Pacific, total	33.78	12.62	14.41	13.10
Washington	1.49	1.54	1.62	1.36
Oregon	0.18	0.98	1.00	0.93
California	31.72	9.60	11.26	10.48
Alaska	0.10	0.13	0.15	0.11
Hawaii	0.29	0.37	0.38	0.31
International and undistributed	0.26			4.04

*Included in Maryland; separate figures not available.

SOURCE: U.S. Department of Commerce, Bureau of the Census, *Statistical Abstract of the United States* 1966; U.S. Department of Commerce, Office of Business Economics, *Survey of Current Business*, vol. 46, No. 12, 1966; U.S. Treasury Department, Annual Report of the Secretary of the Treasury on the State of the Finances, 1965; in U.S. Senate, Committee on Government Operations, *Equitable Distribution of R&D Funds by Government Agencies, Hearings before Subcommittee on Government Research,* July 1967, pp. 649–650.

TABLE 4.7-6   *Scientists receiving federal support, 1966, type of employer*

One-half of the scientists employed by educational institutions and 21 percent of those employed in industry and business reported doing federally supported work.

| | | Registrants receiving federal support | | |
Type of employer	Total registrants	Number	Percentage of total	Percent
All registrants	242,763	104,863	43	100
Educational institutions	87,315	44,089	50	42
Federal government	24,689	24,689	100	24
Other government	8,268	4,240	51	4
Military	5,891	5,891	100	6
Nonprofit organizations	9,813	6,186	63	6
Industry and business	83,990	17,915	21	17
Self-employed	4,914	690	14	1
Other	1,309	541	41	
No report	1,791	622	35	

NOTE: Scientists employed by the federal government and the military services receive their salaries directly from the U.S. Treasury. Scientists employed by other types of employers are supported or sponsored in whole or in part by federal funds through contracts or grants.

SOURCE: National Register of Scientific and Technical Personnel, 1966, in National Science Foundation, *American Science Manpower, A Report of the National Register of Scientific and Technical Personnel, 1966,* December 1967, p. 49.

science. At least some of the work of most of the scientists in meteorology (86 percent), the agricultural sciences (70 percent), and physics and the biological sciences (60 percent each) was supported by federal funds (Table 4.7-7). Forty-three percent of all scientists in the National Register of Scientific and Technical Personnel received some federal support in 1966 (Table 4.7-6). Of the registrants doing federally supported work, 43 percent held a doctorate, 24 percent a master's, and 26 percent a bachelor's degree as their highest degree (Table 4.7-8).

FEDERAL FUNDS FOR RESEARCH AND DEVELOPMENT

Table 4.7-9 gives a summary of federal funds for research, development, and R&D plant for fiscal years 1966 and (estimated) 1967 and 1968. Total federal expenditures on research, development, and R&D plant were $16 billion in 1966 and were estimated to increase to $17 billion in 1968.

TABLE 4.7-7 *Scientists receiving federal support, 1966, scientific field*

At least some of the work of most of the scientists in meteorology (86 percent) and agricultural sciences (70 percent) was supported by federal funds.

| | | Registrants receiving federal support | | |
Field	Total registrants	Number	Percentage of total	Percent
All fields	242,763	104,863	43	100
Chemistry	˙65,917	19,637	30	19
Earth sciences	19,749	5,870	30	6
Meteorology	6,283	5,378	86	5
Physics	29,130	17,496	60	17
Mathematics	22,806	9,862	43	9
Agricultural sciences	10,038	7,044	70	7
Biological sciences	29,633	17,767	60	17
Psychology	19,027	8,149	43	8
Statistics	3,042	1,610	53	2
Economics	13,150	3,981	30	4
Sociology	3,640	1,363	37	1
Anthropology	919	366	40	
Linguistics	1,269	396	31	
Other fields	18,160	5,944	33	6

SOURCE: National Science Foundation, *American Science Manpower, A Report of the National Register of Scientific and Technical Personnel, 1966,* December 1967, p. 48.

Universities and colleges received 8.7 percent of federal R&D funds (excluding R&D plant) in 1966 and were projected to receive 9.2 percent in 1968. Federally funded research centers administered by colleges and universities received 4.2 percent of federal R&D funds in 1966. Universities and colleges accounted for 19.0 percent of federal funds for R&D plant, and federally funded research centers administered by universities and colleges accounted for 3.6 percent.

In fiscal year 1968 (data estimated), basic research accounted for 13 percent, applied research for 20 percent, and development for 67 percent of the $16.2 billion of federal obligations for R&D. Industrial firms performed 60 percent of all federally financed R&D, while colleges and universities performed only 9 percent

(Text continued on p. 780)

TABLE 4.7-8 *Scientists receiving federal support, 1966, government program and highest degree*

Federal support was reported most frequently in defense and health programs. Of all registrants doing federally supported work, 43 percent were doctorate scientists.

		Registrants receiving federal support		
Government program	Total	Ph.D. degree	Master's as highest degree	Bachelor's as highest degree
All programs	104,863	45,192	25,439	27,240
Agriculture	11,468	5,970	2,507	2,742
Atomic energy	11,250	5,526	2,593	2,881
Defense	28,922	9,291	8,224	9,988
Education	13,273	6,836	4,154	1,790
Health	24,487	14,501	2,886	2,772
International	2,511	1,294	552	532
Natural resources	9,079	2,464	2,405	4,033
Public works	1,819	345	470	916
Space	13,905	5,033	3,856	4,553
Other	14,391	6,307	3,492	3,864

SOURCE: National Science Foundation, *American Science Manpower, A Report of the National Register of Scientific and Technical Personnel, 1966,* December 1967, p. 48.

TABLE 4.7-9 *Summary of federal funds for research, development, and R&D plant, fiscal years 1966, 1967, and 1968 (in millions of dollars)*

	Actual, 1966	Estimates	
Item		1967	1968
Total expenditures for research, development, and R&D plant	$16,002.3	$16,506.1	$17,075.8
Research and development	14,944.5	15,754.5	16,309.3
R&D plant	1,057.9	751.6	766.5
Total obligations for research, development, and R&D plant	16,162.4	17,420.3	17,567.5
Research and development	15,304.1	16,508.9	16,733.7
Total research	5,270.8	5,623.4	6,390.2
Basic research	1,843.9	2,074.0	2,331.2
Applied research	3,427.0	3,549.4	4,059.0
Development	10,033.2	10,885.5	10,343.5
R&D plant	858.3	911.3	833.8

TABLE 4.7-9 *(continued)*

Item	Actual, 1966	Estimates 1967	1968
Research and Development			
Performers:			
Federal government	$3,396.6	$3,528.0	$3,583.2
Industrial firms	8,881.3	9,744.5	9,666.8
Research centers administered by industrial firms	359.8	380.8	402.6
Universities and colleges	1,326.7	1,443.8	1,548.5
Research centers administered by universities and colleges	640.2	657.4	698.2
Other nonprofit institutions	395.9	426.2	474.9
Research centers administered by other nonprofit institutions	170.3	185.8	190.1
Other domestic	76.0	80.9	90.2
Foreign	57.1	61.5	79.2
Research:			
Performers:			
Federal government	1,493.3	1,595.4	1,781.2
Industrial firms	1,667.1	1,750.9	2,157.6
Research centers administered by industrial firms	72.0	70.7	70.6
Universities and colleges	1,251.4	1,358.0	1,448.7
Research centers administered by universities and colleges	398.5	418.7	443.9
Other nonprofit institutions	242.5	264.8	297.7
Research centers administered by other nonprofit institutions	35.7	44.9	45.3
Other domestic	66.1	71.4	79.5
Foreign	44.3	48.6	65.8
Field of science:			
Life sciences, total	1,289.8	1,431.2	1,584.4
Biological sciences	369.6	406.3	440.9
Medical sciences	811.5	908.7	1,019.6
Agricultural sciences	108.8	116.2	123.9
Psychological sciences	100.3	107.3	124.4
Physical sciences, total	3,641.5	3,817.2	4,381.5
Physical sciences, proper	1,841.5	1,852.3	2,040.0
Mathematical sciences	122.6	124.4	136.5

TABLE 4.7-9 *(continued)*

Item	Actual, 1966	Estimates 1967	Estimates 1968
Research—continued			
Field of science—continued			
Physical sciences—continued			
Engineering sciences	$1,677.3	$1,840.5	$2,205.0
Social sciences	165.6	177.6	209.3
Other sciences	73.6	90.1	90.6
Basic research			
Performers:			
Federal government	448.7	502.4	548.6
Industrial firms	294.6	359.8	481.4
Research centers administered by industrial firms	30.1	31.1	31.7
Universities and colleges	727.0	790.5	832.6
Research centers administered by universities and colleges	213.3	246.0	269.8
Other nonprofit institutions	89.8	97.8	104.8
Research centers administered by other nonprofit institutions	4.3	4.6	4.5
Other domestic	13.9	15.5	18.0
Foreign	22.1	26.3	39.8
Field of science:			
Life sciences, total	540.4	603.2	669.6
Biological sciences	290.3	326.2	353.4
Medical sciences	208.7	232.9	268.7
Agricultural sciences	41.4	44.2	47.6
Psychological sciences	53.4	58.4	64.3
Physical sciences, total	1,201.7	1,354.0	1,529.8
Physical sciences, proper	973.6	1,093.6	1,279.5
Mathematical sciences	60.4	62.9	63.3
Engineering sciences	167.6	197.5	187.0
Social sciences	44.3	50.8	59.2
Other sciences	4.2	7.6	8.4
Applied research:			
Performers:			
Federal government	1,044.7	1,093.0	1,232.5
Industrial firms	1,372.5	1,391.1	1,676.2

TABLE 4.7-9 *(continued)*

Item	Actual, 1966	Estimates 1967	Estimates 1968
Applied research—continued			
Performers—continued			
Research centers administered by industrial firms	$ 41.9	$ 39.6	$ 38.8
Universities and colleges	524.5	567.5	616.1
Research centers administered by universities and colleges	185.1	172.7	174.2
Other nonprofit institutions	152.7	167.0	192.9
Research centers administered by other nonprofit institutions	31.3	40.3	40.8
Other domestic	52.2	55.9	61.5
Foreign	22.2	22.2	26.0
Field of science:			
Life sciences, total	749.4	828.0	914.8
Biological sciences	79.3	80.2	87.5
Medical sciences	602.8	675.8	751.0
Agricultural sciences	67.3	72.0	76.3
Psychological sciences	47.0	48.8	60.1
Physical sciences, total	2,439.8	2,463.2	2,851.7
Physical sciences, proper	867.9	758.8	760.5
Mathematical sciences	62.2	61.5	73.2
Engineering sciences	1,509.7	1,643.0	2,018.0
Social sciences	121.3	126.8	150.2
Other sciences	69.4	82.5	82.2
Development:			
Performers:			
Federal government	1,903.3	1,932.5	1,802.0
Industrial firms	7,214.2	7,993.6	7,509.2
Research centers administered by industrial firms	287.8	310.1	332.0
Universities and colleges	75.3	85.8	99.9
Research centers administered by universities and colleges	241.7	238.7	254.3
Other nonprofit institutions	153.5	161.4	177.2
Research centers administered by other nonprofit institutions	134.6	140.9	144.8
Other domestic	10.0	9.5	10.7
Foreign	12.8	13.0	13.4

TABLE 4.7-9 *(continued)*

Item	Actual, 1966	Estimates	
		1967	*1968*
R&D plant			
Federal civilian or military installations	$ 629.0	$ 647.4	$ 575.7
Nonfederal site:			
Universities and colleges	162.9	175.2	167.3
Research centers administered by universities and colleges	31.1	27.8	25.0
Other nonfederal sites	34.4	59.8	62.8
Foreign	0.9	1.1	2.9

NOTE: Because of rounding, detail may not add to totals.

SOURCE: National Science Foundation, "Federal Funds for Research, Development, and Other Scientific Activities XVI", in U.S. Office of Education, *Digest of Educational Statistics, 1968,* 1968, p. 111.

(excluding the 4 percent of federally financed R&D performed by federally funded research centers administered by colleges and universities). The Department of Defense and the National Aeronautics and Space Administration (NASA) combined accounted for 75 percent of total federal obligations for R&D in fiscal year 1968 (Figure 4.7-1).

The character of federally financed R&D varies by type of performer. Industrial firms (by far the largest recipient of federal funds for R&D) devoted 85 percent of their federal R&D funds to development and 4 percent to basic research, while universities and colleges devoted 7 percent of their federal R&D funds to development and 52 percent to basic research in fiscal year 1968 (data estimated) (Figure 4.7-2).

Table 4.7-10 gives the major characteristics of R&D obligations of selected federal agencies for fiscal year 1968 (data estimated). Universities and colleges performed 24 percent of the R&D funded by the Department of Agriculture and 53 percent of the R&D funded by the Department of Health, Education and Welfare. This table also shows the percentages of basic and applied research and development performed for these agencies by colleges and universities.

Table 4.7-11 gives the federal obligations for R&D to federally funded R&D centers in fiscal year 1968 (data estimated). Universities and colleges administer the largest share of federal obligations in this sector—53 percent as compared with 30 percent for

(Text continued on p. 784)

FIGURE 4.7-1 *Distribution of federal obligations for research and development,* fiscal year 1968 (estimated)*

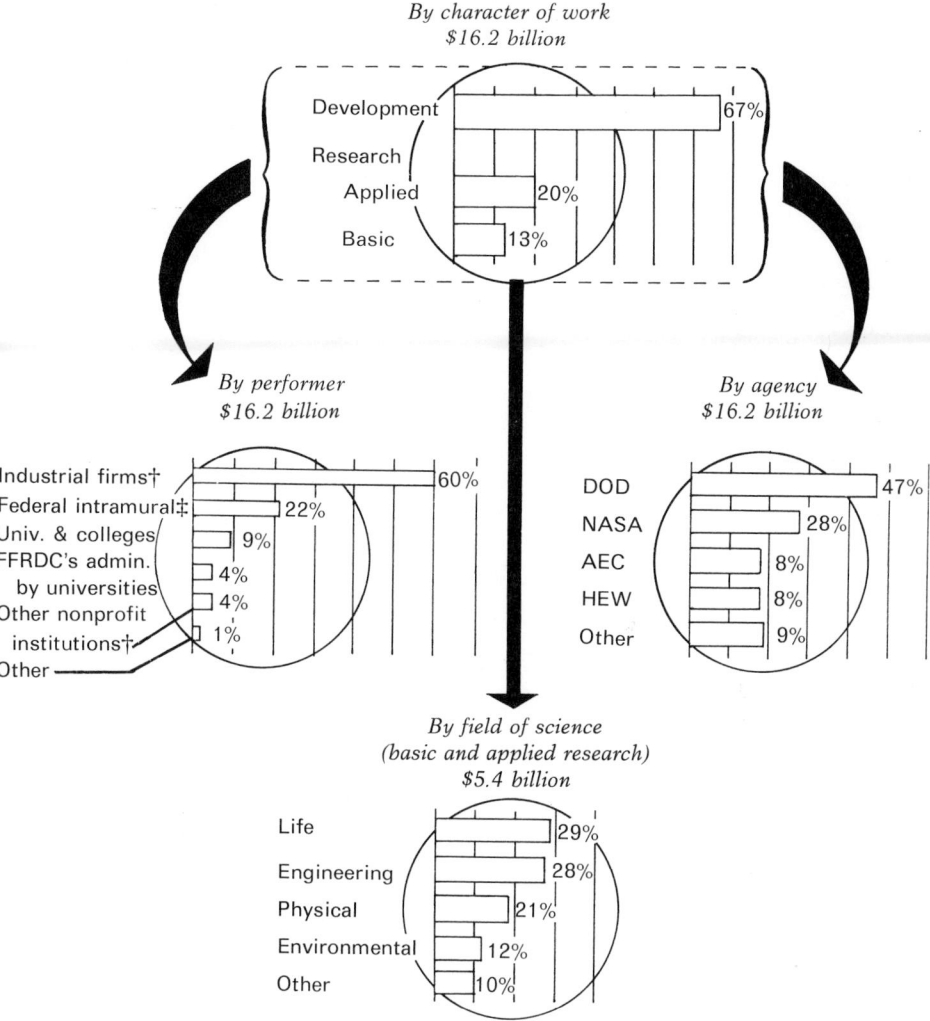

By character of work
$16.2 billion

Development 67%
Research
Applied 20%
Basic 13%

By performer
$16.2 billion

Industrial firms† 60%
Federal intramural‡ 22%
Univ. & colleges 9%
FFRDC's admin. 4%
 by universities
Other nonprofit 4%
 institutions† 1%
Other

By agency
$16.2 billion

DOD 47%
NASA 28%
AEC 8%
HEW 8%
Other 9%

By field of science
(basic and applied research)
$5.4 billion

Life 29%
Engineering 28%
Physical 21%
Environmental 12%
Other 10%

* Excludes R&D plant.
† Includes federally funded Research and Development Centers (FFRDC's) administered by this sector.
‡ Intramural activities cover costs associated with the administration of intramural and extramural programs by federal personnel as well as actual intramural performance.

SOURCE: National Science Foundation, *Federal Funds for Research, Development, and Other Scientific Activities, Fiscal Years 1967, 1968, 1969,* vol. 17, 1968, p. vi.

TABLE 4.7-10 *Major characteristics of R&D obligations of selected federal agencies, fiscal year 1968 (estimated)*

Agency and subdivsion	Total R&D obliga- tions (millions of dollars)	Total research and development			
		Character of work (percentage distribution)			Major performers* (percentage of total)
		Basic research	Applied research	Develop- ment	
Department of Agriculture, total	258.1	40	54	6	72 Intra. 24 Univ.
Department of Commerce, total	89.4	29	42	29	62 Intra. 16 Univ. 11 Ind. 8 Other
Bureau of the Census	2.3	13	53	34	98 Intra.
Department of the Army	1,583.1	3	14	83	58 Ind. 37 Intra.
Department of Health, Education and Welfare, total	1,279.3	32	61	7	53 Univ. 19 Intra. 15 N.P.
Office of Education	90.9	7	39	54	45 Univ. 26 N.P. FFRDC 10 Univ. FFRDC
Public Health Service	1,119.7	36	61	3	55 Univ. 20 Intra. 16 N.P.
Department of the Interior, total	205.5	27	52	21	58 Intra. 23 Ind. 13 Univ.
Bureau of Labor Statistics	3.6	34	31	35	100 Intra.
Federal Aviation Administration	214.4		1	99	83 Ind. 16 Intra.

Basic research		Applied research		Development
Major fields of science* (percentage of total)	*Major performers* (percentage of total)*	*Major fields of science* (percentage of total)*	*Major performers* (percentage of total)*	*Major performers* (percentage of total)*
71 Life 16 Phy.Sci. 8 Soc.	67 Intra. 24 Univ. 9 For.	58 Life 16 Soc. 15 Phy. Sci. 9 Eng.	73 Intra. 26 Univ.	93 Intra.
41 Environ. 39 Phy. Sci. 11 Soc. 8 Eng.	95 Intra.	36 Eng. 22 Soc. 22 Environ. 16 Phy. Sci.	54 Intra. 28 Univ. 11 Other	40 Intra. 34 Ind. 13 Other 12 Univ.
58 Math. 35 Psych.	82 Intra. 10 Univ. 8 N.P.	61 Soc. 30 Psych. 9 Math.	100 Intra.	100 Intra.
35 Life 19 Phy. Sci. 15 Eng. 14 Other 10 Environ.	48 Univ. 39 Intra.	52 Eng. 18 Phy. Sci. 14 Life	68 Intra. 20 Ind.	67 Ind. 32 Intra.
78 Life 10 Psych.	63 Univ. 19 Intra. 15 N.P.	84 Life 8 Soc.	51 Univ. 18 Intra. 16 N.P. 8 Ind.	29 Univ. 24 N.P. FFRDC 23 Intra. 12 N.P. 8 Ind.
50 Psych. 50 Soc.	66 Univ. 27 Univ. FFRDC	59 Soc. 41 Psych.	48 Univ. 17 Univ. FFRDC 14 Other 12 N.P.	45 N.P. FFRDC 40 Univ.
80 Life 10 Psych.	63 Univ. 20 Intra. 15 N.P.	91 Life	52 Univ. 19 Intra. 15 N.P. 9 Ind.	38 Intra. 21 Ind. 21 N.P. 18 Univ.
47 Environ. 21 Phy. Sci. 20 Life	78 Intra. 17 Univ.	39 Eng. 35 Life 13 Environ. 9 Phy. Sci.	60 Intra. 17 Ind. 14 Univ.	67 Ind. 27 Intra.
100 Soc.	99 Intra.	100 Soc. 93 Life	100 Intra. 99 Intra.	100 Intra. 85 Ind. 15 Intra.

TABLE 4.7-10 *(continued)*

Agency and subdivision	Total R&D obligations (millions of dollars)	Total research and development			
		Character of work (percentage distribution)			Major performers* (percentage of total)
		Basic research	Applied research	Development	
National Aeronautics and Space Administration	4,586.8	14	18	68	77 Ind. 18 Intra.
Smithsonian Institution	13.6	100			93 Intra.

*Major is here defined as any performer or field of science which singly accounts for at least 8 percent of total funds.

NOTE: Intramural activities cover costs associated with the administration of intramural and extramural programs by federal personnel as well as actual intramural performance.

Abbreviation	Performer	Abbreviation	Performer
Intra.	Intramural	*Univ. FFRDC*	FFRDC's administered by universities and colleges
Ind.	Industrial firms excluding Federally Funded Research and Development Centers (FFRDC's)	*N.P.*	Other nonprofit institutions excluding FFRDC's
Ind. FFRDC	FFRDC's administered by industrial firms	*N.P. FFRDC*	FFRDC's administered by nonprofit institutions
Univ.	Universities and colleges excluding FFRDC's	*For.*	Foreign

SOURCE: National Science Foundation, *Federal Funds for Research, Development, and Other Scientific Activities, Fiscal Years 1967, 1968, and 1969,* vol. 17, 1968, pp. 38–44.

industrial firms. The Atomic Energy Commission provided 65 percent of the funds for the federally funded R&D centers administered by colleges and universities. Table 4.7-12 is a master list of federally funded R&D centers by administering agency.

BASIC RESEARCH NASA accounts for the largest share of federal agency obligations for basic research—30 percent in 1967. The federal agencies with the next largest shares of total federal obligations for basic research were the Department of Health, Education and Welfare (18 percent), the Atomic Energy Commission (15 percent), and the Department of Defense (14 percent) (Table 4.7-13). From fiscal year 1958 to fiscal year 1968 (data estimated), NASA and the Department of Health, Education and Welfare experienced the largest

Basic research		Applied research		Development
Major fields of science* (percentage of total)	*Major performers* (percentage of total)*	*Major fields of science* (percentage of total)*	*Major performers* (percentage of total)*	*Major performers* (percentage of total)*
45 Phy. Sci.	53 Ind.	64 Eng.	52 Ind.	88 Ind.
30 Environ.	27 Intra.	24 Environ.	39 Intra.	11 Intra.
12 Life	10 Univ. FFRDC			
11 Eng.	9 Univ.			
40 Life	93 Intra.			
35 Soc.				
22 Phy. Sci.				

Abbreviation	*Field of science*	*Abbreviation*	*Field of science*
Life	Life sciences	*Math.*	Mathematical sciences
Psych.	Psychological sciences	*Eng.*	Engineering sciences
Phy. Sci.	Physical sciences	*Soc.*	Social sciences
Environ.	Environmental sciences		

relative increases of all federal agencies in federal obligations for basic research (Figure 4.7-3).

From fiscal year 1958 to fiscal year 1968 (data estimated), intramural obligations (for work performed within the federal agency) for basic research decreased from 37 to 24 percent of total federal obligations for basic research. In this same period the share of federally funded basic research performed by universities and colleges decreased from 38 to 37 percent and the share of federally funded basic research performed by industrial firms increased from 8 to 19 percent (Figure 4.7-4). Federal support of basic research increased approximately 13.5 times from 1956 to 1966—from $157 million to $2,272 million (estimated) (Table 4.7-14).

Universities and colleges are the largest performers of federally

(Text continued on p. 792)

FIGURE 4.7-2 Federal research and development obligations, by performer and character of work, fiscal year 1968 (estimated)

Research and development
$16.2 billion

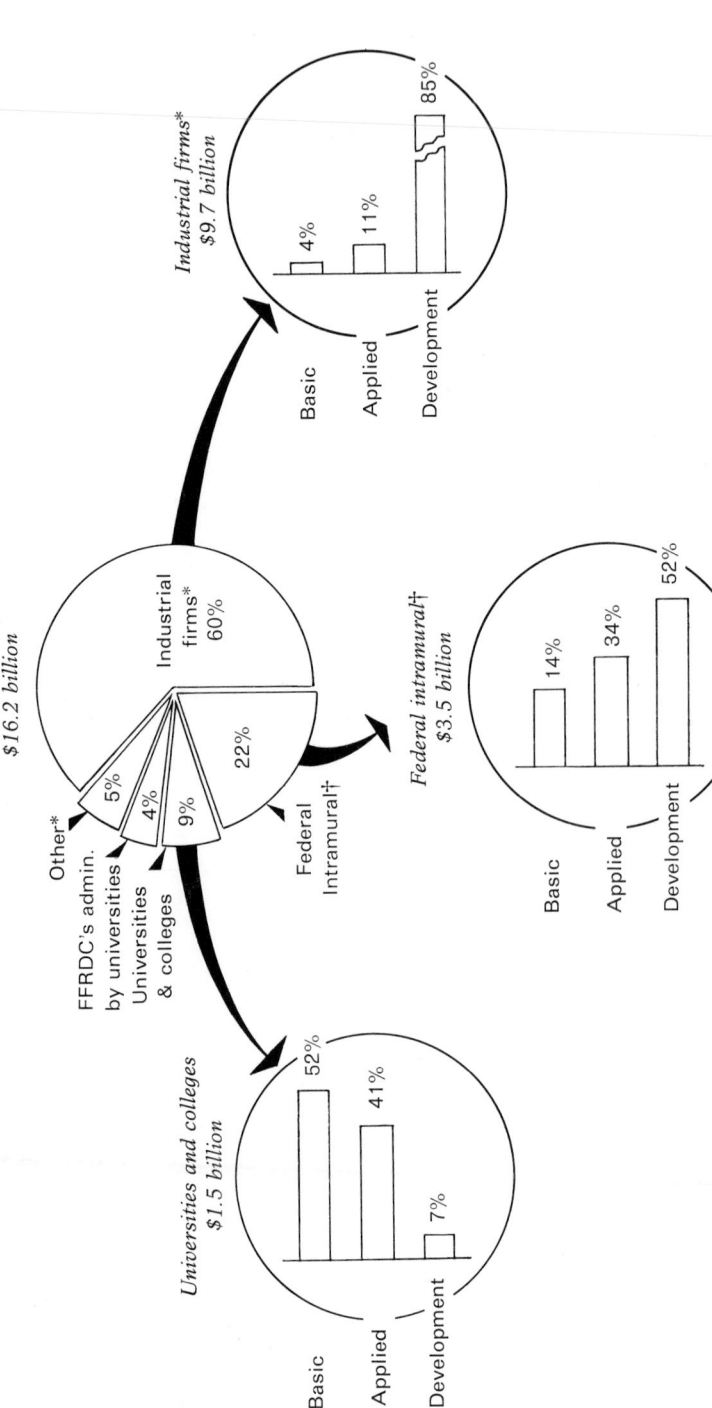

Industrial firms*
$9.7 billion

Basic 4%
Applied 11%
Development 85%

Universities and colleges
$1.5 billion

Basic 52%
Applied 41%
Development 7%

Federal intramural†
$3.5 billion

Basic 14%
Applied 34%
Development 52%

Other*
FFRDC's admin. 5%
by universities
Universities 4%
& colleges 9%
Federal Intramural† 22%
Industrial firms* 60%

* Includes federally funded Research and Development Centers (FFRDC's) administered by this sector.

† Intramural activities cover costs associated with the administration of intramural and extramural programs by federal personnel as well as actual intramural performance.

SOURCE: National Science Foundation, *Federal Funds for Research, Development, and Other Scientific Activities, Fiscal Years 1967, 1968, and 1969,* vol. 17, 1968, p. 7.

TABLE 4.7-11 *Federal obligations for research and development to federally funded research and development centers, by administering sectors and agency, fiscal year 1968 (estimated, millions of dollars)*

	Total	AEC	DOD	NASA	HEW	NSF	Other
TOTAL	$1,343	$871	$306	$107	$34	$22	$4
Industrial firms	402	390	10	1			1
Universities and colleges	711	433	144	106	10	18	
Other nonprofit institutions	230	48	152	*	24	4	2

* Less than $500,000.

NOTE: Detail may not add to totals because of rounding.

SOURCE: National Science Foundation, *Federal Funds for Research, Development, and Other Scientific Activities, Fiscal Years, 1967, 1968, and 1969*, vol. 17, 1968, p. 31.

TABLE 4.7-12 *Master list of federally funded research and development centers (as of June 1, 196u,*

Department of Defense

Office of the Secretary of Defense

Administered by other nonprofit institutions

Institute for Defense Analyses (IDA)

Department of the Army

Administered by universities and colleges

Army Mathematics Research Center (University of Wisconsin)

Center for Research in Social Systems (American University)

Human Resources Research Office (George Washington University)

Administered by other nonprofit institutions

Research Analysis Corporation (RAC)

Department of the Navy

Administered by universities and colleges

Applied Physics Laboratory (Johns Hopkins University)

Applied Physics Laboratory (University of Washington)

Center for Naval Analyses (University of Rochester)

Hudson Laboratories (Columbia University)

Ordnance Research Laboratory (Pennsylvania State University)

Department of the Air Force

Administered by universities and colleges

Lincoln Laboratory (Massachusetts Institute of Technology)

Administered by other nonprofit institutions

Aerospace Corporation

Analytic Services, Inc. (ANSER)

TABLE 4.7-12
(continued)

Department of the Air Force

Administered by universities and colleges

Illinois Institute of Technology, Research Institute (IITRI) at Electromagnetic Compatibility Analysis Center

MITRE Corporation

RAND Corporation

Department of Health, Education and Welfare

Office of Education

Administered by universities and colleges

Center for the Advanced Study of Educational Administration (University of Oregon)

Center for Research and Development in Higher Education (University of California)

Center for Research and Development for Learning and Re-Education (University of Wisconsin)

Center for the Study of the Evaluation of Instructional Programs (University of California)

Center for the Study of Social Organization of Schools and the Learning Process (Johns Hopkins University)

Coordination Center for the National Program in Early Childhood Education (University of Illinois)

Learning Research and Development Center (University of Pittsburgh)

Research and Development Center in Educational Stimulation (University of Georgia)

Research and Development Center in Teacher Education (University of Texas)

Research and Development on Educational Differences (Harvard University)*

Stanford Center for Research and Development in Teaching (Stanford University)

Administered by other nonprofit institutions

Appalachia Educational Laboratory

Center for Educational Policy Research (Stanford Research Institute)

Center for Urban Education

Central Atlantic Regional Educational Laboratory

Central Midwestern Regional Educational Laboratory

Cooperative Educational Research Laboratory, Inc.

Eastern Regional Institute for Education

Educational Development Center, Inc.

The Far West Laboratory for Educational Research and Development

Michigan-Ohio Regional Educational Laboratory

Mid-Continent Regional Educational Laboratory

TABLE 4.7-12
(continued)

Department of Health, Education and Welfare

Office of Education

Administered by other nonprofit institutions

Northwest Regional Educational Laboratory

Policy Research Center (Syracuse University Research Corporation)

Regional Educational Laboratory for the Carolinas and Virginia

Research for Better Schools, Inc.

Rocky Mountain Regional Educational Laboratory

South Central Regional Educational Laboratory Corporation

Southeastern Educational Laboratory

Southwest Educational Development Laboratory

Southwest Regional Educational Laboratory

Southwestern Cooperative Educational Laboratory

Upper Midwest Regional Educational Laboratory, Inc.

Atomic Energy Commission

Administered by industrial firms

Bettis Atomic Power Laboratory (Westinghouse Electric Corp.)

Knolls Atomic Power Laboratory (General Electric Company)

Mound Laboratory (Monsanto Chemical Company)

National Reactor Testing Station (Phillips Petroleum Co. and Idaho Nuclear Corp.)

Oak Ridge National Laboratory (Union Carbide Corp.)

Sandia Laboratory (Western Electric Co., Inc. — Sandia Corp.)

Savannah River Laboratory (E. I. duPont de Nemours & Co., Inc.)

Administered by universities and colleges

Ames Laboratory (Iowa State University of Science and Technology)

Argonne National Laboratory (University of Chicago and Argonne Universities Assn.)

Brookhaven National Laboratory (Associated Universities, Inc.)

Cambridge Electron Accelerator (Harvard University and Massachusetts Institute of Technology)

Lawrence Radiation Laboratory, Berkeley and Livermore (University of California)

Los Alamos Scientific Laboratory (University of California)

Oak Ridge Associated Universities

Plasma Physics Laboratory (Princeton University)

Princeton-Pennsylvania Accelerator (Princeton University and University of Pennsylvania)

Stanford Linear Accelerator Center (Stanford University)

Administered by other nonprofit institutions

Atomic Bomb Casualty Commission (National Academy of Sciences)

Pacific Northwest Laboratory (Battelle Memorial Institute)

TABLE 4.7-12
(continued)

National Aeronautics and Space Administration

Administered by universities and colleges

Jet Propulsion Laboratory (California Institute of Technology)

Space Radiation Effects Laboratory (College of William and Mary)

National Science Foundation

Administered by universities and colleges

Cerro Tololo Inter-American Observatory (Association of Universities for Research in Astronomy, Inc.)

Kitt Peak National Observatory (Association of Universities for Research in Astronomy, Inc.)

National Center for Atmospheric Research (University Corporation for Atmospheric Research)

National Radio Astronomy Observatory (Associated Universities, Inc.)

*Phased as a FFRDC on June 30, 1967.

SOURCE: National Science Foundation, *Federal Funds for Research, Development, and Other Scientific Activities, Fiscal Years 1967, 1968, and 1969*, vol. 17, 1968, pp. 97–99.

TABLE 4.7-14 *Federal government obligations for conduct of basic research, fiscal years 1956–1966 (thousands of dollars)*

Department or agency	1956	1957	1958	1959	1960	1961
National Science Foundation†	15,003	29,999	32,834	54,238	68,417	77,265
Department of Health, Education and Welfare	26,156	38,353	49,647	74,940	103,266	136,818
National Aeronautics and Space Administration (NACA, 1956, 1957)	13,272	16,025	25,600	146,557	213,478	190,300
Department of Defense	27,266	31,101	105,739	120,739	181,032	148,785
Atomic Energy Commission	46,584	56,087	72,034	87,359	103,773	167,146
Department of Interior	10,927	15,670	13,475	19,142	22,876	26,333
Department of Commerce	3,444	3,862	4,787	6,625	9,172	11,118
Department of Agriculture	13,278	16,950	23,865	29,266	33,606	40,556
Other agencies and departments	1,259	2,631	3,081	4,243	5,555	5,194
TOTAL	157,189	210,678	331,062	543,109	741,175	803,515

*Estimated.

† 1956–58 IGY obligations included in total.

SOURCE: U.S. National Science Foundation. "Federal Funds for Science," vols. VI–XI; "Federal Funds for Research, Development, and Other Scientific Activities," vol. XII–XIII; fiscal year 1964–66: "The Budget for Fiscal Year 1966, Special Analysis H"; in U.S. House of Representatives, Committee on Science and Astronautics, *The National Science Foundation: A General Review of Its First 15 Years*, report of the Science Policy Research Division, Legislative Reference Service of the Library of Congress to the Subcommittee on Science, Research and Development, 1965, p. 53.

	Agency	Actual, 1967	Estimates 1968	Estimates 1969
TABLE 4.7-13 **Federal** **obligations** **for basic** **research, by** **agency (millions** **of dollars)**	TOTAL	$2,015	$2,093	$2,354
	National Aeronautics and Space Administration	603	645	745
	Department of Health, Education and Welfare	372	413	438
	Atomic Energy Commission	302	314	330
	Department of Defense	284	246	320
	National Science Foundation	239	251	274
	Other agencies	215	224	247

SOURCE: National Science Foundation, *Federal Funds for Research, Development, and Other Scientific Activities, Fiscal Years 1967, 1968, and 1969,* vol. 17, 1968, p. 11.

1962	1963	1964	1965*	1966*
105,491	143,985	170,000	212,000	290,000
190,421	236,406	265,000	298,000	330,000
316,241	447,177	756,000	910,000	888,000
177,919	198,414	260,000	293,000	324,000
191,565	218,553	238,000	260,000	286,000
29,542	28,889	33,300	37,300	40,600
16,290	21,262	22,200	23,900	27,000
49,666	56,020	62,000	82,000	85,000
8,100	8,804	1,500	1,800	1,400
1,085,235	1,359,510	1,808,000	2,118,000	2,272,000

FIGURE 4.7-3   *Comparisons of federal obligations for basic research, by agency, fiscal years 1958 and 1968 (estimated)*

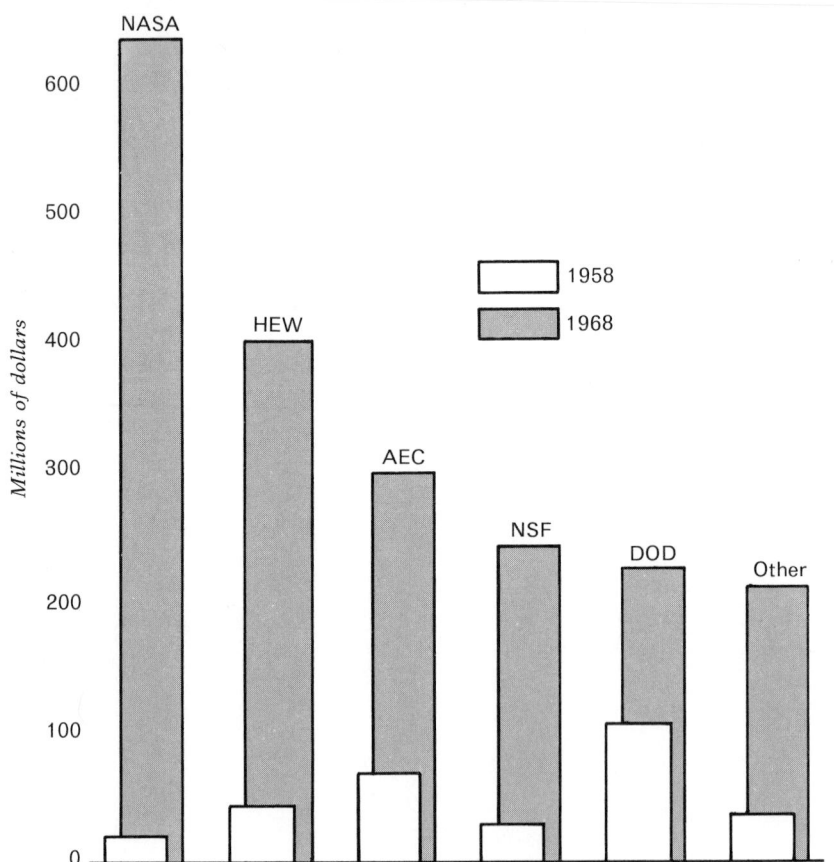

SOURCE: National Science Foundation, *Federal Funds for Research, Development, and Other Scientific Activities, Fiscal Years 1967, 1968, and 1969*, vol. 17, 1968, p. 11.

financed basic research, receiving 37 percent of federal funds for basic research in fiscal year 1968 (data estimated). The Department of Health, Education and Welfare and the National Science Foundation supplied the largest shares of federal funds for basic research to universities and colleges — 33 and 27 percent respectively (Table 4.7-15).

Federal obligations for basic research by field of science are shown in Table 4.7-16. The physical and life sciences combined

FIGURE 4.7-4 *Federal obligations for basic research, by performer, fiscal years 1958 and 1968*

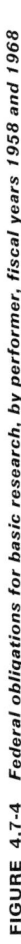

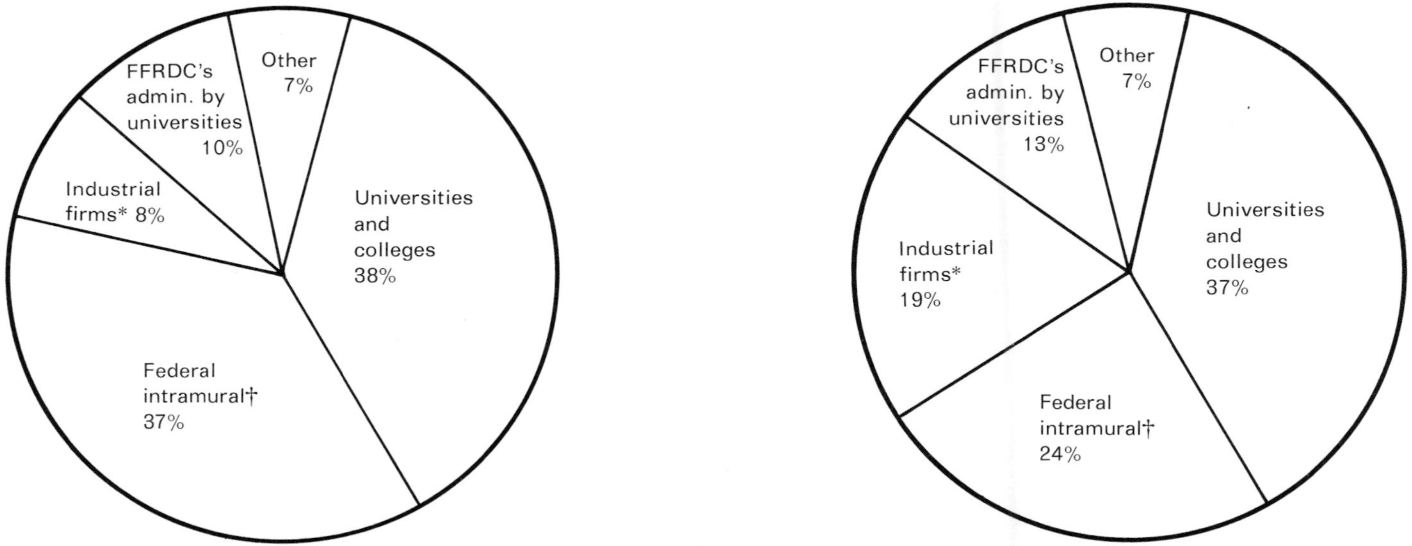

FY 1968: $2.1 billion (estimated)

Universities and colleges 37%

Federal intramural† 24%

Industrial firms* 19%

FFRDC's admin. by universities 13%

Other 7%

FY 1958: $335 million

Universities and colleges 38%

Federal intramural† 37%

Industrial firms* 8%

FFRDC's admin. by universities 10%

Other 7%

* Includes federally funded Research and Development Centers (FFRDC's) administered by this sector.

† Intramural activities cover costs associated with the administration of intramural and extramural programs by federal personnel as well as actual intramural performance.

SOURCE: National Science Foundation, *Federal Funds for Research, Development, and Other Scientific Activities, Fiscal Years 1967, 1968, and 1969,* vol. 17, 1968, p. 12.

TABLE 4.7-15 *Federal obligations for basic research, by performer and agency, fiscal year 1968 (estimated, millions of dollars)*

	Total	NASA	HEW	AEC	NSF	DOD	Other
TOTAL	$2,093	$645	$413	$314	$251	$246	$224
Federal intramural*	503	174	80	5	13	73	163
Industrial firms†	373	342		3	2	25	1
FFRDC's administered by industrial firms	31	‡		31			1
Universities and colleges†	782	58	258	86	208	128	44
FFRDC's administered by universities and colleges	262	65	2	176	18	1	‡
Other nonprofit institutions†	98	6	62	5	11	13	1
FFRDC's administered by nonprofit institutions	9		‡	8		1	‡
Other	30	‡	10	1	1	5	13

*Intramural activities cover costs associated with the administration of intramural and extramural programs by federal personnel as well as actual intramural performance.
† Excluding federally funded Research and Development Centers.
‡ Less than $500,000.
NOTE: Detail may not add to totals because of rounding.
SOURCE: National Science Foundation, *Federal Funds for Research, Development, and Other Scientific Activities, Fiscal Years 1967, 1968, and 1969*, vol. 17, 1968, p. 13.

accounted for 66 percent of federal obligations for basic research in fiscal year 1969 (data estimated).

APPLIED RESEARCH   In fiscal year 1967, federal obligations for applied research were $3.3 billion and were projected to increase to $3.6 billion in 1969.[1] Figure 4.7-5 compares the increases in federal obligations for applied research for selected agencies from fiscal years 1958 to 1968 (data estimated). NASA and the Department of Health, Education and Welfare experienced the largest relative increases, but the Department of Defense had by far the largest share of federal obligations for applied research during this period.

From fiscal year 1963 to fiscal year 1968 (data estimated), the share of federally funded applied research performed by industrial firms decreased from 45 to 31 percent, while the share of federally funded applied research performed by colleges and universities increased from 14 to 19 percent (Figure 4.7-6). In 1967 the De-

[1] National Science Foundation, *Federal Funds for Research, Development, and Other Scientific Activities, Fiscal Years 1967, 1968, and 1969*, vol. 17, 1968, p. 15.

TABLE 4.7-16
Federal obligations for basic research, by field of science (millions of dollars)

Field and discipline	Actual, 1967	Estimates 1968	1969
TOTAL	$2,015	$2,093	$2,354
Life sciences	612	653	717
Psychological sciences	60	65	75
Physical sciences	713	726	828
Astronomy	180	209	254
Chemistry	123	121	129
Physics	381	376	414
Other	28	21	32
Environmental sciences	321	340	382
Atmospheric sciences	179	180	204
Oceanography	39	48	55
Earth sciences	103	113	123
Mathematical sciences	65	57	76
Engineering sciences	184	180	191
Social sciences	57	62	69
Other sciences	4	10	15

NOTE: Detail may not add to totals because of rounding.
SOURCE: National Science Foundation, *Federal Funds for Research, Development, and Other Scientific Activities, Fiscal Years 1967, 1968, and 1969,* vol. 17, 1968, p. 14.

TABLE 4.7-17
Federal obligations for applied research, by agency (millions of dollars)

Agency	Actual, 1967	Estimates 1968	1969
TOTAL	$3,258	$3,313	$3,636
Department of Defense	1,307	1,178	1,338
National Aeronautics and Space Administration	775	831	831
Department of Health, Education and Welfare	710	775	884
Department of Agriculture	137	139	147
Department of the Interior	91	107	118
Other agencies	238	283	318

SOURCE: National Science Foundation, *Federal Funds for Research, Development, and Other Scientific Activities, Fiscal Years 1967, 1968, and 1969,* vol. 17, 1968, p. 61.

FIGURE 4.7-5 *Comparison of federal obligations for applied research, by agency, fiscal years 1958 and 1968 (estimated)*

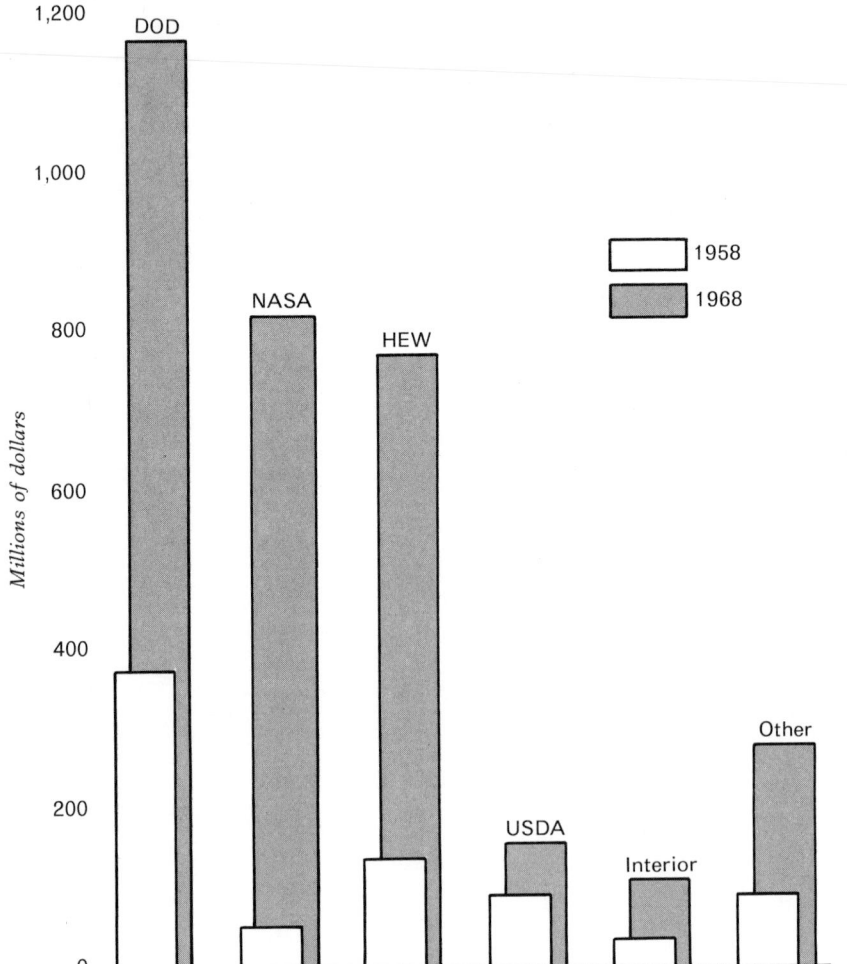

SOURCE: National Science Foundation, *Federal Funds for Research, Development, and Other Scientific Activities, Fiscal Years 1967, 1968, and 1969,* vol. 17, 1968, p. 17.

partment of Defense, NASA, and the Department of Health, Education and Welfare combined accounted for 86 percent of the federal obligations for applied research (Table 4.7-17).

Federal agencies themselves (federal intramural) are the largest performers of federally funded applied research. In fiscal year 1968 (data estimated), they accounted for 37 percent of all federal obligations for applied research, while industrial firms accounted for 30 percent and colleges and universities accounted for 19

FIGURE 4.7-6 *Federal obligations for applied research, by performer, fiscal years 1963 and 1968*

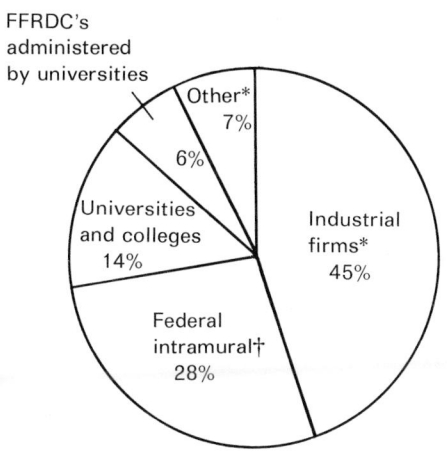
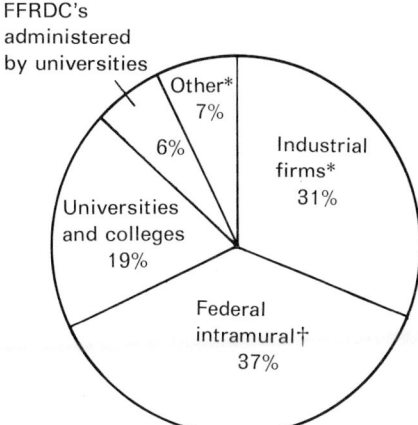

FFRDC's administered by universities

FFRDC's administered by universities

FY 1963: $2.7 billion   *FY 1968: $3.3 billion (estimated)*

* Includes federally funded Research and Development Centers (FFRDC's) administered by this sector.

† Intramural activities cover costs associated with the administration of intramural and extramural programs by federal personnel as well as actual intramural performance.

SOURCE: National Science Foundation, *Federal Funds for Research, Development, and Other Scientific Activities, Fiscal Years 1967, 1968, and 1969,* vol. 17, 1968, p. 18.

TABLE 4.7-18 *Federal obligations for applied research, by performer and agency, fiscal year 1968 (estimated, millions of dollars)*

	Total	DOD	NASA	HEW	USDA	Interior	Other
TOTAL	$3,313	$1,178	$831	$775	$139	$107	$283
Federal intramural*	1,215	494	324	138	102	64	93
Industrial firms†	977	429	434	59	‡	18	37
FFRDC's administered by industrial firms	37	6	1			1	29
Universities and colleges†	615	98	31	397	36	15	37
FFRDC's administered by universities and colleges	185	89	35	6			55
Other nonprofit institutions†	170	27	5	122	1	1	13
FFRDC's administered by nonprofit institutions	31	25	‡	1			4
Other	84	9	1	52		7	15

* Intramural activities cover costs associated with the administration of intramural and extramural programs by federal personnel as well as actual intramural performance.

† Excluding federally funded Research and Development Centers (FFRDC's).

‡ Less than $500,000.

NOTE: Detail may not add to totals because of rounding.

SOURCE: National Science Foundation, *Federal Funds for Research, Development, and Other Scientific Activities, Fiscal Years 1967, 1968, and 1969,* vol. 17, 1968, p. 19.

percent. The Department of Health, Education and Welfare was by far the largest source (65 percent) of federal funds for applied research for colleges and universities. The share of federally funded applied research performed by colleges and universities rises to 24 percent if we include the federally funded R&D centers administered by colleges and universities (Table 4.7-18).

Table 4.7-19 shows federal obligations for applied research by field of science. The life sciences and engineering together received about 70 percent of all federal obligations for applied research in 1969 (data estimated).

DEVELOPMENT Federal agency obligations for development totaled $11.3 billion in 1967. Anticipated budget reductions were expected to bring that amount down to $10 billion by 1969.[2] In fiscal year 1968 (data estimated), the Department of Defense, NASA, and the Atomic (Text continued on p. 808)

[2] Ibid.

TABLE 4.7-19 Federal obligations for applied research, by field of science (millions of dollars)	Field of science	Actual, 1967	Estimates	
			1968	1969
	TOTAL	$3,258	$3,313	$3,636
	Life sciences	839	933	1,048
	Psychological sciences	48	48	56
	Physical sciences	361	410	462
	Astronomy	18	49	63
	Chemistry	119	114	129
	Physics	197	218	237
	Other	27	30	33
	Environmental sciences	349	309	229
	Atmospheric sciences	105	107	112
	Oceanography	30	30	32
	Earth sciences	214	172	85
	Mathematical sciences	65	50	68
	Engineering sciences	1,371	1,345	1,504
	Social sciences	132	146	181
	Other sciences	92	72	87

NOTE: Detail may not add to totals because of rounding.

SOURCE: National Science Foundation, *Federal Funds for Research, Development, and Other Scientific Activities, Fiscal Years 1967, 1968, and 1969*, vol. 17, 1968, p. 19.

TABLE 4.7-20 *Federal obligations for development, by performer and agency, fiscal year 1968 (estimated, millions of dollars)*

Performer	Total	DOD	NASA	AEC	Transportation	HEW	Other
TOTAL	$10,824	$6,274	$3,111	$955	$226	$92	$165
*Federal intramural**	1,822	1,380	327	10	35	21	49
Industrial firms†	7,950	4,598	2,743	364	185	7	53
FFRDC's administered by industrial firms	334	3		329			1
Universities and colleges†	111	34	23	4	3	26	21
FFRDC's administered by universities and colleges	264	54	7	202		2	‡
Other nonprofit institutions†	133	73	12	7	‡	11	30
FFRDC's administered by other nonprofit institutions	191	126		37	1	23	4
Other	20	6	‡	2	2	2	7

*Intramural activities cover costs associated with the administration of intramural and extramural programs by federal personnel as well as actual intramural performance.

† Excluding federally funded Research and Development Centers (FFRDC's).

‡ Less than $500,000.

NOTE: Detail may not add to totals because of rounding.

SOURCE: National Science Foundation, *Federal Funds for Research, Development, and Other Scientific Activities, Fiscal Years 1967, 1968, and 1969,* vol. 17, 1968, p. 24.

TABLE 4.7-21 *Budget estimates of science education programs, fiscal year 1967*

Program	Amount (millions of dollars)
TOTAL	140.0
Fellowships and traineeships	48.0
Institutes	42.0
Research participation and scientific activities for teachers	4.5
Science education for undergraduate students	6.0
Science education for secondary school students	4.5
Specialized advanced science education projects	2.0
Course content improvement	19.0
Instruction equipment for undergraduate education	4.0
College science improvement	10.0

SOURCE: U.S. Congress, Joint Economic Committee, *Federal Programs for the Development of Human Resources,* a compilation of replies from departments and agencies of the U.S. Government to a questionnaire formulated by the Subcommittee on Economic Progress, 1966, p. 1157.

TABLE 4.7-22 *The 25 top recipients of federal funds for research and science education from five principal agencies, fiscal year 1964**

	Amount (thousands of dollars)			
Institution	*NIH*	*DOD*	*NSF*	*NASA*
National total, all educational institutions	577,544	400,977	338,932	88,779
Total, top 25 institutions	336,365	306,318	135,507	57,325
Massachusetts Institute of Technology		98,044	6,267	8,042
University of California	38,729	19,068	20,119	6,072
Berkeley	(7,807)	(7,361)	(8,947)	(3,742)
Los Angeles	(15,768)	(2,793)	(4,642)	(1,444)
San Diego	(379)	(7,876)	(2,748)	(713)
San Francisco	(9,246)	(251)	(75)	(44)
Davis	(3,879)	(266)	(2,058)	(24)
Riverside	(1,344)	(360)	(856)	(35)
Santa Barbara	(105)	(161)	(744)	(70)
Irvine	(200)		(50)	
Johns Hopkins University	15,890	54,989		
University of Michigan	13,071	17,642	4,723	4,510
Stanford University	12,398	14,555	10,670	2,979
Harvard University	21,412	5,852	7,397	2,431
University of Illinois	10,079	8,117	7,573	1,184
Urbana		(7,784)		
Chicago		(333)		
Columbia University	17,522		5,946	916
University of Wisconsin	13,327	3,681	7,241	1,961
University of Chicago	13,437	4,558	4,725	3,367
University of Washington	15,341	4,342	4,316	
University of Pennsylvania	13,302	5,352	3,504	1,177
Cornell University	8,859	6,505	6,313	
Cornell University			(3,128)	
Cornell University—State			(2,992)	
Cornell University—Medical School			(90)	
SUNY College of Agriculture—Cornell University			(81)	
SUNY Veterinary College—Cornell University			(21)	
University of Minnesota	15,350		4,738	1,111
University of Texas	12,773	4,456	4,551	
Main University—Austin	(2,114)	(4,221)	(4,345)	

				Rank		
AEC	*Total*	*NIH*	*DOD*	*NSF*	*NASA*	*AEC*
62,542	1,468,824					
43,404	878,919					
3,158	115,511		1	7	1	3
3,999	87,987	1	3	1	2	2
	70,879	4	2			
1,749	41,695	11	4	11	3	11
	40,602	13	5	2	7	
	37,092	2	10	4	9	
2,608	29,461	18	7	3	17	5
4,679	29,063	3		8	22	1
1,691	27,901	9	21	5	11	12
1,276	27,363	8	15	10	5	13
2,065	26,064	6	17	15		9
	23,335	10	11	19	18	
964	22,641	22	8	6		18
1,195	22,394	5		9	20	14
	21,780	12	16	13		

TABLE 4.7-22 *(continued)*

Institution	Amount (thousands of dollars)			
	NIH	*DOD*	*NSF*	*NASA*
M. D. Anderson Hospital and Tumor Center–				
Houston	(5,035)	(48)	(104)	
Galveston	(2,752)	(139)	(39)	
Dallas	(2,872)	(48)		
Texas Western College			(38)	
Institute of Marine Science			(24)	
Yale University	13,874		3,705	
New York University	12,366	3,926		
Duke University	11,680		2,847	
Illinois Institute of Technology		13,548		
California Institute of Technology		4,611	4,591	909
Princeton University		3,762	3,410	4,179
State University of New York	11,755			
At Buffalo	(4,778)			
Downstate Medical Center (New York City)	(4,067)			
Upstate Medical Center (Syracuse)	(2,686)			
At Stony Brook	(118)			
At Albany	(40)			
Harper College	(33)			
College of Forestry	(28)			
At Plattsburg	(4)			
Washington University	10,010			1,408
Yeshiva University	11,195			
University of Rochester	9,085			
Western Reserve University	9,586			
Pennsylvania State University		5,930	2,962	
University of Pittsburgh	8,825			
Tulane University	8,754			
Purdue University		2,972	3,553	909
University of North Carolina	7,745			
University of Miami		3,299	2,716	
Ohio State University		5,210		
University of Colorado			4,486	
George Washington University		4,731		

				Rank		
AEC	*Total*	*NIH*	*DOD*	*NSF*	*NASA*	*AEC*
3,017	20,596	7		16		4
2,082	18,374	14	19			8
708	15,235	16		22		23
	13,548		6			
2,479	12,590		14	12	24	6
914	12,265		20	20	4	20
	11,755	15				
	11,418	19			13	
	11,195	17				
2,090	11,175	21				7
	9,586	20				
	8,892		9	21		
	8,825	23				
	8,754	24				
1,106	8,540		25	17	25	15
	7,745	25				
	6,015		24	25		
	5,210		12			
666	5,152			14		25
	4,731		13			

TABLE 4.7-22 *(continued)*

Institution	Amount (thousands of dollars)			
	NIH	*DOD*	*NSF*	*NASA*
University of Maryland				3,173
Northwestern University		4,048		
Florida State University			2,838	
Brooklyn Polytechnic Institute		3,576		
University of Denver		3,544		
University of Syracuse			3,540	
University			(3,044)	
Research Institute			(246)	
SUNY College of Forestry			(230)	
Utica College			(20)	
Rice University				2,511
Michigan State University			2,776	
Georgia Institute of Technology				2,384
Rensselaer Polytechnic Institute				1,113
Carnegie Institute of Technology				
Texas A. & M. University				1,441
University of Florida				1,231
University of Alabama				1,195
Auburn University				1,194
University of Arizona				1,018
University of Notre Dame				
State University of Iowa				910
Case Institute of Technology				

*The top 25 universities are not the same for each agency. There are a total of 54 institutions included in the top group of the five agencies.

SOURCE: U.S. House of Representatives, Committee on Government Operations, *Conflicts Between the Federal Research Programs and the Nation's Goals for Higher Education,* report of the subcommittee, 1965, pp. 60–61.

		Rank				
AEC	*Total*	*NIH*	*DOD*	*NSF*	*NASA*	*AEC*
935	4,108				6	19
	4,048		18			
744	3,582			23		22
	3,576		22			
	3,544		23			
	3,540			18		
689	3,200				8	24
	2,776			24		
	2,384				10	
1,008	2,121				19	16
1,764	1,764					10
	1,441				12	
	1,231				14	
	1,195				15	
	1,194				16	
	1,018				21	
1,007	1,007					17
	910				23	
811	811					21

TABLE 4.7-23 *Top 15 producers of science doctorates compared with 15 leading recipients of funds for research and science education from five principal federal agencies, fiscal year 1964*

| 15 top producers of science doctorates | 15 leading recipients of funds | |
	National Institutes of Health	Department of Defense
University of California	University of California	Massachusetts Institute of Technology
Massachusetts Institute of Technology	Harvard University	Johns Hopkins
Purdue University	Columbia University	University of California
University of Wisconsin	Johns Hopkins	University of Michigan
University of Illinois	University of Minnesota	Stanford University
University of Michigan	University of Washington	Illinois Institute of Technology
Stanford University	Yale University	University of Illinois
Harvard University	University of Chicago	Cornell University
Iowa State University	University of Wisconsin	Pennsylvania State University
Columbia University	University of Pennsylvania	Harvard University
University of Texas	University of Michigan	University of Pennsylvania
Ohio State University	University of Texas	Ohio State University
Princeton University	Stanford University	George Washington University
New York University	New York University	California Institute of Technology
Cornell University	State University of New York	University of Chicago
Number of institutions among 15 top producers of science doctorates	8	7

SOURCE: U.S. House of Representatives, Committee on Government Operations, *Conflicts between the Federal Research Programs and the Nation's Goals for Higher Education,* report of the subcommittee, 1965, p. 38.

National Science Foundation	National Aeronautics and Space Administration	Atomic Energy Commission
University of California	Massachusetts Institute of Technology	Columbia University
Stanford University	University of California	University of California
University of Illinois	University of Michigan	Massachusetts Institute of Technology
Harvard University	Princeton University	Yale University
University of Wisconsin	University of Chicago	University of Illinois
Cornell University	University of Maryland	California Institute of Technology
Massachusetts Institute of Technology	Stanford University	University of Rochester
Columbia University	Rice University	New York University
University of Minnesota	Harvard University	University of Washington
University of Chicago	Georgia Institute of Technology	Carnegie Institute of Technology
University of Michigan	University of Wisconsin	University of Michigan
California Institute of Technology	Texas A. & M. University	University of Wisconsin
University of Texas	Washington University	University of Chicago
University of Colorado	University of Florida	University of Minnesota
University of Washington	University of Alabama	Purdue University
10	7	8

Energy Commission combined accounted for 96 percent of total federal obligations for development.

Industrial firms are the largest performers of federally financed development (an estimated 73 percent in fiscal year 1968). Universities and colleges performed only 1 percent of federally financed development in 1968 (or 4 percent if federally funded R&D centers administered by colleges and universities are included) (Table 4.7-20).

RECIPIENTS OF FEDERAL FUNDS FOR RESEARCH AND SCIENCE EDUCATION
In fiscal year 1967 federal programs for the support of science education were budgeted at $140 million. Fellowships, traineeships, and institutes accounted for 64 percent of this $140 million (Table 4.7-21).

Table 4.7-22 shows the top 25 institutions of higher education receiving federal funds for research and science education from each of five principal federal agencies — the National Institutes of Health, the Department of Defense, the National Science Foundation, NASA, and the Atomic Energy Commission — in fiscal year 1964. (The top 25 institutions are not the same for each agency. There are a total of 54 institutions included in the top group of these five agencies.) The Massachusetts Institute of Technology is the leading recipient of federal funds for research and science education, followed by the University of California and Johns Hopkins University. The top dispensing agencies were the National Institutes of Health and the Department of Defense, which provided $577 million and $401 million, respectively, for research and science education.

Table 4.7-23 compares the top 15 producers of science doctorates with the 15 leading recipients of funds for research and science education for the above five agencies. There appears to be a strong correlation between these two lists.

4.8. Expenditures: Various Aspects

Throughout the period 1955–56 to 1975–76, expenditures of institutions of higher education, both public and private, have been projected to rise relatively more than those of public elementary and secondary schools. High projected enrollments and declines in student-teacher ratios (S-T-R) contribute to increased expenditures in both lower and higher education. However, if we choose a conservative estimate of enrollment and assume current S-T-R ratios, we should expect current expenditures for public schools to rise 4.7 times and for higher education, public and private combined, 8.6 times from 1955–56 to 1975–76 (Table 4.8-1).

Assuming improved S-T-R and high enrollment projections, plant expenditures of public schools can be expected to increase 75 percent and those of higher education 213 percent during this same period.

Similar trends were evident from 1950 to 1966, when the increase in expenditures at all levels of education amounted to 253 percent:

Current expenditures for education, by level and control, fiscal years 1950 and 1966 (expenditures in billions of dollars)	1950	1966	Percent increase
All education	10.94	38.52	253
Public	9.39	32.28	244
Private	1.55	6.24	303
Public elementary and secondary	4.71	22.01	367
Higher education			
Public	0.66	5.05	665
Private	0.83	3.45	316

SOURCE: Table 4.8-2.

TABLE 4.8-1 *Educational outlays (in billions of current dollars)*

			1970–71		1975–76	
Expenditures	1955–56	1965–66	A	B	A	B
*Present student/teacher ratios**						
Current funds	11.7	33.5	50.2	53.3	67.7	73.6
Public elementary/secondary	8.3	21.3	31.6	33.7	38.8	43.3
State administration	0.1	0.2	0.3	0.3	0.4	0.4
Higher education†	3.3	12.0	18.3	19.3	28.5	29.9
Capital funds	3.4	7.6	6.0	6.0	6.0	7.0
Public elementary/secondary	2.6	3.8	3.5	3.5	3.5	4.5
Higher education†	0.8	3.8	2.5	2.5	2.5	2.5
Improved student/teacher ratios‡						
Current funds	11.7	33.5		60.7		84.5
Public elementary/secondary	8.3	21.3		39.9		51.5
State administration	0.1	0.2		0.3		0.4
Higher education†	3.3	12.0		20.5		32.6
Capital funds	3.4	7.6		6.0		7.0
Public elementary/secondary	2.6	3.8		3.5		4.5
Higher education†	0.8	3.8		2.5		2.5

* Assumes continuation of present pupil/teacher ratios in elementary and secondary schools; in higher education assumes continuation of trend toward higher student/faculty ratio.
† Public and private.
‡ Assumes a 20 to 1 pupil/teacher ratio in elementary and secondary schools and improvement in student/faculty ratios in higher education to 1959 level.
NOTE: Column A refers to low enrollment and column B refers to higher enrollment projections.
SOURCE: U.S. Office of Education, *Education in the Seventies,* planning papers of the Office of Program Planning and Evaluation, May 1968, p. 6.

These figures clearly demonstrate the much greater increase in outlays on higher education, even though expenditures on private higher education rose less than those on public higher education and less than those on public elementary and secondary schools.

FEDERAL EXPENDITURES One of the factors responsible for the rapid rise in expenditures of institutions of higher education in the late 1950s and the greater part of the 1960s was the pronounced increase in federal expenditures on higher education. Until 1965, federal expenditures were chiefly for the support of academic science, particularly research and development, but from 1965 on expenditures for nonscience activities (chiefly student aid) represented an increasing proportion of the total (Table 4.8-3). However, academic science obligations continued to account for, by far, the greater part of federal expenditures in 1967.

OVERALL TRENDS The various sources of income of institutions of higher education have changed markedly in relative importance since the early part of the present century:

Number of times income of institutions of higher education increased, by source of income, 1909–10 and 1963–64*

Total current fund income	116
Educational and general	107
Student tuition and fees	98
Federal government	451
State government	100
Endowment income	20
Private gifts and grants	16

* For a more detailed analysis, see Chapter 4-1.

SOURCE: Adapted and calculated from U.S. Office of Education, *Higher Education Finances: Selected Trend and Summary Data,* National Center for Educational Statistics, June 1968, p. 3.

The relative contribution of government, especially of the federal government, has increased greatly, whereas the reverse has occurred with respect to the relative contribution of private sources, especially endowment income and gifts.

The pattern of increases of various types of expenditures from 1929–30 to 1963–64 was quite different:

Number of times expenditures of institutions of higher education increased, by type of expenditure, 1929–30 to 1963–64

Administration and general expense	21
Instruction and departmental research	12
Extension and public services	11
Library	24
Plant operation	10
Organized research	108

SOURCE: Adjusted and calculated from U.S. Office of Education data.

Organized research made the largest gains and plant operation the smallest in this period. However, the relatively large increase in expenditures for organized research was closely related to the comparatively large increase in federal government contributions as a source of income shown in the preceding table.

(Text continued on p. 816)

TABLE 4.8-2
Expenditures for education, selected fiscal years, 1949-50 to 1965-66 (amounts in millions)

Program	1949-50	1954-55	1959-60
Total amount	$10,936	$14,338	$22,079
Public expenditures†	9,388	11,999	18,409
Current	8,054	9,438	15,145
Elementary and secondary education	4,706	7,644	12,730
Higher education other than veterans'	659	1,094	2,010
Veterans'	2,689	700	405
Construction	1,334	2,561	3,264
Elementary and secondary education	1,019	2,362	2,869
Higher education	316	199	395
Private expenditures‡	1,548	2,339	3,670
Current	1,266	1,829	3,126
Elementary and secondary education	436	719	1,232
Higher education	830	1,110	1,894
Construction	282	510	544
Public expenditures as percent of—			
Total expenditures	85.8	83.7	83.4
Current expenditures	84.8	83.8	82.9
Elementary and secondary education	91.5	91.4	91.2
Higher education, total	80.1	68.4	56.0
Other than veterans'	41.7	56.8	51.5
Construction	82.5	83.4	85.7

* Preliminary estimates.

† Includes transfers to schools for supervision and training, aside from direct allowances for trainees, under the Manpower Development and Training Act, $147 million in 1965-66; work-study, $64 million; and adult basic education programs, $20 million, under the Economic Opportunity Act; and that portion of expenditures, excluding loans, under the Cuban refugee program that is used for education. Also included (in elementary and secondary education) are Economic Opportunity Act projects Headstart, $147 million in 1965-66, and Upward Bound, $20 million.

‡ Includes expenditures by privately controlled schools, and private expenditures in publicly controlled schools for current educational purposes, in the form of students' tuition and fees and private gifts.

SOURCE: Ida C. Merriam, "Social Welfare Expenditures, 1965-66," Social Security Bulletin, December 1966, table 9 and text, p. 18; in U.S. Congress, Joint Economic Committee, *Federal Programs for the Development of Human Resources,* a compilation of replies from departments and agencies of the U.S. Government to a questionnaire formulated by the Subcommittee on Economic Progress, 1966, p. 44.

1960–61	1961–62	1962–63	1963–64	1964–65	1965–66*
$23,712	$25,584	$27,745	$30,262	$34,424	$38,525
19,654	21,103	22,865	24,944	28,632	32,283
16,314	17,622	19,117	21,190	23,964	27,094
13,796	14,957	16,142	17,602	19,595	22,009
2,265	2,511	2,877	3,522	4,328	5,050
253	153	98	66	41	35
3,340	3,481	3,748	3,754	4,668	5,189
2,968	3,072	3,228	3,204	3,510	3,796
371	410	550	520	1,158	1,393
4,058	4,481	4,880	5,318	5,792	6,242
3,470	3,849	4,218	4,628	5,064	5,466
1,348	1,471	1,622	1,770	1,891	2,011
2,122	2,378	2,596	2,858	3,173	3,455
588	632	662	690	728	776
82.9	82.5	82.4	82.4	83.2	85.7
82.5	82.1	81.9	82.1	82.6	85.8
91.1	91.0	90.9	90.9	91.2	91.6
54.3	52.8	53.4	55.7	57.9	59.5
51.6	51.4	52.6	55.2	57.7	59.4
85.0	84.6	85.0	84.5	86.5	87.0

TABLE 4.8-3
Federal obligations to universities and colleges, by type of program, 1963–1967 (dollar amounts in millions)

| | Total obligations | | Academic science obligations | | | |
| | | | Total | | Research and development | |
Fiscal year	Amount	Percent change from previous year	Amount	Percent of total obligations	Amount	Percent of total obligations
1963	$1,413.0		$1,328.5	94.02	$ 829.5	58.71
1964	1,625.0	+15.00	1,528.6	94.07	975.6	60.04
1965	2,305.5	+41.88	1,816.2	78.78	1,095.0	47.49
1966	3,033.5	+31.58	2,187.0	72.10	1,275.7	42.05
1967	3,311.1	+ 9.15	2,323.8	70.18	1,324.1	39.99

SOURCE: National Science Foundation, *Federal Support to Universities and Colleges, Fiscal Year 1967,* 1968, p. 4.

TABLE 4.8-4
Current fund expenditures of institutions of higher education, by purpose and control, United States and outlying areas, 1963–64 (amounts in thousands of dollars)

| Purpose | Current-fund expenditure, Public and private | |
| | Amount | Percent |
(1)	(2)	(3)
Total current-fund expenditures	$9,224,988	100.0
Educational and general expenditures	7,466,390	80.9
General administration and general expense	964,213	10.5
Instruction and departmental research	2,820,631	30.6
Libraries	237,851	2.6
Physical plant operation and maintenance	689,327	7.5
Organized research	1,982,892	21.5
Other educational and general expenditures	771,475	8.4
Auxiliary enterprise expenditures	1,455,227	15.8
Student-aid expenditures	303,371	3.3

NOTE: Because of rounding, detail may not add to totals.
SOURCE: U.S. Department of Health, Education and Welfare, Office of Education, survey of "Financial Statistics of Institutions of Higher Education, 1963–64"; in U.S. Office of Education, *Digest of Educational Statistics, 1968,* 1968, p. 96.

R&D plant		Other		Nonscience activities	
Amount	*Percent of total obliga- tions*	*Amount*	*Percent of total obliga- tions*	*Amount*	*Percent of total obliga- tions*
$105.9	7.49	$393.1	27.82	$ 84.5	5.98
100.8	6.21	452.2	27.83	96.4	5.93
126.2	5.47	595.0	25.81	489.3	21.22
114.8	3.78	796.6	26.26	846.4	27.90
116.7	3.52	883.0	26.67	987.3	29.82

by control of institution

Public		Private	
Amount	*Percent*	*Amount*	*Percent*
(4)	*(5)*	*(6)*	*(7)*
$5,114,494	100.0	$4,110,494	100.0
4,199,775	82.1	3,266,615	79.5
456,034	8.9	508,179	12.4
1,713,395	33.5	1,107,236	26.9
132,994	2.6	104,857	2.6
392,106	7.7	297,221	7.2
935,906	18.3	1,046,986	25.5
569,340	11.1	202,135	4.9
804,222	15.7	651,005	15.8
110,498	2.2	192,874	4.7

Expenditures for various purposes are distributed differently in public and private institutions of higher education:

	Public	Private
Instruction and departmental research	33.5%	26.9%
Organized research	18.3	25.5
General administration and expense	8.9	12.4
Student aid	2.2	4.7

SOURCE: Table 4.8-4.

Private institutions spend relatively less on instruction and departmental research and relatively more on organized research and the other categories shown in the table than do public institutions. In part, the differences are explained by the larger ratio of graduate enrollment to total enrollment in private institutions.

As a share of current fund expenditures, education and general expenditures accounted for nearly two-thirds in 1955–56, but the trend has been downward (Table 4.8-5). Relative expenditures

TABLE 4.8-5 *Expenditures of institutions of higher education by type of expenditure, academic years 1955–56 and 1965–66*

Expenditure	1955–56*		1965–66†		Ratio: 1965–66 to 1955–56
	Millions of dollars	Percent of expenditure	Millions of dollars	Percent of expenditure	
All institutions					
Total expenditure	4,190		15,018		3.58
Current fund expenditures	3,379	100.0	11,993	100.0	3.55
Education and general‡	2,197	65.0	7,404	61.7	3.37
Organized research	506	15.0	2,190	18.3	4.33
Auxiliary enterprises	580	17.2	1,925	16.1	3.32
Student aid	96	2.8	474	3.9	4.94
Plant fund expenditure	811	100.0	3,026	100.0	3.73
Additions and replacement	753	93.0	2,657	87.8	3.52
Debt reduction	58	7.0	369	12.2	6.36

*Source: NCES.

† Estimated from a probability sample of 100 institutions which had filed financial reports by March 1967.

‡ Excluding organized research.

SOURCE: U.S. Office of Education, *Students and Buildings: An Analysis of Selected Federal Programs for Higher Education,* 1968, p. 10.

TABLE 4.8-6 *Higher education expenditures, projections to 1970 and 1975* (amounts in millions)*

| | Projection A—Low enrollment | | | | Projection B—High enrollment | | | |
| | Low faculty supply† | | High faculty supply‡ | | Low faculty supply† | | High faculty supply‡ | |
Expenditure category	1970	1975	1970	1975	1970	1975	1970	1975
Total expenditures	20,750.0	30,958.3	21,927.3	33,563.9	21,753.9	32,416.3	23,007.1	35,096.4
Current expenditures	18,250.0	28,458.3	19,427.3	31,063.9	19,253.9	29,916.3	20,507.1	32,596.4
Student education	9,035.7	13,828.8	10,213.0	16,434.4	9,681.3	14,784.8	10,934.5	17,464.9
General administration	1,807.1	2,765.8	2,042.6	3,286.9	1,936.3	2,957.0	2,186.9	3,493.0
Instruction	5,423.3	7,973.9	6,365.1	10,058.4	5,818.2	8,569.4	6,820.8	10,713.5
Faculty salaries	(4,609.8)	(6,777.8)	(5,410.3)	(8,549.6)	(4,945.5)	(7,284.0)	(5,797.7)	(9,106.5)
Other	(813.5)	(1,196.1)	(954.8)	(1,508.8)	(872.7)	(1,285.4)	(1,023.1)	(1,607.0)
Libraries	658.7	1,324.9	658.7	1,324.9	704.3	1,395.3	704.3	1,395.3
Plant operation and maintenance	1,146.6	1,764.2	1,146.6	1,764.2	1,222.5	1,863.1	1,222.5	1,863.1
Organized research	3,699.3	5,435.5	3,699.3	5,435.5	3,699.3	5,435.5	3,699.3	5,435.5
Related activities	904.1	1,359.5	904.1	1,359.5	963.4	1,435.0	963.4	1,435.0
Extension	879.6	1,769.1	879.6	1,769.1	936.8	1,863.1	936.8	1,863.1
Auxiliary services	2,892.6	4,450.6	2,892.6	4,450.6	3,082.8	4,693.4	3,082.8	4,693.4
Student aid	838.7	1,614.8	838.7	1,614.8	890.3	1,704.5	890.3	1,704.5
Plant	2,500.0	2,500.0	2,500.0	2,500.0	2,500.0	2,500.0	2,500.0	2,500.0

* Refers to academic year 1970–71 and 1975–76. All fiscal data are in current dollars.

† Assumes a continuation of the trend in student/faculty ratio.

‡ Assumes a lower student/faculty ratio of 13.5/1.

NOTE: Details may not add to totals because of rounding.

SOURCE: U.S. Office of Education, *Education in the Seventies,* planning papers of the Office of Program Planning and Evaluation, May 1968, p. 44.

for students' education have been projected to fall somewhat and those for organized research, auxiliary expenses, and student aid to rise somewhat to 1977–78. Projections on the basis of various alternative assumptions to 1975 are presented in Table 4.8-6.

BREAKDOWN BY CATEGORIES AND STATES

The distribution of expenditures varies greatly from state to state, as the following table shows in the case of four selected states:

Current fund expenditures of institutions of higher education, by purpose and by state, 1963–64 (all states and four states, percentage of national and state totals)

	General administration and general expense	*Instruction and departmental research*	*Libraries*	*Physical plant operation and maintenance*	*Organized research*	*Auxiliary enterprises*	*Student aid expenditures*
United States	10	31	3	7	22	16	3
California	8	25	2	5	46	8	2
Mississippi	9	29	2	7	9	27	2
Missouri	12	32	3	8	13	17	3
New York	14	35	3	9	17	12	4

SOURCE: Adapted and calculated from U.S. Office of Education, *Digest of Educational Statistics, 1968,* 1968, p. 94.

TABLE 4.8-7
Expenditures of institutions of higher education, by purpose and by source of funds, 1956 and 1966 (amounts in millions)

	Current funds				
Year, by source	*Student education (1)*	*Organized research (2)*	*Extension and public service (3)*	*Related activities (4)*	*Auxiliary service (5)*
1956 total	1,788.6	545.0	141.2	208.7	599.6
Federal	86.0	356.6	46.5	1.0	4.2
State	676.5	70.3	38.2	82.0	
Local	85.7	8.4	4.5	9.9	
Other	940.4	109.7	52.0	115.8	595.4
1966 total	6,120.6	2,517.7	437.3	601.3	1,880.0
Federal	612.1	1,940.7	100.5	12.0	20.2
State	2,197.3	219.1	141.5	236.3	
Local	257.0	29.7	16.8	29.5	
Other	3,054.2	328.2	178.5	323.5	1,859.8

SOURCE: U.S. Office of Education, *Education in the Seventies,* planning papers of the Office of Program Planning and Evaluation, May 1968, p. 27.

California is considered a rich state with large public subsidies; Mississippi, an impoverished state with some public support; Missouri, an average state typical of the Midwest, where state subsidies are of some importance; and finally, New York, rich, but with limited, though expanding, public support.

California makes relatively large outlays for organized research, but expenditures are comparatively low in all other major categories, in part because of heavy involvement in research. Mississippi spends heavily for bread and butter items, e.g., instruction and auxiliary, but also makes relatively heavy expenditures on auxiliary enterprises. Missouri's administrative and instructional outlays are large, but research receives modest funding. New York is strong on instructional expenditures, relative to California, and, though heavily involved in research, spends far less than California in this area. New York's low relative auxiliary enterprise expenditures are related to the large number of commuters; its comparatively high student-aid expenditures are associated with the relatively modest role played by public higher education in New York until recently.

BY PURPOSES AND SOURCES OF FUNDS From 1956 to 1966, total expenditures of institutions of higher education rose from $4.1 billion to $15 billion, an increase of 258

Student aid (6)	Total current (7)	Plant funds (8)	Total expenditures (9)
95.6	3,378.7	811.3	4,190.0
11.6	505.9	149.2	655.1
33.7	900.7	257.6	1,158.3
4.0	112.5	17.3	129.8
46.3	1,859.6	387.2	2,246.8
435.6	11,992.5	3,025.9	15,018.4
98.5	2,784.0	754.6	3,538.6
142.4	2,936.6	795.0	3,731.6
17.3	350.3	64.0	414.3
177.4	5,921.6	1,412.3	7,333.9

percent (Table 4.8-7). In these years, federal outlays rose 440 percent, state expenditures about 220 percent, relatively unimportant local outlays also about 220 percent, and other sources 226 percent:

Percentage increase in expenditures of institutions of higher education by purpose and source, 1956 to 1966

	Student education	Organized research	Auxiliary service	Student aid	Total current	Plant funds	Total expenditures
Total	242	362	214	356	255	273	258
Federal	612	444	381	749	450	406	440
State	225	212		323	226	209	222
Local	200	254		332	211	270	219
Others	225	199	212	283	218	265	226

SOURCE: Adapted from Table 4.8-7.

Expenditure trends by sources of income varied greatly from 1956 to 1966. In the case of student education, the percentage increase in federal contributions far exceeded those from other sources. There were also comparatively large increases in the federal government's contributions to organized research and to auxiliary services. Even more pronounced was the percentage increase in federal contributions to student aid, and here again the percentage increase in federal expenditures exceeded those from other sources. The increase in federal contributions to plant funds was also comparatively pronounced. Large federal contributions undoubtedly inhibit contributions from other sources, at least to some degree. Thus, as the federal government increased its *share* of student aid expenditures, the share of state governments dropped somewhat.

From 1956 to 1966, the relative increase in expenditures of the federal government for higher education was roughly twice as great as that of the other three sources of finance. It is also interesting to note that, in the case of organized research, the federal government accounted for $1.58 billion of a total increase of $1.97 billion, or for 80 percent (Table 4.8-7). Large contributions of the federal government tended to restrain other classes of contributions, while at the same time inducing a net increase in total outlays for research.

In general, increasing federal aid to higher education has been correlated with relatively declining contributions from other sources. A comparison of contributions by federal and state governments is helpful here:

Percentage of contributions by federal and state governments, 1956 and 1966, by purpose

	Federal government		State government	
	1956	*1966*	*1956*	*1966*
All	16	24	28	25
Student education	5	10	38	36
Organized research	65	77	13	9
Student aid	12	23	35	44

SOURCE: Adapted and calculated from Table 4.8-7.

An even more pronounced change in relative sources of funds is revealed if we compare *expenditures* by source in 1956 and 1968 (the previous table related to *income*):

Expenditures of institutions of higher education by sources of funds, 1956 and 1968 (percentage of total)

	Federal	*State*	*Local*	*Other*
1956	12.1	26.5	3.0	58.4
1968	24.0	23.0	2.2	50.8

SOURCE: U.S. Department of Health, Education and Welfare: *Trends,* 1966–67 edition, 1968, part 1, p. S-78.

Here one notes the large additional relative responsibilities assumed by the federal government, along with large relative declines for other levels of government and other sources. Whereas the federal share of expenditures doubled, the share of state and local governments (combined) fell from 29.5 to 25.2 percent, and the share of other sources declined from 58.4 to 50.8 percent. The increase in the federal share was much larger for private than for public institutions of higher education—from 12.8 to 29.9 percent for the private institutions and from 11.5 to 19.5 percent for the public institutions (data not shown).

BY CATEGORY AND BY TYPE OF INSTITUTION

It is clear that, as the size of institutions of higher education increases, the percentage of educational and general expense going to general administration, instruction, operating and maintenance expenses, and libraries all drop substantially. But relative outlays on organized research, extension and public services, and organized activities relating to educational departments increase. These relationships are indicated in the following table, which compares a hypothetical public institution with educational and general expenditures of $1 million with a typical public institution having educational and general expenditures of $30 million, and similarly for two hypothetical private institutions in 1959–60:

Educational and general expenditures, 1959–60, by categories and size	*Public*		*Private*	
Percent for E.G.E. with	< *$1 M.*	> *$30 M.*	< *$1 M.*	> *$30 M.*
Administration	15.9	7.7	26.2	9.3
Instruction	60.2	30.2	50.2	22.1
Libraries	3.9	2.3	4.7	2.2
Operation and maintenance of plant	17.1	7.3	16.7	6.1
Organized research	0.1	36.3	0.4	54.8
Extension and public service	1.1	7.7	0.5	0.6
Organized activities	1.6	8.2	1.3	5.0

SOURCE: F. H. I. Lindsay, *Financial Statistics of Institutions of Higher Education: Receipts, Expenditures, and Property, 1959–60,* U.S. Office of Education, National Center for Educational Statistics, 1964, p. 78.

The distribution of expenditures does not differ very much between the public and private institutions, although the private institutions do not participate to any great extent in extension and public services.

Similar trends are evident on the basis of degree-credit enrollment. Thus an institution of higher education with degree-credit enrollment of 1 to 199 allots almost 60 percent of its educational and general expenditures for instruction, whereas an institution of higher education with enrollment of 10,000 to 19,999 allots only about 30 percent.[1]

The breakdown of current expenditures varies with the size and type of institution of higher education. The institution's structure is determined both by size and the services rendered. Variations by type of institution in 1959–60 were as follows:

[1] F. H. I. Lindsay, *Financial Statistics of Institutions of Higher Education: Receipts, Expenditures, and Property, 1959–60,* U.S. Office of Education, National Center for Educational Statistics, 1964, pp. 79–80. See this document for breakdown by important categories related to enrollments.

Percentage of current expenditures by categories of expenditures and by type of institution, 1959–60	All	Univer-sities	Liberal arts colleges	Teachers colleges	Techno-logical	Theo-logical
Administration	10.4	7.9	15.9	11.5	10.8	19.0
Instruction	32.0	28.1	36.9	44.6	26.7	35.3
Plant	8.4	6.7	10.7	12.1	9.9	12.4
Organized research	18.2	25.3	1.9	0.6	35.8	0.2

SOURCE: Adapted from F. H. I. Lindsay, *Financial Statistics of Institutions of Higher Education: Receipts, Expenditures, and Property, 1959–60,* U.S. Office of Education, National Center for Educational Statistics, 1964, pp. 53–57, which includes a breakdown by control.

PER STUDENT The trend has been upwards. Since 1930 expenditures per resident student have increased. Despite the increasing number of students per institution and the deflationary economy of the 1930s, from 1930 to 1950 expenditures per student for all institutions rose 50 percent—51 percent in public and 49 percent in private institutions. By type of institution, expenditures per student rose 57 percent in universities, 39 percent in liberal arts colleges, 46 percent in professional schools, and 62 percent in junior colleges. In constant dollars, however, expenditures per student actually declined by a few percentage points from 1930 to 1950, although there was no net change for universities and an increase for junior colleges of 4 percent. Liberal arts colleges experienced a decline of more than 10 percent. In view of the large gains in per capita income (current and real dollars) these trends reflected a lag of expenditures behind the improved standards of the economy. (Per capita disposable income rose by about one-third between 1930 and 1950.)[2]

By 1960, the adjustment to rising prices and per capita income had greatly improved. Thus, whereas expenditures per resident student for educational and general purposes were only $488 in 1950, by 1960 the figure was $1,515, with a maximum of $3,442 at technological schools and a minimum of $580 in junior colleges.[3] (But in part the difference is explained by the fact that the 1960 figures are for full-time equivalent students. The 1960 figure reduces part-time students to their full-time equivalent and thus

[2] J. D. Millett, *Financing Higher Education in the United States,* Columbia University Press, New York, 1952, pp. 113, 116, and 140.

[3] F. H. I. Lindsay, *Financial Statistics of Institutions of Higher Education: Receipts, Expenditures, and Property, 1959–60,* U.S. Office of Education, National Center for Educational Statistics, 1964, p. 51.

TABLE 4.8-8
Enrollment,
educational
and general
expenditures,
and expenditures
per student, by
control and
level of
institution,
aggregate
United States,*
fiscal years
1965–66 and
1966–67

Control and level of institution	Total enrollment			1965–66
	1965–66	1966–67	Percent increase	
All institutions	5,967,411	6,438,477	8	$10,003,996
Total	3,999,940	4,381,086	10	5,795,253
Universities	1,657,447	1,778,640	7	3,942,519
Public				
Other four-year	1,299,115	1,410,664	9	1,294,662
Two-year	1,043,378	1,191,782	14	558,072
Total	1,967,471	2,057,391	5	4,208,743
Universities	674,688	703,396	4	2,153,522
Private				
Other four-year	1,159,309	1,214,921	5	1,939,401
Two-year	133,474	139,074	4	115,820

*Aggregate United States includes the 50 states, the District of Columbia, United States service schools separately grouped, and outlying areas.

† Increase unless otherwise indicated.

SOURCE: U.S. Office of Education, *Financial Statistics of Institutions of Higher Education: Current Funds, Revenues, and Expenditures, 1966–67,* 1969, p. 10.

the outlay is per full-time student instead of the more numerous part-time student, not corrected to full-time equivalency, of the years 1930 to 1950.)

From 1965–66 to 1966–67, the ratio of the percentage increase in expenditures to the percentage increase in enrollment was 14/8 for all institutions of higher education (Table 4.8-8). In other words, expenditures rose 14 percent and enrollment rose 8 percent. As the ratio of expenditures to enrollment (E/E) rises, unit costs increase. However, there was wide variation among types of institutions. Extremes were 25/9 for other four-year public institutions, 15/4 for public universities, 16/4 for two-year private institutions, and 3/5 for private other four-year institutions. In percentage terms, the largest increase in unit costs was 15 percent for public other four-year institutions.

A gloomy forecast for the financial state of private institutions of higher education has recently been offered by Provost William

Educational and general expenditures (in thousands of dollars)		Average expenditures per student		
1966–67	Percent increase	1965–66	1966–67	Amount of change†
$11,409,979	14	$1,676	$1,772	$ 96
6,796,105	17	1,449	1,551	102
4,479,215	14	2,379	2,518	139
1,622,741	25	997	1,150	153
694,149	24	535	582	47
4,613,873	10	2,139	2,243	104
2,481,611	15	3,192	3,528	336
1,997,701	3	1,673	1,644	−29
134,561	16	868	968	100

Bowen of Princeton University,[4] who asserts that the major cause of impending trouble is the fact that unit costs of private institutions of higher education tend to rise more rapidly than the cost of living. This comparison in itself may be misleading, for allowance should be made for the fact that per capita income has tended to rise more rapidly than the cost of living. But Bowen's data do imply that the rise in income of institutions of higher education has tended to reflect the gains in per capita or per family income. He finds that from 1952 to 1964, the rise in total educational and general expenditures per year *averaged* 12 percent for all universities and 10.9 percent for all private universities, while from 1952 to 1966 the increase averaged 13.9 for Chicago, Vanderbilt, and Princeton. However, particularly disturbing is the large excess of the rate of

[4] William G. Bowen, *The Economics of the Major Private Universities,* Carnegie Commission on Higher Education, Berkeley, Calif., 1968, pp. 8–19, 23, and 54.

TABLE 4.8-9
Trends in direct
costs per
student,
compared with
an economywide
cost index,
selected periods,
1905–1966

Time period	Average annual percentage increase (compound rate)*	
	Direct costs per student at Chicago-Princeton-Vanderbilt†	Economywide cost index
Long-period comparison		
1905–1966	5.2	2.1
Wartime inflations:		
1915–1920	0.8	4.0
1940–1948	1.8	7.7
Depressions:		
1930–1940	0.0	−1.0
"Normal," peacetime periods:		
1905–1915	8.1	1.5
1920–1925‡	7.7	1.5
1949–1966	7.5	2.2

* Calculated between terminal years.
† Chicago is included in the average only for the years since 1955–56.
‡ The rate for the cost index is based on the years 1921 to 1925, to avoid using 1920, when there was an extraordinary peak in the series, as a terminal year.

SOURCE: W. G. Bowen, *The Economics of the Major Private Universities,* Carnegie Commission on Higher Education, Berkeley, Calif. 1968, p. 19.

increase in costs per student at Chicago, Vanderbilt, and Princeton (combined) over costs for the economy as a whole during the long period of years from 1905 to 1966 (Table 4.8-9). Direct costs per student at the three institutions rose at an annual average rate of 5.2 percent, while the cost of living rose at a rate of only 2.1 percent. Bowen projects a deficit of $19.8 million on the basis of a high-income projection and of $27.8 million on the basis of a lower income projection for a typical major private university by 1975–76. Costs tend to rise in relation to income.

As noted elsewhere, institutions of higher education are especially sensitive to inflationary pressures. In wartime inflationary periods, increases in direct costs per student tend to lag behind increases in the price level. However, in peacetime periods, costs tend to rise much more than the general price level. For example, from 1949 to 1966, direct costs per student at Chicago, Vanderbilt, and Princeton (combined) rose at an annual average rate of 7.5

percent, as compared with a 2.2 percent increase in the cost of living.

In Chapter 4.2, we commented on the concentration of federal funds among a relatively limited number of institutions of higher education. The theme merits repetition here: in 1967, of 2,056 institutions of higher education, only 360 (17.5 percent) benefited from federal obligations of $1 million or more (Table 4.8-10).

TABLE 4.8-10
Number of universities and colleges receiving federal obligations, ranked by size of federal program, 1967

Size of federal program	Number of institutions	Percent distribution
TOTAL	2,056	100.00
$10 million or more	85	4.13
$5 million to $9.9 million	53	2.58
$1 million to $4.9 million	222	10.80
$500,000 to $999,000	213	10.36
$100,000 to $499,000	611	29.72
Less than $100,000	872	42.41

SOURCE: National Science Foundation, *Federal Support to Universities and Colleges, Fiscal Year 1967,* 1968, p. 23.

4.9. The Burden
of Educational Finance

This chapter deals selectively with some of the burdens of financing higher education. The burden on students is discussed in the chapters on student aid and student expenses.

At the White House Conference on Education in the early 1960s, the participants considered the nation's ability and effort to finance the public schools. Ability was related to per capita personal income, to personal income per child of school age (5 to 17), and to personal income per pupil enrolled in public elementary and secondary schools. Support was measured by the estimated current expenditures for public schools per pupil in attendance, and effort was measured by total school revenue as a percentage of personal income. We will use some of these same measures in discussing the nation's ability to finance higher education (although some adjustments should be made, such as considering personal income per youth of college age instead of personal income per child of school age).

STATES'
ABILITY AND
EFFORTS TO
FINANCE
EDUCATION

Table 4.9-1 gives several measures of the ability and effort of the 50 states to finance public schools. One measure of ability is personal income per child of school age (5 to 17). In 1963 the average personal income per child of school age for the country as a whole was $9,605. But personal income per child of school age varied widely by state. Nevada ($13,944) and New York ($13,253) had the highest personal incomes per child of school age, while South Carolina ($5,455) and Mississippi ($4,851) had the lowest.

A measure of support is the estimated current expenditures for public schools per pupil in attendance. In 1963–64 this measure of support varied from $705 for New York to $241 for Mississippi.

A frequently used measure of effort is total public school revenue as a percentage of personal income. In 1962–63 this measure

(Text continued on p. 834)

	Ability to finance public schools				
State (1)	Per capita personal income (1962) (2)	State rank (3)	Personal income per child of school age (5–17) 1963 (4)	State rank (5)	Personal income (1962) per pupil enrolled in public elementary and secondary schools in 1962 (6)
United States	$2,366		$ 9,605		$11,580
North New England					
Maine	1,917	38	7,386	35	9,144
New Hampshire	2,206	26	9,256	18	12,294
Vermont	2,005	36	8,079	30	10,381
South New England					
Massachusetts	2,769	8	12,330	6	15,457
Rhode Island	2,372	16	10,663	10	14,854
Connecticut	3,089	3	13,110	3	15,930
Middle Atlantic					
New York	2,930	4	13,253	2	17,770
New Jersey	2,887	6	12,632	4	15,930
Pennsylvania	2,363	18	10,213	13	13,361
Delaware	3,102	2	12,476	5	16,592
Maryland	2,683	9	10,889	9	13,263
East North Central					
Ohio	2,392	14	9,522	15	11,858
Indiana	2,350	19	9,408	17	11,025
Illinois	2,844	7	11,800	8	15,588
Michigan	2,416	12	9,430	16	11,129
Wisconsin	2,283	21	8,901	22	12,325
West North Central					
Minnesota	2,236	24	8,786	26	10,825
Iowa	2,189	27	8,842	25	10,433
Missouri	2,384	15	10,396	12	12,409
North Dakota	2,273	22	7,701	38	9,515
South Dakota	1,065	32	7,265	36	8,911
Nebraska	2,270	23	8,976	21	11,138

TABLE 4.9-1
Ability and effort to finance public schools in the 50 states

	Level of financial support		*Effort**		
			Total public school revenue, 1962–63 as percent of personal income, 1962		*Nonpublic school enrollment as percentage of total elementary and secondary school enrollment 1960*
State rank (7)	*Estimated current expenditures for public schools per pupil in attendance 1963–64 (8)*	*State rank (9)*	*(10)*	*State rank (11)*	*(12)*
	$455		4.3		13.6
34	378	38	4.3	28	14.7
15	427	27	3.5	46	23.9
27	387	36	4.5	20	19.3
6	475	17	2.8	50	22.2
7	500	10	3.5	47	27.9
3	552	4	3.7	43	17.7
1	705	1	4.2	30	22.6
3	568	3	3.8	41	21.1
11	485	15	3.9	36	23.5
2	498	11	4.3	26	18.1
12	489	14	3.8	42	17.2
16	446	25	4.6	16	14.8
19	467	18	4.4	21	11.3
5	479	16	3.7	44	21.9
18	452	23	4.6	18	15.5
14	498	12	4.0	34	25.8
21	509	9	5.3	8	18.9
26	456	21	4.7	15	13.3
13	419	29	3.4	48	15.8
32	420	28	4.1	35	12.4
36	403	30	4.3	27	10.5
17	385	37	3.6	45	15.3

TABLE 4. 9-1
(continued)

State (1)	Per capita personal income (1962) (2)	State rank (3)	Personal income per child of school age (5–17) 1963 (4)	State rank (5)	Personal income (1962) per pupil enrolled in public elementary and secondary schools in 1962 (6)
West North Central cont.:					
Kansas	2,188	28	8,741	27	9,894
South Atlantic					
Virginia	2,018	34	8,000	29	9,554
West Virginia	1,810	41	6,766	44	7,536
North Carolina	1,732	43	6,593	42	7,357
South Carolina	1,545	48	5,455	49	6,290
Georgia	1,759	42	6,961	39	7,497
Florida	2,044	33	8,852	24	10,583
East South Central					
Kentucky	1,712	44	6,793	43	8,365
Tennessee	1,702	46	6,898	41	7,622
Alabama	1,567	47	5,966	48	6,590
Mississippi	1,285	50	4,851	50	5,410
West South Central					
Arkansas	1,504	49	6,175	47	6,622
Louisiana	1,705	45	6,381	46	7,741
Oklahoma	1,905	39	7,977	31	8,468
Texas	2,013	35	7,521	34	9,119
Mountain					
Montana	2,207	25	7,876	33	9,908
Idaho	1,941	37	6,930	40	8,151
Wyoming	2,164	29	8,347	28	9,899
Colorado	2,370	17	9,155	20	10,779
New Mexico	1,824	40	6,468	45	8,022
Arizona	2,097	30	7,906	32	9,243
Utah	2,084	31	7,217	37	7,900
Nevada	3,278	1	13,944	1	14,652

Ability to finance public schools

	Level of financial support			Effort*	
State rank (7)	*Estimated current expenditures for public schools per pupil in attendance 1963–64* (8)	*State rank* (9)	*Total public school revenue, 1962–63 as per- cent of personal income, 1962* (10)	*State rank* (11)	*Nonpublic school enrollment as percentage of total elementary and secon- dary school enrollment 1960* (12)
30	448	24	4.9	12	9.2
31	350	40	3.9	37	6.4
44	300	46	4.2	31	3.5
46	320	41	4.4	24	1.4
49	265	49	4.6	17	2.5
45	306	43	4.2	29	3.0
25	388	34	4.1	32	6.7
38	300	45	3.8	40	11.9
43	291	47	3.8	39	4.1
48	280	48	3.8	38	3.8
50	241	50	5.3	5	3.1
47	302	44	4.4	23	2.7
42	399	32	5.4	3	15.9
37	351	39	4.4	22	3.6
35	387	35	4.6	19	6.5
28	493	13	5.2	9	11.8
39	316	42	4.3	25	4.7
29	540	6	5.3	7	4.8
22	460	20	4.8	14	9.5
40	440	26	5.4	2	9.9
33	455	22	5.1	10	9.2
41	394	33	5.8	1	2.6
8	464	19	3.4	49	5.8

TABLE 4.9-1
(continued)

State	Ability to finance public schools				
	Per capita personal income (1962)	State rank	Personal income per child of school age (5-17) 1963	State rank	Personal income (1962) per pupil enrolled in public elementary and secondary schools in 1962
State (1)	(2)	(3)	(4)	(5)	(6)
Pacific					
Washington	2,485	11	9,525	14	10,952
Oregon	2,333	20	9,184	19	10,775
California	2,898	5	11,932	7	13,498
Alaska†	2,667	10	10,754	11	13,573
Hawaii	2,403	13	8,868	23	10,700

*In column 10 "Total public school revenue" includes varying and inconsistent amounts of federal funds, since methods of designating federal funds received and expended vary from state to state. This would tend to cause possible distortions in the evaluation of the "effort" made by the states. However, the average United States figure for revenue receipts from federal sources for the 1962–63 year is estimated at 3.6 percent of the total. This average United States figure has remained generally the same since 1955–56, at about 4 percent of total revenue receipts. Only Alaska, Hawaii, and New Mexico were above 10 percent. Column 12, "Nonpublic school enrollment," is included to correct possible distortion of the "Effort" column. There are eight states which have a range of 21.1 to 27.9% of their total elementary and secondary school enrollments in nonpublic schools. While these children are not in public schools, and therefore do not involve public tax effort, they do have to be paid for privately. Accordingly, other things being equal, the tax efforts with states with a high percentage of nonpublic school pupils will be lower than those with a low percentage of such pupils.

varied from 5.8 percent for Utah to 2.8 percent for Massachusetts. Another indication of effort is given by state and local taxes as a percentage of personal income (Table 4.9-2). In 1957 this measure of effort varied from 11.7 percent for North Dakota to 4.9 percent for Delaware. Note that Mississippi, which ranked last in personal income per child of school age (in 1963), is the second most heavily taxed state in relation to personal income.

In 1965–66 per capita expenditures for education by state and local governments ranged from $276 for Alaska to $118 for Mississippi and South Carolina (Table 4.9-3). The states with the highest per capita expenditures for education were mainly those

	Level of financial support			Effort*		
State rank (7)	Estimated current expenditures for public schools per pupil in attendance 1963–64 (8)	State rank (9)	Total public school revenue, 1962–63 as per- cent of personal income, 1962 (10)	State rank (11)	Nonpublic school enrollment as percentage of total elementary and secon- dary school enrollment 1960 (12)
20	515	8	4.8	13	8.0
23	549	5	5.3	6	8.3
10	530	7	5.0	11	9.8
9	634	2	5.3	4	4.4
24	402	31	4.1	33	16.6

† Because of the relative purchasing power of the dollar in Alaska, dollar amounts for that state should be reduced by about one-fourth to make them roughly comparable to those of other states.

SOURCES: Columns 2, 3, 8, 9, 10, 11—*Rankings of the States,* 1964; Research Report, 1964-R1, Research Division, National Education Association, Washington, D.C., January 1964, pp. 28, 46, 38. Column 12—*Rankings of the States,* 1963; Research Report, 1963-R1, Research Division, National Education Association, Washington, D.C., January 1963, p. 21. Column 4—*Digest of Educational Statistics,* 1964, U.S. Department of Health, Education and Welfare, Office of Education, Washington, D.C., p. 67. Column 6—*Survey of Current Business,* U.S. Department of Commerce, Office of Business Economics, Washington, D.C., August 1964, p. 16; and *Digest of Educational Statistics,* 1963, U.S. Department of Health, Education and Welfare, Washington, D.C., Office of Education, p. 4. In U.S. Senate, Committee on Labor and Public Welfare, *White House Conference on Education,* prepared for the Subcommittee on Education, 1965, p. 56.

with small populations. The states with the smallest per capita expenditures on education were generally poor Southern states.

Table 4.9-4 shows state and local government revenues and expenditures for selected fiscal years from 1927 to 1964. From 1950 to 1964–65, state and local government expenditures for education increased by 304 percent, while the revenues of state and local governments increased by only 256 percent.

THE BURDEN ON THE STATES   Table 4.9-5 gives some measures of the burden on the states of financing public higher education in 1958. State and local government expenditures for public institutions of higher education as a

State	State tax revenues		State and local taxes	
	As a percentage of personal income	Ranking	As a percentage of personal income	Ranking
Alabama	5.51	14	7.67	36
Arizona	5.38	16	9.21	19
Arkansas	6.16	7	8.77	27
California	4.66	27	9.42	14
Colorado	4.59	29	9.41	16
Connecticut	3.58	40	7.27	42
Delaware	3.72	37	4.90	48
Florida	4.99	21	8.86	25
Georgia	5.82	9	8.69	28
Idaho	4.86	23	9.62	11
Illinois	2.93	46	7.34	41
Indiana	3.27	42	7.01	45
Iowa	4.90	22	9.68	9
Kansas	4.14	33	9.66	10
Kentucky	4.82	24	7.79	34
Louisiana	7.76	1	10.37	4
Maine	4.50	30	8.97	22
Maryland	4.02	35	7.39	40
Massachusetts	3.64	39	8.96	23
Michigan	4.62	28	8.36	31
Minnesota	4.76	26	9.76	8
Mississippi	7.67	2	11.20	2
Missouri	3.22	44	6.70	47
Montana	4.17	32	9.93	7
Nebraska	2.79	47	7.62	37
Nevada	5.45	15	9.21	18
New Hampshire	3.12	45	8.18	31
New Jersey	1.99	48	7.03	44
New Mexico	6.94	3	9.16	20
New York	3.52	41	9.09	21
North Carolina	6.24	6	8.49	28
North Dakota	5.60	12	11.67	1
Ohio	3.26	43	6.77	46
Oklahoma	6.39	5	9.40	17

	State tax revenues		State and local taxes	
TABLE 4.9-2 *(continued)*				
State	As a percentage of personal income	Ranking	As a percentage of personal income	Ranking
Oregon	5.73	10	10.33	6
Pennsylvania	4.22	31	7.62	38
Rhode Island	3.65	38	7.59	39
South Carolina	6.59	4	8.79	26
South Dakota	3.97	36	10.49	3
Tennessee	5.61	11	8.44	30
Texas	4.03	34	7.69	35
Utah	5.32	17	9.48	13
Vermont	5.58	13	10.36	5
Virginia	5.01	20	7.80	33
Washington	6.13	8	8.87	24
West Virginia	5.05	19	7.17	43
Wisconsin	4.80	25	9.56	12
Wyoming	5.20	18	9.42	15

SOURCE: Dexter M. Keezer (ed.), *Financing Higher Education 1960–70.* McGraw-Hill, New York, 1959, p. 63 (by S. E. H.); and U.S. Census, *Compendium of Government Finances, 1957 Census of Governments,* p. 61; in S. E. Harris, *Higher Education: Resources and Finance,* McGraw-Hill Book Company, New York, 1962, p. 349.

percentage of personal income are shown in column 5 of the table. This measure of effort varied from 1.6 percent for Utah to 0.2 percent for Pennsylvania, New York, New Jersey, and Massachusetts. Column 8 of Table 4.9-5 shows adjusted expenditures per student by public institutions of higher education as a percentage of per capita personal income. This figure varied from 84.4 percent for Vermont and Virginia to 29.7 percent for Arizona and 29.4 percent for California.

In a master table for the late 1950s (Table 4.9-6), 12 crucial variables have been put together that relate to (1) the burden of financing higher education, (2) capacity, (3) effort, (4) achievement, and (5) supplementary data. Each state is graded from A+ to E. (The meaning of the grades is given in the table.) To clarify this table, California will be discussed as an example.

(Text continued on p. 844)

TABLE 4.9-3 *Direct expenditures of state and local governments for all functions and for education, by per capita amount and percentage of per capita income, 1965–66*

State (1)	Per capita personal income, 1965 (2)	Direct general expenditures, 1965–66			
		All functions		Education	
		Amount per capita (3)	Percentage of per capita income* (4)	Amount per capita (5)	Percentage of per capita income* (6)
United States	$2,760	$422.97	15.32	$169.95	6.16
Alabama	1,922	341.57	17.77	134.49	7.00
Alaska	3,194	922.64	28.89	275.98	8.64
Arizona	2,371	465.20	19.62	210.21	8.87
Arkansas	1,843	322.90	17.52	122.75	6.66
California	3,261	583.37	17.89	219.10	6.72
Colorado	2,707	513.96	18.99	234.37	8.66
Connecticut	3,430	427.74	12.47	150.87	4.40
Delaware	3,356	578.66	17.24	228.18	6.80
District of Columbia	3,687	517.60	14.04	120.03	3.26
Florida	2,438	379.41	15.56	145.97	5.99
Georgia	2,174	333.15	15.32	132.35	6.09
Hawaii	2,882	564.11	19.57	187.61	6.51
Idaho	2,398	422.15	17.60	162.22	6.76
Illinois	3,302	381.53	11.55	162.24	4.91
Indiana	2,867	383.98	13.39	195.53	6.82
Iowa	2,727	433.47	15.90	198.62	7.28
Kansas	2,669	402.69	15.09	171.57	6.43
Kentucky	2,053	341.49	16.63	129.85	6.32
Louisiana	2,085	415.88	19.95	148.75	7.13
Maine	2,305	346.00	15.01	120.99	5.25
Maryland	3,022	414.20	13.71	172.78	5.72
Massachusetts	3,067	429.97	14.02	133.32	4.35
Michigan	3,060	447.18	14.61	206.40	6.75
Minnesota	2,666	476.04	17.86	197.77	7.42
Mississippi	1,625	326.09	20.07	117.82	7.25

*Percentages were computed by the Office of Education.
SOURCE: U.S. Department of Commerce, Office of Business Economics, "Survey of Current Business," April 1968; and Bureau of the Census, "Governmental Finances in 1965–66," Series GF, No. 13; in U.S. Office of Education, *Digest of Educational Statistics, 1968,* 1968, table 24, p. 21.

| | | Direct general expenditures, 1965–66 | | | |
| | | All functions | | Education | |
State (1)	Per capital personal income, 1965 (2)	Amount per capita (3)	Percentage of per capita income* (4)	Amount per capita (5)	Percentage of per capita income* (6)
Missouri	$2,667	$359.02	13.46	$145.88	5.47
Montana	2,436	491.91	20.19	190.50	7.82
Nebraska	2,626	390.80	14.88	165.43	6.30
Nevada	3,302	661.37	20.03	212.98	6.45
New Hampshire	2,575	377.10	14.64	136.18	5.29
New Jersey	3,258	376.30	11.55	147.35	4.52
New Mexico	2,235	510.32	22.83	237.41	10.62
New York	3,286	530.11	16.13	189.85	5.78
North Carolina	2,060	300.74	14.60	137.12	6.66
North Dakota	2,300	476.46	20.72	190.98	8.30
Ohio	2,845	365.78	12.86	156.59	5.50
Oklahoma	2,310	421.23	18.24	168.09	7.28
Oregon	2,761	501.50	18.16	223.27	8.09
Pennsylvania	2,750	360.65	13.11	151.15	5.50
Rhode Island	2,816	430.67	15.29	152.98	5.43
South Carolina	1,855	267.78	14.44	118.01	6.36
South Dakota	2,204	440.04	19.97	188.21	8.54
Tennessee	2,038	335.03	16.44	121.59	5.97
Texas	2,350	342.78	14.59	150.43	6.40
Utah	2,362	496.01	21.00	255.67	10.82
Vermont	2,340	464.87	19.87	166.47	7.11
Virginia	2,429	347.22	14.29	146.50	6.03
Washington	2,901	489.04	16.86	207.43	7.15
West Virginia	2,034	357.50	17.58	138.83	6.83
Wisconsin	2,740	467.27	17.05	209.11	7.63
Wyoming	2,561	697.09	27.22	275.26	10.75

			General revenues by source†		
			Sales and		
			gross	Individual	Corporation
		Property	receipts	income	net income
Fiscal year*	Total	taxes	taxes	taxes	taxes
1927	7,271	4,730	470	70	92
1932	7,267	4,487	752	74	79
1934	7,678	4,076	1,008	80	49
1936	8,395	4,093	1,484	153	113
1938	9,228	4,440	1,794	218	165
1940	9,609	4,430	1,982	224	156
1942	10,418	4,537	2,351	276	272
1944	10,908	4,604	2,289	342	451
1946	12,356	4,986	2,986	422	447
1948	17,250	6,126	4,442	543	592
1950	20,911	7,349	5,154	788	593
1952	25,181	8,652	6,357	998	846
1953	27,307	9,375	6,927	1,065	817
1954	29,012	9,967	7,276	1,127	778
1955	31,073	10,735	7,643	1,237	744
1956	34,667	11,749	8,691	1,538	890
1957	38,164	12,864	9,467	1,754	984
1958	41,219	14,047	9,829	1,759	1,018
1959	45,306	14,933	10,437	1,994	1,001
1960	50,505	18,405	11,849	2,463	1,180
1961	54,037	18,002	12,453	2,613	1,266
1962	58,252	19,054	13,494	3,037	1,308
1963	62,890	20,089	14,456	3,269	1,505
1962-63¶	62,289	19,833	14,445	3,267	1,505
1963-64¶	68,443	21,241	15,762	3,791	1,695
1964-65¶	74,341	22,918	17,118	4,090	1,929

TABLE 4.9-4
State and local government revenues and expenditures, selected fiscal years, 1927–1964 (millions of dollars)

* Fiscal years not the same for all governments. See ¶ footnote.

† Excludes revenues or expenditures of publicly owned utilities and liquor stores and of insurance-trust activities. Intergovernmental receipts and payments between state and local governments are also excluded.

‡ Includes licenses and other taxes and charges and miscellaneous revenues.

§ Includes expenditures for health, hospitals, police, local fire protection, natural resources, sanitation, housing and urban renewal, local parks and recreation, general control, financial administration, interest on general debt, and other unallocated expenditures.

Revenue from federal government	All other revenue‡	General expenditures by function†				
		Total	Education	Highways	Public welfare	All other§
116	1,793	7,210	2,235	1,809	151	3,015
232	1,643	7,765	2,311	1,741	444	3,269
1,016	1,449	7,181	1,831	1,509	889	2,952
948	1,604	7,644	2,177	1,425	827	3,215
800	1,811	8,757	2,491	1,650	1,069	3,547
945	1,872	9,229	2,638	1,573	1,156	3,862
858	2,123	9,190	2,586	1,490	1,225	3,889
954	2,269	8,863	2,793	1,200	1,133	3,737
855	2,661	11,028	3,356	1,672	1,409	4,591
1,861	3,685	17,684	5,379	3,036	2,099	7,170
2,486	4,541	22,787	7,177	3,803	2,940	8,867
2,566	5,763	26,098	8,318	4,650	2,788	10,342
2,870	6,252	27,910	9,390	4,987	2,914	10,619
2,966	6,897	30,701	10,557	5,527	3,060	11,557
3,131	7,584	33,724	11,907	6,452	3,168	12,197
3,335	8,465	36,711	13,220	6,953	3,139	13,399
3,843	9,252	40,375	14,134	7,816	3,485	14,940
4,865	9,699	44,851	15,919	8,567	3,818	16,547
6,377	10,516	48,887	17,283	9,592	4,136	17,876
6,954	11,634	51,876	18,719	9,428	4,404	19,324
7,131	12,563	56,201	20,574	9,844	4,720	21,063
7,871	13,489	60,206	22,216	10,357	5,084	22,549
8,722	14,850	64,816	24,012	11,136	5,481	24,187
8,663	14,555	63,977	23,965	11,150	5,420	23,442
10,002	15,952	69,302	26,533	11,664	5,766	25,339
11,029	17,256	74,954	28,971	12,221	6,315	27,441

¶ Data for fiscal year ending in the 12-month period through June 30. Data for 1963 and earlier years include local government amounts grouped in terms of fiscal years ended during the particular calendar year.

NOTE: Data are not available for intervening years. Data for Alaska and Hawaii included beginning 1959 and 1960, respectively.

SOURCE: U.S. Department of Commerce, Bureau of the Census; in U.S. Congress, Joint Economic Committee, *Revenue Sharing and Its Alternatives: What Future for Fiscal Federalism?, Hearings before the Subcommittee on Fiscal Policy,* July and August 1967, p. 10.

	Total state and local government expenditures for education (millions of dollars) (1)	Personal income (millions of dollars) (2)	Columns (1)/(2), (percent) (3)	Rank
State				
Alabama	$ 204.4	$ 4,379	4.7	26–27
Arizona	147.0	2,202	6.7	3
Arkansas	109.6	2,152	5.1	18–21
California	1,876.3	37,131	5.1	18–21
Colorado	202.4	3,508	5.8	7–8
Connecticut	224.3	6,506	3.4	46–47
Delaware	62.2	1,248	5.0	22–23
Florida	375.9	8,367	4.5	28–31
Georgia	283.9	5,672	5.0	22–23
Idaho	53.1	1,127	4.7	26–27
Illinois	834.4	24,230	3.4	46–47
Indiana	451.1	9,122	4.9	24–25
Iowa	272.6	5,256	5.2	16–17
Kansas	215.5	4,214	5.1	18–21
Kentucky	184.2	4,336	4.2	36
Louisiana	315.8	4,933	6.4	4
Maine	64.5	1,642	3.9	40–41
Maryland	259.5	6,661	3.9	40–41
Massachusetts	345.0	11,677	3.0	48
Michigan	908.0	16,581	5.5	11–12
Minnesota	369.2	6,486	5.7	9–10
Mississippi	122.1	2,298	5.3	14–15
Missouri	317.1	8,644	3.7	42–43
Montana	60.9	1,342	4.5	28–31
Nebraska	119.0	2,759	4.3	33–35
Nevada	30.6	685	4.5	28–31
New Hampshire	45.2	1,105	4.1	37–38
New Jersey	540.0	14,442	3.7	42–43
New Mexico	105.2	1,554	6.8	2
New York	1,718.3	42,157	4.1	37–38
North Carolina	331.1	6,318	5.2	16–17

TABLE 4.9-5
Measures of public burdens of education, 1958

State and local government expenditures on public IHE* (millions of dollars) (4)	Columns (4)/(2), (percent) (5)	Rank	Public IHE* adjusted expenditures per student, 1958 (6)	Per capita personal income 1958 (7)	Columns (6)/(7), (percent) (8)	Rank
$ 34.4	0.8	24–30	$ 976	$1,355	72.0	6
26.1	1.2	7–9	562	1,893	29.7	47
23.3	1.1	10–15	855	1,200	71.3	7
345.6	0.9	19–23	732	2,493	29.4	48
45.9	1.3	3–6	1,082	2,034	53.2	21
23.6	0.4	41–44	842	2,716	31.0	45
10.5	0.8	24–30	1,225	2,856	42.9	37
44.5	0.5	38–40	982	1,882	52.2	24
33.5	0.6	34–37	785	1,471	53.4	19–20
10.0	0.9	19–23	908	1,723	52.7	22
106.0	0.4	41–44	1,163	2,501	46.5	33
104.8	1.1	10–15	1,400	2,006	69.8	8
50.2	1.0	16–18	1,419	1,918	74.0	4
41.2	1.0	16–18	909	1,983	45.8	35
25.5	0.6	34–37	712	1,456	48.9	29
57.9	1.2	7–9	980	1,537	63.8	10
8.9	0.5	38–40	982	1,707	57.5	16
32.0	0.5	38–40	1,118	2,248	49.7	27
22.8	0.2	45–48	870	2,335	37.3	42
216.5	1.3	3–6	1,211	2,166	55.9	17
73.4	1.1	10–15	1,226	1,942	63.1	12
21.5	0.9	19–23	700	1,070	65.4	9
37.3	0.4	41–44	761	2,021	37.7	41
16.2	1.2	7–9	1,081	2,024	53.4	19–20
21.2	0.8	24–30	944	1,979	47.7	30–31
4.6	0.7	31–33	959	2,575	37.2	43
9.5	0.9	19–23	1,194	1,886	63.3	11
33.8	0.2	45–48	760	2,496	30.4	46
24.0	1.5	2	875	1,748	50.1	26
82.3	0.2	45–48	923	2,586	35.7	44
53.1	0.8	24–30	1,154	1,406	82.1	3

TABLE 4.9-5
(Continued)

State	Total state and local government expenditures for education (millions of dollars) (1)	Personal income (millions of dollars) (2)	Columns (1)/(2), (percent) (3)	Rank
North Dakota	$ 54.4	$ 1,063	5.1	18–21
Ohio	812.8	20,527	4.0	39
Oklahoma	216.4	3,954	5.5	11–12
Oregon	200.8	3,528	5.7	9–10
Pennsylvania	830.4	23,589	3.5	45
Rhode Island	61.8	1,726	3.6	44
South Carolina	155.5	2,924	5.3	14–15
South Dakota	68.5	1,132	6.1	5–6
Tennessee	228.0	5,028	4.5	28–31
Texas	835.0	17,129	4.9	24–25
Utah	109.1	1,516	7.2	1
Vermont	39.2	645	6.1	5–6
Virginia	287.4	6,660	4.3	33–35
Washington	323.8	5,977	5.4	13
West Virginia	129.2	2,960	4.4	32
Wisconsin	329.6	7,648	4.3	33–35
Wyoming	39.4	676	5.8	7–8
Total United States	$15,877.8†	$355,416	4.5	

* Institutions of higher education.

† Because of rounding in the source, details do not add up to totals.

‡ Personal income per capita is an average for the whole nation including District of Columbia, Alaska, Hawaii.

SOURCE: Columns 1, 4—U.S. Department of Commerce, *Government Finances in 1958*. Columns 2, 7—U.S. Department of Commerce, *Survey of Current Business,* August, 1960. Column 6—U.S. Department of Health, Education and Welfare, adapted by S. E. Harris; in S. E. Harris, *Higher Education: Resources and Finance,* McGraw-Hill Book Company, New York, 1962, pp. 354–356.

1   *Burden* is measured by college-age population as a percentage of the total population. California's grade of E+ suggests a very low burden.

2   *Capacity* is measured by per capita income and by net state and local tax revenues per member of the college-age population. California is graded A+ on both, which means it is in the top five states on these measures of capacity.

3   *Effort* is measured by state and local taxes per $1,000 of personal income, by total state tax revenue per capita, by state and local government expenditures on education as a percentage of personal income, and by state and local government expenditures on higher education as a percentage of

State and local government expenditures on public IHE* (millions of dollars) (4)	Columns (4)/(2), (percent) (5)	Rank	Public IHE* adjusted expenditures per student, 1958 (6)	Per capita personal income 1958 (7)	Columns (6)/(7), (percent) (8)	Rank
$ 12.2	1.1	10–15	$ 878	$1,677	52.4	23
90.5	0.4	41–44	926	2,206	42.0	39
49.9	1.3	3–6	728	1,728	42.1	38
39.8	1.1	10–15	1,167	2,017	57.9	15
57.9	0.2	45–48	1,012	2,142	47.2	32
10.9	0.6	34–37	1,218	2,045	59.6	13
24.8	0.8	24–30	919	1,247	73.7	5
15.2	1.3	3–6	883	1,648	53.6	18
31.1	0.6	34–37	736	1,441	51.1	25
111.4	0.7	31–33	715	1,847	38.7	40
24.1	1.6	1	814	1,767	46.1	34
7.0	1.1	10–15	1,410	1,671	84.4	1–2
47.6	0.7	31–33	1,476	1,748	84.4	1–2
54.1	0.9	19–23	1,037	2,173	47.7	30–31
23.1	0.8	24–30	928	1,576	58.9	14
58.2	0.8	24–30	979	1,993	49.1	28
6.7	1.0	16–18	951	2,086	45.6	36
$2,304.6	0.6		$ 930	$2,069‡	44.9	

personal income. Grades of B+, A+, B, and C+ average out to a strong effort for California.

4 *Achievement* is measured by total enrollment at institutions of higher education as a percentage of the college-age population (A+), by enrollment in public institutions of higher education as a percentage of total enrollment in institutions of higher education (B), by adjusted dollar expenditures of public institutions of higher education per enrollee (E+), and by net state and local taxes per enrollee in public institutions (D+). The

(Text continued on p. 850)

TABLE 4.9-6
Twelve crucial
variables (1957
unless otherwise
indicated)

State	Burden CAP^a as a percentage of total population (M-11) (1)	Capacity Per capita income (M-1) (2)	Capacity Net state and local tax revenues per member of CAP (C-17) (3)	Effort State and local taxes per $1,000 personal income,[c] 1959 (4)	Effort Total state tax revenue per capita (M-3)[d] (5)
Alabama	A+	E+	E	D	D
Arizona	B+	C	B+	C+	B+
Arkansas	A+	E	E+	C+	E+
California	E+	A+	A+	B+	A+
Colorado	E	B	B	A	B+
Connecticut	E+	A+	A+	E+	A
Delaware	E	A+	B	E	A
Florida	E	C+	B+	C+	B
Georgia	A	E+	D	C	C+
Idaho	B+	D+	D+	B	C
Illinois	D	A	A	D	D
Indiana	C	B+	D+	D+	E+
Iowa	C+	C	C+	B	B
Kansas	D	C	B+	B+	D+
Kentucky	A	E+	E+	D	E+
Louisiana	B+	D	D+	A+	A+
Maine	B	D+	D+	B+	D+
Maryland	D	A	B	B+	C+
Massachusetts	D	A	A	C+	C+
Michigan	D+	B+	A	C+	B+
Minnesota	C	C+	B	A	C+
Mississippi	A+	E	E	A+	D+
Missouri	C	B	D+	E	E+
Montana	C	C+	B+	A	C
Nebraska	D+	C+	C+	D	E
Nevada	E	A	A+	B	A+
New Hampshire	D+	C+	C	D+	E
New Jersey	D+	A+	A+	E+	E
New Mexico	A	D+	D	C	A+

846

| Educational expenditures, state and local government, as a percentage of personal income, 1959[c] | Higher-educational expenditures, state and local government, as a percentage of personal income, 1958[d] | Achievements | | | | Supplementary |
| | | Total IHE[e] enrollment as a percentage of CAP (M-9) | Enrollment in public IHE as a percentage of total IHE enrollment, 1958 (C-10) | Adjusted dollar expenditures, public IHE per enrollee in public IHE (C-14)[f] | Net state and local taxes per enrollee, public IHE (C-18) | Percentage expenditures adjusted per student, public IHE to per capita income[b], 1957–58[d] |
(6)	(7)	(8)	(9)	(10)	(11)	(12)
C	C	E+	B	C+	D+	A
A+	A	A	A+	E	E	E
B	B+	E	A	D	E+	A
B	C+	A+	B	E+	D+	E
A	A+	A+	B+	B+	D+	C+
E	E+	A	E+	D	A	E
C+	C	C+	A	A	C+	D
C	D	C	D+	B	A	B+
C+	D	E+	C+	D	C+	B
C	C+	D	B+	D+	D+	C+
E	E+	B	E+	B+	A	D+
C+	B+	C+	C	A+	B	A
C	B	C+	D	A+	B+	A+
C	B	A+	A	C	E+	D+
D	D	D	C	E	D+	C
A+	A	D+	C+	B	C	A
E+	D	E+	D	B	A	B
E+	D	C	C	B+	B	C
E	E	A+	E	D+	A+	E+
B+	A+	B	B+	A	C	B
A	B+	A	C	A+	C+	B+
B+	C+	E+	E	E	E+	A
E+	E+	C+	E+	D	B	E+
C	A	D+	A	B+	C	B
D+	C	B+	C+	C+	D	D
C	D+	D	A+	C+	A	E+
D	C+	B+	D	A	B+	B+
E+	E	D+	E+	E+	A+	E
A+	A+	D+	A+	D+	E	C

TABLE 4.9-6
(continued)

| | Burden | | Capacity | | Effort |
| | CAP[a] as a percentage of total population (M-11) | Per capita income (M-1) | Net state and local tax revenues per member of CAP (C-17) | State and local taxes per $1,000 personal income,[c] 1959 | Total state tax revenue per capita (M-3)[d] |
State	(1)	(2)	(3)	(4)	(5)
New York	E+	A+	A+	B	B
North Carolina	A	E	E	D+	C+
North Dakota	B	D	C+	A+	C
Ohio	D	A	B	E+	D
Oklahoma	B+	D	D	B	A
Oregon	C+	B	A	A	A
Pennsylvania	C+	B+	C+	E	B
Rhode Island	E+	B	C	D+	D
South Carolina	A+	E	E	C	D+
South Dakota	B	D	C+	A+	E
Tennessee	A	E+	E+	C	D+
Texas	C+	C	D	D	D
Utah	B	C	C	B+	B
Vermont	B+	D+	C	A+	B+
Virginia	C+	D+	D	E	C
Washington	D+	B+	B+	C	A+
West Virginia	A+	D	E+	D+	C
Wisconsin	C	B	A	B+	B+
Wyoming	B	B+	C	A	A

[a] College-age population.

[b] This relationship reflects the burden of unit expenditures for public higher education in relation to per capita income.

[c] U.S. Census, *Governmental Finances in 1958*, p. 24.

[d] Calculated from ibid. and *Survey of Current Business.*

[e] Institutions of higher education.

[f] General and educational expenditures exclusive of organized research and public services.

(6)	(7)	(8)	(9)	(10)	(11)	(12)
D	E	A	E	C	A+	E+
B	C	E+	D	B+	C+	A+
B	B+	C	A+	D+	E+	C+
D	E+	C+	D	C	B+	D
B+	A+	B+	B+	E+	E	D
A	B+	B+	B	A	C+	B+
E	E	D+	E	B	A+	D+
E+	D	A	E	A	A+	B+
B+	C	E	D+	C	B	A+
A	A+	B	B	D+	D	B
C	D	D	D	E+	C	C+
C+	D+	B	C+	E	D	D
A+	A+	A+	C	D	E	D+
A	B+	B	D	A+	B	A+
D+	D+	D	D+	A+	B+	A+
B+	C+	B+	B	B	C	D+
D+	C	E	B	C	D	B+
D+	C	C	C+	C+	B+	C
A	B	C	A+	C+	D	D

	Rank of state

```
1-5  = A+,  6-10 = A = Very high
11-15 = B+, 16-20 = B = High
21-25 = C+, 26-30 = C = Average
31-35 = D+, 36-40 = D = Low
41-44 = E+, 45-48 = E = Very low
```

SOURCES: M = McGraw-Hill table, in Dexter M. Keezer, ed., *Financing Higher Education: 1960–70,* McGraw-Hill Book Company, New York, 1959; C = current Master Table, pp. 338–341, in Chap. 25; e.g., C-13 = column 13 of Master Table; in S. E. Harris, *Higher Education: Resources and Finance,* McGraw-Hill Book Company, New York, 1962, pp. 361–362.

overall grades on achievement on these measures are less than might be expected.

5 *Supplementary.* California gets a low grade (E) on the basis of adjusted expenditures per student in public institutions of higher education as a percentage of per capita income. Per capita income is relatively high in California, and expenditures per student by public institutions of higher education are relatively low.[1]

Table 4.9-7 shows the average percentage of personal income that each state spent for public higher education from 1952 to 1958. The sparsely populated states tend to spend the largest proportion of personal income on public higher education. This is,

[1] However, the "mix" of types of public institutions is relevant here. California has an exceptionally large proportion of all students in public higher education enrolled in two-year community colleges, which have relatively low costs per student.

TABLE 4.9-7 *Percentage of personal income of the states spent for public higher education, 1952–1958, combined average*

State	Percent	State	Percent	State	Percent
New Mexico	1.34	Mississippi	0.80	California	0.46
Utah	1.34	North Carolina	0.79	Kentucky	0.43
North Dakota	1.17	Oregon	0.77	Maine	0.43
Oklahoma	1.12	Idaho	0.75	Nevada	0.43
South Dakota	1.01	South Carolina	0.74	Maryland	0.42
Colorado	1.00	Alabama	0.72	Vermont	0.42
Minnesota	0.94	West Virginia	0.67	Illinois	0.36
Montana	0.94	Nebraska	0.66	Ohio	0.35
Wyoming	0.94	Wisconsin	0.62	Rhode Island	0.35
Arizona	0.92	New Hampshire	0.61	Missouri	0.32
Arkansas	0.89	Virginia	0.61	Connecticut	0.30
Louisiana	0.89	Delaware	0.58	New Jersey	0.22
Iowa	0.86	Georgia	0.58	Pennsylvania	0.20
Kansas	0.86	Tennessee	0.56	New York	0.16
Indiana	0.85	Texas	0.55	Massachusetts	0.13
Michigan	0.83	Florida	0.51		
Washington	0.81				

SOURCE: Technical Committee, *California's Ability to Finance Higher Education, 1960–1975,* table 29; in Liaison Committee of the Regents of the University of California and the State Board of Education, *Institutional Capacities and Area Needs of California Public Higher Education, 1960–1975,* Sacramento, Calif., February 1961, p. 185.

TABLE 4.9-8 *Personal income, 1963, related to educational and general expenditures for higher education and to educational and general funds received from state and local governments, by state, 1963–64*

State (1)	Personal income 1963 (millions of dollars) (2)	Total expenditures (thousands of dollars) (3)	Percentage of personal income (4)	Received from state and local governments (thousands of dollars) (5)	Percentage of personal income (6)
		Educational and general funds, higher education*			
United States	$463,053	$7,337,891	1.58	$2,350,832	0.51
Alabama	5,660	73,170	1.29	29,295	0.52
Alaska	704	11,731	1.67	4,846	0.69
Arizona	3,366	48,942	1.45	28,252	0.84
Arkansas	3,103	39,001	1.26	20,989	0.68
California	52,615	1,240,480	2.36	419,648	0.80
Colorado	4,750	93,882	1.98	36,970	0.78
Connecticut	8,468	97,873	1.16	20,785	0.25
Delaware	1,446	12,825	0.89	6,046	0.42
District of Columbia	2,669	90,854	3.40	1,144	0.04
Florida	11,865	130,430	1.10	66,036	0.56
Georgia	7,905	97,668	1.24	33,804	0.43
Hawaii	1,776	28,445	1.60	11,184	0.63
Idaho	1,411	18,985	1.35	12,285	0.87
Illinois	30,228	478,487	1.58	151,271	0.50
Indiana	11,813	184,832	1.56	74,474	0.63
Iowa	6,352	124,673	1.96	48,404	0.76
Kansas	5,319	83,739	1.57	43,159	0.81
Kentucky	5,733	75,674	1.32	35,545	0.62
Louisiana	6,284	98,028	1.56	56,291	0.90
Maine	1,932	24,089	1.25	7,176	0.37
Maryland	8,964	166,762	1.86	36,516	0.41
Massachusetts	14,547	414,517	2.85	21,492	0.15
Michigan	20,787	290,761	1.40	120,843	0.58
Minnesota	8,318	135,802	1.63	48,583	0.58
Mississippi	3,291	47,306	1.44	21,561	0.66
Missouri	10,402	147,121	1.41	44,814	0.43
Montana	1,588	21,669	1.36	12,501	0.79
Nebraska	3,342	51,017	1.53	20,424	0.61

TABLE 4.9-8 *(continued)*

State (1)	Personal income 1963 (millions of dollars) (2)	Educational and general funds, higher education*			
		Total expenditures (thousands of dollars) (3)	Percentage of personal income (4)	Received from state and local governments (thousands of dollars) (5)	Percentage of personal income (6)
Nevada	$ 1,268	$ 9,763	0.77	$ 6,141	0.48
New Hampshire	1,516	29,607	1.95	5,235	0.35
New Jersey	19,400	144,206	0.74	35,278	0.18
New Mexico	2,032	36,384	1.79	16,285	0.80
New York	52,697	798,591	1.52	182,079	0.35
North Carolina	8,632	156,907	1.82	44,973	0.52
North Dakota	1,292	22,301	1.73	12,795	0.99
Ohio	25,144	272,519	1.08	72,676	0.29
Oklahoma	4,880	74,242	1.52	34,551	0.71
Oregon	4,578	79,892	1.75	36,701	0.80
Pennsylvania	27,847	394,670	1.42	70,049	0.25
Rhode Island	2,199	35,186	1.60	8,292	0.38
South Carolina	3,948	44,614	1.13	19,268	0.49
South Dakota	1,349	22,421	1.66	10,168	0.75
Tennessee	6,644	108,685	1.64	29,406	0.44
Texas	21,589	261,197	1.21	121,202	0.56
Utah	2,155	55,383	2.57	19,493	0.90
Vermont	799	22,446	2.81	5,385	0.67
Virginia	8,984	114,182	1.27	35,459	0.39
Washington	7,764	124,422	1.60	67,070	0.86
West Virginia	3,233	40,825	1.26	25,333	0.78
Wisconsin	9,654	148,624	1.54	51,324	0.53
Wyoming	811	12,062	1.49	7,331	0.90

*Excludes United States service schools.

SOURCES: U.S. Department of Health, Education and Welfare, Office of Education, "Higher Education Finances: Selected Trend and Summary Data." U.S. Department of Commerce, Office of Business Economics, "Survey of Current Business," April 1968; in U.S. Office of Education, *Digest of Educational Statistics, 1968,* 1968, p. 101.

of course, as much a commentary on the differing income distributions among the states as an indicator of the burdens of financing higher education. (We will see later, however, that there exist variations among the states in the financing of higher education which cannot be explained by differences in income.) Note also the relative neglect of higher education by the governments of three Eastern industrial states—Pennsylvania, New York, and Massachusetts, which spent an average of 0.20, 0.16, and 0.13 percent, respectively, of personal income for public higher education from 1952 to 1958.

In 1963–64, expenditures for all higher education as a percentage of personal income ranged from 3.40 percent for the District of Columbia and 2.85 percent for Massachusetts to 0.74 percent for New Jersey. In the same year state and local government expenditures for higher education as a percentage of personal income ranged from 0.99 percent for North Dakota to .15 percent for Massachusetts (Table 4.9-8).

States are ranked differently according to the measure of effort used. California ranked thirty-fourth on the basis of outlays on public higher education (Table 4.9-7), third on the basis of expenditures on all higher education, and ninth on the basis of state and local government expenditures on higher education (Table 4.9-8), all as a percentage of personal income.[2]

COMPETITION FOR FUNDS From 1934–35 to 1965–66, the ratio of public to private expenditures for health, education, and welfare combined has remained relatively constant at about 2 to 1 (except for 1944–45). But the ratio of public to private expenditures varies with the specific category of health, education, or welfare. In 1965–66 the ratio of public to private expenditures for education was 5 to 1; for health the ratio was 1 to 3, and for social insurance and welfare it was 6 to 1 (Table 4.9-9).

In discussing the competition for funds at the state and local government levels, we look at the relationship between direct general expenditures for all functions and direct general expenditures for education. In 1965–66, per capita state and local government direct expenditures for all functions as a percentage of per capita income varied from 28.9 percent for Alaska to 11.6 percent for Illinois and New Jersey. Per capita state and local government

---

[2] The District of Columbia is excluded from this comparison.

Type of expenditure	1934–35	1939–40	1944–45	1949–50
Total expenditures, net†	$9,590	$12,581	$15,987	$34,905
Public funds	6,417	8,762	8,859	22,973
Private funds†	3,322	4,014	7,375	12,228
Health	3,138	3,881	7,906	12,151
Public funds	559	858	2,571	3,087
Private funds	2,580	3,023	5,335	9,064
Education	2,493	3,161	3,871	10,936
Public funds	2,098	2,647	3,027	9,388
Private funds	395	514	844	1,548
Social insurance and welfare	4,125	5,757	4,486	12,149
Public funds	3,760	5,257	3,261	10,499
Private funds	365	500	1,225	1,650

*Preliminary estimates

† Total and private expenditures adjusted to eliminate duplication resulting from use of cash insurance benefits to purchase medical care and educational services.

SOURCE: U.S. Department of Health, Education and Welfare, Social Security Administration, Office of Research and Statistics; in U.S. Congress, Joint Economic Committee, *Federal Programs for the Development of Human Resources,* compilation of replies from departments and agencies of the United States government to a questionnaire formulated by the Subcommittee on Economic Progress, 1966, p. 8.

direct expenditures for education as a percentage of per capita income ranged from 10.8 percent for Utah and Wyoming to 3.3 percent for the District of Columbia (Table 4.9-3).

It is clear that there are large variations in the per capita expenditures of state and local governments for all functions and for education in particular. These variations exceed the variations that would be caused by the differences in per capita income among the states. Consider Table 4.9-10. In 1966–67 per capita expenditures on education by state and local governments varied from $133 to $322. State and local government expenditures on education per $1,000 of personal income exhibit even a greater degree of variation among the states, with the highest-ranking state spending more than three times as much on education per $1,000 of personal income as the lowest ranking state. Thus, we see that some large variations in expenditures on education by state and local governments are explained by factors other than differences in income among the states. The existence of these ranges points to the possibility of substantial increases in spending for education.

1954–55	1959–60	1962–63	1963–64	1964–65	1965–66*
$50,149	$79,075	$99,933	$107,526	$117,465	$131,030
33,243	52,154	66,543	71,082	77,505	87,578
18,509	28,149	35,046	38,219	41,872	45,608
17,875	26,385	32,668	35,660	39,141	42,967
4,372	6,389	8,328	8,984	9,740	10,896
13,503	19,996	24,340	26,676	29,401	32,071
14,338	22,079	27,745	30,262	34,424	38,525
11,999	18,409	22,865	24,944	28,632	32,283
2,339	3,670	4,880	5,318	5,792	6,242
18,616	31,990	41,377	43,594	46,046	51,944
15,871	27,357	35,351	37,153	39,131	44,399
2,745	4,633	6,026	6,441	6,915	7,545

APPROPRIATIONS OF STATE TAX FUNDS

Table 4.9-11 gives some measures of state government appropriations for the support of public higher education in 1963–64. Appropriations of state tax funds for operating expenses of public institutions of higher education ranged from $263.8 million for California and $174.3 million for New York to $5.0 million for

(Text continued on p. 858)

TABLE 4.9-10 Range of expenditures and revenues of state and local governments, per capita and in relation to $1,000 of personal income, 1966–67

	Range of expenditures and revenue, per capita	Range of expenditures and revenues per $1,000 of personal income
General revenues	$310–$1,067	$118–$320
General revenues from own sources	$250–$541	$99–$182
Expenditures for education	$133–$322	$37–$117
Expenditures for higher education	$3–$109	

SOURCE: Adapted from U.S. Bureau of the Census, *Governmental Finances in 1966–67,* Government Finances Series GF 67, no. 3, 1968, pp. 12–13.

TABLE 4.9-11 *Measures of appropriations for public higher education, 1963–64*

	Appropriations of state tax funds for operating expenses of higher education (millions of dollars)	Appropriations per capita for 18–21 age group	Appropriations per capita for total population	Appropriations as percentage of state personal income	Appropriations as percentage of total state tax revenues
Northeast					
Connecticut	18.6	$130	$ 6.97	0.22	5.52
Delaware	5.8	218	12.24	0.38	5.97
Maine	9.1	161	9.26	0.46	9.31
Maryland	33.6	165	10.20	0.37	7.77
Massachusetts	19.6*	67	3.76	0.13	3.38
New Hampshire	5.1	164	8.21	0.36	10.83
New Jersey	39.8	125	6.15	0.21	8.47
New York	174.3	200	9.79	0.33	6.92
Pennsylvania	59.4*	105	5.20	0.21	4.69
Rhode Island	8.0	136	8.88	0.38	7.53
Vermont	5.0	230	12.82	0.61	9.66
(Averages)		(155)	(8.50)	(0.33)	(7.28)
Midwest					
Illinois	141.4	262	13.89	0.47	13.09
Indiana	70.9	261	15.10	0.61	16.05
Iowa	47.4	339	17.07	0.75	16.34
Kansas	37.9	298	17.04	0.76	15.87
Michigan	109.3	257	13.47	0.53	9.57
Minnesota	48.1	270	13.74	0.59	10.87
Missouri	43.0	184	9.94	0.40	10.40
Nebraska	18.8	249	12.89	0.56	19.08
North Dakota	11.9	350	18.72	0.92	17.29
Ohio	60.5	112	5.94	0.24	6.52
South Dakota	10.1	284	13.74	0.71	15.61
Wisconsin	51.5	250	12.68	0.53	8.59
(Averages)		(260)	(13.69)	(0.59)	(13.27)
South					
Alabama	28.4	139	8.50	0.51	8.69
Arkansas	29.4	208	10.96	0.69	10.74
Florida	57.7	196	10.21	0.48	9.75
Georgia	35.3	136	8.52	0.46	7.97

	Appropriations of state tax funds for operating expenses of higher education (millions of dollars)	Appropriations per capita for 18–21 age group	Appropriations per capita for total population	Appropriations as percentage of state personal income	Appropriations as percentage of total state tax revenues
South cont.:					
Kentucky	32.2	$185	$10.39	0.58	9.55
Louisiana	55.8	278	16.34	0.92	10.97
Mississippi	17.5	130	7.65	0.55	7.90
North Carolina	46.8	152	9.83	0.54	7.95
Oklahoma	33.5	262	13.47	0.69	10.41
South Carolina	17.4	101	7.28	0.44	6.57
Tennessee	28.3	121	7.67	0.43	8.04
Texas	107.0	170	10.36	0.51	10.17
Virginia	34.2	123	7.90	0.38	8.33
West Virginia	22.3	240	12.54	0.67	9.88
(Averages)		(174)	(10.11)	(0.56)	(9.06)
West					
Alaska	4.8	248	19.41	0.69	12.31
Arizona	23.4	283	15.01	0.71	11.28
California	263.8	236	15.00	0.50	10.31
Colorado	33.9	321	17.30	0.73	14.63
Hawaii	13.8	266	19.92	0.82	10.38
Idaho	11.7	325	16.41	0.85	15.37
Montana	12.8	388	18.07	0.81	17.29
Nevada	6.0	337	16.28	0.48	8.82
New Mexico	16.0	282	15.68	0.83	10.71
Oregon	41.0	379	22.48	0.89	18.20
Utah	18.9	306	19.24	0.90	15.48
Washington	60.4	297	19.80	0.79	10.98
Wyoming	6.3	362	18.89	0.76	14.10
(Averages)		(310)	(17.95)	(0.76)	(13.07)
National total	2,077.9				
National averages		$197	$11.07	0.45	9.40

*Estimates based on incomplete data.

SOURCE: A. M. Cartter, "Qualitative Aspects of Southern University Education," *Southern Economic Journal,* vol. 32, no. 1, part 2, July 1965.

TABLE 4.9-12 *Expenditures of state and local government on higher education in relation to tax revenues, 1962*

State	State and local government expenditures for higher education as a percentage of tax revenue	Rank	State	State and local government expenditures for higher education as a percentage of tax revenue	Rank
Alabama	14.49	16	Montana	14.66	14
Alaska	19.65	2	Nebraska	10.81	32
Arizona	15.14	11	Nevada	11.20	31
Arkansas	11.88	24	New Hampshire	9.14	39
California	14.86	12	New Jersey	5.78	46
Colorado	16.23	8	New Mexico	21.50	1
Connecticut	4.25	47	New York	4.03	49
Delaware	12.50	22	North Carolina	11.56	26
Florida	6.87	44	North Dakota	17.12	4
Georgia	9.39	36	Ohio	8.45	40
Hawaii	11.73	25	Oklahoma	14.02	17
Idaho	11.26	29	Oregon	14.77	13
Illinois	7.82	41	Pennsylvania	4.09	48
Indiana	16.25	7	Rhode Island	7.37	43
Iowa	12.64	20	South Carolina	11.39	28
Kansas	13.47	18	South Dakota	12.49	21
Kentucky	16.33	6	Tennessee	9.33	37
Louisiana	11.46	27	Texas	9.82	34
Maine	9.16	38	Utah	19.56	3
Maryland	7.53	42	Vermont	15.16	10
Massachusetts	2.39	50	Virginia	11.24	30
Michigan	13.39	19	Washington	14.51	15
Minnesota	11.99	23	West Virginia	11.15	35
Mississippi	16.48	5	Wisconsin	10.26	33
Missouri	6.67	45	Wyoming	16.01	9

SOURCE: A. H. Bowker, "Quality and Quantity in Higher Education," *Journal of the American Statistical Association,* vol. 60, no. 309, pp. 1–5, March 1965.

Vermont and $4.8 million for Alaska. Appropriations of state tax funds for higher education per member of the college-age population varied from $388 for Montana to $67 for Massachusetts. Appropriations of state tax funds for higher education per capita (for the total state population) varied from $22 for Oregon to $4 for Massachusetts. Finally, appropriations of state tax funds for higher education as a percentage of total state tax revenues varied from 19 percent for Nebraska to 3 percent for Massachusetts. For more recent data, Table 4.9-13 shows state per capita appropriations for higher education for the year 1970–71. Per capita appropriations ranged from $73.70 for Hawaii to $15.13 for New Hampshire.

In 1962 state and local government expenditures for higher education as a percentage of state and local government tax revenues varied from 22 percent for New Mexico to 2 percent for Massachusetts (Table 4.9-13).

INCOME AND EXPENDITURES OF INSTITUTIONS AS A PERCENTAGE OF GNP Educational and general income of institutions of higher education as a percentage of GNP rose from 0.23 percent in 1889–90 to slightly more than 2 percent in the late 1960s and is projected by the Carnegie Commission to increase to 3 percent by 1976–77.[3]

[3] S. E. Harris, *Higher Education: Resources and Finance,* McGraw-Hill Book Company, New York, 1962, p. 7; and Carnegie Commission on Higher Education, *Quality and Equality: New Levels of Federal Responsibility for Higher Education,* McGraw-Hill Book Company, New York, 1968, p. 6.

TABLE 4.9-13
State per capita appropriations for higher education, 1970–71

State	Appropriation per capita	Rank per capita
Alabama	$22.18	47
Alaska	57.70	2
Arizona	47.57	5
Arkansas	29.12	40
California	41.49	14
Colorado	50.38	4
Connecticut	32.58	33
Delaware	37.26	19
Florida	36.18	22
Georgia	33.09	30
Hawaii	73.70	1
Idaho	45.12	7
Illinois	43.52	9
Indiana	33.83	27
Iowa	36.42	21
Kansas	36.91	20
Kentucky	31.23	36
Louisiana	34.18	25
Maine	28.43	41

TABLE 4.9-13 **(continued)**		

State	Appropriation per capita	Rank per capita
Maryland	$31.22	37
Massachusetts	20.62	49
Michigan	39.16	16
Minnesota	38.07	17
Mississippi	33.44	29
Missouri	28.38	42
Montana	42.74	10
Nebraska	32.96	32
Nevada	33.01	31
New Hampshire	15.13	50
New Jersey	21.78	48
New Mexico	41.71	12
New York	41.52	13
North Carolina	35.46	23
North Dakota	38.07	17
Ohio	24.73	46
Oklahoma	27.80	43
Oregon	46.64	6
Pennsylvania	30.25*	38*
Rhode Island	34.05	26
South Carolina	27.26	44
South Dakota	32.06	34
Tennessee	25.68	45
Texas	31.26	35
Utah	42.73	11
Vermont	33.71	28
Virginia	29.96	39
Washington	56.94	3
West Virginia	34.50	24
Wisconsin	41.27	15
Wyoming	44.65	8
Total United States	34.98	

* Estimate.

SOURCE: From *The Chronicle of Higher Education,* vol. V, no. 3, Oct. 12, 1970, p. 1; in Carnegie Commission on Higher Education, *The Capitol and the Campus: State Responsibility for Postsecondary Education,* McGraw-Hill Book Company, New York, 1971, pp. 143–144.

TABLE 4.9-14 *Projection of expenditures of institutions of higher education, total and percentage increase, by control, from 1967–68 to 1977–78*	*Total expenditures (billions of dollars)*		*Percentage increase, 1967–68 to 1977–78*
	1967–68	*1977–78*	
All institutions	$18.8	$30.3	61
Public	11.2	18.4	64
Private	7.6	11.9	57

SOURCE: U.S. Office of Education, *Projections of Educational Statistics to 1977–78*, National Center for Educational Statistics, 1968, pp. 78–79 (author's calculations).

From 1930 to 1966, expenditures on all levels of education as a percentage of GNP rose from 3.3 to 6.3 percent, according to estimates by the American Council on Education. This was an increase of 91 percent. During the same period, expenditures on higher education as a percentage of GNP rose from 0.6 to 2.1 percent—an increase of 250 percent. Expenditures on public institutions of higher education as a percentage of GNP increased by 333 percent and expenditures on private institutions increased by 125 percent from 1930 to 1966.[4]

PROJECTIONS Table 4.9-14 shows Office of Education projections of expenditures of institutions of higher education from 1967–68 to 1977–78. The

[4] American Council on Education, *American Universities and Colleges, 1966*, Washington, D.C., 1966, p. 43.

TABLE 4.9-15 *State and local general revenue, actual and projected, fiscal years 1955–1975*

	Amount (billions)					
	Actual		*Projected,*	*Per*	*Percentage change*	
Source	*1955*	*1965*	*1975*	*capita*	*1955–65*	*1965–75*
Total, general revenue	$31.1	$74.3	$146.9	673	+139	+98
Total from state and local sources	27.9	63.3	116.9	536	+127	+85
Taxes	23.5	51.6	90.2	414	+120	+75
Current charges	3.0	8.4	18.8	87	+183	+124
Miscellaneous	1.5	3.3	7.8	36	+124	+134
From federal grants	3.1	11.0	30.0	138	+252	+172

SOURCE: Actual data from U.S. Department of Commerce, Bureau of the Census. Computations and projections by tax foundation, in U.S. Congress, Joint Economic Committee, *Revenue Sharing and Its Alternatives: What Future for Fiscal Federalism?, Hearings before Subcommittee on Fiscal Policy,* July and August, 1967, p. 72.

expenditures of private institutions show an unexpectedly large increase in these projections—an increase of 57 percent as compared with an increase of 64 percent for public institutions. Yet degree-credit enrollment is projected to rise by 25 percent for private and 65 percent for public institutions in this same period.

TABLE 4.9-16 *Social welfare expenditures under public programs, selected fiscal years, 1928–29 to 1969–70 (millions of dollars)*

Program	1928–29	1939–40	1949–50	1954–55
TOTAL	$3,921.2	$8,795.1	$23,508.4	$32,639.9
Social insurance	342.4	1,271.8	4,946.6	9,834.9
Old-age, survivors, disability, and health insurance		40.4	784.1	4,463.3
Health insurance for the aged				
Railroad retirement		116.8	306.4	556.0
Public employee retirement	113.1	283.4	817.9	1,388.5
Unemployment insurance and employment service		553.0	2,190.1	2,080.6
Railroad unemployment insurance		18.9	119.6	158.7
Railroad temporary disability insurance			31.1	54.2
State temporary disability insurance			72.1	217.5
Hospital and medical benefits			2.2	20.0
Workmen's compensation	229.3	259.2	625.1	943.0
Hospital and medical benefits	75.0	90.0	193.0	315.0
Public aid	60.0	3,597.0	2,496.2	3,003.0
Public assistance	59.9	1,124.3	2,490.2	2,941.1
Vendor medical payments			51.3	211.9
Other	0.1	2,472.7	6.0	61.9
Health and medical programs	351.1	615.5	2,063.5	3,103.1
Hospital and medical care	146.3	343.0	1,222.3	2,042.4
Civilian programs	117.1	297.6	886.1	1,297.6
Defense Department	29.2	45.4	336.2	744.8
Maternal and child health programs	6.2	13.8	29.8	92.9
Medical research				0.2
Medical research		2.6	69.2	132.8

These expenditure trends versus enrollment trends suggest serious financial problems in the future for private institutions.[5]

[5] U.S. Office of Education, *Projections of Educational Statistics to 1977–78,* National Center for Educational Statistics, 1968, p. 16.

Total expenditures					
1959–60	*1964–65*	*1966–67*	*1967–68*	*1968–69*	*1969–70*
$52,293.3	$77,170.5	$99,529.4	$111,829.7	$126,305.6	$143,045.8
19,306.7	28,110.1	37,319.9	42,719.3	48,760.7	54,472.7
11,032.3	16,997.5	24,580.7	28,748.4	33,388.7	36,834.3
		3,394.6	5,347.2	6,597.7	7,149.2
934.7	1,128.1	1,278.4	1,416.6	1,550.7	1,602.5
2,569.9	4,528.5	5,902.7	6,581.9	7,494.2	8,450.0
2,829.6	3,002.6	2,752.1	2,928.4	2,953.3	3,836.9
215.2	76.7	38.5	46.2	45.0	35.0
68.5	46.5	38.4	36.1	57.7	64.6
347.9	483.5	529.6	574.3	648.2	725.0
40.2	50.9	53.7	54.6	57.7	60.0
1,308.5	1,846.7	2,199.4	2,387.4	2,622.8	2,924.4
420.0	580.0	715.0	790.0	875.0	970.0
4,101.1	6,283.4	8,811.0	11,091.7	13,218.5	16,081.3
4,041.7	5,874.9	7,832.4	9,886.6	11,925.9	14,395.2
492.7	1,367.1	2,382.6	3,580.8	4,423.2	5,042.4
59.4	408.5	978.6	1,205.1	1,292.6	1,686.1
4,463.8	6,246.4	7,628.0	8,458.6	9,006.9	9,690.0
2,853.3	3,452.3	4,240.0	4,576.0	4,759.1	5,032.3
1,973.2	2,515.5	2,808.3	2,927.7	3,009.6	3,132.1
880.1	936.8	1,431.7	1,648.3	1,749.5	1,900.2
141.3	227.3	309.9	336.8	408.6	428.6
0.6	4.3				
448.9	1,165.2	1,354.6	1,547.6	1,518.5	1,601.9

TABLE 4.9-16 *(continued)*

Program	1928–29	1939–40	1949–50	1954–55
Health and medical programs cont.:				
School health (educational agencies)	9.4	16.4	30.6	65.9
Other public health activities	88.8	154.5	350.8	383.7
Medical-facilities construction	100.4	85.2	360.8	385.4
Defense Department			1.1	33.0
Other	100.4	85.2	359.8	352.4
Veterans' programs	657.9	629.0	6,865.7	4,833.5
Pensions and compensation	434.7	443.3	2,092.1	2,689.7
Health and medical programs	50.9	75.8	748.0	761.1
Hospital and medical care	46.7	61.5	582.8	721.5
Hospital construction	4.2	14.3	161.5	34.1
Medical and prosthetic research			3.7	5.6
Education			2,691.6	706.1
Life insurance	136.4	77.0	475.7	490.2
Welfare and other	35.8	32.9	858.3	186.5
Education	2,433.7	2,561.2	6,674.1	11,157.2
Elementary and secondary	2,216.2	2,267.4	5,596.2	9,734.3
Construction	377.0	258.0	1,019.4	2,231.9
Higher	182.1	217.6	914.7	1,214.4
Construction	0.2	20.6	310.3	198.6
Vocational and adult	34.9	75.4	160.8	204.9
Housing		4.2	14.6	89.3
Public housing		4.2	14.5	74.7
Other			0.1	14.6
Other social welfare	76.2	116.4	447.7	619.0
Vocational rehabilitation	1.6	4.2	30.0	42.4
Medical services	0.1	0.3	7.4	9.1
Medical research				0.3
Institutional care	74.7	62.4	145.5	195.3
Child nutrition programs		4.0	160.2	239.6
Child welfare		45.0	104.9	135.1
Special OEO programs				
Social welfare, not elsewhere classified		0.9	7.1	6.5

SOURCE: A. M. Skolnik and S. R. Dales, "Social Welfare Expenditures, 1969–70," *Social Security Bulletin,* vol. 33, no. 12, p. 4, December 1970.

Total expenditures					
1959–60	*1964–65*	*1966–67*	*1967–68*	*1968–69*	*1969–70*
101.0	142.2	177.9	204.6	231.0	263.0
401.2	671.0	883.8	1,000.6	1,194.7	1,429.0
518.1	588.3	661.8	792.9	895.0	935.2
40.0	31.1	49.7	26.8	71.8	52.1
478.1	557.2	612.1	766.1	823.2	883.1
5,479.2	6,038.8	6,880.5	7,344.3	7,944.3	8,951.1
3,402.7	4,156.0	4,486.7	4,715.7	4,968.5	5,360.6
954.0	1,239.0	1,346.0	1,464.6	1,540.0	1,739.6
879.4	1,120.9	1,249.5	1,372.3	1,433.9	1,599.2
59.6	81.2	49.4	46.0	53.9	77.5
15.1	36.9	47.1	46.3	52.2	62.9
409.6	43.4	296.9	465.7	707.5	1,046.3
494.1	446.9	548.4	503.8	492.9	502.3
218.8	153.6	202.5	194.6	235.3	302.2
17,626.2	28,107.9	35,667.6	38,498.2	43,018.9	48,822.7
15,109.0	22,357.7	27,741.5	30,207.9	33,850.6	38,884.7
2,661.8	3,267.0	3,970.4	4,219.2	4,654.1	4,873.7
2,190.7	4,826.4	6,488.6	6,704.4	7,371.6	7,960.7
357.9	1,081.4	1,610.1	1,573.5	1,545.1	1,721.4
298.0	853.9	1,296.1	1,434.5	1,636.1	1,795.0
176.8	318.1	377.8	426.3	519.9	699.2
143.5	234.5	275.8	293.8	360.1	472.2
33.2	83.6	102.0	132.5	159.8	226.9
1,139.4	2,065.7	2,844.5	3,291.3	3,836.4	4,328.7
96.3	210.5	410.2	466.0	583.0	697.1
17.7	34.2	67.4	102.0	124.6	152.0
6.6	22.4	27.0	21.6	29.0	29.9
420.5	789.5	860.2	888.2	1,115.4	1,316.4
398.7	617.4	588.5	705.9	754.6	895.6
211.5	354.3	453.2	505.6	565.7	509.7
	51.7	451.7	608.1	700.4	718.0
12.4	42.3	80.7	117.5	117.2	191.9

Table 4.9-15 shows actual and projected state and local government general revenue from fiscal years 1955 to 1975. General revenue is projected to increase by 98 percent from 1965 to 1975, as compared with the above projected increase of 64 percent in the expenditures of public institutions of higher education from 1967–68 to 1977–78.

SOCIAL WELFARE EXPENDITURES FOR EDUCATION

Social welfare expenditures under public programs as a percentage of GNP rose from 2.4 percent in 1889–90 to 9.2 percent in 1939–40 and to 15.0 percent in 1969–70. Public expenditures on education in these same years were 1.1, 2.7, and 5.1 percent of GNP. Public expenditures on insurance and health increased relatively more than public expenditures on education during this period.[6]

Social welfare expenditures under public programs for selected fiscal years from 1928–29 to 1969–70 are given in Table 4.9-16. In 1969–70 public expenditures on social welfare totaled $143 billion. Public expenditures on education increased approximately 19 times from 1928–29 to 1969–70, while public expenditures on higher education increased approximately 43 times. Total public expenditures for social welfare programs increased approximately 35 times during this period.

Table 4.9-17 shows actual and projected per capita expenditures by state and local governments for fiscal years 1955 to 1975. From 1955 to 1965, the relative increase in state and local government expenditures (per capita) on education exceeded the relative increase in all other major categories of per capita expenditures except interest on debt. From 1965 to 1975, however, seven categories of per capita expenditures are projected to increase relatively more than per capita expenditures for education.

Table 4.9-18 gives actual and projected general expenditures by state and local governments for fiscal years 1955 to 1975. From 1965 to 1975 state and local government expenditures for education are projected to increase by 83 percent, as compared with projected increases of 170 percent for public welfare and 97 percent for health and hospitals.

From 1928–29 to 1969–70, the federal government's share of expenditures for social welfare increased from 20.4 to 53.7 percent of the total. During this same period the federal share of expendi-

---

[6] A. M. Skolnik and S. R. Dales, "Social Welfare Expenditures, 1969–70," *Social Security Bulletin,* vol. 33, no. 12, December 1970, p. 9.

TABLE 4.9-17 *Per capita expenditures for selected state and local functions, actual and projected, fiscal years 1955–1975*

Function	Actual amount 1955	1965	Projected, 1975	Increase	Percentage change 1955–1965	1965–1975
Total, general expenditures	$205	$387	$655	$268	+ 89	+ 69
Education	72	150	244	94	+108	+ 63
Highways	39	63	76	13	+ 62	+ 21
Public welfare	20	33	79	46	+ 65	+139
Health and hospitals	15	28	49	21	+ 87	+ 75
Sanitation and sewerage	7	12	20	8	+ 71	+ 67
Police and fire	12	20	33	13	+ 67	+ 65
Housing and urban renewal	3	6	12	6	+100	+100
General control	9	14	22	8	+ 56	+ 57
Interest on debt	5	13	24	11	+160	+ 85
Other general	23	48	96	48	+ 50	+108

SOURCE: Actual data from U.S. Department of Commerce, Bureau of the Census. Computations and projections by Tax Foundation; in U.S. Congress, Joint Economic Committee, *Revenue Sharing and Its Alternatives: What Future for Fiscal Federalism?*, *Hearings before Subcommittee on Fiscal Policy*, July and August 1967, p. 72.

TABLE 4.9-18 *State and local general expenditures, actual and projected, fiscal years 1955–1975 (dollars in billions)*

Function	Actual amount 1955	1965	Projected, 1975	Increase	Percentage change 1955–1965	1965–1975
Total, general expenditures	$33.7	$75.0	$142.0	$67	+123	+ 89
Education	11.9	29.0	52.9	22	+144	+ 83
Highways	6.5	12.2	16.6	4	+ 89	+ 36
Public welfare	3.2	6.3	7.1	11	+ 99	+170
Health and hospitals	2.5	5.4	10.6	5	+112	+ 97
All other	9.7	22.1	44.8	22	+128	+103

SOURCE: Actual data from U.S. Department of Commerce, Bureau of the Census. Computations and projections by Tax Foundation; in U.S. Congress, Joint Economic Committee, *Revenue Sharing and Its Alternatives: What Future for Fiscal Federalism?*, *Hearings before Subcommittee on Fiscal Policy*, July and August 1967, p. 70.

TABLE 4.9-19 Program	1928–29	1939–40	1949–50	1954–55
TOTAL	20.4	39.1	44.8	44.8
Social insurance	16.3	31.0	42.5	64.9
Public aid		62.4	44.2	50.1
Health and medical programs	13.3	15.7	29.2	37.1
Veterans' program	100.0	98.5	93.0	98.7
Education	1.5	2.9	2.3	4.3
Housing		100.0	100.0	83.7
Other social welfare	1.8	9.4	38.9	40.7
All health and medical care†	20.6	22.7	44.4	44.1

TABLE 4.9-19 *Social welfare expenditures under public programs: federal funds as percentage of total, selected fiscal years, 1928–29 to 1969–70*

* Preliminary estimates.

† Combines "health and medical programs" with medical services provided in connection with social insurance, public aid, veterans', vocational rehabilitation, and antipoverty programs.

SOURCE: A. M. Skolnik and S. R. Dales, "Social Welfare Expenditures, 1969–70," *Social Security Bulletin,* vol. 33, no. 12, p. 8, December 1970.

tures for education increased from 1.5 to 11.5 percent (Table 4.9-19).

In the last 40 years, social welfare expenditures from public funds as a percentage of all government expenditures has tended upwards, with an increase of 20 percent from 1928–29 to 1969–70. This relative increase in social welfare expenditures has been particularly large for the state and local government sector. From 1928–29 to 1969–70, state and local government expenditures for social welfare as a percentage of all state and local government expenditures increased by 60 percent. State and local government expenditures for education as a percentage of state and local government non-trust-fund expenditures increased by 43 percent in this period (Table 4.9-20).

1959–60	1964–65	1966–67	1967–68	1968–69	1969–70*
47.7	48.9	53.5	54.1	54.1	53.7
74.1	77.6	81.8	82.8	83.8	82.9
51.6	57.2	59.5	58.2	57.6	57.9
38.9	44.5	48.3	50.0	50.4	51.1
98.0	99.7	99.7	99.6	99.4	99.2
4.9	8.8	14.8	13.2	11.7	11.5
81.2	74.9	74.9	75.9	79.5	84.0
36.6	39.3	47.7	51.7	50.8	51.6
45.6	48.6	62.2	68.9	66.5	66.7

PUBLIC EXPENDITURES FOR HIGHER EDUCATION   Public expenditures for higher education rose from $604 million in 1949–50 to $6,239 million in 1969–70. Private expenditures for higher education rose from $830 million to $6,700 million in this same period. Public expenditures for higher education increased relatively more than private expenditures in these years—a 1,032 percent increase for public as compared with a 806 percent increase in private expenditures for higher education.[7] This was related to the increase in enrollment in public institutions as a percentage of total enrollment in higher education.

[7] Ibid., p. 15.

TABLE 4.9-20
Social welfare
expenditures
from public
funds,* in
relation to
government
expenditures for
all purposes,
by type of
funds, selected
fiscal years,
1928–29 to
1969–70

Item	1929	1940	1950	1955	1960
All social welfare expenditures from public funds:					
Total, as a percentage of all government expenditures	36.3	49.0	37.6	32.7	38.0
Federal, as a percentage of all federal government expenditures	30.9	40.4	26.2	22.3	28.1
State and local, as a percentage of all state and local government expenditures‡	38.2	57.3	60.1	55.3	58.3
Social welfare trust-fund expenditures:					
Total, as a percentage of total government expenditures	2.3	5.7	6.8	9.1	13.1
Federal, as a percentage of all federal government expenditures	1.2	3.5	4.5	9.1	15.2
State and local, as a percentage of all state and local government expenditures‡	2.6	7.9	11.3	8.9	8.8
Social welfare non-trust-fund expenditures:					
Total, as a percentage of total non-trust-fund expenditures	34.9	46.2	35.0	26.2	29.5
Federal, as a percentage of federal government non-trust-fund expenditures:					
All programs	30.2	38.7	24.7	14.7	15.9
Veterans' programs	25.2	7.0	17.0	7.4	6.9
State and local, as a percentage of state and local government non-trust-fund expenditures:‡					
All programs	36.5	53.7	55.0	50.9	54.3
Education	32.4	30.5	36.1	38.9	42.6

* Excluding that part of workmen's compensation and temporary disability insurance payments made through private carriers and self-insurers.
† Preliminary estimates.
‡ Excludes federal grants-in-aid.

SOURCE: A. M. Skolnik and S. R. Dales, "Social Welfare Expenditures, 1969–70," *Social Security Bulletin,* vol. 33, no. 12, p. 11, December 1970.

1965	1967	1968	1969	1970†
42.5	42.4	42.4	44.3	47.0
32.6	35.0	35.3	37.5	39.7
61.7	57.7	57.2	57.7	60.8
14.4	15.0	15.3	16.1	16.8
17.8	19.0	19.5	21.2	21.9
7.9	6.8	6.6	6.2	6.9
33.7	33.0	32.6	34.2	37.0
18.9	20.4	20.2	21.3	23.6
6.2	5.3	5.1	5.3	5.8
58.3	54.6	54.2	54.9	57.9
47.0	44.2	43.5	43.9	46.2

Productivity and Structure

5.1. *The Issue of Productivity*

Any economist who raises the issue of productivity or economical operation of institutions of higher education is likely to be criticized for stressing problems of finance more than problems of education. He is also likely to be told—and the author has been confronted with this charge by a number of college presidents—that he is undermining fund-raising programs of colleges and universities. College administrators seem to believe that a businessman will refuse to open his wallet for them if he hears from an economist that colleges operate inefficiently.

Many college presidents, however, have complained of inefficiencies in administration and of serious wastes of resources. College administrators can correctly contend that inefficiencies exist in all large organizations—business, government, and education. However, the particular structure of the administration of institutions of higher education, which is related to problems of tenure and academic freedom, tends to reduce productivity. Administrators, politicians, bureaucrats, and faculty share the blame for the inefficiencies that could be corrected. But it is my considered opinion that the heaviest responsibility lies with the faculty, for they are generally most reluctant to cut down on waste and modify curricula, teaching hours, and teaching methods.

In the early 1960s I sent a questionnaire to hundreds of economists likely to be knowledgeable in this field, and the response revealed a widespread grasp of the economic problems of higher education. Economists were aware of the costs of an excessive number of courses, small classes, and inefficient use of plant, and were also aware of the heavy costs of teaching poor students. They knew too about the blocks placed by the faculty in the way of needed advances in curriculum.

Many of these economists wanted both more lectures and more

875

small groups to teach. They frequently proposed large classes for average or below average students, and possibly for most students for the first two years, but they also urged greater personal contact between teachers and the able students. Although most of these economists believed that more efficient operation of colleges is possible, they were quite aware of the dangers of treating a college like a business. "Do not allow the efficiency expert to take over!" was a frequent warning.[1]

THE CONTRIBUTION OF EDUCATION TO NATIONAL GROWTH

In the most useful study available on the contribution of education to national growth and productivity, Edward Denison estimated the contribution of education to the growth rate of real national income. He concluded that from 1929 to 1957 education accounted for 23 percent of the total growth rate and 42 percent of the growth rate per employed worker.[2] These results are, of course, only roughly correct. Since some relevant variables such as improved health care were omitted, the importance of education to economic growth is somewhat overstated.

MEASURES OF PRODUCTIVITY IN HIGHER EDUCATION

How productive a college is depends in no small part upon the use to which it is put. If a third-rate college, through modern public relations, attracts first-class students, the loss to the students and to the nation is serious. It is important that the college and the students be matched in a manner that will maximize the product.

However, it is not easy to measure the product or to estimate input-output ratios for higher education. Some often-used measures of the quality of an institution are: the number of Ph.D.'s on the faculty, the number of outstanding books in the library, the number of graduates in *Who's Who,* the number of outstanding books written by graduates, the number of Nobel Prize winners on the faculty, the number of scientists graduated from the college, and the number of students who win a Woodrow Wilson Fellowship or gain access to outstanding graduate schools. Perhaps the most important measure of institutional quality is the quality of the faculty. Unfortunately the above list does not tell us much about the quality of the product turned out. In particular, it does not con-

---

[1] S. E. Harris, *Higher Education: Resources and Finance,* McGraw-Hill Book Company, New York, 1962, pp. 557–558.

[2] E. F. Denison, *The Sources of Economic Growth and the Alternatives before Us,* Committee for Economic Development, New York, January 1962, tables 32, 33.

sider variations in the quality of students entering college. The productivity of colleges and universities depends on input as well as output. Students with serious intellectual interests tend to go to colleges which have the greatest impact in turning out productive graduates.

One simple measure of the quality of an institution is the number of graduates of the institution who go on to receive a Ph.D. R. H. Knapp and H. B. Goodrich studied 18,000 scientists who attended college in the period 1924 to 1934.[3] They found that, in general, the small liberal arts colleges had the largest percentage of their science graduates (with bachelor's degrees) go on to earn Ph.D.'s. A later study by Knapp and Joseph Greenbaum,[4] covering the years 1946 to 1951, was concerned with the production of future Ph.D.'s in all fields. The results of this study showed that large, high-cost institutions had the largest percentage of their graduates go on to earn Ph.D.'s. In 1962 Astin and Holland[5] found a close relationship among the financial resources of a college, student quality, and Ph.D. output. Student quality and Ph.D. output seem to rise with the financial resources of the institution. Austin and Holland concluded that ". . . the scholarly product of a college rests largely on the academic abilities, attitudes and values of the students who enter it." In other words, productivity depends on input as well as output.

The productivity of the college depends also on the extent to which the student can be changed. If no progress is possible after age 17, then the contribution of higher education can be small indeed. But the view is increasingly held that, though many will not gain after 18, growth even after 21 is possible for many others.

Pace and Stern have developed a College Characteristics Index (CCI) which is a scale that attempts to characterize the influences and interrelationships of colleges and their students. Stern has developed an Activities Index (AI) which attempts to measure students' psychological needs. Stern published the results of the applications of the CCI and AI of 75 colleges. On the CCI scale for intellectual climate, 11 institutions of higher education stood out.

---

[3] U.S. Congress, Joint Economic Committee, *The Economics and Financing of Higher Education in the United States,* a compendium of papers submitted to the Joint Economic Committee, 1969, pp. 208–209.

[4] Ibid., pp. 208–209.

[5] Ibid., p. 209.

Among them were Oberlin, Reed, Bryn Mawr, Swarthmore, and Wesleyan.[6]

It is obvious that the quality and operation of the college are crucial. But also important is the capacity of the student to react to what the college offers.

Robert H. Berls summarizes his views in an excellent article on the determinants of effectiveness of higher education:

We can conclude that the possibilities for significant developmental change in college depend on a state of readiness in the student. An intellectual predisposition (as well as ability) is necessary, but the psychological state of readiness that can be traced back to early environmental influence—particularly the family—is also necessary.

Although the predisposition for change in the student is critical, after that it is the nature of the college environment the student enters which will determine how much he will grow and change. The kinds of responses desired in college cannot be made unless the student is ready. The condition of readiness is needed for further development, but it is not itself a sufficient cause of such development—this is where the nature of the college he enters becomes of great importance.

It is true that the distinctive character of colleges with strong intellectual climates is partly dependent on student quality, but it is also dependent on institutional processes and characteristics that are independent of the students who attend those colleges. Lack of ability or lack of an intellectual predisposition in students are not the only characteristics that give a college a weak intellectual climate, and it is not student ability and intellectuality alone that give a college a pervasive intellectual climate. The nature of the faculty and administration, their policies and practices, are just as important.[7]

INCOME DIFFERENTIAL OF COLLEGE GRADUATES   A measure of the benefits of higher education to its graduates is the excess earnings of college graduates over the earnings of high school graduates. In 1961 the Bureau of the Census estimated the lifetime income of college graduates at $361,000, as compared with an estimated lifetime income of $224,000 for high school graduates. Thus, the lifetime income of the average college graduate was approximately 61 percent larger than the lifetime income of the average high school graduate. In 1939 the college graduate was estimated to have a 57 percent larger lifetime income (Table 5.1-1).

[6] Ibid., pp. 237ff.
[7] Ibid., p. 260.

	Elementary–high school differential			High school–college differential		
Year	Elementary school graduates	High school graduates	Ratio	High school graduates	College graduates	Ratio
1961	$169	$224	75	$224	$361	62
1959	169	228	74	228	397	57
1958	146	202	72	202	339	60
1956	146	199	70	199	311	64
1949	107	149	72	149	241	62
1946	85	114	75	114	169	67
1939	(NA)	67	(NA)	67	105	64

TABLE 5.1-1 Estimated lifetime income (earnings) of males 25 to 64 years old, by years of school completed, for selected years, 1939 to 1961 (in thousands)

NOTE: NA = Not available.

SOURCE: H. P. Miller, *Income Distribution in the United States,* U.S. Bureau of the Census, 1966, p. 163.

The relative change from 1939 to 1961 was minimal despite the vast output of college graduates since 1939.

Actually the method of estimating the impact on the college graduate makes a large difference. The graduates under consideration in this table are those already on the labor market. If the estimate were tied to the lifetime differential income of the *current crop* of college graduates, the net gains would be found to be a multiple of $137,000.

Higher education should not receive full credit for the larger income of the college graduate, however. The interaction of the student with his college, the innate ability of the college graduate, and environmental conditions are also important. But it may well be that the ability differential should not be given too much emphasis. Ability without the appropriate education adds little to income. Furthermore, to the extent that the college graduate gets preferential treatment in hiring for jobs not technically requiring a college degree, the income differential may be created by depressing the earnings of those with less education rather than by raising the incomes of college graduates. We should not assume that the only measurement of the benefits of a college education is an earnings differential. Education also contributes to the good life for the graduate and has external benefits for society.

EXPENDITURES, PRICES, AND PRODUCTIVITY

In most sectors of the economy, increases in productivity inhibit price increases. However, in such service markets as medicine and education, increases in productivity are very limited and contribute little to offsetting the rise in costs. The Carnegie Commission on Higher Education has put the problem well:

> For many other activities of society, rising costs are offset in substantial part by accompanying rises in productivity. Unfortunately, higher education has not and perhaps cannot offset its rising costs in this manner. Despite improvements in college management and experiments in programmed learning and other new techniques, no major ways are likely to be found in the short run which will make it possible to educate more students at the same level of expenditures without lowering academic quality. The search for techniques to improve educational productivity without endangering quality should be actively pressed forward; as was indicated in the Foreword to this Report, efficiency in the use of resources is one of the major areas of higher education mapped out for study by the Carnegie Commission. In the meantime, it is inevitable that costs per student will continue to rise.[8]

What is striking in higher education is the relatively rapid increase in expenditures as compared with increases in the cost of living. The large increase in total expenditures, of course, is attributable to increases in enrollment as well as to the rise in the cost of services.

An indication of factors contributing to increases in expenditures on higher education is given by a comparison of changes over almost 100 years:

Income, enrollment, degrees, and number of institutions, 1963–64, as multiple of corresponding item in 1870

Income	362	(1890–1967)
Resident degree-credit enrollment	80	
Baccalaureate and first professional degrees	52	
Number of institutions of higher education	23	

SOURCES: See especially S. E. Harris, *The Market for College Graduates,* Harvard University Press, Cambridge, Mass., 1949; U.S. Office of Education, *Digest of Educational Statistics, 1968,* 1968; and U.S. Office of Education, *Financial Statistics of Institutions of Higher Education: Current Funds, Revenues, and Expenditures, 1966–67,* 1969.

[8] Carnegie Commission on Higher Education, *Quality and Equality: New Levels of Federal Responsibility for Higher Education,* McGraw-Hill Book Company, New York, 1968, p. 6.

The enormous rise in income is explained by the large increases in enrollment and also, of course, by the increase in unit costs. The latter is related to general inflationary pressures as well as to other factors inducing higher costs—e.g., salary increases and increased services provided by institutions of higher education. Wage and salaries comprise a large proportion of expenditures of institutions of higher education, and thus, as wages and salaries rise, the impact on expenditures is great.

The escalation of the budget in recent years is explained both by the rise of numbers—more than 100 percent in the 1960s—and by the increased cost per student. Thus, from 1959–60 to 1965–66, costs per student rose at an annual average rate of 4 percent in public institutions of higher education and 8 percent in private institutions. The consumer price index rose at an annual average rate of less than 1.5 percent in the six-year period.

The contrast in increases of prices and expenditures, a difference that is related to sluggishness in the improvement in productivity, is suggested by the recent experience with library expenditures of institutions of higher education. Thus, from 1950 to 1965, the average price of library books doubled, but the consumer price index rose only 31 percent. In five recent years, library expenditures rose four times as rapidly as the cost of living.

Elsewhere, I summarized the explanation of rising expenditures:

Why Costs per Student Rise.   Continued rises in unit costs in stable dollars over this period of sixty to seventy years—despite the trend toward low-cost education and the increased size of the unit, a factor tending to reduce costs—may surprise many. Among the explanations are the rising standards in the economy which spill over to higher education through competition for goods and services, the difficulties confronting higher education in matching productivity gains in the economy, the rising proportion of students in the upper two years and graduate work, and the change in the product—e.g., the use of expensive equipment, provision of health, social activities, research.[9]

The increase in educational and general income of institutions of higher education since 1889–90 has been many times that of national income, but, over much of this period, educational and

---

[9] S. E. Harris, *Higher Education: Resources and Finance,* McGraw-Hill Book Company, New York, 1962, p. xxi.

general income *per student* rose much less than *per capita* national income:

Enrollment in higher education, educational and general income per student, national income, and national income per capita, 1959–60 as multiple of corresponding item in 1889–90

Enrollment	21
Educational and general income	174
National income	52
Educational and general income per student	8 to 9
National income per capita	17

SOURCE: S. E. Harris, *Higher Education: Resources and Finance,* McGraw-Hill Book Company, New York, 1962, especially pp. 9, 19.

What is striking in the above table is that over a period of 70 years the increase in educational and general income was 8 times that of enrollment and 3⅓ times that of national income, but educational and general income per student rose only one-half as much as per capita national income.

The rise in educational and general income is compounded of the rise in enrollment, and—a more important factor—the large increase in unit costs—in turn related to general inflationary pressures, rising prices of services, expansion of services, and the large increase in the number of graduate students, with their relatively high educational costs. That educational and general income per capita rose only about one-half as much as national income per capita suggests that the standards of higher education, as measured by unit prices, have generally fallen behind overall national standards in the economy.

TUITION, AID, AND PRODUCTIVITY One measure of productivity is the number of students graduating from institutions of higher education. The less the costs of student subsidies per student, the more productive the process, as viewed by the providers of subsidies, public and private.

College administrators increase their enrollments by offering large tuition subsidies. With students paying 40 percent of total institutional costs, overall budgets of $40 billion estimated as needed by 1976–77 imply tuition subsidies of $24 billion. These are large subsidies, compared to estimated needs for student aid of $2 to $4 billion. The problem, which has been mentioned at various points in previous sections, is that tuition subsidies are conferred on many who do not need them.

The provision of student aid makes possible an increase in total tuition income many times the amount spent on aid—thus encouraging the access of students from low-income families to institutions of higher education. A given amount of money used to help students through direct aid is much more productive than a reduction of tuition, which becomes available to all irrespective of need. However, a reservation is needed here. By placing their main emphasis on need, college administrators may sacrifice quality in the students admitted. In selecting graduate students, relatively more attention is paid to the quality of the student, and hence more aid is provided in relation to need than is the case for aid to undergraduates.

Loans are less costly than scholarships for obvious reasons— a given sum will contribute greater increases in enrollment than in the case of scholarships. Loans are especially effective if made available over long periods of time. The financing of a four-year education over 30 to 40 years—the period in which benefits from higher education accrue—is to be welcomed, especially in view of the fact that the burden of repayment is reduced as incomes rise.

ENROLLMENT, DEGREES, AND PRODUCTIVITY

Another measure of productivity is enrollment in relation to a given input of resources.

Enrollment is related to a number of factors: (1) the objectives and philosophy of institutions of higher education, (2) costs per student in relation to resources available to a student, (3) benefits he personally expects to derive, and (4) many other influences. Where tuition is subsidized, the institutions will have to be cautious in accepting additional students if there is a deficit, say, of $1,000 to $2,000 in operating expenses per additional student and if, for example, the contribution of endowment income per student drops by $500 as enrollment rises. Similar caution may be induced if large additional capital outlays are needed per added student.

In its report on the future of private higher education in New York State, the Bundy Committee recommended using degrees awarded, rather than enrollment, as the basis for determining the amount of aid to private institutions of higher education; the institution would receive from the state a given number of dollars per graduate.[10] It was argued that this method would avoid the difficulties involved in measuring enrollment and would provide incentives for completing degrees and concentrating on degrees — "place an emphasis on productivity as against sheer numbers of students."

Other factors also help to determine the level of enrollment. State governments and taxpayers have a tendency to be cautious in increasing facilities because of potential migration of graduates of their institutions of higher education to other states.

NATIONAL SCIENCE FOUNDATION STUDY OF INSTITUTIONAL PRODUCTIVITY
Perhaps the best study of institutional productivity was made by the National Science Foundation.[11] This study deals primarily with the contributions of the federal government to science and manpower production. The inputs are:

> . . . specialized economic and educational resource data based upon the academic institution's total income, the size and character of its student body (with special reference to graduate students and students of science), the size and character of its faculty, and the nature of its facilities. These are the inputs. . . . These techniques must seek out the relationship between the institution's output of trained science graduates at various academic levels and productivity in science and technology.[12]

The study divided colleges and universities into four classes of institutions. Class A institutions awarded at least one doctorate in science or engineering, or at least one degree of doctor of medicine or dentistry. Class B institutions awarded at least one master's degree in science or engineering, but no doctorates in science and technology, nor any degrees in medicine or dentistry. Class C institutions awarded at least one baccalaureate in science or engineering, but neither master's nor doctor's degrees in medicine, dentistry, or veterinary medicine. Class D institutions awarded at least one baccalaureate degree in any field of learning, but no degrees in science or engineering, medicine, dentistry, veterinary medicine, agriculture, or paramedical subjects.[13]

[10] Select Committee on the Future of Private and Independent Higher Education in New York State, *New York State and Private Higher Education,* Bureau of Publications, Albany, N.Y., January 1968.

[11] National Science Foundation, *The Dynamics of Academic Science,* 1967.

[12] Ibid., p. v.

[13] Ibid., p. 28.

A scale was needed for computing institutional productivity in science and technology—the reduction of all degrees in science and technology to a unit system based on a common denominator. The scale adopted—the science and technology degree productivity unit (S&T DP)—uses the baccalaureate degree in science and engineering as the base, with a value of 1. Other numerical assignments were 2.2 S&T DP units for the degree of veterinary medicine, 2.5 units for the master's degree in science and engineering, 4.0 for the degrees of doctor of medicine and doctor of dentistry, and 4.5 for the degree of doctor of science and engineering.[14]

Total enrollment was used as a measure of an institution's total educational capability. Graduate enrollment as a percentage of total enrollment was used as a measure of the extent to which an institution participated in graduate education. The science education index—the degree to which an institution contributes to science education—was defined as the number of science and technology degree productivity units divided by total enrollment.[15]

Table 5.1-2 presents some of the results of the National Science Foundation study. In 1962–63, class A institutions accounted for the majority of the degree-registered students. They enrolled almost 50 percent of the students in the study population and 71 percent of the graduate students. Class A institutions had the largest average enrollment (10,069) and the largest average enrollment of graduate students (1,560). Class A institutions also had the highest ratio of graduate students to total enrollment. In terms of science and technology and degree productivity units, class A institutions accounted for 74.5 percent of the nation's educational productivity in the sciences and engineering. Class B and class C institutions accounted for 14.1 and 11.4 percent of the science and technology productivity units, respectively.

In 1962–63 public institutions enrolled 60 percent of the degree-registered students and 58 percent of the graduate students. Class A public institutions enrolled 33 percent of all degree-registered students and 39 percent of all graduate students and accounted for 46 percent of the science and technology degree productivity units. Class A private institutions, however, had the highest ratio of graduate students to total enrollment and the highest science education index. Class A public institutions appear to carry the

---

[14] Ibid., p. 34.

[15] Ibid., pp. 35–36.

TABLE 5.1-2
Enrollment
and degrees
granted in
science and
technology by
class and
control in 1,063
degree-
accredited
universities and
colleges in
academic year
1962–63

| | Number of institutions | Enrollment | | R_e † |
		Total	Graduate	
TOTAL	1,063	3,425,456	369,964	0.108
Average		3,222	348	
Percent*	100.0	100.0	100.0	
Class A	169	1,701,687	263,699	0.155
Average		10,069	1,560	
Percent*	15.9	49.7	71.3	
Class B	197	875,843	81,372	0.093
Average		4,446	413	
Percent*	18.5	25.5	22.0	
Class C	651	804,718	22,060	0.027
Average		1,236	34	
Percent*	61.3	23.5	5.9	
Class D	46	43,208	2,833	0.066
Average		939	62	
Percent*	4.3	1.3	0.8	
Denominational	480	659,965	39,212	0.059
Average		1,375	82	
Percent*	45.2	19.3	10.6	
Private	229	708,368	115,048	0.162
Average		3,093	502	
Percent*	21.5	20.6	31.1	
Public	354	2,057,123	215,704	0.105
Average		5,811	609	
Percent*	33.3	60.1	58.3	

* Percentage detail may not add to 100 because of rounding.

† R_e = Graduates student enrollment/total enrollment

‡ S&T DP = Science and technology degree productivity.

§ R_s = Science and technology degree productivity/total enrollment.

SOURCE: National Science Foundation, *The Dynamics of Academic Science*, 1967, p. 42.

By class

S&T DP‡	B.A.	M.A.	Ph.D.	D.V.M.	M.D.	D.D.S.	R_s§
277,149	132,436	26,761	7,963	823	6,873	3,181	0.081
261	125	25	7	1	6	3	
100.0	100.0	100.0	100.0	100.0	100.0	100.0	
206,533	71,528	22,902	7,963	814	6,873	3,181	0.121
1,222	423	136	47	5	41	19	
74.5	54.0	85.6	100.0	98.9	100.0	100.0	
38,967	29,259	3,859		9			0.044
198	149	20	0		0	0	
14.1	22.1	14.4	0	1.1	0	0	
31,649	31,649	0	0	0	0	0	0.039
49	49	0	0	0	0	0	
11.4	23.9	0	0	0	0	0	
0	0	0	0	0	0	0	0.000
0	0	0	0	0	0	0	
0	0	0	0	0	0	0	

By control

39,084	27,035	1,776	257	0	885	724	0.059
81	56	4	1	0	2	2	
14.1	20.4	6.6	3.2	0	12.9	22.8	
79,995	31,543	8,674	3,015	107	2,310	924	0.113
349	138	38	13		10	4	
28.9	23.8	32.4	37.9	13.0	33.6	29.0	
158,070	73,858	16,311	4,691	716	3,678	1,533	0.077
447	209	46	13	2	10	4	
57.0	55.8	61.0	58.9	87.0	53.5	48.2	

brunt of the nation's load in higher education; they also carry the heaviest load in the sciences. Class A private institutions are most highly committed in terms of their potential for graduate education and for education in science and technology.[16]

Table 5.1-3 shows enrollment and degrees granted in the sciences, ordered by the educational and general income of institu-

[16] Ibid., pp. 41–45.

TABLE 5.1-3
Enrollment and degrees in the sciences of academic institutions, rank ordered by the educational and general income, academic year 1962–63 (dollars in thousands)

Level of educational and general income (EGI)	Number	EGI†	Enrollment	
			Total	Graduate
TOTAL	1,063	$4,346,393	3,425,456	369,964
Average		4,089	3,222	348
Percent*	100.0	100.0	100.0	100.0
Above $40 million	19	1,040,195	446,340	91,595
Average		54,747	23,492	4,821
Percent*	1.8	23.9	13.0	24.8
$20–$40 million	28	750,107	452,999	66,882
Average		26,790	16,179	2,389
Percent*	2.6	17.3	13.2	18.1
$10–$20 million	52	762,914	598,773	75,250
Average		14,671	11,515	1,447
Percent*	4.9	17.6	17.5	20.3
$5–$10 million	80	576,754	545,101	66,161
Average		7,209	6,814	827
Percent*	7.5	13.3	15.9	17.9
$1–$5 million	469	969,998	1,091,741	64,908
Average		2,068	2,328	138
Percent*	44.2	22.3	31.9	17.5
Under $1 million		246,425	290,502	5,168
Average	415	594	700	13
Percent*	39.0	5.7	8.5	1.4

* Percentage detail may not add to 100 because of rounding.
† EGI = Educational and general income.
‡ S&T DP = Science and technology degree productivity.
§ R_e = Graduate student enrollment/total enrollment.
¶ R_s = Science and technology degree productivity/total enrollment.
SOURCE: National Science Foundation, *The Dynamics of Academic Science*, 1967, p. 46.

tions, for 1962–63. Institutions with educational and general income of from $1 to $5 million accounted for about 2.5 times more enrollment than did institutions with educational and general income greater than $40 million; but institutions with income in the $1 to $5 million range account for less than three-fourths of the graduate enrollment and about three-fourths of the science and technology degree productivity units of the wealthier institutions. The smaller income group produced twice as many bachelor's

S&T DP‡	BA	MA	PhD	R_e §	R_s ¶
277,149	132,436	26,761	7,963	0.108	0.081
261	125	25	7		
100.0	100.0	100.0	100.0		
66,893	20,482	8,116	3,386	0.205	0.150
3,521	1,078	427	178		
24.1	15.5	30.3	42.5		
49,269	16,722	5,284	2,093	0.148	0.109
1,760	597	189	75		
17.8	12.6	19.7	26.3		
54,413	23,615	5,542	1,479	0.126	0.091
1,046	454	107	28		
19.6	17.8	20.7	18.6		
44,406	21,270	4,951	831	0.121	0.081
555	266	62	10		
16.0	16.1	18.5	10.4		
51,487	39,986	2,829	172	0.059	0.047
110	85	6	0.4		
18.6	30.2	10.6	2.2		
10,681	10,361	39	2	0.018	0.037
26	25				
3.9	7.8	0.1			

degrees, one-third as many master's degrees, and one-twentieth as many doctor's degrees as did the institutions with incomes greater than $40 million.

Once an institution embarks on a program of advanced education, it seems to require $112 million of educational and general income for every 1,000 graduate students enrolled—independent of the total size of the student body. Institutions engaged in science education seem to require $17 million for every 1,000 S&T DP units.[17]

PRODUCTIVITY AND INSTITUTIONAL SIZE

Institutional costs per student have increased over the years despite long-term increases in institutional size. Factors contributing to rising costs have more than offset economies of scale.

A useful example of the impact of size differentials is given by the following breakdown:

Structure of costs, institutions of higher education with annual expenditures of $1 million and $30 million

Expenditures		
Amount (in millions of dollars)	$ 1	$ 30
Percent	100	100
Administration	16	7
Instruction	60	30
Library	4	2
Operation and maintenance of plant	17	7
Public services	1	8
Organized activities	1	8

SOURCE: Author's calculations.

As operations increase, the relative cost of some items greatly declines—e.g., administration and plant. The costs of instruction are relatively much higher for the small institution—60 percent versus 30 percent.

Small institutions tend to have small classes and inefficient use of plant. With costs of instruction equal to roughly 60 percent of the budget, small institutions tend to concentrate on "bread and butter education." As an institution becomes larger, the unit cost of instruction decreases and more resources become available for discretionary education. However, public services, research, and organized activities account for a much larger percentage of total expenditures in large than in small institutions.

[17] Ibid., pp. 48–50.

H. H. Jenny and R. Wynn made an interesting study of the growth rates of 31 liberal arts institutions from 1959–60 to 1967–68. The annual growth rate of enrollment ranged from 1.5 to 12.1 percent for the 31 institutions, and the annual increase in costs per full-time equivalent student ranged from 25.7 to 78.2 cents. On the basis of the preceding discussion, it might be expected that expenditures on instruction and administration would rise substantially less than the average rise in total expenditures. This did not happen, although the increase in expenditures on plant operation and maintenance was along expected lines. In this period average total expenditures increased at an annual average rate of 9.20 percent, while expenditures on administration increased by 9.15 percent (Table 5.1-4). Jenny and Wynn conclude:

> . . . It appears as if the colleges with the higher enrollment growth rates *do indeed* pass on to the students (or to those who subsidize the student) a substantially smaller percentage of the marginal total cost than the college with the slower enrollment growth.[18]

OPTIMUM SIZE The problem of determining optimum size is complex. Ph.D. programs, which are highly expensive, provide an example of the difficulties. The output of doctorates has increased exceedingly rap-

[18] U.S. Congress, Joint Economic Committee, *The Economics and Financing of Higher Education in the United States,* a compendium of papers submitted to the Joint Economic Committee, 1969, p. 292.

TABLE 5.1-4
Annual rate of increase in expenditures and income for 31 liberal arts colleges, from 1959–60 to 1967–68

Expenditure	Annual average rate of increase	Income	Annual average rate of increase
TOTAL	9.20	TOTAL	8.41
Student aid	13.37	Gifts for operation	11.11
Library	12.49	Tuition and fees	9.69
Instruction	9.15	Auxiliary	5.70
Administration	10.17	Endowment	6.15
Auxiliary	6.46		
Plant operation and maintenance	6.48		

SOURCE: Adapted from A. M. Cartter and R. L. Farrell, "Academic Labor Market Projections and the Draft," *The Economics and Financing of Higher Education in the United States,* a compendium of papers submitted to the Joint Economic Committee, U.S. Congress, Washington, D.C., 1969, p. 269.

idly. The average annual number of doctor's degrees awarded in the top ten universities (based on quality) rose from 48 in 1920–1929 to 237 in 1960–1962. But even in the latter period, the twenty-sixth to fiftieth schools, in terms of quality, turned out an average of only 76 doctorates per year, and the next 25 only 34. These are indeed small operations for doctoral programs, suggesting that federal stimulation of new centers of doctoral education may have gone too far.[19]

It is generally assumed that unit costs decline with increasing enrollment, but the problem is considerably more complex than this simple inverse relationship suggests. Clearly the location of the institution, the number of professional schools, and the conditions in the area are all relevant. Furthermore, it is important to take account of noneconomic as well as economic considerations in determining optimum size. The Haverford College case underlines the conflict between economic considerations which suggest the desirability of larger enrollment and noneconomic aspects—for example, no more enrollment than the chapel can accommodate. In an earlier discussion of this problem, I have also pointed out that, beyond a certain point, increases in enrollment fundamentally change the nature of the institutions.[20]

Unit costs vary greatly by types of institutions:

In general costs are higher in public than in private institutions.

Once we eliminate research, extension, and public services, unit costs drop substantially, roughly by 20 percent.

Unit costs are particularly high in "other professional schools." It need hardly be said that costs vary by schools in this category; for example, unit costs are especially high in medicine. The costs in public "other professional schools" are roughly about three times as large as in the private schools. Undoubtedly the large enrollments in private urban universities with large professional schools is part of the explanation.

Technological schools also have high unit costs. This is explained by the expensive laboratories and the large number of classes which students are required to attend.

Low-cost operations are especially prevalent in theological schools and in junior colleges. In the former this undoubtedly is due to the low pay of

[19] I am indebted to Chancellor Allan Cartter, New York University, for these data. See also A. M. Cartter, *An Assessment of Quality in Graduate Education,* American Council on Education, Washington, D.C., 1966, p. 120.

[20] S. E. Harris, *Higher Education: Resources and Finance,* McGraw-Hill Book Company, New York, 1962, pp. 573–580.

faculty and persists despite the low enrollment per institution, which should bring high unit costs. In the junior colleges an explanation is low pay and less costly forms of instruction, as suggested by the high student/faculty ratio.

The average cost per student in the liberal arts college is roughly two-thirds of that in the universities. Why should this be so? The answer seems to be that the university is made up of an arts and science college, a graduate school of arts and science, which is an expensive operation, and professional schools. Indeed the average size of a university is much larger than that of a liberal arts college, and undoubtedly many liberal arts colleges are too small to be efficient. But the major factor seems to be the structure of the university and its higher level of pay.[21]

SIZE OF CLASSES

It is a widely held view that small classes are more productive than large classes. Few would question the conclusion that small classes are more costly than large ones; but the recourse to small classes is supposedly justified by the superior product turned out. The late Beardsley Ruml, anxious to make higher education viable, proposed to do away with medium-sized classes and concentrate on large lectures and small seminars. What is striking is that almost every study made of the subject has revealed that the educational product of the large class either exceeds that of the small class, or at least that class size makes no significant difference in the quality of the product. Furthermore, so many other factors are relevant to the productivity of an institution that class size must be a relatively small influence. But costs are important and under financial pressure costs may be decreased significantly by increasing class size. Unfortunately, the definition of a small or large class is a matter of dispute. In comparing the results of classes of varying size, one should allow for teaching aids made available in the larger classes.[22]

After reviewing a vast number of experiments on class size, the Pennsylvania State Division of Academic Research in Services concluded:

Under prevailing methods—class size bears no significant relationship to educational efficiency as measured in terms either of student achievement or any other measurable outcomes. . . . Most of the advantages of the small classes and materialistic methods of instruction accrue to the weaker

[21] Ibid., p. 58.
[22] Ibid., pp. 526–533.

students. . . . If pupil differentiation is a commendable aim, it appears to be more attainable in large classes.[23]

Professor Herbert Simon put some of the issues well, although he underestimates the state of knowledge:

There is no evidence that small classes provide a superior learning environment. I have already pointed out the budgetary importance of the class-size issue. Theoretically, one can point to the greater opportunities for providing feedback in the small class. One can also point, per contra, to its encouraging the student to depend on knowledge of results provided by the teacher.

Further, counterposing small class against large class does not really define a sharp issue in learning design: What goes on in the small class? in the large class? Above all, what is the student *doing:* what is he attending to, thinking of? When we have designed classroom processes carefully enough so that we can answer questions like these, it will be time enough to reintroduce class size as a variable.[24]

My conclusion is that the trend will be toward larger classes, in part because of rising costs and financial threats to higher education now being experienced. In numerous state studies there is already evidence of a rising student-faculty ratio, induced in part by elimination of small classes and an increase in the number of large lecture classes. I do not conclude from all this that there is no place for the tutorial or small discussion groups. But these meetings are expensive, especially in periods when personnel and finance are likely to be scarce. The continuation of the tutorial or classes of less than 10 or 15 people as well as the small classes that are needed in upper-division and graduate courses will be possible only if the wastage in classes of from 30 to 75 can be reduced through large lectures by able and inspiring lecturers.

NUMBER OF COURSES Proliferation of courses is an ancient academic disease, and a costly one. In these days of financial difficulties for higher education, one way of saving money is to reduce the number of courses offered or at least to prevent increases. It might be assumed that, if the student-faculty ratio of 16 to 1 increased to 24 to 1, there

[23] Ibid., p. 532.

[24] A. M. Cartter and R. L. Farrell, "Academic Labor Market Projections and the Draft," *The Economics and Financing of Higher Education in the United States,* a compendium of papers submitted to the Joint Economic Committee, U.S. Congress, 1969.

would be a saving of nearly $7 billion on a total outlay of $20 billion. This could be achieved if the number of courses were reduced by one-third.

However, this is a greatly exaggerated estimate of possible savings. In the first place, the instructional budget is only roughly one-half the total budget. Second, faculty members and their institutions have many responsibilities in addition to teaching. A third consideration is that there are serious obstacles to reducing the number of courses; the rise in the number of courses needed with the explosion of knowledge has been immense. Fourth, and most important, is the resistance of faculty to any attempts to restrain their penchant for more and more courses. Finally, any reduction in the number of courses would result in a disproportionate loss of jobs by young and relatively low-paid faculty. The roughly one-half of faculty members holding tenure would be protected.

A major factor contributing to the increased number of courses is the rising relative importance of enrollment in upper-division and graduate work. At these levels, the number of courses escalates, especially at the graduate level. In a special study of courses from 1902 to 1957, I found that the number of graduate courses rose by 6 times, as compared to 1⅓ times for undergraduate courses. Whereas, in this limited sample, graduate instruction accounted for one-fourth of all courses in 1902, it represented 52 percent in 1957. The graduate curriculum included more than twice as many courses in relation to enrollment as the undergraduate curriculum (Table 5.1-5).

In my 1962 study, I wrote:

TABLE 5.1-5 *Rise in enrollment, faculty, and courses, 1902–1957*

Item	1902–1957	1927–1957
Enrollment:		
Undergraduate	2½ times	½ times
Graduate	4 times	1½ times
Faculty	5 times	1 time
Courses:		
Undergraduate for seven IHL	1⅓ times	
Graduate for five IHL	6 times	
All (seven undergraduate and five graduate)	2½ times	

SOURCE: S. E. Harris, *Higher Education: Resources and Finance,* McGraw-Hill Book Company, New York, 1962, p. 525.

Since 1902, the relative rise in faculty has greatly exceeded that in enroll-ment, a conclusion strengthened when one allows for the relatively small percentage of students in graduate arts and science. This of course means a reduced teaching burden for faculty and a decline in the student/faculty ratio. But when allowance is made for the increase in research, the gains for teachers are reduced to some extent. Relief for teachers would have been much greater had not courses in graduate areas skyrocketed.[25]

President Wriston of Brown University expressed the issues well:

As governments have debased their currency to meet deficits, so have many colleges debased their education for the same purpose. By offering courses in everything, they seek to attract enough students to help balance the budget. Scandalous sophistries have been propagated to make these devices appear to have an educational, rather than a fiscal, basis. Liberal arts colleges give courses in business administration (including stenog-raphy, typing and filing), home economics (one college gives a course in "draping") and many other subjects alien to their history and purpose. None of these additions was really designed to contribute to the pursuit of happiness, one of the basic objectives in the American tradition. Such inflationary courses were concerned with the pursuit of the dollar. . . .[26]

In his able study, *Liberal Education in the Professions,* E. J. McGrath writes:

The catalogues of University-connected liberal arts colleges now display hundreds of courses, many of which have nothing in common. When stu-dents randomly assemble these varied courses in a curriculum, the mem-bers of graduating classes have little more in common educationally than the title of their degrees.[27]

At the end of my discussion, I wrote:

Sounding a warning of the dangers of proliferation of courses, a Columbia committee quotes Charles W. Eliot's forecasts in 1869: "It will be genera-tions before American institutions of education will get growth enough to bear pruning." In the view of the committee the time has arrived. Undue multiplication of courses has resulted, in the view of the committee, in excessive numbers of courses with small registration. In the university in

[25] S. E. Harris, *Higher Education: Resources and Finance,* McGraw-Hill Book Company, New York, 1962, p. 524.

[26] As quoted in S. E. Harris, ibid., p. 526.

[27] Ibid., pp. 533–536.

1956–57, there were 293 courses with zero registration. Of 2,020 courses offered on an advanced level, 404 had a registration of 10 or less, and 36 had a registration of more than 100.

An excessive number of courses is a great evil in higher education. Many college administrators are trying to deal with the problem, though they are often confronted with opposition by faculties. As a minimum, the knowledgeable and courageous administrator demands that a course be dropped when a new one is added; and he insists that small courses be alternated and, if not easily justifiable, be dropped. In the upper division and graduate curricula, a minimum number of courses with small enrollment is a price that has to be paid for necessary specialization. Clarence Faust relates an experience of a department anxious to add three members to its staff. The dean asked each member of the department to list courses considered essential for graduate preparation. The total of courses listed was 11, but the department offered 67 courses.[28]

I also suggested the possibility of saving one-sixth of the budget through a frontal attack on course proliferation. At current budgets, the gains could be $3 billion. In practice, it would probably be a major achievement to save $1 billion.

CRITICAL
ATTITUDES
TOWARD
PRODUCTIVITY
AND
MANAGERIAL
ECONOMIES

Many critics are puzzled by the difficulties encountered by our colleges and universities in increasing productivity, in view of the rising demand for the products of higher education and the downward pressure on costs associated with escalating enrollment. They fail to understand why, with productivity in the nation rising greatly over the last 50 years, higher education has not shared in these gains.

The critics point to the excessive number of courses, the inadequate use of facilities, and curricula that are at variance with objectives of the institutions. They also emphasize the economies that were introduced under the pressures of the Great Depression.

In an earlier study, I pointed out:

Why, it may be asked, in a period of fifty years when the average output per man rose about 2.2 percent per year, has the real cost of higher education increased? The answer lies in part in factors mentioned above and in the difficulty of applying the advances of technology to [institutions of higher learning]. To some extent teaching is a personal matter; it is difficult to mass-produce it. Relevant also is the fact that colleges, and particularly their faculties, have resisted change and new methods of teaching.

[28] Ibid., pp. 533–536.

Some fear that the introduction of machinery may bring about technological unemployment. Many are determined to maintain old teaching methods at all costs. It is difficult for administrations to force change upon teachers who are not employees, as industry can do when confronted with increased competition and falling prices.

In some respects colleges face the same problem as other sellers of services. In the highly mechanized industries, unit costs tend to fall rapidly with the great developments of technology and management. The result is that these industries are able to pay much higher wages out of the increased productivity. But other employments, not equally favored by these advances, must nevertheless meet the competition of more productive employments for labor and materials. Colleges must pay higher prices for all that they purchase, even though these higher prices are not offset by corresponding gains in productivity. This is a most serious aspect of the economics of higher education.[29]

Commentators such as Kiplinger and the *Wall Street Journal* editors comment on the numerous small classes, the wasteful proliferation of courses, the losses associated with the attrition experienced by students from the freshman through the senior year, and the construction of new buildings where excess capacity already prevails.

In a paper before the Conference of Moral Standards in September, 1953, President Hancher of Iowa University, one of the leading educators in the country, had some profound things to say about these issues. One question raised by President Hancher is:

"What educational program is the institution qualified to offer? The question, carefully considered, calls for an accurate, honest, complete appraisal of the institution—its staff, its facilities, its finances, its complete resources—to determine whether or not it possesses the competence and quality essential for the conduct of the program or programs which it offers. It is designed to bring institutions back to a *functional integrity* which is sadly lacking in our system."

President Hancher complains, "Few institutions hesitate to rush into new and presumably popular programs which they were not organized to offer, for which they possess no special competence, and for which the demand has been created by them rather than the public. . . ." Institutions without the requisite scientists or resources should not apply for government research contracts in order to attract staff and acquire facilities. Unrestrained and unintelligent competition reduces standards, and low

---

[29] Ibid., pp. 550–551.

standards tend to drive out high ones. Another waste that President Hancher refers to is that of recruiting new students. He is all for expensive recruiting in order to save the able students who are now left out. What concerns him is that the institution ". . . actively intervenes to affect the choice of the prospective student on grounds other than the true educational worth and attractiveness of the institution." He wants to know whether the information given is fair and accurate. Are students recruited who in their own best interests should go elsewhere? Apparently there are even solicitors who receive a commission or bonus on the basis of students signed up and matriculated. The expenditure of funds for the diversion of students from one institution to another cannot largely be justified.

And President Hancher wants to know whether the student gets the education that he is promised. "This does not preclude the giving of a trade or vocational training but it is not satisfied by such training. The educated man is more than a technician. He not only knows how a thing works but why it works. . . ."[30]

During the Depression of the 1930s, institutions of higher education drastically cut costs by such measures as increasing class sizes, not replacing faculty, and undertaking no new construction unless funds had been provided.

In the Great Depression, President Hutchins of the University of Chicago presented two alternatives: a reduction of courses and staff and maintenance of pay structure, or an unchanged staff and pay cuts. The solution chosen was the former. In some instances the choice was the latter. In North Dakota the salaries of all university teachers, of all normal school teachers, and of teachers in all other state-supported schools were fixed at $1,290 a year.

In a similar vein the president of the University of Pennsylvania writes:

"We must be prepared also to adjust existing academic practices in the interests of efficiency in teaching. For example, without sacrifice of quality, it might be possible to re-deploy the most competent teachers so that a greater percentage of them are assigned to the larger classes; to extend the use of assistance so as to relieve the teaching staff of routine administrative duties; to expand the application of audio-visual aids. At the same time the individual student must be encouraged to assume greater responsibility in the educational process, toward the end that the teacher will be relieved of much of his present duties to transmit hourly fundamental information which is really available in textual form."

In his 1955 report he said that the university would determine which programs are (1) the most central and essential or traditionally the strong-

---

[30] Ibid., pp. 552–553.

est; (2) more peripheral, specialized, or currently less developed at the university; (3) relatively narrowed or highly specialized academic activities making smaller contributions to general education; (4) inappropriate to the general educational objectives of the institution.

He was furthermore prepared to consider trends in income and allocation of resources over the last thirty years and would develop cost information per student by departments and schools, identify the areas in which the major increases have occurred since 1924, and would indicate where possible the services associated with such increases.[31]

LOCATION OF INSTITUTIONS OF HIGHER EDUCATION

The location of colleges and universities is an important factor in determining the proportion of college-age youth who actually attend college. For example, the state of Michigan has roughly twice the relative enrollment in counties in which institutions of higher education are located than in counties in which there are none. This is unfortunate, since those likely to profit from higher education are denied access because of their residence.

On the basis of a questionnaire I sent to 543 institutions in the late 1950s, I studied various aspects of operations of new institutions and of new professional schools.[32] One point was especially clear: the emergence of new institutions tends to be uneconomical in the sense that the new schools tend to be small and, therefore, have large unit costs for several years after they are opened.

These institutions relied first on educational objectives and second on cost considerations in determining their enrollment needs. The crucial variables for the choice of location were, first, the size of the student body, and second, the availability of site and buildings. For about 25 percent of these 543 institutions, the influence of interested groups was important in the determination of location. In general, this survey does suggest impaired productivity associated with the manner in which location and enrollment needs were determined.

The study reveals that economic inefficiency is not marked in those large areas which have a great many professional schools such as New York, Boston, or San Francisco, but rather in those areas of the poorer states where inadequate facilities exist. The problem to be dealt with is usually not one of the existence of a superabundance of professional schools of any

[31] Ibid., pp. 554–555.
[32] Ibid., pp. 602–608.

one type in one area, but rather how the professional school can meet the demands for higher education without placing upon the student the burden of the necessity of extensive travel to reach adequate professional facilities. In less costly methods of instruction—e.g., law and business—the problem is simple. Decentralization is the most economical approach for the institution and student. But in medicine and graduate arts and science centralization, with transportation subsidies for students living outside of large metropolitan areas, seems the most effective approach.[33]

LOCATION OF PROFESSIONAL SCHOOLS

In the rich states, there is a tendency to concentrate professional schools in one or two of the largest cities. Texas is an exception. Hence, as a result, there is frequently excessive capacity in these cities and inadequate capacity elsewhere. The excess capacity is found especially in law schools and graduate schools, but not in medical schools. Here, again, productivity is impaired because of unwise concentration of schools. But in the poorer states, these institutions are more widely distributed, and the issue becomes one of excessive numbers of schools and low utilization, expecially in law. Excess capacity prevails even as these poor states export their graduates to the wealthier states, especially in graduate arts and science. Their graduates, of course, are attracted by the higher incomes available in the wealthier states.

Medical and dental schools were established rather sporadically throughout the country but tended to cluster in three major areas:

1   Middle Atlantic (largely New York)

2   The South

3   The Pacific Coast (largely California)

ENROLLMENT AND POPULATION BY COUNTIES AND STATES

Here again one observes that the larger population centers tend to have high ratios of enrollment to population. This generalization holds for counties in Massachusetts, for counties in a number of other states, and for ten major cities: nine major cities have indices ranging from 1.0 (Cleveland) to 2.9 (New York City). The index is based on the ratio of the city's percentage of the state's total enrollment in higher education to its percentage of the state's population.[34] New York City, for example, had 38.6 percent of

[33] Ibid., pp. 608–611.

[34] Ibid., pp. 614–616 and chap. 1.

total enrollment in the state of New York and 13.2 percent of the state's population.

In other words, places with high population density tend to have greater access to higher education than other places. But this does not, of course, mean that ghetto residents have easy access to higher education.

Historically, institutions of higher education have always found large markets in large cities with intensive economic activity. This is still true today, and even with the recent growth of interregional student mobility, institutions of higher education continue to derive benefits from the so-called tertiary economic development of very large cities.

On the other hand, very large institutions are frequently located in areas of particularly low population. This is the case with agricultural and state universities, which are often located in areas with large spatial accommodations. The land-grant institutions have generally been given locations which were not overly important economically and which provided campus space and farmland when necessary.[35]

Thus, there is geographical maldistribution in the location of institutions of higher education—in part for historical reasons. This has implications for productivity, because students in some areas tend to be barred from higher education simply because of the absence of institutions in their locality.

DEFICIENT UTILIZATION OF PLANT Much waste prevails in the utilization of space. Resistance from faculty and students to afternoon and Saturday classes, for example, contributes to the nonuse of valuable facilities. Improved use would certainly save hundreds of millions of dollars. In a recent year, the operation and maintenance of physical plant involved disbursements of $690 million, or 7.5 percent of current institutional expenditures. Moreover, outlays for capital plant seem to have risen an average of $2 billion in the years 1960 to 1964. Even a saving of one-third could yield close to $1 billion annually. The wastes seem to be at least of these proportions. Not only is it clear that large savings are possible; but even more distressing is the lack of interest of higher-education administrators in these problems.

Moreover, there is evidence of disproportionate plant costs for

[35] Ibid., p. 616.

small institutions. Thus in fiscal years 1965 and 1966, the federal government provided $796 million under Titles I and II of the Higher Education Facilities Act of 1963. Institutions with enrollment of 20,000 or more accounted for 12 percent of enrollment and 4 percent of the funds disbursed.[36]

Large enrollment increases can be achieved through improved use of space. Buildings needs depend, of course, on future enrollment, in turn estimated on the basis of geographical origins of students. Moreover, allowances have to be made for crossovers — for example, the use of arts and science facilities by engineering students.

John Russell and James Doi, using as a base a study by the American Association of Collegiate Registrars and Admissions Officers, published a helpful study of space utilization. Studies of utilization of space are important, according to these writers, because they reveal uneconomic practices. More effective use, achieved by eliminating costly space or increasing the use of available space, or even by *reducing the number of classes,* can greatly reduce costs of maintaining plant.

A committee of registrars in the spring of 1956 sent an inquiry to each of its 1,400 members, asking for reports on studies of space utilization. Only 961 responded, of which number 241, or 25 percent, indicated that a study of plant space utilization had been made. But most studies were inadequate.

Percentage of possible periods during the week the student stations are occupied:

Weekly schedule, 44 hours

Stations in room, 60

Possible student-station periods, 2,640

Group of student stations occupied, 990

Percentage of possible student-station periods, 37.5

"The general impression to be gained from an examination of available space utilization is that relatively few reports showed imaginative planning and skillful execution. For the most part they are limited with respect to the kinds of plant space included, limited in techniques of analysis and generally lacking in interpretative material . . ." [Moose and Rourke, *Campus and the State,* pp. 138–139].

---

[36] U.S. Office of Education, *Digest of Educational Statistics, 1968,* 1968, pp. 96, 102; U.S. Office of Education, *Students and Buildings: An Analysis of Selected Federal Programs for Higher Education,* 1968, p. 66.

Helpful measures of utilization are suggested in the following examples:

1. *Room-period use:* forty-four hour week; 50 instructional room, or 2,200 possible room periods. With 1,100 class meetings scheduled, the average "room-period use" would be twenty-two hours, or 50 percent on a weekly basis.

2. *Student-station-period use* (the number of hours that stations [e.g., seats] are occupied):

Class occupied, 22 hours

Average class, 45

Student-period use, 990

Student-station room with 60 stations

Student hours per week per station $= 16.5 \ (990/60)$[37]

The question of improved utilization has had much study in California: in the *Strayer Report,*[38] in the *Restudy Report,*[39] and in the studies conducted during the formulation of the California Master Plan. For example, the *Restudy Report* recommended that standard room utilization of classrooms in both the state colleges and the University of California should average 36 scheduled hours per week, with class enrollment after the first month of the term or semester averaging 67 percent of room capacity, i.e., the number of student stations the room will accommodate. Five years later the Master Plan reflected doubts that these standards could be achieved, for few colleges had achieved them. Hence, for state colleges and the University of California, the Master Plan urged the maximum practical level, ". . . but in no case shall classrooms average less than 30 scheduled hours per week, with class enrollments after the first month of the term averaging 60 percent of room capacity."

In conclusion, with total costs of existing and new plant approaching $3 billion per year, with improved use of plant—through increased access in unpopular hours, through improved matching of size of class and enrollment, through central control of assign-

[37] S. E. Harris, *Higher Education: Resources and Finance,* McGraw-Hill Book Company, New York, 1962, pp. 617–618.

[38] Committee on Survey of the Needs of California in Higher Education, *A Report of a Survey of the Needs of California Higher Education,* Sacramento, Calif., March 1, 1948.

[39] Joint Staff on the Liaison Committee of the Regents of the University of California and the California State Board of Education, *A Restudy of the Needs of California in Higher Education,* Sacramento, Calif., 1955.

ment of space, through a longer school year, through more carefully considered establishments of new units and location on improved theories of location, and through other means—savings as large as $1 billion a year are within the realm of the possible.

DEGREES Earlier, I commented briefly on the use of degrees as a measure of productivity, but a few additional remarks are relevant here. In general, costs of higher education are unnecessarily increased by the proliferation of degrees. From 1643 to a recent year, American institutions of higher education had given 2,452 *different* degrees, and in this recent year they were still offering 1,600. The differentiation of degrees is wasteful, just as the differentiation of drugs reduces output per item and raises unit costs.

With 1,600 degrees, costs of planning curriculum, of administration generally, and of faculty must be much higher than if we were content, say, with 100 varieties. This is quite apart from the ability of the general public to understand the meaning, significance, and value of these numerous degrees. Undoubtedly, it would be difficult to abandon many degrees; but at the very least, new ones should be discouraged. A cooperative attempt by all the important associations of colleges and universities might well reduce the current number substantially.

The geographical distribution of degrees also raises questions of productivity. A comparison of some areas with high and low per capita incomes reveals twice as many degrees in relation to population for the high-income areas at the baccalaureate level, and five to six times as many at the doctorate level.

Wastage is also involved in accepting students incapable of profiting greatly from higher education. Only about one-half of the baccalaureate candidates get through, and that half only eventually.

THE COSTS OF INFLATION Does higher education thrive in wartime inflationary periods or in normal peacetime periods? In a provocative volume,[40] Provost William Bowen of Princeton deals with this problem. He finds that:

1   In two wartime inflation periods, the economywide cost index rose, in the first period, five times, and, in the second period, four plus times as much as direct costs per student at Chicago, Princeton, and Vanderbilt univer-

---

[40] W. G. Bowen, *The Economics of the Major Private Universities,* Carnegie Commission on Higher Education, Berkeley, Calif., 1968.

sities. The inference is that institutions of higher education are better off in inflationary periods.

2   In three normal peacetime periods from 1905 to 1966, however, direct costs per student, on the average, for the three universities, rose 5.4, 5.1, and 3.4 times as much as the economywide cost index. The inference here is that, in times of peace, institutions of higher education experience difficult financial problems, as costs to the institutions rise much more than the economywide index.

In a volume recently published[41] I studied Harvard's history over 330 years. In all but one case, I found that Harvard's financial crises occurred in inflationary periods. Indeed, in at least two of Harvard's experiences, the degree of inflation was much greater than in the periods discussed by Bowen. The inflation of the first half of the eighteenth century was followed by an 87 percent devaluation. In the Revolutionary War period, the college suffered financially as tuition and income from investments failed to respond to rising prices. Prices rose much more rapidly than Harvard's income. The students aggravated the effects of inflation by postponing payment of tuition and board even as prices escalated. The treasurer's wisdom in frequently tying interest and capital payments due to the college in the eighteenth century to the price of silver, as well as the imposition of the costs of inflation on the faculty (who had to be satisfied with salary increases that were equal to only a small part of the rise in prices), kept the college from falling into a state of bankruptcy. The college treasury also passed a major share of the costs of inflation to the faculty in World War I and World War II.

Indeed, Bowen is correct in analyzing the relationship of rising costs per student to national cost trends, but, at least on the basis of Harvard's experience, I am not prepared to accept the conclusion that inflationary periods are the relatively happy periods for the college treasurer.

FINANCIAL INCOME   Maximizing the yield on investments of institutions of higher education is a highly significant way of making more income available to finance their operations, at least for institutions with large endowments. Hence productivity may be assumed to rise as returns on investments bring increasing incomes. Because prob-

[41] S. E. Harris, *The Economics of Harvard,* McGraw-Hill Book Company, New York, 1970.

lems of gifts and endowment have been considered in Part 4, the discussion here can be brief.

Several years ago, institutions of higher education received about $550 million in private gifts and grants, or 5.8 percent of current income.[42] It was shown in an earlier chapter that there are large differences in the structure of private gifts and that of current expenditures (Table 5.1-6). It might be helpful if the relationship of these variables were closer. For example, the relatively small proportion of gifts for faculty and the large proportion for research are not well adapted to the structure of expenditures of the institutions.

Endowment has become a declining relative source of income. A good part of the explanation for this lies in the growth of national income and of the total income of institutions of higher education, but that is not the whole story. Failure to use expert investment advice; the rise of enrollment and hence reduced amounts of endowment income per student; the abandonment under a sort of legal blackmailing of the allocation of endowment income on the basis of book rather than market value; the failure to seek the maximum long-term income; the fear of using capital gains to meet current needs; the many mistakes of policy pointed out in two studies

[42] The Council for Financial Aid to Education estimated private aid in 1967–68 at $1,570 million (Council for Financial Aid to Education, American Alumni Council, and National Association of Independent Schools, *Voluntary Support of Education, 1967–68,* New York, 1969, p. 4.)

TABLE 5.1-6 Structure of gifts and expenditures, 1950s		
Purpose	Percentage of gifts, three years, 1954–55, 1956–57, 1958–59	Percentage of budget, three years, 1953–54, 1955–56, 1957–58
Faculty and staff compensation	17	41 (instruction)
Basic research	16	19
Student aid	10	3½
Receipts for plant expansion	21	24*

* 1953–54, 1955–56 only.

SOURCE: Council for Aid to Education, *Voluntary Support of America's Colleges and Universities 1958–59,* New York, p. 15; and various issues of U.S. Department of Health, Education and Welfare, *Statistics of Higher Education: Receipts, Expenditures and Property, 1957–58* (preliminary); in S. E. Harris, *Higher Education: Resources and Finance,* McGraw-Hill Book Company, New York, 1962, p. 467.

sponsored by the Ford Foundation;[43] and many other points are relevant.

It is also important to recognize that gifts are excessively restricted as to use. This does not necessarily mean that college administrators know better than potential donors what is needed, but, in fact, this is generally the case. More extensive efforts to provide information on needs to potential donors would help.

COMPENSA-TION OF FACULTY Institutions of higher education can, in some situations, make themselves viable by forcing sacrifices upon the faculty. For example, the reduction in real income experienced by faculty members in the 1940s and early 1950s, while real income of the labor force in general rose by about 50 percent, suggests recourse to pressures on faculty. But if this improves viability, it may have an adverse effect on productivity as faculty members suffer absolute losses of income and even greater relative losses of income.

Resources of institutions of higher education are wasted to some extent because salaries are tied to pay scales to an excessive degree. Hence, as resources increase, the additional funds are used to improve the income of all faculty members, and a little is diverted to increase incomes on the basis of merit. British institutions of higher education have allocated this type of resource better than American institutions. Indeed, in periods of rising prices, it is desirable that all faculty members receive additions at least to offset in part the rise of prices. But some part of available funds should also go for merit increases.

Colleges and universities confronted with financial restraints frequently narrow the range of salaries. Here again viability may be achieved at a cost in productivity if the ratio of instructors' salaries to full professors' salaries is greatly increased. Motivation of higher-ranking faculty is likely to suffer.

Salaries tend to be higher in large institutions than in small ones. Thus in the late 1950s professors in public institutions of higher education with enrollments of less than 500 received an average salary of $5,920, whereas at public institutions with enrollments of 20,000 or more, average salary was $10,420. These relative salaries may seem inconsistent with the evidence of econ-

---

[43] Advisory Committee on Endowment Management, *Managing Educational Endowments,* Ford Foundation, New York, 1969. See also W. L. Cary and C. E. Bright, *The Law and Lore of Endowment Funds,* Ford Foundation, New York, March 1969, especially p. 66.

omies of scale, but the explanation lies in the more advanced work and hence the more highly skilled personnel needed in large institutions and especially in universities.[44]

FRINGE BENEFITS

Fringe benefits contribute to the compensation of faculty, but they are relatively much more important (about 1½ times) in 16 top universities than in all institutions of higher education.

College and university administrators need to determine what share of total compensation should take the form of fringe benefits. The actual pattern reflects the relative strength of various groups seeking fringes. In general, the young prefer cash salary payments, whereas the old tend to prefer fringes. The old are closer to retirement and thus are concerned about prospective retirement income, while at the same time they run a more serious risk of prolonged illness.

Survey data indicate that many important types of fringe benefits are not available in many institutions of higher education or that benefits are not adequate. How can the situation be improved? Emphasis on medical benefits is especially deserved, since adequate health insurance improves the quality of service. The most costly fringe benefits are retirement annuities. At most institutions of higher education, retirement benefits are woefully small. Ordinarily the faculty, as well as the institution, should contribute to the pension plan. When faculty contributes, certain tax advantages may be lost, but the relative importance of contributions by faculty is suggested by a comparison of benefits at Harvard, where the faculty does not contribute, and the University of California, where the faculty does contribute. Until a few years ago, Harvard annuities provided benefits equal to one-third of final salary for a faculty member retiring after 40 years of service; at the University of California, on the other hand, a faculty member retiring after 37 years of service would receive 80 percent of his final salary. However, treatment of the younger faculty has been less than generous at the University of California.

In determining fringe policies, administrators should take advantage of government subsidies. The federal old age and survivor insurance system is especially important. In the last 20 years, this

[44] These points are more fully developed in S. E. Harris, *Higher Education: Resources and Finance,* McGraw-Hill Book Company, New York, 1962, pp. 640, 665–670, 673, 679.

program has paid out tens of billions of dollars beyond sums that would be actuarially justified in the case of private insurance. The current elderly beneficiaries have been treated most generously. Yet a few major universities—the University of California among them—relinquished their stake in the vast contributions of the federal government.

Protection against sickness, permanent disability, high general medical costs, and the vicissitudes of old age should all be available. The resultant impact on recruiting brings an improved product by the faculty members. Moreover, these programs put upon the federal and state governments, as well as on employers, additional responsibilities for financing higher education.

A Columbia survey conducted in 1956–57 indicated large gaps in fringe benefits among 49 highly selective institutions of higher education (Table 5.1-7).

One aspect of fringe benefits needs special emphasis. When the retirement benefit formula relates benefits to the salary at the time of retirement, the faculty is more effectively protected than when it does not, in view of the long-run upward trend in salaries and the fact that faculty members tend to receive their peak salaries just before retirement.

Institutions of higher education, or at least their administrators, tend to be excessively pleased with gifts for endowed chairs. Actually, in no time at all, these endowments pay less than what is needed by the incumbent. With incomes increasing at 5 percent a year, incomes would rise by about 10 times in 50 years. A chair financed with a few thousand dollars in the early eighteenth century paid less than was needed for the chair even before 1750. In the first quarter of the nineteenth century, $20,000 would finance a chair; but the same chair today requires about $30,000 of *income* or $600,000 of capital. Large numbers of endowed chairs become a liability as incomes rise.

Tenure is also a costly device. A decision to give tenure today may well involve a commitment to spend $2 million over the tenured member's lifetime. Is sufficient thought given to the needs of the relevant department and the long-run value of the fortunate tenured member?

GROWTH AND ECONOMIES   As enrollment continues to rise, the opportunity for economies increases. More effective utilization of resources, in particular, can be stimulated. Attitudes toward rising enrollment will be

TABLE 5.1-7 *Numbers of 49 institutions of higher education providing fringe benefits, 1956–57*	

Retirement programs	48
Federal OASI	41
Group life insurance	48
Medical benefits, not insured	8
Medical benefits, insured	46
Salary during disability	47
Group disability insurance	14
Tuition exchange incorporated	21
Tuition exemption, faculty	22
Tuition exemption, families	32
Place to live	35
Travel expense to meetings	48
Grants for summer study and travel	29
Research leaves	42
Money for research and publications	38
Sabbatical leaves	35
Grants for sabbaticals	17
Individual offices	40
Private secretary	0
Research assistance	35
Paper readers	38
Parking facilities	39
Services for retired	43

SOURCE: S. E. Harris, *Higher Education: Resources and Finance,* McGraw-Hill Book Company, New York, 1962, p. 685.

related to objectives of the institution as well as to the efficiency with which the additional resources will be used. On the other hand, some costs will rise disproportionately with growth. A study of 31 liberal arts colleges, for example, reveals disproportionate increases in student aid—a development that offsets to some extent the gains that come with increased outputs.[45]

Greater recourse to technological aids may well yield reduction of costs as the student-faculty ratio is affected. With improvements in technology, more energy is also devoted to the learning process.

[45] A. M. Cartter and R. L. Farrell, "Academic Labor Market Projections and the Draft," *The Economics and Financing of Higher Education in the United States,* a compendium of papers submitted to the Joint Economic Committee, U.S. Congress, Washington, D.C., 1969, pp. 261–294.

Actually, in practice, the gains of increased and improved technology are more likely to result in a better product than in financial gains. So far, the experts on educational psychology have lagged behind those who are mobilizing resources for teaching aids. Faculty members tend to be wary of improvements that may jeopardize their jobs, or, at the very least, change their teaching methods.[46]

As growth proceeds, gains are likely in achieving solutions to problems, and in improved and extended administration both internally and externally. Integration of fund-raising programs, for example, may well increase total funds made available as well as reduce the costs of fund-raising campaigns.[47]

Joint costs are the greatest obstacle to the discovery of costs of services of higher education. For example, faculty members may teach both undergraduate and graduate courses, and may also devote some of their time to research. Buildings are used for both undergraduate and graduate instruction and for research. Thus, it is very difficult to determine the relative costs per student of graduate and undergraduate education. Yet this problem does not get the attention it deserves.[48] Without knowledge of costs, appropriate pricing is difficult. Indeed, institutions of higher education are not wedded to cost pricing, as is industry. Yet, with limited resources, it is important to know what is high-cost education. If a particular course costs 10 times as much per student as does another course, then the administration should weigh this cost against the educational value of the course. Unfortunately, institutions of higher education, like government agencies, concentrate on the allocation of new or additional funds and seldom carefully consider priorities for the expenditure of existing resources. This is unfortunate, because the mix of needed services is always changing.

Capital plant for all institutions of higher education is worth about $35 billion and involves annual use of about $400 per

---

[46] S. E. Harris, *Higher Education: Resources and Finance,* McGraw-Hill Book Company, New York, 1962, part 7.

[47] See especially A. M. Cartter and R. L. Farrell, "Academic Labor Market Projections and the Draft," *The Economics and Financing of Higher Education in the United States,* a compendium of papers submitted to the Joint Economic Committee, U.S. Congress, Washington, D.C., 1969, pp. 261–294.

[48] See S. E. Harris, *Higher Education: Resources and Finance,* McGraw-Hill Book Company, New York, 1962, chap. 42, for a fuller treatment.

student.[49] Yet college administrators do not so much as mention these costs.

COSTS AND ECONOMIES More productive use of faculty for a given outlay can be achieved in various ways. In the first place, faculty members should allocate their time in accordance with their relative abilities. The first-class teacher should devote most of his time to teaching; the star researcher should devote his time primarily, if not absolutely, to research. Resources are seriously wasted if faculty members are required to perform in several areas even though an individual faculty member may have outstanding ability in only one.

Second, more productive use of faculty can be achieved through reductions in course requirements. This will make possible nonreplacement of departing faculty, as Caplow and McGee have well demonstrated.[50] A third approach is through relatively more use of teaching assistants. In addition, allowing students more independent work, which should, of course be adequately supervised, will economize expensive faculty time. Finally, tailoring instruction to the actual requirements of a given course is desirable. Not all instruction, for example, has to cover a semester or a quarter at three hours per week. As I concluded in an earlier study:

If we are to obtain the required resources, we must make effective use of what we have or are likely to get. IHL [institutions of higher learning] are subject to criticism for operating inefficiently. A former president of a major university told me that a great university could perform better at half the cost if the president had a free hand. This may be optimistic. IHL do not operate like the profit corporations. The faculty are not employees, but rather part of the management. They do not accept orders from the administration on such matters as curriculum or the choice of faculty. If they did, the universities would soon lose their freedom and the uninhibited search for knowledge. Yet it is possible to operate more efficiently through cooperation of trustees, administration, and faculty. Most faculty members have a surprisingly limited knowledge of the relation of economical management and the effectiveness of the task they perform or their own economic status. . . .

---

[49] At 5 percent, the annual cost of capital is about $250. On the basis of a 35-year life, capital use would be $1 billion per year, or $133 per student, or $383 in all.

[50] T. Caplow and R. J. McGee, *The Academic Marketplace,* Basic Books, Inc., Publishers, New York, 1958.

Hence the importance of improved planning; of rational choices of sites of new colleges and curricula; of cooperation among colleges to avoid excessive duplication through alternation or elimination of courses where not justified by educational contribution; of eliminating concentration of courses at 10 A.M. to 12 noon on Monday, Wednesday, and Friday (at the pleasure of the instructor); of careful scrutiny of outlays not directly related to the educational process; of exploitation of mechanical aids; of discontinuing the practice of requiring (say) a $20,000 faculty member to spend a substantial part of his time on tasks that should cost at the rate of $2,000 to $4,000 (e.g., research, secretarial, paper grading); of providing cost data for all programs as a guide to administrators in choosing alternative educational programs or the roads to educational objectives; of improved counseling to reduce the attrition of students at college and to enhance the chances of a choice related to the students' abilities and needs; and of adapting the size of the college to minimizing costs, or at least justifying uneconomic size by educational gains.[51]

[51] S. E. Harris, *Higher Education: Resources and Finance*, McGraw-Hill Book Company, New York, 1962, p. 632.

TABLE 5.1-8
Average enrollment, 1955–56; average educational and general expenditures, 1953–54 per resident college student enrolled in November 1953, by control and type of institution; and student-faculty ratio, 1955–56

	Average enrollment, 1955–56			
Type of institution	*All institutions*	*Publicly controlled institutions*	*Privately controlled institutions*	*All institutions*
All institutions, average	1,432	2,247	989	$1,032
Universities	8,544	8,799	8,199	1,334
Liberal arts colleges	973	2,597	768	699
Teachers colleges	1,202	1,318	390	725
Technological schools	1,963	1,508	2,417	1,692
Theological schools	259		259	698
Other professional schools	483	870	448	1,538
Junior colleges*	668	967	258	469

* Includes community colleges, normal schools, technical institutes, and other institutions of higher education restricted to less than four years of work on the undergraduate or terminal-occupational level.

SOURCE: U.S. Department of Health, Education and Welfare, Office of Education, *Statistics of Higher Education: Receipts, Expenditures and Property, 1953–54*, chap. 4, sec. 2, of *Biennial Survey of Education in the United States, 1952–54*, p. 61; U.S. Department of Health, Education and Welfare, *Statistics of Higher Education, 1955–56*, pp. 6–7; in S. E. Harris, *Higher Education: Resources and Finance*, McGraw-Hill Book Company, New York, 1962, p. 581.

STUDENT-
FACULTY
RATIOS
Raising the student-faculty ratio is critical in any attempt to increase the productivity of institutions of higher education. Yet it is extraordinarily difficult. President Gallagher of the City College of New York once said that the student-teacher ratio is sacred.

My study of 11 colleges and universities shows a downward trend in the ratio. Overall figures for the United States also show a tendency for the ratio to decline. Thus from 1919–20 to 1955–56, the number of faculty members increased 5.4 times and students only 3.4 times.

Student-faculty ratios depend on a wide variety of factors: (1) the nature of the curriculum—a 3 to 1 ratio in medical schools is not uncommon, nor is a 40 to 1 ratio in law schools; (2) the course requirements for students—at 15 hours per week, the student-faculty ratio, *ceteris paribus,* will be lower than at 9 hours; (3) the teaching load—the greater the teaching load, the higher the student-

All educational and general expenditures per resident student		Educational and general expenditures except research and extension and public services, per student			Student/faculty ratio, 1955–56
Publicly controlled institutions	*Privately controlled institutions*	*All institutions*	*Publicly controlled institutions*	*Privately controlled institutions*	
$1,106	$ 948	$ 811	$ 841	$ 777	
1,494	1,130	951	1,023	860	16.6
799	661	663	695	651	17.0
727	691	712	713	676	19.2
1,394	1,988	1,043	1,057	1,029	14.3
	698	681		681	16.4
3,194	1,095	1,407	2,741	1,032	11.6
420	678	457	408	669	25.5

faculty ratio; (4) the number and size of classes—the more numerous the courses and the smaller the classes (at given teaching loads), the lower the student-faculty ratio; and (5) the use of teaching assistants—the greater the use of teaching assistants, the higher the student-faculty ratio. Variations among types of institutions are shown in Table 5.1-8.

What is the overall student-faculty ratio? According to a relatively recent study of the National Education Association, the ratio was 13 to 1 in the early sixties and was projected to rise to 15.75 to 1 by 1969–70. However, the study revealed wide variations, with high ratios for junior colleges and low ratios for complex universities with many professional schools. At the University of Pennsylvania, the ratio was 10 to 1; and at Columbia, Cornell, and Yale, 9 to 1, 8 to 1, and 6 to 1, respectively. Variations are also related to differences in categories of faculty members included—for example, graduate assistants or administrative personnel.[52]

The decline that has occurred in the student-faculty ratio is in part the result of the rising relative importance of graduate instruction, which relies heavily on small classes. In my earlier study of 11 institutions—based on data on enrollment, faculty, and courses as revealed by catalogs—I found that the total number of courses rose from 4,072 in 1901–02 to 9,049 in 1926–27 to 14,100 in 1957–58.[53] Over the entire period 1901–02 to 1957–58, undergraduate enrollment rose from 11,830 to 39,314, while graduate student enrollment in arts and sciences rose from 4,516 to 21,682. The relative rise of graduate students was roughly 1⅔ times that of undergraduates. As indicated earlier, the number of faculty members rose 5.4 times, reflecting the large relative increase in graduate instruction, the spread of the elective system, and other factors. The fact that the number of courses increased only one-half as much as the number of faculty members suggests reduced teaching loads and more time spent on nonteaching activities.

[52] For a more detailed discussion, see especially ibid., pp. 525, 527, 543–546, 652.

[53] The study included Harvard, Mount Holyoke, Princeton, Smith, Swarthmore, Vassar, Williams, Wisconsin, Yale, Columbia, and Brown. See S. E. Harris, *Higher Education: Resources and Finance,* McGraw-Hill Book Company, New York, 1962, pp. 14–15, 533–536.

	Under- graduate enrollment	*Graduate enrollment, arts and sciences*	*Number of faculty members*	*Number of courses*	*Student- faculty ratio*
1901–02	11,839	4,516	1,802	4,042	9:1
1926–27	26,621	8,842	5,375	9,049	7:1
1956–57	39,314	21,682	10,673	14,100	6:1

SOURCE: Compiled from catalogs of 11 institutions of higher education.

The student-faculty ratio tends to vary by regions, in part because of differences in economic status. It varies also by size of institution. The larger institutions of higher education seem to have relatively high student-faculty ratios. On the other hand, technical institutions tend to have relatively low ratios. In general, student-faculty ratios vary with size, location, relative enrollments in undergraduate and graduate schools, the "mix" of courses in the curriculum (e.g., science versus humanities), location, control, available resources, and other factors.

As indicated above, the student-faculty ratio also varies according to the definition of faculty. Thus in 1958 the ratios varied as follows with varying definitions of staff:

	Number	*Ratio*
Resident enrollment, college grade	3,585,000	
Total professional staffs	348,500	10:1
Total faculty for resident instruction	260,500	14:1
*Full-time equivalent of that faculty**	194,000	18:1
Full-time equivalent faculty and estimated full-time equivalent students		16:1

* The junior instructional staff is estimated at half-time service, on the average.

SOURCE: B. Berelson, *Graduate Education in the United States,* McGraw-Hill Book Company, New York, 1960, p. 74.

In recent years, under pressure of large increases in enrollment, the student-faculty ratio has tended to rise, although the increase has been relatively greater for public than for private institutions of higher education. In the next chapter, it is noted that the increased relative importance of junior college and four-year public college enrollment has played a role in raising student-faculty ratios. Also relevant has been the financial pressure on all institutions of higher education in recent years, a situation tending to lead to the pruning of curricula and increasing the size of classes. Although these measures obviously will result in a decline of unit costs, this should not be interpreted as necessarily bringing about a corresponding gain in productivity. The impact on the quality of output which results from the above measures must be taken into account.

Because variations in student-faculty ratios are related to so many different factors, as suggested above, changes in student-faculty ratios have to be interpreted with great caution. The decline in the student-faculty ratio that occurred until relatively recent

TABLE 5.1-9 *Funding and manpower characteristics of degree-accredited institutions by class and control, 1963 (dollars in thousands)*

Institutions	Number of institutions	FFAS	EGI	R_{fe}*
All institutions	1,063	$1,099,481	$4,346,393	0.202
Class A	169	1,045,622	2,864,882	0.267
Denominational	24	52,263	174,768	0.230
Private	52	468,727	860,524	0.353
Public	93	524,632	1,829,590	0.223
Class B	197	37,359	725,791	0.049
Denominational	40	7,385	89,726	0.076
Private	43	10,852	153,062	0.666
Public	114	19,122	483,003	0.038
Class C	651	16,306	714,038	0.022
Denominational	404	7,473	347,742	0.021
Private	121	5,117	163,353	0.030
Public	126	3,716	202,943	0.018
Class D	46	194	41,682	0.005
Denominational	12	27	6,283	0.004
Private	13	152	12,593	0.012
Public	21	15	22,806	0.001

*R_{fe} = FFAS/EGI + FFAS.

† R_e = Graduate enrollment/total enrollment.

‡ S&T DP = Science and technology degree productivity.

§ R_s = S&T DP/total enrollment.

SOURCE: National Science Foundation, *The Dynamics of Academic Science,* 1967, p. 68.

years was made possible by prosperity and growth. But under the stress of vast increases in enrollment and serious financial problems, the trend recently has been an increase in the student-faculty ratio, and this is likely to continue, especially for public institutions. Savings in costs result, but to some extent the quality of the product deteriorates.

FEDERAL FUNDS FOR ACADEMIC SCIENCE AND PRODUCTIVITY National Science Foundation publications show that there is heavy concentration of federal funds for academic science, with the 166 institutions of higher education that receive $500,000 or more absorbing 96 percent of federal funds.[54] The text table below (based on data in Table 5.1-9) shows how the ratio of graduate

[54] National Science Foundation, *The Dynamics of Academic Science,* 1967, p. 56.

Enrollment			Science and engineering				
Total	*Graduate*	R_e†	*S&T DP*‡	*B.A.*	*M.A.*	*Ph.D.*	R_s§
3,425,456	369,964	0.108	277,149	132,436	26,761	7,963	0.081
1,701,687	263,699	0.155	206,533	71,528	22,902	7,963	0.121
157,928	22,016	0.139	16,006	5,175	1,293	257	0.101
413,830	97,627	0.236	63,598	17,672	7,675	3,015	0.154
1,129,929	144,056	0.127	126,929	48,681	13,934	4,691	0.112
875,843	81,372	0.093	38,967	29,259	3,859		0.044
115,010	11,991	0.104	5,812	4,594	483		0.051
129,631	13,158	0.102	8,966	6,440	999		0.069
631,202	56,223	0.089	24,189	18,225	2,377		0.038
804,718	22,060	0.027	31,649	31,649			0.039
381,602	5,157	0.014	17,266	17,266			0.045
156,331	3,749	0.024	7,431	7,431			0.048
266,785	13,154	0.049	6,952	6,952			0.026
43,208	2,833	0.066					
5,425	48	0.009					
8,576	514	0.060					
29,207	2,271	0.078					

enrollment and the ratio of science and technology degree productivity are related to the impact of federal funds for academic science on the institution's income.

R_e	$= 0.155$ for class A institutions
	0.093 for class B institutions
	0.027 for class C institutions
S. and T.D.P.	0.121 for class A institutions
	0.044 for class B institutions
	0.039 for class C institutions
R_{fe}	$= 0.267$ for class A institutions
	0.049 for class B institutions
	0.022 for class C institutions
where R_e	$=$ the ratio of graduate enrollment to total enrollment,
S. and T.D.P.	$=$ the ratio of science and technology degree productivity to total enrollment, and
R_{fe}	$= \dfrac{\text{federal funds for academic science}}{\text{educational and general income plus federal funds for academic science}}$

Clearly the class A institutions come out especially well in the impact of federal funds for academic science on their income position.

A National Science Foundation study shows high productivity in 1964 for institutions of higher education granting doctorate degrees. These institutions accounted for seven-eighths of the expenditures for research and development and for 96 percent of the expenditures of institutions of higher education for research and development in that year.[55] In measuring productivity, the National Science Foundation considered both output of highly trained personnel and output of research.

There are a number of institutions in this group whose rank order leads one to believe that they are high producers of research and low producers of scientific manpower. Johns Hopkins, Rochester, the University of Washington at St. Louis, Duke, the University of California at San Diego, Western Reserve, Yeshiva, Tulane, Oregon, Brown, Baylor, and Vanderbilt seem to fall within this group. Does this information mean that these institutions have unused additional capability for training? There are also a number of institutions that appear to be low producers of research and

---

[55] National Science Foundation, *Scientific Activities at Universities and Colleges, 1964,* 1968, tables 1, 3, p. 5.

high producers of scientific manpower. Purdue, Pennsylvania State, Tennessee, Michigan State, Rutgers State, Missouri, Iowa State, Oklahoma State, North Carolina State, and Kansas State seem to fall within this category. Does this information indicate that these institutions are capable of more research than they undertake?

Probing a bit further, Johns Hopkins University may be categorized a high producer of research and a low producer of scientific manpower. It ranks tenth in federal funds for academic science (a high producer of research), sixty-fifth for graduate enrollment, sixty-second for S&T DP, ninety-seventh for the bachelor's degree, one hundred and second for the master's degree, and thirty-first for docorate production (a low producer of scientific manpower). The University of Rochester seems to follow a similar pattern. At the other extreme is Purdue University, which may be said to be a low producer of research and a high producer of scientific manpower. It ranked thirty-fourth according to federal funds and between third and fifth for scientific manpower productivity. It ranks remarkably high in manpower produced considering its own funding characteristics. Is the low Purdue funding characteristic (educational and general income) due to the lack of a medical school? Or is it because Purdue can conduct its training programs in a more efficient fashion? Like Purdue, Pennsylvania State University shows a pattern of low productivity with respect to research as measured by federal funds for academic science, and high productivity with respect to degrees in science and engineering. Pennsylvania State, on the other hand, invests a larger share of its own funds in education. Iowa State University of Science and Technology is a dramatic example of a low producer with respect to research and a high producer with respect to training in the sciences. It ranks sixty-eighth with respect to federal funds, eighteenth with respect to bachelor's degree production in science and engineering, thirtieth with respect to master's degrees, and thirteenth in doctorate productivity.

5.2. Structure of Higher Educational Enrollment

In this chapter I have tried to assemble material that is especially germane to the understanding of the early history and long-term trends of institutions of higher education. To some extent this chapter duplicates material in other parts of the book, and the findings are not always consistent. Unfortunately, aggregate data relating to higher education in the nineteenth century are often incomplete and the coverage of institutions varies from year to year. Thus, any analysis of this material is subject to some reservations.

In 1840 there were only 16,233 students reported enrolled in institutions of higher education (Table 5.2-1). The actual figure was somewhat less. In the succeeding 130 years, enrollment increased more than 400 times, while the population of the United States increased 12 times. Over the years the number of students relative to the population has steadily increased. From 1872 to 1898, enrollment rose from 852 college students per million population to 1,875 college students per million population (Table 5.2-2). In this same period, the number of graduate students per million population rose from 5 to 74.[1]

[1] At the outset, I should warn the reader of the difficulties of finding and putting together the materials for this chapter. The data for the nineteenth century, and especially for the years 1840 to 1880, are scarce. I depended mainly on Bureau of Census studies and on *Reports of the Commissioner of Education* for materials before 1900. Definitions vary from year to year, as does the coverage of institutions and enrollment. Many inconsistencies are found in statistics for identical years from different sources. With the help of officials of the Bureau of the Budget, the Bureau of the Census, and several helpful and able professionals in the Office of Education, I managed to find materials not easily available. I am especially indebted to A. Ross Eckler, director of the Census, and to Kenneth A. Simon, C. G. Lind, and Miss Marie Fullam of the Office of Education.

TABLE 5.2-1
Number of
institutions,
teachers, and
students
in higher
education,
United States,
1840–1902,
various years

Year	Number of institutions	Number of teachers	Number of students
1840	173	NA*	16,233
1850	234	1,651	27,159
1860	467	2,895	56,120
1871†	426	4,125	53,130
1880	591	6,500	85,378
1890	415	7,918	43,638 (118,581)‡
1902§	530	10,700	101,064

* Not available.

† These totals include colleges and universities and colleges for women, but exclude 256 professional schools. For 1872, the estimate was 504 colleges inclusive of women's colleges.

‡ Totals for 1890 include students in collegiate departments. Total enrollment was 118,581. Estimates for 1882 were 372 institutions, 3,839 teachers, and 37,325 students. (This is a partial estimate.) Estimates for 1896 were 484 institutions and 68,507 students.

§ For 1897–98, the Commissioner of Education put collegiate, graduate, and professional enrollment at 144,477, with 5,514 graduate students included. This seems out of line with earlier and later totals. (U.S. Office of Education, *Report of the Commissioner of Education, 1897–98*, p. 1801.) However, note the large enrollment discrepancies compared to the Office of Education estimate (Table 5.2-8 below).

SOURCES: U.S. Bureau of the Census, *Seventh Census of the United States, 1850*, 1853, tables XLII–XLIV; U.S. Bureau of the Census, *Statistics of the United States Compiled from the Eighth Census, 1860*, 1866, table A; U.S. Office of Education, *Report of the Commissioner of Education, 1880*, pp. VI, X; *1889–90*, p. 761; *1903*, p. 1178; U.S. Department of the Interior, *Annual Report of the Secretary of the Interior*, 1872, pp. 54–55.

ENROLLMENT
AT VARIOUS
LEVELS OF
EDUCATION,
1899–1900
TO FALL 1965

From 1900 to 1965 the percentage increase of enrollment in institutions of higher education was much larger than the percentage increase of enrollment in elementary and secondary schools. During this period, as noted earlier, the relative enrollment in public institutions of higher education increased more than three times as much as the relative enrollment in private institutions:

Percentage
increase in
enrollment, by
level of
education,
1899–1900 to
fall 1965

All levels	216
Primary and secondary	188
Higher	2,226
Public	3,897
Private	1,195

NOTE: Decade-to-decade changes are indicated in Table 5.2-3.

	Under-graduate collegiate and technical students	Graduate students	Law students	Medical students	Theo-logical students	Total
TABLE 5.2-2 Number of students in higher education for each 1 million persons from 1872 to 1897–98 (based on the number of students in the colleges of the United States) Year						
1872	573	5	49	142	83	852
1873	739	5	52	176	93	1,065
1874	749	7	61	182	102	1,081
1875	736	8	61	196	120	1,121
1876	706	9	59	194	95	1,063
1877	701	8	61	209	86	1,065
1878	781	9	64	210	91	1,155
1879	775	10	62	231	97	1,175
1880	770	8	62	238	105	1,183
1881	755	9	63	242	83	1,162
1882–83	731	10	57	237	92	1,127
1883–84	741	14	49	230	96	1,130
1884–85	742	15	49	197	103	1,106
1885–86	687	16	53	221	110	1,087
1886–87	690	21	54	208	107	1,080
1887–88	688	22	61	231	109	1,111
1888–89	729	22	64	245	114	1,171
1889–90	850	27	72	266	112	1,327
1890–91	901	83	82	284	115	1,415
1891–92	980	39	94	284	115	1,512
1892–93	1,037	43	105	298	118	1,601
1893–94	1,087	51	107	820	113	1,678
1894–95	1,128	58	130	331	116	1,763
1895–96	1,158	62	139	346	114	1,819
1896–97	1,142	69	146	342	115	1,814
1897–98	1,193	74	163	328*	117	1,875

*Report of President of Cornell University for 1897–98.

SOURCE: U.S. Office of Education, *Report of the Commissioner of Education, 1897–98*, p. 1800.

In 1900 only 1 percent of those enrolled in educational institutions were college and university students, but by the fall of 1965 enrollment in higher education accounted for 10 percent of enrollment at all levels of education:

Enrollment by level of education, selected dates, 1900 to fall 1965	Total (in millions)	All levels	Percentage of total kindergarten to eight grade	Grades 9 to 12	Higher education
1900	17.2	100	95	4	1
1930	29.7	100	80	16	4
1960	45.2	100	72	21	7
1965 (fall)	54.3	100	66	24	10

SOURCE: Computed from data in Table 5.2-3.

TABLE 5.2-3 *Enrollment in educational institutions, by level of instruction and by type of control, United States, 1899–1900 to fall 1965*

Level of instruction, by type of school (1)	1899–1900 (2)	1909–10 (3)	1919–20 (4)	1929–30 (5)	1939–40 (6)
All levels, (elementary, secondary, higher)*	17,198,841	19,999,148	24,061,778	29,652,377	29,751,293
Elementary and secondary	16,961,249	19,643,933	23,463,898	28,551,640	28,257,000
Kindergarten to grade 8	16,261,846	18,528,535	20,963,722	23,739,840	21,127,021
Grades 9 to 12 and post-graduate	699,403	1,115,398	2,500,176	4,811,800	7,129,979
Higher education*	237,592	355,215	597,880	1,100,737	1,494,203
Kindergarten	225,394	346,189	510,949	786,463	660,909
Grades 1 to 8	16,036,452	18,182,346	20,452,773	22,953,377	20,466,112
Grades 9 to 12 and post-graduate	699,403	1,115,398	2,500,176	4,811,800	7,129,979
Higher education*	237,592	355,215	597,880	1,100,737	1,494,203
Publicly controlled	90,689	166,560	315,382	532,647	796,531
Privately controlled	146,903	188,655	282,498	568,090	697,672

* Excludes schools of nursing not affiliated with institutions of higher education.
† Data for first term of the academic year.
‡ Includes resident and extension degree-credit students. Data for earlier years excludes extension students.

SOURCES: U.S. Department of Health, Education and Welfare, Office of Education, "Biennial Survey of Education in the United States"; "Statistics of State School Systems"; "Fall Statistics of Public Schools"; "Statistics of Nonpublic Elementary and Secondary Schools, 1965–66"; comprehensive and fall reports on enrollment in institutions of higher education; and unpublished data. U.S. Department of Commerce, Bureau of the Census, "Current Population Reports," ser. P-20. U.S. Department of the Interior, Bureau of Indian Affairs, "Statistics Concerning Indian Education"; in U.S. Office of Education, *Digest of Educational Statistics, 1968,* 1968, p. 3.

In the years before 1938, however, the largest gains in enrollment occurred in secondary schools, not in institutions of higher education. The ratio of high school students to college students was 2.9 in 1900 and 4.9 in 1938.[2] In this period secondary school enrollment increased from 3 to 25 percent of total enrollment at all levels of education, while higher educational enrollment increased from 1 to 11 percent of total enrollment.

Table 5.2-4 provides additional detail on enrollment in various types of institutions, public and private, by region in 1891–92.

(Text continued on p. 930)

[2] U.S. Office of Education, *Biennial Survey of Education, 1938–40*, p. 2.

1949–50 (7)	1959–60 (8)	Fall 1963 (9)	Fall 1965 (10)
31,319,271	45,227,620	51,191,282	54,306,301
28,660,250	42,012,076	46,957,190	48,779,976
22,207,241	32,412,266	34,701,694	35,759,153
6,453,009	9,599,810	12,255,496	13,020,823
2,659,021	3,215,544†	4,234,092	5,526,325
1,175,312	2,293,492	2,554,576	2,493,296
21,031,929	30,118,774	32,147,118	33,265,857
6,453,009	9,599,810	12,255,496	13,020,823
2,659,021	3,215,544†	4,234,092	5,526,325‡
1,354,902	1,831,782†	2,633,345	3,624,442‡
1,304,119	1,383,762†	1,600,747	1,901,883‡

(1)	Pupils receiving elementary instruction ("primary" and "grammar" grades)	
	Public (2)	*Private (largely estimated)* (3)
The United States	12,966,321	1,198,861
North Atlantic Division	3,092,976	537,815
South Atlantic Division	1,816,722	113,853
South Central Division	2,439,393	151,347
North Central Division	5,012,955	339,099
Western Division	604,275	56,747

	Schools receiving higher instruction			
	In universities and colleges[c]			
(1)	*Public*[d] (6)	*Private* (7)	*Total* (8)	*Public*[e] (9)
The United States	14,070	58,300	72,460	4,768
North Atlantic Division	1,751	20,652	22,403	0
South Atlantic Division	1,452	8,761	10,213	671
South Central Division	1,614	10,559	12,173	582
North Central Division	7,785	16,920	24,705	3,051
Western Division	1,468	1,498	2,966	464

[a] Including pupils in preparatory or academic departments of higher institutions, public and private, and excluding elementary pupils, who are classed in columns 2 and 3.

[b] This is made up chiefly from the returns of individual high schools to the bureau, and is considerably too small, as there are a great many secondary pupils outside the completely organized high schools whom there is no means of enumerating. The whole number of pupils studying secondary branches in public schools is probably near 500,000.

[c] Including colleges for women, agricultural and mechanical (land-grant) colleges, and scientific schools. Students in law, theological, and medical departments are excluded, being tabulated in columns 9 to 11.

[d] Mainly state universities and agricultural and mechanical colleges.

[e] Mainly in schools or departments of medicine and law attached to state universities.

[f] Nonprofessional pupils in normal schools are included in columns 4 and 5.

Pupils receiving secondary instruction ("high school" grade)[a]	
Public[b] (4)	*Private (in preparatory schools, academies, seminaries, etc.)* (5)
247,660	154,420
86,070	45,638
13,577	22,821
15,511	29,797
119,433	47,123
11,069	9,050

In schools of medicine, law, and theology		*In normal schools*[f]		
Private (10)	*Total* (11)	*Public* (12)	*Private*[g] (13)	*Total* (14)
31,297	36,065	33,427	5,710	39,137
12,772	12,772	15,392	418	15,810
4,555	5,226	2,704	312	3,016
3,643	4,225	2,946	1,118	4,064
9,892	12,943	10,736	3,114	13,850
435	899	1,649	748	2,397

[g] Private normal schools are, with one or two exceptions, scarcely superior to the ordinary secondary schools.

NOTE: The classification of states made use of in the above table is the same as that adopted by the United States census, and is as follows: *North Atlantic Division:* Maine, New Hampshire, Vermont, Massachusetts, Rhode Island, Connecticut, New York, New Jersey, and Pennsylvania. *South Atlantic Division:* Delaware, Maryland, District of Columbia, Virginia, West Virginia, North Carolina, South Carolina, Georgia, and Florida. *South Central Division:* Kentucky, Tennessee, Alabama, Mississippi, Louisiana, Texas, Arkansas, and Oklahoma. *North Central Division:* Ohio, Indiana, Illinois, Michigan, Wisconsin, Minnesota, Iowa, Missouri, North Dakota, South Dakota, Nebraska, and Kansas. *Western Division:* Montana, Wyoming, Colorado, New Mexico, Arizona, Utah, Nevada, Idaho, Washington, Oregon, and California.

SOURCE: U.S. Office of Education, *Report of the Commissioner of Education, 1891–92*, vol. 1, p. 2.

The relationship of enrollment to population was discussed extensively in Part 1, but here we shed additional light on historical trends by considering 30-year periods:

*Resident
degree-credit
enrollment as
a percentage
of population,
selected years,
1870 to 1963*

Year	Percentage of total population	Percentage of population aged 18 to 21	Percentage of population aged 18 to 24	Undergraduate enrollment as a percentage of population aged 18 to 21
1870	0.13	1.68	1.14	
1900	0.31	4.01	2.29	3.91
1930	0.90	12.42	7.20	11.89
1963	2.24	38.05	23.33	33.75

SOURCE: Computed from data in U.S. Office of Education, *Digest of Educational Statistics, 1968,* 1968, p. 70.

1   As a percentage of total population, resident degree-enrollment in higher education rose 16 times from 1870 to 1963. However, the most rapid increase in this percentage occurred in the years 1900 to 1930. The increase from 1930 to 1963 was about four-fifths that of 1900 to 1930.

2   As a percentage of the population aged 18 to 21, enrollment rose 22 times in the years 1870 to 1963, with the annual percentage roughly trebling in the years 1930 to 1963, as compared with a similar rate of increase from 1900 to 1930. A similar acceleration in the rate of increase occurred for enrollment in relation to population aged 18 to 24.

3   Enrollment in relation to the 18 to 24 age group amounted to 57, 58, and 62 percent of enrollment as a percentage of the population aged 18 to 21 in the years 1900, 1930, and 1963, respectively. The increase in this percentage reflected the rising relative importance of enrollment in graduate education, in which those aged 22 to 24 are likely to be enrolled. It must be recognized, however, that total enrollment includes persons who are older than 24 years of age. This is especially true for recent years, as a result of the tendency for graduate education to be prolonged and of the increased enrollment of adults in higher education.

Another relevant factor in the interpretation of these data is the dropout rate in elementary and secondary education. A decline in the dropout rate tends to increase the proportion of persons in each cohort from which higher education draws its students. In the last 20 years the dropout rate has decreased greatly, from 65 percent of students entering the fifth grade to 29 percent. Projections of high school enrollment assume a decline in the dropout rate, based on past trends, to 22 percent by 1975. About 900,000 children—22 percent of estimated fifth-grade enrollment in 1968—who could graduate from high school in 1975 are not expected to finish high school.[3]

LEVELS OF ENROLLMENT A highly important difference between institutions of higher education in the nineteenth century and today is that in the last century they enrolled large numbers of preparatory students:

Enrollment, institutions of higher education, by level, 1902 (in thousands)

Preparatory	46.6
Collegiate	83.5
Graduate	6.5
Professional	31.3

SOURCE: U.S. Office of Education, *Report of the Commissioner of Education, 1902*, p. 1392.

More than one-quarter of the enrollment was for preparatory work, a diversion from the collegiate level of instruction that surely reduced the efficiency of operations. The institution did gain, however, in that, by offering preparatory curricula, it could increase its enrollment by promoting to freshman status students who had been in their preparatory program. The types of precollege preparation of a large sample of freshmen in 1896 were distributed as follows:

Type of preparation, large sample of freshmen, 1896

	Percent
Preparation department of college	40
Private preparatory schools	17
Public high schools	41
Private study	2

SOURCE: U.S. Office of Education, *Report of the Commissioner of Education, 1896–97*, p. 1938.

TRENDS IN INSTITUTIONS, ENROLLMENT, AND DEGREES FROM 1869–70 TO 1963–64 From 1869–70 to 1963–64, the number of institutions of higher education rose from 563 to 2,132—a rise of 2.8 times. Resident degree-credit enrollment expanded from 52,286 to 4,234,092 in the same period—a rise of roughly 80 times. Thus, there were large increases in enrollment per institution, because enrollment

[3] U.S. Office of Education, *Education in the Seventies*, planning papers of the Office of Program Planning and Evaluation, May 1968, p. 9.

TABLE 5.2-5 *Historical summary of faculty, students, and degrees, institutions of higher education, United States, 1869–70 to 1963–64*

Item (1)	1869–70 (2)	1879–80 (3)	1889–90 (4)	1899–1900 (5)	1909–10 (6)
Number of institutions	563	811	998	977	951
Faculty*					
TOTAL	5,553†	11,522†	15,809†	23,868	36,480
Men	4,887†	7,328†	12,704†	19,151	29,132
Women	666†	4,194†	3,105†	4,717	7,348
Resident degree-credit enrollment					
TOTAL	52,286†	115,817†	156,756	237,592	355,213
Men	41,160†	77,972†	100,453†	152,254	214,648†
Women	11,126†	37,845†	56,303†	85,338	140,565†
Earned degrees conferred					
Bachelor's and first professional:					
TOTAL	9,371	12,896	15,539	27,410	37,199
Men	7,993	10,411	12,857	22,173	28,762
Women	1,378	2,485	2,682	5,237	8,437
Second level (master's except first professional)					
TOTAL	0	879	1,015	1,583	2,113
Men	0	868	821	1,280	1,555
Women	0	11	194	303	558
Doctor's:					
TOTAL	1	54	149	382	443
Men	1	51	147	359	399
Women	0	3	2	23	44

*Total number of different individuals (not reduced to full-time equivalent).

† Estimated.

‡ Date for first term of the academic year.

§ Data for fall 1963.

NOTE: Beginning in 1959–60, includes Alaska and Hawaii.

SOURCE: U.S. Department of Health, Education and Welfare, Office of Education, "Biennial Survey of Education in the United States"; "Faculty and Other Professional Staff in Institutions of Higher Education"; "Comprehensive Report on Enrollment in Higher Education"; "Earned Degrees Conferred"; in U.S. Office of Education, *Digest of Educational Statistics, 1968*, 1968, p. 69.

1919–20 (7)	1929–30 (8)	1939–40 (9)	1949–50 (10)	1959–60 (11)	1961–62 (12)	1963–64 (13)
1,041	1,409	1,708	1,851	2,008	2,037	2,132
48,615	82,386	146,929	246,722	380,554‡	424,862‡	494,514‡
35,807	60,017	106,328	186,189	296,773‡	332,006‡	385,405‡
12,808	22,369	40,601	60,533	83,781‡	92,856‡	109,109‡
597,880	1,100,737	1,494,203	2,659,021	3,215,544‡	3,726,114‡	4,234,092§
314,938	619,935	893,250	1,853,068	2,079,788‡	2,337,385‡	2,622,787§
282,942	480,802	600,953	805,953	1,135,756‡	1,388,729‡	1,611,305§
48,622	122,484	186,500	432,058	392,440	417,846	498,654
31,980	73,615	109,546	328,841	254,063	260,531	298,046
16,642	48,869	76,954	103,217	138,377	157,315	200,608
4,279	14,969	26,731	58,183	74,435	84,855	101,050
2,985	8,925	16,508	41,220	50,898	58,686	68,969
1,294	6,044	10,223	16,963	23,537	26,169	32,081
615	2,299	3,290	6,633	9,829	11,622	14,490
522	1,946	2,861	5,990	8,801	10,377	12,955
93	353	429	643	1,028	1,245	1,535

increased much more than the number of institutions in this period. The number of bachelor's and first professional degrees awarded rose by 52 times from 1869–70 to 1963–64 — also much less than the increase in enrollment (Table 5.2-5). The difference in the rates of increase of enrollment and degrees is partly explained by the increase in the number of junior colleges not giving degrees and partly by the rising standards for awarding degrees at many institutions.

TRENDS IN ENROLLMENT FROM 1840 TO 1902 Table 5.2-1 shows the numbers of institutions, teachers, and students in higher education from 1840 to 1902 — the first 63 years of coverage of higher education by the U.S. Bureau of the Census. Variations in coverage reduce the comparability of these figures, but they do offer some rough guides gleaned from hundreds of census volumes and reports of the U.S. Commissioner of Education.

From 1840 to 1860 the number of teachers rose relatively less than the number of students (the exact figures are an educated guess). By 1860 the student-faculty ratio was 19 to 1. (Interestingly enough, in 1968 the ratio was 20 to 1.) But from 1850 to 1902 the number of teachers increased almost twice as much relatively as the number of students.

From 1860 to 1871, as might be expected because of the Civil War, the number of institutions declined by 10 percent and the number of students declined by 5 percent. The student-faculty ratio fell sharply because, in addition to the decline in enrollment, the number of teachers rose approximately 40 percent. The declining student-faculty ratio contributed substantially to rising unit costs, as did the inflation associated with the Civil War.

Unfortunately, for the 1880s there is a large discrepancy between the current reports of the Commissioner of Education, which reveal a substantial drop in enrollment during that decade, and data published in more recent years by the U.S. Office of Education, which show a large rise in enrollment for the 1880s. Part of the difference is explained by variations in coverage. The improved economic situation, rising population, and increasing interest in higher education that were evident during the period support the estimates of the Office of Education rather than the earlier estimates of the Commissioner of Education. An increase rather than a decrease of enrollment in the 1880s seems much more probable.

Developments were especially favorable for higher education in the years 1890 to 1902, with the number of institutions increasing by more than 25 percent and the number of teachers increasing by 35 percent. According to the data published by the Commissioner of Education, however, the number of students appeared to decline by about 17 percent. On the basis of these data, the student-faculty ratio appeared to be 9 to 1 in 1902. But, as indicated above, it seems likely that the enrollment data for those years published more recently by the U.S. Office of Education are more accurate. They indicate a student-faculty ratio of 9.9 to 1 in 1899–1900.

What of the entire period 1840 to 1902? Enrollment increased five to six times and the number of institutions doubled. Institutions were becoming larger and more viable. In 1840 average enrollment per institution was a little less than 100. By 1902 average enrollment, on the basis of Commissioner of Education data, was close to 200. The increase by 5 to 6 times in enrollment may be compared with an increase by 3½ times in population. These are comparatively small increases in enrollment relative to population as compared with those for the period 1869–70 to the present. The modest gains of the years 1840 to 1902 reflected the net effects of periods of overextension as well as of variations in economic conditions. Advances made in some parts of the period were not sustainable.

Table 5.2-6 has been assembled from various sources and reveals some relationships that differ greatly from those prevailing

(Text continued on p. 940)

TABLE 5.2-6
Aspects of the structure of higher education, 1891–92 and 1895–96

Type of institution	Ratio*
1891–92:	
Universities and colleges	111.8
Schools and departments of medicine, law, and theology	55.7
Normal schools	60.4
All	227.9
1895–96:	
Collegiate (thousands)	97.3
Professional (thousands)	51.9†

* Number of students in higher education for each 100,000 persons of the total population, by type of institution.

† Includes technology (9.7).

SOURCES: U.S. Office of Education, *Report of the Commissioner of Education, 1891–92,* p. 11; and U.S. Office of Education, *Statistical Review of Higher Education, 1895–96,* p. 1917.

		California	Chicago	Cincinnati	Columbia	Cornell	Harvard
TABLE 5.2-7 *Enrollments of 30 major institutions, 1903, 1908 and 1913*	College, men	1112	936	200	841	} 1120	2350
	College, women	1626	767	419	623		564
	Scientific schools*	828		406	665	1343	76
	Law	142	211		450	267	695
	Medicine	119	191	84	341	107	306
	Nonprofessional graduate schools	408	480	170	1496	315	489
	Agriculture	530				1354	
	Architecture	†			143	143	61
	Art	†					
	Commerce	280	160	97			113
	Dentistry	90					203
	Divinity		125				56
	Forestry	†					9
	Journalism				106		
	Music	†			16		
	Pedagogy	†	287	240	1670		
	Pharmacy	114			441		
	Veterinary medicine	†				122	
	Other courses		808	486			
	Deduct double registration	24	246	231	389	11	
	Total	5225	3719	1871	6403	4760	4922
	Summer session 1913	2363	3771		4539	1392	797
	Deduct double registration	517	656		1013	540	92
	Grand total 1913, November 1	7071	6834	1871	9929	5612	5627
	Grand total 1912, November 1	6457	6351	1924	9002	5412	5729
	Grand total 1910, November 1	4552	5883	1416	7411	5169	5329
	Grand total 1908, November 1	3644	5114	1364	5677	4700	5342
	Grand total 1903, November 1	3477	4146	1068	4557	3438	6013
	Extension and similar courses	638	3182		3644	597	1100
	Officers	525	337	261	907	725	731

Illinois	*Indiana*	*Iowa*	*Johns Hopkins*	*Kansas*	*Michigan*	*Minnesota*	*Missouri*	*Nebraska*	*New York*	*Northwestern*	*Ohio State*	*Pennsylvania*
427	694	610	178	942	1736	639	834	541	486	479	485	} 409
402	423	553		688	784	882	516	733	221	609	412	
1001	248	221	79	372	1282	638	360	306	233	80	811	657
106	85	201		174	553	193	103	200	771	294	181	381
445	132	112	368	107	353	172	75	102	432	178		283
268	83	130	219	99	225	127	123	169	369	85	121	438
792						464	501	423			889	
351				23	120	43		1			65	259
†	58	42		20	†			64		46		
282					†			22	2013	567		1430
94		244			282	268				566		589
										233		
†					†	41	†	36			65	
†	73				†		64		†	39		
78	93	87		130	†	25				407		26
	77	†		181	†	87	182	164	420	122	166	699
255		57		61	96	95		23		135	92	
†										11	163	125
350		86	168			10				296	280	9
16	549	49		489	127	68	211	302	121	360	22	
4835	1417	2294	1012	2308	5304	3616	2547	2482	4835	3776	3708	5305
713	1084	426	347	510	1408	531	810	511	933	193	703	865
289	230	178	48	208	704	215	222	143	260	92	300	202
5259	2271	2542	1311	2610	6008	3932	3135	2850	5508	3877	4111	5968
4315	2192	1944	1058	2403	5620	3737	2871	2811	4543	3632	3608	5287
4659	2132	1957	890	2246	5339	4972	2678	2733	3947	3543	3181	5187
4400	2113	2356	707	2086	5188	4607	2558	3154	3951	3113	2700	4555
3239	1614	1260	694	1319	3926	3550	1540	2513	2177	2740	1688	2644
	242			1185	235	1546	152	902	1676		227	379
737	109	275	208	200	537	465	305	354	425	434	291	564

TABLE 5.2-7
(continued)

	Pittsburgh	Princeton	Stanford	Syracuse	Texas	Tulane
College, men	305	1267	1243	1340	811	166
College, women	87		500		709	152
Scientific schools*	266	156		308	288	164
Law	143		140	291	339	94
Medicine	123		64	96	170	399
Nonprofessional graduate schools	46	176	134	75	77	27
Agriculture				70	38	
Architecture				50	54	25
Art				178		85
Commerce					57	
Dentistry	209					55
Divinity						
Forestry				220		
Journalism						21
Music				925		73
Pedagogy	421			25	443	91
Pharmacy	209				63	7
Veterinary medicine						
Other courses	157			233		
Deduct double registration	60		338	112	676	115
Total	1906	1599	1743	3699	2373	1244
Summer session 1913			38	260	981	1163
Deduct double registration			25	114	248	109
Grand total 1913, November 1	1906	1599	1756	3845	3106	2298
Grand total 1912, November 1	1833	1568	1670	3529	3016	2249
Grand total 1910, November 1		1451	1648	3248	2597	1985
Grand total 1908, November 1		1314	1541	3204	2410	1171
Grand total 1903, November 1		1434	1370	2207	1309	1037
Extension and similar courses	411				757	117
Officers	290	217	218	280		313

*Includes schools of mines, engineering, chemistry, and related subjects.

† Included elsewhere.

‡ 1,220 students in attendance on summer courses.

NOTE: The grand totals of the University of Minnesota prior to 1912 are inclusive of "extension and similar students," which were listed separately in 1912 and 1913, hence the apparent decrease.

SOURCE: R. Tombo, Jr., *University Registration Statistics,* January 1914, p. 2.

Virginia	Washington University	Western Reserve	Wisconsin	Yale
396	152	459	828	1402
	229	358	776	
101	169		775	1133
257	80	109	161	130
102	60	164	79	49
43	57	9	290	334
			968	
	46			
	305			53
			374	
	111	139		
				100
			12	32
			91	
			81	85
			42	
		124	40	
	48	45	45	
14	32	37	112	55
885	1225	1370	4450	3263
‡			2120	
			680	
885	1225	1370	5890	3263
799	958	1378	5141	3265
688	796	1274	4745	3287
757	806	1016	3876	3466
613	761	765	3221	2990
	319		2907	
101	203	252	633	571

today. Professional enrollment plus enrollment in normal schools, for example, was about one-half of total enrollment in 1891–92. In 1895–96 professional enrollment approximated one-half of the total enrollment in higher education, with normal schools excluded from the data.

ENROLLMENT IN 30 MAJOR INSTITUTIONS IN THE EARLY TWENTIETH CENTURY

Some interesting data are available on enrollment in 30 leading institutions of higher education in the years 1903 to 1913 (Table 5.2-7). In 1913, the seven largest institutions in terms of enrollment were Columbia (9,929), the University of California (7,076), the University of Chicago (6,384), the University of Pennsylvania (5,968), the University of Wisconsin (5,380), Harvard (5,627), and Cornell (5,612).

Changes from 1903 to 1913 reflect the influence of various factors. The largest relative increases in enrollment generally occurred in large urban areas—the University of California, 103 percent; Columbia, 118 percent; New York University, 153 percent; and the University of Pennsylvania, 126 percent. The experience of universities in agricultural states was mixed. The University of Minnesota's enrollment increased about one-eighth, as did that of the University of Nebraska. However, enrollment at the University of Kansas doubled, while that at the University of Texas in 1913 was 2.4 times its enrollment in 1903.

The prestigious private universities began to show signs of restrictive policies. With a drop of 7 percent, Harvard was the only one of these institutions to experience a decline. Yale's enrollment gained only 9 percent. But Johns Hopkins, a relative latecomer, had an increase of 90 percent, and Tulane experienced an increase of 122 percent.

Of interest are the data on enrollment of undergraduates. Here Harvard was first, with 2,914, while California, Michigan, Stanford, and Chicago followed in that order.[4]

ENROLLMENT TRENDS AND PROJECTIONS, 1880 TO 1978

Table 5.2-8 provides data on actual enrollment for the years 1880 to 1960 and projected enrollment for 1970 and 1978. Historically, the major increases in enrollment occurred after 1910. In terms of numbers, and percentages, the decade of exceptionally rapid increases, however, was that of the 1960s. The increase turned out to be larger than was suggested by the projected figure for

[4] R. Tombo, Jr., *University Registration Statistics,* January 1914, p. 2.

TABLE 5.2-8 *Percentage increase in resident degree-credit enrollment and enrollment per institution, by 10-year periods, 1870 to 1960, and 1970 and 1978 (projected)* *

Year	Enrollment† Enrollment rise (thousands)†	Enrollment† Percentage rise‡	Institutions Rise	Institutions Percentage rise	Enrollment per institution
1880	64	123	248	44	143
1890	41	35	187	23	157
1900	81	52	−21	−2	243
1910	117	49	−26	−3	372
1920	243	68	90	9	575
1930	503	84	368	35	781
1940	393	36	299	21	875
1950	1,165	78	143	8	1,437
1960	557§	21	157	8	1,601
1970 (projected)	3,345	104			2,406 (1967)
1978 (projected eight years)	2,639 (3,394)¶	40 (52)¶			

* Projected figures deduct an estimated 5 percent for extension enrollment.
† Estimated enrollment before 1910.
‡ Rise is from 10 years previously — e.g., 1880 rise is that from 1870.
§ Data for first term of academic year.
¶ Figures in parenthesis are 1980 totals on assumption of continued growth as from 1970–1978.

SOURCES: Adapted and calculated from U.S. Office of Education, *Digest of Educational Statistics, 1968,* 1968, pp. 68–69; and U.S. Office of Education, *Projections of Educational Statistics to 1977–78,* National Center for Education Statistics, 1968, p. 12.

1970 shown in the table. Actual enrollment in 1970 was 8.5 million.

Projected gains for the 1970s are only about one-half those of the 1960s in percentage terms but about the same in terms of numbers.

In general, the largest relative increases occurred in periods of prosperity—e.g., the 1920s, 1950s, and 1960s. However, the 1930s—the years of the Great Depression—are an exception to the general pattern. Apparently, with jobs unavailable, many sought to improve their capacity to earn through higher education.

The number of baccalaureate and first professional degrees granted declined as a percentage of enrollment from 1870 to 1900 but increased after that:

Baccalaureate and first professional degrees as a percentage of enrollment		
	1870	18
	1900	12
	1930	13
	1960	15

SOURCE: Based on U.S. Office of Education, *Digest of Educational Statistics, 1968*, 1968, p. 69.

NEGRO ENROLLMENT

A comparison of school and college enrollment in 1890 and 1969 indicates some losses in relative positions for Negroes of college age.

In 1890, the percentage of Negroes aged 15 to 19 enrolled was almost as high as for native whites with native parents and in excess of enrollment for native whites with foreign parents. Among those aged 20 and over, however, the proportion of Negroes enrolled was well below the percentage of native whites with white parents who were enrolled:

Enrollment as a percentage of age group, by race and nationality, 1890

Age	*Native white, white parents*	*Native white, foreign parents*	*Negroes*
15 to 19 years	20.44	14.74	18.76
20 years and over	1.78	0.93	1.21

SOURCE: U.S. Bureau of the Census, *Compendium of the Eleventh Census, 1890*, 1892–97, part II, p. 27.

In 1969, the proportion of Negroes of college age enrolled in school was well below that of whites. The Negro percentage was 87 percent of that for whites in the 18 to 19 age group, but only 66 percent of the enrollment rate of whites aged 20 to 21 and 53 percent of that for whites aged 22 to 24:

Percentage of civilian noninstitutional population enrolled in school, by race and age, 1969

Age	*All persons*	*White*	*Negro*
18 to 19 years	50.2	50.9	44.5
20 to 21 years	34.1	35.4	23.3
22 to 24 years	15.4	16.2	8.6

SOURCE: U.S. Bureau of the Census, "School Enrollment: October, 1969," *Current Population Reports*, ser. P-20, no. 206, 1970, pp. 8–9.

However, enrollment rates of college-age Negroes have been rising rapidly in recent years. The gains have been especially pronounced for enrollment in institutions of higher education, although enrollment rates at lower levels have also risen. Just in the years 1967 to 1969, Negroes aged 18 to 19 enrolled in institutions of higher education rose as a proportion of their age group from 18.0 to 23.1 percent; those aged 20 to 21, from 16.2 to 20.5 percent; and those aged 22 to 24, from 6.0 to 8.6 percent.[5]

ENROLLMENT TRENDS BY SEX A substantial part of the rise in enrollment in higher education can be explained by the increased interest of women in educational attainment. However, the increase in women's share of total enrollment has occurred unevenly. There was a large rise from 1870 to 1930, a substantial relative decline from 1930 to 1960 (perhaps explained by the increased number of children to be cared for and by improved employment opportunities for women), and an appreciable recovery since 1960 (possibly explained by declining birth rates and by a changed attitude toward higher education):

Enrollment of women as a percentage of total enrollment in higher education, actual, 1870 to 1970, and projected, 1980*

1870	21
1900	36
1930	44
1960	35
1970	41
1980	44

* Resident degree-credit enrollment before 1970; resident and nonresident degree-credit enrollment for projections.

SOURCE: U.S. Office of Education, *Digest of Educational Statistics, 1968,* 1968, p. 69; U.S. Office of Education, *Projections of Educational Statistics to 1977–78,* National Center for Educational Statistics, 1968, pp. 16, 31; and U.S. Office of Education, unpublished tables on enrollment data for 1970.

In the 1930s, enrollment of women increased only 16 percent, as compared with 30 percent for men. It seems probable that, under the conditions of the Great Depression, limited family resources were more likely to be allocated to higher education for sons than for daughters.

Between 1890 and 1910, the number of women enrolled in co-educational institutions increased relatively more rapidly than the number enrolled in women's colleges, and they represented a rising proportion of all women enrolled in higher education:

[5] U.S. Bureau of the Census, "School Enrollment: October, 1969," *Current Population Reports,* ser. P-20, no. 206, 1970, p. 8; and U.S. Bureau of the Census, "School Enrollment: October 1968 and 1967," *Current Population Reports,* ser. P-20, no. 190, 1969, p. 35.

	Coeducational institutions and men's colleges and universities		Women's colleges	All institutions of higher education	
	Men	Women	Women	Men	Women
1890	38.1	8.1	2.0	44.9	10.8
1900	68.8	20.4	4.9	72.2	26.8
1910	119.6	43.4	8.9	119.6	52.3
Percentage increase, 1890–1910	213.9	435.8	335.0	166.4	384.3

SOURCE: U.S. Office of Education, *Report of the Commissioner of Education, 1910*, vol. 2.

From 1895–96 to 1937–38, women made particularly rapid gains as a proportion of all students enrolled in professional programs in institutions of higher education—from 1 percent in the former year to 34 percent in the latter.[6]

[6] U.S. Office of Education, *Biennial Surveys of Education: Higher Education, 1936–1940*, vol, 1, p. 2.

Year	Graduate enrollment	Graduate enrollment as a percentage of total degree-credit enrollment	Percentage of all degrees	
			Bachelor's and first professional	Master's and doctor's
1872	210	0.5		
1880	411	0.5		
1890	1,717*	1.5*		
1902	6,277	6.0		
1940			86	14
1968	807,924	12.1	77	23

*U.S. Office of Education, *Digest of Educational Statistics, 1968*, 1968, p. 70, gives graduate enrollment for 1902 as 5,831. This difference may be explained by better coverage in the later study and possibly by the use of full-time equivalent enrollment in the earlier study.

SOURCES: U.S. Office of Education, *Report of the Commissioner of Education, 1881*, p. VI; *1889–90*, p. 760; *1891–92*, p. 10; *1896–97*, p. 1536, *1902*, p. 1387; *1903*, p. 1178; U.S. Office of Education, *Digest of Educational Statistics, 1968*, 1968, p. 69; *Digest of Educational Statistics, 1970*, 1970, p. 67; and U.S. Office of Education, *Earned Degrees Conferred: 1968–69, Part A—Summary Data*, 1971, p. 3.

GRADUATE
ENROLLMENT

One of the striking developments in recent years has been the large relative rise of graduate enrollment. Graduate enrollment first began to show a significant increase in the early 1870s. However, even as late as the end of the nineteenth century it was only 6 percent of total enrollment. But by 1968–69, it had risen to 12.1 percent of total degree-credit enrollment, and graduate degrees had climbed to 23 percent of all degrees awarded (Table 5.2-9). With graduate instruction two to four times as costly as undergraduate instruction, the impact of this relative increase in graduate enrollment presents serious problems for university treasurers.

RISING SHARE
OF PUBLIC
INSTITUTIONS
IN TOTAL
ENROLLMENT

Public support of the development of state systems of higher education has been a major factor in the growth of enrollment. By the late 1970s, enrollment in public institutions as a percentage of total enrollment is likely to be at least double what it was in 1900:

Enrollment in public institutions as a percentage of total enrollment in higher education, actual, 1882 to 1960, and projected, 1970 and 1978

Year	Percent
1882	26
1900	38
1930	48
1960	59
1970	69
1978	73

SOURCE: U.S. Office of Education, *Digest of Educational Statistics, 1970,* 1970, p. 67; U.S. Office of Education, unpublished tables on enrollment data for 1970; and U.S. Office of Education, *Projections of Educational Statistics to 1977–78.* National Center for Educational Statistics, 1968, pp. 16, 31. Enrollment data relate to resident degree credit before 1970 and to total enrollment from 1970 on.

In fact, it may be considerably higher than that. Enrollment in private institutions of higher education tended to level off between 1966 and 1970, and the increase in the share of the public institutions in the total accelerated. By 1970 the actual share of the public institutions was 75 percent, as compared with the 69 percent that had been projected by the Office of Education.

Had the share of public institutions in total enrollment been constrained to remain at the 1900 figure of 38 percent, total enrollment today would probably be considerably lower. How much lower would depend on the extent to which private institutions of higher education would have been able to expand to pick up the burden. Two extreme views on this question are shown in Table 5.2-10, which, it should be noted, uses OE projected data for

	1970		1978	
	Thousands	*Percent*	*Thousands*	*Percent*
Actual (projected)				
Private	2,131	31	2,581	27
Public	4,775	69	7,102	73
TOTAL	6,906	100	9,684	100
Alternate projections assuming public at 38%				
Projection A				
Private	4,282	62	6,004	62
Public	2,624	38	3,680	38
TOTAL	6,906	100	9,684	100
Projection B				
Private	2,131	62	2,581	62
Public	1,306	38	1,582	38
TOTAL	3,437	100	4,163	100

SOURCE: U.S. Office of Education, *Projections of Educational Statistics to 1977–78,* National Center for Educational Statistics, 1968, p. 16 (projections A and B are the author's calculations).

1970, rather than the actual data, which have only recently become available. Projection A assumes that private institutions would have picked up all the burden; that is, private institutions would have expanded to accommodate 62 percent of the projected 1970 enrollment of 6.9 million. The probability that this would have happened is not very great.

Projection B assumes that private enrollment in 1970 was 2.1 million—its projected level—but that total enrollment was constrained by the assumption that public enrollment was 38 percent of the total. On this basis, public enrollment would have amounted to only 1.3 million in 1970. Hence, if the massive increase in the relative share of public enrollment since 1900 had not occurred, public enrollment would be from 2.2 million (projection A) to 3.5 million (projection B) less than it actually was in 1970.

For 1963 more detailed data are available (Table 2.2-2). The proportion of college students attending public institutions had reached 64 percent. Roughly the same percentage of all undergraduates and of residential undergraduates and first professional students combined attended public institutions. In contrast, public institutions accounted for only 38 percent of first professional students and 58 percent of graduate students.

The rate of growth of public enrollment is related to the availability of public funds. But that is by no means the whole story. It is also significant that growth has been especially rapid in the types of institutions that have special claims on government, for example, universities because of their research and graduate training, and junior colleges because of their involvement in occupational training. The Commission on Financing Higher Education has provided a breakdown of institutions of higher education that is especially helpful here (Table 5.2-11).

The institutions with the largest enrollment increases are universities, liberal arts colleges, professional schools, junior colleges, and teachers colleges. Universities, junior colleges, teachers colleges, and technological schools are especially likely to receive government aid. Furthermore, liberal arts colleges, which used to be almost entirely private, are now growing rapidly under public auspices, although the number of public liberal arts colleges is still relatively small.

(Text continued on p. 952)

TABLE 5.2-11
Percentage rise in enrollment, 1930–1950

	Percent
All	144
All public	154
All private	128
Universities	125
Public	149
Private	100
Liberal arts	161
Public	223
Private	146
Nonsectarian	72
Protestant	184
Catholic	175
Teachers colleges	64
Technological	180
Junior colleges	424

SOURCE: Commission on Financing Higher Education, *Current Operating Expenditures and Income of Higher Education in the United States, 1930, 1940, and 1950,* Columbia University Press, New York, 1952, p. 3.

	Bachelor's degrees requiring four or five years		
Major field of study (1)	Total (2)	Men (3)	Women (4)
All fields	524,117	301,051	223,066
Agriculture	5,730	5,578	152
Architecture (excluding architectural engineering)*	2,401	2,306	95
Biological sciences	27,010	19,390	7,620
Biology, general	16,866	11,373	5,493
Botany, general	473	309	164
Zoology, general	4,119	3,198	921
Bacteriology, virology, mycology, parasitology, microbiology	996	497	499
Biochemistry	264	195	69
Biological sciences, all other	4,292	3,818	474
Business and commerce	63,500	58,074	5,426
Accounting	15,101	4,203	898
Business and commerce, all other	48,399	43,871	4,528
Education†	118,399	29,256	89,143
Business education, commercial education	6,168	1,731	4,437
Counseling and guidance	4	2	2
Educational administration, supervision, or finance	45	41	4
Elementary education	65,054	6,780	58,274
Music education	5,498	2,347	3,151
Physical education	13,006	8,294	4,712
Secondary education	2,656	1,338	1,318
Education, all other	25,968	8,723	17,245
Engineering*	35,815	35,669	146
English and literature	39,190	13,244	25,946
Fine and applied arts	18,677	7,917	10,760
Art, general	5,244	1,782	3,462
Music, including sacred music (excluding music education†)	3,537	1,531	2,006
Speech and dramatic arts (excluding speech correction†)	5,269	2,266	3,003
Fine and applied arts, all other	4,627	2,338	2,289

TABLE 5.2-12 *Earned degrees conferred by institutions of higher education, by field of study, level, and sex, United States and outlying areas, 1965–66*

First professional degrees requiring at least six years			Second level (master's) degrees			Doctor's degrees (Ph.D., Ed.D., etc.)		
Total *(5)*	*Men* *(6)*	*Women* *(7)*	*Total* *(8)*	*Men* *(9)*	*Women* *(10)*	*Total* *(11)*	*Men* *(12)*	*Women* *(13)*
31,496	30,071	1,425	140,772	93,184	47,588	18,239	16,121	2,118
			1,363	1,295	68	537	530	7
198	190	8	381	365	16	9	8	1
38	38		4,235	3,087	1,148	2,097	1,792	305
			1,546	1,105	441	226	181	45
			316	236	80	203	180	23
			660	485	175	293	246	47
			385	233	152	242	206	36
			231	165	66	315	252	63
38	38		1,097	863	234	828	727	91
			12,988	12,656	332	387	370	17
			862	834	28	34	31	3
			12,126	11,822	304	353	339	14
22	11	11	50,478	25,837	24,641	3,063	2,461	602
			1,170	490	680	43	37	6
7	7		5,881	3,125	2,756	286	232	54
2	2		7,096	5,451	1,645	633	574	59
			8,713	1,772	6,941	140	86	54
			1,392	862	530	48	41	7
9		9	2,765	2,093	672	128	86	42
			3,924	2,360	1,564	114	93	21
4	2	2	19,537	9,684	9,853	1,671	1,312	359
			13,678	13,602	76	2,304	2,295	9
2		2	6,265	2,854	3,411	699	540	159
28	23	5	5,019	2,760	2,259	476	396	80
			940	495	445	25	22	3
28	23	5	1,695	974	721	164	145	19
			1,535	780	755	240	201	39
			849	511	338	47	28	19

TABLE 5.2-12
(continued)

| Major field of study
(1) | Bachelor's degrees requiring
four or five years | | |
	Total *(2)*	*Men* *(3)*	*Women* *(4)*
Foreign languages and literature	15,519	4,545	10,974
French	5,588	1,045	4,543
German	2,061	837	1,224
Latin and/or classical Greek	1,245	634	611
Russian	537	253	284
Spanish	5,039	1,377	3,662
Foreign languages and literature, all other	1,049	399	650
Forestry	1,443	1,441	2
Geography	1,934	1,529	405
Health professions	15,054	3,481	11,573
Dentistry, D.D.S. and D.M.D. only			
Medical technology	2,139	223	1,916
Medicine, M.D. only			
Nursing and/or public health nursing	7,831	96	7,735
Pharmacy	3,311	2,849	462
Health professions, all other	1,773	313	1,460
Home economics (excluding home economics education†)	5,724	145	5,579
Journalism	3,131	1,910	1,221
Law (LL.B., J.D., or higher degrees)	245	235	10
Library science	619	46	573
Mathematical subjects	20,090	13,401	6,689
Mathematics	19,842	13,191	6,651
Statistics (including actuarial science)	248	210	38
Military science	1,979	1,979	
Philosophy	5,024	4,294	730
Physical sciences	17,185	14,852	2,333
Chemistry	9,735	7,934	1,801
Geology	1,307	1,181	126
Physics	4,608	4,384	224
Physical sciences, all other	1,535	1,353	182
Psychology	17,022	10,041	6,981
Religion	4,036	2,744	1,292

First professional degrees requiring at least six years			Second level (master's) degrees			Doctor's degrees (Ph.D., Ed.D., etc.)		
Total (5)	Men (6)	Women (7)	Total (8)	Men (9)	Women (10)	Total (11)	Men (12)	Women (13)
8	8		3,631	1,579	2,052	512	361	151
			1,054	313	741	80	46	34
			514	260	254	93	69	24
			361	187	174	63	51	12
			142	83	59	9	6	3
			867	387	480	82	55	27
8	8		693	349	344	185	134	51
23	23		303	299	4	51	51	
			370	309	61	58	52	6
13,253	12,561	692	2,867	1,610	1,257	251	225	26
3,264	3,229	35						
			7		7			
7,720	7,204	516						
			863	17	846	1		1
452	378	74	187	159	28	78	73	5
1,817	1,750	67	1,810	1,434	376	172	152	20
			740	29	711	54	12	42
			523	395	128	15	12	3
13,442	12,934	508	780	743	37	29	27	2
23	7	16	3,916	1,002	2,914	19	14	5
3	3		4,772	3,771	1,001	782	725	57
3	3		4,387	3,440	947	676	625	51
			385	331	54	106	100	6
12	12		613	504	109	203	181	22
1	1		4,992	4,464	528	3,045	2,914	131
			1,822	1,472	350	1,533	1,442	91
			478	445	33	268	259	9
1	1		1,949	1,869	80	973	952	21
			743	678	65	271	261	10
			2,530	1,680	850	1,046	826	220
4,443	4,260	183	1,946	1,475	471	333	314	19

TABLE 5.2-12
(continued)

Major field of study (1)	Bachelor's degrees requiring four or five years		
	Total (2)	Men (3)	Women (4)
Social sciences	93,669	60,876	32,793
Economics (excluding agricultural economics)	11,585	10,447	1,138
History	28,770	18,829	9,941
Political science or government (excluding internal relations and public administration)	15,375	11,994	3,381
Sociology	15,203	6,139	9,064
Social work, administration, welfare	1,664	476	1,188
Social sciences, all other	21,072	12,991	8,081
Trade and industrial training	2,357	2,334	23
Other broad general curriculums and miscellaneous fields	8,364	5,764	2,600

* Degrees in architectural engineering are included under engineering.

† Degrees in home economics education, music education, and speech correction are included under education.

SOURCE: U.S. Department of Health, Education and Welfare, Office of Education, "Earned Degrees Conferred, 1965–66"; in U.S. Office of Education, *Digest of Educational Statistics, 1968,* 1968, p. 87.

RELATIVE IMPORTANCE OF PROFESSIONAL DEGREES

Professional degrees accounted for about 50 percent of all degrees awarded in 1891–92, but their relative importance has declined dramatically. They constituted only 4.6 percent of all bachelor's and first professional degrees awarded in 1968–69.[7] This sharp decline is largely explained by the fact that in the nineteenth century students were training themselves primarily to become physicians, lawyers, ministers, or teachers. Gradually, however, as industrialization proceeded, the range of occupations for which college and university education was deemed appropriate became much wider.

It should be noted that, among the 524,000 bachelor's degrees awarded in 1965–66, there were substantial numbers of degrees representing professional specialization—for example, education, 118,000; engineering, 35,000; and health professions, 15,000 (Table 5.2-12).

[7] U.S. Office of Education, *Earned Degrees Conferred: 1968–69, Part A— Summary Data,* 1971, p. 3.

First professional degrees requiring at least six years			Second level (master's) degrees			Doctor's degrees (Ph.D., Ed.D., etc.)		
Total (5)	Men (6)	Women (7)	Total (8)	Men (9)	Women (10)	Total (11)	Men (12)	Women (13)
			16,460	11,369	5,091	2,158	1,919	239
			1,528	1,359	169	458	436	22
			3,883	2,800	1,083	599	527	72
			1,429	1,152	277	336	307	29
			981	680	301	244	208	36
			3,912	1,588	2,324	64	34	30
			4,727	3,790	937	457	407	50
			44	42	2	11	11	
			1,878	1,457	421	100	85	15

PROFESSIONAL SCHOOLS It has been observed that professional schools were relatively much more important in the nineteenth century than in recent years, for reasons associated with the decline in the relative importance of first professional degrees. Enrollment in these schools generally accounted for about half of total enrollment in the latter part of the nineteenth century, although the percentage varies with differences in coverage of types of institutions in the data. Law, medicine, and theology accounted for one-half of total enrollment, if normal schools are excluded from the data.

In 1937–38, professional education continued to play a considerably greater relative role than in the 1960s. Eleven major professional schools in that year awarded about 90,000 degrees—a number roughly equal to one-half of bachelor's and first professional degrees.

Professional schools emerged slowly at first; only nine of those in operation in 1915 were established by 1800. Even by 1850, only 25 of the schools operating in 1915 enrolled students in six major

TABLE 5.2-13 *Distribution of the present list (1915–16) of professional and technical and women's colleges with respect to the dates of their opening*

Dates	Theology	Law	Medicine	Dentistry	Pharmacy	Agricultural and mechanical arts	Women's colleges
1761–1765			1				
1766–1779			1				
1781–1785	1		1				
1786–1790		1					
1791–1795	2						
1796–1800	1		1				
1801–1805						1	
1806–1810	2		1				
1811–1815	2	1	1				
1816–1820	5	1	2				
1821–1825	5		5		1		
1826–1830	6	1	1		1		1
1831–1835	4	3	2			1	2
1836–1840	4		3	1	1		5
1841–1845	4	1	6	1	1	1	5
1846–1850	6	4	6		1	1	7
1851–1855	7	2	1			1	16
1856–1860	13	4	5		1	4	15
1861–1865	7		2	1		4	2
1866–1870	18	9	4	4	3	8	11
1871–1875	9	7	4	1	2	9	8
1875–1880	3	5	4	5	2	4	4
1881–1885	14	4	3	5	7	3	5
1886–1890	8	6	5	9	5	5	9
1891–1895	14	16	9	8	15	8	8
1895–1900	5	15	5	7	13		6
1901–1905	9	10	10	6	11	1	8
1906–1910	3	14	6		5	1	2
1911–1915	3	15	3	1	6	—	—
TOTAL	155	119	92	49	75	52	114

SOURCE: Adapted from J. B. Sears, *Philanthropy in the History of American Higher Education,* U.S. Office of Education, 1922, p. 58.

fields, with theology, law, and medicine the most numerous (Table 5.2-13).

A Bureau of the Census report for 1860 indicates that there were 204 literary institutions conferring A.B. and A.M. degrees. Among professional schools, the most numerous were schools of theology (93) and medical schools (46).

By 1915, there were 542 institutions offering seven types of professional training, with theological schools accounting for 155, law schools for 119, and medical schools for 92. It is of some interest that in the years 1871 to 1915, schools of theology received the largest amount from gifts, with medical schools next and law schools receiving the smallest amount. Schools of theology received substantially more than all women's colleges (Table 5.2-14).

TABLE 5.2-14 *Benefactions to different lines of higher education in the United States each fifth year, 1871–1915*

Dates	Higher education of women	Theological schools	Medical schools	National land-grant schools and schools of science	Schools of law
1915		$1,467,055	$2,661,076[a]		$ 90,576[b]
1910	$1,303,431	1,431,028	509,227		86,334[c]
1905	1,107,523	1,890,606[d]	354,210		
1900	588,566	1,123,812	183,500		105,500
1895	625,734	1,385,522	95,260		
1890	303,527	923,831[e]	249,287[e]	$ 205,295[e]	14,663[e]
1885	322,813	681,855	94,250	562,371	40,150[f]
1880	92,372	827,856	11,400	1,371,445	100,000[g]
1875	217,887	404,356	72,395	147,112	
1871	1,600,000	652,265	2,000	285,000	

[a] In 1914 medical schools received $7,113,920.
[b] In 1914 law schools received gifts amounting to $203,067; in 1913, $425,867.
[c] In 1909 law schools received $356,800, and in 1908, $382,000.
[d] In 1906 theological schools received $3,271,480.
[e] In 1891.
[f] In 1886.
[g] In 1878.

SOURCE: Adapted from J. B. Sears, *Philanthropy in the History of American Higher Education,* U.S. Office of Education, 1922, p. 58.

In 1890, students in professional schools were overwhelmingly white (97 percent), but not so overwhelmingly male (68 percent). Among the white faculty, however, 86 percent were male.

Interestingly, by 1890, despite indications that law schools were receiving much smaller amounts in gifts than medical schools, public interest in law schools was much greater than in medical schools. Moreover, the relative importance of private versus public institutions varied greatly among types of professional schools and by region. Theological schools, of course, have always been entirely private. In 1891–92, 11 percent of medical schools and 37 percent of law schools were under public control. Conforming to the regional pattern of development of private versus public higher education, there were only private medical schools in the North Atlantic states, but in the Western Division, 46 percent of enrollment in these schools were in public institutions.

If we use enrollment as a basis, we find that only the normal schools were predominantly public in 1891–92, whereas enrollment in the other types of institutions was predominantly private:

Enrollment in institutions of higher education by type and control, 1891–92

Institutions of higher education	Percentage public	Percentage private
Universities and colleges	19.4	80.6
Schools of law, medicine, and theology	13.2	86.8
Normal schools	85.4	14.6

SOURCE: U.S. Office of Education, *Report of the Commissioner of Education, 1891–92*, p. 13.

Interesting data on student-faculty ratios for five colleges and universities and for their professional schools are available for the year 1889–90:

Student-faculty ratios, five institutions of higher education and their divinity, law, and medical schools, 1889–90

Institution of higher education	College	Divinity	Law	Medical
Boston University	8:1	6:1		3:1
Harvard	12:1	3:1	26:1*	11:1*
Dartmouth	14:1			4:1
Yale	17:1	8:1	9:1	3:1
Columbia	5:1		38:1	18:1

* Additional faculty not included.

SOURCE: Adapted from U.S. Office of Education, *Report of the Commissioner of Education, 1889–90*, pp. 462–63.

The student-faculty ratio was exceptionally low (5 to 1) at Columbia and very high (17 to 1) at Yale. Yale standards were undoubtedly relatively low in that era, although student-faculty ratios are not a complete guide to quality. In law, Harvard and Columbia both had very high student-faculty ratios, although the general view was that Harvard had the top law school at that time. In medicine, there was also a wide range of student-faculty ratios: from 3 to 1 to 18 to 1. Columbia was first in the student-faculty ratio in medicine and law.

Among the various types of professional schools, also, student-faculty ratios varied substantially:

Student-faculty ratios in professional schools, by type of school, 1896–97	
Theology	8:1
Law	14:1
Medicine	6:1
Dentistry	8:1
All other (includes pharmaceutical, nursing, and veterinary schools)	4:1

SOURCE: U.S. Office of Education, *Report of the Commissioner of Education, 1896–97*, p. 1774.

Interesting data are also available for medical, law, and theological schools in 1896–97:

Professional schools: enrollment, student-faculty ratio, endowment, and value of grounds and building—total and per student, 1896–97	*Medical*	*Law*	*Theology*
Student-faculty ratio*	11:1	23:1	11:1
Value of grounds and buildings (thousands of dollars)	$5,377	$1,269	$14,106
Endowment (thousands of dollars)	$344	$434	$18,171
Value of grounds and buildings per student (dollars)	$258	$121	$1,726
Endowment per student (dollars)	$37	$42	$2,228
Number of students	9,441	10,449	8,173

* Part-time faculty omitted.

SOURCE: U.S. Office of Education, *Report of the Commissioner of Education, 1896–97*, pp. 1509, 1775, 1776; see also *Report of the Commissioner of Education, 1902*, pp. 1509–1512.

Law schools had a student-faculty ratio double that of medical and theological schools. Endowment per student was $2,228 for theological schools, as compared with only $42 for law schools and $37 for medical schools. Theological schools also had the highest value of grounds and buildings, both on a total and on a per-student basis.

Growth of enrollment of professional schools has been uneven over the years. From 1887 to 1897, the percentage increases in enrollment of professional schools ranged from 30 percent for theological schools to 284 percent for dental schools. From 1897 to 1937–38, law schools experienced the largest relative increase in enrollment among professional schools (249 percent). The almost imperceptible rise in medical enrollment from 1897 to 1937–38 was attributable in large part to improvements in the quality of medical education and to rising unit costs (Table 5.2-15). It was also attributable to the closing of many proprietary schools following publication of the Flexner Report in 1910.[8]

TABLE 5.2-15
Enrollment in professional schools, 1887 to 1937–38

School	Percentage increase 1887 to 1897	Number enrolled 1897	Number enrolled 1937–38	Percentage increase 1897 to 1937–38
Medicine	108	24,377	25,435	3
Law	228	10,449	36,445	249
Theology	30	8,173	12,814	57
Dentistry	284	3,426	7,527	120

SOURCES: U.S. Office of Education, *Report of the Commissioner of Education, 1897–98*, chap. 38; and U.S. Office of Education, *Biennial Survey of Education, 1938–40*, pp. 4–5.

DENOMINA-TIONAL SCHOOLS

Until the late nineteenth century denominational schools dominated higher education, except for the emergence of land-grant colleges during and after the Civil War. In 1884–85 the government listed colleges under the control of 31 religious denominations. Variations in the student-faculty ratio suggest differences in the quality of denominational institutions. In 1884–85 the average student-faculty ratio for denominational institutions was 8 to 1. The ex-

[8] Abraham Flexner, *Medical Education in the United States and Canada*, bulletin no. 4, report to the Carnegie Foundation for the Advancement of Teaching, D. B. Updike, The Merrymount Press, Boston, 1910.

tremes ranged from 30 to 1 for German Evangelical colleges and 18 to 1 for the Methodist Church South to 2 to 3 (two students to three professors) for reformed German colleges.[9] In comparison, the average student-faculty ratio for nonsectarian institutions was 10 to 1 in 1895–96.

Data on enrollment and endowment per student are available for schools controlled by selected denominations in 1895–96:

Students and endowment per student by denominations, 1895–96

Denomination	Number of students	Endowment per student
Congregational	4,103	2,098
Roman Catholic	30,958	2,090
Baptist	6,800	1,966
Presbyterian	4,542	1,019
Methodist Episcopal	9,268	1,009
Lutheran	1,624	571
Christian	1,611	452

SOURCE: U.S. Office of Education, *Report of the Commissioner of Education, 1895–96*, pp. 1927–1931 (author's adaptation and calculations).

Enrollment at Catholic institutions was more than three times as large as enrollment at any of the other groups of denominational schools. Congregational, Catholic, and Baptist institutions had the largest endowments per student. In the case of denominations with relatively few students, endowment per student tended to be low.

STUDENT MOBILITY With the great improvements in transportation and communication, the proportion of students attending college outside their state of residence has greatly increased. In 1896–97 the percentage of students attending college in their state of residence varied from a maximum of 94 percent for the North Central states to a minimum of 85 percent for the South Atlantic states.[10] From the 1930s to the 1960s, the percentage of students remaining in their home states to attend college was constant at 81 percent. In 1968, however, this percentage rose to 83 percent. In 1968, 90 percent of the students at public institutions were enrolled in their home states,

[9] U.S. Office of Education, *Report of the Commissioner of Education, 1894–95*, p. 219.

[10] U.S. Office of Education, *Report of the Commissioner of Education, 1896–97*, p. 1656.

TABLE 5.2-16 *Historical summary of faculty, students, degrees, and finances in institutions of higher education, United States, 1869–70 to 1965–66*

Item (1)	1869–70 (2)	1879–80 (3)	1889–90 (4)	1899–1900 (5)	1909–10 (6)	1919–20 (7)
Total	563	811	998	977	951	1,041
Total	$5,553^b$	$11,522^b$	$15,809^b$	23,868	36,480	48,615
Men	$4,887^b$	$7,328^b$	$12,704^b$	19,151	29,132	35,807
Women	666^b	$4,194^b$	$3,105^b$	4,717	7,348	12,808
Total	$52,286^b$	$115,817^b$	156,756	237,592	355,213	597,880
Men	$41,160^b$	$77,972^b$	$100,453^b$	152,254	$214,648^b$	314,938
Women	$11,126^b$	$37,845^b$	$56,303^b$	85,338	$140,565^b$	282,942
Bachelor's and first professional:						
Total	9,371	12,896	15,539	27,410	37,199	48,622
Men	7,993	10,411	12,857	22,173	28,762	31,980
Women	1,378	2,485	2,682	5,237	8,437	16,642
Second level (master's except first professional):						
Total	0	879	1,015	1,583	2,113	4,279
Men	0	868	821	1,280	1,555	2,985
Women	0	11	194	303	558	1,294
Doctor's:						
Total	1	54	149	382	443	615
Men	1	51	147	359	399	522
Women	0	3	2	23	44	93
Total current income	g	g	g	g	$ 76,883	$ 199,922
Educational and general income	g	g	$21,464	$35,084	67,917	172,929
Total current expenditures	g	g	g	g	g	g
Educational and general expenditures	g	g	g	g	g	g

1929–30 (8)	1939–40 (9)	1949–50 (10)	1959–60 (11)	1963–64 (12)	1965–66 (13)
Institutions					
1,409	1,708	1,851	2,008	2,132	2,230
Faculty[a]					
82,386	146,929	246,722	380,554[c]	494,514[c]	596,400[bc]
60,017	106,328	186,189	296,773[c]	385,405[c]	464,000[bc]
22,369	40,601	60,533	83,781[c]	109,109[c]	132,400[bc]
Resident degree-credit enrollment[d]					
1,100,737	1,494,203	2,659,021	3,215,544[c]	4,234,092[e]	5,526,325[f]
619,935	893,250	1,853,068	2,079,788[c]	2,622,787[e]	3,374,603[f]
480,802	609,953	805,953	1,135,756[c]	1,611,305[e]	2,151,722[f]
Earned degrees conferred					
122,484	186,500	432,058	392,440	498,654	551,040
73,615	109,546	328,841	254,063	298,046	328,853
48,869	76,954	103,217	138,377	200,608	222,187
14,969	26,731	58,183	74,435	101,050	140,555
8,925	16,508	41,220	50,898	68,969	93,063
6,044	10,223	16,963	23,537	32,081	47,492
2,299	3,290	6,420	9,829	14,490	18,237
1,946	2,861	5,804	8,801	12,955	16,121
353	429	616	1,028	1,535	2,116
Finances (in thousands of dollars)					
$ 554,511	$ 715,211	$ 2,374,645	$ 5,785,537	$ 9,543,514	$12,734,225
483,065	571,288	1,833,845	4,688,352	7,788,446	10,285,252
507,142	674,688	2,245,661	5,601,376	9,177,677	12,509,489
377,903	521,990	1,706,444	4,513,208	7,425,063	9,951,106

TABLE 5.2-16 *(continued)*

Item (1)	1869–70 (2)	1879–80 (3)	1889–90 (4)	1899–1900 (5)	1909–10 (6)	1919–20 (7)
Value of physical property	g	g	$95,426	$253,599	$460,532	$741,333
Endowment and other nonexpendable funds	g	g	78,788	194,998	32,361	569,071

[a] Total number of different individuals (not reduced to full-time equivalent).

[b] Estimated.

[c] Data for first term of the academic year.

[d] Unless otherwise indicated, includes students enrolled at any time during the academic year.

[e] Data for fall 1963.

[f] Opening fall enrollment. Includes resident and extension degree-credit students.

[g] Data not available.

[h] Includes unexpended plant funds.

[i] Excludes student loan, annuity, and trust funds.

NOTE: Beginning in 1959–60, includes Alaska and Hawaii. Data compiled from *Biennial Survey of Education in the United States; Faculty and Other Professional Staff in Institutions of Higher Education; Comprehensive Report on Enrollment in Higher Education; Opening Fall Enrollment in Higher Education, 1965; Earned Degrees Conferred;* and *Financial Statistics of Institutions of Higher Education.*

SOURCE: U.S. Office of Education, *Digest of Educational Statistics, 1970,* 1970, p. 78.

as compared with 65 percent of those at private institutions. Almost 95 percent of the students in two-year institutions stayed in their home states.[11]

SUMMATION   Finally, Table 5.2-16 provides a wealth of data on the development of higher education from 1869–70 to 1965–66, including statistics on the number of institutions, faculty, enrollment, degrees, and finances.

[11] R. L. Jacobson, "Proportion of Students at Colleges in Their Home States Shows Increase," *Chronicle of Higher Education,* vol. 5, no. 5, p. 4, Oct. 26, 1970.

1929–30 (8)	1939–40 (9)	1949–50 (10)	1959–60 (11)	1963–64 (12)	1965–66 (13)
$2,065,050	$2,753,780[h]	$4,799,964	$13,448,548	$21,279,346	$26,851,273
1,512,023	1,764,604	2,644,323	5,571,121	7,295,392	8,766,134[i]

References

Advisory Committee on Endowment Management: *Managing Educational Endowments,* Ford Foundation, New York, 1969.

American Academy of Political and Social Science: "Higher Education under Stress," *The Annals of the American Academy of Political and Social Science,* vol. 301, September 1955.

American Alumni Council: *Symposium: Taxation and Education,* February 1966.

American Association of University Professors: "The Threat of Inflationary Erosion: The Annual Report on the Economic Status of the Profession, 1968–69," *AAUP Bulletin,* vol. 55, no. 2, Summer 1969.

American Council on Education: *American Universities and Colleges, 1966,* Washington, D.C., 1966.

American Council on Education: *A Fact Book on Higher Education,* Washington, D.C., 1967.

Association of American Universities: *The Federal Funding of Higher Education,* Washington, D.C., 1968.

Babbidge, H. D., Jr.: *Student Financial Aid,* American College Personnel Association, Washington, D.C., 1960.

Beazley, R.: *Numbers and Characteristics of Employees in Institutions of Higher Education, Fall, 1966,* U.S. Office of Education, National Center for Educational Statistics, February 1969.

Berelson, B.: *Graduate Education in the United States,* McGraw-Hill Book Company, New York, 1960.

Bogue, J. P.: *American Junior Colleges,* 4th ed., American Council on Education, Washington, D.C., 1956.

Boston Fund: *The 1967 Study of College and University Endowment Funds,* Boston Management and Research Company, Inc., Boston, Mass., 1968.

Bowen, H. R.: *The Finance of Higher Education,* Carnegie Commission on Higher Education, Berkeley, Calif., 1968.

Bowen, W. G.: *The Economics of the Major Private Universities,* Carnegie Commission on Higher Education, Berkeley, Calif., 1968.

Bowen, W. G.: *The Federal Government and Princeton University,* Princeton University Press, Princeton, N.J., January 1962.

Bowker, A. H.: "Quality and Quantity in Higher Education," *Journal of the American Statistical Association,* vol. 60, no. 309, pp. 1–15, March 1965.

Bowles, F.: *Access to Higher Education,* vol. 1, UNESCO, Paris, 1963.

Brown, D. G.: *The Mobile Professors,* American Council on Education, Washington, D.C., 1967.

Bureau of Social Science Research, Inc.: *Five Years After the College Degree,* Washington, D.C., 1966.

Caplow, T., and R. J. McGee: *The Academic Marketplace,* Basic Books, Inc., Publishers, New York, 1958.

Carnegie Commission on Higher Education: *The Capitol and the Campus: State Responsibility for Postsecondary Education,* McGraw-Hill Book Company, New York, 1971.

Carnegie Commission on Higher Education: *The Open-Door Colleges: Policies for Community Colleges,* McGraw-Hill Book Company, New York, 1970.

Carnegie Commission on Higher Education: *Quality and Equality: New Levels of Federal Responsibility for Higher Education,* McGraw-Hill Book Company, New York, 1968.

Carnegie Commission on Higher Education: *Quality and Equality: Revised Recommendations: New Levels of Federal Responsibility for Higher Education,* McGraw-Hill Book Company, New York, 1970.

Cartter, A. M.: *An Assessment of Quality in Graduate Education,* American Council on Education, Washington, D.C., 1966.

Cartter, A. M.: "Qualitative Aspects of Southern University Education," Southern Economic Journal, vol. 32, no. 1, part 2, July 1965.

Cartter, A. M.: "The Supply and Demand for College Teachers," *The Journal of Human Resources,* Summer 1966.

Cartter, A. M., and R. L. Farrell: "Academic Labor Market Projections and the Draft," *The Economics and Financing of Higher Education in the United States,* a compendium of papers submitted to the Joint Economic Committee, U.S. Congress, Washington, D.C., 1969.

Cary, W. L., and C. E. Bright: *The Law and Lore of Endowment Funds,* Ford Foundation, New York, March 1969.

Central Advisory Council for Education: *15–18: Report of the Central Advisory Council for Education,* England, vol. 2, 1959.

Chandler, M. O.: *Opening Fall Enrollment in Higher Education, 1968, Part A—Summary Data,* U.S. Office of Education, National Center for Educational Statistics, 1969.

Chase, J. L.: *Doctoral Study: Fellowships and Capacity of Graduate Schools,* U.S. Office of Education, 1961.

Cliff, N., and R. Ekstrom: *Practices and Attitudes in Paying for College,* Educational Testing Service, Princeton, N.J., 1962.

Cole, C. C., Jr.: *Encouraging Scientific Talent,* College Entrance Examination Board, New York, 1956.

College Entrance Examination Board: *College Admissions,* New York, 1960.

College Entrance Examination Board: *The Economics of Higher Education,* New York, 1967.

Commission on Financing Higher Education: *Current Operating Expenditures and Income of Higher Education in the United States, 1930, 1940, and 1950,* Columbia University Press, New York, 1952.

Committee on Survey of the Needs of California in Higher Education: *A Report of a Survey of the Needs of California Higher Education,* Sacramento, Calif., March 1, 1948.

Council for Financial Aid to Education: *Voluntary Support of America's Colleges and Universities, 1964–65,* New York, 1966.

Council for Financial Aid to Education and American Alumni Council: *Voluntary Support of Education, 1965–66* and *1966–67,* New York, 1967 and 1968.

Council for Financial Aid to Education, American Alumni Council, and National Association of Independent Schools: *Voluntary Support of Education, 1967–68,* New York, 1969.

D'Amico, L. A.: "Salaries of College and University Professors by Rank, Institutional Size, and Control," *Educational Record,* vol. 41, pp. 300–305, October 1960.

D'Amico, L. A., and W. R. Bokelman: *Changes in Tuition Charges to Full-Time Undergraduate Students, 1958–59 to 1962–63,* U.S. Office of Education, March 1964.

Davis, J. A.: *Great Aspirations: Career Decisions and Educational Plans During College,* vol. 1, National Opinion Research Center, The University of Chicago Press, Chicago, 1963.

Davis, J. A.: *Stipends and Spouses: The Finances of American Arts and Science Graduate Students,* The University of Chicago Press, Chicago, 1962.

Davis, J. A.: *Undergraduate Career Decisions: Correlates of Occupational Choice,* Aldine Publishing Company, Chicago, 1965.

Denison, E. F.: *The Sources of Economic Growth and the Alternatives before Us,* Committee for Economic Development, New York, January 1962.

Doehrmann, H.: *Crosscurrents in College Admissions, Institutional Response to Student Ability and Family Income,* Teachers College Press, Columbia University, New York, 1968.

Dunham, R. E., and P. S. Wright: *Faculty and Other Professional Staff in Institutions of Higher Education, First Term 1963–64,* final report, U.S. Office of Education, 1966.

Dunham, R. E., P. S. Wright, and M. O. Chandler: *Teaching Faculty in Universities and 4-Year Colleges, Spring 1963,* U.S. Office of Education, 1966.

Engineering Advisory Council: *An Engineering Master Plan Study for the University of California,* University of California, Berkeley, 1965.

Flexner, Abraham: *Medical Education in the United States and Canada,* bulletin no. 4, report to the Carnegie Foundation for the Advancement of Teaching, D. B. Updike, The Merrymount Press, Boston, 1910.

Folger, J. K., and C. B. Nam: *Education of the American Population,* U.S. Bureau of the Census (1960 Census Monograph), Washington, D.C., 1967.

Great Britain, Report of the Committee Appointed by the Prime Minister under the Chairmanship of Lord Robbins: *Higher Education,* Her Majesty's Stationery Office, London, 1963.

Greenough, W. C., and F. P. King: *Retirement and Insurance Plans in American Colleges,* Columbia University Press, New York, 1959.

Hall, R. C., and S. Craigie: *National Defense Student Loan Program: Student Borrowers, Their Needs and Resources,* U. S. Office of Education, 1962.

Halsey, A. H., J. Flound, and C. Anderson (eds.): *Education, Economy, and Society,* The Free Press of Glencoe, Inc., New York, 1961.

Hanoch, Giora: *Personal Earnings and Investment in School,* dissertation, The University of Chicago Press, Chicago, December 1965.

Harris, S. E.: *The Economics of Harvard,* McGraw-Hill Book Company, New York, 1970.

Harris, S. E.: *Higher Education: Resources and Finance,* McGraw-Hill Book Company, New York, 1962.

Harris, S. E.: *The Market for College Graduates,* Harvard University Press, Cambridge, Mass., 1949.

Harris, S. E., and A. Levensohn (eds.): *Education and Public Policy,* McCutchan Publishing Corporation, Berkeley, Calif., 1965.

Hunter, J. S.: *The Academic and Financial Status of Graduate Students, Spring, 1965,* U.S. Office of Education, 1967.

Iffert, R. E.: *Retention and Withdrawal of College Students,* U.S. Office of Education, 1958.

Iffert, R. E., and B. S. Clarke: *College Applicants, Entrants, Dropouts,* U.S. Office of Education, 1965.

Ingraham, M. H.: *The Outer Fringe: Faculty Benefits Other Than Annuities and Insurance,* The University of Wisconsin Press, Madison, 1965.

Institute of Applied Manpower Research: *Fact Book on Manpower,* Part II—Education and Training , A. J. A. Touro, New Delhi, 1969.

Jacobson, R. L.: "Proportion of Students at Colleges in Their Home States Shows Increase," *Chronicle of Higher Education,* vol. 5, no. 5, p. 4, Oct. 26, 1970.

Jencks, C., and D. Riesman: *The Academic Revolution,* Doubleday and Company, Garden City, N.Y., 1968.

Joint Staff of the Liaison Committee of the Regents of the University of California and the California State Board of Education: *A Restudy of the Needs of California in Higher Education,* Sacramento, Calif., 1955.

Keezer, D. (ed.): *Financing Higher Education,* McGraw-Hill Book Company, New York, 1959.

Keniston, H.: *Graduate Study and Research in the Arts and Sciences at the University of Pennsylvania,* University of Pennsylvania Press, Philadelphia, 1959.

Kerr, C.: "New Challenges to the College and University," in Kermit Gordon (ed.), *Agenda for the Nation,* The Brookings Institution, Washington, D.C., 1968.

Kidd, C. V.: *American Universities and Federal Research,* The Belknap Press, Harvard University Press, Cambridge, Mass., 1959.

Lansing, J. B., T. Lorimer, and C. Moriguchi: *How People Pay for College,* Institute for Social Research, The University of Michigan Press, Ann Arbor, 1960.

Liaison Committee of the Regents of the University of California and the State Board of Education: *Institutional Capacities and Area Needs of California Public Higher Education, 1960–1975,* Sacramento, Calif., February 1961.

Liaison Committee of the Regents of the University of California and the State Board of Education: *A Master Plan for Higher Education in California, 1960–1975,* Sacramento, Calif., 1960.

Lindsay, F. H. I.: *Financial Statistics of Institutions of Higher Education: Receipts, Expenditures, and Property, 1959–60,* U.S. Office of Education, National Center for Educational Statistics, 1964.

Machlup, F.: *The Production and Distribution of Knowledge in the United States,* Princeton University Press, Princeton, N.J., 1962.

McKee, R. C.: *Financial Assistance for College Students: Undergraduate and First Professional,* U.S. Office of Education, 1965.

Medsker, L. L.: *The Junior College: Progress and Prospect,* McGraw-Hill Book Company, New York, 1960.

Medsker, L. L., and D. Tillery: *The Two-Year College in America,* published as *Breaking the Access Barriers: A Profile of Two-Year Colleges,* McGraw-Hill Book Company, New York, 1971.

Merriam, I. C., A. M. Skolnik, and S. R. Dales: "Social Welfare Expenditures, 1967–68," *Social Security Bulletin,* vol. 31, no. 12, pp. 14–27, December 1968.

Mertens, P.: *Financial Statistics of Institutions of Higher Education: Property, 1965–66,* U.S. Office of Education, National Center for Educational Statistics, 1969.

Miller, H. P.: *Income Distribution in the United States,* U.S. Bureau of the Census, 1966.

Millett, J. D.: *Financing Higher Education in the United States,* Columbia University Press, New York, 1952.

Moon, R. G., Jr.: *Student Financial Aid in the United States: Administration and Resources,* College Entrance Examination Board, Princeton, N.J., 1963.

Mushkin, S. J. (ed.): *Economics of Higher Education,* U.S. Office of Education, 1962.

Mushkin, S. J., and E. P. McLoone: *Public Spending for Higher Education, 1970,* Council of State Governments, Chicago, February 1965.

National Academy of Sciences and National Research Council: *Doctorate Production in United States Universities, 1936–56,* Washington, D.C., 1958.

National Association of State Universities and Land-Grant Colleges: *Appropriation of State Tax Funds for Operating Expenses of Higher Education, 1964–1965,* Washington, D.C., 1964.

National Education Association: *Rankings of States, 1968,* Washington, D.C., 1968.

National Education Association: *Teacher Supply and Demand in Universities, Colleges, and Junior Colleges, 1959–60 and 1960–61,* Washington, D.C., 1961.

National Federation of College and University Business Officers Association: *The Sixty College Study . . . A Second Look, A Comparison of Financial Operating Data for 1957–58,* 1960.

National Opinion Research Center: *Graduate Student Finances, 1963,* The University of Chicago Press, Chicago, 1965.

National Science Foundation: *American Science Manpower, A Report of the National Register of Scientific and Technical Personnel, 1960, 1962, 1966,* and *1968,* 1962, June 1964, December 1967, and December 1969.

National Science Foundation: *The Duration of Formal Education for High-Ability Youth,* 1961.

National Science Foundation: *The Dynamics of Academic Science,* 1967.

National Science Foundation: *Federal Funds for Research, Development, and Other Scientific Activities, Fiscal Years 1967, 1968, and 1969,* vol. 17, 1968.

National Science Foundation: *Federal Support to Universities and Colleges, Fiscal Year 1967,* 1968.

National Science Foundation: *Graduate Student Enrollment and Support in American Universities and Colleges,* 1957.

National Science Foundation: *The Prospective Manpower Situation for Science and Engineering Staff in Universities and Colleges 1965–75,* 1967.

National Science Foundation: *Scientific Activities at Universities and Colleges, 1964,* 1968.

National Science Foundation: *Scientific Research and Development in Colleges and Universities: Expenditures and Manpower, 1958,* 1963.

Office of Administration, Management Evaluation Branch: *Fact Book, Office of Education Programs,* U.S. Office of Education, January 1967.

Ohio Board of Regents: *Provisional Master Plan for Public Higher Education in Ohio,* Columbus Blank Book Company, Columbus, Ohio, 1965.

Organization for Economic Cooperation and Development: *Case Studies on Innovation in Higher Education: French Experience Before 1968,* OECD Publications, Paris, 1970.

Organization for Economic Cooperation and Development: *Curriculum Improvement and Educational Development,* OECD Publications, Paris, 1966.

Organization for Economic Cooperation and Development: *Development of Higher Education, 1960–1967: Analytical Report,* OECD Publications, Paris, 1970.

Organization for Economic Cooperation and Development: *Development of Secondary Education: Trends and Implications,* OECD Publications, Paris, 1969.

Organization for Economic Cooperation and Development: *Economic Aspects of Higher Education,* OECD Publications, Paris, 1964.

Organization for Economic Cooperation and Development: *Educational Policy and Planning in Sweden,* OECD Publications, Paris, January 1964.

Organization for Economic Cooperation and Development: *Financing of Education for Economic Growth,* OECD Publications, Paris, 1966.

Organization for Economic Cooperation and Development: *Higher Education and the Demand for Scientific Manpower in the United States,* OECD Publications, Paris, 1963.

Organization for Economic Cooperation and Development: *Resources of Scientific and Technical Personnel in the O.E.C.D. Area,* OECD Publications, Paris, 1959.

Orlans, H.: *The Effects of Federal Programs on Higher Education,* The Brookings Institution, Washington, D.C., 1962.

Rice, M. C., and P. L. Mason: *Residence and Migration of College Students, Fall 1963: State and Regional Data,* U.S. Office of Education, National Center for Educational Statistics, 1965.

Robbins, L. F.: *New Construction and Rehabilitation on College Campuses, 1961–62, 1962–63, and 1963–64,* U.S. Office of Education, 1966.

Rosen, S. M.: *Higher Education in the U.S.S.R.,* U.S. Office of Education, 1969.

Samore, T.: *Library Statistics of Colleges and Universities, 1963–64,* U.S. Office of Education, 1968.

Sears, J. B.: *Philanthropy in the History of American Higher Education,* U.S. Office of Education, 1922.

Select Committee on the Future of Private and Independent Higher Education in New York State: *New York State and Private Higher Education,* Bureau of Publications, Albany, N.Y., January 1968.

Shell, Karl, et al.: *The Educational Opportunity Bank: An Economic Analysis of a Contingent Repayment Loan Program for Higher Education,* Department of Economics, working paper, The M.I.T. Press, Cambridge, Mass., November 1967.

Shell, Karl, et al.: "The Educational Opportunity Bank: An Economic Analysis of a Contingent Repayment Loan Program for Higher Education," *National Tax Journal,* vol. 21, no. 1, pp. 2–45, March 1968.

Skolnik, A. M., and S. R. Dales: "Social Welfare Expenditures, 1969–70," *Social Security Bulletin,* vol. 33, no. 12, pp. 3–17, December 1970.

Tombo, R., Jr.: *University Registration Statistics,* January 1914.

Trimble, V.: "Student Financial Aid: What, Where, How," *American Education,* February 1969.

UNESCO: *Manual of Educational Statistics,* Paris, 1961.

UNESCO: *Statistical Yearbook, 1968,* Paris, 1969.

U.S. Bureau of the Census: *Basic Student Charges, 1962–63,* 1963.

U.S. Bureau of the Census: *Compendium of the Eleventh Census, 1890,* 1892–97.

U.S. Bureau of the Census: "Educational Attainment: March 1966 and 1965," *Population Characteristics, Current Population Reports,* ser. P-20, no. 158, 1966.

U.S. Bureau of the Census: "Educational Attainment, March 1968," *Population Characteristics, Current Population Reports,* ser. P-20, no. 182, Apr. 28, 1969.

U.S. Bureau of the Census: *Estimates and Projections of Educational Attainment in the U.S.S.R., 1950–1985,* International Population Reports, ser. P-91, 1967.

U.S. Bureau of the Census: *Governmental Finances in 1966–67,* Government Finances Series, GF 67, no. 3, 1968.

U.S. Bureau of the Census: "Revised Projections of School and College Enrollment in the United States to 1985," *Population Estimates, Current Population Reports,* ser. P-25, no. 365, May 5, 1967.

U.S. Bureau of the Census: "School Enrollment: October 1968 and 1967," *Current Population Reports,* ser. P-20, no. 190, 1969.

U.S. Bureau of the Census: "School Enrollment: October, 1969," *Current Population Reports,* ser. P-20, no. 206, 1970.

U.S. Bureau of the Census: *Seventh Census of the United States, 1850,* 1853.

U.S. Bureau of the Census: *Statistical Abstract of the United States, 1967, 1968,* and *1969,* 1967, 1968, and 1969.

U.S. Bureau of the Census: *Statistics of the United States Compiled from the Eighth Census, 1860,* 1866.

U.S. Congress, Joint Economic Committee: *The Economics and Financing of Higher Education in the United States,* a compendium of papers submitted to the Joint Economic Committee, 1969.

U.S. Congress, Joint Economic Committee: *Federal Programs for the Development of Human Resources,* a compilation of replies from departments and agencies of the United States Government to a questionnaire formulated by the Subcommittee on Economic Progress, 1966.

U.S. Congress, Joint Economic Committee: *Revenue Sharing and Its Alternatives: What Future for Fiscal Federalism?,* Hearings before the Subcommittee on Fiscal Policy, July and August 1967.

U.S. Department of Health, Education and Welfare: *Accomplishments, 1963–1968, Problems and Challenges and a Look to the Future,* report to President Lyndon B. Johnson, December 1968.

U.S. Department of Health, Education and Welfare: *Toward a Long-Range Plan for Federal Financial Support for Higher Education,* report to the President, Office of Assistant Secretary for Planning and Evaluation, January 1969.

U.S. Department of Health, Education and Welfare: *Trends,* 1966–67 edition, 1968, part 1.

U.S. Department of the Interior: *Annual Report of the Secretary of the Interior,* 1872 and 1890.

U.S. Department of Labor: *Manpower Report of the President and a Report on Manpower Requirements, Resources, Utilization, and Training,* Employment Security Bureau, 1966.

U.S. Department of Labor: *U.S. Economic Report of the President, 1969,* 1969.

U.S. House of Representatives, Committee on Education and Labor: *The Federal Government and Education,* report of a subcommittee, 1963.

U.S. House of Representatives, Committee on Education and Labor: *Higher Education Act of 1965, Hearings before the Special Subcommittee on Education,* February–May 1965.

U.S. House of Representatives, Committee on Education and Labor: *Study of the United States Office of Education,* report, 1967.

U.S. House of Representatives, Committee on Government Operations: *The Brain Drain into the United States of Scientists, Engineers, and Physicians,* a staff study for the Research and Technical Programs Subcommittee, 1967.

U.S. House of Representatives, Committee on Government Operations: *Conflicts Between the Federal Research Programs and the Nation's Goals for Higher Education, Hearings before a Subcommittee,* June 1965.

U.S. House of Representatives, Committee on Government Operations: *Conflicts Between the Federal Research Programs and the Nation's Goals for Higher Education,* report of the Subcommittee, 1965.

U.S. House of Representatives, Committee on Science and Astronautics: *Higher Education in the Sciences in the United States,* report of the Subcommittee on Science, Research and Development, prepared by the National Science Foundation, 1965.

U.S. House of Representatives, Committee on Science and Astronautics: *A National Program of Institutional Grants for Science and Science Education,* study for the Subcommittee on Science, Research and Development, 1968.

U.S. House of Representatives, Committee on Science and Astronautics: *The National Science Foundation: A General Review of Its First 15 Years,* report of the Science Policy Research Division, Legislative Reference Service of the Library of Congress to the Subcommittee on Science, Research and Development, 1965.

U.S. Office of Education: *Academic Degrees,* bulletin 1960, no. 28.

U.S. Office of Education: *Basic Student Charges, 1962–63, 1963–64,* and *1966–67,* National Center for Educational Statistics, 1963, 1964, and 1968.

U.S. Office of Education: *Biennial Surveys of Education, 1928–30, 1936–38,* and *1938–40.*

U.S. Office of Education: *College Aid for Students,* 1963.

U.S. Office of Education: *College and University Endowment: Status and Management,* 1965, 1966.

U.S. Office of Education: *College and University Endowment Investments: A Survey,* 1959.

U.S. Office of Education: *College and University Enrollment and Physical Facilities Survey, 1965–70,* 1970.

U.S. Office of Education: *College and University Facilities Survey,* issued as Department of Health, Education and Welfare circulars, five parts: part 1, 1959; part 2, 1960; part 3, 1964; part 4, 1965; part 5, 1965.

U.S. Office of Education: *Consortiums in American Higher Education, 1965–66,* report of an exploratory study, 1968.

U.S. Office of Education: *Digest of Educational Statistics, 1966, 1967, 1968, 1969,* and *1970,* 1967, 1968, 1969, and 1970.

U.S. Office of Education: *Earned Degrees Conferred, 1966–67: Part A —Summary Data* and *1968–69, Part A—Summary Data,* 1968 and 1971.

U.S. Office of Education: *Education Directory, 1963–64, Part 3: Higher Education,* 1964.

U.S. Office of Education: *Education Directory, 1969–70,* 1970.

U.S. Office of Education: *Education in the Seventies,* planning papers of the Office of Program Planning and Evaluation, May 1968.

U.S. Office of Education: *Enrollment for Advanced Degrees,* Fall 1963.

U.S. Office of Education: *Enrollment for Master's and Higher Degrees, Fall 1964,* final report, National Center for Educational Statistics, 1966.

U.S. Office of Education: *Fact Book, Office of Education Programs,* prepared by the Office of Administration, Management Evaluation Branch, January 1967.

U.S. Office of Education: *Financial Statistics of Institutions of Higher Education: Current Funds, Revenues, and Expenditures, 1965–66* and *1966–67,* National Center for Educational Statistics, 1969 and 1969.

U.S. Office of Education: *Financial Statistics of Institutions of Higher Education: Student Financial Aid, 1965–66,* National Center for Educational Statistics, 1968.

U.S. Office of Education: *Higher Education Finances: Selected Trend and Summary Data,* National Center for Educational Statistics, June 1968.

U.S. Office of Education: *Projections of Educational Statistics to 1975–76* and *1977–78,* National Center for Educational Statistics, 1966 and 1968.

U.S. Office of Education: *Report of the Commissioner of Education,* various years.

U.S. Office of Education: *Retention and Withdrawal of College Students,* 1957.

U.S. Office of Education: *Statistical Review of Higher Education, 1895–96.*

U.S. Office of Education: *Statistics of Higher Education: Faculty, Students, and Degrees, 1953–54,* 1956.

U.S. Office of Education: *Students and Buildings: An Analysis of Selected Federal Programs for Higher Education,* 1968.

U.S. Office of Education: *Students Enrolled for Advanced Degrees, Fall 1968,* National Center for Educational Statistics, 1970.

U.S. Office of Education: *Students Enrolled for Advanced Degrees, Fall 1967: Part A—Summary Data,* National Center for Educational Statistics, 1969.

U.S. Office of Education: *Upper Division Enrollment, Fall 1967,* National Center for Educational Statistics, 1969.

U.S. Office of Education: *Variations in Tuition and Fees Charged Full-Time Undergraduate Students by Denominationally Affiliated Institutions, 1962–63,* 1964.

U.S. Office of the President, Panel on Educational Innovation: *The Educational Opportunity Bank,* report to the Commissioner of Education, Director of National Science Foundation, and Special Assistant to the President for Science and Technology, 1967.

U.S. Senate, Committee on Government Operations: *Equitable Distribution of R&D Funds by Government Agencies, Hearings before the Subcommittee on Government Research,* July 1967.

U.S. Senate, Committee on Government Operations: *Federal Support of Project Grants: Indirect Costs and Cost Sharing, Hearings before the Subcommittee on Government Research,* April–June 1969.

U.S. Senate, Committee on Government Operations: *Research in the Service of Man, Hearings before the Subcommittee on Government Research,* February and March 1967.

U.S. Senate, Committee on Labor and Public Welfare: *Education Legislation, 1963, Hearings before the Subcommittee on Education,* June 1963.

U.S. Senate, Committee on Labor and Public Welfare: *Impact of Federal Research and Development Policies on Scientific and Technical Manpower, Hearings before the Subcommittee on Employment and Manpower,* June and July 1965.

U.S. Senate, Committee on Labor and Public Welfare: *White House Conference on Education,* prepared for the Subcommittee on Education, August 1965.

University of California: *Growth and Distinction: The University of California 1958–66,* University of California Press, Berkeley, 1967.

University of California, Office of the President: *Faculty Effort and Output Study,* University of California Press, Berkeley, 1970.

Williams, R. L.: *The Administration of Academic Affairs,* The University of Michigan Press, Ann Arbor, 1965.

Wilson, K. M.: *Of Time and the Doctorate,* Southern Regional Education Board, Atlanta, Ga., 1965.

Wolfle, D.: *America's Resources of Specialized Talent,* report of the Commission on Human Resources and Advanced Training, Harper & Brothers, New York, 1954.

Wright, P.: *Earned Degrees Conferred, 1963–64: Bachelor's and Higher Degrees,* U.S. Office of Education, National Center for Educational Statistics, 1966.

This book was set in Vladimir by University Graphics, Inc. It was printed on acid-free, long-life paper and bound by The Maple Press Company. The designers were Elliot Epstein and Edward Butler. The editors were Nancy Tressel and Cheryl Allen for McGraw-Hill Book Company and Terry Y. Allen and Verne A. Stadtman for the Carnegie Commission on Higher Education. Alice Cohen supervised the production.

DATE DUE

MAY 4

GAYLORD

PRINTED IN U.S